LATIN AMERICAN WOMEN WRITERS

An Encyclopedia

LATIN AMERICAN WOMEN WRITERS

An Encyclopedia

María Claudia André
Eva Paulino Bueno
Editors

Routledge
Taylor & Francis Group
NEW YORK AND LONDON

Published in 2008 by
Routledge
270 Madison Avenue
New York, NY 10016
USA

Published in Great Britain by
Routledge
2 Park Square
Milton Park
Abingdon
Oxon OX14 4RN
UK

Routledge is an imprint of the Taylor & Francis Group an informa business

10 9 8 7 6 5 4 3 2 1

Printed on acid-free, 250-year-life paper
Manufactured in the United States of America

Library of Congress Cataloging-in-Publication Data:
Latin American women writers : an encyclopedia / María Claudia André, Eva Paulino Bueno, editors.
p. cm.
Includes bibliographical references and index.
ISBN 978-0-415-97971-9
1. Women authors, Latin American–Biography–Dictionaries. 2. Latin American literature–Women authors–Bio-bibliography–Dictionaries. 3. Women and literature–Latin America–Dictionaries. I. André, María Claudia. II. Bueno, Eva Paulino.
PQ7081.3.L37 2008
860.9'928709803–dc22

2007019109

ISBN13: 978-0-415-97971-9

The Editors dedicate this Encyclopedia
to all Latin American women writers, and to the
professors of literature who make them known
in the world.

Contents

Consulting Editors

David Foster
Arizona State University

Jerry Hoeg
Pennsylvania State University

Regina Root
College of William and Mary

Contributors

Daniel Altamiranda
Stephanie Alvarez
University of Texas-Pan American

María Claudia André
Hope College

Yvette Aparicio
Grinnell College

Aída Apter-Cragnolino
Texas Lutheran University

Nara Araújo
University of Havana

Isabel Asensio-Sierra
Weber State University

Vania Barraza Toledo
Central Michigan University

Jorge J. Barrueto
Walsh University

Joanna R. Bartow
St. Mary's College of Maryland

Clara H. Becerra
Mount Union College

Mary G. Berg
Harvard University

Aldona Bialowas Pobutsky
Oakland University

May Bletz
Brock University

Sandra M. Boschetto-Sandoval
Michigan Technological University

Monica Botta
Washington and Lee University

Eva Paulino Bueno
St. Mary's University

Eliana Bueno-Ribeiro
Université Lumière Lyon

Claudia Cabello Hutt
Rutgers, The State University of New Jersey

Susan Carvalho
University of North Carolina at Chapel Hill

Luciana Castro
Skyline College

Ana María Caula
Slippery Rock University

Carlota Caulfield
Mills College

Maria Clark
Carson-Newman College

Margaret Anne Clarke
University of Portsmouth

Karen Cody
Angelo State University

Francesca Colecchia
Duquesne University

Maite Conde
University of Columbia

Elizabeth Coonrod Martinez
Sonoma State University

Miryam Criado
Hanover College

Simone Curi
Texas Christian University

Mónica Díaz
University of Texas Pan-American

Oscar A. Díaz-Ortiz
Middle Tennessee State University

Maria DiFrancesco
Ithaca College

Federica Domínguez Colavita
Università di Trieste

Leandro Mauricio Duarte
University of Pittsburgh

Alice Edwards
Mercyhurst College

Nora Erro-Peralta
Florida Atlantic University

Tina Escaja
University of Vermont

Wilma Feliciano
SUNY New Paltz

Regina Félix
University of North Carolina Wilmington

César Ferreira
University of Oklahoma

Ana Figueroa
Princeton University

Alexandra Fitts
University of Alaska Fairbanks

Dolores Flores-Silva
Roanoke College

Maria Aparecida Rodrigues Fontes
Universidade Federal do Rio de Janeiro

Lucia Fox-Lockert
Michigan State University

Bonnie Frederick
Texas Christian University

Irune del Río Gabiola
University of Illinois at Urbana-Champaign

Myrna García-Calderón
Syracuse University

Antonia Garcia-Rodriguez
Pace University

Anne C. Gebelein
Trinity College

Amalia Gladhart
University of Oregon

Shelley Godsland
Manchester Metropolitan University

Vívien Gonzaga e Silva
Universidade Federal de Minas Gerais

Deborah Gonzalez
FDU – Metropolitan Campus

Miguel González-Abellás
Washburn University

Ángela María González Echeverry
Lake Erie College

Elena González-Muntaner
University of Wisconsin

Myriam González-Smith
University of California, Santa Barbara

Jana Gutiérrez
Auburn University

Anna Hamling
University of New Brunswick

Marguerite Itamar Harrison
Smith College

Marisa Herrera Postlewate
University of Texas, Arlington

Emily Hind
University of Wyoming

Stacey Hoult
Valparaiso University

Carolyn Hutchinson
University of Illinois at Urbana-Champaign

Regina Igel
University of Maryland

Amanda L. Irwin
Rhodes College

Geoffrey Kantaris
University of Cambridge

Anna Katsnelson
University of Texas at Austin

Bryan Kennedy
University of Wisconsin – Milwaukee

Vicki Ketz
Iona College

Luz Angélica Kirschner
Pennsylvania State University

Patricia N. Klingenberg
University of Ohio

Ilka Kressner
SUNY at Albany

Juli A. Kroll
University of North Dakota

Nancy A. LaGreca
University of Oklahoma

Jane Lavery
University of Southampton

Sophie Lavoie
Dalhousie University

Linda Ledford-Miller
University of Scranton

Héctor Fernández L'Hoeste
Georgia State University

Constância Lima Duarte
Universidade Federal de Minas Gerais

Bernardita Llanos
Denison University

Darrell B. Lockhart
University of Nevada, Reno

Clary Loisel
University of Montana

Enrique Ávila López
Mount Royal College

Iraida H. López
Ramapo College

Magdalena Maiz-Peña
Davidson College

H. J. Manzari
Worcester Polytechnic Institute

Gianna Martella
Western Oregon University

Karen W. Martin
Middlebury College

Paloma Martínez-Carbajo
Pacific Lutheran University

María R. Matz
Angelo State University

Ellen Mayock
Washington and Lee University

R. John McCaw
University of Wisconsin-Milwaukee

Sophia A. McClennen
Pennsylvania State University

Isis McElroy
Arizona State University

Kacy McKinney
University of Texas at Austin

Sandra Augusta de Melo
Universidade Federal de Uberlândia

Ana Merino
Dartmouth College

Lisa Merschel
Duke University

Graciela Michelotti
Haverford College

Zulema Moret
Grand Valley State University

Sylvia Verónica Morin
University of Houston

Jeanie Murphy
Rockford College

Eduardo Muslip
Arizona State University

Silvia Nagy-Zekmi
Villanova University

Luciana Namorato
Indiana University

Lyslei Nascimento
Universidade Federal de Minas Gerais

Elizabeth Gackstetter Nichols
Drury University

Dianna Niebylski
University of Illinois-Chicago

Debra Ochoa
Trinity University

Diana Pardo
University of Central Oklahoma

Anne Pasero
Marquette University

Brenci Patiño
University of Illinois at Urbana-Champaign

Ana Peluffo
University of California, Davis

Francisco Peñas-Bermejo
University of Dayton

Susana Perea-Fox
Oklahoma State University

Kenia Maria de Almeida Pereira
Universidade Federal de Uberlândia

Catherine Perricone
Lafayette College

Charles Perrone
University of Florida

Loida Pereira Peterson
Surry Community College, NC

Oralia Preble-Niemi
University of Tennessee at Chatanooga

Maria T. Ramos-Garcia
South Dakota State University

Karen Rauch
Kutztown University

Gerhild Reisner
University Salzburg

Judith Richards
Park University

Barbara D. Riess
Allegheny College

Marcie D. Rinka
University of San Diego

Carolina Rocha
University of Illinois at Urbana-Champaign

Sonia Roncador
University of Texas, Austin

Regina Root
College of William and Mary

Adriana Rosman-Askot
College of New Jersey

Fabiola Fernàndes Salek
York College

César Salgado
University of Texas, Austin

Rafael E. Saumell-Muñoz
Sam Houston State University

Renee Sum Scott
Delta State University

Dawn Slack
Kutztown University

Alexander Steffanell
University of Florida

Rosa Tezanos-Pinto
Indiana University-Purdue University Indianapolis

Aida Toledo
Central Michigan University

Antonio Luciano Tosta
University of Illinois at Urbana-Champaign

Rebecca Ulland
Northern Michigan University

Macarena Urzúa
Rutgers, The State University of New Jersey

Estela Valverde
Macquarie University

Patricia Varas
Wilamette University

Maida Watson
Florida International University

Elizabeth M. Willingham
Baylor University

Keith Woodall
Fort Hays State University

María Magdalena Zalduondo
University of Louisiana at Lafayette

Alphabetical List of Entries

Thematic List of Entries

Argentina

Absatz, Cecilia
Bellessi, Diana
Biagioni, Amelia
Borinsky, Alicia
Bosco, María Angélica
Bullrich, Silvina
Canto, Estela
Diaconú, Alina
Dujovne Ortiz, Alicia
Escofet, Cristina
Gallardo, Sara
Gambaro, Griselda
Glickman, Nora
Gorodischer, Angélica
Gorriti, Juana Manuela
Guerra, Rosa
Guido, Beatriz
Heer, Liliana
Heker, Liliana
Iparraguirre, Sylvia
Jurado, Alicia
Kamenszain, Tamara
Kociancich, Vlady
Lange, Norah
Levinson, Luisa Mercedes
Lojo, Maria Rosa
Lynch, Marta
Mansilla de García, Eduarda
Manso, Juana
Mercader, Martha
Mercado, Tununa
Miguel, María Esther de
Molloy, Sylvia
Mosquera, Beatriz
Navau, Flavia Company
Negroni, María
Ocampo, Silvina
Ocampo, Victoria
Orozco, Olga
Orphée, Elvira
Partnoy, Alicia
Pelliza de Sagasta, Josefina
Pizarnik, Alejandra
Plager, Silvia
Poletti, Syria
Raznovich, Diana
Roffé, Reina
Rosenberg, Mirta
Sarlo, Beatriz
Seibel, Beatriz
Shua, Ana María
Steimberg, Alicia
Storni, Alfonsina
Torres Molina, Susana
Traba, Marta
Valenzuela, Luisa
Walsh, María Elena

Brazil

Almeida, Júlia Lopes de
Archanjo, Neide
Assunção, Leilah
Azevedo Castro, Ana Luisa
Baião, Isis
Bins, Patricia
Bormann, Maria Benedita (Délia)
César, Ana Cristina
Colasanti, Marina
Coralina, Cora
Coutinho, Sonia
Cunha, Helena Gomes Parente
Denser, Márcia
Dolores, Carmen
Floresta, Nisia
Freitas, Emilia
Galvão, Patrícia Rehder, Pabu
Hilst, Hilda
Jesus, Carolina Maria de
Júlia, Francisca
Lajolo, Marisa Philbert
Lispector, Clarice
Lobo, Luiza
Lopes Cançado, Maura
Luft, Lya
Machado, Gilka da Costa Mello
Machado, Maria Clara
Mereiles, Cecília
Miranda, Ana
Moscovich, Cíntia
Piñón, Nélida
Prado, Adélia
Queiroz, Maria José de
Queiroz, Rachel de
Rheda, Regina
Ribeiro Tavares, Zulmira
Savary, Olga Augusta Maria

Preface

Latin American literature, as it is studied in the United States, until recently concentrated mostly on the work of canonical male writers. Except in very specialized literature departments in the biggest universities, very little was included about Latin American women writers, even though each country in Latin America has produced exceptional women writers who have participated in the literary movements of their countries, and contributed to enrich their literature and culture.

To address this initial lack of materials, *Latin American Women Writers: An Encyclopedia* details the works and lives of these and offers a comprehensive vision of Latin American literature by women. Included in *Latin American Women Writers: An Encyclopedia* are women writers from all Latin American countries, both those who wrote originally in Spanish and those who wrote in Portuguese.

Many of the newer writers from Latin America have not been translated into English yet, so we decided that one of the functions of the *Encyclopedia* is to provide an introduction to the work produced by these artists, who speak as women, as well as citizens of their countries. In our experience as teachers of language and literature, there are many examples of students becoming excited about a subject, or an author, if they have an initial contact with that author's work in an English language environment. Even though we know that reading the text in the original language is always preferable, we also believe that a first contact with the literature can well be the first step for a student to decide to study the original language of the novel, poem, or play. Thus, the texts of the *Encyclopedia* will provide both this initial contact for the beginning student, as well as sophisticated information for the advanced student, and a source of information for the general reader. With the thorough, analytical index, the advanced student will be able to follow a thread of information and deepen his/her knowledge of Latin American literature as a whole, and the literature by Latin American women specifically.

The primary audience for the *Encyclopedia* consists of college students working with Latin American literature. It is not unusual for a student—even a college student—to be discouraged by jargon-filled texts that do more to obscure than to clarify a subject. However, we wanted to make the *Encyclopedia* also a tool for a wider audience composed of people interested in learning more about Latin American culture and literature. Therefore, all efforts have been made to keep specialized language to a minimum, and to make all the entries of the Encyclopedia accessible to a wide variety of readers. Each entry contains a short biography of the artist, followed by a concise study of the main aspect of her work, and by Selected Works and References and Further Reading sections. For those interested in more comprehensive criticism, the References and Further Reading section lists the most important sources available at the moment the entry was written. Because most of these writers are increasingly becoming the subject of always newer studies, books, essays, and dissertations, the References and Further Reading cannot be complete. Rather, they give the reader an idea of where to obtain further information on that writer, if needed. A thorough, analytical index increases the ease of navigating this volume. Therefore, the entries of the *Encyclopedia* are at once simple to read and sophisticated in their discussion of the subjects. This will allow the reader to obtain concise and correct knowledge of the wealth of the literature and culture of Latin America.

Scope

This encyclopedia concentrates only on literary works in the genres of fiction, poetry, and drama. Even though there are great examples of the brilliance, talent, and courage of Latin American visual artists, as well as of musicians, singers, songwriters, and actors, these essays focus on literature printed, mostly in books, but also, as was the case of the work from the colonial period until the early twentieth century, in periodicals containing a literary component.

The editors made the decision, early on in the project, to restrict the scope of the encyclopedia to Latin American writers who wrote or write originally in Spanish and Portuguese. We had to make exceptions in a few cases, because in colonial times some writers wrote in other languages, and in some cases were born in European countries. For these writers, the rationale for their inclusion was the fact that their life and work in Latin America warranted them the title of Founding Mothers of Latin American literature by women. In the case of recent Latin American writers who moved to the US early in their lives and who write in English, the decision was to not include them in the Encyclopedia, because their work is more easily available, in English, under Latina literature.

Because a goal of the Encyclopedia is to have a space both for the canonical and the new writers, the editors sought suggestions from colleagues who work with the literature of specific countries, have a more thorough knowledge of that country's literature, and therefore can more authoritatively suggest names of both the newest and the less widely-known writers. To reach these colleagues in the different countries, the editors placed calls for papers in several media and contacted colleges and universities in all Latin American countries. One of the most satisfying aspects of working with this project has been to encounter new young writers, and to discover the writers from previous centuries whose work is just beginning to be studied and understood. The criteria for the acceptance of an entry on a new writer includes her publication of at least three books, and some measure of critical reception either in her birth country or abroad.

Once the text was received, it was read and critiqued by the two main editors and by at least one member of the Editorial Board. On occasions, when the editors considered that other colleagues were better qualified on the subject of the entry, the texts were also sent to them for their suggestions. All writers of the entries for the encyclopedia are, or have been, professors of Latin American literature in the USA or abroad. This project, in its more than a decade in preparation, has been a community effort. This community is composed of male and female professors who speak several languages, teach at different countries, and at different kinds of universities, but they all have the common desire to make the treasure of Latin American women writers' work available to the world. Other efforts will certainly follow this one, and we, the editors, sincerely hope that our contribution becomes an inspiration to younger colleagues. There are many more brilliant Latin American women writers whose work has not crossed their national frontiers. They await a new generation of students and critics to do them justice.

Finally, since this has been a ten-year long project, and many people helped in different ways to make this Encyclopedia a reality, the editors want to thank, first, all the contributors, who have worked through several rewrites, invited their colleagues to participate, suggested new names, and stayed with us throughout the complex process of securing a publisher. We would also like to thank external reviewers Regina Root, David W. Foster and Jerry Hoeg, whose intellectual support and editorial experience have been invaluable for the completion of this encyclopedia. María Claudia André extends her gratitude to Eva Paulino Bueno for welcoming her on board and for sharing her suggestions and her vision. Eva Paulino Bueno thanks Nora Erro-Peralta, of Florida Atlantic University, with whom she first discussed the project in early 1997; Susan McCarthy, of St. Mary's University, who helped her write a grant request in 2005, and her co-editor, María Claudia André, whose energy, generosity and enthusiasm breathed new life into the project since 2000. Eva Paulino Bueno also wants to thank Terry Caesar, who experienced every one of these ten years and the many struggles in each one of them, but never stopped believing the project would become a book.

Eva Paulino Bueno
María Claudia André

Introduction

The principal justification, at this stage of research on Latin American feminist literary production, for *Latin American Women Writers: An Encyclopedia* is the way in which it continues to define research options, as much as it calls attention to what has been done. Earlier compilations may have served to legitimate a field that was barely acknowledged to exist from the perspective of the canon and to chart the beginnings of this rectification, whether through the so-called discovery of unsung women writers or the registry of what was moving from being a trickle of contemporary women's writing to being the veritable outpouring that is currently the case. Problems of recognition and legitimation may continue, but the reader who wishes to read the work of Latin American women writers no longer has a dearth of titles from which to choose.

The task of creating a record of women's writing was always a clear one, even when it had to be pursued against enormous structural oppositions both from within the academy and society at large: (1) to identify who the women writers were, which was an archeological enterprise of enormous dimensions, especially when many texts remain unpublished and others have been lost; (2) to define multiple feminist traditions, to demonstrate that there had always been women who professed literary creation and that these traditions extended those of hegemonic masculinist ones and, more importantly, that these works were written in opposition, resistance, and often outright defiance of masculine hegemony; (3) to pinpoint in the work of those few women who had (always) been included in the canon what it was about their work that enabled such inclusion, but also in what ways their writing was equally in opposition, resistant, and defiant; and (4) to propose models of cultural study in which women's writing (with all the attendant considerations necessary to reflect on the hypostatization of "woman") can exist, in something like a geometrically modeled metaphor of curriculum construction, both in conjunction with and in counterposition to what remains a strongly masculinist cultural hegemony, in literature no less than in other cultural genres.

To be sure, the preparation of volumes such as this one continues to be necessary in order to contest, and eventually overcome, residual tendencies for the masculinist hegemony to reassert itself in the teaching and research in literature and, more broadly, in general culture. Perhaps this is even more so when dealing with all the different cultures that go into the overarching, and ultimately rather ambiguous, category of "Latin America". One would like to believe that "woman as caboose" is not a preferred remedy, whereby aging course syllabi are supposedly revised to include a measure of women's names according to who is receiving space in scholarly journals and academic conferences, who is getting translated into English, or who is getting enthusiastic endorsement from the liberal press as an eloquent spokeswoman for Latin American sociohistorical affairs and (one hopes) women's lives and women's issues. Since such tactics of supplementarity—whether relating to gender, race and ethnicity, national origin, class, sexual identity or preference, or any other dimension of social subjectivity—are to be resisted strenuously, if one has at least a minimal commitment to multiculturalism, projects organized around these matters must continue to be privileged. This is why those of us who have worked to recognize the crucial role that questions of sexual desire play in cultural production are not content to see Manuel Puig and Luis Zapata included and referred to as "gay" writers, or to see Sor Juana Inés de la Cruz or Gabriela Mistral recognized as "lesbian" writers. Rather, one continues to insist energetically on a queering of the curriculum that will not only trace the role of sexual desire throughout cultural history, but will thoroughly question how it is that, first, a patriarchal model of sexual desire comes to be assumed to be the norm (i.e., what is encompassed by the concept of "heteronormativity"), and how, second, that process of normalization comes to be elided from cultural history in such a way that everything else, if recognized at all, is tagged as "marginal," "subaltern," or even "deviant". The extent to which any subaltern or non-hegemonic group continues to require identification and legitimation makes compilations such as this one necessary scholarly tools.

However, to return to the opening assertion, it would now seem that a major function to be fulfilled by this encyclopedia of Latin American women writers is less to establish the validity of the field, with the attendant functions that such legitimation requires. Rather, it is to serve as a status report for research—now often of considerable depth on many writers and issues—and to point to research directions that might yet be taken. In executing this function, this compilation provides a balanced representation along a number of intellectual field lines. Certainly, representation is of course accorded to those figures who have come to dominate the field and, in addition, to those who have made some sort of secure entry into the canon, to whatever degree it might have become multicultural and, indeed, even rejected as an organizing curricular notion. This is unquestionably the case, for example, with Sor Juana Inés de la Cruz, Rosario Castellanos, or Clarice Lispector. Since the presence of these names in Latin American scholarship antedates a specifically feminist enterprise, it will be valuable to assess how the latter has served to reposition them in terms of the concerns of that enterprise. In the process, the opportunity to gauge the difference between different institutions of scholarship will also emerge, whereby the complex feminist enterprise now characteristic of most of the American and many European academic scenes may clash with the disinterest in and, often, frank repudiation of feminism in the country of origin of a particular writer. This is particularly true in the case of Clarice Lispector, who figures in any respectable inventory of feminist writing elaborated in, say, the US or Britain or France, while in her native Brazil the most translated woman writer from Latin America, when studied programmatically, if at all, is almost never framed in terms of a project of scholarly feminism.

One of the most impressive blocks of names represented is those who have always been on the fringes of the criticism of hegemonic masculinism, whether as something like a radical outsider (Delmira Agustini), or as someone who is directly related to masculinist culture (Cuban independence, in the case of Gertrudis Gómez de Avellaneda). Unless one wishes to affirm that any woman cannot by definition stand outside of feminism, and that her resistance to such a label is part of the complex process of subject positioning, the inclusion of individuals such as Victoria Ocampo, Josefina Pla, Beatriz Sarlo is understandably very problematic, and it becomes necessary to assess—and underscore—how a compilation like the present one is enriched by individuals who never showed much commitment to the issues of feminism, no matter in which terms they are defined. Understandably, Ocampo and Pla belong to an earlier generation in which feminism did not carry the far-ranging theoretical weight it has now come to exercise. In the case of Sarlo, it is debatable whether any of her widely cited research, even the writing on sentimental fiction, has come close to significant feminist issues. Or perhaps it can be demonstrated precisely to initiate a debate of when the case of Latin American indifference to feminism (as much by omission as by commission) is itself of considerable concern to the issues of theoretical feminism. At the same time, one must bear in mind the very real, cogent, and legitimate reasons why there are those Latin American writers and scholars who resist the labels of feminism and may even, indeed, question the need for volumes such as this (or volumes on, say, Jewish writers or lesbian and gay writers). These issues cannot be ignored as we situate ourselves, as self-identified feminist scholars, ethically and ideologically within the cultural debates in whose contexts Latin American women write.

Even though so many Latin American women of intellectual and artistic commitment choose to question the parameters of what is understood as feminism—and they often do so primarily as a rejection of the dominance, the imperialism, some would say, of North American academic institutions—it is intriguing to see the degree to which their production does in fact, echo abiding agendas. Writers such as Ana Lydia Vega, Nora Glickman, Alicia Borinsky, Marjorie Agosín, and Rosario Ferrer understand US and international feminist principles very well, even though each individual will position herself differently with respect to them. In fact, her writing will be an implicit critique of them; it is not possible in any meaningful way to say that by calling them feminist, one is going against the grain of their own self-evaluation. Others, like Alicia Steimberg, Ana María Shua, Alicia Yanez Cossío, are perhaps more problematical in this regard—and, therefore, more interesting.

It is important to resist speaking in terms of the convenient, but potentially very distorting, construct of "Latin America". US scholarship needs the denomination for structural and disciplinary reasons, but social and political life is very different from one region to another and even within one single country. Thus, a compilation of this sort, in addition to opening up the Pandora's box of who is included and for what reasons (for example, US Latina writers are excluded), along with the problematics of feminist designations, can also lead to fruitful considerations with respect to exactly how valid the concept of a unified field of Latin American writing really is and how it is to be conjugated with other regional/national definitions.

Finally, this project, as already stated, serves to provide the basis for much needed additional scholarship. Many of these writers, no matter how good the intentions of the multicultural teacher and researcher might be, are not likely to be studied as part of the curricular mainstream. For example, as much of a giant in contemporary Paraguayan culture as Josefina Pla has been, she simply does not exist in terms of the dominant core of studies. If Paraguayan culture is destined to be marginalized, Paraguayan women writers will be doubly so. If queer writing is still either an absent or very fringe component of the central core of the critical enterprise, lesbian writers are likely to remain on those fringes. The same may be said for those who represent ethnic subalternities, such as Jewish culture, a very important emergent component, along with queer studies, of Latin American studies.

Latin American Women Writers: An Encyclopedia represents an important opportunity for writers whose work may fall outside a Spanish (or Portuguese) language core. Flora Tristán may now be read in Spanish translation, but one wonders what will happen as a consequence of Rosario Ferrer's highly controversial decision to write in English. Are these works no longer part of the Hispanic Studies classroom (as English-language Latina writing also customarily is not) because they are in English, irrespective of the question of whether or not they constitute a betrayal of a "real" Puerto Rican identity, held in place by the Spanish language? And, also, popular writing is not likely to make it into the core research and teaching and be only represented in compilations of this sort. Certainly, if women's writing means alternatives to masculinist models, then it is reasonable to include a song writer like Violeta Parra.

Finally, a salient feature of this encyclopedia is the presence of entries prepared by male scholars. While there may still be vibrant discussions regarding "men in feminism," there is a need to question the essentialist premise that only women can profitably engage in feminist scholarship. If it were not for feminism, there would likely not be any masculinist or queer studies, and the totality of the interlocking points of the gender studies triangle are now pretty much understood by newer generations of researchers to be pertinent to both/all genders.

In sum, *Latin American Women Writers: An Encyclopedia* is more than just another contribution to the legitimation of women's writing and scholarship on it. It is much more of a status report: here are those whom we are studying—and here we are, those who are doing that studying—and these are the issues to which we are attending. Here are the writers who have now attracted an impressive bibliography of criticism and who can be said to have found a secure niche in the curriculum. But here are also those writers who may never make it into the classroom, but who flesh out an agenda of the study of women's ever more impressive cultural production.

David William Foster

ABSATZ, CECILIA

Cecilia Absatz was born in 1943 in Buenos Aires, Argentina. Following studies at the University of Buenos she successfully established a career for herself in the fields of publishing, journalism, and advertising in the mid-1960s. She has worked in several capacities – from columnist to editor – for a variety of reputable magazines and newspapers in Buenos Aires in addition to writing for television. Furthermore, Absatz is a professional translator and well- known writer.

Author

As a writer, Absatz has been a constant contributor to Argentine literature since the 1970s. Her first book, *Feiguele y otras mujeres* (Feiguele and Other Women), was published in 1976. It opens with the eponymous novella "Feiguele," which is followed by six short stories about the "other women" mentioned in the title. With this publication Absatz firmly set the foundation for her subsequent works that continue her effort to represent feminine identity within the confines of masculinist Argentine culture and society. Just three months after its publication, *Feiguele y otras mujeres* was banned by the military junta then in power in Argentina. The official justification for proscribing the book was immoral content. Moreover, the military's persecution of the Ediciones de la Flor publishing house may have played a significant role in prohibiting its circulation in bookstores. In "Feiguele" the title character narrates the story of her youth in a middle-class family of Polish-Jewish immigrants in Buenos Aires. Feiguele is an awkward teenager who struggles with issues of insecurity based on her physical appearance and her Jewishness, both of which are sources of alienation for the young girl. Her foreign-sounding name sets her apart and marks her as an outsider. In time she learns to turn the ostracism she suffers into a source of empowerment and independence. Her greatest weapon of self-defense is her humor and talent for sharp sarcasm, which she wields against her peers with great efficiency. The text does an excellent job at portraying both the immigrant Yiddishkeit culture of her family and the character's emerging feminist awareness. Other stories in the collection depict equally resilient female characters, though they are much older and experienced. A common denominator in these stories and other works by Absatz is an overt erotic dimension played out through the open expression of sexuality by the characters. This unapologetically feminine eroticism is what led to the book being labeled, and banned, as immoral. Through the stories, Absatz takes on *machista* Argentine society as her characters struggle with the limitations placed on them and find ways to overcome obstacles in the search for liberation. *Feiguele y otras mujeres* survived its stifled appearance to become somewhat of a classic work from the 1970s, and it was reissued in 2002.

With the publication of two novels in the 1980s Absatz clearly established herself as a literary figure in Argentina. Her 1982 novel, *Té con canela* (Tea with Cinnamon), continued the author's primary thematic concerns, though it is quite different in its structure. The text is comprised of narrative fragments that loosely fit together as a series of the main character's internal meditations as she undertakes an examination of her life following an emotional crisis. As she struggles to come to terms with recent events in her life she learns to reconstruct her identity with a different, more psychologically healthy set of ideals while at the same time rejecting much of society's expectations of her. Absatz's keen sense of humor and penchant for weaving eroticism into her work are also present in this novel. With the publication of *Los años pares* (The Even-Numbered Years) in 1985, Absatz returned to a more conventional novelistic style. The novel is circular in its temporal structure, beginning in 1980, then going back in time to the late 1970s, and returning to 1980 by the end. This time frame clearly situates the novel during the period of brutal repression by the military dictatorship. As in "Feiguele," identity (specifically Jewish and female identity) is central to the development of the plot. When she attempts to renew her national identification card, Clara, the protagonist, encounters difficulty stemming from confusion over her surname, which significantly is Ausländer (German for "foreigner" or "outsider"). Events that follow lead her to scrutinize her European ancestry and, perhaps more importantly, her identity as a woman and the value of her independence.

It wasn't until the mid-1990s that Cecilia Absatz published the next additions to her literary corpus. Her novel, *¿Dónde estás amor de mi vida, que no te puedo encontrar?* (1995, Where Are You Love of My Life, that I Cannot Find You?) is based on a highly successful television mini-series by the same title that she scripted. Juan José Jusid—a well-known contemporary filmmaker in Argentina—directed the television series and also made a feature film version. On the title page, Absatz acknowledges that the novel is based on Jusid's idea. The writing, however, is clearly identifiable as characteristic of Absatz's style, humor, and critical view. Nevertheless, the content does differ quite radically from her previous texts and reflects the time that had passed and the political, social, and economic changes that Argentina had undergone since the publication of *Los años pares* a decade before. This latest novel contains neither the references to the violent past of the dictatorship nor complex positions on issues of identity. The action of the novel revolves around a call-in radio show and its two hosts: Octavio Luz, a famous radio personality, and Liliana Milman, a psychoanalyst. The radio show features calls from the lonely and lovelorn inhabitants of the greater Buenos Aires metropolis. The undefined space of radio provides common ground for callers of different social backgrounds to reach out to one another in search of human companionship through the promise of potential amorous or platonic relationships. These episodes revolve around the core narrative of the budding romantic relationship between the two hosts themselves.

A second book, also published in 1995, is a collection of essays rather than a novel. Absatz's *Mujeres peligrosas: la pasión según el teleteatro* (Dangerous Women: Passion According to the Soap Operas) contains a series of essays on popular culture. Her focus is mainly on the influence of foreign popular culture within Argentine society. To that end, she compares Argentine, Mexican, Brazilian, and American soap operas in an effort to examine the roles of women, feminist issues and passion as they are played out on television. She also looks at American situation comedies like *Murphy Brown* and *Roseanne*, both popular in Argentina in the 1990s. In addition, Absatz compares a wide range of literature from Latin America, Europe and the United States in order to underscore a variety of women's issues. One of the more remarkable aspects of *Mujeres peligrosas* is the author's ability to manage such a diverse body of popular culture samplings (which include the rock lyrics of Pink Floyd, *The Simpsons*, the fiction of Stephen King, the novels of Argentine writer Marta Lynch, and the soap opera *Simplemente María*) in order to provide a compelling and amusing analysis of the situation and image of contemporary women in Western society.

Critical Appraisals

While Cecilia Absatz's work has been widely praised in reviews and well received by the reading public, it has thus far garnered less critical attention than that of many of her contemporaries. Nevertheless, there are a number of fine analytical examinations of her work, which readily lends itself to a feminist critical reading. Almost all critical appraisals of her work focus in some way on the multifaceted main topic of identity (Jewish, feminine, Argentine) that time and again surfaces in her writing. One topic that so far has not been explored in Absatz's work is her utilization of humor as central to her narrative project.

DARRELL B. LOCKHART

Selected Works

Feiguele y otras mujeres. Buenos Aires: Ediciones de la Flor, 1976.

Té con canela. Buenos Aires: Sudamericana, 1982.

Los años pares. Buenos Aires: Legasa, 1985.

¿Dónde estás amor de mi vida, que no te puedo encontrar? Buenos Aires: Espasa Calpe/Seix Barral, 1995.

Mujeres peligrosas: la pasión según el teleteatro. Buenos Aires: Planeta, 1995.

References and Further Reading

Flori, Mónica. "Identidad y discurso de la femineidad en *Los años pares* de Cecilia Absatz". *Explicación de textos literarios* 22(2) (1993–94): 87–97.

——. "Cecilia Absatz". In Mónica Flori (ed.), *Streams of Silver: Six Contemporary Women Writers from Argentina*. Lewisburg, NJ: Bucknell University Press, 1995, pp. 185–213.

Foster, David William. "Buenos Aires: Feminine Space". In David William Foster (ed.), *Buenos Aires: Perspectives on the City and Cultural Production*. Gainesville, FL: University of Florida Press, 1998, pp. 101–31.

Gimbernat González, Ester. "En los nones de *Los años pares*". In Ester Gimbernat González (ed.), *Aventuras del desacuerdo: novelistas argentinas de los 80*. Buenos Aires: Danilo Albero Vergara, 1992, pp. 94–9.

ACOSTA DE SAMPER, SOLEDAD

Soledad Acosta de Samper (1833–1913) is one of the most important Colombian writers of the nineteenth century and her prolific work, like that of many other female writers of her time, has not received the deserved attention. Soledad Acosta de Samper was born in Santa Fe, Bogotá in 1833 when this city was the capital of the Republic of Nueva Granada. She was the only daughter of Joaquín Acosta (a historian, geographer, diplomat and a general who participated in the wars of independence) and Carolina Kemble, an American citizen. Undoubtedly such a lineage was perceived as something positive in her time: her father was one of the founders of the nation, while her mother symbolized the perceived foreign civilizing influence. They provided her with a broad education, from an early age allowing her to lead an intellectual lifestyle, something uncommon for women at the time. She completed her elementary studies in the school La Merced, Bogotá, and in 1845 she traveled to Halifax (Nova Scotia, Canada) where she lived with her maternal grandmother for a year while she continued her education. Between the ages of 13 and 17, she lived in Paris with her parents. There she received part of her formal education and frequently visited social gatherings where she met many important European writers. While she learned English and Spanish at and early age, in Paris she also learned French, an achievement which differentiated her from most other women at the time who were, for the most part, educated only to perform household duties. In spite of her exceptional education she was also subject to a strict tutelage regarding traditional values which distanced her from her parents. Flor María Rodríguez-Arenas tells us of the author's childhood developed in an environment where she had little contact with her parents: "As an only child, she grew up in a quiet and harsh home, isolated mentally from her mother by her strict education and religious inclinations and she was physically distanced from her father due to the many engagements he had taken on as a writer, diplomat, naturalist and military person" (our translation, Rodríguez-Arenas, 2004: 133). In 1850, she returned to Bogotá with her family and in 1855 she married the writer and politician José María Samper Agudelo. Before her marriage, between 1853 and 1855, she kept what became a 750-page diary, where she gives a detailed account of her relationship with José María Samper until the time they married. This narrative which includes current events of her time makes reference to other diaries, which unfortunately have never been discovered. The couple had four daughters, two of whom died at an early age (12 and 15) during an epidemic in October 1872.

During the seven years that they lived in Paris, she wrote her first book *Recuerdos de Suiza* and became a correspondent for two important Latin American newspapers, the *Biblioteca de Señoritas* and *El Mosaico de Bogotá* as well as to the Peruvian newspaper *El Comercio* where she wrote daily accounts of her life and fashion reviews. She also published her own translations in her *Revista Parisina* while she worked with her husband editing and writing for the newspapers he directed. Her first collaborations were penned under different pseudonyms, such as Andina, Betrilda, Aldebarán and Renato. In 1862, the Samper-Acosta family moved to Lima, Peru where José María Samper was contracted as the chief editor of the *El Comercio* newspaper. On his return to Bogotá in 1863, José María Samper was once again named a member of Congress and became an important figure in Colombian politics. It was during these years in Bogotá that Soledad Acosta began publishing short stories and serialized novels in literary magazines.

In 1875, her husband was imprisoned and she was forced to become the sole provider for her family. During these years, using the knowledge and experience she had acquired working with her husband she founded her own magazines, written and directed by women – *El Domingo de la familia cristiana* (1889–90) and *La mujer. Revista quincenal redactada por señoras y señoritas* (1878–81) – which aimed especially at helping and giving advice to women on household matters. They dealt mostly with children's education and fashion but also published romantic novels and biographies of famous women.

When José María Samper died in 1888, Soledad Acosta de Samper returned to Paris. In 1892, she was named the official Colombian delegate to the "IX Congreso Internacional de Americanisistas" which was held in the Rábida Convent in Spain and represented Colombia in the fourth centenary celebration of the discovery of the Americas. She died in 1913 in Bogotá.

As was common for many female writers of her time, although her work was published in newspapers and magazines, she did not lead a public life as one. The education she received distanced her from most women of her time and as a consequence she led what could be described as a double life; on the one hand she was trapped by the condition of being a woman, and on the other she excelled in a trade that was for the most part reserved for men.

Work

As a result of the extraordinary number of newspaper and magazine publications that Soledad Acosta de Samper wrote, there is no complete collection of her works and unfortunately her work is not currently being reedited because of the difficulties in accessing her articles which are only stored either on microfilm or in the few remaining editions that she published. She is supposed to have written over 20 novels, 50 short stories and hundreds of articles on a variety of topics. Among her most important publications we find the magazine *La Mujer* (1878–81) which was written exclusively by women and was published under Soledad de Samper's management. She also directed the publishing of *El domingo de la familia cristiana* (1889–90), a weekly magazine. In Belgium, in 1869, she published a volume titled *Novelas y Cuadros de la vida sud-americana*, with many stories, articles on local customs and traditions and three novels: *Dolores, Teresa la limeña* and *El corazón de la mujer*. Her memories of Switzerland and her travels through Europe, her first literary productions, constitute a series of articles which were published first in the *Biblioteca de Señoritas* in 1858 in Bogotá, later in *El Mosaico*, under the pseudonym *Andina*, and finally they were completed in *La Mujer*. In 1863, she also published *Elementos de higiene general* in *La Revista Americana*, a translation of *Eléments d'hygiène générale* by Doctor Louis Cruveilhier.

From 1880 onwards, Soledad Acosta chose studies of a more historical nature. The following works belong to this period: *Biografía del General Joaquín Paris* (prize-winning work in the *Concurso Histórico-literario* of Bogotá), *Biografías de hombres ilustres ó notables* and *Los Piratas en Cartagena*. She also wrote many historical fictions such as: *La venganza de un piloto, El Almirante Corsario Francisco Drake, Los Filibusteros y Sancho Jimeno, El Obispo Piedrahita y el Filibustero Morgan* and *La expedición del Almirante Vernón*, among others.

Themes

Soledad Acosta de Samper wrote for approximately 60 years in every literary genre: journalism, translations, travel journals, romantic novels, local customs narratives, literary criticism, letters, theatre, historical novels, short stories, biographies and essays. While most male writers of her time focused their work exclusively on the foundation of the nation, Soledad Acosta de Samper also dealt with the daily life and traditions of her native land and the condition of women. She was especially interested in exploring ways in which women could participate in the founding of the nation, breaking away from the stereotypes created by men that relegated them to being only teachers, nurses and mothers. Soledad Acosta de Samper, without distancing herself completely from the ideals of progress and civilization created by men, acquired a place of power and authority (which was reserved for men from the literary elite) to instruct her intellectually neglected female readership. Soledad Acosta de Samper's epistolary style of writing was very effective, as she was able to include letters in her novels with great ability. This genre must have been natural to her as throughout her life she stayed in epistolary contact with many people, both for social reasons and due to her work as an editor. *Dolores. Cuadros de la vida de una mujer* was unfortunately published in 1867, the same year that Jorge Isaac's immensely popular novel *María* appeared and therefore didn't receive much attention. Only in recent years have literary critics discovered the works of this prolific Colombian writer, and have began to recompile and study her extensive body of work. During her last years, the romantic voice of her early texts is replaced by a more didactic one culminating in essays and history books. *La mujer en la sociedad moderna* (1895), a re-edited compilation of articles and writings is one of her most important essays. The two themes that she focuses on are the motherland (the formation of the American nations) and women; especially the way in which women can be a part of national projects in a useful and healthy way.

ANA MARIA CAULA

Selected Works

Conversaciones y lecturas familiares: sobre historia, biografía, crítica, literatura, ciencias y conocimientos útiles. Paris: Garnier Hermanos, 1896.

Novelas y cuadros de vida suramericana. Ed. Flor Maria Rodríguez-Arenas. Bogotá: Universidad de los Andes, 2004.

Soledad Acosta de Samper: escritura, género y nación en el siglo XIX. Ed. Carolina Alzate and Montserrat Ordóñez. Madrid: Iberoamericana, 2005.

References and Further Reading

Ordóñez, Montserrat. "Introducción. Soledad Acosta de Samper: Una nueva lectura". *Soledad Acosta de Samper: Una nueva lectura. Antología*. Bogotá: Fondo Cultural Cafetero, 1988.

Otero Muñoz, Gustavo. "Doña Soledad Acosta de Samper". *Boletín de Historia y Antigüedades* 229 (1933): 169–75.

Rivera Martínez, Edgardo. "*Teresa la limeña*, una desconocida novela de Soledad Acosta de Sam[per]". *Scientia Omni* 1 (Mar. 1997): 201–30.

Rodríguez-Arenas, Flor María. "Soledad Acosta de Samper: Pionera de la profesionalización en la escritura femenina colombiana: *Dolores*, *Teresa la limeña* y *El corazón de la mujer* (1869)". In *¿Y las mujeres? Ensayos sobre literatura colombiana*. Medellín: Editorial U de Antioquia, 1991.

Samper Trainer, Santiago. "Soledad Acosta de Samper. El eco de un grito". In Magdala Velásquez (ed.), *Las mujeres en la historia de Colombia*. Vol. I. Bogotá: Presidencia de la República y Norma, 1995.

AGOSÍN, MARJORIE

Chilean author, academic, and activist, Marjorie Agosín was born in 1955 in Bethesda, Maryland, by an accident of circumstance. Her father, a physician and research scientist, had come to the United States on a grant. Shortly after Agosín's birth, the family moved back to their native Chile where she was raised between Santiago and the southern region of the country. Grandparents on both sides of the family were Eastern European Jewish emigrants who arrived in Chile at the beginning of the twentieth century. In Santiago, Agosín received her early education at the Instituto Hebreo (Hebrew Institute) where she became proficient in Hebrew in addition to her native Spanish. Given the turbulent political situation of the early 1970s that culminated in the *coup d'état* which put General Augusto Pinochet in power, Agosín's parents moved the family back to the United States. The family settled in Georgia where Agosín received an undergraduate degree before going on to complete a PhD in Latin American literature from Indiana University with a doctoral dissertation on Chilean writer María Luisa Bombal (1910–80). Marjorie Agosín has been a professor at Wellesley College for more than twenty years, where she has established a considerable reputation as a scholar and creative writer. In addition to being a prolific literary author, she has published numerous anthologies of Latin American women's writing, and edited various collections of critical essays on a wide range of topics in the field of Latin American studies. She is a tireless advocate of human rights, with a particular emphasis on documenting the struggles of Latin American women's groups such as the Mothers of the Plaza de Mayo in Argentina and the Chilean *arpilleristas*. Much of Agosín's work addresses Jewish issues—from personal family history to the Holocaust—with a primary focus on the Jewish experience in Latin America from a decidedly feminine perspective (Lockhart, "Lo judío"). Reflective of her divided experience between Chile and the United States, the preponderance of Agosín's work is available in both Spanish and English translation with most of her poetry collections being bilingual editions.

The Poet

Marjorie Agosín began her literary career as a poet and the vast majority of her writing pertains to this genre. Indeed, even her prose is heavily influenced by the eloquent lyricism of her poetic voice. Her poetry covers a wide range of topics, but it is defined by Agosín's ability to convey a deep sense of empathy and passion for the human condition in relation, above all, to social matters. Poetry in Agosín's literary universe comprises a diverse geographical, historical, political, and societal map that is at once individual and collective, regional and universal. Her first book of poetry, *Conchalí* (1980), named after Santiago's Jewish cemetery, initiates a global voyage that will take the poet across borders and into territories rich in expression and thematic content. For example, in *Toward the Splendid City* (1994), Agosín's poems take the reader to places both far and near: Jerusalem, Amsterdam, Isla Negra, Baghdad, Odessa, Auschwitz, Boston, Teotihuacán, Valparaíso, Venice, and Virginia City, Nevada, to name but a few. Other poems in the volume explore sites that exist as undefined spaces in the poet's imagination or memory. In *Generous Journeys* (1992), the poet travels throughout Latin America by way of food native to the New World. Here she invokes intertexuality with Pablo Neruda's famous *Odas elementales*, many of which are dedicated to food. Similarly, in many of her poems—as well as in her scholarly work—Agosín turns to Chile's other poet of international fame, Gabriela Mistral. At the heart of her poetic voyage is her attention to detailing women's lives and issues, as can readily be seen in her poems dedicated to other women writers in *Brujas y algo más* (1984) or her representation of the political struggles of women as seen in her *Circles of Madness* (1992) on the Mothers of the Plaza de Mayo in Argentina, as well the effects and circumstances of oppression (*Zones of Pain*; 1988). In other volumes, Agosín provides an intimate perspective on historical figures as revealed in her poetic dialogue with Anne Frank (*Dear Anne Frank*, 1994) or on a more personal level with her own forebears in *The Angel of*

Memory (2001)—with her great-grandmother—and *Poems for Josefina* (2004)—with her grandmother. Another constant in Agosín's writing is the representation of feminine desire and the esthetics of eroticism. While these elements are present in almost all her collections, volumes such as *Hogueras* (1990) and especially *Noche estrellada* (1996) stand out as examples of this type of writing. *Noche estrellada* is particularly noteworthy for its development of erotic desire as a poetic endeavor. Agosín's approach is unique in this volume that at first glance is seemingly a homage to the painter Vincent van Gogh, but upon a closer reading functions as a pseudo-autobiographical exploration of the poet's own erotic agenda.

Jewishness is also at the core of much of Agosín's writing. Poems included in her many collections highlight Jewish themes that fall into several categories, whether it be historical topics on immigration and exile, geographical spaces with Jewish resonance (Prague, Jerusalem, Auschwitz), or persons who represent Jewish strength, suffering or intellect inspired by relatives (grandparents, aunts and uncles, parents), figures from Jewish tradition (Eve, Lilith), or history (Anne Frank). Agosín's relation to the Holocaust is readily apparent in her writing, as an extension of the part it played in altering her family history. She uses poetry – and memoir – as a vehicle for reconstructing lives that were either fragmented or destroyed by Nazi terror. As previously mentioned, Anne Frank occupies the place of privilege in Agosín's poetry, having appeared in several poems even prior to the publication of *Dear Anne Frank*, which is the culmination of her effort to engage the memory of Frank through poetry, not as a martyr, hero or victim, but rather as a way of discovering the young girl lost behind the famous personage. The poetic voice speaks in the second person directing personal questions to Anne Frank that at times are trivial and at others painful. As is common in her poetry, Agosín finds ways to make specific histories universal by linking commonalities. For example, she relates the circumstances of the Holocaust as experienced by Anne Frank to the sociopolitical realities of violence and oppression under neofascist military regimes in Chile and Argentina. In this way, *Dear Anne Frank* becomes a book that is much broader than the focus of the title would indicate and in fact serves the purpose of underscoring the themes of social injustice, suffering, and the beauty of human spirit wherever they may be found. Agosín approaches the Holocaust in a more intimate vein by making her great-grandmother, Helena Broder, the subject of *The Angel of Memory*. By tracing her memory and history from pre-war Vienna to Chile, the poems provide eloquent ponderings on the effects of the Holocaust, those who perished, and the way in which it irrevocably marked the course of history. Poems such as "Unpredictable Northern Train," "Helena Broder Sobs Over Terezin," and "Passover in Chile" are painful but beautifully written texts that bring to the fore the topics of inhumanity, despair, violence, and loss. As a whole the volume is an admirable tribute to Agosín's forebear, but it is also a text that speaks to the universality of the Holocaust as an experience of human disaster and perseverance.

The Memoirist

In addition to being a prolific poet, Marjorie Agosín has written several works of prose, which often are difficult to characterize in terms of conventional narrative forms. *La felicidad* (1991, Happiness) is a volume of texts that conform to the genre of the short story for the most part, but *Las alfareras* (1994, The Women Potters) consists of a series of brief texts that defy such a definition. Both texts continue many of the topics touched upon throughout Agosín's poetry. It is her trilogy of memoirs that have garnered the majority of critical attention and public acclaim. *A Cross and a Star: Memoirs of a Jewish Girl in Chile* (1995), *Always from Somewhere Else: A Memoir of My Chilean Jewish Father* (1998), and *The Alphabet in My Hands: A Writing Life* (2000) are structured as a kind of ongoing family history. The first volume focuses on the memories of Frida, Agosín's mother, but told from the perspective of the daughter. In this way the mother's story is mediated through the daughter's narrative. The reader follows the family's migratory trajectory from Europe to Chile and the struggles in the Southern Cone country upon settling there. The second volume centers on the story of Agosín's father, one of the first Jewish physicians in Chile. Finally, in the third memoir, Agosín writes of her own experience. All three volumes follow the same format of brief narrative pieces that together weave a family history told against the backdrop of Europe, Chile, and the United States. These memoirs may be read as pseudo-novels that combine history, (auto)biography, anecdote, and visual archive (all containing photographs of Agosín and several generations of her family) in a style that is articulate, intimate, and informative. One of the more appealing and interesting aspects of the books is found in the inclusion of the photographs as part of the narrative, which provide an intimate view into the family history and lend a quality of authenticity to the story. Moreover, the photos go beyond the limits of the personal and become part of a larger narrative on history and collective memory.

Critical approaches to Agosín's work were somewhat late in appearing in comparison with the number of years she has been writing and the quantity of books she has authored. The collection of essays edited by Emma Sepúlveda-Pulvirenti represents the most complete examination of her work thus far. Marjorie Agosín's indefatigable efforts to promote women's writing and her particularly feminist articulation of the issues that affect Latin American women in general have made her a prominent figure and earned her a reputation in both academic and non-academic circles. Her own literary project – her many books may be read as a single ongoing work – constitutes a unique talent in women's writing expressed through her lyrical, feminist, and always engaging voice. Further, her contributions to the field of Latin American Jewish studies and literature have been at the forefront of this burgeoning field of academic inquiry.

DARRELL B. LOCKHART

Selected Works

Conchalí. New York: Senda Nueva de Ediciones, 1980.

Brujas y algo más / Witches and Other Things. Trans. Cola Franzen. Pittsburgh, PA: Latin American Literary Review Press, 1984.

Women of Smoke / Mujeres de humo. Trans. Naomi Lindstrom. Pittsburgh, PA: Latin American Literary Review Press, 1988.

Zones of Pain / Las zonas del dolor. Trans. Cola Franzen. Fredonia, New York: White Pine Press, 1988.

Hogueras / Bonfires. Tempe, AZ: Bilingual Press, 1990.

La felicidad. Santiago: Cuarto Propio, 1991.

Circles of Madness: Mothers of the Plaza de Mayo. Trans. Celeste Kostopulos-Cooperman. New York: White Pine Press, 1992.

Generous Journeys / Travesías generosas. Trans. Cola Franzen. Reno, NE: The Blackrock Press, 1992.

Happiness. Trans. Elizabeth Horan. New York: White Pine Press, 1993.

Las alfareras. Santiago: Cuarto Propio, 1994.

Sargazo / Sargasso: poemas. Trans. Richard Schaaf. Tempe, AZ: Bilingual Press/Editorial Bilingüe, 1994.

Dear Anne Frank: Poems. Bilingual edition, trans. Richard Schaaf. Washington, DC: Azul Editions, 1994.

Toward the Splendid City. Trans. Richard Schaaf. Tempe, AZ: Bilingual Press/Editorial Bilingüe, 1994.

A Cross and a Star: Memoirs of a Jewish Girl in Chile. Albuquerque, NM: University of New Mexico Press, 1995.

Noche estrellada. Santiago: LOM Ediciones, 1996.

El consejo de las hadas / Council of Fairies. Falls Church, VA: Azul Editions, 1997.

Melodious Women. Trans. Monica Bruno Galmozzi. Pittsburgh, PA: Latin American Literary Review Press, 1997.

An Absence of Shadows. Trans. Celeste Kostopulos-Cooperman, Cola Franzen and Mary G. Berg. New York: White Pine Press, 1998.

Always from Somewhere Else: A Memoir of My Chilean Jewish Father. New York: The Feminist Press at the City University of New York, 1998.

The Alphabet in My Hands: A Writing Life. New Brunswick, NJ: Rutgers University Press, 1999.

El gesto de la ausencia. Santiago: Cuarto Propio, 1999.

Lluvia en el desierto / Rain in the Desert. Trans. Celeste Kostopulos-Cooperman. Santa Fe, NM: Sherman Asher Publishing, 1999.

The Angel of Memory / El angel de la memoria. Trans. Brigid A. Milligan and Laura Rocha Nakazawa. San Antonio, TX: Wings Press, 2001.

Poems for Josefina / Poemas para Josefina. Santa Fe, NM: Sherman Asher Publishing, 2004.

References and Further Reading

Bornstein-Gómez, Miriam. "Marjorie Agosín: identidad judía y la apertura del espacio". *Taller de letras* 36 (2005): 55–71.

Hall, Nancy Abraham. "Introduction". In Marjorie Agosín, *The Alphabet in My Hands*, 1999, pp. xvii–xxiv.

Horan, Elizabeth Rosa. "Marjorie Agosín". In Darrell B. Lockhart (ed.), *Latin American Jewish Writers: A Dictionary*. New York: Garland, 1997, pp. 7–13.

——. "Introduction". In Marjorie Agosín, *Always from Somewhere Else*, 1998, pp. 11–47.

Kostopulos-Cooperman, Celeste. "Introduction". In Marjorie Agosín, *A Cross and a Star*, 1995, pp. vii–xxi.

Lockhart, Darrell B. "La representación de lo judío en la escritura de Marjorie Agosín". In *Memorial de una escritura: aproximaciones a la obra de Marjorie Agosín*. Santiago: Cuarto Propio, 2002, pp. 45–61.

Rubio, Patricia. "Los discursos de la memoria en la prosa de Marjorie Agosín". *Taller de letras* 25 (1997): 77–90.

Sepúlveda-Pulvirenti, Emma (ed.) *Memorial de una escritura: aproximaciones a la obra de Marjorie Agosín*. Santiago: Cuarto Propio, 2002.

AGUSTINI, DELMIRA

Delmira Agustini (1886–1914) was born in Montevideo, Uruguay. She was the second child of an upper middle-class family with German, Argentinean and French roots. Her mother, María Murtfeldt, was a powerful figure in Agustini's life. A former teacher, María educated her daughter at home, along with private tutors, and her presence is often referred to as possessive towards Agustini and obsessive with her daughter's talents. According to some critics, both parents were indeed involved in what seemed to them the formation of a genius, to the point of consciously deciding not to have any more children, a bold move during the conservative times of the turn-of-the-nineteenth century. However extraordinary, Agustini was trained in the typical fashion of the times for a woman of her social status. She studied piano, painting and French, and rarely left the house without her parents. Her readings were extensive but unsystematic. Kind, polite, and submissive toward her mother, are typical descriptions of Agustini's personality. At a young age, however, she found her passion in poetry, starting to compose poems that soon were inflamed with eroticism. Her father, Santiago Agustini, a devoted Catholic, transcribed these poems in the morning (Delmira composed at night), in the ambience of reverence and silence that saturated their home. Agustini was soon publishing in journals such as *La Alborada*, where she also had a society column under a pen-name typical of the style of the period: "Joujou". Her first collected poems, published in 1907, had an almost immediate positive reception among major intellectuals of her time. Shortly, Delmira Agustini was included in the respected generation of Uruguayan authors termed by Alberto Zum Felde as "la Generación del 900" (the Nine-hundreds Generation). José Enrique Rodó, Florencio Sánchez, Horacio Quiroga, Julio Herrera y Reissig, Eduardo Acevedo Díaz, were part of this influential generation of intellectuals and writers that helped to define modern Uruguayan socio-cultural landscape.

Delmira Agustini's writings followed, while personalizing the prominent Latin American literary movement called *modernismo*, a genuine style inspired by French Parnassians and Symbolists that accentuated linguistic and formal renovation (very different in style and period from Anglo-American "modernism"). Eroticism and exoticism were part of the *modernista*'s mode, often expressed through the literary representation of women as objects of the poet's sumptuous aesthetic experience. Although *modernismo*, a movement that emerged at the end of the nineteenth century, was declining by the time Agustini published her books, it continued its significant influence in Latin America well into the first decades of the twentieth century. In fact, Alberto Zum Felde also noted in his appreciation of "la Generación del 900" that the qualities and complexities of this Uruguayan period extended the turn of the century into the first two decades of the new century, making *modernista* style particularly relevant.

The Myth of "La Nena" (The Baby) and "La Pitonisa" (The Pythoness)

The fundamental contradiction between the moral restrictive values imposed on the women of the period and the literary freedom and recognition that Demira Agustini enjoyed, reflected her own dual projection that would contribute to her myth. In the domestic and social realm she was called among friends and family, "La Nena" (The Baby), an appellation that responded to her projection as a devoted daughter and obedient member of a bourgeois society that was in tune with the European constrictions on women typical of the period. Agustini embraced this designation and portrayed herself as a child in her letters, particularly with her boyfriend of over five years, Enrique Job Reyes, an auctioneer and a man completely removed from the literary arena. In these letters, Agustini mimics the language of children in frivolous messages with erotic undertones that occasionally offered startling metaphors that would appear in her poetry. In fact, this accepting role as "La Nena" seemed to function as a mask that, according to Emir Rodríguez Monegal, hid the real Agustini: la Pitonisa (the "Pythoness"), a strong-minded, energetic and sexual woman who was revealed in Agustini's poems.

This tension in personalities surfaced in a different exchange of letters with her intellectual friends, where Agustini would express herself in a literary manner, stressing her anguish as an artist. This was the case with her brief epistolary exchange with renowned Nicaraguan poet Rubén Darío, the prime representative and promoter of Latin American and Spanish *modernismo*. Delmira Agustini had read the French poets that inspired the *modernista* movement and was familiar with major Latin American and Spanish authors of this style, particularly Darío. The renowned poet visited Delmira Agustini during his Latin American tour in 1912, a decisive encounter for Agustini's life and works. The meeting produced a brief exchange of letters. In Agustini's letters to her admired Darío, she displays her sense of authorship and reveals her inner self as a "confession". The bard's short responses to these letters were respectful but detached. Darío also wrote a "Pórtico" to Agustini's *Cálices vacíos* (Empty Chalices), published in 1913, where the author exalts her writings while calling Agustini, in a typical *modernista* style, "niña bella" (pretty child) and "deliciosa musa" (delicious muse).

This discrepancy between Agustini's own tension of personalities and the paternalistic response from her literary friends and peers was evident upon her marriage. On August 14, 1913, Delmira Agustini married Enrique Job Reyes. Attending the ceremony were some of the most illustrious names of her times such as Juan Zorrilla de San Martín; Carlos Vaz Ferreira; his sister and poet, good friend of Delmira, María Eugenia Vaz Ferreira; and Manuel Ugarte, a writer with whom Agustini had an intense epistolary romance. Prior to the wedding, and during the wedding itself, Agustini expressed doubts to her closest friends and peers: "¿Firmo o no firmo?" (Do I sign [the marriage contract] or not?) (Silva 1968: 108). The answer reported from witnesses such as Manuel Ugarte and André Giot de Badet is of surprise: "¡Escándalo! Todos la hacen razonar, insisten . . ." (Scandalous! Everyone makes her see reason, insists on it) (Silva 1968: 108).

A few weeks after the wedding, Agustini left her husband and returned home famously pronouncing these words: "No puedo soportar tanta vulgaridad" (I cannot stand such vulgarity) (Silva 1968: 62). In November of the same year, Agustini filed for divorce. She was the first to apply under a new law that allowed women to claim divorce as their sole decision. The divorce was granted on June 5, 1914. During all this process, however, the couple continued to exchange passionate notes and had secret sexual encounters. In one of these meetings, on July 6, 1914, Enrique Job Reyes shot Delmira Agustini dead and killed himself. The murder was widely publicized by the press, creating a spectacle and morbid fascination with this tragic event that still prevails.

A Product of her Time

Delmira Agustini's biography and unique literary success had a lot to do with the specific historical moment that the poet used to her advantage, but perhaps also contributed to her tragic end. Agustini was born at the end of a military regime and she matured in a general process of modernization emphasized by the progressive government of José Batlle y Ordóñez (1903–7, 1911–15). Uruguay had abruptly changed from a rural model to an urban model, and Batlle created revolutionary laws that would protect women, such as the law of divorce in 1907, rewritten in 1913. Delmira Agustini's lawyer for her divorce was, in fact, Carlos Oneto y Viana, who designed the first law. This progressive and secular wave promoted by Batlle, that intended to adjust a country in process of industrialization, was in tune with the booming anarchist and socialist ideologies in turn-of-the-century Uruguay. These revolutionary ideas inspired writers such as Roberto de las Carreras, renowned Uruguayan dandy and friend of Delmira Agustini, who in 1902 published a pamphlet entitled "Amor Libre" (Free Love). In this autobiographical work, de las Carreras professed the abolition of the institution of marriage, the sexual liberation of women, and the demise of the traditional Macho in favor of a liberated Lover. Delmira Agustini knew these theories, and her choices seem connected with the anarcho-sexual ideology promoted by her friend.

However, the social mentality of the times was not ready for these dramatic changes. Closely related to Europe, turn-of-the-century Uruguay was molded by the European restrictive societal constructs that denied sexuality to upper-class women. In fact, the Uruguay of this period was particularly moralistic and repressive. In an attempt to distance itself from the previous, reproductive, "barbaric," rural model, the urban regime emphasized the disciplined, the civilized and the emotionally and sexually restrained. This model was particularly demanding for women, whose average age at marriage moved from 18–20 years in the rural model, to 25–27 years in the urban model of Agustini's times, fomenting health problems among women. Seeking to build a comfortable state before the marriage, the bourgeois couples would extend their courtship for years, always expecting from the future bride modesty and restraint.

The relationship between Delmira Agustini and Enrique Job Reyes responded to this socio-sexual paradigm. Their courtship lasted over five years and Agustini married at the age of 27. However, the letters exchanged between them showed an open sexual interest by Delmira quickly neutralized by the more conventional Enrique. In a way, this asymmetric relationship expresses the conflicts and contradictions of the times, and her tragic ending would be the ultimate result of a political experiment that emphasized freedom and reform (embraced by Agustini), within a context of extreme and prevalent social conservatism (represented by Reyes).

Works and First "*Modernista*" Responses

Delmira Agustini published three volumes of poems during her life. In 1907, Agustini published *El libro blanco (Frágil)*

(The White Book (Fragile)), which was very well received by the writers and critics of the period. Her second book, *Cantos de la mañana* (Morning Songs) appeared in 1910, opening with a "Pórtico" by Rubén Darío, and concluding with a selection of reviews of her first book. These comments reflected the mixture of condescension and admiration that intellectuals of her time uttered upon the publication of Agustini's first compositions in the journals of Montevideo. Preeminent intellectuals expressed interest and surprise, noting, however, Agustini's beauty and youth over the quality of her poetry.

Critics continued to refer to Agustini using metaphors that stressed her beauty and virginal qualities, an image that Agustini herself assumed and cultivated in accordance with the *modernista* rhetoric and the restricted roles imposed on the women of that period. She was labeled an "ángel encarnado" (embodied angel) (Medina Betancort, *Poesías Completas* by Delmira Agustini, 1993: 89) and a "joven diosa" (young goddess) (Zum Felde 1944: 27).

Delmira Agustini's third volume of poems was published in 1913 under the title *Los cálices vacíos* (Empty Chalices). This volume presented verses that intensified the powerful, sexual imagery that was emerging in Agustini's previous works. The reception of these poems changed the reactions to the muse. It was at this point that the authors' and critics' delicate epithets changed to address Agustini in terms similar to those later used by Emir Rodríguez Monegal: "pitonisa en celo" (p. 8) (pythoness in heat), "obsesa sexual" (p. 9) (sexually obsessed), "Leda de fiebre" (p. 53) (fevered Leda). Needless to say, this approach was never used when critics addressed male writers. This mechanism of textualization, that is, the conversion of the female writer into a literary or conceptual object, haunted Agustini throughout her career and continued even after her tragic death. Another distorting direction that literary criticism took in response to Agustini was to erase or mask the sexual content of her writings.

In *Los cálices vacíos*, Delmira Agustini announces a new book to be published under the title "Los astros del abismo" (Stars from the Abyss). She was killed before accomplishing what she considered her most mature work, a motive that rejects the theory that Agustini was a willing participant in her death with Enrique. Ten years after her murder, Delmira Agustini's *Obras Completas* (Complete Works) were printed, which included a compilation of unpublished compositions under the name of "El rosario de Eros" (Eros' Rosary).

An Overview of Agustini's Poetry

The three volumes of poems authored by Delmira Agustini, plus the posthumous volume, register a process of maturity and personalization of the dominant *modernista* style. The challenge presented by a literary movement that based much of its aesthetics in the body of women as ornament and fetish, would allow for increasingly surprising images that make Agustini's writing one of the most original of her time.

El libro blanco (Frágil) (1907, The White Book (Fragile)) comprises fifty-two compositions, many of which had appeared in literary journals. The book is introduced by a poem that serves as poetics: "Levando el ancla," or, as stated in subsequent editions: "El poeta leva el ancla" (The Poet Weighs Anchor), where the speaker "sets sail," introducing the journey implied in the book: the poetic creation. A sense of poetic self-reference dominates this book, and this poetic "journey" is revealed through many of the images typical of *modernismo* such as nymphs, lakes, and muses. Given the key influence of French symbolism, colors are also relevant. The color that dominates this book, as stated in the title, is the color white, symbolic of purity, essence, spirituality. Interestingly, this color complements the term "Frágil" (Fragile) that the author issued between parentheses as a subtitle to the book. Both terms, "white" and "fragile," relate to concepts prevalent in the time to represent the ideal woman. Delmira Agustini is using and impersonating through the poetic "I" the values related to this ideal woman. However, the color white will move to a more sensual "pink" in the second and last section of this book: "Orla rosa" (Pink Fringe). These poems start to emphasize the sexual content, a signature of Agustini's style that will blossom in her upcoming compositions.

In *Cantos de la mañana* (1910, Morning Songs) twenty-two poems make up a book that develops some of the most emblematic images of Agustini's style. The "Ophelic discourse," as I interpret the dominant characteristic of *El libro blanco* around themes such fragility and disease (as implied by the Shakespearian figure of Ophelia), moves in *Cantos de la mañana* to a more dramatic and sensual "Orphic discourse," where images of dismemberment, sexuality, and poetic agency prevail (connected to the Greek god Orpheus). Some key images mature in this work in provocative metaphors such as the murdering of God as a way to envision the poetic truth: ". . . Ah, más grande no fuera / tener entre mis manos la cabeza de Dios" (Ah, it would not be greater / To hold in one's hands the head of God), concludes her renowned poem about acquiring, as states the title, "Lo inefable" (the ineffable).

The ambitious book, *Los cálices vacíos* (1913, Empty Chalices), has a deliberate sense of unity and collection emphasized by the fact that within the volume Agustini includes a selection of her first book plus the whole second book, *Cantos de la mañana*. *Los cálices vacíos* matures the key constructions of Agustini's images. One of the most remarkable is the image, previously offered, of an Ideal Lover sometimes identified with the Swan-God (thus, revising the classic myth of Leda and the Swan that obsessed *modernista* writers). One reformulation of this swan figure is apparent in her poem "Nocturno" (Nocturne), where the *modernista* perception of the divinized swan is subverted by the presentation of a poetic speaker that identifies with a swan that stains with blood the pristine waters of a lake, a reference interpreted as a final disrupter of *modernista* aesthetics and its ideal, formal rhetoric-landscape. This disruption is implied by unprecedented images related to the feminine, such as blood staining the literary canon, blood implying menstruation, fluidity, delivery: "Y soy el cisne errante de los sangrientos rastros / Voy manchando los lagos y remontando el vuelo" (I am the wandering swan of the bloody trails, / I go staining the lakes and rising up in flight).

The posthumous volume, *El Rosario de Eros* (1924, Eros' Rosary), appeared as part of the *Obras Completas* (Complete Works) of Delmira Agustini prepared by her father, Santiago Agustini, in collaboration with the editor of the volume, Maximino García, on the occasion of the tenth anniversary of Agustini's death. This group of new works stresses with clarity and precision the sexual imagery within a religious mode that, once again, is recaptured from the *modernista* aesthetics but personalized. Eros is the Ideal God-lover and the "rosary" in the homonymous group of five poems within the volume ("El Rosario de Eros") is sexually explicit. Some of the virtuosity and originality of the author continues and culminates in this work, within an aesthetic of abundance and enjoyment far from the rhetoric of fragility and disease implied in her first volume of poems, *El libro blanco (Frágil)*.

New Directions

Modern research on Delmira Agustini has given special attention to her biography, frequently exploring the idiosyncrasy of the author's family, which certainly facilitated her publishing. Critics have often speculated on the dominant and protective personality of Agustini's mother while the poet's puritan father transcribed her erotic verses (Machado de Benvenuto, Silva). Silvia Molloy comments on the deliberate infantilism that Agustini used as a protective mask. Patricia Varas studies the strategic functions of masks used deliberately by Agustini in order to assure her presence in a literary tradition that the author claims as aesthetic and historic agent.

Doris Stephens has been one of the pioneers of critical exploration of Agustini's work, establishing a close analysis of Agustini's poetic theory through her poems. Asunción Horno Delgado delves into the function of the "eyes" in the construction of Agustini's poetic / self. Sylvia Molloy also compares Agustini's revision of the myth of Leda and the swan with the voyeuristic and misogynist version of Rubén Darío and the *modernistas*. Other feminist and revisionist approaches include the study by Gwen Kirkpatrick, who points out the experimental and subversive character of Agustini's technique that predates the upcoming avant-garde. This subversive mode can be also traced through Agustini's poetic appropriation and redefinition of turn-of-the-century concept of "decadence" (Bruzelius, Escaja). Still to explore is the relation between Delmira Agustini's influential poetic presence and the Spanish and Latin American literary tradition, as well as within its historical context of dissidence, in particular in reference to turn-of-the-century emerging women movements.

TINA ESCAJA

Selected Works

Poesías completas. Edited with an Introduction by Alberto Zum Felde. Buenos Aires: Losada, 1944.

Correspondencia íntima. With an Introduction by Arturo Sergio Visca. Montevideo: Biblioteca Nacional, 1969.

Poesías completas. Edited with an Introduction and Notes by Magdalena García Pinto. Madrid: Cátedra, 1993.

Selected Poetry of Delmira Agustini: Poetics of Eros. Edited with an Introduction and Translation by Alejandro Cáceres. Foreword by Willis Barnstone. Carbondale, IL: Southern Illinois University Press, 2003.

References and Further Reading

Bruzelius, Margaret. "En el profundo espejo del deseo: Delmira Agustini, Rachilde and the vampire". *Revista Hispánica Moderna* 46 (1993): pp. 51–64.

Escaja, Tina. *Salomé Decapitada: Mujer y representación finisecular en la poesía de Delmira Agustini*. Amsterdam: Rodopi, 2001.

——. "Delmira Agustini, ultimación de un proyecto decadente: el batllismo". *Hispania* 89(3) (2006): 501–8.

Kirkpatrick, Gwen. "The limits of *Modernismo*, Delmira Agustini y Julio Herrera y Reissig". *Romance Quarterly* 36(3) (1989): 307–14.

Machado de Benvenuto, Ofelia. *Delmira Agustini*. Montevideo: Ceibo, 1944.

Molloy, Sylvia. "Dos lecturas del cisne: Rubén Darío y Delmira Agustini". *La sartén por el mango*. República Dominicana: Huracán, 1985, pp. 57–69.

Rodríguez Monegal, Emir. *Sexo y poesía en el 900 uruguayo. Los extraños destinos de Roberto y Delmira*. Montevideo: Alfa, 1969.

Silva, Clara. *Genio y figura de Delmira Agustini*. Buenos Aires: Editorial Universitaria, 1968.

Stephens, Doris T. *Delmira Agustini and the Quest for Transcendence*. Montevideo: Géminis, 1975.

Varas, Patricia. *Las máscaras de Delmira Agustini*. Montevideo: Vintén, 2002.

VV.AA. *Delmira Agustini. Nuevas penetraciones críticas*. Ed. Uruguay Cortazzo. Montevideo: Vintén Ed., 1996.

——. *Delmira Agustini y el modernismo: Nuevas propuestas de género*. Ed. Tina Escaja. Buenos Aires: Beatriz Viterbo, 2000.

ALARCÓN FOLGAR, ROMELIA

Romelia Alarcón Folgar was born in Guatemala in 1900. While she did not undertake university studies, she cultivated friendships with intellectuals and artists who introduced her to the aesthetic movements of her day.

Alarcón Folgar worked as a writer for radio journalism, occasionally wrote for newspapers, founded the *Revista Minuto*, and directed the *Revista Pan-Americana*. She married and had seven children. In many respects, she was a traditional Guatemalan middle-class housewife.

Alarcón Folgar was a very prolific writer, publishing during her lifetime a total of thirteen books and two other volumes published posthumously by one of her daughters. In addition to her significant poetic production, she also published four collections of short stories, two for children, *Cuentos de la abuelita* (1950, Grandmother Stories), *Gusano de luz: cuentos infantiles* (1968, Glowworm: Children's Stories), and two collections for adults, *Sin brújula: cuentos* (1964, Without a Compass: Short Stories), and *Vendedor de trinos: cuentos de misterio* (1968, The Trill Vendor: Mystery Stories).

Some critics describe her work as baroque, but others suggest that her poetry reflects the influence of the Spanish Generation of '27, and their brilliant metaphorical trappings. In her first nine books, *Llamaradas* (1938, Blaze), *Cauce* (1944: River Bed), *Clima verde en dimensión de angustia* (1944, Green Weather in Anxiety Dimension), *Isla de novilunios* (1954, Nine Moon Island), *Viento de colores* (1957, Color Wind), *Día vegetal* (1958, Vegetable Day), *Vigilia blanca* (1959, White Vigil), and *Claridad* (1961, Clarity), there is a strong stamp of lyricism. Many of her poems reflect an inner world brimming with tenderness. The imagery of her verses is based on either the exuberant nature of Guatemala or the commonplaces of domesticity. By raising these prosaic symbols and themes to heights of aestheticism, she undermines the patriarchal norms of her place and time. She steps out of the roles considered suitable for a wife and mother by working outside the home and by writing poetry in a household where seven children were clamoring for her attention. Alarcón Folgar subverted the norms of what were deemed appropriate poetic themes by centering her lyricism on the domestic, a topic considered "unpoetic" by contemporaneous literary standards. The main intellectual concern of her poetry in these earlier books is the creative process, the poet's struggle with inspiration and the word. The poet's strife is often expressed in terms of the poetic voice yearning for her beloved, sometimes with slightly erotic overtones. Yet at the end of each of these poems, it becomes clear, that the elusive and yearned-for one is merely a poetic expression.

In her later books, *Poemas de la vida simple* (1963, Simple Life Poems), *Plataforma de cristal* (1964, Crystal Platform), *Pasos sobre la yerba* (1966, Steps on the Grass), *Casa de pájaros* (1967, The Birds' House), *Tránsito terrestre* (1970, Terrestrial Transit), and the two posthumous volumes—*Tiempo inmóvil* (1972, Immobile Time) and *Más allá de la voz* (1976, Beyond the Voice)—the lyrical voice is more subdued. It seems the poet has become reconciled to the fact that exact expression may always elude her, and in turn, she focuses her attention on other matters. In some verses, the poet enunciates the disquiet of a woman who sees herself perceived by others only through the things in her house: her reading chair, her favorite book, the white tablecloth with which she sets the table. She knows she is indispensable, as necessary as the beating of her interlocutor's heartbeat, but also as invisible. So invisible, in fact, that she feels as if she were only a voice within her skin, scattering her poetry to the wind.

The armed conflict in Guatemala moved her to write poems related to social issues. Four poems entitled "Epístola irreverente a Jesucristo," the first three from *Poemas de la vida simple*, and the fourth from *Tránsito terrestre*, stand out as poetry of protest. In these poems, the poetic voice issues a series of direct, familiar commands for Him/Christ to come down from the cross or from his celestial confinement, and get cleaned up and ready to work, for it does no good for him to stay where he is, when injustice is rampant in the world.

Applying motifs from the life and crucifixion of Christ to the oppressed, Alarcón Folgar points out that the world is facing its own "Last Supper," and that it is time for one of His miracles. Alarcón Folgar died in 1970, and she is considered one of the most important Guatemalan poets of the twentieth century.

ORALIA PREBLE-NIEMI

Selected Works

Llamaradas. Guatemala: Imprenta Minerva, 1938.
Cauce. Guatemala: Imprenta Minerva, 1944.
Clima verde en dimensión de angustia. Guatemala: n.p, 1944.
Cuentos de la abuelita. Guatemala: Centro Editorial, 1950.
Isla de novilunios. Guatemala: Centro Editorial, 1954.
Viento de colores. Guatemala: Díaz-Paiz, 1957.
Día vegetal. Argentina: Brigadas Líricas, 1958.
Vigilia blanca. Guatemala: Imprenta Comercial, 1959.
Claridad. Argentina: Brigadas Líricas, 1961.
Poemas de la vida simple. Guatemala: José de Pineda Ibarra, 1963.
Sin brújula: cuentos. Guatemala: Tipografía Nacional, 1964
Plataforma de cristal. Guatemala: Tipografía Nacional, 1964.
Pasos sobre la yerba. Guatemala: Tipografía Nacional, 1966.
Casa de pájaros. Guatemala: Fósforos Publicitarios, 1967.
Gusano de luz: Cuentos infantiles. Guatemala: Editorial del Ejército, 1968.
Vendedor de trinos: cuentos de misterio. Guatemala: Tipografía Nacional, 1968.
Tránsito terrestre. Guatemala: Nuevo Signo, 1970.
Tiempo inmóvil. Guatemala: José de Pineda Ibarra, 1972.
Más allá de la voz. Guatemala: José de Pineda Ibarra, 1976.

References and Further Reading

Berry-Bravo, Judy. *Romelia Alarcón Folgar: Palabra y poesía de Guatemala*. Guatemala: Serviprensa, 1996.
Carrera, Mario Alberto. *Panorama de la poesía femenina guatemalteca del siglo XX*. Guatemala: Editorial Universitaria de Guatemala, 1983.
Carrillo, Hugo. *La alondra iluminada*. Guatemala: Dirección General de Cultura y Bellas Artes, 1982.
Figueroa Marroquín, Horacio. *Las nueve musas del parnaso guatemalense*. Guatemala: José de Pineda Ibarra, 1981.
Méndez de la Vega, Luz. *Poetisas desmitificadoras guatemaltecas*. Guatemala: Tipografía Nacional, 1984.
Ydígoras Fuentes, Carmen. *Compendio de la historia de la literatura y artes de Guatemala*, 5th edn. Guatemala: José de Pineda Ibarra, 1959.

ALEGRÍA, CLARIBEL

Born in Estelí, Nicaragua in 1924 to a Salvadoran mother, Ana Maria Vides, and a Nicaraguan father, Daniel Alegría, a medical doctor and supporter of the rebel Augusto Sandino, Clara Isabel Alegría Vides moved to exile in El Salvador with her family in 1925, where she spent most of her childhood and adolescence. Consequently, despite being born in Nicaragua, she considers herself Salvadoran as well as Nicaraguan. She calls El Salvador her "fatherland" and Nicaragua her "motherland". Though she has written essays, children's literature, testimonial literature and novels, Alegría is best known as a poet. According to *Curbstone Ink*, "her work has been translated into more than 14 languages" (Fall/Winter, 2005: 8). She is one of the best-known writers from Central America, prolific in a range of genres, and an energetic and respected voice of an all too often overlooked region.

Alegría studied at George Washington University, where the well-known Spanish poet, Juan Ramón Jiménez, served as her mentor and provided the impetus for her first published book of poetry, *Anillo de silencio* (1948). She graduated from George Washington with a bachelor's degree in philosophy and letters that same year. In 1947, she married a fellow student, Darwin J. ("Bud") Flakoll, a journalist and future diplomat. The couple had four children; they lived in Argentina, Chile, France, Mexico, Spain, Uruguay, and the United States before returning to settle in Managua, Nicaragua. Their sojourns abroad brought them into contact with major writers such as Juan Rulfo, Mario Benedetti, and Rosario Castellanos. Unable to support American foreign policy towards Latin America, Flakoll left the foreign service. He became Alegría's primary translator to English, and in collaboration they wrote several books, translated the works of others, and edited several anthologies.

Alegría has been honored with several important awards for her work. In 1978, she received the prestigious Premio Casa de las Américas for her volume of poetry, *Sobrevivo* (shared with Gioconda Belli of Nicaragua for *Línea de Fuego*). In 1995, she was featured in the public television journalist Bill Moyers' special program, *Language of Life: A Festival of Poets*. In 2000, she was awarded the Premio de Poesía de Autores Independientes and in 2004, the French government's *Chevalier d'Ordre des Arts et des Lettres*. Most recently Alegría was named 2006 laureate of the Neustadt International Prize for Literature, a $50,000 prize given for a body of work and administered by the University of Oklahoma and its international magazine, *World Literature Today*. She is the nineteenth recipient and the third woman to be so honored with this biennial prize.

Poetry

Sobrevivo ("I Survive") demonstrates the commitment to social and political issues that runs throughout most of Alegría's work. From her exile in various locales abroad, Alegría followed events in Nicaragua. She witnessed the end of the Somoza dynasty and dictatorship; soon after the Sandinista victory, she and her husband returned to Nicaragua to document the revolution in narrative form. But the poems are an earlier recollection of Nicaraguan reality. In "Estelí," a poem to her birthplace, she writes of the river: "your channel has been filled. / With mud and blood / it has been filled / with empty cartridges / with shirts / pants / and corpses". Other poems of *Sobrevivo* address similar themes of torture and disappearances, including "Sorrow," dedicated to Roque Dalton (1935–75), the guerrilla-poet of the revolution in El Salvador, who died in questionable circumstances. But *Sobrevivo* is a testament to survival, and the difficulty of a survival when surrounded by the silenced voices of the unjustly dead.

Flores del volcán/Flowers from the Volcano, translated by the American poet Carolyn Forché, brought Alegría's work to an English-language audience for the first time. Many of the poems in *Flowers* came from *Sobrevivo*, including the title poem. The volcano of the title symbolizes El Salvador and its geographical volcanoes, but also refers to the "volcano" of violence, the civil wars of Central America, the armed struggles of El Salvador, Guatemala, and Nicaragua. Yet from this violence, geographical or political, may spring the flowers of hope. In this collection, Alegría clearly declares herself a poet of "la generación comprometida" ("the committed generation"). In her Preface to the volume, Forché quotes Alegría: "I have no *fusil* [rifle] in my hand but only my testimony" (p. xi). Alegría was profoundly affected by the civil wars in the region, but the 1980 assassination of Archbishop Oscar Romero, shot in the back by a Salvadoran death squad while saying mass, was a life-altering event, making her a more political writer. She supported the overthrow of dictatorships, but she herself espoused non-violence. Thus her writing is her weapon, her *fusil*.

La mujer del río Sumpul (Woman of the River) continues the committed stance of earlier volumes, confronting directly the Central American situation and critiquing US involvement. The pair of poems, "The American Way of Death" and "The American Way of Life," is a harsh indictment of US foreign and domestic policy, the former poem suggesting that whether one chooses "the guerrilla path" or peace, the US response is death, and the latter describing America as a "bitch" that "chews up" Salvadorans and Nicaraguans. "Woman of the River" tells the story of a woman who survives the Salvadoran Sumpul River massacre of 1980 with two of her children by hiding from the security troops who had killed her other three children. In that same year the United States sent at least six million dollars in military aid to support the government side of the civil war, support that including training the very security troops who massacred their own citizens.

In *Fugues*, with the wars over and fledgling democracies underway in Central America, Alegría is much less political, though no less concerned with women's issues. The themes here are love, aging, and death as a natural stage of life rather than a violent end funded by a foreign power. *Fugues* contains a series of poems—like a musical fugue—on the theme of a female figure of importance to mythology or history, such as Odysseus's wife Penelope, Pandora, and the Mexican Malinche. But in Alegría's revisionist interpretations, these are women as subject, not object, and as subject they contest the history in which they are inscribed. The normally patient Penelope writes Odysseus to ask him *not* to come home; Malinche asks, am I not the one who has been betrayed?

Alegría's beloved husband and writing partner, Bud Flakoll, died in 1995, and she felt "mutilated". *Saudade/Sorrow* commemorates the death of her husband and her own grief at his loss. The title comes from Portuguese, and means much more than simply sorrow. *Saudade* implies longing, yearning, a nostalgia for something unattainable, and evokes the presence of an overwhelming absence. Like *Fugues*, *Saudade* incorporates classical figures, including Ariadne, Circe, and Prometheus. Many of the poems are quite brief, and yet deeply evocative, such as "Two Wings in Flight," which immortalizes her loving relationship with her husband: "We were a careless / butterfly / two wings in flight / that folded into one / in repose".

Soltando Amarras/Casting Off is Alegría's most recent book of poetry. She continues the theme of loss and death, again evoking classical female figures (Antigone, Cassandra, Medea) to investigate death and destiny, but this time it is her own aging and death she contemplates: "It's time now / to give up, / my exhausting, / and exhausted body,/ give me the right to escape" ("It's Time Now to Give Up"). Nevertheless, she celebrated her 82nd birthday in May, 2006, at a conference in Granada, Spain, in honor of her first true mentor, José Ramón Jiménez.

Prose fiction

Cenizas de Izalco (Ashes of Izalco)

During her years in exile, Alegría and her husband lived in Paris from 1962 to 1966, where they befriended several of the Latin American "Boom" writers such as Mario Vargas Llosa of Peru, Carlos Fuentes of Mexico, and life-long friend, Julio Cortázar of Argentina. Fuentes would prove to be a decisive influence; after hearing her stories of the 1932 massacre of peasants at Izalco, El Salvador, that Alegría remembered strongly from her childhood, he urged her to tell that story in a novel. Alegría resisted, claiming that as a poet, she knew nothing about narrative. Her husband Bud suggested they write it together, using his experience as a journalist and her memories of the event. Finished in 1964, *Cenizas de Izalco* was a finalist in the Seix Barral Biblioteca Breve competition in Barcelona, but Spanish censorship delayed the publication until 1966. It was the first Central American novel published by the renowned Spanish publisher, Seix Barral. Political conditions in El Salvador delayed its publication there for a decade, but the novel went on to become an official text for Salvadoran schools.

The historical event that serves as the basis of *Cenizas de Izalco* is sometimes called *"La Matanza,"* or "The Slaughter". In January of 1932, Indians and peasants rebelled against the coffee crash and their concomitant unemployment, only to be massacred by the dictator General Maximiliano Hernández Martínez's army and police, and the private militia of the oligarchy, the infamous White Guards, in the name of anticommunism. Among the 30,000 dead were peasants, Pipíl Indians, and students, including Farabundo Martí, the communist revolutionary. The date is said to signal the disappearance of Indians in El Salvador, as any survivors immediately took steps to assimilate and not be recognizably Indian, whether by dress, language, or other cultural markings. Alegría and Flakoll returned to El Salvador to research the novel, and found that Hernández Martínez had performed what Alegría referred to as a "cultural lobotomy," literally erasing as much evidence as possible of the event. Alegría had to rely on her own memories, conversations with a neighbor, and some old newspaper clippings her father had saved. Their novel thus inscribes in history an event that the dictator tried to erase from history, and does so by telling a love story.

The protagonist, Carmen, returns to El Salvador to see her hospitalized mother. But her mother dies just prior to her arrival, bequeathing a diary to her daughter. As Carmen reads the diary, the plot of the novel unfolds, alternating between first person narration and excepts of the diary, which is not her mother Isabel's, but rather the diary of her mother's American lover, Frank Wolff. Carmen thus discovers that her mother was not a contented middle-class housewife as she had assumed, but rather a woman who is unfulfilled by the societal expectations with which she complies. Carmen seeks clarification, and questions friends and family members, only to receive a different response from each of them. The text thus raises questions of history and its multiple interpretations, and creates a link between mother and daughter that did not exist when Isabel was alive. In discovering the "secret history" of her mother's life, Carmen realizes that she too is stifled by a marriage that conforms to the confines of patriarchy.

Cenizas also depicts rural life in El Salvador of the time, clearly indicating the status of the privileged few and the rampant oppression of the indigenous and peasants. Alegría and Flakoll make clear in this novel their preoccupation with the oppressed, whether the peasant by the landowner or the woman by a patriarchal system. Some American reviewers found *Cenizas de Izalco* less than satisfying, neither this nor that, not enough of a historical political novel, but not completely a love story either. Latin American critics, on the other hand, have seen it as a seminal novel, breaking the tradition of social realism, rewriting the history of El Salvador, and presenting perspectives not raised before, including feminist themes such as challenging the patriarchal model.

In *Despierta mi bien despierta* (Awake, My Love, Awake) Alegría takes the challenge to patriarchy yet further, while maintaining the political context of the revolution. The protagonist, Lorena, is middle-aged and middle class, comfortably married to Ernesto, the well-to-do owner of several slaughterhouses. While taking a university writing course, Lorena meets and begins an affair with Eduardo, a young revolutionary. As Lorena writes, keeping a diary and attempting to write a novel, she gains in consciousness. References to newspaper articles and events themselves maintain the link to revolution, such as her husband's refusal one night to stop and assist a naked man on the highway, and the newspaper's report the following day of that man's death. Ernesto discovers his wife's affair through an anonymous note; he strikes her, and she leaves him, taking a step closer to finding her own identity. When she later finds her lover Eduardo's decapitated head in her car (whether as vengeance for being her lover or because of his revolutionary role is unknown), the personal and the political fuse together, and Lorena becomes more fully "awake". Alegría once again uses a love story to reveal the underlying system that oppresses a people into rebellion and oppresses and alienates even middle-class women, but here the female protagonist makes a break from that tradition.

Luisa en el país de la realidad (*Luisa in Realityland*) is perhaps Alegría's most famous novel, a hybrid text whose title plays on Lewis Carroll's *Alice in Wonderland.* Anecdotal vignettes in prose alternate with poetry; notes on real events mix with fantastical fables; Mayan mythology mixes with autobiographical memoir to create a collage-like structure. A montage more than the classic notion of a novel, *Luisa* is told from the point of view of a child narrator-protagonist just seven years old. Nevertheless, the novel manages to address Alegría's on-going concerns with violence, oppression, and the rights of women. One vignette, for example, "The Blue Theater," relates a scene of brutal torture ending in the death of a prisoner in a Chilean prison. And at her "First Communion" Luisa, knowing that on this special day her prayer will be answered, tells God that she doesn't want to get married. "I don't like the way men treat women," she says. But she does want a child, so she prays to get married, have a baby, and as soon as she has the baby, that her husband should die (p. 39). Despite the often negative portrayal of male–female relationships and the background of violence, the English-language edition ends on a hopeful note with the poem "The Cartography of Memory:" "Come, love, let's return / to the future" (p. 152).

Prose Nonfiction

With her husband, Alegría published several testimonial works. The first, *No me agarran viva: la mujer salvadoreña en lucha* (*They Won't Take Me Alive: Salavadoran Women in Struggle for National Liberation*), is dedicated to the women and girls of El Salvador committed to the struggle for liberation. The book follows the *"concientización,"* or consciousness-raising of Eugenia, a middle-class woman who becomes a guerrilla fighter and eventually dies in the war. Eugenia is presented as typical rather than exceptional, and her story is told through testimonies of others, testimonies which reveal as much about them, the situation of their social class, and their ability to survive the hardships of war. The text also describes Eugenia's relationship with her husband and raises the difficult and seemingly inescapable issue of machismo among revolutionaries. With *No me agarran viva*, Alegría has participated in "the deconstruction of the bourgeois 'I' in function of a new collective subjectivity" says the well-known critic of Central American literature, Marc Zimmerman in his "Afterword" to *Claribel Alegría and Central American Literature* (Boschetto-Sandoval and McGowan, 1994: 224).

Their second collaboration also deals with the civil war in El Salvador. *Para romper el silencio: Resistencia y lucha en las cárceles salvadoreñas* ("Breaking the Silence: Resistance and Struggle in Salvadoran Prisons") gives the testimony of a student leader, Toño, who was imprisoned for two years as a political prisoner, along with testimonies of other prisoners, describing their suffering and torture at the hands of their captors.

The couple returned to the war in Nicaragua with their testimonial work on the assassination of the former dictator Somoza, killed in Asunción, Paraguay, in 1980, about a year after being forced to flee Nicaragua after the forty-three-year dictatorship of the Somoza family. *Somoza: Expediente cerrado: La historia de un ajusticiamiento* (*Death of Somoza*) is based on interviews with the remaining members of the Argentine commando group responsible for the assassination. The Spanish title makes clear that this is "the story of a just punishment," rather than simply a terrorist act.

Committed Writer

Whether through her poetry, fiction, or testimonial literature, Claribel Alegría has consistently given voice to the concerns of her people. She has investigated and denounced social and economic injustice; she has challenged the status quo of oligarchies and patriarchies. She contributed to a new direction in Central American writing. Alegría has always been a voice of moral conscience for her people, a voice for survival, and she remains one of the principal voices of Central American literature.

LINDA LEDFORD-MILLER

Selected Works

Poetry

Sobrevivo. Havana: Casa de las Américas, 1978.

Flores del volcán/Flowers from the Volcano. Bilingual edition, trans. Carolyn Forché. Pittsburgh, PA: University of Pittsburgh Press, 1982.

La mujer del río Sumpul. Roldanillo, Valle, Colombia: Museo Rayo, 1987. Trans. Darwin J. Flakoll as *Woman of the River*. Pittsburgh, PA: University of Pittsburgh Press, 1989.

Fugues. Bilingual edition, trans. Darwin J. Flakoll. Willimantic, CT: Curbstone Press, 1993.

Saudade/Sorrow. Bilingual edition, trans. Carolyn Forché. Willimantic, CT: Curbstone Press, 1999.

Soltando Amarras/Casting Off. Trans. Margaret Sayers Peden. Willimantic, CT: Curbstone Press, 2003.

Prose Fiction

Cenizas de Izalco. With Darwin J. Flakoll. Barcelona: Seix Barral, 1966. Trans. Flakoll as *Ashes of Izalco*. Willimantic, CT: Curbstone Press, 1989.

El detén. Barcelona: Lumen, 1977. Trans. Amanda Hopkinson as *The Talisman* in Alegría's *Family Album*. London: Women's Press, 1990.

Album familiar. San José: EDUCA, 1982. Trans. Amanda Hopkinson as *Family Album* in Alegría's *Family Album*. London: Women's Press, 1990.

Pueblo de Dios y de Mandinga. Mexico City: Era, 1985. Trans. Amanda Hopkinson as *Village of God and the Devil* in *Family Album*. London: Women's Press, 1990.

Despierta, mi bien despierta. San Salvador: Universidad de Centro América, 1986.

Luisa en el país de la realidad. Mexico City: Universidad Autónoma de Zacatecas, 1987. Trans. Darwin J. Flakoll as *Luisa in Realityland*. Willimantic, CT: Curbstone Press, 1987.

Prose Nonfiction

Nicaragua: La revolución sandinista: una crónica política. With Darwin J. Flakoll. Mexico City: Era, 1982.

No me agarran viva: la mujer salvadoreña en lucha. With Darwin J. Flakoll. Mexico City: Era, 1983. Trans. Amanda Hopkinson as *They Won't Take Me Alive: Salavadoran Women in Struggle for National Liberation*. London: Women's Press, 1987.

Para romper el silencio: Resistencia y lucha en las cárceles salvadoreñas. With Darwin J. Flakoll. Mexico: Ediciones Era, 1984.

Somoza: Expediente cerrado: La historia de un ajusticiamiento. With Darwin J. Flakoll. Managua: El Gato Negro, 1993. Trans. Darwin J. Flakoll as *Death of Somoza*. Willimantic, CT: Curbstone Press, 1996

References and Further Reading

Aparicio, Yvette. "Reading Social Consciousness in Claribel Alegría's Early Poetry". *Cincinnati Romance Review* 18 (1999): 1–6.

Arias, Arturo. "Claribel Alegría: Los recuerdos del porvenir". In *Gestos ceremoniales*: *Narrativa centroamericana, 1960–1990*. Guatemala City: Artemis & Edinter, 1998, pp. 57–80.

Barbas-Rhoden, Laura. *Writing Women in Central America: Gender and the Fictionalization of History*. Athens, OH: Ohio University Press, 2003.

Beverly, John and Zimmerman, Marc. *Literature and Politics in the Central American Revolutions*, Austin, TX: University of Texas Press, 1990.

Boschetto-Sandoval, Sandra M. and McGowan, Marcia Phillips (eds). *Claribel Alegría and Central American Literature: Critical Essays*. Athens, OH: Ohio University Center for International Studies, 1994.

Craft, Linda. *Novels of Testimony and Resistance from Central America*. Gainesville, FL: University of Florida Press, 1997.

Galindo, Rose Marie. *Novela y crisis política en El Salvador (cuatro momentos)*. La Libertad, El Salvador: Editorial Delgado, Universidad Dr. José Matías Delgado, 2001.

McGowan, Marcia P. "Mapping a New Territory: *Luisa in Realityland*". *Letras Femeninas* 19(1/2) (Spring/Fall, 1993): 84–99.

Rodríguez, Ileana. *Women, Guerrillas, and Love: Understanding War in Central America*. Trans Ileana Rodríguez with Robert Carr. Minneapolis, MN: University of Minneapolis Press, 1996.

Sternbach, Nancy Saporta. "Remembering the Dead: Latin American Women's 'Testimonial' Discourse". *Latin American Perspectives* 18(3) (Summer 1991): 91–102.

Treacy, Mary Jane. "A Politics of the Word: Claribel Alegría's *Album familiar* and *Despierta, mi bien, despierta*". *Intertexts* 1(1) (Spring 1997): 62–77.

Velásquez, Antonio. *Las novelas de Claribel Alegría: historia, sociedad y (re)visión de la estética literaria centroamericana*. New York: Peter Lang, 2002.

ALLENDE, ISABEL

Until the publication of Isabel Allende's (b. 1942) first novel, *La casa de los espíritus* (1982, translated as *The House of the Spirits* in 1985), no woman novelist in Latin America had achieved global visibility equal to that of the best-known male writers. Allende's success, in the popular markets as well as in critical and academic circles, paved the way for—or may have been the first harbinger of—a "boom" of acclaimed novels by women throughout the 1980s and 1990s. Her success can be attributed to several factors: her ability both to capitalize on literary tendencies of the Latin American "boom" novel of the 1960s and 1970s and to realize that the time had come for a significant shift in style and audience; her narration of a political moment that had captured the world's attention; an impressive ability to interweave the national and the personal, the universal and the local, the real and the fantastic; and linking all of these elements, a talent for storytelling that carried her to the top of bestseller lists across the Western world.

Literary Trajectory

Allende's works may be divided into four periods, which correspond to distinct moments in her personal life and literary career. The first consists of the novels structured around the coup of Chilean dictator Augusto Pinochet in 1973 and Allende's subsequent years living in Venezuela (*The House of the Spirits* [1982], *Of Love and Shadows* [1984], *Eva Luna* [1987], *Stories of Eva Luna* [1989]). The second is a transitional period, marked by the seismic events of Allende's second marriage and move to California as well as the tragic death of her daughter Paula; works published during that time include the novel *The Infinite Plan* (1991), the (auto)biographical *Paula* (1994), and a narrative of culinary and erotic celebration entitled *Aphrodite* (1997). The third period consists of historical novels largely emphasizing the role of women in the history of Chile and San Francisco; these novels include *Daughter of Fortune* (1999), *Portrait in Sepia* (2001), *Zorro* (2005), and *Inés of my Soul* (2006). And finally, contemporaneous to the latter novels emerges the trilogy of novels for younger readers, a series comprised of *City of the Beasts* (2002), *Kingdom of the Golden Dragon* (2004) and *Forest of the Pygmies* (2005).

Throughout her literary and autobiographical production, certain themes recur consistently. Positioning her work in contrast to the highly intellectualized and symbolic Latin American novels of the 1960s and 1970s, Allende privileges passion, optimism, and sensuality, borrowing heavily from genres that had been relegated to the realm of the "popular". Allende also maintains an unwavering focus on issues of politics and social justice, in particular the individual's ability and responsibility to resist authoritarianism in all places and throughout all time periods. Elements of the fantastic—the legacy of Latin America's famed "magical realism"—pervade a great deal of Allende's fiction, whether in the form of feminist intuition, cohabitation with the spirits of past generations, an appreciation of the exotic "other," or a general exuberance communicated through exaggeration. In an affirmation of the possibility of happy endings, most of the novels conclude with the triumph of the strong and independent woman protagonist, who has successfully resisted patriarchal authoritarianism. And finally, the structural framework of metafiction ties together Allende's primary body of novels, resulting in a consistent focus on the figure of the woman writer as recorder and repository of both the individual and the collective history. Each of these elements can be best understood in light of Allende's own life and literary trajectory.

Biographical Outline

Isabel Allende was born on August 2, 1942, in Lima, Perú to Chilean parents Tomás Allende and Francisca Llona Barros. Her father, a diplomat, was a cousin of Salvador Allende (1908–73), the man who would become the Socialist president of Chile in 1970, only to be overthrown and assassinated in a violent *coup d'état* three years later. Although Tomás Allende left his family in 1945 and maintained no contact with them, Isabel Allende and her siblings maintained close ties with the family of Salvador Allende, who was her godfather and whom she considered her "uncle". Francisca (Panchita) Llona returned with her three children to Chile, and Allende spent her early years in the home of her maternal grandparents, both of whom played a strong role in her formation as a woman and a writer. It is to her grandmother's influence that she credits her imagination, her appreciation of eccentricity, and her fascination with the permeability of the line between the possible and the impossible. Her relationship with her grandfather is the primary source of her vision of the Chilean patriarchy (in *Paula* she describes him as made of "hard stone" [p. 4]), and her underlying sympathy for many of the men whom she sees as trapped in this element.

Allende established her career as a journalist, first in television and then writing for a feminist magazine entitled *Paula*. While she considers some of her writing to have been focused on traditional women's spheres such as fashion and beauty, her stint there did bring her into contact with the strengthening feminist and socialist movements of that time. Additionally, she credits her journalistic period with the refining of her storytelling craft; in her memoir *Mi país inventado* (2003, My Invented Country) she attributes to her journalistic training her ability to "trap the reader by the neck and not let go until the end of the story" (p. 151).

This career, like so many others, was placed in jeopardy during the 1973 *coup d'état*, when Salvador Allende was overthrown and the right-wing dictator, General Augusto Pinochet, instituted a system of censorship, repression, and disappearances that would control the country's economy and politics until a 1990 plebiscite voted him out of office. Isabel Allende's family ties and published political views, as well as her clandestine activities in support of the resistance, created a situation of increasing vulnerability, until in 1975, one and a half years after the coup, she and her family left Chile to live in Venezuela, a destination chosen specifically because of its long history of democracy. She would not return until 1985, when she cast her vote in the first plebiscite that would determine Pinochet's exit from power.

Between 1975 and 1981, Allende in Venezuela was unable to find her footing either culturally or professionally. With her marriage in decay, she determined that she needed to find a course that would simultaneously lead toward the personal and professional satisfaction she sought.

That opportunity came somewhat unexpectedly when, in 1981, she began to write the story of her family. She claims that in that year, upon being notified that her maternal grandfather was dying, she began to write him a farewell letter in which she would let him know that his stories, and those of her grandmother, would live on. That letter evolved into the novel that ensured Allende's place in the Latin American literary canon, the phenomenally successful *The House of the Spirits*.

Following that success and those of her subsequent novels which also earned best-seller status, *Of Love and Shadows* and *Eva Luna*, Allende ended her marriage to Frías, and soon thereafter fell in love with Willie Gordon, a lawyer in San Francisco. Her next novel, *The Infinite Plan*, is a fictionalized version of his life story, her attempt both to find her new literary voice and to understand him and his cultural context more fully. This transitional phase was radically altered when her 28-year-old daughter Paula, married and living in Spain, suffered an attack of porphyria, a genetic condition whose onset in 1991 left her in a coma; Paula died a year later. Allende considers her next two works, *Paula* and *Aphrodite*, an exorcism of this tragedy; the former work interweaves the chronicle of this traumatic year with Allende's own autobiography, and the latter involves a return to the celebration of living bodies, primarily through the avenues of food and sex.

Returning to the novelistic style that has become her hallmark, Allende has since turned to historical fiction, tracing the role of women in the histories of her two homelands, Chile and California. In *Daughter of Fortune* and *Portrait in Sepia*, she creates two prequels to *The House of the Spirits*, tracing the genealogy of the century preceding the twentieth-century novel. Her subsequent two novels, *Zorro* and *Inés of my Soul*, recreate historical personages that have become national legends, weaving into the historical backdrop stories of passion, intrigue and the triumph of integrity over corruption.

Alongside this steady stream of novelistic successes, Allende has produced a trilogy of adventure novels for young readers, thus acknowledging both the impact of the *Harry Potter* series in prioritizing a new generation of readers, and her own role as the grandmother who tells stories to young listeners.

Debating Popularity

Allende's record of success spanning more than a quarter of a century, combined with a better critical understanding of contemporary cultural shifts, have quietened much of the debate that surrounded her emergence onto the international literary stage. But her early novels created enormous controversy over the question of whether literary quality and popular accessibility were compatible traits. Latin American literature had characterized itself for two decades as experimental, with fragmented narratives that offered a puzzle to those educated readers who took up the challenge of decoding them. Those novels, often referred to as "totalizing" or "encyclopedic," took on themes of international and existential significance, at the same time that they critically assessed the Latin American political and economic situation in a global context. But in the early 1980s, Allende's novels emerged, readable and appealing, offering triumphant endings that challenged the pessimism of this earlier "boom" period.

While her novels met with immense success in the literary market, literary critics, in particular in the United States and Latin America, were harsh in dismissing her work as "popular," written to appeal to mass audiences. Additionally, feminist critics charged her with not being sufficiently radical, since emotions such as love, fear, and horror reigned supreme, particularly for the female characters. And finally, *The House of the Spirits* was criticized for its use of magical realism, the trait trademarked by Gabriel García Márquez in *One Hundred Years of Solitude* and other works. Magical realism involves the blending of the real and the fantastic, often through the incorporation of local legends or through exaggeration, and generally with symbolic value. Other structural similarities with the Nobel Prize-winning García Márquez's work were cited: the use of a four-generation familial genealogy as the basis of the tale, the appearance of women of surreal beauty and fatal attraction, and the blending of family history with national political events.

Allende responded directly to these critiques. In terms of feminism, she has consistently maintained that she writes the story of women as she has known them and as she sees them, instead of creating archetypes that correspond to a particular feminist ethos. As to the question of García Márquez's legacy, she has recognized his influence, but also emphasizes, as he has, that magical realism is part of their cultural reality, not merely a literary technique. She has also pointed out the masculinist bias that attempts to attribute successful women's writing to their male predecessors. And finally, on the issue of accessibility Allende has been unwavering: she claims in her 1988 essay "Por qué y para quién escribo" (*Why and For Whom I Write*), that in a time of political urgency such as the last decades of the twentieth century, Latin American writers do not have the luxury of "contemplating their navels" from an intellectual perspective; instead, they have a responsibility to tell their story to a wide public (p. 158; translation mine).

Her continued success and her confrontation of academic critics work alongside a broader contemporary understanding of the period following the Latin American "boom". The period, often termed the "post-boom," has, in general, involved greater attention to popular culture and a broad-based readership. The post-boom has also brought to center stage a generation of women writers whose acclaim might not have been possible without the groundbreaking work of Allende. These include novelists like Mexicans Laura Esquivel and Angeles Mastretta, Chilean Marcela Serrano, and others who have achieved international visibility in the wake of Allende's success.

Within these contexts, Allende's work is now seen as marking a significant cultural shift. She has consistently asserted that her celebration of passion and melodrama stand in the face of patriarchal intellectualization, and approximate more closely life as it is experienced, instead of as a metaphorical abstraction. She also reminds readers that the magical side of reality plays a major role in many non-Western cultures, only seeming "fantastic" to the more limited US and European imaginations. In her 1988 essay, summarizing her literary ethos and defying her critics, she said:

> I am prepared to challenge the masculine literary discourse, that fears any sign of sentimentalism as a

> subversion in the sacred order of reason and good taste. I do not plan to sidestep sentiment, even if that places me arm in arm with vulgarity. I will write ... with no regard for the stomach of critics, about golden sunsets, selfless mothers, and poets who die of love.
>
> (159; translation mine)

This confrontation with masculinist literary criticism has since been validated by popular acclaim and, increasingly, broader critical appreciation.

Patriarchy and Authoritarianism

Inseparably, the two dominant themes throughout Allende's novels have been the situation of individual women within a patriarchal culture, and the political backdrop of authoritarianism and repression. One key to Allende's success has been her ability to interweave these two themes, to the point that each helps to explain the pervasiveness of the other.

The House of the Spirits tells the story of four generations of the Trueba and del Valle family, focusing on the matrilineage from approximately 1920 to the time shortly after Pinochet's ascent to power in 1973. Symbolically, the names of the women protagonists all convey the idea of light: Nívea, Clara, Blanca, Alba (*snow-white, bright, white, dawn*). The male presence that casts a shadow across the lives of these women is Esteban Trueba, modeled on Allende's own grandfather. After marrying Clara, he assumes the two roles on which the Chilean social system is based: he manages a rural estate and its indigenous workers, and he enters the world of conservative politics. At the same time, he tightly controls the women of the family, opposing Clara's pleas for humanity and tenderness. He opposes his daughter Blanca's love affair with the working-class Pedro Tercero García, eventually maiming Pedro and driving both of them away from his home; and he treats his workers with the same paternal authority, claiming that they would be unable to take care of themselves without his authority and protection. At the same time, his habitual rape of indigenous women leads to the engendering of the cruel Esteban García. When his granddaughter Alba is kidnapped and tortured by the regime of the unnamed dictator (clearly Pinochet), Esteban García is her principal tormentor and rapist, thus bringing the sins of the fathers to bear on the figurative daughters.

The novel thus progresses from a beginning that emphasizes imagination, magical realism, and a focus on the individual, to an ending of brutal realism and strong political activism. This evolution is intentional, as Allende portrays the intrusion of the dictatorship into the individual lives of Chileans; and it reflects her own evolution as a politically committed figure. The novel is credited with increasing the worldwide attention to the brutal Chilean regime and contributing directly to the international pressures that led to Pinochet's stepping down, after nearly two decades in power.

At the novel's end, Alba, having survived her terrifying imprisonment, reveals herself as the narrator of the entire novel, and credits the notebooks of her grandmother Clara, as well as periodic visits from her spirit, as the keys to both Alba's survival and the production of her narrative. Allende's privileging of the woman's narrative voice and the genres of private writing are in themselves a strong feminist statement, and reflect her conceptualization of women's power of resistance to both patriarchy and authoritarian regimes. While other writers have also traced this connection between the personal and national dimensions of machismo, there is general agreement that Allende's *The House of the Spirits*, and her subsequent work, have brought that connectedness to center stage.

Allende's second novel, *Of Love and Shadows*, explores more directly the role of women in resisting dictatorship. Reflecting a true story, the novel chronicles the discovery of a mass grave of "disappeared" victims, along with the exposure of other crimes committed by the government against rural families suspected to be part of the resistance. In that novel, as well as in *The House of the Spirits*, some male figures are viewed sympathetically, as individuals whose appreciation of passion and of freedom align them closely with the novels' female protagonists; but that holds true only for the disempowered men, those who distance themselves from the center held by authoritarianism.

A Passion for Social Justice

This exploration of the ties between patriarchy and authoritarian regimes is taken up again in Allende's later novels, beginning with *Daughter of Fortune*. However, the later group of novels demonstrates a clearer awareness of the role that class distinctions play in the assignment of gender roles, as well as the influence of governmental ideology on the imposition of those roles. Tracing the genealogies that would result in the birth of *The House of the Spirits'* progenitor Clara del Valle, *Daughter of Fortune* and *Portrait in Sepia* at the same time offer Allende the possibility to explore the intertwined histories of California and Chile, through the migrations induced by the Gold Rush of the mid-1800s. Allende explores the marginalized cultures of the US—primarily the Chinese, indigenous, and Hispanic populations—alongside similar class- and race-based oppression in Chile against the indigenous peoples; and always, she exposes the confinement of assigned gender roles and the subversive possibilities offered by rebellion in the name of freedom or love.

Zorro and *Inés of my Soul* apply these same paradigms of gender and class awareness to historical figures, the former applied to California as a Spanish colony and the latter focusing on the Spanish conquest of Chile. While *Zorro* focuses on a male hero, he is nonetheless the kind of hero constructed by popular feminine archetypes—dashing, handsome, passionate, and committed to rescuing women and the oppressed. And in *Inés of my Soul*, Allende elaborates the history of a woman who appears to model many of the characteristics that critics have accused Allende of inventing for her women characters: she is a woman who combines emotional passion with a defiance of societal norms and a strong sense of social justice, resisting the establishment of the authoritarian government that would eventually result in the class divisions that lay at the root of Chile's twentieth-century dilemmas.

The Woman as Writer

Throughout her literary trajectory, Allende has maintained an emphasis on the power of the pen, as wielded by women, and the power of reading to change women's lives. In most of her novels, one finds a chest of books, a private library, a set of notebooks or diaries, forbidden erotic novels, or another textual motherlode that charts potential new paths for the women characters. And through their narratives, many of these protagonists themselves take up the pen, directly addressing an interlocutor or a reading public and insisting on the significance and the power of telling their own stories. In this respect, Allende's metafictional emphasis is a reflection of her own trajectory, as a woman writer who has arguably changed the world. Her exposés of the corruption of Pinochet's regime, and the systems which lay at its roots; her contribution to the creation of a place for women's voices in the Latin American literary canon; and the ardent following she has established in her global readership attest to the power of women who resist through storytelling. Allende has frequently commented on the importance of her own epistolary correspondence with her mother, her journalism, and her private notebooks, alongside her memoirs, short stories and novels, as a way of exorcising her own demons and connecting with the spirits that comprise her own genealogy; and in making these stories public, she has established a legacy of women's writing that now, finally, can be considered mainstream.

SUSAN CARVALHO

Selected Works

La casa de los espíritus. Barcelona: Plaza & Janés, 1982. *The House of the Spirits*. Trans. Magda Bogin. New York: Alfred A. Knopf, 1985.

De amor y de sombra. Barcelona: Plaza & Janés, 1984. *Of Love and Shadows*. Trans. Margaret Sayers Peden. New York: Alfred A. Knopf, 1987.

Eva Luna. Barcelona: Plaza & Janés, 1987. *Eva Luna*. Trans. Margaret Sayers Peden. New York: Alfred A. Knopf, 1988.

"Por qué y para quién escribo". *Araucaria de Chile* 41 (1988): 155–62. http://www.memoriachilena.cl/mchilena01/temas/documento_detalle.asp?id=MC0014382 (accessed 15 January 2006).

Cuentos de Eva Luna. Barcelona: Plaza & Janés, 1989. *Stories of Eva Luna*. Trans. Margaret Sayers Peden. New York: Atheneum, 1991.

El plan infinito. Barcelona: Plaza & Janés, 1991. *The Infinite Plan*. Trans. Margaret Sayers Peden. New York: HarperCollins, 1993.

Paula. Barcelona: Plaza & Janés, 1994. *Paula*. Trans. Margaret Sayers Peden. New York: HarperCollins, 1995.

Afrodita: Cuentos, recetas y otros afrodisíacos. Barcelona: Plaza & Janés, 1997. *Aphrodite: A Memoir of the Senses*. Trans. Margaret Sayers Peden. New York: HarperFlamingo, 1998.

Hija de la fortuna. Barcelona: Plaza & Janés, 1999. *Daughter of Fortune*. Trans. Margaret Sayers Peden. New York: HarperCollins, 1999.

Retrato en sepia. Barcelona: Plaza & Janés, 2000. *Portrait in Sepia*. Trans. Margaret Sayers Peden. New York: HarperCollins, 2001.

Mi país inventado. New York: Random House, 2003. *My Invented Country*. Trans. Margaret Sayers Peden. New York: Harper Perennial, 2004.

Zorro. New York: Rayo, 2005. *Zorro*. Trans. Margaret Sayers Peden. New York: HarperCollins, 2005.

Inés del alma mía. New York: Rayo, 2006. *Inés of my Soul*. Trans. Margaret Sayers Peden. New York: HarperCollins, 2006.

Films

The House of the Spirits. Directed by Bille August; starring Jeremy Irons, Meryl Streep, Winona Ryder. 1994.

De amor y de sombra. Directed by Betty Kaplan; starring Antonio Banderas and Jennifer Connelly. 1996.

References and Further Reading

Bloom, Harold (ed.). *Isabel Allende*. Broomall, PA: Chelsea House, 2003.

Coddou, Marcelo (ed.). *Los libros tienen sus propios espíritus*. Xalapa, México: Universidad Veracruzana, 1986.

——. *Para leer a Isabel Allende: Introducción a* La casa de los espíritus. Concepción, Chile: Literatura Americana Reunida, 1988.

Correas Zapata, Celia. *Isabel Allende: Vida y espíritus*. Barcelona: Plaza & Janés, 1998.

Cox, Karen Castellucci. *Isabel Allende: A Critical Companion*. Westport, CT: Greenwood Press, 2003.

Feal, Rosemary G. and Miller, Yvette E. (eds). *Isabel Allende Today*. Pittsburgh, PA: Latin American Literary Review Press, 2002.

Levine, Linda Gould. *Isabel Allende*. New York: Twayne, 2002.

Ramblado-Minero, María de la Cinta. *Isabel Allende's Writing of the Self: Trespassing the Boundaries of Fiction and Autobiography*. Lewiston, NJ: Edwin Mellen Press, 2003.

Riquelme Rojas, Sonia, and Rehbein, Edna Aguirre (eds). *Critical Approaches to Isabel Allende's Novels*. New York: Peter Lang, 1991.

Rodden, John. *Conversations with Isabel Allende*. Rev. edn. Austin, TX: University of Texas Press, 2004. 1st edn. 1999.

ALONSO, DORA

Dora Alonso (1910–2001) is probably one of the most prolific female authors in Cuba as well as a journalist, war correspondent and radio and television script-writer. During her lifetime, she cultivated a variety of literary genres consecrating herself as a renowned journalist, poet, dramatist and a famous narrator of children's short stories and novels. Born in Máximo Gómez—in the province of Matanzas, Cuba—on December 22, 1910, Alonso was always surrounded and influenced by nature. Her father was a rich cattle breeder and her mother was a housewife of peasant origin. They lived in the rural area and dedicated their lives to work in the fields, maintaining a stable upper-class status. From this experience, she developed an idiosyncratic sense of Cubanness deeply attached to the land—a personal aspect that is recurrent in her work. She wrote her first poem at the age of 16, which appeared in the journal *El Mundo*. In the 1930s and 1940s, she devoted her time to work as a correspondent in the journal *Prensa Libre* and participated in an anti-imperialist organization called Joven Cuba where she met the tobacco trader Constantino Barredo Guerra who became her partner both in life and in the revolutionary fights until 1938.

At the beginning of the twentieth century, Cuba started to develop strong economic relations with the United States through which the island exported most of the sugar produced in the plantations and the mainland could intervene in Cuban political affairs. Since the nineteenth century, the United States had been interested in the annexation of Cuba due to her strategic geographical position and, moreover, they offered Spain a great quantity of money to buy the island—an offer immediately turned down by the European country. With the Teller Amendment enacted on April 19, 1898, that led to the Spanish-American War that same year, the United States promised Cubans freedom and total independence over their own country once the Spanish occupants were defeated. Spain left the island and it was consequently occupied by the United States, which crafted the Platt Amendment in 1901—a replacement of the Teller Amendment. Several agreements were specified in the amendment: the withdrawal of the remaining US troops, the acquisition of the naval base of Guantánamo, the transference of Cuban land restricted to the United States, and the permission to intervene in Cuban political affairs when indispensable. In this manner, Cuba gained formal independence in 1902. At that point, both countries established the basis of their prospective economic and political relations. Cuba's sugar entered the market of the United States and, in exchange, some selected US products appeared in Cuban society. If economic relations were effectively arranged, US cultural and political influence was highly noticeable in the island. Artists and intellectuals perceived the penetration of capitalism as a progressive sign of ruining their aspirations towards a Cuban national identity forged by nineteenth-century leaders such as José Martí. The presence of the United States in the island helped to sustain governmental corruption, the building of casinos and the gambling industry.

During those decades, Dora Alonso started to write scripts for the radio and television, while she composed her first short stories. Her work reflected how passionately she had been involved in cultural transformation as an activist engaged in anti-capitalist social commitments. Her work was also characterized by a skillful and clear handling of emotions with a great simplicity in the narrative style. In 1944, her book *Tierra adentro* received the National Prize Award by the Ministry of Education. Due to its success, *Tierra adentro* was broadcast the following years until the managers of the sponsoring firm voiced their discomfort regarding the social content of the book. As in most of her writings, she demonstrated a preoccupied concern with the increasing social gap between the elite and the working classes. Her aim was to trace the essence of Cuban culture through creole elements (the fields, the blue sky, the sea, the owl, etc.). Apart from this incident, the radio novels of the 1950s grew in popularity and many of them were successfully broadcast over CMQ radio, having an enormous international impact in places such as Puerto Rico and Miami.

In the 1950s, she started to write for children, completing the first Cuban adventure novel for that audience. At that time, Alonso's interests for the dramatic genre increased and in 1956, she started her theatrical production for children with *Pelusín y los pájaros*. Adult audiences received attention with the books *Tierra inerme, Once caballos, Gente de mar, Letras, El año 61, Agua pasada, Juega la dama* and *Escrito en el verano.* The dramatic works of Dora Alonso both for children and adult audiences, are a significant aspect of her literary career, although they have not received the same level of attention as a whole as that given to her narrative fiction and, to a lesser degree, her poetry, criticism and studies of Cuban literature. If her working life was marked by prosperity and success, her personal life was no less intense and productive.

In 1953, she decided to adopt an orphan mulatto boy, hoping to turn the child into the new man forged through the ideals of the revolution: "a Cuban who would work for moral rewards (decorations, public praise) and thus reflect a new, higher level of political consciousness" (Skidmore and Smith, 2005: 279). The following year, she traveled around Mexico and when she came back to Cuba in 1955, Alonso met Fausto Rodríguez Sánchez (Cárdenas, Matanzas, 1928) who had been a militant communist member of the Popular Socialist Party (Partido Socialista Popular) since the age of 16. By the end of the 1950s, her broadcast novels had already been presented in Panama, El Salvador, Mexico, Nicaragua, Colombia, Brazil, Venezuela and other countries. Her enthusiasm and willingness to collaborate in the progress of the nation led to her writing textbooks for primary schools in Cuba. With her publications in the journal *Bohemia*, she aimed to introduce the artistic and literary expression into the lives of Cuban children. She worked as a war correspondent for *Bohemia* where all her chronicles of the Playa de Girón events are compiled. Alonso was the only woman involved in a battle for almost three days of combat during April 1961 near the Bay of Pigs. Cuba's revolutionary militias, police, and armed forces defeated an invasion of Cuban, anti-Castro mercenaries supported by the Kennedy Administration which attempted to bring down the socialist government. The Cold War (1947–91) manifested the division of the world into two opposing blocs, communism and capitalism. And thus, the combat was the consequence of Cuba's agreements with the Soviet Union, the nationalization of Cuba's economy and the establishment of an authoritarian government. As a response to Cuba's alliance with the Soviet Union, the United States reacted by embargoing all trade to Cuba.

Nevertheless, the victory in Playa Girón reinforced an anti-capitalist sentiment and a sense of unity and nationalism among leftist Cubans. It empowered the peasantry sectors and rural workers who had been strongly rejected and disfavored during the second republic that includes the governments of Fulgencio Batista (1940–44), Ramón Grau San Martin (1944–48), Carlos Prío Socarrás (1948–52), and from 1952 to 1954 Batista staged a *coup d'état* becoming a provisional president until he won elections in 1954 to preside over the country for five more years. Alonso's perception of the poverty and misery that affected a huge part of the Cuban society pushed her into defending the ideals manifested by the communist system. Having been deeply involved in the country life, she decided to participate in Playa de Girón where she could empathize with those fighting for their freedom and their rights. In the same year as the victory of Playa de Girón, she published her novel *Tierra inerme* that received the highest recognition at the II Spanish American Literary Contest at Casa de las Américas. Since then, she has continued working on children's books, novels, poetry and journalism. Moreover, Alonso has received numerous prizes and awards for her life-long dedication to her homeland—Cuba; to the development of children's education; and to her prolific career as writer. These prizes include the National Prize of Novel in 1994, conferred by the Education Ministry. In 1981, she was awarded the Honor of National Culture. In 1997, Alonso received the José Martí Infant Literature World Prize and in 1988 the Félix Varela Order (1st grade) and National Prize of Literature, just to mention a few.

Influences and Themes

The social transformations Cuba was undergoing at the beginning of the century made a big impression on the attitude and discomfort of many writers and intellectuals who were in favor of Cuba's emancipation. Foreign intervention and the importation of North American culture and life-style were perceived as a threat to Cuban national identity. Therefore, Alonso and other intellectuals such as Fernando Ortiz, José Antonio Portuondo, Juan Marinello, Dulce María Loynaz, Mariano Brull, Emilio Ballagas or Samuel Feijoo defended Cuban nationalism and highlighted in their work the autochthonous aspects of their culture. They were all influenced by the task José Martí had started during his lifetime. Alonso's attachment to her land reflects Martí's social and cultural preoccupations. Both writers shared a personal commitment to Cuba and situated their work critically against US imperialism. Other writers such as Getrudis Gómez de Avellaneda and José María Heredia became national icons in the exile but were deeply involved in all things Cuban. The cultural background of Spain and Africa was clearly manifest throughout Alonso's works. Besides utilizing Spanish as her mother language, she was also acquainted with a large amount of African culture. In this direction, she knew how to communicate with the Cuban people through the cultural syncretism that characterized and defined the national identity of the Caribbean island.

In this capacity, her work delved into the daily lives of simple men and women who traditionally have remained silent within the official representation of history and culture. It also approached daily events in which a profound connection with nature and with human values was exposed. With respect to the articulation of a feminist discourse in Cuba, Dora Alonso contributed to the literary corpus of female writers that included Countess Merlín (1789–1852), Marchioness Jústiz de Santa Ana (1733–1807), and the renowned Romantic poet Gertrudis Gómez de Avellaneda (1814–73). Bearing in mind this feminist legacy, intellectual women writers born at the beginning of the twentieth century continued to develop a feminist discourse particularly linked to Cuban social concerns. Despite her leftist ideologies in support of the revolution, her feminist discourse demonstrated how the communist system created a mystification of motherhood through the confinement of women to the household. In her work, she represented human and animal mothers as victims of a natural and cultural determinism that perpetuated an ideal mother role which suited patriarchal expectations. In this respect, she opened up in her short stories new possibilities for motherhood that escaped normative models of family and kinship structures.

Along with feminist insights and the deployment of Afro-Caribbean and *criollo* (creole) elements, a philosophical exploration and the use of magic realism permeated her literary works. In particular—and probably her most famous novel—*Tierra inerme* depicted her personal experiences, providing an accurate portrayal of the Cuban fields before the triumph of the revolution in 1959. The characters, setting and situations in the novel mirror the reality she knew very well, including the hopes but also the poverty and misery that permeated that world. Her work condemned the infinite differences between the working class and rich landowners in pre-revolutionary Cuba while also censuring racism against Afro-Caribbean individuals. Similarly, she offered a critical panorama of the corruption that dominated Cuban society through the creation of a marginally exploited peasantry. However, the narrator of the book called into question the conditions of women's life during the revolution. As mentioned before, the revolutionary system idealized motherhood in its traditional sense. Therefore, Alonso's critics not only confronted pre-social status quo, but also the gender inequalities constantly present in society before, during and after the installment of Fidel Castro's government. In her children's novels, she introduced the *criollo* (creole) magic realism in a universal sense. In other words, the Cubanness is examined in its universal dimension while she still resituated the Cuban essence locally. Although her aim was not to create didactic novels, she tried to contribute to the personal and social formation of the child. And in these particular instances, the political messages were absorbed by more concrete life-teaching values that she herself practiced and attempted to infuse into her characters and readers through her narrative, poetry and drama but more importantly, through her everyday activities.

With respect to her personal life, she fought against US policies and the local governments of the first decades. But despite her intellectual and social involvement in pre- and post-revolutionary Cuba, Dora Alonso's adult writings have largely been rejected by the critics. Alonso mostly traced the lives of women and marginal individuals in the poorest social contexts, and the Revolution was not mainly interested in revealing the miseries and the gender inequality perpetuated by culture. She focused on how women were condemned by patriarchy to a social determinism that demanded of them full devotion to children, to the household and, in most cases, to a job they needed in order to escape poverty. Moreover, the critics stressed her children's literature and her role as a national educator. She was even encouraged by the Minister of Education to write literature for children that included Cuban themes and political revolutionary ideologies. Therefore, Dora Alonso's works deserve more critical analysis in the field of cultural studies and theory.

IRUNE DEL RIO GABIOLA

Selected Works

Prose

Tierra inerme. La Habana: Ediciones Casa de las Américas, 1961.
Ponolani. La Habana: Ediciones Granma, 1966.
El caballito enano. La Habana: Editorial Gente Nueva, 1968.
Once caballos. La Habana: Ediciones Unión, 1970.
El cochero azul. La Habana: Editorial Gente Nueva, 1975.
Cuentos. La Habana: Ediciones Unión, 1976.
Una. La Habana: Editorial Arte y Literatura, 1977.
Gente de mar. La Habana: Editorial Gente Nueva, 1977.
El libro de Camilín. La Habana: Editorial Gente Nueva, 1979.
Pelusín del Monte. La Habana: Editorial Gente Nueva, 1979.
Letras. La Habana: Editorial Letras Cubanas, 1980.
Agua pasada. La Habana: Ediciones Unión, 1981.
El valle de la Pájara Pinta. La Habana: Ediciones Casa de las Améŕicas, 1984.
Juega la dama. La Habana: Editorial Letras Cubanas, 1989.
Aventuras de Guille en busca de la gaviota negra. La Habana: Editora Juvenil, 1991.
Tres lechuzas en un cuento. La Habana: Editorial Gente Nueva, 1994.

Poetry

Viaje al Sol. La Habana: Editorial Gente Nueva, 1979.
Palomar. La Habana: Ediciones Unión, 1979.

La flauta de chocolate. La Habana: Editorial Gente Nueva, 1980.
El grillo caminante. La Habana: Editorial Gente Nueva, 1981.
Suma. La Habana: Editorial Letras Cubanas, 1984.
Los payasos. La Habana: Editorial Gente Nueva, 1985.
Escrito en el verano. La Habana: Editorial Letras Cubanas, 1993.

Drama

Espantajo y los pájaros. La Habana: Consejo Nacional de Cultura, 1966.
Doñita Abeja y Doñita Bella. La Habana: Editorial Gente Nueva, 1976.
Teatro para niños. La Habana: Editorial Gente Nueva, 1992.

Journalism

La Revolución Cubana y los niños. La Habana: Ediciones Venceremos, 1962.
El año 61. La Habana: Editorial Letras Cubanas, 1981.
Tiempo ido. La Habana: Editorial Letras Cubanas, 1997.

References and Further Reading

Davies, Catherine. "Beastly Women and Underdogs: The Short Fiction of Dora Alonso." In Catherine Davies and Montserrat Ordóñez (eds), *Women Writers in Twentieth-Century Spain and Spanish America*. Lewiston, NY: Mellen, 1993.

Echebarría Santos, Liset. "El criollismo en los cuentos de Dora Alonso". In Carlos E. Caraballo Vázquez and Salvador Bueno Menéndez (eds), *Acentos cubanos: cinco ensayos*. La Habana: Ediciones Extramuros, 2000.

González López, Waldo. "La flauta". *Casa de las Américas* 20(120) (1980): 166–70.

Saldaña, Exilia. "Cubanía y universalidad en Dora Alonso". *En julio como en enero* 4(7) (1988): 19.

Schlau, Stacey. "Mothers in the Mexican and Cuban Revolutions: Nellia Campobelo, Magdalena Mondragón, and Dora Alonso". In *Spanish American Women's Use of the World: Colonial through Contemporary Narratives*. Tucson, AZ: University of Arizona Press, 2001.

Shea, Maureen. "A Growing Awareness of Sexual Oppression in the Novels of Contemporary Latin American Women Writers". *Confluencia: Revista Hispánica de Cultura y Literatura* 4(1) (1988): 53–9.

Skidmore, Thomas E. and Smith, Peter. *Modern Latin America*. New York: Oxford University Press, 2005.

ALVARADO DE RICORD, ELSIE

Elsie Alvarado de Ricord (1928–2005) was one of the most important writers of poetry in Panama and a well-known academic. As the first woman to head the Panamanian Academy of the Language and the author of many seminal texts on Panamanian literature and language, she opened doors for many Panamanian women to follow in the field of education and the arts. She also reflected in her concern with preserving the purity of the Spanish language in Panama and her interest in studying the main authors of her national literature, a current in Panamanian literature that sought to preserve regional and national values in the face of the growing internationalization of Panama as a result of its geographical location and the existence of the Panama Canal.

She was born in the province of Chiriqui, Panama in 1928, and died in Panama City in 2005. Her life mirrors Panama's change from a newly created nation in the early part of the twentieth century under the political and social control of the United States to a more independent nation in the twenty-first century with control of the Canal. As a native of the western province of Chiriqui which borders on Costa Rica, she represents the conflict in Panamanian literature between the values of the interior provinces, with their emphasis on a more traditional life, and those of the port cities of Panama and Colón, with their varied foreign-born population and their ever-changing lifestyle. She is also one of several women writers from the province of Chiriqui, among them Maria Olimpia de Obaldia, who were known for their poetry and command of the Spanish language.

The Academic

Alvarado de Ricord left her native region of Chiriqui to study at the University of Panama in the capital city where she graduated first in her class in the School of Humanities. She then went abroad, as did many Panamanian scholars of her generation, to earn a doctorate in Romance Philology at the Central University of Madrid and a certificate in Linguistics in Uruguay. Upon her return to Panama, she continued her academic career at the University of Panama where she taught for 40 years and where she rose to be a full professor of Spanish Phonetics and Literary Theory. She became during this time the director of the Panamanian Academy for the Language, correspondent with the Royal Academy of the Language in Spain.

Her academic publications were closely interwoven with her poetic production. Reflecting her constant interest in the spoken language and linguistics, she wrote a book on the Spanish of Panama as well as erudite monographs on the poetry of authors such as Dámaso Alonso and Rubén Darío. But it was to be her studies on the main poets in Panama that were to gain her national recognition and a following among her literature students. Her books on Panamanian poets such as Ricardo Miró (1973), Ricardo Bermudez (1960) and Demetrio Herrrera Sevillano (1952) were to become the seminal texts on the authors. Many of her students, inspired by her works on authors who had largely been ignored by critics both in Panama and abroad, followed in her footsteps to study the literature of Panama. Her careful, albeit traditional, studies on the style and structure of these poets were to be reflected in her own poems.

The Poet

Elsie Alvarado de Ricord's poetry has as its basic theme love. The subject of love in her works evolves from erotic love in her first two books *Holocausto de Rosa* (1953, Rose-Colored Holocaust) and *Entre materia y sueño* (1966, Between Matter and Dreams) to spiritual love in other books such as *Pasajeros en tránsito* (1973, Passengers in Transit) and *Es real y de este mundo* (1978, It is Real and of this World).

In her first book, *Holocausto de rosa* (Rose-Colored Holocaust), love is expressed as sensual, through the expression of the delight of the senses. In contrast to earlier Panamanian women authors who had been forced by social mores to hide their sensuality, Alvarado de Ricord expresses in this book her complete enjoyment of carnal pleasure and the experience of loving and being loved. *Holocausto de rosa* will chart the course for the examination of love which will permeate all her poetry: a roadmap for all the different states of love.

In her first books, the poet uses the images of the lily and the rose to represent purity, chastity and the act of giving herself in love. Another symbol that she uses often is the color blue, under the evident influence of the poet Rúbén Darío, a color that stands for dreams, to which the poet opposes its fierce enemy, time.

Her second book of poems, *Entre materia y sueño* creates the framework within which she will place her poetic creation. The poem "El sueño" (The Dream) introduces us into the spiritual realm, almost forgotten in her first book. The color blue suggests the idea of immensity, liberty, the infinite. Love is seen as a long dream from which the poet does not ever want to wake up. It is her only weapon against the power of time.

Alvarado de Ricord's obsession with the passage of time is seen in her choice of the title for her third book of poems *Pasajeros en tránsito* (1973, Passengers in Transit). It is also the theme of her third and fourth books. Time will unite the second part of her poetic creation, just as love had united the first part. Love is the only force that can combat time, and continues to play a strong role in her poetry. As she says in the poem, "Cuando tu voz me invade" (When Your Voice Invades Me), "with your breath you erase time from my body which is born again in your hands" (*Siempre el Amor. Poesía completa*, Always Love, Complete Poetry, p. 43).

In her last two books of poems, the author discusses social topics. Her poetical language changes so as to transmit her message with cues from the reality which surrounds her. Her reaction to the death of the Panamanian youths in 1964 who were killed by anti-riot police in the Canal Zone when they tried to fly the Panamanian flag in what was then US-controlled territory is reflected in one of her most popular poems, "A los heroes panameños" (To the Panamanian heroes) (*Siempre el amor. Poesía completa*, pp. 146–9). In other poems she contrasts the poverty of the lower classes with that of the affluent lifestyle of the elite.

But these are few variations from her predominant study of the nature of love in its erotic, material and spiritual aspects. Her last book of poetry *Es real y de este mundo* (It is Real and of this World) has as its title the last verse of the final poem. In this book she seems to come to a decision as to the conflict between spiritual and physical love which she presented in her second book. Its name serves as a metaphor for all of Alvarado de Ricord's work on the nature of love. She now comes to the conclusion that love for her is of an earthly nature even though she had debated its spiritual aspect in earlier works.

Critical Interpretations

Critical studies on Elsie Alvarado de Ricord are few and far between. Despite her own valuable contribution to the field of literary criticism on Panamanian authors, she herself has not been the object of many serious academic studies or attracted the attention of foreign critics. Many of the academics who have studied her work in Panama point out the importance of the theme of love in her work but debate its relationship to materialistic philosophy and the topics of death and time. Carlos Manuel Gastezoro in 1952 was the first to point out that the theme of love in Alvarado de Ricord's work was not a subject in itself but instead was presented as an antidote to the ravages of time and death. He also pointed out that her poetry reflected a change in her portrayal of nature from that of the countryside where she grew up to that of the urban city where she lived her adult life.

Victor Fernández Cañizales and Avaro Mendez Franco published essays in the 1970s on Alvarado de Ricord's works. Mendez Franco divides her works into erotic love (the first book) material love (the second book) and political themes (the poems published in 1959). Victor Fernández Cañizales presents the thesis that her poetry in all four of her books is above all materialistic and that Alvarado de Ricord does not distinguish between erotic and spiritual love but, on the contrary, believes that they are both part of the same experience. Fernández Cañizales also examines Alvarado de Ricord's obsession with time, especially in her later books.

Isabel Turner in 1982 points out that Alvarado de Ricord was the first to free herself from the constraints that prevented free expression in poetry on the part of Panamanian women writers. Sonia Riquelme's is perhaps the most useful of all the critical studies on the poet. In 2000, she showed that Alvarado de Ricord's works have influences of Juan Ramón Jiménez, Gabriela Mistral, Rúben Darío and the Panamanian poets Ricardo Miró and María Olimpia de Obaldia among others. She believes that Alvardo de Ricord imposes the order of sensuality over the order of reason and that in her last book, *Pasajeros en tránsito* she changes style dramatically and her work includes much more social commentary.

MAIDA WATSON

Selected Works

Notas sobre la poesía de Demetrio Herrera Sevillano. Panamá: Universidad de Panamá, 1951.

Holocausto de rosa. México: Editorial Humanismo, 1953.

Estilo y densidad en la poesía de Ricardo J. Bermudez. Panamá: INAC, 1960.

Entre materia y sueño. Panamá: author, 1966.

La obra poética de Dámaso Alonso. Madrid: Editorial Gredos, 1968.

El español de Panamá. Estudio fonético y fonológico. Panamá: Editorial Universitaria, 1971

Aproximación a la poesía de Ricardo Miró. Panamá: INCUDE, Editorial de la Nación, 1972.

Pasajeros en tránsito. Panamá: author, 1973.

Rúben Darío y su obra poética. Montevideo: Biblioteca Nacional, 1978.

Es real y de este mundo. Panamá: Talleres de Impresora Panamá, 1978

Usos del español actual(Notas sobre el lenguaje). Panamá: author, 1996.

Siempre el amor. Panamá: author, 2002.

References and Further Reading

Bermudez, Ricardo J. "Pasajeros en tránsito de Elsie Alvarado de Ricord". *Boletín de la Academia Panameña de la Lengua* 4(l) (1973): 97–100.

Fernández Cañizales, Victor. "Elsie Alvarado de Ricord poetisa del amor". *Boletín de la Academia Panameña de la Lengua* 1979: 1–25.

Gasteazoro, Carlos Miguel. "El 'Holocausto de Rosa' de Elsie Alvarado de Ricord". *Revista Nacional de Cultura. Nueva Epoca* 23 (Jan.–Mar. 1991): 182–4.

Gómez de Blanco, Emma. *Ironía de mujer: un espacio para la crítica literaria: ensayos*. Panamá: Fundación Cultural Signos, 2000.

Mendez-Franco, Alvaro. "Las tres facetas del amor en la obra poética de Elsie Alvarado de Ricord". *Revista Cultural Loteria* (Aug.–Sept. 1976): 61–4.

Miro, Rodrigo. "Las mujeres en las letras del Istmo". *Revista Literaria* 296–7 (Nov.–Dec. 1980): 54–60.

Osses, Esther María. "Pasajeros en tránsito". *Boletín de la Academia Panameña de la Lengua* 4(5) (1977): 83–5.

Riquelme, Sonia. "Permanencia de la poesía de Elsie Alvarado de Ricord". *Congreso de Literatura*. Vol. 58. Panama: Universidad Santa Maria La Antigua, 2000.

Turner, Isabel. "Homenaje a Elsie Alvarado de Ricord". *Boletín de la Academia Panameña de la Lengua* 5(2) (1982): 25–7.

ALVAREZ PONCE DE LEÓN, GRISELDA

Born in Guadalajara in 1918, Griselda Alvarez Ponce de León today is considered one of the foremost feminist poets in México. Alvarez hails from a family of politicians; she is both a politician and a poet. Alvarez, however, took the long route of tradition; she went first through marriage and motherhood and only later became the first female governor of the State of Colima (1979–85). Her poetry, meanwhile, ranges from the love poems of her youth to the existential concerns of an elderly person. A teacher by training, Alvarez also holds degrees in Counseling and Letters from the UNAM (National University of México). She has been a teacher of handicapped children and served as the head of the Mexican Office of Child Protection. As an intellectual, she is known as a poet and editor of the magazine *Acá* and had a long involvement with the magazines *Revista de Revistas*, *Ovaciones* and *Excelsior*. Although later in her life Alvarez became more involved in politics, her intense love for poetry has not decreased. She begins her intellectual production with a compendium of love poems in *Cementário de Pájaros* (1956, Birds Cemetery) with which she begins a career that has encompassed more than four decades. Her more recent *Sonetos Terminales* (1997, Terminal Sonnets) and *Erótica* (1999, Erotica) still reflect her ability to express her feelings for a long-gone beauty and her passion for love.

The Erotic as Love

As an accomplished poet, capable of creating an unmatched verbal sensuality, Alvarez owes her fame to the rich erotic lyrics that have characterized much of her work. Alvarez is a poet whose refreshing work gives the reader a glimpse of women's feelings om taboo subjects, especially women's active sexuality. Her erotic poetry not only challenges the notions of the passive, asexual woman, but also calls for sexual femininity to reclaim its active central position in society. Alvarez' lyrics defy long-held beliefs of a traditional society and stress that the erotic should be part of women's lives without parameters, without shame and with no constraints. Alvarez' poetry falls into what Luzmaría Jiménez has called "un erotismo activo" ("active erotic love") with high artistic dexterity which she notes characterizes much of Hispanic women's modern poetry (2003: 8). For Alvarez, however, the erotic in her work is part of love; in fact, for her the erotic might be the highest expression of love. In an interview with Virginia Arzate, Alvarez confesses enjoying this type of love, but clarifies that the erotic does not imply sexual deviations. She confesses that she enjoys "el erotismo" ("the erotic") because it is "la pasión del amor" ("the passion of love"). She later adds that she is convinced that love is "arte y ciencia" ("an art and a science").

Suffering, Law and Affection

In "Pubertad de convento" (Saintly Puberty), she speaks of a youthful sexuality which is under constraints and control; in this poem, sexual self-discovery is quenched partially but not overcome by a nun's panoptic eye. In "Estación sin nombre" (Station without a Name), the lyrics of a maturing sexuality come to fore. In "Eclypse" (Eclipse), for example, the speaker declares to the world her sexual enjoyment of her lover, even qualifying the type of encounters; she confesses how she lives for him and specifies the erotic character of their relationship. The female persona is also the initiator of their lovemaking. Alvarez verbalizes these feelings with a poetic character that takes the initiative and makes her lover aware of her feelings for him. In this poem, women's sexuality is clearly without reserve and without boundaries. The speaker wants her lover to be aware of her desires, especially her wish that he be a perennial part of her own being. Because of this choice of themes, Esther Hernández has called Alvarez the "poeta del amor, del cuerpo y la sensualidad femenina" ("the poet of love, of the body and the feminine sensuality") (quoted in Trejo).

However, not all of Alvarez' poetry is about erotic satisfaction; in some of her poems the lover's sorrow and the inevitability of separation are the unavoidable traits of love. In "Paisaje" (Scenery), the poet gives the reader a glimpse of this dichotomy as she stresses that love entails suffering, which is accentuated by the lover's long absence. The poetic voice acknowledges to her lover that this absence converts love into a punishing desire. To the celebration of women's sexuality, the acceptance of sorrow and happiness as part of the nature of love, Alvarez adds the theme of the irrelevance of laws that forbid affectionate unions. For her, not all erotic relationships need to be sanctified by law. For her, love does not need regulations, judges, or marriage licenses or the acquiescence of culture. It only needs two willing, passionate and unattached individuals. Besides her rejection of legality as the premise of love, Alvarez also writes about the ephemeral yet passionate characteristic of human relationships. We read in "Nido" (Nest), for example, of the swift nature of love, which leaves a deep impression because of its unplanned character and the passionate scars which love leaves in its wake. Nonetheless, one can perceive that regardless of love's fleeting quality, the poet welcomes it as part of life.

Women's Right to Love

Alvarez' own views on erotic poetry clarify the ambiguity of her verses. In the introduction to her anthology of Mexican women poets, Alvarez points out that erotic poetry comes from deep within a woman's soul. For her, this soul is the place where women long for that right to have an active sexuality. This site, however, is not easily reached from the outside. That personal place lies deep within a woman's soul and it is surrounded by "agua profunda" ("deep waters)" where a woman "impredecible como los ciclones" ("unpredictable like the cyclones") searches for the truth which is denied to her. This call for a love without inhibitions and the acceptance of women's sexuality as part of their nature reflects a qualitative development in women's poetry, especially in México where women's sexuality is still controlled by the masculine gaze. In

Latin America, despite old traditions and social constraints, poets such as Cristina Peri Rossi, Delmira Agustini, Gioconda Belli and Clementina Suárez have long championed women's rights to express themselves. Outside México, however, Alvarez is virtually unknown and is still to be "discovered" by the international critics.

JORGE J. BARRUETO

Selected Works

Cementerio de Pájaros. México: Cuadernos Americanos, 1956.
Anatomía Superficial. México: FCE, 1967.
Estación sin Nombre. Barcelona: Ediciones Marte, 1972.
Desierta Compañía. Colima, México: Universidad de Colima, 1980.
Estación sin nombre. Colima, México: Universidad de Colima, 1983.
Cuesta Arriba: Memorias de la primera gobernadora. Colima, México: Universidad de Colima, Fondo de Cultura Económica, 1992.
Sonetos Terminales. México: Fondo de Cultura Económica, 1997.
Erótica. México: Universidad del Claustro de Sor Juana, 1999.
Selección de poemas. Voz de la autora. Colima, México: Universidad de Colima, 1996.

References and Further Reading

Alvarez, Griselda (ed.). *10 mujeres en la poesia mexicana del siglo XX*. México: Colección Metropolitana, 1973, pp. 7–10.
Arzate, Virginia. "El erotismo es la pasión del amor. Interview with Griselda Alvarez". *Etcetera*. http://www.etcetera.com.mx/1999/331/av0332.htm
Cortés, Eladio. *Dictionary of Mexican Literature*. Westport, CT: Greenwood Press, 1992.
Jiménez Faro, Luzmaría. *Breviario de los sentidos: poesia erótica escrita por mujeres*. Madrid: Torremozas, 2003, pp. 5–11.
Manca, Valeria. *El Cuerpo del deseo: poesía erótica femenina en el México actual*. México, D.F.: Universidad Autonoma Metropolitana, 1989.
Ocampo, Aurora M. and Ernesto Prado Velázquez. *Diccionario de escritores mexicanos*. México: UNAM, 1967.
Rodríguez, Victoria Elizabeth. *Women's Participation in Mexican Political Life*. Boulder, CO: Westview Press, 1998.
Trejo, Ángel. "Necesaria y justa, la reivindicación literaria de Pita Amor: Esther Hernández Palacios." http://www.conaculta.gob.mx/saladeprensa/2003/18jul/pita.htm
Villoro, Carmen. *Mujeres que besan y tiemblan: antología mexicana de poesía erótica femenina*. México, D.F.: Planeta, 1999.

ALMEIDA, JÚLIA LOPES DE

Born into an intellectual family, Lopes de Almeida (1862–1934) started writing at a very young age and published in newspapers such as *Tribuna Liberal*, *A Semana*, *O País*, *Gazeta de Notícias* and *Jornal do Comércio*. Her novels, though most first appeared in installments in newspapers (*folhetins*), were later published as books. In a tight market with few publishers and few booksellers, this accomplishment was certainly noteworthy and speaks to the popularity of her work during her lifetime. After her death, however, she was quickly forgotten, due to the change in literary taste, and her work was considered too didactic and conventional. Almeida's works were rediscovered in the 1980s, following a new edition of her novel *Correio da roça* (Letters from the Countryside) in 1987.

Her most important novels were written during a turbulent period in Brazil, in the wake of abolition and the birth of the Republic, when rapid economic and social changes led to feelings of insecurity throughout the nation. In Almeida's work, she is constantly looking for new paths that would help Brazil become a modern country.

Apart from novels, Lopes de Almeida wrote theatre, poetry, journalism, children's books and articles for women's magazines. *Livro das noivas* (1896, The Brides' Book) is a handbook for young brides in which she makes explicit her concept of women's position. Her advice to young brides emphasizes the necessity of subordination to the husband's desires, and she supports the improvement of women's education primarily as a benefit for the better instruction of their children. She advises women to focus on housekeeping and personal hygiene, take up gardening, avoid unnecessary luxury, keep a tight rein on the financial budget and participate in physical sports.

Although in her novels many female characters are faced with similar issues of housekeeping, financial woes and child raising, Lopes de Almeida is much less rigid in her distinction of good versus evil than in *Livro das noivas*. Rejecting deterministic theories on the inferiority of women, she always insists on the relationship between the ills of society and the crisis of gender roles. Although solutions are presented, the reader is nevertheless allowed empathy for the characters who fail to correct their mistakes. It is this empathy, together with her simple and natural language, that makes her a remarkably accessible and entertaining writer for contempory audiences.

More in-depth explorations of Lopes de Almeida's apparently contradictory images of women, such as Sônia Roncador's current research on the figure of the housemaid in Almeida's oeuvre, will hopefully generate more contemporary appreciation of her work.

A fierce republican, Lopes de Almeida spoke in favor of abolition of slavery, as her novel *A família Medeiros* (1891, The Medeiros Family) shows. Abolition is depicted as a humanitarian cause that affects and is influenced by women and men alike. The novel personalizes the issue of abolition by chronicling the effects of slave uprisings, contentious political debate, and the declaration of abolition on one plantation family in the state of São Paulo. The work was written between 1886–88, before the decree of abolition was issued.

The central conflict in the novel focuses on Medeiros, the slave-owning father, and his relationship to his abolitionist son Otávio. However, the hero of the story is not Otávio, but his cousin Eva, a progressive, educated, independent woman who unwittingly threatens her uncle Medeiros' authority. Otávio, fascinated by Eva, learns that she speaks German, an indication of her progressive education. An enlightened woman, Eva has declared she will never marry without love, as her sisters are expected to do, and employs free workers on her farm, following the example of her father. Lopes de Almeida contrasts the two farms: her characters comment on the beauty and prosperity of Eva's Mangueiral, where the workers are free, versus the flawed Santa Genoveva, where the patriarch Medeiros rules, a cold, uncomfortable and unhealthy place, where the despondency of the slaves has led to negligence.

A família Medeiros also includes detailed scenes reflecting Brazilian plantation life at the end of the nineteenth century. The author, in her desire for accuracy, includes lengthy descriptions of flora and fauna, typical of the Realist and Naturalist novels of the nineteenth century.

A viúva Simões (The Widow Simões) concentrates on the limitations faced by one woman in a society clinging to old social norms in times of political transition. Peggy Sharpe, who wrote the Introduction to the reprint of this novel, compares the story to that of a Greek tragedy. In a society with strict social codes, Ernestina, zealously pursuing her own happiness, causes the downfall of her beloved daughter. Still educated in the traditional ways of colonial times, young and intelligent women such as Ernestina are easily seduced by vague romantic ideals and neglect to appreciate the virtues of middle-class existence (20).

The story is set at the beginning of the New Republic in 1891. Ernestina is a virtuous young widow and loving mother. Soon, however, Ernestina's exclusive dedication to home and family is tested by the return of her first love, Luciano, who has been living in France since leaving her without an explanation so many years before. News of his whereabouts reawakens her feelings. Obsessed by her rekindled affections for Luciano and driven by her need to reclaim this love after having sacrificed passionate love during her marriage to the honest but unimaginative Simões, Ernestina's behavior changes quickly and she starts to regret her life with Simões. Luciano, on the other hand, confides in his close friend, Rosas, that he is interested in having a physical relationship with Ernestina but does not want to marry her.

Ernestina, perceiving a change in Luciano's feelings toward her daughter Sara, insists that Sara marry; Sara refuses, admitting that she loves Luciano. Sara, grief-stricken, falls gravely ill. Due to complications resulting from an error made with her medication, Sara will remain in a permanent vegetative state.

Although Ernestina, Sara and Luciano are all flawed characters, the reader is nevertheless allowed a good deal of sympathy for them. Luciano is a playboy but was truly hurt when he discovered Ernestina had quickly married Simões after he was forced to go to France. Sara is upset because of her mother's behavior and remains faithful to her father, but assumes that any kind of change in the household implies a lack of respect for her father's memory. Ernestina feels guilty about her passion and her loveless marriage, but is unable to control her feelings. Eventually, she is grateful that Sara is still alive, and refocuses on her duties as a mother.

A falência (The Bankruptcy) is the account of the unrealistic optimism and subsequent financial ruin of a coffee baron and his family. Francisco Theodoro, a self-made Portuguese immigrant intensely focused on his business, engages in risky, but potentially prosperous, business investments and loses everything. The real tragedy of the narrative is caused not by the bankruptcy but by Theodoro's misunderstanding of his role within, and value to, his family.

Theodoro meets the beautiful Camilla, quickly marries her, and settles into a calm life with her, only interrupted occasionally by his infidelities. Camilla knows that she is expected to ignore her husband's infidelities, but her reflections on contemporary novels indicate her awareness of the moral double standard imposed on her and she has a love affair with Dr. Gervásio. Camilla also tries to hide other problematic situations from Theodoro. She lies to him about their son Mario, a rebellious young man who occupies himself with spending his father's fortune, and is having an affair with an older woman. Camilla is never upset about the loss of the fortune, but complains bitterly that Theodoro did not trust her enough to tell her about his problems. The family follows suit and quickly accepts the loss. But Theodoro cannot accept his new life; he cannot bear to think of Camilla without fine clothes and luxury items and eventually commits suicide. Camilla sees her current misery as the direct result of her adultery. She distracts herself from her problems by focusing on work, inspired by the example of her poor niece Ruth, a talented violinist. Thus she manages to reaffirms her primary role as mother after straying from the correct path.

The plot of *A intrusa* (1908, The Intruder) set in the home of Argemiro, a wealthy lawyer, portrays the effects of the upwardly mobile middle class on the perceived power of the elites. Lopes de Almeida posits a moral tale about the merits of hard work, portrayed as central to the modern Brazilian family, against the backdrop of a leisured aristocracy in decline.

Argemiro endeavors to bring his daughter Maria da Glória back to the city she left after the death of her mother. Citing her need for a better education than that provided on the country estate, he finds a sensible reason to bring her back. He decides to hire a governess in order to raise his daughter at home, knowing, all the while, that his decision as a single father to raise his daughter is unorthodox and that it will cause problems with his stately mother-in-law, the Baroness. Alice, the young governess in her widowed son-in-law's home, is an intrusion, *intrusa* in her life.

Notably, Alice never speaks of her love for her employer, nor is her response to his marriage proposal included in the story. Alice, the lower-class but educated woman, is interesting as a character primarily for her absence from the narrative. She is constantly a topic of conversation and of others' speculation, but almost never speaks herself.

In her Introduction to this novel, Elódia Xavier comments that Lopes de Almeida does not yet manifest a consciousness of women's social situation, but that she rather follows patriarchal ideology. This position seems unattainable when one situates Almeida's ideas in her own time. Women, according to Almeida, are supposed to work, be thrifty and be good mothers, rather than the empty-headed flirtatious creatures they are taught to be.

Correio da roça (1913, Letters from the Countryside) an epistolary novel, details the hardships endured by a widow whose financial security vanished with her husband's death and who is forced to leave Rio and live in a country estate. Maria, disheartened at her current state of affairs, forlornly writes long letters to her friend Fernanda. Fernanda, in her response, immediately asserts that life in the country can be productive, advises Maria to plant potatoes, and affirms her idealization of Brazil's agricultural destiny. Maria thus exemplifies the adaptability of the elite and eventually transforms the melancholic country estate where she is forced to live into a beautiful, happy, successful home where her family has found happiness. Sylvie Paixão has commented in her Introduction how Almeida, who as a woman could hardly be expected to write the same public discourse as her male contemporaries, uses the "feminine form" of personal letters and diaries to express her concerns about the future of her country (p. 10).

Several of Almeida's novels have been reprinted and hopefully English translations will follow. Apart from novels, she also wrote journalism, short stories, children's books, theatre and essays that are also being rediscovered. As Peggy Sharpe observes, the sanctification of the role of mother should be seen as an attempt to position the problem of female education at the center of social, economic and political problems of Brazilian society (pp. 24–5).

Scholarship on Júlia Lopes de Almeida is increasing rapidly, both in Brazil and in the United States. The following bibliography mentions only the more easily available works. The most complete bibliography is by Peggy Sharpe in her 1999 Introduction to *The Widow Simões*.

MAY E. BLETZ

Selected Works

A família Medeiros. Rio de Janeiro, 1892. First published in weekly installments in *Gazeta de Notícias*, from October 16 to December 17, 1891.

A viúva Simões. Lisboa: António Maria Pereira, 1897. First published in installments in *Gazeta de Notícias*, Rio de Janeiro, 1895. This book has been reprinted, with an excellent Introduction by Peggy Sharp. Florianópolis: Editora Mulheres, 1997.

A falência. Rio de Janeiro: Oficina de Obras d'A Tribuna, 1901. Reprinted São Paulo: HUCITEC / Secretaria da Cultura, Ciência e Tecnologia, 1978.

A intrusa. Rio de Janeiro: Francisco Alves, 1908. First published in installments in *Jornal do Comércio*, Rio de Janeiro, 1905. Elódia Xavier has edited an edition published by Departamento Nacional do Livro; Rio de Janeiro: Fundação Biblioteca Nacional, 1994.

Correio da roça. Rio de Janeiro: Francisco Alves, 1913. First published in installments in *O País* from September 7, 1909 to October 17, 1910. Sylvia Perlingeiro Paixão has edited an edition published by INL/Presença, Rio de Janeiro, 1987.

A Silveirinha. Rio de Janeiro: Francisco Alves, 1914. *Jornal do Comércio*, Rio de Janeiro, 1913. Sylvia Perlingeiro Paixão has edited a reprint by Editora Mulheres, Florianópolis, 1997.

Translations

"Les Porcs". *Revue de l'Amérique Latine* XVII(87), March 1929.

"Les Roses". In *Deux Nouvelles Brésiliennes* trans. Jean Duriau. Dunkerque: Imprimerie du Commerce (G. Guilbert), 1928.

"Le lot 587", story trans. Luiz Annibal Falcão, in *Anthologie de quelques conteurs brésiliens*, Paris: Le Sagittaire, 1939.

"Eles e elas" [fragments] translated by Darlene Sadlier, *One Hundred Years after Tomorrow: Brazilian Women's Fiction in the 20th Century*. Bloomington, IN: Indiana University Press, 1992.

References and Further Reading

Arsenault, Natalie C. *Family Upheaval in Selected Works by Júlia Lopes de Almeida*. Gainesville, FL: MA University of Florida, 2002.

Da Costa, Emilia Viotti. The *Brazilian Empire: Myths and Histories*. Durham, NC: University of North Carolina Press, 2000.

Needell, Jeffrey D. *A Tropical Belle Époque: Elite Culture and Society in Turn-of-the-Century Rio de Janeiro*. Cambridge: Cambridge University Press, 1987.

Pereira, Lúcia Miguel. *Prosa de ficção: de 1870 a 1920*. 2nd edn. Rio de Janeiro: José Olympio, 1957, pp. 255–71.

Rio, João do. *O momento literário*. Rio de Janeiro: Fundação Biblioteca Nacional, Depto. Nacional do Livro, 1994, pp. 28–37.

Roncador, Sônia M. "Domestic Fictions: The Nationalist Feminine in Júlia Lopes de Alemeida". Manuscript in progress.

Sadlier, Darlene J. *One Hundred Years after Tomorrow: Brazilian Women's Fiction in the 20th Century*. Bloomington, IN: Indiana University Press, 1992.

Sadlier, Darlene J. "Modernity and Femininity in *He and She* by Júlia Lopes de Almeida". *Studies in Short Fiction* 30(4) (1993): 575–83.

Sharpe, Peggy. "Introduction". In *A viúva Simões*. Florianópolis: Editôra Mulheres, 1999, pp. 9–32.

Soihet, Rachel. "Comparando escritos: Júlia Lopes de Almeida e Carmen Dolores". *Revista do Instituto Histórico e Geográfico Brasileiro* 165(423) (Apr./June 2004).

Telles, Norma. "Fragmentos de um mosaico: escritoras brasileiras no século XIX". *Estudos femeinistas* 2005 http://www.unb.br/ih/his/gefem/labrys8/literatura/norma.htm (accessed October 10, 2006).

Xavier, Elódia. "Introduction". In *A intrusa*. Rio de Janeiro: Biblioteca Nacional, 1994, pp. 3–8.

AMOR, GUADALUPE TERESA

Guadalupe Teresa Amor Schmidtlein (1917–2000), better known during her life as Pita Amor, was the youngest of seven children and one half-brother. As a consequence of the Mexican Revolution, Amor's family lost enormous land holdings in the state of Morelos and was forced to establish exclusive though increasingly impoverished residence in Mexico City. During her childhood, Amor anxiously lived the contradiction between her family's claim to elite social status and the economic limitations that distinguished Amor from her well-heeled schoolmates. This perceived stigma served to fuel Amor's lifelong love for costume and luxury. If Amor's autobiographical accounts are to be believed, even as a child the future poet lived theatrically: she liked to be looked at, often threw dramatic tantrums, showed little interest in studies, and suffered extreme tedium in her enormous house. The death of Amor's father encouraged her eventual, culturally atypical move from the family home as a single woman. Once free of her mother's supervision, Amor engaged in a whirlwind social life, meeting many Mexican painters who used her as a (sometimes nude) model, much to Amor's delight. The poet took many lovers and kept one man in particular over the years as a financial benefactor, though she never married. A late, accidental pregnancy proved an anguishing experience for Amor, and upon giving birth, she entrusted the baby to one of her sisters. When the toddler accidentally drowned on his aunt's property, the writer withdrew for a period from her agitated public life. In the course of her career, Amor published almost a book a year, though the overall quality of this poetry would decline.

Poetic Style

The first period of Amor's poetic production evinces strong concern for rhyme and rhythm in addition to word plays that recall the *conceptismo* of Spanish-language Baroque poetry, the literary conceits that reveal the poet's ingenious games with multiple levels of meaning. Amor's poetic style employs classical forms such as sonnets and ten-line poems. The importance of accessibility and surface stylistics in Amor's work supports itself with reduced vocabulary and tightly controlled thematics. Each collection of poems tends to revolve around a theme, which is announced unambiguously in the title. Amor's word choices sometimes seem to privilege rhyme over meaning, particularly in her artistic decline, and yet the point of her poems is usually understandable with just one reading.

Througout her œuvre, Amor's highly personal writings parallel her contemporary Frida Kahlo's artistic, unapologetic self-examinations. Amor eschews Kahlo's consciousness of politics and history and concentrates on the more general nature of (her) existence. Much of Amor's poetry employs the first-person singular and thus proposes the poet's *yo* (I) as the center of all.

Bestselling Poetry on TV

In her mid-thirties, Amor's fame among the intellectual circle in Mexico spread to the general public when she became nationally famous as poet on television. Her program *Nocturnal*, which lasted about a year and half, featured her readings of classical Spanish religious poetry as well as her own material. The poet favored heavy make-up and low-cut necklines, and this visual appeal along with the accessibility of Amor's poetry and her dramatic oratorical personality, drew an enthusiastic audience. During this period, Amor cultivated crowd-pleasing religious preoccupations in addition to her singular, sexualized appearance. Her book of ten-line poems that alternately questions and admires God, *Décimas a Dios* (Ten-line poems to God), became an instant bestseller with three editions released between 1953 and 1954; the poems also appear in many anthologies of Amor's work during her lifetime. The brief prologue to *Décimas a Dios* allows Amor to develop her artistic persona by, for example, recognizing her vanity and by describing the effortless process of drafting the poems. The prologue and television programs point the way to the most sympathetic critical approach to Amor's literary work: one that takes into account her performance of the role of poet-diva.

Prose, but Not Prosaic

Amor wrote two works of prose, both unusual. Despite the soap-operatic personal life that she nurtured, her narrative largely resists the expected elements of fiction. Instead of the plotted short stories, in *Galería de títeres* (Gallery of Puppets) Amor offers brief character studies. This collection of sketches directly addresses such taboo-for-the-times themes as lesbianism and masturbation. Amor's only novel, the autobiographical *Yo soy mi casa* (I Am my Home), loosely connects numerous domestic scenes from the protagonist's childhood. The novel shares its title with Amor's first collection of poetry and borrows stanzas from that collection to open and close the text. The lengthy novel uses the rooms of the protagonist's childhood home as its organizing principle; occasional exceptions to that organization tend to structure an anecdote around a social ritual, such as first communion or Christmas. The novel ends with 14-year-old Pita Román's self-realization, which occurs when she stands in front of her house, alone for the first time in public. There, she realizes that nothing exists behind the "hypocritical façade" of the house (line 346).

The repetition of the title *Yo soy mi casa* from the poetry volume in the novel suggests that Amor has not quite found her home or is not quite finished with the project of finding herself at ease within her body and social role. For all the defiance of the notion that Amor is her home, she seems troubled by the emptiness behind her façade and appears to live her femininity in ambivalent fashion. In her œuvre, Amor's project is not so much a search for the vertically profound metaphor as the development of horizontally-oriented metonymy in the quest for a better view of the surface of things. After all, if nothing lies beyond the façade, there is no point in delving for meaning behind the symbols. This preference for surface also hints that Amor's artistic understanding of God relates to Amor herself more than to a transcendent entity. Horizontal orientation places Amor on the same level as God, in other words.

The Diva Defense

The racism and classism that Amor wielded openly throughout her life in order to clear her path on sidewalks and perhaps just for the thrill of calling attention to herself takes inspiration from her sharp grasp of the arbitrariness of social categories and the possible void that lies behind them. Possibly, Amor's economically precarious childhood and the financial difficulties of later adulthood fed her need to defend her perpetually threatened status by insulting others. In an essay included in *Las siete cabritas* (The Seven Little Goats), Amor's niece, Elena Poniatowska, relates her aunt's unusual assertiveness on the set of her first television program and Amor's favorite insult: "¡Indio!" (Indian!). The collection of poems, *Fuga de negras* (Flight of Black Women), underscores Amor's racial fetish and her generally unsophisticated approach to issues of class and skin color.

The diva-like behavior, along with late collections of poetry such as the sonnets of *Las amargas lágrimas de Beatriz Sheridan* that celebrates a Mexican play inspired by Rainer Werner Fassbinder's camp-célèbre German-language film, *The Bitter Tears of Petra von Kant*, provide ample evidence that Amor herself harbored a camp aesthetic. In point of fact, Poniatowska recalls unkind popular nicknames for the poet, such as Batman's Granny and the Honorary Queen of Zona Rosa, an area in Mexico City strongly associated with Amor's iconic presence. Amor's public eccentricity inspired both urban legend and female impersonators; these forms of gossipy tribute make legendary Amor's self-obsessed verses, her rude manners, and her over-the-top personality. Select impersonations are found on the Internet page You Tube (keywords "Pita Amor"). A clip of an aging Amor, declaring repeatedly that sex is the only thing that matters in life, appears in Ximena Cuevas's video poem *Medias mentiras* from 1994.

Although Amor could be analyzed as a feminist figure in the style of recent feminist camp studies of Mae West and Madonna, it would be erroneous to describe the Mexican poet as a true social progressive. The diva's feminism seems to have incorporated an individual interest in sexual freedom and artistic success rather than concern for the good of women as a whole. It bears repeating that Amor's performance of female independence exudes ambivalence, perhaps best signaled by her doll-like appearance and act. As the prologue to *A mí me ha dado en escribir sonetos* (I am given to writing sonnets) has it, Amor claims to have begun her career almost by accident at age 27 with an eyebrow pencil and napkin and the spontaneous drafting of the famous poem from her first volume of poetry "Casa redonda que tenía . . ." (I had a round house . . .). In this same volume, Amor describes her "extraordinary" face as that of an "absorbed doll," which formed a huge contrast with her incipient and bold genius ("Mi portentosa cara de muñeca absorta, formaba un alto contraste con mi genio incipiente y temerario") (p. 8). The financial problems that Amor suffered in the later decades of her life demonstrate her inability to assume responsibility for her career and indicate that in some sense Amor expected to be provided for rather than to provide for herself. In the decline of her career, Amor wrote spontaneously on scraps of paper and either gave away the poems or, in recognition of her strained finances, attempted to sell them for a few pesos.

In further support of Amor's ambivalent feminism and play with camp, the poet's adult look with an exaggerated open-eyed gaze and a kewpie curl parallels the kewpie doll Conchis in the novel *Yo soy mi casa*. There, the child Pita Román attempts to open her eyes as wide as the doll's so that adult women will compliment her. Conchis rules Pita's world, and on one Christmas Eve the girl even replaces the Baby Jesus with Conchis in the manger, a scene that culminates in the tiny diva's fainting fit under the Christmas tree. Although Pita Román is not an exact replica of her author, their coinciding aesthetic proves informative. Amor's performance of femininity is at once rebellious and submissive to sexist standards that judge a woman for her body, as her habit of stripping in front of bemused or scandalized acquaintances suggests. Additionally, both the poet and protagonist Pita Román refuse to wear undergarments under their Catholic schoolgirl uniforms.

Criticism, Camp, and the City

To date, the criticism of Amor's work is scant. In addition to Poniatowska's fundamental contribution, Michael Schuessler and Elvira García have published lengthy texts on Amor. These studies weave biographical facts that Amor provides in interviews with quotations from her texts. The interview that an aging Amor gives to Verdugo-Fuentes proves nearly incoherent. Future directions for criticism might take into account the performative aspect of the poet's work and its surprising coherence when viewed through camp sensibilities. Amor's love of artifice, her preference for style over content, and her outrageous declarations bolster analysis of Amor as a consciously assembled work of art whose aesthetic expression is only partially captured in her literature.

EMILY HIND

Selected Works

Personal Anthologies of Poetry

Poesías completas (*Yo soy mi casa* [1946], *Puerta obstinada* [1946], *Círculo de angustia* [1948], *Polvo* [1949], *Más allá de lo oscuro* [1951]). Prologue Margarita Michelena. Madrid: Aguilar, 1951.

Antología poética (*Yo soy mi casa, Puerta obstinada, Círculo de angustia, Máscaras, Polvo, Más allá de lo oscuro, Décimas a Dios* [1953], *Otro libro de amor* [1955]). Buenos Aires: Espasa Calpe, 1956.

Como reina de barajas [1966] *y Fuga de negras* [1966]. Illust. Antonio Peláez. Mexico: Fournier, 1975.

Poesías completas 1946–51 (*Yo soy mi casa, Puerta obstinada, Círculo de angustia, Polvo, Más allá de lo oscuro*). Mexico: CNCA, 1991.

Amor divino (*Décimas a Dios, Sirviéndole a Dios de hoguera* [1958]). Mexico: Planeta, 2000.

Poetry, Not Anthologized

El zoológico de Pita Amor. Mexico: V siglos, 1975.

Las amargas lágrimas de Beatriz Sheridan. Intro. Alberto Dallal. Mexico: Katún, 1981.

A mí me ha dado en escribir sonetos. . . Illust. Susana García Ruiz. Mexico: Katún, 1981.

48 veces Pita. Mexico: Posada, 1983.

Ese Cristo terrible en su agonía. Mexico: Editorial Universidad de Colima, 1984.

Pita por Guadalupe Amor. Mexico: Imposible, 1985.

Mis crímenes. Illust. Ramón Sánchez Lira. Mexico: Federación Editorial Mexicana, 1986.

La sombra del mulato. Mexico: Author's edition, 1989.

Prose

Yo soy mi casa. Mexico: Fondo de Cultura Económica, 1957.

Galería de títeres. Mexico: Fondo de Cultura Económica, 1959.

References and Further Reading

García, Elvira. *Redonda soledad: La vida de Pita Amor*. Mexico: Grijalbo, 1997.

Poniatowska, Elena. "Pita Amor en los brazos de Dios". *Las siete cabritas*. Mexico: Era, 2000, 31–54.

Robles, Martha. "Guadalupe 'Pita' Amor". *La sombra fugitiva: Escritoras en la cultura nacional*. Vol. II. Mexico: Diana, 1989, pp. 79–110.

Schuessler, Michael Karl. *La undécima musa: Guadalupe Amor*. Prologue by Elena Poniatowska. Mexico: Diana, 1995.

Verdugo-Fuentes, Waldemar. "Guadalupe Pita Amor: Que toda morirá cuando yo muera, imposible pensar de otra manera". In *Ocho mujeres del siglo XX*. Mexico: Diana, 1989, pp. 35–53.

ANGEL MARULANDA, ALBALUCÍA

This writer, journalist, art critic, professor, and wandering folksinger in her youth was born in Pereira, Risaralda, in 1939. International literary critics consider her to be one of the most important feminist writers in Latin America today due to the new approaches of feminist literature in the continent. As a result of her ample experience abroad, her naturally rebellious feminine spirit manifests itself in a literary production replete in cultural wealth. Angel Marulanda's work is divided into two periods which can be characterized by changes in her political agenda related to women and their social and gender roles. In the first, the writer claims equality for women in a patriarchal society; in the second, she proclaims the women's liberation and the escape from male dominance. Angel Marulanda is perceived as an insubordinate and subversive writer because she promotes the total liberation of women from the male patriarchy that has marginalized them. For this reason, Angel Marulanda wants to create a space for women where they can take control of their lives and their identity in order to shed their gender role as second-class citizens, although this means breaking with masculine society. She seeks a feminine rebellious discourse by and for women in order to promote solidarity among them. This relationship searches for solidarity as a form of resistance. Her critics consider this cohesion as a distinctly lesbian feature in her cultural production. One of the principal features of Angel Marulanda's narrative production is her tendency to employ a polyphony of feminine narrative voices that replace the presence of a single traditional masculine narrator. She represents, through these voices, women's control over their lives and their right to be recognized as individuals instead of a homogenous grouping. For this reason, she has developed experimental narrative forms in which she undermines punctuation and spelling as a means of transgressing the masculine traditional canon.

Angel Marulanda's works display one of the new thematic tendencies of the Latin American narrative to depict literature as a mirror of reality. In fact, she creates a subversive discourse based on the questioning of gender. This becomes a recurrent theme that she uses in her literary production in order to destabilize patriarchal laws, which impose and control the social norm. Her first work, *Girasoles en invierno* (1968, Sunflowers in Winter), is an analysis of women's reality and their violent inscription into gender roles. The writer wants to establish for her protagonist, Alejandra, a personal identity and existence as a metaphor that extends to all women. She feels herself manipulated and trapped within a reality that she has not chosen for herself. Alejandra faces a society that forces her to repress her own beliefs and adhere to conventional feminine roles. For this reason, Alejandra experiences an internal battle because she must confront not only her desires, but also the social system that acts as a coercive reality. This fact blocks her right to actualize her potential; and, therefore, impedes her from becoming a free woman. Alejandra is bored with the present and portrays the tedium of women who see no escape. Consequently, she wishes to return to the past in order to contemplate women's existence and hopefully uncover a remedy to the social norms that construct their feminine reality.

An analysis of woman's reality, her silence, and her desire to raise the female voice against the masculine word is presented in *Dos veces Alicia* (1972, Alice, Twice Over). This text echoes Lewis Carroll's *Alice in Wonderland*, placing the female protagonist, Alicia, in the traditionally masculine role of a detective. Angel Marulanda seeks to secure writing space in a society controlled by men who subjugate women by means of negating their voice. This domain asserts the feminine existence and marks its validity. For this reason, the death of Mrs. Wilson by "natural causes" according to the medical diagnosis, should be an unquestioned event. Alicia, however, challenges masculine authority by raising the possibility of a crime and casting doubt on the male doctor's opinion. Moreover, Mrs. Wilson's death could be interpreted as a metaphor for the deconstruction of traditional values that the patriarchal system has assigned to women, forcing them to become its best supporter.

Angel Marulanda's third work, *Estaba la pájara pinta sentada en el verde limón* (1975, The Petite Painted Bird Perched on the Green Lemon Limb), focuses on the theme of violence and sexuality, and how it affects women. Angel Marulanda depicts La Violencia, the eighteen years of war (1948–64) in Colombia. *La pájara* is the narrative of Ana's journey through feminine psychology to discover the value of women in society. The protagonist's life is the story of the hundreds of women who were raped and abused during this violent period. Ana is a girl who perceives her existence through two disparate lenses: her own violent experience, and the way in which society justifies it. This reality causes her to feel continually threatened by the image of her father, powerless to question social and familial traditions. The novel is infused with adolescent sexual experimentation, which leads to the protagonist's celebration of adult female sexuality. Because of social morals imposed upon her by society, Ana does not remember experimenting heterosexuality as an act of natural pleasure, but rather as a horrible and sinful experience that she represses. The brutal rape of Ana in her childhood by one of her family's farm workers is an element that shows how masculine society forces her to subscribe to a compulsory heterosexual role. Accordingly, it represents not only an execrable crime against women, but is also a display of man's control over them and their sexuality. However, Ana overcomes her traumatic experiences by discovering that she can take control of her life and imbue it with meaning. For this reason, she enrolls in the guerrilla movement, which offers her, at that moment, a reason to exist and the freedom to be herself.

Angel Marulanda has always tried to present a realistic and panoramic image of the anarchy that exists due to sociopolitical and economic turmoil in Colombian society. To illustrate this, *¡Oh, Gloria inmarcesible!* (1979, Oh, Boundless Glory!) parodies the first line of the Colombian national anthem. In this work, the writer paints different aspects of her nation's everyday life. She presents a collage of reality framed by her country's traditions and customs. Angel Marulanda makes a trip through national geography, revealing the true Colombia and certain phenomena such as drug trafficking which have become an important element in the national reality. For this reason, one can consider this work a portrait of the country with its social and political problems, its festivities, and its beauty contests. In other words, it is an emergence of consciousness that represents a cluster of voices to show Colombian men and women in their social gender roles and also the fight of men for power and control of society.

After presenting the dual gender roles, the women's place in Colombian society, and the empowerment of masculine society, in *Misía señora* (1982, Missus-Lady), Angel Marulanda describes the protagonist, Mariana, in the three stages of her life: childhood, marriage, and madness. Although Mariana fulfills her social obligations as mother and wife (the maximum patriarchal aspiration for women), she experiences complete frustration with the traditional role subscribed to women. The novel focuses on the homosexual identity of the protagonist. Thanks to a mirror, Mariana finds a space to dialogue freely and express dissatisfaction with the stereotypical representation of women in society. Mariana carries a lesbian desire that she had experimented with in her childhood into her adulthood. These desires are contrary to Ana's experience with lesbianism in *La pájara*, in which she represses lesbianism as a sin of her childhood. As a result, Mariana must not only find a space for herself, but also fight against the moralist vision of sex as a sin. Although she embraces lesbianism, she is never free of the guilt that accompanies her choice. Mariana returns to the past in synchronic movements to demythologize that feeling. According to Helena Araújo, synchronism and the wish to return to the past to evoke childhood memories are ways in which the Latin American feminist narrative questions the feminine role in procreation (1989: 52). Mariana is a woman who decides to deconstruct her existence and rebels against the established order, which controls her like a rag doll much like Lilita, the doll she played with in her childhood. With this, Mariana asserts her right to take control of her body, to use it as she desires, and to find refuge for herself in madness as the only alternative to her solitary struggle against the patriarchal system in the economy of power.

Mariana is once again the name of the protagonist in the unpublished play "La manzana de piedra" (1983, The Stone Apple). Here, the main character has three different lives, demonstrating the evolution of women's roles in society in order to liberate women from the patriarchal construct. She is Mariana, the grandmother, whose place is in the kitchen; Mariana, the mother, who worries about social activities; and Mariana, the daughter, who fulfills herself as a writer. This representation of women through space and time shows how women abandon private spaces to invade the exclusive public space of men. Therefore, the last image is the most significant of the three because it can be considered an allegory of a woman who accomplishes a public space where she expresses herself as alternative to the traditional role of mother. As mentioned earlier, Albalucía Angel Marulanda rejects the patriarchal definition of sexuality, which establishes a sexual difference between human beings based upon their reproductive organs and their functions, as a basis for feminine identity. Teresa de Lauretis has proposed creating a new sexual category that does not differentiate between individuals in an effort to rebut this idea. She states that lesbianism should be considered a natural spring of women's sexuality to allow women to claim a lesbian identity (1993: 105). All this demonstrates itself in the core of Angel Marulanda's dismissal of the definition of the feminine identity based solely upon sexuality. As a result of this, a rupture emerges between feminism, which seeks equality in the patriarchal system, and lesbianism, whose objective is to establish a gay category. This rupture is an attempt to establish an identity to counter the patriarchal proposal of man/woman as the only gender categories of society. The representation of this division appears to be the aim of Angel Marulanda in her novel *Las Andariegas* (1984, The Wayfarers) and the play *Siete lunas y un espejo* (1991, Seven Moons and a Mirror). *Las Andariegas* is inspired by a classic of lesbian literature, *Les Guérrillères* (1969, The Women Warriors). *Las Andariegas* splits definitively from the traditional and canonical style of the novel and turns it into poetic prose. This text proposes feminine solidarity among women as a homosocial group in an effort to resist masculine domination. As a result, Angel Marulanda begins the text with the descent from the heavens of a group of women holding hands who will later ascend in the same manner. *Las Andariegas* describes a journey through the history of humanity from prehistoric times toward an indefinite future. This expedition, which starts in Africa and ends on the American continent, presents the subjugated lives of women as represented in myth and legend. The text portrays women's solidarity through advances, retrocession, and circular movements in time throughout the narrative, as a means of gaining autonomy from masculine society. The images of unity at the beginning and the end of this work between the women postulate a total deviation from patriarchal society as the only alternative to gain freedom and demonstrate that they can live without men.

The writer's attempt to deconstruct masculine control of feminine identity is also presented in *Siete lunas y un espejo*, a play in two acts. The play illustrates the barriers that prevent women from being in charge of their lives in order to be transformed into a subject of their own history. For this reason, Angel Marulanda chooses in her play seven women who have been subjugated by men at different times in history. These women are Virginia Woolf, George Sand, Alice (in Wonderland), Marie Antoinette, Juliet, and Joan of Arc. This group of women appears in a forest scene as an interpretation of freedom, but the scenario will change as each of these women confronts her personal romantic interest, demonstrating with it that women have always been economically and socially marginalized. In addition, the play argues, each woman strives to unmask the social construct which has victimized her. Therefore, Angel Marulanda shows the imaginative power of women to create multiple areas for themselves by moving away from the exclusive reproductive role that the patriarchy has assigned to them. This role has converted them into "little females with little tits and butts" ("hembritas, tetoncitas y culoncitas") which represents the object of masculine erotic desire as is expounded by the character of the Zorro in the play. In the final scene, Joan of Arc confronts the Soldier as the writer constructs an allegory of the woman who faces patriarchy and defies this system to recover her own authority and freedom.

In conclusion, Angel Marulanda's productions show the construction of gender in patriarchal society as seen through its foundation as well as its rules. Thus, the writer attempts to establish a semiotic representation of men's control over women. Consequently, one might define her work as a subversive discourse that challenges masculine supremacy and its abuse of power. These conditions lead the writer to claim men's oppression as an unpunished and abominable crime against women. As a result, she postulates gay liberation and sexual dissidence as true alternatives for women to break with centuries of male domination and as a way to establish their own identity. For this reason, she rejects an enforced sexual human behavior based on biological gender and its traditional roles. With this, she argues for recognition of women not only as free beings, but also as gender dissidents who choose their sexual preferences in order to transgress the hegemonic patriarchal laws and norms and its compulsory heterosexual discourse.

Oscar A. Díaz-Ortiz

Selected Works

Los girasoles en invierno. Bogotá, D.E: Linotipia Bolívar, 1970.

Dos veces Alicia. Barcelona: Seix Barral, 1972.

Estaba la pájara pinta sentada en el verde limón. Bogotá: Instituto Colombiano de Cultura, 1975.

!Oh, gloria inmarcesible! Bogotá: Instituto Colombiano de Cultura, 1979.

La manzana de piedra. Unpublished play.

Misía señora. Barcelona: Argos, 1982.

Las andariegas. Barcelona: Argos, 1984.

"Siete lunas y un espejo". In Nora Eidelberg and María Mercedes Jaramillo (eds), *Voces en escena/Antología de dramaturgas latinoamericanas*. Medellín: Universidad de Antioquia, 1991.

References and Further Reading

Araújo, Helena. *La Sherezada criolla/Ensayos sobra escritura femenina latinoamericana*. Bogotá: Universidad Nacional de Colombia, 1989.

De Lauretis, Teresa. "Sexual Indifference and Lesbian Representation". In Henry Abelove *et al.* (eds), *The Lesbian and Gay Studies Reader*. New York: Routledge, 1993, pp. 141–58.

Diaz, Oscar A. "Gustavo Alvarez Gardeazábal y Albalucía Angel: Insubordinación del género sexual para establecer una identidad gay". In María Mercedes Jaramillo, Betty Osorio and Angela Robledo (eds), *Literatura y cultura: Narrativa colombiana del siglo XX*. vol. III: *Hibridez y alteridades*. Bogotá: Ministerio de Cultura; 2000, pp. 225–57.

Jaramillo, María Mercedes. "Albalucía Ángel: El discurso de la insubordinación". In *¿Y las mujeres? Ensayos sobre literatura colombiana*. Medellín: Editorial Universidad de Antioquia, 1991, pp. 203–38.

Filer, Malva E. "Autorescate e invención en *Las andariegas*, de Albalucía Ángel". *Revista iberoamericana* 132–3 (1985): 649–55.

Goldman, Karen S. "Angel, Albalucía". In David William Foster (ed.), *Latin American Writers on Gay and Lesbian Themes*. Westport, CT: Greenwood, 1994, pp. 13–15.

Osorio, Myriam. "Albalucía Angel Marulanda". In Cynthia Margarita Tompkins and David William Foster (eds), *Notable Twentieth-Century Latin American Women: A Biographical Dictionary*. Westport, CT: Greenwood Press, 2001, pp. 14–17.

Williams, Raymond L. "Albalucía Ángel". In Diane Marting (ed.), *Spanish American Woman Writers: A Bio-Biographical Source Book*. Westport, CT: Greenwood Press, 1990, pp. 31–40.

ANTILLANO, LAURA

Laura Antillano (b. 1950), one of Venezuela's most prolific writers, has written short stories, novels, essays and children's stories. Her family and social surroundings make up her early literary universe. She began writing at a young age and published her first short stories as a teenager. She has been a university professor, a coordinator for creative writing workshops, and has created an extensive network of cultural relationships regarding literature as a creative practice. Her recognizable essays on reading, literary creation, the feminine universe and child and youth creation are impossible to pigeonhole. She holds a Bachelor's degree in Spanish Studies and a Master's degree in Venezuelan Literature. Laura Antillano could be considered part of the generation of Venezuelan female writers with Ana María Torres, Stefanía Mosca, Milagros Mata Gil, whose literary works pay special attention to the treatment of history.

The Universe of her Short Stories

The evocative tone of the stories in *La bella época*, about childhood and adolescent memories, begins in a certain manner the cycle of the *Bildungsroman*, or coming-of-age stories. Using a descriptive and at times reminiscent style, the author turns childhood and adolescent memories into a point of departure for development, which may be a collection of impressionistic objects in some cases, or an evocative list inhabited by a set of objects that organize the story in fragments. The evolution of the adolescent voice that re-enacts interior places and landscapes is the voice that visits family and personal history through the conjunction of autobiographical work. And it is this intimacy that multiplies into stories throughout her literary production, from an "I" that turns into "we" and "the others," from an intimate space which is transformed by the magic of her writing into the home, community or national space; into a map that covers Caracas, Maracaibo, and Valencia and extends to other cities in Latin America and Europe.

Childhood is another of the great themes throughout her work, the perspective of an adult world narrated from the voice of children, or from the childhood of characters who meet and part ways throughout life. This treatment is not just a nostalgic look that organizes the narration, it is a construction of history, which, observing the character's development, acquires another dimension and allows intimate elements to be woven with exterior elements, private life with public life. It is here that we find one of the greatest successes of this author's literary work and one of the most original literary projects of her generation. This sort of counter-history, a history of what is private, allows for the reconstruction of family trees and voices, and segments of society, which – like a drawn line disappearing into a vanishing point – can be recognized in the interstices of family and social history. The student movements of the 1960s and 1970s with their dreams and utopias are reflected in some of the stories where the student youth, the idealist youth, clash with the adult world, with the values established by the system in accounts included in later short stories, and somehow close with the extensive short story named "La luna no es pan de horno" in which the narrator addresses, in a form close to a soliloquy, her dead mother. This text demonstrates what the critic Charles Mauron describes as the author's "personal myths". In this case, we can create a certain chain of association or classification of obsessive images that recurrently appear in both Laura Antillano's stories and novels, among them some significant examples are: her grandmother's death, her father's imprisonment, her mother's death. Later, another element that feeds her narrative is the reference to cinema, and some of these youthful short stories serve as a precursor for literary projects that will be resolved with greater literary complexity in later stories such as those included in the volume *Cuentos de Película*. Through the creation of these stories, Antillano is not "writing" cinema, she is "reading" it, and that gives her an unheard-of formal experience, showing how subjectivity unwinds the threads of where the narrator's life mixes with cinematographic characters turned into literary characters. From there, cinema appears through her narrative work insistently and in many different ways.

The Perfumes of Memory and the History

Antillano's writing becomes a more experimental work very close to that of Latin American Boom writers – where the reader can enjoy discovering a plurality of voices and elements – weaving into the game of writing both high and popular elements, expressed through very diverse subject matters. An entire universe of quotations, book references, films, graffiti, songs, and the inclusion of journalistic elements reinforce narrative parts. The interspersed elements quoted in the text, the wide range of poems, songs, and news articles show some of the cultural devices which describe 1970s Latin American narrative and the close relationship between literary creation and the mass media. These quotations, these types of texts constitute what Bernard Mouralis has dubbed "counter-literatures," that is, stories where these interwoven elements permit a fictional reconstruction of official history. This includes elements from advertisements, all types of pamphlets, newspaper headlines and articles, and business letters, that is, an entire system of elements that enter the text, weaving it together by a complex process of intertextualization, a procedure Antillano begins in her novel *La muerte del monstruo come piedra* and takes to its highest point of experimentation in the novel *Perfume de Gardenia*.

Perfume de Gardenia is not just a simple representation of the past, it's the reconstruction of three chronotopos in the precise intersection of time/space: the grandmother, the mother and the granddaughter with their requests, characters, and as a backdrop, a dynamic and ever-changing set: Venezuela's history. From agrarian to oil-rich Venezuela these three women fragmentarily show their lives on different narrative planes. What is more, in the novel *Solitaria solidaria*, the autobiographic genre appears in the diary and letters of Leonora Armundeloy, a young girl belonging to Venezuelan society, who tells her life-story at the end of the nineteenth century and the marginal circumstances that affected her existence. In the same way, Zulay Montero, a university professor in the present, offers the key to reading the narrative text of her own story to the reader, a story constructed from Leonora's diary. The structure of the novel is dual in nature and it shows that expression on a level of literary creation, a procedure that proves the self-reflexive value of the act of writing.

The protagonists of her novels belong to different eras, but we can definitely state that the woman, presented in her different functions, is one of the profoundly original elements of her work because, beyond what is personal and private, we can see an axis structured around the possibilities that show the protagonists choosing a lifestyle different from what is traditional, and showing the multiple ways in which the woman manages to resolve her conflicts. So much of the maternity, or the loving relationships, and of the professional choices of the women depicted by Antillano is constructed with immense humanity, unparceled, with the whole array of doubts and contradictions demanded by modern life in a Latin American country, not free from pain, but in no way anchored to suffering, somehow showing the limits marking the social realities for freedom.

Reconstructing Home

In 2004, Laura Antillano presented her first book of poems under the title of *Migaja* and with this work won the Premio "José Antonio Pocaterra" at the Latin American Biennial of Literature, which is organized by the Atheneum of Valencia. With an almost elemental language, stripped of any ornament, the book is structured as a dialogue between the poetic voice and an absent subject. The loneliness, the memory, and the ache of a break-up infuse Antillano's text. Later, she worked on two books of poems: *El verbo de la madre* (2004) and *La casa del Milagro* (2005). These three books make up the recently published *La casa de la madre* anthology. According to José Napoleón Oropeza in the epilogue to the anthology, "In her work there is always a passing eye, looking and probing, that nostalgically evokes the figures and beings of space. The mother brings order to that mythic space, drawing and cooking" (2005: 146). The different sections of this anthology show the detailed treatment of daily life. Nature and culture combine in a kind of catalogue of daily life. The flowers of the house of childhood, the activities of the mother and the family members organize their universe plenty of contrasts. She composes her poetry as a delightful game of sensuality, paying attention to the tiny details of domestic history, childhood and motherhood.

ZULEMA MORET

Selected Works

Short Stories

La bella época. Caracas: Monte Avila, 1969.

Un carro largo se llama tren. Caracas: Monte Avila, 1975.

Los Haticos, casa Nro. 20. Maracaibo: Dirección de Cultura, Univ. del Zulia, 1975.

Si dentro de ti oyes tu corazón partir. Caracas: Edit. Fundarte, 1983, re-edited in 1992.

Cuentos de película. Caracas: Ed. Selevén, 1985, re-edited in 1997 in Caracas: la Fundación Cinemateca Nacional.

La luna no es pan de horno. Caracas: Monte Avila; 1988.

Tuna de mar. Caracas: Edit. Fundarte, 1991.

Las paredes del sueño. (Textos-Miradas), Maracaibo: Edit. Lagoven, 1991.

La luna no es pan de horno y otros cuentos. Caracas: Ed. Monte Avila, 2005.

Novels

La muerte del monstruo come piedra. Caracas: Monte Avila, 1971, re-edited in Maracay: La Letra Voladora, 1996.

Perfume de gardenia. Caracas: Ed. Selevén, 1982 and 1984, re-edited in 1996 in Valencia: el Rectorado de la Univ. de Carabobo y La Letra Voladora.

Solitaria Solidaria. Caracas: Edit. Planeta, 1990, re-edited in 2001 in Mérida: Ediciones El otro @ el mismo.

Children and Teenagers' Books

¿Cenan los tigres la noche de Navidad? Caracas: Monte Avila, 1990.

Jacobo ahora no se aburre. Maracay: La Letra Voladora: 1991.

Diana en la Tierra Wayuu. Bogotá: Ed. Santillana, 1992.

Una vaca querida. México: 1996.

Las aguas tenían reflejos de plata. Caracas: Edit. Alfaguara, 2002.

Poetry

El verbo de la madre. (Anthology) Edit. El otro @ el mismo, Mérida, 2005.

References and Further Reading

Carrillo, Carmen Virginia. "Albores y ocasos del siglo, una mirada femenina". *Cifra Nueva: Revista de Cultura* 8 (July–Dec. 1998): 83–8.

Cunha-Giabbai, Gloria da. "En búsqueda de la utópica plenitud humana: Malena de cinco mundos". In Luz Marina Rivas (ed.), *La historia en la mirada: La conciencia histórica y la intrahistoria en la narrativa de Ana Teresa Torres, Laura Antillano y Milagros Mata Gil.* Ciudad Bolívar, Venezuela: Fondo Editorial del Centro de Estudios Literarios, 1997.

Esteban, Angel. "La narrativa solidaria de Laura Antillano". *Cuadernos Hispanoamericanos* 597 (Mar. 2000): 83–8.

Fernández, Edmée Source. "El guzmancismo en la novela venezolana". *Venezuelan Literature and Arts Journal/Revista de Literatura y Artes Venezolanas* 2(1) (1996): 71–84.

Gary, Edith Dimo. "La marginalidad como autorrepresentación en la escritura de Laura Antillano". *Alba de América: Revista Literaria* 14 (26–7) (1996 July): 373–9.

González Stephan, Beatriz. "Escritura de memorias subalternas". *Texto Crítico* 5(10) (Jan.–June 2002): 21–34.

Moret, Zulema. "Los perfumes de la memoria: *Perfume de Gardenia* de Laura Antillano". In Edith Dimo and Amarilis Hidalgo de Jesús (eds), *Escritura y desafío. Narradoras venezolanas del siglo* XX. Caracas: Monte Avila, 1996.

Rivas de Wesolowski, Luz Marina. "La perspectiva marginal de la historia en la obra de Laura Antillano". *Venezuelan Literature and Arts Journal/Revista de Literatura y Artes Venezolanas* 2(1) (1996): 15–31.

Zambrano, Gregory. "Narrar desde la memoria. La historia posible (Laura Antillano, Ana Teresa Torres y Milagros Mata Gil)". *Texto Crítico* 5(10) (Jan.–June 2002): 243–53.

ARAÚJO, NARA

Born in Havana in 1945, this literary scholar is an important figure in a variety of academic spheres. Educated internationally, in both French (University of Havana and the Sorbonne University) and Philological Science (University of Moscow, Lomonosov), she has always maintained a home in Havana and held a position at the University of Havana for many years. Employing this international perspective and dismissing the polarized extremes frequent in the definition and study of Cuban culture, Araújo's work suggests a textual rather than politicized ethic in her professional life. Her most significant contributions to academic activity in and on the region are in the dissemination of "western" theory in Latin America, the comparative application of these theories to ongoing debates on gender, genre, and national identity, and the scholarly treatment of Cuban and Caribbean women's literature.

Her work has been recognized by the French (Palmas Académicas de Francia, 1993) and Cuban governments (1992, 1994), and by universities in Cuba (University of Havana, 1997, 2004) and Mexico (Autonomous University of Mexico-Iztapalapa, 2001). She has been active internationally as a scholar, receiving grants from the Rockefeller and the Ford Foundations (1995, 1998), and giving lectures at universities in Russia, France, Mexico, Venezuela, the United States, Brazil and England. Araújo has also given conference papers at the Autonomous Metropolitan University of Mexico, Iztapalapa (UAM-I) and the Mexican National Autonomous University (UNAM).

Comparative "Others"

From the outset, Araújo looked for "other" readings of canonical texts. Her first book, *Visión romántica del otro* (Another Romantic View) does not focus on what the "other" sees during the Romantic period. Rather, she argues that similar constructions of Indians and slaves in two European and Latin American novels do differ when considering the historical context and the geographical origin of the texts. With Marxist interventions into the structuralist and formalist praxis of comparative literature (V.M. Zirmunski, D. Durisin, H. Markiewicz) as her theoretical framework, Araújo seeks to undo the unidirectional notion of "influence" and "analogy" from the metropolis to the colony, treating the relationship between these two positions of power as dialectical. The French imaginary, she suggests, is fundamentally influenced by the "New World" before the latter adopts its romantic literary forms. In this way, Araújo practices a textual criticism that gives rise to alternative views of French Romanticism as constituted by the colonial process.

This early work forms the foundation of Araújo's further contributions to contemporary criticism and cultural studies. By privileging textual theory as the main apparatus for the praxis of literary criticism, Araújo has become a significant voice in Latin American and Caribbean Studies, warning of the limitations to applying identity theories to cultural production in the search for "truth" in fiction.

Gender and Genre

Araújo's work figures prominently in the field's move to reconfigure its canonical exclusion of women's writing. Not caught up in the debates surrounding subaltern identity and the ability of the subaltern "to speak," her writing foregrounds the specificities that compel a more inclusive configuration of literary history. "A feminist reading of the relation between gender and genre can enrich and subvert the traditional focus of literary history," she writes in the introduction to her book *El alfiler y la mariposa* (The Pin and the Butterfly). In her extensive study of autobiography, Araújo argues that the institutional processes that create an essentialist model of feminine autobiography mark possible fissures where such texts produce and reproduce the so-called subaltern discourse. The author's narrative strategy, she finds in her reading of Dolores María de Ximeno y Cruz's (Lola María's) autobiography, reaffirms a feminine genealogy, rather than the subaltern discourse as a source of "truth". Her analysis, therefore, not only highlights a textual "difference" in relation to canonical autobiographies. It also proves that this "difference," in turn, alters Latin American literary historiography.

While theoretical, *El alfiler y la mariposa* is also very literary. The book's title pays homage to Cuban poet and novelist Dulce María Loynaz. Araújo's essay on this author's texts (*Jardín*, *Bestiarium* and *Versos*), regarded as one of the salient essays in Cuban culture during the twentieth century, reconstructs the mythical Edenic feminine in a celebration of its subversive power, suggesting an "imagery in which the pin holds the butterfly, but the shadow escapes the light" (p. 132). The text, permeated with such metaphors, reflects Araújo's diverse reinscription of the sex/gender binary, fundamental in her search for the *huella del género* (gender's footprints) in Caribbean women's narrative production.

The writer's footprints join with the readers' in *La huella y el tiempo* (The Footprint and Time). As she does in her first collection, Araújo sketches out both an important typology for women's travel writing – in "Truth, Power and Knowledge. Women's Travel Writing" – and a textual praxis that questions the literary historiography surrounding the genre. But this text, as its title suggests, is also a complex sort of meta-*mise en abîme*. "La huella y el tiempo" is also both the title of her essay on Dulce María Loynaz's *Un verano en Tenerife* and *Fe de vida* and a conceptual metaphor for writing. Araújo's writing fixes her attempts as a critic to capture a meaning in Loynaz's writing which in turn attempts to capture a certain meaning in her novel. The relationship between the paradoxical fixedness of the written word and the ephemeral nature of meaning frames Araújo's conclusions about the "truth" of travel writing.

Araújo's second collection of essays is also an example of the postmodern blurring of theory and literature at the center of debates in post-colonial Caribbean cultural criticism. It becomes the object it presumes to study. One could use Araújo's typology to analyze the critic's representation of her own literary travels or the fictitious travelogue that mimics those she has so frequently analyzed. Conflating literary and theoretical texts, her "creative" writing thus exposes the textual nature of the "truth" these works ostensibly offer.

The theoretical praxis at the heart of Araújo's writing extends to her efforts to spread literary theory in Latin America and the Caribbean. Her collaborative work on *Textos de teorías y crítica literarias (del formalismo a los estudios poscoloniales)* (Texts on Literary Theory and Criticism—from Formalism to Postcolonial Studies) presents texts, some for the first time in translation, necessary for an understanding of twentieth-century literary criticism. Araújo traces advances in theory from its nineteenth-century positivist roots to the post-structuralist epistemological shift and its consequences. In light of this synthesis, Araújo approaches Latin American theory's advances in *Diálogos en el umbral/Dialogues on the Threshold* (2003).

A collection of essays written between the last years of the twentieth century and the first of the twenty-first, *Diálogos . . .* is just that: comparativist, feminist, and theoretical literary essays that converse with each other and provide a comprehensive example of the integrity of Araújo's work. Her essay on critical theory in the twentieth century dialogues with her essay on Latin American cultural theory, which, in turn, is informed by her analysis of how feminist critical inquiry has transformed Latin American Studies. Her textual analyses of Margarita Mateo's *Ella escribía poscrítica*, Constancias de Rosalba Campra's autobiography, Ena Lucía Portela's poetics and the novels of Puerto Rican author Luis Rafael Sánchez, put Araújo's theoretical hypotheses to the test/text, and posit new ways of reading for the new century.

Cuban Feminist Literary Criticism

Araújo is one of the pioneers in Cuban literary feminist criticism. Her study of Cuban women's autobiography and travel writing revives this field both internationally and on the island. Cuba's revolution in 1959, while discursively liberating women under the rubric of constructing a socialist society, made feminism obsolete. For the nearly thirty years that second wave feminism has been transforming all fields of academic inquiry, feminist literary criticism languished under the broader debates in revolutionary cultural politics.

The first professor of a course on women's literary discourse at the University of Havana, Araújo established the diachronic study of texts that constitute women's literature as a field of study in the Cuban scholarly sphere. Most importantly, Araújo used her formalist training to carve out a historiographic space for women prose writers vis-à-vis the dominant (male) view since 1959. Her inventory of thematic and stylistic currents in women's prose configured a textual typology in literary terms, thus begging the question of whether there exists a literary corpus worthy of study. Together with her gender/genre studies, her promotion of the *novísimas* (the newest) women writers, in particular Ena Lucía Portela, has undoubtedly changed the face of women's writing and feminist criticism on the island and abroad.

Araújo does not work with feminist literary criticism in a vacuum. She connects her analysis of Cuban women's writing with the intense debates on Cuban national identity and postmodernity. Her reading of Cuban-American women's fiction places the texts within the framework of borderland cultural production or production in the "contact zone," instead of debating notions for establishing this hyphenated ethnic identity. Thus, Araújo's commitment to introducing Cuban women's literature into the academic sphere promotes the same textual ethic underlying her contributions to advancing comparative literary studies in the Latin American and Caribbean context.

BARBARA D. RIESS

Selected Works

Novels

(ed.) *Viajeras al Caribe*. Havana: Casa de las Américas, 1983.

El alfiler y la mariposa. Genero, voz y escritura en Cuba y el Caribe. Havana: Letras Cubanas, 1997.

Visión romántica del Otro: Estudio comparativo de Atala y Cumandá, Bug-Jargal y Sab. Havana: Facultad de Artes y Letras, 1993. 2nd edn, México: Universidad Autónoma Metropolitana, Iztapalapa, 1998.

Diálogos en el umbral. Santiago de Cuba: Editorial Oriente, 2003.

La huella y el tiempo. Havana: Editorial Letras Cubanas, 2003.

O tempo e o rastro. Florianópolis: Universidad Federal de Santa Catarina, 2003.

Textos de teoría y crítica literarias (del formalismo a los estudios post coloniales). (intro. and ed. with Teresa Delgado). México: Universidad Autónoma Metropolitana, 2003.

Essays

"La escritura femenina y la crítica feminista en el Caribe; otro espacio de la identidad". *UNION* VI(15) (1993): 17–23.

"Naturaleza e imaginación: el Bestiarium de Dulce María Loynaz". *Plural* 23(274) (1994): 26–9. Also in *Anthropos (Barcelona)* 151 (1993): 65–7. Translation, "Nature and Imagination: The Bestiary of Dulce María Loynaz". In Alvina Ruprecht (ed.), *The Reordering of Culture: Latin America, the Caribbean and Canada in the Hood.* Ottawa: Carleton University Press, 1995, pp. 187–98.

"The Contribution of Women's Writing to the Literature and Intellectual Achievements of the Caribbean: *Moi, Tituba Sorciere* and *Amour, Colère et Folie*". *Journal of Black Studies* 25(2) (1994): 217–30.

"Literatura femenina, feminismo y crítica literaria feminista en Cuba". *Letras femeninas* 21 (1995): 150–3.

"L'œuvre de Maryse Condé: à propos d'une écrivaine politiquement incorrecte". *Actes du Colloque sur l'œuvre de Maryse Condé.* Montréal: L'Harmattan, 1996, pp. 14–18.

"The Sea, the Sea, Once and Again: *Lo Cubano* and the literature of the *novísimas*". In Madeline Betancourt and Damián Fernández (eds), *Cuba, the Elusive Nation: Interpretations of National Identity.* Miami, FL: University Press of Florida, 2000, pp. 224–39.

"El mar, el mar, una y otra vez. Lo cubano en la literatura de las novísimas". In Johanna von Grafenstein and Laura Muñoz (eds), *El Caribe region. Frontera y relaciones internacionales II*. Mexico: Instituto Mora, pp. 238–56.

"I Came All the Way from Cuba So I Could Speak Like This? Cuban and Cuban American Literatures in the U.S". In Ashok Bery and P. Murray (eds), *Comparing Postcolonial Literatures: Dislocations.* New York: Macmillan, 2000, pp. 93–103.

"Desterritorialización, posdisciplinariedad y posliteratura". In *Geografías literarias y culturales: espacios y temporalidades*. Porto Alegre: University of Río Grande del Sur, 2004, pp. 19–34.

"Zonas de contacto. Narrativa femenina cubana de la diáspora". In Laura P. Gallo and Fabio Murrieta (eds), *Guayaba Sweet. Literatura cubana en los Estados Unidos*. Cádiz: Aduana Vieja, 2004.

"Truth, Power and Knowledge: Women's Travel Writing". In *Homenaje a Alejandro de Humboldt. Literatura de viajes desde y hacia Latinoamerica*. Oaxaca: Humboldt University and University of Oaxaca, 2005, pp. 31–42.

References and Further Reading

Durán, Diony. "El Otro habla: la escritura femenina en el cuento cubano". In Janette Reinstädler and Ottmar Ette (eds), *Todas las islas la isla. Nuevas y novísimas tendencias en la literatura y cultura de Cuba*. Madrid: Iberoamericana, 2000.

Hernández, Rafael and Rojas, Rafael (eds) *Ensayo cubano del siglo XX*. México: FCE, 2002.

Irralegui, Gladys. "Review of *Textos de teoría y crítica literarias ... Ciberletras*". http://www.lehman.cuny.edu/ciberletras/v12/ilarreguy.html

Méndez Rodenas, Adriana. *Gender and Nationalism in Colonial Cuba: The Travels of Santa Cruz y Montalvo, Condesa de Merlin*. Nashville, TN: Vanderbilt University Press, 1998.

ARCHANJO, NEIDE

A poet, lawyer, and psychologist, Neide Archanjo (b. 1940) is considered one of the most important poets of Brazilian literature of the 1960s generation. Her poetry is influenced by Jorge de Lima's poetry, as well as Carlos Drummond de Andrade, Ilka Brunhilde Laurito, Olga Savary, and Renata Pallottini. She is regarded as a modernist poet interested in both subjective and discursive forms, and an explorer of a variety of the tendencies and directions of her time. As we know, the greatest accomplishment of modernism has been precisely its openness, its critical view and clarity, its unceasing aesthetic exploration and its deepening of consciousness. Neide Archanjo's work is testimony to this movement as she balances historical reality with emotional myth, often referring to the meaning and function of poetry, capable of expressing what it would not be possible to express through other mediums.

Archanjo was born in São Paulo in 1940, where she attended law school at the Universidade de São Paulo (University of São Paulo), and studied psychology at Faculdades Metropolitanas Unidas de São Paulo. In 1967, the year she graduated from college, she moved to Rio de Janeiro to work for Petrobrás, the Brazilian Oil Company, where she served as a lawyer until 1992, even after her career as a writer was established.

Archanjo was only 24 years old when she published *Primeiros Ofícios da Memória* (First Duties of Memory) in 1964, the year of Brazil's military coup. Despite her age, her debut was celebrated by significant poets and critics such as Hilda Hilst, Paulo Bonfim and Domingos Carvalho da Silva, who praised the author's work for its intellectual density as well as its simple and yet refined poetic form. Both in *Primeiros Ofícios da Memória* and her next book, *O Poeta Itinerante* (The Itinerant Poet) published in 1968, she explores her very personal universe, but in the latter she takes up the tradition of the long, unified poem made up of chants (*Telurica*, *Onirica*, *Ascese*, *Mistica* and *Epuras*), introduced by Vilém Flusser. Her poetry is permeated with metaphysics and a dense reflection on the universals. Making use of abundant metaphors and images, Archanjo seeks the sublime and the timeless present in everyday life, while the historical is translated into exercises in contemplation.

In 1969, one of the hardest years of the dictatorship under Médici's rule, together with her brother José Luiz Archanjo, Ilka Brunhilde and Renata Pallottini, Archanjo created the literary movement Poesia na Praça (Poetry at the Square). Poesia na Praça embodied socio-political concerns and the resistance to censorship. Although the group did not participate in guerrilla movements, they were engaged in cultural protests, hanging poems written on cardboard and hung on clotheslines strung between trees at the Praça da República (Republic Square) in São Paulo. *Poesia na Praça* was also the title of her third book, published in 1970. The book received critical acclaim, and was awarded the Prêmio Pen Clube de São Paulo (Pen Club Award of São Paulo) and recognition by *Jornal do Brasil* (Journal of Brazil) as one of the ten best books of the year. *Poesia na Praça* brings the elements of oral language to Archanjo's poetry.

Her next book, *Quixote Tango Foxtrote* (1975) is a mature piece, and one of the most significant poetry books of the 1970s. The book is highly emotional and rhythmic, written in an oral and colloquial language. Written in a concise and direct language, rarely making use of more complex metaphors, *Quixote Tango Foxtrote* addresses the usual affective relations – love, human destiny, art and poetry – but now lived as tangible experiences, integrated in everyday life, and not as privileged spaces for rare spirits. What articulates the poem is a dialogue between the poet, Quixote and Sancho Pança.

In 1980, Archanjo set up a literary workshop at the Mário de Andrade Library (Oficina Literária da Biblioteca Mário de Andrade) and published *Escavações* (Excavations), where she developed one single theme: memory. Managing once again to escape from conventional forms, making use of a transparent, simple and concise language, she received the APCA prize (Associação Paulista dos Críticos de Arte) for *Excavations.*

In 1983, she moved to Lisbon, Portugal, to spend a year as a student supported by the Calouste Gulbenkian Foundation, further developing her project for an epic poem, which resulted in *As Marinhas* (The Marines). In Portugal, she was awarded an Honors position by the Portuguese government and participated at the Festival de Poesia da Cidade (Festival of Poetry in of the City) in the town of Afife. *The Marines* is a long epic-lyric poem exploring the interior odyssey of a contemporary being in search for his/her Ithaca. The ocean is the context for the construction of the individual and collective unconscious. The poem is also autobiographical, as Archanjo describes her personal journey in search of her individuality.

Her next two books were *Poesia, 1964–1968*, (Poetry 1964–84, collected works), a compilation of all of her writings; and *Tudo é Sempre Agora* (All is Always Now), published in 1994 and short-listed for the Prêmio Jabuti (Jabuti Award) of poetry, one of the most prestigious awards in Brazil. Three years later, she published *Pequeno Oratório do Poeta para o Anjo* (Brief Oratorio from the Poet to the Angel), translated into French in 2003 and recorded on a CD by the famous Brazilian singer Maria Bethania, who had recorded only Fernando Pessoa's poetry at that time. *Epifanias* (Epiphanies), her tenth book, was published in 1999, presenting a collection of her writings divided into five sections, with a Preface by Carlos Nejar.

Archanjo was the first woman to occupy a chair in the traditional *Largo do São Francisco* tribune. She also founded the feminist newspaper *A Presença* (The Presence), in which she published political poems and commented on some of the main pillars of her poetic initiation such as Neli Dutra, Mira Schendel, Vilém Flusser and José Luiz Archanjo. She also served as a member of the editorial committee of the magazine *Poesia Sempre.* Together with others poets like Hilda Hilst and Henriqueta Lisboa, she reaffirms the high quality of the feminine contribution to Brazilian poetry. Addressing a wide range of themes, she has been an inspiration for many poets, actors and writers in Brazil and abroad. For José Nêumanne, author of *The Best Hundred Poets of the 20th Century* (*Os cem melhores poetas do século XX*), she is a "deep intellectual and poetic genius". For Ignácio de Loyola Brandão, Neide Archanjo "screams with images, signs and symbols, being able to express dense occurrences through her ability to use exact words". For Nelly Novaes Coellho, "Her work is a celebration of the real, the visible and the invisible".

The form of her work is free, but with a rigorous rhythm. In Archanjo's poems there are few rhymes, if any, and it is the sonority that dictates the reading pace. In *A Poesia na Praça*, she writes with no punctuation and still produces a coherent discourse, located between the rhythms of everyday speech and chant. And she capitalizes, adds spaces, all to stress the importance of rhythm in her poems. Her body of work encompasses several themes and forms, from the short poem to long epic pieces. She reveals full command of poetic styles, traditional and non-traditional lyrical poetry, profoundly addressing the ambiguities of the feminine and masculine, sexual and erotic energy, human emotions and the historical facts of the world in most of her pieces, as *Quixote, Tango e Foxtrote* so clearly demonstrates.

The Academia Brasileira de Letras (Brazilian Academy of Letters) awarded Neide Archanjo the Prêmio ABL de Poesia (ABL Poetry Prize) for *Todas as Horas e Antes: Poesia Reunida* (All the Hours and Before: Collection of Poems), in 2005, when she was also a recipient of the prestigious Prêmio Jabuti (Jabuti Award) for this work.

LUCIANA CASTRO

Selected Works

Primeiros Ofícios da Memória. São Paulo: Ed. Massao Ohno, 1964.
O Poeta Itinerante. São Paulo: Ed. I.L.A.Palma, 1968.
Poesia na Praça. São Paulo: Ed I.L.A.Palma, 1970.
Quixote Tango e Foxtrote. São Paulo: Ed. do Escritor, 1975.
Escavações. Pref. Carlos Felipe Moisés. Rio de Janeiro: Nova Fronteira, 1980.
As Marinhas. São Paulo: Ed. Salamandra, 1984.
Poesia, 1964/1984: Antologia. Sel. e est. crít. Pedro Lyra. Rio de Janeiro: Guanabara, 1987.
Tudo é Sempre Agora. São Paulo: Ed. Maltese, 1995.
Pequeno Oratório do Poeta Para o Anjo. São Paulo: Ed. do Autor, 1997.
Neide Archanjo por Neide Archanjo. São Paulo: Ed. Luz da Cidade, 1998.
Todas as Horas e Antes: Poesia Reunida. Rio de Janeiro: A Giraffa, 2005.

References and Further Reading

Bishop, Elizabeth and Brasil, Emanuel. *An Anthology of Twentieth-Century Brazilian Poetry.* Middletown, CT: Wesleyan University Press, 1972.
De Faria, Alvaro Alves. *Palavra de Mulher.* São Paulo: Ed. SENAC, 2003.
Neinstein, José and Cardozo, Manoel (eds). *Poesia Brasileira Moderna: A Bilingual Anthology.* Washington, DC: Brazilian American Cultural Institute, 1972.
Stern, Irwin. *Dictionary of Brazilian Literature.* New York: Greenwood Press, 1988.
Valdes, Mario J. and Djelal, Kadir (eds). *Literary Cultures of Latin America: A Comparative History.* New York: Oxford University Press, 2004.
Homepage: http://poezibao.typepad.com/poezibao/2005/09/neide_archanjo.html
Homepage: http://www.geocities.com/~rebra/autoras/11ingl.html

ARIAS, OLGA

Despite a writing career that has spanned over 40 years and produced over 100 volumes, Mexican writer Olga Arias (1923–94) is rarely anthologized and little known outside of her home country. Born in Toluca, in the state of Mexico, on October 25, 1923, Olga Esther Arias Elenes spent the majority of her life in Durango, the capital city of the north-central Mexican state of the same name. Arias is best known as a poet, though she also authored numerous short stories, novels, essays, children's stories, and tributes to distinguished Duranguenses. Arias' revolutionary spirit, which permeates much of her work, can be traced to both sides of her family. Her mother was a direct descendant of the sister of Guadalupe Victoria, revered revolutionary fighter and the first president of Mexico; her father fought alongside Francisco "Pancho" Villa and later became a general in the Mexican Army. After an itinerant childhood owing to her father's military career, Arias moved to Durango permanently in 1942. She married businessman Enrique Weber Lozoya and together they had four children.

Alongside her prolific literary career, Arias earned a degree in elementary education from Benemérita y Centenaria Escuela Normal del Estado de Durango and served as director of the Departamento de Extensión Universitaria de la Universidad Juárez del Estado de Durango for over twelve years. She also labored vigorously and tirelessly to promote the arts in Durango in her role as cultural advisor for the state government. She has received diplomas from the Universidad de Juárez del Estado de Durango, the Centro Cultural Durangueño, and other cultural and literary institutions. She was also granted many Mexican awards, such as the "Francisco Villa," "Orquídea de Plata," "Francisco Zarco," and "Salvador Nava Rodríguez," as well as the "Coronilla de Oro" from Italy. A few of her works have been translated into Italian, French, Portuguese, and German. Her sister Irene Arias, a well-known artist, illustrated many of her published writings. Olga Arias died on April 8, 1994, in her beloved city, Durango.

Durango's Adopted Daughter

Durango was a source of pride, hope, and love for Arias and is a common subject in her writing. In *Cuatro preludios para una ciudad* (1962, Four Preludes for a City), Arias traces the city through its diurnal cycle, showing how Durango promises progress, beauty, and possibility throughout—and despite—its various tribulations and metamorphoses. Here, she also calls Durango "ciudad paloma" (dove city), a term of endearment that appears in several of her works. Arias wrote *A Durango* (1963, To Durango) to commemorate the quadricentennial of the founding of the city. In it, she bemoans the dark periods of the city's 400-year history (the Conquest, slavery, despotism), while celebrating Independence for planting the seeds that will surely bear a fruitful future. *En la espiga del viento* (1959, In the Spike of the Wind) is a collection of poems in which Arias shouts her battle cry of liberty and justice, hoping to galvanize the Duranguense people. She describes Durango's important historical events, highlights its prominent geographical features, decries its social injustices, and praises its most venerated heroes. She also articulates her own affection for the city, writing in "Declaración de amor y gratitud" (Declaration of Love and Gratitude), "Tu voz / me ha enseñado / el inextinguible lazo del amor más alto" (Your voice has taught me the eternal bond of the highest love, (lines 23–5)).

Just as Arias adopted Durango as her hometown, Durango itself warmly embraced the poet as its own daughter—a metaphor carried out by Arias herself in the many instances where she refers to Durango as a mother or endows the city with maternal qualities. In addition to the numerous local awards bestowed upon Arias, there are many other signs of Durango's admiration and pride for its adopted daughter. Several of her poems have been engraved in public monuments and buildings; two schools, a fountain, a street, and a neighborhood are named in her honor; the Premio Estatal de Poesía Olga Arias is one of the highest prizes a writer from Durango can receive; and the Centro Literario Olga Arias del Instituto de Cultura del Estado de Durango houses books, letters, awards, paintings, and photographs of the poet, in addition to sponsoring cultural and educational activities that carry on Arias' work of fostering Duranguense society.

Glimmers of Hope

Durango represents one form of the hope that often (if faintly) rises up from the maelstrom of pessimism and despair depicted in much of Arias' work. Indeed, solitude and alienation are two of the main leitmotifs that run throughout her literary corpus. She questions man's place in the modern world, denounces continued victimization of the marginalized, and laments the repetition of sadness, exploitation, and destruction. *Fragmentario* (1963, Fragmentary), for example, paints the world as a dark, post-modern wasteland rife with amputations, truncations, stumps, and ripped-open chests; yet there are also glimpses of shining suns, flowers, and stars, offering just enough promise to continue on: "un lucero de mirar obscuro / ensarta sueños con una centella" [a shadowy star links dreams with a spark] (7.13–14). In her poem *Presente de indulgencia* (Present of Indulgence) in the collection *Mínima Galaxia* (1958, Tiny Galaxy), dawn is a caress of optimism that pours out over the pain of the Mexican landscape ("esa alborada / que inunda como una caricia de optimismo / el dolor del paisaje" (lines 31–3)).

Las pupilas (1960 Pupils), whose name reflects one of the poet's favorite images, poignantly reveals Arias' maternal anguish over how to answer life's largest and most difficult questions—questions brimming in the eyes of her young child. How can she explain a horror like the atomic bomb, for instance, to someone whose very being embodies freshness and life? Hopes, dreams, and nature's beauty can all be easily consumed by the science, machinery, and heartless capitalism of the modern world. Arias expands on this idea in *El cornetín de los sueños* (1965, Bugle of Dreams) when she warns that fine-tuned systems and machines have dehumanized man: "Los hombres se habían convertido en engranajes y todo sucedía puntual y exactamente" [Men had turned into gears and everything happened punctually and exactly] (p. 28). While mankind tries to reach the heavens with spaceships and airplanes, Arias finds the cosmic in earthly things, often using stars, suns, moons, galaxies, and angels to describe everyday objects, landscapes, and human emotions. In *El grito* (1960, The Scream), for example, the poet resolves to capture the light of the moon and spread it like multiplying bread to nurture and inspire others:

La alcanzaré con un grito
y la pondré en mis pupilas
como un pan en una canasta,
como un pan multiplicado
que mañana
será presente de amor
en todas las panaderías.

(111–17)

[I will grasp it with a scream
and put it in my pupils
like bread in a basket
like multiplied bread
that tomorrow
will be a gift of love
in all the bread shops.]

The same passion for hope seen in this poem seeps out from the whole of Mexican writer Olga Arias' bountiful literary œuvre – despite the dark and dreary images that often dominate. There are undeniable pains and sufferings in her world, but also beacons of love and promise.

CAROLYN HUTCHINSON

Selected Works

Mínima galaxia. México: Métafora, 1958.
En la espiga del viento. México: Impresiones Zarco, 1959.
Las pupilas, y El grito. Durango: Talleres Salas Impresores y Fotograbadores, 1960.
Cuatro preludios para una ciudad. Durango: Universidad Juárez del Estado de Durango, Departamento de Extensión Universitaria, 1962.
A Durango. Durango: Universidad Juárez del Estado de Durango, Departamento de Extensión Universitaria, 1963.
Fragmentario. Durango: Universidad Juárez del Estado de Durango, Departamento de Extensión Universitaria, 1963.
El cornetín de los sueños. México: Pájaro Cascabel, 1965.
Espejos y espejismos. Palencia: Editorial Rocamador, 1977.
Poesía. México: Editorial Oasis, 1982.
Casa encantada: relato. Colección Cuadernos del Fuego Nuevo 8. México: Signos, 1983.

Lluvia de pétalos. México: Editorial Praxis, 1993.
Antología de la poesía cósmica de Olga Arias (1923–1994). Ed. Fredo Arias de la Canal. México: Frente de Afirmación Hispanista, 2004.

References and Further Reading

Álvarez, Griselda (ed.). *10 mujeres en la poesía mexicana del siglo XX*. Colección Metropolitana 22. México: Departamento del Distrito Federal, Secretaría de Obras y Servicios, 1974, pp. 23–36.
Bello, Francisco R. "Review of *Poesía*, by Olga Arias". *Repertorio Latinoamericano* 9(55) (July–Sept. 1983): 16.
Durán Rosado, Esteban. "Poesía en prosa de Olga Arias. Review of *El cornetín de los sueños*, by Olga Arias." *Revista Mexicana de Cultura* 947 (23 May 1965): 15.
González, Otto-Raúl. "Poemas duranguenses. El mundo de Olga Arias. Review of *Duranguenses*, by Olga Arias." *Excelsior* (6 August 1982): 1.
Hernández, Esteban. *Olga Arias, semblanza biográfica*. Durango: Gobierno del Estado de Durango, Secretaría de Educación, Cultura y Deporte, 1995.
Jiménez Luna, Oscar. *Olga Arias, la contemplación amorosa de la realidad*. Durango: Gobierno del Estado de Durango, Secretaría de Educación, Cultura y Deporte, Revista de Creación Contraseña, Grupo Cultural Analco, 1997.
Lerín, Manuel. "Preludios poéticos. Review of *Los preludios*, by Olga Arias." *Revista Mexicana de Cultura* 944 (2 May 1965): 15.
——. "'Sueños Bufonescos'. Review of *El cornetín de los sueños*, by Olga Arias". *Revista Mexicana de Cultura* 947, 23 May 1965, 1.
Montenegro, Manuel Roberto. "La coronilla de oro italiana para la duranguense Olga Arias". *Excelsior*, 25 May 1984, sec. 8B, 1.
Ocampo, Aurora M. "Olga Arias". In Aurora M. Ocampo (ed.), *Diccionario de escritores mexicanos, siglo XX: desde las generaciones del Ateneo y novelistas de la Revolución hasta nuestros días* Tomo I (A–CH). México: Universidad Nacional Autónoma de México, Instituto de Investigaciones Filológicas, Centro de Estudios Literarios, 1988, pp. 79–81.
Semblanza de Olga Arias. Durango: Desarollo Integral de la Familia, 1989.

ARREDONDO, INÉS

Life and Literary Beginnings

Inés Arredondo is unique in the world of twentieth-century Mexican letters in that she achieved critical acclaim in her homeland mostly on the strength of her writing in the short story genre. Her famous works include the collections *La señal*, *Río subterráneo*, and *Opus 123*. Born in Culiacán in the state of Sinaloa on March 20, 1928, Arredondo studied Spanish language and Hispanic literature at the National Autonomous University of Mexico (UNAM) in Mexico City from 1947 to 1951, receiving her Licenciatura with a thesis on twentieth-century Mexican theater. She was married to the author Tomás Segovia from 1953 to 1965, and they had three children: Inés, Ana and Francisco Segovia. Her writing career blossomed in the 1960s, when in 1961 and 1962 she was awarded grants from the Centro Mexicano de Editores and the Fairfield Foundation in New York, respectively. In the 1960s and 1970s, she also worked for the Biblioteca Nacional, as an editorial consultant, and as a researcher in the humanities. Branching out into multiple media for artistic expression after the publication of *La señal* in 1965, Arredondo won an award for experimental cinema in 1966 for her filmed version of her story "La Sunamita". She also briefly served as professor in Golden Age Spanish literature and in cinema at the UNAM from 1965 to 1968, and participated in professional activities as a lecturer, scholar, and in cinema and radio productions.

Arredondo's career continued to flourish in the 1970s until her death in 1989. She married a surgeon, Carlos Ruíz Sánchez, in 1972, and in 1979 won the prestigious Premio Xavier Villaurrutia in Mexico. She earned a Master's Degree in Spanish letters in 1981 with a dissertation entitled "Acercamientos a Jorge Cuesta," and was paid tribute in various displays of appreciation in the year of her sixtieth birthday, 1988, when she accepted an Honorary Doctorate from the Autonomous University of Sinaloa, her home state. Due to decreased mobility resulting from a spinal column injury, Arredondo remained mostly homebound for the last eight years of her life. She died November 2, 1989, in Mexico City.

Literary Contexts in Mexico

Arredondo forms part of the mid-century generation, characterized as departing from the nationalist concerns of post-revolutionary literature (Albarrán, 2000), and as preceding the Generation of 1968's disillusionment with social utopias. Along with their commitment to literary and cultural criticism, the mid-century authors formed artistic communities through cultural institutions like the Centro Mexicano de Editores and various literary journals such as the *Revista Mexicana de Literatura* and *Cuadernos del Viento*. Claudia Albarrán notes the significance of their cosmopolitanism and cultural pluralism, which allowed for the influx of international literary undercurrents in the 1960s. Other mid-century authors include those who formed the *Revista Mexicana de Literatura*, among them Arredondo's spouse, author Tomás Segovia, and Juan Vicento Melo, Huberto Batis, José de la Colina, Salvador Elizondo, and Juan García Ponce.

Sociocultural Criticism in Inés Arredondo's Writing

Reading Arredondo, it becomes evident that her powerful short stories reveal the intense psychological effects of interpersonal conflicts between characters even as they address harrowing social problems of Mexico. These include sexism, class struggle, urban alienation in the capital ("2 de la tarde" from *Río subterráneo*), the racist aftermath of colonialism, and birth defects and the abandonment of orphans ("La orfandad" from *Río subterráneo*). Many of her stories focus on a repeated action or gaze whose meaning changes throughout the narrative. The result can be a harrowing confrontation with oppression that results in a transformative revelation or resistance, often marked by what the reader will readily recognize as the narrator's ambiguity or ambivalence toward the perceived aggressor.

"2 de la tarde"

"2 de la tarde" from the collection *Río subterráneo,* is an example of a story that could be said to typify Arredondo's use of sustained tension within a brief, linear narrative, employment of repeated – yet evolving – actions or gazes, and, similar to many mid-century authors, setting the story against the backdrop of repressive social conditions in Mexico. The narrative begins describing a 1970s Mexico City bus stop at rush hour; gradually we enter the internal monologue of the "*pelado*" (stereotypical macho) Silvio, whose sexist fantasies at the bus stop culminate as he runs his hand along a woman's thigh with a sardonic remark of "Completo" ("All Woman") as the two attempt to board a packed bus. When she responds by returning his sneer with a serene and blank stare of recognition, Silvio re-examines his poor socio-economic state, feels the shame of the other's gaze, and finally re-perceives the woman, again waiting for the bus, as occupying an escapist fantasy of marine breezes, free of victimhood. When they approach the bus to attempt boarding a second time, Silvio extends his hand to assist the woman, who accepts his chivalrous gesture. The two part ways subsequently, with the knowledge of having conquered "2 in the afternoon".

Whether the apparent (negative) force of the other in tales like the incestuously eroticized "Apunto gótico" and "La sunamita" is transformed through the protagonist's perception remains to be analyzed by the reader; clearly "2 de la tarde" resists giving a simple solution to hierarchical social relationships by replacing one prescribed treatment of women (machismo) with another (chivalry). Throughout, the intimacy of the *pelado*'s perspective provides a brief psychological portrait and shows his absorption of the woman's passive resistance.

Ambivalence, Desire, and Alienation

In various Arredondo stories, ambivalence marks the narrator's perception of social behaviors (incest, child sexuality, adultery, necrophilia) that, according to Michel Foucault, have been both condemned and exhaustively addressed in Western legal and medical practice since at least the inception of the nineteenth century (*The History of Sexuality:* Vol. I). Like the tales of the famed Brazilian author Clarice Lispector, Arredondo's narratives demonstrate each protagonist's imaginative force, which becomes a vehicle for negotiating the compromised situations in which they find themselves physically and psychologically. Often, an imagined, shared national condition of existential angst, alienation, and psychological disintegration leads to a sense of powerlessness in the face of injustice, as expressed in *Río subterráneo*'s chaotic "En la sombra": "Qué significa injusticia cuando se habita en la locura?" ["What does injustice mean when one is crazy?"]. In *Río subterráneo*, the rejection of public political spheres and shared agency—caused by disillusionment with the integrity of the subject—leads each narrative to explore the affective ruptures caused by absence and loneliness. In "Apunte gótico," for example, a father's corpse is embodied with sensuality as through the eyes of the daughter who sits with him, eventually transforming her conjuring of *eros* into *thanatos* (Lillian von der Walde, 1991: 114). Also focusing on the other's perception, "Atrapada" shows an abused wife isolated by her husband, convinced that the "gaze of the other takes away your authenticity".

"La sunamita"

"La sunamita" is also a psychological *tour de force* in which, in Alfredo Pavón's reading, polar opposites annihilate one another through the contrasting egos of the characters Luisa and Apolonio. In "La sunamita," Luisa's first-person narrative insists on an inflated self-valorization based on the hypocritical flattery she accepts as truth from those around her, a perspective that grants her an artificial power and subjectivity. Her manic delusion lasts as long as she inhabits a privileged and edenic world of her own imagining. Hence, when Luisa is summoned home to attend to her dying uncle, Apolonio, she expects a sunny reconciliation with happy childhood scenes of familial harmony, benevolence, and paternalistic indulgence. Yet the encounter with her uncle and with her father unmasks the paternal giants of the past as withered remnants of their former, idealized selves, while her town and home seem hollow environs where good and evil weigh equally on the psyches of their inhabitants. Pavón claims nature itself disappears, as the "paradise" of childhood cedes to the eventuality of perdition—which we may interpret as Luisa's horror before moral and social relativism, and emotional disappointment that becomes linked to the depressing, naturalistic physical details of caring for the dying (fecal matter, bodily fluids, etc.). Limited to negotiating her role in the depressed household according to prescribed feminine roles and male approval, Luisa imagines herself alternately as wife, daughter, and mother; this equally inauthentic self-positioning negates the possibility of imagining actual, self-motivated and individual agency based on a sense of personal purpose outside of gendered familial, social, and religious hierarchies (Pavón, 1990). In a development influenced by these arbitrary hierarchies, Luisa's self-integrity is further abraded when to her abject horror, her depraved uncle eventually fondles her and demands that she, his "wife," fulfill her duty as defined by God – by servicing him sexually. Her last recourse is to flee the household, yet the priest to whom she confesses her uncle's shocking demands advises her that she would commit a greater sin by not returning to the household: that of murderer. Convinced that only sin will bring Apolonio back from the grave, Luisa acquiesces; her moral victory is that he "dies in peace," a rationalization that proves she is unable to escape her self-definition according to sexist expectations and male approval. Accordingly, her self will never be rescued from the absolute depravity through which she has been forced, which convinces her that all men henceforth will view her as "worse than a prostitute".

Deconstructing Social Hierarchies

We can interpret Arredondo's focalization of moral, physical, and psychological abjection as constituting both feminist and deconstructive critique of the patriarchal, repressive hierarchies inherent to the primary socializing institutions of Mexican society. These institutions—the Catholic Church, the nuclear family, and the government/the State—have been criticized as positioning the powerless in ways that challenge subjectivity, agency, and cross-cultural solidarity. In studying Arredondo's work, the reader must revel at the intense creation of sustained, yet compressed and seething emotional and intellectual energy, which plays out in each story's direct expression of the human experience through dire circumstances that are first most myopically viewed by paralyzed protagonists, and then magnified in the narrative. In the Mexican canon, true to the aims of the mid-century generation, Arredondo marks a summit of aesthetic and technical achievement in the short narrative genre combined with a biting and pluralistic social and cultural criticism.

JULI A. KROLL

Selected Works

La señal. México: Era, 1965.
Río subterráneo. México: Joaquín Mortiz, 1979.
La sunamita y otros cuentos. México: Secretaría de Educación Pública, 1981.
Acercamientos a Jorge Cuesta (Master's Thesis). México: SepSetentas Diana, 1982.
Opus 123. México: Oasis, 1983.
Historia verdadera de una princesa. México: Reloj de Cuentos/CIDCLA/SEP. 1984.
Mariana. México: UNAM, Material de Lectura, serie El Cuento Contemporáneo No. 2, n.d.
Los Espejos. México: Joaquín Mortiz, 1988.
Obras completas. México: Siglo XXI/DICOFUR Sinaloa, 1988.

References and Further Reading

Albarrán, Claudia. *Luna Menguante. Vida y obra de Inés Arredondo*. México: Ediciones Casa Juan Pablos, 2000.
Amatto, Alejandra. "*La señal* de señales: El juego de la ambigüedad en Inés Arredondo". http://www.tuobra.unam.mx/publicadas/050707220141.html (10 July 2006).
Corral, Rose. "Inés Arredondo: La dialéctica de lo sagrado". In Aralia López González, Amelia Malagamba and Elena Urrutia (eds), *Mujer y literatura mexicana y chicana: Culturas en contacto, II*.
Escalante, Evodio. "Inés Arredondo: Entre la pureza y la pornografía". *Texto Crítico* 4(7) (July–Dec. 1998): 9–24.
García Castro, Ma Guadalupe. "'Sombra entre sombras' o el desenfreno de los sentimientos". *La Palabra y el Hombre: Revista de la Universidad Veracruzana* 91 (July–Sept. 1994): 166–75.
Martínez-Zalce, Graciela. *Una poética de lo subterráneo; la narrativa de Inés Arredondo*. México: Tierra Adentro, 1996.
Mendoza Aguirre, Carlos Iván. "Naufragios en el río metafísico de Inés Arredondo." http://www.difusioncultural.uam.mx/revista/dicolene02/mendoza.html (accessed 10 July 2006).
Pavón, Alfredo. "La anulación del 'yo' en 'La sunamita.'" *El presente insoportable {Soliloquio de la solterona}: Lectura y análisis a obras de Sergio Galindo, Rosario Castellanos, Juan Vicente Melo, Aline Pettersson e Inés Arredondo*. Veracruz: Manantial en la Arena, 1990, pp. 235–54.
von der Walde, Lillian. "*Apunte gótico*, de Inés Arredondo". In Alfredo Pavón (ed.), *Te lo Cuento otra vez. (La ficción en México)*. México: Universidad Autónoma de Tlaxcala-Universidad Autónoma de Puebla, 1991, pp. 109–19.

ARVELO LARRIVA, ENRIQUETA

Arvelo Larriva (1886–1962) did not write the traditional sort of poetry expected of Venezuelan women of her day. Rather she threw herself into the breach, not only risking the immoral selfishness of writing, but seeking to discover a new type of barbarous, rebellious, independent voice that sought inspiration from nature and communion with the natural world.

Life and Literary Formation

Enriqueta Arvelo Larriva grew up, the daughter of a respected family, in the rural province of Barinas, Venezuela, a place where the plains meet the Andes. Her formation and early career as an author took place under the dictatorship of Juan Vicente Gómez, who from 1908 to 1935 ruled Venezuela as if it were his private hacienda. Her brother, Alfredo Arvelo, was also a noted poet, and is still considered one of the best practitioners of the nativist poetry of the time. His verse shows the rigors of the metrical art required of a poet of the day, the strictness of both rhythm and rhyme. Politically, Alfredo was even more renowned, fighting the Gómez dictatorship, serving time in prison for his efforts and dying in exile. The success and fame of Alfredo cast an early shadow over the literary efforts of Enriqueta in the traditionally *machista* Arvelo household.

Enriqueta's life was dominated by her father and brother. She never married, and lived in her father's home all her life, caring for him until his death. Where she shows her rebellion from the patriarchal structures of family and literary society is by being one of the first poets in Venezuela to abandon the formal poetic precepts of the time. Enriqueta disdained the metric arts and is credited by some with founding modern poetry in Venezuela with her use of wider subject matter and form.

Living in Barinas kept Arvelo Larriva outside the round of vanguardist experimentation taking place in the cultural epicenter of Caracas. While literary groups organized around the specific movements and schools of thought that reigned in the capital, Arvelo Larriva worked alone in the provinces. She aligned herself with no literary movement or generation, having no access to the dialog that formed such groupings. Her isolation was nearly total. Indeed, the family's hacienda was 25 kilometers from the nearest small town of Barinitas.

This position, however, afforded creative freedom to the nascent poet. As an outsider, Arvelo Larriva was able to experiment with a wider range of modes and styles, unencumbered by the weight of a poetic manifesto of the type that drove the groups in the capital. As carer for her father, living in a time and place where women were discouraged from studying or writing poetry, Arvelo Larriva read whatever came her way, whenever she had the time. Completely self-taught, she used the family's library, becoming an avid reader of the classics.

The poet began her career writing for regional newspapers and magazines, using the popular press to reach a wide audience. This led to her association with the scholar Julián Padrón who edited her first collection of poetry in 1939. Arvelo Larriva eventually began a correspondence with Juana de Ibarbourou and Nobel Laureate Gabriela Mistral as well as other international names in poetry. As her reputation grew and the value of her work became recognized, Arvelo Larriva became a congresswoman for Barinas in 1945 after the death of Gómez, at which time she moved to Caracas. During her years in Caracas, where she lived until her death, she served as a representative at the constitutional congress of 1947, as a contributor to the newspaper *El Nacional* and as a member of the governing board of the Ateneo of Caracas.

Work: Themes and Form

Arvelo Larriva is the first female poet in Venezuela to discover the possibilities of a barbarous voice, one that exists outside the strictures of strict rules of syllabification and rhyme and also of societal expectation. Her poetry highlights the search for a mode of expression purely her own, and to achieve this objective she was willing to explore uncharted territory. An overall view of Arvelo Larriva's poetry shows the consistency of her insistence in maintaining her own voice. The speaker of her poetry always asserts itself, using active verbs to demand freedom or to describe future plans and actions. In addition, she calls to others to join her, famously extending the invitation: "let us enter into the barbarous with fearless steps".

Where the reader does glimpse the price to be paid by the speaker in her search for an independent and personal voice is in the isolation she suffers as a result. While the poetic voice remains steadfast, it does portray a speaker totally alone, one who at times feels isolated from the rest of society's discourse. This position of the poetic voice may be seen as a product of the isolation of the poet herself from the mainstream of literary thought within the nation, but also as a result of her efforts to write herself and her feminine voice into the mainstream of patriarchal literary communication.

Another element of note in Arvelo Larriva's work is the connection between the poetic voice and the natural world. Sometimes attributed to Arvelo Larriva's rural life, her work shows a particular interest in the description of themes of fertility and fecundity, often represented in floral or aquatic imagery. The speaker in Arvelo Larriva's poetry is indeed often identified with water. The water in these cases is free flowing: a river, a waterfall, a storm, the surf—underlining the poetic voice's desire to break free of restrictions and confinements.

In the same way, the appearance of flora in the work is many times set against a hostile environment. The trees, plants and gardens of Arvelo Larriva's work are representative of resistance and triumph over adversity as they struggle to show their colors to the world, just as the poet struggled to show her poetic talent in an arid environment of rural neglect. Many critics note the depth of the relationship between the speaker in the poetry and the natural world. The verse shows a desire to intimately connect the interior existence of the poetic voice with the power and sweep of the countryside and the life that it represents.

Criticism

In the main, Arvelo Larriva's poetry was ignored by the intellectual establishment of the day. Her avenue to public discourse was the popular press, including the weekly magazines in Barinas and in Barquisimeto. While she did not gain early scholarly attention, however, she won popular support, municipal poetry awards and several national awards, among them the first prize in a women's writing competition sponsored by the Inter-American Cultural Association.

More recently, however, there has been an upsurge in interest in the works of Arvelo Larriva. Especially in her native Venezuela, she has been the subject of much intense study in the past twenty-five years. The list of recent research and criticism of her work extends for pages. Perhaps more importantly, Arvelo Larriva continues to serve as a guiding light for her poetic descendants. Indeed, contemporary poet and critic Yolanda Pantín has used the idea of "entering into the barbarous" as an organizing idea for the breadth of women's poetry in the twentieth century, as women continue to assert an independent voice. In this way, Arvelo Larriva's voice no longer walks the path alone.

ELIZABETH GACKSTETTER NICHOLS

Selected Works

Voz aislada (Poemas 1930–1939). Preface by Julián Padrón. Caracas: Cuadernos Literarios de la Asociación de Escritores Venezolanos, 1939.

El cristal nervioso: poemas 1922–1930. Caracas: Publicaciones de la Asociación Cultural Interamericana, Colección Biblioteca Femenina Venezolana, No. 4, 1941.

Poemas de una pena. Caracas: unedited, 1942.

Canto de recuento. (In Memory of Alfredo Arvelo Larriva on the occasion of the repatriation of his remains) Caracas: López y Bosque, 1949.

Mandato del canto: poemas 1944–1946. Caracas: Cuadernos Literarios de la Asociación de Escritores Venezolanos, 1957.

Poemas perseverantes. Caracas: Ediciones de la Presidencia de la República, 1963.

Antología poética. Selection and preface by Alfredo Silva Estrada. Caracas: Monte Avila, 1976.

Poesías. Valencia: Universidad de Carabobo, 1976.

Obras de Enriqueta Arvelo Larriva. 2 vols. Barinas: Fundación Cultural Barinas, 1987.

Refrences and Further Reading

Anzoa Arvelo, Luis Alejandro. "Biografía de Enriqueta Arvelo Larriva". *Obras de Enriqueta Arvelo.* Vol. II. Barinas: Fundación Cultural Barinas, 1987, pp. 201–7.

Gerbasi, Vicente. "Enriqueta Arvelo Larriva: *Voz aislada*". *La rama del relámpago.* Caracas: Ediciones Casa de Bello, Colección Zona Tórrida, 1992, pp. 166–9.

Liscano, Juan. "Enriqueta Arvelo Larriva". *Panorama de la literatura venezolana actual.* Caracas: Alfadil, 1995, p. 135.

Mandarino, Carmen. "Enriqueta Arvelo Larriva y su poesía". In *Poesías.* Caracas: Dirección Cultural de la Universidad Central de Venezuela, 1994, pp. 7–48.

Pantin, Yolanda. "Entrar en lo bárbaro: Una lectura de la poesía venezolana escrita por mujeres". In Kart Kohut (ed.), *Literatura venezolana hoy: Historia nacional y presente urbano.* Madrid: Vervuert, 1999, pp. 305–20.

Pantin, Yolanda and Torres, Ana Teresa. "Enriqueta Arvelo Larriva". In *El hilo de la voz: Antología crítica de escritoras venezolanas del siglo XX.* Caracas: Fundación Polar, 2003, pp. 53–62.

Russotto, Márgara. *Bárbaras e ilustradas: Las máscaras del género en la periferia moderna*. Caracas: Fondo Editorial Tropykos, 1997.

Tamayo, Francisco. "Enriqueta Arvelo Larriva y Santa Teresa". In *Obras de Enriqueta Arvelo.* Barinas: Fundación Cultural Barinas, 1987, pp. 222–5.

ASSUNÇÃO, LEILAH

Leilah Assunção (b. 1943) is considered to be one of the foremost Brazilian playwrights, and she was one of the young authors to begin their careers in the period of Brazilian theater sometimes called the *Nova Dramaturgia* or *Teatro Novo* (New Theater) of the late 1960s. Leilah has since become a key figure in the history of Brazilian theater. Born in Botucatu, São Paulo, as Maria de Lourdes Torres de Assunção, she became known as Leilah at an early age. Her works have been signed as Leilah (or Leila) Assumpção, but Leilah Assunção is the most frequently used spelling.

Playwright, Actress and Author

Leilah began her studies at the Catholic University of São Paulo, but graduated with a degree in education from the University of São Paulo (USP) in 1964. She completed courses in theater (with Eugênio Kusnet at Teatro Oficina), literary criticism (with Antônio Cândido de Mello e Souza), and several other theater-related courses in Brazil and in England. She began her career working as a fashion model and actress both nationally and internationally. As an actress she performed in *Vereda da Salvação* (The Path of Salvation) by Jorge de Andrade in 1963, and in *The Three-penny Opera* by Bertolt Brecht in 1964. She has published stories in magazines, and has written television series and *telenovelas* (soap operas). Her first work of prose was published in 1998, *Palma da Minha Mão* (The Palm of My Hand), and comprises a collection of short letters addressed to her young daughter. Her work has been translated into Spanish, French and English. While she has produced some of her own plays, and has written for other formats, she is best known for her work as a playwright.

Leilah's third play, *Fala Baixo Se Não Eu Grito* (Speak Quietly or I'll Scream) was performed in São Paulo in 1969. For that play she received the Molière Prize and Author of the Year from the Associação Paulista de Críticas Teatrais (Association of Theater Critics of São Paulo). Her first major success, this play launched her career and with it she became known throughout Brazil. Her play *Roda Cor de Roda* (The Circle Game) was banned by the censors for two years before it finally received authorization to show in São Paulo in 1975. That work, which played for a year, was not only successful with audiences in Brazil, but it is also considered to have been socially and politically significant for the cause of women's rights in Brazil. *Roda Cor de Roda* received awards for Leilah, the director and for the lead actress. Her play *Kuka de Kamaiorá* (The Boogeyman of Kamaiorá), 1975, won the publishing prize of the Serviço Nacional de Teatro (National Theater Service), and was a struggle with the censors that lasted nearly a decade, finally being produced in 1983. Many of her plays were delayed by the strict censors of the Brazilian military regime (1964–85), making the first two decades of her career a struggle that involved the protection of the content of her plays and the fight to have them authorized for performance.

Historical Context and Influences

The playwrights who began their careers in theater in the years after the military coup of 1964 faced new political and social challenges that were not experienced by previous generations. The coup of 1964 became a dictatorial military regime in 1968 with the creation of the Institutional Act (AI-5). This repressive regime continued in power until the *Abertura* (democratization) of 1985, and all but ended the artistic, political and other forms of expression of Brazilian society until well into the 1980s. Leilah's first works were produced during that period of severe political, social and cultural repression and censorship. Many artists, intellectuals and activists had little choice but to go into exile in order to avoid persecution. Those who stayed in Brazil, and who continued to produce and be active faced continuous censorship and threat of persecution by the regime. During that period, Leilah worked to have her plays liberated and produced. As many authors who have written about Leilah's work have noted, she was not to be deterred by censorship, and worked diligently and often successfully to have her plays authorized, while still retaining in them a perspective of the issues of that time.

Themes and Significance

The themes of Leilah's plays have fluctuated throughout her career, but have remained centered primarily on the reality of the Brazilian middle class. In her earliest works of the late 1960s and 1970s she focused on questions of the egalitarian values of the period and the role and status of women. In *Fala Baixo Senão eu Grito*, the lead character, Mariazinha, is a middle-aged unmarried woman who expresses extreme frustration with the limits of her existence and is repressed by her own (and society's) moral standards. In an evening with an unknown stranger who breaks into her room, she is able to lift herself out of her situation through fantasy. In the end, however, she is unable to make real change in her life. With this play, and many of her subsequent works, the author brought to the Brazilian stage the dialogue surrounding feminism and feminist issues, and did so in a manner that was not necessarily linked to political resistance. In several of her plays, she examined the newly modern and emancipated woman of the post-1960s in her search for a new identity in society and in the home. She has pointed to the necessity of a much broader feminism that would examine the root causes of the problems discussed within feminist critiques of society.

While Leilah has not defined herself or her works as feminist, her plays have examined political and social repression, gender roles and divisions, and the role of women in the home and in society. They have included themes such as national identity, prostitution, homosexuality, women and aging. Her plays have critiqued traditional values as well as modern attempts to shift them. The expectations and limitations of the Brazilian housewife have appeared repeatedly as a key theme, as has the difficulty of creating lasting, and effective, social change. Leilah's play *Amanhã, Amélia, de Manhã* (Tomorrow Amelia, in the Morning) was performed in Rio de Janeiro in 1973, but it was so distorted by censorship that the author was inspired to write the play *Roda Cor de Roda*, including in it the character of Amelia. In that play, a traditional romantic triangle between a wife and husband and his mistress unexpectedly shifts into a tale of prostitution, homosexuality, and bisexuality, and it turns traditional gender divisions upside down. This surprising comedy of role-reversals is considered to have been significant for the cause of women's rights in Brazil and internationally. Discussion of this play, after the UN decree of that year emphasizing egalitarian values, was important to the cause of the status of women. As Margot Milleret notes, international discussion of the play was significant within Brazil because it "directly contradicted the repressive Brazilian military dictatorship that promoted traditional patriarchal family values" (2004: 69). According to Vincenzo (1992: 10), *Roda Cor de Roda* has also been acknowledged as a contribution to the efforts leading to the *Novo Estatuto da Mulher* (New Civil Statute for Women) of 1984.

During the 1980s, Leilah's work featured a movement away from political themes and the question of the traditional role of women, and toward the dynamics of the relationships of men and women as couples. At that time, Leilah expressed her view that some progress had been made since the 1960s in terms of women's rights and equal rights between men and women, and that she found less pressing the critique of the social expectation of women, thus shifting her attention to other elements of the male/female relationship. Two of Leilah's plays from the 1980s reflect that shift towards the examination of the dynamics of middle-class married couples, *Lua Nua* (1986, Naked Moon) and *Boca Molhada, Paixão Calada* (1988, Moist Lips, Quiet Passion). In the 1990s much of Leilah's work returned to the theme of female frustration with traditional values and the difficult development of women's autonomy in the face of such a value system.

Leilah's plays are considered to have contributed directly to the improvement of women's rights in Brazil. Her career began with the struggle of an artist for expression in a time of great repression and censorship. She has written numerous plays that question the traditional roles and expectations of housewives, unmarried men and women, couples and others. Thus she has brought to the Brazilian stage, throughout her career, innovative and socially and politically relevant discussions of women and gender roles. Her later works have continued to expand and diversify in terms of themes and styles. Her original and powerful works have created space on the stage for new representations of women and she has earned a place in the history of Brazilian theater.

KACY MCKINNEY

Selected Works

Da Fala ao Grito. Preface by Sábato Magaldi. São Paulo: Edições Símbolo, 1977. Includes *Fala Baixo Senão Eu Grito, Jorginho, o Machão*, and *Roda Cor de Roda.*

A Kuka de Kamaiorá. Rio de Janeiro: Ministério da Cultura e Educação, 1978.

Boca Molhada, Paixão Calada. In Elzbieta Szoka and Joe Bratcher III (eds), *3 Contemporary Brazilian Plays in Bilingual Edition.* Austin, TX: Host Publications, 1988, pp. 293–361. *Moist Lips, Quiet Passion*, English trans. Lydia Gouveia Marques.

Lua Nua. Introduction by Yan Michalski. São Paulo: Editora Scipione, 1990.

Na Palma da Minha Mão (as Leilah Assumpção). 2nd edn. São Paulo: Editora Globo, 1998.

References and Further Reading

Andrade, Ana Lúcia Vieira de. *Nova Dramaturgia: Anos 60, Anos 2000.* Rio de Janeiro: Quartet Editora, 2005.

——. *Margem e Centro: A Dramaturgia de Leilah Assunção, Maria Adelaide e Ísis Baião.* São Paulo: Perspectiva, 2006.

Bissett, Judith. "Leilah Assunção: Marginal Women and the Female Experience." In C. Larson and M. Vargas (eds), *Latin American Women Dramatists: Theater, Texts, and Theories.* Bloomington, IN: Indiana University Press, 1998, pp. 202–14.

Magaldi, Sábato. "Prefácio". In *Da Fala ao Grito.* By Leilah Assunção. São Paulo: Edições Símbolo, 1977, pp. 11–19.

Michalski, Yan. "Leilah Doce Guerreira". In *Lua Nua.* By Leilah Assunção. São Paulo: Editora Scipione, 1990, pp 5–6.

Milleret, Margo. "Entrapment and Flights of Fantasy in Three Plays by Leilah Assunção". *Luso-Brazilian Review* 21(1) (1984): 49–56.

——. "Introduction". In Elzbieta Szoka and Joe W. Bratcher III (eds), *3 Contemporary Brazilian Plays by Plínio Marcos, Leilah Assunção and Consuelo de Castro: in Bilingual Edition.* Austin, TX: Host Publications, 1988.

——. *Latin American Women On/In Stages.* New York: State University of New York Press, 2004.

Pelegrini, Sandra C.A. "A Sociabilidade Feminina nos Palcos Brasileiros – Um Destaque à Produção de Leilah Assunção". *Estudos Históricos* 28 (2001): 1–16.

Vincenzo, Elza Cunha de. *Um Teatro de Mulher.* São Paulo: Editora Perspectiva, 1992.

AZEVEDO CASTRO, ANA LUÍSA

Ana Luísa de Azevedo Castro (c.1823–69) was a poet and fiction writer, as well as an educational reformer interested specifically in the plight of women and girls. Her life has not been well documented, only recently have the important dates and some details pertaining to her work been ascertained. Azevedo Castro was born in São Francisco do Sul, in the state of Santa Catarina in Brazil around 1823. Details about her family and childhood are missing. After attaining an education where she was trained as an educator, she moved to Rio de Janeiro, and married. She then established a school for young women, where she became a teacher and a highly gifted principal, who devoted herself to her pupils and their futures.

Sometime before 1858, Azevedo Castro wrote her only work of fiction *Dona Narcisa de Villar: Legenda do Tempo Colonial* (Dona Narcisa de Villar: The Legend of Colonial Times). The work was written under a pseudonym, as Indígena do Ipiranga (Native of Ipiranga). It was published first in serialized form in the periodical, *A Marmota* from April 13 to July 6, 1858. In the following year, 1859, the novel was published as a book by the journalist Paula Brito. The author chose to maintain her anonymity in the book form as well; because of this the author is mistaken for other authors. In the 1899 *Mulheres Ilustres do Brasil* (Famous Women of Brazil) the author Inês Sabino attributes the work to Ana Bárbara de Lossio e Seilbitz, while Sacramento Blake, the author of *Diccionario Bibliographico Brazileiro* (Brazilian Bibliographical Dictionary), attributes the work to the name in the title, Dona Narcisa de Villar.

In 1860, Azevedo Castro published poems in *A Marmota*, which can be accessed in the National Library in Rio de Janeiro. On April 16, 1866, she became an honorary member of the Sociedade Ensaios Literários (The Society for Literary Studies). She also wrote the *Alegoria ao Sete de Setembro* (The Allegory for the 7th of September); was read at the Sociedade Ensaios Literários on the same date in 1866. She also published it in 1866 in the journal of the same society, the *Revista Mensal da Sociedade Ensaios Literários.* Finally, *Dona Narcisa de Villar* was republished in 1997 by Editora Mulheres, Florianópolis. Azevedo Castro died on January 22, 1869, in Rio de Janeiro.

Dona Narcisa de Villar: Legenda do Tempo Colonial

The novel is a story within a story, the first and last chapters form the frame of the story, which hinges on the explanation for a haunted island, Ilha do Mel. The frame story is a clever and much used introduction for legends. Azevedo Castro distances herself from the story not only through the introduction of the Indígena do Ipiranga but also through the two Indian women, Micaela and Simoa, who relate the story to her. The legend is told to the narrator, the Indígena do Ipiranga, by two old Indian women. The narrator states that she wrote the story when she was only 16; she apologizes for the inelegance of her prose and attributes it to her age. For critics of the novel, it is important that Azevedo Castro is thrice removed from her novel and that her prose cannot be judged fully because she has chosen a young narrator.

This novel or novella is the love story of a beautiful young Portuguese woman and a Brazilian Indian youth. The story takes place in the 1600s when the young Narcisa de Villar comes to join her brothers in Brazil. Her parents have died in Lisbon, and her only relatives are three elder brothers. The brothers leave the rich and noble Narcisa in the care of an Indian woman, Efigênia, who raises Narcisa as if she were her own. Narcisa's youth is spent in the happy company of Efigênia's son Leonardo. She begins to educate Leonardo, even though they are of the same age, and her care transforms him from a poor Indian youth into a beautiful, intelligent man worthy of everyone's admiration. It is then that Narcisa's brothers choose to use her for their means, planning to marry her to a Portuguese Colonel, who falls in love with her. When the brother's plan is revealed, Narcisa and Leonardo pledge their love to each other. The day before the wedding takes place Narcisa has a confrontation with her brothers, in which she begins to propound ideas of a feminist nature. She pleads with them to allow her to choose her own life, as only she can. She explains that a woman cannot be a material possession that is used to barter or sell or exchange. Narcisa's brothers do not listen to her, and as the wedding begins to take place Leonardo comes to rescue her. Narcisa is certain that she will commit suicide before her bridal night with her groom, but Leonardo convinces her to run away. The couple take a canoe out on the ocean, but a huge storm forces them to circle back to the area belonging to her brothers. Cruel fate conspires with the tyrannical Villars, and the lovers are brought to Ilha do Mel where Narcisa first met her brothers' intended fiancé for her. The brothers find them on the island, and kill the impetuous Leonardo who will not part with his beloved. Efigênia appears then to announce that Leonardo is really the son of one of the brothers. Unlike a Greek tragedy though, the brothers do nor repent, but also kill Narcisa, leaving Efigênia to lament the death of her two beloved children. In the epilogue the narrator explains that the island has been haunted from then on, and that the brothers who were cursed by Efigênia suffered terrible deaths and agonies. In the chapter that finishes the frame story, the author explains that the two lovers now fly in the sky as pigeons and are trailed by three crows, the brothers whose cruelty ended the lives of Narcisa and Leonardo.

Themes and Influences

Azevedo Castro's work reflects the influences of the Greek myths and the Romantic preferences of the day. Towards the end of the story Efigênia announces that a filicide has taken place, Leonardo was sacrificed by his own father; this harks back to the story of the original Iphigenia sacrificed by her father Agamemnon. This plot is repeated with the fratricide of Narcisa. At the same time the novel the repetition of other themes popular in Romanticism, stories of unrequited, fatal and unequal loves.

The nuances of descriptions in the novel are also typical of Romanticism; the language constantly uses comparisons of natural wonders, the tempest is described as a waterfall coming from the sky; the heroine resembles an angel, a goddess, a queen. Almost every other physical description uses flowers, birds, and trees to define the atmosphere and hint at the characters' nature. These descriptions mimic the novel's preoccupation with the native population of Brazil. The author wants to contrast the naturalness, health, and vigor of the indigenous with the stale reality of the Portuguese who will not succeed in the new world unless they become more like the natives. Reminiscent of José de Alencar, Azevedo Castro seems to advocate the perfect union of the Indian and the white to make way for a better, more cohesive Brazil. In the beginning of the novel, Micaela notes that the story is about Anhangá, an evil spirit who was portrayed as white with eyes of fire, which was known to protect animals from the Indians. Yet the novel does not specifically deal with the Anhangá, and there is only the suggestion that the spirit has become Leonardo, the half Indian-half white, perfect noble savage. Azevedo Castro reflects the preoccupations of Alencar that can be seen in *Iracema*; she champions the primitive goodness and the innate superiority of the indigenous population of Brazil, and chooses it over the incestuous, cruel European culture.

Azevedo Castro is as concerned with the just portrayal of women as she is with writing the story of the noble savage and the limitations of colonialism. The novel reflects the author's own experiences as a pedagogue; initially Narcisa teaches Leonardo proper Portuguese, manners and etiquette. She portrays the feminist struggle in much the same way that she shows the struggle against colonialism; she seems to imply that women and the indigenous population of Brazil face many of the same problems. The novel shows that a combination of the two struggles in the future can pull society away from the patriarchal system. Narcisa knows that she is subordinate to her brothers, and their interests, and she voices many of the concerns of her sex. Her character criticizes the system of marriage as a commercial enterprise. She does not understand why women must while away their lives in servitude, and she presents a worthy opposition to her brothers' intention to suppress her own interests.

ANNA KATSNELSON

Selected Works

D. Narcisa de Villar: Legenda do Tempo Colonial. Florianópolis: Editora Mulheres, 1997.

A Marmota. Rio de Janeiro, 1860.

"Discurso". *Revista Mensal da Sociedade Ensaios Literários*, Rio de Janeiro, 1866.

References and Further Reading

Almeida, Augusto de. "Carta à Exma. Sra. D. Guiomar Torrezão". *Re Annavista Mensal da Sociedade Ensaios Literários.* Rio de Janeiro, 31 May 1873.

Muzart, Zahide Lupinacci. "Narrativa feminina em Santa Catarina (do século XIX até meados do século XX)". *Organon: Revista do Instituto de Letras da Universidade Federal do Rio Grande do Sul* 16(16) (1989): 227–35.

——. "Uma precursora: Ana Luísa de Azevedo Castro". In Ana Luísa de Azevedo Castro, *D. Narcisa de Villar*. Florianópolis: Editora Mulheres, 1997, pp. 5–15.

——. "Ana Luísa de Azevedo Castro". In Zahide Lupinacci Muzart (ed.), *Escritoras Brasileiras do Século XIX*. Florianópolis: Editora Mulheres, 1999, pp. 250–5.

Simoẽs, Jerônimo. "Necrologia". *Revista Mensal da Sociedade Ensaios Literários* 4 (1872): 674–6.

Soares, Iaponan. "Pequena história de um encontro". In Ana Luísa de Azevedo Castro, *D. Narcisa de Villar*. Florianópolis: Mulheres, 1997, pp. 132–5.

Sousa, J. Galante de. "Duas escritoras e um problema de autoria". In *Machado de Assis e outros estudos*. Rio de Janeiro: Cátedra, 1979, pp. 217–20.

B

BAIÃO, ISIS

Social satire, irony and a feminist critique of Brazil's patriarchal structure highlight the works of playwright Isis Baião (b. 1941). Isis Maria Pereira de Azevedo was born in 1941 in Belo Horizonte in the state of Minas Gerais, but was raised in the northeastern state of Piauí. She moved to Rio de Janeiro to study journalism, and graduated in 1970 with a degree from the Pontifícia Universidade Católica in Rio. She fell in love with the theater, adopted the nom de plume Isis Baião, wrote her first play in 1975, and saw her first staged production performed two years later.

Baião's earlier works demonstrate a critical portrayal of Brazilian society during the military dictatorship. Living under the military *censura*—censorship—until 1979 and the eventual opening up of free speech rights, Baião gently poked fun at the government, the Catholic Church and Brazilian society in general through the use of social satire and irreverence. By the mid-1980s, Baião's works began a transition to a sardonic feminist critique of society. Fred Clark has described the phases: "The plays written between 1975 and 1982, imbued with an incisive and irreverent humor, deal with contemporary Brazilian social realities. Although always present in her texts, the woman and her restricted position in Brazilian society becomes the focal point beginning in 1982. ... Since 1982, Baião's theater has contained a marked preoccupation with the woman and the notion of feminine identity" (1998b: 89). Ms. Baião's understanding of a number of foreign tongues also enables her to use plays on words and euphemisms to disguise social and political commentary.

Cabaret da crise: As da vida também votam (1982) examines the life of the lower classes through the feminine voices of actresses and prostitutes. These marginalized female figures reflect on the corruption of government and the ills of society, all the while feeling unempowered by their newfound ability to vote. Clark explains: "Elections are portrayed here as nothing more than promises made through empty rhetoric". He adds, "One bad candidate has replaced another, and nothing has changed for the people" (1998b: 93). Thus, the piece serves as an introduction to Baião's search for feminine identity, while also providing a social and political critique during a troubling era of political transition.

In *Essas mulheres, ou She by three of them* (1993), the main character She, "played by three actresses, passes from monologue to soliloquy, creating a multifaceted entity that is woman" (Clark 1998b: 93). She appears in three distinct periods of her life—various stages of youth, then as a mature woman in her forties, and finally in old age. Each stage serves as a building block in the construction of a strong female protagonist. By the end of the work, she will decline a marriage proposal, thereby declaring her independence and preventing her shackling to the patriarchal order. She serves as a type for the modern woman, who can experience love and personal accomplishment on her own terms.

One of Baião's later plays, *Clube do leque* (1997), is illustrative of both social and feminist commentaries. The play tells of two warring ladies' social and philanthropic organizations in the fictional town of Maria Mole. One club, the Clube do Leque of the title, is composed of the *madames*—society ladies—who come from old money, have aristocratic mentalities, and use their organization for socializing and gossiping. The other club, the Champã Clube, founded by *nouveaux riches*, is concerned much more with charitable matters and working with the poor. The play is a series of farcical interactions between the two organizations and their leadership.

The piece culminates in an irreverent display of dark humor. Forced to compete with the Champã Clube, the ladies of the Clube do Leque decide to host a benefit for the starving, poor children of a fictional Third World country. During the event, it begins to rain heavily and the club slowly fills with water. Because it would be impolite to criticize anything at the event, no one speaks of the rising floodwaters. They merely move to standing on chairs and eventually on the tables. Finally, everyone drowns rather than break social customs of the elite. The audience laughs at an event in which it really wants to cry. Friesen explains: "The absurdity of the characters standing around ignoring the rising flood waters challenges the audience to question the absurdities of the rigid systems that shape society" (1998: 29).

Isis Baião has also been instrumental in promoting the theater among young people and opening doors for young women to write and act. In 1983, she created the Drama Academy (currently, the Dramatic Text Academy—Theater and TV), which eventually became a part of the Universidade Estácio de Sá. She has helped many to get their first experiences in the theater and television industries in Rio de Janeiro. Her organization has also worked together with others like it in the state of Rio and throughout Brazil to collaborate on projects destined for the stage. Her work has been recognized by winning several major awards, including the esteemed Onassis International Cultural Competition for Theatrical Plays for her piece *Casa de Penhores* in Athens, Greece, in 1997.

BRYAN KENNEDY

Selected Works

Theater

Maria Manchete. Not performed and unpublished, 1975.
Chá de panelas. Not performed and unpublished, 1976.
Instituto Naque de Quedas e Rolamentos. Performed in Rio de Janeiro, production of Júlio Wolguenmuth. Unpublished, 1978.
Maria Manchete Navalhada e Ketchup. Performed in Rio de Janeiro. Unpublished, 1979.
A via crucis nossa de cada dia. Performed in Rio de Janeiro. Unpublished, 1979.
As chupetas do Senhor Refém. Performed in Rio de Janeiro, production of João das Neves. Unpublished, 1981.
Casa de Penhores. Performed in Rio de Janeiro, production of Ana Maria Taborda. Unpublished, 1982.
Cabaré da crise – As da vida também votam. Performed in Rio de Janeiro, production of Ana Maria Taborda. Unpublished, 1982.
As bruxas estão soltas. Performed in Rio de Janeiro, production of Maria Lúcia Vidal. Unpublished, 1984.
Doces fragmentos de loucura. Performed in Rio de Janeiro, production of Ana Maria Taborda. Unpublished, 1989.
Só dói a primeira vez ... Performed in Porto Alegre, production of Ana Maria Taborda. Unpublished, 1991.
El comedor. Not performed and unpublished, 1992.
Espelho, espelho meu ... Performed in Teresina, Piauí, production of Lari Sales. Unpublished, 1993.
Essas mulheres ... ou She, by Three of Them. Performed in Rio de Jenairo, production of Thaïs do Amaral Balloni. Unpublished, 1995.
Sob o signo da estrela. Performed in Rio de Janeiro. Unpublished, 1995.
Clube do leque. Performed in Rio de Janeiro, production of Ivonne Hoffman. Unpublished, 1997.
Casais "mudernos". Performed in Rio de Janeiro. Unpublished, 1997.
A atriz e o cantor e mais alguém. Performed in Rio de Janeiro, production of Nildo Parente. Unpublished, 1998.
Quem matou Madame Silva? Performed in Rio de Janeiro. Unpublished, 1998.
Cenas curtas. Performed in Rio de Janeiro, production of Joaquim Vicente. Rio de Janeiro: Ed. Achiamê, 2001.

Fiction

Tresloucado gesto. Rio de Janeiro: Memórias Futuras Edições, 1983.

Works on the Theater

Em cenas curtas. Rio de Janeiro: Achiamé, 1989.
"Como trabalhar com mulheres". In *Costurando estórias.* Rio de Janeiro: Ed. Vozes, 1988.
"A mulher en-cena". In *A transgressão do feminino.* Rio de Janeiro: Projeto Mulher/IDAC, 1989.

References and Further Reading

Clark, Fred. "'Essas mulheres' de Isis Baião: Do social ao feminino". *Anais do Quinto Congresso do ABRALIC.* Vol. III. Rio de Janeiro: UFRJ Press, 1998a, pp. 941–5.
——. "Actress, Woman, Theater: Isis Baião's 'As da vida também votam' and 'Essas mulheres.'" *Luso-Brazilian Review* 35(2) (1998b): 87–97.
Friesen, Jana. *The Development of a Feminist Perspective in the Plays of Isis Baião.* MA thesis. UNC, Chapel Hill, 1998.

BARRAGÁN DE TOSCANO, REFUGIO

Born in Tonila, in the state of Jalisco in Mexico, Refugio Barragán de Toscano (1843–1916) was the first woman to publish novels in Mexico. Researchers interested in Barragán's biography will note that most bibliographic entries cite 1846 as her date of birth. However, literary historian of the state of Jalisco, Gabriel Agraz García de Alba and José María Muría who is affiliated with the Carmen Toscano Foundation, a non-profit organization initiated by the daughter of Salvador Toscano and granddaughter of the author, both confirm the 1843 date.

Barragán's obscure novelette of one hundred and forty-seven pages, *Premio del bien y castigo del mal* (1884, Goodness is Rewarded and Evil is Punished) was first published in Ciudad Guzmán; a subsequent edition appeared in 1891, printed by J.F. Jens in Mexico City. Barragán's most popular novel, *La hija del bandido o los subterráneos del Nevado* (1887, The Bandit's Daughter or the Subterranean Caves of the Snowcapped Mountain), was originally sold in serialized form in Ciudad Guzmán for eleven Mexican *centavos* per fascicle and was later published as a book in Guadalajara the same year. The novel still enjoys popularity in Ciudad Guzmán (formally Zapotlán el Grande), the location of most of the action in the novel. The Municipal Historical Archive of Zapotlán el Grande in the state of Jalisco continues to publish editions for its readers, thus ensuring that the legend of the buried bandit treasures in the caves of the Colima volcanoes remains a vivid local lore.

The town of Colima had an important role in the professional formation of the author. After living in several towns in the region the author's parents, Antonio Barragán Sánchez and Doña María Francisca Carillo Aguilar, settled there and in 1863 Refugio entered the *Escuela Normal para Señoritas de Colima* (Training School for the Young Ladies of Colima). The famed Colima educator Rafaela Suárez provided the young women with instruction. At this teacher training school Barragán studied pedagogy, calculus, Castilian grammar, cosmology, calligraphy, history, religion/morality, etiquette, and other courses deemed necessary for a skilled, educated teacher. After finishing her studies in 1865, Barragán lived in Ciudad Guzmán with her parents and taught at the Municipal School. In 1869, she married Esteban Toscano Arreola, a professor. The two moved to Guadalajara a year later where they each pursued professional careers as teachers: he taught at the *Colegio Inglés* (English Elementary School) and she at the *Sociedad Lancasteriana* (Lancaster Society). Refugio had four children but only two survived infancy. Barragan's husband died in 1879, leaving her to care for their two sons: Salvador Toscano (1872–1947) and Ricardo Toscano. Salvador is considered an important initiator of Mexican filmmaking and produced several films, including important footage of the Mexican Revolution of 1910. In early 1900s Puebla, Barragán managed Cine Pathé, a cinema owned by her son.

Barragán initiated her literary career towards the end of the nineteenth century when it was no longer necessary for women to enter a convent for a socio-physical space in which to write and publish. Beginning in the 1880s Porfirio Díaz made education one of the essential elements of his administration's positivist campaign for order and progress, creating the space for women to become professional teachers and writers. Carmen Romero Rubio, Díaz's young wife, promoted Mexican women writers and showcased their œuvre for the Chicago World's Fair of 1893. Barragán's lithographed image and poetry appear in that collection edited by José María Vigil entitled *Poetisas Mexicanas* (Mexican Women Poets). With her numerous publications, Barragán de Toscano became part of a generation of women who not only became known as poets but published novels, edited weekly journals and emerged as important cultural producers in their respective states.

Poet, Educator, Novelist and Publisher

Barragán de Toscano's literary career began in the 1860s with the publication of her poetry in a local Colima journal, *La Aurora*. Laurena Wright de Kleinhans documents Barragán's first poem in a short biography written for *Mujeres Notables Mexicanas* (1910, Notable Mexican Women). The verses are a nostalgic tribute, written at the age of 14, to the land of her childhood years, a land she will miss and describes with great affection. In 1873, her play *Diadema de perlas, o los bastardos de Alfonso XI* (The Crown of Pearls or Alfonso XI's Bastards), premiered in the Teatro Apolo of Guadalajara. Barragán continued to write poetry, at times religious in nature, such as *La hija de Nazaret, poema religioso dividido en dieciocho cantos* ... (1880 The Daughter of Nazaret, a religious poem divided into eighteen cantos). The Catholic Church often commissioned poets to compose verses and *cánticos* or chants for a modest remuneration; for Barragán, a widow after 1879, this became a source of income in the early 1880s. The author published several books, including plays, novels and children's stories. A collection of her work up to the date of publication is *Celajes de occidente: composiciones líricas y dramáticas* (1880, Western Cloudscapes: Dramatic and Lyric Creations) which includes the drama *Diadema de perlas, o los bastardos de Alfonso XI*, a moral tale condemning infidelity. Another play, *Libetinaje y virtud o El verdugo del hogar* (Licentiousness and Virtue or The Executioner of the Home) was published in Ciudad Guzman in 1881. Her first novel, *Premio del bien y castigo del mal* (1884) was followed by the popular (perhaps fifteen editions to date) *La hija del bandido o los subterráneos del Nevado* (Guadalajara, 1887). She was the editor and co-publisher (with her father Antonio Barragán) of *La Palmera del Valle: periódico quincenal de carácter religioso, científico y literario* (The Palm Tree of the Valley: A Bimonthly Newspaper of Religious, Scientific and Literary Orientation), a periodical whose first volume circulated from February 5, 1888 to June 16, 1889. The second volume circulated beginning August 15, 1889, and it is unclear when it ended; the last number at the Hemeroteca at UNAM in Mexico City is dated November 1, 1889. A note in the second volume identifies Barragán as the printer, which explains why it is smaller in size and lacks the elaborate lithograph that accompanied the masthead in the first volume. Although the journal claimed to be partly scientific, it was mostly a family-oriented publication aimed at providing moral guidance to young women. *La Palmera* included poetry, short stories, articles and religious announcements. Article topics ranged from how to identify a potential suitable husband to an opinion piece on the futility of suicide, a theme that plagued modernist Mexico.

Eleven years before her death in 1916, Barragán published a small collection of short stories for children, *Luciérnagas: Lecturas amenas para niños* (Fireflies: Enjoyable Readings for Children); the work was reprinted with additional stories and entitled simply *Luciérnagas* in 1940. Didactic in orientation, this latter collection of short stories well captures Barragán's persistent role of educator and source of maternal guidance.

Bandits and Barragán de Toscano

La hija del bandido o los subterráneos del Nevado (1887) appeared during the Porfiriato (1876–80; 1884–1911) when bandits captured the imagination of Mexican writers. Ignacio M. Altamirano (1834–93) wrote *El Zarco* (El Zarco, Bandit) between 1885 and 1888 but the novel was published posthumously in 1901 (Barcelona, Spain). Manuel Payno (1810–94) also published his *Los Bandidos de Río Frío* (1888–91; The Bandits of Cold River) in Barcelona. His complex and lengthly novel was inspired by the life of Colonel Juan Yáñez, an associate of President Antonio López de Santa Ana, who was executed for criminal activities in 1839. Barragán's novel was published in Mexico yet received scant national attention. This romantic novel was tinged with historical references and hints of *costumbrismo* (the portrayal of local customs). Her portrayal of Vicente Colombo, a fictional bandit who terrorizes the Mexican countryside near the volcanoes of Colima, is of a complex paternal figure who commits crimes to ensure a viable future for his daughter, María. It is precisely this representation of a bandit as concerned father, and the depiction of his daughter as an independent subject that distinguishes Barragán's banditry narrative from her male counterparts. The narrative follows the coming-of-age experiences of a young woman who learns that her father is a bandit and takes action to undo his criminal activities. María Colombo is a female character with unusual agency and self-determination. She is a rival to the Domestic Angel ideology prevalent in nineteenth-century social discourse. That ideology limited women's societal contribution to the private sphere (as dutiful wives, mothers, daughters) and exalted their spiritual nature. María's independence in action, her rescue of the romantic hero, and choice of working against her father all obviate this paradigm. This provocative portrayal of womanhood situates Barragán as a pioneer in Mexican letters. Her life's cultural work and literary production not only championed the education of young women but consequently authorized Mexican women to write.

Scholarship on Barragán de Toscano

Critical inquiry into the work of Barragán de Toscano has been minimal perhaps because her literary production has not been translated into English. In the early 1990s a recovery project of nineteenth-century Mexican women writers was initiated by a group of women scholars at the Colegio de Mexico in Mexico City. Their efforts were published in 1991 in *Las voces olvidadas* (The Forgotten Voices) and a chapter on Refugio Barragán de Toscano was included. Two dissertations from the University of Texas at Austin in 2001 and 2004 dedicated chapters to Barragán and contributed critical approaches to the bandit novel. However, the present dearth of critical essays on Barragán challenges feminist scholars to re-discover this significant writer and thinker.

MARÍA MAGDALENA ZALDUONDO

Selected Works

Celajes de Occidente: Composiciones, líricas y dramáticas de Refugio Barragán de Toscano. Ciudad Guzmán, Mexico: Imprenta Agapito Ochoa, 1880.

La Palmera del Valle: periódico quincenal de carácter religioso, científico y literario. Guadalajara, February, 1888–November, 1889.

"Los ángeles". *Poetas Hispano-Americanos: México. Entrega Cuarta*. Lázaro M. Pérez and José Rivas Groot. Bogotá: J.J. Pérez, 1889, pp. 229–31.

Premio del bien y castigo del mal. 1884. Mexico City: Imprenta de J.F. Jens, 1891.

"El 16 de septiembre". *Poetisas Mexicanas, Siglos XVI, XVII, XVIII y XIX. Antología formada por encargo de la junta de señoras correspondiente de la Exposición de Chicago*. Edited by José María Vigil. Mexico City: Secretaria de Fomento, 1893, pp. 139–41.

"Prólogo". *Fray Antonio de la Concepción*. 1888. Juan S. Castro. Guadalajara: Fortuno Jaime, 1918.

Las cuatro estaciones. Zarzuela de fantasía dividida en tres actos y en verso. Mexico City: n.p., 1933.

La hija del bandido o los subterráneos del Nevado. Guadalajara, 1887. Mexico City: Editorial México, 1934.

Luciérnagas: Cuentos para niños. Mexico City: n.p., 1940.

References and Further Reading

Agraz García de Alba, Gabriel. "Refugio Barragán de Toscano". *Bio-bibliografía de los Escritores de Jalisco*. Mexico City: Universidad Nacional Autónoma de México, 1980, pp. 76–82.

El Pensamiento Libre. Quincenal Independiente. Ciudad Guzmán, Mexico. 3(11) (1887): 3.

González Casillas, Magdalena. *Historia de la literatura Jalisciense en el siglo XIX*. Guadalajara: Gobierno de Jalisco/Secretaría General Unidad Editorial, 1987.

La Bandera Liberal. Periódico independiente, de política y variedades. Ciudad Guzmán, Mexico. 1(10) (1884): 4.

Morán, Diana and Cázares, Laura. "Doña Refugio Barragán de Toscano: *Luciérnagas* y *La hija del bandido*". In Ana Rosa Domenella and Nora Pasternac (eds), *Las voces olvidadas: Antología crítica de narradoras mexicanas nacidas en el siglo XIX, 1991*. Mexico City: El Colegio de México, 1997, pp. 77–115.

Muría, José María. "En busca de Salvador Toscano". In *Correspondencia*. Mexico City: Carmen Toscano Institute, 1996, pp. 7–13.

BARROS, PÍA

Pía Barros (b. 1956) features among the major authors of the Generation of 1980, the youngest group of Chilean novelists, as well as one of the most prominent leaders of feminism in Chile and Spanish America. Although her works have been widely acclaimed in Chile, she continues to gain recognition in international literary circles. After majoring in Spanish Language and Literature at the University of Santiago, Barros published her first collection of short stories, *Miedos transitorios* (1985, Transitory Fears, 1993), at the age of 29 and since then she has developed an intense literary work, periodically publishing short fiction, novels, and scholarly articles. Other short fiction collections include *A Horcajadas* (1990, Astride), *Signos bajo la piel* (1994, Signs under the Skin), *Ropa usada* (2000, Used Clothes), and *Los que sobran* (2002, The Remaining Ones). *El tono menor del deseo* (1991, The Lower Pitch of Desire) is her first novel and she is the author of the first Chilean digital novel, *Lo que ya nos encontró* (2001, What Already Found Us).

Barros's narrative work won first prizes in the following literary contests: "Juegos Literarios Gabriela Mistral" in the city of Santiago (1977), "Concurso de Literatura Juvenil" in the city of Providencia (1982), and "Concurso Nacional Antonio Pigafetta" (1986). She has been the recipient of a number of scholarships and literary awards on several occasions: the Fondart prize, two scholarships from the Fondo para el Desarrollo de la Cultura y las Artes del Ministerio de Educación, a scholarship from the Fundación Andes, and the Beca del Escritor del Consejo Nacional del Libro y la Lectura. Anthologies from around the globe (published in the United States, Italy, Germany, Hawaii, Russia, France, Venezuela, and Costa Rica among other countries) have included her work, and her short stories and novels have been translated into English. All this proves what a favorable reception her prose has had not only in Chile but also abroad.

Being a firm feminist and defender of women's literary expression, Barros founded the Ergo Sum literary workshops in 1976 and she has directed them since then. She created Ergo Sum as a response to the Agrupación Cultural Universitaria. This group of workshops was mainly formed by men and ignored the work of women writers. Thus, the Ergo Sum workshops have always focused on the development and promotion of women's literature in Chile and they have witnessed the emergence of outstanding writers such as Ana María del Río, Andrea Maturana, and Sonia Guralnik to name but a few.

Barros and the Generation of 1980

The Generation of 1980 emerged at a time of political repression, violence, and constant vigilance. This context inevitably influenced the work of renowned Chilean authors such as Gonzalo Contreras, Arturo Fontaine, Juan Mihovilovich, Antonio Ostornol, and Alberto Fuguet. These writers' didacticism encouraged them to follow a great variety of readings, from the Classics to the North American and European narrative masterpieces to the great works of Spanish American narrative. Such a political and cultural context favored literary innovation and enrichment of themes, styles, and language in an attempt to escape the government's effort to completely control literary production. For example, the theme of eroticism became an unorthodox strategy against patriarchy and conventionalism. The preference for the erotic during this decade was because a group of prominent women writers emerged, among whom Pía Barros excels. Other women writers from this group are Lilian Elphick, Juana Gallardo, Sonia González, Silviana Riqueros, Carolina Rivas, Diamela Eltit, and Marcela Serrano. These women writers had a determined agenda: to develop a vision of the world from the woman's perspective showing the problems, sensibility, and language, as well as to explore the notion of what being a woman and being Spanish American is. A central feature of Barros's work, which she shares with other women writers of this generation, is the use of a narrative discourse where sexuality and politics intertwine. Barros's *El tono menor del deseo* exemplifies this unique narrative discourse, where the author also addresses her women readers from the specificity of the condition of the Chilean woman.

Style, Characters, and Themes

Barros utilizes literary motives recurrent in women's literature such as the re-evaluation of masculine and feminine roles, sexual initiation, the extra-marital affair, and erotic desire. What makes her use unique is her talented ability to conjugate the private space of women and their social role in the public sphere. In her prose, one can find a gallery of female portraits characteristic of a new generation of women. These women participate in the history of Chile, have a social and political commitment, and are eager to redefine the female identity beyond the conventionalism of patriarchy. For Barros, individuals are cultural constructions with particular ideologies. Thus, it is difficult to ignore the historical reality of Chile that is present in her narrative. Throughout the years, however, and as a new maturity developed, Barros's narrative style has experienced a process of detachment from the political commitment that featured in her earlier writings. In fact, in her most recent works, Pía Barros affirms, she does not write with an explicit ideological agenda in mind (García-Corales 2005: 20).

A major theme in Barros's prose is the mother–daughter relationship. With this theme, the writer ponders the debate on the role of the family in contemporary Chile and explores the mother–daughter, woman–man, and woman–society relationships in a fuller context. Another theme that Barros develops in her work is that of women and power. It is only by controlling their bodies that women can survive the repressive systems exerted on them, that is, dictatorship and patriarchy. In general, Barros's work offers the reader passionate, dramatic human experiences expressed through a variety of styles and linguistic registers.

Works

El tono menor del deseo, Barros's first novel, narrates the stories of three women during the dictatorship in Chile. The three narrated lives interweave indistinctly, which helps portray the disjointed nature of women's experiences under repression. The author accentuates the significance of these broken lives through the use of a fragmented narration, dividing the text into sections rather than chapters. Set during the military regime, the novel has a tone of denunciation; in particular, it revolves around the metaphor of torture which is a recurrent topic in Barros's work. This complex metaphor functions as the link between the political and the sexual conflicts. In other words, through the expression of women's sexuality, Barros proposes the subversion of norms of traditional institutions and patriarchal values that are commonly reinforced during authoritarian regimes.

Clearly related to the dictatorship, the first volume of short stories *Miedos transitorios* is a book of political denunciation—in fact, it was published clandestinely during Pinochet's regime. Many of the short stories show the terror of the military government and the arbitrariness of political repression. Others deal with the theme of oppression in a wider sense. Some stories, for instance, describe the lives of young women who feel an anguished frustration and are confined in conservative and patriarchal environments. Desire, one of Barros's favorite themes, is the central subject matter of her second collection of short stories, *A horcajadas*. In this work, desire is not only expressed through sexual impulses but also through the volition of controlling, abusing, and marginalizing others by exerting power. For example, Latin America is presented in the text through the metaphor of a woman's distraught body.

The next book that Barros published was *Signos bajo la piel*, a collection of short stories in which the writer continues to develop the theme of desire, in particular the erotic impulse as the foundation of life and death. After this publication, Barros shifted gears and experimented with a new subgenre, the "microcuento," a very brief short story with a story line that leaves the reader in suspense and disturbed. The outcome of such experimentation was *Ropa usada*, a book that reveals one of her obsessions in life, that is, used clothes. Always interested in formal experimentation, Barros published in 2000 the digital novel *Lo que ya nos encontró*, also known as the book-object. Because of the nature of the novel, the reader experiences it through written text, a series of video images, and an audio soundtrack. This virtual novel intends to be a physical representation of modern-day Chile. Cultural, national, and sexual marginality are the main themes of Barros's next collection of short stories, *Los que sobran*. With this book Barros was nominated for the Altazor Prize in 2003, which is awarded to the best four books of the year. Current literary projects include *Políticas de olvido* (Politics of Oblivion) and an erotic novel, *Maica* (Maica).

ISABEL ASENSIO-SIERRA

Selected Works

Miedos transitorios: de a uno, de a dos, de a tres. Santiago de Chile: Ergo Sum, 1986.
A horcajadas. Chile: Editorial Mosquito Comunicaciones, 1990.
Microcuentos. Santiago de Chile: Editorial Mosquito, 1990.
El tono menor del deseo. Santiago de Chile: Editorial Cuarto Propio, 1991.
Signos bajo la piel. Santiago de Chile: Grijalbo, 1994.
Lo que ya nos encontró. Santiago de Chile: Pía Barros, 2001.
Los que sobran. Santiago de Chile: Asterión, 2002.
Ropa usada. Santiago de Chile: Asterión, 2003.

References and Further Reading

Bell, Andrea L. "Creating Space in the Margins: Power and Identity in the *cuentos breves* of Pía Barros and Cristina Peri Rossi". *Studies in Short Fiction* 33(3) (1996): 345–53.
Galarce, Carmen. "Pía Barros: la generación del desencanto y la pérdida de utopias". *Confluencia* 13(1) (1997): 221–7.

García-Corales, Guillermo. "Pía Barros y los senderos del deseo: una perspectiva feminista de la Nueva Narrativa Chilena". In *Dieciséis entrevistas con autores chilenos contemporáneos: la emergencia de una nueva narrativa*. Lewiston, NY: E. Mellen Press, 2005, pp. 9–26.

Muñoz, Willy O. *Polifonía de la marginalidad: la narrativa de escritoras latinoamericanas*. Providencia, Chile: Editorial Cuarto Propio, 1999.

Pélage, Catherine. "Pía Barros y Diamela Eltit: transgresión y literatura femenina en Chile". *La palabra y el hombre* 114 (2000): 59–77.

Spiller, Roland. *Memoria, duelo y narración: Chile después de Pinochet: literatura, cine, sociedad*. Frankfurt am Main: Vervuert, 2004.

Trevizán, Liliana. "Retazos de mujeres en *El tono menor del deseo* de Pía Barros". In *Albricia: la novela chilena del fin de siglo*. Santiago de Chile: Cuarto Propio, 2000, pp. 127–45.

BELLESSI, DIANA

Born in Santa Fe, Argentina in 1946, to poor immigrant Italian parents, Diana Bellessi is considered one of contemporary Argentina's preeminent poets. Although her family did not have the means to provide her with abundant resources, Bellessi was intellectually driven to achieve. She studied philosophy at the Universidad Nacional del Litoral but never graduated from college, having failed to take two required courses. Between 1969 and 1975, she backpacked across the South and North American continents and published her first book, *Destino y propagaciones* (1972, Destiny and Propagations). While traveling through the United States, Bellessi taught herself English. In New York, the poet lived the life of a drifter, finally finding a place to stay among Ecuadorian friends of friends who lived in the Bronx. By day, Bellessi worked as a factory worker and learned to speak English by conversing with the mostly African-American and Hispanic women who worked beside her. At night, she used a dictionary to translate and read contemporary American women poets whose powerful, feminist voices would come to influence her own writings. She spent her spare time borrowing books from the public libraries, reading the *Village Voice* and writing.

On returning to Argentina in 1975, Bellessi lived in Fuerte Apache and Constitución. There, she experienced, at first hand, the military coup against Isabel Perón, the National Reorganization Process and the beginning of the "Dirty War" led by Jorge Rafael Videla, Roberto Viola, Leopoldo Fortunato Galtieri Castelli and Reynaldo Benito Antonio Bignone Ramayón.

In 1984, the Cultural Center of San Martin invited Bellessi to direct a project she proposed that would give voice to prisoners in the jails of Buenos Aires. As a result, Bellessi coordinated and led creative writing workshops among inmates. She chronicled her experiences in *Paloma de contrabando* (1988, Smuggling Dove), an edited collection of writings produced by the incarcerated.

Although largely recognized as a poet, Bellessi has held positions on the editorial boards of prestigious literary journals. Until 1991, she was an editor of Argentina's *Diario de Poesía* (Journal of Poetry), and she currently serves on the editorial board of *Feminaria*, a magazine dedicated to the dissemination of feminist theory, essays, bibliographic information and creative writing. Bellessi is also highly regarded as a translator, having completed and published professional translations of a great number of North American and European authors. Perhaps most significantly, Bellessi worked together with the acclaimed American science fiction writer Ursula Le Guin on *The Twins, the Dream*, a collection of poems the two writers translated for each other.

In 1993, Bellessi was awarded a Guggenheim Fellowship for her poetry, and in 1996, she received a fellowship from the Antorchas Foundation, a prestigious non-profit organization that fosters education and scientific research as well as cultural and community development in Argentina. George Washington University's Columbian College of Arts and Sciences recently named Bellessi their 2006 Writer in Residence.

Poet/Translator

Diana Bellessi, who began writing as a child, came to think of herself as a poet while still an adolescent. A prolific writer of no less than 14 volumes of poetry, Bellessi has been called an "outsider". In interviews, she has stated that it is her duty as a poet to be a magician: to locate herself outside the laws of culture. This position uniquely privileges the poet to relate the human condition. She defends human rights, speaking for those who would otherwise remain silent: the indigenous poor, the weak, the defenseless. Bellessi demonstrates her commitment to telling the truth of the society in which she has lived in works such as *Tributo del mudo* (1982, Tribute to the Mute). The title of this collection dually refers to Bellessi's mute neighbor and friend, Ramón, as well as to the experience of the poet living under the bloody violence of the military regime of the mid-1970s and early 1980s. Inspired by political terror and a growing number of disappeared friends, the author wrote these poems to confront her own fears as well as to expose the existing culture of fear. In *Eroica* (1988, Eroica), the author similarly defended the expression of the feminine Eros, erotic love shared between women. Dealing with lesbian eroticism as well as the textual construction of lesbian subjectivity, this writing challenged heterosexual cultural norms by shedding light on the interplay between lesbian desire and discourse.

For Bellessi, translation is a practice intimately related to the creative production of poetry. A slow process demanding linguistic precision and the internalization of the poem by the individual, Bellessi demonstrates that it is incumbent on the translator to be uniquely attuned to one's native language if one is to successfully decipher the signs, signifiers (sounds) and signifieds (concepts) of a poem. What's more, as a translator Bellessi participates in the structural and historical destabilization of language by interrogating the semantics and syntax of poetry, thereby contributing to the revisioning process of culture.

Themes and Influences

The themes that run throughout Bellessi's works reflect the main socio-cultural concerns of many contemporary women. Of these, perhaps the most salient are: life as an existential journey of becoming, writing the female body and the creation of feminine subjectivities, erotic love and the garden as a symbol of stability as well as of rebellion. Bellessi alludes to travel and space as metaphors used not only to symbolize the very real travels of the young author as she crossed the South and North American continents, but also to represent life as a journey without a destination. For the poet, one's life journey is paradoxical: it leads to both a sense of belonging to a place as well to as a sense of estrangement from the known, the intrinsic or natural state of being. Nowhere is this motif better expressed than in *Buena travesía, buena ventura pequeña Uli* (Good Crossing, Good Fortune Little Uli). Though published in 1991, the collection was written during the Bellessi's backpacking days and chronicles the poet's encounter with herself as well as with the "other," those whom she met on the road.

With regards to writing the female body, to the extent to which the act of writing creates subjectivities, Bellessi sees her poetry as a means by which she not only captures herself on the page, but by which other women might come to see their own stories, experiences, emotions and lives legitimated through text. Through the mirror of her poetry, Bellessi strives to make it possible for women to see themselves not as marginalized second-class citizens within a predominantly patriarchal culture, but as powerful agents capable of creating and articulating their own genealogies. *Danzante de doble máscara* (1985, Dancer with a Double Mask), *Sur* (1998, South) and *La rebelión del instante* (2005, Instant Rebellion), among other works, carefully detail the production of this feminine history.

Related to both the journey motif and the creation of a feminine genealogy is the theme of erotic, Sapphic, love, showcased in *Eroica*. An openly lesbian poet, Bellessi employs geographic references, drawing a parallel between the female body and the writer who dares to search and explore this territory. The female bodies depicted often evoke the landscape of Latin America as well as the indigenous myths of its native peoples.

Garden imagery, thematically tied to love, natural beauty and the fall from grace, has more recently served as a politically charged symbol representing the limits and rules placed on individuals by governments. In *El jardín* (1993, The Garden), the well-tended garden dually symbolizes the control of political authority as well as the imminent danger of impending revolution and civil disobedience. Here, the unbridled power of the lush forest that is Nature rebels against social law.

Bellessi acknowledges having been inspired by a wide range of writers from the Baroque Spanish poet Quevedo to the turn-of-the-century American poet Walt Whitman. Among her earliest influences, she claims the writings of Spanish Renaissance poets, especially San Juan de la Cruz, whose marked effect can be read in *La edad dorada* (2003, The Golden Age). Other influential writers are the nineteenth-century Spanish Romantic poet Gustavo Adolfo Bécquer, Generation of '27 poet Pedro Salinas, the Afro-Cuban poet Nicolás Guillén and Nicaraguan poet Rubén Darío. Of the Argentine writers with whom Bellessi feels a strong kinship, she names Gabriela Mistral, Ricardo Molinari, Juan L. Ortiz, Alberto Girri, Amelia Biagioni, Alejandra Pizarnik and Olga Orozco, among others.

Bellessi recognizes several American women whose works resonate in her writings. Among these women, she counts Adrienne Rich, Denise Levertov, Ursula K. Le Guin, Diane Di Prima, and H.D., all of whom Bellessi translated in the anthology *Contéstame, baila mi danza* (1984, Answer Me, Dance My Dance).

Modern Interpretations

Bellessi has been called one of the most important Argentine poets of her generation and a guide for future generations. In as much as critics foreground the lyrical nature of her largely biographical poetry, they also emphasize Bellessi's meticulous attention to rhyme and verse. Rather than perceive such poetic devices as likely impediments to her artistic production, critics note that these provide the author with coveted boundaries. Rhyme and verse serve as figurative prisons through which she paradoxically encounters an unequivocal freedom of expression. This freedom further corresponds to the subversive nature of her poetry. Critics note that the poet's lyricism conceals the space of confrontation and social activism that is her poetry.

MARIA DIFRANCESCO

Selected Works

Destino y propagaciones, Guayaquil: Casa de la Cultura Ecuatoriana, 1972.

Crucero ecuatorial. Buenos Aires: Ediciones Sirirí, 1981.

Tributo del mudo. Buenos Aires: Ediciones Sirirí, 1982.

Contéstame, baila mi danza. Antología de poetas norteamericanas. Buenos Aires: Último Reino, 1984.

Danzante de doble máscara. Buenos Aires: Ediciones Último Reino, 1985.

Eroica. Buenos Aires: Libros de Tierra Firme/Ediciones Último Reino, 1988.

Paloma de contrabando. Textos escritos en las cárceles de Buenos Aires. Ed. and Intro. Diana Bellessi. Buenos Aires: Torres Agüero Editor, 1988.

Buena travesía, buena ventura pequeña Uli, 1991. Buenos Aires: Nusud, 1991.

Las malas lenguas: Antología del cancionero tradicional picaresco. Selección y estudios de *Diana Bellessi y Noemí Diez*. Buenos Aires: Ediciones del sol, 1992.

El jardín. Buenos Aires: Bajo la Luna Nueva, 1993.

Crucero ecuatorial/Tributo del mudo. Buenos Aires: Libros de Tierra Firme, 1994.

The Twins, the Dream. Written with Ursula K. Le Guin. Houston, TX: Arte Público Press, 1996.

Días de seda. Antología y traducción de poemas de Úrsula K. Le Guin. Buenos Aires: Nusud, 1996.

Colibrí, lanzarelámpagos. Buenos Aires: Libros de Tierra Firme, 1996.

Sur. Buenos Aires: Libros de Tierra Firme, 1998.

Gemelas del sueño. Buenos Aires: Grupo Editorial Norma, 1998.

Leyenda. Barcelona: Nuevas Ediciones de Bolsillo, 2001.

Antología poética. Buenos Aires: Fondo Nacional de las Artes, 2002.

Mate cocido. Buenos Aires: Nuevohacer, 2002.

La rebelión del instante. Buenos Aires: Edición a secas, 2002.

La edad dorada. Buenos Aires: Adriana Hidalgo, 2003.

La rebelión del instante. Buenos Aires: Adriana Hidalgo Editora, 2005.

References and Further Reading

André, María Claudia. "Entrevista a Diana Bellessi". *Agulha, Revista de Poesía* 15, August 2001. http://www.secrel.com.br/jpoesia/ag15bellessi.htm (accessed July 21, 2006).

Bellessi, Diana. "Gender and Translation." In Daniel Balderston and Marcy Schwartz (eds and trans.), *Voice-Overs: Translation and Latin American Literature*. Albany, NY: SUNY Press, pp. 26–9.

——. "La diferencia viva". *Nuevo texto crítico* 2(4) (1989): 7–9.

Bello, Javier. "Diana Bellesi: Inmóvil transparente: Crucero Ecuatorial". *Cyber humanitatis* 19 (Winter 2001). http://www2.cyberhumanitatis.uchile.cl/19/jbello.html (accessed July 21, 2006).

Chatzivasileiou, Litsa. "Somatografías o el patos de Ecce Soma en dos episodios y un epitafio." In Lady Rojas-Trempe and Catharina Vallejo (eds), *Celebración de la creación literaria de escritoras hispanas en las Américas*. Ottawa: GIROL, 2000, pp. 71–80.

Colombo, María del Carmen and Genovese, Alicia. "Entrevista: Del viaje sin límites a la profundidad del detalle". In Diana Bellessi, *Colibrí, ¡lanza relámpagos*. Buenos Aires: Libros de Tierra Firme, 1996, pp. 169–86.

Friera, Silvina. "Diana Bellessi habla de *La rebelión del instante*". *Página 12*. September 13, 2005. http://www.pagina12.com.ar/diario/suplementos/espectaculos/2-422-2005-09-13.html (accessed July 21, 2006).

Mallol, Anahí. "Entrevista a Diana Bellessi, Palermo, 17 de mayo de 1999". *Inti: Revista de Literatura Hispánica* 52–3 (2000): 683–700.

Monteleone, Jorge. "La utopía del habla". In Diana Bellessi, *Colibrí, ¡lanza relámpagos!* Buenos Aires: Libros de Tierra Firme, 1996, pp. 9–27.

——. "La palabra como casa y familia". *Suplemento Cultura La Nación*, Feb. 9, 2003.

Ortega, Eliana: "Travesías bellessianas". *Revista Chilena de Literatura* 42 (1993): 183–91.

BELLI, GIOCONDA

Gioconda Belli (b. 1948) is perhaps the best-known contemporary writer from Nicaragua. Though originally known primarily for her poetry, Belli has increasingly dedicated herself to prose.

Gioconda Belli Pereira was born in Managua, Nicaragua, to Humberto Belli, a prominent businessman, and Gloria Pereira, founder of the Teatro Experimental de Managua. She attended Catholic school in Managua before being sent abroad to complete the education considered appropriate to her social class. She studied at a Catholic boarding school in Spain and summered in England. She then studied journalism and advertising in the United States, returning to Managua as the first woman to be an advertising account executive. Despite her marriage in 1966 to Mariano Argüello, and contrary to all expectations of the time for women of her background, Belli continued working, taking only a short leave of absence after the birth of her daughter, Maryam, in 1967.

Poet and Revolutionary

A colleague at work introduced her to members of the Frente Sandinista de Liberación Nacional (the Sandinista National Liberation Front, or FSLN), such as Camilo Ortega, brother of the future president of Nicaragua, Daniel Ortega. As a result of her friendships with Camilo Ortega and other Sandinistas, Belli became steeped in a critique of class structure and the need for social change through political, even armed, revolution. In 1970, she began to take an active role in the Sandinista movement, whose goal was to to bring the decades-long Somoza dictatorship to an end. She eventually joined the underground, leading a double life as an upper-class wife, mother, and professional while involved in clandestine revolutionary activities. She also wrote the poetry of her first book of poems, *Sobre la grama* (On the Grass), which won the Mariano Fiallos Gil Prize for Poetry in 1972.

Her second daughter, Melissa, was born in 1974, but Belli maintained and intensified her involvement with the Sandinistas to such an extent that she was forced into exile for her own safety, leaving her two daughters behind with her disillusioned husband, who had not been aware of her political activities. She was tried and condemned in absentia and sentenced to seven years' incarceration for treason. She lived in Costa Rica and Mexico, working in advertising and writing on behalf of the FSLN. With Sergio De Castro, a Brazilian journalist, she had a son named Camilo, but De Castro died in an airplane accident. She published her second collection of poems, *Línea de fuego* (Firing Line) in 1978, intertwining political, revolutionary, and erotic themes. The book won the Casa de las Américas Prize for Poetry that same year.

Post-revolutionary Poet and Novelist

The Sandinistas came to power on July 19, 1979, and Belli returned to Nicaragua. She divorced her husband and became director of communications and public relations for the revolutionary government and later was director of an advertising company. In 1987 she published her fourth books of poems, *De la costilla de Eva* (From Eve's Rib), demonstrating a feminism tied to eroticism. In 1987, she married an American journalist, Charles Castaldi, who covered the news in Nicaragua for National Public Radio during the electoral campaign of 1984. She left her job to dedicate two years to writing her first novel, *La mujer habitada* (The Inhabited Woman). She published her second novel, *Sofía de los presagios* (Sophie and the Omens) two years later, and moved to the United States with her husband in 1990, after the Sandinistas lost the presidency. Her fourth child, Adriana, was born in 1993. She ended her membership of the Sandinist Party in 1994, dedicating herself to writing rather than politics. She published her third novel, *Wasala: Memorial del futuro* in 1996 (Wasala: Memoir of the Future). The following year she published a collection of poems written in the preceding decade, *Apogeo* (1997, Apogee). In 2000, she published *El país bajo mi piel: Memorias de amor y guerra*, a semi-autobiographical memoir of the Sandinista revolution. Her most recent work is *El pergamino de la seducción* (2005, The Parchment of Seduction), her first historical novel, about Juana la Loca ("Joan the Mad"), Queen of Castile.

Themes and Influences

Poetry

Clearly, the Sandinista movement was a major influence on Belli. The revolutionary political stance she gained from her education and involvement as a Sandinista led to the poems of her early collections, in which Woman was the Nation of Nicaragua, to be loved, possessed, even rescued by the Man/Revolutionary. And Love would ignore the boundaries of class. But even in these early poems she also questioned the traditional role of women, and charted a different course for herself. Indeed, the focus on political resistance and ideology of the early collections gives way to a new kind of resistance in her last two collections, in which she speaks with a more feminist, and yet still feminine, voice to critique patriarchy as a system, with its privileged role for men. "How would it be, I ask myself / not to feel incessantly / that one ought to occupy several spaces at the same time? / Not to think, while lying down with a book / that one ought to be doing something else? / To assume, as men do / the importance of the time we spend on self-enrichment. / We women / tenaciously feel / that we are stealing time from someone. . . . We need / complete training / to not erase ourselves, minimize ourselves, / constantly" (from "Culpas obsoletas," in *Apogeo*, my translation).

Prose

Structured with two narrative planes, Belli's first novel, *La mujer habitada*, presents the mythic perspective of Itzá, a young Indian woman of the time of the Conquest of Spanish America, along with the contemporary perspective of Lavinia, whose story recalls some of Belli's own history. Itzá's spirit inhabits an orange tree in Lavinia's garden and thus she can observe events that take place in Lavinia's home, but it is Lavinia who becomes "inhabited" by the spirit of Itzá. The novel creates a parallel between two historical periods of resistance: the resistance of the indigenous peoples of the sixteenth and seventeenth centuries against the Spanish conquerors, and the Sandinista revolution that toppled the Somoza dictatorship. Despite the revolutionary priniciples of the Sandinistas, however, Lavinia is disappointed to discover that her revolutionary friends and even her lover subscribe to traditional views of women and their role, and a desire for social equality does not lead to gender equality. Like her ancient counterpart, Lavinia dies while taking part in the armed revolution designed to save her country.

Sofía de los presagios, the protagonist of Belli's second novel, is daughter of a gypsy mother and a Nicaraguan campesino. As a child she is left behind by the gypsies in the town of El Diriá, where she is adopted by Eulalia y Ramón. Sofía is both pitied for being abandoned, and reviled, as potentially dangerous because of her gypsy blood.

Sofía's childhood passes quickly, and she marries young. Her husband, René, is extremely jealous and requires her to stay at home unless he accompanies her. After her adopted father dies, Sofía leaves her husband, running away to the mountain home of Xintal, the good witch. When she returns to El Diriá, she takes control of the lands inherited from her father. Unlike women of her time, she divorces her husband and takes control of her own life. In doing so, she takes on a man's role and suppresses her own sexuality, which she sees as an obstacle to her freedom. Samuel, a good witch, makes love to her to free her from her false concept of female identity. Sofía later chose to conceive a child with Jerónimo, a man she does not love, because she no longer believes in love and certainly does not want a man to attempt to control her as her husband René did. Sofía manages to take control of herself, of her own body, and embrace her identity as woman, mother, gypsy, and free.

In *El país bajo mi piel*, Belli writes a memoir of the Sandinista revolution. Though not an autobiography, the work contains many elements of Belli's own life, such as exile, leaving her children behind, and an affair with "the Poet". She chronicles her typical female trajectory for that time and place: school, marriage, children, while also revealing the "new woman" in process, the woman who would leave her husband, risk her status, and eventually her life, in clandestine political activities. Like her earlier books of poetry, Belli weaves together the political and the personal, the ideology of the intellect with the passion of the body. As a woman in the process of becoming a New Woman, Belli confronts gendered traditions and sometimes transcends them. In her introduction to the text she comments about being someone who "yearned for the privileges men enjoyed: independence, self-reliance, a public life, mobility, lovers" (*The Country Under My Skin*, p. x). Her memoir narrates the stages of the Sandinista revolution in step with the stages of her personal revolution, a woman moving toward a "masculine" freedom of self.

Belli's latest novel, *El pergamino de la seducción*, interweaves a first-person narration by a twentieth-century Nicaraguan, Lucía, with the story of the sixteenth-century Queen of the Kingdom of Castile, Spain, Juana the Mad, who was declared insane and confined from the age of 29 until her death more than four decades later. Lucía is studying at a convent in Spain, where her history professor, obsessed with Juana the Mad and finding an uncanny resemblance between his student and the historical queen, fuses them into a kind of single object of desire, seducing the student while narrating Juana's story. Though *El pergamino* is Belli's first historical novel, it continues the eroticism seen in her other work. In addition to political considerations, Juana's passion for, and jealousy of, her philandering husband Philip the Handsome, suggests Belli, were the true cause of Juana's confinement and diagnosis.

Though Belli has dedicated herself to prose in recent years, the poetic language of her latest novel reminds us that she remains a poet as well. Belli's writing ranges from poetry to memoir to historical novel, but the twin themes of politics and passion and an ardently feminine feminism pervade all her works.

LINDA LEDFORD-MILLER

Selected Works

Sobre la grama. No place; no publisher, 1974.

Línea de fuego. Havana: Casa de las Américas, 1978. Translated into German.

De la costilla de Eva. Managua: Nueva Nicaragua, 1987. Translated into Dutch and German.

La mujer habitada. Managua: Vanguardia, 1988. Translated into Dutch, Finnish, German, Italian, and Persian.

Sofía de los presagios. Managua: Vanguardia, 1990. Translated into Dutch and German.

El país bajo mi piel: Memorias de amor y guerra. Barcelona: Plaza y Janés, 2000. Translated into Dutch.

The Country Under My Skin: A Memoir of Love and War. New York: Knopf, 2002.

El pergamino de la seducción. Barcelona: Seix Barral, 2005.

References and Further Reading

Barbas-Rhoden, L. *Writing Women in Central America: Gender and the Fictionalization of History*. Athens, OH: Ohio University Press, 2003.

Craft, Linda J. *Novels of Testimony and Resistance from Central America*. Gainesville, FL: University Press of Florida, 1997.

De Fays, Hélène. "The Revolutionary Empowerment of Nature in Gioconda Belli's *The Inhabited Woman*". *Mosaic: A Journal for the Interdisciplinary Study of Literature* 38(2) (June 2005): 95–110.

Ferman, Claudia (ed.). *The Postmodern in Latin and Latino American Cultural Narratives*. New York: Garland, 1996.
Ghosh, Bishnupriya and Bose, Brinda (eds). *Interventions: Feminist Dialogues on Third World Women's Literature and Film*. New York: Garland, 1997.
Hansen, Suzy. "Sex, Lies and Revolution." Interview. http://dir.salon.com/story/books/int/2002/12/10/belli/index.html
Kearns, Sofia. "Una ruta hacia la conciencia feminista: la poesía de Gioconda Belli". *Ciberletras* 9 http://www.lehman.cuny.edu/ciberletras/v09/kearns.html
Krugh, Janis. *Afrodita en el trópico: Erotismo y construcción del sujeto femenino en obras de autoras centroamericanas*. Potomac, MD: Scripta Humanistica, 1999.
Lorente-Murphy, Silvia. "De las ideas a la práctica: la complejidad de las propuestas éticas en *La mujer habitada* de Gioconda Belli". *Ciberletras* 5 http://www.lehman.cuny.edu/ciberletras/v05/lorente.html
Rodríguez, Ileana. *House/Garden/Nation: Space, Gender, and Ethnicity in Post-colonial Latin American Literatures by Women*. Durham, NC: Duke University, 1994.
Salgado, María A. "Gioconda Belli, novelista revolucionaria". *Revista Mongráfica* 8 (1992): 229–42.

BERENGUER, AMANDA

Amanda Berenguer Bellán was born in Montevideo, Uruguay on June 24, 1921. At the age of 20, she married José Pedro Díaz, who would become a distinguished literary writer and professor. In 1940, Berenguer published her first book, *A través de los tiempos que llevan a la gran calma* (Across the Times that Lead to the Great Calm) that she later decided not to include in her bibliography as she considered it a production of her youth. When Díaz and Berenguer were living with her parents, they acquired some printing equipment and set up the publishing house La Galatea in their garage. The first book published by La Galatea was Berenguer's *Elegía por la muerte de Paul Valéry*, 1945 (Elegy to the Death of Paul Valéry), which appeared the same year as the death of this French poet whom she admired and acknowledged as one of her poetic models. In time, Berenguer would publish three additional books with La Galatea as well as many of those of her fellow writers who became known as the *Generación del 45* (Generation of 45).

In 1950, when Pedro Díaz received a grant and was named Honorary Cultural Attaché to Belgium, Berenguer had the opportunity to live in Europe for two years, where she came into contact with many Latin American and European literary figures. During this period she wrote *El río* (1952, The River) that won the First Prize of the Ministry of Public Instruction of Uruguay, the first of many prizes she would receive. Back in Montevideo, many of her poems appeared in the renowned weekly *Marcha,* and she founded the French-Uruguayan literary journal *Maldoror* with French poets Paul Fleury and Lucien Mercier. From 1979 to 1980, Berenguer lived in United States where she gave audiovisual presentations of her poems in several universities. In 2006, she was inducted as an Honorary Member into the National Academy of Literature.

Berenguer's long and distinguished career attests to her many intellectual interests and to her constant desire to find new forms to express them. As the Uruguayan critic Alejandro Paternain has observed: "We don't hesitate to ascertain that in the framework of the *Generación del 45*, Amanda Berenguer is the figure that is working best, with a deep sense of experimentation and with a sharp restlessness for innovative invention". Critics agree that *El río*, in which the river becomes a metaphor for life's journey, signals Berenguer's poetic maturity. The book intertwines autobiographical information with rich imagery, resulting in a self-sufficient poetic structure. Additionally, it shows Berenguer's preoccupation with death and her sense of existential anguish that take center stage in her poetic production: "Llévame, madre, a morir a solas, / junto al hondo rincón de tu memoria" [Take me mother, to die alone / by the deep corner of your memory]. In the 1950s, as Latin American poets were experimenting with avant-garde methods of composition, Berenguer published *La invitación* (1957, The Invitation) in which she uses striking images that join together dissimilar ideas and elements: "Un adonde de sombra, un pozo vivo / graznando como un pájaro violento" [a site of shade / a live well / squawking like a violent bird]. She also breaks from the traditional presentation of poetry by employing typographical innovations, such as in *Suficiente maravilla* (1953, Sufficient Marvel) and *Composición de lugar* (1976, Composition of Place) where some words are not aligned and the characters are of diverse fonts and sizes. Berenguer also turned to everyday activities for inspiration. In *Quehaceres e invenciones* (1963, Chores and Inventions), she utilizes kitchen utensils and domestic activities: "Me arrepiento. Bajo hasta la negra / olla donde preparo día y noche / un alimento para condenados en rebeldía". [I regret. I descend to the black / pan where I prepare night and day / a meal for those condemned / for being rebellious]. Likewise in *Identidad de ciertas frutas* (1983, Identity of Certain Fruits), the characteristics of twenty-five fruits offer a point of departure to express her views about human existence: "Ser como la manzana / es estar-en la alta fiesta del día-toda de raso rojo y diamantes / y llevar en el índice enguantado / un anillo de sombra". [To be like the apple / is to be – in the best party of the day– / all dressed up with red satin and diamonds / and wearing in the gloved index finger / a shadow ring].

Starting with *Materia prima* (1966, Raw Material), Berenguer elaborated on the concept of what she called "kinetic poetry" to express the movement and speed that exist in real life. This can be seen, for instance, in the circular structure of "Las nubes magellánicas" (Magellan-like Clouds) or "La cinta de Moebious" (Moëbius Strip). In addition, she has integrated scientific and technical elements in her compositions, such as in *La botella verde* (1995, Green Bottle), inspired by the Klein Bottle, a spatial figure that passes through itself without the presence of a hole. This bottle represents the many angles from which one can observe the universe, a central theme throughout Berenguer's work. By then she had joined her fellow writers of the *Generación of 45* and was writing poems that expressed her views on Uruguay's swiftly deteriorating socio-political and economic conditions. *Declaración conjunta* (1964, Joined Declaration) has been called by Uruguayan writer and critic Mario Benedetti "a true work in progress". The reader is aware of the creation of the poem by observing how each of its verses subtly differs from the previous one with the addition of an adjective, an adverb, or a preposition. This book-length poem, in which the poetic female voice "Yo" [I] addresses a masculine "Tú" [You]: "tú esperma/yo araña . . . tú bandera/yo huelga" [you sperm/I spider . . . you flag/I strike], also reflects Berenguer's awakened political consciousness. Then, in *Los signos sobre la mesa* (1987, Signs on the Table), she condemned the torture that many Uruguayans had suffered during the twelve years of military dictatorship known as *Proceso* that had begun in 1973.

Time has not slowed down Berenguer's poetic ventures. In 2002, she published *Constelación del Navío. Poesía 1950–2002* (Ship Constellation. Poetry 1950–2002) that includes both new and previously published poems. In 2005, she published two books. *Casa donde viven criaturas del lenguaje* (House Inhabited by Language Creatures) deals with grammatical and rhetorical terms: "Tardé mucho / en hallar la Casa del Sr. Substantivo-/ no era fácil–por las vueltas y vueltas del camino . . ." (It took me a long time / to find the House of Mr. Noun – it was not easy because of the bends upon bends of the path). In that same year she also issued *Las mil y una preguntas y propicios contextos* (A Thousand and One Questions and Favorable Contexts) which contains a series of poems and questions for the reader: "¿Por qué no escribes – tú lector – en otra hoja – lo que piensas de esto?" (Why don't you write – you reader – in another page – what do you think about this?). These questions further indicate Berenguer's intellectual curiosity and her quest to engage the reader in a never-ending dialogue in search of all the answers.

RENEE SUM SCOTT

Selected Works

A través de los tiempos que llevan a la gran calma. Montevideo: La Industrial, 1940.
Canto hermético. Montevideo: Sagitario, 1941.
Elegía por la muerte de Paul Valéry. Montevideo: La Galatea, 1945.
El río. Montevideo: La Galatea, 1952.
La invitación. Montevideo: La Galatea, 1957.
Contracanto. Montevideo: La Galatea, 1961.
Quehaceres e invenciones. Montevideo: Arca, 1963.
Declaración conjunta. Montevideo: Arca, 1964.
Materia prima. Montevideo: Arca, 1966.
Dicciones. Montevideo: Ayuí, 1973.
Composición de lugar. Montevideo: Arca, 1976.
Poesía (1949–1979). Montevideo: Calicanto, 1980.
"En eso llegó". In *Maldoror*. Montevideo 16 (1981): 64–5.
Identidad de ciertas frutas. Montevideo: Arca, 1983.
La dama de Elche. Madrid: Edhasa-Banco Exterior de España. 1987; 2nd edn. Montevideo: Arca, 1989.
Los signos sobre la mesa. Montevideo: Universidad de la República, 1987.
El monstruo incesante (expedición de caza). Montevideo: Arca, 1990.
La botella verde. Montevideo: Cal y Canto, 1995.
El pescador de caña. Caracas: Fondo Editorial Pequeña Venecia, 1995.
La estranguladora. Montevideo: Cal y Canto, 1998.
"Fondo de ojo". *Mujeres de mucha monta. Fábulas eróticas de féminas uruguayas*. Montevideo: Arca, 2000, pp. 35–7.
Constelación del Navío. Poesía 1950–2002. Montevideo: H Editores, 2002.
Casas donde viven criaturas del lenguaje. Montevideo: Artefato, 2005.
Las mil y una preguntas y propicios contextos. Montevideo: Libreria Linardi y Risso, 2005.

References and Further Reading

Apprato, Roberto. *Antología crítica de la poesía uruguaya*. Montevideo: Projección, 1990, pp. 10, 45–55.
Benedetti, Mario. *Literatura uruguaya: siglo XX, ensayo*. 2nd edn, Montevideo: Alfa, 1969.
Blixen, Carina. "Amanda Berenguer. Poeta en metamorfosis". In Heber Raviolo and Pablo Roca (eds), *Historia de la literatura uruguaya contemporánea*. Vol. 2. Montevideo: Ediciones de la Banda Oriental, 1997, pp. 127–41.
Guimaraes Ferreira, Izacyl. "La poesía enciclopédica de Amanda Berenguer". *Hermes criollo* 2–5 (2003): 108–12.
Paternain, Alejandro. *36 años de poesía uruguaya*. Montevideo: Alfa, 1967, pp. 41–3, 149–56.

BERMAN, SABINA

Sabina Berman Goldberg (b. 1956) is an accomplished director, producer, journalist, screenwriter, novelist, essayist and poet who also has written and performed several plays for children. Berman is Mexico's most commercially successful and critically acclaimed female playwright.

Born in Mexico City on August 21, 1956, daughter of Jewish immigrants fleeing persecution, Berman studied psychology at the Universidad Nacional Autónoma de México, where she also took classes in scenography, theater and playwriting. The final project of one of these classes resulted in her monologue *Esta no es una obra de teatro* (1976, This Is not a Play). During this time she worked with director Abraham Oceransky and dramatists Héctor Azar and Hugo Arguelles. Berman also wrote children's theater, including *Caracol y Colibrí* (1996, The Snail and the Hummingbird) and *El árbol de humo* (1994, The Tree of Smoke). According to Ronald D. Burgess, Berman began to write theater during a time in which Mexican theater was in crisis; but despite this unfavorable atmosphere, she continued her creative work, and between 1975 and 1993 wrote nine new dramas, four of which won important national awards (*Sabina* 146).

Berman also is a published poet. In 1986, she published *Poemas de agua* (Poems of Water), followed in 1988 by a collection of lesbian poems, *Lunas* (Moons). Among her narrative works, her most well-known is her novel *La Bobe* (1990, Bubbeh), in which she describes the life of a young woman in Mexico and the opposition she encounters from her very traditional Jewish grandmother.

Sabina Berman has been awarded prizes in several of the genres in which she creates. She received the award for Poesía Pluridimensional Juguete (Multi-dimensional Toy Poetry) for *Mariposa* (Butterfly) in 1974, and in 1975 for *Máscaras* (Masks). That year, *Máscarus* also received the award for the Latin American Short Story. Her theatrical work has been recognized four times with the National Theater Award, bestowed by the Instituto Nacional de Bellas Artes (National Institute of Fine Arts), five times with the Critics' Award for her dramas, and three times for stage direction. In 1999, she was awarded the Premio Nacional María Lavalle Urbina (María Lavalle Urbina National Prize) for her contributions to the cultural world; in addition, she received, along with Isabelle Tardán, the Premio Nacional de Periodismo (National Journalism Award) for the series *Mujeres y Poder* (Women and Power), broadcast on television.

The plays she created in the 1990s focus on her two main themes: gender roles and the struggle for power. In 1993, Berman staged and directed *Entre Villa y una mujer desnuda* (Between Villa and a Naked Woman), a highly successful play that was subsequently transformed into a film in 1996. The two protagonists of the play, Gina and Adrián, are on-again off-again lovers. The plot revolves around Gina's growing desire to change the casual, ritualized nature of her relationship with Adrián to a more involved and committed one. After a particularly long absence, Adrián returns to find Gina has moved on to a younger, more emotionally available partner. Adrián fails to win Gina back, and after attempting unsuccessfully to commit suicide by jumping out the first-floor window, he is left forlornly, and unsuccessfully, trying to recapture his sexual relationship with a Gina-substitute, her business partner Andrea. Plot enrichment appears in the guise of the history book Adrián is writing about Pancho Villa. In the conversations between Adrián and Gina, Adrián's re-telling of his Villa story appears enacted on the stage as he narrates, with Villa even interacting with the Adrián–Gina level of the play. The two worlds — the modern-world stage, and the historical stage — intersect on a verbal and physical level (Gina doesn't see Villa, but Adrián does).

Directed more to an international audience than to a purely Mexican one, the film has been seen as foregrounding gender as the site where revolutions still need to happen. Scenes that do not appear in the stageplay frame the film. An even greater difference between the cinematic and theatrical versions of the story is the conclusion of the film, which contains an entire act that is not in the play. Berman points out to the audience how powerfully myths influence gender and gendered behavior, making clear that fictionalized recreations of images of history can have a huge impact on the receiver of those images.

In the plays written in the past ten years — *Molière* (1998), *¡Feliz nuevo siglo, doctor Freud!* (Happy New Year, Dr. Freud! 2000), and *65 contratos para hacer el amor* (2000, 65 Contracts for Lovemaking) — Berman makes use of European literary and scientific history to again develop her two main themes of gender and power. Most recently, spurred by her outrage about the murders of many young women and determined to call the world's attention to the lack of appropriate governmental response, Berman has written a new screenplay. The first scene of "Backyard" is set outside the Mexican border town of Juárez. A woman's body is found half-buried in the sand. Although the mangled and decomposing corpse is unrecognizable, the uniform she wears reveals the name of the multinational corporation which owns the *maquiladora* or assembly plant where she worked. While photographers, reporters and investigators circle the body, the camera pulls away to gaze out at the incongruous backdrop of trans-national corporate office buildings and juxtaposed shantytowns that make up a large part of Juárez, perched just below El Paso. Talking about this screen play, in a recent interview, Berman was quoted as saying: "Creo que nos debemos dar cuenta de que a las mujeres de Juárez, del estado de México, de Guatemala, de Texas o de cualquier rincón del país y del mundo, las están asesinando por el solo hecho de ser mujeres" [I believe that we have to come to terms with the fact that these women from Juarez, Mexico, from Guatemala, from Texas or from any corner of the country and the world, are being murdered just because they are women.]

Ronald Burgess has called Berman one of the "new dramatists of Mexico," along with Oscar Villegas, Víctor Hugo Rascón Bada, Jesús González Dávila, Miguel Angel Tenorio y Oscar Liera, all born between 1954 and 1973. All these playwrights share as common characteristics the predominant use of one-act plays, socio-political criticism, humorous use of colloquial speech, and the overarching influence of the dramatic giants of the preceding generation Rodolfo Usigli, Emilio Carballido, Vicente Leñero, and Luisa Josefina Hernández, among others. Berman distinguishes herself from her peers by a "flair for dialogue, a predilection for black humor and irony, a distrust of all official discourse, an interest in personal and national identity, a need to transgress sexual and theatrical boundaries, and a profound awareness of the inherently theatrical nature of Mexican history and politics" (Bixler xxi). While later in her career, she has publicly acknowledged the influence of a number of American and European playwrights, she claims affiliation with no single dramatic school or group. Jacqueline E. Bixler notes the difficulty of classifying and studying Berman's work because of the perfectionism, which drives her to continuously re-evaluate and re-edit her plays. Because of her background as a stage director, Sabina Berman's dramatic text is difficult to understand without considering the stage text. In other words, her theatrical skill matches the depth of her dramatic design whether it is the variety of techniques that appear in *El suplicio del placer* (1978, The Agony of Ecstasy); the physicalization of what it means to be interrogated and to interrogate in *Yankee* (1979); the accentuation of gender differences through the androgynous couple in *Uno/El bigote* (1985, 1/The Moustache); the tragic triangle of *Muerte Súbita* (Sudden Death); the final enigmatic image of a soldier alone on stage, silently aiming his firearm at an undefined threat that potentially emanates from the audience in *Rompecabezas* (1981, Puzzle); or the manner in which the family narrates its own "heretical" actions in *Herejía* (1983, Heresy).

When Berman writes, she uses gender roles within the society to illustrate her feminist point of view. Her work speaks to us of the difficulty of being a minority (lesbian, Jew) in Mexico, and she uses her work as a weapon to win the battle of discrimination. It is her combination of theatrical technique with universal themes of self-definition that cuts across cultures.

MARIA R. MATZ AND KAREN CODY

Selected Works

Teatro de Sabina Berman. Mexico: Gaceta, 1994.

El suplicio del placer. El gordo, la pájara y el narco. Mexico City: Consejo Nacional para la Cultura y las Artes, 1994.

"Krísis". *Tramoya* 52 (1997): 51–100.

Bubbeh. Trans. Andrea G. Labinger. Tempe, AZ: Latin American Literary Review Press, 1998.

"Berman. Entre Villa y una mujer desnuda. Muerte súbita/ El suplicio del placer". In Edgard Ceballos (ed.), *Col. Escenología/drama*. Vol. 10. *Escenología*: Mexico, DF, 1998.

¡Feliz nuevo siglo, doktor Freud! In Felipe Galvan (ed.), *Teatro, mujer, país*. Puebla, Mexico: Editorial Tablado Iberoamericano, 2000.

Mujeres y Poder. Mexico City: Hoja Casa Editorial, 2000.

The Theatre of Sabina Berman: The Agony of Ecstasy and Other Plays. Trans. Adam Versényi. Carbondale, IL: Southern Illinois University Press, 2003.

References and Further Reading

Bixler, Jacqueline E. "The Postmodernization of History in the Theatre of Sabina Berman". *Latin American Theatre Review* 30(2) (1997): 45–60.

——. "Krísis, Crisis and the Politics of Representation". *Gestos. Teoría y Práctica del Teatro Hipánico* 13(26) (1998): 83–97.

——. "Sabina Berman y la posmodernización de la historia". In Osvaldo Pellettieri (ed.), *El teatro y su critica.* Buenos Aires: Galerna, 1998, pp. 83–9.

Burgess, Ronald D. *The New Dramatists of Mexico. 1967–1985*. Lexington, KY: University Press of Kentucky, 1991.

——. "Sabina Berman's Undone Threads". In Catherine Larson and Margarita Vargas (eds), *Latin American Women Dramatists*. Bloomington, IN: Indiana University Press, 1998, pp. 145–58.

Cypess, Sandra M. "Ethnic Identity in the Plays of Sabina Berman". In Robert DiAntonio and Nora Glickman (eds), *Tradition and Innovation: Reflections on Latin American Jewish Writing*. Albany, NY: SUNY University Press, 1993, pp. 167–77.

Hind, Emily. "Entrevista con Sabina Berman". *LATR* 33(2) (2000): 133–9.

Nigro, Kristen. "Sabina Berman and Her Theater". *Theatre Forum* 14 (1999): 88–90.

Rojas, Mario. "Sabina Berman". In David Foster (ed.), *Latin American Writers on Gay and Lesbian Themes: A Bio-Critical Sourcebook*. Westport, CT: Greenwood Press, 1994: 59–63.

BIAGIONI, AMELIA

Amelia Biagioni was born in Galvez, Santa Fe province in Argentina in 1916. There is some conjecture whether her father was part of the Italian immigration boom to Argentina at the end of the nineteenth century, hence her very common Italian surname of Biagioni. Biagioni studied literature and earned her degree as a professor of literature in the Dr. Nicolas Avellaneda School of Professors in the Rosario province of Santa Fe in 1936. She taught Spanish and Spanish literature to high school students in Santa Fe until 1955 when she moved to Buenos Aires and continued to teach there. Biagioni first had her poetry published under a pseudonym until she published her first collection of poetry – *Sonnet of Solitude* – in 1954 under her own name due to the influence of the poet José Pedroni. Pedroni would be instrumental in having Biagioni awarded the Sash of Honor by the Argentinean Society of Writers (SADE).

Biagioni would go on to win various awards for her poetry including: Second Municipal Prize for Buenos Aires for "The Key" in 1957; First Municipal Prize for "The Smoke" in 1967; the Jorge Luis Borges Argentinian Foundation Award for Poetry in 1967 for her book *The Hunts*; the Esteban Echevarría Award in 1985; the Second Award in National Poetry for *Stations of Van Gogh* in 1987; and the José Manuel Estrada Award from the Archdiocese Commission on Culture in 1993.

Biagioni's poetry is known for its extensive use of symbolism and literary expression which create an interesting web of allegories. She is lost in her world of words and hidden meanings, a reflection of her solitary life and primary dedication to the art of poetry. In fact, Biagioni would often edit and re-write portions of her poems, even after they were published. She felt she had a responsibility to her poetry because she felt "selected by poetry". Biagioni is also known for the scarcity of her literary work – having only published six books of poetry and one epic poem posthumuously in her fifty-plus year career. She was a perfectionist in her selection of poems to be published and she worked in isolation, taking pains to stay away from literary events and other writers. The question is often asked as to why she isolated herself. Considering the lack of personal information on Biagioni, it is surmised that she was a private person and did not want to be distracted from her work.

Themes in Biagioni's poetry include reflection on the hostile nature of this world and a search for enlightenment of what is essential for survival, as well as isolation and natural strength. Her work is usually classified as neoromanticism but with modernist primitivism used liberally, as she explores naturalistic themes. Many of her poems are autobiographical. Her first book, *Sonnet of Solitude* is a collection of 22 poems where Biagioni explores her feelings of loneliness and her longing for escape. For example in her poem, "The Window," she writes:

> One window and nothing else do I want
> A fervent prologue to flight . . .
> So much did I dream it, one morning?
> I find in my room the window
> Which calls out to me with a luminous cry.

What is interesting to note in these lines is her desire for the window, a means of escape, but she never goes as far as the escape itself.

"The Key," on the other hand, brings us closer to Biagioni's relationship with her poetry: she is its subject and what she wants to explore is imminent death: "to sing is to die. I sing . . . everything that lasted ended in my song". Biagioni's identification with language is made even more explicit in the poem "Drizzle" from the book *The Smoke*:

> I think that on the earth
> I do not exist
> I am only falling
> Like that, from the nostalgia of a poem.

So for Biagioni, she exists only in the words of her poems, but not outside of them. Perhaps this is another insight as to why she isolated herself – she feels she has nothing to offer as a person, but only as words.

This theme of Biagioni's nonexistence would culminate in her last book of poetry *Region of Escapes*. In the poem "In the Wood," she writes:

> I am my own unknown
> Maybe your messenger without memory
> Or your evasion (escape),
> Blow the bird
> Mirror (mirage)
> Cancel me.

Biagioni again emphasis her unimportance – here she asks the reader to "cancel" her – like smoke in the mirror – one can blow it away.

Biagioni also took an innovative turn by assuming the voice of the famous painter, Vincent Van Gogh, in her book *Stations of Van Gogh*. Using her extensive studies of the painter and his work, Biagioni attempts to make sense of Van Gogh's unique style of painting with curves and heavy brushstrokes that for some art experts were indicators of an unstable mind. For Biagioni, Van Gogh's style is due to his passion – he is lost in his work as she is lost in her poetry: "As much as you configure or paint it is always an ardent mysterious mistake".

The Hunts is Biagioni's only book of poetry to be translated into English (by Renata Treitel). In this collection we see the use of primitive images – in this case, a hunter on the hunt, complete with horse, pack of dogs and prey. Biagioni describes the elements of the hunt in an effort to define universal belief – the hunt has purpose but also has senseless moments; God is the supreme hunter; everyone is chasing, eating and being chased: "becoming a self that eats up another self".

For Biagioni, there is no creation without sacrifice, without action. In the poem "Forest" Biagioni indicates that the universe is soothed with deeds, that "the universe is a dark light wandering the forest where every movement is a hunt". In other words, the hunt is the deed; the hunt is what we do here, why we are here, our purpose; to the extent that we complete it subconsciously. In another poem, "The Hunter in a Trance," she shows her extraordinary ability to set rhythm with her words. As we read the poem, we feel the rhythm of a galloping horse.

Another interesting aspect of these poems is Biagioni's comprehensiveness in exploring all aspects of the hunt, including the perspectives of other creatures in the forest as they bear witness to what is happening around them. No creature is too small – Biagioni even assumes the persona of an ant who "bears the paradox of being minimal and minus charisma but with enormous powers". She also becomes a jaguar, who talks with pride about her spots and a frog, who although it knows Shakespeare and Stravinsky, states:

> And I shall set out to straighten the nations
> With the original truth
> Learnt in the mud.

The novelty of a little frog straightening out great nations not with great art or music but with the dirty truth learned from a life of experience may have been Biagioni's reflection that it is the lowly of a country who have the wisdom to run a country for its citizens.

Throughout this collection we see Biagioni's style of listing words and phrases without punctuation or conjunctions, leaving the reader to make the connections. As an example, look at "Carved on Thighbone:"

> The voice that leads and bestows
> The solar glance
> The rhythm of lion
> The rhumb of ruby
> The infinite posterity.

We see another aspect of Biagioni in terms of the political persecutions of her country. Biagioni's first book of poetry coincides with the military coup which overthrew Juan Domingo Perón's government in 1955. Perón, an army officer who seized power in 1944, was a contentious political figure described as a fascist by some, or as a revolutionary supporting the working class by others. Biagioni understands she is a different writer from the rest in terms of her content but she feels no guilt in this fact. In her poem "Warning," she writes:

> You must flee
> They are searching for you
> Passing judgment on your profile.
> I feel no guilt.
> They will hunt you because you feel no guilt.

Biagioni also refers to religious persecutions, becoming the disciple Paul in "Aguae Salviae" who "at the foot of my beheading thank you for this victorious seal" and Saint Simon in "Saint Simon Stylites" who for forty years celebrated the maker waiting for the "compassionate vulture". Again, Perón is significant here. In 1954, Perón accused a group of Roman Catholic clergymen of inciting protests against the government. His government would then begin to enact a series of legislation against church doctrine – abortion, prostitution and granting benefits to children born out of wedlock.

Literary critics and fellow poets, such as Claudia Schvartz, would describe Biagioni's work as valiant and subtle. Melanie Nicholson would praise Biagioni's semantic elements and poetic techniques that set up rhythm and meaning. Valeria Melchoire would emphasize Biagioni's connection between identity and language. All agree that Biagioni was a consummate wordsmith, who could tantalize her readers with a well-placed word or two.

DEBORAH GONZALEZ

Selected Works

Sonnet of Solitude. Argentina: Editorial Castelivi, 1954.
The Key. Buenos Aires: Editorial Emece, 1957.
The Smoke, Buenos Aires: Emece, 1967.
The Hunts. Buenos Aires: Sudamericana, 1976.
The Stations of Van Gogh. Buenos Aires: Sudamericana, 1981.
Hunter in a Trance and Other Poems. Centro Editor de America Latina, 1989.
The Region of Escapes. Buenos Aires: Sudamericana, 1995.

References and Further Reading

Melchiore, Valeria. "Amelia Biagioni: Una Identidad en fuga por el languaje errante". *Espéculo: Revista de estudios literarios.* Universidad Complutense de Madrid, 2003. http://www.ucm.es/info/especulo/numero23/biagioni.html

Negroni, Maria and Bonzini, Silvia. *La maldad de escribir: 9 poetas latinoamericanas del siglo XX*, Montblanc: Editorial Igitur, 2003.

Nicholson, Melanie. "Soy el cazador: the Function of the Primitive in the Poetry of Amelia Biagioni". *Confluencia: Revista Hispánica de Cultural y Literatura* 20(1) 2004: 165.

Piña, Cristina. *Poéticas de lo incesante: Sujeto, Materialidad y escritura en Amelia Biagioni y Nestor Perlongher.* Buenos Aires: Botella al Mar, 2005.

Sobon, Rosa Maria. *Amelia Biagioni: Esplandor y Silencio.* Prometeo Digital, 2006. http://www.prometeodigital.org/Descarga/Fondo_Documental/FDP2003_SOBRON_Biagioni.doc

BINS, PATRICIA

Patricia Doreen Bins was born in Rio de Janeiro, on July 24, 1928, one year after her parents, Andrew and Iris Holliday Stroh, settled in that city, arriving from Europe. Speaking English at home, the child was raised in an international atmosphere, since her father was Hungarian and her mother was British. Growing up in a privileged family situation (her father was president of an American enterprise in Brazil), starting at age 5 she attended prestigious private schools where she developed her precocious talent for music, dance, and painting.

When she was 6 years old, the family moved to Belo Horizonte, capital of the state of Minas Gerais, where her younger sister, and only sibling, was born. After six years, the family moved again and settled definitely in Porto Alegre, Rio Grande do Sul. In that city, which became the background of many of her narratives, the author completed her studies in Art History and Painting, before meeting and marrying, at age 22, Roberto Bins, an architect and Art History instructor. They had two sons; one of them graduated in Architecture, while the other became a fine arts craftsman. The family expanded with the addition of three grand-children by one of them. Mr. Bins passed away in 1997.

After earning the "Certificate of Competency in English" from the University of Michigan through exams taken in her hometown, she became instructor of English at the *Instituto Cultural Brasil-Estados Unidos* (ICBEU) of Porto Alegre, besides giving private classes. In that same city, she attended the School of Journalism, and even without having completed the courses, she became coordinator of the cultural section of *Correio do Povo,* a Porto Alegre newspaper, for 16 years (1968–84). Besides contributing with weekly chronicles to the same, she also published short stories in dailies printed elsewhere in Brazil, and contributed with translations of literary works from English to Portuguese. Painting was another of her activities, having participated in art exhibitions in the School of Fine Arts of Porto Alegre and in other galleries. Her biography as painter is included in the *Dicionário de Artes Plásticas do Rio Grande do Sul* (Dictionary of Fine Arts of Rio Grande do Sul, 2000). She dedicated most of her time, however, to writing, having published nine novels, two collections of short stories, and two booklets for children. She also co-edited a book of culinary recipes, contributed by renowned Brazilian writers.

Patricia Bins's novels and short stories revolve round a woman's perception of the world, re-creating, in each female character, a psychological profile committed to solving their existential issues. In an interview, the author stated that the main influences in her fictional career were the writings by Virginia Woolf and James Joyce. Indeed, the atmosphere of intimacy found in Woolf's fiction, and the variety of symbols and metaphors built in Joyce's texts may have found a niche in Bins's literary creativity.

Her formative years were surrounded by non-Brazilian writers, as she indicates in one of her chronicles: "As a child raised in a foreign idiom up to her 10th birthday (my parents intended to return to England) with habits totally different from the Brazilian customs, books and stories were, for a long period of time, my most frequent companions. The first one I read from beginning to end, I remember it well, was *Little Women*, by Luisa May Alcott. I then became an inseparable friend of the four March sisters, idolizing and identifying myself with the character Josephine, who was (as I wanted to be) an unrelenting writer. I think that my attempts in the kingdom of writing-desks are rooted at that time". (Chronicle "Alimentando o espírito" (Nurturing the Spirit), November 14, 2006, in *CS Zona Azul Gazette*.)

The publication of her first book was a Christmas gift from her husband, who had collected most of the chronicles published in newspapers as an edited book: *O assassinato dos pombos – Cronicontos* (1982, The Assassination of the Pigeons – Chronistories). With an introduction by the poet Heitor Saldanha, the book was illustrated with drawings by Roberto Bins. Notwithstanding its neologism ("Chronistories"), the book had a successful reception among readers, mainly because the author was already known for her chronicles and short stories in newspapers.

Patricia Bins's bibliography depicts three Trilogies, whose themes are: Solitude, Passion and Eroticism. *Jogo de fiar* (1983, Spinning Threads), the first book of the Trilogy of Solitude, was awarded the Grande Medalha da Inconfidência – Ouro (Grand "Inconfidência" Golden Medal, 1984), personally handed over by Tancredo Neves, then governor of Minas Gerais. In that novel, the author portrays a female's German heritage as a descendant of immigrants to Brazil's Southern region along her spiritual journey as an individual who questions her feelings, passions, renunciations and attempts to overcome life predicaments. *Janela do Sonho* (1987, A Window to Dreams), the third book in the trilogy, was awarded the Afonso Arinos Prize by the Brazilian Academy of Letters (1986), having received a "*Menção Especial*" (Special Mention) from the *União Brasileira de Escritores* (Brazilian Writers Association), in the following year. In the novel, the myth of Penelope is subtly folded into the plot as a way of interpreting the suffering felt by the female protagonist when faced with loneliness.

For *Pele nua no espelho* (1989, Naked Skin on the Mirror), the first book of the Trilogy of Passion, the author was awarded the *Coelho Neto Prêmio* by the Brazilian Academy of Letters (1990). As in the other narratives, this novel conveys an obsessive search by a woman for answers to inquiries related to her life. From simple basic questions related to situations that filled her past, she goes into elaborated queries about the purpose and the mission, if any, of existence and, ultimately, the hypothetical need to be alive. A play of imaginary and real mirrors is incorporated in the narrative, reflecting diversified images – some real, some imaginary – of the protagonist in search of her real and dreamy-like personalities, realizing that both are the same, although each one is different from the other. The third volume of the trilogy, *Sarah e os anjos* (1993, Sarah and the Angels), was also awarded a prize by the Academy of Brazilian Letters. As in the second volume of the same trilogy (*Theodora*, 1991), the author places a female as the center of her inquiries about passions, illusions, triumphs, deceptions and death. The main character revolves around these existential topics as if mesmerized by the beauty and horror of her search, preventing her from enjoying or simply understanding the possibly small pleasures of her daily life.

The "Trilogy of Eros" comprises two novels (the third one, promised by the author in interviews, should be a collection of short stories). In the first volume, *Caçador de memórias* (1995, Hunter of Memories), as in her previous novels, the protagonist is in search of answers to questions related to her life. The structure of the book is based on letters, therefore the epistolary style may indicate the not so subtle message that one has to look for the past in order to better inform the carriers of the future. In this case, the role of the messenger was interpreted by a character named Lobinho, who wrote the letters to the receiver of them, who could be readers at large.

In 1998, Patrícia Bins was invited by a committee composed of writers of Rio Grande do Sul to be the "honorable hostess" at the 44th International Book Fair, an annual celebration for writers, editors, the general public and young readers to meet at book exhibits, conferences and interviews. She gracefully accepted the honor, granted to other highly prestigious Brazilian writers, before and after that year.

In *Instantes do mundo* (1999, Instants of the World), the second volume of the Trilogy of Eros, the author emphasizes psychoanalytical sessions where the protagonist, Anadia, is a middle-aged woman suffering from depression and the effects of a bad marriage. Contemplating death, the woman is shown recovering and reconstructing her life through threads of hope along a narrative mostly consisting of fragments of memory.

The author diversified her literary contributions through books for children: *O dia da árvore* (1995, Tree's Day), which was awarded a "Special Prize" by the Brazilian Writers Association (UBE), and *Pedro e Pietrina* (1995, Peter and Pietrina), also winner of the "Joaquim Norberto Award" by the same Association (1997). Eventually, she and co-editor Dileta S. Martins compiled a collection of recipes sent out by 55 Brazilian writers, *Brasil: receitas de criar e cozinhar* (1998, Brazil: Recipes for Creativity and Cookery). It contains texts and recipes by renowned authors for their favorite food, who explain how they link culinary to literary creativeness. The author's entire collection of publications is now part of the *Centro de Memória Literária* (Literary Memory Center), of the Catholic University of Rio Grande do Sul (PUCRGS).

Patricia Bins's style infuses a tone of reality into the spiritual searches conducted by her characters which are mostly done in the rarefied atmosphere of spiritual inquiries, existential questions and a search for solutions, while life is actual and present. Her contributions to Brazilian literature are embedded in the artistic handling of the Portuguese language, the insertion of psychological situations represented mostly by women. Their dilemmas are of universal recognition through their transcendental symbolism and factual approach to their problems. In Bins's novels and short stories, women, more than men, are the carriers of the burden of understanding human existence.

REGINA IGEL

Selected Works

Stories

O assassinato dos pombos – Cronicontos. Editora Metrópole, 1982.

Chronicles published in the *CS Zona Azul Gazette* (most of them are illustrated with drawings by her late husband) – Internet: www.cszonasul.com.br

Novels

Trilogy of Solitude.

Jogo de Fiar. Rio de Janeiro: Editora Nova Fronteira, 1983.

Ante que o amor acabe. Rio de Janeiro: Nova Fronteira, 1984.

Janela do Sonho. Rio de Janeiro: Nova Fronteira, 1987.

Trilogy of Passion.

Pele nua no espelho. Rio de Janeiro: Bertrand Brasil (after 1996: Grupo Editorial Record), 1989.

Theodora. Rio de Janeiro: Bertrand Brasil, 1991.

Sarah e os anjos. Rio de Janeiro: Bertrand Brasil, 1993.

Trilogy of Eros.

Caçador de Memórias. Rio de Janeiro: Bertrand Brasil, 1995.

Instantes do mundo. Rio de Janeiro: Bertrand Brasil, 1999.

For children and young adults

O dia da árvore. Rio de Janeiro: Bertrand Brasil, 1995.

Pedro e Pietrina. Rio de Janeiro: Bertrand Brasil, 1995.

Edited (with Dileta S. Martins): *Brasil: receitas de criar e cozinhar*.

Translations

"Destination", In Marjorie Agosín (ed.), *Landscapes of a New Land: Fiction by Latin American Women*. Buffalo, NY: White Pine Press, 1989.

References and Further Reading

Dicionário de Artes Plásticas do Rio Grande do Sul, entry on Patricia Bins, ed. Rosa Renato and Decio Presser. Porto Alegre: Universidade Federal do Rio Grande do Sul, 1997 and 2000.

Mattos, Cyro de. "*Pele nua no espelho*" *Jornal da UBE* 101 (December 2002): 25.

Nunes, Maria Luiza. "The Novels of Patricia Bins". In G. Sabat-Rivers and Lou Charnon-Deutsch (eds), *Estudios sobre Escritoras Hispánicas en Honor de Georgina Sabat-Rivers*. Madrid: Editorial Castalia, 1992.

Tutikian, Jane Fraga. "Sobre o *Assassinato dos Pombos*. (About *The Assassination of the Pigeons*)". *Letras de Hoje* 47 (1982): 181–2.

——. "Sobre *O Jogo de Fiar*. (About *Spinning Threads*)". *Letras de Hoje* 53 (1983): 125–6.

——. "*Antes que o amor acabe*, segundo Patrícia Bins." *Imprensa Oficial do Estado de Minas Gerais/ Suplemento de Minas, Belo Horizonte* November 17, 1984.

Valenzuela, Stella Máris. Interview with Patricia Bins. *Extra-Classe*, 3(25) (September 1998). (Internet: www.sinprors.org.br)

BLANCO CASTILLO, YOLANDA

Yolanda Blanco Castillo was born in 1954, in Managua, Nicaragua. She attended the Universidad Nacional Autónoma de Nicaragua, in León, during 1970 and 1971 and there she promoted the first recitals of women poets. In 1975, she went to France to study Art History and Literature at the University of La Tourine (Tours). Blanco graduated with a degree in Humanities from the Universidad Central de Venezuela. From 1981 to 1983, she was a member of the literary group "Cal y Canto" in Venezuela. Blanco moved to New York and has resided there since 1985. She designs programs for bilingual education and is invited frequently to read her poetry and to conduct seminars in many universities in the United States, Central and South America. Her anthology *De lo urbano y lo sagrado* (Of the Urban and the Sacred) won the "Mariana Sansón" Prize for poetry written by women in 2005. She currently directs the Nicaraguan poetry web page, *Dariana*: www.dariana.com.

Poet

Yolanda Blanco's poetic writing reveals a route of intimate spaces that intensify the experience of the female apprehension of reality, of Nature, and of language through the articulation of a discourse coinciding with the feminist postulates of the *difference*. Her poems also represent a testimony of the revolutionary fight that culminated with the triumph of the Sandinista Front of National Liberation (FSLN) in Nicaragua.

Blanco's poetry has defined her insistence on recreating the female subject as a fundamental priority in the vindication of various fronts: her identity, the recognition of the essential role of women in the advancement and attainment of equality in society, and in the unfair subordination to the traditional conception of what it is to be a woman. In her poems, an increased awareness exists of the importance of respecting and using different linguistic expressions in order to solidify the coexistence of ethnic plurality in Nicaragua. Also, there is a concern to recognize the genuine elements of Nature by their names through celebrating the rain, the summer, the insects, the flowers and the trees. Woman, language, and Nature become, therefore, the combined constituents of the personal and national identity that the poet seeks to formulate.

Blanco's poetic discourse incorporates a complex physical and psychological framework that comprises historicity and individuality to display a mode of expressing a female reality. The focus of her first collection, *Así cuando la lluvia* (Thus When the Rain), is on May and June, months of the rain and of the tree. The poet affirms the creative power of the rain identified with that of the woman and welcomes it with affection and happiness. The water brightens up the colors and dissipates monotony. It also creates a bucolic vision in which time is only present and the woman is actualized in love and in memories establishing the foundation of her existence. In addition, the rain, personified in a woman who dances similarly to the indigenous ahuaini, fulfils the symbolic function of originating a poetic discourse with a feminine dimension and, therefore, inaugurating a process of cultural reconstruction from the perspective of the female subject: "I am here / I exist / the rain soaks / my soul / and my red lips". The woman, identified with natural elements, brings a desire for embedding and understanding herself in landscapes, trees, leaves, corn, ducks, beetles, rocks. The tree is a powerful emblem of the second part of this collection. The woman asserts her pride of *being* and her common nature with the tree through the sensuality of the touch and the eroticism of the body.

In *Cerámica sol* (Sun Ceramics), Blanco tries to rescue the power of the primeval word, the language rooted in the symbol and in rites. The poet becomes the sun's priestess to extol its meaning in the human life, in the humbleness of the harvests and fruits, in the activity of the bees, in the chant. In her poetry, a magic animation of Nature palpitates along with the prayer to the sun-god for the feeling of love. The harmony of human and natural elements is revealed and the sun turns into a child at sunrise, a ram climbing mountains in the afternoon, and a figure who pulls his curls and feathered beard to describe the passing of the day. It is the life-giving sun who becomes impressionistically green or yellow to display the happiness found in life in communion with the rain, a perfect conciliation attained in the fertile embrace of Nature: "Thus the happiness of the tigüilote was born / and thus the happiness of the cortez was born / and thus the fruits were ripe".

Penqueo en Nicaragua (Fight in Nicaragua) was written during the revolutionary fight of the Nicaraguan people that ended with the regime of Anastasio Somoza. It constitutes the testimony of a call for action against injustice and a chant for the hope of liberation. With an enormous emotive force, the poet depicts the heroism and courage of the indigenous neighborhood of Monimbó that led the vanguard in the war against the *Sower of the Flowers of Evil*. The transformation of peace, work, music and dance into shrapnel, bombs, destruction and death originated the uprising against the Somocist army. Blanco remembers the dead Sandinista guerrilla fighters and the faith in the cause for Nicaragua. Pain, hope, guns and guitars alternate in the poet's affirmation of having been "impregnated" by the love for the Revolution. The colors of Sandinism, black and red, appear in most of the poems to verbalize the conflict generated by oppression and liberty. The denouncement of atrocities, the imprisonments for insurgency, the voices of witnesses, the poverty, orphanhood, mutilation, hunger, and affliction create a multiple cry for solidarity in the fight guided by the motto "Free Country or Death". In this book, the attention resides also in the presence of the woman in the revolutionary forces. The testimony includes the voices of the guerrilla woman, the woman poet, the mother, as a means of introducing a bi-textual discourse which, on one hand, confronts the patriarchal tradition and, on the other, opens up and vindicates a new space for feminine expression.

Blanco's awareness of being a woman is the dominant theme in *Aposentos* (Lodgings). A quotation by French poet Arthur Rimbaud, declaring that a woman poet will exist when the woman is independent of the male's yoke and she lives by herself and for herself, introduces the poems. The first part of the book is entitled "Mistagogia," the revelation of a hidden and marvelous doctrine which penetrates in the sacred mysteries of the female reality and narrative. This doctrine brings a different conception of the world and, therefore, it articulates a new language which is independent from the patriarchal discourse, as the poem "Initiation" illustrates: "And I was given this prayer / only to be said / at the hours of the blood: I learn from my menses / I forge my contiguity with the moon / from the ubiquitous land / I draw my force / I know that every month there is a son who is dreaming me". Using a subversive language that praises sensuality and sexuality, the poet glorifies each part of the female body. Her objective is to install a new sociological and cultural space confronting the prevalent stereotypes that limit female expression: "I initiate the alphabet of a woman. / Ignoring the meters / I propose others: / strange / repulsive / delightful / others".

Blanco's poetic expressivity concentrates in the woman's corporal fertility to form a utopian realm in the center of Nature and of cosmic forces, as the eco-feminist criticism advocates. Sex becomes the symbolic seed and creative source of the universe and of artistic imagination in her discourse, which also incorporates the ethnic plurality of Nicaragua as reflected in the variety of its languages and idiosyncratic lexicons. At the same time, the identification of the poet with moon cycles and natural elements lays the foundation for a new discourse as a confluence of biography, psychology and culture, escaping, thus, from the essentialist definition advocated by traditional patriarchism which limits the possibilities of change and of social reorganization. Blanco will, then, assert the acceptance of the female beyond conventionalisms: "Same as a moon risen in a high night / you should see me . . . / same and different / in curved / ecstatic / mysterious happening".

The identification of woman and Nature emerges continuously in Blanco's poems to communicate their essential creative commonality. It becomes a double discursive axis of universal denouncement: the subordinated role of women in society, and the generalized repression of their emotions, their experience of love, and writing, as her recent anthology *De lo urbano y o sagrado* (Of the Urban and the Sacred) attests. Blanco's poetry vindicates the validity of a female discourse, the synthesis of a personal and historical process: "In the name of the pubis / of the breasts / and of the holy mind / May I grow as woman / Amen".

FRANCISCO J. PEÑAS-BERMEJO

Selected Works

Así cuando la lluvia. León, Nicaragua: Editorial Hospicio, 1974.
Cerámica sol. León, Nicaragua: Editorial UNAN, 1977.
Penqueo en Nicaragua. Managua, Nicaragua: Editorial Unión, 1981.
Aposentos. Caracas: Pen Club de Venezuela, 1985.
De lo urbano y lo sagrado. Managua, Nicaragua: Asociación Nicaragüense de Escritoras, 2005.

References and Further Reading

Angleysey, Zoë. *Isok amargo: poesía de mujeres centroamericanas por la paz. Central American Women's Poetry for Peace*. Penobscot, ME: Granite Press, 1987.
Arellano, Jorge Eduardo (ed.). *Open to the Sun*. Van Nuys, CA: Perivale Press, 1981.
——. *Four Central America Women Poets*. Cambridge, MA: Woodberry Poetry Room, 1986. Recording.
——. *Antología general de la poesía nicaragüense*. Managua, Nicaragua: Distribuidora Cultural, 1994.
Peñas-Bermejo, Francisco J. "Mujer y revolución: dinámica de una síntesis en la poesía de Yolanda Blanco". *Hispanic Research Journal* 2(3) (October 2001): 235–44.
Ramos, Helena. "Tercera es la vencedora". *7 Días On Line* 459 (20 March 2005). http://www.7dias.com.ni/
Silva, Fernando Antonio. "Presentación del libro *De lo urbano y lo sagrado* de Yolanda Blanco". http://www.dariana.com/diccionario/yolanda_blanco4.htm
White, Stephen. "La poesía de Yolanda Blanco: Cantos de vida y experiencia." http://www.dariana.com/diccionario/yolanda_blanco3.htm
Zamora, Daisy (ed.) *La mujer nicaragüense en la poesía. Antología*. Managua, Nicaragua: Nueva Nicaragua, 1992. 37, 49, 51–52, 421–40.

BOBES LEÓN, MARILYN

Marilyn Bobes León (1955), poet and fiction writer, was born in Havana, Cuba. She began studying history and spent much of her professional life as a journalist, working for *Prensa Latina* and the magazine *Revolución y cultura*. Bobes' vast record of published interviews, articles, and reviews is a testament to her extensive cultural knowledge and her importance as an intellectual in contemporary Cuba. Moreover, her fiction and poetry are key to the growth of Cuba's visibility in the corpus of contemporary Latin American and Caribbean women's writing.

Bobes' work has been recognized in many different ways. She won the "David" Literary Award for Poetry at age 25 for her collection of poems entitled *La aguja en el pajar* (1979, The Needle in the Haystack). Later, she entered the literary arena with her prose, for which she won awards in Mexico (The Edmundo Valadés Prize for Latin American Short Story, 1993), Peru (the Magda Portal Prize for Latin American Women's Short Story Prize, 1994), and Cuba (the Casa de las Américas award for her short story collection *Alguien tiene que llorar* (1995, Somebody Has to Cry) and her novel *Fiebre de invierno* (2005, Winter Fever)). In addition, she is recognized as one of the Cuban intellectual elite, joining other well-known figures in group projects that commemorate Cuban authors (Miguel Barnet and Pablo Armando Fernández), the capital city ("¡Oh, La Habana!" *La Gaceta de Cuba*, vol. 2, 1999), and the twentieth century (*Siglo Pasado* (2003) [Last Century]). She served for a short time as president of the Writers' Association of Cuba's Union of Cuban Writers and Artists (UNEAC) and is an editor of that organization's editorial branch UNIÓN.

Bobes has demonstrated a strong commitment to increasing women's literary publication. With Mirta Yáñez, she edited the groundbreaking panorama of Cuban women writers, *Estatuas de sal* . . . (1996, Salt Statues). She then compiled multiple anthologies of Cuban women's short fiction and poetry published in Cuba and abroad, such as *Eros en la poesía cubana* (1995, Eros in Cuban Poetry), *Cuentistas cubanas de hoy* (2002, Cuban Women Short Fiction Writers Today), and *Las musas inquietantes: antología sobre infidelidad* (2003, Restless Muses: An Anthology about Infidelity), as well as specific collections of work by Alfonsina Storni, *Entre el largo desierto y la mar* (1999, Between the Long Desert and the Sea) and Carilda Oliver Labra, *Sombra seré que no dama: Antología poética* (2000, A Shadow I May Be, Not a Lady). This same commitment to the female voice infuses her own creative writing, which is characterized by intertextual dialogue and a plurality of voices that speak to the contingent nature of women's identities and self-representation.

A Poet, Not a Poetess

The most salient characteristic of Bobes' poetry and prose is a creative consciousness of the act of writing and its relationship with the act of reading, both the reader's and her own. While Bobes agrees with the grammatical specificity of gendering her work as that of a poetess, she rejects the notion that the feminine title encompasses the multiple textualities in her poetry. We see this distinction in the generic naming of her voice, *Alguien está escribiendo su ternura* (1978, Someone is Writing Tenderly), the search for the image and poetic language in *El aguja en el pajar* (The Needle in the Haystack), and finally a consciousness of a feminist voice in *Hallar el modo* (1989, To Find the Way), a title referring to Rosario Castellanos' famous poem. By contrast, the titles of her later collections suggest the postmodern notion of poetic voices and ideals as simulacra, and the transience of images, for example, in her collections *Revi(c)itaciones y homenajes* (2001, Re(-)citations and Ref/verences) and *Impresiones y Comentarios* (2003, Impressions and Observations).

More specifically, the central theme in Bobes' early poetry is the consequences of writing, specifically of writing (as) women. She pays homage to predecessors who suffered the consequences of being women and writers: Sor Juana, Gertrudis Gomez de Avellaneda, Gabriela Mistral, and Alfonsina Storni. Heroic women are frequently the subjects of her poems (Micaela Bastidas, Haydée Santamaria, Amalia Simoni). In addition, Bobes' more feminist poems take to task the traditional roles assigned to women – "Hablan los viejos conceptos" (Antiquated Concepts Speak) – and adopt the male critic's voice speaking about women writers, as in "Triste oficio" (A Sad Trade). Her appropriation of this voice serves to expose its abusive power and women's marginal position within the literary institution, as the poem concludes, "Y pensemos después cómo callarla" [and later we'll figure out how to silence her].

Bobes' challenge to women's marginality is also explicit in her textual rewriting of canonical authors. Not simply a novel *poetisa*, she also sees herself as a member of a broader community of poets and intellectuals. Her *Revi(c)itaciones* ... plays with language usage and canonical figures and concepts. For example, she rewrites some of Juan Clemente Zenéa's most famous verses in a section playfully entitled "Romanticidios" (Romanticides). Blaise Pascal, Thomas Edison, and Edgar Allan Poe motivate her own images of reason, emotion, individuality, and beauty. Robert Louis Stevenson's Mr. Hyde evokes the image of repressed desire. Finally, appropriating Marguerite Duras and Susan St. John evokes Bobes' own poetic expression, and playful poems in honor of Rilke, Quevedo, Borges, and José Martí (in a poem called "Variaciones sencillas") round out the collection. More than just revering or referring to these artists, her poems bear witness to the postmodern notion of the logic and succession of images (Baudrillard), especially her reading of José Lezama Lima's reading of the Cuban poet in his "Oda a Julián de Casal".

Fiction: Major Themes

Perhaps better known for her prose, Bobes is considered one of her generation's most accomplished female narrators. Her prized collection, *Alguien tiene que llorar* attests to Bobes' preoccupation with women's agency in society. The first edition of the collection has six stories (the second has ten). The multiple voices in the story "Alguien tiene que llorar" speak throughout the collection, in "Esta vez tienes que hacerme caso" (This Time You Have to Do What I Say) and "Y hace bien" (It's a Good Thing). Identifiable by the characters' names and the particular way they view themselves and their girlfriends throughout the book, this repetition gives the collection the feeling of an organic whole. By creating unity in form through a multiplicity of gendered voices, Bobes dismantles monolithic social gender constructions and reveals the rift between the ideal and the real perpetuated by her female characters.

In "Alguien tiene que llorar," someone has to cry for the death of the protagonist, who has taken her only tragic alternative – suicide. Through the other characters' interior monologues, the protagonist's feminist stance – repeating the story's leitmotif "Si alguien tiene que llorar, que sean ellos" [If someone has to cry, let it be them (referring to men in general)] – is interpreted as both supportive and threatening. The heterogeneous voices both criticize and admire the deceased for her open bisexuality, career ambitions, and lack of family. In all of Bobes' stories, the choices, frustrations, and doubts that plague her female characters are intertwined with contemporary Cuba's material crisis, and in "Pregúntaselo a Dios" with exile's cross-cultural confusions and painful repercussions.

Bobes also treats the relationship between gender, voice, reading and power in this collection. For example, in "¿Te gusta Peter Handke?," Bobes places reading the German writer's reading of F. Scott Fitzgerald and her own rewriting of Handke's novel *Short Letter, Long Farewell* on the same narrative plane as peeling a potato or packing a suitcase. Domestic tasks motivate the plot that hinges on the acts of reading and writing. Similarly, her symbolic reinscription of Dante's inferno in "Ellas in el gimnasio," suggests Bobes' feminist transgression of literary conventions through her intertextual dialogue with canonical male representations of female subjectivity. Edited a second time in Cuba, Argentina and Italy, the collection has had international impact and its stories appear in numerous Cuban, Latin American and Caribbean anthologies and in translation.

Bobes' first novel, *Fiebre de invierno*, is thematically similar to her short story collection. The title is taken from a Dylan Thomas verse: "muda para decirle a la rosa encorvada / que doblega mi juventud la misma fiebre de invierno" [And I am dumb to tell the crooked rose / My youth is bent by the same wintry fever]. The lyrical yet realist novel artistically embraces all of the conflicting connotations implied in the metaphorical winterish fever through the perspective of a menopausal narrator: ageing, youthful passion, cold fear, heated emotion, fantasy, mortality, and future possibility. In the process of writing a novel of the same name, the protagonist struggles to overcome her insecurities, reconcile her memories and begin anew. Impressionistic representations of the protagonist's life and historical events (The 10,000 ton Harvest, Mariel) mix with references from Raymond Carver to The Beatles to *Sex and the City* and lend the novel an autobiographical feel. Writing, memory, and feminine difference are themes more compelling than the plot, which takes a back seat to Bobes' artful prose. An interesting experiment in gendered voices, her most recent short story "La feminista, la postmoderna y yo, el burlador prevenido" (The Feminist, the Postmodern Chick and I, the Forewarned Fool) works the same plot from the masculine point of view to a much different effect.

Bobes' rich artistic production, as Eliana Rivero suggests, has contributed to defining the *corpus* of Latin American women's literature. Her characters and her feminist positioning of her poetic and narrative voices reveal a creative self-awareness of writing as a woman in contemporary Cuba. Moreover, she has used her important position in Cuba's cultural sphere to promote other women's fiction and poetry thereby advancing the broader cause of legitimizing women's production of cultural meaning in the contemporary Cuban context.

BARBARA RIESS

Selected Works

Alguien está escribiendo su ternura. In *Cuatro poetas jóvenes*, Serie Literatura y Arte. University of Havana: Dept. de Actividades Culturales, 1978.

La aguja en el pajar. Havana: Ediciones UNION, 1980.

Hallar el modo. Havana: Editorial Letras Cubanas, 1989.

Alguien tiene que llorar. Havana: Casa de las Américas, 1995.

"Somebody has to Cry". Trans. Dick Cluster. In Mirta Yánez (ed.), *Cubanas, Contemporary Fiction by Cuban Women*. Boston, MA: Beacon Press, 1998.

"Ask the Good Lord". Trans. Peter Bush. *The Voice of the Turtle*. New York: Grove Press, 1998.

"This Time Listen to What I Say" and "It's a Good Thing". Trans. Anne Fountain. In Mary Berg (ed.), *Open Your Eyes and Soar: Cuban Women Writing Now*. Buffalo, NY: White Pine Press, 2003.

Alguien tiene que llorar: otra vez. Córdoba, Argentina: Ameghino Editora, 1998.

Revicitaciones y homenajes. Havana: Ediciones Unión, 1998. Havana: Ediciones Unión, 2001. Milano: Editore Frassinelli, 2003.

Impresiones y comentarios Havana: Letras Cubanas, 2003.

Fiebre de invierno. Havana: Casa de las Américas, 2005. San Juan: Editorial Isla Negra, 2005.

"La feminista, la postmoderna y yo, el burlador prevenido" in Riverón, 153–59.

"She". Trans. Pamela Carmell and Anne Fountain. In Mary Berg *et al.* (eds), *Cuba on the Edge. Short Stories from the Island.* Nottingham: Critical, Cultural and Communications Press, 2006, pp. 169–73.

References and Further Reading

Babbit, Susan E. "Stories from the South: a Question of Logic". *Hypatia*. 20(3) (2005): 1–21.

Cruz, Zuleika. "Muchas (y muchos) tienen que agradecerlo". Rev. of *Alguien tiene que llorar. Casa de las Américas* 36(203) (1996): 152–5.

Davies, Catherine. *A Place in the Sun? Women Writers in Twentieth Century Cuba*. London: Zed Books, 1997.

Lindstrom, Naomi. Review of *Alguien tiene que llorar. World Literature Today* 71(2) (1997): 351–2.

Riess, Barbara. "Escritora/Escritura y la idiosincrasia cubana: La posicionalidad textual en Marilyn Bobes". In Lady Rojas Trempe and Catharina Vallejo (eds), *Celebración de la creación literaria de escritoras hispanas en las Américas*. Ottawa: Girol–Enana Blanca, 2000, pp. 193–202.

Rivero, Eliana. "Hacia una definición de la lírica femenina en Hispanoamérica". *Revista/Review Interamericana* 12(1) (1982): 11–26.

Riverón, Rogelio. *Conversación con el búfalo blanco. Selección de cuentos y entrevistas*. Havana: Editorial Letras Cubanas, 2005, pp. 145–53.

BOMBAL, MARÍA LUISA

The details of María Luisa Bombal's life (1910–80) parallel in interesting ways the lives of the women she narrates in her fiction. Not only are the facts murky, but much contradictory information exists, meaning that the following description of her life must be read provisionally. María Luisa Bombal was born in Viña del Mar, Chile, into a family of Argentines who had left their homeland because of political persecution in the mid-nineteenth century. At the age of 12, after the death of her father, she traveled to Paris to study until 1931. After graduating from the Sorbonne, she returned briefly to Santiago, Chile, where she became friends with Pablo Neruda and other emerging writers of the period. She also was active in theatrical productions in Viña del Mar and in Santiago. During this time she fell in love with Elogio Sánchez, who did not share her passion for literature. Her relationship with Sánchez caused her to become increasingly depressed and she attempted suicide. When that failed, she shot him (he survived). As a consequence of the scandal, Bombal fled Chile for Argentina with the help of friends. In 1933, she moved to Buenos Aires where she lived for two years in the home of Pablo Neruda. While there she made contacts with intellectuals involved in the literary magazine *Sur,* which was founded by Victoria Ocampo and published the work of important literary figures such as Jorge Luis Borges and Alfonsina Storni. During this period she met and later married Jorge Larco, who unfortunately died shortly thereafter. As Neruda was writing *Residencia en tierra* (Residence on Earth), Bombal shared the same table with him and wrote *La última niebla* (The Last Mist)—two texts that would have an enormous impact on poetry and prose in the region. In 1944, she married for the third time and moved to the United States where she lived until her husband's death in 1970. During this period she had a daughter and continued to work on a full-length novel that was never completed, possibly because of problems with alcoholism. She then returned to Chile by way of Argentina for the remainder of her life. In her last years she lived alone and out of touch with literary society. She read a great deal, wrote two unpublished plays, and an unfinished novel. As her published works were few, she never received the National Award for literature in Chile. Other reasons for her lack of recognition as a Chilean writer during her life may be the fact that she lived primarily abroad, that her writing was originally published in Argentina, or that she did not write prose in the regionalist manner popular in Chile at the time. Ironically her work is now widely recognized as both innovative and highly significant to the development of Latin American modern fiction. There is now a Chilean national literary prize in her name; this prize honors the contributions of one of Chile's most significant writers.

A Small Body of Work with a Tremendous Impact

Bombal's literature, published from 1934–40, consists of the short novella *La amortajada* (The Shrouded Woman), the collection of short stories *La última niebla* (The Last Mist) and *La historia de María Griselda* (The Story of María Griselda). Her first novella appeared in 1935 and her second in 1938. While her work was not copious, its influence on the development of literary approaches in Latin America was tremendous. Many consider her work, as well as that of William Faulkner, to have been a precursor to the work of "boom" authors such as Gabriel García Márquez, Carlos Fuentes, and José Donoso. Bombal's writing includes a mix of the fantastic, the naturalistic, and a feminist perspective, which all combine to form a unique style. Her work focuses on female protagonists and the way in which their identity is both socially constructed and integrally tied to their natural surroundings. For instance in the short story, "El árbol" (The Tree), the protagonist marries due to social expectations, but remains in her unhappy marriage because of the tree she is able to view from her bedroom. When the tree is cut down, she leaves her husband explaining that she had tolerated his mature age and cold manner because of the beautiful tree that had brought her peace.

It is this interesting combination of women's free will, their essential tie to the natural world, and their fantastic lives that runs through Bombal's narrative. Her unique style can be noted in the work of "boom" writers who continued to seek the connections between their identity, their environmental surroundings, and their place in history. For instance, in the story "Trenzas" (Braids) the connection between a woman's way of wearing her hair and her position in life are narrated as naturally bound. When a woman with long hair dies, a ranch burns down simultaneously and the ties between these events are narrated as being naturally and integrally connected, much in the way that later writers working in the styles of "magical realism" and the "marvelous real" made famous.

The genre of her work is also often hard to place. What some consider novellas, are also called short stories or novels. Nevertheless, her first publication *La última niebla* is a "sentimental drama" (according to Bombal) that depicts the life of a bourgeois woman in a bad marriage. The protagonist, Helga, consistently questions why women center their lives on those of men. The first person narrative reflects both the outside world and the interior passions and desires of the protagonist. The role of nature is also strong in this text as the mist itself has the ability to allow the protagonist's imagination to reconstruct reality around a non-patriarchal system. As a consequence of the way in which the narrator, through nature, retreats from reality, the protagonist is presented as socially alienated: she has only fragmentary ties to the world, is lost between fantasy and fact, and wavers between accepting and rejecting the norms of a male-dominated society.

In her second text, *La amortajada* (The Shrouded Woman), the protagonist is a dead woman. The reader receives information from an unknown narrator who often appears to be the dead woman, Ana María. The text recounts the life of Ana María as she remembers (or as someone else remembers) her life while her body lies shrouded awaiting burial. The visits of significant men from her past give the reader insight into the way in which gender is once again a primary concern of Bombal. Each visit is the motivation for a journey back in time where the relationship between the visitor and Ana María is described. Through the "spinning of threads" (the text has numerous references to weaving) the narrator demonstrates the way in which this woman's life was subject to the constraints of patriarchal society. Only through her own mental escape is she able to relive her life on different terms which ultimately leads to her ability to accept death as a better way to live when compared to her previous "lifeless" existence as a woman ruled by men.

Throughout Bombal's work there is a pattern of themes that relate the tragic and painful loves of women and the cold, distant men they desire. Rather than narrate these tales in a romantic style, however, Bombal weaves a complex style that combines the fantastic with the sentimental. In almost all of her works natural elements such as trees or fog function as vehicles for women's imaginations at the same time that they draw a material link between women's feelings and the world they live in. The lack of regionalist details or orientating information made her work a novelty in an era when many novelists worked in a style that was very specifically situated in concrete Latin American locations.

La amortajada

The short novel, *La amortajada* (The Shrouded Woman), is arguably Bombal's most important work. The novel opens during the wake of Ana María. As people in her life come to pay their respects, the reader learns of her perspective on her relationship with each one of them. The reader meets the important people in her life, but the lyrical style and the blending of past and present make it difficult for the reader to pinpoint the details of their relationships. The reader literally has the sense of watching her ideas flow across her mind, scattered, fragmented, and highly personal. From these glimpses the reader watches her life unfold through the people who come to pay respects to her dead body and her still active mind. In her immediate family there is her husband Antonio who frivolously married her and does not really love her, her 20-year-old daughter Anita, her son Fred, who was her husband's favorite, and her son Antonio who is married to María Griselda and who always tried to control his mother. Later there are the sounds of horses and Ricardo, her first love, arrives. The reader learns that when Ana María became pregnant with his child, he abandoned her, causing her to suffer a breakdown and lose the baby. Another key figure in Ana María's life is her lover Fernando. As he sits by her side, she learns that he finds some comfort in her death since he will now no longer need to solve her problems. She is shocked at the cold ways he speaks about her and also his dead wife, Inés. As the novel closes she hears the voice of Padre Carlos which allows her to reflect on her ideas about religion and the future of her soul. Over the course of the novel almost all of Ana María's thoughts have been coded through her relationships with men. In fact, in the opening sequence she asks why men are always the axis around which women's lives revolve. Throughout the text she struggles with this dilemma and it is never fully resolved. Bombal's protagonist does not end the novel triumphantly claiming her own independent identity. Instead, after taking stock of her life and of those close to her, observing them observing her, she obtains a sense of self that is not entirely dependent on what others think of her. For the first time, she is the one who is assessing the men in her life, and even though her thoughts about herself continue to be connected to others, she becomes conscious of herself in an entirely new way. In a bittersweet and touching conclusion, Bombal narrates this awakening at the moment when she finally prepares to lose consciousness forever.

By writing a novel from the perspective of a dead protagonist, Bombal radically broke with any form of realism. The novel's dream-like style and fluid stream of consciousness link it with later novels like Juan Rulfo's *Pedro Páramo*. In addition to the stylistic innovations of the novel, the text is one of the best examples of gynocentric feminist writing. Centered in a woman's essential difference from men and her constant need to struggle against patriarchy, Bombal's novel creates a dream-like world where women's desires are always removed from real possibility. The effect is a novel that is haunting and tragic at the same time that it is lyrical and moving.

One of the most innovative women writers from Latin America, Bombal stands out as a significant writer for the richness of her work and the legacy it left behind. It is also important to note that she is consistently one of the few Latin American women to hold a firm standing in the literary canon both in Latin America and internationally. Her work has played a central role in feminist studies of Latin American literature and also in studies of Latin American modernism, magical realism, the avant-garde, and the fantastic.

SOPHIA A. MCCLENNEN

Selected Works

New Islands and Other Stories. Trans. Richard and Lucia Cunningham. Ithaca, NY: Cornell University Press, 1982.

Breviario de La playa de Miramar: fragmentos. Valparaiso: Universidad de Valparaiso, 1994.

La Historia de María Griselda. Santiago de Chile: Andrés Bello, 1994.
House of Mist and The Shrouded Woman. Austin, TX: University of Texas Press, 1995.
La última niebla, La amortajada. 6th edn. Barcelona: Seix Barral, 1995.
Obras completas. 2nd edn. Santiago de Chile: Andres Bello, 1997.

References and Further Reading

Agosín, Marjorie. "Un cuento de hadas a la inversa: *La historia de María Griselda* o la belleza aniquilada". *Hispanic Journal* 5(1) (1983a): 141–9.

——. *Desterradas del paraiso, Las: protagonistas en la narrativa de María Luisa Bombal*. New York: Senda Nueva, 1983b.

——. *Hacedoras, Las: mujer, imagen, escritura*. Santiago de Chile: Cuarto Propio, 1993.

——. "María Luisa Bombal o el lenguaje alucinado". *Symposium* 48(4) (1995): 251–6.

Articles by and about María Luisa Bombal. Chapel Hill, NC: University of North Carolina Library, Photoreproduction Service, 1959.

Baker, Armand F. "El tiempo y el proceso de individuación en *La última niebla*". *Revista Iberoamericana* 52(135–6) (1986): 393–415.

Bente, Thomas O. "María Luisa Bombal's Heroines: Poetic Neuroses and Artistic Symbolism". *Hispanofila* 28(1) (1984): 103–13.

Cortés, Dario A. "Bibliografía de y sobre María Luisa Bombal". *Hispanic Journal* 1(2) (1980): 125–42.

Díaz, Gwendolyn. "Desire and Discourse in María Luisa Bombal's *New Islands*". *Hispanofila* 112 (1994): 51–63.

Fernández, Magali. *El discurso narrativo en la obra de María Luisa Bombal*. Madrid: Pliegos, 1988.

Galvez Lira, Gloria. *María Luisa Bombal, realidad y fantasía*. Potomac, MD: Scripta Humanistica, 1986.

Gligo, Agata. *María Luisa: sobre la vida de María Luisa Bombal*. 2nd edn. Santiago de Chile: Andrés Bello, 1985.

Guerra-Cunningham, Lucía. "Entrevista a María Luisa Bombal". *Hispanic Journal* 3(2) (1982): 119–27.

——. *La narrativa de María Luisa Bombal: una visión de la existencia femenina*. Madrid: Playor, 1980.

——. "Visión de lo femenino en la obra de María Luisa Bombal: Una dualidad contradictoria del ser y el deber ser". *Revista Chilena de Literatura* 25 (1985): 87–99.

——. "La marginalidad subversiva del deseo en *La última niebla* de María Luisa Bombal". *Hispamérica* 21(62) (1992): 53–63.

Kostopulos-Cooperman, Celeste. *The Lyrical Vision of María Luisa Bombal*. London: Tamesis, 1988.

Levine, Linda Gould. "María Luisa Bombal from a Feminist Perspective". *Revista/Review Interamericana* 4 (1974): 148–61.

López Castaño, Oscar. "La alucinación como forma de vida en *La última niebla*". *Lingüística y Literatura* 13(21) (1992): 84–94.

Loubet, Jorgelina. "María Luisa Bombal y el realismo mágico". *Boletín de la Academia Argentina de Letras* 53(207–8) (1988): 125–34.

Méndez Rodenas, Adriana. "El lenguaje de los sueños en *La última niebla*: la metáfora del Eros". *Revista Iberoamericana* 60(8) (1994): 935–43.

Mora, Gabriela. "Rechazo del mito en *Las islas nuevas*, de María Luisa Bombal". *Revista Iberoamericana* 51(132–3) (1985): 853–65.

Munnich, Susana. *La dulce niebla: lectura femenina y chilena de María Luisa Bombal*. Santiago de Chile: Universitaria, 1991.

Ostrov, Andrea. "*La última niebla*: la locura de una mujer razonable. Lectura de la novela de María Luisa Bombal". *Acta Literaria* 19 (1994): 39–48.

Oyarzun, Kemy. "Ecolalía e intertextualidad en *La última niebla*". *Discurso Literario* 4(1) (1986): 163–83.

Piñones L., Julio. "Lectura de *La amortajada*, de María Luisa Bombal". *Logos 2* (1989): 71–85.

Rodríguez-Peralta, Phyllis. "María Luisa Bombal's Poetic Novels of Female Estrangement". *Revista de Estudios Hispánicos* 14(1) (1980): 139–55.

Sánchez, Hernan. "El trasfondo místico en *La última niebla* de María Luisa Bombal". *Revista Hispánica Moderna* 44(2) (1991): 238–46.

Schulz, Barbara. "La visión andrógina en *El árbol* de María Luisa Bombal". *Estudios Filológicos* 27 (1992): 113–22.

Scott, Nina M. "Verbal and Nonverbal Messages in María Luisa Bombal's *El árbol*". *Modern Language Studies* 17(3) (1987): 3–9.

Spanos, Tony. "Spatial Dimensions in the Fiction of María Luisa Bombal". *Revista de Estudios Hispánicos* 17–18 (1990–91): 259–66.

Vidal, Hernan. *María Luisa Bombal: la feminidad enajenada*. San Antonio de Calonge, Spain: Hijos de Jose Bosch, 1976.

BORINSKY, ALICIA

Background

Argentinean poet, writer, and critic Alicia Borinsky (b. 1946) grew up in a Polish exiled family. As a student of the Buenos Aires' public school system, she learned English as a second language and was able to read classical authors of English literature while taking pleasure in local literary production. Both aspects of her personal life would create a particular framework for the creative and critical contribution to the twentieth-century women's literature in Argentina and the United States. She moved to the United States in 1967 to complete her doctorate studies at the University of Pittsburgh. Since then, she has been teaching comparative literature at Boston University.

In 1989, Borinsky published her first novel *Mina cruel* (Mean Woman) in which a nameless country is the setting for a revolution that never takes place. Totalitarianism is present in the argument through the most brutal imagery derived from coercion and a restrictive system. However, this uncontrolled political dynamic seems to infuse not only civil, political, and military actors who participates directly in the brutal situation, but also women who participates as dissidents or subordinates. In this sense, women in the private and public spheres provoke individual questioning that would result in further dichotomies between tyranny and groundbreaking projects.

From the mid-twentieth-century Latin American context and beyond, it is necessary to see that Argentina together with other countries such as Colombia and Chile suffered from historical periods of violence, where repression and expatriation provided the equilibrium required to establish further economic and political ideologies currently in crisis. Nevertheless, it was not until several decades later that fascist governments fell, giving the chance to rebuild the countries democratically. However, personal frustrations and social disappointment due to the lack of action of social segments were there for Borinsky and other writers who incorporated this corpus in their creative duties. In this sense, it is possible to find books such as *El otoño del patriarca* (The Autumn of the Patriarch) a novel by Gabriel García Marquez, and *Señor presidente* (Mr. President) by Miguel Angel Asturias as references for this dissenting literature. *La pareja desmontable* (1994) is a collection of poems in which lovers and their everyday experiences are used in order to express with irony and humor the insensate and complex feelings beyond romance. Absence is perhaps one of the most relevant themes within this compilation since between some of the characters there is a lack of engaging relationships, even when they share their lives. In other words, common mistakes, burnt letters, leavings, conflicts, and seduction are seen from the perspective wherein the spectacle of seduction and power relations are always active human subject memories.

Works

Madres alquiladas (Rented Mothers) (1996), published by Ediciones Corregidor in Buenos Aires, has on its front cover a photograph taken by Borinsky in which there is a naked blond doll barely hidden behind green tree branches. This picture refers to other Borinsky front book covers such as *La pareja desmontable*, *La mujer de mi marido* (My Husband's Woman) and *All Night Movie* where women's bodies, seduction and gender issues introduce the reader into the fallacy of normative feminine roles and its life projects. *Madres Alquiladas* (Rented Mothers) is about disenchantment at the end of the maternity experience because of the futility of the care and love shared with children as those children will eventually take part of their mothers' bodies with them to fight others' battles. Additionally, Borinsky explores through several poems, on the one hand, the issue of women writing within the context of the traditional history written by men and addressed to administrate and maintain their interests, and, on the other hand, how women's political, social and literary participation needs justification under these terms.

Cine continuado (1997) has been surrounded by criticism because its story embraces the journey of a young woman displaced from her hometown to the metropolis where urban living allows the protagonist to engage in a life devoted to finding her own space within this chaotic setting. Accordingly, the author scrutinizes an ordinary character taking into consideration the complexity of being under the vigilance and desires of others. Here, classical aesthetics are disrupted by Borinsky when applying a veil of magnificence to events that, more often than not, would be taken as disturbing. From the reader's perspective, it is not easy to trace the concordances between language and reality in this text because the author expresses with an extreme sensitivity the significance of details while fragmenting their sequences. In addition, Borinsky inserts a whole gallery of irreverent characters that give the novel a polyphonic texture framed by popular cultural references that bring this literature closer to a new understanding of the picaresque novel as acknowledged by several critics. *Dreams of the Abandoned Seducer* (1998), the English translation of *Sueños de un seductor abandonado* originally published in 1995, is a blend of different narrative choices within a city's chronicle. Borinsky according to Cola Franzen, the translator, incorporates dialogues and monologues, but also conversations between the author and the reader that allow the text to be both humorous and imaginary. In the last pages of that edition, Borinsky clarifies her conception of the novel with the interviewer Julio Ortega. As a result we can firstly, find out how Borinsky's platform refers to a city which is transformed through humor into a spectacle (p. 207) and secondly, it points out ugly women's fascination with beauty and fitness. Both elements form a whole where there is no interest in verisimilitude. On the contrary, Borinsky explains her use of hyperbole to link urban behaviors to gender issues. At the same time, Julio Ortega reminds us about Borinsky's literary and academic interest, Borges and Puig, who have influenced not only this novel, but also others in the way they access dialogue, fiction, and popular cultures.

A Focus on Gender

Borinsky summarizes her motive as follows: "I am fascinated by the shapes that lives acquire in present-day cities, the possibilities for confusion and love in a space where fragmentation of family life and the new social incarnation of women suggest prospects for criss-crossed stories" (p. 209). *La mujer de mi marido* (My Husband's Woman) (2000) continues exploring what Borinsky had already suggested in earlier publications, in which women have been portrayed as targets for others. In this sense she defines *los piropos* during an interview with Julio Ortega as a "gallant remark, or an aggressive erotic comment". In recent text, Borinsky creates parodies by using the style of a diary including the most common flirtations used in the streets. In this sense, this manual draws attention to different levels of this popular form of expression where meaning and its intricacies are substantial for both the emissary and the receptor. In the praxis those parties work as a dichotomy that gives the voice and the active role to the male and the passive task to women. Thus, [*piropos*] flirtatious comments portray social prejudices regarding women's bodies and performance generally through humiliation and sexual harassment. In contrast, city diversity is a recurring reference for Borinsky in her literature. Sometimes it is possible to apply the connections between some of those urban elements to the specific city of Buenos Aires. However, there are other elements that take this literary approach of the city to a more universal stage such as the presence of marginality and the fear of minority groups. Consequently, the reader can recognize segments of crowded cities that during the twentieth century provided scarce shelter for rural immigrants, leaving cities, at least in Latin America, to deal with the issues of race, identities, and nation. In addition, anger, persecution, romantic encounters, domestic violence, insanity, and commercial relationships compose a local kaleidoscope that relates to what it is going on in the streets. This displacement and mobility are Dianna Niebylski's starting point for understanding Alicia Borinsky's contribution to literature. Niebylski states that nomadism, as a trope, lets Borinsky stress female subjectivity within the scope of the process of "transition or becoming". This critic focuses her interpretation on Deleuze and Guattari's theories wherein instability permits a subversive potentiality to the female idea of "morphing" bodies. These bodies that eventually modify their features as occurs in *Cine continuado*, when women become taller or smaller depending on their partners, establish pastiche, humor, and a satirical style in order to avoid monotony. According to Niebylski, Borinsky not only goes beyond literary genres but also looks for epistemological exercises while letting her writing flow without a predetermined direction.

In conclusion, Alicia Borinsky is one of the most relevant figures to understanding the Latin American literary constellation of the past thirty years in Argentina and the United States. As Borinsky has spent her life between those nations, it is relevant at this point to recognize how literature in Spanish has lost the mandatory bond between writing and territories. As a result, the study of Borinsky's work provides a better knowledge of those gaps and at the same time traces how to bridge the experience of reading Latin American Literature from an inside/outside perspective. Finally, there are two less analyzed texts *La ventrilocua y otras canciones* (1975) and *Mujeres timidas y la venus de China* (1987) and a great number of academic articles in Spanish and English that reveal the literary passions of Alicia Borinsky such as Jorge Luis Borges and Alejandra Pizarnik among others. Alicia Borinsky received the Latino Literature Award for Fiction in 1996 and the John Simon Guggenheim Fellowship. She is currently professor of Latin American and Comparative Literature at Boston University. She also has held visiting professorships at Harvard University and Washington University, St. Louis, and received the Boston University Metcalf Award for Excellence in Teaching in 1985. Her literary work has been translated by Cola Franzen.

Ángela María González Echeverry

Selected Works

Mina cruel. Buenos Aires: Corregidor, 1989.
Timorous Women. Peterborough: Paul Green Press, 1992.
Mean Woman. Lincoln, NB: University of Nebraska Press, 1993.
Theoretical Fables: The Pedagogical Dream in Latin-American Fiction. Pittsburgh, PA: University of Pennsylvania Press, 1993.
La pareja desmontable. Buenos Aires: Corregidor, 1994.
Sueños del seductor abandonado. Buenos Aires: Corregidor, 1995.
Madres Alquiladas. Buenos Aires: Corregidor, 1996.
Cine Continuado. Buenos Aires: Corregidor, 1997.
Dreams of the Abandoned Seducer. Lincoln, NB: The University of Nebraska Press, 1998. Translated into English in collaboration with Cola Franzen.
Golpesbajos. Buenos Aires: Corregidor, 1999.

References and Further Reading

Borinsky, Alicia. "Palabras, cosas, desastres: José Donoso y sus juegos con la materialidad". *Anthropos* 184–5 (1999) 87–91.

——. "In Barbieland: The Triumph of Wardrobes". *Hopscotch: A Cultural Review* 2(2) (2000): 60–3.

——. *All Night Movie*. Chicago, IL: Northwestern University Press, 2002.

Granados, Pedro. "La poesía de Alicia Borinsky: Algunas aproximaciones". *Revista de Literatura Hispánica (Inti)* 49–50 (1999): 225–30.

Niebylski, Dianna. "Spectacle and Nomadic Bodies in Alicia Borinsky's *Mina cruel* and *Cine continuado*". *Letras Femeninas* 27(2) (2001): 54–67.

Tompkins, Cynthia M. "Re/presentación/es: Entrevista con Alicia Borinsky". *Confluencia* 17(1) (2001): 112–16.

BORMANN, MARIA BENEDITA (DÉLIA)

Maria Benedita Câmara Bormann (1853–95) was born in Rio Grande do Sul to Patrício da Fontoura Lima and Luísa Bormann de Lima. In 1863, the Lima family and daughters Maria Benedita and Julieta moved to Rio de Janeiro, capital of the Second Brazilian Empire (1840–89). Her family lived in comfortable middle-class style, and as a mid-level civil servant, Patrício Lima managed to raise his children according to standards somewhat beyond the family's means providing both daughters with an education fit for refined young ladies.

At the age of 19, Maria Benedita Bormann married her maternal uncle José Bernardino Bormann (1844–1919) whose military prowess in the Paraguay War (1864–70) brought him to the rank of Marshall and the post of War Secretary (1910–14). Little is known about her life but contemporaries allude to some unhappiness, possibly caused by her husband's long periods of absence. Intellectual work must have been Bormann's strategy to overcome marital disappointment. Very tellingly in this connection, she published her first novel between the time her husband was coming back from military training in Europe and preparing to leave again for his greatest undertaking: to resolve a frontier issue between Brazil and Argentina. Away between 1882 and 1899, as the director of Chapecó colony in Southern Brazil, Marshall Bormann survived his wife. The couple did not have any children, but descendants of his second marriage with Ernestina Bormann live in Paraná state today.

Novelist and Press Contributor

Maria Benedita Bormann spoke English and French and demonstrates considerable erudition in her books. Writer Inês Sabino mentions her sophistication and poise, as a woman who frequented the cultured salons of her time and occasionally accompanied herself on the piano with a pleasant mezzo-soprano voice. Bormann drew and wrote from an early age but destroyed the materials she did not want to be published. Aged 28, active during the Second Wave of Brazilian Feminism (1870–1920), she joined efforts with the flourishing feminist media making her presence known in the press by publishing *Magdalena* in *O Sorriso* (1881).

Her oeuvre includes *feuilletons*, short stories and essays in prestigious periodicals, such as *Gazeta da Tarde*, *Gazeta de Notícias*, *O Paiz*, and has been reedited in the last decades but a number of pieces are still unknown. Among those recovered by researchers the most substantial portion comprises narratives in which a distinct project may be discerned. The following assessment takes into consideration her five novels *Magdalena* (1881), *Uma Victima* (1883), *Duas Irmãs* (1884), *Lésbia* (1890) and *Celeste* (1894).

Thematics and Point of View

An aura of mystery surrounds Bormann and her work that led some commentators to attribute to her features that belong to her fictional characters, or conversely, to interpret her writing as purely autobiographical. But the author herself warns against such interpretations and rejects the facile reduction of fiction in favor of real life. Her use of *Délia* as a pen name suggests more properly that interlacing autobiographical details, artistic self-identity and imaginative narrative must be seen as an expression of the author's outlook. Bormann was a meticulous writer who deliberately sustained ambiguity so as to further dissolve the truth/art opposition thus exploring the fictional dimension of veracity. More exactly, Bormann was concerned with crafting her image as a woman-writer among men, who ruled the literary field. Oddly enough, she showed a sensibility similar to the *fin-de-siècle* European aesthetes and was as aware as they were about the persuasive power of appearance, and so controlled the degree of exposure of her biography to the public.

At the risk of simplifying the singularity of her individual works, one may delineate two cycles in Bormann's novelistic, a family one (*Magdalena*, *Uma Víctima*, *Duas Irmãs*) and an intellectual cycle (*Lésbia*, *Celeste*), with one permeating the other. Bormann's novels often represent a progressive narrative of subjective elucidation from youth to adulthood; from idealism and illusion to knowledge and some times disenchantment. Her work thus shares aspects of the novel of education or *Bildungsroman*.

In its conservative form, such a novel generally presents the coming of age of a male protagonist who leaves his family behind to become an integrated member of a society, which is seen as a positive and productive environment. A more elaborated illustration of this genre will intensify the clash between self-volitions and the barriers imposed by social rules. Bormann's novels present this complication which is aggravated by the fact that the desires and acts of her protagonists are bound to be contradicted and not nurtured by her surroundings. In a society dominated by men's values, which in turn structure the limiting realm of the family, women are assigned the sole functions of mothers and daughters. They are not supposed to grow by means of a personal quest in the world.

As a general rule, Bormann's protagonists are women of petit-bourgeois lifestyle, always of rare beauty and intelligence, frequently voracious and shrewd readers. These characters consistently have an intense relationship with their parents, either challenging or cherishing them. In *Magdalena*, *Uma Víctima*, *Duas Irmãs*, one parent will be exposed as a fraud. In *Celeste*, both will eventually be condemned. Bad parents are shown as ill principled and as failing in their parental role to encourage their children toward an expression of their own talent. The protagonist always connects with the good parent but the existence of a clash at home is linked to the daughter's inability to overcome difficulties. In contrast, *Lésbia* (1890) shows that unconditional parental support for the protagonist's artistic inclination results in the development of a contented person who becomes a successful writer. Further, *Duas Irmãs*, *Lésbia* and *Celeste* insinuate a new social order that must take into consideration more than women's intellectual aspiration, for such an ambition in these novels is linked to the protagonist's sensual desires. Astonishingly then, Bormann's discussion addresses the issue of the mind–body divide and its historical usefulness for keeping woman in bondage as child-bearing and child-rearing, a concern that has led to an enduring debate in feminist theory.

Contemporary Assessment

Perhaps because the sexual desire of some of her protagonists is not presented as an aberration, as with characters in novels written by male authors of that period, but is integrated into the life of an otherwise genteel youngster, two critics bluntly expressed their discontent with Bormann's work. Inês Sabino, for instance, alludes to her as a female version of Emile Zola. Also, Araripe Júnior censored the protagonist of her novel *Celeste* as a madwoman suffering from erotomania. Esteemed by a few and for the most part not fully understood, her work was ignored until the 1980s, when Women's Studies revisionist projects set out to recover women's intellectual works. Thus only the observation afforded by a retrospective standpoint will accurately assess such a woman writer's condition and properly demarcate her mode of artistic production.

From a twenty-first-century vantage point, Bormann is revealed as an author with a keen insight into female subject formation vis-à-vis the family. She parts company with writers such as José de Alencar and Machado de Assis, who present the middle-class family as a safe haven to which a select few of the disadvantaged may aspire. In their portrayals of upper mobility, marriage is the key for the advancement of the few favored ones. A secure place in polite society will distinguish these uncommonly beautiful or clever, but not necessarily moral, individuals and so rescue them from a life of grinding poverty perceived as fit only to the lower classes of Brazilian slavery society.

Bormann's narratives also go beyond the American and European *domestic fiction* which usually promotes women's taming of their own passions in order to achieve a most correct, happy-ending marriage. Her narratives also avoid Emma Bovary-like escapism. Bormann exposes the domestic realm as an arrangement that primarily sustains men's privileges. Breaking with this paralyzing ideology, her characters are thinking women in trouble with the marriage market and the family as the founding structure of patriarchy. By trying to be freed from family and marriage, through premature sex relations or an overtly libertine life, her characters collapse. But there remains the indication of a desire to become the cultured individual who can play a role in the continuous reshaping of society.

Compared to the European literary fashions reflected by most Brazilian writers of the period, Bormann's work is still not easy to classify. Bormann points toward the position of a well-read woman of intellectual ambition who perceived her constraints both as someone from a society on the periphery of cultivated Europe, and also as a woman in relation to patriarchy. Bormann responded to the limitations of her cultural context with unconventional ideas that she, like all other Brazilian writers, acquired from European literature and philosophy. Only the understanding of the fact that she responded to both the colonial and the patriarchal horizons of *fin de siècle* Brazil will justify her ideological choices which in turn may help enhance evaluations of her work. Bormann's originality thus rests on her narrative allegories of women's passage from domesticity on the way to the open field of socio-cultural innovation.

REGINA R. FÉLIX

Selected Works

"Magdalena (*feuilleton*)". Rio de Janeiro: *O Sorriso*, 1881.

"Uma Vítima (*feuilleton*)". Rio de Janeiro: *Gazeta da Tarde*, 1883.

Duas Irmãs. Rio de Janeiro: Tipografia Central, 1884.

Celeste. Ed. Nanci Egert. 2 edn, Rio de Janeiro: Presença, 1988.

Lésbia. Ed. Norma Telles. 2 edn, Florianópolis: Editora Mulheres, 1998.

References and Further Reading

Araripe Júnior, Tristão Alencar. *Obra Crítica*. Rio de Janeiro: Casa de Rui Barbosa/MEC, 1958.

Cesar, Guilhermino. *História da Literatura do Rio Grande do Sul*. Porto Alegre: Editora Globo, 1955.

Duarte, Constância Lima. "Feminismo e Literatura no Brasil". *Revista Estudos Avançados* 17(49) (Sept./Dec. 2003): 151–72.

Félix, Regina. *A modernidade escrita por mulheres* (working title). Monograph accepted for publication. Florianópolis: Editora Mulheres, 2007.

Martins, Ari. *Escritoras do Rio Grande do Sul*. Porto Alegre: Instituto Editorial do Livro, 1978.

Martins, Wilson. *História da inteligência no Brasil*. vol. 3. São Paulo: Cultrix/Edusp, 1977.

Mott, Maria Lúcia de Barros. *Calendário: escritoras brasileiras do passado*. São Paulo: Conselho Estadual da Condição Feminina, 1985.

Sabino, Inês. *Mulheres Ilustres do Brasil*. Fac Simile edn. Florianópolis: Editora Mulheres, 1996.

Telles, Norma. "Maria Benedita Câmara Bormann". In Zahidé Lupinacci Muzart (ed.), *Escritoras Brasileiras do Século XIX*. Florianópolis: Editora Mulheres, 1991.

——. "Caelum ou 'tinctura azul'". Suzana Borneo Funk. *Trocando idéias sobre a mulher e a literatura*. Florianópolis: Edeme, 1994.

——. "Escritoras, escritas, escrituras". In Mary Del Priori (ed.), *História das Mulheres no Brasil*. São Paulo: Contexto, 1997.

——. *Encantações*. São Paulo: Nat Editora, 1998.

Schimid, Rita Terezinha. "Da exclusão, da imitação e da trangressão: o caso do romance Celeste de Maria Benedita Bormann". In Michel Patersen (ed.), *As armas do texto: literatura e a resistência da literatura*. Porto Alegre: Editora Sagra, 1998.

BORRERO, JUANA

Juana Borrero (1878–96) was born in Havana, Cuba. She was a member of a family of renowned Cuban authors and patriots. Her father, Esteban Borrero Echevarría, was a prominent member and intellectual of the revolutionary arena. Juana Borrero herself excelled in poetry and painting and benefited from the *tertulias*, gatherings of prominent writers, revolutionaries and artists that her father hosted at their well-known home of Puentes Grandes. In these *tertulias*, Juana was exposed to the *fin-de-siècle* decadent and *modernista* trends, as well as to the political struggle for independence of Cuba from Spain, all of which informed Juana Borrero's sensibility and writings.

In 1892, Juana Borrero traveled with her father to the United States to study painting. The official reason for this trip disguised a clandestine meeting with the Cuban Revolutionary Committee in New York. Within this context, Juana Borrero had the opportunity to meet the influential poet and revolutionary José Martí, according to accounts by her sister and poet Dulce María Borrero. After a brief return to Cuba, Juana Borrero traveled again to the United States where she visited the World's Columbian Exposition in Chicago, gave readings of her poems, and continued her work as an accomplished painter.

Poet and Patriot

In 1891, Juana Borrero met the influential poet Julián del Casal, with whom she shared the dark and melancholic images that informed the aesthetic sensibilities of the times. Julián del Casal was conveying this forlorn vision in rich verses that would shape the emerging Latin American literary movement called "modernismo". Their friendship produced an exchange of letters and compositions that cemented the spiritually tortured image of Borrero. Her poems expressed this sentiment in works that moved between the aesthetic emphasis of the *modernista* poetics, often with undertones from the Romantic movement, and the need to serve the national cause for independence. Supported by her privileged position, Borrero introduced her literary and political voice within the *modernista* style in a moment of definition of the national identity at its revolutionary stage, something particularly unique for a woman of her time.

In 1893, the year of the abrupt ending of their friendship, Julián del Casal published in the prestigious journal *La Habana Elegante* a poem about Borrero: "Virgen triste" (Sad Virgin). This poem promoted Borrero while reinforced her image of a tormented person. In the final verses, Casal prophesied Borrero's premature demise. In October of the same year, Julián del Casal died, which made Borrero dedicate heartrending poems to her lost friend. Immersed in these feelings of pain and anguish, she took solace in her friendship with the writer Carlos Pío Uhrbach, whom she met in 1895. A passionate romance between Carlos and Juana flowered in their letters.

In January of 1896, because of their revolutionary involvement, the Borrero family was exiled to Key West, Florida. Once in Key West, Juana was diagnosed with typhoid fever, but she continued to write and conduct an intense correspondence with Carlos who remained in Cuba engaged in the war for independence. Juana Borrero died in exile, in March of the same year, at the age of 18.

Works and Critical Reception

Beginning in 1891, Juana Borrero published poems in the most prestigious journals in Havana. Many of these compositions maintained romantic themes and modes, while stressing patriotic messages. The debt to Romanticism is explicit in the title of her only book of poems, *Rimas* (Rhymes) (1895), homonymous of the influential book written by post-romantic Spanish writer Gustavo Adolfo Bécquer and published in 1871. However, Borrero's best work was written in the innovative new style of *modernismo* that Casal promoted. This presented a problem of authority since *modernista* style based much of its aesthetics in the perception of women as ornament and fetish. The same could be said about the representation of the national identity on the female body, its most recurrent metaphor, a representation staged in this time of political conflict. One way that Juana Borrero challenged these perceptions was by implementing a woman's voice within the masculine trends of the period, both in terms of politics and poetics. Tina Escaja argues that, by taking advantage of a historic moment of crisis, Juana Borrero was able to introduce her voice and authority within the literary and political hegemonic discourse that often reduced women to objects/muses or to allegories of the nation. Juana Borrero was able to insert her voice by using strategies such as duplication and self-representation. One example argued by Escaja is Borrero's series of passionate poems dedicated to women artists and friends. The use of conventional images in these poems favors a certain homoerotic reading, while allowing the author to reveal her own female self. In her patriotic poems, Borrero implies a desire to be a participant as a public figure, willing to die for the cause, and not just a mere allegory of the nation, reduced to the private realm and excluded from history.

However, the trends of the period emphasized a different perception of Borrero. The preface of Borrero's *Rimas* was written by Count Kostia, pseudonym of the poet Aniceto Valdivia, who again reinforces the image of the "niña-musa" (child-muse) and "vestal soñadora" (dreamy vestal virgin), an image that Casal had contrived and which Borrero herself fomented perhaps to ensure her legitimacy within the hegemonic discourse. This rhetorical insistence that converted Borrero into a textual object in the new *modernista* style, would prevail after her death. Rubén Darío distinguished Juana from other women whom he considered "inconscientes, uterinas" (mindless, uterine), emphasizing the spiritual and virginal values of Borrero. Some decades later, Angel Augier would coin the popular designation of Borrero as the "adolescente a tormentada" (tormented teenager).

Modern Interpretations

While *Rimas* is Juana Borrero's only book of poems, five other unpublished volumes are reported to have been destroyed after the family went into exile. *Rimas* also includes poems that had appeared in a volume of works written by members of the Borrero's family entitled *Grupo de familia* (Family Group) (1895). In 1966, the government of Cuba published *Epistolario* (Epistolary), a compilation of passionate letters exchanged between Juana Borrero and Carlos Pío Uhrbach that reveal the spirited and independent personality of Juana, a discourse considered subversive for the times (Jiménez 1997). The appearance of *Epistolario*, and subsequent publishing of Borrero's letters, emphasized the critical interest in the biography over Borrero's works of poetry. Ottmar Ette notes the inversion of the models implied by Borrero when she makes Carlos the object of her personal and literary desires, an ideal of masculinity that also connects with the Romantic movement. Life and literature intertwine in what seems a conscious construction of the self in Borrero's letters, which makes *Epistolario*, according to critics like Cintio Vitier, "her major work," "a true confession". Luis A. Jiménez observes in *Epistolario* a literary self-portrait that makes Borrero a complex example of the *Mujer Nueva* (New Woman), a figure antagonist and counter-point of the male figure of the decadent. In this sense, Jiménez places Borrero between the movements of Romanticism and *modernismo*, and also between the generation of Cuban women writers born in the mid-nineteenth century and those born in the twentieth century. Her self-presentation within these parameters of a "New Woman," that is based, according to Jiménez, on Borrero's actual participation in the decadent Cuban school of "Kábala," breaks the myth of the child-poet, a rupture also pointed out by Ileana Rivero. Rex Hauser likewise mentions the duality of Borrero and her contribution to a legend centered on the poetics of disease and despair. Ana Rosa Núñez's study extols the exiled and patriotic Borrero. Fina García Marruz documents the bibliographic and artistic course of the author.

Few critics have delved into Borrero's poetry. Ivan A. Shulman stresses the *modernista* quality of her poetry that makes Borrero a participant of the modern sensibility that is imprinted in the works of recognized Latin American *modernista* authors such as Rubén Darío, Manuel Gutiérrez Nájera and José Asunción Silva. According to Shulman, Borrero's poems insert within the Parnassian sculpting of the poem the need for introspection, the expression of anguish, a tension that informs modernity. Shulman argues that this expression of discomfort moves to the socio-political realm in many of Borrero's poems, a transition that unites the desire for national independence with her own creative and personal freedom. Intimacy, patriotism, independence, and striving for perfection intertwine in Borrero's works, making her a clear example of the modern writer in the new cultural and social fabric of Latin American emerging nations. Other analyses of Borrero's poetry include Gladys Zaldívar's interpretation of Borrero's use of *modernista* themes in symbolic contrasts that reflect the aesthetics of the *art nouveau*. Luis A. Jiménez also refers to the plastic nature of Borrero's poems in her "Siluetas femeninas" (Feminine Silhouettes), a group of eight poems by Borrero dedicated to women of her period. Nonetheless, the remarkable work of Juana Borrero still lacks an in-depth study of her poetry, which would secure a place for this first *modernista* of Latin America in the canon of modern letters.

TINA ESCAJA

Selected Works

Poesías. La Habana: Academia de Ciencias de Cuba/Instituto de Literatura y Lingüística, 1966.

Epistolario. 2 vols. La Habana: Academia de Ciencias de Cuba/Instituto de Literatura y Lingüística, 1966–67.

Poesías y cartas. La Habana: Editorial Arte y Literatura, 1978.

Espíritu de estrellas. Nuevas cartas de amor de Juana Borrero. La Habana: Ed. Academia, 1997.

References and Further Reading

Augier, Angel. *Juana Borrero, la adolescente atormentada*. La Habana: Cuadernos de Historia Habanera, 1938.

Escaja, Tina. "Autoras modernistas y la (re)inscripción del cuerpo nacional". In Daniel Balderston (ed.), *Sexualidad y nación en América Latina*. Pittsburgh, PA: Instituto Internacional de Literatura Iberoamericana, 2000, pp. 61–75.

Ette, Ottmar. "*Gender Trouble*: José Martí y Juana Borrero". In Annette Paatz (ed.), *Texto social: Estudios pragmáticos sobre literatura y cine: Homenaje a Manfred Engelbert*. Berlin: Tranvía-Frey, 2003, pp. 79–96.

García Marruz, Fina. "Introducción." In *Poesías de Juana Borrero*. La Habana: Academia de Ciencias de Cuba / Instituto de Literatura y Lingüística, 1966, pp. 7–56.

Hauser, Rex. "Juana Borrero: The Poetics of Despair". *Letras Femeninas* 13(1–2) (1990): 113–20.

Jiménez, Luis A. "Dibujando el cuerpo ajeno en 'Siluetas femeninas' de Juana Borrero". *Círculo: Revista de Cultura* 26 (1997): 73–79.

——. "Juana Borrero en el autorretrato de la 'Mujer Nueva' fin-de-siglo". In *Estudios en honor de Janet Pérez: El sujeto femenino en escritoras hispánicas*. Potomac, MD: Scripta Humanistica, 1998, pp. 77–89.

Núñez, Ana Rosa. "Juana Borrero: Portrait of a Poetess". *The Carrell Journal of the Friends of the University of Miami Library* 16 (1976): 1–21.

Rivero, Eliana. "Pasión de Juana Borrero y la crítica". *Revista Iberoamericana* 56 (1990): 829–39.

Schulman, Ivan A. "Una voz moderna: La poesía de Juana Borrero". *Torre: Revista de la Universidad de Puerto Rico* 1(1–2) (July–Dec. 1996): 191–203.

Vitier, Cintio. "Prólogo". In *Epistolario*. Vol. I. La Habana: Academia de Ciencias de Cuba / Instituto de Literatura y Lingüística, 1966, pp. 7–31.

Zaldívar, Gladys. "Juana Borrero: Paradigma de la vertiente femenina del modernismo". *Círculo: Revista de Cultura* 26 (1997): 80–6.

BOSCO, MARÍA ANGÉLICA

María Angélica Bosco was born in Buenos Aires, Argentina, in 1909, though for a number of years it was thought she was born in 1917. Although she began writing at a young age and publishing a collection of stories in her twenties, her literary career did not begin in earnest until she became divorced at the end of the 1940s. Her novel, *La muerte baja en el ascensor* (Death Takes the Elevator) was published in 1954 in *Séptimo círculo* (Seventh Circle), a prestigious detective series created by Jorge Luis Borges and Adolfo Bioy Casares. She was awarded the Premio Emecé for this text, making Bosco one of the first and preeminent women writers of detective fiction in Latin America. She also has written essays and other fiction, though these works have not achieved the same recognition as her detective fiction.

La muerte baja en el ascensor

While Argentina has a respected tradition of the *novela negra,* "black novel," or noir tinged detective fiction, María Angélica Bosco stands out as one of the few women writers to make a name for themselves in the genre. *La muerte baja en el ascensor* (Death Takes the Elevator), remains Bosco's best-known work for its tightly interconnected plot. In this text, the residents of a Buenos Aires apartment building become potential suspects in the murder of the mysterious Frida Eidinger, whose poisoned body is discovered in the building's elevator. While the novel has many characteristics of classic detective stories, such as murder, a detective, and a series of clues, the text is most notable for its attention to characters and the relationships between them. The characters are complex and nuanced, each with his or her own secret to be uncovered such as shared desires, control, and deceitfulness. Typical of Argentinean detective novels of the time, the investigators are male, however Bosco's female characters play strong, essential roles in the novel. The male characters, even the detectives to some extent, are portrayed as fallible and human, driven by their desire for love and power.

An interesting facet of *La muerte baja en el ascensor* is that its plot is set in post-war Buenos Aires. Argentina was a popular destination for Spanish and Italian immigrants during the late nineteenth and early twentieth centuries and saw an influx of European immigrants after World War II. The novel reflects the complex dynamics between older-established families and newer immigrants. *La muerte baja en el ascensor* investigates the implication of the link between the immigrants' personal and political histories as they try to establish new identities independent of these histories.

Other Detective Fiction

Bosco published other successful detective novels after *La muerte baja en el ascensor,* such as *La muerte soborna a Pandora* (1956, Death Bribes Pandora) and *En la estela de un secuestro* (1977, In the Wake of a Kidnapping). In 1979, she published *Muerte en la costa del río* (Death on the River Coast). These later books demonstrate the increasing quality and craftsmanship of her work which discusses the relationships between the characters in depth and thoroughly explores the motives of the crime more than her counterparts of the time. Bosco does this to such a degree that the crime becomes almost secondary to its motives and its effects on the characters.

Muerte en la costa del río takes place in the wealthy circle of residents and vacationers in the coastal town of Colonia, Uruguay. In this novel, the investigation and detective almost become lost in the background of the novel as the cast of characters, particularly the women, are written into more prominent roles. Bosco's plot includes wealthy women who feel trapped by their designated place in society and as a result, rebel against motherhood as a way of confronting oppression by the constraints of class and tradition. The pampered existence of these upper-class women masks their boredom and anxiety. The rigid social roles limit the possibilities of individuality for women and their frustration at the lack of creative outlets manifests itself as gossip and petty deception. Bosco's interpretation and expression of the social roles of the women in her texts are intentionally limiting and debilitating. These roles are constructed in such a way that even when female characters who don't fall within traditional roles try to exhibit authority and autonomy, they often fail, drawing attention to the absence of empowerment.

Later Works

Bosco once said that despite her fame as a detective novelist, relatively few of her works fall into that category. As her career has progressed, she has continued to develop characters instead of plot twists, drawing the readers' attention to the complexities and implications of female characters in general. Representative of this trend in her work is the 1996 novel, *Tres historias de mujeres* (Three Stories of Women). The novel is divided into three sections, each set in Colonia, Uruguay. Because Colonia was the only Portuguese settlement on the Rio de la Plata, it is historically a site of colonial battles for control between the Portuguese and Spanish. Bosco uses the historical framework of Colonia and includes it in the story of the three women's narratives. María's story takes places in 1542, Sancha's in 1680, and lastly Bernabela's in 1799. María's story is of a native girl who becomes the lover of a conquistador. This tale parallels the dynamics of Sancha's situation, who is a poor young woman who becomes the mistress of an officer. Bernabela, however, is positioned as an affluent, powerful colonial woman. Despite the differences in their ethnic and socio-economic positions, each woman struggles to find her place in society, and does so through necessity, as the companion of a more powerful man. These women are united in their socially constructed destiny, as the reader sees history repeating itself in a cycle of dependence, rejection, and ultimately strength.

Themes and Critical Reception

Though Bosco is one of the few recognized Latin American women writers of detective fiction, her work has received relatively little critical attention. A handful of articles on Bosco have been published, and she is frequently mentioned in comparison to other writers in the genre, such as Syria Poletti. The critical works on Bosco focus almost exclusively on the feminine nature of her detective fiction, largely ignoring her forays into more traditional or non-detective fiction. Critics name her attention to characters and relationships as "feminine" instead of the "masculine" tendency to concentrate on plot and the actions and reactions of the detectives. Bosco herself has stated that she began writing detective fiction for women readers, who she thought might want an alternative to traditional women's literature as women were often alienated by the works of many male writers.

María Angélica Bosco's work, while easy to classify as detective fiction, also goes beyond that categorization. Her work avoids overt political content in spite of the political unrest that occurred in Argentina during her career. She has continually focused on subtle issues of class and gender with a particular attention to the lives of women who struggle for legitimacy and authority in a limiting society. Her work has grown increasingly more centered on women as her career has progressed. This transition is clear when considering her female characters in *La muerte baja en el ascensor* and the stronger, more proactive women in works like *Muerte en la costa del río* and the exclusively female protagonists of *Tres historias de mujeres*.

Alexandra Fitts

Selected Works

La muerte baja en el ascensor. Buenos Aires: Emecé, 1954.
La muerte soborna a Pandora. Buenos Aires: Conjunta, 1956.
En la estela de un secuestro. Buenos Aires: Emecé, 1977.
Muerte en la costa del río. Buenos Aires: Emecé, 1979.
La muerte vino de afuera. Buenos Aires: Editorial Belgrano, 1982.
Las burlas del porvenir. Buenos Aires: Atlántida, 1993.
Tres historias de mujeres. Buenos Aires: Vinciguerra, 1996.

References and Further Reading

Azzario, Esther A. "María Angélica Bosco and Beatriz Guido: An Approach to Two Argentinian Novelists between 1960 and 1970". In Yvette E. Miller and Charles M. Tatum (eds), *Latin American Women Writers: Yesterday and Today.* Pittsburgh, PA: Latin American Literary Review, 1977, pp. 59–67.

Martella, Gianna M. "Pioneers: Spanish American Women Writers of Detective Fiction". *Letras Femeninas* 28(1) (June 2002): 31–44.

Schiminovich, Flora. "María Angélica Bosco". In Darrell B. Lockhart (ed.), *Latin American Mystery Writers: An A–to–Z Guide.* Westport, CT: Greenwood Press, 2004, pp. 44–7.

——. "Two Argentine Female Writers Perfect the Art of Detection: María Angélica Bosco and Syria Poletti". *Review: Latin American Literature and Arts* 42 (June 1990): 16–20.

Simpson, Amelia. *Detective Fiction from Latin America.* Cranbury, NJ: Associated UP, 1990.

BOULLOSA, CARMEN

A Public Intellectual Life

Carmen Boullosa (b. 1954) is one of the most important living Mexican authors, dedicating her craft to exploring gender and subjectivity, sociocultural criticism and historiography in her poetry, theater, narrative and essays. She is also a collaborator in art books. Her work has inspired literary conferences, dozens of doctoral dissertations and praise from literary critics and fans. Roselyn Costantino and Susan Wehling, for example, comment on the hybrid, feminine space and negotiation of female identities in Boullosa's *Teatro herético* (1987). Examining Boullosa's early novels, *Mejor desaparece* (1987) and *Antes* (1989), published criticism has recognized the trope of the absent mother, and various theorists have focused on *Mejor desaparece*'s chaotic, apparently non-linear structure and the importance of found documents in the novel *Papeles irresponsables* (1989). Considering Boullosa's fiction that focuses on Mexican history and identity, Carrie Chorba identifies the metafictive and historiographic technique and thematic of the novel *Duerme* (1994), a tale set in Mexico's colonial era that ends with the heroic cross-dressed protagonist sleeping and the narrator doomed to die; the text suggests that the reader could be responsible for creating the next strand of narrative.

Carmen Boullosa was born into an era of rapid modernization and shifting values in Mexico. Born in 1954 in Mexico City, Boullosa and her sisters received a Catholic education in an all-girls school; Boullosa's parents worked as missionaries for a year with the conservative Opus Dei. The death of Boullosa's mother when she was a child was an especially traumatic event, after which followed her father's remarriage and a resulting troubled home life. These events were probable influences for the dysfunctional household of the 1987 novel *Mejor desaparece* and the ghost-like girl narrator whose mother has died in *Antes* (1989).

According to a remark made by Boullosa in an address at the University of Minnesota in 2006, her father's remarriage caused the young Carmen to turn her creative energy to rediscovering the Mexico City that had been transformed, even as she reached puberty in a household that seemed inhospitable. By the time she was a teenager, Boullosa knew she wanted to be a writer; she began publishing poetry in the late 1970s (*El hilo olvida*, 1979; *Ingobernable*, 1979; *Lealtad*, 1981; *Abierta*, 1983) and in the mid-1980s started producing her own plays at the Mexico City theater/bar El Cuervo, which she owned with then-husband Alejandro Aura. She and Aura had two children, María Aura and Juan Aura. In 1989, Boullosa was awarded the prestigious Premio Villaurrutia in Mexico; she has been a Guggenheim Fellow, has received rave reviews from fellow authors and critics, and her work has been translated into many languages. While Boullosa's early work in theater and narrative focuses on young women and subjectivity, her mid-1990s novels turn to historiographic topics, especially examining Mexican colonialism and post-colonialism in *Llanto: novelas imposibles* (1992), *Duerme* (1994), and *Cielos de la Tierra* (1997).

In addition to publishing novels centering on magic, storytelling, female creativity ("Isabel" 1992; *La milagrosa*, 1993 and *Treinta años,* 1999), and historical topics such as seventeenth-century Caribbean pirates (*Son vacas, somos puercos,* 1991) and the Egyptian Cleopatra (*De un salto descabalga la reina*, 2002), Boullosa is a prolific poet. She has published more than a dozen books of poetry, among them *La salvaja* (1988), *Sangre* (1992), *Envenenada: antología personal*, (1993), and *La delirios* (1998). Boullosa has given classes and lectures at numerous universities around the world, and in 2001 she was named a fellow of the New York City Center for Scholars and Writers. Boullosa was in New York during the attacks to the World Trade Center on September 11, 2001, and the event caused her to investigate the topic of religious wars. Her research, combined with her love of Cervantes, led her to flesh out a minor character from the *Quijote*, set against the background of a Moorish/Christian Spain in her novel *La otra mano de Lepanto* (2005), which was named Best Novel Published in Mexico in 2005 by the publication *Reforma* critic Sergio González Rodríguez. Boullosa's recent book of poems *Salto de mantarraya* (Illustr. Philip Hughes) was designated the Best Book of Poems published in Mexico in 2004 by *Reforma*. Since 2001, Boullosa has lived in New York City, where she has been Visiting Professor and Distinguished Lecturer at NYU, Columbia University, and CUNY; she also has befriended numerous artists and writers, including Jean Franco and the Pulitzer Prize-winning author Mike Wallace, whom she later married. With Salman Rushdie, Boullosa co-founded the Mexico City House for Persecuted Writers; she and her colleagues are looking into a similar venture under the CUNY auspices. Boullosa continues to lecture in the United States, Mexico and abroad, and she writes articles and reviews for publications such as the *New York Times*. Her *La novela perfecta* was published in 2006.

Female Subjectivity, Magic and Desire

Carmen Boullosa's early works focusing on girls and women tell of females learning to signify through the body, dreams, the elements, and language. Through storytelling and the imagination, they express lack, absence, repression and sensuality, effecting what could be called a feminist critique of Catholic morality, patriarchy, and the nuclear family in Mexico. The ambivalence that repressive socializing institutions create in the would-be subject causes Boullosa's characters to elaborate representational strategies that do not simplify the often conflicting needs that exist between the intellect and the need to be socially recognized. The three plays of Carmen Boullosa's *Teatro herético,* for example, combine a satirical attitude with serious social issues in Mexico, humorously presenting Boullosa's own critique of Catholicism's effects on girls and women. In *Aura y las once mil vírgenes*, Catholicism and western capitalism are shown to be complementary discourses that demand unreasonable perfection, purity, and correctable sins or aesthetic flaws in women. *Cocinar hombres* shows two girls awakening to find that they have aged from 12 or 13 to 23 years old in the space of one evening, as a result of a special witches' ceremony. The ensuing dialogue between characters Ufe and Wine illustrates their negotiation of their fears about having women's bodies, about sexism, patriarchy, marriage, and motherhood. Together they create or "cook up" various incarnations of the ideal mate, and end by incarnating their own creative sisterhood and signifying space. The third play of *Teatro herético*, *Propusieron a María* consists of the "found" tape recording of the Virgin Mary discussing the banality of married life on the eve of the Assumption.

Several novels, poetry, and a novella continue to forge new womanly identities and express the problems of repressed desire, emotion, and disappearing maternal ties to the past and to female power. The disjointed narrative fragments and multiple speaking voices of *Mejor desaparece* portray the Ciarrosa sisters' chaotic home life disrupted by the presence of a mysterious male figure who disciplines them. A ghostly mother figure can hear the action from a central room but cannot intervene; eventually, the sisters – all of whom are named after flowers – disappear from the dinner table forever and the father figure shrinks into the grass one evening as the house refuses him. The 1989 novel *Antes* continues *Mejor desaparece's* dreadful climate, showing a young girl who claims to be a ghost narrate what she calls the approaching sounds that come for her – and which turn out to be puberty and menstruation, events that are surrounded by taboo and embarrassment. Concomitant with her approaching maturity, the narrator awakens to the power of telling stories. Boullosa's later novel *Treinta años* (1999) links rural political violence, sexuality, religion, and the conflicts of an all-female household.

While two of the aforementioned novels link signifying to the body's creativity, Boullosa's poetic collection *Sangre* (1992) and the novella "Isabel" (1993) plumb European folk tales and myth for monstrous female images and fairy tale maidens. *Sangre* weaves the voices of fairy tale maidens such as the Perfect Bride and Snow White with the demonized woman werewolf and the Evil Queen; each expresses romantic fantasy, desire and disillusionment. In "Isabel," the title character finds that she has devoured the man that she adores who repudiated her; in turn she becomes a lustful female vampire who carries a horrible plague to various urban areas, ending in New York City.

Historiography and the Novel

Boullosa's trilogy of historiographic novels: *Llanto: novelas imposibles* (1992), *Duerme* (1994) and *Cielos de la Tierra* (1997) re-read Mexican identity through a postcolonial optic; each demands reader participation in the interpretation of their significance for global survival in an age of ongoing conquests, territorialism, and nuclear armament. In *Llanto*, a revived Aztec emperor Moctezuma II tours the modern-day Mexican capital and is reduced to dust when the three women escorting him translate his presence into an anthropological exercise and re-enactment of cultural and ethnic *mestizaje,* or blood-mixing. Moctezuma becomes an ethnographic and sexual fantasy to serve the present-day's dearth of historical responsibility to its many indigenous victims when his language and his adornments are stripped from him in order to be studied as national heritage – and when one of the women has sex with the emperor. *Duerme* relates the colonial adventure of a cross-dressed daughter of a French prostitute who escapes death in the gallows in Mexico City and then becomes immortal via an infusion of water from Lake Texcoco in a wound to her chest. Doomed to fall asleep if she strays from the Aztec/colonial capital of Tenochtitlán/Mexico City, the protagonist, Claire, plans indigenous uprisings and ends up asleep in the forest outside of Potosí, awaiting a future awakening.

In the philosophical and metaphysical novel *Cielos de la Tierra*, narrators representing the Mexican colony, contemporary modern era, and the apocalyptic future share space in the novel's pages and are able to read and react to each previous authors' texts. When the present-day narrator is unable to sufficiently insert her own tale into the novel's textuality, the future narrator's intrepid efforts to interpret twentieth-century Mexico lead the reader to question whether she could have helped record a rapidly changing nation in her own time, thereby re-interpreting what Mexicanness means in the present era.

Cielos de la Tierra proves that, in the wake of successively more grave human catastrophes, palimpsestic layers of textual interpretation and historical archeology are required in order to save memory, the Earth, and humanity itself.

JULI A. KROLL

Selected Works

El hilo olvida. México: La Máquina de Escribir, 1979.
Teatro herético. Puebla, México: Universidad Autónoma de Puebla, 1987.
Mejor desaparece. México: Océano, 1987.
La salvaja. México: Taller Martín Pescador, 1988.
Papeles irresponsables. México: Juan Pablos, 1989.
Antes. México: Vuelta, 1989.
Son vacas, somos puercos. México: Era, 1991.
Llanto: novelas imposibles. México: Era, 1992.
Sangre. México: Universidad Autónoma Metropolitana, 1992.
Envenenada: antología personal. Caracas: Fondo Editorial Pequeña Venecia, 1993.
La milagrosa. México: Era, 1993.
Duerme. México: Alfaguara, 1994.
Cielos de la Tierra. México: Alfaguara, 1997.
La delirios. México: Fondo de Cultura Económica, 1998.
Treinta años. México: Alfaguara, 1999.
"Isabel". In *Prosa rota*. México: Plaza & Janés, 2000. Orig. published 1993.
De un salto descabalga la reina. Madrid: Debate, 2002.
Salto de mantarraya. Illus. Philip Hughes. Trans. Psiche Hughes. London: The Old School Press, 2004.
La otra mano de Lepanto. México: Fondo de Cultura Económica, 2005.
La novela perfecta. México: Alfaguara, 2006.

References and Further Reading

"About the Author". *Carmen Boullosa*. 2005. www.carmenboullosa.-net/about/index.html. 26 July 2006.
Boullosa, Carmen. Address. University of Minnesota Graduate Symposium in Romance Studies. University of Minnesota, Minneapolis, MN. 25 March 2006.
Chorba, Carrie. "The Actualization of a Distant Past: Carmen Boullosa's Historiographic Metafiction". *INTI: Revista de literatura hispánica* 42 (Autumn 1995): 301–14.
Costantino, Roselyn. "Carmen Boullosa's Obligingly Heretic Art: New Challenges for Criticism". In Catherine Larson and Margarita Vargas (eds), *Latin American Women Dramatists: Theater, Texts, and Theories*. Bloomington, IN: Indiana University Press, 1998.
Dröscher, Barbara and Rincón, Carlos (eds) *Acercamientos a Carmen Boullosa: Actas del Simposio "Conjugarse en infinitivo – la escritora Carmen Boullosa"*. Berlin: Walter Frey, 1999.
Kroll, Juli. "(Re)Opening the Veins of the Historiographic Visionary: Clothing, Mapping and Tonguing Subjectivities in Carmen Boullosa's *Duerme*". *Hispanófila* 141 (2004): 105–27.
Machoud Nivón, Corinne. "Transgresión del espejo: traducciones, figuraciones, y migraciones en *Llanto: Novelas imposibles* de Carmen Boullosa". In Carlos Véjar Pérez-Rubio (ed.), *La Otredad: Los discursos de la cultura hoy: 1995*. México: Universidad Autónoma Metropolitana-A, 1997, pp. 35–43.
Pirott-Quintero, Laura. "El cuerpo en la narrativa de Carmen Boullosa". *INTI: Revista de literatura hispánica* 45 (Spring 1997): 268–75.
Wehling, Susan. "Cocinar hombres: Radical Feminist Discourse". *Gestos* 16 (Nov. 1993): 51–62.

BRUNET, MARTA

One of Chile's most acclaimed novelists and short story writers of the twentieth century, Marta Brunet was born in Chillán, Chile, on August 9, 1897, and died in Montevideo, Uruguay on August 9, 1967. She was the only child of Ambrosio Brunet and his Spanish wife, María Presentación Cáraves de Cossío. Brunet's childhood was spent in the small town of Victoria, where she studied at home with various tutors. She read every book within reach, and she began to write at an early age. She was fascinated by the lives of the country people around her, and she wrote of their daily struggles, legends, beliefs, speech patterns, and customs. When Brunet was 14, the family traveled in Europe and South America for three years and she was introduced to many European writers. Back in Chile, she became part of an active literary group and began to publish poems and stories. Her first novel, *Montaña adentro* (Back Country) was published in 1923 and was greeted enthusiastically by critics. In 1925, she moved to Santiago, worked as a journalist, and published literary notes and short stories in a variety of periodicals. Her first collection of short stories, *Don Florisondo*, appeared in 1926, as well as her second novel, *Bestia dañina* (Treacherous Beast). A third novel with rural characters and setting, *María Rosa, Flor del Quillén* (María Rosa, Flower of Quillén) appeared in 1927. In 1929, Brunet won an important literary prize, and published a fourth rural novel, *Bienvenido* (Welcome). Her second short story collection, *Reloj de sol* (Sundial) was published in 1930. Winner of the prestigious Sociedad de Escritores de Chile best novel prize in 1933, Brunet turned next to stories for children. She published *Cuentos para Mari-Sol* (Stories for Mari-Sol) in 1934, and she was the editor of the Santiago magazine *Familia* until 1939, when the government appointed her to a consular position in Buenos Aires. She was welcomed into Buenos Aires literary circles and began to publish in prominent periodicals like *La Nación* and *Sur*. A new prize-winning short story collection, *Aguas abajo* (Downstream), appeared in 1943, and two important novels were published in 1946: *Humo hacia el sur* (Smoke on the Southern Horizon) and *La mampara* (The Outer Door). While in charge of cultural affairs and cultural relations at the Chilean Embassy in Buenos Aires, Brunet worked to expand Argentine awareness of Chilean culture until she was recalled in 1952. A collection of short stories, *Raíz del sueño* (Root of the Dream) was published in 1949 and her most popular novel, *María Nadie* (María Nobody) in 1957. She lectured extensively, published a volume of stories in verse for children, *Aleluyas para los más chiquitos* (Hallelujahs for the Smallest Ones), in 1960 and won the major Chilean literary prize, the Premio Nacional de Literatura in 1961. In 1962, Brunet's last novel, *Amasijo* (Lump of Dough) was published. That same year she was designated cultural attaché of the Chilean Embassy first in Río de Janeiro and then in Montevideo. Her *Obras completas* (Complete Works), including many previously unpublished texts, appeared in 1963 with a prologue by her close friend and mentor, Hernán Díaz Arrieta. She was in the middle of giving a lecture at the Uruguayan Academy of Letters in Montevideo when she died suddenly of a cerebral hemorrhage on August 9, 1967, at the age of 70.

Marta Brunet's eight novels and over sixty short stories were controversial during her lifetime, and remain so. Among other more conventional topics, she wrote about poverty, injustice, squalor, immoral behavior, and homosexuality, and many of her readers were shocked. She has never fitted into any of the usual categories of literary grouping, but she is a major figure in twentieth-century Chilean fiction, and her books continue to be published in new editions.

In all her fiction, Brunet analyzes the components of individual human identity and the extent to which people manage to find fulfillment in the circumstances of their lives. She is fascinated, too, with how whole communities function: rural ranch and village inhabitants in the early novels, and larger towns and cities in her later books. She is especially interested in the significance of gender, race and social class in individuals' life trajectories. Brunet's first three novels (*Montaña adentro, Bestia dañina* and *María Rosa, Flor del Quillén*) and many of her early stories (1923–27) are set in the primitive countryside of southern Chile where Brunet spent her childhood. Local settings are described in detail: forests, mountainous terrain, simple farmhouses and outbuildings, pastures and fields. The inhabitants of this untamed land are country people, struggling to survive economic hardships, extremes of climate, and their own fatalistic passions, sensuality and pride. In *Montaña adentro*, a young woman who is a ranch cook, pregnant by a man who left her, falls in love only to have her new lover killed by the one who abandoned her. *Bestia dañina* focuses on the young women who suffer when their widower father marries a woman he eventually kills for her infidelity, and the protagonist of *María Rosa, Flor del Quillén*, lonely in her marriage to an older man, has only her pride to sustain her.

Within a few years of Brunet's move from southern Chile to Santiago, her narratives (1929–43) reflect a greater interest in educated, articulate protagonists although rural settings still affect and limit individual choices and opportunities. The central characters in *Bienvenido* and many of the stories of *Reloj de sol* are sophisticated urban people relocated to the southern countryside, where they feel lonely and even alienated. *Aguas abajo* is a trilogy of powerful tales of rural survival: two stories of mothers and daughters who confront bitter realities, and "Soledad de la sangre" (Solitude of Blood), Brunet's most anthologized and translated story, which depicts the loneliness of an educated, sensitive woman isolated on a ranch in a loveless marriage.

In her later fiction (1946–63), urban settings play an important role: claustrophobic, isolated small towns in *Humo hacia el sur* and *María Nadie* and disorienting big cities in *María Nadie, La mampara, Amasijo* and many stories. The emphasis of her later fiction (with the exception of her stories for children) is a gradual psychological unfolding of what motivates the central characters, what paralyzes them, and what enables them to function in their families, jobs and towns. Many of the main characters of these later books are children and women. The protagonist of Brunet's last novel, *Amasijo*, is a man, but he is so warped by his experiences with strong women (his mother, his housekeeper, his only friend) that he is dysfunctional, as are many male characters in Brunet's novels and stories. *Humo hacia el sur*, Brunet's most ambitious novel and the one most highly praised by critics, describes the lives of women who live in a lumbermill town in 1905, a boom town while it is the southernmost stop on a new railroad line. The women are strong and interesting characters: among them are energetic, aggressive Batilde, who has built up the town; María Soledad, who seeks refuge in being a traditional wife; and her daughter Solita who sees through all the hypocrisies and shams. Brunet is fascinated by the ways personality and behavior are molded by social influences. The differences between "good women" and "bad women" and the social dynamics of these perceptions interest her in each of her books.

La mampara also depicts several contrasting women, examining closely how they are shaped and changed by their circumstances and by social pressures. As they confront economic desperation, the lives of two sisters and their mother are recounted from within the consciousness of each woman. Each must live with the painful disparities of how society views them, how they define themselves, and how they would like to have others regard them. The stories of *Raíz del sueño* also describe women in anguish and solitude, who become increasingly isolated and alienated from the families and towns that suffocate them. *María Nadie*, like *Humo hacia el sur*, dissects the social organization and dynamics of a small town in the south. María López, arriving in town as the operator of the new phone sytem, is viewed first through various perspectives of the town, and then through her own consciousness. By the end she feels like "María Nobody," trapped within her emotions, isolated from the community. María López and Julián García, of *Amasijo*, Brunet's last novel and the one that stirred up the greatest outrage from critics (because of its depiction of homosexuality) both suffer from social ostracism and personal desperation, and the two books analyze the various social and psychological causes of these.

Children are portrayed in Brunet's writings with extraordinary skill; they figure as protagonists in *Bestia dañina, Humo hacia el sur, María Nadie* and in many of the best stories of *Reloj de sol* and *Raíz del sueño. Solita Sola* includes a set of stories about the child of *Humo hacia el sur*, the little girl Brunet referred to as her favorite fictional character of all those she created. Brunet's fiction, poetry and plays for and about children are very different from her texts meant for adult readers. *Cuentos para Mari-Sol, Aleluyas para los más chiquitos* and *Las historias de Mamá Tolita* (Mama Tolita's stories) are collections written for children. They are magical, lyrical tales of fantasy worlds filled with personified animals and Chilean folklore, good humor and joy.

Although Brunet won major literary prizes and her books circulated widely, her novels and stories have always seemed out of synchrony with critical fashions. Her first books' strong language and depictions of violence, sexuality, superstition and crude behavior were felt by early critics to be unladylike and a threat to civilized values. Her refusal to idealize rural situations and characters was often viewed as distasteful and even pornographic. Later she and many other writers of the early twentieth century were swept aside by the popularity of Boom fiction and magical realism in the late 1960s and 1970s, just when Brunet's feminism and directness might have seemed acceptable. Occasional critics, such as Kemy Oyarzun, have reevaluated Brunet's work in recent years, but many of her books have slipped out of print and out of critical awareness.

MARY G. BERG

Selected Works

Montaña adentro. Santiago de Chile: Nascimento, 1923. Other editions: Santiago: Nascimento, 1933; Buenos Aires: Losada, 1953, prol. Guillermo de Torre; Buenos Aires: Losada, 1965; Santiago: Editorial Andrés Bello, 1978, prol. Hugo Montes Brunet; Santiago de Chile: Editorial Universitaria, 1997, prol. Kemy Oyarzun.

Bestia dañina. Santiago de Chile: Nascimento, 1926. Other editions: Buenos Aires: Losada, 1953, prol. Guillermo de Torre; 1965, Buenos Aires: Losada.

"Don Florisondo". Santiago de Chile: *Lectura Selecta* #15, 1926. Included in *Reloj de sol*. Santiago de Chile: Nascimento, 1929. "Don Florisondo" and "Doña Santitos" appear in many anthologíes.

María Rosa, Flor del Quillén. *Atenea* 2 (1927): 119–43 and 3 (1927): 217–40. Other editions: Santiago de Chile: La Novela Nueva, Vol. 4, Dec. 1929; Santiago de Chile: Nascimento, 1929; Buenos Aires: Losada, 1953, prol. Guillermo de Torre; Buenos Aires: Losada, 1965.

Bienvenido. Santiago de Chile: Nascimento, 1929.

Reloj de sol. Santiago de Chile: Nascimento, 1930.

"Americanismo también es obra femenina". *Repertorio Americano* 36 (1939): 279–85.

Cuentos para Mari-Sol. Santiago de Chile: Zig-Zag, 1941.

Aguas abajo. Santiago de Chile: Cruz del Sur, 1943. Other editions: Santiago de Chile: Editorial Cuarto Propio, 1997, prol. Kemy Oyarzun.

Humo hacia el sur. Buenos Aires: Losada, 1946. Other editions: Buenos Aires: Losada, 1967.

La mampara. Buenos Aires: Emecé, 1946. Other editions: Santiago de Chile: Editorial Universitaria, 1987, prol. Hugo Montes Brunet.

Raíz del sueño. Santiago: Zig-Zag, 1949.

María Nadie. Santiago: Zig-Zag, 1957. Other editions (all Santiago de Chile: Zig-Zag): 1961; 1962; 1962; 1965.

"El mundo mágico del niño". *Atenea* 130–2 (1958): 265–76.

Aleluyas para los más chiquitos. Santiago: Editorial Universitaria, 1960.

Antología de cuentos. Santiago de Chile: Zig-Zag, 1962, prol. and bio-bibliography by Nicómedes Guzmán.

Amasijo. Santiago de Chile: Zig-Zag, 1962.

Obras completas de Marta Brunet. Santiago de Chile: Zig-Zag, 1963, prol. and bio-bibliography by Alone (Hernán Díaz Arrieta). Includes all the novels and stories indicated here, and additional texts, including *Solita Sola* and *Las historias de Mama Tolita*.

Soledad de la sangre. Montevideo: Editorial Arca, 1967. Prologue by Angel Rama.

References and Further Reading

Balart, Carmen. *Marta Brunet C.: Narrativa chilena femenina*. Santiago de Chile: Santillana, 1999.

Berg, Mary G. "The Short Stories of Marta Brunet". *Monographic Review/Revista Monográfica* 4 (1988): 195–206.

——. "Marta Brunet (1897–1967) Chile". In Diane E. Marting (ed.), *Spanish American Women Writers: A Bio-Bibliographical Source Book*. Westport, CT: Greenwood Press, 1990, pp. 53–63. Updated in *Escritoras de Hispanoamérica*, ed. Montserrat Ordóñez. Bogotá: Siglo XXI, 1991, pp. 56–67.

——. "Marta Brunet's *La mampara*". In Claire J. Paolini (ed.), *LA CHISPA '97: Selected Proceedings*. New Orleans, LA: Tulane University, 1997, pp. 39–48.

López Morales, Berta. *Orbita de Marta Brunet*. Concepción, Chile: Municipalidad de Chillán/Universidad de Concepción, 1997.

Melón de Díaz, Esther. *La narrativa de Marta Brunet*. Rio Piedras, Puerto Rico: University of Puerto Rico, 1975.

Orozco Vera, María Jesús. *La narrativa femenina chilena, 1923–1980: escritura y enajenación*. Zaragoza, Spain: Anubar Ediciones, 1995.

Oyarzun, Kemy. "Género y canon: la escritura de Marta Brunet". In Fernando de Burgos (ed.), *Studies in Honor of Myron Lichtblau*. Newark, NJ: Juan de la Cuesta, 2000, pp. 251–64.

BUITRAGO, FANNY

Born in Barranquilla, Colombia in 1944, Buitrago's writing career started in 1963 with the novel *El hostigante verano de los dioses* (The Harsh Summer of the Gods). In 1964, her theatrical piece *El hombre de paja* (The Straw Man) received the National Theatre Prize at the IV Cali Theatre Festival. Her ballet *La garza sucia* (The Dirty Heron) received the Summer Season Prize in Buenos Aires in 1965. Buitrago was also a runner-up for the Seix Barral Award for *Cola de zorro* (1970, Fox Tail), and in 1974 she won prizes awarded by three different newspapers from Colombia, Venezuela and France for her short story "Pasajeros de la noche" (Night Travelers). She also received the Villa de Avilés Prize in Spain in 1984 for "Tiquete a la pasión" (Ticket to Passion) as well as the Premio Felipe Trigo de Narraciones Cortas in Spain in 1987 for her short novel *Los fusilados de ayer* (1986, The Ones who Were Shot Yesterday), and second prize in the UNESCO contest for children's fiction in 1988.

Buitrago's critics often stress the rich intertextuality between her texts and fairy tales, courtly love, western mythology, the sentimental novel, as well as authors such as Shakespeare, Machuiavelli and Cervantes. Others notice the influences of William Faulkner, Rabelais, Gabriel García Márquez and Laura Esquivel (Jaramillo, 1991: 269; Muñoz, 1996: 54, Montes Garcés, 1997: 1), considering Buitrago a precursor of postmodern writing in Colombia, as well as a feminist in her criticism of women's conventional upbringing and their limiting role in marriage.

The concept of the dysfunctional family is a fundamental trope in Buitrago's writing, where homes are broken, children abandoned, couples divorced, and lovers married to someone they do not love. As Teresa R. Arrington puts it succinctly, her themes "can be reduced to a single dichotomy: absence/presence, which can also be expressed as lack/fulfillment" (1990: 66). For example, the story of Dalia Arce and her twins in *El hostigante verano de los dioses* (1963) exhibits hatred among family members, paternal despotism, and sexual abuse. *Cola de zorro*, on the other hand, presents despotic husbands who treat their wives instrumentally, as well as women married for convenience or financial necessity. The paradigmatic triad of a husband, wife, and a child inevitably falls apart, testifying to the instability of human relations. For instance, the unnamed heroine of the short story "Camino de los buhos" (1967, The Path of the Owls) narrates the tale of her family's dissipation upon the arrival of her oldest brother's bride-to-be. Defying the accepted family structure, the newcomer seduces and marries the widowed father, and she returns to the oldest son only after he murders his father in a jealous rage. Soon after, during her second lover's absence, she submits to the younger brother, which leads to another death in a mortal duel between the siblings. In the end, the narrator is happy when the woman elopes with one of the youngest brothers, together with the family's money and its best horse, because her disappearance breaks the cycle of ludicrous deaths caused by such a problematic woman.

Buitrago's writing is not always explicitly political but her obsession with familial chaos along with the ever-present depictions of violence serves as a metaphor for civil unrest and political upheaval, experienced by the writer during her youth in Colombia during the 1960s. Within the parameters of dysfunctional family ties and violent alliances, Buitrago explores the issues of racial injustice, legitimate and illegitimate relationships, the harmful imposition of gender roles in contemporary culture, as well as woman's place in family and society, with a particular emphasis on her sexuality. Buitrago's work often revolves around specific female concerns, such as rape, unwanted pregnancies, abortion, a desire for a child in the face of infertility, as well as woman's relation to her spouse and children. *Los amores de Afrodita* (1983, Aphrodite's Loves) brings together five short stories of heroines who suffer from betrayal and/or the dissolution of their relationships. Their expectations, fed on sentimental novels and maudlin soap-operas, appear to be ridiculous in the face of reality, a fact which demystifies women's stereotypical *education sentimentale*. Buitrago views her female protagonists as manipulated by a cultural system which converts them into dependent, weak, and submissive individuals who seek only amorous fulfillment, putting aside personal ambition and individual desires. Thus, the romantic arrangements of Buitrago's narratives invariably end up badly, as they disclose double standards and the impossibility of a positive, healthy heterosexual bond. Husbands either lead double lives, or hide steamy romances with their own adopted daughters. Women lust after power, engaging in ruthless manipulations with the opposite sex, and hide their modest past, all the while avoiding contact with the people who loved and supported them when they were unknown. Physical beauty hides grotesque psychological characteristics, intensifying the contrast between the domains of appearances and the truth. Buitrago's latest novel, *Bello animal* (Beautiful Animal), takes place precisely in such an environment of beautiful and pampered individuals, of modeling and advertising agencies, where corruption and hedonism define all human relationships.

Parody and the grotesque rescue Buitrago's eye-opening texts from utter pessimism, however, creating a unique blend of strong symbolism and biting reality. Her texts bespeak existential angst, attesting to the absurdity of life and the innate cruelty of humanity. The anxious residents of the town of Opalo in the 1964 play *El hombre de paja*, for example, passively succumb to the onslaught of certain unfamiliar attackers, rejecting any idea of active defense. Paralyzed by terror, they sacrifice a newcomer in a substitute act of misled revenge. This fictional event, which historically coincides with the era known as "La Violencia," is a parable of Colombian history of the past half-century. Similarly the play "El final del Ave María" (1991, The End of the Hail Mary), set in the public space of Bogotá, cuts through various layers of society, pointing to strong class contrasts and the general atmosphere of fear and violence. The main theme is the death of the archbishop Simón Mayoral, whose solitary yet resolute voice of social critique makes him the target of aggressive suppression. The sinister presence of violence is palpable at every level of society, including the most basic, familial cell. Esteban and Fernando, legitimate brothers in *El hostigante verano de los dioses*, conduct an unending war between themselves. Fernando abhors his brother so much that he harms those who hold Esteban in respect and marries the woman loved by his brother. What is more, it is suggested that the brothers murdered their own father to free themselves from his tyranny and to take over his wealth.

Fanny Buitrago's most translated novel, *Señora de la miel* (1993, The Mistress of Honey), reveals a more positive *Weltanschauung* despite the presence of the usual leitmotifs of unrequited love, unfaithfulness and familial abuse. In a parodic recreation of Laura Esquivel's sensual culinary ambience and García Marquéz's trademark magical realism, Buitrago tells the story of the highly contagious sexual awakening of a woman, an arousal that transforms other characters who come into contact with the power of her sexual energy. Here, impotent men suddenly become healthy and sexually active, sexually inhibited people dare to seek out erotic pleasures, and neglected wives recapture their husbands. The novel is a humorous subversion of traditional values in terms of woman's role in marriage (Eugenia Muñoz, 1996: 50). It also pokes fun at Colombian coastal macho stereotypes who, supported by their mothers, continue to lead the lifestyle of a playboy, squandering their wives' money and cheating on them incessantly.

Whereas the images of dysfunctional families pervade Buitrago's narrative world in her works intended for mature readers, her stories for children represent the opposite because they valorize the warmth of large extended families, with the presence of loving grandparents, uncles, and cousins. Such friendly and secure environments create the image of an idyllic childhood, filled with recollections of innocent games intertwined with myths and legends. They also promote equality and respect for all races and creatures of the world, encouraging young readers to love and cherish their surroundings. For instance, *Cartas del Palomar* (Letters of Palomar) traces a correspondence between two cousins, Laura and the 12-year-old Tomás, a boy who, as a result of an accident, is forced to spend a couple of weeks with one leg in a cast. Laura encourages Tomás to become a writer, as they exchange different fantasy tales together with brief notes on what is going on in their lives. Thus their letters are populated with dancing rabbits and frogs, friendly unicorns, fish who befriend little girls, and mice who fall for sweet and caring cockroaches. Similarly, *La casa de arco iris* (The Rainbow House) takes us back to blissful childhood of a group of little children who get to spend time in their grandfather's magical country house. There, they become owners for life of different stars in the sky, learn to differentiate between numerous flowers and herbs, grow to understand that love and happiness are not necessarily linked with wealth, and, most importantly, they listen to fascinating stories about their family's past, narrated by their aunt Feíta. *La casa del verde doncel* (The Green Page's House) combines the themes of both novels, as it goes back to the world of little children and their favorite aunts spending a holiday together by the ocean, accompanied by various magical creatures and sea animals. All in all, Buitrago's children's stories teach that there is a child in every one of us regardless of our age, and that to be happy, we need to remain linked to the candid innocence of our youth.

ALDONA BIALOWAS POBUTSKY

Selected Works

Novels

El hostigante verano de los dioses. Bogotá: Tercer Mundo, 1963.
Cola de zorro. Bogotá: Monolito, 1970.
Los pañamanes. Barcelona: Plaza y Janés, 1979.
Los amores de Afrodita. Bogotá: Plaza y Jánes, 1983.
Señora de la miel. Bogotá: Arango Editores, 1993.
Bello animal. Bogotá: Planeta Editorial, 2002.

Short Fiction

La otra gente: cuentos. Bogotá: Instituto Colombiano de Cultura, 1973.
Bahía Sonora, relatos de la isla. Bogotá: Plaza y Janés, 1975.
"Mammy deja el oficio". *El cuento colombiano: Generaciones 1955–1970*. Ed. Eduardo Pachon Padilla. Bogotá: Plaza y Janes, 1985.
Eduardo Padilla. Bogotá: Plaza y Janés 2 (1980), pp. 169–79.
"Tiquete a la pasión". *El Espectador* (Dominican Magazine) 56 (April 22, 1984): 7–10.
(Villa de Avilés de Asturias Prize, Spain, 1984).
Los fusilados de ayer. Badajoz: Diputación Provincial de Badajoz, Ayuntamiento Villanueva de la Serena, 1986.
¡Líbranos de todo mal! Bogotá: Carlos Valencia Editores, 1989.

Theater

El hombre de paja y *Las distancias doradas*. Bogotá: Espiral, 1964.
"A la diestra y a la siniestra". *Latin American Theatre Review* 20(2) (1987): 77–80.
"Al final del Ave María". *Gestos. Revista de teatro hispánico de la Universidad de California*. 6(12) (1991): 115–63.

Ballet

"La garza sucia," unpublished in Spanish, 1964.

Children's Literature

La casa del abuelo. Bogotá: Voluntad Unesco, 1979.
La casa del arco iris. Bogotá: Carlos Valencia Editores, 1986.
Cartas del palomar. Bogotá: Carlos Valencia Editores, 1988.
La casa del verde doncel. Bogotá: Carlos Valencia Editores, 1990.

Works in Translation

"The Dirty Heron". *Américas* 17(3) (1965): 31–2 (Trans. the author).
"The West Side of the Island". *Américas* 18(4) (1966): 36–8 (trans. the author).
Señora Honeycomb: A Novel. Trans. Margaret Sayers Peden. New York: HarperCollins, 1996.
"The Sea from the Window". In Psiche Hughes (ed. and Trans.), *Violations: Stories of Love by Latin American Women*. Lincoln, NB: University of Nebraska Press, 2004, pp. 33–8.

References and Further Reading

Arrington, Teresa R. "Fanny Buitrago". In Diane E. Marting (ed.), *Spanish American Women Writers: A Bio-Bibiographical Source Book*. New York: Greenwood Press, 1990, pp. 64–71.

Jaramillo, María Mercedes. "Fanny Buitrago: la desacralización de lo establecido: *El hostigante verano de los dioses*, *El hombre de paja* y *Los amores de Afrodita*". In María Mercedes Jaramillo *et al.* (eds), *¿Y las mujeres? Ensayos sobre la literatura colombiana*. Medellín: Otraparte, 1991, pp. 239–83.

Montes Garcés, Elizabeth. *El cuestionamiento de los mecanismos de representación en la novelística de Fanny Buitrago*. New York: Peter Lang, 1997.

Muñoz, Eugenia. "Fanny Buitrago y la parodia de la construcción social de la realidad femenina latinoamericana". *MACLAS* 10 (1996): 49–56.

Tedio, Guillermo. "*Los pañamanes* o la resignificación del mito y la leyenda como valores identitarios". *Espéculo* 11(32) (2006): no pagination.

BULLRICH, SILVINA

Silvina Bullrich was born in Buenos Aires, on October 4, 1915. Her father, Rafael Augusto Bullrich, the son of German parents, was an outstanding cardiologist and received his education in Paris. Her mother, María Laura Meyrelles y Torres Sáenz Valiente, was the daughter of the Portuguese ambassador in Argentina.

Raised in a favorable cultural environment with a humanistic background in French, Silvina Bullrich became a poet, a novelist, a short story writer, a translator, an essayist, a journalist and a screen writer. In her youth, she published a few poems in the *Atlântida* magazine. As a journalist, she wrote reviews for a number of periodicals, especially *La Nación*. As a teacher, she taught French Literature at the Universidad Nacional de La Plata and at the Instituto Francés de Estudos Superiores (French Institute of High Studies). She translated a number of books from French, including works by contemporary women writers as Natalie Sarraute, Simone de Beauvoir, or by Béatrix Beck, Louis Jouvet, George Sand, among others. Still in French, she wrote the play *Les Ombres* (1938). She assisted the Argentinean writer Jorge Luis Borges in the compilation of the anthology *El compadrito*.

She was part of the Argentinean *intelligentsia* in the 1940s, an elite identified with the European culture, though connected to the autochthonous culture, and which included members of the Revista Sur group, like Borges, Bioy Casares, the sisters Silvina and Victoria Ocampo, Manuel Mujica Láinez, Beatriz Guido, and Sara Gallardo. Together with the writer Alicia Jurado, she is considered a liberal novelist, since both supported divorce and abortion, the body and consumerism, polemical elements not only in the reception of literature at that time, but still controversial fifty years later. With Martha Lynch, she is acknowledged as a hypermedia writer, for the success achieved by her work in the 1960s. Both writers developed a style that transcended the realm of intimacy to become a criticism of reality, which brought them recognition and editorial success.

In 1961, she was awarded the Prêmio Municipal (Municipal Prize) for *Un momento muy largo* and for *El hechicero*. In 1972, she won first place in the second Prêmio Nacional (National Prize), in the creative prose category for the 1969–71 triennium. In 1982, she won the Palmas Acadêmicas, in France.

The author of a wide range of works, among her many works one finds: *La redoma del primer ángel* (1943), *Bodas de cristal* (1952), *Un momento muy largo* (1961), *Los burgueses* (1964), *Los salvadores de la patria* (1965), *La creciente* (1967), *Mañana digo basta* (1968), *Los pasajeros del jardín* (1971), *Los despiadados* (1978), *La mujer postergada* (1982), *Cuento cruel* (1983), *Floria Tristán, la visionaria* (1982), *La Bicicleta* (1983), *Georges Sand* (1984, biography); a number of her books have been translated into many languages and some were adapted to film. She lived her last years alone in Punta del Este (Uruguay), and died in 1990, in Switzerland.

Bullrich's narrative, especially in her short stories and novels, is notable for discussing social themes. From a critical perspective, the narrative of the Argentinean writer is divided into two themes: the feminist and the sociopolitical. In the first, from a realist approach, she identifies issues related to the feminist universe as she portrays the condition lived by women in those environments, as her works translate the incommunicability of marriage, submission, passion, love, treason, and the generational gap between mothers and daughters. Some of her works, which fit into that first theme include: *Bodas de cristal* (1951), *Teléfono ocupado* (1956) and *Mañana digo basta* (1968).

In *Mañana digo basta*, a view is offered of the mother who is victimized by her children, a mother who is characterized by an unlimited availability; an availability that comes close to slavery, which submits her both to authority and to the realm of the family. Most certainly, Bullrich conceives a feminine stereotype. In relation to feminine models in the representation of the Argentinean oligarchy, the writer meets again her own experience in the form of an autobiography (*Mis memórias*, 1980), as she reports the financial difficulties she had to face when she divorced her husband and became solely responsible for raising her only son. It states the enormous amount of work she had to do, her obligations, and the strict schedule for her intellectual production.

Bullrich – who translated Simone de Beauvoir untiringly – is accused by her fiercest critics of using a pragmatic and bourgeois mode of feminist thought, which she advanced in her works, as sexual independence and professional voracity. On the other hand, her erotic narratives, whether in delicate suggestions, or for subtle teasing, or for the eroticism that constitutes the axis of her argument, place her on a par with other national paradigmatic narrators: from Julio Cortázar to Silvina Ocampo, from David Viñas to Adolfo Bioy Casares, from Luisa Valenzuela to Dalmiro Sáenz, among others.

Openly inspired by the style of the *Nouveau Roman*, the narrative in *Los Burgueses* (1964) comprises what one calls the second theme. It is the first novel of the "sociopolitical" trilogy, completed with *Los Salvadores de la Pátria* (1965) and *Los Monstruos Sagrados* (1971), obeying a determinate thematic organization. There, an analysis of Argentinean society is shown to be facing class issues, but especially the issue of identity in that country; in combination, the three books show a disposition to uncover the three corrupt pillars that supported the Argentinean society of the 1950s and 1960s: the oligarchy, the parliament, and the intellectuals. In those narratives, Silvina Bullrich does not forgive the bourgeois society, that is, her own class, stating that personal interests had overcome the best interests of the country. Particularly in *Los Burgueses*, whose structure of an interior monologue together with a polyphonic observation surprises the "Bullrichian" reader, the focus is on the social and cultural devaluation that results from the hegemonic landowners due to their ambition, their hypocrisy and the loss of identity.

Los Salvadores de la Patria, preceded by a quotation from Bertold Brecht ("Unhappy the land that needs heroes"), describes the ridicule and the impudence of those legislators, men who hold power uselessly, sold out to personal interests and to lobbies of uncertain origins. In such a narrative, once again one appreciates the undermined shock between the oligarchy and middle class, social results from the old dichotomy between fellow-countrymen and the immigrants. The former, however, do not prove worthy of the legacy of their predecessors, from whom they inherited only a surname and a position that undervalues their acts, but which carry the flag of favoritism and self-indulgence. Within such a sociopolitical reading, one can also include *La creciente* (1967) and *Será justicia* (1976).

In *Mal don* (1973), the writer deals with the delicate theme of the homosexual mafia, which, according to her, dominates the literary circles in Argentina. She also examines the hierarchical structure of these relations; in the novel, they follow asymmetric social, economic and educational parameters. The "dominant" in the relation is usually the oldest one, more educated and occupying a better social position than the "subordinate". By dealing with a theme marginal in itself, she shapes an inclusive canon of the Latin American homosexual literature.

Another controversial theme appears in the work of the writer before the period of the military dictatorship in the country – that of the Nazi as the image of the prototype of evil – as in *Te acordarás de Taormina* (1975), taking part in a certain tradition in Argentinean literature that includes books like *Sobre héroes y tumbas* (1962), by Ernesto Sábato; *El Amor, los Orsinis y la Muerte* (1971) by Néstor Sánchez; and *Dormir al sol* (1973) by Adolfo Bioy Casares.

Thus, still without receiving the proper attention from the critics, the work of Silvina Bullrich can be found sometimes unwittingly hidden on the best-seller shelves. In contrast to such careless classification, her work remains relevant for its themes, from the reflection on the voice and memory, with evident signs of servility or of domination, which situates her within the literary trend of Latin American feminine tradition, to the resolute protests of a writing politically marked against sectors of power as the Argentinean bourgeoisie and its intellectuals.

SIMONE CURI

Selected Works

Las sombras (play in verse, published in *La Nación*, in 1938).
La tercera versión. Buenos Aires: Emecé, 1944.
Georges Sand (fictionalized biography, 1946). Buenos Aires: Emecé, 1963.
Teléfono ocupado. Buenos Aires: Goyanarte, 1955.
Mientras los demás viven. Buenos Aires: Sudamericana, 1958.
Un momento muy largo. Buenos Aires: Editorial Sudamericana, 1961.
Los Monstruos Sagrados. Buenos Aires: Sudamericana, 1961.
Los Burgueses. Buenos Aires: Sudamericana, 1964.
Los Salvadores de la Patria. Buenos Aires: Sudamericana, 1965.
La creciente. Buenos Aires: Sudamericana, 1967.
La redoma del primer ángel (1943). Buenos Aires: Santiago Rueda, 1967.

Carta a un joven cuentista. Buenos Aires: Santiago Rueda, 1968.
El compadrito. Su destino, sus barrios, su música (in collaboration with Borges, 1968). Buenos Aires: Compañía General Fabril, 1968.
Carta abierta a los hijos. Buenos Aires: Emecé, 1970.
La aventura interior. Buenos Aires: Merlín, 1970.
Mañana digo basta. Buenos Aires: Sudamericana, 1970.
El hechicero (1961). Buenos Aires: Merlin, 1971.
Entre mis veinte y mis treinta años. Buenos Aires: Emecé, 1971.
El calor humano. Buenos Aires: Merlin, 1971.
Cuento cruel. Buenos Aires: Lectorum Publications Inc., 1973.
Mal don. Buenos Aires: Emecé, 1973.
Historias inmorales (1965) Buenos Aires: Sudamericana, 1973.
Su excelencia envió el informe. Buenos Aires: Emecé, 1974.
Bodas de Cristal, en Tres Novelas. Buenos Aires: Sudamericana, 1975.
El mundo que yo ví. Buenos Aires: Emecé, 1976.
Historia de un silencio (1949). Buenos Aires: Monte Avila, 1976.
Los Pasajeros del Jardín. Buenos Aires: Círculo de los lectores, 1976.
Te acordarás de Taormina. Buenos Aires: Emecé, 1976.
Será Justicia. Buenos Aires: Sudamericana, 1976.
Reunión de directorio. Buenos Aires: Emecé, 1977.
Los despiadados. Buenos Aires: Emecé, 1978.
Silvina Bullrich by Silvina Bullrich. Buenos Aires: Ministerio de Cultura y Educacion: 1979.
Calles de Buenos Aires (first novel, 1939). Buenos Aires: Emecé, 1979.
Mis Memorias. Buenos Aires: Emecé, 1980.
Después del escándalo. Buenos Aires: Emecé, 1981.
Escándalo Bancario. Buenos Aires: Emecé, 1981.
Floria Tristán, la visionaria. Buenos Aires: Riesa, 1982.
La Mujer Postergada. Buenos Aires: Sudamericana, 1982.
A qué hora murió el enfermo. Buenos Aires: Emecé, 1984.
Más vida y gloria del Teatro Colón (In collaboration with Aldo Sessa). Buenos Aires: Cosmogonias, 1985.
La Argentina contradictoria. Buenos Aires: Emecé, 1986.
La Bicicleta. Buenos Aires: Emecé, 1986.
Cuando cae el telón. Buenos Aires: Emecé, 1987.
Mis novelas escogidas. Buenos Aires: Emecé, 2001.

References and Further Reading

Aira, César. *Dicionário de autores latinoamericanos*. Buenos Aires: Emecé, 2001.
Balderston, Daniel. "Los escándalos de Silvina Bullrich". Paper presented at the symposium on *Culture and Democracy in Argentina*, Yale University, 11 April 1987.
——. "Dos literatos del proceso H. Bustos Domecq y Silvina Bullrich". *Nuevo Texto Crítico* 5 (1990).
Barcia, Pedro Luis. *La Catarsis del autor: de lo autobiográfico a lo ficcional, estudio introductorio a "Los Pasajeros del Jardín"*. Buenos Aires: Nuevo Siglo, 1995.
Cócaro, Nicolas. *Silvina Bullrich*. Buenos Aires: Ediciones Culturales Argentinas, 1979.
Gonzáles López, María Cristina. *Visión sociopolítica en la novelística del Silvina Bullrich*. Doctoral thesis, Universidad Complutense de Madrid, 2004.
Lindstrom, Naomi. *Women's Voice in Latin American Literature*. Boulder, CO: Lynne Rienner Publishers, 1989.
López Lavali, Hilda. "Silvina Bullrich y el discurso de apoyo al régimen militar argentino 1976–83". Paper presented at the Symposium Seventh International Conference of the Asociación de Literatura Femenina Hispánica. Hispanic Women's Integration in History: Writing and Historicity, University of Colorado at Boulder, Oct. 1996.
McCard, Victoria L. "Feminine Psychology in Four Novels of Silvina Bullrich". Thesis. Master of Arts, Spanish, University of Georgia, 1990.
Mucci, Cristina. *La gran burguesa: biografia de Silvina Bullrich*. Buenos Aires: Grupo Editorial Norma, 2003.
Villanueva-Collado, Alfredo. "Homo sexualidad y periferia en la novelística de Marta Brunet y Silvina Bullrich". In Juana Alcira Arancibia (ed.), *El descubrimiento y los desplazamientos: la literatura hispanoamericana como diálogo entre centros y periferias*. Westminster, CA: Instituto literario y cultural hispánico, 1990.

BURGOS, JULIA DE

A Poetic Naturalism and Nationalism

Julia de Burgos (1914–53) was a Puerto Rican poet, journalist, feminist, and independence advocate whose work celebrated Puerto Rican identity, the self, and romantic love. Most widely recognized for her poem "Río Grande de Loíza" and for her tragic death in New York City at the age of 39, Burgos nevertheless published poems and articles throughout her life and was a vocal advocate of Puerto Rican nationalism and women's rights.

In the mountain town of Carolina, Puerto Rico, Julia de Burgos was born on February 17, 1914. She was the first of thirteen children born to Paula García, a woman of African and Spanish descent, and Francisco Burgos Hans, a man of partly Germanic heritage. Burgos's childhood combined poverty, creativity and closeness to nature. On the one hand, six of the thirteen children born to Paula and Francisco died, and although the family cultivated a parcel of land, they suffered hunger. Burgos's father was said to have been a heavy drinker who sometimes wandered the fields at night. On the other hand, despite poverty, Julia led a richly imaginative life. Her father told tales from *Don Quixote* and other epics. Paula García, meanwhile, shared stories of nymphs, naiads and other natural spirits during visits to the *pozo hondo* (deep well) where the women washed the clothes against stones. Burgos's poetry would reflect the influence of her father's sense of adventure and her mother's naturalism.

In her neighborhood, Burgos attended six years of rural elementary school between 1920 and 1926, and then transferred to a school in Carolina. In 1928, the Burgos family sold their land and moved to the city of Río Piedras, where Julia and her sister Consuelo played basketball, ran track, and swam at their high school. The bright, tall, and athletic Julia had enjoyed climbing trees in her youth; now she received a scholarship to high school, skipped grades, and graduated ahead of schedule. In 1931, she enrolled at the University of Puerto Rico to study education as part of a two-year program to prepare teachers, receiving her teaching credentials two years later, at the age of 19.

Political Consciousness and Early Writing

While at university, Burgos developed her political consciousness. She learned about the Puerto Rican independence movement and its leader, Pedro Albizu Campos; the knowledge spurred her lifelong commitment to abolishing colonialism on the island. However, harsh economic times befell Puerto Rico, and in the early 1930s the median family income declined by two-thirds, and Julia struggled to find work. She found temporary employment at the Puerto Rican Economic Rehabilitation

Agency (PRERA) distributing breakfast to poor children as part of a program stemming from Roosevelt's New Deal (Estevez, 1995). She also wrote copy for a radio program called the *School of the Air*, where some say her employment was terminated because of her nationalist beliefs (Agüeros, 1996). In 1934, Burgos married fellow nationalist Rubén Rodríguez Beauchamp, a journalist and/or radio announcer whose name she used to sign her poems, "Julia Burgos de Rodríguez" until the couple's divorce in 1937.

By the 1930s, Julia had begun to submit her poems for publication in flyers, journals and newspapers, and several had been published. Possibly her first published poem, "Gloria a tí" appeared on April 16, 1934, in the journal *Alma Latina.* The Spanish sonnet chronicled the death of nationalist leader Rafael Suárez Díaz in the Río Piedras massacre, in which three nationalist demonstrators were killed and forty plus were wounded by federal soldiers on October 24, 1935. Federal repression of nationalists was ever-present: on Palm Sunday – March, 1937 – governor Blanton Winship ordered an attack that resulted in twenty-one dead and over two hundred nationalists injured. Pedro Albizu Campos, who was imprisoned in Old San Juan, was transferred to a jail in Atlanta, Georgia, where he was incarcerated for the next ten years; Julia's friend Juan Antonio Corretjer was also jailed there. To commemorate the cumulative losses and fight political repression, Burgos wrote her poem "Domingo de Pascua" (Estevez, 1995: 225).

Shortly after her first publication, Julia penned what would become her most famous and popular poem, "Río Grande de Loíza," written after she moved to the town of Naranjito to teach school in 1935. Tragically, Julia's mother was diagnosed with cancer of the leg and endured several operations before losing the limb; to raise money for her medical expenses, Burgos toured the country reciting "Río Grande de Loíza" and trying to sell copies of her book, *Poema en veinte surcos* (Poem in Twenty Furrows). As work became available first in Comerío, then Naranjito and San Juan, Julia followed; she supported the nationalist cause and took two courses at the University of Puerto Rico in San Juan. In 1937, despite their political similarities, Burgos and Rodríguez parted. This same year, Julia completed what is considered to be a collection of her earliest poems, *Poemas exactos a mí misma* (Exact Poems to Myself), which was never published and is presumed lost.

By 1937, Burgos and her poetry had gained admirers. In November, her friend, lawyer and poet Luís Lloréns Torres, had read a draft of *Poema en veinte surcos* and compared Burgos to Gabriela Mistral of Chile, Argentinean Alfonsina Storni, Uruguayan Juana de Ibarbourou, and Clara Lair, who was also from Puerto Rico (Agüeros, 1996: xvii). In November, Burgos published "Cortando distancias" in the journal *Renovación* and in December, *El Imparcial* published "Interrogaciones," "Paisaje interior," "Ronda nocturna," "Ya no es canción," "Pentacromía," and "Ven". Finally, *Poema en veinte surcos* hit the presses in December of 1938. Puerto Rican journalist, lawyer and editor Nilita Vientós Gastón reviewed the book and called Burgos's work, especially "Río Grande de Loíza" "magnificent" and endowed with "evocative beauty" (Agüeros, 1996: xix).

In 1939, Paula García died. Two days after her mother's death, a poetry reading in tribute to Julia was held at the Ateneo Puertorriqueño, and Burgos read the poem "Mi madre y el río". Burgos was becoming a mythologized public figure. She was reading the work of César Vallejo, Federico García Lorca, and Pablo Neruda, whose "Twenty Poems of Love" she had memorized. She met Cuban Nicolás Guillén, Dominican Juan Bosch, who requested copies of her poems, and Pablo Neruda, who said that she had been called to be a great poet of Puerto Rico. She belonged to a literary circle, El Chévere, along with Puerto Rican poet Luís Palés Matos, and she continued to read poems by Alfonsina Storni, whom she deeply admired. She met the man who would become the love of her life, Juan Isidro Jimenes Grullón, a medical doctor and political figure from the Dominican Republic. Burgos's second book, *Canción de la verdad sencilla* (Song of the Simple Truth) was published in December, 1939, and for it she was awarded a literary prize from the Instituto de Literatura Puertorriqueña.

Poet in New York City

After her love, Jimenes Grullón, moved to New York City in November, 1939, Julia followed two months later. In New York, she found a second home, as the city soon welcomed her with interviews, reviews of her work appeared in *La Prensa*, and the Master Theater hosted a reading of her poetry. She had difficulty selling her work, however, and in April 1940 Burgos went to work for the United States Census Bureau. Jimenes Grullón departed for Cuba, where his influential family had relocated. Burgos followed in June, 1940. During two years in Cuba – June, 1940 to June, 1942, Burgos wrote most of her third book, *El mar y tú* (The Sea and You), then sent it for publication with poet Carmen Alicia Cadilla, who was returning to Puerto Rico in early 1941. The book would go through a series of revisions, and publication would evade the author for the rest of her life.

Eventually, Burgos's relationship with Jimenes Grullón ended, as his social standing and familial influence superseded his desire to remain with Burgos – a divorcée. She returned to New York City in 1942, worked in various jobs, dealt with emotional strain, and declined into despair, alcoholism, and ill health. She worked as a reporter for the short-lived weekly *Pueblos Hispanos* and organized its cultural section, which gave her ample opportunity to sample New York's artistic life. In a proliferation for which her stint at the School of the Air surely had prepared her, she published her poems, reviews, interviews, essays, and one short story in the weekly paper.

In 1944, Julia married Armando Marín, a public accountant and musician with whom she moved to Washington, DC, for a year; she returned to New York in August, 1945. Her essay "Ser o no ser es la divisa" was published in the weekly *Semanario hispánico* and won an award for journalism from the Instituto de Literatura Puertorriqueña in 1946. The essay voiced Burgos's moral imperative that human beings stand against the fascism brought by repressive regimes like those of Somoza, Trujillo, Carías and Francisco Franco.

Declining Health and Last Days

By 1946, Julia de Burgos had developed cirrhosis of the liver. Sometimes, she was recognized on the street by fellow Puerto Ricans, who called her "Puerto Rico's greatest poet". Her "Río Grande de Loíza" had made her famous: schoolchildren read the poem, made popular by Argentinean Berta Singerman, a touring performer whose one-woman show included a recital of the poem.

Julia's romantic attachments and heartbreaks contributed to her status as a mythologized figure, made more concrete as she sank into alcoholism and was hospitalized various times between 1947 and 1953. She worked sporadically, but was depressed and despairing because of the failure to publish her third book, her poor health, and poverty; she almost died in July, 1951. This same year she participated in a radio homage to Luís Lloréns Torres. Finally, in July, 1953, Julia left the home of some friends; deathly ill, she collapsed on the street, and was found unconscious at the corner of 5th Avenue and 105th Street on July 5th, 1953. She was pronounced dead minutes after arriving at Harlem Hospital, and since no identification was found on her, was buried in a common plot at Potter's Field. One month passed, and she was exhumed, identified, and transported to her native Puerto Rico as she had requested, finally returning to be interred in her home town of Carolina, near the beloved Río Grande de Loíza. Ironically, one year after her death, her third book, *El mar y tú*, was finally published.

Selected Prose

Julia de Burgos's journalistic writing during her time in New York lends itself to a reading of her anti-fascism, multiculturalism, eclecticism, hispanism, and feminism, especially the award-winning "Ser o no ser es la divisa". Burgos also actively promoted multiculturalism in specific portrayals of Caribbean women, such as her published interview of Haitian singer/dancer "Con Josephine Premice" (*Pueblos Hispanos*).

In addition to these publications, Burgos reviewed Hispanic cultural events in New York City. Carmen M. Rivera Villegas reads Burgos's articles on art in New York – ranging from poetry readings and theater to piano recitals – as promoting a multicultural identity through art. According to Rivera Villegas, Burgos believed that multicultural and national affirmation is achieved when we "recognize ourselves in the diversity of others" (Rivera Villegas, 1998: 217); Burgos's cultural eclecticism was broader than Antonio S. Pedreira's nationalism (*Insularismo*, 1934) or the negritude of Luís Palés Matos (*Tuntún de pasa y grifería*, 1937), which were seen as contrasting conceptualizations of Hispanic identity (Rivera Villegas, 1998: 222).

The Poems

Julia de Burgos wrote about 200 poems that are in existence. Evaluating the poems, we find that her individualistic style is influenced by nineteenth-century Latin American Romanticism with its emphasis on identity and idealization of the soul's suffering, romantic attachment, and nature. Carlota Caulfield explains that Burgos "eroticizes" nature as a way to extend her praise of her lover to nature and then to the universe; thus the individual's experience relates to the totality of the world via the work of art. Julia also schematized existential questions of identity and metafictive problems such as how to confess to creating – a thematic seen in Latin American *vanguardia* poets like Pablo Neruda. She commemorated life events in verse, penning odes to imprisoned political figures and to her mother. Her love of Puerto Rico and her various heritages is evident, too, in her famous "Río Grande de Loíza" and the wonderful "Ay, ay, ay de la grifa negra" (Lament of the Kinky-Haired Negress). Finally, her confession to mortality and unapologetic art shines in "Yo misma fui mi ruta" (I Was My Own Path).

"Río Grande de Loíza"

Several of Julia de Burgos's early poems are powerful celebrations of an identity that announces its Puerto Ricanness and connection to nature, to the seasons, to the mother, to the self. It is said that after her first divorce, Julia Burgos began signing her poems "Julia de Burgos" – literally, Julia of Burgos or Julia belonging to Burgos, to herself – as part of her intimate self-song that was her life and work. "A Julia de Burgos," for example, describes the schism between the social identity of "Julia de Burgos" and the private self, saying "You are the cold doll of social lies, / and me, the virile starburst of human truth". The confident feminism asserts that only her heart and mind, not social expectations, govern all of her behaviors and the truth. Another poem, "Íntima," portrays an internal voyage to selfhood and self-knowledge. "Dame tu hora perdida" is a romantic expression of the intimacy between two who find one another; "Se me ha perdido un verso" elaborates the power of a single verse to be the totality – and perhaps not – of the writer's voice and self and ultimately, to express truth. "Pentacromía" jolts the reader when, after the speaking voice describes its desire to explore the world as a man such as adventurer Don Quixote or rogue Don Juan, the voice concludes by saying that it would like to "violar" (rape) Julia de Burgos.

"Río Grande de Loíza" is similar to the abovementioned poems, with daring comparisons and clever manipulation of subject-object dichotomies that reveal the intimate relationship between reader and verse, self and other, the nation and the poet. Masculine forces' similarity or complementarity to feminine force also pervades much of Burgos's work. In "Río Grande de Loíza," the speaking voice relates the river's meanderings to her body and the earth's growing seasons. She says "Río Grande de Loíza! ... Elongate yourself in my spirit / and let my soul lose itself in your rivulets," (v. 1–2) after which the speaker expresses her desire that the river spiritually "make love" to her: "... I was yours a thousand times, and in a beautiful romance / you awoke my soul and kissed my body" (v. 21–2). Celebrating the colors, the spirit of the river that unites the Puerto Rican people, sorrowful under colonialism, the poem ends in a romantic dream and in popular solidarity:

> Río Grande de Loíza! ... My wellspring, my river
> since the maternal petal lifted me to the world;
> my pale desires came down in you from the craggy hills
> to find new furrows
> Most sovereign river mine. Man river. The only man
> who has kissed my soul upon kissing my body.
> río Grande de Loíza! ... Great river. Great flood of tears.
> The greatest of all our island's tears
> save those greater that come from the eyes
> of my soul for our enslaved people.
>
> (v. 13–16, 39–44)

"Ay, ay, ay de la grifa negra" and Negritude

Burgos's "Ay, ay, ay de la grifa negra" may be compared to the work of fellow Puerto Rican Luís Palés Matos and Cuban Nicolás Guillén – especially their respective poems "Pueblo negro" and "Canción del bongo". All three poems celebrate the Caribbean's African heritage, in a celebration of negritude that at times essentializes Africanness.

"Ay, ay, ay de la grifa negra" is different than Palés Matos' connection of the African woman's sexuality with the African landscape's musicality in that Burgos's poem self-consciously elaborates the first-person perspective of an African woman singing her beauty, pain and hope. Taking possession of racial description in an emphatic declaration of selfhood, the first-person voice exclaims her physical attributes: "Ay, ay, ay, that I am kinky-haired and pure black; / kinks in my hair, Kafir in my lips; / and my flat Mozambiquean nose". The poem continues, condemning slavery, and then asserting that the "black queen" could cleanse the white master's shameful sins via her forgiveness. The poem ends describing the "fraternity of America" whereby the races unite biologically and culturally, forming a bronzed identity.

"Yo misma fui mi ruta" and Other Poems

Various other Burgos' works merit considerable study for their power, grace, and insistence on Puerto Rican identity, the poetic self's voice, and the woman's independence and intelligence. "Yo misma fui mi ruta" describes the self's response to initial "feminine" attempts at obedience:

> I wanted to be like men wanted me to be:
> an attempt at life;
> a game of hide and seek with my being.
> But I was made of nows,
> and my feet level upon the promissory earth
> would not accept walking backwards,
> and went forward,
> mocking the ashes to reach the kiss
> of new paths.
>
> (v. 1–9)

The magnetic voice throughout Burgos's work is energetic, sincere, and filled with dreams, idealism, the consciousness of self ("Poema para mi muerte" and "Poema para una muerte que puede ser la mía"), love ("Mi madre y el río" and "Oferta"), and political solidarity ("Canción a los Pueblos Hispanos de América y del mundo").

Among so many good poems, the reader must also investigate "Réplica," "Despierta," "A plena desnudez," and "El cielo se ha visto su traje de horizontes". This last poem divulges a deep secret for the poet whose life was a work in progress, and who communicated her emotional and intellectual truth so directly. Speaking to her lover or the imagined other, the narrator asks "Can the sky navigate me / to this entire infinity?" The poem's last line responds "You are the universe". Burgos captured the instantaneity of the universal and the eternality of the lived instant, between Puerto Rico and New York City, a promise of accompaniment between her own voice and those of her readers.

JULI A. KROLL

Selected Works

Poema en 20 surcos. San Juan, Puerto Rico: Imprenta Venezuela, 1938.
Canción de la verdad sencilla. San Juan, Puerto Rico: Imprenta Baldrich, 1939.
El mar y tú. San Juan, PR: Puerto Rico Printing and Publishing Co, 1954.
Criatura del agua, Obra Poética. San Juan, Puerto Rico: Instituto de Cultura Puertorriqueña, 1961. Compiled by Consuelo Sáez and Juan Bautista Pagán.
Agüeros, Jack, ed. *Song of the Simple Truth: The Complete Poems of Julia de Burgos*. Willimantic, CT: Curbstone Press, 1996. Bilingual ed. Trans. Jack Agüeros.

References and Further Reading

Agüeros, Jack (ed.) *Song of the Simple Truth: The Complete Poems of Julia de Burgos*. Willimantic, CT: Curbstone Press, 1996. Bilingual edn, Trans. Jack Agüeros.
Barradas, Efraín. "'Entre la esencia y la forma:' El momento neoyorquino en la poesía de Julia de Burgos". *Explicación de Textos Literarios* 15(2) (1986–87): 138–52.
Calderón, Gustavo Adolfo. *El mar metafórico de Julia de Burgos como voz moduladora: Actas de la decimotercera conferencia anual de literatura hispánica en Indiana Univ. of Pennsylvania*. Miami, FL: La Escritora Hispana, 1990.
Caulfield, Carlota. "*Canción de la verdad sencilla*: Julia de Burgos y su diálogo erótico-místico con la naturaleza". *Revista Iberoamericana* 59(162–3) (1993): 119–26.
Estevez, Carmen. "Julia de Burgos: Woman, Poet, Legend". In Marjorie Agosín (ed.), *A Dream of Light and Shadow: Portraits of Latin American Women Writers*. Albuquerque, NM: University of New Mexico Press, 1995, pp. 221–36.
Jiménez de Báez, Yvette. *Julia de Burgos: Vida y Poesía*. San Juan, Puerto Rico: Editorial Coquí, 1966.
Lockert, Lucía Fox. "Vida, pasión y muerte de Julia de Burgos". *Letras Femeninas* 16(1–2) (1990): 121–4.
Mascia, Mark: "Selfhood and National Identity in Julia de Burgos". *Textos: Works and Criticism* 5(2) (1997): 48–52.
Rivera, Félix, Tirado, Amilcar and Pérez, Nélida (eds), *Julia de Burgos, 1914–1953*. New York: Centro de Estudios Puertorriqueños, Hunter College, City College of New York, 1986.
Rivera Villegas, Carmen M. "Sobreviviendo en la metrópoli: El multiculturalismo en la prosa de Julia de Burgos". *Bilingual Review/ Revista Bilingüe* 23(3) (1998): 214–22.
Springfield, Consuelo López. "'I am the Life, the Strength, the Woman:' Feminism in Julia de Burgos' Autobiographical Poetry". *Callaloo* 17(3) (1994): 701–14.
Zavala Martínez, Iris. "A Critical Inquiry into the Life and Work of Julia de Burgos". In Cynthia T. Coll and María de Lourdes Mattei (eds), *The Psychological Development of Puerto Rican Women*. New York: Praeger, 1989.

C

CABELLO DE CARBONERA, MERCEDES

Mercedes Cabello de Carbonera (1842–1909) is considered the founder of the modern novel in nineteenth-century Peru. She is part of a generation of professional women writers who emerged in the public sphere after the War of the Pacific (1879–83). Although she is best known as a novelist, she was also a very prolific critic, poet, and journalist. For many years scholars believed, following Cabello de Carbonera's own assertions, that she was born in 1845 or 1848. However, a recently discovered baptismal certificate places her birth on February 17, 1842 in the city of Moquegua, Peru. Her real name was Juana Mercedes Cabello de la Llosa.

Cabello de Carbonera occupied a marginal position in society because of her gender but she had a privileged status in terms of class and race. Her parents, Gregorio Cabello and Mercedes Llosa belonged to the land-owning Creole aristocracy and they possessed vineyards in Moquegua. Her father had been to France and was a chemistry teacher in one of the local schools. Most of Cabello's education took place in her father's library where she familiarized herself with the leading French writers of the day (Flaubert, Balzac, Comte, Zola, Hugo, and Stendhal, among others). At a time when women could not aspire to an education that went beyond the elementary school level, Cabello de Carbonera acquired on her own a knowledge that was superior to that of her more educated male colleagues. During her formative years, her family's liberal and scientific leanings had a significant influence on her early literary training.

Essays on Women's Education

In 1864, Mercedes Cabello moved to Lima where she married a distinguished physician, Urbano de Carbonera, two years later. He was also from Moquegua and had written a controversial thesis in favor of the cremation of dead bodies that offended the sensibility of the church. In 1874, she published in *El Álbum* a series of short essays on the education of women signed under the pseudonym of Enriqueta Pradel. In these early reflections she defended the need to secularize women's education and argued against the idea that educated women tended to be arrogant and vain.

In order to promote women's intellectual rights, Cabello de Carbonera invoked the dominant ideology of republican motherhood, according to which women needed an education to become better mothers. Later in her career, she stopped using the sacred figure of the mother to advance her feminist views. In *La religión de la humanidad. Carta al señor Don Juan Enrique Lagarrigue* (1893), she argued that it was mostly widows and women without children like herself who most needed education because they had to build their identity away from the sanctuary of the home. In an essay entitled "Necesidad de una industria para la mujer," she associated civilization and progress with the professionalization of women and their access to paid work. These ideas went against the views of her liberal and conservative colleagues who prescribed through the doctrine of the spheres (private–public, domestic–political, home–streets) a domestic role for women as sentimental educators of future male citizens.

In 1876, Mercedes Cabello de Carbonera joined the literary salon of Juana Manuela Gorriti where she became one of its most conspicuous participants. It was in the context of these weekly cultural events that she became acquainted with other women writers of her generation such as Clorinda Matto de Turner, Teresa González de Fanning, Carolina Freyre de Jaimes, and the Wilson Baroness. It was also at one of Gorriti's inter-disciplinary encounters that Cabello de Carbonera read an essay comparing female intelligence and beauty in which she favored the life of the mind over the body. At the same time, she thought that only through education women would be able to transcend the limits of their assigned domestic role ("Estudio comparativo de la inteligencia y la belleza en la mujer"). In another text that she read at Gorriti's salon, Cabello de Carbonera asserted that novels had an important role in the process of nation-building and that they could become tools to combat materialism and religious fanaticism in women.

Mercedes Cabello de Cabonera published many of her pieces on literature, positivism, and women's education in Latin American journals. She collaborated on a regular basis with publications such as *El correo de Ultramar*, *El Álbum Ibero-Americano*, *La revista literaria de Bogotá*, *El correo de Europa*, *El correo ilustrado de Lisboa*, *La Habana Elegante*, and *La ilustración de Curazao*, among many others. She associated sentimental and romantic poetry in her early essays with a colonial past that had to be defeated by modernity. In a piece entitled "Importancia de la literatura," she advocated the use of literature to teach readers to become better citizens. She also thought that it was the duty of the writer to portray virtues and vices so that readers would be able to discriminate between both. She later rejected *fin-de-siècle* modernism and decadence as proposed by Clemente Palma and José Santos Chocano, claiming that those French schools were out of place in Latin America.

Anticlericalism, Positivism and Gender

Mercedes Cabello de Carbonera, like many women writers of her generation, started writing novels professionally when she became a widow in 1885. In the short span of six years (1886–92) she published six novels (*Eleodora*, *Sacrificio y recompensa*, *Los amores de Hortensia*, *Las consecuencias*, *El conspirador*, *Blanca Sol*) and three books of essays (*La novela moderna*, *El conde León Tolstoy*, *La religión de la humanidad*). For the most part, her books were very successful and they received important prizes and awards. *Sacrificio y recompensa*, a novel that expressed her support for the independence of Cuba, won a gold medal at the Ateneo de Lima's competition; an essay entitled "Influencia de las bellas artes en el progreso moral y material de los pueblos," won a gold medal at Lima's municipality competition; and *La novela Moderna*, one of her most important theoretical books, was awarded a Golden Rose at the Literary Academy in Buenos Aires. In recognition for her distinguished publications she was invited in 1893 to the Universal Exposition in Chicago.

Mercedes Cabello was, like Gonzalez Prada, a secularist and a liberal. However, women's duty in the nineteenth century was to defend religion and the church against the advances of science and modernity. The idea of an anti-clerical woman was taboo in the republican imagination because the angel of the house was supposed to be religious. At the beginning of her career, Mercedes Cabello embarked in double discourse to defend her secular views so that they would be perceived as less threatening by the literary establishment. She emphasized morality and spiritualism while defending the advances of scientific thought. Her ideas were sometimes contradictory and paradoxical as when she asserted in *La religión de la humanidad* that women needed to acquire a scientific education so that they could teach men to be more religious.

The turn of the century was a time of frequent battles between liberals and conservatives, religious faith and scientific progress. Mercedes Cabello was on the side of secularism, anti-clericalism, and modernity although she tried to act as a bridging figure between the two factions. She introduced her readers to the positivist ideology of Auguste Comte and she corresponded with Juan Enrique Lagarrigue, a Chilean philosopher who was one of Comte's greatest advocates in Latin America. What attracted Cabello to Comte's "secular religion" was his desire to reconcile tensions between spiritualism and science. She agreed with Comte's impulse to replace God with humanity and she also subscribed to his idea that society in its ideal form should be a fraternal space ruled by altruism, order, and progress. However, in *La religión de la humanidad* she was extremely critical of the limitations that positivists placed on women by assigning them an angelic role as moral guardians of men. She rightly believed that feminism was the peaceful revolution that would change the future of nations. In spite of the disagreement on women's rights, Cabello de Carbonera became one of the few female advocates of Comte's humanist religion in Latin America.

Naturalism, Realism and the Eclectic Novel

In the Preface to *Blanca Sol* (1889), one of her most successful and polemical novels, Cabello de Carbonera declares herself a reader of Cambaceres, a writer who had imported Zola's theories about the novel to Argentina. At the same time in *La novela moderna* (1892), she expresses her admiration for Balzac and Flaubert. Later in her life she became interested in Russian writers and she wrote an important biographical essay entitled *El conde León Tolstoy* (1896) in which she was very supportive of the mysticism of Tolstoy's later years. In the discussion of Tolstoy's novels, she focuses almost exclusively on *The Kreutzer Sonata* and *Anna Karenina*, two novels that were very critical of marriage as an institution.

The fictional heroine of one of her first novels, *Los amores de Hortensia* (1887) shares with Anna Karenina and Emma Bovary a desire to escape the confinement of an unhappy marriage through the acquisition of a refined lover. This theme reappears with a vengeance in *Blanca Sol*, a novel in which an ambitious coquette marries a wealthy man whom she despises out of economic necessity. Although Blanca Sol is in many ways an anti-model of republican virtue, the reader cannot help but admire the way in which she manipulates her admirers to gain access to political power. At the same time, when Blanca Sol takes a resounding fall from the heights of the upper classes, the narrator puts the blame on a patriarchal society that makes marriage the only option for women. Thus Blanca Sol's tragedy is not the consequence of genetically determined defects but of poor choices caused by social conditioning and a bad Catholic education. At one point in the novel, Cabello even goes so far as to say that marriage without love is a form of institutionalized prostitution in which women gain economic security in exchange for sexual favors.

Blanca Sol was a huge best-seller when it came out in 1889. Two editions appeared in quick succession (1890, 1894) and the publishers had a difficult time keeping up with the readers' demands. Part of the commotion caused by the novel had to do with the fact that critics accused Cabello of basing her characters on real life as Zola had advocated in his theories about the experimental novel. Speculations flourished as to who the model for the corrupt Blanca Sol was and there was a lot of finger pointing in the small urban world of the Peruvian aristocracy. To appease her critics, Mercedes Cabello wrote a prologue for the second edition of the novel in which she compared her literary tactics with those of Zola, Daudet and Cambaceres. By defending these authors from unjust accusations, she found a way of distancing herself from her critics. All she wanted was to create fictional hybrids or literary composites that would function as archetypes for certain traits.

The extent to which Cabello de Carbonera was a naturalist writer remains a point of controversy among her critics. At the turn of the century, Cabello de Carbonera's name was frequently associated with that of other naturalist writers such as Emilia Pardo Bazán and Emile Zola but she frequently called herself a "social realist". What adds to the confusion is that naturalism was at the time an extremely polemical aesthetic trend caused by its associations with sexuality, secularism and vice. It was considered immoral for women even to read naturalist novels and Emile Zola was thought to be a pornographer in his own country.

Mercedes Cabello de Carbonera asserted in her theoretical writings about the novel that she opposed the "excesses" of naturalism. In *La novela moderna*, she advocates an eclectic and conciliatory approach to the novel in which writers mix different aspects from opposing cultural trends. At the same time, she rejected the hyperbolic idealism of the romantic imagination and the extreme pessimism of Zola's experimental method. She modeled the realist-social novel on Balzac's œuvre and she frequently juxtaposed romantic, realist and naturalist themes. Thus, the sentimental character of the suffering seamstress in *Blanca Sol* is in direct tension with the more naturalist profile of Blanca Sol as evidenced by the entropic movement of her downfall. All the scandalous themes that had been controversial in Zola's novels (alcoholism, adultery, gambling, prostitution) appeared in her novels. However, it was morality as a subtext that justified the inclusion of these vices. Ultimately, it was the duty of the woman writer to educate readers even if in the process of doing it she put her own respectability in danger.

El conspirador (1892) was Cabello's last and most polemical novel. It shared with *Blanca Sol* a successful trajectory fueled by political scandal. Although it has been argued that the narrator of this political autobiography is a fictional mix of the main conspirators of the day (Vivanco, Cáceres, Piérola), the general consensus was that Jorge Bello, like Blanca Sol before him, was a fictionalization of the historical character of Nicolás de Piérola. Readers also thought that the character of Ofelia Olivas in the novel was modeled on Piérola's French lover, Madame Garreaud. Politically speaking, Cabello de Carbonera was a supporter of Cáceres, like Clorinda Matto de Turner, and when Piérola took power in 1895, both Matto and Cabello were made to suffer. Clorinda Matto de Turner went into exile and Mercedes Cabello de Carbonera became increasingly isolated. As Jorge Basadre points out in *Peruanos del siglo XIX*, if Cabello had wanted to punish Piérola by fictionalizing his demise in the novel, in reality, Piérola was victorious, strong and thirsty for revenge (1981: 37). When he staged a revolution against Cáceres in 1895, he became president until 1898.

The occasion for vengeance presented itself when Mercedes Cabello de Carbonera gave a speech at a girls' private school directed by Elvira García y García in 1898. In this incendiary speech that she delivered as the special guest of an oral public examination, she declared herself an enemy of religious education. She asserted that religious schools did not teach girls anything about science, physiology and the body. She also added that nuns were the most inappropriate teachers for girls because they did not have enough worldly experience, a criticism that she had already made in *Blanca Sol*. Cabello's anticlerical ideas created an uproar in Catholic circles and even González Prada who had similar liberal views did not come to Cabello's defense. Another woman writer of the time, Lastenia Larriva de Llona, silenced her by saying that she had no right to talk about the education of girls because she was not a mother. Ricardo Palma said that she suffered from megalomania, and Piérola, the resentful politician now in power, denied in one of the daily newspapers that he had named her a representative of his government's educational policies as Cabello had claimed. In the meantime, Cabello's health began to deteriorate rapidly. Some biographers believe that she had contracted syphilis from her husband many years ago.

In the middle of what had already become a very turbulent year, Mercedes Cabello decided to take a long trip to Buenos Aires via Chile, two countries where she had friends that she corresponded with. After a year in Chile and Argentina that was not as fruitful and positive as she thought it would be, she returned to Lima where her enemies had not forgotten her. The mysterious illness for which she took all kinds of medications had worsened during the trip, and a year later, on January 27, 1900, her family locked her up in "El cercado," a somber mental institution that also functioned as a jail. It is not very clear the extent to which Cabello needed medical attention since a clear diagnosis for mental illness did not exist at the time. However, for her contemporaries, declaring Cabello de Carbonera crazy was a way of silencing one of the most lucid minds of the nineteenth century. After several years in the mental institution, she died in solitary confinement on October 12, 1909.

Ana Peluffo

Selected Works

Sacrificio y recompensa. Lima: Imprenta de Torres Aguirre, 1886.

Los amores de Hortensia (Una historia contemporánea). Lima: Imprenta de Torres Aguirre, 1887.

Eleodora. Lima: Imprenta de Torres Aguirre, 1887.

Las consecuencias. Lima: Imprenta de Torres Aguirre, 1889.

Blanca Sol. Lima: Imprenta y librería del Universo de Carlos Prince, 1889.

El conspirador. Autobiografía de un hombre público. Lima: Imprenta de La Voce d'Italia, 1892.

La novela moderna. Lima: Imprenta Bacigalupi, 1892.

La religión de la Humanidad. Carta al señor. D. Juan Enrique Lagarrigue. Lima: Imprenta de Torres Aguirre, 1893.

El conde León Tolstoy. Lima: Imprenta de El Diario Judicial, 1896.

References and Further Reading

Basadre, Jorge. *Peruanos del siglo XIX*. Lima: Ediciones Rikchay, 1981.

Batticuore, Graciela. *El taller de la escritora. Veladas Literarias de Juana Manuela Gorriti*. Lima-Buenos Aires (1876/7–1892). Rosario, Argentina: Beatriz Viterbo, 1999.

Denegri, Francesca. *El abanico y la cigarrera. La primera generación de mujeres ilustradas en el Perú*. Lima: Centro de la mujer peruana Flora Tristán, 1996.

Gamarra, Abelardo. "Mercedes Cabello de Carbonera". In *Rasgos de pluma*. Lima: Librería Francesa Cientifica, 1902, pp. 46–9.

Guerra Cunningham, Lucía. "Mercedes Cabello de Carbonera: estética de la moral y los desvíos no-disyuntivos de la virtud". *Revista de Crítica Literaria Latinoamericana* 26 (1987): 25–41.

Martínez-San Miguel, Yolanda. "Sujetos femeninos en *Amistad Funesta* y *Blanca Sol*: El lugar de la mujer en dos novelas Latinoamericanas de Fin de siglo XIX". *Revista Iberoamericana* 174 (1996): 2–45.

Peluffo, Ana. "Las trampas del naturalismo en *Blanca Sol*: Prostitutas y costureras en el paisaje urbano de Mercedes Cabello de Carbonera". *Revista de crítica literaria latinoamericana* 28 (2002): 37–52.

——. "Chismes, rumores y traiciones epistolares en Mercedes Cabello de Carbonera". In *Brújula* 3. Special issue on Working Gender: Cultural Representations of Women and Labor. eds Febe Armendáriz and Vanessa Yvette Pérez, 2004.

Pinto Vargas, Ismael. *Sin perdón y sin olvido. Mercedes Cabello de Carbonera y su mundo. Biografía*. Lima: Universidad de San Martín de Porres, 2003.

Ruiz Zevallos, Augusto. *Psiquiatras y locos. Entre la modernización contra los andes y el Nuevo proyecto de modernidad. Perú: 1850–1930*. Lima: Instituto Pasado & Presente, 1994.

Tamayo Vargas. Augusto. *Literatura Peruana*. Lima: Universidad Nacional Mayor de San Marcos, 1965.

Voyssest, Osvaldo. PhD thesis. Berkeley, CA: University of California, 1997.

CABRERA, LYDIA

Born in Havana, on May 20, 1900, Lydia Cabrera was the youngest of eight children in a socially and financially privileged family in pre-revolutionary Cuba. Her father, Raimundo Cabrera Bosch, was a writer and a former fighter for Cuba's independence, and her mother, Elisa Marcaida Casanova, was a devoted housewife and mother. The family's many black servants, including nannies for the children, introduced the young Lydia to the magical world brought to Cuba by the African slaves. It is possible that it was through them that she first learned about African myths, stories, religions and the supernatural world.

Because young women were not allowed to attend high school or the university, Cabrera did not receive a formal education, however, she did complete her studies independently. As a way to earn money so that she could study art in Paris, she organized an exhibit of Cuban art and opened an antique shop. She moved to Paris in 1927, and attended the École du Louvre and the École des Beaux Arts. Her stay in Paris coincided with a growing European interest in what was then called "primitive civilizations," and especially African art. At the time, the work of many European intellectuals and artists was heavily influenced by this "primitive art". Lydia Cabrera became interested in Cubism and Surrealism, and Asian civilizations. What especially attracted her was Eastern folklore, which reminded her of the stories she had heard in her childhood. It was then that she recognized the slaves that had been brought from Africa to Cuba were central to the national folklore because the indigenous peoples of Cuba had disappeared early in the country's history. Helped by Omí Tomí, one of the former servants in her home, she started to put down in writing some of the stories she had been told as a child. The publishing house Gallimard had these stories translated into French, and the volume entitled *Contes nègres de Cuba* appeared in 1936. Lydia Cabrera returned to Cuba before the Second World War and became completely involved in the study of Afro-Cuban languages and traditions. She left Cuba in 1960, and first moved to Spain and then to Miami, Florida, where she remained until her death on September 19, 1991.

Ethnographic Work, Traditional Stories and their Use

Cabrera devoted her life to the study of Africans in Cuba and their influence on the development of Cuban folklore, a development that was also influenced by the Spanish culture brought to the island during the Conquest. As an author, Cabrera proved to be extremely versatile, since she was a writer of fiction and an ethnographer. Among her publications as an ethnographer is her well-known book *El Monte* (The Forest), which has become a bible for practitioners of Santería and is a very important work on cultural and religious syncretism. According to the Afro-Cuban tradition, "el monte" (forest or jungle) is the place where the African gods and the spirit of the African ancestors of the slaves live. She also published *La Sociedad Secreta Abakuá*, a study of the rites and traditions of the secret society Abakuá (its members were known as "ñáñigos"). This society was not only secret but membership was limited to males. It must be stressed that the fact that Cabrera, a white woman, was permitted access to this knowledge speaks highly of the trust her informants had in her. It is also important to note that she never distanced herself from her topic, or criticized them, instead providing the information as if she herself believed in the religious practice being described.

Cabrera described her stories as "transpositions," and yet they were much more than a simple retelling. She not only recreated elements, characters, and themes of African and universal folklores, but she also modified the traditional stories by adding details of Cuban customs of the nineteenth and early twentieth centuries. In addition, she represented well-known themes within universal folklore from a different perspective. One example of this process can be seen in Cabrera's use of a magical object such as a saucepan, a salt shaker, a tablecloth that provides endlessly for its owner. This technique was popular at the time and with it, she re-created this use of an object to represent characters and people from Colonial Cuba, such as intelligent slaves, white owners, and European and local slave merchants. Themes of universal folklore such as cruel stepmothers, lost children, and magical fish who have the power to grant wishes are also present in some of the stories she tells. Contrary to the traditional folktale in which many characters are not individualized by their name but by their idiosyncrasies, Cabrera always personalizes them, whether they are gods, humans, or animals, by giving them their own name. Some of her descriptions are obviously influenced by Surrealism. One of her most interesting characters is Jicotea, a little water turtle with whom many Afro-Cubans identify, because it belongs to the lowest rung in the social ladder and because of this, it has a very hard life. In the traditional stories, the little water turtle adapts and confronts its aggressive environment in order to survive. In Cabrera's stories, the little water turtle doesn't just confront the unkind environment, instead it actively engages with it, deceiving its stronger adversaries and because of this adaptability, cleverness, and ingenuity is admired.

Fiction

In her works of fiction, Cabrera draws from her ethnographic interests and knowledge when she tells fables, legends and religious myths that originated in Africa. Recurring themes are the relationships between humans, animals and nature, and supernatural explanations of unusual phenomena. Many of the stories tell about the hardships suffered by slaves, as well as their thoughts about white Europeans. Cabrera's narratives are colorful and original; she uses many African onomatopoeic terms, repetitions, and refrains that lend her texts the rhythm and the feel of the original stories as told in the oral tradition. Another technique she uses that recalls the style of oral literature is the repetition of an action or a fact. This repetition emphasizes the cyclical nature of both their story and the universe. Cabrera was at her best when dealing with time and space in her stories, and it has been said that her representation of the real and the fantastic heralded many of the techniques used later in magical realism.

Critics have pointed out the fact that many of Cabrera's stories are told from a typically feminine point of view, and that most of her male characters are presented as weak and easily manipulated by their smarter female counterparts. The matter of sexuality is complicated because it is used as a weapon, especially by mulatto women, as a means to escape oppression. This can be explained in part because her characters are usually slaves who are far from the favorable situation of "cimarrones," former slaves who had escaped their servitude and created free communities in the forests. Another aspect several critics have pointed out is that in Cabrera's narratives there is no denunciation of social inequalities, and only few, if any, direct references to the oppression suffered by the Africans and Afro-Cubans.

Lydia Cabrera's work is part of a larger attempt, on the part of other Latin American writers and intellectuals such as Esteban Picardo, Fernando Ortiz, Rómulo Lachatañeré in Cuba, and Arthur Ramos, Gilberto Freyre and José Lins do Rego in Brazil, to reinstate the voices of the former slaves, their language and their culture. As such, her ethnographic, as well as her fictional work, is invaluable for a better understanding of the African experience not just in Cuba, but in all the Americas.

GIANNA M. MARTELLA

Selected Works

Cuentos Negros de Cuba. La Habana: Imprenta La Verónica, 1940.

Por Qué . . . Cuentos Negros de Cuba. La Habana: Ediciones C.R., 1948.

El Monte: Igbo-Finda; Ewe Orisha, Vititi Nfinda (Notas sobre las religiones, la magia, las supersticiones y el folklore de los negros criollos y el pueblo de Cuba). La Habana: Ediciones C.R., 1954.

Refranes de Negros Viejos: Recogidos por Lydia Cabrera. La Habana: Ediciones C.R., 1955.

Anagó: Vocabulario Lucumí (El Yoruba que Se Habla en Cuba). La Habana: Ediciones C.R., 1957.

La Sociedad Secreta Abakuá: Narrada por Viejos Adeptos. La Habana: Ediciones C.R., 1959.

Otán Iyebibé: Las Piedras Preciosas. Miami, FL: Ediciones C.R., 1970.

Ayapá: Cuentos de Jicotea. Miami, FL: Ediciones Universal, 1971.

La Laguna Sagrada de San Joaquín. Madrid: Ediciones R., 1973.

Yemayá y Ochún: Kariocha, Iyalorichas y Ororichas. Madrid: Ediciones C.R., 1974.

Anaforuana: Ritual de Símbolos de la Iniciación en la Sociedad Secreta Abakuá. Madrid: Ediciones R., 1975.

Francisco y Francisca: Chascarrillos de Negros Viejos. Miami, FL: Peninsular Printing, 1976.

Itinerarios del Insomnio: Trinidad de Cuba. Miami, FL: Ediciones C.R., 1977.

La Regla Kimbisa del Santo Cristo del Buen Viaje. Miami, FL: Ediciones C.R., 1977.

Reglas de Congo. Palo Monte-Mayombé. Miami, FL: Ediciones C.R.; Peninsular Printing, 1979.

Koeko Oyawó, Aprende Novicia: Pequeño Tratado de Regla Lucumí. Miami, FL: Ediciones C.R., 1980.

Cuentos para Adultos Niños y Retrasados Mentales. Miami, FL: Ultra Graphics Corp., c. 1983.

Vocabulario Congo (El Bantú que Se Habla en Cuba). Miami, FL: Ediciones C.R., 1984.

La Medicina Popular en Cuba. Médicos de Antaño, Curanderos, Santeros y Paleros de Hogaño. Miami, FL: Ediciones C.R., 1984.

Supersticiones y Buenos Consejos. Miami, FL: Ediciones Universal, 1987.

La Lengua Sagrada de los Ñáñigos. Miami, FL: Ediciones C.R., 1988.

Los Animales en el Folklore y la Magia de Cuba. Miami, FL: Ediciones Universal, 1988.

Páginas Sueltas. Ed., intro. and notes by Isabel Castellanos. Miami, FL: Ediciones Universal, 1994.

Arere Marekén: Cuento Negro. Illustrated by Alexandra Exter. Ed. Facsimilar (México, D.F.) Artes de Méjico, in collaboration with the University of Miami, c. 1999.

References and Further Reading

Bolívar Aróstegui, Natalia. *Lydia Cabrera en Su Laguna Sagrada*. Santiago de Cuba: Editorial Oriente, 2000.

Di Le, Octavio. *El descubrimiento de África en Cuba y Brasil, 1889–1969*. Madrid: Editorial Colibrí, 2001.

Gutiérrez, Mariela A. *Lydia Cabrera: Aproximaciones Mítico-Simbólicas a su Cuentística*. Madrid: Editorial Verbum, 1997.

Perera, Hilda. *Idapo: El Sincretismo en los Cuentos Negros de Lydia Cabrera*. Miami, FL: Ediciones Universal, 1971.

Romeu, Raquel. "Dios, Animal, Hombre o Mujer: Jicotea, Un Personaje de Lydia Cabrera". *Letras Femeninas* 15(102) (1989): 29–36.

Soto, Sara. *Magia e Historia en Los "Cuentos Negros," "Por Qué" y "Ayapá" de Lydia Cabrera*. Miami, FL: Ediciones Universal, 1988.

Valdes-Cruz, Rosa. "The Short Stories of Lydia Cabrera: Transpositions or Creations?" In Yvette E. Miller and Charles M. Tatum (eds) *Latin American Women Writers: Yesterday and Today*. Pittsburgh, PA: Latin American Literary Review, 1977, pp. 148–54.

CÁCERES, ESTHER DE

Esther de Cáceres (1903–71) received her doctorate in Medicine at the Universidad de la República in Montevideo, Uruguay, in 1929. Her passion for literature and poetry grew alongside her medical studies and her first collection of poetry, *Las islas extrañas* (The Strange Islands), was published in the same year. During her ensuing tenure as Professor of Medicine at Montevideo, the aspiring poet began teaching literature at local high schools and eventually also became professor of literature at the university.

In 1933, 1934, and 1941, she was the recipient of the Premio Nacional de Literatura (Uruguayan National Book Award). In spite of her fame in the Southern Cone, none of her works have been translated into English.

Esther de Cáceres is primarily known as a poet. Her lyrical work is characterized by a deep mysticism. In many ways, her verses convey a yearning for a communication with the divine and an ultimate fusion with the transcendental beyond language. In this respect, her poems take their place in the tradition of Teresa de Ávila and Sor Juana Inés de la Cruz. Aside from the religious theme and the use of mystical metaphors, such as the duality of light and darkness or music as a transcendental force, the poetry of Esther de Cáceres gives evidence of her familiarity with Western Classical and Renaissance poetry. Her poems elaborate on well-known imagery and allegorical metaphors from the Renaissance (roses, the sea, birds, stones, and mirrors). Her intricate vocabulary and rich inner rhymes and assonances often recall the verses of the Spanish-American and Peninsular "modernista" movement, e.g. Rubén Darío's *Cantos de vida y esperanza* (Chants of Life and Hope) and Miguel de Unamuno's "Salmos" ("Psalms"). Most of de Cáceres' texts are composed in free verse.

Her publications are numerous. After *Las islas extrañas* (1929), Esther de Cáceres' collections of poetry comprise *Libro de la soledad* (1933, Book of Solitude); *Los cielos* (1935, Heavens); *El alma y el ángel* (1938, The Soul and the Angel); *Espejo sin muerte* (1941, Mirror Without Death); *Concierto de amor y otros poemas* (1951, Concert of Love and Other Poems); a second and enlarged edition of *Concierto de amor* edited by de Cáceres' friend, the Chilean Nobel Laureate Gabriela Mistral; followed by *Paso de la noche* (1957, Passage of the Night); *Los cantos del destierro* (1963, Chants from Exile); *Tiempo y abismo* (1965, Time and Abyss); *Evocaciones de Lauxar* (1965, Evocations of Lauxar); and *Canto desierto* (1969, Solitary Song). Aside from poetry, de Cáceres wrote two volumes of cantatas and madrigals: *Cruz y éxtasis de la pasión cantada* (Cross and Ecstasy of the Sung Passion, 1937) and *Mar en el mar. Madrigales, trances, saetas* (1947, Sea in the Sea: Madrigals, Trances, and Saetas). 1945 saw the publication of her first and only anthology of poetry, *Antología de Esther de Cáceres, 1929–1945*.

In addition to her literary work, de Cáceres also made a name for herself as an influential critic of Uruguayan, Spanish-American and Peninsular literature. She had a predilection for the poetry of the 'Generación del '98, the "modernista" movement, and the work of various individual poets, particularly Delmira Agustini, Susana Soca, and María Eugenia Vaz Ferreira. She was the author of numerous book introductions and the editor of several critical editions and anthologies, including *Antología de Delmira Agustini* (1965); *Poesía completa de Gabriela Mistral* (1966, Complete Poetry of Gabriela Mistral); Francisco Espínola's *La recuperación del objeto – lección sobre plástica* (1965, The Recuperation of the Object: Lesson on Sculpture) as well as his *Raza ciega y otros cuentos* (1967, Blind Race and Other Stories); the prologue to María Eugenia Vaz Ferreira's *La isla de los cánticos* (1956, The Island of the Canticles); and Enrique Casaravilla Lemos' *Partituras secretas* (1967, Secret Scores). De Cáceres was one of the first female members of the Uruguayan "Academia Nacional de Letras" (National Academy of Literature) and a prominent member of literary circles in the Southern Cone. In 1974, the "Academia Nacional de Letras" published the posthumous *Selección de ensayos de Esther de Cáceres* (Selection of Essays by Esther de Cáceres).

Her poetry, in the words of the critic Julio J. Casal, is a creation of "canciones religiosas, ardientes en soledad y silencio" [religious songs, burning in solitude and silence] (1940: 534). Similarly, the poet Juana de Ibarbourou describes the common motif of de Cáceres' work as a deep yearning for "todo lo que pueda traerle un eco de la Divina Palabra" [all that might carry an echo of the Divine Word] (1959: 321); In this way, according to de Ibarbourou, all of de Cáceres' lyrical writings become "monólogo[s] frente al Ser que ama ... [sin] una palabra ni una imagen que no tengan un profundo y radiante significado de alma en el dogma" [monologues directed at the beloved Being ... without a single word or image that does not convey a deep-seated and radiant connection between the soul and Christian dogma] (ibid.: 321).

A good example of her mystical mood and her allusions to classical and biblical themes with a strong "modernista" undercurrent is "Antiguo espacio" (Ancient Space) from *Tiempo y abismo*. The poem invokes a melancholic image in which ancient ruins, Greek gods and biblical characters stand in marked contrast to the figure of the resurrected Christ. Like many other of de Cáceres' texts, this poem is written in free verse, with rich inner assonances and enjambements. These poetic techniques highlight the phonetic qualities of the words:

> Antiguo espacio
> En sus quebrantos sueña
> la luz tranquila.
> Cada columna, cada estatua erguida
> vive como una lámpara
> de pausados recuerdos
> y de melancolía.
> Piedra de Apolo y piedra de San Pablo
> como puentes de sangre
> ya remota y perdida
> tienden sus invisibles
> hiedras hacia el abismo
> ...
> Mientras Cristo, transido,
> sangre en flor, flor de sangre,
> pasa vivo y fragante entre las ruinas.
>
> [The quiet light / dreams in its shadows. / Every column, every towering statue / resides like a glow / of slow remembrances / and of melancholy. / Stone of Apollo and stone of Saint Peter / like bridges of blood / already far and lost / reach out their invisible / ivy stems towards the abyss ... / While Christ, suffering / blood in flower, flower in blood, / wanders vibrant and sweet-scented between the ruins.]

The most remarkable feature of de Cáceres' poetry is the combination of religious themes characterized by an echoing of different poetic traditions and imagery. Her reliance on traditional themes contrasts with the idiosyncratic manner of her lyrical expression in free verse. Her poetry of yearning transports the solitary search for an encounter with the divine, which is yet endowed with the promise of communion with God. For de Cáceres, poetry is a central means to convey this yearned-for reality beyond language and solitude. In this vein, the lines "¡y ya estoy en el ámbito / de la gran noche sola!" [And I am already in the ambit / of the great lonely night!] from an untitled poem from *Libro de la soledad* are transformed into the jubilant exclamation in the final lines: "Vienen las Soledades y juntas contemplamos. / ¡Los mares del día cantan!" [And here come the Solitudes and together we contemplate. / The seas of the day are singing!].

ILKA KRESSNER

Selected Works

Cruz y éxtasis de la pasión cantada. La Plata, Argentina, 1937.
El alma y el ángel. Montevideo: Impresora Uruguaya, 1938.

Espejo sin muerte. Montevideo: Reuniones de Estudio, 1941.
Antología de Esther de Cáceres, 1929–1945. Buenos Aires: Ediciones Correo Literario, 1945.
Concierto de amor y otros poemas. Buenos Aires: Losada, 1951 (second and enlarged edition of the earlier *Concierto de amor*).
Evocaciones de Lauxar. Montevideo: Impresora Uruguaya, 1965.
Canto desierto. Montevideo: Ediciones de Teseo, 1969.
Las islas extrañas. Santiago del Estero, Argentina: Brasa, 1929.
Libro de la soledad. Montevideo: Imprenta germano-uruguaya, 1933.
Los cielos. Montevideo: Impresora Uruguaya, 1935.
Mar en el mar. Madrigales, trances, saetas. Montevideo: Reuniones de Estudio, 1947.
Paso de la noche. Buenos Aires: Losada, 1957.
Los cantos del destierro. Buenos Aires: Losada, 1963.
Tiempo y abismo. Montevideo: Ediciones Río de la Plata, 1965.
Selección de ensayos. Montevideo: Academia Nacional de Letras, 1974.
"Introducción a la lectura de Susana Soca". *Revista Nacional (Montevideo)* 9: (1964): 16–45.

References and Further Reading

Casal, Julio J. (ed.) *Exposición de la poesía uruguaya desde sus origenes hasta 1940*. Montevideo: Editorial Claridad, 1940, pp. 534–7.
de Ibarbourou, Juana. "La poesía de Esther de Cáceres". *Revista Nacional (Montevideo)* 4(201) (1959): 321–6.
Rosario Fernández Alonso, María. "Sor Juana Inés de la Cruz y Esther de Cáceres: Dos poetisas de religiosidad vivida y honda trascendencia en sus respectivos ámbitos socio-culturales," in *XVII Congreso del Instituto internacional de Literatura Iberoamericana: El barroco en América*. Madrid: Ediciones de la Universidad Complutense de Madrid, 1999, pp. 239–56.

CALDERÓN, TERESA

Teresa Calderón (b. 1955) is considered one of the most important women poets from the 1960s and an important active member of the movement of women writers during the 1980s. Born in La Serena, Chile, Calderón hails from a family of poets. Her father is Alfonso Calderón, recipient of the National Prize of Literature and her sister, Lila is also a poet. Teresa Calderón has dedicated her life to the study, the teaching, and the writing of literature. She is a Spanish teacher and has also received a degree in Aesthetics from the Universidad Católica de Chile.

During her time as a student of education at the Instituto de Letras, she won the Literary Contest sponsored by the Universidad Católica in 1978 and 1979, and her first book of poetry was published as a result of this prize.

Teresa Calderón produced her work under the dictatorship regime in Chile (1973–89) and she belongs to the post-1973 generation that has been called *Dispersa* (Disperse) by the Chilean critic, Soledad Bianchi. This group of poets, whose work spans from 1973 through the 1980s, has been called by Bianchi a "Diaspora generation", or a group that lived in a state of internal exile. As with any classification, it is difficult to establish to which generation she belongs, but it is easier to identify some of the concrete circumstances surrounding her work. She stayed in Santiago during the dictatorship and developed her poetic style and voice during those years, and published her first book in the 1980s.

During this period this group did not publish their poetry due to censorship, so at that time there were many self-published and independently published editions, but most of all there was an orality about poetry that was cultivated through many group readings in cultural centers and meetings. The idea of community among those poets who stayed in Chile at the time of dictatorship persisted, as did the necessity of writing and listening to those poems that were contingent to that period.

As Calderón stayed in Chile, her fame grew as one of the most important voices of poetry of the 1980s, and in 1992 she won the Pablo Neruda Prize. During this time feminine voices started to emerge in Chilean literature and generated new movements, represented by authors such as Carmen Berenguer, Elvira Hernández, Eugenia Brito and Diamela Eltit. This growing movement of women in literature also represents the change in their subjectivity in Chilean society; women began to exhibit more agency in the 1970s and the 1980s, and started to have a place in history, as is observed through women's active roles in the Association of Relatives of the Disappeared and in the rise in the number of feminine leaders who appeared in opposition to the dictatorship. These women's voices are an important part of social and political movements of this period. They also developed a feminine criticism from their works in which they talked about politics, sensuality, the erotic, etc. at the moment of the "apagón cultural" (cultural blackout). Their work acquired importance and strength at this moment, and became valued in the world of Chilean literature.

Women of the World: Unite

Calderón's work has been widely recognized for the change in feminine voice toward an historical "you", a recourse traditionally employed by women poets. Calderón does so, but changes this relation and dependence towards this poetic "you" and shows an attitude of strength, irony and antagonism. This started with her book *Causas perdidas* (1984). Composed almost as epigrammatic poems, Calderón attempts to portray a new kind of relationship between man and woman that is more conflictive in nature and shows a totally different attitude. In these poems the space of marriage is destroyed through the use of acidic humor and everyday language. In a very personal and nostalgic tone, she shows her perspective toward those subjects, as is seen in the poem: "A diez rounds", where the rounds are the marriage fights that end up being a battlefield. As in another of her most quoted poems, "Guerrilla doméstica" (Domestic Battles), where this "you" and "me" fight in the home space, "A diez rounds" ends by alluding to the loss of love as a lost battle, or like "Bodas" (Marriage) in which the end of the relationship is announced from the beginning of the poem.

Calderón plays with the traditional roles of men and women and the expectations of marriage and family to make a statement about all that has changed and still needs to change in order to empower women with strong voices under the patriarchal regime. She creates a metaphor for the country through domestic space.

For Calderón, the experience of dictatorship made her write about contingency, as seen in the poems, "Asuntos de la memoria" (Affairs of Memory), and "Estado de sitio" (State of Siege), included in *Género Femenino* (1989, Feminine Gender).

These poems respond to the dictatorship period in Chile and her critical vision toward politics at that moment. The mixture of political context with the relationship theme is common in her poetry. Calderón often employs irony to refer to the roles of women in society, a central focus in all her writing, and in most of the poems included in this book. The poem "Mujeres del mundo: Uníos" (Women of the World: Unite), paraphrases the ready-made slogan made popular in relation to working men. In this famous poem she addresses all different kinds of women to lend a perspective on gender roles and society. Calderón's discourse is not explicitly feminist, but her writings do address a diverse group of women, united in one common discourse, as the title of the poem points out.

Calderón uses many ready-made phrases, as well as song lyrics and black humor in order to dismantle the patriarchal discourse and the established place of women, usually expressed through explorations of domesticity, marriage, and relationships. The poet appeals to her readership through engagement with orality and everyday language.

Género Femenino is perhaps one of her most significant books, in terms of exposing the subjects of her poetry (women) and the relationship between men and women, but from the perspective of irony, and pain, that ends up being just life itself, as is seen in the poems "Dispareja" (Uneven) and "Bodas" (Marriage), both poems that talk about loss or its possibility.

Aplausos para la memoria (1998, Applause for Memory) and *El poeta y otras maravillas* (2003, The Poet and other Wonders) are examples of her most recent books of poetry that deal more with experimentalism. She has also made an incursion into narrative with the publication of the volume of short stories, *Vida de perras* (2000, Bitch's Life) and the novel *Amiga mía* (2003, Friend of Mine), which received very good critical reviews and led her to win the National Book Council Prize (2004) for the best novel published in 2003.

In 2003, she also edited a volume of poetry called *Obra poética* (Poetic Works). This compilation reunites all five of her previously published books and shows the consistency of her poetic writing in the past twenty years. Her work has been translated into English, Swedish, German, French, Italian and Portuguese.

In general, Teresa Calderón's writing is autobiographical and confessional, but in a way that addresses many women and readers universally. Teresa Calderón has become a writer and a fundamental feminine voice in Chilean literature. Since the 1980s, she has been a witness to Chilean history and to the changes in society which she depicts in her works.

MACARENA URZÚA

Selected Works

Publicación de autores premiados. Concurso Literario Universidad Católica, 1978.

Uno X Uno: Nueve poetas jóvenes. Antología. Santiago de Chile: Editorial Nascimento, 1979.

Publicación de autores premiados. Concurso Literario Universidad Católica, 1979.

Causas Perdidas. Santiago de Chile: Ediciones Artesanales, 1984.

Arteche, Massone, Scarpa (eds) *Poesía Chilena Contemporánea*. Santiago de Chile: Editorial Andrés Bello, 1984.

Villegas, Juan (ed.) *Nueva poesía femenina chilena*. Santiago de Chile: Editorial La Noria, 1985.

Poets of Chile: A Bilingual Anthology 1965–1985. Trans. Steven White. Greensboro, VA: Unicorn Press, 1986.

Género Femenino. Santiago de Chile: Editorial Planeta, 1989.

Díaz, Erwin (ed.) *Poesía chilena de hoy. De Parra a nuestros días*. Santiago de Chile: Ediciones Documentas, 1993.

Marjorie Agosín (ed.) *These are Not Sweet Girls: Latin American Women Poets*. Fredonia, NY: White Pine Press, 1994.

Imágenes Rotas. Santiago: Editorial Red Internacional del Libro, 1995.

Calderón, Teresa, Harris, Tomás and Calderón, Lila (eds) *Veinticinco años de poesía chilena (1975–1995)*. Santiago de Chile: Fondo de Cultura Económica, 1996.

Seis poetas de la República: Antología de Poesía Inédita. Santiago de Chile: Ediciones Altazor, 1997.

Esto es el Amor. Antología de poemas de amor. Versos de 100 poetas chilenos. Edited by Teresa Calderón, Lila Calderón and Tomás Harris. Santiago de Chile: Editorial Planeta, 1997.

Voces de Eros. Antología de Cuentos Eróticos. Diez cuentos eróticos de escritoras chilenas. Edited by Mariano Aguirre. Santiago de Chile: Editorial Grijalbo, 1997.

No me arrepiento de nada. Santiago de Chile: Editorial Xerox, 1999.

Aplausos para la memoria. Santiago: Red Internacional del Libro, 1999.

Vida de perras. Santiago de Chile: Editorial Alfaguara, 2000.

Aventuras de Super Inti y Analfabruja. Santiago de Chile: Editorial Alfaguara, 2000.

Amiga mía. Santiago de Chile: Editorial Alfaguara, 2003.

Obra poética. Santiago de Chile: Al Margen Editores, 2003.

Mi amor por ti. Santiago de Chile: Editorial Alfaguara, 2005.

References and Further Reading

Arteche, Miguel (ed.) *Antología de la poesía religiosa chilena*. Santiago de Chile: Universidad Católica, 1989.

Bevingade Lejon Sun, Axelsson (ed.) *Antología de poetas chilenos traducidos al sueco*. Suecia: Editorial Bonniers, 1991.

Bianchi, Soledad. "Un mapa por completar: La joven poesía chilena" (1983). In *Poesía Chilena (Miradas Enfoques Apuntes)*. Santiago de Chile: Ediciones Documentas, CESOC, 1990.

Brito, Eugenia (ed.) *Antología de poetas chilenas. Confiscación y silencio*. Caracas and Santiago de Chile: Editorial Dolmen, 1998.

Corsen, Inge (ed.) *La mujer en la poesía de los 80*. In *Antología*. Santiago de Chile, 1987.

Díaz, Erwin (ed.) *16 poetas chilenos. Antología de poesía chilena*. Santiago de Chile: Talleres Gráficos GRAFICOM, 1987.

Hernández Sender, Juan (ed.) *Poetry from Chile: 26 New Voices*. The Translators' Workshop, Long Beach, CA: California State University, 1993.

Levitin, Alexis (ed.) *Beacons 8: Publication of the American Translators Association*. Trans. Justin Bland, Sylvia Mello and Tia Rabine, 2002, pp. 20–7.

"Poesía femenina en la década de 1980. Causas Perdidas". Memoria chilena. Portal de la cultura de Chile. http://www.memoriachilena.cl/mchilena01/temas/dest.asp?id=vocesfemeninascausas. June 5, 2006.

Villegas, Juan. *El Nuevo discurso lírico de la mujer en Chile: 1975–1990*. Santiago de Chile: Mosquito Editores, 1993.

"Visions from Within: Contemporary Chilean Literature and Arts". *Review: Latin American Literature and Arts*. 49 (1994).

CAMPESINO, PILAR (PILAR RETES, ALIAS LY SETER)

Pilar Campesino was born in Mexico City on June 15, 1945, but her identity is clearly entrenched in the state of Morelos, land of the revolutionary Emiliano Zapata. She grew up in

Cuernavaca, Morelos, where she attended local schools. Campesino reports barely surviving the profusion of pinches dutifully administered by the Catholic nuns who did not appreciate her religious unruliness. Or perhaps she was targeted for asking too many existential questions at a very young age. In college, she decided to study psychology. However, since the field was quite nascent in 1960s Mexico, and the local state university did not provide this curriculum, she traveled to Mexico City's UNAM (National Autonomous University of Mexico). Young Pilar felt overwhelmed by the enormity of the nation's largest university and decided instead to pursue her studies at the Universidad Iberoamericana. There she became interested in literature and creative writing. In those early college years she wrote *Sabotage*, a novel inspired by Daphne Du Maurier's *Rebecca* (1935). Ironically, the work was destroyed, a result of the author's own overly critical gaze.

She met Gabriel Retes in 1965 and married him two years later. He is the son of the prolific writer, and theatre and cinema actor, Ignacio Retes. This marriage facilitated Campesino's entry into the intriguing and innovative world of Mexican theatre where young dramatists were experimenting with theatrical techniques and themes. During that time her father-in-law Ignacio was an important mentor and inspiration to her. In 1967, she premiered her first play: *Los objetos malos* (The Evil Objects) in the Hidalgo Theatre under the nom de plume Ly Seter. Her husband Gabriel initiated his directorial debut with this play. It was presented in the *Primer Festival de Autores Inéditos del INBA* (The First Festival of Unpublished Authors of the Institute of Fine Arts). Campesino proposed the work in fulfillment of her thesis requirement in psychology. The play explores the Oedipal complex in the context of a modern Mexican family. In it she demonstrates a keen understanding of the dynamics of repression, jealousy and desire implicit in this psychological phenomenon. Though the play was soundly rejected as an experimental thesis, it received accolades and honorable mention at the aforementioned *Primer Festival*.

The author's subsequent drama, *Verano negro* (1967, Black Summer) premiered in 1968 at the Teatro Estudiantil de la Universidad de Mexico, but was interrupted because of the mass student protests of 1968. Tragically, the Mexican student movement was truncated on October 2, 1968, at the Plaza de las Tres Culturas in Tlatelolco. This is a day most Mexicans of the era remember as the massacre of unarmed and defenseless university students by the military police. The student protestors were gunned down as Mexico, host to the 1968 summer Olympics, prepared to present itself as a modern nation. *Verano negro*, with its portrayal of American Black Power activism and civil rights movement, seemed to portend the violent encounters that were to stun Mexicans throughout the republic.

Many writers in Mexico, influenced by the massacre of October 2nd, sought to denounce and purposely expose what the government tried to disclaim and conceal. (See Elena Poniatowska.) Pilar Retes, as she was known then, received a grant in 1969 from the Centro Mexicano de Escritores (Center for Mexican Writers) and as a consequence wrote what is her most famous play *Octubre terminó hace mucho tiempo* (October Ended a Long Time Ago). As an artist, Campesino's response to the events was to document what occurred through the interplay of gender relations in a heterosexual couple engaged in political activism. Although the drama ostensibly explores the lack of communication and its relation to domestic violence, it is immersed in the events that tragically surrounded Tlatelolco.

The drama's performance was censored in Mexico City because it violated Articles 6 and 7 of the Constitution. The simulated sex scenes and smoking of cannabis on stage upset bourgeois sensibilities and the play was prohibited to Mexican audiences. It premiered in New York City at the Community Center Theatre in 1971 under the direction of Ignacio Retes. The local Spanish-language theatre association bestowed upon the drama a prize in the category of Best Foreign Theatre Group. However, the play did not premiere in Mexico City until September 26, 1974. *Octubre* was directed by her husband Gabriel Retes and appeared in the Galeon Theatre. There it enjoyed one hundred shows and more accolades. The play continues to be a favorite among university student theatre groups, enjoying a variety of informal representations. Indeed, among students of performance and theatre, it is a well-established work.

In the 1970s, Campesino began script-writing for various creative projects involving Mexican films, dramatic/historical programs for television and *telenovelas* (soap operas). She was a scriptwriter for the 1973–74 *telenovela* "Nosotros los pobres" (We, the Poor) and the screenwriter for *Chin-Chin El Teporocho* (1975, Chin-Chin, the Drunkard), a film directed by her husband Gabriel Retes. Personal vicissitudes forced the writer to engage in more lucrative and predictable employment as copyeditor and writer for the private sector. Intermittently the dramatist returns to her true vocation to explore the complexities of women's sexual, maternal and political identities. After a decade long hiatus she published a new play, *ese 8* (Super8mm), in a collection of her work simply entitled *Teatro* I (1980, Cihuacóatl Editoras). An adventurous artist of many talents, she appears in her ex-husband's commercially successful film *El Bulto* ("The Load," Gabriel Retes, Dir. 1992).

Subsequently in the 1990s and thereafter, her plays appeared in various anthologies aimed at students of Mexican theatre. One collection, for example, cites *El Tinglado* (Street Theatre) as an excellent piece for directing students with a propensity towards experimentation. Another includes *Las tres siempre seremos las tres* (The Three of Us Will Never Change) in its collection of children's plays because of its lyric qualities, brevity and representational malleability. In this experimental work the author collapses the boundaries of theatre as representation and theatre as text by transforming the stage directions into poetry.

In 2003, Pilar Campesino was hospitalized for a debilitating bout of emphysema, forcing her to abandon Mexico City and semi-retire to the salubrious environment of Tepoztlán, Morelos, a picturesque town just a few kilometers from her childhood home of Cuernavaca. In Tepoztlán, she can be found working at a local bookstore and always imagining the next experimental theatrical representation, the next incursion into the psychology of women, the next conflation of the real with the unreal.

Gender, Psychology and Resistance

Mexican theatre enthusiasts acknowledge Pilar Campesino as an audacious, experimental writer whose creative work explores the dynamics of psychology, gender, violence and political action. Campesino's first play *Los objetos malos* documents her early interest in psychology and psychiatry. As part of her continued interest in the field, she attended two separate conferences in Cuernavaca, later editing two compilations based on the presentations. A socially committed writer, plays such as *Verano negro* and *Octubre* set her apart from her contemporaries, the generation of 1969. The playwright is the only one in her generation to directly mention the unspeakable events of Tlatelolco in 1968. In *Octubre*, the stage directions demand that Mario, one of two characters, project 8mm film images of the student movement, including the detentions, repression and demonstrations. Fellow playwrights Jesús González Dávila, and Claudio Patricio mention the events indirectly. Hints of an absurdist aesthetic can be found when the two characters engage in child's play and "ride" a newspaper now transformed into a skateboard. In *eSe 8* the conflation of reality with the unreal punctuates the dialogue as the characters try to decipher if they are actors in a film about a play or vice versa. This anxiety about reality and the desire to create it permeate the creative productions of dramatists in the 1980s. Subsequent to *Octubre*, her dramatic endeavors concentrate on the complex psychological dynamics between mothers and daughters/sons, at times offering unexpected renditions of traditional characterizations of motherhood. This approach is evident in plays such as *Mi pequeño Tristán, tú eres el amo* (My Little Tristán, You Are the Master), *La partida* (The Departure) and *Las tres siempre seremos las tres*. However, *El Tinglado* signals the playwright's constant preoccupation with the theme of Mexican politics and art as resistance. The work is a parodic one-act piece written at the end of the Salinas de Gortari *sexenio* (six-year rule) that is critical of the administration's disdain for the Constitution (one of the characters *is* the Mexican Constitution personified). Without doubt, Campesino is a talented experimental writer whose work is just beginning to be noticed. Ultimately, it is Campesino's courageous depiction and denunciation of the Mexican government's repression of the 1968 student movement that willl remain as a testament to the power and importance of the writer as politically engaged activist.

MARÍA M. ZALDUONDO

Selected Works

Octubre terminó hace mucho tiempo. Mexico City: Colección Teatro Social Mexicano INFONAVIT, 1979.

"Verano negro". In *Teatro jóven de México*. Ed. Emilio Carballido. Mexico City: Mexicanos Unidos 1979, 2006, pp. 249–67.

I Teatro: *Los objetos malos. Verano negro. Octubre terminó hace mucho tiempo. eSe 8*. Mexico City: Cihuacoatl Editoras, 1980.

Ed. *Antipsiquiatría y Política. Alternativas a la psiquiatría*. IV Encuentro Internacional. Cuernavaca: Mor, 1978. Mexico City: Editorial Extemporáneos, 1980.

"Octubre terminó hace mucho tiempo". *Más teatro jóven*. Mexico City: Mexicanos Unidos, 1982.

Ed. *Manicomios y prisiones: Alternativas a la Psiquiatría*. I Encuentro Latinoamericano y V Internacional. Cuernavaca: Mor, 1981. Mexico City: Red-ediciones, 1983.

"La partida" (preludio en un solo acto). *Doce a las doce*. Mexico City: Editorial Obra Citada, 1989, pp. 37–57.

"Mi pequeño Tristán, tú eres mi amo". Ed. Dante del Castillo, *Teatro de humor para jóvenes*. Mexico City: Árbol Editorial, 1996, pp. 155–75.

"El Tinglado". *Teatro para estudiantes de teatro*. Mexico City: Árbol Editorial, 1996, pp. 61–74.

Las tres siempre seremos las tres. In Miguel Ángel Tenorio (ed.), *Teatro para niños*. Mexico City: Árbol Editorial, 2000, pp. 17–30.

Octubre terminó hace mucho tiempo. Mexico City: Arte y Escena Ediciones, 2003.

References and Further Reading

Álvarez, Noguera and Rogelio, José (eds) "Campesino, Pilar". In *Enciclopedia de México*. Mexico City: Instituto de la Enciclopedia de México, 1987, p. 1263.

Bissett, Judith. "The Revolution and the Role of Women in the Plays of Consuelo de Castro and Pilar Campesino". *Latin American Theatre Review* 33(1) (1999): 45–53.

Burgess, Ronald D. "The Generation Gap: The First Wave". *The New Dramatists of Mexico, 1967–1985*. Lexington, KY: Kentucky University Press, 1991, pp. 30–44.

Ceballos, Edgar, Ostoa, Alejandro and Porras, Yalma Hail (eds). "Retes, Pilar". In *Diccionario enciclopédico básico de teatro mexicano*. Mexico City: Escenología, 1996, p. 390.

Dell Adams, Monty. "Introducción". In *Teatro I. Pilar Campesino*. Mexico City: Cihaucoatl, 1980.

Larson, Catherine and Vargas, Margarita (eds) "Introduction". In *Latin American Dramatists: Theatre, Texts and Theories*. Bloomington, IN: Indiana University Press, 2000, pp. XI–XXV.

Milleret, Margo. "Questioning Motherhood". *Latin American Women On/In Stages*. New York: State University of New York Press, 2004, pp. 85–152.

Olson Buck, Carla. "Power Plays/Plays of Power: The Theatre of Pilar Campesino". In Catherine Larson and Margarita Vargas (eds), *Latin American Dramatists: Theatre, Texts and Theories*. Bloomington, IN: Indiana University Press, 1998, pp. 55–73.

Tenorio, Miguel Ángel. "Prólogo". In *Teatro para niños*. Mexico City: Árbol Editorial, 2000, pp. v–vi.

CAMPOBELLO, NELLIE

Nellie Campobello (1900–86) is widely recognized in Mexico for her dedication to arts, culture, and dance, and is less known for her efforts to dispel the "lies" of the government about the Revolution in the North with her published recollections of events and people. Campobello's testimonial literature of the Mexican Revolution (1910–20) was rediscovered in the second half of the twentieth century; her two best-known works, *Cartucho* (Cartridge or Bullet, a young soldier's nickname) and *Las manos de mamá* (My Mother's Hands) continue to be read and studied for their unique eyewitness perspective of the Revolution and of Mexican culture of the period. As a mark of affection, kinship, and esteem, critics and journalists, as well as the Mexican public, often refer to Campobello as "Nellie".

Creating a Revolutionary

Campobello was born in Villa Ocampo in the state of Durango in the mountains of Northern Mexico. Irene Matthews affirms that the date for Campobello's baptism given in the official acts of the parish church of San Miguel de Bocas is September 8, 1901, for the child "María Francisca, hija natural de Rafaela Luna," (natural [illegitimate] daughter of Rafaela Luna), who had given birth to the baby on November 7, 1900 (1997: 23).

Oscar Mata provides her baptismal name as Nellie Francisca Ernestina Moya Luna ("La Revolución Mexicana escrita en mirada de niña". ["The Mexican Revolution Written through the Gaze of a Child," 2006: 45]), suggesting that she may have been the *tocaya* (namesake) of the General. Elsewhere, her name is given María Francisca "Xica" Moya Luna.

Campobello's mother was Rafaela Luna, and her father is assumed to have been Felipe de Jesús Moya, but no father's name is given in this or in any other document pertaining to the "seis, siete u ocho" (six, seven, or eight) children of Rafaela Luna, from whom Campobello apparently took her love of dance, folklore, and narrative as well as her independent approach to the world (Mathews 1997: 24 ff.). Some biographers provide Campobello with the surname "Morton," from Jesús Campbell Morton who may have been the father of Campobello's younger half-sister, Gloria. Campobello passed her early years in Durango, where Francisco "Pancho" Villa was the military and folk hero of the period—and of times to come.

In 1919, Campobello bore a son, Raúl, who died at the age of 2, and her mother, Rafaela Luna, died shortly after (Mathews 1997: 37). *Abra en la roca* (Abra on the Rock) contains a poem "Ella y su hijo" ("She and her son") dedicated to Campobello's mother. The first-person voice of the narrator is perhaps intended to point to Rafaela Luna, but the poem is a deeply experienced maternal lament for the death of a young child. Also contained in this section, collated immediately before "Ella y su hijo," is "Regalo" ("Gift"), a poem that addresses an absent man who arrived unexpectedly and in whom the speaker has had great hopes for the future, but the man's promise remains unfulfilled, and the lament for the child concludes in a similar recognition of irreparable absence.

At this juncture of loss, Campobello and her siblings relocated to Mexico City in the early 1920s, and Campobello imposed Spanish phonology on the English name Campbell and took it as a surname (1997: 46). The Spanish version of the name also recalls Campobello's Villa Ocampo (see Matthews, 1997: Chapter 2).

Ballet Lessons and Literary Beginnings

Campobello and Gloria attended the Colegio Inglés (English School) in Mexico City, and there, an opportunity of viewing a performance of ballerina Ana Pavlova in 1924 inspired Gloria to take up ballet. Campobello went along, but preferred singing and riding to dance. Nevertheless, both sisters received instruction, and by 1927 their accomplishments were being praised in newspaper notices. Campobello continued working in the arts, particularly in dance, through the 1970s.

At about the same period, Campobello's literary career began with a minor foray into journalism (see "Hemerografía" in Dávila Valero 2000: 209) and her first creative literary work, *¡Yo!*, (I! 1929) published under the name "Francisca". At least two editions were issued, the second of which was titled *Yo, por Francisca* (I, by Francisca; see Matthews 1997: 57). Matthews notes that the "frescura e intimidad" (freshness and intimacy) of the collection went unappreciated in the Mexican capital where the literary public sought a different kind of poetic voice.

A few years afterward, Campobello released *Cartucho* which Emmanuel Carballo records was written in Havana, Cuba, between 1929 and 1930. In 1930, Campobello returned to Mexico, and the first of many editions of *Cartucho* was printed the following year in Xalapa by Ediciones Integrales. Indeed, Campobello's works have been published repeatedly, and the prologues included in these editions form valuable critical material on Campobello, for whom there is relatively limited critical work. Editions also may vary in text, so textual comparisons are worthwhile.

Literary Reputation

Campobello recognized that her version of history was not likely to be well received by mainstream history or criticism. She comments on her expectations in the "Prólogo" (Prologue) to her collected works, *Mis libros* (My books): "Mi tema era despreciado, mis héroes estaban proscritos. A Francisco Villa lo consideraban peor que el propio Atila" (p. 14). [My theme was despised; my heroes were forbidden. They considered Francisco Villa to be worse than Attila himself.] In spite of the contrary position in which she found herself, Campobello felt compelled to record her memories because they were "the truth": "Comprendí que decir verdades me ponía en situación de gran desventaja frente a los calumniadores organizados. Me ponía en peligro de que me aplastaran aquellas voces enemigas . . ." (14). [I understood that to tell these truths was putting me in a very disadvantageous position against the organized slanderers. I was putting myself in danger of having enemy voices crush me.] She notes that she could have continued to live comfortably without writing her version of history, but that she would not have then been true to the ideals of her own family, nor to all the people who participated in the Revolution.

In fact, *Cartucho* won praise from unexpected quarters. Campobello recalls that the second wife of Mexican president and Revolutionary general Elias Plutarco Calles once confided to Campobello, "Tu libro . . . debe ser muy bueno. Mi viejo lo tiene en su buró" (*Mis libros* p. 26). [Your book . . . must be very good. My husband has it in [on] his bureau.] Others, as Campobello had expected, reviled it: "Comenzaron las calumnias en mi contra; me disfiguraban como si no me conocieran" (26). [The slanderous gossip began against me; they altered me so much that I did not recognize myself.] More recent critics have been generous in their praise of Campobello's contribution to Revolutionary Mexican literature. It is an error, though, to regard her prose in *Cartucho* or in *Las manos de mamá* as immature or rustic and unpolished. It is much more likely that the wide-eyed, child-like style of those two works is intentional. Campobello's prose in her "Prologue" to *Mis libros* and her narrative of Villa's career (*Apuntes* [*Notes*]) is distinct from her "child witness" works in style, vocabulary, and structure. Clearly Campobello matched her voice with her narrative aim and wrote with the ear of a reader to achieve the sensuous and suggestive prose of *Cartucho* and *Las manos de mamá*.

Final Years

Campobello's last years are sketched by Matthews in "Querida Nellie, ¿Dónde estás?" (Beloved Nellie, Where Are You? in *La Centaura del Norte* [*Female Centaur of the North*, meant to refer to Villa as "Centaur of the North"]). Matthews saw Campobello immediately before Campobello came to be under the absolute power of her unscrupulous former dance student (1980), who sought to profit from Campobello's possessions, including jewelry and papers and artifacts related to Mexico's leading artists of the first half of the century. Just before Campobello disappeared from the Mexican intellectual and cultural scene, the State of Durango awarded her the "Francisco Zarco" medal of achievement in 1983 (Matthews 1997: 19) or 1984 (State of Durango website).

Matthews visited Campobello for the last time in 1984, at the beginning of her enforced confinement (Matthews 1997: 18–19), and Campobello was seen for the last time in public in 1985 at the age of 85, as Luis de la Barreda Solórzano notes (see also Matthews 1997: 160). Eventually a private organization "¿Dónde está Nellie?" ("Where is Nellie?") was formed by her admirers to investigate Campobello's disappearance. Long after Campobello's death, her kidnappers were sentenced to prison for their role in holding her under conditions of abuse and neglect until her death, which, according to a death certificate issued for Francisca Moya Luna, occurred on July 9, 1986, and which the pair concealed (Luis de la Barreda Solórzano "El escalofrío" ["Shiver"]).

Current Editions and Biography

¡Yo! (1929) has recently has been re-edited in light of renewed critical interest in Campobello's prose works, and its fifteen poems are included in *Mis libros* (My Books) (1960). Additional works of poetry are contained in *Abra en la roca* (Abra on the Rock, contained in *Mis libros*). Campobello's prose includes *Cartucho* (1937) a series of short sketches of persons and events related to the Revolution; *Las manos de mamá* (1937), an homage to Campobello's mother; and *Apuntes sobre la vida militar de Francisco Villa* (Notes on the Military Life of Francisco Villa) (1940), in which Campobello details the General's career. Campobello's accounts of the Revolution were long relegated to a subordinate position in the literature of the period, overshadowed by such luminaries as Martín Luis Guzmán, a personal friend of Campobello's; Mariano Azuela, the first writer of a novel of the Mexican Revolution; and other male authors.

Irene Matthews' biography of Campobello is definitive, and Elena Poniatowska's "Prologue" presents an invaluable perspective of historical and cultural background on Campobello's work. Patricia Davila Valero's work on Campobello is singular for its unique photographs and for its detailed discussion and documentary evidence related to Campobello's disappearance, including letters in facsimile and a chronology.

ELIZABETH MOORE WILLINGHAM

Selected works

Mis libros. "Prologo" Nellie Campobello. 1st edn. Mexico: Compañía General, 1960.

Cartucho and My Mother's Hands. Trans. Doris Meyer and Irene Matthews. Austin, TX: University of Texas Press, 1988.

Las manos de mamá. Mexico: Grijalbo, 1991.

Cartucho. "Prólogo" by Fernando Tola de Habich. México: Factoría Ediciones, 1999.

Cartucho. Relatos de la lucha en el Norte de México. "Prólogo" by Jorge Aguilar Mora. México: Ediciones Era, 2000.

Further Reading

Davila Valero, Patricia. *Nellie Campobello*. Durango, Mexico: CISA, 2000.

Carballo, Emmanuel. "Nellie Campobello" in *Protagonistas de la literatura mexicana*. Series Lecturas Mexicanas, 2(48) (1986): 408–19.

Garcia, Clara Guadalupe. *Nellie: El caso Campobello*. Mexico: Cal y Arena, 2000.

Martinez Reynosa, Emilia Elena. *Nellie Campobello y su obra literaria*. Mexico: UNAM Press, 1965.

Mata, Oscar. "La Revolución Mexicana escrita en mirada de niña." http://www.azc.uam.mx/publicaciones/tye/okcart.htm (November 16, 2006).

Matthews, Irene. *La centaura del Norte*. Mexico: Cal y Arena, 1997.

Meyer, Doris. "Nellie Campobello's *Las manos de mamá*: A Rereading". *Hispania* 68(4) (1985): 747–52.

Rodríguez, Blanca. *Eros y violencia*. Mexico: UNAM Press, 1998.

CAMPOS, JULIETA

Julieta Campos was born in La Habana, Cuba, on May 8, 1932. Campos left Cuba to study French literature at the Sorbonne from 1953–54, upon graduating from la Universidad de la Habana in 1952. Her stay in France resulted in her marriage in 1954 to Enrique González Pedrero, a Mexican political scientist. In 1955, the two moved to Mexico, where she has since resided. Campos is a critic, essayist, novelist, short story writer, and playwright. Both Cuba and Mexico have proved to be profound influences in her work.

Campos' career as a writer began in 1956 as a literary critic. Her role changed from critic to novelist in 1964 when she wrote her first novel *Muerte por agua,* the same year her mother passed away. Campos tells that the writing of this novel was her way of dealing with her mother's illness and subsequent death. Campos, in 1968, published her second work of fiction, *Celina o los gatos*, a collection of short stories that once again reflect upon the process of writing and the construction of identity. These early works, and subsequent ones as well, are radically different from the fiction being produced at this time in Latin America, which concentrated on presenting the social reality of the continent. However, Campos herself, later in her career does explore the circumstances of Latin American society in both her fiction and essays. However, during the 1960s and 1970s, her essays are of a purely literary nature. *La imagen del espejo*, published the same year as *Celina,* and *Función de la novela*, published in 1973, provide the reader with key insights to her fiction, particularly her analysis of writing as a self-reflexive process.

Campos, in 1974, returns to fiction with the publication of *Tiene los cabellos rojizos y se llama Sabina* for which she received the distinguished Xavier Villarutia award for her novel. Then, in 1979, the first production of her play *Jardín de invierno* took place. Throughout her career as an author of fiction, she has continued to produce literary criticism as well as over thirty-eight translations of books in history, psychoanalysis, and the social sciences. She taught literature at the Universidad Nacional Autónoma de México from 1976 to 1982 and was president of the P.E.N. club of Mexico from 1978 to 1982. From 1981 to 1984, she edited *Revista de la Universidad de México*. She has been involved in other literary and cultural journals such as *Novedades, ¡Siempre!, Revista mexicana de literatura, Plural,* and *Vuelta*. The main theoretical preoccupations present in her criticism appear frequently in her literary works as themes and narrative strategies.

Recurring symbols in Campos' work include; the ocean, water, islands, ships, roses, Venus, cats, and mirrors. Symbols chosen to reflect life, love, death and their dual and ambivalent nature are constant themes in her fiction. Other frequent themes in her fiction include the search for order, intertextuality, isolation, and emptiness. However, the process of writing itself is perhaps the most constant and important theme in her early works of fiction. This is particularly evident in *Tiene los cabellos rojizos y se llama Sabina* in which Campos tells the story of a woman who gazes at the sea before returning from a vacation and listens to voices that desire to speak through her, creating a novel that perhaps will never be written. In essence, the novel elaborates on understanding the process of writing while seeking the solution to the problem of mortality detailed in her previous fiction. Important to this process is the narrator's efforts to capture a single moment in time. In *Sabina*, one finds that the author's literary criticism and fiction intersect and the novel is replete with intertextual references to her previous works as well as the works of others that have influenced her. The unique form of this novel have led some to label it an anti-novel and its publication brought Campos to the attention of Latin American literary critics and placed her in the company of the great experimental writers of Latin America in the second half of the twentieth century. To this date, *Sabina* is the most-often studied work of Campos. However, *El miedo de perder a Euridice* (1979) is perhaps her most understudied work of fiction. In this novel, as in *Sabina*, once again intertextuality becomes an important component as does the immobilized protagonist. In fact, characters confined to one singular space are characteristic as well in the novel, *Muerte por agua*, the collection of short stories *Celina o los gatos* (1968), and the drama *Jardín de invierno* (written in 1979 and published in 1988). In *Euridice*, the locus of the immobilization is a Mexican café where the protagonist, a professor of French, sits and reads a novel, draws an island on a napkin, and writes a diary of a love story related to the characters of the novel he reads. Again, Campos continues with the experimental style that characterizes her earlier works, yet the narrative in this case is more cohesive. The author also continues with the theme of writing about the writing process appears, this time while searching for a utopia. *Euridice,* published in 1979, closed an important cycle in Campos' work; she did not publish another work of fiction until 2003.

The most notable reason for the lack of fiction published until 2003 is the election of her husband in 1982 to a six-year term as governor of Tabasco. Her experiences in Tabasco took her away from literary concerns and toward the analysis of anthropological, psychological, philosophical, and socioeconomic concerns. These concerns are reflected in *La herencia obstinada* (1982), an analysis of Nahuatl stories using the theoretical frameworks of psychoanalysis and structuralism. Other works that reflect this new focus on the part of the author include *Bajo el signo de IX Bolon* (1988) and *El lujo del sol* (1988). In *El lujo del sol*, Campos explores the customs and lives of Chontal Indians. In the 1990s, Campos explored the issue of poverty in Mexico in *¿Qué hacemos con los pobres? La reiterada querella por la nación* (1995), and *Tabasco: un jaguar despertad. Alternativas para la pobreza* (1996). In *¿Qué hacemos con los pobres?* Campos presents almost one thousand pages detailing poverty. In the latter, she describes her role in the creation of and work with the Laboratorio de Teatro Campesino e Indígena in Tabasco.

After a twenty-five-year absence, Campos returned to fiction in 2003 with the publication of *La forza del destino*. Campos' fiction has led some critics to categorize her among the best of postmodern writers in Latin America for her use of experimental narratives that reject linear time and plot, her use of multiple narrative voices, and the creation of psychologically fragmented characters. Campos has described her writing as a means of recuperating from the fragmentation in her own life, a means of bringing order to chaos. This fragmentation can be attributed to her dual Cuban/Mexican identity. *La forza del destino*, therefore, could be read as an attempt by the author to bring order to her Cuban past. In this novel, Campos recounts fourteen generations of the Cuban de la Torre family, and their relationship to Cuba from the sixteenth century until 1956. Campos stops referring to dates after 1956 and describes the island as living under a fog. Undoubtedly, the fog exists as a metaphor for her own relationship with the island since that same year, as well as the political situation of the island caused by the Cuban Revolution and the dictatorship that followed.

Julieta Campos has revealed in a number of interviews that her fiction is an attempt to bring order to chaos, a means of organizing one's life. Today, she is revered as one of the most important contemporary writers in Mexico and Latin America, but she is relatively unknown and unstudied in the United States. However, in the 1990s more and more attention was given to Campos and some have begun to read her in the light of the French feminist ideas of *l'écriture féminine*. Additionally, Campos is considered by a number of critics to be at the forefront of Latin American postmodernism. However, the question and problems related to the defining of postmodernism in a Latin American context have caused many to overlook Campos' literary contributions. In conclusion, Campos' body of work reflects that of the great writers of Latin America who engage not just in the production of fiction, but also criticism and essays, reflecting on the reality of the region.

STEPHANIE ALVAREZ

Selected Works

Fiction

Muerte por agua. México: Colección Popular, 1965.

Celina o los gatos. México: Siglo Veintiuno Editorial, 1968.

Tiene los cabellos rojizos y se llama Sabina. México: Editorial Joaquín Mortiz, 1974.

El miedo de perder a Euridice. México: Editorial Joaquín Mortiz, S.A. 1979.

Jardín de invierno. México: Ediciones del Equilibrista, 1988.

Reunión de familia. México: Fondo de Cultutra Económica, 1997.

La forza del destino. México: Editorial Alfaguara, 2003.

Translations in English of Fiction

She Has Reddish Hair and Her Name Is Sabina. Trans. Leland Chambers. Alabama, GA: University of Georgia Press, 1993.

The Fear of Losing Eurydice. Trans. Leland Chambers. Normal, IL: Dalkey Archive Press, 1994.

Celina or the Cats. Trans. Leland H. Chambers and Kathleen Ross. Pittsburgh, PA: Latin American Literary Review Press, 1995.

Nonfiction

La imagen en el espejo. Mexico: UNAM, 1965.

Oficio de leer. México: Fondo de Cultura Económica, 1971.

Función de la novela. México: Joaquín Mortiz, 1973.

La herencia obstinada. Análisis de cuentos nahuas. México: Fondo de Cultura Económica, 1982.

"Mi vocación literaria". *Revista Iberoamericana* 51(132–33) (1985): 467–70.

Un heroísmo secreto. México: Editorial Vuelta, 1988.

El lujo del sol. México: Fondo de Cultura Económica, Gobierno del Estado de Tabasco, 1988.

Bajo el signo de IX Bolon. México: Fondo de Cultura Económica, 1988

¿Qué hacemos con los pobres? La reiterada querella por la nación. México: Aguilar, 1995.

Tabasco: un jaguar despertado: Alternativas para la pobreza. México: Aguilar, 1996.

References and Further Reading

Beard, Laura J. "Navigating the Metafictional Text: Julieta Campos' *Tiene los cabellos rojizos y se llama Sabina*". *Hispanófila* 129 (2000): 45–58.

Bruce-Nova, Juan. "Julieta Campos' *Sabina:* In the Labyrinth of Intertextuality". *Third Woman* 22 (1984): 43–63.

Castellanos, Rosario. "Tendencias de la novelística mexicana contemporánea". *Revista de la Universidad de México* 20(7) (1966).

Castillo, Debra. "Surfacing: Rosario Ferré and Julieta Campos, with Rosario Castellanos". *Talking Back: Towards a Latin America Feminist Literary Criticism*. Ithaca, NY: Cornell University Press, 1992.

Fallon, Ann Marie. "Julieta Campos and the Repeating Island". *The Review of Contemporary Fiction* 26(2) (2006): 36–65.

Picon Garfield, Evelyn (ed.). *Women's Voices from Latin America: Interviews with Six Contemporary Authors*. Detroit, MI: Wayne State University Press, 1985, pp. 73–96.

González, Olympia. "Un orden en el caos: Visión crítico-narrativa de Julieta Campos". *Letras femeninas*, Special Commemorative Issue, 1974–94: 107–14.

Martínez, Martha. "Julieta Campos o la interiorización de lo cubano". *Revista Iberoamericana*. 51(132–3) (1985): 793–7.

Rivero Potter, Alicia. "La creación literaria en Julieta Campos: *Tiene los cabellos rojizos y se llama Sabina*". *Revista Iberoamericana* 51(132–3) (1985): 899–907.

Tompkins, Cynthia M. "Intertextuality as Différance in Julieta Campos. *El miedo de perder a Eurídice*: A Symptomatic Case of Latin American Postmodernism". In Claudia Ferman (ed.), *The Postmodern in Latin and Latino American Cultural Narratives*. New York: Garland, 1996.

CAMPUZANO, LUISA

Born in Havana in 1943, Luisa Campuzano has played a fundamental role in promoting women's studies in Cuba and in Latin America. Her work illustrates a commitment to using knowledge of the past to inform contemporary studies. Such a methodology has supported perhaps her most important contribution to Latin American Studies: the construction of a legitimate and legitimized space for the scholarly investigation of women's cultural production and Women's Studies in Cuba and the region.

Campuzano received her degree in Classics from the University of Havana in 1966 and her doctorate in Classical Philology from the University of Bucharest in 1979. She held a number of administrative positions during her more than thirty years of teaching Latin and Latin literature at the University of Havana. Nonetheless, during the early years of the revolution, when most intellectuals on the island were concerned with the appraisal of Cuban history and cultural production, Campuzano used her administrative and secretarial positions at the Consejo Nacional de Cultura (National Cultural Council) and the National Library to amass her profound knowledge of Cuban culture—which would shape the trajectory of her career from the mid-1980s onward. Having become the director of the Women's Studies Program at Casa de las Américas in 1994, and of the cultural magazine *Revolución y cultura* in 1998, she decided to retire from the university in 2000.

Campuzano's work in Classics and in Women's Studies has been recognized internationally. Her doctoral thesis *Las ideas literarias en el Satyricon* (Literary Ideas in the Satyricon) was awarded the Cuban National Critic's Prize in 1985, as was her collection of essays *Las muchachas de La Habana no tienen temor de Dios* (Havana Girls Aren't God-Fearin') in 2004. She has served on the Social Science Research Council, received support from the Rockefeller Foundation, and been invited to teach at many universities in the US, Latin America and Europe. She has also played an important part in extending Women's Studies Programs in Latin America (Rio de Janeiro and Chile). Her professional trajectory as researcher and proponent of Women's Studies is the quintessential example of the way women who achieve institutional power can effect change in women's struggle for an interpretative cultural voice.

A Scholar and Founder

In 1986, Campuzano was asked to direct the Center for Literary Research at Casa de las Américas. There, when asked to research women's writing in the revolution, she inaugurated contemporary feminist literary criticism on the island. The resulting essay's title is telling: "La mujer en la narrativa de la revolución: ponencia sobre una carencia" ("Women in the Narrative of the Revolution: An Essay on Scarcity"). In it, Campuzano juxtaposes the immense transformation of women's roles in Cuban society (their integration into the workforce, discursive legal rights, etc.) with a survey of women's prose fiction and narrative written by men dealing with women's issues. Her results exposed a controversial social contradiction: that despite decades of the construction of a more egalitarian society, between 1965 and the date of the article, only two novels had been published by women, apart from science fiction, a testimonial novel, and children's literature – as compared with the 170 novels published by men. Later, noting the "boom" of women's writing and inquiry from Latin America in the 1980s and the continued lack of the same in Cuba, Campuzano would dedicate her research to "recuperating the memory, models, and examples that will allow us to create a new identity for ourselves and to contribute to Cuban women's better self-awareness and self-esteem" ("Ser cubanas . . .": 5).

In 1990, Campuzano wrote: "In Cuba, there has not been feminist criticism: we are now just beginning" (*Las muchachas* ... *I*:13). That same year, through Casa de las Américas and a connection with the Colegio de México's Programa Interdisciplinario de Estudios de la Mujer (PIEM) (The Interdisciplinary Women's Studies Program), Campuzano organized the first conference on women's literature in Cuba. In March of the following year, a dozen Cubans went to Mexico to the second conference organized between the two institutions. Dedicated entirely to Cuban women's writing, this 1991 meeting was the first of its kind. Coupled with the changes in revolutionary cultural politics upon the fall of the Soviet bloc in 1989, these two historic events would set in motion a process that would bring Cuban women's writing and feminist inquiry to the attention of critics and scholars on the island and abroad.

Campuzano founded the Women's Studies Program at Casa de las Américas. Inaugurated in 1994 (the centenary celebration of Camila Henríquez Ureña's birth), the program instituted the periodic Extraordinary Prize for Essays on Women's Studies, to be awarded as part of Casa de las Américas' international literary competition. In order to create a forum for collaboration, Campuzano instituted the yearly Coloquio Internacional [International Colloquia] at Casa de las Américas that brings together scholars from around the world dedicated to Women's Studies. Her collaboration with other feminist scholars in articulating the program's goals led to the publication of two volumes of essays on women's history and cultural analysis (*Mujeres latinoamericanas* ...) and *Yo, con mi viveza*, an anthology of texts from the colonial period. These are essential resource materials for understanding women's roles in history and culture in the region.

Research Themes

Campuzano's scholarly research on women covers centuries. She works both archeologically, collecting and analyzing colonial and nineteenth-century texts, and systematically, charting the salient themes in contemporary Cuban women's writing. Perhaps due to her early training and years of teaching classics, history is a recurrent theme in all her work, both in the broader diachronical review of women's roles in Cuba's history and in the synchronic or contextual elements that influence the enunciation of the texts. Connecting this "antiquity" with our contemporary (feminist) gaze is another theme in Campuzano's writing. Analyzing women's writing, she finds, reveals the contradictions and antagonisms in gender relations in their intersection with race and class, and therefore brings a new perspective to transitional times in a nation's history.

Her analysis of both colonial and revolutionary texts illustrates this analytical process. First, in *Las muchachas de La Habana* ... (Havana Girls), Campuzano reads the texts of perhaps Cuba's first woman writer Beatriz de Jústiz y Zayas. De Jústiz y Zayas wrote a scathing letter to the King exposing the Spaniards' negligence during the English takeover of the port of Havana in 1762, thereby transgressing the gendered boundaries of conduct of the emergent ruling class that would consolidate colonial rule for nearly another 150 years. In subjecting her letter to a feminist analysis and exposing the tensions and backlash it caused, Campuzano is able to add a woman's voice to the larger historical narrative of difficult colonial rule.

In a similar fashion, Campuzano explores the nature of US/Cuba relations through her recovery of texts written by women who traveled to North America during the second half of the nineteenth century ("A Valiant Symbol ..."). The authors' representations of views on the abolition of slavery, debates about secession, the suffragist movement, etc., bring other voices to the hot-button issues of the years leading to the formation of the Cuban Republic in 1902. And, in "Cuba 1961 ...," her reading of women's narrative texts written in the early years of the revolution, Campuzano lays bare dominant (genre and gender) editorial bias. The authors' palimpsest-forming transformation and fictionalization of personal memoirs, Campuzano suggests, speak to the pressures to conform to the more legitimate (masculine) genre of the novel. Thus, Campuzano innovatively exposes the gendered unifying historical and cultural objectives of the consolidation of revolutionary rule.

Campuzano's work on contemporary women writers follows this same socio-historical approach. She reads contemporary fiction with the idea that "as we know, cultural forms not only reproduce but also produce reality" ("Literatura de mujeres ..." 41). Not surprisingly, she finds marginalization, prostitution, emigration, and scarcity as themes in women's fiction written during the "Special Period" (1991–). More importantly, Campuzano illustrates the historical forces at work in women's increased literary production such as the questionable existence of a free press on the island and the problematic flood of market forces that make the *realidad cubana* a sought-after product. Campuzano takes advantage of these market forces herself. She served as the director of a grant awarded to *La Gaceta de Cuba* by the International Humanist Institute for Cooperation with Developing Countries (HIVOS) to produce the journal's first issue entirely dedicated to women's cultural production and analysis (January 2004).

More broadly, Campuzano's latest work exemplifies the organic nature of her use of antiquity to inform her literary criticism. In *Narciso y Eco: Tradición clásica y literatura latinoamericana* (Narcissus and Echo: Classic Tradition and Latin American Literature), Campuzano reads the powerful reappropriation of rituals and symbols turned upon themselves as transgressive translations of Western traditions to the Latin American context. In this way, Campuzano is a participant in the current shift among cultural scholars who critically examine the mutual effects of the colonial imposition of cultural forms—in the contact zones where cultures meet, the dominant as well as colonized cultural forms are both transformed. Her work also makes evident more recent developments in Cuban literary analysis, which has incorporated a plurality of sociological discourses, rather than adhering solely to Marxist or formalist aesthetic considerations.

As a critic, and through her efforts to open Cuban literary studies to feminism and Latin American feminist criticism to Cuban women writers, Campuzano has contributed to the introduction of gender studies in the Hispanic Caribbean and their specific application to the Cuban literary canon. Like many others who worked to incorporate women's studies into the academy during the latter part of the twentieth century, her career exemplifies women's use of knowledge and institutional power to transform notions of legitimate cultural expression.

BARBARA RIESS

Selected Works

Books

Breve esbozo de poética preplatónica; con antología de fragmentos y testimonios. Havana: Editorial de Arte y Literatura, 1980.

Las ideas literarias en el Satyricon. Havana: Editorial Letras Cubanas, 1984.

Quirón o del ensayo y otros eventos. Havana: Editorial Letras Cubanas, 1988.

Ed. *Mujeres latinoamericanas: historia y cultura (siglos XVI al XIX)*. 2 vols. Havana: Casa de las Américas; México, D.F.: Universidad Autónoma Metropolitana-Iztapalapa, 1997.

Carpentier entonces y ahora. Havana: Editorial Letras Cubanas, 1997.

Ed. and comp. *Cartas de México/Aurelia Castillo de González*. Mexico: Redacta, 1997.

Ed. *Mujeres latinoamericanas del siglo XX: historia y cultura*. Havana: Casa de las Américas; México, D.F.: Universidad Autónoma Metropolitana-Iztapalapa, 1999.

Ed., with Catharina Vallejo. *Yo y mi viveza: textos de conquistadoras, monjas, brujas y otras mujeres de la colonia*. Havana: Casa de Las Américas; Montreal: Concordia University, 2003.

Las muchachas de La Habana no tienen temor de Dios . . . Escritoras cubanas (s. XVIII– XXI). Havana: Ediciones UNIÓN, 2004.

Narciso y Eco en nuestra América. Buenos Aires: La Bohemia, 2005.

Essays

"La mujer en la narrativa de la revolución: ponencia sobre una carencia". In Ana Cairo (ed.), *Letras. Cultura en Cuba*. Havana: Editorial Pueblo y Educación, 1992, vol. VII, 85–102. Also in Mirta Yánez and Marilyn Bobes (eds), *Estatuas de Sal. Cuentistas cubanas contemporáneas*. Havana: Ediciones Unión, 1996, pp. 351–71.

"Ser cubanas y no morir en el intento". *Temas* 5 (1996): 4–10.

"Cuba 1961: los textos narrativos de las alfabetizadoras: conflictos de género, clase y canon". *Unión* IX(26) (1997): 52–8.

"Narciso y Eco: Tradición clásica y literatura latinoamericana de autoría femenina". In Lady Rojas Trempe and Catharina Vallejo (eds), *Celebración de la creación literaria de escritoras hispanas en las Américas*. Montreal: Girol–Enana Blanca, 2000.

"A 'Valiant Symbol of Industrial Progress'? Cuban Women Travelers and the United States". Trans L. Paravisini-Gebert. In L. Paravisini-Gebert (ed.), *Women at Sea: Travel Writing and the Margins of Caribbean Discourse*. New York: Palgrave, 2001, pp. 161–81.

"Cuban Women Writers Now". In Mary G. Berg (ed.), *Open Your Eyes and Soar: Cuban Women Writing Now*. New York: White Pine Press, 2003, pp. 9–17.

"Literatura de mujeres y cambio social: narradoras cubanas de hoy". *Temas* 32 (2003): 38–47.

References and Further Reading

Araújo, Nara. "Otra habanera sin temor de Dios". *Casa de las Américas* 46(244) (2006): 151–2.

Davies, Catherine. *A Place in the Sun? Women Writers in Twentieth-Century Cuba*. London: Zed Books, 1997.

Díaz Mantilla, Daniel. "Hebras del mismo tejido" review of *Las muchachas* . . . http://www.lajiribilla.co.cu/2005/n224_08/ellibro.html

Grant, María. Interview. *Opus Habana*. 6(3) (2002): 16–25. Or *Mujeres en line@* 29 July, 2005 http://www.opushabana.cu/noticias.php?id_brev=366

Scott, Nina. "Review of *Yo, con mi viveza*". *Colonial Latin American Review* 14(2) (2005): 331–44.

CANETTI DUQUE, YANITZIA

Yanitzia Canetti Duque (b. 1967) was born in Havana, Cuba, of Spanish and Swiss-Italian ancestors. In Cuba, she studied Journalism at the University of Havana, and later on, after moving to the United States with her husband, an American journalist, she obtained a Master's in Linguistics and a PhD in Literature at Harvard University. Fluent in English, Italian and Spanish, she is currently an author, editor, and translator. She has received many awards for her work, including the National Literature Award three years in a row in Cuba (1984, 1985, and 1986); as well as the "Rosa Blanca" (White Rose) Literature Award (Best Literature of the Year, Cuba) in 1994; and an Honorable Mention (National Association of Hispanic Publications, California) in 1997 for *novelita Rosa*. Canetti is considered one of the younger members of the 1980s generation.

Writing as a Vital Need

She began to write little poems for school at age 5, because she felt she had things to say, although she never thought she would become a writer. For Canetti, writing is mostly a nourishing act, in search of self-fulfillment. By age 8, she had begun to write and illustrate books. She first published children's literature, and then poems, articles, and her two novels to date. As an author, she loves the power of creation, like a little goddess, able to convey a world, give life to different characters, and organize their world.

Canetti is an avid reader, and all she reads leaves a mark on her. Therefore, the list of influences is endless: from Rabindranat Tagore to Italo Calvino, going through Mercé Rododera, Clarice Lispector, Jorge Luis Borges or William Faulkner, among many others, not to mention Cuban writers such as Virgilio Piñera, José Martí o Lezama Lima. She still continues her work as journalist, writing for several newspapers in the United States and, occasionally, abroad. She is thankful to journalism because it gives her all the valuable skills for writing fiction.

An Author of Children's Literature

The main corpus of her production is in the field of children's literature. The first book she wrote was called *Los fantásticos viajes de Fantasía* (Fantasy's Fantastic Adventures), a book for children she wrote at age 8, then rewrote later on, and was finally published recently; and her first published book was *Secretos de palacio* (Secrets of the Palace), in 1993 in Cuba, which was a children's book of short stories. Later, she wrote some plays for school, and several other children's books, more than fifty to date, both in English and Spanish. As well as developing educational programs for leading publishers in bilingual education and English as a Second Language (ESL), she has taken part in the creation of various educational programs. She has also worked as an author, editor, writer, translator, and literary consultant for student anthologies, teachers guides, workbooks, and collections of books for young readers.

Adventures in Adult Fiction

However, her reputation is based on the two novels for adults that she has published so far, both different in style but original and entertaining. *novelita Rosa* (Through Rose-Colored Lenses), with lower case n at the beginning, was the first to be published, although it was written after the other one, *Al otro lado* (On the Other Side). *novelita Rosa* narrates the bittersweet life of a Mexican immigrant in the United States, Rosa Barril, who lives two realities: on the one hand, she is trying to adapt to a new culture; and on the other hand, she "lives" the surreal and false reality of the soap operas. Although the novel is easy to read and very comical, its simplicity hides a complex and well-crafted structure, in which the narrative voice, hired by the author, argues with her and takes the liberty of inserting her own comments, until her contract expires close to the end of the novel, forcing the author to finish it. Canetti, in a prose that incorporates Mexican expressions, reveals the dangers for the lonely and uneducated of the false world of television, whose influence Canetti considers pernicious for the mind. In fact, TV becomes another protagonist in the novel, together with the Barril family, representing the excess of the consumerism of the American way of life. Canetti got the idea from television, watching soap operas, a topic of conversation for many immigrants, who regard them as their daily bread.

Her next published novel, *Al otro lado*, established a radical change. It is a brilliant and solid novel, whose elaboration took several years (she began to write this novel in Cuba, and finished it years later in Boston), and which shows a literary maturity that came as a surprise for those critics who have only read *novelita Rosa*. In a lyrical, charming and carefully elaborated prose, with a subtle sense of humor and plenty of lyricism and eroticism, the novel tells the story of a woman who goes to confess to a church that may or may not exist and may be only the product of her imaginings throughout the novel, until she makes peace with herself (with her "other side") and moves to another country. This ethereal novel is set for the most part on an island in the Caribbean (most likely Cuba, although it is never mentioned), and later another place (maybe the United States, but no names are given). The book was unanimously celebrated by critics and has been praised as an extremely important work of contemporary Cuban narrative. It has been read as part of the boom in Cuban literature at the end of the twentieth century. Although some critics have seen the novel as autobiographical, Canetti insists that it is not, despite the fact that some passages match her own experiences.

Themes and Criticism

Canetti explores the human soul in her novels: the internal struggle between good and evil, the human perception of sin, the search for identity, loneliness, fear, death and love. No wonder that some critics have seen a new variation of mysticism in her narratives, especially in *Al otro lado*. Her novels are full of contradictions: reality clashes with fantasy, eroticism is subverted by humor, and solemnity mixed with impudence. As a Cuban, she is used to the paradoxes and contrasts of life, and she faces them with humor and *choteo* (the Cuban art of making fun of everything). In fact, critics have mentioned humor itself as one of the themes in her two novels.

Her Cubanness is also reflected not only in *Al otro lado*, where one can find a subtle criticism of Cuban reality in its pages, but also in *novelita Rosa*, with the constant *choteo* of Rosa and her family, as well as the image of the Cuban friend of Rosa, a sharp criticism to the Cuban-American community. However, she is aware that she writes against the current of contemporary Cuban literature, something the critics have noted, because her narratives do not address the issues and conflicts of Cuba today, something she considers difficult since she cannot achieve impartiality; but despite this independence, she considers herself part of Cuban literature because that's what flows out of her when she writes, since she is Cuban.

MIGUEL GONZÁLEZ-ABELLÁS

Selected Works

Novels

novelita Rosa. Andover, NH: Versal, 1997.
Al otro lado. Barcelona: Seix Barral, 1997.

Children's Books (selection)

Secretos de palacio. La Habana: Gente nueva, 1993.
En mi nuevo barrio. Boston, MA: Houghton Mifflin, 1997.
Carlita Ropes the Twister. Austin, TX: Steck-Vaughn, 1997.
Completamente diferente. León, Spain: Everest, 2000.
Los fantásticos viajes de Fantasía. Orlando, FL: Harcourt, 2001.
Doña Flautita Resuelvelotodo. Madrid: Edebé, 2002.
How Many Climates Does One Island Need? Austin, TX: Steck-Vaughn, 2003.
The Curse of the Jungle Treasure. New York: Scholastic, 2004.
Un poquito más. León, Spain: Everest, 2005.
El príncipe azul. León, Spain: Everest, 2006.
Ay luna, lunita, lunita. León, Spain: Everest, 2006.

References and Further Reading

Cámara, Madeline. *La letra rebelde: estudios de escritoras cubanas*. Miami, FL: Universal, 2002.

Canetti, Yanitzia. *Yanitzia Canetti* (Author's webpage). http://www.yanitziacanetti.com

Espinosa Domínguez, Carlos. *El peregrino en comarca ajena*. Boulder, CO: Society of Spanish and Spanish-American Studies, 2001, pp. 253–4.

Fernández-Vázquez, Antonio A. "Humor y erotismo en las novelas de Yanitzia Canetti Duque". In Jorge Chen Sham and Isela Chiu Olivares (eds), *De márgenes y adiciones: Novelistas latinoamericanas de los 90*. San José, CR: Ediciones Perro Azul, 2004, pp. 259–81.

Fuentes, Yvette. "En medio de dos aguas: Yanitzia Canetti y la literatura cubana en Estados Unidos". In Laura P. Alonso Gallo and Fabio Murrieta (eds), *Guayaba Sweet: Literatura cubana en Estados Unidos*. Cádiz, Spain: Aduana Vieja, 2003, pp. 197–216.

Thiem, Annegret. "*Al otro lado*: Yanitzia Canetti entre la mística y el postmodernismo". *Espéculo* 26 (March 2004) http://www.ucm.es/info/especulo/numero26/o_lado.html

CANTO, ESTELA

Estela Canto (1919–94), an accomplished novelist and short story writer, is inevitably associated with Argentina's most famous author, Jorge Luis Borges, for two important reasons: first, Borges dedicated one of his best-known stories, "El Aleph," to her; and, second, she wrote a fascinating biography of him called *Borges a contraluz* (1989).

Borges a contraluz (1989)

Canto's account of her friendship with Borges and other writers of his intimate circle is an invaluable insider's view of both the man, the creative genius, and his work. Both Edwin

Williamson in a recent comprehensive biography of Borges and Daniel Balderston (see Further reading) credit Canto with providing insightful glimpses into his personal life and intelligent readings of the numerous works she mentions.

Canto relates her personal experiences with Borges, divided into several periods. The most important is certainly the first. They met in 1944 at the house of Adolfo Bioy Casares and Silvina Ocampo where Borges and other writers, such as Canto's brother, poet Patricio Canto, were frequent guests. Borges dedicated "El Aleph" to her, and gave her the manuscript as a special gift. Canto believes that "El Zahir" and "La escritura de dios" also belong to this same set of literary impulses, which she describes as Borges's version of a mystic experience. Her nascent feminism and his timid, conventional approach to sexuality produced an impasse which could not be overcome, and she eventually refused his proposal of marriage. Nevertheless, they remained distant acquaintances and eventually reclaimed a real friendship which lasted until his death. Canto offers fascinating glimpses into Borges's relationship with his mother, his sister Norah, his first wife, and his ultimate period of happiness with María Kodama. Canto also provides a convincing interpretation of Borges's politics, which offended so many and cost him the Nobel Prize in Literature. She argues that his hatred of Perón and his isolation from everyday political realities in his later life pushed him to support anyone who would counter what he considered Perón's nefarious influence, including the infamous military officers who overthrew the Perón government and undertook what has become known as "the dirty war" of 1976–84. Canto's disagreements with Borges, both at the personal and political levels, find their way into her novels.

El muro de mármol (1945), *El retrato y la imagen* (1950), and *El hombre del crepúsculo* (1953)

Canto's first novel won the Premio Municipal in 1945. It depicts a "perfect" crime in which the murderer, a young boy, seems to kill his victim almost by accident. The extreme ambiguity of the shooting, a kind of "accident on purpose," leaves the ending open to a number of readings. Like José Bianco's *Las ratas* (1943), the novel's ending strongly suggests the homoerotic forces at work on the boy narrator, but leaves the motivation behind the murder/accident undecided and undecidable. The ambiguity of desire and therefore of plot remain constants in Canto's fiction.

The main plot thread of the second novel again produces an accidental death and a strange mystical union of murderer and victim by way of a photograph. More interesting for the modern reader, perhaps, is the important feminist subplot involving the character, Ida Ballentén. Ida's unprecedented personal freedom, her refusal of conventional marriage within a context of a defense of economic independence and the pursuit of creative work identify her as the most overtly feminist of Canto's characters.

Alberto Moreiras considers both these early novels as nothing less than rewritings of Borges's "El Aleph". Moreiras argues that Borges suggests in two similar stories, "El Aleph" and "El Zahir," that sexual passion is the price of literary genius, situating both within the context of the death of the beloved. Borges's characters, Beatriz Viterbo and Teodelina Villar, are parodies of *arriviste* women whose social pretensions are part of the fun. Canto's serious, passionate characters, especially the working-class woman of her second novel who finds a unique road to transcendence, unrelated to sexual sacrifice, seem the perfect opposite of those dedicated to her by Borges.

Estela Canto's subsequent novels have received little if any critical attention. If anything, however, her third novel seems the most pointed attack on Borges's puritanical notions of female sexuality to be found in any of her works. Here the issues of conventional masculine morality and a feminist concept of sexual freedom are overtly juxtaposed in ways which echo the situation she describes with Borges in her biography of him. What all three early novels have in common is their crime novel structure. The subsequent works veer from this plot pattern and become more pointedly political in character.

Los otros, las máscaras (1973), *La hora detenida* (1976), and *El jazmín negro* (1978)

The three novels published in the 1970s bring Canto's understanding of the general sexual discomfort experienced in Argentine culture to a broader, national arena. Canto continues to explore women's sexual and artistic expression, but now turns her attention to a critique of Argentine class structure, and an increasingly pessimistic view of the political and moral climate. All three novels open the crime of passion to a broad cultural critique, making each a study of a disintegrating Argentine society rather than of one aberrant individual.

Certainly the most interesting of these is *La hora detenida*. The novel's setting in 1952, around the day of Eva Perón's death, provides the context noted in the title. However, the novel tells us more about the moment of its production, 1976, than about 1952; it attempts what Tulio Halperin Dongui suggests is necessary to reread the past in light of the present. Canto uses the knowledge granted to hindsight to revisit a key moment of the past, and writes in the midst of terror to decry her country's present.

La hora detenida transforms the theme of female sexual transgression by way of various scenes of rape, and more overtly creates the self-destructive, sexual child that she clearly views as symbolic of political chaos, marking their sexual freedom as symptoms of national disease. While her biography of Borges offers an extended recognition of the misogyny and sexism which dominate her era of Argentine history, her fiction presents a more ambiguous reading of the national problem, often seeming to identify her precocious young characters as the cause, not the result, of moral collapse. The very construction of feminine subjectivity makes her characters, especially in the final two novels, conscious, and thereby appear to be complicit in their fate.

Canto has been unacknowledged until now as an important precursor to other writers who make such overtly political and historic commentary—Puig, Viñas and Piglia, for instance—because, perhaps, she couches the issues of Argentine politics within the specific realm of women's bodies and sexuality. Her novels should be read with those of her male contemporaries if only because she situates her political allegory within the feminine spaces completely left out of their better-known works.

PATRICIA N. KLINGENBERG

Selected Works

El muro de mármol. Buenos Aires: Losada, 1945.
Los espejos de la sombra (short stories). Buenos Aires: Claridad, 1945.
El retrato y la imagen. Buenos Aires: Losada, 1950.
El hombre del crepúsculo. Buenos Aires: Sudamericana, 1953.
Los otros, las máscaras. Buenos Aires: Losada, 1973.
La hora detenida. Buenos Aires: Emecé, 1976.
El jazmín negro. Buenos Aires: Emecé, 1978.
Borges a contraluz. Buenos Aires: Espasa Calpe, 1989.

References and Further Reading

Balderston, Daniel. (ed.) *The Historical Novel in Latin America.* Gaithersburg, MD: Ediciones Hispamerica, 1986.
——. "'Beatriz Viterbo c'est moi': Angular Vision in Estela Canto's *Borges a contraluz*". *Variciones Borges: Revista del Centro de Estudios y Documentación Jorge Luis Borges* (Aarhus, Denmark), 1 (1996): 133–9.
Borges, Jorge Luis. *El Aleph.* Buenos Aires: Emecé, 1990
"Canto, Estela". www.me.gov.ar/efeme/jlborges/amigos.html
Fares, Gustavo. "This Text Which is Not One: Escritoras Argentinas Contemporáneas". *Hispanic Journal* 12(2) (1991): 277–89.
Halperín Dongui, Tulio. *El espejo de la historia: Problemas argentinos y perspectivas latinoamericanas.* Buenos Aires: Sudamericana, 1987.
Klingenberg, Patricia N. "Against Borges: Mapping the Feminine in Estela Canto". Forthcoming from *Bulletin of Hispanic Studies.*
Moreiras, Alberto. "Borges y Estela Canto: La sombra de una dedicatoria". *Journal of Interdisciplinary Literary Studies* 5(1) (1993): 131–46.
Williamson, Edwin. *Borges: A Life.* New York: Viking Penguin, 2004.

CÁRDENAS, NANCY

Nancy Cárdenas (1934–94) was a playwright, poet, journalist, film critic, actress, director, political activist, and gay rights pioneer. Cárdenas was born on May 29, 1934, in the northern Mexican town of Parras. She attended primary and secondary school in her hometown, completed preparatory studies in Celaya, and earned her bachelor's and master's degree in Dramatic Arts at the Universidad Nacional Autónoma de México (UNAM) in Mexico City. She also pursued doctoral work at UNAM. In the early 1960s, Cárdenas studied film and theater at Yale University, and Polish language and literature in Lodz, Poland. Upon her return to Mexico, she worked as a radio announcer, actress, journalist, and translator. Though an active member of the Communist Party during the 1950s, Cárdenas intensified her activism in the 1960s, and was arrested in 1968 while participating in student protests against police violence. Over the next three decades, Cárdenas continued much of her activism on stage, as she wrote, adapted, and directed several plays, primarily reflecting the political and social struggles of women, homosexuals, and AIDS victims. Nancy Cárdenas died in Mexico City of breast cancer on March 23, 1994. Though Cárdenas's life and works have not garnered the scholarly attention they deserve, an internet archive of lesbian history (*El Centro de Documentación y Archivo Histórico Lésbico de México y América Latina "Nancy Cárdenas"*) has been established in her memory.

Early Works

Cárdenas began her literary career in the 1960s with a couple of plays and a couple of theoretical works on film and theater. In 1960, she published *El cántaro seco*, a one-act play that explores the social and political hardships endured by impoverished Amerindians in a small, drought-stricken village in rural west-central Mexico. Several villagers with pitchers in hand congregate near a mud wall on the outskirts of town in order to wait for a water delivery truck. The ensuing conversation reveals the hopes, fears, and stark realities of the village's women, men, and children. The villagers discuss a wide array of pressing concerns, ranging from crop yields and pregnancies to illnesses and economic woes. Also a topic of conversation is don Eulogio, the powerful overlord who financially preys upon the village's neediest people, just as his male assistants regularly victimize the village's young women. Eventually, the water truck arrives, but Eulogio decides which villagers may receive water, and which may not. This position creates tension and worry among the assembled villagers, though Eulogio's driver tries to mediate in favor of the villagers. In the end, the villagers receive water, but not without some dramatic and unfortunate concessions on their part. This play's treatment of class conflict and ethnic divisions anticipates the strong social and political bent of Cárdenas's later work as an activist and playwright.

In 1962, after her stay in Poland, Cárdenas published *El cine polaco*, a study of the history of Polish film from the end of World War I through the 1950s. The following year she wrote and staged her second play, *La vida privada del profesor Kabela*, and in 1965 she published her master's thesis, *Aproximaciones al teatro de vanguardia.* Though Cárdenas's subsequent literary output was not very extensive, she nonetheless achieved some important milestones in theater, film, and poetry.

A Life in Theater

In the 1970s and 1980s, Cárdenas's literary interests focused on translating and adapting canonical and non-canonical literary works for the stage. Her highly acclaimed adaptation and direction of Paul Zindel's *The Effects of Gamma Rays on Man-in-the-Moon Marigolds* (*El efecto de los rayos gamma sobre las caléndulas*, 1970) was followed by many other triumphs, including theatrical versions of Lope de Vega's *La Dorotea* (1978), Dario Fo's *Misterio Bufo* (1978 and 1989), Juan Rulfo's *Pedro Páramo* (1979), and George Bernard Shaw's *Pygmalion* (1979). Though Cárdenas's literary output during these years focused less on original works and more on the works of other writers, she nevertheless published a collection of poetry (*Vuelo acordado*, 1971), and she collaborated with Carlos Monsiváis on a script for an influential film on the history of Mexican cinema (*México de mis amores*, 1979), which she directed.

Social and Political Activism

During the 1970s, Nancy Cárdenas emerged as a major voice of lesbian and gay awareness in Mexico and abroad. In 1973, she publicly came out as a lesbian during a discussion of homosexuality on Jacobo Zabludovsky's *24 Horas*, a popular television program aired throughout Mexico. The following year, Cárdenas founded the Frente de Liberación Homosexual (FLH), the first gay and lesbian organization in Mexico. She not only continued to advocate for the visibility and rights of lesbians and gays in Latin America throughout the rest of her life, but she also championed other causes such as women's rights and the rights of adults and children with HIV/AIDS. Cárdenas's literary and dramaturgical work during this period heavily reflects her social and political interests. She adapted for the stage several literary works with overt or subtle homosexual themes, such as Mart Crowley's *Boys in the Band* (*Los chicos de la banda*, 1974 and 1982), Rainer Werner Fassbinder's *The Bitter Tears of Petra von Kant* (*Las amargas lágrimas de Petra von Kant*, 1980), Radclyffe Hall's *The Well of Loneliness* (*El pozo de la soledad*, 1985), and William M. Hoffman's *As Is* (*Sida, así es la vida*, 1988).

Cárdenas's own literary creativity surged during this era, as she wrote several original plays and published poetry. However, because of conservative social attitudes in Mexico toward lesbianism and other sexual themes, almost all of these works remain unpublished and untranslated. The plays *El día que pisamos la luna* (first performed in 1981) and *Las hermanitas de Acámbaro* (first performed in 1983) openly explore lesbian themes, including the psychological and social struggles of lesbians who seek to create a woman-centered world for themselves, in spite of the patriarchal and heterosexual norms of society in general. Near the end of her life, Cárdenas wrote *Sexualidades I* (first performed in 1992) and *Sexualidades II* (first performed in 1993), plays which boldly examine homosexuality, heterosexuality, and related themes from a variety of personal and social perspectives.

Among Cárdenas's poetic achievements during the 1980s and 1990s are *Amor de verano* (1985) and her posthumously published *Cuaderno de amor y desamor* (1994). *Cuaderno* features scores of short, free-verse poems loosely arranged in a lyrical, first-person narrative that refers to a wide range of discursive traditions, such as creation stories and international cinematography, in order to examine the ecstasy of affection, the erotic timelessness of sexual intimacy, and the pain of love lost. Cárdenas playfully and subtly develops the lesbian nature of these relationships while simultaneously ensuring a sensitive and universal look at the triumphs and failures of love in general. In spite of its erotic richness and verbal nuance, *Cuaderno* awaits the serious attention of readers and scholars that it deserves.

Throughout her life, Nancy Cárdenas faced numerous challenges in publishing her works, staging controversial plays, and fighting for political and social causes. In many important respects, Cárdenas's activism and artistic boldness have cleared the path for other Mexican writers to explore controversial topics such as homosexuality and AIDS in their work. Though relatively little is known about Nancy Cárdenas and her work, her impact on literature and drama in the Spanish-speaking world has been significant, and her iconic status in Latin America's gay and lesbian movement is well deserved.

R. JOHN MCCAW

Selected Works

El cántaro seco. Mexico: UNAM, 1960.
El cine polaco. Mexico: UNAM, 1962.
Aproximaciones al teatro de vanguardia. Mexico: UNAM, 1965.
Cuaderno de amor y desamor. Mexico: Hoja Casa, 1994.

References and Further Reading

Aldama, Frederick Luis. "Nancy Cárdenas". In Tom and Sara Pendergast (eds), *Gay and Lesbian Literature*. vol. 2. Detroit, MI: St. James Press, 1994, pp. 73–4.

Martínez, Elena M. "Nancy Cárdenas: Mexican Poet and Playwright". *Connexions* 47(4) (1995): 4–6.

——. *Lesbian Voices from Latin America: Breaking Ground*. New York: Garland, 1996.

Monsiváis, Carlos. "Recado para Nancy Cárdenas". In *Cuaderno de amor y desamor. 1968–1993*. Mexico: Instituto Coahuilense de Cultura, 2004, pp. 9–21.

CARTAGENA PORTALATÍN, AÍDA

The most anthologized Dominican Republican woman writer, Aída Cartagena Portalatín (1918–94) authored fourteen books and edited several literary and academic journals as well as a short story collection. Initially known for her surrealist poetry, which she wrote as the only female member of the group called "La Poesía Sorprendida" (Surprised Poetry), Cartagena Portalatín transcended that movement in order to forge a very personal style of poetry in her later years. In the 1970s and 1980s, Cartagena Portalatín cultivated other literary genres, including the short story, the novel and the monographic essay. Despite critical acclaim for her work, however, she remains an understudied figure in academic circles and rarely appears in general studies of twentieth-century Latin American literature. Hers is, nonetheless, a formidable voice that "must be considered, studied, and understood, if one is to write about Dominican literature in the twentieth century" (de Filippis, 2003: 85).

Born in the northern city of Moca to a family of limited economic means, Cartagena Portalatín attended local schools before enrolling in the Universidad Autónoma in Santo Domingo, where she eventually earned her doctorate in 1941. She completed post-doctoral work in Museum Studies and the Plastic Arts at the Louvre in Paris, the first of many trips to a city that was to become her second home. Fiercely independent, Cartagena Portalatín traveled widely and alone, an uncommon practice for a woman in the early twentieth century. Daisy Cocco de Filippis, a scholar of Dominican literature who has studied Cartagena Portalatín's work extensively, observes, "To a younger generation of Dominican women writers, Portalatín's travels have come to symbolize Dominican woman's flight from her imposed surroundings, her home, and her taking on a world until then closed off from women's experience" (2003: 78).

After her return home in the 1950s, Cartagena Portalatín emerged as an important figure not only in literary and academic circles, but also in the public sector. She founded several journals (*La Isla Necesaria* and *Brigadas Dominicanas*) and served as editor for the *Anales* publication of the Humanities Division of the Universidad Autónoma of Santo Domingo, where she also worked as a professor. Following the 1965 Revolution, Cartagena Portalatín became the Dominican representative at UNESCO, a post she filled at the request of the institution's regional office in Havana. By the early 1970s, Cartagena Portalatín's growing interest in archaeology led her to a position at the Museum of Anthropology at the Universidad Autónoma in Santo Domingo. In 1977, she was appointed a jury member for the prestigious *Casa de las Américas* literary prize (Cuba). An indefatigable writer, researcher, teacher and intellectual, Cartagena Portalatín was preparing an essay on the indigenous peoples of the Caribbean at the time of her death in 1994.

Poetry

Cartagena Portalatín's early poetry must be read in the context of the work of the Dominican literary group called "La Poesía Sorprendida," as well as in the broader, international context of the artistic *avant-garde* of the first half of the twentieth century. Indeed, the group known as "La Poesía Sorprendida" attempted to end the isolation of the literary production on the island by exploring more universal themes and by embracing the tenets of surrealism. Although the group never published a poetic manifesto, it did set down some formal concepts that gave shape to the movement. In particular, the group advocated, "una poesía nacional nutrida en la universal, única forma de ser propia; con lo clásico de ayer, de hoy y de mañana . . ." (Gutiérrez, 1998: 28). Cartagena Portalatín's first poetry collections (1945, *Víspera del sueño* (Eve of a Dream), *Del sueño al mundo* (From the Dream to the World) and *Llámale verde* (Call him Green)) all appeared in the group's journal, published from 1943 until 1947, when the dictator Rafael Leónidas Trujillo ordered the magazine to be closed. As especially the first two titles indicate, an oneiric mood, typical of surrealism, predominates in these early lyrical poems.

The theme of solitude, a thread that binds all of Cartagena Portalatín's work, becomes more prevalent in her two collections from the 1950s: *Mi mundo el mar* (My World the Sea) and *Una mujer está sola* (A Woman is Alone). While some of the elements of her early poetry remain, Cartagena Portalatín began to transcend the "Sorprendida" aesthetic in order to lay claim to her own poetic voice during this period. In addition, these two works share another theme; as Marcano-Ogando asserts, both of these collections are characterized by "la centralidad que adquiere la mujer como sujeto y objeto de la escritura" [the centrality that woman has as subject and object of writing] (2005: 22). Furthermore, with these two books, the poet substitutes prose poems for her polymetric verse, thus initiating a formal experimentation that will continue throughout her career. In *Mi mundo el mar*, a dense poem consisting of six untitled movements, the protagonist, Aída, journeys to the sea, which, according to Marcano-Ogando, represents, "un espacio alternativo a la falta de amor en la tierra, al mismo tiempo que sirve como puente para la configuración del yo y la exploración poética" [an alternative space to the lack of love in the world, at the same time it works as a bridge for the configuration of the "I" and of the poetic exploration] (2005: 22). *Una mujer está sola* distances the poet even further from her surrealist roots. The collection's initial poem, "Estación en la tierra" (Season on Earth), declares Cartagena Portalatín's literary independence:

> NO creo que yo esté aqui demás.
> Aquí hace falta una mujer, y esa mujer soy yo.
> No regreso hecha llanto. No quiero conciliarme
> con los hechos extraños.
> Antiguamente tuve la inútil velada de levantar las tejas
> para aplaudir los párrafos de la experiencia ajena.
> Antiguamente no había despertado.
> No era necesario despertar.
> Sin embargo, he despertado de espalda a tus discursos,
> definitivamente de frente a la verídica, sencilla y clara
> necesidad de ir a mi encuentro.
>
> (Collado 103)

[I do NOT believe that I am useless here. / A woman is necessary here, and I am that woman. / I do not return dissolved in tears. I don't want to reconcile myself / to others' accomplishments. / Formerly I had the useless vigil of lifting up tiles / to applaud the paragraphs of others' experience. / Formerly I had not awakened. / It wasn't necessary to wake. / Nevertheless, I have awakened with my back to your discourses, / definitively facing the truthful, simple and clear necessity of going to my own encounter.]

Having come to terms with herself as a woman and as a writer, in this poem Cartagena Portalatín asserts her identity through the use of the first person and proclaims her right to pursue her own path, renouncing the need to adhere to the male literary tradition. The poet envisions her newly discovered autonomy as an awakening or a rebirth. In effect, the concept of being reborn is echoed throughout the collection in her insistence on the image of blood, which for the poet becomes "madre de la voz que toca con su voz / el aire de la luna" [mother of the voice that touches with her voice / the airo of the moon] ("Estación de la sangre"). Despite Cartagena Portalatín's lifelong rejection of feminism, it is clear why Dominican critic and sociologist Sherezada Vicioso has deemed *Una mujer está sola*, the "First Feminist Manifesto" on the island (de Filippis, 2003: 79).

Fortified by her inner journey to discover her unique poetic voice, Cartagena Portalatín began to expand her vision to include the social and economic problems affecting the Dominican people and indeed the oppressed peoples of the world. Her last four collections of poetry chronicle this journey outward. As the poet herself confessed in her final interview, these books caused an uproar in the Dominican Republic, not only because of their break with traditional poetic form, but also, and more particularly, because of their frank exploration of racism and bigotry. In a well-known, untitled poem from *La tierra escrita*, the poet writes, "MI MADRE FUE UNA DE LAS GRANDES MAMA (sic) DEL MUNDO / De su vientre nacieron siete hijos / que serían en Dallas, Menphis (sic) o Birminghan (sic) un problema racial" [MY MOTHER WAS ONE OF THE GREAT MAMA (sic) OF THE WORLD / From her womb seven sons came forth / who would be in Dallas, Menphis (sic) or Birminghan (sic) a racial problem] (Collado 207). Her penultimate book of verse, *Yania Tierra* (Yania Earth), consists of a long narrative poem that retells the history of the Dominican Republic by highlighting women's participation in the historical process, while it excoriates centuries of violence and exploitation against females, the indigenous and those of African descent.

Prose

Although best known as a poet, Cartagena Portalatín produced several narrative works and essays in her later years. Her first novel, *Escalera para Electra* (Ladder for Electra), was a finalist for the Seix Barral prize. The few critical studies that focus on this work agree on the novel's narrative complexity and rich intertextuality, as the novelist weaves together diverse threads that include travelogue, Greek myth, psychoanalysis, the story of an incestuous Dominican family and a self-reflective meditation on the genesis of her own work. The novel transgresses many of the genre's conventions in order to affirm an important role not only for the author, but also for Dominican literature and history in world culture. Indeed, Cartagena Portalatín's narrator calls attention to the link, not between the novel and literary tradition, but rather between the words "novela" and "novedad," thus emphasizing that the novelistic art is that of creating something new and utterly unconventional. In this way, Cartagena Portalatín continued her experimentation with literary form that she initiated with *Mi mundo el mar*. At the end of the 1970s, despite the success of her short story collection, *Tablero* (Chessboard), Cartagena Portalatín discontinued her work in this genre in order to finish her second novel, *La tarde en que murió Estefanía* (The Afternoon Estefania Died), a narrative in verse that explores the Trujillo dictatorship and its effects on the lives of Dominican citizens, in particular the country's women. Like *Escalera para Electra*, this second novel relies on a subtext from ancient Greek tragedy, in this case the plight of Aeschylus' Antigone, in order to underscore the tragic features of twentieth-century Dominican history.

Conclusion

Although there is some academic debate as to which is Cartagena Portalatín's finest poetic moment, with some scholars favoring the lyricism of her "Sorprendida" poetry, while others point to *Una mujer está sola* or her final, more politically engaged collections as the pinnacle of her craft, there is no argument over her significance to Dominican literature. In light of her long, prolific writing and editing career, her anthropological research on the Caribbean and her contribution to women's struggles for visibility and voice, the majority of critics agree that Aída Cartagena Portalatín is the most important female writer and intellectual in twentieth-century Dominican history.

KAREN RAUCH

Selected Works

Víspera del sueño. Ciudad Trujillo: Ediciones *La Poesía Sorprendida*, 1944.

Mi mundo el mar. Ciudad Trujillo: Editorial Stella, 1953.

Una mujer está sola. Ciudad Trujillo: Editorial Stella, 1955.

La tierra escrita. Elegías. Santo Domingo: Ediciones Brigadas Dominicanas, 1967.

Escalera para Electra. Santo Domingo: Colección Montesinos, 1970.

Tablero. Santo Domingo: Editora Taller, 1978.

Yania tierra. Poema Documento. Santo Domingo: Colección Montesinos, 1981.

La tarde en que murió Estefanía. Santo Domingo: Colección Montesinos, 1984.

En la casa del tiempo. Santo Domingo: Editora Universitaria, 1984.

Culturas africanas: rebeldes con causa. Santo Domingo: Editora Taller, 1986.

Del consuelo al compromiso:/From Desolation to Compromise: Bilingual Anthology of the Poetry of Aída Cartagena Portalatín. Ed. Daisy Cocco de Filippis. Trans. Emma Jane Robinet. Santo Domingo: Editora Taller, 1988.

Obra Poética Completa (1955–1984). Ed. Miguel Collado. Santo Domingo: Colección de la Biblioteca Nacional, 2000.

References and Further Reading

Cocco de Filippis, Daisy. "Aída Cartagena Portalatín: A Literary Life". In Miriam DeCosta-Willis (ed.), *Daughters of the Diaspora: Afro-Hispanic Writers*. Kingston, Jamaica: Ian Randle Publishers, 2003, pp. 76–87.

González, Carolina. "A Poet on Her Own: Aída Cartagena Portalatín's Final Interview". *Callaloo* 23(3) (2000): 1080–5.

Gutiérrez, Franklin (ed.) *Antología histórica de la poesía dominicana del S. XX (1912–1995)*. 2nd edn, San Juan, PR: Editorial de la Universidad de Puerto Rico, 1998.

Marcano-Ogando, Ramonita. *La configuración del sujeto en la poesía de Aída Cartagena Portalatín*. Ann Arbor, MI: ProQuest, 2005.

Sosa, José Rafael (ed.) *La mujer en la literatura. Homenaje a Aida Cartagena Portalatín*. Santo Domingo: Editora Universitaria, 1986.

Williams, Lorna V. "The Inscription of Sexual Identity in Aída Cartagena's *Escalera Para Electra*". *MLN* 112(2) (1997): 219–31.

CASAS, MYRNA

Dramatist, director, producer, and professor, Myrna Casas (b. 1934) began to study drama at the University of Puerto Rico (UPR) where she met René Marqués and Emilio Belavel, two giants of Puerto Rican theater. She transferred to Vassar College, completed a BA in 1954, and did a short stint with the Little Theater of New York. The following year, Casas joined the faculty of UPR as a costume designer, her academic base until 1985. She completed her formal education (MFA, Boston University, 1961; PhD, NYU, 1973) while teaching dramatic construction and representation. In 1963, she directed *Waiting for Godot* in Spanish, a peek at the experimental-absurdist vision that defines her dramaturgy. That same year she founded Producciones Cisne, began to produce plays from the national and world repertoire, and tour with them throughout the island.

Puerto Rico's divided history has affected all the arts. After four centuries of Spanish colonialism, it became a territory of the United States in 1898. Citizenship and the military draft came in 1917. Commonwealth status in 1952 – the current *Estado Libre Asociado* – increased the island's political and economic ties to the mainland, but most of its 3.8 million inhabitants remain Spanish monolingual. This duality of Spanish heritage and American sovereignty plays out as the struggle between the heart and the stomach, called "la problemática puertorriqueña".

Themes and Style

Like her fellow playwright Luis Rafael Sánchez, Myrna Casas represents this cultural fracture through mordant satire. Her favorite structure is the *theatrum mundi* or play-within-a-play. The outer play depicts the caricatures and farces of daily life; the inner play peels back the socio-psychological conflicts of Puerto Ricans, especially women trapped between machista islanders and imperious mainlanders.

Casas began to write by experimenting with the polarities of a "well-made play". Set in a dilapidated colonial home turned brothel, *Cristal roto en el tiempo* (1960, Glass Shattered Though Time), her first play, dwells on the romantic fantasies of an aging prostitute. *Cristal* bemoans the island's moral decay with poetic sentimentality. In contrast but still in a realistic style, the title character of *Eugenia Victoria Herrera* (1963) is a strong woman of wealth surrounded by mendacity, incest and genetic determinism, a naturalistic jab at the social pathologies. After *Eugenia*, Casas cast realism aside.

Absurdos en soledad (1963, Absurdities in Solitude) marked her turn to farce and metadrama, the transparent interplay between illusion and reality, actor-character and spectator. Buffeted by hostile social mores, an aspiring actress looks for the stage door. Her travails provoke uneasy laughter; even old ladies attack her. The stage is set in a dead park; the cast awaits an old actor still learning his lines – in Latin, Hebrew, English – amid chattering incomprehension and relentless rot. Although the actress gains the stage, her obstacles symbolize the neuroses of a people with an unstable identity.

The anguish of feeling trapped in a stagnant marriage and dysfunctional family defines Nena (girl), the protagonist in *La trampa* (1964, The Trap). A docile wife and dutiful daughter, Nena fantasizes about playing house with another lover, as does her husband. Nena foresees their married future in her parents; her mother is a fat materialist; her father, a jack-in-the-box puppet, sits atop of the garbage can, an image of emasculation and cuckoldry in Puerto Rico. Nena leaves home to search for life in all its contradictory richness.

Nena's personal confinement expands to symbolize Puerto Rico's helpless political conditions in *El impromptu de San Juan* (1966). Like *Absurdos* and later *Este país no existe* (1993), *Impromptu* recreates the world-as-stage metaphor. Thematically the action lampoons the docility of *Boricuas* who yield to American values; theatrically the farce subverts the facile formulas of comedy. Humor arises in the outer play when the shifting identities of the women (muses, nieces, actresses, spectators) clash with the authoritarian director. Unable to salvage the rehearsal in the inner play, the actors dance away while a flamboyant "estar" beats a drum as he takes center stage. The Elvis-imitator banging on the primal instrument of Caribbean culture implies that island people must affirm their cultural identity or risk dancing off into an abyss.

Casas' style changed again with *No todas lo tienen* (Not All of Them Have One 1974, rewritten 1994). Hereafter her plays retained their zany antics, but the story gained plot cohesion, the jokes became more situational than linguistic, and the cultural void deeper. As the action begins, an urban middle-class couple, dulled by liquor and consumerism, bickers. Gaby, the mousey martyred housewife, despairs about her husband's womanizing. She abandons him, travels to Europe, and returns converted into her glamorous twin. Predictably, Luis starts to lust for the new Gaby. Unpredictably, the play sets up a spoof.

Represented without backdrops to reveal stage machinery, deliberate mistakes in staging provoke bewildered laughter. As the plot advances, the stage manager interrupts the action; lights, music, and props are mis-timed; characters move into and out of their roles. Just when the ludic knot starts to unravel, the protagonist rips off her wig and refuses to act. Her co-actors insist that the play must go on. By suddenly dropping her mask, Gaby invites spectators to examine their own behavior, their own role-plays and lies. The plastic flowers on stage are perfect; real flowers are not. *No todas* starts as a domestic farce that evolves into a parody of theater, especially its artifice and surprise.

El gran circo eucraniano (1988, The Great Ukranian Circus) begins with barkers inviting passers-by to see their souls on stage. Again, the conventional comedy blurs into metadrama: the action trips against vignettes inserted to break the story line and characters unfold into multiple roles. They serve as actors, narrators, spectators, or revert suddenly to their personal identity – on stage and off. Nomadic players with no other home than a tent, no other family than each other, they yearn for places and loved ones left behind. Instead, they wander about seeking local issues to improvise their scenes: the despair of people dependent on welfare programs and beset by crime, corruption, and drugs.

The erratic behavior of the characters mirrors their shifting identities. Gabriela José, the circus owner, is an able administrator, but her name implies gender conflict. She pines for the child she left behind, but refuses to embrace the young man who might be her son. Freedom and shame fix the mask of the vagabond to her. Implicitly, the scene liberates women to choose between motherhood and a profession.

Beyond the recursive structure of circus-mirror-society, one perceives the political and psychic confusion of the people. Gabriela José insists on pronouncing the name "E-U-craniano" not "Ucraniano". That stress suggests, *Estados Unidos*, United States, in Spanish; *Eucraniano* recalls the Soviet Ukraine. The title alludes to political hegemonies. It also invites reflection about the *Estado Libre Asociado,* Commonwealth status: a political invention; Puerto Rico is neither a state nor free. The Theater Critics' Circle of San Juan selected *Circo* for their National Dramaturgy Award in 1988; it is Casas' most compelling play.

Another prizewinner, *Este país no existe* (1993, This Country Does Not Exist) won the Miami Circle of Critics Award in 1993. The production crew's failure to even stage a thwarted rebellion against colonial rule reproduces contemporary political failures. The country does not exist because, just as *Boricuas* loyal to the Spanish crown betrayed the rebels in 1868, today's acculturation diminishes their national identity.

Voces (2000, Voices) projects the degradation of love and civility in Puerto Rico. Set in milieux that emphasize communications – the psychologist's office, university, and radio station – the characters speak past each other and muffle their inner voices with chatter. As in much of Casas' drama, a theater-mirror metaphor reflects back to a better past and forward inviting the spectators to examine their lives. *Voces* won the Theater Critics Circle of San Juan's National Dramaturgy Award in 2000.

Versatility and experimentation mark the comedies of Myrna Casas. Her farces mock social mores, privileges, and pathologies with humor and satire. The *theatrum mundi* structure conforms to the theme of psychic and cultural fragmentation within a confined space. Unexpected turns in the action keep the audience alert to surprises. Her theatricality exposes the artful guises of stagecraft to reveal the solitude of people trapped in a chaotic world. Her use of narrators, episodic development and self-referential images remind the audience to see themselves. Her female characters range from self-confident girls to lonely women broken by past mistakes; their shifting identities symptomatic of their divided psyches. The open endings call for action. Just as players must collaborate to craft a meaningful performance, Puerto Ricans must cooperate to create a healthy society.

The 14th *Jornadas Internacionales del Teatro Latinoamericano*, an annual drama conference in Puebla, Mexico, honored Myrna Casas in 2006, and the City of Puebla granted her *la Célula Real*; their royal seal. Antonio García del Toro, professor and theater director at the University of Puerto Rico, directed a retrospective that combined a dozen or more of her forty plays in *Casas y más casas: un revolú bien hecho* (Casas and more Casas: a well-done chaos). The wordplay starts with her last name; *casas* means house or home in Spanish. *Revolú*, a truncated form of revolution, imagines home as a well-done chaos and a final spoof on the well-made play.

WILMA FELICIANO

Selected Works

Cristal roto en el tiempo, Teatro puertorriqueño, tercer festival. San Juan, PR: Instituto de Cultura Puertorriqueña, 1961: 259–349. Also in *Tres obras de Myrna Casas.*
Santurce, PR: Playor, 1987.

Absurdos en soledad and *Eugenia Victoria Herrera.* San Juan, PR: Editorial Cordillera, 1964.

La trampa and *El impromptu de San Juan.* Rio Piedras, PR: Editorial Universitaria, 1974. *La trampa* also in *Tres obras de Myrna Casas.* Santurce, PR: Playor, 1987.

Teatro de Vanguardia: Contemporary Spanish American Theatre. Editor and prologue. Lexington, MA: D. C. Heath, 1975.

Eugenia Victoria Herrera 2nd edition. Hato Rey, PR: Borikén Libros, 1987.

Tres obras de Myrna Casas. Santurce, PR: Editorial Playor, 1987 – includes *Cristal roto en el tiempo*, *La trampa*, and *Tres.*

The Great USkranian Circus. Women Writing Women: An Anthology of Spanish-American Theater of the 1980's. Ed and trans. Teresa Cajiao Salas and Margarita Vargas. Albany: SUNY Press, 1997.

Voces. San Juan: Plaza Mayor, 2001.

El gran circo eukraniano. San Juan, PR: Plaza Mayor, 2004.

Selected First Performances

Cristal roto en el tiempo: pausa dolorosa en dos actos y una voz. San Juan, Third Festival of Puerto Rican Theater, Tapia Theater, 5–8 May 1960.

Absurdos en soledad, San Juan, Experimental Theater of the Ateneo, 22–24 Feb. 1963.

La trampa, San Juan, first act, Teatro Bar La Tierruca, 1963; whole play, Ateneo Theater, 1964.

Eugenia Victoria Herrera, San Juan, Tapia Theater, 31 January, 1964.

El impromptu de San Juan, Río Piedras, PR: Experimental Theatre at University of Puerto Rico, 1973.

Tres comprises a series of satirical skits: *Loa*, *No se servirá almuerzo a Anita Millán o La historia triste de las plantas plásticas*, *Quitatetu*, *Eran tres y ahora son cuatro;* San Juan, Sixteenth Festival of Puerto Rican Theater, Tapia Theater, 23 May 1974.

No todas lo tienen, San Juan, Seventeenth Festival, Sylvia Rexach Theater, 13 November 1975; revised Mayagüez, Yagüez Theater, February 1994.

Cuarenta años después: drama sin son ni ton, San Juan, Seventeenth Festival, Silvia Rexach Theater, 1975.

El gran circo eucraniano, San Juan, PR, Tapia Theater, 1988.

Este país no existe, Quebradillas, PR, Liberty Theater, 1993.

Al garete, San Juan, PR, Fine Arts Center, 1995.

Voces, San Juan, PR, Carlos Marichal Theater of Luis A. Ferré Center of Fine Arts, 24 March 2000.

¡Qué sospecha tengo! San Juan, PR, Tapia Theater, March 2001.

References and Further Reading

Aguilú de Murphy, Raquel. "Hacia una teorización del absurdo en el teatro de Myrna Casas". *Revista Iberoamericana*, 162/163 (1993): 169–76.

Cajiao Salas, Teresa and Vargas, Margarita. "Voices in Hispanic Theater". In Anna K. Frances and J. P. Corso (eds), *International Women Playwrights: Voices of Identity and Transformation.* Metuchen, NJ: Scarecrow Press, 1993, pp. 213–21.

Cypess, Sandra M. "Eugenia Victoria Herrara and Myrna Casas' Redefinition of Puerto Rican National Identity." In K. Nigro and S. Cypess (eds), *Essays in Honor of Frank Dauster.* Newark, DE: Juan de la Cuesta Monographs, 1995, pp. 181–94.

Dávila-López, Grace. "Discurso dramático femenino e historia del teatro nacional en Puerto Rico". *Gestos*, 14 (November 1992): 141–55.

Feliciano, Wilma. "Myrna Casas: la mujer y el juego metadramático". *Revista del Ateneo Puertorriqueño*, 4(10–11–12) (1994): 147–54.

García del Toro, Antonio. *Mujer y patria en la dramaturgia puertorriqueña.* Madrid: Playor, 1987.

Montes Huidobro, Matías. *Persona: vida y máscara en el teatro puertorriqueño.* San Juan, PR: Centro de Estudios Avanzados de Puerto Rico y el Caribe, 1986.

Phillips, Jordan B. "Chapter IV: 1960–68". In *Contemporary Puerto Rican Drama.* Madrid: Playor, 1973, pp. 135–41.

Rivera de Alvarez, Josefina. "Otros autores teatrales". In *Literatura puertorriqueña, su proceso en el tiempo.* Madrid: Partenón, 1983, pp. 802–5.

Umpierre, Luz María. "Inversiones, niveles y participación en *Absurdos en soledad* de Myrna Casas". *Latin American Theatre Review*, 17(1) (Fall 1983): 3–13.

Unruh, Vicky. "A Moveable Space: The Problem of Puerto Rico in Myrna Casas's Theater". In Catherine Larson and Margarita Vargas (eds), *Latin American Women Dramatists: Theater, Texts, and Theories.* Bloomington, IN: Indiana University Press, 1998, pp. 126–42.

Waldman, Gloria. "Myrna Casas: Dramaturga y directora". *Revista del Instituto de Cultura Puertorriqueña*, 21(78) (January–March1978): 1–9.

CASTELLANOS, ROSARIO

One of the most multifaceted writers of twentieth-century Mexico, Rosario Castellanos (1925–74) published poetry, novels, short stories, essays and plays during her nearly thirty-year literary career. She is considered to be among contemporary Mexico's most important thinkers and writers. Her personal biography, marked by great intellectual achievement as well as painful personal experiences of rejection and solitude, is central to understanding and appreciating her literature.

Castellanos was born in Mexico City on May 25, 1925. When she was just one year old she returned with her parents, Adriana Figueroa and César Castellanos, to their native Chiapas. She spent her childhood on the family ranch, in the quiet town of Comitán, near the Guatemalan border. Her father's family had been part of the privileged landowning class for generations and the young Castellanos grew up with the material comforts to be expected in that social milieu. She did not, however, experience the parental affection and attention that would have made her early years less lonely. She was looked after by her indigenous nanny, Rufina, while her parents showered the family's male heir, Castellanos' younger brother Benjamín, with their care and protection. When her brother died unexpectedly at a very young age, her parents lost themselves in grief and regret and Castellanos retreated further into her own isolation.

The large-scale sociopolitical transformations that took place in Mexico after the Revolution played a decisive role in Castellanos' intellectual formation. With President Lázaro Cárdenas' sweeping land reforms of 1941, the Castellanos family lost their vast landholdings and decided to migrate to Mexico City. The geographic change provided more educational opportunities for Castellanos and, at the age of 16, she enrolled in a preparatory school in the capital. Upon graduating from the Luis G. Leon School, she matriculated in the National University of Mexico where she studied philosophy and regularly attended the *tertulias*, a weekly opportunity to engage in intellectual conversation with her friends and classmates. Her interlocutors at these meetings were some of the most gifted future writers of Latin America and who, along with Castellanos, would form the "Generation of 1950": Ernesto Carballido, Jaime Sabines, Augusto Monterroso, Sergio Galindo, Ernesto Cardenal and Dolores Castro, among others.

The late 1940s and early 1950s mark the beginning of Castellanos' career as a writer and cultural critic. In 1948, the year in which both her parents died, Castellanos published her first two books of poetry, *Trayectorio del polvo* (Trajectory of Dust) and *Apuntes para una declaración de fe* (Notes for a Declaration of Faith). In 1950, she completed her master's thesis in philosophy, entitled *Sobre la cultura femenina* (On Feminine Culture). Although the text has been criticized as being too pessimistic and lacking a strong scientific base, the study is important in that it clearly signals the beginning of Castellanos' pointed examination and questioning of the role of women in a male-dominated cultural tradition. Her interest in women's issues was recognized and, in 1953, she was awarded a grant from the Mexican Writers Center in order to research and write an essay on the contributions of women to Mexican culture.

As Castellanos continued to explore the possibilities of giving a voice to women in Mexican culture, she also began to cultivate what would become her other great literary interest: the history and current reality of the Indigenous peoples of southern Mexico. She was named Director of Cultural Activities in the Chiapanecan Institute of Arts and Sciences in 1951. Later, from 1956–58, while working with the Guiñol Theater for the National Indigenist Institute, she traveled extensively throughout the region and helped to produce the performances of the puppet troupe as they presented plays in various indigenous languages. These experiences allowed Castellanos to once again come into contact with the indigenous cultures she had first known as a child in Comitán. A fellowship from the Rockefeller Foundation (1954–55) further enabled her to study and re-evaluate the indigenous experience and influence in her native Chiapas. As a result, in 1957, she published her first novel, *Balún Canán* (The Nine Guardians). The novel, narrated in part by a 7-year-old girl whose family fears expropriation of their lands after the 1941 reforms, examines the changing power relations between the white minority and the indigenous majority in Chiapas. The novel denounces the social structures that have left the indigenous population in poverty and submission. It also narrates the transition from the Cárdenas reforms of the early twentieth century to the mid-century consolidation of national politics. Castellanos' second novel, *Oficio de tinieblas* (1962, Rites of Darkness), is based on actual historical events. It, too, explores the inevitable clash of cultures in southern Mexico as well as the secret rites and defensive religious practices of the indigenous people.

Castellanos' professional life continued along its diverse course throughout the decade of the 1960s. She worked as Director of Information Services for the National University of Mexico while also writing cultural essays for several magazines and publishing more poetry in volumes such as *Lívida luz* (1960, Livid Light) and *Materia memorable* (1969, Memorable Material). Many of the poems in these collections express the sadness and sense of loss that the poet experienced when her brief marriage began to fall apart after the birth of her son, Gabriel, in 1961. During this time, Castellanos also had the opportunity to teach Latin American literature at various universities in the United States and, upon returning to Mexico, she accepted a position in the department of Comparative Literature at the National University of Mexico.

In 1971, Castellanos was named Mexican Ambassador to Israel. She and her son moved to Tel Aviv and there she was able to thrive not only in her diplomatic post but also at the Hebrew University where she lectured on literature. That same year saw the publication of a collection of short stories, *Álbum de familia* (Family Album), which narrated the frustrating and truncated experiences of women in Mexico trying to conform to cultural standards. A compilation of essays, *Mujer que sabe latín* (A Woman Who Knows Latin), published in 1973, was well received and widely distributed, in part because it closely coincided with the celebration of the International Year of the Woman (1975) and the subsequent public discussions on feminist issues. The essays reveal Castellanos' interest in and influence from other women writers such as Virginia Woolf, María Luisa Bombal, Silvina Ocampo and Betty Friedan. Castellanos' writings also reflect a keen analysis of topics such as the expectations placed on women in terms of physical beauty and the use of language as a tool of domination. While in Israel, Castellanos also wrote the play *El eterno femenino*, a satirical look at love, marriage and a woman's place in society.

Rosario Castellanos died on August 7, 1974. She was electrocuted in her home in Tel Aviv when she switched on a lamp after leaving the shower. She received a state funeral in Mexico and was memorialized in a number of other countries in Europe and Central America as well as Israel and the United States.

The "Chiapas Cycle"

Early in her career, Rosario Castellanos demonstrated an interest in documenting life in rural Chiapas. The novels and short stories she produced at this time belong to what Joseph

Sommers has called "el ciclo de Chiapas". Having grown up in southern Mexico and later working on various projects related to the region, Castellanos had an intimate knowledge of its people, traditions and history. In particular, she was drawn to the legends and beliefs as well as the suffering of the indigenous groups of Chiapas. Her commitment to the cause of the indigenous is central to the novels already mentioned, *Balún Canán* and *Oficio de tinieblas* in addition to the short stories of *Ciudad Real* (1960, Royal City) and *Los convidados de agosto* (1964, Guests of August). The texts rely to a certain degree on the myths and folklore of the original inhabitants of Chiapas and, in this way, create a more authentic voice for the people portrayed. The fictional world is infused with a magical quality without denying the repression of the indigenous. *Oficio de tinieblas* is considered by many critics to be her narrative masterpiece. Based on a Chamula revolt that took place during the presidency of Benito Juárez, it details a racial conflict that ends with the crucifixion of one of the indigenous leaders. Beyond the extreme violence of the scene, the novel chronicles the tragic reality of a fragmented society sustained by racial division. *Ciudad Real*, which Castellanos referred to as a collection of "Chiapanecan sketches", also probes the strained relations and different perspectives present in San Cristóbal de las Casas, a city in Chiapas that had been known as Ciudad Real during the colonial period.

In a 1965 essay translated as "Discrimination in the United States and in Chiapas", Castellanos invokes the tensions and strict racial separation of 1960s America in order to contemplate the other extreme of discrimination: forced assimilation. The essay summarizes the ideas of a nineteenth-century lawyer, Vicente Pineda, who, after witnessing the rebellion of various indigenous communities in Chiapas, proposes new methods for achieving racial unity and avoiding future conflicts. The strategies, while presented as humanitarian measures, actually reveal a desire to erase all traces of the indigenous culture through intermarriage and the placement of native orphans in the care of white families. In examining the views of Pineda, Castellanos demonstrates that there are various ways in which racial discrimination can manifest itself.

During the 1950s, in her private letters and published works, Castellanos insists on the need to change the conscience of the white population. She believed that the exploitation and other injustices to which the indigenous peoples were subjected would only be ameliorated when the dominant culture ceases to see itself as superior and, therefore, would no longer be able to justify its abusive policies.

Creating a Feminist Discourse

Most of Rosario Castellanos' work is marked by a noticeable feminist ideology. Although her writing reflects a deep concern with what it means to be a woman in Mexico, it also transcends national boundaries to become universal. Castellanos sees the cultural constructs of patriarchal society as the source of much of the repression suffered by women. She criticizes the idealized version of love that strips women of their individuality and she strives to put into perspective the reality of marriage, motherhood and other roles assumed by women. In all the literary genres she cultivated, she explores the female experience in order to give a voice to women and to give value to their cultural contribution. The themes of "otherness" and silence, with respect to women's reality, are central to her writings and the domestic arena often becomes the space in which androcentric symbols and ideas are questioned and subverted.

One of her best-known poems, "Poesía no eres tú" ("You Are Not Poetry"), challenges the traditional concept of women as passive beings, objectified by men. The title is an ironic reference to the verses of the nineteenth-century Spanish poet, Gustavo Adolfo Bécquer in which the lyric voice proclaims to his love and muse that she herself is poetry. Castellanos, in contrast, rejects the romantic view of woman as the silent, idealized other and instead calls for dialogue and mutual understanding. In a similar vein, the poem "Meditación en el umbral" ("Meditation on the Brink"), by invoking such women as Sor Juana, Emily Dickinson and Mary Magdalene, examines the image of women in Western culture and calls for a radical change that will allow creative, independent women to thrive without the rebuke of a patriarchal society.

In the essay, "La mujer y su imagen" ("Woman and her Image"), Castellanos criticizes the tendency of a male-dominated world to elevate the ideal of feminine beauty and character to near mythic proportions. The author insists on a rejection of the false images that trap women and lead to her social alienation. The essay demonstrates a desire on the part of Castellanos to challenge the myths surrounding women and redefine their role in society.

Many other works of Castellanos also examine the stereotypes and behavioral norms governing women's lives. The author often employs household metaphors in order to evaluate and deconstruct these models. The short story "Lección de cocina" ("The Cooking Lesson") is an ironic look at a newlywed's despair as she attempts to prepare a meal for her husband. The interior monologue of the narrator, as she watches the steak dinner burn reveals, in a comic tone, the problematic conditions of her life as she tries to meet society's expectations. This same need to comply with the rules imposed by society is the cause of much anguish in poems such as "Economía doméstica" ("Home Economics") and "Valium 10". Both poems present the image of women who, to outsiders, would appear to be well in control as they tend to domestic tasks like keeping the house in order and carefully reviewing household expenses. However, disappointment and discontent lurk beneath the perfect façade; there are repressed cries and secret moments of nostalgia as well as the need to chemically balance one's life when the feelings of failure are overwhelming. The poem "Recordatorio" ("Reminder") also questions the price to be paid for obeying the dictates of society. The lyric voice, a quiet, submissive woman, at the end of the poem must remind the "señores" of her presence and request their permission to leave.

As another approach to creating a feminine discourse, Castellanos often appropriates the symbols of masculine culture in order to insert her own distinct point of view. Poems such as "Lamentación de Dido" ("The Lament of Dido"), *Salomé* and *Judith* enter the realm of Western mythology and debunk the traditionally accepted readings and lessons of these stories. In the case of the two dramatic poems, the action is transported to Chiapas and the two protagonists are not portrayed as sinners so much as rebels seeking liberty from social constraints.

Similarly, "Malinche" is a poem in which the lyric voice assumes the personality of this archetypal Mexican figure and, thus, is able to rewrite history. A new perspective on the life of la Malinche, one emphasizing the tragedy and betrayal of her early life and her strength in facing her destiny, emerges in these verses.

The critics who have analyzed Castellanos' work also point out her ability to address typically taboo subjects such as female sexuality. Most notably, her poem "Kinsey Report", in a reference to the famous survey of the sexual behavior of men and women, gives voice to six different women answering questions about their intimate lives. Although the questions are not part of the text, a dialogue is implied and each voice reveals a different life experience and attitude towards sex. Taken as a whole, they reflect feelings of disillusion and a certain amount of naïveté on the subject.

Castellanos as Playwright

Rosario Castellanos was also attracted to theater for its ability to reach a wider audience but it was not a genre in which she worked very much. She had written pieces for the puppet troupe in Chiapas but it was not until she was living in Israel that she was persuaded to fully apply her wit and intelligence to playwriting. Responding to a request from her friends, the actress Emma Teresa Armendáriz and the director Rafael López Miarnau, Castellanos wrote a three-act farce entitled *El eterno femenino* (The Eternal Feminine).

The action of the play begins in a space very often associated with women, the beauty salon. From there, it takes a humorous and quite radical look at the stereotypes and myths influencing both men and women in contemporary Mexico. The play signals the responsibility both sexes share in perpetuating a questionable status quo.

The second act has been characterized as both the most interesting and the most controversial aspect of *El eterno femenino*. Presented as a dream, induced by a new device attached to hair dryers, the young protagonist, Lupita, finds herself at a carnival about to witness a show based on the "sacred, moral principles" of the nation. What follows is a clever exploration and subversion of many of the ideas and events that helped to shape Mexican identity. Giving voice to several quintessential female figures of Mexican history such as Sor Juana, la Malinche, the Empress Carlota and la Adelita, among others, Castellanos is able to challenge the beliefs and symbols of Mexican culture. Official history is displaced as the traditionally silent voices of women are permitted to tell their own story and, thus, suggest a new reading of formerly accepted beliefs.

The play concludes with a call to all Mexican women to discover their true identity within their own culture. The ultimate message is that a feminist movement in Mexico cannot follow foreign models but, rather, must come from within, transforming society at every level.

Castellanos and the Literary Canon

Many of the works of Rosario Castellanos have been incorporated into the canon of Latin American literature. A number of her poems, short stories and essays have been included in literary anthologies and her name is on the reading list of any scholar of Mexican literature. Several of her works have been translated into French, German, English, Hebrew, Polish and Russian. Among her most widely read books are *Mujer que sabe latín, Poesía no eres tú: Obra poética 1948–1971* and *Álbum de familia*.

In a prologue to *El uso de la palabra* (1975, Use of the Word), José Emilio Pacheco observed that, in her time, no one knew how to appreciate the works of Castellanos. She understood the significance of the "double condition of being a woman and Mexican" and this was a completely new perspective in mid-twentieth-century Mexican writing. In all of her poetry, fiction and drama, the experience of being female informs her creativity and fuses with her perspective on Mexico and its culture. Although she was adorned with many honors and awards during her lifetime (Mexican Critics Award in 1957 and the Chiapas Prize in 1958 for *Balún Canán*; Xavier Villaurrutia Prize for Literature, 1961; Sor Juan Inés de la Cruz Prize for *Oficio de tinieblas*, 1962; Carlos Trouyet Prize for Literature, 1967 and Mexico's Woman of the Year, 1967), it was not until after her untimely death that she received the critical national and international attention and recognition she deserved as a clever and witty writer.

JEANIE MURPHY

Selected Works

Trayectoria del polvo. Mexico City: Colección el Cristal Fugitivo, 1948.
Apuntes para una declaración de fe. Mexico City: Ediciones de América: Revista Antológica, 1948.
Balún Canán. Mexico City: Fondo de Cultura Económica, 1957.
Salomé y Judith: Poemas dramáticos. Mexico City: Editorial Jus, 1957.
Ciudad Real: Cuentos. Xalapa: Universidad Veracruzana, 1960.
Lívida luz: Poemas. Mexico City: Universidad Nacional Autónoma de México, 1960.
Oficio de tinieblas. Mexico City: Joaquín Mortiz, 1962.
Los convidados de agosto. Mexico City: Ediciones Era, 1964.
Juicios sumarios: Ensayos. Xalapa: Universidad Veracruzana, 1966.
Materia memorable. Mexico City: Universidad Nacional Autónoma de México, 1969.
Álbum de familia. Mexico City: Joaquín Mortiz, 1971.
Poesía no eres tú: Obra poética, 1948–1971. Mexico City: Fondo de Cultura Económica, 1972.
Mujer que sabe latín. Mexico City: Sepsetentas, Secretaria de Educación Pública, 1973.
El uso de la palabra. Prologue by José Emilio Pacheco. Mexico City: Ediciones de Excélsior-Crónicas, 1974.
El eterno femenino: Farsa. Mexico City: Fondo de Cultura Económica, 1975.
Meditación en el umbral: Antología poética. Compiled by Julian Palley. Foreword by Elena Poniatowska. Mexico City: Fondo de Cultura Económica, 1985.

References and Further Reading

Ahern, Maureen and Vásquez, Mary Seale (eds) *Homenaje a Rosario Castellanos.* Valencia: Albatros-Hispanófila Ediciones, 1980.
Baptiste, Victor N. *La obra poética de Rosario Castellanos.* Santiago de Chile: Ediciones Exégesis, 1972.
Bonifaz, Oscar. *Remembering Rosario: A Personal Glimpse into the Life and Works of Rosario Castellanos.* Trans. Myralyn F. Allgood. Potomac, MD: Scripta Humanistica, 1990.

Gil Iriarte, María Luisa. "Invasión del silencio: la voz de la mujer en la poesía de Rosario Castellanos". *Revista de estudios hispánicos* 23 (1995): 65–82.

López, González, Aralia. "*Oficio de tinieblas:* novela de la nación mexicana". *Palabra y el Hombre: Revista de la Universidad Veracruzana* 113 (2000): 119–26.

Miller, Beth. *Rosario Castellanos: Una conciencia feminista en México.* Tuxtla Gutiérrez, Chiapas: Universidad Autónoma de Chiapas, 1983.

Miller, Yvette. "El temario poético de Rosario Castellanos". *Hispamérica* 10(29) (1981): 107–15.

Nigro, Kirsten F. "Rosario Castellanos's Debunking of the Eternal Feminine". *Journal of Spanish Studies: Twentieth Century* 8 (1980): 89–102.

Pérez, Laura Lee Crumley de. "*Balún Canán* y la construcción narrativa de una cosmovisión indígena". *Revista Iberoamericana* 50 (1984): 491–503.

Schwartz, Perla. *Rosario Castellanos: Mujer que supo latín.* Mexico City: Editorial Katún, 1984.

Scott, Nina M. "Rosario Castellanos: Demythification through Laughter". *Humor: International Journal of Humor Research* 2(1) (1989): 19–30.

Sommers, Joseph. "El ciclo de Chiapas: Nueva corriente literaria". *Cuadernos Americanos* 133(2) (1964): 246–61.

CASTILLO, MARÍA JOSEFA DEL

Madre Castillo (1671–1742) is considered the second most famous nun in Spanish America, after Sor Juana Inés de la Cruz. She is well known for her mystical writings, particularly in Colombia, where she lived. She was born as Francisca Josefa de Castillo y Guevara Niño on October 6, 1671 in Tunja, a small town in the mountains of the *Nuevo Reino de Granada* (today Colombia). She was a legitimate daughter of Francisco Ventura de Castillo y Toledo, who was Spanish by birth. He traveled to Tunja to act as lieutenant to the district governor, and he also served as councilor for Tunja. Madre Castillo's mother, María Guevara Niño y Rojas, was born to a politically and socially powerful family of Tunja. Francisca Josefa de Castillo lived in a highly religious environment, where monasticism was considered an honorable option for girls. Her family attended mass regularly, and as a young woman, she was encouraged to look for the spiritual guidance of priests. According to her spiritual autobiography, she went to confession frequently with the priests of the Jesuit order, a practice that shaped her desire to become a nun. Francisca Josefa del Castillo decided to enter the *Convento Real de Santa Clara* (Royal Convent of Saint Claire) in 1689. Her choice of convent might have had to do with the fact that she was related to one of the founder nuns of that convent. An aunt of Madre Castillo was living in the convent as a professed nun at the time of her entrance. She changed her name to Francisca Josefa de la Concepción upon entering the convent, and became a black-veiled nun on September 4, 1694.

Writing Nun

From the beginning of her monastic life, Madre Castillo started writing short spiritual pieces at the behest of Father Francisco de Herrera. Those papers were later gathered together and published, first under the title of *Sentimientos espirituales* (Spiritual Sentiments) in 1843 and later as *Afectos espirituales* (Spiritual effects) in 1942. Her confessor, Father Diego de Tapia, ordered her to write the account of her life, *Su vida*, some time around 1713, and she concluded the account around 1723. These dates were gathered from information given in the account of her life and in the *Afectos espirituales*; there are no certain dates of when she started and ended her manuscript.

To understand the kind of narrative that Madre Castillo wrote, it is necessary to understand the context in which it was produced. The genre of the *vida espiritual* (spiritual life) emerged from the relationship of the nun with her confessor. In the context of the Spanish Counter-Reformation, the Church sought to control its subjects, in particular, women. This control was exercised through writing. Confessors put into effect their authority by demanding their spiritual daughters, the nuns, to write their innermost thoughts and spiritual experiences in order to better know their lives and be assured of the orthodoxy of their religious practices. However controlling the practice of writing was intended to be, the women living in the cloister between the fifteenth and eighteenth centuries found a space for self-affirmation and creativity. These women writers were able to develop strategies and rhetorical devices to escape censorship and to be the subjects of praise and admiration. Most writing nuns followed accepted models within the Church such as the writings of Saint Teresa of Ávila, reformer of the Carmelite order in Spain during the sixteenth century; Saint Teresa followed the model set by Saint Augustine in his *Confessions*. Hundreds of nuns in Spain and Spanish America during this period wrote their autobiographies, plays, poetry, theological treatises, prayers, and other kinds of writings allowed for women. There were certain genres available only to men, but even then, a few women writers found their way into these prohibited genres, like Sor Juana Inés de la Cruz in her *Carta Atenagórica* (Athenagoric Letter).

Vida and *Afectos espirituales* (Life and Spiritual Effects)

Within this context, it is important to identify the many filters to which the text was subjected. Madre Castillo was writing her *Vida* as commanded by her confessor, who was going to be the ultimate reader of the text. Thus, she had to conform to the model of perfection and to the life of *imitatio Christi* (imitation of Crist) the Church expected religious women to follow. The story of the *Vida* follows a chronological order. It begins with the birth of Francisca Josefa de Castillo and ends a few years after her first term as abbess of her convent. Madre Castillo portrays herself as a child aware of the many sins surrounding her. She relates that she looked for solitude and a life of prayer but her weaknesses made her sin repeatedly. She struggled to live a life of perfection within the world until finally she is able to enter the convent, but the struggles continued during her life there too. She recounts that she was the butt of criticisms and envies, and she was treated with scorn by many of her sisters in the convent. At the same time, she received mercies from God in the form of mystical experiences. Some of the short writings that comprise the *Afectos espirituales* were introduced into her *Vida* and represent her spiritual journey. The rest of her narration is about her daily efforts to succeed in her quest to reach perfection.

From archival research conducted by several scholars in the field, it is known that she held several important positions within the hierarchy of the convent, five times as mistress of novices and three times as abbess.

Critics such as Darío Achury Valenzuela and María Teresa Morales Borrero consider Madre Castillo to be a mystical nun not for her *Vida* but for her *Afectos espirituales*. Madre Castillo called the *Afectos, papeles* (papers) and they were composed as individual pieces that she submitted to her confessors for approval. Madre Castillo writes in these papers about the moments in which her soul was united with God and the knowledge that she acquires from that experience. She also comments on prayers, psalms and other biblical passages. There is a third work by Madre Castillo known as *Cuaderno de Enciso*; Enciso was her brother-in-law's last name. It contains revised pieces from the *Afectos*, as well as some devotional texts and poems of unknown authorship.

Madre Castillo died at the age of 70 in 1742.

Scholarship

Madre Castillo's works were published for the first time during the nineteenth century. Darío Achury Valenzuela compiled the latest and most complete edition of her works in 1968. He provides a critical edition and has published critical studies of her works. María Teresa Morales Borrero published analyses of some of Madre Castillo's writings in the same year. There are also a number of studies about Madre Castillo's works in Spanish and mostly from Colombia. In 1997, Kathryn Joy McKnight published a study of Madre Castillo in English, which to date is the most comprehensive study of her works. She places Madre Castillo in the tradition of conventual writing and develops a theoretical framework to understand Madre Castillo's writing. McKnight also conducted archival research in Colombia and demonstrated that Madre Castillo's autobiography could not be read as a modern narration of her life but as a convention within Church practices. McKnight's path-breaking research opened possibilities for future studies of Madre Castillo's works and other kinds of colonial discourse through a critical analysis of genre, gender and culture.

MÓNICA DÍAZ

Selected Works

Vida de la venerable Madre Francisca Josefa de la Concepción escrita por ella misma. Philadelphia, PA: T. H. Palmer, 1817.

Sentimientos espirituales de la venerable Madre Francisca Josefa de la Concepción de Castillo. Santafé de Bogotá: Bruno Espinosa de los Monteros, 1843.

Afectos espirituales. Bogotá: Editorial A.B.C., 1942.

Obras completas de la Madre Francisca Josefa de Castillo. Edited by Darío Achury Valenzuela 2 vols. Bogotá: Banco de la República, 1968.

References and Further Reading

Achury Valenzuela, Darío. *Análisis crítico de los Afectos espirituales de Sor Francisca Josefa de la Concepción de Castillo. Texto restablecido, introducción y comentarios del autor.* Santafé de Bogotá: Biblioteca de cultura colombiana, 1962.

——. "Un manuscrito de la madre de Castillo: El llamado Cuaderno de Enciso". *Boletín Cultural y Bibliográfico* 19(1) (1982): 47–86.

Galaz-Vivar Welden, Alicia. "Francisca Josefa de Castillo una mística del Nuevo Mundo". *Thesaurus: Boletín del Instituto Caro y Cuervo* 45(1) (1990): 149–61.

Hernández-Torres, Ivette N. "Escritura y misticismo en los Afectos espirituales de la madre Castillo". *Revista Iberoamericana* 69(204) (2003): 653–65.

McKnight, Kathryn Joy. *The Mystic of Tunja: The Writings of Madre Castillo, 1671–1742*. Amherst, MA: University of Massachusetts Press, 1997.

Morales Borrero, María Teresa. *La Madre Castillo: Su espiritualidad y su estilo*. Bogotá: Instituto Caro y Cuervo, 1968.

Robledo, Ángela. "Género y discurso místico autobiográfico en las obras de Francisca Josefa del Castillo y Francisco Castillo". *Texto Crítico* 15(40–1) (1989): 103–21.

——. "La Madre Castillo: Autobiografía mística y discurso marginal". *Letras Femeninas* 18(1–2) (1992): 55–63.

CAULFIELD, CARLOTA

Carlota Caulfield was born in 1953 in Cuba and is a poet. She divides her time between Berkeley, California and London, and is a Professor of Spanish and Spanish-American Studies as well as a member of Mills College Women's Studies Advisory Council. In 1981, she left her native country and has since lived in Dublin, New Orleans, Zurich, Barcelona, and London. Caulfield defines herself as a poet, and has created a multimedia book of "hyper poetry" (*XXXIX Steps*, 1995, CD, 1999). In Cuba, she was a publisher for the Editorial de Ciencias Sociales, and was in charge of editions of eighteenth-century French political and literary figures Charles de Montesquieu (1689–1755) and Maximilien de Robespierre (1758–94), and nineteenth-century Cuban writer José Antonio Saco (1797–1879). Her literary career as a poet, scholar and translator began only after she left Cuba. Since 1984, she has published several books of poetry in the United States, Italy and Spain. As a poet, she has been recognized in Puerto Rico (Honorable Mention in "Mairena" International Poetry Prize); Italy ("Ultimo Novecento," 1988; "Ricardo-Marchi-Torre di Calafuria," 1995); Spain (Honorable Mention in the Spain–USA poetry prize "Federico García Lorca," 1994); Mexico (Honorable Mention in "Premio Plural," 1993); United States (Latino Literature Prize Honorable Mention of the Latin American Writers Institute of New York, 1997; and the First Hispanic-American Poetry Prize "Dulce María Loynaz," Spain, 2002).

The concept that best defines Caulfield's poetic is multiplicity. From her first book (*Fanaim*, 1984) to the most recent (*Ticket to Ride*, 2005), she has been constructing her own poeticism by incorporating into her writing a vast collection of female voices she considers her precursors. Her themes include eroticism, sensuality, myths, legends, histories, alchemy, Jewish mysticism, and paintings from different periods and cultures. Jack Foley states that "memory functions as the key to Carlota Caulfield's complex subjectivity". John Goodby points out that "as ever in Caulfield's work there is an insistence upon the body as physical presence and as a mode of knowledge". Jaime D. Parra defines Caulfield's poetic as follows: "first, a passion for travels and travelers, cities, a cult for the arts, praise of memory, mysticism, recreation of different landscapes (outer and inner) and above all this immense task of bringing up to date different times and spaces".

In this sense, she cannot be considered a typical Latino female poet whose work is mostly focused on the loss of motherland, the acquisition of a Cuban-American ethnicity, or the challenges of social and gender discrimination. Also, some male critics have pointed out that she does not fit the stereotypical pattern attributed to feminist poets as her poetry revives the feminine tradition through different historical, national and literary masks.

Nevertheless, scholars who study Cuban poetry in exile have contested this multiplicity. They argue that her construction of referential labyrinths seems to be eccentric and that her Cuban poetic voice is hollow because of its lacking definition. On the other hand, Caulfield has explained that, like herself, her readers have many voices: friends, students of Latino/a and Latin American literature in the United States, Italian and Spanish readers. Female critics of Caulfield's works have noted that she reviews history from a feminist standpoint.

María Jesús Mayans says that "the lyricism of Caulfield's poetry comes from the intensity of the language, its rhythm and cadence, as well as the lucid language that illuminates the images. There is no doubt that this is the work of a poet of great maturity who also possesses an extraordinary esthetic sensibility". Other female scholars argue that while men take femininity as a source of poetical enigma, the female poet exalts, precisely, the enigma as a positive aspect of her totality. Rather than accepting the notion of the "universal feminine," they state that Caulfield's numerous poetic voices express *what* Hélène Cixous calls the imagination of women, those who prefer to explore possible languages instead of describing the existing language. Caulfield's *Oscuridad divina* is a collection of poems where these ideas can be tested. Neria de Giovanni, for instance, emphasizes how important they are for the literary representation of women and the fact that in this book the reader is exposed to several female voices taken from numerous cultural and historical contexts.

RAFAEL E. SAUMELL-MUÑOZ

Selected Works

Fanaim, 1984.
Oscuridad divina, 1985 and 1987.
A veces me llamo infancia/Sometimes I Call Myself Childhood, 1985.
El tiempo es una mujer que espera, 1986.
34th Street and Other Poems, 1987.
Angel Dust/Polvo de Ángel/Polvere d'angelo, 1990.
Visual Games for Words and Sounds, Hyperpoems for the Macintosh, 1993.
Libro de los XXXIX escalones/Libro dei XXXIX gradini, 1995.
Estrofas de papel, barro y tinta, 1995.
Libro de los XXXIX escalones/Book of the XXXIX Steps, 1997.
Books of the XXXIX Steps, A Poetry Game of Discovery and Imagination. Hyperpoems for Macintosh, 1995.
A las puertas del papel con amoroso fuego, 1996.
Book of the XXXIX Steps, A Poetry Game of Discovery and Imagination, CD-ROM, 1999.
Quincunce, 2001.
Autorretrato en ojo ajeno, 2001.
At the Paper Gates with Burning Desire, 2001.
Movimientos metálicos para juguetes abandonados. Premio Hispanoamericano de Poesía "Dulce María Loynaz", 2002.
The Book of Giulio Camillo/El libro de Giulio Camillo/Il libro di Giulio Camillo, 2003. La Laguna, Tenerife: Gobierno de Canarias, 2003.
Ticket to Ride. Essays and Poems, 2005.

References and Further Reading

Barquet, Jesús. "Lo cubano en la poesía de Carlota Caulfield". In Yara Montes-Huidobro (ed.), *Anthology of Women Cuban Writers*. Manoa, HI: University of Hawaii, 1998.

——. "Lo cubano en la poesía de Carlota Caulfield: Una poética en busca de su autora". *Banda Hispanica, Jornal de Poesia*, Brazil, May 2001. (http://www.secrel.com.br/jpoesia/bhcaulfield1.htm)

Cámara, Madeline. "Autorretrato con Carlota Caulfield". *El Nuevo Herald*, Sunday, 20 Jan. 2002.

Cavallari, Héctor Mario. "Review of Autorretrato en ojo ajeno (2001)". *Caribe. Revista de Cultura y de Literatura,* 4(2)–5(1) (2001–2): 143–9.

Foley, Jack. "Carlota Caulfield, 34th Street and Other Poems". *Linden Lane Magazine,* 6(4) (October–December 1987).

Hernández, Librada. "Review of *Oscuridad Divina* (1987) and *34th Street and Other Poems* (1982–84)". *The Americas Review* 17(3–4) (Winter 1989): 187–9.

Mayans-Natal, María Jesús. "La poesía de Carlota Caulfield o el lenguaje de la posmodernidad". *Explicación de Textos Literarios* 24(1–2) (1995–96): 123–35.

Montilla, Patricia. "Review of *The Book of Giulio Camillo (A Model for a Theater of Memory)*".

Parra, Jaime D. "Poesía en Anolecrab. Poetas en la Barcelona de entre siglos," *Corner*, 5 (Fall 2001–Spring 2002). http://www.cornermag.org/corner05/page03.htm

Rodolfo Häsler. "Review of *Quincunce. Lateral*". (March 2001): 24–5.

Rodríguez, Carlos Espinosa. *El peregrino en comarca ajena*. Boulder, CO: University of Colorado at Boulder, 2001, pp. 130, 177–9, 337, 339.

Silva-Rodríguez, Graciela. "Review of *Autorretrato en ojo ajeno.*" *Feministas Unidas Newsletter* 22(1) (2002): 17–18.

——. *El libro de Giulio Camillo (Maqueta para un teatro de la memoria)*; *Il libro di Giulio Camillo (Modello per un teatro della memoria)*. *Caribe. Revista de Cultura y de Literatura* 8(1) (Spring 2005): 123–6.

Zapata, Miguel Angel. "Breve lectura de la poesía de Carlota Caulfield". *Latinos in the U.S. Review 1994*. Middlebury College, 1994.

CERDA, MARTHA

A role model and emissary for regional women writers, Martha Cerda (1945) was born and lives in Guadalajara, Jalisco, Mexico, where she earned a law degree before embarking on a literary career. A prolific writer of fiction, she published her first collection of short stories, entitled *Juegos de damas*, in 1988 and has been consistently active in a creative and professional career. Her awards and recognitions on the international level include a scholarship from the National Endowment for the Arts (1993, USA), a prize from the Association of Italian Booksellers for her novel *Toda una vida* as the Best Book of Fiction in 1998, and the nomination of her novel *Ballet y Mambo* as finalist for the prestigious Premio Casa de las Américas (2000, Cuba). In 2002 Cerda was invited to the selection committee for the Library of Universal Literature in Norway, an honor she shared with Carlos Fuentes as the only two writers representing Mexico. While gaining international recognition for several of her books in translation, Cerda has also been instrumental in promoting the work of regional Mexican writers. As the founder and director of the General Society for Writers in Mexico, SOGAM (1988–97), and in her position as president of the Guadalajara Centre for the International Pen Club (1994–97), she has coordinated and organized writing workshops and scholarly conferences and advanced the professional development of Mexican as well as international women writers. During her time in office as chair of the International Pen Women Writers Committee (2000–3) Cerda facilitated the dialogue between writers of Spanish and English literature and established the Elena Garro Prize in 2003 to honor accomplished women writers in these languages.

An International Bestseller

The complexity and dynamic nature of Cerda's professional engagement with literary production, reception and recognition also characterize the scope of her creative work which invites the reader's active engagement with each text and its multiple portraits and voices. The female protagonists of her stories and novels speak from the margins of the private domestic sphere or represent minorities who otherwise remain unheard or are silenced in the hierarchical structure of their social context. While the postmodern strategies at work in Cerda's narrative discourse have attracted the attention of numerous scholarly studies, her novel entitled *La señora Rodríguez y otros mundos* (1990; Señora Rodriguez and Other Worlds 1997) has achieved critical and popular recognition in Mexico and on the international scene. Literary reviews enthusiastically highlight the playful and often humorous narrative style as well as the fragmentary structure of the text. Consisting of thirty untitled chapters that depict non-chronological and episodic moments in the protagonist's life, an equal number of seemingly unrelated vignettes creates bridges by association that add surprising twists and puns to each theme. The narrative offers the reader a spectrum of insights on cultural, historical and political aspects of Mexican life seen through the eyes of Señora Rodriguez, a middle-aged housewife, mother and obedient daughter-in-law who randomly recovers accumulated objects from the magically unlimited space of her purse. The objects turn gateways to interior and imaginary worlds and bring to light a feminine consciousness that may seem overtaxed, surreal and even absurd to the rational mind but nonetheless depicts convincingly the complicated network of family ties, religion, history, politics and sexuality this Señora juggles in her daily life. A full-length mirror, when consulted, becomes a vehicle for political, philosophical and existential deliberations, and though humorous or even grotesque at times, they are also the universal themes of the literary canon. Memory and time, cause and effect, the double and the other, and the act of writing itself emerge in Cerda's fictional universe playfully yet provocatively each time Señora Rodriguez reaches into her purse.

Interactive Voices on Culture and Sexuality

The most provocative array of Cerda's alternate creations appears in the collection of short stories entitled, *Las mamás, los pastores y los hermeneutas* (1995) that Mexican writer Carlos Arredondo describes in the prologue as a salvaging of those characters, stories and fragments that, in our Western tradition, have come to be considered as the "other". Thus the title story elaborates the cultural commonplace of the Lord's role in Genesis as benign and grandfatherly creator and takes a gleeful delight in the description of his fumbling efforts to reconcile the necessities of the first human couple with the more lofty designs spelled out in Scripture. Many of the stories are visually reinforced with art reproductions that decorate the elegant volume and provide a backdrop for the text as important markers of Western civilization. Albrecht Dürer's "Four Apostles" appear in faded silhouettes behind the printed words of a story entitled, "La última cena," which, in turn, plays with the relationship between the Gospel description of the "Last Supper" and the creative process behind Leonardo da Vinci's completion of his masterpiece with the same title. With striking irreverence, Cerda cannibalizes these canonized texts and images to assemble her visual and literary collage. The playful character of many of the stories is, however, not the dominant trait of the collection but rather helps to ease the tension arising from the alternating ironic or sarcastic, and sometimes stark and repulsive portrayals of human nature. The theme of motherhood takes on ominous tones in an Oedipal scenario or in a downright virulent account of sexual depravation in the final story of the book, entitled "Los dos abriles (1786–1992)". As the longest piece, it also goes to the greatest length in drawing a parallel between the hyperbolic dimensions of sexuality and the hypocrisy and corruption implicit in the official moral code of a society. The female body under colonial rule and its socialization through an official discourse on sexual conduct and perversion are themes that provide the outline for a narrative discourse driven by the energy of attraction and repulsion.

National Gestation and Fantastic Transformations

The theme of national identity and the fantastic depiction of historical events and cultural characteristics take an important place in Cerda's prizewinning novels *Toda una vida* (1998) and *Ballet y Mambo* (2000). They illustrate her talent for a brand of social criticism that debunks national myths and icons through exaggeration and fantastic interpretation. Both novels structure history through music, the Bolero and the Mambo respectively, while the female protagonists pursue dreams of romantic love and artistic recognition from their marginalized positions. Unable to fulfill satisfactorily the conventional roles of motherhood and marriage, these women nonetheless develop active fantasy lives in which the historical calamities of the twentieth century play a major role in trapping them in a limbo of broken promises and lost opportunities. Thus the narrative voice of a fetus in *Toda una vida* may postpone the event of being born for decades while waiting for a nation to improve the living conditions of its population, while in *Ballet y Mambo*, Mexico and its mestizo population become the ground for British stock to take roots and to develop hyperbolic dimensions in the youngest female member of a racially diverse family tree. In spite of the tragic overtones of these life stories, their dominant characteristic is the boundless energy and creative force of a fantastic discourse that invents its bizarre subversions of natural laws by taking its images and symbols literally.

MARIA B. CLARK

Selected Works

Juegos de damas. México: Joaquín Mortiz, 1988.

La señora Rodríguez y otros mundos. México: Joaquín Mortiz, 1990. Translated into Croatian, English, French, Greek, Italian, and Norwegian.

Y apenas era miércoles. México: Joaquín Mortiz, 1993. Translated into English.

Las mamás, los pastores y los hermeneutas. Monterrey, NL: Ediciones Castillo, 1995.

Señora Rodríguez and other worlds. Trans. Sylvia Jiménez-Anderson, Durham, NC: Duke University Press, 1997.

Toda una vida. Barcelona: Ediciones B, 1998. Translated into Italian and Norwegian.

Ballet y Mambo. Monterrey, Nuevo León: Ediciones Castillo, 2000. Translated into German.

En el nombre del nombre. Salta, Argentina: Editorial Biblioteca de Textos Universitarios, 2001.

References and Further Reading

Aguilera Garramuño, Marco Tulio. "Humor, erotismo y lenguaje en tres cuentistas latinoamericanas". *La Palabra y el Hombre: Revista de la Universidad Veracruzana* 92 (Oct.–Dec. 1994): 178–84.

Duncan, Patricia J. (trans.) "A Lifetime: The Fetus Speaks Out". *Hopscotch: A Cultural Review* 2(2) (2000): 114–19.

Loustaunau, Esteban E. "Imaginarios interculturales en los límites de la integración latinoamericana". *Revista Iberoamericana*, 70(207) (Apr.–June 2004): 545–64.

CÉSAR, ANA CRISTINA

Ana Cristina Cruz César (1952–83) is one of the most important names in the "marginal poetry" movement that emerged in Rio de Janeiro in the 1970s through the 1980s. She was born on July 2, 1952, in Rio de Janeiro, to a politicized intellectual family. Her mother was a literature teacher at the renowned Bennet Methodist high school. Her father, a prominent Protestant intellectual, was the director of the magazine *Paz e Terra* (Peace and Land) and, according to a critical-biographical study by Italo Moriconi, representative of the FAO in Latin America. Ana Cristina César or Ana C., as she liked to sign her name, had a more solid cultural and literary background than most from her generation. Her intellectual and poetic gifts appeared early in childhood, when she composed her first poems. Upon entering the PUC (Pontificia Universidade Católica) in Rio de Janeiro, which at the time was one of the best institutions of higher education in Brazil, she already spoke English, French and Spanish, having enjoyed a stay in England on a scholarship from a Protestant religious organization. As a teacher of Portuguese and English, as well as essayist and translator, Ana Cristina César took full advantage of the intellectual opportunities offered to her.

Literary Critic, Translator and Poet

By 1976, she was already relatively well known by readers of the vanguard Brazilian press as a literary critic, translator and poet when she participated in the *26 poetas hoje* (26 Poets Today), anthology of Editorial Labor Publishing. In 1979, she published two books of poetry at her own expense, *Cenas de Abril* (Scenes from April) and *Correspondência Completa* (Complete Correspondence). In September of the same year, with a scholarship from the Rotary Club, she returned to England, where she would remain until January 1981 and obtain a diploma in Literary Translation from the University of Essex. She also printed the book *Luvas de Pelica* (Kid Gloves) and wrote the texts that would become her next book, *A teus pés* (At Your Feet), published in Brazil by Editora Brasiliense in a volume that would unite the three previous books. Victim of severe depression, she committed suicide on October 29, 1983, at the height of her success, just a few days after the publication of the second edition of her book. According to Vera Queiroz, her work is inextricably linked to her premature demise and cannot be interpreted otherwise. Her suicide thus became an internal element of her work insomuch as it conferred it with a certain dynamic, lending it an irremediably inconclusive nature.

Themes and Modes

Her work has enjoyed cult status since its emergence and stands out with regard to two aspects. First, as with a large part of the poetry of the time, it has strong feminist, erotic and homoerotic content. Second, under the spontaneous appearance that characterizes "marginal" poetry, her work distinguishes itself from that of her contemporaries by introducing themes by means of procedures that demand of the reader intimate knowledge of the international literary canon.

Erudite and carrying with it the mark of the author's translation activities, the work is replete with references to poets and poems; steeped in the time and space of Rio de Janeiro in the 1970s and 1980s, we frequently find in this work references to popular music and other elements of Brazilian popular culture. Utilizing different poetic forms and diverse linguistic references, the work can be considered both spontaneous and affected.

For a myriad of reasons, the theme of identity emerges saliently. The poetic subject here seeks to establish itself both in terms of the individual and the poet, which are presented as two inseparable dimensions. The work exhibits the recurring themes of death, love and heterosexual, autoerotic and homoerotic sexuality, as well as essays on the organization of literary values and the reader's place in the constitution of the poem. In her blank verses, which seek the transgression of gender, there is ample use of irony, parody and quotations. Her "letters" and "diary entries" mark the emergence of new poetic subjects, such as women, adolescents and homosexuals, as well as issues of female eroticism, auto-eroticism and homosexual eroticism. While presenting changes in both the moral and behavioral standards of the 1970s regarding the concepts of modesty and privacy, such texts take the literature-document as reference. It is poetry on poetry, which cannot be read without an understanding of its intertextuality and ironic tone. For Ana Cristina César, literature is never an expression of the direct experience of reality, but a re-creation and appropriation of linguistic material.

Reading and Influences

The poet's understanding of writing as an interpretation of a world already placed into words, of art not as an interpretation of life but of her numerous linguistic translations, was constructed from her academic upbringing and literary preferences. In a study entitled *Atrás dos olhos pardos: uma interpretação da poesia de Ana Cristina César* (Behind Brown Eyes: An Interpretation of the Poetry of Ana Cristina César),

Maria Lúcia de Barros Camargo shows how her readings of Manuel Bandeira and Carlos Drummond de Andrade, as well as Eliot, Pound, Emily Dickinson, Katherine Mansfield, Sylvia Plath, Marianne Moore, Virginia Woolf, Gertrude Stein, Walt Whitman, Victor Hugo and even Baudelaire, led her to consider the literary canon as an infinite house of mirrors. Following the footsteps of Eliot, she considered the world as a bustling blend of numerous voices. Palimpsest, her work deliberately made up of other works, requires an interpretation that takes into account the references that compose it. If every writer is, above all, a translator and every poet writes from what he/she reads, intertextuality can be considered the main characteristic of the poetry of Ana Cristina César, which she herself defined in one of her poems as a "castillo de allusiones/ forest of mirrors" and has images of the "vampire" and "thief of verses" in the center of its metaphoric structure: "As I read, my texts make discoveries. It is difficult to hide them amid these letters. Thus, I suckle on the teats of the poets in my breast".

Poetry and Deconstruction

In her article "Gênero e performance na narrativa latino-americana contemporânea de mulheres" (Gender and Performance in the Contemporary Latin American Narrative of Women), Graciela Ravetti sees the poetry of Ana C. as an act of rebellion against norms and using the concepts of John Austin, characterizes it as a "performance narrative", which implies the radical exposure of the self of both the subject and the locale of enunciation, evidencing the mechanisms that constitute the subject through the intervention of the different instances that question it (educational, social, geographic, medical and sexual criteria) and characterize it as cultured or uncultured, of good or bad taste, socially well situated or outsider, cosmopolitan or provincial, physically or mentally fit or ill, heterosexual or homosexual. The poetry of Ana Cristina presents one of the characteristics of performance writing, an interruption in the collective imagination of the placid, continuous course of the empire of law, which creates an impasse, an interval that can become the realm of perception and the creation of new forms of being. She seeks the discussion of social criteria in the constitution of identity, exposing the self of the poet in her discourse, purposely blending the person and the poetic *persona*.

Universal and Local

Like other "marginal" poets, her work follows the lessons of the Brazilian Modernism of 1922 and uses the Portuguese language in its oral, colloquial form. The poetry of Ana Cristina César is radical and is made to be heard in the accent of the posh neighborhoods on the south side of Rio de Janeiro in the 1970s and 1980s. It is necessary to have knowledge of the slang employed at the time in this section of the city from where the poetic subject speaks, as well as subtle intonations with which certain expressions are pronounced. The poem "Mocidade Independente" ("Independent Youth"), from *A teus pés* (At Your Feet), serves as an example, demanding to be heard in the characteristic rhythm and diction of the neighborhoods of Rio de Janeiro regarding both the title and certain phrases, a diction ironically used by the "jeunesse dorée" of the "South Zone", "I flew upwards: it is now, my heart . . .".

Similarly, one must "hear" the use of the at times crude language and vulgar terms that seek not only to "épater le bourgeois" but also, in the spirit of the times, "naturalize" expressions linked to sexuality, as in "Arpejos" ("Arpeggios"): "I awoke with an itching in my hymen. On the bidet, I examined the locale with a mirror . . . I rubbed in a white pomade until the skin (wrinkled and withered) began to shine. With this, my projects to go to the Strikers point withered as well. The bicycle seat might bring back the irritation . . .". For its poetic references, this poem seeks to situate itself in the ideal world of literature, firmly anchored in daily life filled with references to personalities as well as the manner of speaking and living in the city of Rio de Janeiro, blending biography and chronicle with the abovementioned poetic influences. In this poem, the reader is seduced not only intellectually by the plethora of interlacing voices, but also in a mundane manner by the presence of an entire intellectual, bohemian group, known through various means of communication.

Reading Ana Cristina César to some extent signifies pertaining to her "gangue" in the space of a moment. In her elliptic and allusive style, her poetry demands of the reader knowledge on the biography of its author as well as its historical and cultural context. It functions as an inscription of a group in a broader social realm, an inscription that requires reflection. For it is extremely elaborate poetry that, in linking the local and the universal, its time and a-historical time of the universe of "great works" for its own construction, it chooses the reader, seeming more to address "the small audience of the soirée", as the author says in one of her texts to an unknown reader. Contrary to most poets that take the local to the universal, Ana Cristina César, who invokes so many voices in her texts, channels the reader's attention of shared literary references to a particular circumstance, from different great cities to the city of Rio de Janeiro, from different languages to a particular use of the Portuguese language. At this time of the globalization of culture, this somewhat "provincial" aspect of the work of such a cosmopolitan poet is perhaps one of its greatest merits.

ELIANA BUENO-RIBEIRO

Selected Works

Poetry

Cenas de abril. Rio de Janeiro: author, 1979.

Correspondência completa. Rio de Janeiro: author, 1979.

Luvas de pelica. England: author, 1980.

A teus pés. (*Cenas de Abril, Correspondência completa, Luvas de pelica* unedited). São Paulo: Brasiliense, 1982.

Inéditos e dispersos. Ed. Armando Freitas Filho. São Paulo: Brasiliense, 1985.

Other Texts

Literatura não é documento. Rio de Janeiro: MEC/FUNARTE, 1980.

Escritos da Inglaterra. Ed. Maria Luiza César. São Paulo: Brasiliense, 1988.

Escritos no Rio. Ed. Armando Freitas Filho. São Paulo and Rio de Janeiro: Brasiliense/UFRJ, 1993.

Correspondência incompleta. Ed. H. Buarque de Hollanda and A. Freitas Filho. Rio de Janeiro: Aeroplano/instituto Moreira Salles, 1999.

Portmouth/Colchester (caligrafia/desenhos). São Paulo: Duas Cidades, n.d.

Participation in Collective Works

26 poetas hoje. Ed. H. Buarque de Hollanda. Rio de Janeiro: Editorial Labor, 1976.

Quingumbo: Nova poesia norte-americana. Ed. Kerry Shawn Keys. São Paulo: Escrita, 1980.

References and Further Reading

Barbosa, Adriana Maria de Abreu. "Transgressão, identidade feminina e outricidade na poesia marginal de Ana Cristina César". In H. Cunha (ed.), *Desafiando o cânone. Aspectos da literatura de autoria feminina na prosa e na poesia (anos 70/80)*. Rio de Janeiro: Tempo Brasileiro, 1999, pp. 53–61.

Camargo, Maria Lúcia de Barros. *Atrás dos olhos pardos. Uma leitura da poesia de Ana Cristina César*. Chapecó: Argos, 2003.

Duarte, C. L., Ravettie, G. and Alexandre, M.-A. "Gênero e performance na narrativa latino-americana contemporânea de mulheres". *Gênero e representação em literaturas de línguas românicas*. Col. Mulher e Literatura, vol. V. Belo Horizonte: UFMG, 2002, pp. 31–7.

Habkost, N. M. "Luvas de pelica ou a máquina intersubjetiva de visibilidade". In Rita de Cássia Barbosa (ed.), *Revista Travessia* 24, Poesia Brasileira Contemporânea, PG/UFSC. Florianópolis: EDUFSC, 1 semestre, 1992, pp. 113–23.

Lima, Regina Helena Souza da Cunha. *O desejo na poesia de Ana Cristina César, 1952–1983*. Apresent. Lúcia F. de Almeida. 2nd edn. São Paulo: Annablume, 1993.

Maia, Cristina Mota. "E que dialeto é esse para a pequena audiência de serão? Aspectos lingüísticos e textuais de *A teus pés*". Doctoral thesis, Instituto de Letras da UFF, 1993.

Moriconi, Italo. *Ana Cristina César: O sangue de uma poeta*. Rio de Janeiro: Relume-Dumará/Prefeitura, 1996.

Queiroz, Vera. "Pactos do viver e do escrever: Ana Cristina César". *Pactos do viver e do escrever. O Feminino na literatura brasileira*. Fortaleza: 7 Sóis Editora, 2004, pp. 5–34.

Santiago, S. "Singular e anônimo". In *Nas malhas da letra*. São Paulo: Companhia das Letras, 1989.

Sussekind, Flora. *Literatura e vida literária. Polêmicas, diários & retratos*. Rio de Janeiro: Jorge Zahar, 1985.

——. *Os cadernos de Postmouth*. São Paulo: Augusto Massi, 1993.

——. *Até segunda ordem não me risque nada. Os cadernos, rascunhos e poesia-em-vozes de Ana Cristina César*. Rio de Janeiro: Sete Letras, 1995.

Viegas, Ana Claudia Coutinho. *Bliss & Blue – segredos de Ana C.* São Paulo: Annablume, 1998.

CHAVIANO, DAÍNA

Daína Chaviano (1957) was born in Havana, Cuba where she grew up reading fairy tales and, at a young age, also read Jules Verne, Ray Bradbury, and William Shakespeare on the one hand, and, on the other, Sigmund Freud, Jean Piaget, and Carl Jung (her mother was a psychiatrist). In fact, she pursued her university studies in English literature to read Bradbury and Shakespeare in their original language. Thus, unlike other members of the 1980s generation, she did not grow up reading Cuban authors like Lezama Lima and Cabrera Infante. Besides writing, she has also been an actress and has held executive positions at the Spanish language editions of *Newsweek*, *Prevention*, and *Architectural Digest*. She is a popular author worldwide, and is considered to be among the best science fiction writers in Spanish, with her work translated into several languages.

From Havana to Miami

While Chaviano was still attending the University of Havana, she submitted a manuscript to the first science-fiction contest organized on the island for unpublished authors in the science-fiction genre, the David Prize, and she won it with *Los mundos que amo* (The Worlds I Love), a collection of five stories for young readers, the longest of which served as title to the whole work. The book was very successful and that allowed Chaviano to keep publishing more collections of short stories, until the publication in 1988 of her first full-length novel, *Fábulas de una abuela extraterrestre* (Fables from an Extraterrestrial Grandmother), a book that became a classic in Latin American science-fiction and was even recognized abroad, winning the Anna Seghers International Prize (that annually recognizes the works of young writers) in Germany. During the 1980s she also wrote TV scripts and even hosted a radio and a TV program dedicated to science fiction; and it was during these years that she was also an actress in a few films by director Tomás Piard.

However, despite this success, she was becoming disillusioned with the regime and with the absence of creative freedom. In 1991, taking advantage of an invitation to the University of Quito, Ecuador, to give a series of lectures, she decided not to return to the island and, two months later, she moved to Miami. Her defection caused the cancellation of the publication of two of her works in Cuba, one of them, *País de dragones* (Land of Dragons), winner that year of the National Prize of Children's and Young People's Literature "La Edad de Oro".

Once in the United States, Chaviano found out that some Spanish publishing houses were only interested in Spanish or Anglo-Saxon authors, and she was unfamiliar with the American and international mechanisms of publishing. However, she kept writing, and spent more than two years dedicated exclusively to writing and exploring a new direction in her fiction: a combination of fantastic-realism with science fiction in a well established context: Cuba at the end of the twentieth century. The result was the tetralogy "La Habana oculta" ("The Occult Side of Havana"), a series of four novels (*Gata encerrada* [Cat in a Cage], *Casa de juegos* [House of Games], *El hombre, la hembra y el hambre* [Man, Woman, and Hunger], and *La isla de los amores infinitos* [The Island of Endless Loves]), independent from one another, but whose main foundation is the city of Havana at times real, at times unreal and peopled by ghosts. Havana serves as a point of departure for journeys into other dimensions and other worlds. Finally, a few years later, one of the novels (the third in the series and the one with a more realistic plot) won the prestigious Azorín prize in Spain and was published by Planeta: *El hombre, la hembra y el hambre*. This book was the first novel where she explores the possibility of creating without censorship, of reflecting on the circumstances of Cuba at the end of the twentieth century without the repression of living there. The success of this novel opened the way to the publication of the other ones and established Chaviano as a major author of Cuban letters.

Master of Science Fiction

Chaviano is synonymous with science fiction in Cuban letters. Her approach to the genre is not so much a technological point of view as a mythological one: her trademark is the fusion of science fiction with mythology, magic, and the supernatural. The universe, in Chaviano's view, is more than the physical environment we can see; therefore her novels go beyond daily life to explore paranormal perceptions, ghosts, spirits, and time travel. In most of her novels, Chaviano includes Celtic and North European gods and myths, such as reincarnation (a Celtic belief) or mediums and spirits (also very British), but she also includes Cuban santería and the orishas, especially in *Casa de juegos*.

"The Occult Side of Havana" novels include a new theme in her narrative: eroticism (more explicit in *Casa de juegos*); this theme, almost absent in her previous work, is treated as a way of self-knowledge and it transcends to the point of becoming a quasi philosophy. Eroticism permeates her poetry as well: *Confesiones eróticas y otros hechizos* (Erotic Confessions and Other Spells) contains, according to some critics, some of the best examples of erotic literature written by women in Latin America today, vindicating women's right to satisfy their own needs, in a direct and humorous tone. Together with eroticism, love is another issue. In her work, love has a redeeming power and is a sign of intelligence. Her characters are moved by their faith in love as a universal form of relationship.

Havana also becomes a protagonist in these novels: the reader finds not only the physical geography, but the social and human geography as well, sometimes incomprehensible even to those who live in it. The depiction of the city raises doubts about the daily and familiar world, and the characters in the novels share the tragedy of being strong individuals who happen to populate an environment which forces them to hide that individuality; fortunately for them, magical and mysterious worlds await, full of possibilities to fulfill all they can.

Chaviano and Criticism

Chaviano's initial work has been compared to that of authors like Ursula K. LeGuin and Angelica Gorodischer for the universal character of its esthetic and philosophical values. On the one hand, her poetic language has been praised as a natural ally to create the sensual and surreal atmospheres of her narratives, populated not only by human beings, but by gods, wizards, and ethereal creatures; and on the other hand, her plots show the complexity of human relations and the human need to look for answers in search of identity and purpose, ultimately, in search of a creator.

Her work has been fundamental in opening Latin American letters to high quality science fiction, incorporating the new ideas in quantum physics and string theory that made possible the idea of parallel universes and the possibility of space and time travel, but not with technology as much as with the power of the mind. She is also important for showing a vision of Havana rich in details and history.

Her most recent work—the tetralogy "The Occult Side of Havana," and in particular *El hombre, la hembra y el hambre*—has created a debate among critics: some reacted in a negative way to what they perceive as commercial novels, written to satisfy Western readers by showing a series of clichés about the dire situation in Havana during the special period, whereas other critics considered these novels fascinating and full of symbolism, rich language, and sharp socio-political criticism towards Cuba's regime. Either way, Chaviano's success makes her an important writer nowadays and guarantees her presence in the future of Cuban literature.

MIGUEL GONZÁLEZ-ABELLÁS

Selected Works

Los mundos que amo. Havana: Unión, 1980.
Amoroso planeta. Havana: Letras Cubanas, 1983.
Historias de hadas para adultos. Havana: Letras Cubanas, 1986.
Fábulas de una abuela extraterrestre. Havana: Letras Cubanas, 1988.
El abrevadero de los dinosaurios. Havana: Letras Cubanas, 1990.
Confesiones eróticas y otros hechizos. Madrid: Betania, 1994.
El hombre, la hembra y el hambre. Barcelona: Planeta, 1998.
Casa de juegos. Barcelona: Planeta, 1999.
Gata encerrada. Barcelona: Planeta, 2001.
País de dragones. Madrid: Espasa Juvenil, 2001.
La isla de los amores infinitos. Madrid: Grijalbo, 2006.

References and Further Reading

Calvo Peña, Beatriz. "Entre la memoria y el deseo: Daína Chaviano y la creación de *puentes de encuentro* cubanos". In Laura P. Alonso Gallo and Fabio Murrieta (eds), *Guayaba Sweet: Literatura Cubana en Estados Unidos*. Cádiz: Aduana Vieja, 2003, pp. 331–49.

Chaviano, Daína. "Science Fiction and Fantastic Literature as Realms of Freedom". *Journal of the Fantastic in the Arts* 15(1) (2004): 4–11.

——. *Daína Chaviano* (Autor's Webpage). No date. http://www.dainachaviano.com/

Fernández Olmos, Margarite. "El erotismo revolucionario de las poetas cubanas". *Explicación de textos literarios* 24(1–2) (1995): 137–48.

Kanev, Venko. "Las significaciones del paisaje y el espacio en *El hombre, la hembra y el hambre* de Daína Chaviano". *Anales de literatura hispanoamericana* 28 (1999): 833–45.

Whitfield, Esther. "The Novel as Cuban Lexicon: Bargaining Bilinguals in Daína Chaviano's *El hombre, la hembra y el hambre*". In Doris Sommer (ed.), *Bilingual Games: Some Literary Investigations*. New York: Palgrave Macmillan, 2003, pp. 193–201.

COLASANTI, MARINA

Marina Colasanti was born in Asmara, Eritrea, in 1937. She lived with her family in Libya and then Italy before moving to Brazil in 1948. After having studied at the Escola Nacional de Belas Artes (the National School of Fine Arts) in Rio de Janeiro, she began her multifaceted career as a visual artist, primarily in printmaking, before venturing into the fields of journalism and literature. Her publications are often accompanied by her own illustrations. Colasanti's writing career spans many genres, including essays, short stories, poetry, and literature for children and young adults. In addition to other book awards, she has received Brazil's prestigious literary prize, the Jabuti, three times. She won twice for her books of children's literature, *Entre a espada e a rosa* (Between the Sword and the Rose) in 1993 and *Ana Z, aonde vai você?* (Where Are You Going, Ana Z?) in 1994, and once for her poetry collection *Rota de colisão* (Collision Course) in 1993. As Susan Quinlan has aptly highlighted in the 2005 volume *Brazilian Writers*, Colasanti's talents as an artist and writer are complemented by her active commitment to contemporary women's issues in Brazil.

Women's Issues Unveiled

Marina Colasanti's literary works combine an erudite attention to language and formal precision with the ability to reach out to women of all ages and socioeconomic conditions through simplicity and candor. According to Quinlan's profile of Colasanti in *Brazilian Writers*, the author draws from personal experience while at the same time touching upon common themes universal to all women. In both literary and journalistic form, she has been outspoken about women's rights and fought against gender oppression, speaking publicly about intimate, private matters. Her work on all fronts is dedicated to empowering women.

Colasanti's book of essays entitled *Mulher Daqui Pra Frente* (Women from This Point Forward), of 1981, posits transformations in the lives of Brazilian women at the end of the twentieth century. It remains an important and frequently cited feminist text in both academic and popular contexts. She has made significant contributions to women's issues by publicly addressing a variety of subjects that question women's traditional roles in society. In 1975, Colasanti helped found the pioneering women's magazine, *Nova*, to which she served as Editor at Large for eighteen years. A collection of letters in the style of "Dear Abby," called *Intimidade Pública* (Public Intimacy), was published in 1991. The collection, highlighted in an essay by Cristina Ferreiro Pinto, in which she compares the works of Colasanti with those of fellow Brazilian writer, Marcia Denser, lends voice and public attention to women's concerns regarding private matters, particularly heterosexual intimacy.

Literary Gems

Marina Colasanti embarked on her literary career in the 1970s and gained instant fame through her "mini-contos" (mini short stories) printed in the Rio-based newspaper *Jornal do Brasil*. These short fictional pieces were subsequently published in such collections as *Zooilógico* (Zoo-illogic) of 1975, *Contos de Amor Rasgado* (Stories of Torn-up Love), of 1986, and *O Leopardo é um animal delicado* (The Leopard Is a Delicate Animal), of 1998. Stylistically, Colasanti's work often fuses more than one genre, such as fiction and travel narratives, an example of which is her 2005 publication *23 Histórias de um Viajante* (23 Stories by a Traveler). The twenty-three short narratives depict a traveler's visit to a fictional kingdom shut off from the world. The traveler, a kind of male Sheherazade, is introduced to the king, to whom he relates a series of enlightening tales. The collection has the dual effect of underscoring both the importance of storytelling and that of the direct cultural exchange derived from travel. These inter-linked elements are essential to Colasanti's own worldview, and are drawn from her personal experiences.

As Peggy Sharpe has emphasized in her essay "A Tropical Utopia?" included in the volume, *Daughters of Restlessness: Women's Literature at the End of the Millennium,* Marina Colasanti's works are frequently portrayed in fantastical, fairytale-like settings that lend her fiction a universal, timeless quality. Colasanti's classic tale for young adults, entitled "A moça tecelã" (The Young Woman Weaver), for instance, presents an enchanted setting through storybook language, in order to recount a young woman's ability to determine her own destiny. As the fable unfolds, the young protagonist literally weaves a husband into being from scratch, only to later unweave him out of her life when he proves to be too demanding and forceful. Through Colasanti's literary skillfulness, the magical, legend-like quality of the story does not undermine the reality-based, modern-day punch-line: that life as a single woman is not only acceptable, but preferable to that as the wife of an abusive husband. Marina Colasanti's works thus also evoke contemporary experience, particularly from a woman's perspective. The themes Colasanti addresses as an essayist, columnist, fiction writer and poet often focus on women's concerns and insecurities in regard to their bodies, including issues of self-image, such as weight gain or aging. Her works also give consideration to domestic concerns and sexuality in general, as well as more serious topics such as jealousy, adultery, incest, and rape.

Marina Colasanti's most recent collection of poetry, *Fino Sangue* (Thin Blood), of 2005, embodies her creative approach and world vision. In a refreshingly innovative manner, her poems unveil experiences that embrace both worldly and mundane points of view. Her images and metaphors are extraordinarily rich with meaning and almost mythical in tone, yet themes drawn from daily life and common experiences—breakfast scenes at a Venice hotel from the poem "Lua-de-mel em Veneza" (Honeymoon in Venice), or a man's whimsical tie collection in "A todos igualmente" (To Each Equally)—anchor her work and maintain its accessibility. Her humorous poem "Livres à noite" (Free at Night), centers on the act of removing one's bra at the end of the day in order to unleash pent-up breasts, which are depicted as ships sailing out onto an open sea. This poem contrasts to the serious tone and sharpness of "Chamava-se Gina" (She Called Herself Gina), which draws on a young woman's inability to fully recover from an incident of male gang violence during war-time. Whereas both poems rely on a third-person perspective, they nonetheless masterfully establish a sense of proximity or commonality between subject and narrator, and consequently, between subject and reader.

Travel is a recurrent theme in Colasanti's work, and several poems included in the collection borrow from the insights one gains from travel. They capture beauty in landscape—such as vibrant bougainvillea petals lining a street after a rainstorm in "Águas de verão" (Summer Rains)—as well as the extraordinary moments of revelation we experience away from home. For instance, listening in the night to age-old furniture unleash phantom sighs and murmurs, in the poem "Respiram à noite" (They Breathe at Night). There are numerous poems in *Fino Sangue* that reflect Colasanti's own travels by revealing her impressions and responses to places, people or objects. For instance, a majestic row of cypress trees on a hillside gains artful prominence in "Na encosta são" (On the Hillside Are). The private act of rescuing a turtle from a street market in New York's Chinatown becomes a sign of peaceful protest in "Nunca se perguntou" (She Never Asked Herself). With elegant simplicity and a contemplative approach, Colasanti's poem entitled "Pontos de vista" (Points of View) compares the Roman Emperor Nero's view of the world to her own, word-based philosophy. Other examples, such as "Ao nosso" (To Our) or "Sobre a cama" (On the Bed), unabashedly portray sexual intimacy and passion. Colasanti's poem entitled "Desde que" (Ever Since) critically and ironically, with a climactic, vindictive edge, confronts a woman who has undergone a nose job. Another poem, aptly entitled "Para poder" (In Order To) seems to be a song of resistance and renewal, summoning women to action.

Professional Prowess

Marina Colasanti's professional career is marked by versatility and resourcefulness. Beyond the print media she has also served as television editor and newscaster, particularly in the 1980s and 1990s. In 1985, she was nominated to the National Committee on Women's Rights in Brazil. She continues to serve as a regular contributor to the *Jornal do Brasil*. As a tribute to Colasanti's contributions as a *Jornal do Brasil* columnist, Editora Leitura published in 2006 *Os últimos lírios no estojo de seda* (The Last Lilies in the Silk Case), a collection of forty-five of her essays previously printed in the newspaper. Many of Colasanti's works have been published in translation, in Argentina, Colombia, and Mexico, as well as in Spain and France. In English, her work is represented in *One Hundred Years After Tomorrow: Brazilian Women's Fiction in the 20th Century* (1992), edited by Darlene J. Sadlier. Colasanti is married to poet and essayist Affonso Romano de Sant'Anna.

MARGUERITE ITAMAR HARRISON

Selected Works

Short Stories

Zooilógico. Rio de Janeiro: Imago, 1975.
Contos de Amor Rasgado. Rio de Janeiro: Rocco, 1986.
O Leopardo é um Animal Delicado. Rio de Janeiro: Rocco, 1998.
Penélope Manda Lembranças. São Paulo: Ática, 2001.
23 Histórias de um Viajante. São Paulo: Global, 2005.

Essays and Short Narratives

E Por Falar em Amor e Outros Contos. Rio de Janeiro: Rocco, 1984.
Eu Sei, Mas Não Devia. Rio de Janeiro: Rocco, 1996.
A Casa das Palavras. São Paulo: Ática, 2002.
Fragatas para Terras Distantes: Ensaios. Rio de Janeiro: Record, 2004.
Os últimos lírios no estojo de seda. Belo Horizonte: Leitura, 2006.

Poetry

Rota de Colisão. Rio de Janeiro: Rocco, 1993.
Gargantas Abertas: Poesia. Rio de Janeiro: Rocco, 1998.
Fino Sangue:Poesia. Rio de Janeiro: Record, 2005.

Literature for Children and Young Adults

Entre a Espada e a Rosa. Rio de Janeiro: Salamandra, 1992.
Ana Z., aonde vai você? São Paulo: Ática, 1993.
A moça tecelã. São Paulo: Global, 2004.

Articles in Anthologies

Mulher Daqui Pra Frente. Rio de Janeiro: Nórdica, 1981.
Aqui Entre Nós. Rio de Janeiro: Rocco, 1988.
Intimidade Pública. Rio de Janeiro: Rocco, 1990.

Novellas

Eu, Sozinha. Rio de Janeiro: Graf/Record, 1968.

References and Further Reading

Pinto, Cristina Ferreira. "Female Agency and Heterosexuality in the Works of Márcia Denser and Marina Colasanti". In *Gender, Discourse, and Desire in Twentieth-Century Brazilian Women's Literature*. West Lafayette, IN: Purdue University Press, 2004, pp. 143–58.

Quinlan, Susan Canty. "Marina Colasanti". In Monica Rector and Fred M. Clark (eds), *Brazilian Writers*. Detroit, MI: Thomson Gale, 2005, pp. 136–40.

Sharpe, Peggy. "Imagens e Poder: Construindo a Obra de Marina Colasanti". In Peggy Sharpe (ed.), *Entre Resistir e Identificar-se: Para um Teoria da Prática da Narrativa Brasileira de Autoria Feminina*. Goiânia, Florianópolis: UFG; Mulheres, 1997, pp. 43–55.

——. "A Tropical Utopia? The Brazilian Fairy Tales of Marina Colasanti". In Sabine Coelsch-Foisner, Hanna Wallinger and Gerhild Reisner (eds), *Daughters of Restlessness: Women's Literature at the End of the Millennium*. Heidelberg: Universitätsverlag Winter, 1998, pp. 71–9.

CONDE, ROSINA

Hilda Rosina Conde Zambada was born in 1954, in Mexicali, Baja California. She studied elementary and middle school in Tijuana, and spent 1968 to 1969 at San Luis Rey Academy in Oceanside, California. She returned to Tijuana for her remaining high school studies, and throughout her adolescence cultivated practical interests that her father did not approve of, such as typing, drawing, pastry-making, and clothes tailoring. Conde overcame her father's prejudice for a business career and in 1971 the single mother moved to Mexico City with her six-month-old son. Once enrolled in the capital's National Autonomous University of Mexico (UNAM), Conde studied Hispanic language and literature until 1977. In order to support her family, Conde worked in many jobs, from receptionist and costume designer to translator, university professor, writer, and editor for numerous academic publishing houses. Conde's involvement with art beyond the written page has led her to design Mexican performer Astrid Hadad's costumes since 1994, and Conde herself has performed as a jazz singer since returning to Tijuana at the beginning of the 1980s. A move back to Mexico City facilitated her integration into the band Follaje in 1996, and the group has recorded two albums, released in 1998 and 2000, with Discos Phoenix. Conde has sung in the original performances of "Cilicios de amor" (Tortures of love) and "Señorita maquiladora" (Miss Assembly Plant). On the more academic side, Conde has directed the magazines *El Vaivén*, *Tercera Llamada, La línea quebrada/The Broken Line*, and *Revista de Humanidades*. Conde founded two independent publishing houses, Panfleto y Pantomima and Desliz Ediciones. She regularly publishes short journalistic pieces with the Baja California newspaper, *Diario 29, El Nacional*. In 2000, Conde received a writer's grant from the State Fund of Baja California for Cultura and the Arts. Today, Conde works full time as a professor of literature with the University of Mexico City.

Principal Themes and *Women on the Road*

The principal themes in Conde's work, whether short story, novel, or poetry, contemplate social problems from the point of view of the individual as s/he relates to a sex partner, a family, or an even larger community, such as client/performer relationships in sex shows or employee/employer interactions. Dissatisfaction with the possibilities for communication with these ever-widening social circles often drives the anecdote, regardless of genre. This is to say that Conde's poetry often contemplates an autobiographical or otherwise realistic social conflict from a woman's point of view. The short story collection *Arrieras somos . . .* (Women on the Road) indicates this tension between individual and group from the very title: the ellipsis points to the suppressed ending of the familiar refrain, whose first word Conde has changed to the feminine: "Arrieros somos; en el camino nos veremos" (We're mule-drivers; we'll see each other on the road). Thus, a sense of both community *and* individuality emerges as these "women on the road" anticipate a future encounter despite their individual responsibility in following the path.

Arrieras somos . . . won the National Literature Prize "Gilberto Owen" in 1993 and contains one of Conde's most technically successful tales, "Arroz y cadenas" (Rice and Chains) which narrates the thoughts of a pregnant, single young woman who knits a sweater for her unborn child and contemplates her parents' disapproval of her situation. The self-aware young woman meditates on the traps that bind her mother and that she herself may soon experience. The jargon for knitting, literally the words for "rice," "chains," and "enough," forms a parallel with the actions of tying knots, taking one step back, and then taking one step forward in an ultimately constructive though repetitious enterprise. The ambivalence contained in this story comprises a common recourse in Conde's literature: the writer is often less interested in breaking stereotypical role patterns than in simply exploring them. Her literature is feminist for its sympathy toward women affected by patriarchal oppression and recognizable for its psychological realism, but Conde does not necessarily aim for a literature of optimistic triumph or solutions.

Novel Techniques

One of the happiest endings in Conde's œuvre occurs in the slim novel *La Genara*. The title refers to Tijuana locals' habit of placing a definite article before personal names, hence: "The Genara". The novel's epistolary form imitates in a fashion its original mode of serial publication, from 1994 to 1995 in *Diario 29, El Nacional*. Letters from female readers over the course of the newspaper publication influenced the plot, or so Conde claims (Magdaleno, 1998: 26). The novel certainly evinces a popular taste for melodrama, and the characters by turns suffer and perpetuate divorce, infidelity, family conflict, and even anorexia. Conde's style in the novel attains a colloquial naturalness that seems effortless, a literary achievement that is perhaps marred by the occasionally tedious nature of the information relayed in the realistic mode, including phone numbers and computer jargon for a failed email message. The latter has earned critics' attention, including Debra Castillo's intelligent and enthusiastic commentary. Possibly, the failed email exemplifies a new sort of writing in the Information Age, though one wonders if the non-critic finds unintelligible strings of data as compelling as the critics do. Whether for better or worse, *La Genara* spares the reader few details.

Border Questions

The Tijuana setting of much of *La Genara* gives rise to analysis of Conde's work as a meditation on the national border between Mexico and the United States. However, Debra Castillo wonders if it is possible for mainstream critics to read Conde's work from a truly regional viewpoint rather than one conditioned by the center, whether for instance Mexico City-based or US-based. Conde herself abandoned work with self-conscious border-performer Guillermo Gómez de la Peña because she felt that his group pressured her to adopt a border identity as Chicana, or pseudo Chicana. Conde often declares in the Mexican press that she does not believe that there is such a thing as "border literature" and that to the extent that a literary formula exists for such a phenomenon, it has been self-consciously created in order to please critics who do not hail from or reside on the border.

Additional Texts

Another short story collection, *En la tarima* (Onstage) which shares texts with *El agente secreto* (The secret agent), includes the piece "Viñetas revolucionarias" (Revolutionary vignettes), which refers not to the Mexican Revolution but rather to the main avenue in Tijuana, "Revolución" (Revolution). Accordingly, the anecdotes concern performers in a Tijuana strip club: the performance of a sexy virgin, a pregnant-in-denial siren, a transvestite, and other complex personalities reveal the conscious enactment of gender and the accompanying struggle for personal integrity. "Sonatina" from this collection also tends to receive critics' favorable review. This story sympathizes with a Tijuana-native adolescent who leaves her family to become a prostitute, and then leaves prostitution for a bullying, macho lesbian partner. Conde shows that games of power and oppression involve more than male-to-female abuse, when in "Sonatina" gender becomes an individually chosen, consciously elaborated stance that serves to oppress a same-sex partner. The melodramatic turns that make *La Genara* less interesting for critics may fade in "Sonatina" due to the novelty of the characters: a bisexual, passive younger, (ex)prostitute contemplates her predicament regarding her older female rescuer/jailer. A final notable tale from *En la tarima* displays Conde's brilliant talent with dialogue. "Señora Nina" proves that although her plots are often predictable, Conde's language nearly always strikes pitch-perfect believability and achieves a deceptive "transparency" in its seeming straightforwardness.

Criticism

Besides the central contribution of Debra Castillo's readings, three writers take up Conde's work in dissertation projects that eventually became an article. Jeffrey Norman Lamb, Santiago Vaquera-Vásquez, and María Socorro Tabuenca Córdoba treat aspects of feminism and Tijuana society in their dissertations, each approved in 1997. The relative lack of critical attention accorded to Rosina Conde may stem from centrist prejudice, as Castillo and Tabuenca Córdoba suggest. The other possibility, of course, is that Conde's work does not require intensive critical labor to decode. Even if the reader leans toward the latter interpretation, it is helpful to note that Conde's "natural" yet literary language in conjunction with her simple, recognizable plots means that critics' successful discussions of her work are even more impressive. Whether using postcolonial, feminist, or border theory, critical analyses often problematize Conde's work and thus indicate greater complexity in the texts than the casual reader might suspect.

EMILY HIND

Selected Works

Poetry

Poemas de seducción. Mexico: Ediciones de la Máquina de Escribir, 1981.
De amor gozoso (textículos). Tijuana, Mexico: Desliz, 1991.
Bolereando el llanto. Mexico: CONACULTA, 1993.

Short Stories

En la tarima. Mexico: UAM, 1984. New edition, Desliz/Ariadne, 2001.
El agente secreto. Mexicali, Mexico: Universidad Autónoma de Baja California, 1990.
Embotellado de origen. Mexico: Coordinación Nacional de Descentralización, Aguascalientes, Mexico: Instituto Cultural de Aguascalientes, 1994.
Arrieras somos ... Mexico: Dirección de Investigación y Fomento de la Cultura Regional, 1994.
"El silbido". In Edmundo Paz Soldán and Alberto Fuguet (eds), *Se habla español: Voces latinas en* USA. Miami, FL: Alfaguara, 2000, pp. 103–8.

Novel

La Genara. Tijuana: Centro Cultural Tijuana; Mexico, CONACULTA, 1998.

Translations

Excerpt from "Como cachor al sol". In Harry Polkinhorn (ed.), *Border Literature, Literatura Fronteriza: A Binacional Conference*. San Diego, CA: Institute for Regional Studies of the Californias, San Diego State University, 1987, pp. 7–31.
Women on the Road. (*Arrieras somos* ...) San Diego, CA: San Diego State University Press, 1994.
"Round Four". (*En esta esquina*.) In *In this Corner: Short Plays*. Trans. Bertha Hernández. San Diego, CA: San Diego State University Press, 1996.
"Morente". In Mónica Lavín and Gustavo Valentin Segade (eds), *Points of Departure: New Stories from Mexico*. San Francisco, CA: City Lights Books, 2001.
"Arroz y cadenas". In Ethel Krause and Beatriz Espejo (eds), *Atrapadas en la casa: Cuentos de escritoras mexicanas del siglo* XX. Mexico: Selector, 2001.
Across the Line/Al otro lado: The Poetry of Baja California. Ed. Harry Polkinhorn and Mark Weiss. San Diego, CA: Junction Press, 2002, pp. 166–73.

References and Further Reading

Castillo, Debra A. "http://www.LAlit.com". In Edmundo Paz-Soldán and Debra A. Castillo (eds), *Latin American Literature and Mass Media*. New York: Garland, 2001a, pp. 232–45.
——. "Unhomely Feminine". In Carl Good and John V. Waldron (eds), *The Effects of the Nation: Mexican Art in an Age of Globalization*. Philadelphia, PA: Temple University Press, 2001b, pp. 178–95.
Castillo, Debra A. and Córdoba, María Socorro Tabuenca. "Unredeemed: Rosina Conde". *Border Women: Writing from La Frontera*. Minneapolis, MN: University of Minnesota Press, 2002, pp. 124–48.
Conde's webpage: http://www.rosinaconde.com.mx/
Magdaleno, Víctor. "Conde: apropiarse de un lenguaje, imperativo actual de las mujeres". *La Jornada* 8 July 1998: 26.

CORALINA, CORA

Cora Coralina (1889–1985) was the pseudonym of Ana Lins dos Guimarães Peixoto Bretas, who is now considered one of the greatest female poets of Brazil, and the most prominent poet of the Brazilian Midwest. Ana Peixoto, or "Aninha," as the author affectionately refers to herself in works that depict her childhood, was born in the town of Vila Boa de Goiás, in the state of Goiás, Brazil, on August 20, 1889. She was the daughter of Judge Francisco de Paula Lins dos Guimarães Peixoto and Jacinta Luiza do Couto Brandão.

Cora Coralina published her first short story *Tragédia na Roça* (Tragedy in a Small Plantation) in 1910 in the *Anuário Histórico Geográfico e Descritivo do Estado de Goiás* (Historical, Geographical, and Descriptive Yearly Review of the State of Goiás), a collection of works compiled by Francisco Ferreira dos Santos Azevedo. She left Goiás for the interior of the state of São Paulo in 1911 with the lawyer Cantídio Tolentino Brêtas, whom she married in 1926. She lived in several cities in the state of São Paulo, such as Jaboticabal, Penápolis, Andradina, and São Paulo, and her six children were born and raised in this state. Cora Coralina returned to her hometown in 1956, more than twenty years after her husband's death. Her re-encounter with Goiás prompted her to explore local themes, traditions, and stories, often through her own memories. Her first book *Poemas dos Becos de Goiás e outras histórias mais* (Poems of the Alleys of Goiás and Other Stories) was published in 1965, when she was 76 years old. Her work only achieved national recognition after it reached the acclaimed Brazilian poet Carlos Drummond de Andrade. Drummond publicly acknowledged his admiration of Cora Coralina's poetry in the newspaper *Jornal do Brasil* in 1980, when the writer was almost 90 years old.

Cora Coralina never managed to study beyond the elementary school level, but her poetry granted her the title of Doctor Honoris Causa by the Federal University of Goiás in 1983. The Art Critics Association of São Paulo awarded her the *Grande Prêmio da Crítica* (Great Criticism Award) in 1984. That same year, the Brazilian Union of Creative Writers (*União Brasileira dos Escritores*) honored her with the Juca Pato Trophy, and the federal government of Brazil awarded her the *Comenda da Ordem do Mérito do Trabalho* (Award of Distinction of the Guild of Merit of Labor) for her dedication to social and cultural activities in Goiás. After her death on April 10, 1985, her hometown house was turned into the museum Casa Cora Coralina (Cora Coralina's House). Since then, scholars, students, townspeople, and tourists have visited it in search of her manuscripts, or just to learn a little more about this amazing Brazilian poet.

A Poet of the Land, for the Land

If one had to explain what Cora Coralina wrote about, the simplest and most straightforward answer would be that she wrote about her land, her small town in Goiás. Titles such as "Minha Cidade" ("My Hometown"), "Coisas de Goiás" ("Peculiarities of Goiás"), "Coisas do Reino da Minha Cidade" ("Peculiarities of the Kingdom of Goiás"), and "Becos de Goiás" ("Alleys of Goiás") reveal her explicit intention to portray her homeland. The city of Goiás in Cora Coralina's writing is a mirror that reflects her own image and identity. Her personal history and the city's history are often one and the same, which is curious since she spent a large part of her life in the São Paulo state. Perhaps it was exactly this geographical and temporal distance which allowed her to return her gaze to the past of her community and which brought about her need to re-locate herself within the space that she had physically left, but never truly distanced herself from.

In the poem "Minha Cidade" ("My Hometown"), Cora Coralina links her past and her present. She addresses the city as if she were introducing herself. More precisely, the poem is a depiction of a re-encounter in which the poetic voice needs to reveal its identity, as time has changed its appearance. One notes, therefore, a slight—but not trivial—fear of being unrecognized in the poem. The poetic voice introduces itself both as "Aninha," Cora Coralina's autobiographical childhood persona, and as an old woman, which is no doubt a reference to a more contemporary version of the character/author. The autobiographical and meta-fictional characteristics of this poem are clear in its first two stanzas:

> Goiás, minha cidade . . . / Eu sou aquela amorosa
> de tuas ruas estreitas,
> curtas,
> indecisas,
> entrando,
> saindo
> uma das outras.
> Eu sou aquela menina feia da ponte da Lapa.
> Eu sou Aninha.
> Eu sou aquela mulher
> que ficou velha,
> esquecida,
> nos teus larguinhos e nos teus becos tristes,
> contando estórias,
> fazendo advinhação.
> Cantando teu passado.
> Cantando teu futuro.
>
> (1–18)

> [Goiás, my hometown . . . / I am that loving one
> from your narrow,
> small,
> undecided streets,
> that go in
> and out
> of each other.
> I am that ugly girl from the Lapa's bridge.
> I am Aninha.
> I am that woman
> Who got old,
> forgotten,
> in your small squares and sad alleys,
> telling stories,
> telling fortunes.
> Singing your past.
> Singing your future]

There are descriptions of the city, as in the mention of streets, squares, and alleys; however, the poetic voice does not situate itself as a mere *flâneur*, gazing at the scenery from a distance. The observer, whether as a child or an old woman, is also a participant. She interacts with the streets and alleys of the city, as if sharing their "narrowness" and "sadness". In fact, outside spaces such as streets and alleys are personified in the poem, themselves becoming a mirror of the townspeople, and of the poetic voice. Later, poetic and authorial voices merge as the character becomes a storyteller/singer who sings the past to give it a future—that is, to prevent it from being forgotten, as the old woman in the poem has been. The interface between the individual and the city becomes even stronger in the rest of the poem. The poetic voice is ubiquitous, dwelling in churches, roofs, and walls (19–22). The thin line between poet and place is then obliterated: the voice becomes the city, its walls, houses, trees, and hills (23–56). The poem ends with the child, "Aninha," which is also a reference to the beginning, to the roots of the character/author. The poem, therefore, ends as it begins, by stating the identity of the author. The poet's mission is declared right before the end in these meta-fictional lines: "Minha vida / meus sentidos / minha estética/ todas as vibrações / de minha sensibilidade de mulher / têm, aqui, suas raízes" [My life / my meanings / my aesthetic / all vibrations / of my female sensitivity / have its roots here] (57–62). The city is the source of writing, as it is the cultural foundation of the character/author. It is not only a geographical space, but the symbol of origin and the setting from which person, author, and text come to life all at once.

The connection that Cora Coralina makes with the city is, in fact, an extension of her relationship with the land. In several of her poems, the poetic voice sees in the land its own reflection as well. In "O Cântico da Terra" ("The Ode of the Land") is celebrated as the source not only of the protagonist's roots, but also of all life. It is from the land that one's identity springs out. Beginning with biblical overtones, the poem expresses that land is not only a foundation, but also what bonds and connects people and places. For that reason, the character offers all that is hers—including her chest as a cradle—to the farmhand, the one who works the land. At the end, the poetic voice grows to be both the land and the farmhand—it is a provider like the former, and a caretaker like the latter. The title of "A Gleba Me Transfigura" ("The Land Transfigures Me") indicates another characteristic of the land that Cora Coralina sees: its ability to undergo and generate change. As the farmhand in "O Cântico da Terra" ("The Ode of the Land"), the poetic voice now chooses another image of work that is connected to the land: a bee. Working the land is associated with the poet's own work, to which the bee as a symbol adds a collective dimension. The voice identifies with and declares pure love for natural elements, sounds, fauna, and flora. Writing and the land become one and are given regenerative roles. They are responsible for the community's sense of renewal, to which a call for preservation should be attached: "Sou a espiga e o grão que retornam à terra" ("I am the corncob and the grain that return to the land") (33); "Minha pena (esfereográfica) é a enxada que vai cavando, / é o arado milenário que sulca" [My pen (ballpoint) is the spade that keeps digging, / it is the millenary plow that furrows] (34–5). Like the land, writing—poetry in particular—allows one to search for and eventually find oneself, as it brings back the past and memories of experiences that were formative in developing one's personality and identity: "Em mim a planta renasce e floresce, sementeia e/ sobrevive" [The plant is reborn and blossoms, gives seeds and survives in me] (83–4). Writing also makes a record of the past available for the new generations, those who need to learn from their predecessors in order to understand who they themselves are: "Sou a espiga e o grão fecundo que retornam à terra. / Minha pena é a enxada do plantador, é o arado que vai / sulcando / para a colheita das gerações" [I am the corncob and the fertile grain that return to the land. / My pen is the spade of the one who plants, it is the plow that moves / furrowing / for the harvesting of the generations] (85–7). The beginning of the poem "Sou Raiz" ("I am Root") brings a similar suggestion: "Sou raiz, e vou caminhando / sobre as minhas raízes tribais" [I am root, and I keep walking / over my tribal roots] (1–2). For Cora Coralina, roots—and writing—must be firm and deep. But the past, which is fragile like memory, must be told in order to generate a cyclical movement that promotes not only remembering, but also rethinking: "Seguro sempre nas mãos cansadas a velha candeia / de azeite valetudinária e vitalícia do passado" [I always hold the old, feeble, and lifelong oil lamp of the past / in my tired hands] (21–2).

As we can see, Cora Coralina's writing does go beyond the depiction of a place, or of her past. It is true, however, that she often departs from her own childhood memories to portray a bygone era. The city of Goiás is the stage from which Cora Coralina delves into human nature, aspirations, uncertainties, desires, frustrations, anxieties, and accomplishments. She explores the local context which is so familiar to her in order to encourage reflections which, while personal and even intimate, are truly universal in nature. This is the case in the poem "Coisas de Goiás: Maria" ("Peculiarities of Goiás: Maria"). Although the title refers to a specific person, a "Maria" who lived in Cora Coralina's hometown, the poem asserts that it is also about all "Marias," destitute, homeless women whose life histories are unknown by most people, but who exist in Goiás and elsewhere. Cora Coralina uses the story of a Maria, who, whether fictional or not, lived in her hometown, wandered around the city collecting buttons and clips, and used to live in Cora Coralina's house, as just one example of these women. The poetic voice turns to the defense of this Mad-Maria-type character by enumerating her qualities and criticizing those who mock her. Furthermore, the poem provides her with a story, even alluding to her origins. The reader learns, then, that Maria once had a regular life, enjoyed skills such as reading and sewing, and even cared for a child named Salma who is now a young woman and indebted to Maria. With her story told, Maria loses the otherness—and strangeness—that the townspeople used to mark her with, and her life story becomes more similar to so many others' whose lives for one reason or another end up full of adversities. The poem goes even farther, commenting on social inequality and human solidarity as well.

The social awareness and apprehension present in Cora Coralina's depictions of her small hometown frequently mirror national concerns, and, as the example of "Coisas de Goiás: Maria" ("Peculiarities of Goiás: Maria") shows, often demonstrate a genuine care for humanity. In her introduction to *Melhores Poemas: Cora Coralina* (Best Poems: Cora Coralina), Cora Coralina scholar and enthusiast Darcy França Denófrio aptly notes the presence of the "poema engajado" ("engaged poem") in Cora Coralina's work. She argues that Cora Coralina's poetry "flows, frequently, to the social commitment aspect" (2004: 27). Such political quality can be observed in her depiction of characters that are not from the mainstream of society, those with whom she always sides. For instance, she calls a prostitute her "sister" in "Mulher da Vida" ("Working Woman"), and a prisoner her "brother" in "Premunições de Aninha" ("Aninha's Predictions"). In the former, a poem written for the year 1975, the "International Women's Year," Cora Coralina writes about all prostitutes, "De todos os tempos / De todos os povos / De todas as latitudes" [Of all times / Of all peoples / Of all places] (261). She stands up for them, showing how they are in many ways victims of society: "Pisadas, espezinhadas, ameaçadas. / Desprotegidas e exploradas. / Ignoradas da Lei, da justiça e do Direito" [Stepped on, oppressed, threatened. / unprotected and exploited. / Ignored by law, justice, and human rights] (16–18). She takes up the defense of a group that is usually only seen through a negative lens: "Nenhum direito lhes assiste. / Nenhum estatuto ou norma as protege" [No right assists them. / No statute or norm protects them] (27–8), and she shifts their traditional image as offenders to one of victims, a surprising reversal for someone writing at the elderly age she was. The poem "Sou Raiz" ("I am Root") ends with a dedication to the oppressed: "esta página é toda de vocês" [this page is all yours] (33). More evidence of her concern for and solidarity with the subaltern groups of society in this poem lies in the fact that the poetic voice "mixes" (4) with the "small and illiterate, the poor and the sick" (5), and the "humble ones" (6), who, for her, are all "heroic and anonymous" (24). As Drummond put it in the *Jornal do Brasil*, "Throughout the highway that Cora Coralina is, the Brazil of then and now, and today's children and miserable people pass by" (8).

Children are indeed a common presence in Cora Coralina's poems. For her, children represent the future, and the possibility of change and improvement. This is why she emphasizes education so much. "Menor Abandonado" ("Abandoned Child") for instance, is a cry for help for children. Written for celebrations of the "International Children's Year" in 1979, the poem explores the many facets of the hard life that abandoned children face in Brazil and elsewhere, criticizes society's apathy and prejudice against them, and blames urban life for the poor conditions that these ill-fated children cope with. The poetic voice seems to be the only one that cares for them: "Estou sozinha na floresta escura / e o meu apelo se perdeu inútil / na acústica insensível da cidade" [I am alone in the dark forest / and my useless cry has gotten lost / in the insensitive acoustics of the city] (38–40). It feels hopeless, as its cry does not reach very far. Although the poem finishes with a celebratory tone, asking the child to wake up because it is the "International Children's Year," one cannot fail to notice the deterministic and pessimistic aura that surrounds the whole poem:

> Passa criança . . .
> Segue o teu destino.
> Além é o teu encontro.
> Estarás sentado, curvado, taciturno.
> Sete 'homens bons' te julgarão.
> Um juiz jogado dirá textos de Lei
> que nunca entenderás

—Mais uma vez mudarás de nome.
E dentro de uma casa muito grande
e muito triste—serás um número.
E continuará vertendo inexorável
a fonte poluída de onde vens.

(60–70)

[Go on child . . .
Follow your destiny.
You will find it far over there.
You'll be sitting, leaning down, and taciturn.
Seven 'good men' will judge you.
A relaxed judge will read Law excerpts
That you will never understand
—Once again you will change your name.
And inside a fairly large
And sad house—you will be a number.
And the polluted source from which you come
Will continue to overflow steadily.]

These two stanzas reveal not only a strong sense of determinism, but also an acute criticism of the way that society, and in particular the judicial system, handles the cases involving abandoned children. The system is portrayed as fallible, meaningless, and unable to make the changes that these children need to truly transform their lives. Though the poem suggests that education is the way to save these children from their horrible fate: "pedindo para ti—menor abandonado, / Escolas de Artesanato—*Mater et Magistra* / que possam te salvar, deter a tua queda" [Requesting for you—abandoned child, / Arts and Crafts Schools—*Mater et Magistra* / that may save you, prevent your fall] (28–30), it does not show any true optimism for real future changes in these children's lives, as its tone is distrustful. Education is a common theme in Cora Coralina's poetry. Poems such as "Mestra Silvina" ("Teacher Silvina"), "A Escola da Mestra Silvina" ("The School of Teacher Silvina"), and "O Beco da Escola" ("The School's Alley") depict events that happened at schools, and "Normas de Educação" ("Educational Norms"), "Pai e Filho" ("Father and Son"), and "Antiguidades" ("Antiquities") meditate on the real meaning of upbringing and parenthood.

The critical and universal aspects of Cora Coralina's work do not diminish the importance of the local feature in her verses. Her poetry is no doubt an important referent in the cultural history of the city of Goiás and in the representations of that same history. These are her words in the opening of *Poemas dos becos de Goiás e estórias mais* (Poems of the Alleys of Goiás and Other Stories): "Alguém deve rever, escrever e assinar os autos do Passado antes que o Tempo passe tudo a raso. É o que procuro fazer para a geração nova" [Someone must review, write, and sign the events of the Past before Time erases it all. That is what I try to do for the new generation] (25). She documents her people's traditions, values, and ways of thinking as her work tells personal histories that almost always intersect with collective events or concerns. Her writing is personal, intimate, and subjective, and—despite its sensitivity and lyric quality—often sounds like everyday conversation, as if it is attempting to emulate those whose stories it tells. By expressing universal ideas with a local voice, Cora Coralina's poetry continues to attract readers in Goiás and all over Brazil. Through writing, Cora Coralina fulfilled her role as cultural preserver and shall continue to do so for many generations still to come.

ANTONIO LUCIANO DE ANDRADE TOSTA

Selected Works

Poemas dos becos de Goiás e estórias mais. Rio de Janeiro: José Olympio, 1965.

Meu livro de cordel. Goiânia: Livraria e Editora Cultura Goiana, 1976.

Vintém de cobre. Goiânia: Editora da Universidade Federal de Goiás, 1983.

Estórias da casa velha da ponte. São Paulo: Global, 1985.

O Tesouro da casa velha. São Paulo: Global, 1989.

Villa Boa de Goyaz. São Paulo: Global, 2001.

Melhores poemas: Cora Coralina. Org. Darcy França-Denófrio. São Paulo: Global, 2004.

References and Further Reading

Barbosa, Maria José Somerlate. "A via-láctea da palavra: Adélia Prado e Cora Coralina". In C. L. Duarte, A. D. Eduardo and K. da C. Bezerra (eds), *Gêneros e representação na literatura brasileira*. Coleção Mulher e Literatura. 2. Belo Horizonte: Letras/UFMG, 2002.

Brasil, Assis. *A poesia goiana no século XX*. Rio de Janeiro: Imago; Goiânia: Fundação Cultural Pedro Ludovico Teixeira, 1997.

Camargo, Goiandira de F. Ortiz de. "Poesia e Memória em Cora Coralina". *Signótica* 14 (2002): 75–85.

Coelho, Nelly Novaes. *Dicionário crítico de escritoras brasileiras: (1711–2001)*. São Paulo: Escrituras, 2002.

Fernandes, José. "Telurismo e cosmologia em Cora Coralina". *Dimensões da literatura Goiana*. Goiânia: Cerne, 1992.

França-Denófrio, Darcy and Camargo, Goiandira F. Ortiz (eds), *Cora Coralina: celebração da volta*. Goiânia: Cânone Editorial, 2006.

Machado, Marietta Telles. "Depoimento sobre Cora Coralina". *Coletânea*. Goiânia: Instituto Goiano do Livro/Agepel, 2000.

Ramón, Saturnino Pesquero. *Cora Coralina: o mito de Aninha*. Goiânia: Eds. da UFG and UCG, 2003.

Santos, Wendel. "O universo imaginário de Cora Coralina". *Crítica Sistemática*. Goiânia: Oriente, 1977.

Tahan, Vicência Brêtas. *Cora Coragem, Cora Poesia*. São Paulo: Global, 1989.

Teles, Gilberto Mendonça. *A poesia em Goiás: estudo/antologia*. Goiânia: Ed. da UFG, 1964.

Teles, José Mendonça. *No santuário de Cora Coralina*. Goiânia: Kelps, 1991.

COUTINHO, SÔNIA

Novelist, short-story writer, journalist, and translator, Sônia Walkíria de Sousa Coutinho (b. 1939) was one of the first Brazilian fiction writers to problematize Brazilian women's revision of their traditional roles from the late 1960s on. While this phenomenon has been common in the major cities of Brazil, rural regions have remained rather conservative and patriarchal. Like Coutinho herself, her characters are often women who have exchanged suffocating surroundings for the cosmopolitan and (supposedly) liberating Rio de Janeiro. Economically independent and living a relatively comfortable life, these women now face new problems: solitude, isolation, loneliness, and the invisibility that the mass media society imposes on middle-aged women.

Born in Itabuna, a small town in the Northeastern Brazilian state of Bahia, Coutinho moved to Salvador, the colonial capital of the same state, as a child. She first encountered books in the library of her father, who was a poet. At the age of 18, Coutinho had to abandon her studies in order to start working, and she would only be able to resume them almost twenty years later, receiving a degree in Letters (1975) and a Master's degree in Communication Theory (1994).

In the 1960s, Coutinho began her literary activities by joining a literary group in Salvador, and by publishing short stories in newspaper literary supplements and in the volumes *Reunião* (Reunion, 1961) and *Histórias da Bahia e doze contistas da Bahia* (Stories from Bahia and Twelve Short-Story Writers from Bahia, 1965). At this time, she started working as a journalist, and in 1968, Coutinho moved to Rio de Janeiro, where she worked as a translator for Reuters, and as a journalist for various newspapers. She also contributed to the magazines *Nova* and *Status*, and received the *Status Prize* for erotic literature in 1977 for the short story "Cordélia, a caçadora" (Cordelia, the Hunter), later published in *Os venenos de Lucrécia* (1978, Lucretia's Poisons), which received the *Jabuti Prize* in 1979. In 1977, Coutinho was Visiting Writer at the University of Texas at Austin, and in 1983, she was a Writer in Residence in the International Writing Program at the University of Iowa. In 1989, Coutinho abandoned journalism in order to dedicate herself to the translation of literary works by writers such as Doris Lessing, Agatha Christie, Michael Crichton, and Danielle Steel. She currently lives in Rio de Janeiro. Since 2003, she edits the online magazine and blog *Sidarta*.

After her collection of short stories *Do herói inútil* (1966, On the Useless Hero), Sonia Coutinho published *Nascimento de uma mulher* (Birth of a Woman) in 1971, a book of short stories that thematizes female protagonists in a rapidly changing society, and that Coutinho considers to be her literary debut. The kaleidoscopic Copacabana, in Rio de Janeiro, reappears in *Uma certa felicidade* (1976, A Certain Happiness) as a place where women find a useless sense of freedom. Salvador, on the other hand, is described as a place where the characters' roots remain, a lost city that the protagonists attempt to rescue through memory. In *Uma certa felicidade*, one sees an affinity with one of the main themes of the Latin American novel: the rescuing or reinvention of a land violated by the conquerors through both the memory of its inhabitants and the very act of writing. In *Os venenos de Lucrécia* (1978), Coutinho examines family relations. At the same time fragile and dangerous, the female protagonists suffer from an endless search for happiness. But as in the story "Doce e cinzenta Copacabana" (Sweet and Gray Copacabana), these women recognize the value of experiencing something that is theirs, and not the product of a law that they did not help to institute.

Most of Coutinho's works include references to Afro-Brazilian culture. The novel *O jogo de Ifá* (1980, Ifá Game), for example, derives its title from a Yoruban divination rite. This polyphonic novel combines metafictional interferences, intertextual references, and an androgynous form of writing that interweaves the voices of both a male and a female protagonist in order to disrupt traditional sexual binaries and to recall a collective human experience.

In *O último verão de Copacabana* (1985, The Last Summer of Copacabana), Copacabana is not only the setting but also the object of desire. The stories reveal the complexity of Brazil's subcultures, many of which, like women's culture, have been forced into a marginal position. References to icons from popular culture, such as Lana Turner and Billie Holliday, compose a mosaic of the different facets of women in a metropolis. The famous beach district stands for a culture centered on the body and physical pleasures, an environment where the female character can become reacquainted with her body and sexuality, but which also exposes a woman's diminished sense of self and a feeling of mediocrity. By focusing on the sexuality of aging women, Coutinho presents a transgressive and disruptive female body that deconstructs myths of femininity.

In seeking to give expression to female subjectivity, Coutinho makes use of different thematic elements, such as lesbian desire and the adaptation of the detective novel. In *Atire em Sofia* (1989, Shoot Sofia), a murder investigation is intertwined with the depiction of the writing process of a detective novel written by one of the victim's friends. Both in *Atire* and in *O caso Alice* (1991, The Alice Case), there is a strong emphasis on fantastic elements. In *O caso Alice*, the city, sustained by references to popular culture, is presented as a text built over other texts. Amidst murder, betrayal, and incest, the narrator investigates the disappearance of a woman, while deconstructing the detective novel genre by questioning the very possibility of dealing with objective events. Similar dilemmas reappear in the life of Dora Diamante, the female detective of *Os seios de Pandora* (1998, Pandora's Breasts, *Jabuti Prize* 1999), who travels to a small Brazilian town in order to investigate the murder of an artist. The detective novel as a genre is also the scholarly focus of Coutinho's critical study *Rainhas do crime: Ótica feminina no romance policial* (1994, Queens of Crime: Feminine Point-of-view in the Detective Novel), which examines the extent to which women writers have transformed this genre, as well as the subversion of patriarchal social codes by female detective protagonists.

Guilt is an element with which Coutinho's protagonists constantly struggle. Looking for ways to escape from the marginal position of an older single woman, some of them resort to superficial and provisory loves and friendships, while others are able to break away from the patriarchal ideology and embrace their own maturity, sexuality, and independence. In Coutinho's works, capital letters and hyphenated phrases are frequently used in order to emphasize the banality and emptiness of myths that inform the expectations imposed on the female subject. Sound structures and strong imagery are employed in order to achieve a synaesthetic sensual effect.

In Coutinho's most recent collection of short stories, *Ovelha negra e amiga loura* (2006, Black Sheep and Blond Friend), explorations of solitude, aging, family disintegration, sexual trauma, and the loss of belief in love as salvation still recognize the redemptive potential of small things and unassuming facets of life. Responding to a society in which material profit is fetishized and women and artists are labeled "unproductive," Coutinho presents art as a possible source of relief.

LUCIANA NAMORATO

Selected Works

Do herói inútil. Salvador de Bahia: Macunaíma, 1966.

Nascimento de uma mulher. Rio de Janeiro: Civilização Brasileira, 1971.

Uma certa felicidade. Rio de Janeiro: Francisco Alves, 1976.
Os venenos de Lucrécia. São Paulo: Ática, 1978.
O jogo de Ifá. São Paulo: Ática, 1980.
O último verão de Copacabana. Rio de Janeiro: José Olympio, 1985.
Atire em Sofia. Rio de Janeiro: Rocco, 1989.
O caso Alice. Rio de Janeiro: Rocco, 1991.
"Every Lana Turner Has Her Johnny Stompanato". In Darlene J. Sadlier (ed. and trans.), *One Hundred Years After Tomorrow*. Bloomington, IN: Indiana University Press, 1992, pp. 228–35.
Rainhas do crime: Ótica feminina do romance policial. Rio de Janeiro: Sette Letras, 1994.
Os seios de Pandora. Rio de Janeiro: Rocco, 1998.
"Last Summer in Copacabana". In *Urban Voices: Contemporary Short Stories from Brazil*, ed. Cristina Ferreira-Pinto, trans. Tanya T. Fayen. Lanham, MD: University Press of America, 1999, pp. 35–47.
Mil olhos de uma rosa. Rio de Janeiro: 7Letras, 2001.
"Summer in Rio". In *Fourteen Female Voices from Brazil: Interviews and Works*, ed. Elzbieta Szoka, trans. Elzbieta Szoka with Shanna Lorenz. Austin, TX: Host, 2002, pp. 229–35.
Guerreira Maria: Presença de Maria Quitéria. Rio de Janeiro: Dublin, 2004.
Ovelha negra e amiga loura. Rio de Janeiro: 7Letras, 2006.

References and Further Reading

Brink-Friederici, Christl M. K. "Sonia Coutinho: *Atire em Sofia*, um romance policial?" *Travessia* 22 (1991): 51–62.
Carvalho, Luiz Fernando Medeiros de. "Configurações do fragmento: Análise do romance *O caso Alice*, de Sonia Coutinho". In *Literatura e promessa: Figuração e paradoxo na literatura brasileira contemporânea*. Rio de Janeiro: EdUFF, 2002, pp. 68–76.
Costa, Sérgio. "*O último verão de Copacabana*: A cidade impossível de Sonia Coutinho," Afterword to *O último verão de Copacabana*, by Sonia Coutinho. Rio de Janeiro: 7Letras, 2004, pp. 103–6.
Ferreira-Pinto, Cristina. "Sonia Coutinho's Short Fiction: Aging and the Female Body" and "Contemporary Brazilian Women's Short Stories". Chapters 4 and 5 in *Gender, Discourse, and Desire in Twentieth-Century Brazilian Women's Literature*. West Lafayette, IN: Purdue University Press, 2004, pp. 93–112, 113–42.
Lobo, Luiza. "Sonia Coutinho Revisits the City". In Anny Brooksbank Jones and Catherine Davies (eds), *Latin American Women's Writing: Feminist Readings in Theory and Crisis*. Oxford: Clarendon Press, 1996, pp. 163–78.
Patrício, Rosana Ribeiro. *As filhas de Pandora: Imagens da mulher na ficção de Sonia Coutinho*. Rio de Janeiro: 7Letras, 2006.
Szoka, Elzbieta. "Sonia Coutinho". In Elzbieta Szoka (ed.), *Fourteen Female Voices from Brazil: Interviews and Works*. Austin, TX: Host, 2002, pp. 221–8.

CRESPO DE BRITTON, ROSA MARÍA

Rosa María Crespo de Britton (b. 1936) is a successful gynecologist and oncologist in Panama where she also is a prolific, and equally successful, writer. Crespo de Britton is the leading contemporary woman writer of Panama and arguably the best Panamanian author of the late twentieth and early twenty-first centuries excelling in three genres—novel, short story, and drama. Crespo de Britton enjoys both a high critical reputation and a large readership in Panama, in part, because she writes an accessible fiction that enables her to communicate her social concerns to a wide and receptive audience. This excellence is attested not only by critical recognition—six Miró awards—but also by book sales, as she continues to be a perennial best-selling author. Crespo de Britton won the Golden Pen Award in Panama for having sold more books than any other national author. Panama, a melting pot of cultures and ethnicities, presents Crespo de Britton with a rich source of material as she draws not only inspiration from native peoples, but also from Orientals, African Hispanics, Spaniards, and Gringos with emphasis on the Canal Zone.

Crespo de Britton's father, Matías Crespo Evora from Cuba and her mother, Carmen Justiniani from Panama, were both unsatisfied and ambitious, causing them to leave their respective countries for a better education and the American dream in New York. The stock market crash of 1929 interrupted her mother's schooling at Columbia University and caused her to seek employment at a clothing factory where she met Crespo de Britton's father. In 1931, several years after their marriage, the couple decided to open a clothing factory in Panama. Crespo de Britton was thus born into a middle-class family and, although not wealthy, her childhood was comfortable and included access to her father's library where she read constantly. From her parents Crespo de Britton received an ambitious nature, progressive thinking, and a love for reading. With her mother's encouragement, Crespo de Britton left Panama to study at the best high school in Havana, Cuba, where she graduated valedictorian. After graduation her medical studies were temporarily interrupted by the Cuban Revolution in 1959. Crespo de Britton left Cuba to study in Madrid where she earned her medical degree and married a US engineer, Carl Crespo de Britton. She then continued her studies in gynecology and oncology in New York City after spending one year in Canada. In 1966, Crespo de Britton established a successful practice in Queens where her two children, Walter and Gabrielle, were born. In 1973, she returned with her family to Panama following her husband who had accepted a position in the Canal Zone the previous year. Some five years later Crespo de Britton began her literary career by pretending to take notes during endless bureaucratic meetings. These efforts resulted in the historical novel, *El ataúd de uso* (The Used Coffin).

In *El ataúd de uso,* and other novels, Crespo de Britton allows her characters the free will to choose life's various options and they tend to do so in opposition to society's chosen roles. The theme of blacks and racial discrimination, although subtle in the first book, is more pronounced in later efforts, especially her plays. Crespo de Britton's second novel, *El señor de las lluvias y el viento* (The Lord of the Rain and the Wind) also initiates and develops themes and preoccupations that appear in later works. Both of these early works are set in imaginary towns, the first in Chumico and the second in Chirico. Crespo de Britton's fifth novel—*Laberintos de orgullo* (Labyrinths of Pride) also takes place in Chumico. Covering the years between 1953 and 1998, the reader, due to auto-intertextuality—the use of the same town, characters and incidents in several works of an author—learns the rest of the story of Chumico. In a contemporary version of Chumico, political concerns, drug trafficking, and the daily lives of certain characters and their descendants are divulged. It is in the "social laboratory" of Crespo de Britton's imaginary Chumico, a remote and all but forgotten little town along the Pacific coast of Panama near Colombia, where Crespo de Britton addresses one of her concerns: blacks in Panama. Crespo de Britton often treats themes common to both Panama and the United States such as racial discrimination and interracial marriages. Some of the Panamanian characters in her books spend time in the US, while others, US citizens, live and work in Panama. Crespo de Britton addresses negritude and also gives the Colonial black an important role in the narrative. Manuel, the principal character of *El ataúd de uso*, is a black who rises from humble beginnings as a fisherman to become a successful merchant, city mayor, war hero, and ultimately the most respected and important citizen in Chumico. *No pertenezco a este siglo* (I Don't Belong to This Century) is a historical literary discourse on US expansion in Colombia and Panama. It deals with the independence of Panama from Colombia, as did her first novel, but in this work the perspective is through the eyes of a conservative Colombian politician. Her following novel, *Todas íbamos a ser reinas* (We Were All Going to Be Queens) is set, initially, in a girls' school in Cuba. This novel is both autobiographical and historical. The action unfolds during the Batista era in Cuba just prior to, and briefly into, the Castro period and moves on to Spain during the Franco regime. Years later the group of classmates reunite in the US to review their lives revealing accomplishments and tragedies. Crespo de Britton's sixth and latest novel, *Suspiros de fantasmas* (Sighs of Phantoms) treats a common contemporary problem—the deterioration of the family and its consequences. It reveals that today's parents are more involved in shopping, taking trips, and organizing and attending social events than they are in their children's lives.

Crespo de Britton's literary successes in the novel continue with the short story genre beginning with the first collection *¿Quién inventó el mambo?* (Who Invented the Mambo?) that treats life in Panama during the 1940s. The title of the book refers to the king of mambo—Dámaso Pérez Prado. *La muerte tiene dos caras* (Death Has Two Faces) contains stories inspired by her work with cancer patients and is followed by *Semana de la mujer y otras calamidades* (Women's Week and Other Calamities) that deals with problems of contemporary Panamanian women who attend a conference dedicated to women. The latest short story collection, *La nariz invisible y otros misterios* (The Invisible Nose and Other Mysteries) explores contemporary women victimized by the effective abandonment by their family, resulting in a feeling that their own existence is jeopardized.

The dominant themes of Crespo de Britton's socially oriented theatre are racism, the problem of bureaucracy in modern life, and low self-esteem of women. The work that best exemplifies the latter theme is *Mi$$ Panamá, Inc.* followed by *Los loros no lloran* (Parrots Don't Cry). *Esa esquina del paraíso* (That Corner of Paradise) treats racism while *Banquete de despedida* (Farewell Banquet) deals with bureaucracy. All four plays tend to depict women in a dominant role while men are portrayed as lesser individuals as regards character, motivation, and the ability to accomplish their goals.

Crespo de Britton, who considers herself a novelist first, has also written commendable short stories and plays. She writes in an engaging and accessible style and treats themes that are relevant not only to Panamanians but also for a more universal reading public making her one of Panama's outstanding writers.

LEE A. DANIEL

Selected Works

El ataúd de uso. Panamá: Editorial Oveja Negra, 1983.
El señor de las lluvias y el viento. Panamá: Editora Sibauste, 1984.
Esa esquina del paraíso. Panamá: Editorial Mariano Arosemena, 1985.
¿Quién inventó el mambo? Panamá: Editorial Mariano Arosemena, 1986.
Banquete de despedida/Mi$$ Panamá, Inc. Panamá: Editorial Mariano Arosemena, 1987
No pertenezco a este siglo. San José: Editorial Costa Rica, 1992.
Semana de la mujer y otras calamidades. Madrid: Torremozas, 1995.
Todas íbamos a ser reinas. Bogotá: Plaza & Janés Editores, 1997.
La muerte tiene dos caras. Panamá: Editora Sibauste, 1997.
Teatro. Panamá: Editorial Mariano Arosemena, 1999.
La nariz invisible y otros misterios. Madrid: Torremozas, 2000.
La costilla de Adán. Panamá: Editora Sibauste, 2000.
Laberintos de orgullo. Cali, Colombia: Alfaguara, 2002.
Suspiros de fantasmas. San José, Costa Rica: Alfaguara, 2005.

References and Further Reading

Daniel, Lee A. "Centroamérica y sus poblados míticos: Un acercamiento cartográfico". *El pez y la serpiente* 42 (2001): 91–113.
——. "Explorando nuevos espacios: los pueblos imaginarios de Rosa María Crespo de Britton". In Humberto López Cruz (ed.), *Encuentro con la literatura panameña*. Panamá, 2002, pp. 61–80.
Jaramillo Levi, Enrique. *When New Flowers Bloomed: Short Stories by Women Writers From Costa Rica and Panama*. Pittsburgh, PA: Latin American Literary Review Press, 1991.
——. *Ser escritor en Panamá: entrevistas a 29 escritores panameños al finalizar el siglo XX*. Panamá: Fundación Cultural Signos y Fundación Pro-Biblioteca Nacional, 1999.
López Cruz, Humberto. "Factores discursivos en la narrativa de Rosa María Crespo de Britton: feminismo y negritud". *SECOLAS Annals* (1998): 55–60.

CROSS, ELSA

Elsa Cross (b. 1946) is one of the mostly widely translated, prolific, and prize-winning poets in Mexico today. Cross is an inveterate traveler, fluent in English and French, and with translating skills in Italian. She has published in the best Mexican presses and from an early age. Despite Cross's continued residence in Mexico City, nature is perhaps the single most consistent thematic underpinning of her poetry. Cross's parents—her father was a commercial airline pilot and her mother an amateur painter, moved to Mexico City when they married, though they returned to their hometown of Matamoros, Mexico, for vacations. Perhaps it was during those vacations in Matamoros that Cross developed her abiding interest in nature.

Poetic Approach and Education

Cross's work tends to stress the importance of inner vision and of experiencing nature in order to see beyond it. Her poems celebrate rhythm and image and tend to avoid strict patterns of syllable count and rhyme. Through a blend of details regarding local nature and a more universal, often genderless spiritual thematic, Cross's poetry operates independently of the identity politics that might stress her perspective as a Mexican woman. In fact, Cross's academic background stresses male philosophers. Her undergraduate and Master's theses for her philosophy degrees from the National Autonomous University of Mexico (UNAM) concern Nietzsche's theories on tragedy. A version of the Master's thesis, directed by Ramón Xirau, was published in Spanish in 1985. Cross's dissertation for the philosophy department at the UNAM studies the life and works of the Hindu saint Jñaneshwar Maharaj. Cross lived in India for two years and occasionally returns for shorter visits. In 1976, she began to practice Siddha Yoga under the guidance of Swami Muktananda in Ganeshpuri, an ashram located north of Mumbai. The act of daily meditation strongly affects Cross's poetry.

Prizes and Major Publications

In 1967, Cross won the Diana Moreno Toscano Prize for literary promise. The jury included Octavio Paz, whose work bears a noticeable influence on her poetry, and Juan José Arreola, whose literary workshop began Cross's poetic career. Arreola's workshop led to the publication of *Naxos*, a collection of prose poems that reveals world-weariness and romantic solitude. Cross also earned the National Prize from the Secretariat of Public Education in 1972 for *La dama de la torre* (The Lady in the Tower), a work inspired in medieval Italian poetry. In 1971–72, Cross received a grant from the Mexican Center for Writers and consequently drafted a study of Shakespeare's dramatic work. In 1979–80, she received another grant from the Mexican Center for Writers and this funding produced *Tres poemas* (1981, Three Poems). After *Tres poemas*, Cross destroyed her writing over a nine-year period because she felt that her possibilities for expression were tapped out. The apprenticeship in Siddha meditation eventually refreshed Cross's poetic energies, and in 1989 she won the Aguascalientes Poetry Prize for *El diván de Antar*. This long poem creatively recognizes poetic tradition, and even the title shows Cross's literary cosmopolitanism. The word "diván" means "poetry" in Arabic, and Antar was an important warrior and poet in sixth-century Islamic culture. In 1992, Cross received the Jaime Sabines Poetry Prize for *Moira*, a word that refers to the Greek fates. In 1991, Cross published a lyrical collection titled *Jaguar* that turns the thematic axis from India to Mexico. Since 1993, Cross has belonged to the National System of Creators, which supplements her income as a Professor of Religion at the UNAM.

Over Cross's prolific poetic trajectory, two collections of meditative poetry stand out, *Baniano* (1986; the title refers to a kind of tree important in Cross's ashram experience) and *Canto Malabar* (1987, Malabar Song). The Octavio-Paz influenced *Baniano* also reflects Cross's study with her meditation teacher Muktananda; his death produced the meditative *Canto Malabar*. Frank Dauster offers the most comprehensive review of Cross's work. He views *Baniano* as reflecting a western perspective on experience in India, while he reads *Canto Malabar* as adopting an Indian native's point of view. Additional criticism has yet to comment on this possible distinction between the works. Both collections cultivate tensions in stasis. Thus, instead of resolving the tensions, Cross relates the process of a search that revels in the experience of the present moment. In other words, *Baniano* and *Canto Malabar* articulate perceptions of this world that might lead to knowledge of the transcendent. Cross called her second personal anthology *Espirales* (Spirals) in recognition of recurring themes in her poetry. Across her work, Cross favors images that involve the sea, fire, and light. She infuses these universal themes with contradictions, such as a fire that does not consume itself, a sea that moves and yet does not break its waves, and a light that shines when eyes are closed. Light is not always illuminating and sight is not always gained through physical eyes in Cross's work because her meditative poetry registers an inner vision. For Cross, poetry serves as a vehicle for spirituality that does not necessarily result in goal-oriented accomplishment, but rather facilitates heightened consciousness as an experience valuable in itself. In some ways, her meditative poetry seems to reflect an experiential paradox, something on the order of "thought before thinking". The poetic paradox is furthered through her tendency to court silence through words.

Eroticism and Mysticism

Not all of Cross's poetry corresponds to the contemplative process of meditation. Some of her work focuses on amorous and erotic topics. As Cross reveals in an interview with Erna Pfeiffer, the poem "Canción de Arnaut" (Song of Arnaut) employs a masculine voice that speaks of a homosexual love, as signaled by the epigraph from Dante. Cross's preferences for spiritual and erotic themes are interrelated, as suggested by *Los dos jardines* (2003, The Two Gardens), a collection of short essays on fellow Mexican poets. There, Cross analyzes mysticism and eroticism as two aspects of the same literary search. By applying this principle to Cross's poetry, it would seem that if, for example, *Canto Malabar* leans toward mysticism, Cross's earlier *Bacantes* (Followers of Bacchus) favors the erotic side of the duality by inventing a marijuana-smoking, Hindu-inspired figure who seduces the women of the poem from their homes and responsibilities. Typically, however, Cross does not indulge in straightforward celebrations of the sexual nor does she favor explicitly mystical poetry: her literary awareness of the body and of the spirit tends to find expression through more philosophical concerns.

Future Directions

Cross's poetry is at once erudite and accessible. Her poetry looks beyond the page and does not engage in intellectual games nor precious language. The complexity of her work appears in the ideas and not so much the language itself, which tends to be syntactically simple and straightforward. Aside from the thematic constants, Cross's work consistently enters into dialogue with literary traditions that span eastern and western, contemporary and ancient poetry. Forthcoming texts by Cross include *Cuaderno de Amorgós* (Notebook of Amorgós) due for release in 2006 and her complete works with the Fondo de Cultural Económica. The translation of her selected poems into English by Tony Frazer is also due to appear with Shearsman Press.

EMILY HIND

Selected Works

Poetry

La dama de la torre. Mexico: Joaquín Mortiz, 1972.

Espejo al sol: Poemas, 1964–1981. (Includes selections from *Naxos* (1966), *Verano* (previously unpublished), *Amor el más oscuro* (1969),

La dama de la torre (1972), *Destiempo* (previously unpublished), *Espejo al sol* (from *Tres poemas*, 1981), *Las edades perdidas* (from *Tres poemas*, 1981), and *Bacantes* (1982).) Mexico: SEP, Plaza y Valdés, 1988.

El diván de Antar. Mexico: Joaquín Mortiz, 1990.

Moira. Mexico: Gobierno del Estado de Chiapas, CEFIDC-DIF Chiapas, Instituto Chiapaneco de Cultura, 1993.

Espirales: Poemas escogidos 1965–1999. (Includes selections from *Verano*, *Amor el más oscuro* (1969), *La dama de la torre* (1972), *Espejo al sol* (from *Tres poemas*, 1981), *Pasaje de fuego* (1987), *Bacantes* (1982), *Destiempo*, *Baniano* (1986), *Canto Malabar* (1987), *Poemas desde la India* (1993), *El diván de Antar* (1990), *Jaguar* (1991), *Casaurinas* (1992), *Moira* (1993), *Urracas* (1995), and *Cantáridas* (1999).) Mexico: UNAM, 2000.

Jaguar y otros poemas (1985–2000). Mexico: CONACULTA, 2002.

Los sueños: Elegías. Mexico: CONACULTA, 2000.

Ultramar: Odas. Mexico: Fondo de Cultural Económica, 2002.

El vino de las cosas: Ditirambos. Mexico: Era, CONACULTA, 2004.

Puerto Bagdad: Antología poética. Mexico: Libros del Estero, 2004.

Naxos: Antología personal. Mexico: Red Utopía, Jitanjáfora Morelia Editorial, 2005.

Philosophy and Criticism

Los dos jardines: Mística y erotismo en algunos poetas mexicanos. Mexico: Sin Nombre, CONACULTA, 2003.

Translations

Acosta, Juvenal. *Light from a Nearby Window: Contemporary Mexican Poetry.* San Francisco, CA: City Lights, 1993, pp. 86–105.

de la Torre, Mónica and Wiegers, Michael. *Reversible Monuments: Contemporary Mexican Poetry.* Port Townsend, WA: Copper Canyon Press, 2002, pp. 134–57.

Fick, Marlon L. *The River is Wide: Twenty Mexican Poets, a Bilingual Anthology/El río es ancho.* Albuquerque, NM: University of New Mexico Press, 2005, pp. 80–111.

Gander, Forrest. *Mouth to Mouth: Poems by Twelve Contemporary Mexican Women.* Minneapolis, MN: Milkweed Ed, 1993, pp. 139–53.

McWhirter, George. *Where Words Like Monarchs Fly: A Cross-Generational Anthology of Mexican Poets (1934–1955) in Translations From North of the 49th Parallel.* Vancouver: Anvil Press, 1998.

References and Further Reading

Dauster, Frank. "La poesía de Elsa Cross: El círculo de la iluminación". *Revista de Literatura Mexicana Contemporánea* 3(8) (1998): 37–44.

Ochoa Sandy, Gerardo. "Elsa Cross: Uno no puede dar nada si está vacio." In *La palabra dicha: Entrevistas con escritores mexicanos.* Mexico: CONACULTA, 2000, pp. 157–66.

Pasternac, Nora. "Hermetismo y transparencia: Elsa Cross y José Emilio Pacheco". In Maricruz Castro and Laura Cázares Hernández (eds), *Escrituras en contraste: Femenino, masculino en la literatura mexicana del siglo XX.* Mexico: Aldus, UAM, 2004, pp. 259–91.

Valdivia, Benjamín. "Aproximación al *Canto Malabar* de Elsa Cross." In *Presencia del sueño: Cinco poetas de México hacia el nuevo siglo: Huerta, Rivas, Cross, Hernández y Morábito.* Veracruz, Mexico: Instituto Veracruzano de la Cultura, 2003, pp. 69–55.

Vázquez Valdez, María. "Elsa Cross: Todo cede a la luz/Everything Dissolves into the Light". In *Voces desdobladas, Unfolded Voices: Retratos de mujeres poetas de México y Estados Unidos.* Mexico: Alforja, Casa Abierta al Tiempo, UAM, 2004, pp. 25–61.

CRUZ, SOR JUANA INÉS DE LA

Sor Juana Inés de la Cruz (c. 1648–95) was a Mexican poet, dramatist, feminist and nun, who was known also as "The Tenth Muse," "The Phoenix of Mexico" and "The Mexican Nun". Sor Juana is one of the foremost figures of Latin American letters of the seventeenth century.

Juana Inés de Asbaje y Rairez de Santillana was born at 11:00 p.m. Friday, November 12 in San Miguel de Nepantla, Amecameca. The legitimacy of her birth is a matter of debate among scholars. Her mother, Isabel Ramirez de Santillana, in her will, described her marital status as not married, but Sor Juana, in 1669 described herself as the legitimate daughter of Don Pedro de Asbaje y Vargas Machuca and Isabel Ramirez. Little is known about her father other than that he was a Basque from Guipuzcoa (Vergara). There has been some controversy as to her father's name given the lack of consistency in spelling during this time. Asbaje is sometimes written Asuaje or Asuaxe y probably pronounced /asßaše/. Another matter of debate is the year of her birth. Diego Calleja, a Spanish Jesuit and friend of Sor Juana, was her first biographer and gives the year of her birth as 1651 although a baptismal document believed to be hers gives the year as 1648.

Juana Inés was raised by her mother as her father had abandoned the family when she was 3 years old. She grew up with two older sisters, three younger half-siblings and her maternal grandfather, Pedro Ramirez, on the hacienda of Panoayan outside of Mexico City. Having learned to read at the age of 3, she later asked to be sent to study at the university dressed as a boy when she was 7. At 9, she wrote a *loa* (a short dramtic prologue) to the Holy Sacrament. In her *Carta respuesta a Sor Filotea de la Cruz* (Reply to Sor Filotea de la Cruz), she described this period of her life as a time devoted to reading and studying. In her determination to learn, she would often cut her hair and not allow it to grow back until she had mastered the task at hand: "... And so my hair grew, but I did not yet know what I had resolved to learn, for it grew quickly and I learned slowly. Then I cut my hair right off to punish my dull-wittedness for I did not think it reasonable that hair should cover a head that was so bare of facts" (Arenal and Scklau 1989: 51).

Upon the death of her grandfather in 1656, her mother sent her to the capital to live in the home of her sister, María Ramirez, wife of the affluent Juan de Mata, where Juana studied Latin with a tutor, Martín de Olivas. Twenty lessons were sufficient for her to master the language as she demonstrates in several of her works, overall in her *villancicos* (carols) which contain Latin verses.

In 1664, she entered into the service of the court of the Viceroys of New Spain and wrote extensively for its members. She became a favorite of the Marquis of Mancera and his wife Leonor María Carreto de Toledo, who is referred to in some of Sor Juana's poems as "Laura". In admiration of her intellectual capacity and the novelty of her being a woman, the Viceroy convened a diverse group of forty of the most knowledgeable scholars of New Spain to submit Juana to an exam which she ably passed.

Juana remained at court until she decided to enter a religious order as she explained in her autobiographical reply to Sor Filotea:

> Given my complete aversion to marriage, this was the most seemly and decent choice I could make, for the security I wished and my salvation ... wanting to live

alone, not wanting to have any obligations that would disturb my studies, or doings in the community that would interrupt the quiet calm of my books.

She first entered into the convent of the Discalced Carmelites of Saint Joseph in 1667 but left after a few months because of the severity and rigor of the order, which damaged her health. She convalesced for two years and, having recovered her health, thanks to the help of the vicereine, she was able to get monetary support from Pedro Vázquez de la Cadena that allowed her to enter the convent of the Sisters of Saint Heironymus where, on February 24, 1669, she became a nun with the name Juana Inés de la Cruz. At the convent, she worked as treasurer, archivist and secretary, among other tasks.

Sor Juana was allowed a personal and spacious cell along with a servant (a mulatta slave given to her by her mother) where she collected more than four thousand volumes in her library along with musical instruments, maps and medical instruments and where she pursued studies in astronomy, mathematics, languages, philosophy, mythology, history, theology, music and painting. She performed scientific experiments, composed musical works and wrote extensively. Her living quarters became a place for meetings of groups of poets and intellectuals like Carlos de Sigüenza y Góngora, a relative of the poet Luís de Góngora y Argote, who introduced Góngora's poetry to New Spain. Also among the group were the new Viceroy, Tomás Antonio de la Cerda, Marquis of la Laguna, and his wife doña María Luisa Manrique de Lara y Gonzaga, Marquise of la Laguna and Countess of Paredes. The Marquise would later appear in the poems of Sor Juana as "Lysis" (or "Phyllis") while Sor Juana took the pseudonym of "Julia". For eight years the patronage of the Marquises allowed Sor Juana the freedom and protection she needed to accomplish what would be the bulk of her work. During this period she wrote both religious and secular poetry as well as plays, one of which, *Los empeños de una casa* (The Trials of a Noble House), was performed for the public.

Her confessor, the Jesuit Antonio Núñez de Miranda, a powerful, intelligent and extremely ascetic man, criticized Sor Juana for her writings which he believed to be a task prohibited to women. For him, the use of reason was an exclusively masculine privilege. His criticism grew sharper with her increased fame and contact with the prominent political, academic and artistic personalities of the era. At first, Sor Juana endured the humiliation of his remarks, but due to the political protection of the Marquise of la Laguna, Sor Juana renounced Núñez de Miranda as her confessor, as she states in her *Autodefensa espiritual* (Spiritual Self-defense).

In 1688, the Lagunas returned to Spain where they published the many works of Sor Juana as *Inundación castálida* ("Muses' Flood," also known as "Castalian Inundation") the following year. An expanded version was published in 1690. A second collection was published two years later which contained later works that she had sent from Mexico (including the religious play *El cetro de José* [José's Sceptre]); and a third was published after her death.

After her patrons and protectors returned to Spain, Sor Juana continued to write, co-authoring a secular play, *Amor es mas laberinto* (Love, the Greater Labyrinth), which was performed for the new Viceroy in 1689. A religious play, *El divino Narciso* (The Divine Narcissus), was published in Mexico in 1690. Lacking the protection she had previously enjoyed, Sor Juana came under public criticism from the Bishop of Puebla in 1690. A former friend, the Bishop published a letter that Sor Juana had written to him which he entitled *Carta Atenagórica* (Athenagoric Letter) with an introduction under the pseudonym of Sor Filotea in which he urges her to abandon all secular studies and writing so as to concentrate on religious works. Sor Juana responded with what would become one of her better-known works, *Respuesta a Sor Filotea* (The Answer to Sor Filotea), a defense of herself and her studies that critics regard as an early feminist manifesto of the New World.

The last five years of her life have been the subject of as much debate as her birth. Given the constant pressure from the Church and growing social unrest owing to epidemics, food shortages and natural disasters, Sor Juana retreated from public life. An investigation into her conduct was initiated by the Church in 1693. The following year, celebrating the twenty-fifth anniversary of her vows, Sor Juana signed documents with her own blood. Scholars debate whether this can be seen as a conventional act of contrition, or, along with her donation of the majority of her library and scientific instruments for sale to raise money for the suffering, as a rejection of her past life. She died soon after on April 17, 1695, at 44 years of age, along with most of the nuns in her monastery as a result of an epidemic.

Her literary work is primarily poetry, her sonnets prominent for their intellectual expression and irrefutable logic. At least two of Juana's sonnets can be dated before 1669, and other poems may be from her time at court. It is hard to be sure, because in her monastery she continued to write secular poetry in the tradition of the Baroque lyric. Love is one of the themes of her poems that has created much speculation and debate about her personal life among scholars, given the very tender and personal nature of her words.

In 1674, the Manceras left Mexico City, and for the next six years the Archbishop of Mexico would act as viceroy. Her best religious work can be seen in the *villancicos* written in this period for various Mexican cathedrals under ecclesiastic commissions. In these *villancicos*, Sor Juana defends marginal social groups and makes fun of masculine clerical types.

According to Sor Juana, almost everything she wrote was commissioned by someone and the only thing written for her own pleasure was a philosophical poem "El sueño" sometimes published under the title "*Primer sueño*" (The First Dream). This poem is an allegory of several hundred lines in which the soul expresses its passion to acquire knowledge and, in the process, ultimately to find the absolute Truth or God. The poem is a compendium of the scientific thinking of her day and unites the classic world and Renaissance poetic topology, with cult issues and concepts. Octavio Paz, author of the essay *Sor Juana Inés de la Cruz o Las trampas de la fe,* has expressed admiration for this work.

Sor Juana also wrote significant works for the theatre. Among her theatrical works are three *autos sacramentales* (an allegorical play in one act that refers to the Eucharist): *El cetro de José*, based on a story from the Bible, *El mártir del sacramento, San Hermenegildo* (The Martyr of the Sacrament, Saint Hermenegil) based on a hagiography, and *El divino Narciso* based on the Greek myth of Echo and Narcissus. *El divino*

Narciso has received more critical attention than the others. In addition to these three plays which contain elements of the creole society to which Sor Juana belonged, she also composed fifteen others. Her secular theatre is composed of two plays of the type "cloak and dagger" in the tradition of Lope de Vega: *Los empeños de una casa* and *Amor es mas laberinto.* Even though her theatre follows the model of Calderón, subtle differences can be observed in outlook, heritage and inflection, as well as the use of satirical elements that give a critical edge to a talent employed in the service of orthodoxies and hierarchies of power.

In prose, she wrote *Explicación del arco, Razón de la fábrica alegórica y aplicación del fábula* as well as some meditations: *Rosario* (Rosary) and *Encarnación* (Incarnation). Other smaller works and manuscripts known collectively as *El equilibrio moral* (Moral Equilibrium) and one musical treatise *El caracol* (The Snail) are known to have existed but have been lost. Commissioned to design one of two architectural-theatrical triumphal arches to welcome a new viceroy to Mexico, she also wrote a pamphlet explaining the allegorical meaning of her design, which was published as *Neptune alegórica.* Sor Juana presents Neptune allegorically as a model for the new Marquis in an erudite text full of Latin quotations.

Incited by the Bishop of Puebla to criticize a sermon given by a famous theologian of the era, the Portuguese Jesuit Antonio de Vieyra, Sor Juana composed a letter later published as *Carta Atenagórica* (Athenagoric Letter) in 1690. In this letter she refutes the thesis put forth by the Jesuit in which he criticizes the positions of the Saints Augustine, Thomas and John Chrysostom regarding which of Christ's gifts to mankind was greatest, an ongoing theological debate. Sor Juana first summarizes the priest's arguments then, defending the arguments of those he had attacked, refutes his position. Woven into her careful argument in the *Carta Atenagórica,* Sor Juana tries to create a space born from the intersection of diverse conventions (conventual, inquisitorial, of friendship and suspicion) that regulate the thinking in New Spain and the freedom of reason and the intellectual freedom to which she aspires.

The letter was published by the Bishop with his own critical introduction charging Sor Juana with intellectual vanity and scolding her to put her intelligence to better use in the study of religious matters instead of worldly concerns. The Bishop cited her obligation to devote her intelligence exclusively to the service of God and, failing this, her immortal soul could be in danger of condemnation. But she answered in 1691 in her extraordinary *Respuesta a Sor Filotea de la Cruz*, in which she presented her views on the rights of women and their intellectual endeavors. "Not to have written much about matters sacred has not been due to lack of faith," she wrote, "but to great fear and the reverence that is due those sacred writings". She wrote with great pain that her church superiors "have gone so far as to prohibit me from studying". She obeyed, but in her own way. She did not study from books but from "all the things that God created," since there is nothing "that does not focus the mind if it is considered in the proper way". In her answer she cites the example of educated women prior to her time, citing those found in the Bible, classical antiquity, the history of her own era, thereby defending the education of women. Asunción Lavrin, in "Vida conventual: rasgos históricos" (in *Convent Life: Historical Traits*) says that the *Respuesta a Sor Filotea* is a mixture of both challenge and contrition. She concludes: "el cuerpo de la Respuesta es una mezcla de expresión de libre albedrío y de reiteración de obediencia" ("The body of the *Answer* is a mixture of an expression of free will and of a reaffirmation of obedience") (Lavrin, 1995: 56–63). Sor Juana had previously used a similar argument in her *Autodefensa espiritual* (also known as the *Letter of Monterrey*, discovered in 1980) where she complains to her confessor, Núñez de Miranda, who wanted to mold her to his norms of spiritual direction, and informs him that if he does not want to help her, there are other confessors and, lacking this, God will guide her.

Her intellectual capacity was remarkable, given the nature of her education: feverish, reflexive and self-taught. She was persistent in her pursuit of knowledge, which she did through texts and personal observation without the benefit of classrooms, teachers or the collaboration of other students. Her accomplishments would be extraordinary enough at any time but all the more remarkable given the era in which such an education was denied to women. Her fame while alive was immense and the publication of her works in Spain, various editions of three separate volumes from 1689 to 1725, as well as the numerous published debates inspired by her works is sufficient proof of her celebrity. The closing decades of the eighteenth century saw a diminishing of her stature which continued throughout most of the nineteenth century. In the early twentieth century interest in her work grew, given the attention paid to her extraordinary life and works by contemporary authors like Amado Nervo and Pedro Henríquez Ureña among others. Her work was later rediscovered and embraced by a new generation of scholars and intellectuals when Alfonso Méndez Plancarte began to publish her *Obras completas* (Complete Works) in 1951, culminating with the essay *Las trampas de la fe* (The Traps of Faith) by Octavio Paz in 1982. Contemporary scholarship has been advanced by the finding of previously unknown documents carrying the field a considerable distance beyond Paz. Recent scholarly interest in the fields of Gender Studies and Colonial Studies has greatly increased the amount of critical literature published about her life and works. Often regarded as the Americas' first feminist, critics are now reevaluating her works and positions on women's abilities and their right to individuality and independence.

The literary production of Sor Juana can be seen as a rare exception to the stylistic decadence of the seventeenth century. She uses the elaborate excesses of the time to create a space in which to express the concerns of a female intellectual. While religious themes abound in her works, secular themes form the majority of her poetry. Her works not only reflect the Baroque influences of Góngora but, particularly in her theatre, one can see the influence of Pedro Calderón de la Barca and of Agustín Moreto. Within her work can be seen elements, influences and anticipations of the Renaissance, the baroque and of the philosophy of modern science with the overall unifying approach of an Aristotelian scholarship. Her prose, poetry, and drama represent the pinnacle of literary creativity from both the viceregal court and Catholic convents in New Spain whose excellence remained unmatched throughout the entire colonial period.

MARIA R. MATZ AND KEITH WOODALL

Selected Works

Obras completas. Edited by Alfonso Méndez Plancarte. 4 vols. Salceda. México: Fondo de Cultura Económica, 1957.

A Sor Juana Anthology. Edited by Alan S. Trueblood. Cambridge, MA: Harvard University Press, 1988.

Poesía lírica. Edited with an Introduction and Notes by José Carlos González Boixo. Madrid: Cátedra, 1992.

Sor Juana Inés de la Cruz. The Answer/La Respuesta. Including a Selection of Poems. Critical ed. and trans. Electa Arenal and Amanda Powell. New York: Feminist Press, 1994.

Fama y obras póstumas. Introduction by Antonio Alatorre. México: Facultad de Filosofía y Letras, UNAM, 1995.

Inundación Castálida. Edited by Gabriela Eguia-Lis Ponde. México: México: Facultad de Filosofía y Letras, UNAM, 1995.

Segundo tomo de las obras de Sor Juana Inés de la Cruz. Edited by Fredo Arias de la Canal. México: Frente de Afirmación Hispanista, 1995.

Poems, Protest, and a Dream: Selected Writings. Edited by Margaret Sayers Peden and Ilan Stavans. New York: Penguin Books, 1997.

"*The Sor Juana Inés de la Cruz Project*": http://www.dartmouth.edu/~sorjuana/

References and Further Reading

Arenal, Electa and Schlau, Stacey (eds). *Untold Sisters: Hispanic Nuns in their Own Works.* Trans. Amanda Powell. Albuquerque, NM: University of New Mexico Press, 1989.

——. "Sor Juana Inés de la Cruz: Speaking the Mother Tongue". *University of Dayton Review* 16(2) (1983): 93–105.

Careaga, Delfina and Gutiérrez, Antonio Cardoso. *Sor Juana Inés de la Cruz: tres siglos de inmortalidad, 1695–1995.* Toluca, México: Instituto Mexiquense de Cultura, 1995.

Flynn, Gerard. *Sor Juana Inés de la Cruz.* New York: Twayne, 1971.

Franco, Jean. *Plotting Women.* New York: Columbia University, 1989.

Glantz, Margo (ed.). *Sor Juana Inés de la Cruz y sus contemporáneos.* Mexico: Facultad de Filosofía y Letras, UNAM; Centro de Estudios de Historia de México, CONDUMEX, 1998.

——. *La destrucción del cuerpo y la edificación del sermón: La razón de la fábrica: Un ensayo de aproximación al mundo de Sor Juana.* México: Colegio de México, 1995.

Jurado, Alicia. "Sor Juana Inés de la Cruz". *Boletín de la Academia Argentina de Letras* 1995.

Kirk, Pamela. *Sor Juana Inés de la Cruz: Religion, Art and Feminism.* New York: Continuum, 1998.

Lavrín, Asunción. "Vida conventual: rasgos históricos". In Sara Poot Herrera (ed.), *Sor Juana y su mundo.* México: Universidad del Claustro de Sor Juana, 1995, pp. 33–91.

Merrim, Stephanie (ed.) *Feminist Perspectives on Sor Juana Inés de la Cruz.* Detroit, MI: Wayne State University Press, 1991.

Miller, Beth (ed.). *Women in Hispanic Literature: Icons and Fallen Idols.* Berkeley, CA: University of California Press, 1989.

Paz, Octavio. *Sor Juana or, The Traps of Faith.* Trans. Margaret Sayers Peden. Cambridge, MA: Harvard University Press, 1988.

Salazar, Norma. *Foolish Men! Sor Juana Inés de la Cruz as Spiritual Protagonist, Educational Prism, and Symbol for Women.* DeKalb, IL: LEPS Press, Northern Illinois University, 1994.

Sayers Peden, Margaret. *A Woman of Genius: The Intellectual Autobiography of Sor Juana Inés de la Cruz.* Salisbury: Lime Rock Press, 1982.

Schmidhuber, Guillermo (ed.) *The Three Secular Plays of Sor Juana Inés de la Cruz: A Critical Study.* Trans. Shelby G. Thacker. In collaboration with Martha Peña Doria. Lexington, KY: University Press of Kentucky, 2000.

CUNHA, HELENA GOMES PARENTE

Helena Parente Cunha (1930), contemporary Brazilian novelist, short-story writer, poet and academic, is a native of Salvador in the Northeastern state of Bahia, an environment which has appeared in various guises in her work, and where she spent her early years and completed her primary education. She returned to her native city in order to study for her bachelor's degree in Neo-Latin Literatures which she completed in 1952, and, after obtaining a further qualification from the University of Perugia in Italy, began her long and distinguished career as an academic and educator with a position as tutor in Italian and French at the Federal University of Bahia. Parente Cunha moved to Rio de Janeiro on her marriage in 1958, where she has continued to reside and work. She also began to publish poetry, essays and literary translations. In 1968 she accepted a position as Professor of Literary Theory at the Federal University of Rio de Janeiro, which she held until formal retirement. She continues to write, publish and participate in academic life.

Themes and Influences

Although Helena Parente Cunha began her literary career in the 1960s as a poet and essayist, it was not until the end of the 1970s that she began to write and publish the fiction which brought her much critical acclaim and international attention. While all of her work, whether poetry or prose, is characterised by a high degree of formal and theoretical experimentation and linguistic innovation, the content itself is highly relevant and contemporary, depicting the lives, personal experiences and emotions of individuals – chiefly women – and their often problematic position within a patriarchal society which imposes rigid and authoritarian rules and norms of behaviour. This central theme has evolved and developed throughout each of Parente Cunha's publications. Her first collection of poems, *Corpo no Cerco* (Body under Siege), published in 1978, and her subsequent collections, treat questions on the nature of existence, human identity and personal relationships, but the formal structures of the works themselves develop the methods established by the Brazilian concretist and visual poetry movements, in which meaning is isomorphic with form: typographical experiments, semantic and spatial arrangements of words on the page dissolve into each other, mutate and acquire new meanings within a progressive sequence. The same is true of Parente Cunha's collections of short stories, which, in common with her other writings, transgress the formal limits of the genre. *Os Provisórios* (The Impermanents), published in 1980, and *Cem Mentiras de Verdade* (1985, One Hundred Truthful Lies) consist of very short, minimalist micro-narratives in which, once again, the reader's attention is focused on the visual and semantic properties of the word itself, and meaning and sequence of thought is generated by geometrical arrangements of lines and columns on the page.

In 1983, Helena Parente Cunha published her first long work of fiction, *Mulher no Espelho* (translated in the English version as *Woman Between Mirrors*) which brought her wider attention from the national Brazilian reading public, and international critical recognition. The protagonist of *Mulher no*

Espelho is a woman who must rebuild her life after many years of enduring a difficult family situation caused by an authoritarian and oppressive father and an equally difficult marriage. The anonymous heroine draws on her inner reserves of imagination, insight and creativity to reinvent herself and come to terms with her situation. As in all Parente Cunha's works, the novel features many formal innovations, the most striking of these being the introduction of three narrative voices: the actual author of the work, a first-person narrator who recounts her story from her own hard-won personal experience, and a second narrator, a sophisticated Westernised author and critic, 'the woman who writes me', who analyses the heroine's position as a case study of the oppression of woman in patriarchal society. The narrative oscillates in a process of dynamic evolution and exchange between these two voices until the two perspectives represented by the narrators – the need to reconcile first-hand experience of life with more analytical insights into the nature and context of woman's position in society – are finally reconciled. Thus the novel, in common with so much contemporary Brazilian writing, also illustrates a preoccupation with metafiction, the authentic – or otherwise – representation of reality and the nature of writing itself. These concerns are developed still further in Parente Cunha's subsequent work of prose fiction, *As doze cores do vermelho* (1989, The Twelve Colours of Red), which defies classification as a novel: the protagonist is a woman artist, again striving to create and express herself, but from a fundamental state of confrontation and conflict with patriarchal structures and norms of society. Once again, the story is told within a formal structure of great narrative complexity: an interplay of voices and perspectives, suggesting the multidimensional nature of human identity, linked also to rich visual symbolism and multilayered and multifaceted imagery.

Critical Interpretations

As the author's Brazilian peers and colleagues and international critics have invariably commented, Parente Cunha's work is self-consciously and explicitly informed and underpinned by concerns of a theoretical and academic nature concerning the nature of literary representation; indeed, Carmen Chaves Tesser reads *Mulher no Espelho* as a specific response to French theorists and the post-structuralist movement in general, commenting that the experience of reading *Woman Between Mirrors* bears some resemblance to attending a literary theory class. Yet the author herself, in an interview published in 2002, and in other interviews also, has identified herself and her work as belonging to the contemporary generation of women authors in Brazil who seek to address social and psychological problems of deep-rooted alienation, self-identity, or never-expressed identity, and strive towards the authentic expression of emotions, desires and needs within a fundamentally patriarchal society which imposes clearly delineated social roles. The social purpose of Parente Cunha's writing has become ever more evident in both her last novel published in 2002, *Claras manhãs de Barra Clara* (Clear Mornings of Barra Clara) which treats themes of solidarity and the need to build an alternative society based on communal love, and the work *A casa e as casas* (1996, The House and the Houses), which, as the title suggests, depicts the house as a multivalent symbol of women's lives, existence and language. Parente Cunha's solidarity with fellow women authors is further reinforced and complemented by her published academic studies of women's and other literature, sometimes written in collaboration with other colleagues. Thus, according to other commentators such as Laura Beard and Naomi Lindstrom, the formal and theoretical concerns which are so evident in Parente Cunha's work must be seen in the context of these fundamental aims: it is also important to challenge power structures on a linguistic level, to strive constantly for new narrative and poetic models adequate to express social and individual conflicts, disrupting in the process chronological time and linear narrative. The fundamental aim of the author is to develop multivocal and multifaceted perspectives which transgress the traditional boundaries of linguistic expression and literary genre, and thus challenge the traditional authority of master narratives produced by the omniscient author. Helena Parente Cunha's crowning achievement, then, is her tireless and always pioneering contribution to the present situation of women's writing as the most relevant, contemporary and linguistically innovative in Brazil today.

MARGARET ANNE CLARKE

Selected Works

Corpo no Cerco. Rio de Janeiro: Tempo Brasileiro, 1968.
Os provisórios. Rio de Janeiro: Antares, 1980.
Maramar. Rio de Janeiro: Tempo Brasileiro, 1980.
Mulher no espelho. Florianópolis: Fundação Catarinense de Cultura, 1983.
Cem mentiras de verdade. Rio de Janeiro: José Olympio, 1985.
As doze cores do vermelho. Rio de Janeiro: Espaço e Tempo e Editora da Universidade Federal do Rio de Janeiro, 1989.
A casa e as casas. Rio de Janeiro: Tempo Brasileiro, 1996.
Vento Ventania Vendaval. Rio de Janeiro: Tempo Brasileiro, 1998.
Desafiando o cânone: aspectos da literatura de autoria feminina na prosa e poesia (anos). Rio de Janeiro: Tempo Brasileiro, 1999.
Além de estar. Antologia Poética. Rio de Janeiro/ Salvador: Imago/ Fundação da Bahia, 2000.
Claras Manhãs de Barra Clara. Rio de Janeiro: Mondrian, 2002.
Cantos e cantares. Rio de Janeiro: Tempo Brasileiro, 2005.

References and Further Reading

Beard, Laura J. "The Mirrored Self: Helena Parente Cunha's *Mulher no Espelho*". *College Literature* February (1995).
Campbell, Elizabeth. "Re-visions, Re-flections, Re-creations: Epistolarity in Novels by Contemporary Women". *Twentieth-Century Literature* 41 (1995).
Coelsch-Foisner, Sabine, Wallinger, Hanna and Reisner, Gerhild (eds) *Daughters of Restlessness: Women's Literature at the End of the Millennium*. Heidelberg: Universitätsverlag C. Winter, 1998.
Franco, Jean and Szoka, Elzbieta (eds) "Interview with Helena Parente Cunha". In *Fourteen Female Voices from Brazil: Interviews and Works*. Austin, TX: Host Publications, 2002, pp. 40–50.
Godsland, Shelley. *Writing Reflection, Reflecting on Writing. Female Identity and Lacan's Mirror in Helena Parente Cunha and Sylvia Molloy*. Valladolid, Mexico: Universitas Castellae, 2006.
Hardin, Michael. "Dissolving the Reader/Author Binary: Sylvia Molloy's *Certificate of Absence*, Helena Parente Cunha's *Woman Between Mirrors*, and Jeanette Winterson's *Written on the Body*". *International Fiction Review* 29 (2002).
Lindstrom, Naomi. "Narrative Experiment and Social Statement: Helena Parente Cunha". *Luso-Brazilian Review* 33(1) (1996): 141–50

Parsons, Nívea Pereira. "Discussion of and Interview Answers from Parente Cunha. Escritos de mulheres: Nívea Pereira Parsons entrevista escritoras brasileiras". *Hispania* 71(2) (1988): 347–8.

Tesser, Carmen Chaves. "Post-structuralist Theory Mirrored in Helena Parente Cunha's *Woman Between Mirrors*". *Hispania* 74(3) (September 1991): 594–7.

Valente, Luis Fernando. "Review of *Woman Between Mirrors*. Trans. Fred P. Ellison and Naomi Lindstrom. Austin, TX: University of Texas Press, 1989". *Hispania* 74(3) (September 1991): 697–8.

CUZA MALÉ, BELKIS

Belkis Cuza Malé was born 1942 in Guantánamo, Cuba. She moved to Santiago de Cuba at the age of 12 and later studied Humanities at the Universidad de Oriente. From 1964 to 1979, Cuza Malé lived in Havana where, at one time, she was Director of the Office of External Relations and Literature and Publications of the Provincial del C.N.C. in the province of Oriente. She served as editor of the Cultural Section of *Granma*, the official newspaper of the Cuban Communist Party, from 1966 to 1968 and, also, of *La Gaceta de Cuba*, published by the Unión de Escritores y Artistas de Cuba-UNEAC (Cuban Artists and Writers Union). Her poetry won honorable mentions from La Casa de las Américas literary group (1962, 1963, 1970) and from UNEAC (1968). Cuza Malé married Cuban poet Heberto Padilla in 1967. Though initially a supporter of the Castro Revolution, Cuza Malé later became a critic of his regime, causing her and her husband's lives to come under official scrutiny. She was jailed for over a month in 1971 charged with what the Cuban government defined as "subversive writing". After that, Cuza Malé and Padilla were closely watched and were not allowed to publish their poems in Cuba. She went into exile in the United States with her husband in 1971, where she continued to write poetry, fiction and also published the life stories of Juana Borrero, Elvis, and Selena. Cuza Malé founded *Linden Lane Magazine*, a review of Latin American and North American writers in 1982, and has served since then as its director. She has contributed numerous articles to newspapers and journals in Argentina, France, Mexico and Spain.

Poet

Belkis Cuza Malé's poetry is distinguished by powerful images resulting from a synthesis of alternating interior and external realms. In her poems, the reader is drawn into an ambience of absurdity and existentialist asphyxia, in which signs of childhood surface continuously, relaying abandonment and sadness. However, later in her work, an affirmation of existence emerges (along with a declaration of authenticity, of justice, of independence and poetic personality) from within herself that opposes exterior social conformations. To reconcile these two realities, Cuza Malé uses a language composed of irrational images from surrealism that facilitate new dimensions of perception. An array of representations, existing only in the poet's imagination, converges into a unified impression, which is then conveyed to the readers, producing an evocative simultaneity. This recourse promotes a confrontation with conventionality, with lack of creativity, and with the negativity of life. At the same time, it originates a metamorphosis of daily occurrences to stylistically enhance her strangeness from life.

In her collection, *El viento en la pared* (The Wind on the Wall), Cuza Malé immerses herself in silence and solitude to recreate the turmoil of an unfair children's world, characterized by affliction and alienation. Ingenuity, innocence and love for animals contrast with the hardened reality of the adult. From the perspective of her childhood in which her poetic vocation was born, the poet initiates a search for truth that leads her, occasionally, to an existential nihilism and to the experience of fatigue and vertigo in the face of passing time. The dynamic between the sun, a fundamental symbol in her early collections, and the darkness of night, determines her quest for personal identity, her yearning for liberty, and her acceptance of life's anguish as a necessary component in the creative process.

Tiempos de sol (Times of Sun) relapses into the same agonizing tone of her former collection although, in certain moments, the sun and the hope shine. Cuza Malé's radical sadness is depicted through themes that include a sometimes welcome death, destruction, the intent to preserve the innocence of childhood, and the denunciation of children's hunger and misery. She also finds in Nature the realm opposite from war and advocates the need for global peace. This idea reflects the human race's power to reconcile the material and the immaterial in a threatening world. The poet calls for action and sings an anthem to construct a new future overcoming the instinct for violence: "Upwards! Let's sing, let's sing: / We will have the expansion of the bird / to beat time in this game. / Today everything exists . . . and tomorrow".

Cartas a Ana Frank (Letters to Anne Frank) enters again into the children's world but now tragically individualized in the figure of Anne Frank (1929–45), the Dutch Jewish girl who kept a diary during the Second World War until she died in a concentration camp. The first poem, dated June 12, 1962, the day on which Anne Frank would have turned 33, represents the death of children and of the innocent by a totalitarian system. Memory becomes actuality to universally denounce violence, the stigmatization of beliefs and ideas, the suppression of freedom, the suffering, and the subsequent death of victims. In Cuza Malé's voice, Anne Frank warns against the consequences of war, criticizes the passivity of those alive who do not fight for their liberty, and questions the destiny of the human being involved in hostilities for centuries. Anne, finally, becomes the dramatic representation of all those who died in concentration camps. Throughout the book, an emotional identification between Anne Frank and Belkis Cuza Malé is achieved, asserting the eternity of childhood: "During seven centuries, I was Anne Frank / and today, I continue to be / despite being afraid of the dentist / my name being belkis / and my obsession for collecting crows. / The strange thing is not the tree but rather its roots / not the death but rather the life / not the eyes but rather the silence / not Anne Frank but rather me".

Woman in the Front Lines, which includes the books *Game Pieces* and *The Patio at my House*, was published when Cuza Malé was in exile. The female is the unquestionable protagonist of poems in which, with the background of a mordant irony, the vindication of a real woman is declared. The poet evidences her opposition to the prevailing patriarchal influences on society, which have contributed to the implementation of traditional canons defining female beauty in contests, the suppression of feminine instincts and coerced passivity, the stereotyped and unnatural demands on the modern woman, and the absence of women from recorded history. The feminist voice of the poet questions with irony the traditional conceptualization of God and how patriarchy has impacted women in "The Piety of Teresa de Cepeda": "God is everywhere, / her master, / her advocate, / her husband, / her son, / her lover, / her amulet . . . All women belong to God, / but He belongs to none of them". Absent from this world, Saint Teresa's desire to believe hovers over "the rest of us, / poor country girls, / whose work is in the home, / who're visited from time to time by the Devil, / and left among dry leaves / falling from the shadows of the trees". In other poems, Cuza Malé's solidarity with the humble and silenced is combined with the painful memory of Cuba and of those in exile who are trying to overcome the anxiety over loss of their homeland and isolation from cultural roots and families while struggling to find their destiny in a new country. The exiled search inwardly for refuge, unfolding memories which will bring sense to a sometimes chaotic world. All of these themes lead to a reflection about the creative activity that allows the poet "sometimes to catch a glimpse / of a real landscape". For Pamela Carmell, the codes, allegories and fables in Cuza Malé's poetry are a kaleidoscope of angles and perspectives, of images which are "cryptic, those half-formed of dreams or of something seen out of the corner of one's eye".

FRANCISCO J. PEÑAS-BERMEJO

Selected Works

El viento en la pared. Poemas. Oriente: Universidad de Oriente, 1962.

Los alucinados. Santiago de Cuba, 1963.

Tiempos de sol. La Habana: Ediciones El Puente, 1963.

Cartas a Ana Frank. La Habana: Ediciones Unión, 1966.

El clavel y la rosa: biografía de Juana Borrero. Madrid: Ediciones Cultura Hispánica, 1984.

Woman on the Front Lines. Includes *Juego de damas* and *El patio de mi casa*. Trans. Pamela Carmell. Greensboro, NC: Unicorn Press, Inc., 1987.

Elvis: la tumba sin sosiego (Elvis: The Unquiet Grave). Miami Lakes, FL: E. Press, 1994.

En busca de Selena. (*In Search of Selena*.) Ft. Worth, TX: E. Press, 1995.

References and Further Reading

Agosín, Marjorie and Franzen, Cola. *The Renewal of the Vision: Voices of Latin American Women Poets, 1940–1980*. Peterborough: Spectacular Diseases, 1987.

Anhalt, Nedda G. de and Mendiola, Víctor (eds) *La fiesta innombrable: trece poetas cubanos*. México: Ed. El Tucán de Virginia, 1992, pp. 145–50.

Cardenal, Ernesto (ed.) *Poesía cubana de la Revolución*. México: Extemporáneos, 1976.

Carmell, Pamela. "Belkis Cuza Malé: Translating an Exile". Thesis, Fayetteville, AR, University of Arkansas, 1984.

Collmann, Lilliam O. "*Juego de damas* de Belkis Cuza Malé: El otro caso Padilla". *La Torre* 9(34) (Apr.–June 1995): 313–27.

Cuza Malé, Belkis. "Lo que no se ha dicho". In Pedro R. Monge Rafuls (ed.), *Poesía y exilio. Essays Commissioned by Ollantay Center for the Arts*. Jackson Heights, NY: Ollantay, 1994, pp. 194–8.

Hoz, León de la (ed.) *La poesía de las dos orillas. Cuba (1959–1993)*. Selección y prólogo de León de la Hoz. Madrid: Libertarias/Prodhufi, 1994.

Lázaro, Felipe (ed.) *Poesía cubana contemporánea*. Madrid: Catoblepas, 1986.

Levine, Linda G. and Waldman, Gloria F. "No más máscaras: un diálogo entre tres escritoras del Caribe: Belkis Cuza Malé–Cuba, Matilde Daviu–Venezuela, Rosario Ferre–Puerto Rico". In *Literatures in Transition: The Many Voices of the Caribbean Area: A Symposium, Gaithersburg, MD*. Upper Montclair, NJ: Hispamérica, 1982, pp. 189–97.

Martínez Sobrino, Mario. *Cuatro leguas a La Habana*. La Habana: UNEAC, 1978.

Peñas-Bermejo, Francisco J. "Belkis Cuza Malé". *Poetas cubanos marginados*. El Ferrol: S.C.V-I, 1998: 29–30, 191–212.

Robinson, Marc (ed.) *Altogether Elsewhere: Writers on Exile*. Winchester, MA: Faber and Faber, 1994.

D

DÁVILA, AMPARO

Amparo Dávila (b. 1928) is best known for her short stories that range from familiar spooky tales to the experimental. Autobiographical writing and interviews reveal Amparo Dávila's lonely, sickly childhood in the somber town of Pinos, Zacatecas. Her relatively wealthy family kept her interest in books though her father discouraged Dávila from a literary career. In defiance of that skepticism, Dávila published three slim volumes of poetry in San Luis Potosí and in 1954 moved with her mother to Mexico City. In the national capital, Dávila worked as Alfonso Reyes's secretary, and Reyes encouraged her talent as a short story writer. In 1958, Dávila married the painter Pedro Coronel, gave birth to two girls, and divorced in 1964. Over her brief writing career, Dávila produced three collections of short stories. In 1977, her last book, *Árboles petrificados* (1977, Petrified Trees) won the Xavier Villaurrutia prize. Another claim to inner-circle status for Dávila is her exchange of letters with Julio Cortázar, who admired her work for its similarity to Edgar Allen Poe's stories, which Dávila had not read at the time. In 1978, Dávila's two previous volumes of short stories, *Tiempo destrozado* (1959, Destroyed Time) and *Música concreta* (1964, Concrete Music), were published together as *Muerte en el bosque* (1985, Death in the Woods).

Circular Criticism

Criticism of Dávila's work often reviews the writer's biography and plots. The tendency to rehash the plots in lieu of analyzing them may relate to the relative dearth of Mexican fantastic literature and the consequent assumption of the reader's ignorance of Dávila's work. In fact, during the 1980s, Dávila disappeared from Mexico's literary scene. Around 1989, Mexican and US criticism rediscovered Dávila's writing, and today her short stories figure prominently in anthologies. In 1998, Mexican writers paid homage to Dávila in Mexico City's Fine Arts Palace. This tribute called for new editions of Dávila's out-of-print prose. Still, criticism has not achieved much of interest regarding Dávila. Some exceptions to the criticism based on plot summaries are the articles by Erica Frouman-Smith, who reads Dávila's stories by way of the analysis of English-language literature in Gilbert and Gubar's *The Madwoman in the Attic*. Susan A. Montero examines Dávila's stories through the notion of the "alter": alteration, alternative, altercation, and alternate. Montero explores the notion of marginality in Dávila's texts by noting that these elements affect a variety of characters, independent of sex, age, ethnicity, and class. Cristina Rivera Garza's novel *La cresta de Ilión* (2002, The Iliac Crest) has also made significant progress toward Dávila's resuscitation. Rivera Garza's novel excerpts quotations from Dávila's short stories and writes Dávila into the plot as a character split among many bodies though suffering from her condition as "disappeared". Rivera Garza's innovative dialogue with Dávila indicates the latter's continued relevance and points to an alternative form of engaging in literary criticism.

Narrative Haunts

In Dávila's description, her fundamental themes are love, death, and insanity. The latter thematic complements Dávila's narrative tendency to defy reason: from story to story, a character might see his or her double, a character might remember his origin as a tree, or enigmatic monsters such as "Oscar" and "Moisés and Gaspar" in their eponymous stories might terrorize caregivers. Dávila often resorts to imprecise language to create a sense of dread. In "El húesped" (The Guest) and "La celda" (The Cell), a mysterious figure named *"él"* (he) threatens the protagonists. In "Señorita Julia" (Miss Julia) and "Alta cocina" (Haute Cuisine), the mysterious *"ellos"* (they) perturb characters. The vague language coincides with lightning flashes and creaking furniture typical of the horror genre. Clearly, Dávila's settings sometimes make use of gothic details, especially in stories that express physical enclosure, sexual repression, and the uncanny.

Dávila also portrays scenes from tedious daily life—a monotony not necessarily linked to just Mexico. Other cosmopolitan elements include the US-related themes that sometimes weave through Dávila's texts, such as "Arthur Smith" and "El pabellón del descanso" (The Rest Ward). Other texts focus on particular Mexican contexts: for example, "El desayuno" (The Breakfast), composes Dávila's most political story and deals with the Mexican student uprisings in the late

1960s. The tale describes one young woman's uncanny prescience of violence. Characters' despair over their daily twentieth-century tedium and their inability to realize authentic communication with others recall existential themes. Besides the blend of gothic and existential topics, the recourse to psychoanalysis—especially the notion of the subconscious, seems to inform Dávila's studies of troubled relationships among families. The existential and psychoanalytical themes perhaps explain Dávila's fondness for employing male protagonists. As regards gender, Dávila treats despair as an equal opportunity thematic. However, Dávila does distinguish between sexes in her preference for showing female characters' inner torment through details about untidy physical appearance and careworn, aging faces.

Though Dávila often recurs to traditional short story structures that leave the surprise to the final plot twist, she is not afraid to experiment. With "El Patio cuadrado" (Square Patio), Dávila incorporates poetic technique by omitting logical connections from the consequently unrelated fragments of the story. Indeed, from her experience as a poet, Dávila seems to have recognized the effectiveness of leaving the most important ideas unwritten, requiring the reader to fill in absent explanations, transitions, and descriptions. This flexibility allows Dávila to rework a given concept in surprising maneuvers that point out the possibly arbitrary nature of plotted narrative. In a fragment from "El Patio cuadrado" and in the story "Final de una lucha" (End of the Struggle), the double supplies a source of terror for the character, while in "El espejo" (The Mirror), the *absence* of a double in the mirror image terrorizes viewers. In "El Pabellón del descanso" the protagonist intends to commit suicide rather than leave an asylum, while in "Detrás de la reja" (Behind the Bar) the protagonist finds to her horror that she has been unjustly committed to an asylum. Dávila may continue to publish and stimulate renewed critical attention, as anticipated in a comment that she offers a Mexican newspaper in July 2005, that claims the existence of a manuscript of stories, *Con los ojos abiertos* (With Eyes Open). In terms of future directions for criticism, it is interesting to note that while critics often detect political themes in Dávila's friend Julio Cortázar's short stories, such as the eerie "Casa tomada" (House Taken Over), Dávila's stories do not often receive politically motivated readings.

EMILY HIND

Selected Works

Salmos bajo la luna. San Luis Potosí, México: Estilo, 1950.
Meditaciones a la orilla del sueño. San Luis Potosí, México: El Troquel, 1954.
Perfil de soledades. San Luis Potosí, México: El Troquel, 1954.
Tiempo destrozado. México: Fondo de Cultura Económica, 1959.
Música concreta. México: Fondo de Cultura Económica, 1964.
Árboles petrificados. México: Joaquín Mortiz, 1977.
Muerte en el bosque. México: Fondo de Cultura Económica, 1985.

Autobiographical Essay

"Amparo Dávila". *Los narradores ante el público*. México: Joaquín Mortiz, 1966, pp. 129–34.

Translations

"Haute Cuisine". In Alberto Manguel (ed.), *Other Fires: Short Fiction by Latin American Women*. New York: Clarkson Potter, 1986, pp. 122–4.

"The Guest," "Tina Reyes," "Concrete Music," "Oscar," "Petrified Trees". Trans. Jennifer Elaine Hammond-Fernández. Master's thesis. Arizona State University, 1988, pp. 56–123.

"The End of a Struggle". In Celia Correas de Zapata (ed.), *Short Stories by Latin American Women: The Magic and the Real*. Houston, TX: Arte Público Press, 1990, pp. 52–5.

References and Further Reading

Cardoso Nelky, Regina. "Amparo Dávila y Juan José Arreola: Alternativas a la realidad." In Maricruz Castro, Laura Cázares and Gloria Prado (eds), *Escrituras en contraste: Femenino/masculino en la literatura mexicana del siglo XX*. México: Aldus and UAM, 2004, pp. 109–29.

Frouman-Smith, Erica. "Entrevista con Amparo Dávila". *Chasqui* 18(2) (1989a): 56–63.

——. "Patterns of Female Entrapment and Escape in Three Short Stories by Amparo Dávila." *Chasqui* 18(2) (1989b): 49–55.

Montero, Susan A. "La periferia que se multiplica". In Aralia López González (ed.), *Sin imágenes falsas, sin falsos espejos: Narradoras mexicanas del siglo XX*. México: Colegio de México, 1995, pp. 285–96.

Oyarzun, Kemy. "Beyond Hysteria: 'Haute cuisine' and 'Cooking Lesson' Writing as Production". In Lucía Guerra Cunningham (ed.), *Splintering Darkness: Latin American Women Writers in Search of Themselves*. Pittsburgh, PA: Latin American Literary Review Press, 1990, pp. 87–110.

DEL RÍO, MARCELA

Marcela del Río (b. 1932) poet, playwright and novelist is a versatile and prolific writer. To date, she has produced three novels, two volumes of poetry, eight plays (five of them published) and a number of essays in which she engages contemporary issues, employing a variety of techniques to portray Mexican society. Del Río's work is deeply rooted in México and embodies the country's cultural and historical preoccupations.

Marcela del Río was born in México City, on May 20, 1932. Her father, mother and brothers were all writers and her great uncle was the renowned humanist Alfonso Reyes, who became her first literary critic. Del Río studied Language and Hispanic Literature at the National Autonomous University of México, and Dramatic Art at the Academy of Cinematography in México, which led to a nearly ten-year career as a theater and television actress.

Invited to participate in a theater Festival in Moscow in 1957, she wrote a monologue entitled *Fraude a la tierra* (The Defrauded Land). It was then that del Rio discovered that her true vocation was writing. She worked as a drama critic for the newspaper *Excelsior* from 1959 to 1968, and wrote under the pseudonym Mara Reyes. Del Río also wrote original scripts and adaptations for Mexican television and has taught drama classes at the Cultural Institute and at the National Institute of Fine Arts.

In 1972, she entered the diplomatic corps as the Mexican cultural attaché to Czechoslovakia, a post that she filled until 1977. From 1980 to 1983, she served as the cultural attaché to the Mexican Embassy in Belgium, and it was during this period that she wrote several of her novels and plays.

In 1988, after obtaining a B.A. in Hispanic Language and Literature from the National Autonomous University of

México, she moved to Irvine, California, to continue her studies at the University of California. Her doctoral dissertation *Perfil y muestra del teatro de la Revolución Mexicana* (Overview and Selected Works of the Theater of the Mexican Revolution) was later published in México by Fondo de Cultura Económica. In 1990, she accepted a position to teach Latin American Literature in the Spanish Department at the University of Central Florida. Del Río has dedicated much of her career to teaching literature and conducting workshops in theatre and creative writing.

Novels

In her works, del Río focuses on the lives of women and explores themes of love, identity and solitude. Her fiction is a profound inquiry into human relationships. She began her literary career with *Proceso a Faubritten* (1976, Trial to Faubritten), a science fiction work which was published with a prologue by Ray Bradbury. The novel narrates the story of a scientist, Dr. Faubritten who invents a bomb that makes everyone immortal. The narrative begins in the sixteenth century, and continues to recount the true horrors of Hitler's Germany and ends in an imagined future where no one dies and where the overpopulated earth and the endless aging create numerous practical problems. In the course of describing past, present and inconceivable future events, del Río poses many philosophical, social and religious questions employing a complex structure, various narrative voices, and creative language.

Del Río's second novel, *La cripta del espejo* (1988, The Crypt in the Mirror) is the story of a Mexican family residing in Czechoslovakia, following the father's appointment as ambassador there. The novel is presented by three narrative voices, the first of which narrates events related to embassy life, the diplomatic and political world of Prague, and includes the interior monologue of the ambassador. The second voice belongs to the ambassador's son, an idealistic young man who secretly joins the Communist Party, and is confronted with a new reality in Prague. The third voice is that of the maid who has been uprooted and moved to Czechoslovakia and has difficulties adjusting to her new environment. The novel, narrated chronologically, begins when the father is appointed ambassador and ends when the family returns to México five years later.

Most recently, *La utopía de María* (2003, María's Utopia), a "bionovel," according to the subtitle, narrates the life of María Vélez Marrón, a talented painter, pianist and writer of newspaper articles, that defends women's role in society. The novel recreates the social and cultural life in México from the end of the nineteenth century through World War II and up to the presidency of Ávila Camacho (1940–46), emphasizing the impact that the protagonist's grandfather General Vélez's tragic death had upon her life as well as that of her family. Del Río inter-weaves María's diary with letters, photographs, newspaper articles, drawings, paintings and official family documents in order to portray Mexican society and reveal the protagonist's struggle to survive in a patriarchal society.

Theatre

Although she has proved herself as a novelist and has been recognized for her achievements in poetry, del Río is chiefly known for her work in the theatre, notably for her imaginative use of the fantastic and her depiction of historical characters and ordinary individuals trapped by their circumstance.

El pulpo (1970, The Octopus), her first documentary drama, dramatizes John F. Kennedy's life between January 20, 1961 and November 22, 1963. Divided into three acts, it includes flashbacks to the past as well as events that occurred after his assassination. *El pulpo* begins on Kennedy's inauguration day, quoting memorable phrases from his inaugural speech, and goes on to portray national conflicts with labor and industrial leaders and the military in the United States, as well as his highly publicized confrontation with Nikita Kruschchev, and the failed invasion of Cuba at the Bay of Pigs.

Entre hermanos (1972, Between Brothers), which premiered in 1974 at the Second International Cervantine Festival in Guanajuato, again deals with an historical figure. The author presents three key moments in the life of the Mexican president Benito Juárez: his ascendancy to the presidency, the signing of the Treaty McLane-Ocampo, and Juárez's refusal to forgive Emperor Maximilian, thereby eliminating a future threat to México.

De camino al concierto, (1984, On the Way to the Concert) dramatizes the last moments of the life of a violinist who was killed in a car accident on the way to a concert. In this story of a man who deeply loves his wife and his music, the writer uses expressionistic, magical realist and erotic techniques to capture the protagonist's obsession with life and music. The play is a tribute to del Río's husband Hermilo, one of Mexico's premier violinists.

Marcela del Río, a distinguished and talented writer, has received many awards for her works. In 1968, she was awarded the International Poetry Contest Award for her book *Thirteen Skies,* as well as an honorary mention in the León Felipe contest. *El pulpo* (The Octopus) received the National Prize Juan Ruiz de Alarcón, from the Mexican Theater Society of Critics, and in 1991, del Río was awarded the Prize *Letras de Oro* for a book of poems *Homenaje a Remedios Varo* inspired by the well-known Spanish painter, Remedios Varo. Presently she resides in México and continues to write.

NORA ERRO-PERALTA

Selected Works

Narrative

Cuentos arcaicos para el año 3000. Monterrey, México: Sierra Madre, 1972.
Proceso a Faubritten. México: Aguilar, 1976.
La cripta del espejo. México: Joaquín Mortiz, 1988.
La utopía de María. México: Fondo de Cultura Económica, 2003.

Poetry

Trece cielos, poemas. México: Unión Internacional de Escritoras, 1982.
Homenaje a Remedios Varo. Coral Gables, FL: Iberian Institute, 1993.

Theatre: Published Plays

Fraude a la tierra. México: n.p., 1957.
El pulpo. México: Aguilar, 1971.
Opus nueve. México: UNAM, 1978.
De camino al concierto. México: Universidad Autónoma Metropolitana-Xochimilco, 1986.
Tlacaélel, México, 1988.

Theatre: Plays Performed

Miralina. México City, 1965.
El pulpo. México City, 1970.

Entre hermanos. México City, 1974.
De camino al concierto. México City, 1985.
Una flor para tu sueño: Felipe Carrillo Puerto. Mérida, Yucatán, México, 2000.

Criticism

Perfil y muestra del teatro de la Revolución Mexicana. México: Fondo de Cultura Económica, 1997.

References and Further Reading

Arancibia, Juana A. "Entrevista con Marcela del Río". *Alba de América: Revista Literaria* 9(16–17) (1991): 395–401.
Correas de Zapata, Celia. "La violencia en *Miralina* de Marcela del Río y *Los siameses* de Griselda Gambaro". *Plural: Revista Cultural de Excelsior* 212 (1989): 46–52.
Hodge, Polly. "Una mirada hacia la identidad: La visión multifacética en *Miralina* de Marcela del Río". *Alba de América: Revista Literaria* 13(24–25) (1995): 83–93.
Shafer, Ivonne. "Interview with Marcela del Río". *Journal of Dramatic Theory and Criticism* 8(2) (1994): 157–62.

DELMAR, MEIRA (OLGA ELJACH)

Meira Delmar (b. 1922), considered not only one of Colombia's but also one of Latin America's premier poets, and often compared to such Hispanic women poets as Mistral, Ibarbourou, Agustini, and Storni, was born to Lebanese parents in 1922 in Barranquilla, Colombia. A family trip to Lebanon when she was 9 heightened the budding poet's awareness and appreciation of her Middle Eastern heritage. She studied music at the Universidad del Atlántico's Conservatorio Pedro Biava. In 1962, she traveled to Rome where she studied Italian Literature as well as Art History, courses which she taught later at her alma mater. For thirty-six years she served as the director of Barranquilla's Biblioteca Pública Departamental which now bears her name.

Her literary achievements have earned many honors for Delmar. She received, among other awards, the *Medalla Simón Bolívar* (Simón Bolivar Medal) from the Ministerio de Educación, and an honorary doctorate from the Universidad del Atlántico. In 1995, the Universidad de Antioquia granted her its *Premio Nacional de Poesía* (National Poetry Prize), an honor awarded every four years. On May 15, 1989, she was one of three women admitted to the Academía Colombiana de la Lengua which, in its 118 years of existence, had accorded this honor to only three other women. Recognition of her many contributions also included service on the Interamerican Commission on Women of Zonta International.

The Writer

In a 1997 essay entitled "Sobre la poesía" (About Poetry), the poet cites an event from her childhood as the moment of her awakening to the beauty of poetry which was to define her life. At school one day, she noticed a sunbeam filter through the windowpane, replicating the colors of the rainbow. The moment brought her to the realization that beauty could be found in the most unexpected places, even within the modest confines of a grade school classroom.

The Cuban review *Vanidades,* published Delmar's first literary efforts in 1937—four poems: "Tú me quieres piedra" (You Want Me of Stone), "Promesa" (Promise), "Cadena" (Chain), and "El regalo de la lluvia" (The Gift of Rain). To spare her father cause for concern, the 16-year-old poet submitted these initial efforts using the penname Meira Delmar, a name combining her love of the sea with her ethnic origins. Though individual poems appeared in countless publications, in Delmar's volumes of verse we have the author's foremost poetic opus.

In 1942, her first book *Alba de olvido* (Dawn of Oblivion) appeared. *Sitio del amor* (Locus of Love) followed in 1944 and *Verdad del sueño* (Dream's Truth), in 1946. The latter garnered the author an award that year from the Sociedad de Mejoras Públicas de Barranquilla. Five years elapsed until the publication in 1951 of her fourth book, *Secreta Isla* (Secret Isle). Here we have a less tentative, more confident author. It has been suggested that her first four collections of poetry be read in chronological order so as to comprehend Delmar's aesthetic evolution. In his prologue to her anthology *Huésped sin sombra* (The Shadowless Guest), the Colombian critic Javier Arango Ferrer observed that these four volumes are "like the four seasons in which a great poet matures" (como las cuatro estaciones en que madura un gran poeta. [13])

Eleven years passed until *Poesía* (Poetry), the Spanish/Italian edition of her poems, was published, and another nine, until *Huésped sin sombra.* Meanwhile, Delmar remained actively engaged in the cultural and academic spheres. Besides her work as library director, she participated in poetry readings and conferences, and continued to write. In 1981, she published *Reencuentro* (Re-encounter), a compilation of her first four volumes, then out of print. *Laúd memorioso* (Memorable Lute) appeared in 1995, followed three years later by *Alguien pasa* (Someone Goes By). Her most recent volume, *Pasa el viento* (The Wind Passes), came out in 2000. The Corporación Universitaria de la Costa produced a CD-Rom, *Antología Poética: Meira Delmar* (Poetic Anthology: Meira Delmar) in which Delmar reads selections from her poetry.

While Delmar's greatest fame derives from her verse, recent attention has focused on her prose. Topics range from observations on life, friends, and colleagues, to speeches delivered on special occasions, to philosophical reflections on life and death, to recollections of travels and views on nature. Their tone varies from the question, "What is love?" in "De amor" (About Love) to the feminist argument advocating the advancement of women pronounced on her reception into the Academia. These musings, gathered for the first time in the Jaramillo *et al.* (2003) work, afford a more intimate view of the private Delmar rather than the public persona of the poetry, thus providing the reader with new perspectives to a fuller appreciation of her poems.

Themes and Influences

In "Sobre la poesía," Delmar mentions diverse authors as inspirations, starting with Solomon whose "Song of Songs" she considers unequaled as a love poem. From biblical writers to less distant ones she cites various authors including, among them, of Spanish authors, John of the Cross and Garcilaso, to Jiménez and Lorca, and of Latin American authors, Darío, Mistral and Neruda as influences upon her.

A thoughtful consideration of her work suggests more pervasive affects, including the dual aesthetic and philosophical impact of the Lebanese/Colombian environment into which she was born and raised, and which serves as the bedrock of her life and work. It is echoed in poems such as "Elegía de Leyla Kháled" (Elegy of Leyla Kháled), "Romance de Barranquilla" (Ballad of Barranquilla), and "Regresos" (Homecoming).

Meira Delmar utilizes several traditional Spanish meters in her poetry such as the *alejandrino*, the *endecasílabo* and the *eneasílabo*. Her verse forms range from the sonnet to haiku and blank verse. The poet's creativity prevails over these technical elements which serve simply as the entree to her poetic world.

An all-encompassing love is the underlying theme of Delmar's verse. This emotion prompts the many evocative and unique images characteristic of her poetry, stated in simple rather than abstruse words. This sentiment ranges from the love of her birthplace in "Romance de Barranquilla" to children in "Canción para dormir a un niño" (Song to Lull a Child to Sleep), to her family in "Regresos".

The love of nature and the relationship of love to nature appear as constants in Delmar's work. She not only associates love with nature, but the colors in nature reflect her response to love. In "Romance del recuerdo" (Ballad of Remembrance), published in *Vanidades*, the poet links the gray skies with the gray of her soul. Delmar incorporates other aspects of nature throughout her verse, presented not from the external viewpoint of the observer, but as an extension of the author and her affinity with nature.

The relationship with her "bienamado" (her beloved), informs a substantial portion of her verse. Rather than the superficial love of youth, we find the confident love of maturity—a love in which the author retains her own individuality.

Additional Considerations

From a careful reading of Delmar's writings a portrait of the author emerges, disclosing the oneness of the person with her opus, which results from her complete surrender to poetry and persistent striving for perfection in her art. Though this oneness appears in various guises in the poet's work, one poem, "Huésped sin sombra", is central to understanding Delmar. While acknowledging her own uniqueness here, she assesses her life in light of the inevitability of death. This poem closes the volume of the same name, as well as *Poesía*, *Reencuentro, Secreta isla* and the above-mentioned CD-Rom, suggesting that Delmar considers it pivotal to comprehending her and her deceptively simple opus.

FRANCESCA COLECCHIA

Selected Works

Alba de olvido. Barranquilla, Colombia: Editorial Mejoras, 1942.
Sitio del amor. Barranquilla, Colombia: Editorial Mejoras, 1944.
Verdad del sueño. Barranquilla, Colombia: Ediciones Arte, 1946.
Secreta Isla. Barranquilla, Colombia: Ediciones Arte, 1951.
Poesía. (Bilingual edition—Spanish/Italian). Mario Vitale, trans. Introduction by Javier Arango Ferrer. Siena: Casa Editrice Maia, 1962.
Huésped sin sombra (Antología). Prologue by Javier Arango Ferrer. Bogotá: Editorial Kelly, 1971.
Poesía. Prologue by Ignacio Reyes Posada. Bogotá: Carlos Valencia Editores, 1981.
Reencuentro. Bogotá: Carlos Valencia Editores, 1981.
Laúd memorioso. Bogotá: Carlos Valencia Editores, 1995.
Alguien pasa. Bogotá: Carlos Valencia Editores, 1998.
Pasa el viento (Antología poética 1942–1998). Prologue by Fernando Charry Lara. Supplement "Meira Delmar o la secreta isla de la poesía" by Juan Gustavo Cobo Borda. Bogotá: Instituto Caro y Cuervo, 2000.
Los más bellos poemas de Meira Delmar (Antología). Barranquilla, Colombia: Fundación para el Desarrollo Tecnológico Científico y Cultural de Colombia, 2001.

References and Further Reading

Castillo Mier, Ariel. "Las palabras en prosa o el magisterio (sin cátedra) de Meira Delmar." *La casa de Asterión: Revista trimestral de estudios literarios.* IV(14) (2003).
——. "El oasis poético de Meira Delmar". *La casa de Asterión: Revista trimestral de estudios literarios* III(9) (2002).
Colecchia, Francesca. "The Poetry of Meira Delmar: Portrait of the Woman". In Nora Ero Orthman, and Juan Cruz Mendizábal (eds), *La escritora hispánica.* Miami, FL: Ediciones Universal, 1990, pp. 227–36.
——. "Motivos e imágenes artísticos en la poética de Meira Delmar". In María Mercedes Jaramillo, Betty Osorio and Ariel Mier Castillo (eds), *Meira Delmar: Poesía y prosa.* Barranquilla, Colombia: Ediciones Uninorte, 2003, pp. 56–62.
Crespo Escorcia, Cielo Cecilia (ed.) *Meira Delmar: una vida a la poesía.* Barranquilla, Colombia: Fundación para el Desarrollo Tecnológico, Científico y Cultural de Colombia, 2000.
Jaramillo, María Mercedes. "La poética amorosa de Meira Delmar". In María Mercedes Jaramillo, Betty Osorio and Angela Inés Robledo (eds), *Literatura y diferencia. Escritoras colombianas del siglo XX.* Bogotá: Ediciones Uniandes, 1995.
Jaramillo, María Mercedes, Osorio, Betty and Castillo Mier, Ariel (eds) *Meira Delmar: Poesía y prosa.* Barranquilla, Colombia: Ediciones Uninorte, 2003.
Romero Fuenmayor, Campo, E. "La presencia del ángel o el ángel de la presencia". *El Heraldo Revista Dominical.* Barranquilla, Colombia, February 14, 1999. http://www.elheraldo.com.co/revistas/dominical/99–03–14/noti6.htm

DENSER, MÁRCIA

Proud of being a fourth-generation paulistana (from the city of São Paulo, Brazil), Márcia Denser was born on May 23, 1949. She obtained a B.A. in Communications from Universidade Mackenzie, and pursued her graduate studies in Literature and Semiotics in the Pontifícia Universidade Católica in São Paulo. She has been working for the Idart Cultural Center in São Paulo for ten years, where she manages the research on contemporary Brazilian literature. Denser achieved recognition as a writer towards the middle of the 1970s when she published her first book of short stories *Tango fantasma* (1976, Ghost Tango), a book that fluctuates between a vulgar realism and eroticism. However, it was not until the decade of the 1980s, when Denser's literary reputation was definitely established. Parallel to her literary writing, Denser has also accomplished an important journalistic career throughout her life. Her first experience with journalism was the magazine *Nova*, for which she worked as editor and columnist from 1977 to 1979. Since then, she has worked and collaborated for such well-known magazines as *Folha de São Paulo*, *Interview*, *Vogue*, and *Salles Interamericana de Publicidade*.

As a writer of short stories and novels, not only has Denser been well recognized among national literary circles but she has also received international acclaim. For example, her works have been translated into German, Dutch, and English, and have been published in Germany, Switzerland, Holland, and the United States. Her contributions as editor deserve to be noticed since Denser organized, edited, and co-authored two important anthologies of erotic short stories written by women, *Muito prazer* (1982, "Much Pleasure") and *O prazer é todo meu* (1984, "The Pleasure Is All Mine"), which were published in Germany and Switzerland with the title of *Tigerin und Leopard: Erotische Erzählungen brasilianischer Autorinnen* (Amman, Zurich, 1988 and Rowoholt Verlag, Switzerland, 1992), and re-edited in 2003 by Unionsverlag. Moreover, her short stories are included in numerous anthologies of women's literature published inside and outside Brazil. In fact, Denser has gained herself a place among the best one hundred Brazilian short story writers of the twentieth century, and many know her as the dark muse of Brazilian literature. Márcia Denser herself confesses to being a writer with a great deal of influence from the language of Clarice Lispector, Julio Cortázar, and William Faulkner (Denser, *Toda prosa*, 2001: 13).

Her main works are *Tango fantasma* (short stories, 1976), *O animal dos motéis* (a novel in episodes, 1981, "Animal of Motels"), *Exercícios para o pecado* (short novels, 1984, "Exercises for Sin"), *Diana caçadora* (1986, "Diana, the Huntress"), *Cronologia da literatura em São Paulo 75/95* (essay, 1996; "Chronology of literature in São Paulo"), *Toda prosa* (2002, "All Prose"), *Os apóstolos* (anthology, 2002, "The Apostles"), *Diana caçadora/Tango fantasma* (erotic short stories, 2003 edition, Ateliê Editorial; "Diana, the Huntress/Ghost Tango"), and *Caim* (novel, 2005, "Cain"). Although her literary trait is eroticism, Denser changed gears in 1990 and wrote the novel *A ponta das estrelas* ("The Tip of Stars") which is an allegory of the human tragicomedy.

Denser's Narrative within the Brazilian Cultural Scene

In order to better understand the narrative of Márcia Denser is necessary to examine the sociopolitical and cultural context in which she developed and achieved recognition as a writer. Denser's work may be situated in two literary frames: the existential literature produced in Latin America since the 1950s, and the literature written by women since the 1970s. In her narrative, Denser cultivates the hallmarks of this type of existential literature, such as self-fragmentation and mutilation, with the purpose of illustrating the emotional and intellectual state of her characters who inhabit a chaotic world. This sort of writing is inevitably and intrinsically related to the feminine (and feminist) issues that are present in her narrative and that put her in the spectrum of post-1970 women's literature. Denser's protagonists are women who live in a self-centered world that functions according to the norms imposed by others. These are women who desperately need to be at peace with their selves, and to be sure of who they really are, before they can even ask themselves what "being a woman" means in this frantic world in which they live. Only then, will they be able to redefine their use of power in an inherently male system.

Eroticism and Denser's Prose

Márcia Denser is among the representatives of the flourishing of erotic literature written by women in the last quarter of the twentieth century. In general, the theme of eroticism serves as a channel to examine the ideology of power, and to reflect on the power relations between men and women and the abuse of power. In Denser's work, the theme of women's eroticism is also a release from female traditional stereotypes, and a vehicle to establish a new differentiated identity. The female characters in her narrative stem from the traditional images of the "fallen woman". These women's inner selves are dislocated (here is the self-fragmentation that is also characteristic of her narrative) from the socially accepted, conventional model of the chaste woman. Denser employs eroticism manifested from the woman's perspective only to de-objectify women's stereotypes and to recreate a new archetype of women as subject. Nevertheless, this is a difficult task to fulfill because the contemporary urban female protagonist typical of Denser's short stories feels both alienated from the imposed traditional norms and hesitant with herself. In other words, the female protagonist needs to clarify the misconceptions that reinforce the fallen woman imagery as well as explore the contradictions of women's dual nature.

An Overview of Style, Language, and Themes

In her fiction, the traditional male protagonist is replaced by a contemporary, urban heroine. Denser's novels are urban and portray the harshness and loneliness of depersonalized city life. In fact, Denser describes her literary work as intent to capture women's daily life pleasures in a frenzied, turbulent Brazilian society. Nevertheless, the city she writes about may be São Paulo or any other major metropolis in the world since Denser writes about the urban middle class, the business executives, and the bohemian artists in cafés. In other words, her characters may be found in any of the major capitals of the world.

Her books *Tango fantasma* and *O animal dos motéis* reveal Denser's literary compromise: to make literary discourse a fundamental element in the fight in which women have been engaged for decades to elucidate the contradictions of the dual nature that traditional ethics has enforced upon women (chaste woman vs. tainted woman). Denser lucidly articulates in her prose that, in order to achieve this goal, one needs to comprehend that it does not affect only one woman, but rather, it is a collective problem. In fact, the sense of collectivity is a relevant element in Denser's narrative. The individual persona of the female protagonist becomes a representative of a collective search for identity. That is, Denser's protagonist is not only Brazilian but she may also be Argentine, Chilean, and Mexican. In other words, the female protagonist is a citizen of the world. At the same time, Denser searches for a particular literary discourse: one that is feminine, one that can register the intimate experiences specific to women in today's world.

Some recurrent themes in Denser's works are: the woman's alienation from the traditional norms and uneasiness with her self in today's society, the contrasts between what is wished for and what actually happens, truncated love relationships (especially affairs outside of marriage), and lack of communication in human relationships. These themes harmonize with the sort of atmosphere that surrounds Denser's characters. It is the sordid environment of urban life, the impersonal atmosphere of the office cubicle, the dehumanized setting that city cement buildings reveal. Her main characters are not too different from these artificial locales, but rather, they strive for maintaining interpersonal contact, and for compromising with others. However, the latter is impossible if no intimacy and real emotions exist between two people. In Denser's narrative, resistance against reigning power manifests at both a thematic level and linguistic level. In other words, Denser opts for the language of the body and the right to the body's pleasure, in particular women's body pleasure, which was prohibited by traditional morals. In such a context, then, sexual lexicon, the purely carnal and vulgar swearwords function as weapons.

O animal dos motéis

Written with a non-traditional structure, *O animal dos motéis* contains eight interrelated, but semi-independent, stories that tell about the daily life of the female protagonist. Although the language of this novel is quite sexually explicit and violent at times, it comes closer to poetic prose at other times. As for technique, Denser does not emphasize plot development, but rather, the events are told through the stream of consciousness of the female protagonist and narrator, Diana Marini. Throughout the various episodes in the book, Diana struggles to have control over herself and her relationships with men. However, her attempts end up in frustration with herself and with others because the abuse of power only dehumanizes people. Thus, Denser maintains that reversing the power relations does not grant personhood to women, that is, instead of desiring to dominate others, one should first be able to understand and have control over him or herself.

Any piece of writing on Márcia Denser is not complete without her most famous quote found in her "Auto-retrato" (self-portrait) in *O animal dos motéis* (1981) and which most of the scholarly articles on her work include. Denser affirms:

> As mulheres da minha geração perambulam pelo castelo em ruinas do casamento. E se possuem a chave da liberdade conferida pela pílula, nada podem fazer com ela. Deram-nos a chave mas esqueceram de construir a porta. Nada mais inútil que uma chave num castelo sem portas, não acham?
>
> [women from my generation wander around the castle of marriage in ruins. And if they have the key of freedom granted by the (birth control) pill, there is nothing they can do with it. They gave us the key but they forgot to build the door. There is nothing more useless than a castle's key with no doors, don't you think?].

This statement metaphorically articulates the interior conflict of the twentieth-century woman, and identifies the dilemma of the liberated but also disillusioned woman. In the 1960s and 1970s, a liberated woman is born who challenges the traditional male establishment. However, the initial euphoria becomes cynicism when she realizes that her freedom won't be legitimate as long as the same patriarchal principles continue governing the system's structure and norms. This disillusioned woman's voice is what the readers hear in Denser's works.

ISABEL ASENSIO-SIERRA

Selected Works

Tango fantasma: contos. São Paulo: Alfa-Omega, 1976.
O animal dos motéis: novela em episódios. Rio de Janeiro: Civilização Brasileira, 1981.
(ed.) *Muito prazer: contos eróticos femininos*. Rio de Janeiro: Record, 1982.
Exercícios para o pecado: duas novelas. Rio de Janeiro: Philobiblion, 1984.
(ed.) *O prazer é todo meu: contos eróticos femininos*. Rio de Janeiro: Record, 1984.
(ed.) *Histórias de amor infeliz: contos*. Rio de Janeiro: Nórdica, 1985.
Diana caçadora. São Paulo: Global Editora, 1986.
A ponte das estrelas: uma superprodução de aventuras. São Paulo: Editora Best Seller, 1990.
Toda prosa: inéditos e dispersos. São Paulo: Noval Alexandria, 2001.
Diana caçadora e Tango fantasma: duas prosas reunidas. Cotia, SP: Ateliê Editorial, 2003.

References and Further Reading

Betto, *O decálogo: dez mandamentos, dez histórias*. São Paulo: Nova Alexandria, 2000.
Canty Quinlan, Susan. "Writing with Intent: Márcia Denser's *O animal dos motéis: novela em episódios*". *Luso-Brazilian Review* 26(2) (1989): 87–101.
——. "*O animal dos motéis: novela em episódios*. I Write to Describe All Sides of Myself". In *The Female Voice in Contemporary Brazilian Narrative*. New York: Peter Lang, 1991, pp. 103–37.
Faria, Alvaro Alves de. *Palavra de mulher*. São Paulo: Senac São Paulo Editora, 2003.
Ficções feminino. São Paulo: SESC, Lazuli Editora, 2003.
Moriconi, Italo. "Uma erótica da escrita". In *Toda prosa: inéditos e dispersos*. São Paulo: Nova Alexandria, 2001, pp. 5–11.
Novaes Coelho, Nelly. "Márcia Denser. *O animal dos motéis*: O discurso feminino sobre o sexo reinventado" in *A literatura feminina no Brasil contemporâneo*. São Paulo: Siciliano, 1993, pp. 249–55.
——. *Coleção e ficções femininas*. São Paulo: SESC, 2003.
Pinto, Cristina Ferreira. *Urban Voices: Contemporary Short Stories from Brazil*. Lanham, MD: University Press of America, 1999.
Sadlier, Darlene J. "Introduction". In *One Hundred Years after Tomorrow. Brazilian Women's Fiction in the 20th Century*. Bloomington, IN: Indiana University Press, 1992, pp. 1–12.

DIACONÚ, ALINA

The life and work of Alina Diaconú (b. 1949) have been marked by the experience of travel, entering new environs and new forms of political repression. The only child of an art critic and a native of Bucharest, Romania, Diaconú was raised in an atmosphere of intellectual debates both in Romanian and French. When the Soviet puppet government of Gheordhiu-Dej (1961–65) began to curtail her father's intellectual pursuits, the family left Eastern Europe and through France emigrated to Argentina, then under the government of Arturo Frondizi (1958–62). In Argentina, the 14-year-old Diaconú entered school and this period turned out to be a groundbreaking era in terms of her intellectual development. Diaconú's first novel, *La señora*, appeared in 1975. Her second novel, *Buenas noches, profesor* (1978), was awarded the 1979 Argentine Society of Writers' Honor Band and soon after, it was censored by the regime reigning in Argentina during the "Proceso" or "Dirty War" (1976–82). As a result, Diaconú became her own strictest censor, departing from realistic settings in favor of symbolism, metaphor, and open endings. Her allegorical prose resists patriarchal authoritarianism, simultaneously recovering the peripheral voices of individuals who are silenced by the state. Her characters—whether men, women or hermaphrodites—live on the fringe of society, refusing reintegration into the symbolic, even under the threat of annihilation. Aside from novels, Diaconú has also written short stories and articles for numerous magazines and the newspapers *La Nación*, *Clarín* and *La Gaceta*. She has also organized many cultural events for various foundations in Buenos Aires.

Long journeys and state persecution brand Diaconú's narratives much as they have marked her life. The theme of travel is a metaphor for the human condition and one's destiny, a journey which inevitably leads to death. Aside from the mythic voyage, Diaconú's narratives explore the concept of identity, deconstructing simplistic binarisms in their analysis of the complexity of human nature. For Diaconú, "reality isn't clear-cut, it is always composed of facets" (Flori, 1995: 136); thus her literary worlds and characters are often ambiguous and ambivalent. Her narrative environs originate from the marginal spaces of society and, eventually, destabilize and replace the presumed center, with peripheral characters, repulsive bodies, and desperate souls searching hopelessly for their proper place. Her protagonists, as Flori asserts, "are fallen heroes or antiheroes who have failed in life," experiencing a physical or emotional confinement "felt by an alienated mind marked by loneliness, isolation, despair, and madness" (*Streams* 1995: 100).

The protagonist of Diaconú's first novel, *La señora*, seems to be a typical, middle-aged bourgeois housewife; yet, deep inside, she abhors her monotony and empty existence and finally rebels against conventions, changing everything around her. She contributes to the disintegration of her family by taking her daughter's boyfriend as a lover, then prostituting herself, and finally by attempting to kill her own child. In the end, the protagonist is put away in an asylum, as threatening to her surroundings and unable to live in society.

Buenas noches, profesor introduces an aging high school teacher who falls in love with an adolescent student who visits him at home. Motivated by his feeling of increased infatuation, the hero regains his youthful vigor and intellectual spark, becomes outgoing, prolific in writing, and successful in his other academic endeavors. This lucky turn in life, however, turns out to be nothing more than a construct of his delusional imagination. In reality, the man remains locked up in his house and unable to work, still in shock after his wife's death.

The novel *Enamorada del muro* (1981), depicts the dilemmas of 18-year-old Bruma, who rejects her parents' life and roams the streets of Buenos Aires in search of true love. This text explores compulsive behaviors, such as uncontrollable cravings for certain types of foods—ice cream in Bruma's case—or biting her nails. Bruma falls for a young man King Kong, and tries to have a relationship with him, ignoring his homosexual tendencies and the criminal activities of a sect he actively represents.

Through the theme of bodily needs, the novel inaugurates another important trait in Diaconú's writing, namely, corporeality in an atmosphere of the grotesque, excess, and abjection. For the critics Flori and Gimbernat, this negative perspective in Diaconú's characters comes from an internalization of horror and abuse experienced during the "Dirty War". These allegorical novels express the terror of oppression through the images of bodily abjection rather than the realistic depiction of historical events. With each subsequent narrative, the corporeal theme takes on a bigger role; Diaconú packs her fiction with characters whose bodies and minds refuse to be average: they are obsessive, aging, disfigured, hermaphrodite and grotesque. Marginal and extraordinary, they fail or refuse to comprehend the norm, a norm which in Diaconú's literary world stands dangerously close to state order and oppressive regimes.

The defiled female body constitutes the gist of *Los ojos azules* (1986), dedicated to Diaconú's close friend and fellow writer, Marta Lynch, who committed suicide in 1985. The heroine is a secretary in her thirties, whose husband has abandoned her for another woman. Feeling devastated and rejected, she decides to spend all her savings on a one-night trip to a distant island. There, the protagonist hopes to experience something magical, perhaps a passionate encounter with Prince Charming, before she commits suicide. Her experiences in the resort stand in a stark contrast with what she hoped to find. The island promotes sexual relations only between people of the same sex and all the men she meets are revoltingly old and obscene.

As the blue-eyed secretary embarks on her journey towards death, so does Amapola, the protagonist of *El penúltimo viaje* (1989), who travels by train from Buenos Aires, recalling another trip from twenty years ago, when she emigrated with her family from Eastern Europe to Argentina. Memories of her childhood bring back the influential figures from her past: her long-gone mother and her domineering father. At some remote station the girl is dragged out of the compartment by two individuals and she joins her dead mother in what, presumably, is her own death.

Los devorados (1992) presents a panoramic view of the inhabitants of a desolate and alienating city. Three distinct characters, whose life stories are woven separately, converge in time and space to mirror the existential dramas of one another. Ian Grabski, a sybarite and the owner of numerous carnivorous plants, a 60-year old diva who hides her age under the cloak of luxury and cosmetic surgeries, and a beggar living in a gutter, become the protagonists of this story. Both Grabski and the woman have strong emotions concerning the homeless man; they see his fate as a premonition of their own defeat and the beggar himself as their alter ego.

The plot of *Cama de ángeles* (1983) focuses on two distinct, yet similarly self-exiled individuals whose fates converge in an affluent apartment building in Buenos Aires: Ángel/a, a reclusive hermaphrodite, and Morgana, a famous but already aging actress who fears losing her beauty. Despite their great differences in characters and life styles, they decide to go on a trip to Paris in order to forget Morgana's failed comeback in a recent theatrical production that was supposed to resuscitate her career. This intention, however, goes awry, since they fail to find their taxi, lose their luggage, miss the plane, and accidentally end up in a desolate zone of the city, trying in vain to reach the airport on foot.

The second part of the novel traces the descent of both protagonists into the hellish neighborhoods of the city. In a matter of hours, they run the full gamut from the luxurious settings of their domicile to the filthy, destitute and perilous ruins of what surrounds their small section of comfort. As the resigned protagonists try to find a place to eat and sleep, they are robbed of whatever money they have left and finally encounter a makeshift hospital set up in an enormous tent in the middle of nowhere. Run by a tyrannical doctor, the place retains infirm citizens, yet it does not bother to cure them. As the patients get sicker and die, their bodies are thrown away and their cots are immediately offered to ill newcomers. Once rested, the protagonists escape and accidentally reach familiar surroundings, managing to find their way home. Curiously, this peregrination allows for their self-discovery and re-definition within the tyrannical systems of signification. On a more recondite level, the novel reveals the wounds of society, with its individuals and organizations shattered by political oppression.

Overall, Diaconú concocts a world divested of structure, safety, and human warmth. Traditional sites of security become nests of instability and dissolution. Marriages represent a dreadful routine, while parents give rise to their children's traumas by disciplining and alienating them. Men and masculinity are closely related to authority and violence. Fathers, physicians, neighbors and, in fact, all male figures who symbolically stand in charge represent the enemy and military rule. For example, the doctor in *Cama de ángeles* is ominously reminiscent of torturers recorded by the victims of the "Dirty War," while the heroine's transient lover recalls the military officials who seized power in Argentina and terrorized its citizens for the ensuing years. But as paternalistic ideology relinquishes force and meaning in the novel, so do men become powerless and inessential. They lose their say, surrendering to women's marginal discourse. The state, the patriarchy, and the sovereignty of the father are questioned and exposed in their inadequacy and corruption. Instead, the marginal and the feminine move to the forefront, challenging the symbolic (male) order. They go against the grain of accepted practices, highlighting the precariousness of civil safety, family security and gender identity.

Diaconú's texts disclose the monstrosity of the center, which has individuals browbeaten by discipline, misled by deception, abject and tortured. Life is often too hard to bear; tormented protagonists thus find comfort in insularity, escapism, insanity or even death. In contrast, their peripheral standing confers on Diaconú's characters an awareness of the distortion of their lives, ceaselessly imposed by hostile state institutions. While others are blindly stranded in a discourse that obscures the act of social and political enslavement, Diaconú's desperate rebels reject the "norm", knowing that sometimes there is only one, negative, way out.

ALDONA BIALOWAS POBUTSKY

Selected Works

La señora. Buenos Aires: Rodolfo Alonso, 1975.
Buenas noches, profesor. Buenos Aires: Corregidor, 1978.
Enamorada del muro. Buenos Aires: Corregidor, 1981.
Cama de ángeles. Buenos Aires: Emecé, 1983.
"Soliloquio ante una ausencia". In *Libro del padre*, ed. Antonio Requeni. Buenos Aires: Torres Agüero, 1984.
"Con Ciorán, en París". Suplemento Literario de *La Nación,* 17 November 1985: 1–2.
Los ojos azules. Buenos Aires: Fraterna, 1986.
"Victoria Ocampo: Historia de un apasionamiento". Suplemento Literario de *La Nación*, 22 January 1989: 6.
El penúltimo viaje. Buenos Aires: Javier Vergara, 1989.
Los devorados. Buenos Aires: Atlántida, 1992.
(ed.) *Alberto Girri: Homenaje*. Buenos Aires: Sudamericana and Fondo Nacional de las Artes, 1994.
"Autogeografía". *Alba de América* 12(22–23) (1994): 111–15.
¿Qué nos pasa, Nicolás? Buenos Aires: Atlántida, 1995.
Calidoscopio. Buenos Aires: Atlántida, 1998.
Preguntas con respuestas: Entrevistas a Borges, Cioran, Girri, Ionesco, Sarduy. Buenos Aires: Vinciguerra, 1998.
Intimidades del ser: Veintisiete poemas y algunos aforismos. Buenos Aires: Vinciguerra, 2005.

References and Further Reading

Fares, Gustavo and Cazaubon Hermann, Eliana (eds). "Alina Diaconú". *Contemporary Argentinean Women Writers: A Critical Anthology*. Gainesville, FL: University Press of Florida, 1998, pp. 45–59.
Flori, Mónica. "Madres e hijas y creatividad femenina en *La señora* de Alina Diaconú". *Confluencia* 8–9(2–1) (1993): 229–35.
——. "La articulización de lo inexpresable: Metaforización del cuerpo femenino en *Los ojos azules* de Alina Diaconú". *Alba de América* 12(22–3) (1994): 351–60.
——. "Alina Diaconú". In *Streams of Silver: Six Contemporary Women Writers from Argentina*. Lewisburg, PA: Associated University Presses, 1995, pp. 99–147.
Gimbernat González, Ester and Tomkins, Cynthia (eds). *Utopías, ojos azules y bocas suicidas. La narrativa de Alina Diaconú*. Buenos Aires: Fraterna, 1994.
López-Cabrales, María del Mar. "La escritura como respuesta a la intolerancia histórica. Alina Diaconú entre Bucarest y Buenos Aires". *Revista Iberoamericana* 62(175) (1996): 585–97.
Pobutsky, Aldona Bialowas. "Postmodern Cityscape: Living in 'the Zone' in Alina Diaconú's *Cama de ángeles*". *Chasqui* 33(2) (2004): 3–17.
——. "Subversive Masquerades: Performing Gender and Age in *Cama de ángeles* by Alina Diaconú". *Confluencia* 21(2) (2006): 11–23.
Tompkins, Cynthia. "*Los devorados* de Alina Diaconú: ¿Vía mística? ¿Atracción tanática? Alegoría social?" *Confluencia* 9(2) (1994): 88–97.

DOLORES, CARMEN

Brazilian writer Emília Moncorvo Bandeira de Melo (1852–1910) adopted a number of pseudonyms throughout her literary career, but it was as Carmen Dolores that she became best known. It was under this name that she published novels, plays, short stories, literary criticism and numerous journalistic essays or *crônicas*, making her one of the most important female writers during Brazil's *belle époque*.

Emília Moncorvo Bandeira de Melo was born in Rio de Janeiro on March 11, 1852. She was the daughter of Dr. Carlos Honório de Figueiredo and D. Emília Moncorvo de Figueiredo and was raised in a traditional upper-class family. She married Jerónimo Bandeira de Melo with whom she had a number of children, including Cecília Bandeira de Melo

(1887–1948), who became a well known and commercially successful writer in the 1920s under the pseudonym Madame Chrysanthème.

Journalist and Writer

Initially an amateur writer, contributing articles to journals for fun, it was the financial difficulties that followed her husband's early death that prompted Moncorvo to embark on writing as a professional career. In order to support her home and children, Moncorvo wrote for a number of newspapers and magazines. She published a series of short stories using the pseudonym Júlia de Castro for the newspaper *O País*; in *Tribuna* she published literary criticism under the male name Leonel Sampaio, and in the publication *Etoile du Sud* she wrote articles using the names Mário Vilar and Célia Márcia. It was not until 1905 that she adopted the pen name Carmen Dolores under which she would achieve considerable fame and success. In 1908, writing as Carmen Dolores, Moncorvo penned a weekly column called "A semana" in *O País*, and became the newspaper's highest paid writer, earning more than her male counterparts.

Dolores' early journalistic work was characterized by lively portraits of Brazilian society. Focusing on Rio de Janeiro, she depicted the animated life of the city and its affluent upper-class members, presenting readers with entertaining vignettes typical of the *belle époque* of Brazilian literature. These lighter social portraits, however, soon changed to encompass contemporary political issues, especially the struggle for women's rights. Articulating and responding to the broader feminist struggle, Dolores championed a number of social and political changes. She strenuously promoted and defended women's education. Female education in Brazil was largely non-existent or restricted to only a few elite women. Feminists began to campaign for an improved public education as a means of ensuring the progress of Brazil, although they defined education as that which would make women good wives and competent mothers. Dolores' essays strongly emphasized the need to broaden instruction to women, articulating the writer's belief that education would help to make women independent and free from their husbands or fathers. This emphasis on female freedom from male dependency differed from mainstream feminist discourses of the time. Dolores allied the cause for female education, not to traditional ideologies of motherhood, but rather to her belief in women's right to salaried work. These arguments were strongly influenced by Dolores' own personal experiences that led her to professional writing. In her essay entitled "Protesto," she refers to unfortunate and unforeseen circumstances that force independence upon many women, evoking her own history in which the death of her husband left her financially destitute and alone. By calling upon her own past and highlighting the real presence of strong and independent working mothers, Dolores' writing shattered the idealistic image of women as domestic angels dominant in Brazil.

Dolores' journalistic work also fervently promoted the legalization of divorce in Brazil. This period saw the start of the campaign for divorce led by female lawyer Mirtes Campos. Dolores supported Campos' work and in numerous *crônicas*, published collectively in 1910 as *Ao esvoaçar da idéia,* she articulated intelligent arguments against those who opposed legalizing divorce. She skillfully manipulated fashionable liberal and republican discourses to defend divorce as an individual right and freedom. Further, she argued, divorce would strengthen progress and civilization, as it would dissolve ineffectual marital unions, and thus benefit not just women and men but also the country as a whole. It was another, more logical argument for divorce, however, that gained Dolores most attention. Observing that the only legally recognized form of marriage in Brazil was civil, Dolores noted the paradox of a law that was based on and upheld the Catholic Church's tenets. Dolores' pragmatic stance towards divorce highlighted her staunch anti-clericalism, and led to a controversial debate in 1908 with journalist Carlos Laet. The debate was sparked by Dolores' outspoken criticism of Padre Júlia Maria and his renowned religious sermons. Dolores accused the priest of vanity, superficiality and hypocrisy, values she attributed to the clergy in general. In the following issue of *O País*, Laet defended the priest's traditional views and condemned Dolores as a radical feminist. Surprisingly, in her reply, Dolores forthrightly denied being a feminist and stated clearly that she was above all a mother.

Dolores' denial reveals wider ambiguities regarding her political and social views. On the one hand, the writer ardently championed changes for women, on the other hand, she promoted traditional patriarchal structures, even criticizing modern women as superficial and as dangerous to the stability of the family. Similarly, her strong anti-clerical beliefs coincided with Republican sentiments, yet Dolores referred to herself as a monarchist and bemoaned the advent of the Republican regime in Brazil. Maria Angélica Lopes views this ambivalence as tied to the socio-historical moment in which Dolores lived and wrote, a reflection of broader contradictions regarding change in Brazil. Dolores' incongruous stances can also be interpreted as part of the writer's independence; rather than strictly adhering to a cause or party, Dolores always defended her own beliefs and values. It was this strong independent spirit that earned her respect among her readers and other writers of the time. Journalist Gilberto Amado noted Dolores' passion, enthusiasm and independence and author Coelho Neto referred to her work as evidencing her own robust commitment to art and to truth.

The contradictory views evidenced in Dolores' journalism figured in her creative work. In 1897, she published *Gradações*, a collection of short stories, followed in 1907 by another collection *Um drama na roça*. Both works display an acute perception of the social status of bourgeois women in Brazil and reveal the writer's dexterous criticism of their condition. Shortly after *Um drama na roça*, Dolores turned her attention to the theatre. She wrote the play, *O desencontro*, which was staged in Rio in October, 1908. The following year, however, she returned to prose fiction, writing her only novel called *A luta.* The narrative focuses on the lives of young Celina, her sisters and her mother Dona Adozinda, the owner of a hostel in Rio's fashionable district, Santa Teresa. It depicts the women's passionate encounters with the hostel's male guests and charts the aging mother's uneasy relationship with her younger more attractive daughters, highlighting the pernicious effects of a society that values women's physical attributes, their beauty, above all else. Published in serialized form in *O País* in 1909, Dolores referred to *A luta* as her most accomplished piece of work. The novel was published as a book in 1911. Sadly Dolores herself never saw its release. She died in 1910, months before *A luta*, the book, appeared in Brazil.

Themes, Style and Influences

Carmen Dolores' work reflects the influence of the transitional moment of Brazilian history in which she was writing, the advent of Republican fervor and the changes facing traditional social and patriarchal structures. Her writing embraced a variety of genres, essays, short stories, plays, novels and *crônicas*. As a *cronista*, Dolores' acute reports of urban life parallel those of authors such as João do Río, who also depicted social life in Brazil's *belle époque*. Her *crônicas*, like her other works, display an awareness of how this society impacts the role and place of women, revealing the influence of international feminist writers such as Virginia Woolf as well as domestic writers like Nísia Floresta, who also merged literature together with feminism. Dolores' work displays a strong belief in writing as a tool that can help to effect those changes. This belief in the political potential of the writer evidenced the strong social role that writing assumed in Brazil at the end of the nineteenth century and that marked the so-called *Geração de 1870*. Dolores inflects this political impetus with questions revolving around gender, her writing seeking to empower women in Brazilian society.

The major themes of her prose fiction coincide with those she championed in her newspaper articles and essays. Female characters dominate the stories, with a prevalence toward showing how family relationships, love and marriage can weaken their independent character and resolve. These portraits display the role that journalism had on Dolores' prose work. Yet the observation of women as they are affected by their wider milieu reveals the influence of realism and especially naturalism on Dolores' writing and the impact of writers such as Emile Zola, Eça de Queiroz, Honoré de Balzac and Brazil's Aluísio de Azevedo. In her novel *A luta*, she merges social observation with questions of gender, comparing the attitudes and values of women from differing classes. Published in 1909, the novel's strong naturalist style and its debt to past masters contrast starkly to contemporary prose authors in Brazil who had started to experiment with modern styles as evidenced in the work of Lima Barreto. Nevertheless, *A luta* stands as a document of turn-of-the-century Brazilian society, women's complex place in it and Dolores' dexterous literary representation in depicting both.

Contemporary Reappraisals

Publishing the majority of her work in the mainstream press, Dolores' work has until lately received little critical and scholarly attention. Much of her prose fiction was published posthumously with her own daughter, Cecília Bandeira de Melo, organizing a collection of essays and stories, published as *Almas complexas* in 1934. The re-evaluation of Brazilian women and literature in the 1980s, especially its focus on the Republican years, has brought Dolores' writing renewed attention in recent years. In 2001, Brazil's Editora Mulheres published a new edition of *A luta* that includes a critical essay of Dolores' work. Through her life and work Dolores undertook the new crusade of vindicating women's roles in Brazilian society, emphasizing women's rights to receive an education and to work. Her essays are radical testimonies of her campaigns for these basic freedoms and provide a deeper understanding of women's place in turn-of-the-century Brazil as well the country's literary traditions.

Selected Works

Gradações, 1894–1986. Rio de Janeiro: Tipografia Leuzinger, 1897.
Um drama na roça. Introduction by Coelho Neto. Rio de Janeiro: J. Laemmert, 1907.
Ao esvoaçar da idéia. Porto: Chadron, 1910.
A luta. Rio de Janeiro and Paris: Garnier, 1911.
Almas complexas. Introduction by Cecília Bandeira de Melo. Rio de Janeiro: Calvino, 1934.
A luta. Florianópolis: Editora Mulheres, 2001.

References and Further Reading

Brito, Cândida de. *Antologia feminina*. Rio de Janeiro: A dona da casa, 1937, pp. 22–3.
Broca, Brito. *A vida literária no Brasil*, 1900. Rio de Janeiro: J. Olympio, 1975, pp. 241–2.
Erse, Armando. "Carmen Dolores". In *Elogios*. Porto: Renascença, 1916, pp. 63–70.
Lopes, Maria Angélica. "Carmem Dolores: Jornalismo, literatura e feminismo na Bela Época brasileira". *Luso-Brazilian Review* 26(2) (1989): 75–85.
——. "O crime da Galeria Cristal em 1909. A jornalisa como árbitro". *Travessia (Revista do Curso de pós-graduação em Letras da UFSC)* (1992): 167–77.
——. "Desafio materno. A luta de Carmen Dolores". In *A luta*. Florianópolis: Editora Mulheres, 2001.
Magalhães Júnior, Raimundo. "Carmem Dolores". In *O conto feminino*. Rio de Janeiro: Civilização Brasileira, 1959, pp. 33–48.
Pereira, Lúcia Miguel. *História da literatura Brasileira. Prosa de ficção (de 1870 a 1920)*. Rio de Janeiro: José Olympio, 1957, pp. 138–9.

DOMECQ, BRIANDA

Brianda Domecq is a novelist, essayist, and journalist. She was born on August 1, 1942 in New York City to a Spanish father, Pedro Domecq, and a North American mother, Elizabeth Cook. At 9 years of age, after living in New York and Connecticut, her family moved to Mexico. At 15, she attended boarding school in Massachusetts. Afterward, she attended college for a year in New York, then moved back to Mexico, married, and had two children. In 1972, Domecq began studies in Hispanic Language and Literatures at the Universidad Autónoma Nacional de México (UNAM); she received her degree in 1979. Throughout the 1970s, Domecq balanced the demands of school and family with a variety of other activities, including a stint as editor-in-chief of the *Revista de Bellas Artes* in 1972 and 1973. It was not until the end of the 1970s, however, that she launched her literary career. Domecq has published two novels, two collections of short stories, and many other works of fiction and non-fiction. Though she currently lives in Spain, she continues to identify as a Mexican writer.

Kidnapping and *Once días*

In 1978, on her way home from the university, Domecq was kidnapped and held for ransom for eleven days. Though the kidnappers attempted to extort several million dollars from her father, a wealthy wine producer, she was rescued and her captors were caught. Domecq's first novel and literary debut, *Once días . . . y algo más* (1979, Eleven Days), fictionalizes this experience.

Once días portrays the kidnapping and captivity of Leo del Río, the daughter of a wealthy wine producer, over a period of eleven days. In this novel, Leo struggles with fear, boredom, uncertainty, and powerlessness as she becomes acquainted with her captors, and as she tries to understand and adjust to them. In addition to studying the delicate balance of social power between the boss and his four assistants, and in addition to examining the social dynamics between a woman and five men, the novel explores how Leo's imagination and self-identity compel her to assert a degree of conversational and gestural power in her interactions with her captors. As Leo remains blindfolded throughout her ordeal and never sees her captors, she relies on touch, smell, and sound in order to make sense of her new world. Sound, ranging from ambient noise to human discourse, plays a particularly important role in Leo's imagination, understanding, and self-control. Specifically, Leo uses rhetoric and language to her advantage, as she quickly gains the trust and respect of her captors through humor, wordplay, and discussion. As the ordeal continues, the boss and his assistants show increasing frustration as ransom negotiations with Leo's family proceed more slowly than anticipated. The boss fears that the conversations between captive and captors will reveal incriminating information, so he orders his assistants and Leo to remain silent in their interactions. But this directive has only partial success. By the time Leo is rescued, she has gained varying degrees of confidence with three of her captors, and has managed to diminish somewhat the control that the boss held over them.

Fiction and Non-Fiction in the 1980s

Though *Once días. . .y algo más* effectively began Domecq's literary career, her subsequent work not only shows a remarkable depth and breadth with regard to genre and themes, but also exhibits a strong interest in understanding the lives of women in Mexico. Her collection of widely acclaimed short stories, *Bestiario doméstico* (1982; English translations included in *When I Was a Horse*), features eleven pieces that examine a variety of themes, including the struggle of women to develop their own identity and cultural autonomy in modern society. Some of the stories, such as "(YO) ¡Clonc!" (Mr. Clunk!) and "El eterno teatro" (The Eternal Theater), contain a strong autobiographical element; other stories in the collection draw loosley from historical, mythical, and legendary sources. The piece entitled "Trilogía" (Trilogy), really more a poetic novella than a short story, creatively rewrites the late medieval version of the Jewish legend of Lillith, Adam's first wife. Domecq inventively retells Lillith's refusal to submit to Adam's sexual authority, as well as her willful departure from Eden and subsequent relationship with Sammaël.

After the publication of *Bestiario doméstico*, Domecq's attention shifted to projects of a more investigative nature. She was commissioned to research and write *Voces y rostros del Bravo* (1987, Voices and Faces of the Bravo), a photo essay on the culture and history of the people living on the borderlands of the Río Bravo (known as the Río Grande in the United States). Shortly afterward, Domecq edited *Acechando al unicornio: La virginidad en la literatura mexicana* (1988, Stalking the Unicorn: Virginity in Mexican Literature), an anthology of stories and excerpts dealing with the theme of virginity in Mexican literature and culture.

La insólita historia de la Santa de Cabora

Domecq's most significant work since *Once días* is the novel *La insólita historia de la Santa de Cabora* (1990, The Astonishing Story of the Saint of Cabora). This novel recreates the life and times of Teresa Urrea (1873–1906), a Mexican woman and popular legend who developed her powers as a mystic and faith healer. Though born into poverty as the illegitimate daughter of a wealthy landowner (Don Tomás) and a poor Amerindian woman (Cayetana), Teresa learned to read and write, and gradually established herself in her father's household. At the age of 16, Teresa became gravely ill, and her family duly planned for her death. She revived several days later. Not only did her unexpected recovery gain popular attention, but also the news of her power as a visionary and healer began to spread across Mexico. Teresa became popularly known as the Saint of Cabora, and with her father's support, she dedicated herself to healing the sick and physically impaired. Eventually, Teresa's mission acquired political overtones, as she began to advocate for social reform. Teresa's popularity and beliefs ultimately led to conflict with the regime of Porfirio Díaz, and she and her father were exiled for instigating rebellion. They sought asylum in the United States, where Teresa continued to work as a healer until her death at 33 years of age.

Brianda Domecq's gift for dialogue, description, and psychological detail turn Teresa de Urrea's life, fascinating in its own right, into a gripping and suspenseful story. Against the backdrop of Mexico's multicultural society, this novel explores an array of complex themes, including wealth and poverty, youth and adulthood, life and death, rural customs, relations between women and men, and family relationships. Domecq also succeeds in showing the tangled interconnections between history and fiction, as she incorporates a variety of discursive levels and points of view into the novel in order to underscore the composite nature of Teresa's reconstructed story. Perhaps the most notable feature of Domecq's novel, however, is the multifaceted connection between the life of a young individual, such as Teresa, and the socio-political upheavals and conflicts on a national scale that eventually lead to the Mexican Revolution. Ultimately, Domecq triumphs not only in creating a lively sketch of a popular Mexican heroine; she also succeeds in showing how transformative, national forces play out at local levels.

Though most of Domecq's literary work, including *Once días* and *Bestiario doméstico*, still awaits scholarly attention, *La insólita historia de la Santa de Cabora* has been the subject of several critical studies. One scholarly tendency has been to examine Domecq's novel in light of the known history of Teresa de Urrea, and a couple of studies have even explored the relationships between narrative technique, historical discourse, and national identity in the novel. But the most popular scholarly tendency has been to investigate elements of the novel—the female characters, motherhood, patriarchy, and misogyny—within the context of feminism. Indeed, much of Domecq's reputation as a feminist writer stems from the scholarly attention given to *La insólita historia*, and future studies of Domecq's work will likely enhance Domecq's status as a significant woman writer concerned with experiences and issues that are unique to women.

Recent Works and Themes

Domecq's interest in describing and analyzing female identity, the role of women in society, and the lives of specific women is evident throughout her literary career, starting with *Once días* and continuing with *Bestiario doméstico*, *Acechando al unicornio*, and *La insólita historia de la Santa de Cabora*. Since the publication of *La insólita historia*, women and womanhood have occupied an even more explicit place in Domecq's literary career, and her publications in the 1990s and afterward show her increasingly focussed interest in the challenges faced by women in a world ruled by men. Her autobiography, *Brianda Domecq: De cuerpo entero* (1991; In Full View, published in English as *Truth, Lies and Other Inventions: An Autobiography*), reveals her personal struggle to come to terms with her childhood, adult life, and self-identity. The following year, Domecq published *A través de los ojos de ella* (1992; Through Her Eyes), a critical anthology of woman-themed short stories by Mexican women writers. In the middle of the decade, Domecq published *Mujer que publica, mujer pública* (1994; Woman Who Publishes, Public Woman), a collection of original essays on women writers such as Virginia Woolf, Inés Arredondo, and Georges Sand. Her second collection of short stories, *Un día fui caballo* (2000, *When I Was a Horse*), is also her most recently published work. In this collection, Domecq emphasizes familiar themes related to women and their role in a male-dominated society, but the stories nonetheless show considerable variation in subject matter and context.

Though Brianda Domecq started her literary career relatively late in life, she has not only earned distinction as one of Mexico's most important women writers, but she also has emerged as one of contemporary Mexico's most creative and versatile writers in general. Domecq's importance as a woman writer and feminist comes chiefly from *La insólita historia de la Santa de Cabora*, but her less studied works—both fictional and non-fictional—reveal equally interesting and multifaceted perspectives on women and their roles in society. Given her wide range of literary and critical publications, and given her special interest in understanding the nuances of women's lives, Brianda Domecq has undeniably earned a place among Latin America's most important women writers.

R. John McCaw

Selected Works

Once días . . . y algo más. Xalapa, Mexico: Universidad Veracruzana, 1979.

La insólita historia de la Santa de Cabora. Mexico City: Planeta, 1990.

Brianda Domecq: De cuerpo entero. Mexico City: Coordinación de Difusión Cultural, Dirección de Literatura, Universidad Nacional Autónoma de México: Ediciones Corunda, 1991.

Bestiario doméstico. Mexico City: Fondo de Cultura Económica, 1992.

Un día fui caballo. Mexico City: Biblioteca del Instituto de Seguridad y Servicios Sociales de los Trabajadores del Estado, 2000.

References and Further Reading

De Beer, Gabriella. "Brianda Domecq". In *Contemporary Mexican Women Writers: Five Voices*. Austin, TX: University of Texas Press, 1996.

García, Kay S. *Broken Bars: New Perspectives from Mexican Women Writers*. Albuquerque, NM: University of New Mexico Press, 1994.

Merithew, Charlene. *Re-Presenting the Nation: Contemporary Mexican Women Writers*. New Orleans, LA: University Press of the South, 2001.

Strand, Cheryl. "Conversation with Brianda Domecq". *Bilingual Review* 16(3) (1998): 248–54.

DORNBIERER, MANÚ

Born in 1932 in Mexico City, Mexico, to a Swiss-born father and the daughter of French immigrants, Manú Dornbierer married at a young age, had three children and after fourteen years of marriage to an architect, divorced. In an interview published in *Excelsior* on April 30, 1989, Dornbierer speculates that this marital relationship bequeathed her interest in home remodeling, which she claims to be a more lucrative enterprise than her journalism and fiction writing. The Mexican public best knows Dornbierer for her prolific criticism of national politics, which spans a dozen or so texts. Dornbierer's literary interest began when she translated an article from French to Spanish for a women's magazine. Soon, Dornbierer began publishing her own articles and short stories. The scant literary criticism on her work tends to celebrate Dornbierer's use of science fiction in her short stories. Today, Dornbierer lives in Acapulco and maintains a webpage rich in information on her past and current activities.

Career in Journalism

From 1977–88, Dornbierer produced a weekly article for the political magazine *Siempre!*. She wrote three weekly columns for the newspaper *Novedades* from 1973–84, two weekly columns for *Excélsior* 1984–91 and returned to this paper from 2001–2, and wrote for *El Financiero* from 1994–99. Starting in 2004, she published in the newspaper *Diario Monitor*. During the height of her involvement with journalism, her opinion pieces appeared in dozens of local Mexican newspapers from coast to coast and even in Los Angeles. In addition to radio broadcasts, Dornbierer has also shared her frank opinions and investigative journalism with the Mexican television audience. From 1980–84 she appeared on the program *Para Gente Grande* on Televisa. As with her exit from *Excelsior* in 1991, Dornbierer attributes the end of her work with Televisa to political pressure exerted by powerful men who objected to her candid coverage of Mexican politics.

Most of Dornbierer's journalism has been collected in a series of books, which proliferate thanks to her habit of issuing expanded re-editions. Four volumes titled *Satiricosas* (1984; 1985; 1987; 1989; 'Satirica-things') have given birth to a recycled version of the series that incorporates old columns with new material, distinguishable by typeface. Dornbierer's journalistic style is accessible, with a limited vocabulary, straightforward sentences, and short paragraphs. Dornbierer may find success in the Mexican book market for her willingness to communicate with the lowest common denominator among her readers. For example, she is not above defining such potentially confusing words as "oligarchy" within a sentence that employs the term. Often her books use large print, perhaps in anticipation of a general reading audience likely to buy a graphic novel or colorful daily tabloid. Dornbierer habitually relies on undocumented personal opinion and, in the instances that require a bibliography, on simple informative texts.

Novels

The social criticism expressed in plain language that is characteristic of her journalism also defines Dornbierer's fiction. Her first novel, *El bien y el mal* (1986, Good and Evil) was republished with slight changes as *Matacandela* (1996) ten years after its debut. Both the first novel and Dornbierer's second novel, *Los indignos* (1988, The Undeserving), explore a theme based on the tenets of second-wave feminism, namely that women should enjoy their sexuality and that housework and child-rearing duties for middle-class and upper-middle-class women are unfulfilling in the absence of a profession outside the home. Dornbierer's thesis calls for female characters based on type who emerge in relation to men characters, whether husbands, lovers, or fathers. The novels tend to be circular, in part because—feminist principles aside, Dornbierer is in many ways a conservative writer and because the thesis anticipates the characters' destinies from the beginning of the novel. *Los indignos* is the superior of the two novels as far as innovation goes. Among the sections of character exposition, Dornbierer intercalates segments of journalistic opinion pieces on politics, art, and western lifestyles in the 1960s that serves to shake up the familiar thesis novel.

Short Stories

Like the recycled and expanded tomes of *Satiricosas*, Dornbierer republished the short-story collection *La grieta* (1978, The Fissure) with five new stories under the title *Nuevas dimensiones* (1996, New Dimensions). In the only English-language criticism catalogued on Dornbierer's work, Gabriel Trujillo Muñoz enthusiastically reviews the stories and discovers in them strong women protagonists, adequate attention to characters' psychological perception, and a range of genres, from fantastic to fairy tales to gothic. It can be added that in her short stories Dornbierer habitually explores the notion of two, equally authentic realities and meditates on the disastrous consequences of war. Perhaps Dornbierer's least sophisticated collection is *Sonrío, luego existo* (1983, I Smile, Therefore I Exist) which presents a series of ironic anecdotes purported to derive from believe-it-or-not episodes from daily life.

A Truth that Sells

Perhaps Dornbierer's greatest strength as a journalist is her indignation. Though she seems to lack specialized knowledge of areas beyond Mexican politics and general history, her condemnation of corruption, censorship, economic crises precipitated by political ineptitude and other crimes creates a tone of earnestness. This sincerity, while helping to win commercial success, limits the viciousness of her sarcasm and sometimes makes her less witty than righteous. Her most sustained attempt at political satire, *Los periodistas mueren de noche* (1993, Journalists Die at Night) springs from a vow that Dornbierer took after leaving *Excélsior* in 1991. Though she promised not to publish journalism again until Carlos Salinas's presidency ended, she released the hybrid *Los periodistas*, which contains thirty-three political anecdotes that comment on contemporary Mexico, as told by journalist Gil Duarte, who argues for his life before a tribunal of saints. In segments concerning such current topics as drug trafficking, the environment, and child prostitution, Duarte describes a "Banana Republic" that bears many parallels to the Salinas administration, including an Emperor Nasilas (a reference to Salinas), the Party of Infernal Reactionaries (referring to the PRI, the Institutional Revolutionary Party), the media monopoly Teletrinca (Televisa), and the governmental program *Falicidad* (fallacy), a reference to Salinas's program *Solidaridad* (solidarity). The legislation that Nasilas wishes to pass, the Transaction of Free Purchase of the Country, is a send-up of NAFTA. Here, Dornbierer shows her dislike of neoliberalism, her preference for a secular state, and her ideal brand of feminism that supports birth control and in cases of rape, abortion. The rigid structure of Duarte's anecdotes and the saints' reactions become tedious after the first hundred pages or so.

Limitations

Dornbierer does not convey a broad sense of Mexican politics and its historical resonances in the way that more famous cultural critics such as Carlos Monsiváis manage. In general, her journalism focuses on the daily event, on the scandal at hand without greater reflection, which jeopardizes the longevity of Dornbierer's work. Dornbierer is a brave writer, however, and she has persevered in her fight for democracy, freedom of speech, accountability for public figures, and greater economic equality among Mexican citizens. She appears to believe sincerely that journalism provides a superior form of historical narrative, for the fresher, fairer, more real and authentic expression innate to journalism that history books cannot manage (*Ave César* [1982, Hail Caesar] 13). Her faith and ambition in the Mexican populace and national promise never waver, even over thousands of pages.

EMILY HIND

Selected Works

Fiction

La grieta y otros cuentos. Mexico: Diana, 1978. Rev. edn with 5 additional stories, *Nuevas Dimensiones*. Mexico: Grijalbo, 1996.
Sonrío, luego existo. Mexico: Diana, 1983.
El bien y el mal. Mexico: Océano, 1986. 2nd edn as *Matacandela*. Mexico: Grijalbo, 1996.
Los indignos: Novela autobiográfica. Mexico: Diana, 1988.
Non-fiction in the original *Satiricosas* series
Satiricosas I. Mexico: Katún, 1984.
Satiricosas II. Mexico: Katún, 1985.
Satiricosas III. Mexico: Posada, 1987.
Satiricosas IV (Epílogo). Mexico: Posada, 1989.
Revised collection of *Satiricosas*

Ave César: López Portillo (1976–1982), Emperador de México. Mexico: Grijalbo, 1982.
El hombre gris: El sexenio de Miguel de la Madrid (1982–1988). Mexico: Grijalbo, 1999. (Though this text was published in 1999, its contents pertain to the second of the revised series.)
Los periodistas mueren de noche. Mexico: Grijalbo, 1993.
El Prinosaurio: La bestia política mexicana. Mexico: Grijalbo, 1994.
La Neta. Mexico: Grijalbo, 1995.
La Neta II. Mexico: Grijalbo, 1997.
Sexenio terminal. Mexico: Grijalbo, 2000.
Foxtrot: De cómo Vicente nos lleva al baile global. Mexico: Grijalbo, 2002.
Updated information on "*Satiricosas*" can be found on Dornbierer's *webpage:* http://www.manu-dornbierer.com.mx/ (31 July 2006)

References and Further Reading

Galicia Miguel, Renato. "Manú Dornbierer: 25 años de periodismo político". *El Financiero* 2 Oct. 1998: 46.
Güemes, César. "Manú Dornbierer reedita *Los indignos*". *El Financiero* 19 Apr. 1995: 57.
Juárez Madrid, Jesús. "*Sexenio Terminal*, de Manú Dorbnierer, apareció". *Excélsior* 27 Nov. 2000: B1.
Trujillo Muñoz, Gabriel. "Manú Dornbierer". In Darrell B. Lockhart (ed.), *Latin American Science Fiction Writers: An A–Z Guide*. Westport, CT: Greenwood Press, 2004, pp. 77–8.

DUJOVNE ORTIZ, ALICIA

Of Ukrainian and Jewish descent, Alicia Dujovne Ortiz (1940) was born in Buenos Aires, Argentina, and grew up in Peronist Argentina in a household with anti-Peronist parents. Her father, Carlos Dujovne, was one of the founders of the Argentinean Communist Party. He was imprisoned for two years by the Perón government and the Party later revoked his membership when he abandoned it because of disillusionment, effectively preventing his daughter's adherence the movement in the mid-1960s. Daughter of ex-landowners of Italian descent, her mother Alicia Ortiz, was a novelist and feminist, author of a history of literature in 20 volumes and a study of women in Russian literature, among others.

Alicia Dujovne Ortiz studied literature at the University of Buenos Aires. The budding writer made a notable appearance in a fake interview of herself by Julio Cortázar published in an Argentinean magazine as a "vehement revolutionary that questionably uses a double last name" ("Estamos como queremos o los monstruos en acción," *Crisis*, Buenos Aires, 11, 1974). Four years later, the young journalist emigrated with her young daughter from Argentina to France, because of the difficult situation created by the military dictatorship.

A cultural journalist at *La Opinión* (Argentina), *Excelsior* (Mexico), *La Vanguardia* (Spain) and *Le Monde* (France), Dujovne Ortiz has maintained a frequent column for the Argentinean newspaper *La Nación* since the 1970s. She has directed writing workshops in France and Argentina as well as prepared radio programs for *France Culture*. From 1978 to 1995, Dujovne Ortiz was also an editorial adviser on Spanish and Italian language books for the French editorial house Gallimard. The writer received a Guggenheim Foundation prize in 1986 as well as four creative bursaries from the French Centre National du Livre. After more than 20 years of exile, Dujovne Ortiz attempted a return to Buenos Aires in 1999, but three years later returned to France and compiled a guide for the emigrant: *Al que se va* (To the One Who Goes), in which she reflects on the difficult question of exile for Argentineans and the resulting situation for the country's society and culture. She again returned to Buenos Aires in 2006.

Dujovne Ortiz' first books were published in the 1960s, when she first released a collection of poems written during the admittedly difficult passage from adolescence to adulthood, entitled *Orejas invisibles para el rumor de nuestros pasos* (1967, Invisible Ears to the Sound of Our Steps), and *Mapa del olvidado tesoro* (1969, Map of the Forgotten Treasure). Her third collection of poetry, *Recetas, florecillas y otros contentos* (Recipes, Little Flowers and Other Happiness), contains the origins of the eroticism that will appear in later novels and biographies. Furthermore, according to Carolina Rocha's study of the text, it is a potential precursor to Laura Esquivel's culinary eroticism of *Like Water for Chocolate*.

Although she published poetry in later years, Dujovne Ortiz' focus shifted towards the novelistic genre in 1977 with the publication in Argentina of *El buzón de la esquina* (The Mailbox on the Corner), a series of poetic and fantastic stories told about a character named Jacinta. In 1980, she published *El agujero en la tierra* (The Hole in the Earth) in which she recreates life in rural Argentina using various immigrant characters, in a poetic and richly imaginative language that often borders on the experimental.

El árbol de la gitana (1997, The Gypsy's Tree) is, according to the author, the step between her earlier, often surrealist fiction, and the new reality, exile. In this book, and for the first time, Dujovne Ortiz is intensely personal in a text that she qualifies as auto-fiction in the sense that she "invents herself" and her new identity as an exile. In her unpublished study of this work, Kelly Jensen finds that Dujovne Ortiz is attempting to explore and define the "exilic identity" of one who is caught between two cultures which to call home. That first collection of stories on exile and identity was followed almost ten years later by *Las perlas rojas* (2005, The Red Pearls), written with a similar goal.

Alicia Dujovne Ortiz is also the author of a number of biographies in which she desacralises mythical characters from Argentinean history and society. This is a distinctive vision that she asserts stems from the apparent objectivity afforded by her exile. At the petition of the Argentinean singer and poet, Alicia Dujovne Ortiz researched and prepared the biography *María Elena Walsh* (1979). This was her first official incursion into the biographical genre, one that she embraces to this day with remarkable success. The second character to occupy Dujovne Ortiz' creative sphere is the soccer player Diego Maradona, also the solitary masculine protagonist present in her biographical series. She wrote *Maradona c'est moi* (1992, I Am Maradona) originally in French and it was translated by the author herself and published in Spanish a year later (1993).

Perhaps her most famous work is *Eva Perón: La Biografía* (1995), translated into more than twenty languages to date and celebrated by some as one of the authoritative versions of Evita Duarte's life despite the fictionalised biography intriguingly being considered to be "written for entertainment rather than fact" (Kate Jennings, "Two Faces of Evita", *New York Times Review*, Nov. 24, 1996). Thanks to the meticulous techniques she had acquired in previous biographies, Alicia Dujovne Ortiz researched her manuscript through interviews of people who surrounded the famous figure, whose death she had admittedly mourned, a sentiment she had concealed from her anti-Peronist parents at the time. In writing the book, the author admits having wanted to expose the numerous inconsistencies that existed in the different ways the legendary woman's life had been manufactured, especially in the preparation for Tony Parker, movie, *Evita*.

The author continued the biographical series with two fictionalized (and impeccably researched) biographies about other women who regrettably lived in the shadow of legendary men but whom Dujovne Ortiz reveals as remarkable. The first novel is titled *Anita cubierta de arena* (2003, Anita Covered in Sand) and explores the life of Ana Maria de Jesus Ribeiro. She was better known as Anita Garibaldi, the Italian revolutionary Guiseppe Garibaldi's Brazilian spouse who left everything (including her then-husband) to follow Garibaldi in his various illustrious travels. For *Dora Maar, prisionera de la mirada* (Dora Maar: Prisoner of the Gaze), Dujovne Ortiz explores and tells the story of Henriette Theodora Markovitch, the surrealist photographer and muse of Man Ray and Pablo Picasso who, like the author, had spent her childhood in Argentina.

Dujovne Ortiz is herself a purveyor of myths; the novel *Mireya* (1998) is the completely fictional biography of a prostitute and model from one of Toulouse Lautrec's paintings, "Le Salon de la Rue des Moulins", whom Julio Cortázar had imagined traveling to Argentina and becoming the legendary *Rubía Mireya* of assorted tango lyrics. Alicia Dujovne Ortiz garnered a nomination for the French Médicis Prize for Best Foreign Book for *Mireya*. Apart from putting out volumes almost simultaneously in French and Spanish (often showcasing her own translations), Dujovne Ortiz has also published various novels exclusively in French including essays on the cities of *Bogotá* and *Buenos Aires*, as well as three novels for adolescents in which she presents her socially conscious views in ways that they can be understood by that demographic grouping.

SOPHIE M. LAVOIE

Selected Works

Recetas, florecillas y otros contentos. Buenos Aires: Editorial Rayuela, 1973.

Eva Perón: A Biography. Trans. Shawn Fields, New York: St. Martin's Press, 1996.

Mireya. Buenos Aires: Alfaguara, 1998.

Al que se va. Buenos Aires: Libros del Zorzal, 2002.

Dora Maar, prisionera de la mirada. Buenos Aires: Editorial Tusquets, 2003.

References and Further Reading

Kaplan, Caren Jane. "The Poetics of Displacement: Exile, Immigration and Travel in Contemporary Autobiographical Writing". PhD dissertation, University of California, Santa Cruz, 1987.

Mariani, Philomena (ed.). *Critical Fictions: The Politics of Imaginative Writing*. Seattle, WA: Bay Press, 1991.

Partnoy, Alicia (ed.). *You Can't Drown the Fire: Latin American Women Writing in Exile*. San Francisco, CA: Cleiss Press, 1988.

Rocha, Carolina. "A partir del exilio: la exploración de la identidad en la narrativa de Alicia Dujovne Ortiz". In Birgit Mertz-Baumgartner and Erna Pfeiffer (eds), *Aves de paso. Autores latinoamericanos entre exilio y transculturación (1970–2002)*. Madrid: Iberoamericana; Frankfurt: Vervuert Verlag, 2005, pp. 117–30.

Senkman, Leonardo. "La Nación imaginaria de los escritores judíos latinoamericanos". *Revista Iberoamericana*, LXVI(191) (April–June 2000): 202–29.

E

ECHEVERRÍA DE LARRAÍN, INÉS

Inés Echeverría de Larraín (1868–1949) or Iris, her literary pen name, is one of the most productive and renowned Chilean women writers of the first half of the century. She published over a dozen books during her life as well as numerous articles in major newspapers and magazines. A public intellectual, she was appointed to the Faculty of Philosophy and Sciences of the University of Chile in 1922. Earlier that same year, Iris' friend Amanda Labarca Huberson had become the first woman to hold a university faculty position in Chile.

Born on December 22, 1868, in Santiago, Chile, to an aristocratic family that included Andrés Bello (her grandfather), Iris was a controversial figure who transgressed the limitations imposed on upper-class women of her time. Shortly after she was born, her mother, Inés Bello, died, and her aloof and unstable father, Felix Echeverría, left Inés in the care of her paternal grandparents and a single aunt who raised her according to strict conservative and Catholic principles. Like most girls of her social class, she was instructed privately at home by a French governess who introduced her not only to French grammar, but also French literature and culture. She later claimed that she became so fascinated with French that she ultimately never learned English or any other language. To the disapproval of some middle-class women writers of her time, Iris declared that French was the language she associated with literature because of its richness and wide range of tones. Her writing made frequent resort to French expressions and sentences. Two of her books, *Entre deux mondes* (1914, Between Two Worlds) and *Au Delà* (1948, Farther Along) were originally published in French.

In 1892, at the age of 24, she married Joaquín Larraín Alcalde, with whom she had four daughters. Iris was an unconventional wife and a distant mother with an intense public life that included long trips abroad, political activism and public exposure that sometimes strained her family. Nevertheless, when Rebeca, the second of her daughters, was murdered by her husband Roberto Barceló in 1933, Iris called on all her contacts in the media and the government to make sure her son-in-law received the severest sentence. After a long public legal battle, she convinced her close friend, President Arturo Alessandri not to commute Barceló's sentence. In spite of his aristocratic origins and Iris's suffering public image, he was condemned to death by firing squad in 1936.

Birth of the Writer

Inés Echeverría claimed that Iris, her literary persona, was born only after she had lived for over thirty years in a state of mental slavery and social repression. Her decision to write, to actively participate in politics and to challenge social and religious norms can be understood as the result of the influence of certain figures and events that left a deep impression on Inés as a young girl. Her maternal grandmother, Rosario Reyes, whom she visited regularly, was well known for her literary salons and liberal life style. As a girl, Iris was fascinated by this world and recited French poetry in front of her grandmother's guests. Afterwards, in her late teens, she was sent to Europe with her uncle and his family. There she developed new ideas about aesthetics and the role of women and witnessed cultural events such as the opening of the Eiffel Tower during the Paris Exposition of 1889. Once back in Chile, she began frequenting literary gatherings at which she met middle-class writers and political leaders who were viewed with fear and contempt by the conservative ruling class to which she belonged. By this point Iris had discovered oriental philosophy, which, along with her readings of Ibsen, Bergson, Maeterlinck, Tagore and Emerson, laid the foundation for her own particular spiritualism. She rejected the excessive positivism that dominated the nineteenth century and instead identified with a literary and aesthetic sensibility that her critics have called avant-garde spiritualism.

Following a trip to the Holy Land in 1900, Iris wrote her first book, *Hacia el Oriente* (Towards the Orient), published anonymously in 1905. It narrated her experience in Palestine in an intimate and reflective tone that went behind place description, providing an insight into her own interiority. After enjoying a favorable critical reception, Iris dedicated the following years to writing intensely and hosting literary gatherings that brought together well-known writers and politicians. In 1910, she published *Tierra Virgen* (Virgin Land), *Perfiles Vagos* (Vague Portraits), *Hojas Caídas* (Fallen Leaves) and *Emociones Teatrales* (Theatrical Emotions). Submitted for publication a week before Iris left for Europe, these books created a scandal among the upper class and the church because of their sarcastic tone and sharp criticism of individuals, aristocratic families, well-known priests and various aspects of Chilean culture. Despite her family's request for a retraction and the threat of excommunication by the Catholic Church, Iris ignored her critics and kept writing. *La hora de queda* (Time of Stillness), a collection of novellas, was published in 1918. Between 1930 and 1946, she published a six-volume historical novel, *Alborada* (Dawn). This monumental work, which is narrated by several generations of women, tells the story of Chile as a nation, from its birth to Iris's era. Although this novel is not regarded as having high literary value, its strong female characters who leave the domestic space to become involved in social and political events offer a perspective that diverges significantly from the rest of the novels written by contemporary Chilean writers in the 1930s and 1940s.

Feminist and Public Figure

A declared feminist and founder of the Ladies' Club, the first Chilean women's organization formed outside the Church, Iris was a key figure in her country's liberation movement. She wrote about the condition of women in newspapers and magazines: even her literary critical pieces challenged traditional gender roles. She actively defended women's civil rights in her writings, lectures, and by supporting politicians that worked to improve women's social and legal status. However, Iris's feminism was limited to upper-class women and did not extend to poor and working-class women, as Gabriela Mistral argued when she refused to participate in her aristocratic organizations. Iris was more of an intellectual feminist, whose writing sharply analyzed the relationships between women's ignorance, religious fanaticism, legal negligence and male domination.

Current critics agree that the most interesting and original part of her production consists of the many non-canonical genres she cultivated, such as her memoirs, essays, diaries, travel journals and innumerable articles on art, literature and culture. The last of these were published mainly in the newspaper *La Nación* and the magazine *Zig-Zag*; some of them are included in the anthology *Inés Echeverría (Iris): Alma femenina y mujer moderna*. (Inés Echeverría (Iris): Feminine Soul and Modern Woman). In her writing, Iris analyzed the limitations women writers had to confront, but at the same time made use of her female identity as a source of empowerment which offered her a knowledge that she believed originated in her sensitivity and gave her a unique and deeper understanding of reality.

Published in 2005, Iris's memoirs, covering the period from 1889 to 1925, comprise a valuable testimony to the process of women's liberation, together with an intimate view of some key historical events. Iris died in Santiago, Chile, on January 13, 1949, a few days after receiving an invitation to the official declaration of Chilean women's right to vote.

CLAUDIA CABELLO HUTT

Selected Works

Hacia el Oriente. Santiago de Chile: Imprenta Universitaria, 1905.
Tierra virgen. Santiago de Chile: Imprenta Universitaria, 1910.
Perfiles vagos. Santiago de Chile: Imprenta Universitaria, 1910.
Emociones teatrales. Santiago de Chile: Imprenta Universitaria, 1910.
Hojas caídas. Santiago de Chile: Imprenta Universitaria, 1910.
Entre deux mondes. Paris: Bernard Grasset, 1914.
Cuando mi tierra nació. Santiago de Chile: Nascimiento, 1930.
Cuando mi tierra fue moza. Santiago de Chile: Nascimiento, 1943.
Inés Echeverría (Iris): Alma femenina y mujer moderna. Edited by Bernardo Subercaseaux. Santiago de Chile: Cuarto Propio, 2001.
Memorias de Iris. 1899–1925. Santiago de Chile: Aguilar, 2005.

References and Further Reading

Echeverría, Mónica. *Agonía de una irreverente*. Santiago de Chile: Sudamericana, 1997.
Labarca Hubertson, Amanda. "La vida del espíritu: Conversando con la señora Inés Echeverría de Larraín". http://www.memoriachilena.cl/mchilena01/temas/documento_detalle.asp?id=MC0010831 (9 October 2006).
Ovalle Castillo, Francisco Javier. *Inés Echeverría de Larraín: Iris en la república de las letras*. Santiago de Chile: Imprenta Universitaria, 1918.
Prado Traverso, Marcela. "Inés Echeverría Bello (Iris) (1868–1949)". In Patricia Rubio (ed.), *Escritoras Chilenas: novela y cuento*. Santiago de Chile: Cuarto Propio, 1999.
Subercaseaux, Bernardo. "Las mujeres también escriben malas novelas (Sujeto escindido e híbrido narrativo)". *Revista Chilena de Literatura* 56 (2000): 93–103.
——. "Sujeto femenino y voces en conflicto: el caso de Inés Echvrría-Iris (1869–1949)". *Revista de crítica cultural* 22 (2001): 62–6.

ELTIT, DIAMELA

Diamela Eltit (b. 1949) is famous for her innovative and experimental cultural work. A novelist and essayist, she has also worked extensively in the visual and performance arts. Writing in response to the stifling conditions of Augusto Pinochet's dictatorship of Chile (1973–90), Eltit's work was critical, inventive, disturbing, and bold. During the Pinochet years, Eltit lived in Santiago and she was involved in various cultural efforts to protest and challenge the regime. In an attempt to bring her writing and work into a public space she formed an artistic collective entitled, CADA (Colectivo de Acciones de Arte/Art Actions Collective), which she founded in conjunction with the Chilean poet Raúl Zurita and the visual artist Lotty Rosenfeld. In one example of a CADA project from 1980, Eltit washed the street in front of houses of prostitutes as a symbolic gesture meant to restore dignity to the community and to protest the "zones of pain" created by the dictatorship.

Eltit forms part of the 1980s Post-Coup Generation of Chilean writers (born between 1948–57) who published innovative and daring work during the dictatorship and that tended to use complex and experimental aesthetics, a neo-avant-garde, as a means of intense social critique. The recipient of numerous literary prizes and honors, she was awarded a Guggenheim grant in 1985. Much of her work investigates the construction of gender and specifically the treatment of women and she was one of the key organizers of the Congreso Internacional de Literatura Femenina Latinoamericana (International Congress on Latin American Women's Writing) held in Santiago in 1987, which—during the dictatorship—brought together writers and scholars from the region and the

United States to analyze the marginalization of women's writing. After the election of Patricio Aylwin in 1990, she became the cultural attaché at the Chilean Embassy in Mexico. She has taught at various universities including Brown University, the National University of Chile, and Mexico's Metropolitan University of Technology.

The Pinochet Years

When Augusto Pinochet led the violent coup in 1973 to overthrow the democratically elected Socialist president, Salvador Allende, the Chilean nation suffered the most extreme forms of authoritarian repression. Many were forced into exile and the secret police detained, tortured, and murdered thousands of "subversives" extra-judicially with no official accounting for their arrests. Thus began a reign of terror that paralyzed the Chilean populace and that effectively silenced, through murder, detention, and exile, much of the Chilean intellectual elite. By the late 1970s, though, there emerged a growing population of artists and writers who sought creative ways to be critical of the dictatorship. A group of these writers and artists, including Eltit, distanced themselves from traditional forms of leftist protest art, such as protest songs and testimonials, seeking instead a mode of critique that was aesthetically innovative and artistically complex. In this sense Eltit's critical project during the Pinochet years went beyond a mere protest against the state and she used her art to challenge the ways that society attempts to categorize and define identity. Focusing on segments of society that were being systematically marginalized, oppressed, and abused, Eltit's work during the Pinochet years attempts to reveal the ties between regimes of power and regimes of meaning. For this reason, her work centers on women, the poor, and the insane while simultaneously critiquing the possibility of representing such groups. On the one hand, she shows how the marginalized sectors of society stage rebellion and, on the other hand, she dismantles the language with which she tells her stories. According to Eltit, any challenge to social and political structures requires attention to the marginalized and to the linguistic and symbolic systems that represent these groups.

Her first novel, *Lumpérica* (*E. Luminata*) published in 1983, set the tone for a dramatically distinct narrative style. This highly experimental style makes it exceedingly difficult to provide plot summaries of any of her novels since at a fundamental level her novels are efforts to deconstruct the language of the state and the traditional ways of structuring meaning and identity. This means that any effort to describe the content of her novels must be understood within a larger aesthetic project that is committed to providing a counter-discourse to official rhetoric and to radically critiquing traditional forms of knowledge production. Eltit's first novel revolves around a female figure who is among the "lumpen" of Santiago and who has been afflicted with convulsions and bleeding. Through the optic of this woman Eltit examines the marginalized in the city, employing a style that is designed to shock and which is similar to visual narrative. Focusing on a plaza where performance art is mixed with debauchery, the novel consists of fragments and vignettes that are united in their investigation of writing's relationship to power and sexual desire.

Of her novels during the dictatorship, *Por la patria* (1986, For the Fatherland) is considered to be one of the most compelling narratives of cultural resistance during the Pinochet regime. This novel, like her first, centers on a female protagonist, alternately named Coya/Coa, who is a marginalized victim of society. This figure, however, is more a symbol or semantic field, than a "character" in the traditional narrative sense. The figure of Coya/Coa serves to transmit a critical voice of opposition to the structuring narratives of Chilean society. As a mestiza and a social outcast, Coya/Coa performs a violent rejection of linguistic norms, as evidenced by her alternating names: Coya refers to the original queen of the Inca Empire and symbolizes collective memory and Coa means slang in Chilean Spanish and signifies the delinquent language of the marginalized class. Yoking these two groups of social outcasts together through her protagonist's polyphonic voice, Eltit's novel embarks on a series of linguistic protests that suggest that social resistance can only be a force for change via a radical critique of modes of communication. In conjunction with the novel's interest in language and communication is an intense scrutiny of gender norms. The protagonist is obsessed with incest and patriarchy, which ultimately leads to her encounter with her jailor, Juan, an impotent "macho". Through the figure of Juan, Eltit analyzes masculine forms of power to reveal the ways in which they can undergo crisis and destruction. The ambiguous relationship between Coya/Coa and Juan further hints at Coya/Coa's fragmented and dispersed identity. She is at once victim and aggressor, marginal and central, a subject of official discourse and a creator of her own voice.

Eltit's novels during the Pinochet period are characterized by a radical rupture with traditional narrative form. They represent diverse linguistic usage as well as a break with modernist forms of writing. Gender, family relations, and cultural identity are carefully critiqued through the use of language that is revealed to have multiple meanings that are constantly in flux. Insanity, passion, and illness are represented as forces which envelope her characters in a storm of chaos, isolation, and social neglect. For example, in *El cuarto mundo* (1988, The Fourth World), Eltit uses the metaphor of the family to reveal a persistent social crisis that has specific implications for understanding the complexities of Chilean history in the last years of Pinochet's dictatorship. The novel recounts the incestuous relationship between two twins and over the course of the novel the linguistic distinctions between the feminine and the masculine break down.

In her last novel of the Pinochet period, *Vaca sagrada* (1991, Sacred Cow), a female protagonist is the reader's guide through the confusion of authoritarian society. Beginning with a scene where the reader witnesses the protagonist bathing in her menstrual blood, the protagonist challenges all traditional expectations for gender roles. Her relationship with Manuel who decides to leave the city and travel South, her connection to the tortured Francisca, and her wandering in the streets all serve as backdrops for an investigation into the relationship between the female body, sexuality, violence, power, and official discourse.

Testimonials

As evidence of her commitment to make her art provocative and socially relevant, Eltit has also worked on testimonials that give first-hand accounts of the most marginalized segments of society. In particular, she recorded the voice of a homeless man suffering from delusions in *El padre mío* (My Father). She also worked in conjunction with the photographer Paz Errázuriz on *El infarto del alma* (1995, Soul Attack), a collection of text and images that represent romantic couples living in a mental hospital. In both cases, Eltit sought the most abject, abandoned, and ignored segments of society and imagined that these voices represented Chile itself in all of its horror and beauty. For while these texts illuminate the extreme ways in which certain sectors of the Chilean population have been forsaken, the voices and images presented are also ones of love and spirited resistance. These testimonials uncover the obscure and frightening space of the other, while giving voice to their discursive innovation.

Literature of the Transition

Eltit has written three novels since the official end to Pinochet's rule that represent the social context of Chile's transition to democracy: *Los vigilantes* (1994, Custody of the Eyes), *Los trabajadores de la muerte* (1998, The Death Workers), and *Mano de obra* (2002, Manual Labor). Each of these directly confronts the official discourse of the transition, which has described Chile as a model nation of economic progress and democratic ideals. In contrast, Eltit characterizes the Chilean transition as complicit with the dogma of the Catholic Church and subservient to the neoliberal economic logic of hyper-capitalism. Whereas during the Pinochet era she focused on the violence of the authoritarian state, since the transition to democracy, she has focused on the violence of historical amnesia and political apathy. Like her earlier work, she funnels this critique through the female body, especially through the figure of the mother, and she posits the fractured family as a symbol for social decay and devastation. This technique is especially visible in the first two novels of this period, which recount the letters from a single mother to the absent father of her son and a tragic tale of incest respectively. Her third novel of the transition, *Mano de obra,* is situated in one of the most poignant examples of global postmodern culture—the mega-supermarket—where the lives of the workers are less important than the dazzling display of products to consume. Eltit continues to seek an innovative and radical form of writing that engages and disturbs while reminding readers of the most oppressed and alienated members of society.

SOPHIA A. MCCLENNEN

Selected Works

Lumpérica. Santiago de Chile: Las Ediciones del Ornitorrinco, 1983.
Por la patria. Santiago de Chile: Las Ediciones del Ornitorrinco, 1986.
El cuarto mundo. Santiago de Chile: Planeta, 1988.
El Padre Mío. Santiago de Chile: Francisco Zegers Editor, 1989.
Vaca sagrada. Buenos Aires: Planeta, 1991.
Elena Caffarena: el derecho a voz, el derecho al voto. México: Casa de Chile en México, 1993.
El infarto del alma. With photos by Paz Errázuriz. Santiago de Chile: Francisco Zegers Editor, 1994.
Los vigilantes. Santiago de Chile: Editorial Sudamericana, 1994.
The Fourth World. Trans. Dick Gerdes. Lincoln, NB: University of Nebraska Press, 1995.
Sacred Cow. Trans. Amanda Hopkinson. New York: Serpent's Tail, 1995.
E. Luminata. Trans. Ronald Christ. Sante Fe, NM: Lumen, 1997.
Los trabajadores de la muerte. Santiago de Chile: Seix Barral, 1998.
Emergencias. Escritos sobre literatura, arte y política, ed. y pról. Leónidas Morales T. Santiago de Chile: Planeta /Ariel, 2000.
Mano de obra. Santiago de Chile: Seix Barral, 2002.
Custody of the Eyes. Trans. Helen Lane and Ronald Christ. Sante Fe, NM: Lumen, 2005.

References and Further Reading

Agosín, Marjorie. "Diamela Eltit o la vocación de lo marginal". *Las hacedoras: mujer, imagen, escritura.* Santiago: Editorial Cuarto Propio, 1993.
Avelar, Idelber. *The Untimely Present: Postdictatorial Latin American Fiction and the Task of Mourning*. Durham, NC: Duke University Press, 1999.
Brito, Eugenia. *Campos minados (literatura post-golpe en Chile)*. Santiago de Chile: Editorial Cuarto Propio, 1990.
Castro-Klarén, Sara. "Del recuerdo y el olvido: el sujeto en *Breve cárcel* y *Lumpérica*". In *Escritura, sujeto y transgresión en la literatura latinoamericana.* México: Premiá, 1989.
Cróquer, Eleonora. *El gesto de Antígona o la escritura como responsabilidad: Clarice Lispector, Diamela Eltit y Carmen Boullosa*. Santiago de Chile: Editorial Cuarto Propio, 2000.
Labanyi, Jo. "Topologies of Catastrophe: Horror and Objection in Diamela Eltit's *Vaca sagrada*". In Anny Brooksbank-Jones and Catherine Davies (eds), *Latin American Women's Writing: Feminist Readings in Theory and Crisis*. New York: Oxford University Press, 1996.
Lagos, María Inés (ed.) *Creación y resistencia: la narrativa de Diamela Eltit, 1983–1998*. Santiago de Chile: Editorial Cuarto Propio, 2000.
Lértora, Juan Carlos (ed.) *Una poética de literatura menor: la narrativa de Diamela Eltit*. Santiago: Para Textos/Editorial Cuarto Propio, 1993.
Loach, Barbara. *Power and Women's Writing in Chile*. Madrid: Editorial Pliegos, 1994.
Luttecke, Janet A: "*El cuarto mundo* de Diamela Eltit". *Revista Iberoamericana* 60 (1994).
Malverde Disselkoen, Ivette. "Esquizofrenia y literatura: El discurso de padre e hija en *El Padre Mío* de Diamela Eltit". *Acta Literaria* 16 (1991): 69–76.
Morales, T. Leonidas. "*Los trabajadores de la muerte* y la narrativa de Diamela Eltit". *Atenea: Revista de Ciencia, Arte y Literatura de la Universidad de Concepción* 478 (1998).
Neustadt, Robert. *CADA Día: la creación de un arte social*. Santiago de Chile: Editorial Cuarto Propio, 2001.
Niebylski, Dianna C. "Against Mimesis: *Lumpérica* Revisited". *Revista Canadiense de Estudios Hispánicos* 25(2) (2001): 241–57.
Norat, Gisela. *Marginalities: Diamela Eltit and the Subversion of Mainstream Literature in Chile*. Wilmington, DE: University of Delaware Press, 2002.
——. "Diálogo fraternal: *El cuarto mundo* de Diamela Eltit y Cristóbal Nonato de Carlos Fuentes". *Chasqui: Revista de Literatura Latinoamericana* 23(2) (1994): 74–85.
Olea, Raquel. *Lengua víbora: producciones de lo femenino en la escritura de mujeres chilenas*. Santiago de Chile: Editorial Cuarto Propio, 1998.
Richard, Nelly. *Residuos y metáforas (ensayos de crítica cultural sobre el Chile de la Transición)*. Santiago: Editorial Cuarto Propio, 1998.
Tierney-Tello, Mary Beth. *Allegories of Transgression and Transformation: Experimental Fiction by Women Writing under Dictatorship*. Albany, NY: State University of New York Press, 1996.

ERAUSO, CATALINA DE

Catalina de Erauso (1592–1650) was an intrepid Basque woman who, disguised as a man, traveled around the world, and actively participated in the conquest of the Americas. One of the main "disguised" women of the Renaissance, she crossed all varieties of sexual, social, religious and territorial borders. Her adventures have always intrigued historians, provoking an air of legendary mystery that still surrounds her life.

Even though she claimed to have been born in 1585 on the first paragraph of her alleged autobiography, *Historia de la monja alférez escrita por ella misma* (1624, History of the Nun Ensign, Written by Herself), her baptismal certificate contrarily indicates that she was baptized on February 10, 1592, in San Sebastián. Her parents were Captain Miguel de Erauso and María Pérez de Galarraga y Arce, also from San Sebastián.

She is known for having written her memoirs, probably upon her return from the Americas, in 1624. In 1626, Juan Pérez de Montalbán wrote the play *La monja alférez* (The Nun Ensign), possibly even read by Catalina herself. Two centuries later, it would be translated into French and German, and into English by Thomas de Quincey. However, the first documented edition of her autobiography appeared in 1829 and was the work of Joaquín María de Ferrer.

Life

According to her autobiography, she was raised at home until the age of 4, when she was placed in the Dominican convent of San Sebastián the Elder, where her aunt, Úrsula Unzá y Sarasti, was prioress. She remained there until aged 15, when she escaped from the convent after having tricked her aunt, from whom she literally took the keys and ran to the woods, hiding for three days. Once beyond the convent's walls, she immediately changed her appearance and, considering her habit useless, symbolically threw it away, along with her hair, which she had cut short. Discarding her habit may indicate her separation from the Catholic Church, which she found inadequate. Also, in abandoning her hair, she rejected something conventionally associated with femininity and notions of beauty.

Additionally, the adoption of a masculine identity in a patriarchal society meant to enter a privileged world. Catalina must have realized the importance of creating a visual illusion of a complete and balanced being. Cohesion between both her interior and external appearance was essential in the process of adaptation.

Catalina's next important step toward conversion was to create a name that would identify, even temporarily, her new being. Thus, she first used the name Francisco Loyola, which she adopted in Valladolid. After that, around 1603, she pursued adventures overseas. In the colonies, passing as a man named Antonio, Catalina complemented this new personality with a traditionally natural attraction toward the opposite sex. This implied that not only was Catalina a woman transformed into a man, but she was also a woman attracted to other women. Again and again in her autobiography, she bragged about her various relations with women. Early on, masters and superiors tried to marry her off to desirable ladies of the new colonies. Thus, in Saña, Peru, Catalina was under the orders of Juan de Urquiza, who attempted to arrange a marriage between Catalina and his own mistress. Interestingly enough, the lady did not seem to mind this arrangement and repeatedly implored Catalina to stay with her overnight, to the point that, on one occasion, Catalina had to force her way out the lady's house and flee.

Her experiences with women continued, and she also had to deal with another situation in Tucumán, Argentina, where she was welcomed into the home of a *mestiza* woman who wanted Catalina to marry her daughter, but the girl was unattractive and undesirable to Catalina. Failing to succeed in her masculine role and fearing discovery, Catalina's only solution was to escape once again.

Her passion for women complemented her stereotypical masculine personality with its military courage. She confessed that she was naturally inclined to see the world and that she had chosen to become a mercenary to do so. Enhancing the role, she overdid her military duties by being excessively violent and aggressive, and mistreating prisoners. She was aware of partaking in an exterminatory process where men were expected to conquer and plunder.

However, in Guamanga, Peru, seeing her life in danger, she literally sought shelter in a sacred temple, and was eager to relate her experiences to the archbishop. Seeking an audience with him, she decided to reveal the truth about her life and journey: her escape from the convent, her travels, her criminal sprees and her problems with justice. The bishop's reaction was surprisingly sympathetic toward Catalina due to her "virginal" state. Esteeming her as a remarkable person, he asked her to make a true confession and promised to help her in whatever possible. Pledging to do something about her salvation, Catalina shifted easily from a criminal to an almost repentant Christian. Consequently, Catalina had to re-enter the religious life she had left twenty years before. The feminine rehabilitation was, therefore, to return to one of the traditional female roles. Nonetheless, after spending only two years at a convent, she headed back to Spain and arrived there on November 1, 1624.

Back in Europe, Catalina's search for forgiveness led her to confront the trinity of power that governed life in general: the canonical, the Christian pastoral, and the civil law. Although she had not shown any intention of repenting until that moment, Catalina's remorse may be an authentic redeeming act or, simply, a strategy to obtain some money from King Philip IV. He actually granted her a pension of about 500 pesos, with which she was not satisfied. She then headed to Rome. As it was the holy year of the great Jubilee, she hoped the Pope would forgive her. Her reputation took her to Urban VIII, to whom she related her life and travels, and the fact that she had kept her virginity. The Pope allowed her to continue wearing men's clothing, with the condition that she would lead an honest existence. Once again, her virginal state absolved her of any doubt about her virtue. At this point, her security restored and the papal blessing in hand, Catalina finishes her narrative in the Port of Naples, where she has a word exchange with two prostitutes.

She went back to the New World in 1645, under the name of Antonio, worked as a muleteer, and died five years later, presumably on the road to Veracruz, Mexico. Until then, she continued her escapades, dueling, gambling, and falling in love with women.

Significance

For Jerome R. Adams, in *Notable Latin American Women: Twenty-Nine Leaders, Rebels, Poets, Battlers and Spies*, and equally, for James and Linda Henderson, in *Ten Notable Women of Latin American*, Catalina de Erauso is a subject of interest, and relevant enough to be considered part of, and to be included among, women of such appeal and influence as La Malinche, Sor Juana Inés de la Cruz, Evita Perón and Gabriela Mistral, to mention a few.

The originality of her questionable behavior resides in the fact that both as a woman and as a man, she transgressed all varieties of barriers and still had the courage to tell her adventures. Her peculiar picaresque voice, together with some comments on the female condition, is heard. Catalina, whether a subaltern or a selfish aggressor, is an attractive character, even to the most traditional critics. She was able to colonize, rob, kill, and seduce, under the privileged form of a man. In fact, becoming and acting as one made it possible for Catalina to take an active part in the history being written before her own eyes. At a time and place where women were subjected to masculine authority, and whose participation in the colonizing project was limited, Catalina appears rebellious, aggressive, temperamental, and yet, brave, patriotic, and loyal.

PALOMA MARTÍNEZ-CARBAJO

Selected Works

Historia de la monja alférez escrita por ella misma. Edited by Jesús Munárriz. Madrid: Hiperión, 1986.

Lieutenant Nun: Memoir of a Basque Transvestite in the New World. Trans. Michele Stepto and Gabriel Stepto. Boston, MA: Beacon Press, 1996.

References and Further Reading

Adams, Jerome R. *Notable Latin American Women: Twenty-Nine Leaders, Rebels, Poets, Battlers and Spies, 1500–1900*. Jefferson, NC: McFarland & Company, Inc., 1995, pp. 45–53.

Foster, Jeannette H. *Sex Variant Women in Literature*. Tallahassee, FL: The Naiad Press Inc, 1985.

Henderson, James D. and Henderson, Linda Roddy. *Ten Notable Women of Latin America*. Chicago, IL: Nelson Hall, 1978, pp. 49–72.

Lucena Salmoral, Manuel. "Hispanoamérica en la época colonial". In Luis Íñigo Madrigal (ed.), *Historia de la literatura hispanoamericana. Época colonial*. Madrid: Ediciones Cátedra, 1982.

Masiello, Francine. "Gender, Dress, and Market. The Commerce of Citizenship in Latin America". In Daniel Balderston and Donna J. Guy (eds), *Sex and Sexuality in Latin America*. New York: New York University Press, 1997.

Merrim, Stephanie. "Catalina de Erauso: From Anomaly to Icon". In Francisco Javier Cevallos-Candau, Jeffrey A. Cole, Nina M. Scott and Nicomedes Suárez-Araúz (eds), *Coded Encounters: Writing, Gender, and Ethnicity in Colonial Latin America*. Amherst, MA: University of Massachusetts Press, 1994, pp. 177–205.

Stoler, Ann Laura. "Carnal Knowledge and Imperial Power". In Joan Wallach Scott (ed.), *Feminism and History*. Oxford: Oxford University Press, 1996, pp. 209–66.

Trexler, Richard C. *Sex and Conquest. Gendered Violence, Political Order, and the European Conquest of the Americas*. Ithaca, NY: Cornell University Press, 1995.

EROTICISM

In her introduction to *Intimidades: Dez contos eróticos de escritoras brazileiras e portuguesas*, Luisa Coelho joins an important tradition of philosophers, psychologists, anthropologists and artists in claiming that eroticism is the creative force at the heart of all art forms. A distinguished scholar of Portuguese and Brazilian erotic writings by women, Coelho addresses the problematic distinction between pornography and eroticism by arguing that the line between the two can be fluid and subtle. She further qualifies this distinction by adding that eroticism requires a degree of mystery and therefore a certain distance from the embodied object of sexual pleasure. Speaking specifically of Mexican art and letters, Elena Poniatowska also identifies the erotic as the place from whence the Mexican imaginary surfaces, but her equation of eroticism with a strictly biological and even bestial urge appears to be both more raw and less devoid of mystery than civility or culture would prescribe. Speaking of the photographer/painter Tina Modotti, the cross-dressing, bisexual artist who is the subject of the author's fictional biography *Tinísima*, Poniatowska describes the erotic as a "feroz exhibición de la intimidad" (1996: 59), noting that the sexually adventurous but troubled Modotti failed to understand that pleasure, or "paradise," meant accepting "the momentary flash of the gorilla flaring under our armpits" (1996: 59). Between Coelho's and Poniatowska's seemingly disparate conceptions of the erotic experience there is a vast and varied spectrum of contemporary Latin American women writers whose incursions into the subject of female sexuality and pleasure have helped to produce a substantial and highly diverse literature on the subject.

"Escribí con el cuerpo ... el secreto es *res*, non verba" ["[w]rite with your body ... the secret is *res*, non verba"] (1991: 16), advises the protagonist of Luisa Valenzuela's mystery-cum-political thriller *Novela negra con Argentinos* (Black Novel with Argentines). Valenzuela's character, like most of her female narrators, insists on the intimate relationship between eroticism and writing. Stated as an imperative for a woman writer, this notion of writing as a nearly erotic secretion is most frequently equated with first-wave French-Algerian feminist Hélène Cixous. Along with Julia Kristeva and the Belgian philosopher Luce Irigaray, Cixous's reflections on the subject of sexuality, eroticism and motherhood had profound and lasting effects on Latin American women writers during the last three decades of the twentieth century. So did the influence of North American feminist thinkers and writers of the 1970s and 1980s and that of Latin American literary critics based largely in the US, women critics who were deeply committed to theorizing about issues of gender, sexuality and power. Partly as a result of sociopolitical gains made during the decade of the 1960s, partly out of concern from seeing those same gains threatened by repressive regimes in the 1970s and early 1980s, Latin American women writers who published some of their earlier work in the 1960s and 1970s were among the first crop of pro-feminist Latin American women to approach the subject of women's sexuality and eroticism openly and explicitly, even if a number of them resisted having their texts grouped under feminist labels. Emboldened by this first wave of women writing openly about sexuality, a younger, often more aggressively pro-feminist generation has continued to explore the erotic throughout the 1980s and 1990s through the present. At times the erotic experience is at the center of their novel or short stories, as in Nélida Piñón's *A casa da paixão* (1972), Griselda Gambaro's *Lo impenetrable*

(1984), Cristina Peri Rossi's *Solitario de amor* (1988), Fanny Buitrago's *Los amores de Afrodita* (1984), Gioconda Belli's *La mujer habitada* (1988), Alicia Steimberg's *Amatista* (1989), or in the erotic stories by Brazilian women Hilda Hilst, Márcia Denser or Myriam Campello. More frequently, the exploration of women's sexuality in these works is a key element of a larger plot, one that generally includes political, ideological and social concerns. "The truly erotic book," notes novelist Alicia Steimberg in a 1993 interview, "is one that reaches the place of the erotic through unexpected corridors . . . and exits from it with the same ease with which it reached it" ["El libro verdaderamente 'erótico' es el el que llega al erotismo por caminos imprevistos, incluso para el autor mismo, y sale de él con la misma naturalidad con la que entró"].

A diverse but necessarily partial list of the Latin American women writers who have explored or continue to explore female eroticism in their narratives includes the Argentines Luisa Valenzuela, Alicia Borinsky, Angélica Gorodischer, Griselda Gambaro, Ana María Shúa, Mexican women writers Inés Arredondo, Margo Glantz and Elena Poniatowska, Puerto Ricans Rosario Ferré and Ana Lydia Vega, Brazilians Marina Colasanti, Nélida Piñón, Márcia Denser, and Sonia Coutinho, Colombians Fanny Buitrago and Laura Restrepo, Ena Lucía Portela in Cuba. Exiled authors Isabel Allende (Chile), Cristina Peri Rossi (Uruguay), Teresa Ruíz Rosas (Peru) and Zoé Valdés (Cuba) owe the notoriety of at least some of their published works to their treatment of eroticism, one that ranges from the lyrically sensual to the quasi-pornographic. A number of Latin American women poets have also made important contributions to the field of erotic literature, condensing glimpses of sexual desire or moments of erotic pleasure in their verses. Among them are Nancy Morejón and Clementina Suárez (Cuba), Gilka Machado (Brazil), Gioconda Belli (Nicaragua), Alejandra Pizarnik (Argentina), and the aforementioned Cristina Peri Rossi. A substantial number of Latina writers of the 1970s, 1980s and 1990s engaged the erotic partly as a means to illustrate how their ethnically, culturally and linguistically-borderline experience affected their sexuality; partly so as a means of engaging and entering a more mainstream feminist discourse of sexuality that often left them marginalized. Among the first wave of Latina writers to find a border/migrant discourse of the erotic, Gloria Anzaldúa, Ana Castillo, Sandra Cisneros, Denise Chávez, Cherríe Moraga and Judith Ortiz Cofer relate heterosexual, bisexual and lesbian desire to issues of race, ethnicity and class.

Foucault noted in *The History of Sexuality* that sexuality may not be the most rigid mechanism of domination, but it is certainly one of the most manipulative and pervasive ones. Armed with this knowledge, many of these women writers who explore the sexual mysteries of female libido do so out of an even broader and more basic need: the need to explore how female subjects can constitute, re-discover or reconstruct themselves as subjects of their own story rather than objects in male-authored scenarios of power and pleasure. Similarly, while many contemporary feminist theorists and writers resist the psychological and biological essentialism characteristic of some early feminist thinkers like the afore-mentioned Cixous, they distance themselves just as critically from philosophers, psychoanalysts and theorists like Jacques Lacan or Georges Bataille with their insistence on denying the particularities (and even the ontological possibility) of a recognizably feminine sexuality. Arguing for the possibility of fluid and/or performative subjectivities, most postmodern feminist philosophers and cultural theorists maintain that sexuality is indeed an important—if shifting—ground on which to try out facets of one's subjectivity. In a paper presented in 1996, cultural theorist Teresa de Lauretis returns to an idea she had explored in her earlier work on cinema and eroticism when she notes that "sexuality is the site upon which the subject elaborates its image of itself, its own corporeal awareness [and] . . . its modes of relating and acting in the world". In many of the narratives and works of poetry cited in this entry, the erotic experience has the effect of exploding or imploding the subject. In this way, the exploration of eroticism becomes part of the complexity and, at times, the ambiguity that characterizes the larger project of identity construction or recovery. In this way, Luisa Valenzuela's characters are often undone by the initially blinding glare of sexual discoveries before they begin to remember and reshape their own identity. In many of Cristina Peri Rossi' stories, coyly ironic narrators and sexually adventurous characters find ways to defer the revelation of their own and other characters' sexual preference, so that the mystery of their sexuality becomes part of the larger challenge of being able to construct or reconstruct a fictional identity. In *The Margarita Poems* (1987), Puerto Rican/Latina poet Luz María Umpierre weaves a sexually explicit poetic language to explore ways in which the poetic persona's lesbian sexuality complicates her project of defining her multi-sided identity as a transplanted Puerto Rican and a bilingual Latina in the US.

Latin American women writers of the 1970s and 1980s had no Hispanic Colette or Anaïs Nin to provide models for writing about women's erotic dreams or adventures. Brazil had Hilda Hilst and Lygia Fagundes Telles as well as Clarice Lispector in the 1930s, 1940s and 1950s, but only Lispector's influence succeeded in crossing the language barrier in time to leave an imprint on many of the Hispanic writers mentioned in the above paragraph. Hilst and Fagundes Telles proved crucial influences for later generations of Brazilian women writers who chose to explore female eroticism, but they remained relatively unknown in Spanish-speaking circles. For women writers writing in Spanish-speaking Latin America there were, nevertheless, subtle and restrained yet instructive earlier models for exploring women's desire from a feminine-centric perspective. The passionate but languid and self-eclipsing eroticism of the Latin American women poets of the 1920s, 1930s and 1940s paved the way for some of the more lyrical erotic incursions of women writers who followed. The eroticism present in the poems of Alfonsina Storni (Argentina), Juana de Ibarbourou, Delmira Augustina (Uruguay) and Gabriela Mistral (Chile) is masked by these poets' obligatory adherence to rules of propriety as well as by the self-censorship imposed by their peripheral status vis-à-vis their much better known male contemporaries, yet echoes of these poets' erotic imagery reappears frequently in contemporary women writers' more daring sexual scenarios, as in the ebullient lyrical eroticism of the Nicaraguan poet and novelist Gioconda Belli, and in some of the earlier novels of Isabel Allende, for example. One might argue that Augustini's phantom vampires, sphinxes and Salomés slink their way (less as phantoms than as monsters) into some of Alejandra Pizarnik's darkly erotic early poems.

An even more significant precedent is the guarded but arguably subversive eroticism of several Latin American women writers of the 1930s and 1940s. Chilean María Luisa Bombal's ghostly yet abject eroticism lurks behind some of Pía Barro's most successful stories of troubled sexual encounters. Bombal's exacerbated and oddly macabre sensuality can still be felt also in recent women writer's texts with an erotic edge, as in *El rastro* (2002) by the highly prolific Margo Glantz. There are echoes of Silvina Ocampo's erotic cruelty in Alejandra Pizarnik's violently gothic novella *La condesa sangrienta*, while the influence of Ocampo's flawless sense of erotic timing and verbal foreplay is palpable in Luisa Valenzuela's more openly erotic passages. Mexican essayist, poet and novelist Rosario Castellanos' earthy yet comic-ironic take on heterosexual eroticism resonates differently but in recognizable ways in writers as disparate in their approach to the female body as are Elena Poniatowska and Margo Glanz, as well as in the more recent Mexican women writers mentioned later in this essay.

Notably, the most pervasive influence on the generation of women writers mentioned in the last paragraph was a writer more interested in textual than sexual experimentation. Clarice Lispector's alienated female characters are better known for their erotic failures than for any celebration of their sexuality. Even Lispector's lesser known *Uma Aprendizagem ou O Livro dos Prazeres* (1969), the author's most mystical book, is more preoccupied with epistemological than with corporeal or existential questions. Nevertheless, Lispector's better-known "writerly" texts and their Moëbius strip practice of textual-sexual unveilings proved to be an indelible influence on the way in which future Latin American women writers like Armonía Somers, Luisa Valenzuela, Elena Poniatowska, Margo Glantz, and Nélida Piñón approached both the sexual or sexualized female body. Registering this trend among women-authored texts that entail an exploration of erotic desire Sylvia Molloy writes:

> What one often finds in women writers, in terms of erotic desire, is a slippage from sex to text: the text itself is an erotic encounter in which the poet [or the writer] makes love to her words . . . Not limited to the physical body, and certainly not repressing it, desire in these cases extends to the body of writing.
>
> (1991: 120)

Brazilian and Latin American writers of the 1970s and 1980s struggled to escape the phallocentric sexual scenarios so characteristic of traditional pornography and porno-eroticism by frequently resorting to parodies of reversal or inversion. The gendered use of parody in the context of experimenting with a discourse previously associated almost exclusively with male-authored texts lies in parody's potential to subtly or radically alter readers' perceptions of gender relations. As such, parodic erotic writings by these women authors were often boldly transgressive. Yet the limitation of parody as a textual approach is lodged in the fact that parodic texts tend to be caught within the same bi-polar or binomial terms as the original model parodied. In this respect, despite its potential for overturning narrative layers, parody is rarely truly subversive. Nevertheless, the frequent use of parody among Latin American women writing about sexuality during these decades is significant in that it signaled the urgency with which a generation of women writers sought to dismantle a discourse that had been dominated almost exclusively by male heterosexual writers for centuries. Moreover, the broad range of parodic genres present in women's sexual or erotic narratives during these two decades is worth noting. The spectrum is broad enough to encompass the carnivalesque and garrulous bawdiness of Ana Lydia Vega's "Letra para salsa y tres soneos por encargo", the courtly burlesque in Gambaro's *Lo impenetrable*, the lyrically ironic in Peri Rossi's *Solitario de amor*, and the farcical and campy passages of Borinsky's first novel, *Mina cruel*, to name only a handful of possible examples.

While the use of parody in these women-authored texts was not a trait exclusive to or even predominantly characteristic of Latin American women authors, what does appear to be a cultural trait present in a significant number of the erotic texts and passages by many of the authors mentioned thus far in this essay is their recognizably picaresque edge. The erotic tradition in Spain can be traced back to the fourteenth century and the Arcipreste de Hita's *Libro del buen amor*—a comic-satiric treatise that features a cast of lascivious women. Yet it is with the enormously popular picaresque genre that flourished from the fifteenth to the late seventeenth centuries that female sexuality (presented as insatiable for the most part) became a recurrent *leitmotiv* of a literary genre. From its inception, the picaresque tradition portrayed female sexuality prominently as an all-consuming and socially disruptive force. No wonder, then, that picaresque traits tend to be found—in varying degrees and modalities—in writers as stylistically and thematically antithetical as are Alicia Borinsky and Zoé Valdés. A notable number of stories and novels written by Latin American women writers in the 1990s center on picaresque female characters who relish the sexual discoveries that are tied to more or less happy adventures with food and/or travel.

Among the best known of these erotic-picaresque narratives in the last two decades are Laura Esquivel's *Como agua para chocolate* (Mexico), Laura Restrepo's *La novia oscura* (Colombia), and Isabel Allende's *Eva Luna.* The adventure-filled plot and the quasi-pornographic detail of the picaresque are openly in evidence in the novels of exiled Cuban author Zoé Valdés (*La nada cotidiana*), and in narratives by Latina writers Sandra Cisneros (*The House on Mango Street*; *Caramelo*) and Ana Castillo (*Loverboys*), or the Cuban-American Achy Obejas (especially in *Days of Awe*), whose female characters often exhibit the unlawful bravado of seventeenth-century *pícaras*. Much like the latter, these contemporary female characters practicing various kinds of civil and uncivil disobedience too are tripped, or tricked, by the surprises of border, trans-national geographies. More postmodern or less mimetic traces of the picaresque can be found in the work of Alicia Borinsky's work. A Jewish-Argentine writer who resides and writes in the US, Borinsky's novels and poems contain explicitly sexual and even pornographic passages that succeed in highlighting the fetishistic commodification of sexuality in a world where desire can be simulated, packaged and consumed. Sexually explicit but anti-erotic, Borinsky's novels manage to illustrate the degree to which popular culture deflates the erotic impulse by depriving sexuality of all mystery.

No less interesting in this body of erotic literature by Latin American and Latina women is the conjunction of eroticism and mysticism in many contemporary Latin American women's narratives that portray erotic experiences. As Bataille's work on eroticism reminds us, the conjunction of eroticism and the sacred was never far from the Western imagination. Yet there is little doubt that this relationship has been especially present in Catholic—and mostly Mediterranean and Latin—countries with a long-established cult of the Virgin Mary, one that often breaks the barriers between transcendent mysticism and a fetishistic secular eroticism. In *Dulce compañía* by Colombian novelist Laura Restrepo one finds echoes of her countryman García Márquez's long-lasting fascination with both fallen angels and otherworldly creatures with superhuman sexual powers. Restrepo's novel features a white, middle-class female reporter intent on covering the apparitions of a rebel mixed-race angel. Instead she soon finds herself sexually seduced by the supposedly other-worldly creature. Armonía Somers's much anthologized story "El derrumbamiento" turns the reader into a voyeur who has no choice but to witness the seduction of a male criminal at the hands of a not so holy Virgin. Teetering between the grotesque and the sublime, Somers' story is disturbingly perverse in its exploration of the cultural and religious taboos. What makes these fictional encounters even more daring in their exploration and representation of subversive sexuality is the fact that the otherworldly being plays the aggressive role in the seduction. Some of the earliest experimentations in the explosive field of the sacred or anti-sacred erotic take place in the deeply troubling stories of Inés Arredondo, where incest is sometimes an added complication to an already taboo scenario. Less openly transgressive of religious and social taboos but intent on exploring the relationship between the erotics of mysticism and the transcendent aspirations of all-too human eroticism, Margo Glantz's (2001) novel *Apariciones* experiments with a double-helixed narrative in which seventeenth-century nuns' fetishistic surrender to their divine savior is read against the narrative of a contemporary woman consumed by her lust for her all too human lover. An attentive review of some of these taboo-breaking narratives soon confirms and perhaps exceeds Bataille's assumptions about eroticism. Indeed, few other dramatizations of the erotic could pose more of a threat to cultural and religious proscriptions than those that seek to break the walls between the all too viscous erotic jungle of the eroticized human body and the petrified forest of religious symbols or sacred icons.

Despite the sociological and cultural pressures to silence lesbian desire in Latin American and Latino contexts, the last three decades have seen a significant increase in texts that center or address lesbian and bisexual eroticism. In her Introduction to David William Foster's *Gay and Lesbian Themes in Latin American Writing*, Lilian Manzor-Coats writes that "the lesbian exists in the vacuum of unreadability and unnameability both socially and sexually" (1994: xxii). Although many of the Spanish-speaking Latin American writers mentioned in this essay thus far write largely about heterosexual eroticism, a growing number of women writers in Latin America and of Latina writers in the US are committed to writing lesbian sexuality into our literary erotic imaginary. Among Brazilian and Latina authors, however, the 1980s and 1990s witnessed a proliferation of stories and novels about lesbian sexuality and eroticism. More recent collections of erotic stories by Brazilian women writers include lesbian eroticism. Examples are "A mulher de ouro" (1984) by Myriam Campello, "Tigresa" (1986) by Marcia Denser, and "Fátima e Jamila" (1976), by Sonia Coutinho. Lesbian eroticism also accounts for a significant number of texts (narratives, plays and collections of poems) by Latina, Puerto Rican-American and Cuban-American writers of the 1980s and 1990s. The late Gloria Anzaldúa spoke insistently on the need to rescue the lesbian subject from exclusion and silence; her autobiographical fictions frequently seek to challenge iconic heterosexuality. In Judith Ortiz Cofer's fiction, the erotic experience reveals a vindication of the ways in which lesbian sexuality re-negotiates the power imbalance inscribed in traditional heterosexual sexual relations. On the other hand, Chérrie Moraga's *Giving Up the Ghost* shows how patterns of emotional and physical abuse common in heterosexual relations can reinscribe themselves in the context of lesbian desire, thus proving that same-sex erotic unions are not immune to abuses typical of heterosexual liaisons. Further complicating and expanding definitions of Latina sexuality, Latina writers like Denise Chávez and Ana Castillo have written texts that engage the complex and sometimes confused eroticism of bisexual subjects. Chávez's *The Last of the Menu Girls* (1986) and Castillo's *The Mixquiahuala Letters* (1986) and *Sapagonia* (1990) fall into this category. For all these writers, the exploration of alternative or socially proscribed sexuality or bisexuality is often inseparable from larger discussions about the Latina subject's cultural, ethnic, linguistic and even religious identity.

Despite the breadth and diversity of these writings on the erotic by women authors, articles and editorials on the subject of "mainstream" erotic literature continue to ignore or eschew the growing presence of women's writings in an area that was once an exclusively androcentric enclave. A June 2004 article by Juan Carlos Ubilliz, published in "Identidades," the cultural supplement of the official newspaper *El Peruano*, on perversions, mysticism and the influence of Bataille and Klossowki's notion of the sacred on Latin American literary representations of eroticism, fails to mention a single woman-authored text as an example of this phenomenon. Until this kind of selective myopia to the erotic scripts and scenarios in texts by women writers is corrected, it will remain the responsibility of women critics and scholars to note the abundant and diverse presence of women's voices in writings about eroticism.

DIANNA NIEBYLSKI

Selected Works

Allende, Isabel. *Eva Luna*. New York: Knopf, 1988.

Anzaldúa, Gloria. *La Prieta*. San Francisco, CA: Aunt Lute Books, 1992.

Arredondo, Inés. "Mariposas nocturnas". *Río subterráneo*. Mexico, DF: Joaquien Mortiz, 1979.

——. "La sunamita". *La señal* [1969]. México: Universidad Nacional Autónoma de México, 1980.

Barros, Pía. *Signos bajo la piel*. Santiago de Chile: Grijalbo, 1995.

Belli, Gioconda. *La mujer habitada*. Managua: Editorial Vanguardia, 1988.

Borinsky, Alicia. *Mina cruel*. Buenos Aires: Corregidor, 1989.

——. *Cine continuado*. Buenos Aires: Corregidor, 1997.

Buitrago, Fanny. *Los amores de Afrodita*. Bogotá: Plaza & Janes, 1983.

——. *Señora de la miel*. Bogotá: Arango Editores, 1993.

Campello, Myriam. "A mulher de ouro" [1980]. *O prazer é todo meu: contos eróticos femininos*. Márcia Denser, ed. Rio de Janeiro: Record, 1984, pp. 59–63.

Castillo, Ana. *Sapogonia: An Anti-Romance in 3/8 Meter.* Tempe, AZ: Bilingual Press, 1990.
——. *Loverboys*, New York: W. W Norton & Co., Inc., 1996.
Chávez, Denise. *The Last of the Menu Girls*. Houston, TX: Arte Público Press, 1986.
——. *Loving Pedro Infante*. New York: Farrar, Straus & Giroux, 2001.
Cisneros, Sandra. *The House on Mango Street*. New York: Knopf, 1983
——. *Loose Woman: Poems*. New York: Vintage, 1995.
——. *Caramelo, or, Puro cuento: a Novel.* New York: Knopf, 2002.
Coelho, Luísa (ed.) *Intimidades: antología de contos eróticos femininos*. Preface by Luísa Coelho. Lisbon: Roma Editora, 2005.
Coutinho, Sonia. "Fátima e Jamila". *Uma certa felicidade* [1976]. Rio de Janeiro: Rocco, 1994, pp. 131–35.
Denser, Márcia (ed.) *Muito prazer.* Rio de Janeiro: Record, 1980.
——. (ed.) *O prazer é todo meu: contos eróticos femininos*. Rio de Janeiro: Record, 1984.
——. "Tigresa". *Diana Caçadora*. São Paulo: Global, 1986, pp. 119–36.
Esquivel, Laura. *Como agua para chocolate.* Barcelona: Mondadori, 1989.
Ferré, Rosario. *La muñeca menor y otros cuentos.* Río Piedras, PR: Ediciones Huracán, 1980
Gambado, Griselda. *Lo impenetrable*. Buenos Aires: Grupo Editorial Norma, 1984.
Glantz, Margo. *Apariciones.* México, DF: Alfaguara, 1996.
——. *El rastro*. Barcelona: Editorial Anagrama, 2003.
Lispector, Clarice. *A Paixão segundo G.H*. Rio de Janeiro: Ed. do Autor, 1964.
——. *Uma aprendizagem ou O Livro dos prazeres*. Rio de Janeiro: Sabiá, 1969.
Machado, Gilka. *Poesias completas*. Rio de Janeiro: Cátedra; Brasília: INL, 1970.
Morejon, Nancy. *Mirar Adentro/Looking Within: Selected Poems, 1954–2000*. Ed. Juana Maria Cordones Cook. Detroit, MI: Wayne State University Press, 2002
Obejas, Achy. *Days of Awe*. New York: Ballantine Books, 2001.
Ocampo, Silvina. *Viaje Olvidado*. Buenos Aires: Sur, 1937.
Peri Rossi, Cristina. *El libro de mis primos*. Montevideo: Biblioteca Marcha, 1969.
——. *Diáspora*. Barcelona: Lumen, 1976.
——. *Una pasión prohibida*. Barcelona: Seix Barral, 1986.
——. *Solitario de amor.* Barcelona: Grijalbo, 1988.
——. *Otra vez Eros*. Barcelona: Lumen, 1994.
——. *Desastres íntimos*. Barcelona: Lumen, 1997.
Piñón, Nélida. *A casa da paixão*. Rio de Janeiro: Mario de Andrade, 1972.
Pizarnik. Alejandra. *La condesa sangrienta*. Buenos Aires: Aquarius, 1971.
Poniatowska, Elena. *Tinísima*. London: Instituto Cervantes, 1996.
Portela, Ena Lucía. *El pájaro: pincel y tinta china*. La Habana: Ediciones Union, 1999.
Savary, Olga. *Magma*. São Paulo: Massao Ohno-Roswitha Kempf Editores, 1981.
——. *Carne viva: 1ª antologia brasileira de poemas eróticos*. Rio de Janeiro: Anima, 1984.
Shúa, Ana María. *Los amores de Laurita*. Buenos Aires: Editorial Sudamericana, 1984.
Somers, Armonía. "El derrumbamiento". *El derrumbamiento*. Montevideo: Salamanca, 1953.
Steimberg, Alicia. *Amatista*. Barcelona: Tusquets, 1989.
Telles, Lygia Fagundes. "Tigrela". In *Seminário dos ratos*. Rio de Janeiro: Nova Fronteira, 1977, pp. 131–7.
——. "A Escolha". *Histórias de amor infeliz*. Rio de Janeiro: Nórdica, 1985, pp. 129–33.
Umpierre, Luz María. *The Margarita Poems*. New York: Third Woman Press, 1987.
Valdés, Zoé. *La nada cotidiana*. Barcelona: Emecé, 1995.
Valenzuela, Luisa. *Cambio de Armas*. Hanover, NH: Ediciones del Norte, 1982.
——. *Novela negra con argentinos*. Barcelona: Plaza y Janés, 1990.
Van Steen, Edla. "Intimidade". *Antes do amanhecer.* São Paulo: Editora Modema, 1977. 65–8.
Vega, Ana Lydia. *Encancaranublado*. Río Piedras, PR: Editorial Antillana, 1983.
——. *Pasión de historia y otras historias de pasión*. Río Piedras, PR: Editorial de la Flor, 1987.

References and Further Reading

Anzaldúa, Gloria. "To(o) Queer the Writer-Loca, escritora y chicana". In Betsy Warland (ed.), *In Versions: Writings by Dykes, Queers and Lesbians*. Vancouver: Press Gang, 1991, pp. 249–63.
Cixous, Hélène. "The Laugh of the Medusa". In Keith Cohen and Paula Cohen (eds), *The Signs Reader: Women, Gender and Scholarship.* Trans. Elizabeth Abel and Emily K. Abel. Chicago, IL: University of Chicago Press, 1983, pp. 279–97.
De Lauretis, Teresa. *The Practice of Love: Lesbian Sexuality and Perverse Desire*. Bloomington, IN: Indiana University Press, 1994.
——. "Irriducibilità del desiderio e cognizione del limite", quoted in María Rosa Cutrufelli (ed.), *In the Forbidden City: An Anthology of Erotic Fiction by Italian Women*. Chicago, IL: University of Chicago Press, 2000, p. 3.
Faderman, Lillian. "What Is Lesbian Literature? Forming a Historical Canon". In George E. Haggerty and Bonnie Zimmerman (eds), *Professions of Desire: Lesbian and Gay Studies in Literature*. New York: MLA, 1995, pp. 49–59.
Foster, David William. *Gay and Lesbian Themes in Latin American Writing*. Austin, TX: University of Texas Press, 1991.
Kristeva, Julia. "Stabat Mater". In Susan Rubin Suleiman (ed.), *The Female Body in Western Culture: Contemporary Perspectives*. Cambridge, MA: Harvard University Press, 1986, pp. 99–118.
Manzor-Coats, Lillian. "Introduction". In David William Foster (ed.), *Latin American Writers on Gay and Lesbian Themes: A Bio-Critical Sourcebook*. Westport, CT: Greenwood Press, 1994, pp. xv–xxxvi.
Molloy, Sylvia. "Introduction. Female Textual Identities: The Strategies of Self Figuration". In Sara Castro, K. Klarén, Sylvia Molloy and Beatriz Sarlo (eds), *Women's Writing in Latin America: An Anthology.* Boulder, CO: Westview Press, 1991, pp. 107–24.
Steimberg, Alicia. "Como escribir literatura erótica." http://www.literatura.org/ Steimberg/ asTexto2.html.
Ubilliz, Juan Carlos. "El erotismo místico francés en la literatura latinoamericana" "Identidades," *El Peruano,* 4–7.

ESCOFET, CRISTINA

Cristina Escofet (b. 1945), actress, playwriter, philosopher, poet, novelist and declared feminist, is one of the better known Argentinian dramatists of the past thirty years. She is part of a generation of Argentine women playwrights—like Diana Raznovich and Susana Torres Molina—interested in dismantling conventional categories of gender.

Escofet was born in Caleufú, La Pampa, Argentina, on October 8, 1945. She began working in theater at an early age as an actress and dancer in La Plata Independent Theater from 1960–67. In 1969 she graduated with a degree in Philosophy from the University of La Plata, where she taught Modern Philosophy between 1970 and 1975. Because of the political situation in Argentina during this period, she was a victim of the general repression that plagued the universities. As a result, she lost her position and suffered persecution by the *Asociación Anticomunista Argentina* (Argentine Anticommunist Association), a right-wing organization. Escofet moved to

Buenos Aires, resulting in what she calls an internal exile from the city of La Plata where she now resides.

Seeking refuge in writing, Escofet began to write children's literature and later published *Llueve en la ciudad* (1981, It is Raining in the City), *Cyrano de la colina* (1981, Cyrano of the Hill), *Mariana* (1986), and *Las vanillas de Ulises y otras historias* (1991, Ulysses' Dinnerware and Other Stories). In 1984, she published *Primera piel* (First Skin), a novel dedicated to her generation and a point of departure for her later theatrical work.

In 1979, Escofet's work began to focus on feminist issues. According to Escofet, her work from this moment on "is that of a woman who will no longer retreat from an education and profession that seeks to explore the enigmas – truths of the genre" (personal correspondence, 2002). From her studies of various feminist authors, she rejected traditional patriarchal approaches to literature and criticism as limited by their binary and restrictive nature. She began to develop a new model based in part on Carl Jung's concepts of *animus* and *anima* "with the certainty that these could provide a new intellectual framework" (personal correspondence, 2002). It is from this new perspective that, in 2000, she published her critical work *Arquetipos, modelos para desarmar palabras desde el género* (Archetypes, Patterns to Dismantle Words through Gender). This work describes the critical models through which Escofet approaches art and society and, as a consequence, some important insight into her work for the theater.

Influenced by the theories of Eugene Ionesco and the Theater of the Absurd, Cristina Escofet has written exclusively for the theater since 1985. Her debut as playwright occurred in 1985 with her play *Té de tías* (Aunt's Tea time) performed as part of *Teatro Abierto* (Open Theater) a resistant movement within the Argentinean theater, expressing resistance to military dictatorship. *Té de tías* presents in one act "lo que no debe decirse de las relaciones familiares," (that which is not talked about within the family) (*Teatro* 15). This play was Escofet's first big success and was unanimously praised by the critics.

In June 1988, she received a national Funds for the Arts grant, and the same year she premiered *Solas en la madriguera* (Women Alone in the Burrow, 1988), her first feminist monologue. *Solas en la madriguera* presents a variety of vignettes inter-woven in the style of Bertolt Brecht. In 1989, Escofet presented *Nunca usarás medias de seda* (You Will Never Wear Silk Stockings), another short play in which the main character, a traditional middle-class housewife, denounces the educational system that maintains women's subordinate roles within society in a series of dreams. *Ritos del corazón* (1992, Rites of the Heart) presents the constant struggle to redefine oneself amid the limitations imposed by the past. Her most staged and popular piece is *Señoritas en concierto* (1993, Young Ladies in Concert), which Escofet describes as a production variety (music-hall) in thirteen scenes. The play is about a group of actresses traveling the road in an old wagon sweeping away age-old feminine archetypes. Each scene is completely independent of the others but an understanding of the play itself depends upon linking the various feminine voices into one unifying voice.

Las que aman hasta morir (Women Who Love to Death), first presented in 1985 and later published in 2001, is also a monologue. The main character is a nameless, 40-year-old actress who represents all women who dedicate themselves to the search for love. The protagonist's search leads to the realization that it is man who defines the terms for success and only by rejecting these terms is she able to move forward with her life. Unable to justify her failed relations, the actress decides that only after becoming a woman true to her own terms will she ever be complete. Cristina Escofet takes on the myths of her childhood in *Los fantasmas del héroe* (2000, The Ghosts of the Hero) which explores some of the contradictions of history. Escofet has called this work an epilogue to *Primera piel.* In the same year she also presented *Frida*, a work of *teatro semi-montado* (spoken theater), inspired by some of the works of the painter Frida Kahlo. *Eternity Class* (2001), along the lines of her first theater piece *Té de tías*, marks Escofet's return to the demythification of family roles through strong social criticism. In this work the author attempts to acknowledge that although the concept of the eternal femine is the ideal sought by society, it too imposes demands on those who seek it. In *¿Qué pasó con Bette Davis?* (2001, Whatever Happened to Bette Davis?), through a meta-theatrical structure, Escofet presents a series of historical female characters. On a metaphorical level the author puts forward the idea that it is the option and the responsability of each woman to define herself and not acknowledge any fixed roles imposed by others. In *La doncella de Ámsterdam (El diario de Anne Frank)* (2002, Amsterdam's Maiden: The Diary of Anne Frank), the most significant aspect is Escofet's having converted a personal diary into a theatrical piece without losing the freshness and innocence of the original narrative voice.

Escofet is currently focusing on what she calls "ontological healing," seeking to heal ontological damage by exploring archetypal masks, and developing these ideas in creative workshops in which the goal is to reconstruct, through conscience confrontation, the archetypes that each individual has assimilated in order to redefine reality.

Throughout her body of work, the theme of feminine identity is dominant. What distinguishes the plays of Escofet from other feminine writers is the variety of forms of presenting these ideas. She employs styles that compare to those of Brecht and Ionesco, presenting characters who are in various stages of personal development and function as stereotypes for the presentation of each work's message: the destrucion of imposed roles and archetypes as part of the process of constructing one's own identity. For Escofet, identity is a series of repetitive acts which can change and deconstruct themselves and thus allow women the opportunity to recreate and define their own reality. In the plays, the actresses are given meaning by the signifiers (props, scenery, the audience and other characters) which surround them. Escofet uses these characters to expose the roles that society has offered women (virgin, wife, mother and prostitute) and with the plays she dissects, subverts and destroys these limitations.

Escofet seeks to communicate, through the theater, that the concept of "feminine" is nothing more than a social construct or archetype imposed at birth. In order to fully realize one's potential and discard these social restrictions it is necessary to be able to recognize these archetypes and abandon those which oppress and objectify thus allowing one to identify new models which permit us to define our gender for ourselves. Her plays stress the necessity of abandoning the traditional stereotypes of masculinity and femininity in order to redefine these concepts in a new manner in which neither is exclusive to any group. Using Escofet's own words we can end saying that her goals are to know to what extent we are made of stereotypes and to die in order to be born again.

MARIA R. MATZ AND KEITH WOODALL

Selected Works

Llueve en la ciudad. Buenos Aires: Plus Ultra, 1981.
Cyrano de la colina. Buenos Aires: Plus Ultra, 1981.
Primera piel. Buenos Aires: Riesa, 1984.
Mariana. Buenos Aires: Plus Ultra, 1986.
Teatro Completo. Volumen 1. Buenos Aires: Torres Agüero, 1994.
"Señoritas en concierto". *Gestos* 19 (1995): 222–59.
"Los fantasmas del héroe". *Diálogos dramatúrgicos México-Argentina*. Ed. Felipe Galván. México: Tablado Iberoamericano, 2000, pp. 291–319.
Arquetipos, modelos para desarmar (palabras desde el género). Buenos Aires: Nueva Generación, 2000.
Tres obras de teatro de Cristina Escofet. Buenos Aires: Ed. Nueva Generación, 2001.
"La doncella de Ámsterdam (el diario de Anne Frank)". *Dramaturgas/1*. Buenos Aires: Ed. Nueva Generación, 2001.
"Eternity Class". *Obras argentinas premiadas en Nueva York*. Buenos Aires: Fundación Autores, 2001.
"Género Mujer y Teatralidad. Realidad y ficción en la construcción de una nueva subjetividad". *Revista de Teatro CELCIT* 19–20 (2001). 14 May 2002 http://www.celcit.org.ar

References and Further Reading

Argentores Cristina Escofet, 2001. http://www.autores.org.ar/cescofet
Castellví DeMoor, Magda. "Monólogo dramático y narración: *Las que aman hasta morir* de Cristina Escofet". In Osvaldo Pelletieri (ed.), *Tradición, modernidad y postmodernidad*. Buenos Aires: Galerna, 1999.
——. "Dramaturgia argentina: *Ritos del corazón* de Cristina Escofet y la escritura del sujeto". In Fabiana Inés Varela, Magdalena Ercilia Nállin and María Graciela Romano (eds), *Homenaje a Carlos Orlando Nállin*. Mendoza, Argentina: Facultad de Filosofía y Letras de la Universidad de Cuyo, 2001.
——. *Dramaturgas argentinas. Teatro, política y género*. Mendoza, Argentina: Facultad de Filosofía y Letras de la Universidad Nacional de Cuyo, 2003.
Dubatti, Jorge. "Review of *Arquetipos, modelos para desarmar (palabras desde el género)*, by Cristina Escofet". *Gestos* 31 (April 2001): 213–15.
Frega, Graciela. "Cristina Escofet: la obsesión de escribirse mujer". In Halima Tahan (ed.), *Dramas de mujeres*. Buenos Aires: Ediciones ciudad argentina, 1998.
Matz, Maria R. "La dramaturgia de Cristina Escofet: deconstrucción de los arquetipos femeninos de todos los tiempos." Dissertation, Texas Tech University, 2002.
Proaño-Gómez, Lola. "De la inmanencia a la trascendencia: una conversación con Cristina Escofet". *Gestos* 17 (1994): 215–19.
——. "El humor feminista de Escofet: una ironía militante". In Jorge Dubatti (ed.), *Nuevo teatro. Nueva crítica*. Buenos Aires: Atuel, 2000, pp. 161–79.
——. "Cristina Escofet (8 October 1945–)". In Adam Versényi (ed.), *Latin American Dramatists: First Series*. Detroit, MI: Gale, 2005, pp. 138–42.
Rathbun, Jennifer "Mirando a través de las máscaras: Una entrevista con Cristina Escofet". *Latin American Theatre Review* 36(1) (2002): 133–8.
——. "Atravesando el inconsciente femenino: Una conversación con Cristina Escofet". *Gestos* 17(34) (2002): 165.
——. "The Dramatic Feminine Discourse of Cristina Escofet". Dissertation, Arizona State University, 2002.
Zatlin, Phyllis. "Feminist Metatheatricalism: Escofet's *Ritos del corazón*". *LATR* Fall (2001): 17–26.

ESCUDOS, JACINTA

Jacinta Escudos (b. 1961) is part of the literary generation born between 1961 and 1970, and also part of a group who revitalized ideas, language and literature in El Salvador, Central America. She is considered a very qualified writer since she has written several novels, short stories, journal reports and poems. Her work has also been published in several newspapers, magazines and anthologies in Central America, United States, Mexico, France and Germany.

She was attracted to literature from the age of 13, when she started writing short stories and poems. "I always wrote and wrote with only one purpose in mind: becoming a professional writer", she said in an interview with the electronic journal *El Faro*. Her first contact with literature happened in 1979, when she began working on a short novel called *Apuntes de una Historia de Amor que No Fue* (Notes for a Love Story that Didn't Happen), published by UCA (San Salvador) in 1987. The following year, she moved to Germany, where she lived for more than two years. Later on, she lived in Nicaragua and El Salvador from 1992 to 1999. In 2000, she was an invited lecturer at the Heinrich Böll Stiftung (Germany) and in La Maison des écrivains etrangers et des traducteurs in Saint-Nazaire (France). In 2001, she went back to San Salvador. Other works by this author are the short stories compiled in *Contra-corriente* (1993, Against the Grain) (a book that appeared in the post-war period of transition), and *Cuentos Sucios* (1997, Dirty Stories), the novel *El Desencanto* (2001, The Disenchantment), and the short stories in *Felicidad Doméstica y Otras Cosas Aterradoras* (2002, Domestic Happiness and Other Terrifying Things).

That same year, she was the winner of the National Award "Décimos Juegos Florales de Ahuachapán" with a book of short stories called *Crónicas para sentimentales* (Chronicles for Sentimental People). With her latest novel, *A-B-Sudario*, she won the "Mario Monteforte Toledo" Novel Award of Central America in 2002. This novel was published the following year by Alfaguara (Guatemala, 2003), making her the first author from El Salvador ever to be published by the Spanish publishing house. In April 2004, Escudos received a commemorative plaque for her literary work in the World-Wide Copyright Day, granted by several institutions in the private sector and the Economic Ministry of El Salvador.

Her publications also include the non-authorized *Letter from El Salvador* (1984), a bilingual edition—English-Spanish—of her poems under the pseudonym Rocío América. In addition to those texts are *Crónicas para Sentimentales* and *El Diablo Sabe mi Nombre* (The Devil Knows My Name), the novel *Cuarteto contra el Ángel* (Quartet against the Angel), and the book of poems *Novia de Cuchillos* (Bride of Knives).

The literature of Jacinta Escudos can be classified under terms such as testimony, feminism and post-war literature. In Jacinta Escudos' work, some critics have found a new idea of the function of literature. These critics believe that she is discussing literature as a social and cultural function; an example of this is the book, *Apuntes de una Historia de Amor que no Fue*. This book, published in 1987, explained how the testimonial novel of Central America is going to change its paradigm; in other words, how literature is going to capture reality. However, the writing of this Salvadoran writer sometimes resists being considered or labeled by these literary terms. Her work has different registers, depending on genre, or the time when the short story, poem or novel was written. In a certain sense, her literature is unclassifiable. According to the Salvadoran critics, her texts tend to explore themes that are hidden on the dark side of human nature. These texts also work with trivial and melodramatic tones, but they never ignore the possibility of finding other borders of the human condition. Jacinta Escudos' literary work is characterized by asking herself about the established conditions for the appropriate behavior. In Central American societies, that behavior often requires the individual to define, in a very clear, rigid and permanent manner, his/her class and gender identity. In her books of short stories like *Contracorriente* (1996) and *Cuentos Sucios* (1998), Escudos questions sacred and important institutions in Central American culture, such as the family and the maternal figure. In this way, Escudos symbolically discusses themes like the humanization of this figure, a woman's desire, and violence in the private sphere, particularly inside the family, among others; the short story, "Costumbres pre-matrimoniales" (Prematrimonial Customs) is a perfect example of this behavior in her second book of short narratives. On the other hand, her work itself fights for the literacy of the female discourse and also for the modification of the usual topics treated in literature. The Salvadoran writer opens the collection *Contracorriente* (Counter-current) with "Hirohito, mi amor," a text in which she creates an emblematic portrayal, making some parallels between human beings and animals which the critics called "animalism". She also uses, in another piece, the word "zoociedad" in order to describe contemporary society in Central America. In this way, Escudos is discussing themes and issues that are more related to intellectual analysis in post-war San Salvador, in that she brings to the table of discussion the theme of this new violence, which is a continuation of the political violence experienced during the war.

The longer stories work with similar issues and introduce other elements that connect the political world with people's private world in Central America. The critics certainly point out that the personal becomes political in Escudos' work. The Central American post-war fiction also pays attention to the private space of normal people, working on topics that were untouched before the war. Therefore, contemporary texts are marked by the disenchantment and rejection of rules that restrict human beings, both in the public and private spheres. For example, the novel *El desencanto* was published immediately after the peace agreements with the guerrillas in El Salvador and Guatemala. Taking all this into account, the critics received this novel as daring and refreshing. In Salvadoran society it is certainly not common to find texts in which a woman thinks about desire and defines pleasure from a female point of view. In this way, the novel is successful. However, the ending leaves us with a real disappointment: the protagonist is unable to feel any kind of pleasure. In the last novel, *A–B–Sudario* (A–B–Sweating), Escudos deals with a young woman, Cayetana, and her attempt to write a novel. Cayetana's struggle consists of adapting her private life to literature. She does it through reflections, writings and dialogues with her friends. The novel is an experimental piece using language and certain expressions, which make the text a particular word game. The author also mixes several literary genres, such as poetry, drama, diary and narrative. Sometimes, all this mixture proves to be incoherent, senseless, like life itself. Some critics compared this work to Charles Bukowski's texts; he is also quoted in the novel itself. At the same time, there are some connections with a revisited magical realism and surrealism in the Latin American arenas.

The Salvadoran critics agree that the most important literary constant observed in Jacinta Escudos' work is her compromise with the Spanish language over the course of twenty years. In her work, the reader does not find empty words or a ready-made literature. Her writing has an obsession for the authentic artistic expression.

AIDA TOLEDO

Selected Works

Apuntes de una historia de amor que no fue. San Salvador: UCA Editores, 1987.

Contra-corriente. San Salvador: UCA Editores, 1993.

Cuentos Sucios. San Salvador: Dirección de Publicaciones e Impresos, 1997.

El Desencanto. San Salvador: Dirección de Publicaciones e Impresos, 2001.

Felicidad doméstica y otras cosas aterradoras. Guatemala: Editorial X, 2002.

A-B-Sudario. Guatemala: Alfaguara, 2003.

References and Further Reading

Aguirre, Liz. "Jacinta Escudos presenta 'El Desencanto'". *El Diario de Hoy* 13 August 2001. URL: http://www.elsalvador.com/noticias/2001/8/13/ESCENARIOS/escen3.html

Alfaro, Alma. "Women Writers and Central American Literature: Politics, Sexuality, and Gender in the Writings of Daisy Zamora, Jacinta Escudos, and Lety Elvir". Dissertation Abstracts International, Section A: The Humanities and Social Sciences, 2004 Dec.; 65 (6): 2399. University of California, Santa Barbara, 2004.

Campos, Orsy. "Conflictos de una escritora". *Hablemos on line*. 11 May 2003. http://www.elsalvador.com/hablemos/110503/110503–7.htm

Carballido Gómez, Armando. "*A-B-Sudario* de Jacinta Escudos." *Fundación CLIC, Arte y Nueva Tecnología*. October 2006. http://www.clic.org.sv/espacio_plantilla.php?id=11

Cortez, Beatriz. "Los *Cuentos sucios* de Jacinta Escudos: La construcción de la mujer como sujeto del deseo". In Oralia Preble-Niemi (ed.), *Afrodita en el trópico: Erotismo y construcción del sujeto femenino en obras de autoras centroamericanas*. Potomac, MD: Scripta Humanistica XI, 1999, pp. 111–22.

——. "El desencanto de Jacinta Escudos y la búsqueda fallida del placer." *Istmo* 3 (October 2006). http://www.denison.edu/collaborations/istmo/n03/articulos/desencanto.html

Escudos, Jacinta. "¿Subversión, moda o discriminación? Sobre el concepto de literatura de género". *Istmo* (October 2006). http://www.wooster.edu/istmo/foro/subversion.html

Gringerg Pla, Valeria. "Entre el desconocimiento, la pasión y la academia: ¿Dónde está la literatura centroamericana? Entrevista a Jacinta Escudos, Dante Liano y Anacristina Rossi". *Iberoamericana, América Latina, España, Portugal* 2(8): (2002): 176–83.

Mackenbach, Werner and Wallner, Alexandra Oritz. "Jacinta Escudos: La continuidad en la discontinuidad". *Istmo* 2005. http://www.denison.edu/collaborations/istmo/n10/foro/escudos.html

Schroeder, Regina. "Monólogos en la madrugada: la obra narrativa de Jacinta Escudos". *Revista Tatuana* 1. University of Alabama. 2004. http://bama.ua.edu/~tatuana/numero1/monologos.pdf

Torres-Recinos, Julio. "Desconciertos, desencantos y otros malestares: La narrativa de Jacinta Escudos". *Ístmica: Revista de la Facultad de Filosofía y Letras* 7 (2002): 169–89.

Urioste, Carmen. "Minimalismo y suciedad en la narrativa de Jacinta Escudos." *Revista del Consejo Nacional Para la Cultura y el Arte* May–Aug 85 (1999): 124–9.

Villalta, Nilda. "De la guerra a la post-guerra: Transición y cambios en la literatura salvadoreña". *Ístmica: Revista de la Facultad de Filosofía y Letras* 5–6 (2000): 94–102.

——. "Historias prohibidas, historias de guerra: el testimonio de Jacinta Escudos". *LASA*. October 2006. http://lasa.international.pitt.edu/LASA98/Villalta.pdf

ESPEJO, BEATRIZ

Beatriz Espejo, born in Mexico in 1939, has written essays, articles, and translations. Nevertheless, her short stories distinguish her as a writer. Her protagonists are predominantly bourgeois middle-aged women experiencing a crisis, often alone, lamenting the loss of their youth, and in search of an identity. She is also highly critical of the double morality and the customs of the disappearing Mexican bourgeoisie. She has reflected on her own life experience to represent her characters' social and cultural background. At the same time, Espejo does not shy away from topics that other modern female writers have traditionally disdained and considered too domestic, such as cooking and embroidering. Indeed, she has embraced such topics recurrently in her writing and also included them as titles in her work, e.g., *Alta costura* (1997, High Fashion) and *De comer, coser y cantar* (1997, On Eating, Sewing, and Singing).

Born in Veracruz in 1939, she found her calling in literature at the age of 12. She studied Literature at the Universidad Autónoma de México (UNAM) and started publishing at an early age. Her first book, a collection of fifteen short stories entitled *La otra hermana* (The Other Sister), was published in 1958 in the first number of Cuadernos del Unicornio, directed by Juan José Arreola. Arreola's initial influence on Espejo's work is evident in the mini short stories *Muros de azogue* (1979, Quicksilver Wall). These twenty stories are inspired by Espejo's own family and portray the life of the Príncipe Beltrán family, the wealthy owners of a hacienda in Veracruz. In these short stories she denounces the hypocrisy of the bourgeoisie and the excessive importance that is given to social conventions. In this society people hide their own perversions, while condemning those of others. Thus, this society, through their inability to change, fosters paralysis and ignorance.

Although Espejo has been influenced by Jorge Luis Borges, Julio Torri, Katherine Mansfield, and Luisa Josefina Hernández; she found her own writing style. Her work received numerous awards such as Premio Nacional de Periodismo in 1984; Premio Magda Donato in 1986; Premio Nacional Colima de Navarra in 1993; and Premio Nacional de Cuento INBA-San Luis Potosí in 1996. Two short-story awards carry the "Beatriz Espejo" name; one in Mérida, and the other in Tlaxcala. In 1959, she founded, and for ten years ran, the journal *El rehilete*. Additionally, Espejo was a professor at Escuela Nacional de Maestros, UNAM, and Universidad Iberoamericana.

Espejo describes the style in some of her books as "realismo milagroso" (miracle realism). A prime example is *El cantar del pecador* (1993, The Sinner's Song), a collection of ten short stories where she recalls *Muros de azogue.* Using some of her mother's stories from Veracruz, she retells her family's saga.

"El cantar del pecador," which gives the book its title, is based on a prayer for sinners. After her wedding is cancelled, the protagonist goes to Perote to live with her aunt and her two spinster daughters. The family lives haunted by the spirits of the past; especially by Nena, who supposedly died after an abortion. We later discover she is the protagonist's mother, and that she has been locked in a room to conceal her shame. "La casa junto al río" (The House by the River) deals symbolically with her father's death and the subsequent collapse of her family life. According to her, in this book Veracruz is limbo, Perote equals hell, and Tlacotalpan equals heaven.

Alta costura (1997) received the Premio Nacional de Cuento. It contains fifteen short stories about mature modern bourgeois women; struggling with the loss of their youth, money, and love. In "Alta costura," which gives the book its title, a Russian seamstress makes a delicate scarf which later plays a central role in the death of writer Isadora Duncan. In "Don't Try This Home," the protagonist must hold back her primal instincts, since she feels an animal attraction for a homeless man. In "Una mujer altruista" (An Altruistic Woman), the main character refrains from smashing the maid's daughter against the wall. One of her best stories, "Entrevista con una leyenda" (Interview with a Legend), is really a chronicle, retelling Espejo's conversation with Pita Amor. Espejo dedicates "Los delfinios blancos" (The White Delphiniums) to Emmanuel Carballo, the famous literary critic, to whom she was married for many years. In fact, each of the stories is dedicated to different Mexican writers, such as Inés Arredondo and Elena Garro.

In *Marilyn en la cama y otros cuentos* (Marilyn in Bed and Other Short Stories, 2004), she strays from her usual irony and reflects on her sadness, perhaps because this book was written after the death of her nephew. It deals with more contemporary stories than those in former collections, which reminisce about Mexico's old-style bourgeoisie. In the story "Marilyn en la cama," Espejo portrays the dead sex symbol in the morgue as an obese drunkard addicted to pain killers, pregnant, and with a fetid odor. The journalist covering the story is at the same time moved and repulsed by her. The collection also pays homage to Anthony Quinn, Vincent Van Gogh, and Elena Garro.

Additionally, Espejo and Ethel Krauze have compiled three short-story anthologies by Mexican women: *Atrapadas en la casa* (Trapped in the House, 2001), *Atrapadas en la cama* (Trapped in Bed, 2005), and *Mujeres engañadas* (Betrayed Women, 2004). The selections include well-established as well as emerging writers. The idea behind these anthologies, that they will continue publishing in the future, is to give a voice to the numerous Mexican women writers, whose publications are still underrepresented under current editorial policies (*Mujeres engañadas,* pp. 9–29).

In *Atrapadas en la cama* Espejo's story is "El espejo lateral" (Lateral Mirror), and for *Atrapadas en la casa* she reprints "El cantar del pecador". Espejo's own short story for *Mujeres engañãdas* is "Nina". The protagonist, Nina, is a wealthy middle-aged housewife in crisis. Her daughter is about to marry, and she has a strained relationship with the husband, whom she married very young. Later we find out that the husband is leaving her for his life-long business partner, Carlos.

Espejo's only novel, *Todo lo hacemos en familia* (2001, We Do Everything in the Family), coincidentally takes the format of many intertwined short stories. The central character, Sara, is the crazy matriarch of an impoverished bourgeois family. She is a modern-day Penelope who through her embroidery recreates the family history. Different family characters become protagonists at some point in the novel; including the favorable portrait of the General, one of the few male characters in Espejo's work. Her current work revisits the initial influence of Arreola, as can be seen in her work in progress provisionally entitled "Sobre héroes impuros" (About Impure Heroes).

For Espejo, the language used in her short stories needs to be detailed, elaborate, and rounded. She is ironic and strongly critical of the bourgeoisie and social conventions, which she believes hinder the real feelings of human beings. A careful observer of human nature, Espejo portrays women as full of flaws, exhibiting only self-compassion, motivated only by their own instincts, and without their social coating. She loves the ability of a short story to capture the psychological depth of a character in a limited space.

FABIOLA FERNÁNDEZ SALEK

Selected Works

La otra hermana. México: Cuadernos del Unicornio, 1958.
Breve biografía de Leonardo da Vinci. México: Secretaría de Educación Pública, 1968.
La prosa española de los siglos XVI y XVII. México: UNAM, 1971.
Muros de azogue. México: Diógenes, 1979; 1986.
Mariano Silva y Aceves / selección y nota de Beatriz Espejo. México, D.F.: UNAM/ Coordinación de Difusión Cultural, 1986.
Historia de la pintura mexicana. 3 tomos. México: Armonía, 1989.
Julio Torri, voyeurista desencantado. México: UNAM, Instituto de Investigaciones Filológicas, Centro de Estudios Literarios, 1987; México: Diana, 1991.
Oficios y menesteres: crónicas. México, D.F.: Universidad Autónoma Metropolitana Departamento Editorial, 1988.
Palabra de honor. Villahermosa, Tabasco: ICT Ediciones, 1990.
De cuerpo entero. Viejas fotografías. México: Ediciones Corunda, 1991.
El cantar del pecador. México, D.F.: Siglo Veintiuno Editores, 1993.
Dr. Atl, el paisaje como pasión. México: Fondo Editorial de la Plástica Mexicana, 1994.
En religiosos incendios. Estudio preliminar y notas. México, D.F.: UNAM–Dirección General de Publicaciones, 1995.
La hechicera. Toluca, México: Instituto Mexiquense de Cultura, 1995.
Alta Costura (Andanzas). México, D.F.: Tusquets Editores, 1996.
Antología personal. Xalapa, Veracruz: Universidad Veracruzana—Serie Ficción, 1996.
De comer, coser y cantar. México, 1997.
Cómo mataron a mi abuelo el español. México, D.F.: ISSSTE, 1999.
José García Ocejo o el gozo de vivir. México: CONACULTA, 2000.
Todo lo hacemos en familia. México: Ed. Aldus, 2001.
Marilyn en la cama y otros cuentos. México: Nueva Imagen, 2004.
Cuentos reunidos. México: Fondo de Cultura Económica USA, 2005.
Espejo, Beatriz and Krauze, Ethel. *Atrapadas en la casa/Trapped in the House.* México, D.F.: Selector, 2001.
——. *Mujeres engañadas.* México, D.F.: Alfaguara, 2004.
——. *Atrapadas en la cama.* México, D.F.: Alfaguara/Santillana, 2005.
Espejo, Beatriz, *et al. Los siete pecados capitales.* México: SEP/CONACULTA/INBA, 1989.

References and Further Reading

Bradu, Fabienne. "Crónica de dos crónicas". *Vuelta* 12(144) (1988): 46–7.
Carballo, Emmanuel (ed.) *Confiar en el milagro.* Colima, México: Universidad de Colima, 1998.
Gil, Eve. "La humedad del milagro". *La trenza de Sor Juana*, October 20, 2006.
http://evetrenzas.blogspot.com/2006/10/la-humedad-del-milagro.html
Pfeiffer, Erna. *Entrevistas. Diez escritoras mexicanas desde bastidores. Interviews. Ten Women Writers of Mexico in the Wings.* Frankfurt: Vervuert, 1992.
Rojas, Carlos. "La nostalgia de lo femenino." CONACULTA-INBA. http://www.literaturainba.com/escritores/bio_beatriz_espejo.htm
Tafoya, Jesús. "Ruptura y continuidad del discurso hegemónico en *Cómo mataron a mi abuelo español* de Beatriz Espejo". *Revista de Literatura Mexicana Contemporánea* 5(11) (1999): 65–9.

ESQUIVEL, LAURA

Though she began as a writer of film scripts, Laura Esquivel (b. 1950) exploded into best-seller status with her first novel *Como agua para chocolate*, which was made into an equally popular film, and translated into many languages. Though her later works have not met with similar popular or critical success, Esquivel remains a popular writer and, with the Chilean Isabel Allende, is probably the best-known Latin American woman writer.

Born in Mexico City to Josephina and Julio Caesar Esquivel, the third of four children, Laura Esquivel grew up near and attended the Escuela Normal de Maestros, the national college for teacher preparation. She taught young children for several years, and then founded the Taller de Teatro y Literatura (Literature and Theater Workshop) with some friends, and wrote for children's theater. She met Alfonso Arau, her first husband, while he was still an actor rather than the film director he would become. They married and in 1976 had their daughter, Sandra. In 1985, she wrote the screen play for a children's film directed by Arau, *Chido Guán y Tacos de oro*, and in 1989 she published her first novel, *Como agua para chocolate*. Her marriage to Arau ended in 1993–94. She spends most of her time in Mexico City with her second husband, Dr. Javier Valdez, a dentist.

Themes and Influences

Esquivel's family is a major influence on her writing: her grandmother taught her the medicinal and culinary arts reflected in later works; her mother was a traditional homemaker; the death of her aunt, who cared for her mother rather than marrying, inspired the character of Tita in *Como agua para chocolate*; her father inspired the character of Júbilo Chi, a telegraph operator in *Tan veloz como el deseo*, her third novel.

Como agua para chocolate

A charming novel, *Como agua para chocolate* (1989; *Like Water for Chocolate*, 1992; translated into Chinese, Dutch, English,

Finnish, French, German, Hebrew, Italian, Japanese, Korean, Persian, Polish, Portuguese, Russian, Serbo-Croatian, and Turkish) began as an idea for a film. Because of the expense of producing a period piece, Esquivel was discouraged from writing a film script and decided to write a novel instead.

Como agua para chocolate was a best-seller in Mexico in 1990. Despite the publisher's hesitance, Esquivel insisted that Doubleday release the English translation simultaneously with a Spanish version in 1993. The release of the novel coincided closely with the 1992 release of the film of the same name, with the script written by Esquivel. By May, 1994 the film had become the largest grossing foreign film in US history. The Spanish version of the novel was on the bestseller list in San Francisco, and the English version was on the *New York Times* list of bestsellers for over a year. The novel was among the top ten bestsellers for 1993, along with such popular authors as Tom Clancy and John Grisham; Esquivel was the only first-time author among them. Esquivel was awarded the ABBY (the American Booksellers' Book of the Year) in 1994. The film won ten Ariel awards (the Mexican Oscar), including one for Best Screenplay for Esquivel and Best Direction for Arau. The film was nominated for the Golden Globe for Best Foreign Film, and won several other awards from international film festivals.

Como agua para chocolate: *novela de entregas mensuales con recetas, amores, y remedios caseros* (*Like Water for Chocolate: A Novel in Monthly Installments, with Recipes, Romances, and Home Remedies*), as its full title suggests, is a hybrid work, combining the medicinal and culinary arts that Esquivel learned from her grandmother with elements of a historical novel set during the Mexican Revolution and a love story that both depends on and parodies the romance novel. The novel is divided into twelve chapters, one for each month of the year, beginning with January and ending with December. Each chapter opens with a recipe relevant to the events that will unfold in that chapter. After the list of ingredients, the narrative begins with "Manera de hacerse," or instructions for the preparation of the recipe for that month.

The heroine of the novel, Tita de la Garza, is born in the kitchen and raised there by the Indian Nacha. The third and youngest daughter of Mamá Elena, she is required to take care of her mother until her death, forsaking a life of her own. She falls in love with Pedro, but this tradition of care taking (invented by Esquivel) prevents their marriage. He marries her sister Rosaura in order to be close to Tita, but Tita is jealous of the intimacy that Pedro shares with Rosaura and cannot share with her. Tita is forced to prepare the very cake to be served at her beloved's wedding to another. Her tears season the cake and transfer her sorrow to all the wedding guests, who sob uncontrollably and become very ill.

Tita's most (in)famous recipe is "Quail in Rose Petal Sauce," which causes all those who eat it to become consumed with the same passionate desire with which Tita crushed the rose petals. Mamá Elena sends Rosaura and Pedro, with their son, to the United States to separate Pedro and Tita. The child dies and Tita, who had nursed him despite having never been pregnant, suffers a nervous breakdown. She goes to Texas in the care of a kind but boring American doctor, John Brown, whose offer of marriage she accepts after her mother's death. But Rosaura has died, and finally Tita and Pedro can be together. She and Pedro spend one glorious night in an embrace so passionate that it spontaneously causes a fire that destroys the two lovers and the ranch.

Esquivel has commented in interviews about the importance of the kitchen—her grandmother's kitchen in particular, and her own kitchen as well. She began cooking with her mother and grandmother when she was seven years old, and she observed the power of these women who became priestesses, alchemists of the home. The "womanly" arts of care taking, healing, and cooking are here elevated to nearly mythical proportions, as Tita's culinary creations cause magical reactions. And kitchen magic is just one aspect of the magical realism in this novel. In addition to elements of magical realism already mentioned, Tita's tears are equally magical. Even before birth, she cries in the womb when onions are cut. At her birth, her tears when dried are swept up to be used for salt. While recovering in Texas her sorrow is so great that her tears run down the stairs of Dr. Brown's house like a river.

The female characters in *Como agua para chocolate* are much more powerful than the male characters. Pedro is handsome, but weak-willed; Dr. Brown is kind, but boring. Tita's sister Gertrudis runs off with a soldier, but eventually takes the male role and becomes a soldier herself.

The unprecedented success of all versions of *Como agua para chocolate* led publishers to recognize the market potential for books in Spanish for a previously ignored Hispanic population and the increasing number of Hispanics in the United States. Though some reviewers of the novel claim that translations were done in some twenty-four to thirty-three languages, the novel has been translated definitively into sixteen languages. Critics consider the novel a "bestseller," a work of popular, rather than great literature. The novel and film remain popular choices for literature classes in English or Spanish, as well as Spanish language classes.

La ley del amor

Esquivel calls her second novel, *La ley del amor* (1995; *The Law of Love*, 1995; translated into Chinese, English, Italian, Polish, and Portuguese), the first multi-media novel. The action of the novel occurs from the Mexico of Moctezuma and the city of Tenochtitlan in the sixteenth century, to the Mexico City of the twenty-third century built over the site of the Aztec city. The novel comes packaged with a compact disc of musical selections and color comic book panels illustrate sections of the text.

The protagonist, Azucena Martínez, is an astro-analyst in the future Mexico City, who uses music in her practice and is herself looking for her "Twin Soul," her one true love, Rodrigo Sánchez. Both characters have led many previous lives, beginning with Aztec times, when Rodrigo, captain for Hernán Cortés, conqueror of the Aztecs, was married to Isabel and raped the Indian Citlali on the pyramid of the Aztec goddess of love. When Citlali gives birth to his child, Rodrigo murders the child. Citlali avenges herself by killing Rodrigo's son with Isabel. The Law of Love dictates that acts of brutality upset the cosmic order, which must be realigned. A single lifetime is insufficient to the task, so through reincarnation the players must meet again and again in order to eventually achieve spiritual cleansing. Azucena has settled the karmic debts of her 14,000 lives, but Rodrigo has not. For his crime, Rodrigo is sent to another planet; Azucena follows to save him, and restore the balance of the universe. *La ley del amor* combines magic realism, New Age philosophy, and science fiction with popular and high culture – comics, opera – and thus is highly imaginative. But the plot is intensely complicated and finally, perhaps, unbelievable, in contrast to *Como agua para chocolate*, which is highly believable despite its many elements of magic realism.

Tan veloz como el deseo and *Malinche*

Tan veloz como el deseo (2001; *As Swift as Desire*, 2001; translated into English, Polish, and Portuguese) is inspired by the life of Esquivel's father, a telegraph operator who died in 1999 after suffering from Parkinson's disease. The protagonist, Júbilo, is a telegraph operator of Mayan Indian heritage who had the ability to comprehend the feelings that people cannot express. The story is told in flashbacks, beginning with Júbilo as a bedridden old man who cannot communicate at all. His daughter Lluvia finds an old telegraph machine and, using Morse code, manages to communicate with her silent father and find out what had caused the rift between him and her mother, Lucha. The novel is a homage to her father and to the telegraph, once as important as the Internet is now.

Malinche (2006; *Malinche*, 2006; translated into English and Russian), written at the suggestion of editors at Santillana publishing in Mexico and published simultaneously in Spanish and English translation, is the fictionalized biography of the woman who is the mother of the Mexican race. Given to Cortés as a gift, Malinche was the slave who became Cortés's lover, and the mother of his son Martín, thus creating the first Mexican. But perhaps most importantly, she was his "lengua," his tongue. As a translator, Malinche helped Cortés conquer the powerful Aztecs. Malinche is a fascinating and enigmatic figure in Mexican history and for Mexican identity. Mexicans see Malinche as either a traitor, someone who betrayed her own people for a foreign invader, or a victim, a woman "occupied" by the enemy.

Esquivel spent two years researching the novel, but so little is definitively known about Malinche herself that most of the research relates to the historical setting. Esquivel begins her novel with Malinche's birth and the religious naming ceremony that gives her the name Malinalli. Historical research surfaces in the presentation of Cortés, and in sometimes didactic passages on Mayan religious beliefs or aspects of Mexican folklore. Esquivel presents the known details of Malinche's life—being given to Cortés and then taken by him in the carnal sense, giving birth to Cortés's son, considered the first Mexican, the first mestizo—but the characters are undeveloped and the writing is uneven. Nonetheless, Esquivel does attempt to vindicate, or at least explain, Malinche's role in the conquest of Mexico.

Considered a best-seller rather than a serious writer, Esquivel is known for the lyricism and New Age spirituality of her writing. Each of her novels centers on a creative concept that drives the narrative, whether the recipes of *Como agua para chocolate* or the multi-media, multi-century foundation of *La ley del amor*, for example, but the concept is truly successful only in her first novel. Nevertheless, *Como agua para chocolate* alone assures Laura Esquivel's place in Mexican and Latin American literature.

LINDA LEDFORD-MILLER

Selected Works

Como agua para chocolate: novela de entregas mensuales con recetas, amores, y remedios caseros. Mexico: Editorial Planeta Mexicana, 1989. Trans. Carol Christensen and Thomas Christensen as *Like Water for Chocolate: A Novel in Monthly Installments, with Recipes, Romances, and Home Remedies*. New York: Doubleday, 1991.

La ley del amor. With CD. Mexico: Grijalbo, 1995. Trans. Margaret Sayers Peden as *The Law of Love*. New York: Three Rivers Press, 1996.

Tan veloz como el deseo. Barcelona: Plaza y Janes Editores, 2001. Trans. Stephen A. Lytle as *Swift as Desire: A Novel*. New York: Anchor Books, 2001.

Malinche. New York: Atria Books, 2006. Trans. Ernesto Mestre-Reed as *Malinche*. New York: Atria Books, 2006.

References and Further Reading

Contreras, Marta. "La novela: *como agua para chocolate*, de Laura Esquivel; La película: *como agua para chocolate*, dirección de Alfonso Arau". *Acta literaria* 21 (1996): 117–22.

Cruz-Lugo, Victor. "The Poet & the Visionary: A Conversation with World-Renowned Writer Laura Esquivel". *Hispanic* 19(4) (April 2006): 28–30.

Fernández-Levin, Rosa. "Ritual and 'Sacred Space' in Laura Esquivel's *Like Water for Chocolate*". *Confluencia: Revista Hispánica de Cultura y Literatura* 12(1) (Fall 1996): 106–20.

Ibsen, Kristine. *The Other Mirror: Women's Narrative in Mexico, 1980–1995*. Westport, CT: Greenwood Press, 1997.

Jaffe, Janice. "Hispanic American Women's Recipes and Laura Esquivel's *Como Agua Para Chocolate*". *Women's Studies* 22 (1993): 217–30.

Pout, Ryan. "Cosmic Weddings and a Funeral: Sexuality, Techno-science, and the National Romance in Laura Esquivel's *La ley del amor*". *Journal of Iberian and Latin American Studies* 6(1) (2000): 43–54.

Taylor, Claire. "Body-Swapping and Genre-Crossing: Laura Esquivel's *La ley del amor*". *Modern Language Review* 97(2) (April 2002): 324–35.

Valdés, María Elena de. "*Like Water for Chocolate*: A Celebration of the Mexican Pre-Aesthetic". In *The Shattered Mirror: Representations of Women in Mexican Literature*. Austin, TX: University of Texas Press, 1998, pp. 183–90.

Zubiaurre, Maite. "Culinary Eros in Contemporary Hispanic Female Fiction: From Kitchen Tales to Table Narratives". *College Literature* 33(30) (Summer 2006): 29–51.

F

FERNÁNDEZ, ADELA

Adela Fernández was born in Mexico City on December 6, 1942. Fernández was the daughter of the famous Mexican actor and director Emilio "El Indio" Fernández and his 16-year-old wife, Gladys Fernández. "El Indio's" artistic world of using film for cultural acknowledgement and preservation would greatly influence his daughter's work, cultivating a desire in her to learn about her people's history and mythologies and communicate it through story, theater and film.

Fernández's life was one of a nomad. She traveled extensively throughout the Mexican Republic and experienced the life of a Mexican migrant worker in various occupations including: tomato planter, sugar cane cutter, sea fisher, miner and wandering artist. When not traveling, Fernández lived in Valles del Mesquital, one of the aridest places in Mexico. She did, however, spend time at her father's grand colonial home. Known as "The Fortress of the Indian" the house on Zaragoza Street in the borough of Coyoacan in Mexico City's capital, was built to impress in the architectural style of Spanish colonialism. "El Indio" would use his home as a cultural center and meeting place for some of the most influential people during the Golden Age of Mexican Cinema, including: Diego Rivera, Frida Kahlo, Dolores del Río, Arthur Rubenstein, and many others.

Fernández would commemorate her memories of this grand home in a tribute to her father in 1989 with her recipe book "The Traditional Mexican Kitchen and Its Best Recipes". Fernández offers us a first-hand account of the daily life in her father's kitchen, as well a brief history of Mexican cooking and some delicious recipes based on what was served in the Fortress. El Indio was a traditionalist and the kitchen was constructed to resemble the old cooking spaces of colonial times, complete with tiles, bricks and murals. Fernández learned that the kitchen was the "most animated place in the house, always in movement, in agitation, full of colors, of smells and flavors". Fernández also learned that the kitchen was so animated because of the women who occupied it—always cooking, always preparing meals and coffee and tacos beginning at four in the morning. She comments "the result was a kitchen too small for so many women who work in it".

The importance of culinary arts, which, according to Fernández, was to "adorn the tables as if you were preparing to serve the gods," is a good indication of the beginning of Fernández's interest in Mexican mythology. Taking her cues from her father's work and kitchen, Fernández would study and explore Nahuatl mythology and its influences on contemporary Mexicans, culminating in her being in charge of the National Indian Institute's information bulletin "Indigenous Mexico".

Published in Spanish in 1983 and subsequently published in English in 1984, Fernández's "Prehistoric Gods of Mexico: Myths and Deities from Nahuatl Mythology" would become a standard in the field of Mexican cultural anthropology. Joel Davila Gutierrez, in his *Literatura hispanoamericana: Rumbo y conjeturas,* would describe her work as essential to understanding indigenous literature from Mexico. Fernández compiles information about the gods of the people of Mesoamerica including the Nahuas, Zapatecs, Mayan and Tarascans. Using the hierarchy of Aztec gods as her model, she discovers that the gods are the same, just the names are different; "despite the different names given by the various civilizations to their deities, their gods nevertheless represented the same forces of nature and fulfilled similar divine roles".

Underlying the mythology is the belief that the world has been created and destroyed several times, the people feared the metaphysical, they wanted to understand the cosmos and they were preoccupied with spirituality in terms of the afterlife. Fernández traces the evolution of the belief system, for example, how the civilizations divided the universe, whether into two—heaven and earth—or three—heaven, earth, underworld. Using mythology as her base, she brings to life the distinct characteristics of ancient civilizations and their intellectual growth in understanding the world they lived in.

It is not surprising that Fernández combined her varied experiences while growing up and her in-depth studies of Mexican culture in her literary and cinematic work. She authored nine books, eleven plays, various short stories and films, and won the Sor Juana Inés de la Cruz award.

Fernández's stories, compiled in three collections, *The Dog* (1975), *Of These Days* (1981) and *Duerme Velas* (1986), have a dark sense about them, sometimes even described as morbid.

But what she does in her stories is tell tales of life by contrasting it with pain and death. For example, in her short story "You Do Not Have to Ascend to Death," her protagonist Mateo knows he is alive because he is "vomiting, coughing and has fever". In the opening paragraph, Fernández shows us that nature is supreme, "men, trees, bulls and rocks all do the will of the current". Mateo arrives to his ranch after surviving a flash flood—and his women—all eight of them—scurry to his side to help. Fernández introduces the women by their interaction with Mateo—the supreme king—and one imagines the similarities between what is happening in the story and what Fernández experienced in the kitchen of her father's grand house. "Jesusa takes off his wet clothes and covers him with seven blankets. Ruperta puts his feet in a pan of hot water. Anastasia makes him breathe in a vapor of eucalyptus and mint. Gertrudis has him drink sugar cane alcohol and punches of cinnamon and herbs. Victoria puts warm towels on his temples. Palmira puts hot towels on the soles of his feet. Agustina gives him a tablespoon of viper oil and Gervasia prays in the back". Everyone has their place.

What also makes the story so convincing is its fast pace expressed through the intermittent prayers and pleadings to the saints. It is also interspersed with the superstitions of the eight women since they believe that "death enters through the feet and goes up" and so as Mateo grows cold from the feet first the women's lamentations escalate. We experience the women's race against time and the cold and hence against death. In the story they lose Mateo to death, as in life, we all do.

Another of Fernández's stories, "The Burnt One," brings the issue of superstition to its ultimate climate of mass hysteria and murder, when it is confronted by the truth of a new religion. A curandero—witch doctor—is deceived into a trap by villagers spurred on by a priest. His child watches as he and others like him are brought into a pit to be burned. All the others change into animals such as snakes and eagles and escape except for the father. The child returns home despondently "lamenting the father's weakness of power" only to discover the father waiting and singing. The themes of transformation, old tradition vs. new beliefs, and spirituality are beautifully incorporated in such a short story.

But Fernández does not believe that new beliefs replacing old ways of thinking are necessarily bad, and she recognizes that there are times when the older generation needs to move aside for the younger one to come to power. In her short story "The Initiated" she turns the tables as the great priest of a village puts a 9-year-old to a test. The old priest and leader asks the boy to bring the sun bitten by the tiger over a piece of earth dominated by fire". The boy leaves and brings back a plate containing a "fried egg bathed in ground chilli". The priest realizes that the boy understands that "symbols are to be applied to everything in our daily life". The priest gives his power stick to the boy who then becomes the high priest.

Critics analyzing Fernández's work put her in a category of new Mexican voices—specifically a feminine voice—that explores the female role in society, past and present. Literary critic Brianda Domecq cites Fernández as an example of how the "voice" in the story (or "message") is one that reflects the author's persona, for in publishing her stories, the female author become a public entity. So, for Brianda, the melancholy, pain and suffering of Fernández's characters are a reflection of Fernández's own life struggles.

Adela Fernández is considered soft-spoken and does not seek the limelight as her father did. But her stories, infused with the influence of pre-Hispanic Mexican mythology and life with her father, express vividly and bring to life a culture rich in symbolism, passion and delicious taste.

DEBORAH GONZALEZ

Selected Works

The Dog. Mexico: Edicion El Hábito por la Rosa, 1975.
Of These Days. Mexico: UAM, 1981.
Pre-historic Gods of Mexico: Myths and Deities from Natuatl Mythology. Mexico: Panorama Editorial, 1984.
El Indio Fernández, Life and Myth. Mexico: Panorama Editorial, 1986.
Duerme Velas. Mexico: Editorial Katun, 1986.
The Traditional Mexican Kitchen and its Best Recipes. Mexico: Panorama Editorial, 1989.

References and Further Reading

Davila Gutierrez, Joel (ed.). *Literatura hispanoamericana: Rumbo y conjeturas.* Tlaxcala, Mexico: Universidad Autonoma de Tlaxcala, 2005.
Domecq, Brianda. *Mujer que publica, mujer pública.* Mexico: Diana, 1984
Adela Fernández, Breve Biografía Hasta 1984, Online Magazine Sensibles #104, 2001. http://www.paginadigital.com.ar/articulos/2001seg/sensibles/sensibles104.html
Mercedes, María. *Amena Conversación con Adela Fernández.* Hoy Digital, 2004. http://www.hoy.com.do
Terrero, Miguelina. *Adela Fernández: La Vida de mi Padre Fue Muy Dura.* El Nacional, Sept. 2004. www.elnacional.com.do

FERNÁNDEZ DE JUAN, ADELAIDA

Cuban novelist and short story writer, Adelaida Fernández de Juan (b. 1961), whose latest books are published under the name Laidi Fernández or Laidi Fernández de Juan, was born in Havana. She is the younger of two daughters of Roberto Fernández Retamar and Adelaida de Juan, two of Cuba's most prominent intellectuals and writers. She received a medical degree from the University of Havana in 1985 and served as a volunteer doctor with an international Cuban mission in Zambia from 1988 to 1990. She had no intention of becoming a writer, but as she wrote letters home from Zambia, letters which piled up because she rarely had any way to send them to Cuba, she discovered her literary vocation. These letters, about the people and situations she encountered, and the stories they helped her to discover, became the basis for her first collection of short fiction, *Dolly y otros cuentos africanos*, published in Havana in 1994 and translated into English as *Dolly and Other Stories from Africa*, published in 1996. In these early stories, Fernández reveals her fascination with the nuances of language and the absurdities of cultural collision as she describes her experiences in Zambia.

After she returned to Havana in 1990, Laidi Fernández continued to work as a doctor, specializing in Internal Medicine, practicing now at the Rampa Polyclinic and the Fajardo Hospital. After describing the unfathomable disparities of African life, upon her return she began to write vividly of similar incomprehensible contradictions in Cuban life. Her stories display reverence for the unexpected, the spontaneous and the apparently trivial, moments when truths are revealed and the authenticity of emotion is validated. Fernández often writes about women characters who are energetic and impassioned, aware of the incongruities of their situations, but determined to do what they feel is important. The humor with which these women's quests for fulfillment are told is sympathetic, never mocking. Fernández has spoken frequently, as in her interview with Maribel Duarte González, of feeling that she is part of a longstanding Cuban tradition of humor, one which laughs with rather than at others as it recognizes the absurdities of life.

In 1996, she won the important Cecilia Valdés Prize for her story "Clemencia bajo el sol" ("Clemencia Under the Sun"), which was later adapted for the theater on two occasions, in Cuba in 1997 and in Italy in 2002, and widely anthologized. Recognized as one of the group of extraordinarily fine writers who began to publish in the 1990s, Fernández has continued to write fiction, both long and short stories. These have appeared in many magazines, and in two volumes. The first collection of stories written after her return from Africa was published as *Oh Vida* (Oh Life), and received the National Union of Cuban Writers and Artists (UNEAC) Short Story Prize in 1998. Stories from *Oh Vida* are frequently included in anthologies focusing on the material scarcities of the Cuban "Special Period" of the 1990s and the creative—and often comic—survival strategies of this era. In "Antes del cumpleaños" (Before the Birthday Party), one of the better known and frequently anthologized stories in *Oh Vida*, Fernández recounts a young mother's obsession with assembling all the components of birthday celebration for her young son during the time of scarcities when acquiring candles and balloons and a birthday cake required highly developed organizational skills and weeks of intrigue.

In 2004, her story "El beso" (The Kiss) was published and received an honorable mention in the Julio Cortázar International Short Story Competition. "El beso" is a multilayered and deliberately ambiguous tale of childhood memory reevaluated by an adult narrator. Laidi Fernández's second collection, *La hija de Darío* (Darío's daughter), which includes thirteen short stories, received the prestigious Alejo Carpentier Short Story Prize in 2005, and was published that same year. In this book, she includes stories with a young child as narrator, and in interviews she ascribes her experiments with children's perspectives of the adult world to her many conversations with her two young sons, Robin and Rubén. The child narrator's honesty, as he tries to figure out the odd behavior of the adult world, is both hilarious and revealing of the surreal scarcities, bureaucracies, contradictions and passions of present-day Cuban life. "Comando perro" (Operation Dogbite) is a boy's account of his mother's epic pursuit of a stray dog that bit him, in order to ascertain that it is not rabid. Eventually an entire community of determined women manages to coerce an unwilling male bureaucracy into the effort and the mother triumphs, to the boy's relief. The child is both embarrassed by his mother's increasingly public exertions, and proud of her tenaciousness on his behalf. This story is one of many that involve travel across the city of Havana, describing contemporary urban panoramas.

In 2003, in collaboration with a photographer, Errol Daniels, Fernández wrote the text that accompanies Daniels' pictures in *Nani: Documentary Project*. Nani is a severely disabled child whose courage and positive attitude toward life impress those who meet her, both in real life, and in this tribute by Laidi Fernández, Nani's doctor. A lifelong admirer of the descriptive writing of Eladio Secades, a popular Cuban chronicler and story teller of the 1940s and 1950s, Fernández collected many of his best texts in 2004, and they were published under the title of *Estampas:1941–1958* (Scenes 1941–58). Laidi Fernández's first novel, *Nadie es profeta* (No One is a Prophet) was published in 2006 and featured in the 2007 Havana Book Fair. It tells the story of a Cuban family over the course of some seventy years, set in the panorama of dramatic twentieth-century historical and social changes. The family lives through years of unrest and intrigue, under the Batista regime, suffering under increasing undercover protest and militarism, and temporary exile in New York before returning to the excitement of revolutionary change in 1959, and the euphoria of building a new society. The novel is a creative mirror image of changing times in Cuba from the 1950s on. The story alternates between a chronological third person account of four generations of Natacha Sockler's family and a first person emotional series of letters between Natacha and a friend whose identity becomes clear only at the very end of the book, thus adding an element of mystery and gender ambiguity in its suspenseful counterpoint to the more traditional narrative. The insights into the lives (and particularly the education) of important participants in the revolutionary changes of the 1960s, and the hopes and beliefs that sustain them are depicted with particular effectiveness. A recurring subtext of the presence of Afro-Cuban religious beliefs and ceremonies is important in this novel as well as in Fernández's recent stories, which feature a central character named María E., who is expected to be the protagonist of Fernández's next collection.

MARY G. BERG

Selected Works

Dolly y otros cuentos africanos. La Habana: Pinos Nuevos, 1994. Translated into English as *Dolly and Other Stories from Africa*. Trans. Lucy Robinson, Esperanza Devesa and Zilpha Ellis. Toronto: Lugus Books, 1996.

Oh Vida. La Habana: Ediciones Unión, 1998

"El juego de las palabras". *Revista Casa de las Américas* 228 (July–Sept. 2002),104–6.

Nani: Documentary Project. With Errol Daniels. Buffalo, NY: Errol Daniels Photography, 2003.

"El beso". In *Reliquia familiar de Horacio Verzi y otros relatos. Premio Iberoamericano de Cuento Julio Cortázar, 2004*. La Habana: Instituto Cubano del Libro, 2004, pp. 37–41.

Prologue and selection, Eladio Secades, *Estampas (1941–1958)*. La Habana: Ediciones Unión, 2004.

La hija de Darío. La Habana: Editorial Letras Cubanas, 2005.

Nadie es profeta. La Habana: Ediciones Unión, 2006.

References and Further Reading

Araújo, Nara. "Zonas de contacto: narrativa femenina de la diáspora y de la isla de Cuba" in her *Diálogos en el umbral*. Santiago de Cuba: Editorial Oriente, 2003, 112–60.

Berg, Mary G. (ed.). *Open Your Eyes and Soar: Cuban Women Writing Now.* Buffalo, NY: White Pine Press, 2003.

Berg, Mary G., Carmell, Pamela and Fountain, Anne (eds). *Cuba on the Edge: Short Stories from the Island.* Nottingham: CCC Press, 2007.

Bobes, Marilyn. "Todas las vidas de Adelaida Fernández". *El tintero*, supplement of *Juventud Rebelde*, Jan. 30, 2005: 3.

Campuzano, Luisa. "La mujer en la narrativa de la Revolución: ponencia sobre una carencia". In Luisa Campuzano (ed.), *Quirón o del ensayo y otros cuentos*. La Habana: Letras Cubanas, 1988, pp. 66–104.

——. "Ser cubanas y no morir en el intento". *Temas* 5 (Jan.–March, 1996): 4–10.

——. "Literatura de mujeres y cambio social: narradoras cubanas de hoy". *Temas* 32 (Jan.–March, 2003): 38–47.

Davis, Catherine. *A Place in the Sun? Women Writers in Twentieth Century Cuba*. London: Zed Books, 1997

Duarte González, Maribel. "Entrevista a Adelaida Fernández de Juan". *Librínsula* 2(92) (Oct. 7, 2005). www.bnjm.cu/librinsula/2005/octubre/92/entrevistas/entrevistas232.htm

López-Cabrales, María del Mar. *Arenas cálidas en alta mar. Entrevistas a escritoras contemporáneas en Cuba*. Santiago de Chile: Editorial Cuarto Propio, 2007.

Strausfeld, Michi (ed.). *Nuevos narradores cubanos*. Madrid: Siruela, 2002.

Vallejo, Catharina. "El bumerang de las cuentistas novísimas cubanas: Adelaida Fernández de Juan y *Oh Vida* (1998)". In Lady Rojas-Trempe and Catharina Vallejo (eds), *Celebración de la creación literaria de escritoras hispanas en las Américas*. Ottawa: Girol Books, Inc., 2000, pp. 203–12.

Yáñez, Mirta and Bobes, Marilyn (eds). *Estatuas de Sal. Cuentistas cubanas contemporáneas. Panorama Crítico (1959–1995)*. La Habana: Ediciones Unión, 1996.

Yáñez, Mirta (ed.). *Cubana: Contemporary Fiction by Cuban Women*. Boston, MA: Beacon Press, 1998.

Zubieta, María José. *Madre patria/madre revolución: la maternidad en el discurso oficial de la revolución cubana y en tres cuentistas cubanas contemporáneas (Dora Alonso, Adelaida Fernández de Juan, Anna Lidia Vega Serova)*. Dissertation, UCLA, 2002. DAI, March 2003. UMI Publication AAT 3063952.

FERRÉ, ROSARIO

Rosario Ferré (b. 1938) is Puerto Rico's leading woman of letters. To date, she has produced a body of essays, novels, short fiction, poetry, children's books and literary criticism in Spanish and English that places her at the forefront of the Puerto Rican literary scene. A leading feminist writer, Ferré's work focuses on the role of women in a patriarchal society, and on the colonial status of the island.

Biography

Ferré was born (28 September 1938) in the city of Ponce, on the southern coast of Puerto Rico, to one of the island's most prominent families. Her mother, Lorenza Ramírez Ferré, came from an elite, landowning family while her father, Luis A. Ferré, a representative of the upper-class industrial and banking interests, served as governor of the island from 1968 to 1972. As a child, she was so deeply influenced by the fairy tales and stories related by her black nanny, Gilda, that she took to composing stories of her own at an early age. She studied in Puerto Rico and the United States, and after graduating from Manhattenville College, Rosario Ferré returned to her native land to continue her graduate studies in literature at the University of Puerto Rico. There she met the Uruguayan critic Angel Rama and the Peruvian novelist Mario Vargas Llosa, both of whom encouraged her to pursue writing. In 1974, she graduated from the University of Puerto Rico in Río Piedras with an M.A. in Hispanic Studies. While pursuing her studies at the University of Puerto Rico, Ferré co-founded and directed a literary journal, *Zona de carga y descarga* (1972–75, Loading and Unloading Zone), in which some of her first essays and short stories appeared. Her (Master's) thesis, an analysis of the works of the Uruguayan short-story writer and a comprehensive study of the nature of fantastic literature was later published in book form: *El acomodador: Una lectura fantástica de Felisberto Hernández.* Some years later (1987), she received a Ph.D. from the University of Maryland, writing her dissertation on the work of the Argentinian writer Julio Cortázar.

Short Stories

In 1976, Ferré published her first book *Papeles de Pandora* (translated by the author as *The Youngest Doll*, 1991). The book, which contains short stories and poems, has been considered a kind of a feminist manifesto because of its depiction of the plight of Puerto Rican women and the denunciation of their dependent and marginal position in society. Through the symbol of a doll, a recurring motif in this book, she underscores the confining, and deforming nature of this image, and criticizes how this passive role is imposed upon women by a patriarchal society.

In these short stories the Puerto Rican writer experiments with language, fantastic elements, symbols, literary and stylistic strategies to portray her feminist and social concerns. "La muñeca menor" (The Youngest Doll), one of Ferré's most reviewed short stories, relates the life of a beautiful woman who after being bitten by a prawn that remains lodged in her leg, totally devotes herself to taking care of her nieces and making life-sized dolls for them. Years later, when the family doctor bring his son to meet the family, she realizes that the doctor diagnosed the condition as incurable so that he could pay for his son to attend medical school. Eventually the doctor's son marries her youngest niece. As a representative of the old sugarcane aristocracy she will be instrumental for him to acquire social status and earn money. The aunt makes her a special doll with diamonds for eyes as a wedding present. After the wedding the husband removes the diamond eyes, sells them and replaces the doll on top of the piano. He also insists that his bride sit on the balcony so that their neighbors can see that he has married well. As time passes he notices that his wife never ages, and one evening as he watches her sleep, he realizes that her chest is not moving. Intrigued he puts his stethoscope on her chest and as he does so she opens her eyes and out of her empty sockets several prawns emerge. The end of the story suggests that the niece has become the doll and the prawns now lodged in her eyes will attack the greedy, materialistic and controlling husband. Ferré uses the doll motif to epitomize the passive, mute role to which women have been reduced in Puerto Rican society, and the prawn as an instrument of revenge against the men that condemn women to submissiveness and silence. In *"La bella* durmiente"

(Sleeping Beauty) Ferré uses fairy tales and classical ballet to reveal and subvert women's conditions. The story, structured in three parts named after three classical ballets: *Coppelia, Sleeping Beauty* and *Giselle,* recounts the life of María de los Angeles Fernández, a member of the elite who loves to dance. She leaves the convent where she has been studying to pursue dancing, although both her father and the Reverend Mother are opposed, because it does not suit the image of a proper young lady. María de los Angeles marries Felisberto, believing that he will support her desire to become a first-class prima ballerina and respect her wish to remain childless so that she can attain her goal. However, he rapes her in order to have an heir for his fortune. When her father, the Reverend Mother and her husband enforce their views on marriage and motherhood and forbid her to dance she rebels and plots her own death by writing letters to her husband implying that she is unfaithful. The story ends when the husband kills both himself and María de los Angeles.

Ferré weaves a collage of letters, social columns, newspapers clippings, captions written in a photo album, a birth announcement, fragments of an interior monologue and comments by an omniscient narrator to reveal the struggle between María de los Angeles and the oppressive forces of the church and patriarchy. In this story, the Puerto Rican author demythologizes the myths and taboos construed by men to manipulate women and compel them to observe the virtues of submission and silence.

The dislocation of time, the doubling of personality, the multiplication of levels, the shifting points of view, and the introduction of fantastic elements contribute to the creation of a tense, phantasmagorical atmosphere in many of the stories in this collection. *Papeles de Pandora* surprised many readers in Puerto Rico with its aggressive denunciation of the bourgeoisie, its irreverent language, innovative techniques and feminist perspective.

Ferré became interested in children's folklore, and created critical versions of tales such as *El medio pollito* (The Half Chick), 1977; *Los cuentos de Juan Bobo* (The Tales of Juan Bobo), 1977, and *La mona que le pisaron la cola* (The Monkey Whose Tail Was Stepped On), 1981, most of which were later collected in a book called *Sonatinas* (1989).

Essays

Alongside her narrative and lyric production, Ferré has assiduously cultivated the essay, above all the essay of literary and artistic criticism. In 1980, she published *Sitio a Eros* (Eros Besieged), a book of literary essays about women writers of the nineteenth and twentieth centuries. In this volume, Ferré examines the life and works of women artists who profoundly influenced her. She summarizes the experiences of Mary Shelley, Georges Sand, Flora Tristán, Jean Rhys, Anaïs Nin, Tina Modotti, Alexandra Kollontai, Sylvia Plath, Julia de Burgos, Lillian Hellman, and Virginia Woolf.

In "La cocina de la escritura" (1986, The Writer's Kitchen) the first and most extensive essay in the book, Ferré describes her own creative process. Relating her initial literary attempts to the precepts of her "mentors," Simone de Beauvoir and Virginia Woolf, the Puerto Rican author deals openly with such controversial and contemporary questions as the existence of feminine writing. Although Ferré concurs with the widely-held view that women's literature often focuses on interior or intimate experiences while men tend to write about historical, social or political issues she asserts that "there does not exist a women's way of writing different from that of men," and concludes that "the secret of writing, like the secret of cooking has nothing to do with gender. It has to do with the skill with which we mix the ingredients over the fire". This volume, together with *Papeles de Pandora*, established her as an influential Puerto Rican feminist writer.

In 1986, Ferré published her second collection of short stories, *Maldito amor* (translated as *Sweet Diamond Dust*, 1988) that received the Liberatur Prix in Germany in 1992. This volume consists of a short novella "Maldito amor," and three additional short stories, "El regalo" (The Gift), "Isolda en el espejo" (Isolda's Mirror), and "La extraña muerte del capitancito Candelario" (Captain Candelario's Heroic Last Stand). All four pieces examine different periods of Puerto Rican history: beginning at the turn of the century with the transition from the sugar-cane aristocracy to a professional middle class in "Maldito amor," to an imaginative creation of a futuristic Puerto Rico fragmented by the struggle for independence in "La extraña muerte del capitancito Candelario". A common theme ties these stories together: the revision and appropriation of official history by the marginalized and oppressed groups of society, women, the poor, and people of color.

In the title story "Sweet Diamond Dust," Ferré narrates the history of the De La Valle family through four generations, from the end of the nineteenth century to the 1950s. The plot is centered around Sweet Diamond, the family sugar-cane *hacienda* and mill. Don Hermenegildo Martínez, the primary narrator, is a lawyer who sets out to write the history of the mythical town of Guamaní and its hero, his friend Ubaldino De La Valle who saved his ancestral sugar-cane plantation from being taken over by American corporations. His narrative is repeatedly interrupted throughout the story by several characters who give disparate and conflicting views of the story that he is telling. Arístides, one of the hero's sons, explains his family's failures; Titina, the loyal housekeeper of the De La Valle family, confronts Hermenegildo with the unfortunate events that have taken place in the family, contradicting his utopian view of the town and its hero; and Gloria, the mulatto nurse and mistress of the hero, destroys the elegiac nostalgic vision of Guamaní as the vanished paradise described by the narrator. Finally, Laura, the hero's dying widow reveals that Ubaldino's father was not a handsome Spaniard, but a black man from a nearby town who tamed horses. This use of contrasting points of view challenges the official version of the text and finally destroys the male narrator's discourse. The marginalized women, oppressed by both the old sugar-cane feudal system and the new industrial society, rebel against the oppressors and, led by Gloria, set the house on fire, burning down the plantation with Don Hermenegildo and all De La Valle's family inside.

The story of *Sweet Diamond Dust* plays with perspectives and voices, the authority of the narrator is subverted by the intruding voices of female characters. By introducing conflicting accounts of the family history, the authority of the male narrator is called into question, and his discourse is stripped of its power. The novella demystifies the official history by replacing the patriarchal male discourse with a rebellious feminine discourse, cleverly rewriting Puerto Rican history from a woman's perspective.

Novels

In her first novel, *La casa de la laguna* (1995, The House on the Lagoon), Ferré returns to her preoccupation with the role of women in Puerto Rican society. Questioning women's marginal position in the socio-historical processes of the country, she associates their subordination and marginalization to the political situation of the island of Puerto Rico, which, as a territory of the United States, remains outside the mainstream of American society and politics.

The novel chronicles the life of the Mendizabals, an upper-class bourgeois family, from the fourth of July, 1917, when the Puerto Ricans celebrate their United States citizenship, until the beginning of the 1980s, when a plebiscite is held to decide the political status of the island. Incorporated into the saga of this rich and prestigious family is the story of their servants of African origin, men and women whose lives are intertwined with those of the family's descendants.

In several flashbacks Isabel recounts the life of three families: the Mendizabals, the Monforts and the Avilés, presenting her own version of the family deeds and shedding light on the shortcomings and prejudices of the patriarchal system as it is reflected in the official history of Puerto Rico. Her narration is based on her own remembrances and on what she has been told by her husband Quintín, by Buenaventura and Rebecca (her father-in-law and mother-in-law), and by Petra, Buenaventura's loyal black servant.

The story of this oligarchic family is narrated by two conflicting voices, one feminine and one masculine, that present contradictory versions of the same events. Isabel's and Quintín's accounts constitute diametrically opposed readings of the history of the Mendizabal family and also of the history of Puerto Rico. The female protagonist's primary text is interrupted by the masculine voice which comments, and even attempts to impose its own version of events. Thus, throughout the novel the masculine voice which criticizes and destroys the woman's role alternates with the feminine voice that creates and defines woman's contribution to society.

The use of a shifting point of view in the novel establishes a connection between the political conflict in Puerto Rico, and the position of women in society. The text suggests that there are similarities between the oppression and exploitation imposed on female characters by the patriarchal system and the exploitation and oppression of Puerto Rico by the United States and the dominant upper classes.

In *The House on the Lagoon*, the Puerto Rican author fuses social and historical issues with the interior world of emotions, intuition and passion. She dramatizes the dilemma of the woman artist who struggles for her freedom; for a room of her own. The narrative presents the conflict of an inventive woman against a society that frustrates her desire to create and fulfill herself. In this novel the woman character plays a subversive role, undermining the authority of patriarchal society by revealing the hollowness of the male version of history. Here, as in many of her works, Ferré rewrites Puerto Rican history from a female, if not a feminist, perspective, using irony and parody to dismantle the hegemonic discourse and to denounce and subvert the ways that the patriarchy silences women.

In her second novel, *Vecindarios excéntricos* (1998, Eccentric Neighborhoods), Ferré traces the lives of three generations of two upper-class families, the Rivas de Santillana and the Vernets, through the eyes of one of its descendants, Elvira Vernet.

Over the course of fifty-eight chapters, Elvira, the narrator, reveals the lives and fortunes of both sides of her family. She begins by narrating the trials and tribulations of her plantation owners relatives to survive and keep their land: her grandfather Alvaro Rivas de Santillana, his wife Valeria, their son Alejandro, and their four daughters, all named after their mother's favorite literary heroines: Dido, a fragile poet; Artemisia, a business tycoon and religious fanatic; Lakhme, a beautiful divorcee; Siglinda, whose only aspiration is to be a housewife and Clarissa, the most intelligent and independent of all the children and Elvira's mother. The following chapters describe the struggles of her paternal relatives to establish themselves by promoting industry on the island: her grandfather Santiago (Chaguito) Vernet, his wife Adela and their six children: Aurelio, an engineer and talented pianist and the father of the narrator; Ulises, a business wizard; Roque, a collector of relics of the Taino Indian tribe; Damian, an ethereally sensitive art collector; Celia, a devout Catholic like her mother, becomes a nun, and Amparo, the happiest and most optimistic member of the family. As in *La casa de la laguna*, the narrator intertwines the history of Puerto Rico with the lives of the characters, emphasizing the role they played in the development of the Puerto Rican nation. The protagonist, Elvira Vernet, records the family history from the turn of the century to the present, a history that reflects the coinciding political and economic changes of Puerto Rico itself. The stories of the two families mirror Puerto Rico's shift from a primarily agrarian society to an industrial one. The Rivas Santillanas represent the insular and finally obsolete world of the sugar plantation owners while the Vernets' construction and cement companies contribute to the industrialization of the island.

The novel's central core, however, lies in the troubled relationship between Elvira and her mother, Clarissa, who insists that Elvira adhere to accepted and traditional patterns of behavior and conform to the role imposed by society. Determined to escape from her mother and father's control Elvira marries Ricardo Cáceres. Her hope of finding freedom soon fades as she finds herself stuck in a loveless marriage, unable to pursue her dreams. Elvira's inheritance from Clarissa finally allows her to divorce and become her own person. Although not autobiographical in the strictest sense of the word, *Eccentric Neighborhoods* undoubtedly derives much of its inspiration from Ferré's own family experiences and some details do parallel the author's life.

This family saga is strongly anchored in history through innumerable references to Puerto Rico's historical events such as the North Americans' arrival on the island in 1898, the San Felipe Hurricane of 1928, the Costigan-Jones Law that set a quota for sugar production in Puerto Rico in 1934, the plebiscite of 1966, Theodore and Eleanor Roosevelt's visits to Puerto Rico and the real persona of the Spanish poet Juan Ramón Jiménez who appears in the novel as a friend of one of the characters.

Vuelo del cisne (2001, Flight of the Swan), Ferré's third novel, is the captivating tale of Madame (as the narrator calls her), a world-famous Russian ballerina. In this novel Ferré recreates the life of Anna Pavlova, the Russian prima ballerina, emphasizing the character's commitment and devotion to dance, and her willingness to forsake everything for it. Moreover, she captures in a rich poetic language the magic created when the Russian ballerina performs her favorite ballet *The Dying Swan*.

In 1917, Madame's dance company embarks on a South American tour while Russia is entrenched in World War I. Just as the troupe arrives in San Juan, Puerto Rico, they learn that Russia has suffered a *coup d'état* and that the Bolsheviks are in power. They also discover that their passports are invalid and all of them must remain on the island while Victor Dandré, the company's manager, travels to New York to obtain English passports for the troupe. At this time Madame meets Diamantino Márquez, a poet, journalist and violinist struggling against colonial dependence and falls desperately in love with the much younger man.

After Madame's death in 1932, her loyal, loving assistant and confidant Masha undertakes the narration of Madame's life based on her own recollections of what Madame had confided to her, as well as what she had been told by others. As Masha narrates the events that take place on the island, she intertwines Madame's life story with the personal accounts of other characters: Diamantino, Madame's lover; Juan Anduce, Masha's husband; Victor Dandré, Madame's husband; Pedro Bastini, a millionaire landowner and Diamantino's godfather and others.

Grounded in Puerto Rico's rich history and culture, *Flight of the Swan* weaves the tumultuous love affair between the charismatic ballerina and the Puerto Rican revolutionary with the political events of the period. This was the time when Puerto Ricans were granted citizenship and the United States entered World War I drafting these new citizens to fight in the war.

One of the most talented and versatile authors in Latin America today, Rosario Ferré belongs to a group of writers engaged in demystifying patriarchal values, subverting traditional forms, debunking societal myths and norms, and rewriting the official histories of their countries. In her fiction, written both in Spanish and English, Ferré links her feminist concerns to the social and cultural problems of Puerto Rico, deconstructing the myths of the controlling system to appropriate a dominant voice that parodies and undermines the phallocentric and colonial ideologies prevalent in that society. Yet, one could say that her creation of an innovative and highly poetic language to convey and explore her characters' psyche and milieu remains her greatest literary achievement.

NORA ERRO-PERALTA

Selected Works

Papeles de Pandora. México: Joaquín Mortiz, 1976.
La muñeca menor. Río Piedras, PR: Huracán, 1980.
Sitio a Eros: Trece ensayos literarios. México: Joaquín Mortiz, 1980.
Fábulas de la garza desangrada. México: Joaquín Mortiz, 1982.
Maldito amor. México: Joaquín Mortiz, 1986.
Sweet Diamond Dust. New York: Ballantine, 1988.
Sonatinas. Río Piedras, PR: Huracán, 1989.
El árbol y sus sombras. México: Fondo de Cultura Económica, 1989.
El coloquio de las perras. Río Piedras, PR: Editorial Cultural, 1990.
The Youngest Doll and Other Stories. Lincoln, NE: University of Nebraska Press, 1991.
Las dos Venecias. México: Joaquín Mortiz, 1992.
La batalla de las vírgenes. San Juan, PR: Universidad de Puerto Rico, 1993.
The House on the Lagoon. New York: Farrar, Straus and Giroux, 1995.
La casa de la laguna. Barcelona: Emecé Editores, 1995.
Eccentric Neighborhoods. New York: Farrar, Straus, and Giroux, 1998.
Vecindarios excéntricos. New York: Vintage, 1998.
Flight of the Swan. New York: Farrar, Straus, and Giroux, 2001.
Vuelo del cisne. New York: Vintage, 2002.
A la sombra de tu nombre. México: Alfaguara, 2001.

References and Further Reading

Caballero, María. "*La casa de la laguna*: familia y nación en Rosario Ferré". In *Ficciones isleñas: estudios sobre la literatura de Puerto Rico.* San Juan, PR: Editorial de la U de Puerto Rico, 1999, pp. 103–27.
Gutiérrez, Mariela. A. *Rosario Ferré en su Edad de Oro: heroínas subversivas de Papeles de Pandora y Maldito amor.* Madrid: Verbum, 2004.
Hintz, Suzanne. *Rosario Ferré: A Search for Identity.* New York: Peter Lang, 1995.
Palmer-López, Sandra. "Rosario Ferré y la Generación del 70: evolución estética y literaria". *Acta Literaria* 27 (2002): 157–69.
Pino-Ojeda, Walescka. "Rosario Ferré: familia e historia nacional". In *Sobre castas y puentes: conversaciones con Elena Poniatowska, Rosario Ferré y Diamela Eltit.* Santiago de Chile: Editorial Cuarto Propio, 2000, pp. 77–135.

FERRER, RENÉE

One of the most published of the new generation of women writers in post-Stroessner Paraguay, Ferrer has garnered for herself an unusually extensive international readership. Hers is one of the strongest female voices in Paraguayan literature today, expressing the role of women as defenders of the family, society, and environment. Many of her works reveal the hidden strengths of women who endure oppression, injustice and abuse. Her works include poetry, novels, short stories and plays. She holds a Doctorate in History from the National University of Asunción and has published several scholarly works in this area. Her creative writing has earned her the recognition of numerous literary prizes in Paraguay, among them: *Amigos del Arte*, *El Lector*, *La República* and *Los 12 del Año*. Internationally, she has received awards from the *Pola de Lena* competition in Spain, from UNESCO, and from the *Fundación del Libro* in Buenos Aires. Ferrer travels regularly to give conferences and present her work, and her books are translated into English and Portuguese.

Themes and Technique

Many of Ferrer's literary pieces focus on the experience of women—solitude, love, suffering and sensuality. History, oppression and the abuse of power, the environment, and the world of children are also central to specific works. Her poetry deals with a variety of topics, from the bold sexual exploration of the feminine voice to the humble act of writing, which is characterized by its sonorous quality, rhythm and rich imagery rising from the realms of sensuality and nature.

Poetic elements are also consistently present in Ferrer's narrative. Her language tends to be intimate and personal, and the narration frequently progresses through the sequencing of visual and other sensory images. Music has an important role in all of Ferrer's works. In her poetry, it can be observed in the resonance and rhythm of the word, as well as direct musical references, such as the title *Nocturnos*. Musical instruments are frequently used in her narratives to define atmosphere and tone, and their sounds and effects emerge repeatedly, in such a way that they filter through the characters' actions, words and thoughts.

In contrast to the musical quality of her work, silence is also a constant theme, in Ferrer's poetry as well as her narrative. In numerous poems, silence contrasts with noise, voices and music in the construction of synesthetic images, imitating the play between light and shadow. In narrative pieces, silence appears in multiple forms, representing the lack of communication between female and male characters, opening the way to alternative means of expression and sensation (such as music), or signaling the effects of oppression on women, as partners and as citizens, whose voices are not heard.

Los nudos de silencio

In the novel *Los nudos del silencio*, Ferrer alternates the obsessive, seductive music of the saxophone with moments of profound and prolonged silence to reflect the characters' actions, thoughts and emotions in the dominant spaces of the novel. As the reader follows the female protagonist through a process of self-discovery and eventual liberation from oppression—as a wife, a citizen, and a member of society—the scenes are marked either by music, dialogue, or interior monologue. In this way, silence is expressed literally through pauses in the music and non-spoken words directed to a character, as well as figuratively, in the lack of communication between husband and wife, in the oppressive force of an intolerant authoritarian government, and in the secret rebellion that awakes in the central character.

Vagos sin tierra

The theme of the subjugation of women and of society under oppressive government also appears in the historical novel *Vagos sin tierra*. Set in the eighteenth century, it follows the members of a family as they migrate to northern Paraguay as part of the vice-regal policy of colonization of the borderlands. Interior monologue and stream of consciousness emerge, as they do in other narrative pieces, as the primary means of expressing the characters' pain and suffering. The rhythms and emotions of the lives of the characters are expressed through alternating sounds (crying, arguing, barking of dogs) and silences, much in the same way as in *Los nudos del silencio*.

Poetry

The collection of poems entitled *Itinerario del deseo* develops the interplay between sound and silence into an ironic complex of contrasts on a number of levels. Images frequently combine sound with other perceptions in synesthesia—hearing perfume, a singing flower, light dwelling on lips. And the music of the saxophone appears again, as in *Los nudos del silencio*, in contrast to the silence of non-communication. The poem "Sonido" is perhaps the most expressive of the dynamic between sound and silence in this collection. Alliteration in the form of the repeating sound of *s* throughout the poem underlines the whispering sea breeze that echoes the poetic voice's whispering heart, and the sounds of the universe that unite to put an end to the silent waiting for love. The image of the ocean in this poem is repeated throughout the collection, as the predominant metaphors revolve around the sea—there are images of calming sunsets, crashing waves, sharp cliffs. Considering the geographic context of Paraguay's insularity, this creates an additional level of imagery, setting the conflictual dynamic of love and sexuality in a space beyond everyday experience.

Ferrer has combined some of her poems into a performance piece, in which she recites poetry from the collection *Nocturnos* accompanied by the music of Chopin's *Nocturnes*. The alliteration, rhyme and rhythm of the spoken word play off the melody and rhythm of the piano pieces to create a kind of sonorous voice dance, in which the primary expressions are of desire and darkness. "Fecundación" corresponds to the second Nocturne, and recreates the act of love through the rhythmical movement of ocean waves against the shore. The lines of the poem are spaced in a back-and-forth pattern across the page, so that the reader's eyes move with the waves, and the spaces separating the words echo the same movement by imposing a silence with each blank space. The feminine poetic voice speaks to a masculine second person, represented as a small boat that journeys out into the world while the shore awaits. Words in opposition—to part/to wait, yours/mine, estuary/wave, silence/song, tremulous/anchor—repeat the to and fro of the waves in an additional level of representation. The live performance of this poem, with the corresponding musical piece, creates an additional dimension that ties together the multiple elements of the piece in one unique spatial-temporal experience.

Like many women writers of her generation, Renée Ferrer finds common cause among women, children, the poor and the oppressed. Her work is critical of the patriarchal society and the oppressive government that has surrounded her during a significant period of her life. Perhaps as a result of the intolerant character of this socio-historical context, her criticism bypasses direct references and is expressed through rhetorical techniques that imbue her message with an expressive force that penetrates beyond the reader's intellect and deep into his or her intuitive consciousness.

AMANDA L. IRWIN

Selected Works

Hay surcos que no se llenan. Asunción: Edición de la Aurora, 1965.
Voces sin réplica. Asunción: author's edition, 1967.
Cascarita de nuez. Asunción: Gráfica Zamphirópolos, 1978.
Desde el cañadon de la memoria. Asunción: Escuela Técnica Salesiana, 1982.
Galope: libro infanto-juvenil. Asunción: Mediterráneo, 1983.
Campo y cielo: poemas y relatos. Asunción: Cromos, 1985.
Peregrino de la eternidad. Asunción: Alcándara, 1985.
La seca y otros cuentos. Asunción: El Lector, 1986.

Nocturnos. Asunción: Arte Nuevo, 1987.
Los nudos del silencio. Asunción: Arandurá, 1988.
Sobreviviente. Madrid: Ediciones Torremozas: 1988 (Spanish-English edition, Asunción, 1999).
Viaje a destiempo. Asunción: Universidad Católica Nuestra Señora de la Asunción, 1989.
De lugares, momentos e implicancias varias. Asunción: Ediciones Ñandutí Vive/Intercontinental Editora, 1990.
El acantilado y el mar. Asunción: Arandurá, 1992.
Por el ojo de la cerradura. Asunción: Arandurá, 1993.
Itinerario del deseo. Asunción: Arandurá, 1994 (Spanish-English edition, 2002).
La voz que me fue dada. Asunción: Don Bosco, 1996.
El resplandor y las sombras. Asunción: Arandurá, 1996.
De la eternidad y otros delirios. Asunción: Intercontinental Editora, 1997.
La mariposa azul y otros cuentos – Panamby hovy ha ambue mombe'uranguera (Spanish-Guaraní edition). Asunción: Intercontinental, 1997.
Desde el encendido corazón del monte – Ka'aguy pa'u rendy ruguaite guive (Spanish-Guaraní edition). Asunción, 1998.
Escape al río, La partida y dados, El burdel, Se lo llevaron las aguas. Asunción, 1998.
El ocaso del milenio. Asunción: Colección del Corcel, 1999.
Vagos sin tierra. Asunción: RP Ediciones, 1999.
Poesía completa hasta el año 2000. Asunción: Arandurá, 2000.
Desmenuzando cuentos. Asunción: Editiones Alta Voz, 2001.
La colección de relojes. Asunción: Editiones Alta Voz, 2001.
Las cruces del olvido. Asunción: Intercontinental, 2001.
Entre el ropero y el tren. Asunción: Ediciones Alta Voz, 2004.

References and Further Reading

Cunha-Giabbai, Gloria de. "Ecofeminismo latinoamericano". *Letras femeninas* 22(1–2) 1996 (Spring–Fall); 51–63.
——. *La cuentística de Renée Ferrer: continuidad y cambio de nuestra expresión*. Asunción: Arandurá, 1997.
Méndez-Faith, Teresa. *Breve diccionario de literatura paraguaya*, Asunción: El Lector, 1996.
——. *Poesía paraguaya de ayer y de hoy, Tomo I*. Asunción: Intercontinental Editora, 1995.
Partyka, Betsy. "Viaje íntimo al *Itinerario del deseo*". *Itinerario del deseo/Itinerary of Desire*. Asunción: Alta Voz, 2002.
Rodríguez Alcalá, Guido and Villagra, María Elena. *Narrativa paraguaya (1980–1990)*. Asunción: Editorial Don Bosco, 1992.

FLORESTA, NISIA

The name of Nísia Floresta is noteworthy among those famous people who wrote the history of women in Brazil, both for her courage and for her innovative ideas. This is the pseudonym of Dionísia Gonçalves Pinto, born in 1810 in Rio Grande do Norte, who lived in some other Brazilian states, such as Pernambuco, Rio Grande Do Sul and Rio de Janeiro. Afterwards, she moved to Europe where she remained until her death in Rouen, France, in 1885.

Nísia Floresta lived at a time when the vast majority of women were constrained by prejudice, without having any rights other than being obliged to follow men's will. However, not only did she open a school for girls in Rio de Janeiro, but she also wrote several books defending the rights of the women, the Native Brazilians, and the slaves. Moreover, Nísia Floresta was one of the first women in Brazil to break out of the limits of her private life, publishing stories, poems and essays in important newspapers of the time. Actually, her constant presence in the national press, discussing the most controversial questions since 1830, emphasizes Nísia Floresta's modernity.

Nísia Floresta published about fifteen works, including poems, novels and essays, written not only in Portuguese, but also in French, English, and Italian. Her first book is also the first in Brazil to deal with the rights of women to education and to work, and to demand that they be considered intelligent human beings. This book, published in 1832 in Recife (PE), has the suggestive title of *Direito das mulheres, injustiça dos homens* (Women's Rights, Men's Injustice). It was inspired by authors such as Mary Wollstonecraft, Poulain de La Barre, Sophie, and even by Olympe de Gouges, the author of the *Declaração dos direitos da mulher e da cidadã* (Declaration of the Rights of Women and of the Female Citizen). However, instead of simply translating the new ideas circulating in Europe, the Brazilian author wrote a text which in addition to denouncing the prejudice against women that existed in Brazil, demystified the dominant idea of men's superiority.

In other works, such as *Conselhos à minha filha* (1842), *Opúsculo Humanitário* (1853), *A mulher* (1859), and in novels dedicated to the girls from the school she had founded, she points to the importance of women's education for society. In these writings we find bits of information ranging from advice on how girls should behave, to the duties expected of a daughter, as well as moralistic and didactic stories, and even a detailed explanation of the history of women's conditions in several different civilizations and different times.

In *Opúsculo Humanitário*, for example, Nísia Floresta puts together sixty-two articles on education, commenting on Asia, Africa, Oceania, Europe and North America, before dealing with Brazil. These comments establish a relationship between the intellectual and the material development of a country, or the lack of it, with the position occupied by women in that society. In accordance with the intellectuals of her time, Nísia defends the thesis that the progress of a society depends on the education that it offered to its women. Moreover, only through instruction and moral education would women achieve dignity and thus become better wives and mothers.

Nísia was also a precursor in broaching other questions such as that of the Native Brazilians. In the poem called "A lágrima de um Caeté," of 1849, the author takes a position regarding the indigenous people. Besides honoring their values and nature, she also criticizes the Portuguese. What is new about the poem is that it is not written from the standpoint of the Native Brazilians as heroes who fight, as in the majority of texts on this topic, but rather from the standpoint of them as losers who are miserable because of the oppression of the invading white people.

Another important story is "Páginas de uma vida obscura," which was first published in chapters in the newspaper *O Brasil Ilustrado*, in 1855, and still has not been published as a book. It tells the life story of a slave, since having been brought as a child from Africa, and depicts his acts of heroism and devotion to work until his death. The first glimmers of Nísia Floresta's thoughts on slavery can be noted in the text. As well as exalting the qualities of the Afro-Brazilian man, she vigorously defends a humanitarian treatment of slaves, revealing how sincerely she felt about their suffering. Some years later, in 1870, the author would feverishly defend the abolition of slavery.

In the same year as the publication of *A lágrima de um Caeté*, Nísia Floresta went to Europe, and for some years she traveled around Italy, Portugal, Germany, Belgium, Greece, France and England. Consequently, she established a relationship with some of the greatest writers of the time, such as Alexander Herculano, Alexander Dumas (the father), Lamartine, Duvernoy, Victor Hugo, Georges Sand, Manzoni, Azeglio and Auguste Comte.

Some books are the result of her many trips to Europe and, as used to be fashionable in those days, they contain impressions of the places that she knew. Nísia Floresta, however, does not simply describe her trips. What she does is describe in detail the cities, churches, museums, parks, libraries and monuments, as well as the people; commenting on everything with both sensibility and knowledge. *Itinerário de uma viagem à Alemanha* (1857), and *Três anos na Itália, seguidos de uma viagem à Grécia* (in two volumes, 1864 and 1872) are the titles of these books, which were originally written and published in French, and only recently have been translated into Portuguese. The latter, for example, contains notes of the year before the Italian unification, describing the fight, the popular feelings, and the revolutionary climate. Furthermore, it reveals the author's admiration for the leaders, Garibaldi and Azeglio, with whom she had corresponded for some time.

Another significant work is *Cintilações de uma alma brasileira*, published in Florence, in 1859. This book contains five essays about the education of the young, the European woman, and about how homesick the author felt after being away from her country for a very long time. In one essay, for example, called "A mulher," she describes the Frenchwomen in the mid-nineteenth century, and criticizes their superficial and mundane behavior. Actually, in this essay, Nísia was ahead of the government in condemning the Frenchwomen's custom of abandoning newborn babies to be breast-fed and raised by peasants in the countryside. In another essay, "O Brasil," she summarizes the history of the Brazilian nation, and writes about its economic strength and about its best-known writers. Her intention was, beyond advertising her native land abroad, to undo the prejudice and lies about Brazil which prevailed in Europe then.

Despite living abroad, Nísia Floresta Brasileira Augista was always committed to publicizing her country, and displayed, even in her name, how proud she felt of her homeland.

Selected works

Direito das mulheres, injustiça dos homens. Recife, 1832.
Conselhos à minha filha. 1842.
Opúsculo Humanitário. 1853.
A mulher. 1859.
Cintilações de uma alma brasileira. Florence, 1859.
Três anos na Itália. Trans. Francisco das Chagas Pereira. Natal: Editora da UFRN, 1999.

CONSTÂNCIA LIMA DUARTE

References and Further Reading

Duarte, Constância L. *Direitos das mulheres e injustiça dos homens*. 4th edn. São Paulo: Cortez, 1989.
——. *A lágrima de um Caeté*. Natal: Fundação José Augusto, 1997a.
——. *Cintilações de uma alma brasileira*. Trans. Michelle Vartulli. Florianópolis: Editora Mulheres, 1997b.
——. *Itinerário de uma viagem à Alemanha*. 2nd edn. Trans. Francisco das Chagas Pereira. Florianópolis: Editora Mulheres, 1998.

FOX LOCKERT, LUCIA

Lucia Ungaro was born in Lima, Peru on March 29, 1928. Her literary career began when she started writing poetry at the early age of 9. Eight years later her first literary work, *Intimate Preludes*, was published (1945) while she was still in high school. A collection of 40 poems depicts the discovery of the world through the dreams, thoughts and experiences of a young adolescent. The self-biographical undertone pervades all of Fox's poetry.

After completing elementary and secondary education in Catholic schools in Peru, Fox completed two bachelor degrees: a B.A. in Literature from the National University of San Marcos (1949) and a B.A. in Education with a minor in philosophy, also from the National University of San Marcos (1951). Fox attended and completed her Master's degree in Latin American and Spanish Literature at Washington University, in St. Louis, Missouri (1955) after winning a scholarship from the Institute of International Education in a Peruvian competition, the first woman to win the competition. Her studies culminated in a Doctorate of Philosophy in Latin American and Spanish Literature from the University of Illinois (1961). Fox entered academia in 1964 and continues as a professor in the Department of Romance and Classical Languages at Michigan State University.

Fox (her married name) has received numerous awards throughout her career, including: Gold Medal from the Peruvian Ministerial, Peru (1984); Diane Creative Award, YMCA, Michigan (1985); Michigan Association of Governing Boards Award for Extraordinary Contribution to Higher Education (1990); Poetry Award, The American Association, California (1991); The Rockefeller Foundation Creative Award, Bellagio, Italy (1991); Editor's Choice Award, National Library of Poetry, Maryland (1993); The National Poetry Award, California (1995), as well as a number of arts and travel grants.

Fox is a prolific writer: poet and playwright, author and artist, professor and advocate. She has written poems about legendary princesses, plays of revolution, research studies on women novelists of Spanish descent, and memoirs praising the country of her birth, Peru. Her themes encompass historical facts, flights of fancy, distant nostalgia, and political philosophy on gender and equality.

Fox's poems show the dichotomy between the ideal and the real, as they reflect her anguish and confusion in trying to understand the worlds she finds herself in—first Peru; then Ohio, California, Rhode Island, Illinois, in the United States; Mexico, Venezuela, and Argentina; a brief stay in Italy; back to California; and finally in Michigan. The poems follow her psychological development as she changes from adolescent to young lover, mother, divorcee and finally, academic professor. She formed part of a group of Latin American poets in California called "La Frontera"—The Frontier—where they believed that "to be a poet is to be a witness". Fox's eloquent style makes witnesses of all her readers.

Sometimes the witnessing is a visceral sensation such as in *The Risk of Living* (1992), a three-act drama set in revolutionary Peru. In this theatrical play Fox explores what happens when social conflict between classes arises because of government fallacy. She shows us the symptoms and manifestations of violence through the interactions of the characters. Literary techniques in the dialog include irony and humor to emphasize the social tension and the results of living in constant fear of death. Blackouts are scheduled throughout the play, playing on the contrast of the darkness with the name of the guerillas *Sendero Luminoso*—The Luminous Messenger.

Fox is known for her depictions of strong women, as Latin American feminism is vitally important to her. Unlike other authors, however, her women, although strong, usually end up in situations not of their own choosing and struggling with the inner conflicts of traditional roles vs. new independent thinking. A recurrent theme is the social restrictions placed on women because of marriage which places limits on women's aspirations. Ana Matos, the central female character of *Risk of Living*, is a good example. A self-proclaimed guerilla fighter, after being raped, after a culminating scene ending in an earthquake that could lead to her escape from prison, goes back to help her friend, Raul. In one scene in *Seeds of the Gods* (2000), various leading female characters—Cappa, Clara, Isabel, Zaira, Luisa and Ana—question their "choices" in their male partners as to whether it was luck, destiny or choice and whether it matters if it was one of those three or not. In addition, these characters face adventures on their own, finding inner strength and power and overcoming obstacles in their quest for their identities.

Indigenous roots of her Peruvian culture are another theme Fox explores in her work. *Legends of an Indian Princess* (1979) is a collection of twelve poems following events in an Indian princess's life. Based on Peruvian folklore and legend, fantasy is predominant in these poems which include monsters, the invisible world protector, and a magical dancer who changes his surroundings as he dances.

Indian Visions (1997) also comes into this category. *Visions* offers a look at present Peru through the lens of the past by combining traditions and legends with doubts and questions of the actual world. As a final example, the character of an indigenous prisoner, Yupanqui, in *The Risk of Living*, serves as a symbol representing the superiority of the past through ritual and harmony with nature. Yupanqui liberates himself through his beliefs and transcends his bodily restrictions through mind control.

Fox's poetry is autobiographical, but her dramas allow her to express her creativity through the integration of researched fact and pondering fiction. A good example is *Sor Juana, the Tenth Muse* (1988). This three-act play is based on the life of Sor Juana Inés, and covers her time as part of the Mexican Royal Court, to her decision to enter a convent. Fox admits that although she did a lot of research in preparation for writing the play, fictional elements abound in order to emphasize the conflict between civil and religious authorities. Again we find Fox portraying a strong female character by focusing on the characteristics of Sor Juana that were in opposition to the current mindset of a woman's place—it is implied that Juana joins the convent to prevent scandal associated with her illegitimacy and Juana is constantly ridiculed and criticized by the priests for her continuous writing. Juana's response is that "she was born a poet". Referring back to Fox's poetry, one can ask, is this Fox herself defending who she is—a poet?

Fox's writings about history are not limited to legends. The first group of poems in *Atonal Time* (1968) focuses on historical discovery and includes "The Fourth Voyage of Columbus" where she contrasts the Spanish and native cultures and touches on the topic of slavery. This group also includes a poem on the conquest of Mexico. The second group of poems in this collection focuses on trips she took to Ecuador, Peru, Chile and Bolivia, and her insights into their peoples and cultures. Insights into other countries are also expressed in *Images of Caracas* (1965) and *Latin America in Evolution* (1974), where she speaks about the possible unity of Latin America. The third group of poems recollects her childhood in Peru.

Her scholarly publications have made a great contribution to the field of Latin American and Spanish Literature Studies and include biographical and critical essays on women novelists (*Women Novelists in Spain and Spanish America*, 1979) as well as male authors (*The Face of the State in Peruvian Literature*, 1970). *Women Novelists* covers more than four centuries of women authors whose work focus on family, social class and sexuality. Various articles, presentations and conference papers on Hispanic-American topics round out Fox's literary production. Fox was a professor at Michigan State University for over thirty years, retiring as professor Emeritus.

In the 1980s, Fox retuned to Peru and conducted a series of interviews and investigations to evaluate the activities and status of women in "shanty towns". The research she conducted would serve as the basis for various works including *Feminist Centers in Lima, Peru* and *Grass Roots Feminist Organizations in Lima, Peru*. Fox's last published work was a collection of poems where she explores the cosmos and our place in it. Entitled *Nova*, it was published in 2004. Fox claims that the "creative process is a mysterious thread that unites the creator and the reader". Her work is a collage of personal metaphysical ponderings within a context of transplanted feminism, *Redes* (1968).

DEBORAH GONZALEZ

Selected Works

Preludios Intimos. Lima: Editorial Condor, 1945.

Images of Caracas. Caracas: Garcia Hermanos, 1965.

Atonal Time. East Lansing, MI: La Nueva Crónica, 1968.

Ghost Dance. East Lansing, MI: La Nueva Crónica, 1969.

The Face of the State in Peruvian Literature. Buenos Aires: Ediciones Continente, 1970.

Latin America in Evolution. East Lansing, MI: Superspace, 1974.

Women Novelists in Spain and Spanish America. Metuchen, NJ: The Scarecrow Press, 1979.

Legends of an Indian Princess. East Lansing, MI: Shamballa Publications, 1979.

Latin American Women Writers in the United States: Lucia Fox Speaks about Her Creative Work. Michigan State University, 1984.

"Male and Female Poets". In *Concerning Contemporary International Poetry*, Vol. 17, No. 2, Michigan State University, 1985, pp. 180–1.

Sor Juana, the Tenth Muse. East Lansing, MI: Pachacamac, 1988.

"Personal Universe". *Re-Visions* (Fall 1992): 16.

The Risk of Living. East Lansing, MI: La Nueva Crónica, 1992.

Indian Visions. East Lansing, MI: La Nueva Crónica, 1997.
Seeds of the Gods. East Lansing, MI: La Nueva Crónica, 2000.
Interviews and email correspondence, January–July, 2006.

References and Further Reading

Castillo, Susan. *Women Writers of Spanish America*. Westwood, CT: Greenwood Press, 1987.

Elissondo, Guillermina, "Lucia Fox". *Concerning Contemporary International Poetry*. 17(2) (1985): 177–9.

Grimes, Katherine. "A Flight of Words: Book Review on Odyssey of the Bird". *Americas* (April 1974): 37.

Krakusin, Margarita. "The Reality of Fiction". *Confluencia* (Fall, 2001): 141–2.

Petro, Antonia. "Life and Poetry: Review of Indian Visions, Poetry Book". *La Nueva Crónica*. East Lansing, MI, 1997.

Rojas-Trempe, Lady. "The Risk of Living by Lucia Fox: The Dramatization of Peruvian Violence". *La Escena Latinoamericana*. Iberoamerican University of Mexico, 1993, pp. 14–17.

Ward, Thomas. "Lucia Fox: Seeds of the Gods". Loyola College, *Inti* 54 (Fall, 2001).

FREITAS, EMÍLIA

Born in Aracati, Brazil, Emilía Freitas (1855–1908) was the daughter of Maria de Jesus Freitas and Tenente Coronel Antônio José de Freitas, a man described as "a valorous soldier of democracy and a distinct and important liberal" (Colares 1976: 47). Although there is little information available about the Freitas family, it is logical to conclude that Freitas' family belonged to the upper classes of nineteenth-century Brazilian society and had considerable wealth. When Antônio José de Freitas was assassinated in 1869 for his liberal political beliefs (Colares 1976: 47), Emília and her family moved to Fortaleza. Although the death of the family patriarch was certainly devastating for the family, it does not seem to have had adverse effects on the family finances. In Fortaleza, Emília attended a private school, the Escola Normal, where she studied French, English, Geography and Arithmetic (Lima Duarte 1999: 724).

Emília seems to have been profoundly influenced by her father's social and political ideas. Like him, she believed in the democratic ideals of liberty, equality and fraternity. While living in Fortaleza, the first city in Brazil to liberate the slaves, Emília became an active member of the abolitionist group, the Sociedade das Cearenses Libertadoras. In the inaugural meeting, Freitas gave a speech in which she pledged her time and her talents to the abolition of slavery (Lima Duarte 1999: 724).

Emília's literary career began in 1873 when she started to collaborate on diverse literary journals such as *Libertador*, *Cearense*, *O lyrio e a brisa*, *Amazonas commercial* and *Revolução*. Many of the poems published in these journals were later collected and republished in a single volume of poetry, entitled *Canções do lar* (1891). Although primarily known as a poet, Emília also published two novels, *O renegado* (c. 1890) and *A rainha do ignoto: um romance psicológico* (1899). Copies of *O renegado* appear to be lost (Lima Duarte 1999: 724).

After her mother's death in 1892, Emília and her brother, Alfredo, moved to Manaus. In Manaus, Emília began to work as a primary and secondary school teacher at the Instituto Benjamin Constant. In 1900, she married journalist Antônio Vieira, editor of the *Journal de Fortaleza*, and the two returned to Ceará. Emília Freitas died in October of 1908 in Manaus, where she had lived since the death of her husband.

Freitas has been lauded as a pioneer of fantastic literature in Brazil for her unique and innovative novel, *A rainha do ignoto* (1899) and her literary style has been described as a mixture of late nineteenth-century Romanticism and regionalism (Colares 1976: 45). While some critics attribute Freitas's use of the fantastic to her familiarity with North American writers such as Poe (1809–1949), Hawthorne (1804–64) and Stephenson (1850–93) (Colares 1976: 28), the introduction to Freitas' novel indicates a very different reason for the appearance of fantastic elements; her interest in the nineteenth-century Brazilian Spiritualist movement.

Spiritualism, or the belief that the dead can communicate with the living, as through a medium, was introduced to Brazil at the end of the nineteenth century by members of the intellectual elite who discovered the work of Allan Kardec, the pseudonym of French educator, Hippolyte Léon Denizard Rivail (1804–69). Inspired by the Fox sisters' ability to communicate with the dead, Kardec set out to elaborate a doctrine that would provide scientific proof of the existence of the spiritual world. In the process, Kardec not only presented empirical research on the spirits of the dead, but outlined a moral philosophy of life and a code of conduct based on benevolence and social justice.

In late nineteenth-century Brazil, Kardec's doctrine developed two variants. While some Brazilian Spiritualists became more interested in the legacy of psychical research that developed in France and Britain and attempted to study the phenomena associated with mediums, ghosts and telepathy from a scientific perspective, others became more interested in the practical application of Spiritualist principles and endeavored to carry out charitable activities including providing food and medical services to the poor and running orphanages and mental hospitals. For these "humanitarian" Spiritualists, Spiritualism became a moral, philosophical doctrine that advanced such qualities as tolerance, liberty, equality, evolution and progress. In Brazil, Spiritualism was closely associated with progressive movements such as abolitionism and the women's rights movement, and attracted social idealists who looked to the "other world" as a harmonious model for this one.

Freitas seems to fit squarely in this tradition. Much in the same way that earlier Utopian socialists such as Saint-Simon, Charles Fourier and Robert Owen sought to establish a more perfect version of society, Freitas envisions Brazil as an educated, industrial society in which men and women of different races and ethnicities work together for the greater good. In her novel, *A rainha do ignoto*, Freitas critiques the monarchy, the *latifundia* and the Catholic Church and suggests that Spiritualism's moral and ethical code provides a solution for the problems of late nineteenth-century Brazilian society, including racism, sexism, slavery and the abuse of clerical and administrative power.

A rainha do ignoto is the story of Dr. Edmundo Lemos' journey to the rural village of Aracati in Ceará, where he discovers an underground cave called the Ilha do Nevoeiro, home of a community of women, the paladins, who fight injustices alongside their leader, the Queen of the Humble. Described as a modern, industrialized city, complete with factories, workshops, an observatory, a laboratory and charitable organizations, the island is inhabited by people of various races, who live and work together harmoniously. Read as a model for a Republican form of government in which slavery and class distinctions are abolished, Freitas' vision of Brazil is radical. Although the Republican ideals of liberty, equality and fraternity were imported from Europe to Brazil during the nineteenth century, they were only selectively adopted by the governing elite. Under the constitutional monarchy, entire groups of people were excluded from exercising their rights as citizens, including the poor, women, minors, and slaves.

In her novel, Freitas criticizes the status quo and introduces liberal ideals. Instead of limiting herself to offering a solution to the social, political and economic problems of Brazil, which can only be envisioned in a separate and distinct place, she empowers her heroines with the ability to effect a change in the exterior world by granting them the power of being mediums. Through their medium powers, the Queen of the Humble and her followers leave their underground community and actively participate in a restructuring of nineteenth-century Brazilian society. As ardent Spiritualists, the Queen and her followers hold seances and use their medium powers to prefigure the miscarriage of justice. Through the powers of transfiguration, the Queen and her followers travel throughout Brazil, righting the many wrongs committed by the slavocracy, the Catholic Church and a corrupt government system.

Freitas' novel can also be read as critique of the limited social role of women in late nineteenth-century Brazilian society. Although the curious subtitle of Freitas' novel, *um romance psicológico*—a psychological novel—can be read as a reference to Freitas' familiarity with the latest scientific and psychiatric theories (Lima Duarte 1999: 724), Freitas' novel appears to be a case study of feminine psychology which redefines traditional definitions of feminine behavior. In the underground community of women founded by the Queen of the Humble, Freitas presents alternative social arrangements of women and inscribes a place for women in the world, which was largely denied them during the nineteenth century. Removed from the control of men, the women in the Queen's community have achieved a level of autonomy unattainable in the world outside. Free from the restrictions of nineteenth-century Brazilian society and the control of masculine relatives, the Queen and her followers are independent women who live as they please. Within the Ilha de Nevoeiro, they enjoy a sense of intellectual freedom and their underground community is a place to freely discuss art, literature and politics. Likewise, the women earn their living working in professions traditionally defined as masculine during the nineteenth century; they are doctors, engineers and members of the military.

Through her use of Spiritualism, Freitas reconfigures the social role of women. By introducing a belief system, which revalorized women's innate passivity, frailty, and moral and spiritual sensibility, Freitas is able to level a criticism against nineteenth-century Brazilian society for the way in which it defines femininity and limits female social roles. By revalorizing female spirituality and sensitivity and demonstrating the way in which female power of medium can be used to improve nineteenth-century Brazilian society, Freitas is able to promote a more active social role for women in the construction of the nation.

MARCIE D. RINKA

Selected Works

A rainha do ignoto: um romance psicológico. Fortaleza, Brazil: Tipografia Universal, 1899.

References and Further Reading

Colares, Otacílio. *Lembrados e esquecidos: ensaios sobre literatura cearense*. Fortaleza, Brazil: Imprensa Universitária da Universidade Federal do Ceará, 1976.

Lima Duarte, Constâcia. "Emília Freitas". In Zahidé Muzart (ed.), *Escritoras brasileiras do século XIX*. Florianópolis: Editora Mulheres, 1999, pp. 723–7.

G

GALLARDO, SARA

Sara Gallardo is one of the most important Argentine authors of the twentieth century. A novelist, storyteller, essayist, journalist, and screenwriter, Gallardo was born to a prominent family in Buenos Aires, Argentina, in December 1931. Her family had ties with the prestigious newspaper *La Nación;* this connection along with her elitist upbringing would later manifest itself in her novels and short stories. As a child, she was an avid reader with a very vivid imagination, factors that moved her to start writing at the age of 11.

In the 1950s, Gallardo launched her career in journalism, married Luis Pico Estrada, and published *Enero* (1955, January), her first novel, inspired by her childhood experiences in the country and her family *estancia* (ranch). The story narrates the hardships of a young woman, who becomes pregnant, and is forced by the rancher's wife to marry the man who raped her in order to comply with social mores.

Her second novel, *Pantalones azules* (Blue Slacks, 1963), also deals with social issues of exploitation, discrimination, and the heavy weight of the Catholic Church. Five years later, Gallardo wrote *Los galgos, los galgos* (The Greyhounds, The Greyhounds, 1968), a groundbreaking novel for which she received two important awards. In this novel, 30-year-old Julián inherits some family land. Unwillingly, but attracted by the romantic idea of a secluded life in the country, he takes possession of the property. However, unfit to run it appropriately, and frustrated by financial pressures, he abandons his lover, his house and his ranch, and moves to Paris, secretly wishing that time and distance will help him overcome his failure. While in Paris, he marries Adelina, an aristocratic widow. His marital life is dull and oppressive to the point that he becomes irritable and abusive. At the end of the novel, Julián finds himself estranged and alienated from everyone and everything he once loved.

In the 1970s, Gallardo divorced, and married renowned writer and philosopher Héctor A. Murena, with whom she had a third child. During this time, she worked as a journalist for two cutting-edge magazines *Atlántida* and *Confirmado.*

Eisejuaz (Eisejuaz), her fourth novel, was published in 1971, and is regarded by literary critics as one of her best works. *Eisejuaz* is the extensive monologue of an indigenous shaman in his quest for enlightenment and sanctity. The merit of the narrative, though, resides in the innovative creation of a pseudo-language with which Gallardo portrays the particular expressions and vocabulary of these local tribes. This interest in the oral tradition is also reflected in her collection of short stories, *El país de humo* (1977, The Country of Smoke).

After her second husband's death in a tragic accident in 1975, Gallardo traveled extensively to Córdoba, Barcelona, Switzerland and Rome where she sought to make a new life for herself. In her fourth novel, *La rosa en el viento* (The Rose in the Wind) published in 1979 while she was living in Barcelona, Gallardo recreates the hardships of European foreigners who settled in the Patagonia region in the south of Argentina, at the turn of the century. Once again, Gallardo reflects upon the country life, and pays homage to its people and their cultural legacy.

In recent years, some of Gallardo's admirers and colleagues, Griselda Gambaro, María Moreno and Ricardo Piglia, have rekindled an interest in her narratives and published some of her works in anthologies and literary collections.

María Claudia André

Selected Works

Enero. Buenos Aires: Editorial Sudamericana, 1958.
Pantalones azules. Buenos Aires: Editorial Sudamericana, 1963.
Los galgos, los galgos. Buenos Aires: Editorial Sudamericana, 1968.
Eisejuaz. Buenos Aires: Editorial Sudamericana, 1971.
El país de humo. Buenos Aires: Editorial Sudamericana, 1977.
Narrativa breve completa. Buenos Aires: Emecé, 2004.

References and Further Reading

Brizuela, Leopoldo. "Escrito en llamas". *Página/12* http://www.pagina12.com.ar/diario/suplementos/libros/10-881-2004-01-04.html

Martínez, Esteso, Santiago. "Sentidos bárbaros. Nación y sexualidad en disputa." *Río de la Plata: Culturas* 29(30) (2004): 391–403.

Pérez, Alberto Julián. "Eisejuaz y la gran historia americana". In Juana Arancibia (ed.), *La mujer en la literatura del mundo hispánico.* Westminster, CA: Instituto Literario y Cultural Hispánico, 2005, pp. 239–49.

GALVÃO, PATRÍCIA REHDER—'PAGU'

Patrícia Rehder Galvão (1910–62), better known as Pagu, is considered an important writer and intellectual of modern Brazilian literature, whose life and work embodied the revolutionary and rebellious spirit of early twentieth-century Brazil. Yet it is only recently that her literary and journalistic work has received critical attention for its combination of politics, aesthetic experimentation, and feminist focus.

Galvão was born on June 9, 1910, in São Paulo, Brazil, and was raised in Braz, a working-class district of the city, home to a number of textile workers and immigrant laborers. She attended São Paulo's prestigious Normal School, where girls typically received an education that prepared them to be wives and mothers. From an early age, however, Galvão flaunted her disdain for traditional canons of female behavior, wearing scandalous clothes—transparent blouses, short skirts—and heavy makeup and smoking in public. In 1925, at the age of 15, Galvão wrote articles for the *Braz Jornal* using the pseudonym Patsy.

From Modernist Muse to Political Rebel

Galvão's rebelliousness caught the attention of São Paulo's artistic and intellectual community. In the 1920s, São Paulo was a major cultural center in Brazil, a cauldron of artistic experimentation. Brazilian culture came of age here, with the installation of the avant-garde movement known as 'modernismo' in an event held in 1922 in São Paulo's municipal theatre. The movement radically questioned traditional Brazilian cultural styles and aesthetics, seeking to modernize artistic production.

In 1928, Galvão became affiliated with the radical wing of the modernist movement—*antropofagia*—led by Oswald de Andrade and constituted in the *Manifesto antropófago* (The Cannibalist Manifesto) and the *Revista de antropofagia* (The Cannibalist Magazine). The *Antropófagos* called for a modern Brazilian art of exportation that would cannibalize European values in order to wipe out traditional Brazilian society with its rigid social boundaries. The group adopted the defiant Galvão and transformed her into their muse. In 1928, poet Raul Bopp rechristened her 'Pagu' in a poem entitled 'Coco'. It was under this name that Galvão became well known in Brazil.

Galvão's status within the modernist movement was consolidated by her romance with Oswald de Andrade, followed by their marriage and the birth of their son Rudá in 1930. Yet it was at an event at São Paulo's municipal theatre in 1929 that she captured critical attention. Dressed in an extravagant dress and cape, Galvão recited Bopp's poem about her. Journalists noted Galvão's strange appearance and cold-blooded quality in accounts that suggested that the performance was a parody of her own role as a passive female muse, accentuating a profound questioning of her ascribed identity. This questioning of her identity as a modern muse was present in a work of self-representation entitled *O album de Pagu: Nascimento vida paixão morte.* Published in 1929, *O album de Pagu* was collection of a series of texts—poems, drawings and prose—grouped in four stages of the artist's experience: birth, life, passion, death. The work's format, its synthesis of visual scenes with lyrical and prose captions and use of first person monologues highlight *O album de Pagu*'s emphasis on self-portrayal, a radical attempt to register her own voice within the movement and defy the objectification implicit in her role as muse.

By the time *O album* was published, Brazil was witnessing a climate of political and social agitation. Successful labor organization by anarchist and anarcho-syndicalist trade unions led to waves of strikes during the late 1910s and in 1922 the Brazilian Communist Party was formed, reflecting a growing tide of left-wing politics in the country that called for broad social and political reforms. 1930 saw the installation of a new political regime led by Getúlio Vargas that would lead to the harsh *Estado Novo* dictatorship. In 1931, Galvão joined the Communist Party and was jailed for the first time at a demonstration in support of dockworkers, obtaining the dubious honor of being the first Brazilian woman imprisoned for political reasons. That year she and Oswald published a newssheet called *O homem do povo* for which she wrote the column "A mulher do povo," where she criticized bourgeois society and attacked mainstream feminism for its lack of recognition for issues confronting working women.

This convergence of class and feminists politics strongly marked her most well known novel *Parque industrial*. Published in 1931, *Parque industrial* was a series of sketches that presented life in São Paulo. The novel focused on the lives of a number of characters, from working-class women to upper-class intellectuals, displaying the varied and complex nature of the city and its inhabitants. Central to this display was a harsh critique of modern Brazilian society, where poverty, oppression, and exploitation were inherent to the daily experiences of workers and in particular working-class women. The critical portrait of Brazilian society was deemed offensive even to the Communist Party who insisted Galvão publish the novel under pseudonym, Mara Lobo, and subsequently expelled her from the party.

After completing *Parque industrial*, Galvão traveled as a journalist and joined international political causes, spending time in Hollywood, China, Germany, Russia and France. She returned to Brazil in 1935, ended her relationship with Oswald and became further engaged in politics. She was jailed for four and a half years by the fascist *Estado Novo* regime and was tortured. Galvão left jail in 1940 and resigned from the Communist Party. Nevertheless, she continued her political commitment to improve society, as well as her literary activities. She met her second husband Geraldo Ferraz in 1940 and together they wrote her second novel, *A famosa revista*. The novel was a mordant satire of the authoritarian character of Brazil's *Estado Novo* as well as the Communist Party, denouncing its bureaucratization, corruption and debasement of human values. At the same time that she and Ferraz wrote *A famosa revista*, Galvão published detective stories for the magazine *Detetive*, using the pen name of King Shelter, in which she parodied the all-knowing (male) detective figure of the popular genre. She was a prolific writer throughout the 1940s and 1950s, writing numerous literary criticism, theatre reviews and commentaries for newspapers. She also published poems under the name Solange Sohl. In 1950, she produced a political pamphlet called *Verdade e liberade*, part of her (unsuccessful) campaign for the legislature of São Paulo. She died in 1962 after a battle with cancer.

Influences and Themes

Galvão's work represents the confluence of a commitment to art and politics that characterizes the vanguard and especially 1930s Brazilian literature. Her work encompassed a variety of genres, journalistic criticism, political commentary, poetry and prose fiction, often merging the boundaries between them in a linguistic and stylistic innovation typical of the times. The formal construction of her novel *Parque industrial* reflects the influence of Brazilian modernism's rejection of traditional realist characterization and styles. Stylistic lines of cinematographic, fragmentary and documentary images conveyed in a stark synthetic language serve to juxtapose the differences and inequalities between social classes that make up modern Brazil. The emphasis on modern experimentation with political observation places Galvão in the Brazilian tradition of social realistic writers of the 1930s such Gracialiano Ramos.

The themes of Galvão's work cannot be separated from her aesthetic intentions: the rejection of traditional norms and conventions. This rejection extends to society, and her work harshly attacks Brazil's traditional elite and highlights the exploitation of workers and the lower classes in a questioning of official ideologies of progress and modernity. Gender questions are firmly explored within this social focus and Galvão's work is committed to discussing the sexual exploitation of women. While this exploration intersects with the contemporary campaign for female suffrage, her journalistic work and her novel *Parque industrial* attack feminism in Brazil as a bourgeois movement, blind to the problems facing working-class women and women of race. Her work thus problematizes the clear-cut divisions between oppressors and oppressed that can characterize social realist prose of the 1930s.

Contemporary Revisions and Reappraisals

The political militancy of Galvão's work placed her novels outside of the nationalist framework acceptable even to the circles that had supported innovation in the arts and letters. As a result, Galvão's prose passed without notice and was not mentioned in any subsequent major history of Brazilian literature or Brazilian modernism. In the 1980s, however, Galvão's work was rediscovered. *Parque industrial* was reprinted in 1981, the fiftieth anniversary of its composition, followed a year later by an edited anthology of her other literary endeavors by poet and critic, Augusto de Campos. Since then Galvão and her three decades of journalistic, literary and political work have generated a full-length film, stage productions, two documentaries as well as a feminist study group at Brazil's Campinas University, whose journal *Cadernos Pagu*, bears her name. Galvão is now admired as a figure of courageous political protest and one of Latin America's most dramatic female intellectuals.

MAITE CONDE

Selected Works

Patrícia Galvão and Geraldo Ferraz. "A famosa revista". In *Dois romances*. Rio de Janeiro: José Olympio, 1959.

O album de Pagú: Nascimento vida paixão e morte. São Paulo: Duas Cidades, 1978.

(as Mara Lobo). *Parque industrial: Romance proletário*. São Paulo: Alternativa, 1981.

Parque industrial. Porto Alegre and São Paulo: Mercado Aberto, EDUFSCar, 1994.

(as King Shelter). *Safra macabre, contos policiais*. Introduction by Geraldo Ferraz. Rio de Janeiro: José Olympio, 1998.

References and Further Reading

Besse, Susan. "Pagu: Patricia Galvão – Rebel". In William H. Beezley and Judith Ewell (eds), *The Human Tradition in Latin America*. Wilmington, DE: Scholarly Resources, 1987, pp. 103–17.

Bloch, Jayne H. "Patricia Galvão: The Struggle Against Conformity". *Latin American Literary Review* 14(27) (1986): 188–201.

Campos, Augusto de. *Pagu vida obra*. São Paulo: Brasiliense, 1982.

Daniel, Mary L. "Life in the Textile Factory: Two 1933 Perspectives". *Luso Brazilian Review* 31(2) (1994): 97–113.

Guedes, Thelma. *Pagu, Literatura e revolução*. São Paulo: Atelier/ Nankin, 2003.

Jackson, David K. "Patricia Galvão and Brazilian Social Realism of the 1930s". *Proceedings of the Pacific Northwest Council on Foreign Languages* 28 (1977): 95–8.

Owen, Hilary. "Discardable Discourses in Patricia Galvão's *Parque Industrial*". In Solange Ribeiro de Oliveira and Judith Still (eds), *Brazilian Feminisms*. Nottingham: University of Nottingham, 1999, pp. 68–84.

GAMBARO, GRISELDA

Daughter of Italian immigrant parents, Griselda Gambaro was born in Buenos Aires, Argentina, in 1928. Married with two children, she is one of Argentina's foremost contemporary dramatists, although she began her writing career as a novelist. She has travelled extensively to teach and write, and was obliged to spend the years between 1977 and 1980 in Spain in political exile following the banning of one of her books in Argentina.

Her theatre reveals the influence of the principal European dramatists of the 1950s, although themes are adapted to the contemporary Argentinean reality lived by Gambaro. Primary among these concerns are the existentialism that characterised the work of Camus and Sartre, and which is apparent in Gambaro's work through her portrayal of profound human solitude, anguish, and absolute lack of communication between its characters, while critics have also observed parallels with Becket in that he too presented characters condemned to perpetual loneliness. Similarities with Pinter have also been suggested, particularly in the violent cruelty engaged in by Gambaro's characters, a cruelty which the protagonist of the piece is incapable of comprehending. Concerns with the inefficiency of language as a means of communication characteristic of Ionesco's theatre are also apparent in Gambaro's work, manifesting themselves in the absolute inability for communication characterising human relationships. Dark humour, another element of European avant-garde theatre of the 1950s, is incorporated into Gambaro's theatre, while she also has recourse to parody of the type deployed by Genet and Arrabal. It is of note, however, that although many of these elements lead to an association of her work with that of the Europeans mentioned here, particularly the notion of a scenic universe entirely divorced from reality, the denouncement of socio-political realities and practices in fact makes her drama closer to moral theatre, rather than avant-garde. Clear parallels with the theatre of the absurd also suggest themselves, although Gambaro has rejected critical characterisation of her plays as such.

Although more recently critics have begun to address the representation of the female and women's issues in Gambaro's work, it is of note that her early theatre was apparently devoid of concern for the widespread oppression of women perceived to characterise Latin American society. Her more contemporary productions, however, have tended to present more female characters, recognising that it is more often the woman than the man who is the victim of the kinds of brutality and repression that are the hallmark of her work, and Gambaro herself has discussed the representation of the feminine in critical essays. Despite this lack of a specifically female or feminist focus, two of her early works in particular did explore the role and experiences of women in inter-personal relationships. *Viejo matrimonio* (1965, Old Couple) analyses the fundamental lack of communication and comprehension that can exist between a married couple, while the violence and degeneration of familial relationships is explored in *Los siameses* (1967, The Siamese). Two works written during the 1970s, *Ganarse la muerte* (1976, Earning Death) and *Dios no nos quiere contentos* (1979, God Does Not Want Us Happy), situate female protagonists in horrifyingly abusive situations where their sexuality becomes commodity. In the novel *Ganarse la muerte*, a young girl, Cledy, becomes the victim first of those who would abuse her adolescent body, and later of a husband and a society which televise the first night of her married life in a bizarrely voyeuristic and frighteningly intrusive manner. María, the central character of *Dios no nos quiere contentos*, also becomes the victim of child abuse, and, upon reaching maturity, of a horrifyingly predatory male sexuality, a situation for which she is encouraged to perceive herself, and particularly her female sexuality, as responsible. Sexual issues and the commodification of women are also revealed in a work first produced in 1981, *El despojamiento* (The Dispossession). Protagonised by a former actress and model, the one-act piece explores the fate of the female who, in response to patriarchy's overtures, has constructed her persona on her image and sexuality alone, and who ultimately finds herself in a harrowingly exploitative situation. More recently the negative female stereotype of the 'bad mother' has been portrayed in *La malasangre* (1984, Bitter Blood). A derelict mother–daughter bond and the betrayal and oppression of the child by the parent are all portrayed as the result of the mother's own subjugation and violent repression at the hands of society, although the daughter's ultimate rebellion against patriarchal norms may serve as a more positive female model. In fact, in several interviews, Gambaro has noted that her work is not conditioned by gender issues, but by her compromise as a social subject; however, in *Real envido* (1983, Real Envy), *Del sol naciente* (1984, The Rising Sun) and *Antígona furiosa* (1986, Angry Antigone), female characters take center stage by becoming agents of their own destiny. According to the author, if Emma from *El Campo*, suffered all the infamies of power, the other protagonists do too, but unsubmissively, "they assume their defeat as a learning process. They know where they want to go and what they want. Even Antigone's suicide in *Antígona furiosa,* is a response to the lies and the silence" (Andrade and Hilde 1991: 149). Inspired by Sophocles' drama, *Antigona furiosa* presents a vivid metaphor on the significant role women played during the military regime in Argentina (1976–83). The play renders tribute to their moral strength and their courage to challenge the status quo, in their search for the whereabouts of their beloved ones.

In the 1990s, Gambaro turned back to narrative, publishing several well-received novels such as *Después del día de fiesta* (1994, After the Holiday), awarded the Giacomo Leopardi Medal by the University of Buenos Aires and the Centro Nasionali de Studi Leopardiani, Italy; *Lo mejor que se tiene* (1997, The Best We Have), First Prize of the Argentine Academy of Letters 1996/98; *Escritos inocentes* (1999, Innocent Writings), *El mar que nos trajo* (2002, The Sea that Brought Us) and *Promesas y desvaríos* (2004, Promises and Ravings). Some of these novels have been translated into English, French and Polish.

Gambaro is, unquestionably, one of the most prolific and well-respected female playwrights in contemporary Latin American theatre.

SHELLEY GODSLAND

Selected Works

Madrigal en ciudad. Buenos Aires: Goyanarte, 1963.
Las paredes. Buenos Aires, 1963.
El desatino. Buenos Aires: Instituto Di Tella, 1964.
Una felicidad con menos pena. Buenos Aires: Sudamericana, 1967.
Los siameses. Buenos Aires: Insurrexit, 1967.
El campo. Buenos Aires: Insurrexit, 1968.
La gracia, in *El Urogallo* 17 (1972).
Información para extranjeros, 1972.
Nada que ver con otra historia. Buenos Aires: Noé, 1972.
La cola mágica. Buenos Aires: La Flor, 1976.
Conversaciones con chicos: sobre la sociedad, los padres, los afectos, la cultura. Buenos Aires: Timerman, 1976.
Ganarse la muerte. Buenos Aires: La Flor, 1976.
Dios no nos quiere contentos. Barcelona: Lumen, 1979.
Cuatro ejercicios para actrices. 1980.
Decir sí. Buenos Aires: Teatro Abierto, 1981.
El despojamiento, in *Tramoya: Cuaderno de Teatro* 21/22 (1981): 119–27.
La malasangre. 1982.
Nada que ver. Sucede lo que pasa. Ottawa: Girol, 1983.
Del sol naciente. 1984.
Lo impenetrable. Buenos Aires: Torres Agüero, 1984.
Nosferatu. 1985.
Antígona furiosa, in *Gestos* 5 (1988).
Efectos personales. 1988.
Desafiar al destino. 1990.
Atando cabos. 1991.
Information for Foreigners: Three Plays. Evanston, IL: Northwestern University Press, 1992.
Después del día de fiesta. Buenos Aires: Seix Barral, 1994.
Lo mejor que se tiene. Buenos Aires: Norma, 1997.
Escritos inocentes. Buenos Aires: Norma, 1999.
El mar que nos trajo. Buenos Aires: Norma, 2002.
Teatro (Cinco piezas). Buenos Aires: Norma, 2002.
Promesas y desvaríos. Buenos Aires: Norma, 2004.

References and Further Reading

Andrade, Elba and Hilde, Cramsie. *Dramaturgas latinoamericanas contemporáneas: Antología crítica*. Madrid: Verbum, 1991.

André, María Claudia. "Entrevista a Griselda Gambaro: Feminismos e influencias en su narrativa". *Confluencia: Revista Hispánica de Cultura y Literatura* 14(2) (1999): 115–20.

Boling, Becky. "Reenacting Politics: The Theater of Griselda Gambaro". In Catherine Larson and Margarita Vargas (eds), *Latin American Women Dramatists: Theater, Texts, and Theories*. Bloomington, IN: Indiana University Press, 1998, pp. 3–22.

Boorman, Joan R. "Contemporary Latin American Women Dramatists". *Rice University Studies* 64(1) (1978): 69–80.

Bulman, Gail. "Moving On: Memory and History in Griselda Gambaro's Recent Theater". *Studies in Twentieth and Twenty-First Century Literature* 28(2) (2004): 379–95.

Castro, Marcela and Jurovietzky, Silvia. "Decir no: Entrevista a Griselda Gambaro". *Feminaria Literaria* 6(11) (1996): 41–5.

Contreras, Marta. *Griselda Gambaro, Teatro de la Des-composición*. Concepción: Universidad de Concepción, 1994.

——. "Diagnosis teatral: Una aproximación a la obra dramática de Griselda Gambaro". *Acta Literaria* 22 (1997): 19–25.

Foster, David William. "Pornography and the Feminine Erotic: Griselda Gambaro's *Lo impenetrable*". *Monographic Review/Revista Monográfica* 7 (1991): 284–96.

Franco, Jean. "Self-Destructing Heroines". *The Minnesota Review* 22 (1984): 105–15.

Gambaro, Griselda. "¿Es posible y deseable una dramaturgia específicamente femenina?" *Latin American Theatre Review* 13(ii) (1980): 17–21.

——. "Algunas consideraciones sobre la mujer y la literatura". *Revista Iberoamericana* 51(132–3) (1985): 471–3.

Garfield, Evelyn P. *Women's Voices from Latin America: Interviews with Six Contemporary Authors*. Detroit, MI: Wayne State University Press, 1985.

Gladhart, Amalia. "Playing Gender". *Latin American Literary Review* 24(47) (1996): 59–89.

Gnutzmann, Rita. "Casa-hogar-cámara de tortura en el teatro de Griselda Gambaro". *Río de la Plata: Culturas* 29–30 (2004): 487–96.

——. "El teatro de Griselda Gambaro: De la pasividad a la rebelión". *Insula: Revista de Letras y Ciencias Humanas* 715–16 (2006): 30–3.

Lasala, Malena. *Entre el desamparo y la esperanza. Una traducción filosófica a la estética de Griselda Gambaro*. Buenos Aires: Biblos, 1992.

López-Calvo, Ignacio. "Lesbianism and Caricature in Griselda Gambaro's *Lo impenetrable*". *Journal of Lesbian Studies* 7(3) (2003): 89–103.

Mazziotti, Nora. *Poder, deseo y marginación: Aproximaciones a la obra de Griselda Gambaro*. Buenos Aires: Puntosur, 1989.

Méndez-Faith, Teresa. "Sobre el uso y abuso de poder en la producción dramática de Griselda Gambaro". *Revista Iberoamericana* 51(132–3) (1985): 831–41.

Morales Ortiz, Gracia María. "Estrategias visuales en la dramaturgia de Griselda Gambaro: Los personajes 'defectuosos' en sus obras de los años sesenta y setenta". *La literatura hispanoamericana con los cinco sentidos: V congreso internacional de la AEELH / Actas del V congreso internacional de la AEELH. Cursos, Congresos e Simposios. 78*. Ed. Eva Valcárcel. La Coruña: Universidade da Coruña, 2002, pp. 447–55.

Mundani, Liliana. *Las máscaras de lo siniestro. El caso Gambaro*. Córdoba: Alción Editora, 2002.

Paz, Marcelo. "La domesticidad del horror en dos novelas de Griselda Gambaro". *Ciberletras* 14 (2005): n.p.

Roffé, Reina. "Entrevista a Griselda Gambaro". *Cuadernos Hispanoamericanos* 588 (1999): 111–24.

Taylor, Claire L. "Bodily Mutilation and the Dismemberment of Discourse in the Novels of Griselda Gambaro". *Forum for Modern Language Studies* 37(3) (2001): 326–36.

Taylor, Diana. "Border Watching". In Peggy Phelan (ed.), *The Ends of Performance*. New York: New York University Press, 1998, pp. 178–85.

Trastoy, Beatriz. "Madres, marginados y otras víctimas: El teatro de Griselda Gambaro en el ocaso del siglo". In Osvaldo Pellettieri (ed.), *Teatro argentino del 2000. Cuadernos del GETEA (Grupo de Estudios de Teatro Argentino e Iberoamericano) 11*. Buenos Aires: Galerna/Fundación Roberto Arlt, 2000, pp. 37–46.

Yehenson, Myriam Y. "Staging Cultural Violence: Griselda Gambaro and Argentina's 'Dirty War'". *Mosaic: A Journal for the Interdisciplinary Study of Literature* 32(1) (1999): 85–104.

GARCÍA MARRUZ, FINA

Fina García Marruz was born on April 28, 1923, in Havana, Cuba, where she was educated and continues to live with her husband, the well-known poet and critic Cintio Vitier (1921–). She received her doctorate in Social Sciences from the Universidad de la Habana in 1961. She joined the editorial board of the journal *Clavileño* (1943) and, together with Vitier, participated actively in the Orígenes group and their eponymous journal (1944–56), contributing essays, poetry and criticism. Among the many other journals to which she has contributed are the *Revista de la Biblioteca Nacional* and the *Anuario Martiano*. The couple have worked as researchers at the Colección Cubana of the Biblioteca Nacional José Martí and its Centro de Estudios Martianos. García Marruz has published numerous studies of Martí's works, both alone and in collaboration with Vitier. She has been the recipient of numerous honors including membership in the Orden Alejo Carpentier, the Medalla 30 Aniversario de la Academia de Ciencias de Cuba, and the Premio Nacional de Literatura in 1990. In spite of accolades received in her own country, García Marruz's poetry has failed to receive the critical attention it merits, though a series of events (including her Premio Nacional, the fiftieth anniversary of the beginning of Orígenes in 1994 and her eightieth birthday in 2003), along with her more prominent appearances in major critical studies of Cuban and Caribbean literature, have raised her international profile. Her poem "Mediodía" (Noon) inspired a 1995 composition of the same name by Joyce Orenstein for the Cygnus Ensemble, and an issue of the *Revista de la Biblioteca Nacional* was dedicated to García Marruz in her eightieth year. In 1998, she and her husband were invited to participate in a program with the Residencia de Estudiantes de Madrid in which they shared the title of Poets in Residence. Their travels have also taken her to other countries, including the US and the former Soviet Union. Her cultural legacy is continued in the work of her and Vitier's two sons, the noted musician/composers José María and Sergio Vitier.

Poetry

She began publishing her poetry in journals at an early age, inspired by a meeting with Juan Ramón Jiménez when she was just 13. Her first collection, *Poemas* (Poems), was published in 1942, followed by *Transfiguración de Jesús en el Monte* (Transfiguration of Jesus on the Mount) in 1947. She gained some measure of critical recognition with the publication of *Las miradas perdidas* (1951, The Lost Looks), a collection distinguished by its poignant recollections of lost childhood. *Visitaciones* (1970, Visitations) sees the broadening of her thematic concerns to include more reflections on motherhood and the motherland, as well as tributes to historical figures such as Ernesto "Che" Guevara, Ho Chi Minh and Martin Luther King, Jr. In 1977, her writings dating from the previous twenty years were gathered and published as *Habana del centro* (Havana Downtown), a wide-ranging collection that includes, among other works, the entirety of *Viaje a Nicaragua* (Trip to Nicaragua), a collaboration with Vitier inspired by their 1979 trip to that country; the Premio de la Crítica-winning *Créditos de Charlot* (Charlie [Chaplin]'s Credits), consisting of poems inspired by the life and works of Charlie Chaplin; *Viejas melodías* (Old Melodies), which re-creates the songs of her childhood, and *Los Rembrandt de l'Hermitage* (The Rembrandts of l'Hermitage), a series of poetic responses to works held by the famous St. Petersburg museum, which she visited in 1976. Two anthologies, *Poesías escogidas* (1984, Selected Poetry, edited by Jorge Yglesias) and *Antología poética* (1977, Poetic Anthology, edited by Jorge Luis Arcos) contain useful introductions to general characteristics of her poetry. 2002 saw the release of a compact disc, *Visitaciones*, featuring García Marruz reading her own work. A new *Antología poética* was also released in 2002, and a collection entitled *El peso de las cosas en la luz* (The Weight of Things in the Light) was presented by fellow Cuban poet Nancy Morejón at the Buenos Aires Book Fair in 2006. Her work appears in numerous anthologies, among them *Once grandes poetisas hispanoamericanas* (1967, Eleven Great Spanish American [Women] Poets).

Among the widely acknowledged constants throughout García Marruz's work are the clarity and simplicity of her writing and the central importance of visual detail. Frequently observed themes include the nature of memory, transcendentalism and Catholicism, Cuba, music and the arts, particularly portraits. Memory is most often associated with the theme of childhood, presented in poem after poem as an unrecuperable paradise lost. She pays touching tribute to the cities and landscapes, the history and politics, and, above all, the people of Cuba in poems which often present a unique perspective on the material poverty so prevalent in that country. The best-known example of her religious poetry remains the long poem *Transfiguración de Jesús en el Monte*. Poems inspired by paintings and films often focus on the "behind the scenes" activity that led to their creation. Other, less frequently studied thematic concerns include an interest in creating portraits of women who appear marginalized in one way or another with respect to the poetic voice, and the related theme of maternity, which receives a distinctly ambivalent treatment in her work. Her poetic portraits make revealing use of objects, articles of clothing, and cinematic props. Throughout her work, recurring imagery of darkness and light adds to the visual impact of her verse. The development of her poetic language over her long career has been observed as a move towards a more simplified and stripped-down, almost colloquial language. She works in a wide range of poetic forms, ranging from sonnets, such as her celebrated "En la muerte de una heroína de la patria" (On the Death of a Heroine of the Fatherland), to the free verse that becomes more prevalent later in her career.

Prose

García Marruz's poetic theory is elaborated in her essays on the poetic process as well as in her critical responses to writers from myriad countries and historical periods. On José Martí alone she has published *Temas martianos* (1969, Martían Themes, with Vitier), *A cien años de Martí* (1997, At Martí's One Hundredth Year, with Vitier and others), *El amor como energía revolucionaria en José Martí* (2003, Love as Revolutionary Energy in José Martí), *Darío, Martí y lo germinal americano* (2001, Darío, Martí and the American Germinal) and various journal articles, in addition to contributing to the critical edition of *Obras completas de José Martí* (2001, Complete Works of José Martí) and compiling 1990's *Textos Antiimperialistas de José Martí* (Anti-imperialist Texts of José Martí). She and Vitier selected texts for Martí's *Obra literaria* (1978, Literary Works) and for *Ideario: Selección de Cintio Vitier and Fina García Marruz* (1987, Ideology: Selection by Cintio Vitier and Fina García Marruz). Other studies include the prologues to Juana Borrero's *Poesías* (1966, Poetry) and Cleva Solís's *Obra poetica* (1998, Poetic Works), *Bécquer o la leve bruma* (1971, Bécquer or the Light Mist), *Sor Juana Inés de la Cruz: Dolor fiero* (1999, Sor Juana Inés de la Cruz: Fierce Pain), and *Quevedo* (2003). Together with Vitier, she co-authored *Estudios críticos* (1964, Critical Studies) and the compilation *Flor oculta de poesía cubana* (1978; Hidden Flower of Cuban Poetry). In "Hablar de la poesía," from the collection of her studies of the same name (1986, Speaking of Poetry), she treats the themes of beauty and the poetic, asserting that beauty is less a constantly apparent characteristic of an object than an essence that may or may not be revealed to the viewer/poet. One of her most-quoted declarations about poetry appears in this essay, in which she declares herself in opposition to both "pure" and "committed" art and the worn-out polemic between the two. The relationship between poetic subject and object is addressed in "Lo exterior en la poesía" (The Exterior in Poetry), included in *Poesía y poética del Grupo Orígenes* (1994, Poetry and Poetics of the Orígenes Group). This essay focuses on the necessary distance between the eye and that which is seen; the importance of this magical distance is illustrated in one of her best-known poems, "Una dulce nevada está cayendo" (A Sweet Snow is Falling). Finally, the paradoxical role of silence in poetry, a key theme in her tributes to Chaplin and other poems, is addressed in "Hablar," in which she writes of silence as a means of expression and of the importance of blank spaces denoting silence to the understanding of a poem. Other collections of essays include *La literatura en el Papel Periódico de la Habana* (1991, Literature in the Papel Periódico de la Habana, with Vitier), *La familia de Orígenes* (1997, The Family of Orígenes) and *El libro de Job* (2000, The Book of Job). *Ensayos* (Essays) was published in 2003 as part of the Colección Premio Nacional de Literatura.

STACY HOULT

Selected Works

Temas martianos (with Cintio Vitier). Havana: Biblioteca Nacional José Martí, 1969.

Poesías escogidas. Edited by Jorge Yglesias. Havana: Letras Cubanas, 1984.

Hablar de la poesía. Havana: Letras Cubanas, 1986.

Antología poética. Edited by Jorge Luis Arcos. Havana: Letras Cubanas, 1997.

Habana del centro. Havana: Ediciones Unión, 1997.

References and Further Reading

Arcos, Jorge Luis. *En torno a la obra poética de Fina García Marruz*. Havana: Ediciones Unión, 1990.

Davies, Catherine. "Fina García Marruz: Love of Mother and God". In *A Place in the Sun? Women Writers in Twentieth-Century Cuba*. London and New Jersey: Zed Books Ltd, 1997, pp. 90–115.

Hernández, Wilfredo. "Entre Orígenes y la Revolución: Introducción a la poesía de Fina García Marruz". *Monographic Review/Revista Monográfica*. 13 (1997): 340–54.

Instituto de Literatura y Lingüística de la Academica de Ciencias de Cuba. "Fina García Marruz". *Diccionario de la literatura cubana*. Havana: Letras Cubanas, 1980, p. 369.

Méndez Martínez, Roberto. "Fina García Marruz: El desciframiento de la superficie". In *La dama y el escorpión*. Santiago de Cuba: Editorial Oriente, 2000, pp. 221–74.

GARCÍA RAMIS, MAGALI

Magali García Ramis is one of several female writers whose work began appearing in the 1970s in Puerto Rico. She was born in 1946 in Santurce, Puerto Rico. Raised by a single mother (her parents were divorced), growing up she was part of her mother's extended family comprised of six aunts, an uncle, many cousins and her grandmother, admittedly the matriarch of the family. Her father fought in World War II and later worked as a park ranger in Puerto Rico's rainforest, El Yunque. Her mother and aunts worked in a laboratory that her oldest aunt established.

In spite of the fact that her family was not exactly wealthy, García Ramis studied in an elite Catholic school in Miramar called Colegio de Nuestra Señora del Perpetuo Socorro (School of Our Lady of Perpetual Help) where one of her classmates would be another future Puerto Rican writer, Ana Lydia Vega. As with most private parochial schools in Puerto Rico, the teachers and students believed that American and Catholic ideas were better than those of Puerto Rican culture. This might explain why in several interviews García Ramis has said that, growing up, she read and wrote primarily in English, and that she didn't particularly like Spanish. Ironically, both her grandfathers were from Spain, and her family world was very Spanish. García Ramis always struggled with this contradiction. It would not be until many years later, while a graduate student, first in New York, and later in Mexico City, that she would encounter a completely Puerto Rican reality that would come into sharp contrast with her previous perceptions. This theme would later appear in her literary work.

Education and Literary Contribution

After graduating from high school in 1964, Magali García Ramis enrolled at the University of Puerto Rico, Río Piedras where she majored in History; however, she soon became interested in writing. While still an undergraduate student she worked as a reporter for the daily newspaper *El Mundo*. The president of this publication, Ángel Ramos, granted her a scholarship to study journalism. In 1968, after concluding her undergraduate degree, García Ramis moved to New York to study journalism at Columbia University. This experience changed her life in unexpected ways. First, she came into contact with a number of Puerto Rican and Latin American students who introduced her to Latin American literature, especially the writers of *Boom*. At 22, she began to understand her identity as a Puerto Rican, Caribbean, and a Latin American. In addition to her school work and involvement in journalism during this time, she worked as a waitress at a restaurant called *The Golden Rail*, an experience that inspired her third book.

It was in New York City that García Ramis wrote her first story, "Todos los domingos" ("Every Sunday"), which was also her first story in Spanish. She won first prize in the literary contest of the *Ateneo Puertorriqueño* with this short story. (Puerto Rican Athenaeum). She returned to Puerto Rico in 1971 and began working for the newspaper *El Imparcial*. She wrote for this newspaper until 1972 and until 1973 worked for a cultural magazine called *Avance* as well. During this period she continued to write short stories, some for a literary journal called *Penélope,* published by Zoraida Barreto. It was Barreto who collected and edited a few of her stories and published them in the book entitled *La familia de todos nosotros*.

Already a fiction writer, García Ramis submitted a book composed of four short stories to the *Casa de las Américas* literary contest (House of the Americas) in Cuba. She received an honorary mention for one of the stories "La viuda de Checho el Loco" (The Widow of Chencho, the Crazy) which was published in 1974. Years later in 1999, Casa de las Américas invited her to be part of the panel of established and recognized writers who acknowledged notable up-and-coming writers. To her, this position signified that she had come full circle. In 1974, this same year, García Ramis moved to Mexico to pursue graduate studies in Literature and Latin American Studies at the Universidad Nacional Autónoma de México (National Autonomous University of México). She returned to Puerto Rico in 1977, and published her book of short stories called *La familia de todos nosotros* in the same year. She also started to work for the then newly created School of Communications of the University of Puerto Rico, Río Piedras. In spite of her obligations as a university professor, she routinely collaborated with and contributed to several Puerto Rican newspapers. In 1985, she finished her famous semi-autographical novel *Felices Días, Tío Sergio* (Happy Days, Uncle Sergio) and it was published in 1986, to great critical and popular acclaim. In 1988, she received a prestigious Guggenheim Fellowship that allowed her to work on her second novel, *Las horas del Sur* (The Hours of the South). In 1993, García Ramis published *La ciudad que me habita* (The City that Inhabits Me), a collection of journalistic essays that she wrote while she worked for several local newspapers: *El Mundo*, *El Imparcial*, *Avance*, *Claridad* and *La Hora*.

Themes and Influences

Many critics have written about how García Ramis's stories, novels, and chronicles are depictions of Puerto Rican culture, family and politics. While it is true that in many of her earlier texts she wrote about interactions within a family, and Puerto Rican identity and women's identity, she has also dealt with a number of other issues and themes. Several of her writings explore the delicate negotiations between history and fiction; gender roles, and gender performance; urban imaginaries, space and place; fragmentation and spatial disruptions.

Her most celebrated work is her novel *Felices Días, Tío Sergio* (1986), about growing up in Puerto Rico in the 1950s. This is a loosely autobiographical *Bildungsroman* where the quiet power of real life is recreated with warmth, tenderness, and simplicity against the backdrop of a rapidly developing society. Her short story collections, *La familia de todos nosotros* (1977) and *Las noches del Riel de Oro* (1995) have a couple of common threads such as fragile negotiations within family life and between family members, and an array of characters that allow the author to chronicle multiple identities. While *La familia de todos nosotros* is anchored in the immediate Puerto Rican reality, *Las noches del Riel de Oro* grew out of the author's experiences in New York City. *La ciudad que me habita*, is García Ramis's impassionate and affectionate reflection on space and place. These urban chronicles celebrate San Juan as profoundly and sincerely as *Felices días, Tío Sergio* paid homage to Santurce, where she was born and raised. This book evocatively reveals the importance that location and everyday life have in her work. There is also a great degree of social commentary and criticism in this collection. Her latest novel *Las Horas del Sur* (2006) is a historical fiction that spans from the end of the nineteenth century to the beginning of the twentieth in Puerto Rico. The protagonist, a journalist who appears to have no social consciousness, is a *dilettante* who must change when his cultural identity is revealed. Appearing once again is the theme of cultural identity, which is central to this text, and a constant preoccupation in all García Ramis' work, as is the theme of reconciliation in all its forms.

García Ramis has also written movie scripts (*La flor de piel,* 1989) and collaborated in books about architecture and the city. Recently she has begun working on a book about her aunts and on another novel tentatively entitled *Matadero Road.*

MYRNA GARCÍA-CALDERÓN

Selected Works

La familia de todos nosotros. Río Piedras, PR: Editorial Cultural, 1976.
Felices Días, Tío Sergio. Río Piedras, PR: Editorial Cultural, 1986.
La Ciudad que me habita. Río Piedras, PR: Ediciones Huracán, 1993.
Las noches de Riel de Oro. Río Piedras, PR: Editorial Cultural, 1995
Las Horas del Sur. San Juan, PR: Ediciones Callejón, 2006.

References and Further Reading

Adán-Lifante, Virginia. "Elementos disruptivos en 'Una semana de siete días' de Magali García Ramis". *Explicación de Textos Literarios* 31(20) (2002–3): 21–30.

Díaz, Luis Felipe. "Ideología y sexualidad en Felices días, tío Sergio de Magali García Ramis". *Revista de Estudios Hispánicos* 21 (1994): 325–41.

Esteves, Carmen C. "Literature/Journalism: The Frontier: An Interview with Magali García Ramis". *Callaloo: A Journal of African American and African Arts and Letters* 17(3) (1994 Summer): 862–9.

Fernández Olmos, Margarite. "Growing Up Puertorriqueña: The Feminist Bildungsroman and the Novels of Nicholasa Mohr and Magalí García Ramis". *Centro* 2(7) (1989–90 Winter): 56–73.

Figueroa, Alvin Joaquín. "Feminismo, homosexualidad e identidad política: El lenguaje del otro en *Felices días, tío Sergio*". *La Torre: Revista de la Universidad de Puerto Rico* 5(20) (Oct.–Dec. 1991): 499–505.

García-Calderón, Myrna. "La añoranza histórica en las obras de Magali García Ramis". *Explicación de Textos Literarios* 23(2) (1994–95): 5–63.

Gelpí, Juan G. "René Marqués y Magali García Ramis: Dos acercamientos a la novela de aprendizaje". *Revista de Estudios Hispánicos* 17–18 (1990–91): 353–68.

La Fountain-Stokes, Lawrence. "Tomboy Tantrums and Queer Infatuations: Reading Lesbianism in Magali García Ramis's *Felices días, tío Sergio*". In Lourdes Torres and Inmaculada Pertusa (eds), *Tortilleras: Hispanic and U.S. Latina Lesbian Expression*. Philadelphia, PA: Temple University Press, 2003.

López, Ivette. "Minute and Fragrant Memories: *Happy Days, Uncle Sergio* by Magali García Ramis". In Lucía Guerra Cunningham (ed.), *Splintering Darkness: Latin American Women Writers in Search of Themselves*. Pittsburgh, PA: Latin American Literary Review Press, 1990.

Matos Freire, Susana. "El sujeto femenino y la escritura: *Felices días, tío Sergio* de Magali García Ramis". *Revista de Estudios Hispánicos* 20 (1993): 327–33.

Negrón-Muntaner, Frances. "*La familia de todos nosotros* y algunos que somos huérfanos: Una entrevista a Magali García Ramis". *Nuez: Revista Internacional de Arte y Literatura* 5(13) (1994): 64–6.

Sotomayor, Aurea María. "Si un nombre convoca un mundo ... , *Felices días, tío Sergio*". *Revista de Estudios Iberoamericanos* 11(2) (Jan.–June 1994): 161–74.

GARRO, ELENA

Elena Garro (1916–98) is best known for a single novel, *Los recuerdos del porvenir*, yet she was one of Latin America's most prolific and versatile writers, male or female, of the twentieth century. Her poetic and probing prose reconstructed the past with its cruelties and injustices, suggested the power of memory to shape the future, and challenged official accounts of history. Garro rejected the notion of "magic realism" and affirmed that she wrote what she had observed. Mexico, which was most often the setting of her fiction and drama, first celebrated, then ostracized, and later ignored Garro's work, but in the end, her native country recognized and honored her genius. Although Garro's associates have described her ability to write a creative piece on demand, in a single draft, it appears that Garro's most celebrated novel, as well as many plays and short fiction, emerged from long periods of physical illness and isolation; it is a commonplace that Garro laid her writing aside "in trunks" for years before publishing it. Two of her works have been published posthumously.

Shaping the Writer

Garro was born Elena Delfina Garro Navarro on 11 December 1916, in the Mexican colonial city of Puebla de los Ángeles (in the State of Puebla), where her mother, Mexican native Esperanza Navarro Benítez had arrived, traveling there from Spain through the port of Veracruz and thence by train to the home of her sister in Puebla. Garro's father, José Antonio (Pepe) Garro Melendreras, was a native of Cangas de Onís, Asturias, Spain; thus, Garro held a Spanish, as well as a Mexican passport. Garro's year of birth was given erroneously for most of her public life, but she provided 11 December 1916 as her birth date in one of her last interviews; her will records the same date (Toruño 2004: 13–14). See Prado (2002) and Toruño (2004) for authoritative biographical information on Garro.

From Puebla, the family went to Mexico City and lived there but a brief time before settling in Iguala, Guerrero, where, to all appearances, Garro's childhood was centered on books and education. There, she learned to love reading and dance, both of which informed the passions and professions of her adult life. Garro's father owned a varied library from which he taught her and her sisters in a variety of languages. Garro recalled that her mother was an entertaining story-teller who encouraged her daughters to read. The predilections of both parents contributed in important ways to Garro's development as a writer and to her causes as a political activist. Garro's parents supported the Revolution (1910–20), and two of her maternal uncles fought in the conflict.

Around 1934 (Toruño 2004: 16), Garro and her sisters were sent to Mexico City to live with their mother's sisters to be educated. There, Garro went to school and studied ballet, and eventually began her university education at the Universidad Autónoma de Mexico (UNAM), where she worked as a choreographer and wrote for the theater. As a journalist, Garro wrote pieces for periodicals such as *México en la Cultura* (Mexican Culture), *La Palabra y el Hombre* (Word and Man), and *Revista de la Universidad* (University Review) (Universidad de Guadalajara, Feria Internacional del Libro de Guadalajara, 25 Nov.–3 Dec. 2006 www.fil.com.mx/sor/garro.asp). At a family party, she met poet Octavio Paz (Rosas Lopátegui 2000: 27), whom she married in 1937 while she was still a student at UNAM. Her father opposed the marriage, attempted to annul it, and sought a convent which would admit Garro (Toruño 2004: 20–2). None of these efforts succeeded.

Garro enlarged her world through her marriage to Paz, who was already recognized as a writer, and who later became a member of the Mexican diplomatic service. Their travels acquainted her with the US, Japan, France, and Spain, and foreshadowed her long exile from Mexico. The marriage also provided Garro with her prototypes of certain characters. Paz and his mother, doña Pepa Delgado Lozano, are portrayed in Garro's fiction and plays as elements of control and evil, sometimes in ironic tones. These types appear in *Un traje rojo para un duelo* (A Red Mourning Suit), where Paz's father's suicide, which occurred the year before Garro and Paz were married, is a plot element (Toruño 2004: 22–3). Paz and Garro had one daughter, Helena (b. Laura Elena) Paz Garro, whose birth year is given as 1948 (for example, by Princeton University), but who was born on 12 December 1939 according to Toruño (2004: 26). Photographs of Garro and Helena taken in 1947, 1953, 1957, and 1960 appear in the family-authorized work of Lopátegui (2000: 54–5; 69–77) and suggest 1939 is correct.

Garro's return to Mexico in the late 1960s led to events that shaped the rest of her life and that briefly influenced Mexican reception of her fiction and theater writing. Following the massacre of student protesters in the Plaza de Tres Culturas at Tlatelolco, Mexico City, on October 2, 1968, student detainees named Garro as a "mastermind," and the government held her for nine days beginning October 5. Garro's terse public response to this accusation put the blame for the tragedy on other intellectuals, those who had come out in support of the students, and essentially exculpated herself.

Public outrage greeted her denial and opened a rift between Garro, who had been divorced from Paz since the early 1960s, and Mexican intellectuals that would endure for many years, causing her to seek exile and influencing critical response to her work. Despite the fact that Garro was deprived of her passport following her release, she left Mexico for the US, and resided in New York for several years before going, first, to Spain for several years, where she obtained a Spanish passport, and then to Paris. Garro experienced great personal suffering at this period: "So many atrocious things were said about me that I have felt as if I had been marked with a branding iron . . . I was ashamed to call myself Elena Garro . . . I was embarrassed to say my name" (Muncy 1990: 32). Garro's decision to live abroad and the resultant emotional and financial privation fostered themes of exile, isolation, failure of communication, and desperation in her work.

Garro visited Mexico in 1991 to attend a conference programmed around her plays and to be honored in cities around Mexico for her work. Garro's exile ended permanently in 1993 when she returned to Mexico to live. Eventually debilitated by lung cancer and supported medically by the Mexican Consejo Nacional para la Cultura y las Artes, Garro died in Cuernavaca on 22 August 1998.

Playwright and Novelist

Garro was first recognized as a writer in 1957 for her plays *Andarse por las ramas* (Beating around the Bush), *Los pilares de doña Blanca* (The Pillars of Doña Blanca), and *Un hogar sólido* (A Solid Hearth). These one-act, single-scene pieces depend for their irony on a playful subversion of language and convention, and they treat themes of feminism, romantic love, traditional values, and domestic life. They were staged under the auspices of the "Poesía en Voz Alta" ("Poetry Read Aloud") program of the Universidad Nacional Autónoma de México (UNAM) in that year. It is said that these theatrical pieces are products of Garro's singular genius, written quickly, and released in the first draft. *Andarse por las ramas* depends for its irony on a male stock character, conventional in all respects, dressed (as are many of Garro's male characters) all in black, and faced with a bizarre, rebellious household. *Los pilares de doña Blanca* also treats romantic conventions. It closes with a *Caballero* (Gentleman) retrieving a souvenir representing the deceased *doña* Blanca and tucking it away, like a love relic, near his heart. In *Un hogar sólido*, Garro parodies manners and domestic problems that survive death. The title is ironic in that the Mexican capital has not offered the play's dead family members a "good" place to live, yet their "home" (*hogar*) is "solid" in the sense that a crypt is a concrete form—even though the characters are not.

Garro's most highly praised work is the novel *Los recuerdos del porvenir*, written in Berne, Switzerland, supposedly during a period when Garro was recuperating from a serious illness in the early 1950s. It was not published until 1963 in Mexico, where she was working at the time as a journalist. *Los recuerdos del porvenir* is a singular novel in its approach to space and time. Its focus is a southern Mexican *pueblo* (small community) that retains its pre-Columbian name—Ixtepec—and that has a mixed Colonial and pre-Columbian world view. Garro's themes are the universals of struggle, moral compromise, resignation, suffering, and resistance, but the time of the novel is specific: the period of the Cristero rebellion, 1926–29. Garro mingles past and present time and juxtaposes images of stark violence and raw political power against those of custom, love, and community, creating a world of ambiguities and contradictions.

Isabel Moncada and Julia, Garro's principal women characters in *Los recuerdos del porvenir*, represent starkly opposed codes of morality and justice within the hermetic environment of the novel, yet Isabel and Julia coincide ironically and significantly as women who fight for autonomy, identity, and freedom in dehumanizing circumstances. Much critical discussion of *Los recuerdos del porvenir* has centered on these juxtaposed female characters, examining the ways that other characters respond to their actions, and, particularly, probing the ambiguities of Isabel's character. Critics have viewed Julia and Isabel as re-creations of the Mexican mother-whore, La Malinche. The parallels between Julia and Isabel (who both consort with Rosas, Ixtepec's military strongman) and La Malinche, who became the mistress of Cortez, are obvious, but Garro's meaning is more subtle than such superficial conventions.

Critics have connected this theme in Garro's novel with the essay by Octavio Paz, "Los hijos de la Malinche" (Sons of Malinche) from *El laberinto de la soledad* (1959, Labyrinth of Solitude), in which Paz locates the weakness of the Mexican nation in the Indian woman who is "open" and capable of "treason," and in which he asserts that the nation's strength lies in the stalwart, indigenous male. Garro's treatment of the woman who takes up with the oppressor offers a different reading from the "La Malinche" tradition promulgated by Paz, but the townspeople of Ixtepec, including Isabel's family, read the signs in the standard way, failing to notice who the traitors are and who contests their power. *Los recuerdos de porvenir* assured Garro's enduring critical reputation as a major Mexican writer and made her a favorite of Mexican intellectuals for a time.

It should be noted that *Los recuerdos del porvenir* and other of Garro's works have frequently been observed to possess "surreal" elements. Garro's treatment of characters and fictional space in *Los recuerdos del porvenir*, indeed, has the effect of making the ordinary appear fantastic and ephemeral. When questioned about this quality of her fiction, however, Garro objected vehemently, especially against the view that her work embodied so-called "magic realism," and she denied that her writing reflected anything other than a reality that she or others had experienced; moreover, she asserted that "magic realism" did not exist and placed her entire body of work "con ironía y gracia" (with irony and humor) in the category of "realism" (Prado 2002: 35).

Later Fiction, Film, and Theater

Garro's first collection of short fiction, *La semana de colores* (The Week of Colors), largely biographical, was published in 1964 with eleven stories in which the protagonists are sisters Lelinca (Leli) and Eva. During the period of her exile, Garro recreates the sisters as adults in a second collection, *Andamos huyendo Lola* (1980, We Go Around Fleeing Lola), which contains stories that may have been written decades before they were published together. *Andamos huyendo Lola*, dealing ironically with the futility of the struggle for truth and justice, is darker in outlook than *La semana de colores*. The 1970s, which intervened between the publications of these related short-story collections, included a difficult exile in Spain, followed by a highly productive period of fiction writing, with the second short-story collection and three novels released in the 1980s.

In addition to her fiction, Garro wrote screenplays, teleplays, and stage plays. Muncy (1990) records that Garro wrote "many" screen plays in the 1950s that were never produced. Garro's screenwriting credits include *Solo de noche vienes* (You Only Come at Night) and *Las señoritas Vivanco* (The Vivanco Girls). Garro's stage work includes her early one-acts (mentioned above), along with *El Rey Mago* (The Wise Man), *Ventura Allende* (the name of the main character), *El encanto* (The Spell), *Los perros* (The Dogs), *La dama boba* (The Foolish Lady), *La señora en su balcón* (The Lady on her Balcony), *Felipe Ángeles*, *La verdad sospechosa* (The Suspected Truth), and *El coloquio de los perros* (The Colloquy of the Dogs). Only *Un hogar sólido*, *Los perros*, and *La señora en su balcón* have been translated into English (1958).

Garro's last novel, *Mi hermanita Magdalena* (My Little Sister Magdalena), remained unpublished during her lifetime, but makes a fitting epitaph for Garro's life and work, characteristic of her previous fiction in important ways—the innocent are misled and oppressed by the cruel and unscrupulous—yet the darkness of earlier work is lifted in this novel with a victory for the decent and doughty female protagonists. *Mi hermanita Magdalena* is an ironic view of Garro's coming-of-age experience in which three sisters—Rosa, Estefanía, and Magdalena, the youngest—play out Garro's early struggle for freedom, clarity, and identity. The Mexico City of *Mi hermanita Magdalena* is the clean and fragrant city of the 1930s where three young girls live under the rule of their puritanical and conventional maternal aunts. Magdalena, at 17, marries against the wishes of her family and also contests her strong-willed mother-in-law, but she soon regrets having left the university to marry and recognizes that the marriage has been a mistake. When she disappears, Rosa and Estefanía search for her using English detective novels, Fyodor Dostoevsky's *Crime and Punishment*, and US film as their models for investigation. Estefanía eventually travels to Europe to rescue Magdalena, and the search ends triumphantly.

Political Themes

In addition to the thematic constants already mentioned, Garro's activism toward Mexican domestic policy dealing with agrarian reform and social justice was formative in her life and fiction. Her first works, the novel *Los recuerdos del porvenir*, and the three-act play *Felipe Ángeles*, written in 1954 (Muncy 1990: 24), take the Revolution as their setting and reinvent those whom history has forgotten. Her 1991 novel, *Y Matarazo no llamó . . .* (Matarazo Didn't Call) was begun in 1957 as a short story and re-edited through several versions that fictionalized the brutal reality of Mexican politics. A dramatic work written in 1969, *Sócrates y los gatos* (Socrates and the Cats), published in 2003 (after Garro's death) treats the 1968 events at Tlatelolco (Toruño 2004: 95–6, 107–8).

Garro experienced Spanish fascism when she accompanied Paz and other Mexican members of the Liga de Escritores y Artistas Revolucionarios (the League of Revolutionary Writers and Artists) to Valencia, Spain, for a stay of several months in 1937 in order to participate in the II Congreso Internacional del Escritores para la Defensa de la Cultura (Second International Congress of Writers and Artists for the Defense of Culture), an anti-fascist group. *Casa junto al río* (The House Beside the

River) takes the house of Garro's grandparents in Cangas de Onís for its title, and in *Memorias de España 1937* (Memories of Spain 1937), Garro records a spirited memoir of her experience, with frank impressions of Spanish and Latin American intellectuals.

Critical Reception

In the 1960s, comparatively early in Garro's career, Carlos González Peña mentioned her work in his history of Mexican literature, emphasizing the poetic quality of her fiction and the originality of her stage plays. He praised *La semana de colores* as rich in poetic quality and "not inferior to her novel [*Los recuerdos del porvenir*]" (454). Octavio Paz described the novel as "una obra de verdad extraordinaria, una de la[s] [*sic*] creaciones más perfectas de la literatura hispanoamericana contemporánea" [a work of extraordinary truth, one of the most polished creations of contemporary Spanish American Literature] (Stoll 1990: 11). A recent critic has described her work in its portrayal of Mexican culture most aptly as "cinematográfica" (cinematic), an apt assessment for the work of a writer who might well have thought in terms of staging, movement, and film as she framed her fictions.

Garro's Mexican honors included the Premio Villaurrutia (1964) for *Los recuerdos de porvenir*; the Premio Juan Grijalbo (1980) for *Testimonios sobre Mariana* (Testimony about Mariana), which caused a stir in Mexican intellectual circles; and the Premio Sor Juana Inés de la Cruz (1996) for *Busca mi esquela* (Look for My Obituary), a slender volume of two short novels, that of the title and *Primer Amor*. Garro also experienced rejection for her work and was unable at times to have her work published. Both Mortiz and Grijalbo, publishing houses that had repeatedly brought out her work, refused to publish *Mi hermanita Magdalena*, which was published after her death (Castillo 1998).

Garro's principal papers, including manuscripts of creative work, journals, family correspondence, photographs, and other documents are housed at Princeton University (Princeton, New Jersey). Manuel Barbachano Ponce produced *Las dos Elenas* (The Two Elenas. José Luis Ibáñez, dir. 1965), based on Carlos Fuentes' novel of the same title, whose protagonists are meant to be Garro and her daughter. A black-and-white documentary entitled *La cuarta casa, un retrato de Elena Garro* (José Antonio Cordero 2002) offers a brief view of Garro's last years in Mexico and retraces her early years (www.habanafilmfestival.com). In 2006, the Mexican government reopened archives (1962–70) related to Garro and Octavio Paz (Coordinación Nacional de Literatura. July 2006; www.literaturainba.com). The International PEN Foundation has honored Garro with a literary award in her name.

ELIZABETH MOORE WILLINGHAM

Selected Works

Los recuerdos del porvenir. Mexico: Joaquín Mortiz, 1963.
La semana de colores. Xalapa, Mexico: Universidad Veracruzana, 1964.
La señora en su balcón. Teatro mexicano del siglo XX. Vol. V. Antonio Magaña-Esquivel, (ed.) Mexico: Fondo de la Cultura Económica, 1970, pp. 59–71.
Felipe Ángeles. Colección textos de teatro. Mexico: UNAM, 1979.
Andamos huyendo Lola. Mexico: Joaquín Mortiz, 1980.
Testimonios sobre Mariana. Mexico: Joaquín Mortiz, 1981.
Reencuentro de personajes. Mexico: Grijalbo, 1982.
La casa junto al río. Mexico: Grijalbo, 1982.
Un hogar sólido y otras piezas. 2nd edn. Xalapa, Mexico: Universidad Veracruzana, 1983.
Recollections of Things to Come. Trans. R. L. C. Simms. Austin, TX: University of Texas Press, 1986.
Y Matarazo no llamó ... Mexico: Grijalbo, 1991.
Memorias de España 1937. Mexico: Siglo Veintiuno, 1992.
Inés. Mexico: Grijalbo, 1995.
Busca mi esquela; Primer Amor. Mexico: Castillo, 1996.
First Love and Look for My Obituary. Trans. David Unger. Willimantic, CT: Curbstone Press, 1997.
El accidente y otros cuentos inéditos. Mexico: Seix Barral, 1997.
Mi hermanita Magdalena. Edited by Patricia Rosas Lopáategui. Monterrey, Mexico: Castillo, 1998.

Further Reading

Beucker, Verónica. "Encuentro con Elena Garro." In Lucía Melgar and Gabriela Mora (eds), *Elena Garro: Lectura múltiple de una personalidad compleja*. Puebla, Mexico: BUAP and Fomento Editorial 2002, pp. 37–52.
Castillo, Debra A. *Easy Women: Sex and Gender in Modern Mexican Fiction*. Minneapolis, MN: University of Minnesota Press, 1998.
González Peña, Carlos. *History of Mexican Literature*. Trans. G. B. Nance and F. J. Dunstan. Dallas, TX: SMU Press, 1968.
Kaminsky, Amy. "Residual Authority and Gendered Resistance". In Steven M. Bell, Albert H. LeMay, and Leonard Orr (eds), *Critical Theory, Cultural Politics, and Latin American Narrative*. Notre Dame, IN: University of Notre Dame Press, 1993, pp. 103–21.
Melgar-Palacios, Lucía. "Lights and Shadows: Elena Garro's Lasting Legacy". *PLAS Boletín* [Princeton University's "Program in Latin American Studies"] (Fall 1998): 15–16.
Melgar, Lucía and Mora, Gabriela. *Elena Garro: Lectura múltiple de una personalidad compleja*. Puebla, Mexico: BUAP and Fomento Editorial, 2002.
Méndez Rodenas, Adriana. "Tiempo femenino, tiempo ficticio: *Los recuerdos de porvenir* de Elena Garro". *Revista Iberoamericana* 51(132–3) (1985): 843–51.
Muncy, Michèle. "The Author Speaks. ... ". In Anita K. Stoll (ed.), *A Different Reality: Studies on the Work of Elena Garro*. Lewisburg, PA: Bucknell University Press. 1990, pp. 11–37.
Prado, Gloria. "Lazos de familia." In Lucía Melgar and Gabriela Mora (eds), *Elena Garro: Lectura múltiple de una personalidad compleja*. Puebla, Mexico: BUAP and Fomento Editorial. 2002, pp. 23–36.
Princeton University Library, Department of Rare Books and Special Collections. "Elena Garro Papers." http://libweb.princeton.edu/libraries/firestone/rbsc/aids/garro.html#bio (accessed27 November 2006).
Rosas Lopátegui, Patricia. *Yo sólo soy memoria" Biografía visual de Elena Garro*. Monterrey, Mexico: Castillo, 2000.
Stoll, Anita K. *A Different Reality: Studies on the Work of Elena Garro*. Lewisburg, PA: Bucknell University Press, 1990.
Toruño, Rhina. *Cita con la memoria: Elena Garro cuenta su vida a Rhina Toruño*. Buenos Aires: Prueba de Galera Ediciones, 2004.

GLANTZ, MARGO (MARGARITA)

Margo Glantz, born in Mexico City on January 28, 1930, is one of Mexico's most important contemporary essayists, translators, educators and writers. Her parents, Jacobo Glantz and Lucía Shapiro, Ukrainian-Jewish immigrants to México, instilled in her an interest in both the Mexican culture and their own traditional roots and customs. With her family, Glantz learned to enjoy and appreciate fine arts, music, and literature. At the National Autonomous University of Mexico (UNAM) she studied English Literature, Hispanic Literature, Theater and Art History. She received a doctorate degree in Literature from the Sorbonne in Paris. She traveled extensively while in Europe. Her travels and her experiences deeply influenced her autobiography and works.

Professional Career

Her professional career has been notably productive. Glantz was a professor at UNAM from 1958 to 1994. She was chair of the Department of Letters and Philosophy (1968). Upon her retirement, she became an emeritus professor. She also taught at the Escuela Nacional Preparatoria (1958–66), at the University Center for Theatre (1962–65), and at other institutions such as Casa del Lago, and the National Institute for the Fine Arts (INBA). She has been a visiting professor at numerous universities around the world, such as Cambridge, Princeton, Harvard, Yale, Complutense of Madrid and many others in the USA, Perú, Argentina and Chile. Glantz directed the Mexican-Israeli Cultural Institute (1966–70), became General Director of Libraries of the Public Education Agency (SEP) in 1982, Director of Literature in 1986, and Cultural Attaché to the Mexican Embassy in England (1986–88), since 1989 has been a member of the National System of Investigators (III Level), and in 1995 she became a member of the Mexican Academy for Language. She founded and directed the magazine *Punto de Partida* (1966–70), and served as a member and/or editor of literary journals such as *Voices* (1986), *Revista de la Universidad* y *Deslinde* (1989–90), *Poéticas del Nuevo Milenio* (1995), *Travesias de Chile* (1996), *Hispanic Review* (1988), and *Ciberletras* (1999). She has also collaborated with *Unomásuno* (1977–85), and *Siempre* (1962–69), and since 1986 has collaborated with *La Jornada*, *Cuadernos Hispanoamericanos, Revista Iberoamericana, Letras Libres*, *Vuelta, México en Marcha, El gallo ilustrado, Sábado, Thesis, Diálogos*, among others.

Honors and Recognitions

Glantz has received several prizes and recognitions. In 1982, she received the Magda Donato Prize for her autobiographical novel *Geneaologías* (1981), translated into English as *Family Tree* (1991) by Susan Bassnett, and in 1984 she received the Xavier Villaurrutia Prize for *Síndrome de naufragos*; in 2002, she was runner-up for the Herralde Prize for her novel entitled *El rastro* (2002), and in 2003, she won the Sor Juana Inés de la Cruz Prize for the same novel. This novel has been translated into English and is entitled *The Wake* (2005). Glantz won the National University Prize in 1991, and received both a Rockefeller and Guggenheim Scholarship. Glantz received the prestigious Mexican National Prize for the Sciences and the Arts in Linguistics and Literature in 2004, only the fourth woman to receive this award since its endowment fifty years ago.

Nonfiction Work

Travel and the conquest of America comprise two of the major themes of her *oeuvre*. Glantz emphasizes that she inherited a fondness for travel from her parents, who traveled extensively. Her first book, *Viajes en México. Crónicas extranjeras* (1964), is a study and a translation of the chronicles of several French travelers in Mexico during 1821 to 1875. She also examines the reasons why Spaniards became writers in colonial times. She has researched early chronicles and the writings of Bernal Díaz del Castillo, Hernán Cortés, Cristobal Colón, Cabeza de Vaca, Oviedo and Malinche. *La aventura del Conde de Rousset Boulbon* (1973) closes this first important cycle of her writings. She translated and wrote the prologue for two books of Georges Bataille: *Story of the Eye* (*La historia del ojo,* 1979), and *The Impossible* (*Lo imposible,* 1981). Glantz considers Bataille's works as essential reading, particularly on the subject of the body. She has translated the following works into Spanish: *The Spanish Tragedy* (*La tragedia española*) by Thomas Kyd, *Los primeros filósofos* (1959), by Thomson George, *Hacia un teatro actual,* by E.A. Wright (1962), and *Hacia un teatro pobre,* by Jerzy Grotowski (1970). Her essay *No pronunciarás* (1980) exhibits a cosmic preoccupation that includes the religious and the sacred, explores Biblical questions, and the relationship among the name, the writing, the signature and the biography of a person. Glantz has also worked with various plays of Spanish drama. In one of her most important compilations of essays, *De la erótica inclinación de enredarse en cabellos* (1984), she examines fourteen plays where hair represents one of the mayor themes; she also dedicates almost one hundred pages to the works of Calderón de la Barca. Her *Erosiones* (1984) explores personages and topics such as Anaïs Nin, Frieda Kahlo, Coco Chanel, fashion, etc.; *El día de tu boda (Your Wedding Day)* (1982), has something of Barthes and Benjamin and deals with Mexican life in the 1920s and 1930s and the adaptation of European influences to Mexican life; *La lengua en la mano* (1983), and *Borrones y borradores* (2002) compiles essays on Colonial Literature from Bernal Díaz del Castillo to Sor Juana Inés de la Cruz, and on the art of writing. Her most recent work entitled *Walking Dreams* (2006), explores the life and works of the well-known Italian shoe designer, Salvatore Ferragamo.

Although she admires writers such as Nellie Campobello, Elena Garro, and Rosario Castellanos, Margo Glantz refers to herself as "sorjuanista" and has devoted approximately 15 years of her life to the study of this famed Mexican writer. According to critics, Glantz's interpretation of Sor Juana's *oeuvre* is among the finest. When discussing Sor Juana's works and the writings of other contemporary nuns of Sor Juana, Glantz assures us that, contrary to normal feminine activities, feminine writing is "ambiguous and suffers the ups and downs impressed on the nuns by their confessors. It is a suspicious activity carefully observed, that can be intermittent and may even disappear completely". Her major texts on Sor Juana include: *Sor Juana Inés de la Cruz, ¿hagiografía o autobiografía?* (1995), *La destrucción del cuerpo y la edificación del sermón*: *La razón de la fábrica: Un ensayo de aproximación al mundo de Sor Juana* (1995), *Sor Juana Inés de la Cruz: Saberes y placeres* (1996), and *Sor Juana: La comparación y la hipérbole* (2000). These texts have become essential reading for the study of Sor Juana's *oeuvre*.

Glantz has written journal articles on a great variety of topics, many of which have been published in *La Jornada* and *El País Babelia*. Some of her most recent articles published between 2005 and 2006 include: "Gran investigadora: Dolores Bravo," "La celosa de sí misma," "Reivindicar ciencia y cultura," "Catástofes y desaguisados," "Berlín, una extraña fascinación," "Mi amigo Sergio Pitol," and "¿Cómo matar a una mujer?" among others.

Fiction

Glantz also writes fiction – novels and short stories – although she did not begin to write until well into her forties. In many of her works she uses the themes and ideas of well known writers from all over the world such as Foucault, John dos Pasos, Steinbeck, Faulkner, Proust, Stendhal, Dostoyevski, Flaubert, Quevedo, and Calderón de la Barca, just to mention a few. Glantz first published *Las mil y una calorías* in 1978, and then published *Las genealogías* (1981). *Las mil y una calorías* ties topics such as myth with the search of a feminine being left behind the omnipresence of the masculine. Her family autobigraphy *Las genealogías* stands out for the decisive role that memory plays in it. This novel tells the journey from Odessa, USSR, to Mexico City by a Jewish woman in search of her family roots, the forced emigration of her parents, and their settlement in Mexico. Glantz's fiction presents a synthesis of her occupations as an essayist, a journalist, and an educator. Her didactical research may become essays, her essays may become fiction or vice versa. This amalgam of many forms of expression transforms as if in an equilibrium tube and takes on a new life. It should not come as a surprise that intertextuality represents one of her main literary techniques. Her novel *Apariciones* (1996), for example, permutes and transforms her non-fictional studies on Sor Juana Inés de la Cruz and other contemporary nuns. This technique is also illustrated by the recurrence of the main character, Nora García, in *Zona de derrumbe* (2001), *El rastro* (2002), and *Historia de una mujer que caminó por la vida con zapatos de diseñador* (2005). Although Glantz's work and interests have evolved through time, the themes of the body and knowledge constantly emerge in her fiction and in the non-fictional *oeuvre*. Nora's body and soul bind and give sense to a series of different events and texts published over a long period of time (such as is the case of *Zona de derrumbe*). In *El rastro*, Nora García returns to a Mexican town to attend the funeral of her ex-husband, who has died of a heart attack. His dead body incites memories and reminiscences. Throughout this work Nora experiences all sorts of emotions, and therefore the novel, according to the Peruvian critic Julio Ortega, "runs through the life, passion and the death of the heart," blending heart motifs, music, and poetry, that suggest states of mind, emotion and life in the twentieth century. Glantz says that this novel is the fictionalization of one of her essays on Sor Juana Inés de la Cruz's sonnets, the ones that deal with the language of love. *Historia de una mujer que caminó por la vida con zapatos de diseñador*—another version of the previously published *Zona de derrumbe*, rewritten, extended and more unified—has been labeled by the author a "fictitious autobiography". A collection of short stories linked by the adventures of Nora García, it explores the connections between the body and language. Nora's discourse both isolates and joins apparently mundane events that become profoundly important in relation to each other and to the life of the protagonists. Glantz has two other collections of stories: *Síndrome de naufragios* (1984) and *Doscientas ballenas azules* (1979); in the latter Glantz explores her fascination with the natural life of whales, especially with the remaining blue whales left in the world.

SUSANA PEREA-FOX

Selected Works

Tennessee Williams y el teatro norteamericano. México: Universidad Nacional Autónoma de México, 1964.

Viajes en México. Crónicas extranjeras. México: Secretaría de Obras Públicas, 1964.

Onda y escritura en México: jóvenes de 20 a 33. (Prologue) México: Siglo XXI, 1971.

La aventura del Conde de Rousset Boulbon. México: SepSetenta, 1972.

Las mil y una calorías, novela dietética. México: Premiá Editores, 1978.

Doscientas ballenas azules. México: La Máquina de Escribir, 1979.

Intervención y pretexto. Ensayos de literatura comparada e iberoamericana. México: Universidad Nacional Autónoma de México, 1980.

No pronunciarás. México: Premiá Editores, 1980.

Repeticiones: Ensayos sobre literatura mexicana. Xalapa, Veracruz, México: Centro de Investigaciones Lingüístico-Literarias, Instituto de Investigaciones Humanísticas, Universidad Veracruzana, 1980.

Las genealogías. México: Martín Casillas, 1982.

El día de tu boda. México: Secretaría de Educación Pública (SEP)/ Martín Casillas, 1982.

La lengua en la mano. México: Premiá Editores, 1983.

De la erótica (amorosa) inclinación de enredarse en cabellos. México: Ediciones Océano, 1984.

Erosiones. Toluca: Universidad Autónoma del Estado de Toluca, 1984.

Síndrome de naufragios. México: Joaquín Mortiz, 1984.

Alvar Núñez Cabeza de Vaca, Notas y documentos. México: Conaculta, 1992.

Borrones y borradores. Ensayos sobre literatura colonial. México: UNAM/ El Equilibrista, 1992. Re-printed as *La desnudez como naufragio: borrones y borradores.* Madrid: Iberoamericana, 2004.

Esguince de cintura (ensayos sobre narrativa mexicana del siglo XX). México: Consejo Nacional para la Cultura y las Artes, 1994.

La Malinche, sus padres y sus hijos. México: Universidad Nacional Autónoma de México, 1994.

Huérfanos y bandidos. Los bandidos de Río Frío. Toluca: Instituto Mexiquense de Cultura, 1995.

La destrucción del cuerpo y la edificación del sermón: *La razón de la fábrica: Un ensayo de aproximación al mundo de Sor Juana.* México: Colegio de México, 1995.

Obra selecta de Sor Juana Inés de la Cruz (selección y prólogo de Margo Glantz y cronología y bibliografía de María Dolores Bravo Arriaga). Caracas: Biblioteca Ayacucho, 1995.

Sor Juana Inés de la Cruz, ¿hagiografía o autobiografía? México: Grijalbo/Universidad Nacional Autónoma de México, 1995.

Apariciones. México: Alfaguara, 1996.

Del fistol a la linterna: homenaje a José Tomás de Cuéllar y Manuel Payno en el centenario de su muerte, 1994. México: Universidad Nacional Autónoma de México, 1997.

Sor Juana Inés de la Cruz: Saberes y placeres. Toluca: Instituto Mexiquense de Cultura, 1996.

Sor Juana: La comparación y la hipérbole. México: Consejo Nacional de la Cultura y las Artes, 2000.

Zona de derrumbe. Rosario, Argentina: Beatriz Viterbo Editora, 2001.

El rastro. Barcelona: Anagrama, 2002.

Historia de una mujer que caminó por la vida con zapatos de diseñador. Barcelona: Anagrama, 2005.

Walking Dreams: *Salvatore Ferragamo 1898–1960.* México: Museo del Palacio de Bellas Artes, 2006.

References and Further Reading

Academia Mexicana de la Lengua. Margarita (Margo) Glantz Shapiro. http://www.academia.org.mx/Academicos/AcaCurriculos/Glantz/Glantz.htm (28 August 2006).

Biblioteca Virtual Miguel de Cervantes. Margo Glantz. http://www.cervantesvirtual.com/bib_autor/margoglantz/pcuartonivel.jsp?autor=margoglantz&conten=obra (19 August 19, 2006).

Diccionario de Escritores en México. Artes e Historia México. Margo Glatz. http://www.arts-history.mx/feeds/ilce/sitio.php?id_sitio=7851&id_seccion=3426&id_subseccion=5339&id_documento=1329 (26 August 26 2006).

Eidelberg, N. "Glantz, Margo". In Eladio Cortés (ed.), *Dictionary of Mexican Literature.* Westport, CT: Greenwood Press, 1992, pp. 275–6.

García Pinto, Magdalena. "Margo Glantz". In Trudy Balch and Magdalena García Pinto. (eds), *Women Writers of Latin America*. Austin, TX: University of Texas Press, 1991, pp. 105–22.

Huberman, Ariana. "Threading Layers of Memory into Family Trees: Family Collective Memory and Jewish Memory by Two Contemporary Latin American Writers". *Cincinnati Romance Review* 23 (2004): 117–30.

Lindstrom, Maomi. "The Heterogeneous Jewish Wit of Margo Glantz". In Majorie Agosín (ed.), *Memory, Oblivion, and Jewish Culture in Latin America*. Austin, TX: University of Texas Press, 2005, pp. 115–30.

Lorenzano, Sandra. "El viaje de la memoria: Entre recuerdos y ciudades (Sobre las genealogías)". *Lucero: A Journal of Iberian and Latin American Studies* 10 (1999): 12–17.

Maíz-Peña, Magdalena. "Sujeto, género y representación autobiográfica: Las genealogías de Margo Glantz". *Confluencia* 12(3) (1997): 75–87.

Mazoni, Celina (ed.) *Margo Glantz: Narraciones, ensayos y entrevista. Margo Glantz y la crítica*. Valencia: Excultura, 2003.

Ortega, Julio. "Margo Glantz en cuerpo y alma". *Cuadernos Hispanoamericanos* 640 (2003): 79–83.

Perilla, Carmen. "La escritura como arca. Síndrome de naufragios de Margo Glantz". *Revista de Crítica Literaria Latinoamericana* 29(57) (2003): 185–92.

GLICKMAN, NORA

Nora Glickman was born in 1944, in La Pampa, Argentina. She is the descendant of Jewish immigrants who arrived in the country as part of the so-called flood of European immigration that Argentina experienced at the turn of the twentieth century. She studied in Israel, Great Britain, and the United States, where she currently resides and works as a university professor at Queens College in New York. A good portion of her scholarly and creative work focuses on Jewish themes in Latin American literature. A secondary topic recurrent in her work is that of feminine identity and women's issues. As a literary author, she has published both narrative and dramatic works. Her scholarly work includes anthologies, collections of critical essays, numerous articles, and an important historical-cultural monograph on the Jewish white slave trade in South America.

Jewish Issues

Starting with her first work of fiction, *Uno de sus Juanes y otros cuentos* (1983, One of Her Johns and Other Stories), Nora Glickman has shown a preoccupation with writing the Jewish experience in Argentina. This collection of eighteen stories opens with "El último de los colonos" (The Last of the Colonists) and recounts the early Jewish experience in Argentina in the agricultural colonies where the vast majority of Jewish immigrants settled. Most of the stories in this collection do not address this topic, but cover a wide array of themes and take place in both Argentina and the United States. Glickman continued her portrayal of Jewish life in the colonies in her second work of fiction, *Mujeres, memorias, malogros* (1991, Women, Memories, Failures), in which the first grouping of stories returns to the topic of Jewish-Argentine life. One of the most striking of these stories is "Incendio en la chacra" (Fire on the Farm), which tells the story of a devastating fire that threatens both property and life and underscores the trials of the early Jewish immigrants as they tried to eke out a living on the unforgiving pampas. A third collection of stories, *Puerta entre abierta* (2004, Half-Open Door), also contains several stories that may be included as part of her effort to address Jewishness in her work.

After having written mostly prose fiction, Glickman turned her creative efforts to the theater and she has been highly successful as a playwright. Many of her works have been both published and performed in Spanish, English, and other languages in the United States, Latin America, Europe, and Israel. Her first four major plays are published together in the volume *Teatro: Cuatro obras de Nora Glickman* (2000). Two of the plays in the volume focus specifically on Jewish themes: *Una tal Raquel* (A Certain Raquel) and *Liturgias* (Liturgies). A third play, *Dos Charlottes* (2004, Two Charlottes), joins the previous two in forming a corpus of works that are as diverse and they are fascinating in their representation of Jewishness. *Liturgias* focuses on the story of Blanca Dias, a young married woman from New Mexico, who slowly begins to discover her Sephardic roots. The play vacillates between the present and the past, evoking scenes of Jewish persecution at the hands of the Inquisition and intertwining them with the story of the modern-day Blanca Dias as she seeks to embrace her Jewish identity and negotiate family and marital resistance to it. *Dos Charlottes* is a two-act play that recounts the experience of two real women: Charlotte Salomon, a German Jewish painter, and Charlotte Delbo, a French Christian writer. Both shared the similar fate of being sent to Auschwitz, but ultimately their destinies were different. Glickman's play on the lives of these two remarkable women is an eloquent achievement.

Una tal Raquel, the third play in this category, in reality belongs to a much wider scope of investigation carried out by Glickman. It tells the story of Raquel Liberman, the Polish-Jewish immigrant to Argentina who is largely credited with bringing about the downfall of the infamous Zwi Migdal—a Jewish organized crime group that operated a widespread white slavery ring in Argentina at the turn of the twentieth century. Liberman herself was one of the many *polacas*, or young Jewish women who were deceived, exploited and forced into prostitution in the Buenos Aires brothels managed by the Zwi Migdal. Glickman is responsible for bringing her story to light, first in her historical studies on the *trata de blancas* (the Jewish white slave trade) and finally in her play *Una tal Raquel*, published in English as *A Certain Raquel*. Glickman first took up the topic of this rather infamous chapter in Argentine and Jewish history in her monograph *La trata de blancas* (1984), which also included a Spanish translation of the Yiddish dramatist Leib Malach's play *Regeneration*. This study was later greatly expanded and published in English as *The Jewish White Slave Trade and the Untold Story of Raquel Liberman* (2000). While the book contains information on the social phenomenon of the *trata de blancas* as it has been portrayed in Yiddish and Latin American fiction and film, the majority of the book is dedicated to constructing a biography of Raquel Liberman. There is a significant amount of documentary materials incorporated into the content of the volume including a good selection of photos, letters handwritten in Yiddish, personal documents, and newspaper clippings. These items, together with Glickman's narrative piecing together of Liberman's story provides the reader with an intimate glimpse into the life of this woman who overcame remarkable odds. Seemingly not content to have reconstructed Liberman's life in biographical documentary form, Glickman also wrote the play *Una tal Raquel* based on the topic. It has proven to be one of the author's most well-developed works and has enjoyed a great deal of praise from critics and audiences alike. The play functions on memory as Liberman engages in a conversation with her granddaughter who urges her to tell her story. The play then reconstructs her voyage to Argentina from Poland, the tragic death of her husband, the way in which the Zwi Migdal deceived her and forced her into a life of prostitution, and finally her personal victory. Long a taboo topic within the Argentine Jewish community, Glickman manages to effectively portray the story of Raquel Liberman—and by extension, of all the *polacas*—not as one of shame, but rather one of triumph over tragedy and oppression. Glickman's innovative text and staging directions make use of photos, fragments of Liberman's personal letters, music, intertexual references to other works on the subject (namely Leib Malach's play), and a variety of other devices to reconstruct the pivotal moments in Raquel Liberman's life.

Women's Lives

While Jewish issues are a central part of much of Glickman's work, there are other significant components to both her fiction and her theater. Primary among them is the author's portrayal—often a thinly veiled version of her own life—of the challenges women face on a day-to-day basis as they struggle to balance career, family life, relationships, and sundry other responsibilities. Her characters, more often inhabitants of New York than Buenos Aires, find themselves caught up in the hectic pace of urban life, trying to survive between cultures, but finding solidarity and solace in their social relationships with other women. These circumstances are exemplified in the plays *Un día en Nueva York* (1994, A Day in New York) and *Noticias de suburbio* (1993, Suburban News). Glickman's dramatic works have garnered the most attention from critics, though there are several good studies of her prose fiction. Mónica Detrick's edited selection of critical articles on Glickman is the most complete appraisal of her work to date.

DARRELL B. LOCKHART

Selected Works

Uno de sus Juanes. Buenos Aires: Ediciones de la Flor, 1983.
La trata de blancas. Regeneración: drama en cuatro actos de Leib Malaj. Buenos Aires: Pardés, 1984.
Mujeres, memorias, malogros. Buenos Aires: Milá, 1991.
The Jewish White Slave Trade and the Untold Story of Raquel Liberman. New York: Garland, 2000.
Teatro: Cuatro obras de Nora Glickman. Una tal Raquel; Un día en Nueva York; Noticias de suburbio; Liturgias. Buenos Aires: Editorial Nueva Generación, 2000.
Dos Charlottes. In *Dramaturgas en la escena del mundo*. Buenos Aires: Editorial Nueva Generación, 2004, pp. 47–75.
Puerta entre abierta. Buenos Aires: Corregidor, 2004.
A Certain Raquel. In Ellen Schiff and Michael Posnick (eds), *Nine Contemporary Jewish Plays*. Austin, TX: University of Texas Press, 2005, pp. 75–110.

References and Further Reading

Baumgarten, Murray. "Urban Life and Jewish Memory in the Tales of Moacy Scliar and Nora Glickman". In Robert DiAntonio and Nora Glickman (eds), *Tradition and Innovation: Reflections on Latin American Jewish Writing*. New York: SUNY Press, 1993, pp. 61–72.
Bausset-Detrick, Mónica. "Nora Glickman: Diaspora and Identity in Liturgies and Blanca Días". *Yiddish* 12(4) (2001): 98–107.
——. (ed.) *Claves del teatro de Nora Glickman*. Buenos Aires: Editorial Nueva Generación, 2007.
Cordones-Cook, Juanamaría. "*Liturgias*: Máscaras de identidad sefardita". *Latin American Theatre Review* 37(1) (2003): 105–16.
Holte, Matilde Raquel. *Teatro contemporáneo judeoargentino: una perspectiva feminista bíblica*. Buenos Aires: Editorial Milá, 2004.
Schiminovich, Flora. "*Noticias de suburbio*: una visión utópica de relación entre mujeres". In *En un acto: antología de teatro femenino latinoamericano*. Medellín, Colombia. University of Medellín.
Schneider, Judith Morganroth. "Nuevas mestizas: Hibridismo y feminismo en el teatro de Nora Glickman". *Alba de América* 21(39–40) (2002): 181–90.

GÓMEZ DE AVELLANEDA, GERTRUDIS

An Independent Life

Gertrudis Gómez de Avellaneda y Arteaga (1814–73), a poet, novelist, and playwright who defines a unique vector of aesthetic achievement in nineteenth-century Cuban historical and romantic literature, lived according to her own credo of steadfast independence coupled with bouts of romantic abandonment. The author of nineteen plays, nine novels, volumes of letters, poems, articles, and an autobiography, Avellaneda was born on March 23, 1814, in Santa María de Puerto Príncipe (today Camagüey) in central Cuba to a wealthy Creole Cuban mother and a distinguished Spanish soldier. Her father died when Avellaneda was only 8 years old. The fact that her mother remarried just ten months after her father's death may explain Avellaneda's resistance to forming any attachment to her stepfather. She began writing verse at the age of 9 and her early adoration of literature was influenced by her tutor, the Cuban romantic poet and patriot José María Heredia; each wrote works celebrating the flora and fauna of Cuba and the majesty of the United States' Niagara Falls. Avellaneda's developing confidence, intellect, and adventurous spirit led her to pursue literature in Spain starting at age 22 at Instalada la Coruña, then in Seville in 1839 and Cádiz where she wrote for the periodical *La Aureola* directed by Manuel Canete. In

Madrid in the 1840s, Avellaneda was welcomed in the literary circle of José Zorilla, José de Espronceda, and Manuel José Quintana. In his *Recuerdos del tiempo viejo*, Zorilla remarks that he was impressed by her handsomeness and her evocative, "masculine" poetic craft. Her Cuban compatriot José Martí claims, "There is not a woman in Gertrudis Gómez de Avellaneda: everything in her announced a potent and masculine *animus*; she was tall and robust, like her poetry brisk and energetic" (*Luisa Pérez*).

A series of romantic relationships would cause Avellaneda to rediscover her underlying solitude and independence. These qualities appear to directly complement her desire for romantic attachment and her love of symbolic flights of fancy in her own writing, as well as what some critics describe as a "narcissistic" quality in her autobiographical descriptions of her own soul's superiority of feeling. In Cuba, the author was disinherited by her family when she refused an arranged marriage. In Seville she became enamored of the wealthy Ignacio de Cepeda, after which followed a 15-year correspondence. These letters, which both parties agreed were to be kept secret—even destroyed upon receipt—were published by Cepeda's wife after his death; it is due to this betrayal that we know much of Avellaneda's—or "Tula's" thoughts about writing, love, and society.

Avellaneda's mid-1840s relationship with the poet and diplomat Gabriel García Tassara ended when he abandoned her and their newborn daughter María—whom Avellaneda called "Brenilde"—refusing to return even as the child lay dying. After her infant's death, an 1846 marriage to an already-ill politician, Pedro Sabater, left Avellaneda widowed several months later, after which she sought refuge in a convent. The author competed to be inducted into Spain's Real Academia but was not selected, probably due to her female sex and to the fact that she was competing with the President of the Council of Ministries, Luís Sartorius (d. 1871). While Avellaneda was designated an "autora ilustre" (illustrious author), that she was not inducted into the Real Academia counters the expectations for one so talented and seemingly well connected in the Royal Court and in literary circles. In 1855 Tula wed Domingo Verdugo, a politician and coronel who died in 1863. Returning to Cuba where Verdugo was stationed in 1859, Avellaneda was paid homage by the Lyceum in Havana, an event that deeply moved the author. In 1860, she founded and edited the short-lived journal *Album cubano de lo bueno y lo bello*. In 1864, Avellaneda traveled to the United States; she returned to Seville in 1865 and then to Madrid where she died on February 1, 1873, from complications of diabetes. She is buried in Seville.

Nineteenth-Century Contexts and the Literary Canon

According to Alexander Roselló Selimov ("La verdad vence apariencias: hacia la ética de Gertrudis Gómez de Avellaneda a través de su prosa"), Avellaneda's autobiography and letters to Cepeda indicate a firm belief in the nineteenth-century ideal of the "noble soul" of natural virtue, an idea influenced by Jean-Jacques Rousseau's *Social Contract*. This "natural man"—often considered to be the indigenous American—possessed inclinations and passions not restricted by the social mores of the city or by social law. In fact, Avellaneda's letters illustrate her belief in the opposition between natural virtue—the feeling and actions that spring from a pure soul—and social virtue—the adherence to the mere appearance of goodness, often through marriage, motherhood, and religion. It is evident that Avellaneda considered natural virtue far superior to social virtue in a society corrupted by falseness and hypocrisy. The reader must recall that Avellaneda chose her own path of literary romanticism and independent thinking and action during an era in which a woman's virtue was associated almost exclusively with the proper preparation for domestic service; her "education" was to instruct her in the chores of wifehood and motherhood—in that order—coupled with lessons in the catechism so that she could attend church and instruct her children in religious matters. A woman of intellect who wrote poetry was presumed unfit for domestic duties—hence, not virtuous.

These are the preconceptions against which Avellaneda worked throughout her illustrious literary career. Curiously, we note unpredictable variations in the manner in which her success affected others' perceptions of her gender, identity, and their own reactions' social acceptability. It is almost as if the author's intellect and confidence upset every assumption about what a woman could be in the nineteenth century, and surely, Avellaneda redefined the applications of gender to writing. What was "masculine" or "men's" writing was successfully dominated and expanded by a woman who could manage any style of writing in all of the genres; we can see what both José Ortega y Gasset and Terry Eagleton refer to as the historicism of literary genres (Roselló Selimov 1999) in her work's relationship to the literary canon and in the assumption that passionate, independent-spirited, erudite writing in the "high art" mode is the property of men only.

Avellaneda lived in Spain for thirty years, and her incorporation into the literary canon during the reign of Isabel II (1843–68) contrasts with her deliberate marginalization or decanonization during the Spanish "Restoration" of 1874–1931. We can again see the ways in which the formation and valorization of literary genres responds to the cultural needs of specific historical moments in Íñigo Sánchez-Llama's description of the change in reception and categorization of Avellaneda's work over time. In "*Baltasar* (1858) de Gertrudis Gómez de Avellaneda: Análisis de una recepción institucional," Sánchez-Llama explains that during the era of Isabel II, theorists identified the author's writing as "high culture" as defined during an era of "literary eclecticism," historical romanticism in the Schlegelian mode, and neo-Catholicism, which was identified with the literary sublime—all influenced by the ruling Moderate Party (72–73). Concomitant with Avellaneda's popularity, critics attribute to her a "masculine" identity, evidenced in Zorilla's, Martí's, and many others' remarks about Avellaneda. This prestige enjoyed during the court of Isabel II was lost during the "liberal secularization" and the triumph of alternative aesthetic principals after the Revolution of 1868 and the subsequent Restoration, during which time critics attributed to Avellaneda's writing what they deemed a "feminine"—and subsequently, less valuable—quality. Perhaps they focused on her privileging of passion and romantic sentiment in an era that valued reason over religiosity and the sublime. This in turn provided the pretext for the marginalization of her work, which has since been re-evaluated in the twentieth century.

Edith Checa tells how the famed Spanish poet and Avellaneda's contemporary, Carolina Coronado, reflected upon Tula's "masculinization". In an analysis of Avellaneda published in the "Galería de Poetisas" in the Madrid-based periodical *La America* in 1861, Coronado laments "How is it possible, now that a shining star has appeared in our sex's poetry, that they want to take her away from us?" Coronado simultaneously seems to celebrate Tula's duality, and she examines several of Avellaneda's poems that, for Coronado, demonstrate elements of the author's identity as either "poetess" or "poet" (*La Améŕica*, 24 March 1861).

A Highly Honed Historical Romanticism

Not one to be beholden to prescribed social and literary roles, Avellaneda sometimes responded to the straitjacket of gendered responses to her work by using these preconceptions to her benefit. On the one hand, she occasionally used the pseudonym Felipe Escalada to gain advantageous academic posts (Checa, p. 6) and when publishing poems in Spanish periodicals; her reasons may have been as varied as increasing her chances of publication, deferring sexist criticism, or as a buffer when experimenting with voice. More significantly though, during her writing of Isabel II's time, Avellaneda cultivated a middle ground of stylistic romanticism, somewhat in the mode of her tutor Heredia. This is due to the fact that, prior to 1868 in Spain, Gómez de Avellaneda faced the dilemma that "demanded of the writer two options whose end results were mutually exclusive: to fully integrate herself into the feminine model traced by the conventional Carolina Coronado (1823–1911) or to articulate, on the other hand, aesthetic tendencies similar to those of male contemporaries. The Hispano-Cuban author resolved the disjuncture by adopting literary models of the triumphant Peninsular 'historical romanticism'" (Sánchez-Llama 71). Her historical romanticism is evident in her works' lush description and elaboration of religious and historical topics, such as in the play *Hernán Cortés* (1835) and biblical *Baltasar* (1858) and the novel *Guatimozín: ultimo emperador de México* (1846).

Students of Avellaneda's romantic poetry may immediately note their passionate personae—even in the poems of a religious nature—can be traced to the electrifying sensibilities expressed in her autobiographical letters, with her adoration of Cepeda a probable impetus for mercurial romantic rants such as "A Él". Her poems tend to connect the sensitive soul's topography and religious sentiment to the terrain, flora, and fauna of Cuba, leading to frenzied and vibrant poetic landscapes and symbolic voyages in the mid Romantic style. Raúl Ianés signals Mary Louise Pratt's identification (*Imperial Eyes: Travel Writing and Transculturation*) of the "Humboldtian fascination with volcanoes and the forces of volcanic energy" in the poem "El viajero americano," and points to the "narcissistic narrative" (Linda Hutcheon) of her highly self-reflective novels *Guatimozín, ultimo emperador de México* (1846), *Dolores, páginas de una crónica de familia* (1851) and the tale *El artista barquero o Los cuatro cinco de junio* (1861). This quality is considered a prerequisite for the romantic style and as prefiguring the postmodern. Ianés contextualizes Avellaneda's historical novel *Guatimozín* among other nineteenth-century historical fiction using Peter Brooks' assertion (*Reading for Plot: Design and Intention in Narrative*) that the nineteenth-century novelist's anti-technological and anti-industrial attitude is matched by a fascination with forces and engines. In Avellaneda's novels, this can appear as a pastoral nostalgia for the country plantation of the colonial era. After the historiographic, Mexican colonial novel, *Dolores* (1851) adopts a "medieval, Castilian tone," while *El artista barquero* takes place in the Paris of Louis XV.

Sab and *Dos mujeres*

Avellaneda's most important novels for modern readers are most likely her early works *Sab* (1841) and *Dos mujeres* (1842), whose anti-slavery and feminist themes predate the publication of related works such as Harriet Beecher Stowe's *Uncle Tom's Cabin*. Other abolitionist works of the era are *Petrona y Rosalia* by Felíx Manuel Tanco y Bosmoniel (1797–1871), *Francisco* by Anselmo Suárez y Romero (1818–78), the *Autobiografía de un esclavo* by José F. Manzano (1797–1854), the famous *Cecilia Valdés* by Cirilio Villaverde (1812–94), and the French Romanticist Victor Hugo's (1802–85) novel *Bug Jargal*.

Sab was published despite Cuba's turbulent political climate tinged by fear of slave revolt and ingrained in the economic gains of slave labor, which ensured the dominant class's privileges. Analyzing *Sab*, Evelyn Picon Garfield notes that Avellaneda exposes the hegemonic forces of power and sexuality in the nineteenth century (1993: 17). The novel traces the love of the mulatto protagonist Sab for the white hacienda owner's wife, Carlota. The fates of Sab, Carlota, and the servant Teresa are intertwined as the text relates the powerlessness suffered under slavery by females lacking agency under authoritative, traditional mandates about masculinity and femininity. This is especially notable given Avellaneda's privileged perspective as a white woman from a slave-holding family who had experienced both the relative advantages and disadvantages of her own gender, race and class positioning in Cuban society. *Dos mujeres* is also a theoretically pathbreaking text; Susan Kirkpatrick claims that it creates the first womanly subjectivity in nineteenth-century fiction, that of a sexually and intellectually independent Spanish woman.

In *Sab*, Sab and Carlota enjoy a mutual, romantic affinity that remains platonic, probably because of the racial and class boundaries that, though they are socially constructed, prevent Sab's naturally elevated soul from achieving a high social status equal to his spirit's capacity of feeling. Neither he nor Carlota actively seeks consummation of their feelings. At various points in the novel, Sab fails to respond to offers of his freedom, a self-denigration that Roselló Selimov reads as a continuation of his social condition, which both the character and narrator have adopted as metaphors of his passionate/romantic subjugation: Sab cannot have the married Carlota. The slave's superior use of self-restraint—consciously exercised so as not to upset Carlota's social standing—and his depth of feeling together ensure both his and Carlota's social virtue and allow them to explore their natural virtue. At the end of the novel, Carlota realizes her husband's lack of virtue and

Sab's elevated natural virtue, but by this time, Sab has martyred his love to ensure what he supposes will be Carlota's future happiness. The conclusion indicates the triumph of natural virtue over social, or false, virtue (Roselló Selimov 1999: 229).

Like Avellaneda's 1839 *Autobiography* and her letters, *Dos mujeres* openly criticizes the hypocritical constraints that matrimony imposes on women (Miller) and it examines the conflicting interests and concepts of morality in the would-be love triangle formed by characters Carlos, his traditionally educated wife, Luisa, and the naturally virtuous Countess Catalina. *Dos mujeres* sets the pure and affectionate relationship between Carlos and Catalina against the hypocritical and stultifying atmospheres of Seville and Madrid, where self-interest and arbitrary moralizing reign. Similar to *Sab*'s climax, in *Dos mujeres* the naturally virtuous soul is sacrificed in order to spare the apparently virtuous social construct of marriage, which is then revealed to be built of falsehood; the conclusion annihilates the perceived rivalry between characters Luisa and Catalina.

Roselló Selimov says that the naturally virtuous characters of both *Sab* and *Dos mujeres* function as stand-ins or metaphors for the sentiment that Avellaneda expresses in her autobiography and letters, especially expressing the idea that arbitrary, restrictive social rules nullify the woman's talent and individuality. For him, it is clear that the author conceived of social virtue as built upon appearances, convenience and self-interest and, therefore, counter to nature. It is a shame, as Avellaneda herself wrote, in that each type of woman—she who is trapped in an adherence to tradition and she who is demonized for following her own path—would remain unknown to herself and/or society, "both unhappy, and maybe also, both equally noble and generous" (*Dos mujeres* 210, quoted in Roselló Selimov 1999: 239).

Narrative and Theatrical Production

Both *Sab* and *Dos mujeres* became controversial enough in Cuba that Avellaneda excluded them from her volume of collected works. Her later short story, "El cacique de Turmequé," written in 1860 and published in 1871, combines her tendency toward the historiographic, the political, and the aesthetic as it reworks the textual and sexual politics of the misogynist seventeenth-century text by Juan Rodríguez Freire, *El carnero o conquista y descubrimiento del Nuevo Reino de Granada,* a text that was only first published in Bogotá in 1859 (Picon Garfield 1993: 99).

The commercially successful theatrical works of Avellaneda are numerous, including *Hernán Cortés* (1835), *El príncipe de Viana* (1844), *Egilona* (written in 1844 and presented in 1846), *Oráculos de Talía o las Duendes en palacio* (1855), *Baltasar* (1858)—a hybrid work of romantic and tragic force considered by many her best dramatic work—and *Catilina* (1867). These political works destabilize power hierarchies and often revise Spanish history. *El príncipe de Viana*, for example, inverts the roles of masculine and feminine in order to explore the motivations of the weak or "feminized" Spanish king and the conversely strong, "masculinized" queen in the fifteenth century (Picon Garfield 1993: 85). This subversive feminist and anti-hegemonic undercurrent has led Avellaneda to be compared with her contemporary, the Spanish poet Carolina Coronado.

A Life in Letters

A series of dialectic tensions underlies Avellaneda's life and works; her texts are marked by a powerful drive to reveal problematic social, political and sexual/romantic dynamics, constrained at times by a reticence to fully condemn the societies—Spanish and Cuban—in which she herself risked retribution if she were to anger the centers of power that could injure her literary career and reputation: "masculine" bourgeois literary society, the Catholic Church, the Spanish Royal Court, and by extension the economic system of exploitation in Cuba. Further, Gómez de Avellaneda's own life is fraught with ambivalence owing in part to her passionate nature that grew to mistrust both conservative social codes and the promises of "inferior" souls who could not return her depth of feeling. Throughout, Avellaneda managed to navigate the polar opposites that defined her era's social and political organization as her poetic force and intellect contradicted the imposed social subjectedness of women that she was forced to endure. The results in both her autobiographical statements and her texts are powerful and uncompromising self-reflection and critical commentary about the Spanish and Cuban societies whose national identities continue to be influenced by her prolific talent.

JULI A. KROLL

Selected Works

El gigante de las cien cabezas (1822), short story.
Hernán Cortés (1835), drama.
Memorias (1838, published in 1929), memoirs.
Autobiografía (1839, published in 1928), autobiography.
Leoncia (1840, published in 1914), drama.
Sab (1841) novel.
Poesías líricas (1841), lyric poems.
Dos mujeres (1842), novel.
Espatolino (1844) novel.
Alfonso Munio (1844) drama.
El Príncipe de Viana (1844) drama.
Egilona (1845) drama.
Saúl (1845, published in 1849) drama.
Una anécdota de la vida de Cortés (1845, pub. in 1869) legend.
Guatimozín (1846) novel.
Hortensia (1851) drama.
Dolores (1851) novel
Errores del corazón (1852) dramatic comedy.
La aventurera (1854) drama.
La sonámbula (1854) drama.
Baltasar (1856 pub. 1858) drama.
Catilina (1856 pub. 1857) drama.
El cacique de Turmequé (1860 pub. 1869) Colombian legend.
La mujer (1860) articles.
Devocionario nuevo y completísimo en prosa y verso (1867) devotionary.
El artista barquero o Los cuatro cinco de junio (1861) novel.

References and Further Reading

Checa, Edith. "Gertrudis Gómez de Avellaneda en la prensa española del siglo XX." http://www.ucm.es/info/especulo/numero19/avellane.html (accessed 13 July 2006).

Coronado, Carolina. "Galería de poetisas contemporáneas". *La América* 24 March–8 April 1861.

Ianés, Raúl. "Metaficción y 'elaboraciones al vapor': la novela histórica de Gertrudis Gómez de Avellaneda". *Letras Peninsulares* 10: 2 (1997 Fall): 249–62.

Kirkpatrick, Susan. *Las Románticas: Women Writers and Subjectivity in Spain, 1835–1850*. Los Angeles, CA: University of California Press, 1989.

Martí, José. "Luisa Pérez". http://www.damisela.com/literatura/pais/cuba/autores/marti/proceres/zambana.htm (13 July 2006). Orig. published in José Martí, *Obras de Martí*. Edición de Gonzalo de Quesada, vol. 13, Crítica y libros, 96–9.

Miller, Beth. "Gertrude the Great: Avellaneda, Nineteenth-Century Feminist". In Beth Miller (ed.), *Women in Hispanic Literature: Icons and Fallen Idols*. Los Angeles, CA: University of California Press, 1983, pp. 201–14.

Picon Garfield, Evelyn. *Poder y Sexualidad: El discurso de Gertrudis Gómez de Avellaneda*. Atlanta, GA: Rodopi, 1993.

Roselló Selimov, Alexander. "La verdad vence apariencias: hacia la ética de Gertrudis Gómez de Avellaneda a través de su prosa". *Hispanic Review* 67 (1999): 215–41.

Sánchez-Llama, Íñigo. "*Baltasar* (1858), de Gertrudis Gómez de Avellaneda (1814–73): Análisis de una recepción institucional". *Hispanófila* 133 (Sept. 2001): 69–94.

Simón Palmer, María del Carmen. "'*Lego a la tierra, de que fue formado, este mi cuerpo mortal* . . .': Últimas voluntades de Gertrudis Gómez de Avellaneda". *Revista de Literatura* (Madrid) LXIII(124)(2001): 525–70.

Ward, Thomas. "Nature and Civilization in *Sab* and the Nineteenth-Century Novel in Latin America". *Hispanofila* 126 (1999 May): 25–40.

GORODISCHER, ANGÉLICA

Born Angélica Beatriz Arcal in 1928 in Buenos Aires (Argentina) to Fernando Felix Arcal, a businessman, and María Angélica Junquet de Arcal, Angélica was exposed to fiction at an early age. Her mother, the poet Angélica de Arcal (1905–75), engaged Angélica in composing oral stories. In 1936, Gorodischer's family moved to Rosario (Santa Fe, Argentina) where she was raised and has lived ever since then. Gorodischer, a voracious reader, was first tutored at home. She completed her elementary and high school in the Escuela Normal number 2, a prestigious public institution. Gorodischer also studied Literature at the National University of the Litoral for several years, but she did not complete her studies.

Angélica married architect Sujer Gorodischer, and together they had a daughter and two sons. At the age of 30, Gorodischer began writing professionally. Her first short story "En verano, a la siesta y con Martina" (In Summer during Naptime with Martina) was printed in 1964. The following year, a collection of realist short stories, *Cuentos con soldados* was published. Gorodischer is recognized as one of the most important science fiction writers of Latin America. Often compared with Borges for her use of fantastic elements in her narrative, Gorodischer is a prolific author and a staunch feminist. In the 1990s, she chaired and organized colloquiums and symposia about Latin America's women writers. She has also written essays: *Escritoras y escritura* (1992, Women Writers and Writing), edited anthologies like *Mujeres de palabra* (1994, Women of Words) and compiled collections of feminist short stories by Latin America writers such as: *Esas malditas mujeres* (1998, Those Evil Women) and by Argentine authors: *Locas por la cocina* (1998, Crazy for the Kitchen). She has lectured extensively both in Latin America and abroad.

In recognition for her work, she has received several awards, among them the Award of the Order (1984), Emecé Award (1984–85), the Gilgamesh Prize (Spain), in 1986 and 1991; the Konex Platinum, in 1994, in 2000, the Esteban Echeverria award, granted by Gente de Letras in Buenos Aires, Argentina, among others. She has twice won the Fullbright Fellowships and has taken part in the Writers residence Program in Iowa City in 1987. Her works have been translated into German, English, French, and Italian.

Science Fiction

With the publication in 1967 of *Opus 2*, a novel, Gorodischer switched from realism to science fiction, a genre in which she would become widely known. Two books inspired her in this transition: Arthur Clarke's *Childhood's End* (1953) and Isaac Asimov's *The End of Eternity* (1955). Another collection of science fiction short stories, *Bajo las jubeas en flor* (1973, Under the Yubayas in Flower), marked her consecration as a professional writer. From this collection, critics have chosen the short story "Los embriones del violeta" (The Embryos of the Violet) as one of the best Argentine science fiction short stories. In this short story, Gorodischer employs science fiction to write about the discovery of new worlds alternating time and space. The short story opens with the rescue of a crew lost in the planet Salari II where women do not exist as they have been replaced by transvestites. Thus, all characters are men who have the ability to wish for anything when they stand in the violet dots of Salari II, but choose not to wish for women. This short story also calls the readers' attention to issues of sexism and engages the reader in identifying prejudices about homosexuality. While most of the rescuers object to the way of living of the lost crew and have their memories erased, the narrator of this short story, Leo Sessler does not condemn the adaptation of the survivor, and is thus able to write what he witnessed in Salari II. "Bajo las jubeas en flor" has also been acclaimed because of its totalizing effect, and the dialogue it establishes through the deployment of parable with the narrative of the best-known Argentine storyteller, Jorge Luis Borges (1899–1986).

In *Trafalgar* (1979), a collection of short stories unified by the presence of an Argentine businessman, Trafalgar Medrano, Gorodischer uses parody to subvert the traditional perspective of the male hero by presenting strong female characters and the point of view of the female narrator. Written as an epic story, *Trafalgar* gathers the accounts of this explorer of other worlds, using the Spanish dialect of the River Plate region. Moreover, Gorodischer who had cultivated soft or a socially preoccupied science fiction up to that moment, adopts the tenets of scientific or hard science fiction when she describes the shuttles that were used by Trafalgar during his intergalactic voyages.

With the publication of *Kalpa Imperial* in 1983, Gorodischer delves deeper into philosophical matters and fantasy. The short stories that composed this collection are narrated by different storytellers, and center on the ways men and women use power. Continuing her examination of gender roles and relations, Gorodischer portrays female characters, who have access to power, but are not necessarily better than men. As in *Trafalgar*, in *Kalpa Imperial* science fiction allows Gorodischer to separate herself from the more immediate political events taking place in Argentina during the military dictatorship of 1976–83, when both these collections were written. With *Las repúblicas* (1991), a collection of five short stories, Gorodischer returns to the combination of fantastic elements with science fiction that were features of her earliest works.

As a writer of multiple science fiction narratives, Gorodischer has explicitly rejected the tenets of hard science fiction with its emphasis on technology. However, some scholars have noted her use of both variants of science fiction: the soft one that privileges the revaluation of reality, the control of man over machines and an examination of myths, and the technological one.

Feminism

The concern about women's rights and roles became noticeable in her collection of short stories *Mala noche y parir hembra* (1983). The title of this collection was taken from Victoria Sau's book and is attributed to General Castaños who, in the nineteenth century spent a sleepless night in Bailén, awaiting the birth of the heir to the Spanish crown only to be informed that a girl had been born. *Mala noche y parir hembra* gathers short stories in which women are the protagonists of the events narrated. From this collection, scholars have paid special attention to "La perfecta casada" (The Perfect Married Woman). Gorodischer borrows Fray Luis de Leon's title to depict the double life led by a dutiful mother, wife and homemaker who enters into other locations and times just by opening doors. Critics have read the contrast between the unnamed protagonist's actions in other settings and her dull domestic life as a denunciation of women's oppression in a patriarchal society.

The exploration of power and its effects on the genders also appear in her novels, *Floreros de alabastro, alfombras de Bokhara* (1985) and *Jugo de mango* (1988). These novels portray middle-aged, conventional women who undertake the solution of international enigmas foiling the domination plans of pseudo-scientists and terrorists. Their adventures take them from their familiar and comfortable environments to situations in which they face the examination of their long-held beliefs and end up choosing a new way of living their lives according to what they have experienced. Critics have detected in *Jugo de mango* a liberation of the female protagonist not only from patriarchy but also from political corruption. A distinct sign of this liberation is Gorodischer's use of a female language to provide the point of view of the narrators, which includes elements of popular culture (soap operas), allusion to feelings and attention to details. In addition, Gorodischer used humor and irony, particularly in the dialogues as a way to deconstruct the authority and power of the protagonists' opponents.

Experimental Writing

Gorodischer has written fiction using the different literary genres. In *Prodigios* (1994, Prodigies) the novel lacks a plot, but is organized around a house that serves as a solid structure that reacts against the transient lives of the six guests that inhabit it. *Tumba de jaguares* (2005, Jaguars' Tombs) consists of three novelas that are linked by narrators. A different narrator tells each novela, and the three novelas have in common the fact that the main characters have all lost close family members.

Starting with her thriller novel, *Fábula de la virgen y el bombero* (1993, Fable of the Virgin and and the Firefighter), Gorodischer sets her novels *La noche del inocente* (1996, The Night of Innocence) and *Doquier* (2002, Everywhere) in the past. In *Fábula*, using a humorous tone and colloquial language, Gorodischer narrates the lives of characters belonging to different social classes and nationalities during the first decades of twentieth-century Rosario. As a port city, Rosario had tumultuous history when gambling and prostitution made it comparable to Chicago. *La noche del inocente*, a suspense novel based in the Middle Ages, the author uses a different register from Fábula. *Doquier,* another suspense novel, is set on the last months of the eighteenth century in an unspecified location in America. Written from the first person perspective, *Doquier* presents the hidden lives of a respected pharmacist and an accomplished young aristocrat, impersonated by his sister in a reversal of gender roles.

Nonfiction

Gorodischer has penned numerous essays about women's writing. In "Señoras" (Ladies), which appeared in *Escritoras and Escritura*, she makes the distinction between feminine literature and literature written by women. She holds that the former is the one that "denies, rejects and condemns the hero's cult" (p. 45). Moreover, in *Historia de mi madre* (2004, History of My Mother) she traces her mother's life as a way to preserve her memory. By chronicling her mother's accomplishments and shortcomings, the author also provides a look at the constraining gender roles in Argentina during the 1940s and 1950s.

Themes and Influences

Gorodischer possesses a very vivid imagination and this has led her to experiment in many different genres such as science fiction, suspense and fantastic fiction, using both contemporary and historical settings to locate both her short stories and novels.

Gorodischer is internationally known for her science fiction. In this genre, critics have detected the influence of English writers James G. Ballard, Aldous Huxley and American Ray Bradbury, particularly his *Martian Chronicles* (1950), and Italo Calvino in her deployment of speculative hypothesis and the preoccupation for the fantastic.

Among the feminist writers that have influenced her work, Gorodischer acknowledges the inspirations found in Virginia Woolf, Simone de Beauvoir and Victoria Sau.

Common themes in Gorodischer's work are love, death and the ab/use of power. Worth highlighting is the latter as many of her short stories from *Trafalgar, Kalpa Imperial* and *Cómo triunfar en la vida* display the tension between those who have power and those who suffer its effects.

Another concern that often appears in Gorodischer's narrative is the limits of written word to convey a clear and transparent meaning. Gorodischer understands that words, as an artificial sign, can and do trigger misunderstandings.

CAROLINA ROCHA

Selected Works

Cuentos con soldados. Santa Fe, Argentina: Premio Club del Orden, 1965.
Opus dos. Buenos Aires: Minotauro, 1967.
Pelucas. Buenos Aires: Sudamericana, 1968.
Bajo las jubeas en flor. Buenos Aires: Ediciones de la Flor, 1973.
Casta luna electrónica. Buenos Aires: Ediciones Andromeda, 1977.
Trafalgar. Buenos Aires: El Cid Editor, 1979.
Mala noche y parir hembra. Buenos Aires: Ediciones La Campana, 1983.
Kalpa Imperial. Buenos Aires: Minotauro, 1983/4.
Floreros de alabastro, alfombras de Bokhara. Buenos Aires: Emecé Editores, 1985.
Vases of Alabaster, Carpets from Bokhara. Lyndhurst, NJ: Lectorum Publications, 1985.
Jugo de mango. Buenos Aires: Emecé Editores, 1988.
Las Repúblicas. Buenos Aires: Ediciones de la Flor, 1991.
Fábula de la virgen y el bombero. Buenos Aires: Ediciones de la Flor, 1993.
Prodigios. Barcelona: Editorial Lumen, 1994.
Técnicas de supervivencia. Rosario; Editorial Municipal, 1994.
La noche del inocente. Buenos Aires: Emece, 1996.
Cómo triunfar en la vida. Buenos Aires: Emecé Editores, 1998.
Menta. Buenos Aires: Emecé Editores, 2000.
Doquier. Buenos Aires: Emecé Editores, 2002.
Kalpa Imperial: The Greatest Empire that Never Was. Trans. Ursula K. Le Guin. Northampton, MA: Small Beer Press, 2003.
Historia de mi madre. Buenos Aires: Emecé Editores, 2004.
Cien islas. Rosario: Fundación Ross, 2004.
Tumba de jaguares. Buenos Aires: Emecé Editores, 2005.

References and Further Reading

Cano, Luis. "Angélica Gorodischer y Jorge Luis Borges: la ciencia ficción como parodia del canon". 87(30) *Hispania* (2004): 453–63.
Dellepiane, Angela B. "Contar=mester de fantasía o la narrativa de Angélica Gorodischer." *Revista Iberoamericana* 51 (1985): 627–40.
Gimbernat de González, E. and Echeverría, M. Balboa. *Boca de dama: la narrativa de Angélica Gorodischer*. Buenos Aires: Feminaria, 1995.
Godsland, Shelley. "Enajenadas, endiabladas, envidiosas: La mujer delicuente en los cuentos de Angélica Gorodischer". *Alba de América* (41) (2003): 263–75.
Urraca, Beatriz. "Angélica Gorodischer's Voyages of Discovery: Sexuality and Historical Allegory in Science-Fiction's Cross-Cultural Encounters". *Latin American Literary Review* 23 (1995): 85–102.

GORRITI, JUANA MANUELA

Juana Manuela Gorriti (1818–92) is one of the most famous Latin American women writers of the nineteenth century. She was born in Horcones, Salta, in Argentina, into an upper-class family of Spanish descent that played an important role in the Independence of Argentina. She started her formal education in a convent, but she could not bear the discipline and returned to her family very soon after. Gorriti did not have any additional formal education, but she was an avid and curious reader. She took advantage of the family library as well as of the stories told by the servants in the Gorriti household. As a result, she became a woman with an unusually high level of education for her time, even if it was heterogeneous and not systematic. During the political conflicts that emerged after Argentina's independence, the Federalist Facundo Quiroga defeated her father, General José Ignacio Gorriti. In 1831, the entire Gorriti family had to flee the country. They settled in Tarija in Bolivia where Juana Manuela met a young army officer named Manuel Belzú, whom she married at an early age (according to some accounts at 14). They had two daughters, Edelmira and Mercedes, but they had a tumultuous marriage and separated several years later. In the meantime, Belzú advanced in positions of power, and became President of Bolivia by means of a military coup in 1848. When he came to power he reclaimed their daughters, who were at the time living with their mother in Lima, Peru. Gorriti refused to be reconciled with him, but moved temporarily to Bolivia to be near her daughters. Later she moved back to Lima where she founded a school for boys and girls—co-education being a very unusual practice in the nineteenth century—and a school for "young ladies". She also began writing and in 1845 published her first short story, "La quena". From this point on, Gorriti's literary activity never stopped. In her home she hosted the *Veladas literarias*, social gatherings that included many Peruvian intellectuals of her time, such as Clorinda Matto de Turner and Ricardo Palma. She continued to write, edited several magazines and founded more schools. Refusing to accept help from her estranged husband, Gorriti supported on her own her two daughters and two other children she had out of wedlock, Clorinda and Julio. Gorriti was an untiring traveler, and in her trips she returned to Argentina several times—especially after she was granted a pension—finally moving permanently to Buenos Aires for the last ten years of her life. In Argentina, as in Peru, she published fiction and magazines and opened her well-known *Veladas literarias*. But in spite of the requirement to stay in the country (as a stipulation of her pension), she requested several permits to return to Peru. Juana Manuela Gorriti died in Buenos Aires at the age of 75.

Gorriti's life was novelesque, and, as such it has inspired some recent fictional biographies, especially the best-seller *Juanamanuela muchamujer*, by Martha Mercader (1980). She was in many instances a woman ahead of her time and a respected intellectual in spite of her unconventional behavior. She raised her illegitimate children and spoke openly about them, although she always refused to reveal the identity of their fathers; she traveled extensively, in some cases dressed as a man; and legend has it that she had what in nineteenth-century Latin America were considered strange customs in an upper-class woman, such as sitting on top of cushions on the floor, in her famous *veladas*. But, as Liliana Zuccotti notes, she managed to be diplomatic and avoided ostracism. Upper-class families would send their daughters to her schools and her works were published in spite of her unconventional lifestyle.

Works

Most of her early literary works, scattered in magazines, were compiled in two collections, *Sueños y realidades* (1865) and *Panoramas de la vida* (1876), and later in *Misceláneas* (1878). These are miscellaneous works of fiction, memoirs, essays and biographies. She also published a biography of General

Dionisio de Puch, whom she met in her childhood, in 1868, the novel *Oasis en la vida* (1888), several books of memoirs, and a cookbook, *Cocina ecléctica* (1890). Memory is very important, not only in her memoirs, but also in her narrative, which includes old Inca legends, and historical fictions, most of them set at the time of the Independence and subsequent civil war that ended with Rosas' brutal dictatorship. Her work is numerous and varied. What follows is a brief description of some of the works most mentioned by critics.

"La quena", her first story, already shows many of the staples of Gorriti's fiction. The mestizo illegitimate son of an Inca princess and a noble Spaniard tells the woman he loves the sad story of his childhood including the mention of a secret treasure the Incas have kept underground (a theme that will be repeated in "El tesoro de los Incas"). The woman is also loved by a nobleman who pays a black slave who had been separated from her own children in Africa to make her mistress believe her loved one has died and the Inca heir that she has been unfaithful. Later on, and after the woman has married her second suitor, the lovers discover the truth and they finally end up living together, only to be found by the treacherous husband who stabs his estranged wife to death. The Inca prince goes mad and, with a "quena," a musical instrument, constantly serenades the decomposing body of the woman he loved. In this story we find a story within a story, gothic and eerie elements, the use of indigenous legends, the representation of different races and nationalities, and the violence of men against women as well as two cases of forced separation of children from their mothers. All of these elements intertwined in a story that covers two generations, and that takes place in Spain, Lima, and the Peruvian Sierra and also mentions the Philippines and Africa. These elements are constant in most of her fictional work all through her life.

Oasis de la vida, a late work, can be interpreted as a commercial for the insurance company that sponsored the publication. In this story, a poor but talented young man in love finds the solution to his problems thanks to the foresight of his father who had set an insurance policy for him. Still much of the story is devoted to represent the varied talents of a group of working women who support themselves with their work. *Cocina ecléctica* is a compilation of cooking recipes edited by Gorriti that includes contributions from many of her friends.

Gorriti's fiction belongs to the Romantic literary movement, even though she continued writing for many decades and many of her works were published at a time when realism and naturalism were well established as the predominant writing style. Many of her stories contain fantastic elements, making her the first practitioner of this genre in Argentina, with some incursions into the Gothic (Meehan 1981). What make her work outstanding are the roles of women and her vision of history and society in the complex, tumultuous, and ever-changing situation of South America in the nineteenth century, at odds with the foundational fictions that were written by her more prominent male colleagues (Sommer 1991).

Criticism

As Gorriti was the most prolific and prominent woman writer of her time in Argentina, many critics in the past included her in their literary histories; however, her work is usually dismissed for lacking literary quality, following the path set by Ricardo Rojas when he published the first literary history of Argentina. Her work shows the improvisation that comes with publication in periodicals, but the reasons of her critics had more to do with her romantic style and the subversion in her work of masculine models of fiction and nation. Since the late 1980s a new wave of literary criticism from a predominantly feminist approach has shed some new light on her work.

Her writings are always very connected to her life, and in her fiction she intertwines autobiographical and historical elements (Batticuore 1996). Her stories constantly revolve around the themes of history, exile, travel, and women in unusual situations. Those themes are very directly related to her own experience as an exile, her numerous travels, and the changing circumstances of her life. Change is ever present in her fiction, but her focus is on the individual. Marzena Grzegorcyk points out that what really matters to Gorriti is not the change "per se", but the ways in which women deal with that change.

As in Gorriti's own life, many of her heroines are women who take—or try to take—control over their destiny. One example is *Peregrinaciones de una* [sic] *alma triste* (1875), one of her most studied short novels. In this text, the protagonist has to flee her home and be in constant movement to avoid dying of tuberculosis. In other cases, women are victimized by men, and by men's lust and constant political and military conflicts, in which women very often play the role of mediators (see Lucía Guerra-Cunningham 1987).

In Gorriti, travel and space are related to the female identity, and the search for a defined feminine subject. Grzegorcyk observes that this lack of a defined, stable space expresses the lack of a real space for women as citizens of the new Latin American republics. Gorriti's concept of national identity is different from that of her male counterparts. Contrary to the general preference for European models and isolated national identities, she proposes a vision for a more unified Latin America, as many critics have noted. Her characters have different national origins, her works were published in different countries and she directed magazines with a transnational audience in mind. In one of her articles she asked the Peruvian elite to educate their children in the motherland, instead of sending them to Europe, as was customary. In social terms, she seems to defend the boundaries of race and class, but she shows a very compassionate view of the lower classes, the Indians and the blacks, and the oppressed in general (Salgado 1996).

María T. Ramos-García

Selected Works

Sueños y realidades. Buenos Aires: Imprenta de Mayo, 1865.

Biografía del General Don Dionisio de Puch. Paris: Imprenta Hispano-Americana de Rouge Hermanos, 1868.

Panoramas de la vida. Buenos Aires: Librería e Imprenta de Mayo, 1876.

Misceláneas. Buenos Aires: Imprenta de M. Biedma, 1878.

El mundo de los recuerdos. Buenos Aires: Félix Lajouane, 1886.

Oasis en la vida. Buenos Aires: Félix Lajouane, 1888.

La tierra natal. Buenos Aires: Félix Lajouane, 1889.

Cocina ecléctica. Buenos Aires: Félix Lajouane, 1890.

Perfiles. Buenos Aires: Félix Lajouane, 1892.

Veladas literarias de Lima 1876–1877. Vol. 1. Buenos Aires: Imprenta Europea, 1892.

Lo íntimo. Buenos Aires: Ramón Espasa Ed., 1892.

Obras completas. Salta: Fundación del Banco del Noroeste, 1992–99 (6 vols).

Dreams and Realities: Selected Fictions of Juana Manuela Gorriti. Ed. Francine Masiello, trad. Sergio Weisman. Oxford: Oxford University Press, 2003.

La tierra natal. Buenos Aires: Stock Cero, 2005

Peregrinaciones de una alma triste. Ed. Mary G. Berg. Buenos Aires: Stock Cero, 2006.

El pozo del Yocci. Buenos Aires: Stock Cero, 2006.

References and Further Reading

Batticuore, Graciela. "Itinerarios culturales. Dos modelos de mujer intelectual en la Argentina del siglo XIX". *Revista de crítica literaria latinoamericana* 22 (1996): 163–80.

Berg, Mary G. "Rereading Fiction by 19th-Century Latin American Women Writers: Interpretation and Translation of the Past into the Present". *Translation Perspectives* 6 (1991): 127–33.

——. "Escritoras hispanoamericanas del siglo XIX y su importancia hoy". *Actas del X Congreso de la Asociación de Hispanistas, I–IV.* Barcelona: Promociones y Publicaciones, 1992, pp. 449–58.

Denegri, Francesca. "Desde la Ventana: Women 'Pilgrims' in Nineteenth-Century Latin-American Travel Literature". *Modern Language Review* 92(2) (1997): 348–62.

Fletcher, Lea (ed.) *Mujeres y cultura en la Argentina del siglo XIX*. Buenos Aires: Feminaria, 1994.

Grzegorczyk, Marzena. "Lost Space: Juana Manuela Gorriti's Postcolonial Geography". *Journal of Iberian and Latin American Studies* 8(1) (2002): 55–69.

Guerra-Cunningham, Lucía. "Visión marginal de la historia en la narrativa de Juana Manuela Gorriti". *Ideologies and Literatures* 2(2) (1987): 59–76.

Iglesia, Cristina (comp.) *El ajuar de la patria. Ensayos críticos sobre Juana Manuela Gorriti*. Buenos Aires: Feminaria, 1993.

Meehan, Thomas C. "Una olvidada precursora de la literatura fantástica argentina: Juana Manuela Gorriti". *Chasqui* 10 (1981): 3–19.

Mercader, Martha. *Juanamanuela muchamujer*. Buenos Aires: Sudamericana, 1980.

Pratt, Mary Louise. "Las mujeres y el imaginario nacional en el siglo XIX". *Revista de crítica literaria latinoamericana* 19(38) (1993): 51–62.

Rojas, Ricardo. *Historia de la literatura argentina*. Buenos Aires: La Facultad, 1925.

Salgado, María A. "Juana M. Gorriti: una escritora decimonónica ante el discurso de la enfermedad". *Hispanic Journal* 17(1) (1996): 56–67.

Sommer, Doris. *Foundational Fictions. The National Romances of Latin America*. Berkeley, CA: University of California Press, 1991.

Vergara, Magda Teresa. "In Defense of Motherhood: J.M. Gorriti's Ambivalent Portrayal of a Slave Woman in *La quena*". *Romance Notes* 36(3) (1996): 277–82.

Zuccotti, Liliana. "Gorriti, Manso: de las Veladas literarias a 'Las conferencias de maestra'". In *Mujeres y cultura*, ?, pp. 96–107.

GRAMCKO, IDA

For a child born in a rural backwater, never the recipient of any formal education, Ida Gramcko (1924–94) achieved a remarkable literary, professional, political and educational career. Gramcko spent her childhood in Puerto Cabello in Carabobo state in the central northern part of Venezuela with her family. She received no formal education to speak of and always maintained that all of her knowledge until adulthood was self-taught. Indeed, her only formal instruction came at the age of 38 when she decided to pursue primary education through a government program. She continued assiduously with the independent study, and was awarded a high-school diploma by the government at the age of 40 in 1964. She then entered university and obtained a degree in philosophy in 1968.

Despite the gaps in her education, Gramcko had managed to teach herself to read and write. Indeed, Gramcko maintains that by the age of 3 she told her mother "she had things inside her" and began writing poetry at the age of 8. By the age of 11, she had published poetry in several regional magazines. At the age of 17, she won a special mention in a national women's poetry contest for her collection *Umbral* (Threshold).

In 1939, at the age of 15, she began a career as a freelance journalist with various magazines and newspapers in her native Carabobo State. She also began working on radio programs, specializing in short scenes in verse and sentimental dialogs. In 1943, she started writing for the recently founded national newspaper *El Nacional*, where she continued until 1946. It was here she met her husband, the Spanish journalist José Beavides, and became acquainted with the famous Venezuelan author Rómulo Gallegos, who would later become President of the Republic.

In 1948, Gramcko was named ambassador to Russia by Gallegos and traveled to Moscow, where she stayed for a brief time until the Gallegos government was overthrown. Gramcko took advantage of her stay in Europe, however, to make contact with the literary world and several of her works were translated. During this period she became very interested in philosophy as well, reading the works of Plato, Kierkegaard, Bergson and Nietzsche.

Upon her return to Venezuela, Gramcko received various national awards for her novels, drama, poetry, and essay including Venezuela's highest award, the National Literature Award. Before her death, Gramcko served as dean of the school of letters at the Central University of Venezuela, the Director of the Center for Visual Arts, and Professor of Venezuelan Literature at the Pedagogical University of Caracas, and also coordinated poetry workshops at the Centro de Estudios Rómulo Gallegos.

Work

Gramcko is respected for her work in both poetry and prose in Venezuela, but her contributions in poetry are perhaps the more substantial. The elaborate structure and symbolic imagery evident in Gramcko's early poetry invites comparison to that of the Spanish baroque poets of the seventeenth century. Like the baroque poets, Gramcko wrote during this period in a very strict style, favoring the sonnet. The structure evident in her first three collections was a departure from her contemporaries who were writing in a simpler, more expressive and emotional style. Like the Spanish baroque, Gramcko's poetry avoided the sentimental, seeking inward toward a pure interior and intellectual space. Visual imagery was privileged over subjective experience in these poems.

This early poetry, for its inward-seeking rejection of the sentimental, may then alienate the reader, who finds it hard to connect with the poetic voice. The message and the imagery of the poem may remain ephemeral or abstract, dancing beyond the reach of the reader. Communication is not the main goal of this early work.

Also of interest in Gramcko's early work is her interest in the mythic. We can see this in her re-figuring of traditional fairy tales in the collection *La vara mágica* (The Magic Wand). In the collection, Gramcko takes stories from the collections of Perrault and the brothers Grimm and refigures them in modern settings, deconstructing the mythic tales in terms of lost innocence. It is here that Gramcko's interest in philosophy becomes apparent, as she investigates man's relationship with his (or her) mythic past. Gramcko's drama *María Lionza*, which refers to the nation's indigenous cult, also explores this mythic past, while questioning the patriarchal dictatorship of Pérez Jiménez.

Standing out later as a departure from the mythic and the baroque is the collection *Poemas de una psicótica* (Poems of a Psychotic) of 1964. This work shows a radical willingness to treat the messy world of everyday life, and in particular sexual themes. In this work Gramcko lets her unconscious speak, allowing repressed and hidden desires and emotions flow into the poetry. This work also leaves behind the formal constraints of syllabification and rhyme and moves into experimentation with poetic prose and stream of consciousness. In this, the work of this collection stands in sharp contrast to her other poetry, and paves the way for some of the confrontational work of women writing in Venezuela in the 1970s and 1980s.

Gramcko's later work returns to a more sparse and abstract style that, while still showing a willingness to treat the world of human emotion, does so in minimalist language. Where earlier works experiment with prose poetry and a great deal of text on the page, later collections show a desire to express emotion and thought in as few words as possible.

Criticism

Many critics believe that Gramcko's early poetry was influenced by the works of the baroque poet Luis de Góngora and San Juan de la Cruz, who was also known for elaborate poetry with more attention to impersonal detail. Critics often use the verb "weave" to describe Gramcko's tendency to braid diverse ideas, lines of thought and difficult concepts within one poem, creating a complex intellectual whole.

The literature on Gramcko has also highlighted the tendency in Gramcko's collected work to "ascend" in a spiral toward an abstract ideal of pure beauty that disdains the mundane everyday of human emotion and sentimental thought. This is the same process championed by baroque poets in the image of the nautilus, with each poem representing a chamber in an ascending spiral reaching toward poetic perfection. The desire to move toward this type of perfection has been attributed to a desire to compensate for a reality that was, with its turbulent political and social climate, not in itself controllable or fixed. Her work has been called by some critics a "new Latin American baroque".

The example of *Poemas de una psicótica* represents a different position for both poet and critics of Gramcko's work. It has been called a wholly unique work in the history of Venezuelan poetry, comparable only to the writings of the Uruguayan author, Marosa di Giorgio. Critics point to it as one possible starting point for the exploration of women's sexuality in Venezuelan literature. It has also been called the first "hallucinogenic" work of poetry in Venezuela. As such, it has been seen alternately as threatening or enlightening, the product of a demented or enlightened mind, depending on the gender, generation and politics of the critic.

Elizabeth Gackstetter Nichols

Selected Works

Poetry

Umbral. Caracas: Publicación de la Asociación Cultural Interamericana, 1942.
Cámara de cristal. Caracas: Editorial Suma, 1943.
Contra el desnudo corazón del cielo. Caracas: Garrido, 1944.
La vara mágica. México: Editorial Orbe, 1948.
La baguette magique. Paris: Edit. Jean Paul Vibert, 1950 (later trans. into Spanish).
Poemas (1947–52). México: Editorial Atlante, 1952.
Poesía y teatro. Madrid: Ediciones Aguilar, 1955.
Poemas de una psicótica. Caracas: Editorial Grafos, 1964.
Lo máximo murmura. Maracaibo: Ediciones de LUZ, 1965.
Sol y soledades. Barquisimeto, Venezuela: Nieves, 1966.
Salmos. Caracas: Voluntad, 1968.
Sonetos del origen. Caracas: Vargas, 1972.
Quehaceres, conocimientos, compañías. Caracas: Concejo Municipal del DF, 1973.
Salto Angel. Caracas: Fundarte, 1985.
Treno. Valencia: Ateneo de Valencia, 1993.

Prose

Juan sin miedo. Madrid: Editorial Mediterráneo, 1956.
La dama y el oso. México, Editorial Interamericana, 1959.
El jinete de la brisa. Caracas: Arte, 1967.
Tonta de capirote. Caracas: Biblioteca Popular, 1972.

Theater

La hija de Juan Palomo. México: Editorial Atlante, 1948.
Teatro. Caracas: Ediciones Ministerio de Educación, 1961.
María Lionza. Caracas: Monte Avila, 1976.

References and Further Reading

Castillo, Susana. "La revisión de un mito: María Lionza de Ida Gramcko." In *Las risas de nuestras medusas: Teatro venezolanos escrito por mujeres*. Caracas: Fundarte, 1992.
Liscano, Juan. "Ida Gramcko y Juean Aristigueta". In *Panorama de la Literatura venezolana actual*. Caracas: Alfadil, 1995, pp. 158–9.
Medina, José Ramón. "Ida Gramcko". In *Antología venezolana*. Madrid: Gredos, 1962, pp. 288–9.
Monasterios, Rubén. *Un enfoque crítico del teatro venezolano*. Caracas: Monte Avila, 1998.
Picón Salas, Mariano. "Símbolos de caracol". Prologue to Ida Gramcko, *La andanza yel hallazgo: Antología*. Caracas: Monte Avila, 1970, pp. 7–11.
Schön, Elizabeth. "Relato sentimental sobre Ida Gramcko". In Ida Gramcko, *Ida teatro*. Valencia: Edicones del Gobierno de Carabobo, 1997, pp. 7–10.
Stolk, Gloria. "Poemas". *37 apuntes de crítica literaria*. Caracas: Edime, n.d., pp. 125–8.

GUARDIA, GLORIA

Gloria Guardia was born in 1940 in Venezuela, where her Panamanian father had gone to work. She published her first novel in 1961, *Tiniebla Blanca* (White Darkness), a book that critics have compared to the novels of the French author Françoise Sagan. The novel tells of the love affair between an upper-class Latin American girl who graduates from Vassar College, where Gloria graduated, and her uncle.

During the years before she published her next novels, *El Último Juego* (1976, The Last Game), *Libertad en Llamas* (1999, Freedom on Fire) and *Lobos al Anochecer* (2006, Wolves at Sunset), Gloria Guardia wrote several in-depth critical studies which included books and essays on Pablo Antonio Cuadra, Miguel Hernández, Carmen Laforet, Rubén Darío and various Panamanian writers. She traveled to Nicaragua in 1977 and became involved in the Sandinista movement. Later on Guardia worked for several important newspapers and was the ABC representative in Panama. For many years she wrote an opinion piece in a Panamanian newspaper. Gloria Guardia has been a member of the Panamanian Academy of Letters since 1984, a corresponding member of the Spanish Royal Academy of Language since 1989 and a corresponding member of the Colombian Academy of Language since 1997.

Themes and Influences

Gloria Guardia's life and works mirror Panama's role as an international gateway as well as Guardia's interest in two themes: the politics of Panama and Nicaragua, her father and her mother's nations respectively, and modern philosophy and literary theory. Guardia's cosmopolitan background as well as her education at some of the best universities in Europe and the United States is reflected both in her literary criticism and her creative works

In her novels Guardia chooses historical periods such as the negotiations for a new Canal treaty in the case of Panama in 1977, the assassination of Panamanian President José Remon in 1955 and the 1927–28 struggles of Sandino in Nicaragua to explore the topic of each country's political and social autonomy in view of its dependent relationship to the United States. Her novels are examples of the new historical novel, a hybrid genre halfway between fiction and non fiction

Guardia's novel *El Último Juego* (The Last Game) is in itself a complex play between time and space. The author tell us the events that take place in 12 hours of the life of the main character, Roberto Garrido, the Panamanian diplomat in charge of negotiating the new treaty for the Canal, who is made a prisoner in his own house by a group of left-wing terrorists. The novel describes the internal conflicts within Garrido who not only has to face the problem of the attack by the terrorists but who has within himself a conflict between his love for his mistress and his feelings for his socially proper wife. The stream of consciousness of the main character is expressed through two discourses, one related to love and the other to politics, both aspects of the game of life which he so falsely plays.

In *El Último Juego*, we can see the relationship between the microcosm of the invaded house and the macrocosm of the nation. From the time of the colony, as a result of its geographical location, Panama has been prey to the commercial interests of the rest of the world. As a result of this, the country is defined as a transit area, a meeting place for different powers, which varies constantly as a result of the fluctuations of the international market. The invasion of Garridos's house by left-wing guerillas parallels the invasion of Panama by foreign interests from the very beginning of its creation. In both cases there is an invasion of space by an exterior force whose arrival produces a permanent change in that interior space. The Panamanian nation is conceived as a bridge, not just between two oceans, as it says in many of its official slogans, but between the past and the future. It is a land which constantly experiments the struggle between its desire for national autonomy and the ambitions of foreign economic powers.

The character of Garrido in *El Último Juego* also serves as a means of portraying the role of women in Panamanian society, a constant theme in Guardia's literary creation. Garrido's monologue underlines the contrast between the character of his wife Queta who represents the passive and superficial woman of the elite class and his lover, Marina, who, although she belongs to that same social class, is nevertheless an independent person who expresses her own autonomy and breaks the behavioral rules of her social class.

Guardia's great interest in literary criticism caused her to publish in 1996 a fictional work called *Cartas Apócrifas* (False Letters) which received the Premio Nacional de Cuento de la Ciudad de Bogotá (Short Story prize of Bogotá, Colombia), in which she combined the creative task of writing fiction with that of the literary critic. This book, which consists of a series of short stories, each in the form of a letter from a famous woman, comes the closest of all her works to combining literature with literary criticism. In an interview with Professor Frances Yaeger, the author says that this book was perhaps the most ambitious of anything that she had written up to this date. She herself says that she had mixed both criticism and literary creation in it and created a new genre.

In *Libertad en Llamas* (Freedom on Fire), published in 1999, the author experiments with literary techniques but continues her interest in national identity and Latin American politics. She is constantly changing from time and place and from one narrative voice to another. The preparation of a festival to celebrate the arrival of a North American president is told sometimes in the voice of the main character Esmeralda and sometimes by her uncle. The events related to the war with Sandino are also sometimes described by Esmeralda and sometimes by other narrators. The novel ends with the arrival of the American president, in this case Herbert Hoover, in Nicaragua where he is greeted in the port of Corinth by a live statue, a girl dressed as the Statue of Liberty who, forgotten by everyone, dies as a result of the sun and the harsh weather

Lobos al Anochecer (Wolves at Dusk) published in 2006, is the second book along with *El Último Juego* of a trilogy that Guardia has announced will be called *Marabierto*. The trilogy will deal with different periods in Panamanian political history, starting with the 1970s in *El Último Juego*, the 1950s in *Lobos al Anochecer* and with the period of the beginning of the republic of Panamá in the early 1900s for the last book.

The assassination of President Jose Remon at the racetrack in Panama in January 1955 in *Lobos al Anochecer* is the pivotal event that structures the book's other subplots. The novel changes continually in time and place and narrates the event from the point of view of various speakers, some involved in the actual murder, others just observers. The main character is a young woman from the oligarchy, daughter of a prominent Panamanian politician who is married to an Argentine military officer and who recounts the events of the assassination. Her former lover, another prominent member of the oligarchy, is involved indirectly in the assassination. Again, a member of the elite is the one who narrates the story just like Garrido in *El Último Juego* and Esmeralda in *Libertad en Llamas.* Meticulously researched and documented, the novel provides another example of Guardia's ability to fuse history with literature and create an example of the new historical novel.

In conclusion, we can say that Gloria Guardia's literary creation brings to contemporary Panamanian literature the perspective of a woman whose work is the result of an in depth study of universal literature and of a committed ideology. Her interest in presenting political topic and in analyzing the role of women in this society is the keynote of her writings. Her interest in the world of ideas, philosophy and literary theory is reflected in her essays, novels and short stories.

Critical Interpretations

Guardia's works have attracted the interest of foreign critics much more than that of Panamanian critics, perhaps because of her own experience of living in many parts of the world. Her novels and short stories have been examined from many different perspectives, including that of traditional critics who study her work in relation to national literary movements and thematic concerns, and those who examine her work from the perspective of feminism, national identity and cultural studies. Many critics are fascinated by Guardia's perspective on the Panamanian and Nicaraguan elites, which she examines in her works from her vantage point as a member of both of these groups.

In 1994, several articles about Guardia's work appeared in a book dealing with Central American literature entitled *Cambios Esteticos y Nuevos Proyectos Culturales en Centroamerica.* Carmen Alverio published an article in this book in which she placed Guardia in the context of Central American and Panamanian literature and found a heavy influence of the 1960s "boom" authors on Guardia's writings. In another article published elsewhere that same year, Alverio related Guardia's prose to the studies of national identity and use of the symbol of the female body to express this identity.

Ramón Luis Acevedo published in 1994 also in *Cambios Estéticos y Nuevos Proyectos Culturales* a study of Guardia in which he studied her political ideology but saw her more as a reformer than a revolutionary. Two other articles which appeared in this same volume are useful in understanding Guardia's work. Maria Roof provided a feminist study of Guardia's novel *El Último Juego* and Elizabeth Otero-Krauthammer examined Guardia's collection of short stories, *Cartas Apócrifas,* from a feminist viewpoint.

Arturo Arias published in 1998 an excellent in-depth analysis of Guardia's works, particularly of *El Último Juego.* He believes that the reversal of the male/female roles in the novel as a result of the invasion of the house by the left-wing guerillas is expressed through the multiplicity of narrative voices, particularly the use of the authorial voice in contrast to Garrido's voice, which reflects the official voice and that of his social class. Arias also sees Garrido as a symbol of globalization and as a representative of an older form of Panamanian nationalism which is being counteracted by the radical-populism represented by the guerillas in the novel under the leadership of Comandante Urraca.

Gloria's novel *El Último Juego* continued to attract in the late 1990s and early twenty-first century the interest of critics. In 1999, Barbara Droescher studied *El Último Juego* in relation to other novels by Central American women and found that the theme of women who are orphans is prevalent in several of them. In 2001, Ana Maria Camargo studied *El Último Juego* using a phenomenological approach and the theories of Eric Fromm.

In the early 2000s, Frances Yaeger applied the theories of Benedict Anderson and Homi Bhabha to the study of national identity in Guardia's novel *Libertad en Llamas.* Yaeger published several studies on different aspects of Guardia's work and other Panamanian writers.

MAIDA WATSON

Selected Works

Tiniebla Blanca. Madrid: Editorial Clásica y Moderna. 1961.
Estudio sobre el pensamiento poético de Pablo Antonio Cuadra. Madrid: Editorial Gredos, 1971.
Rogelio Sinán: una revisión de la vanguardia en Panamá. Panamá: Litho-Impresora Panamá, S.A. 1975.
El Último Juego. San José: Editorial Universitaria, 1976.
La búsqueda del rostro Panamá: Editorial Signos, 1984.
La mujer en la academia. Discurso de recepción en la Academia Panameña de la Lengua. Panamá: Editorial Myriam Bermúdez, 1989.
Aproximación a Libre y Cautiva de Stella Sierra. Panamá Impresos López, 1990.
Rogelio Sinán: una reflexión crítica en torno a la contribución del libro Onda a la poesía panameña del siglo XX. Panamá: Impresora de la Nación, 1994.
Cartas apócrifas. Bogotá: Tercer Mundo Editores, 1997.
La carta. Salta: Biblioteca de Textos Universitarios, 1997.
"Aspectos de creación en la novela centroamericana". *Colección Encuentros.* Washington, DC: Centro Cultural del Banco Interamericano de Desarrollo, 1998.
Libertad en llamas. México and Barcelona: Plaza y Janés, 1999.
Lobos al anochecer. Bogotá: Alfaguara, 2006.

References and Further Reading

Acevedo, Ramón Luis. "El Último Juego de Gloria Guardia: Novela premiada por EDUCA". *Hispania: Review of the American Association of Teachers of Spanish and Portuguese*, 61(3) (September, 1978).
——. *Gloria Guardia y Rosario Ferré: Dos visiones burguesas de la burguesía caribeña.* Río Piedras, PR: Universidad de Puerto Rico, 1992.
Alverio, Carmen. "Gloria Guardia, una biografía". In Janet Gold (ed.), *Volver a imaginarlas. Retratos de escritoras centroamericanas.* Tegucigalpa: Editorial Guaymuras, 1998, pp. 80–97.
Alverio, Carmen and Acevedo, Ramón Luis. "Gloria Guardia". *Exégesis: Revista del Colegio Universitario de Huamacao* 7(19) (1994): 10–13, 77–83.
Arias, Arturo. "Gloria Guardia: el paródico socavamiento de la guarida de la cansada élite panameña". In *Gestos ceremoniales: narrativa centroamericana 1960–1990.* Guatemala: Artemis & Edinter, 1998, pp. 159–83.
Araya, Seidy. *Seis narradoras de centroamérica.* Heredia, Costa Rica: Editorial de la Universidad Nacional, 2003.
Balderston, Daniel and González, Mike. *Encyclopedia of Latin American and Caribbean Literature 1900–2003.* New York: Routledge, 2004.

Correa, Pedro. "Cuando se enferma el amor: a propósito de dos cuentos de Gloria Guardia". *Revista Lotería* (Jan.–Feb. 1992): 69–71.

Dröscher, Barbara. "No tienen madres: deseo, traición y desaparición en la literatura centroamericana escrita por mujeres". *Scripta Humanistica* 140. Potomac, MD, 1999, pp. 183–95.

Hidalgo, Linde Lichte. "Tres facetas en la joven narrativa panameña (1966–1981)". Dissertation, The University of New Mexico, Alburquerque, NM, December, 1983.

Menton, Seymour. "La identidad nacional en el cuento panameño, Cartas apócrifas de Gloria Guardia". *Caminata por la narrarativa latinoamericana*. México: Fondo de Cultura Económica, 2002, pp. 33, 339–46.

Mondragón, Amelia (ed.) *Cambios estéticos y nuevos proyectos culturales en Centroamérica, (Testimonios, entrevistas y ensayos) en torno a la obra de Manlio Argueta, Arturo Arias, Gloria Guardia, Carmen Naranjo, Sergio Ramírez y Roberto Sosa*. Washington, DC: Literal Books, 1994, pp. 107–44.

Watson, Maida "Una nueva relación entre la crítica y la literatura: Gloria Guardia". In Laura P. Alonso Gallo (ed.), *Voces de América*. Cádiz, Spain: Editorial Aduana Vieja, 2004, 417–33.

Yaeger, Frances. "Novela y Nación: el caso de Rosa Maria Britton y Gloria Guardia". *Revista Iberoamericana* LXVII(196) (July–Sept. 2001): 451–61.

——. "El poder polivalente de las metáforas en *Libertad en llamas* de Gloria Guardia". *Explicación de Textos Literarios* 31(1) (2002): 5–20.

GUERRA, ROSA

Rosa Guerra (unknown–1864) was a pioneering Argentine novelist, poet, and essayist whose publications in the 1850s and early 1860s helped establish the role of the woman writer in the tumultuous years following the end of the Rosas dictatorship. Women's public voice, which had begun to flourish after Independence from Spain, was effectively silenced by Rosas during the 1830s; after his defeat in 1852, there was a pent-up explosion of women's writings in which Guerra was a well-known participant. Guerra modeled an intellectual life that many women writers adopted throughout the second half of the 1800s: like Guerra, they earned their living through teaching, frequently wrote essays for periodicals, and wrote literary works that incorporated many of the ideas they expressed in their journalism.

Teacher and Journalist

Not much is known about Guerra's early years; some give her birth date as 1834, but it was probably earlier. She was educated in a girls' school established by the Sociedad de Beneficencia, and later became a schoolteacher herself. It is believed that Guerra was one of the anonymous editors of *La Camelia*, a short-lived women's newspaper that appeared after the defeat of Rosas in 1852. This journal defended women's rights, especially the right to education, citing the suffering and self-sacrifice of women during the dictatorship as justification for their demands. Soon after *La Camelia* folded, Guerra founded and edited (in her own name) *La Educación*, dedicated to the Sociedad de Beneficencia; its title reflected its content. However, after a half dozen numbers, this periodical also disappeared. Abandoning editing, Guerra continued to publish her essays in general circulation newspapers and magazines, sometimes using the pseudonym "Cecilia". Her constant theme was the betterment of women's situation through education (by this she meant intellectual formation, not the needlework, music, and sermons of dames schools). With the bitter memory of the oppression of women by Rojas still fresh in her mind, Guerra believed that only an educated populace could resist future dictatorships. Her reader for girls, *Julia o la educación: libro de lectura* (1863), continues this theme.

Novelist, Dramatist, and Poet

In 1860, Rosa Guerra published a groundbreaking novel, *Lucía Miranda*. The work is notable for its early date; few Argentine women in that era wrote novels, which were published at the author's own expense. But more importantly, the novel employs a folkloric figure, Lucía Miranda, to re-envision Argentina's creation mythology. The Miranda legend was first published in 1612 in Ruy Díaz's *La Argentina*. According to Díaz, Lucía and her husband, Sebastián, sailed to Argentina in 1532 as colonists. Two indigenous men, Siripo and Mangoré (in Guerra's version, Mangora), fall in love with the beautiful Lucía. She speaks of friendship's love, which the Indians hear as romantic love. When Lucía rejects their advances, they attack the fort and take the Mirandas captive. To save Sebastian's life, Lucía agrees to become Siripo's wife. However, the Spanish couple cannot disguise their love for each other, and Siripo orders their death. Díaz describes their end in the language and imagery of traditional saints' tales.

In Guerra's version of this legend, she shows sympathy for the Indians, particularly Mangora; she even allows Lucía to say that, if she weren't married to Sebastián, she would consider marrying Mangora. Lucía herself is portrayed as a woman of natural intelligence whose lack of education leads to the indiscretions that produce such fatal results. Guerra's novel was published the same year as Eduarda Mansilla's *Lucía Miranda*; the two novels, different in their interpretation of the legend, were among the first of many versions of the Miranda tale that proliferated in the late 1800s and early 1900s.

Again, Rosa Guerra was a genre pioneer in 1862, when she wrote *Clemencia: drama en 3 actos y en verso*. Guerra's final book, *Desahogos del corazón: poesías,* was published the year of her death, 1864. In these last works, she is still concerned with (1) the role of women in the national identity; and (2) expressing women's subjectivity on its own terms. Written in an emotional, idealizing style that has since fallen out of favor, these works are not ordinarily studied today.

Rosa Guerra died on August 18, 1864, in Buenos Aires. (The literary history by Ricardo Rojas gives Guerra's death date as 1894, and that date is often repeated in error.) The obituary published in *El Nacional* a few days later mentions that her death came after a long illness. It also includes passages from the funeral oration. A photograph of Guerra is available at the Archivo General de la Nación in Buenos Aires.

Modern Interpretations

Among today's scholars of literature and women's culture, Rosa Guerra is remembered mainly for three reasons: (1) she has historical significance for her career at a time when Argentina had not yet established models for women's authorship; (2) her essays defending women's rights are important documents in the history of Argentine feminism; and (3) her novel, *Lucía Miranda*.

Feminist literary historians, in their efforts to rewrite Argentina's canonical literary histories, have rescued Rosa Guerra and her works from obscurity, and have restored her to her place as one of the few well-known female public voices during the critical years of the post-Rosas era. In surveys of women's periodical activities—for example, those of Lily Sosa de Newton—Guerra's journals are now routinely included.

But scholarly attention to Rosa Guerra is not limited to mentions in chronologies; contemporary critics examine her works for insight into the intellectual life of women during a turning point in Argentina's national identity. Guerra's essays make a significant contribution to the understanding of how carefully the role of the woman author had to be constructed in order to be acceptable to a public who generally frowned on women who deviated from the idea of the self-effacing "angel in the house". Nancy Saporta Sternbach's study is an example of critics' interest in Guerra's rhetorical construction of the female author; her analysis of Guerra's use of irony is especially valuable. Moreover, as Francine Masiello points out, Guerra's essays reveal that the demand for education was interwoven with seeking a larger role in Argentine national life, particularly in political matters.

Of all her works, though, Guerra's *Lucía Miranda* has brought the author the most critical attention. Several scholars have compared Guerra's presentation of the legend with those of other writers, particularly Eduarda Mansilla's. Among these are Kathryn Lehman, Susana Rotker, and Nancy Hanway. These studies have revealed how problematic the Miranda literature is, including Guerra's contribution, especially in the ways it places gender at the center of revisionist versions of Argentine history and identity.

BONNIE FREDERICK

Selected Works

La Camelia. Buenos Aires: April 11–May 11, 1852. Available at the University of Texas at Austin's Benson Library.

Lucía Miranda. Buenos Aires: Imprenta Americana, 1860. The complete text is available on several online sites.

References and Further Reading

Hanway, Nancy. *Embodying Argentina: Body, Space and Nation in 19th Century Narrative*. Jefferson, NC: McFarland, 2003.

Lehman, Kathryn. "Naturaleza y cuerpo femenino en dos narrativas argentinas de origen nacional". *Revista Iberoamericana* 70(206) (2004): 117–24.

Masiello, Francine. *Between Civilization and Barbarism: Women, Nation, and Literary Culture in Modern Argentina*. Lincoln, NB: University of Nebraska Press, 1992.

Rotker, Susana. *Cautivas: Olvidos y memoria en la Argentina*. Buenos Aires: Ariel, 1999. English translation: *Captive Women: Oblivion and Memory in Argentina*. Trans. Jennifer French. Minneapolis, MN: University of Minnesota Press, 2002.

Sternbach, N. "'Mejorar la condición de mi secso': The Essays of Rosa Guerra". In Doris Meyer (ed.), *Reinterpreting the Spanish American Essay: Women Writers of the 19th and 20th Centuries*. Austin, TX: University of Texas Press, 1995, pp. 46–56.

GUERRA CUNNINGHAM, LUCÍA

Lucía Guerra Cunningham (b. 1943) was born in Santiago, Chile. She is a professor of Latin American Literature at the University of California, Irvine. In addition to her work as a professor, she is an award-winning writer and an outstanding literary critic. As a critic, she specializes in critical theory, gender studies, and creative writing. After receiving a degree in teaching in Chile at Universidad de Chile in 1965, she came to the United States and continued her studies. In 1975, she obtained a Ph.D. in Latin American Literature from the University of Kansas.

Her article entitled "Cultural Identity and the Dilemma of the Self in Latin American Women's Literature" won the Plural Essay Award Prize in 1987. Her book *La mujer fragmentada: Historias de un signo* (1994, Fragmented Woman: History of a Sign), a theoretical critique of the meanings ascribed to the sign "woman", both in philosophy and religion as the prevalent patriarchal metanarratives in Western culture was awarded the Casa de las Américas Prize in 1994. In 1979, she won the Annual Translation Award sponsored by Columbia University and the Council of the Arts for her translation of María Luisa Bombal's book, *New Islands*, published by Farrar, Straus & Giroux in 1981. In her groundbreaking essay, "La narrativa de María Luisa Bombal: Una visión de la existencia femenina" (Narrative by María Luisa Bombal: A Vision of Feminine Existence), Lucía Guerra placed this complex Chilean author in the international spotlight she deserves, in 1980, the year of her death.

Guerra was intrigued by women's writing from the beginning of her career. In 1980 she published an edited volume, entitled *Mujer y Sociedad en América Latina* (Woman and Society in Latin America) in which she articulates the problematic nature of the representation of female subjectivity. In her analysis – echoing Luce Irigaray's *Ce sexe qui n'en est pas un* (This Sex Which is not One), Guerra recognizes that a woman does not simply "exist" as does man within the "symbolic" Lacanian order. Therefore, women must struggle to oppose the patriarchal system and its depiction of women in order to acquire an identity recognizable to themselves. The critic describes the role of the female body in the representation of women within the system in which the female becomes a commodity.

Guerra's edited volume, *Splintering Darkness: Latin American Women in Search of Themselves* (1990) reveals a specific double agenda in the selection of the articles compiled in it: namely, the subversion of the discourses and the "de-authorization of patriarchal concepts" (Jehensen 1992: 337) manifest in the traditional representation of women. The extensive foreword to this volume may be considered as the precursor to *La mujer fragmentada: Historias de un signo*, a thorough analysis of the constructions of alternative feminine/feminist discourses in Latin American literature. However, Lucía Guerra cannot be labeled "a feminist critic" as many critics who wrote about women's writing have been.

Guerra's critical and scholarly works embrace many other aspects of Latin American literature and cultural studies. She co-edited with Juan Villegas a volume, entitled *Tradición y marginalidad en la Literatura Chilena del Siglo XX* in 1982 (Tradition and Marginality in Twentieth-Century Chilean

Literature). More recently she has been working on the literary representation of urban space under the title, "Imaginaries of the City in Latin America". This work started *à propos* the "crónicas urbanas" by the controversial Chilean performance artist and writer, Pedro Lemebel. Analyzing Lemebel's work and borrowing the terms from it, Guerra distinguishes the "ciudad neoliberal" (neoliberal city) and the "ciudad anal" (anal city) that lies in its margins suggesting that economic and social marginalization that go hand in hand are located in specific urban zones (see Pastén 2005).

In addition to being an eminent critic, Lucía Guerra is also a recognized fiction writer in the Hispanic world who has won many literary honors. Her collection of short stories entitled *Frutos extraños* (Strange Fruits) in 1991 won the *Premio Letras de Oro* and the Municipal Prize of Literature in Chile. Her short story entitled "Emboscadas de la memoria" (Memory's Traps) was awarded the First Prize in the *Certamen Bienal del Cuento '94* sponsored by the Centro Cultural Mexicano and the Spanish Press. In 1997, she received the Gabriela Mistral Award (*Coté-femmes éditions* in Paris) for the outstanding quality of her fiction. Her thematic preferences range from the testimonial: *Más allá de las máscaras* (1990, Beyond the Masks), to the erotic: *Frutos extraños* (1991 Strange Fruits). *Muñeca brava* (1993, translated into English as *The Street of Night* 1999, by Lucía Guerra's husband, Richard Cunningham, a translator and writer), *Los dominios ocultos* (1998, Hidden Spheres) and *Las noches de Carmen Miranda* (2002, Carmen Miranda's Nights) may be characterized by what Jonathan Culler defines as an "appeal to a sexual identity defined as essential and privileging experiences associated with this identity" (1982: 48). The feminist poetic strategy the author follows gives back the confidence to manifest their identity and voice to those women who have been silenced and whose identity was questioned by patriarchal oppression, for Guerra considers women's writing as a "proceso interior de la adquisición de una identidad" (an inner process of acquiring an identity). But beyond feminism, it is her ideological commitment that may also be observed in these works. Nevertheless, her open expression against oppression and brutality does not render these novels and short stories aesthetically unsound (as it happens in many cases of "*écriture engagée*" whereby works become political demagoguery), on the contrary: it gives them uncommon vigor and vitality.

The intellectual coherence of Guerra's work, both critical and creative, is remarkable for its focus on gender inequality. As many feminist critics, Guerra also sees the subordination of women as caused by patriarchy and attempts to represent the empowerment of women in the candid depiction of female eroticism, among other means, such as the subversion of patriarchal values through irony. In *Más allá de las máscaras* (1984), Guerra attempts to lay bare the social construction of upper middle-class femininity. Cristina, a journalist tells her story, her rebellion against her comfortable, middle-class life after 10 years of a hollow marriage, and her "moment of truth" when, for the first time, she takes a close look at the lives of poor women she encounters through her work, who fight for their survival.

In *Muñeca brava* (1993), her representation of women goes beyond class boundaries and examines the anatomy of political participation and resistance. The resistance of women develops in parallel fashion on two narrative axels, the one that deals with the political and the other that deals with the feminine through which the female subject is articulated against the backdrop of the Pinochet dictatorship years in Chile. The author creates a "counter-history" that not only puts in doubt the so-called "official history", but also focuses on women's experiences in active political participation. The originality of her writing lies in the frankness of her discourse and also in the poetic quality of the imagery she employs.

Las noches de Carmen Miranda (2002) is a tragic tale of a great Hollywood sensation, the singer of Portuguese origin who, ironically, becomes the emblematic image of Latin America in Hollywood, where the diva's successes are juxtaposed by her constant suffering in a sad parallel to Billie Holiday and Edith Piaf, both of whom are mentioned in the novel. In her scrutiny of Miranda's life, the author untangles the anatomy of an apparent success story through the careful construction of an idol as a money-making machine. Thus she condemns not only patriarchy that exploits women, but also the cruelty of the system that encourages such exploitation motivated by greed and power. After several books of fiction, Guerra returned to scholarly writing. In Spain, her new book, entitled *Bases Teóricas de la Crítica Feminista* (Theoretical Basis of Feminist Criticism) was published in Spain by the Editorial Orto and is about to reappear published by the Universidad Nacional Autónoma de México (UNAM). This book offers a review of feminist criticism from its earliest stages, that includes the most current critical trends, including post-feminist and post-colonial perspectives.

Guerra is very active in academe as well. She is the vice-president of the Instituto Internacional de Literatura Iberoamericana, the most prestigious organization of the study of Latin American literature. She continues to serve on the editorial board of the *Revista Iberoamericana,* published by the Instituto Internacional de Literatura Iberoamericana, currently in its 72nd year of publication.

Lucía Guerra Cunningham's contributions to Latin American literary criticism and narrative are of great importance. He works have been translated into half a dozen languages and are quoted in numerous studies about feminist criticism.

SILVIA NAGY-ZEKMI

Selected Works

La narrativa de María Luisa Bombal: Una visión de la existencia femenina. Madrid: Editorial Playor, 1980.

(ed.) *Mujer y sociedad en América Latina*. Santiago de Chile: Editorial del Pacífico, 1980.

Tradición y marginalidad en la literatura chilena del siglo XX. Los Angeles, CA: Ediciones de la Frontera, 1984.

Texto e ideología en la narrativa chilena. Minneapolis, MN: The Prisma Institute, 1987.

(ed.) *Splintering Darkness: Latin American Women in Search of Themselves*. Pittsburgh, PA: Latin American Literary Review Press, 1990.

La mujer fragmentada: Historias de un signo. Bogotá: Editorial CoCultura, 1994. Santiago de Chile: Editorial Cuarto Propio, 1995.

(ed.) *Obras completas de María Luisa Bombal*. Santiago de Chile: Editorial Andres Bello, 2000.

Mujer y escritura: Fundamentos teóricos de la crítica feminista. Madrid: Orto Ediciones, 2004. Second edition: Mexico: UNAM-PUEG, 2007.

Fiction

Más allá de las máscaras. Five editions. Mexico: Premiá Editora, 1984; Pittsburgh, PA: Latin American Literary Review Press, 1986; Santiago de Chile: Editorial Cuarto Propio, 1990, 1994; Bogotá: Indigo, 1997.

Frutos extraños. Three editions. Caracas: Monte Avila Editores, 1991; Miami, FL: Iberian Studies Institute, 1992; Santiago de Chile: Editorial Cuarto Propio, 1997.

Muñeca brava. Caracas: Monte Avila Editores, 1993.

Los dominios ocultos. Bogotá: La Oveja Negra, 1998.

Las noches de Carmen Miranda. Santiago de Chile: Editorial Sudamericana, 2002 with a simultaneous edition in Argentina.

Texts Published in English

"The Virgin's Passion". *Short Stories by Latin American Women: The Magic and the Real*. Houston, TX: Arte Público, 1990, pp. 93–100.

"In the Beginning". *The Latin American Report* (South Africa), vol. 8, 1992, pp. 102–10.

"Encounter on the Margins". *What Is Secret: Stories by Chilean Women*. New York: White Pine Press, 1995, pp. 194–7.

"Cuba: A Special Situation". *Confrontation*, 1996, pp. 63–70. Reproduced in *The Latin American Report* (South Africa), vol. 12, 1996, pp. 58–62.

The Street of Night (trans. of *Muñeca brava*). Berkshire: Garnet Publishing, 1997.

Texts Published in Other Languages

"Von Spiegel und Satyrn". In *America Latina: Mein Kontinent–Mein Körper. Erotische Texte Lateinamerikanischer Autorinnen*. Vienna: Wiener Verlag, 1991, pp. 331–45.

"Von Hexen und Märtyrerinnen". In *Torturada: Von Schlächtern und Geschlechtern*. Vienna: Wiener Frauenverlag, 1993, pp. 35–52.

"Alba". *L'immaginazione* 198 (May 2003): 18–21.

"Do amore e outras ficcoes". In *Crime de mulheres*. Porto: ASA Editores, 2003, pp. 23–41.

Swedish translation of "The Virgin's Passion". In *En färd mot vindens ansikte*. Stockholm: En bok för alla, 1998. It has also been adapted for a play by Maria Grahn.

References and Further Reading

Culler, Jonathan. *On Deconstruction: Theory and Criticism after Structuralism*. Ithaca, NY: Cornell University Press, 1982.

Gálvez-Carlisle, Gloria. "Si nos permiten hablar: los espacios silenciados y la deconstrucción del discurso del silencio en la narrativa de Lucía Guerra". *Revista Iberoamericana* 168–9 (1994): 1073–9.

Jehensen, Yvonne. "Review of *Splintering Darkness*". *Hispania* 75(2) (1992): 337.

Lagos, Ramona. *Decir lo indecible: Gioconda Belli, Lucia Guerra y Angeles Mastretta*. Santiago de Chile: Editorial Cuarto Propio, 2004.

Muñoz, Elías Miguel. "La mujer y la historia en *Más allá de las máscaras* de Lucía Guerra". In E. Mayers and G. Adamson (eds), *Continental, Latin American and Francophone Women Writers*. Lanham, MD: University Press of America, 1987.

Nagy-Zekmi, Silvia. "Representaciones de resistencia en las novelas de Lucía Guerra". *Revista Monográfica*. Special issue: *Beyond Postmodernism in the Hispanic Novel*. XVI 2001: 237–51.

Owens, Craig. "El discurso de los otros: Las feministas y el postmodernismo". In Hal Foster (ed.), *La postmodernidad*. Barcelona: Kairós, 1985, pp. 93–124.

Pastén, Agustín: "Neither *Gro*balized nor *Glo*calized: Fuguet's or Lemebel's Metropolis?" *AmeriQuests* 2(1) (2005) http://ejournals.library.vanderbilt.edu/ameriquests/viewarticle.php?id=55&layout=html

Peralta, Elva. "Lucía Guerra". In Patricia Rubio (ed.), *Escritoras chilenas*. Vol. III. Santiago de Chile: Cuarto Propio, 1999, pp. 469–85.

Sefamí, Jacobo. "Un continente metonimizado en la cabeza: *Las noches de Carmen Miranda*, de Lucía Guerra". *Revista Chilena de Literatura* 64 2004: 125–9.

GUIDO, BEATRIZ

Beatriz Guido (1925–88) is one of the most prolific, controversial, published, and widely read female writers of twentieth-century Argentina. She was born to Rosario's elite, where her family was deeply involved in the political and intellectual concerns of the era. Her father, the architect Angel Guido, supervised important public works, such as the Flag Monument in Rosario, and held other governmental positions. Her mother, Uruguayan actress Bertha Eirin, came from a traditional family. Such connections with high society—variously real, imagined, or exaggerated by Guido—significantly influenced the author's image and had a strong presence in her literary world. Throughout her life, Guido elaborated a kind of personal mythology of appearing connected to all central figures of Argentine culture.

After writing a couple of fictional works and essays in her early youth, *Regreso a los hilos* (1947, Return to the Threads) and *Estar en el mundo* (1950, Being in the World), Beatriz Guido wrote the novel for which she won the Emecé award: *La casa del ángel* (1956, The House of the Angel). She was by then already romantically involved with Leopoldo Torre Nilsson, the movie director who would make several of her stories into movies. With Torre Nilsson she co-wrote screenplays, and she promoted him on both the national and international scenes. Their joint creative efforts led to several movies of a remarkable thematic and stylistic homogeneity: among others, *La casa del ángel* (1957; The House of the Angel), *La caída* (1959, The Fall), *La mano en la trampa* (1961, The Hand in the Trap), *La terraza* (1963, The Terrace). They are *Bildungsromane*, with a morose but sustained rhythm, and an intense look at the fantasies and fears of adolescence in the midst of a repressive adult world. Beatriz Guido's characters rarely offer unambiguous keys to their own experience. Processes of self-conscience, or even epiphany-like revelations seem to be inaccessible. Trauma is seen in its origin, but never in its resolution. Guido's position among generations of Argentine writers initially situates her closer to the group gathered around the literary magazine *Sur* than to the so-called "parricides" grouped around the *Contorno*. The first works of Beatriz Guido show the influence of the existentialist generation; the fictional world, starting with *La casa del ángel*, resembles that built in Spain by Carmen Laforet. In fact, Laforet's novel *Nada* (Nothing), adapted into the movie *Graciela* (1956, Graciela), precedes Guido's earlier works, and shows a strong similarity with Guido's female adolescence amid a decadent and repressive adult's world, the keys of which are difficult to manage and understand.

Beatriz Guido attempts to approach a more politically committed style within a realistic narrative with *Fin de fiesta* (1956, The Party is Over), and *El incendio y las vísperas* (1964, End of a Day). The former shows the environment of Argentine caudillist politics prior to the advent of Peronism; this work would also receive a film adaptation by Leopoldo Torre Nilsson. The latter represents a love story under Peronism's "totalitarian" political context. This novel was one of the most resounding successes in the history of Argentine publishing business. Its essentially realistic setting articulates romantic, even melodramatic topics. The story recreates the basic plot of José Mármol's *Amalia,* the novel that condenses the romantic and liberal ideology opposed to the caudillist system of Rosas: the nineteenth-century story of frustrated love of a liberal couple persecuted during Rosas' dictatorship is rewritten in *El incendio y las vísperas* as a romance between a young college student opposed to Peronism, and a young woman from a traditional family. The pair fall in love as she hides him in her parents' house. Guido's novels is thus located at the center of a literature strongly connected with local political events, on the "liberal" side of history (high-level, educated, Europeanizing sectors of society) as against the populist authoritarianism and the tradition of "barbarism" that permeates Argentina's history from Rosas in the nineteenth century, to General Perón, a century later.

After this novel, Guido engaged a less controversial revision of historical facts in *Escándalos y soledades* (1970, Scandals and Solitudes). This novel enlists more experimental narrative forms, reflecting the influence of the *nouveau roman*, the *novela del lenguaje* and the intertextual games characteristic of the "boom" and "postboom". This aesthetic approach failed to achieve the circulation of her prior works. Although Guido never gained a place among the more successful group of Latin American writers of the 1960s, Guido continued to experiment with diverse genres and styles. In *Soledad y el incendiario* (1982, Soledad and the Arsonist), for example, she plays with female pulp fiction, while *Apasionados* (1982, Impassioned), is a historical novel. *Una madre* (1973, A Mother), presents a homage to and book of memories dedicated to Bertha Eirin. Here, Guido constructs the image of her mother as a function of her own place in terms of gender, class and intellect. She wrote "Esperando a los Castro" (1971, Waiting for the Castros), a closet drama, and, in the context of the political violence of Argentina in the 1970s and early 1980s, *La invitación* (1979, The Invitation), a mystery, as *Rojo sobre rojo* (1987, Red on Red). Her book *¿Quién le {sic} teme a mis temas?* (1977, Who Is Afraid of My Themes?) proposes a tour of the history of her literary works. This text mixed references to the impact and influence of her texts, her interaction with other intellectuals, and her public image. Further, her stories and screenplays for film productions are experiments in which literary and cinematographic languages converge; she thus publishes *El Pibe Cabeza (crónica cinematográfica)* (1975, Kid Head, Cinematographic Chronicle), and includes a "story line" for the film version of *Piedra libre* (1976, Free for All), at the end of the anthology of the same title.

Her books of short stories do not lend themselves to an easy chronological classification. The author's variety of interests shows her sometimes revisiting themes from her earlier novels and her lifelong literary explorations. She also reorganizes and works on new editions of some of her short stories in successive anthologies. Her first volume of short stories, *La mano en la trampa* (1961, The Hand in the Trap), opens with the novella that gives the collection its title. This book is followed by *El ojo único de la ballena* (1971, The Only Eye of the Whale), *Los insomnes* (1973, The Insomniacs), *Piedra libre* (1976, Free for All), and *Todos los cuentos el cuento* (1979, All the Tales, the Tale).

The literary life of Beatriz Guido, and her place within the Argentine intellectual field, were strongly influenced by the country's political circumstances and her attitude towards them. After youthful involvement with intellectual groups that opposed the then-governing Peronist regime, the fall of Peronism in 1955 and the subsequent political climate elevated Beatriz Guido's profile among the most virulent anti-Peronist sectors. This position, along with her self-confessed belonging to her country's social elite, made her the target of frequent criticism by the most "progressive" intellectual groups of the day. Argentina's deeply polarized polical life—marked for many years by a Peronist/anti-Peronist dichotomy—resulted in these themes driving the reception and evaluation of both the author and her works. Essayist Arturo Jauretche thus sees her as the symbol of the mediocrity and elitism of Argentina's oligarchic sectors. Critics apparently disregarded Guido's attempts to build a body of literary work that delineates the country's social and political history. Her more experimental efforts received scant attention. Beatriz Sarlo sees Guido's historical novels as a "race towards absurdity", and her attempts of formal renewal as a mere "cultural prejudice". Guido enjoyed little of the prestige that surrounded figures such as Borges, Bioy Casares, or Silvina Ocampo.

During the last military dictatorship (1976–83), Guido had a less active public image: Leopoldo Torre Nilsson's illness and subsequent demise contributed to her withdrawal. With the return to democracy in 1983, she resumed her political participation, actively supporting the governing party, which had defeated Peronism for the first time in Argentine history. She was appointed cultural attaché to the Argentine Embassy in Madrid, the city in which she later died.

In summary, Beatriz Guido was among the most renowned figures in twentieth-century Argentine narrative. At the same time, she is among the least known of Argentina's major writers in the rest of the Hispanic world, and her work is rarely translated. The fictional world she created in her first novels that Torres Nilsson brought to the screen is nowadays recognized as one of the most original artistic achievements of her country during the late 1950s and early 1960s. Currently, less attention is paid to the political evaluation of her work, as opposed to other aspects, such as genre. Guido represents, in the words of Mizraje, "the most potent female voice in an emphatically masculine generation". Other, more contemporary topics of interest, such as her work with hybrid literary genres, deserve a more detailed, sustained analysis.

EDUARDO MUSLIP

Selected Works

La caída. Buenos Aires: Losada, 1956.

La casa del ángel. Buenos Aires: Emecé, 1955. trans. J. C. MacLean, *The House of the Angel*. New York: McGraw-Hill, 1957.

Fin de fiesta. Buenos Aires: Losada, 1958.

La mano en la trampa. Buenos Aires: Losada, 1961.

El incendio y las vísperas. Buenos Aires: Losada, 1964. Trans. A. D. Towers *End of a Day*. New York: Scribner's, 1966.

Escándalos y soledades. Buenos Aires: Losada, 1970.

El ojo único de la ballena. Buenos Aires: Merlín, 1971.

Los insomnes. Introduction by Reina Roffé and J. C. Martini Real. Buenos Aires: Losada, 1973.

Una madre. Buenos Aires: Emecé, 1973.

BG, L. Pico Estrada, L. Torre Nilsson. *El pibe Cabeza, crónica cinematográfica.* Buenos Aires: Schapire, 1975.
Piedra libre. Buenos Aires: Galerna, 1976.
¿Quién le teme a mis temas? Buenos Aires: Fraterna, 1977.
Todos los cuentos el cuento. Buenos Aires: Planeta, 1977.
La invitación. Buenos Aires: Losada, 1979
Soledad y el incendiario. Buenos Aires: Abril, 1982.
Apasionados. Buenos Aires: Losada, 1982.
Rojo sobre rojo. Buenos Aires: Losada, 1987.

References and Further Reading

Alonso, F. Y A. Rezzano. "Beatriz Guido". In *Novela y sociedad argentinas.* Buenos Aires: Paidós, 1971, pp. 184–92.

Barcia, Pedro Luis. "Introducción. Beatriz Guido: la narrativa como testimonio y espionaje". In Beatriz Guido, *El incendio y las vísperas.* Madrid: Castalia, 1989.

Bioy Casares, Adolfo. "Beatriz Guido: *La caída.*" *Sur* 243 (1956): 82–3.

Clifford, Joan. "The Female Bildungsromane of Beatriz Guido". *Hispanófila* 132 (2001): 125–39.

Domínguez, Nora. "Familias literarias: visión adolescente y poder político en la narrativa de Beatriz Guido". *Revista Iberoamericana* 70(206) (Winter 2004): 225–35.

Jauretche, A. "Una escritora de medio pelo para lectores de medio pelo". *El medio pelo en la sociedad argentina.* Buenos Aires: Peña Lillo, 1966, pp. 193–216.

Jitrik, Noé. *Seis novelistas argentinos de la nueva promoción.* Mendoza: Cuadernos de Versión, 1959, pp. 55–9.

Mahieu, José A. "Beatriz Guido: Las dos escrituras". *Cuadernos Hispanoamericanos* 437 (1986): 153–68.

Mizraje, María Gabriela. "Beatriz Guido: otra pantalla para las mujeres". In *Argentinas de Rosas a Perón.* Buenos Aires: Biblos, 1999, pp. 251–67.

Rodríguez Monegal, Emir. "Beatriz Guido". *El arte de narrar.* Caracas: Monte Avila, 1968, pp. 199–217.

Sarlo, Beatriz. "Beatriz Guido y el simulacro de lo peligroso". *Los libros* 14 (1970): 6–7.

Viñas, David. "Niños y criados favoritos: de *Amalia* a Beatriz Guido a través de *La gran aldea.*" *Literatura argentina y realidad política.* Buenos Aires: Jorge Álvarez, 1964, pp. 81–121.

H

HEER, LILIANA

Liliana Heer was born in Esperanza, Province of Santa Fe, Argentina in 1943. She is a writer, psychologist and literary critic. Heer studied psychotherapy at the University of Litoral (1959–63), and completed internships at a psychiatric hospital, a prison, and the Institute of El Buen Pastor, a correctional institution for women. In 1963 she was awarded a two-year scholarship in scientific research and methodology. While working on this project, Heer developed an interest in the underlining fictional characteristics of psychiatric patient's testimonies and chronicles. After completing her research, Heer moved to Buenos Aires to pursue a graduate school at the *Escuela de Psicoterapia para Graduados,* a three-year project conducted by members of the prestigious Asociación Psicoanalítica Argentina. From 1967 to 1969, she was Assistant Professor at the University of Belgrano, where she taught introductory courses in psychology, and in 1968, she joined the teaching staff at the University of Buenos Aires. In 2001, Heer was appointed the General Secretary of SADE, the prestigious Sociedad Argentina de Escritores. Her work at SADE consisted in coordinating the Human Rights Commission in charge of gathering and classifying material for an anthology of writers who disappeared during the years under military dictatorship (1976–83). While working at SADE, she also directed *A río revuelto: instantáneas de la realidad*—a collection of lectures, essays and testimonies on the dramatic reality of this period. For her extraordinary performance as pavilion director of a center of highly contagious diseases, in 1993 Heer was accepted as an active member to the International School of Lacanian Orientation. Her national recognition in the field of psychotherapy soon opened the doors to international travel; subsequently, she presented conferences, workshops and lectures in Germany, Ecuador, Spain, Ireland, Italy, Puerto Rico, Yugoslavia, the United States and France. Most recently, in 2002, she organized the Jornadas de Literatura y Psicoanálisis: Autopistas de la Palabra at the National Library in Buenos Aires.

Heer's first novel, *Bloyd* (1984), received the Boris Vian Prize, a highly prestigious award created during the military regime in Argentina as a form of resistance and opposition to the official discourse. In 1988, while working with terminal patients, she wrote and published *La tercera mitad*, an outstanding novel in which psychoanalysis and literature combine to recreate the complex mechanisms of the human mind. Most of the characters in this work were born out of Heer's hospital experience.

After reading James Joyce, she became interested in linguistics and philology, and, with the collaboration of J. C. Martini Real, she published *Giacomo*: *El texto secreto de Joyce* (1993). This collection of essays was first introduced at New York's Americas Society and later presented in Paris, Zurich, Trieste and Dublin. In the last decade, Heer has published: *Frescos de amor* (1995), *Ángeles de vidrio* (1998), *Repetir la cacería* (novella, 2003), and *Pretexto Mozart* (2004). Throughout her career as a psychiatrist, Heer kept writing short stories and critical essays for literary magazines such as *Sitio*, *Utopías del Sur, Pierre Menard, El grillo de papel, Graffiti* and *Espacios*, and has presented critical works on Argentine authors in Berlin (1991), New York (1991–92), Amsterdam, Utrecht and Germany (1993).

Interested in challenging Argentina's suppressive patriarchal system, Heer belongs to a group of Argentine women writers from the 1980s and 1990s—such as Luisa Valenzuela, Liliana Heker, Angélica Gorodischer and Ana María Shúa—who consciously explore and subvert the margins of censored language as an attempt to release it from the rigid parameters of canonical discourse. The confidential tone and fragmented structure of Heer's narrative echo the sound of a feminine voice calling for an active and an intuitive reader unafraid of pouring the soul into the text. A reader willing to dive into a highly poetic narrative where images of madness, incest and *jouissance* (eroticism) form the pattern of a cosmological wheel of life and death. Heer's experimental techniques ascribe to the French feminist concept of *écriture féminine* (feminine writing) which seeks to question the capacity of inherited language to properly articulate women's experiences and perceptions in relation to the world. French critics, Hélène Cixous and Luce Irigaray, have analyzed and compared both practical and political implications of *écriture féminine* and *jouissance* as strategic practices for women to go beyond the theory into the actual expression of desire and sexuality in itself and for themselves.

Using language as a malleable and organic material, the author works with it to produce a highly sophisticated imagery full of symbolism and meaning. By displacing and replacing inherited structures, her prose liberates the flow of a much deeper voice that speaks from within. Heer's complex discourse constantly aims to reflect upon the intricacies of the human psyche bringing forth its darkest fears and thoughts. According to the writer herself, "during authoritarian regime, when silence, death and torture impregnated society, I could not reflect on a full body but a fragmented and mutilated one. Literature deals with art and death, the act of writing is but a means to deciphering death" (author's website). Framed within the characteristics of psychological representation, Heer's works tackle a whole spectrum of human interrelationships in which the individual searches not only to give meaning to existence, but also strive to come to terms with the dramatic reality of a country facing political turmoil and social decadence.

According to the writer, her love for both traveling and cinematography has influenced her writing style, allowing her to further develop her narrative freedom. As she explains on her website, visual imagery became a tool to enhance her work: "*Frescos de amor* and *Ángeles de vidrio* are an attempt to narrate how frontiers of the soul fall. How, from the void, other traditions emerge forcing us to invent unusual styles of cohabitation. I wrote these two novels through the eye of a camera, prioritizing the relevance of montage" (www.lilianaheer.com.ar).

Heer's novels take place within microcosmic worlds such as a hospital, a run-down brothel or a psychiatric institution; all these scenarios provide metaphorical spaces of displacement in which individuals are able to disassociate themselves from society and become free to explore their personal inner paths. Madness, alienation, obsession, and eroticism are the proposed alternatives to escape the unbearable weight of repression and patriarchal domination. Both Lacanian as well as Joycean influences are evident in all of Heer's works, both in her deconstructive approach to social and sexual identities, and in her reformulation of canonical discourse. In an interview with Juana María Cordones-Cook, the author notes that in addition to Lacan and Joyce, other influential theorists in her works are: Derrida, Deleuze, Guattari and Barthes.

Heer's texts synthesize a whole literary aesthetic, metaphysical and socio-political vision that is shared by contemporary intellectuals of Argentina. Her constant experimentation with diverse forms of artistic expression make of her a unique and innovative writer whose creative talent makes of literature a cathartic practice to live out the daily contradictions and conflicts of being alive.

María Claudia André

Selected Works

Dejarse llevar. Buenos Aires: Editorial Corregidor, 1980.
Bloyd. Buenos Aires: Legasa, 1984.
La tercera mitad. Buenos Aires: Legasa, 1988.
Giacomo. El texto secreto de Joyce. Rosario: Luna Nueva, 1992.
Frescos de amor. Buenos Aires: Seix Barral, 1995.
Verano rojo. Buenos Aires: Taller de Copistas de la Letra Muerta, 1997.
Ángeles de vidrio. Buenos Aires: Editorial Norma, 1998.
Repetir la cacería. Buenos Aires: Grupo editor latinoamericano, 2003.
Pretexto Mozart. Buenos Aires: Alción Editora, 2004.

References and Further Reading

André, María Claudia. "Entre el psicoanálisis y la literatura: Conversación con Liliana Heer". *Alba de América* 19(35–6) (July 2000): 555–61.

Cordones-Cook, Juana María. "Entrevista con Liliana Heer". *Alba de América* 24(25) (July 1995): 505–17.

Gimbernat de González, Ester. "The Eloquence of Silence: Argentine Women Writers after the Proceso." *Fiction International* 19(10) (1990): 72–82.

——. *Aventuras del desacuerdo: Novelistas argentinas de los 80.* Buenos Aires: Danilo Albero Bergara, 1992.

Dellepiane, Angela B. "El aporte femenino a la narrativa últma argentina." In Nora Erro-Orthman and Juan Cruz Mendizabal (eds), *La escritora hispánica.* Miami, FL: Universal, 1990.

HEKER, LILIANA

Liliana Heker was born in Buenos Aires, Argentina, in 1943, where she continues to live today. After graduation from high school, at age 17, Heker started to work as an editor of the literary periodical *El grillo de papel* (The Paper Cricket), which also became the platform for the publication of her first short story, "Los juegos" (1960, The Games). Alongside her editorial work, Heker took classes in physics at the University of Buenos Aires (1961–63). After several semesters of simultaneously working as an editor, studying, and writing, she quit the university in order to dedicate all her time to literature. Over the past thirty years, Liliana Heker has contributed to a wide range of literary and political journals and has served as a prominent participant in the main cultural debates in her home country, Argentina.

Heker was the editor-in-chief of the two influential literary journals, *El escarabajo de oro* (The Golden Beetle) from 1961 to 1974, and *Ornitorrinco* (Duck bill) from 1977 to 1986. In 1966, she published her first collection of short stories, *Los que vieron la zarza* (Those Who Saw the Thornbush), for which she was awarded the prize of the Cuban "Casa de las Américas" during the same year. The following years saw the publication of three collections of short stories: *Acuario* (Aquarium) in 1972, *Un resplandor que se acabó en el mundo* (A Glow that Died in the World) in 1977, and *Las peras del mal* (The Pears of Evil) in 1982.

In 1986, Heker published her first novel, *Zona de clivaje* (Cleavage Zone; in Spanish, the title is ambiguous, besides the erotic connotation, it is also used as a term in physics, where it refers to an unconsolidated structure of atoms within a crystal), for which she received the Primer Premio Municipal of the city of Buenos Aires. The volume *Los bordes de lo real* (The Edges of the Real) from 1991 comprised all her short stories up until that time. In the 1990s, Heker devoted herself to the analysis of political repression during the military dictatorship in Argentina from 1976 to 1983. Her second novel, tellingly titled *El fin de la historia* (The End/Purpose of History), which was published in 1996, is the product of her research on the strategies of repression, kidnapping, torture, and murder of the *Junta* during the period of the "Guerra sucia" (Dirty War).

Las hermanas de Shakespeare (Shakespeare's Sisters) from 1999 contains a re-edited selection of articles and essays that were composed between 1971 and 1999. Included among these texts is her famous correspondence with Julio Cortázar about the role of the intellectual during times of repression (1981), which was published under the title "Polémica con Julio Cortázar" (Polemic with Julio Cortázar), as well as a re-edited version of Heker's essay "Las hermanas de Shakespeare," in which she analyzes challenges faced by women writers. The year 2000 saw the publication of *Diálogos sobre la vida y la muerte* (Dialogues on Life and Death), a compilation of essays and interviews with Argentinean artists and intellectuals. In *La crueldad de la vida* (The Cruelty of Life), Heker's most recent publication (2001), she returned to the genre of short fiction and presented literary snapshots of everyday experiences from surprising and often humorous points of views.

In her home country, Heker is best known for her socially committed journalistic work; outside Argentina, in contrast, her primary reputation derives from her work as a fiction writer. While her journalistic work is naturally geared towards more local audiences, the international reception of her literary work was furthered by her contract with the Spanish publishing house Alfaguara, which maintains subsidiaries in several Spanish American countries. In the wake of her success with Alfaguara, many of her short stories have been translated. In this way, Heker became one among the new Argentinean short fiction authors of the so-called "post-boom" movement, who wrote in the period after the literary giants Adolfo Bioy Casares, Jorge Luis Borges and Julio Cortázar.

The fact that Liliana Heker is both a journalist and a fiction writer is reflected in the hybrid quality of many of her texts – articles and literary works that recount ongoing events but spill over into fiction, as well as literary works that are inspired by contemporary events or everyday encounters. As the author states in the prologue to *Las hermanas de Shakespeare*, all her writings are the fruit of a passion to "polemizar, discutir, urdir impresiones rápidas sobre cosas o gente que me rodea . . . [construir] un cuento o una novela . . . [Estos textos] fueron compuestos para un presente . . . dialogan con ese presente" [to polemize, to discuss, to jot down quick impressions about things or people that surround me . . . to construct a short story or a novel . . . These texts were written for a present, and are dialoguing with this present] (p. 9).

Notwithstanding their similarity in inspiration, Heker distinguishes between the divergent intentions behind her journalistic and literary writings. According to Heker, articles and essays, on the one hand, enable the reader to face different constructions of a given reality—"[es una] confrontación de posiciones . . . entre las cuales [el] lector podrá construir su verdad" [a confrontation of positions . . . from which the readers can choose their truth] (p. 11). Fiction, on the other hand, allows the writer to draw out a coherent pattern or image from the chaotic accumulation of the everyday world. In several essays, Heker insists on the individual and often solitary effort of the author to mold a fictional world of her own. In the essay, "Las hermanas de Shakespeare" (the title refers to Virginia Woolf's conjecture about William Shakespeare's anonymous sister from *A Room of One's Own*), Heker argues that the expressive potential of literature arises independent of gender differences and social positions. She denounces the "confortable jaulita de la mirada femenina" [comfortable cage of the feminine point of view]. She also highlights that, "la mujer, al igual que el hombre, mira el mundo. Sola. Si es una artista, será desde esa intersección propia, absolutamente personal y de posibilidades infinitas, que construirá su obra" [A woman, just as a man, looks at the world. If she is an artist, it will be from a unique junction, absolutely personal, yet containing infinite possibilities that she will construct her work] (p. 123).

Heker's fictional writing is rooted in quotidian observations and experiences. Quite often, her material is drawn from human interactions and the wealth of minute gestures, routines, and expectations they contain. In "El sur" (The South), she recounts in lapidary words, not the encounter of a man with his mythologized *raison d'être*, as did Borges in the famous short story of the same name, but a trip to a local store in the San Telmo neighborhood of Buenos Aires in search for a particular nacre button: "Basta un botón para conocer el sur . . . Uno decide comprarlo por la calle Chile, yendo hacia el río, podrá internarse en la anarquía campechana del sur, en su desvencijada belleza" [A button is enough to get to know the south . . . One decides to purchase it in Chile Street; reaching in the direction of the river, one enters the vivacious anarchy of the south, with all its faded beauty] (*Las hermanas*, p. 240). While revising a huge collection of single buttons of all shapes, sizes, and colors on the sales counter, the shop owner and the customer engage in a lively conversation on buttons, fatality, football, and life in general.

In the novel *Fin de la historia*, Heker describes the lives of two young girls who grow up in Buenos Aires of the 1950s, the timid narrator Diana and her friend, the intrepid Leonora, who becomes a *montonera* (leftist militant) and suffers persecution during the dictatorship. The narration consists of Diana's diary notes and inner monologues and is written in a strikingly different tone from Heker's short fiction and her first novel *Zona de clivaje*. Fragments from different streams of consciousness alternate with detailed accounts of isolated episodes that cannot be assigned to a single character's point of view, the description of body parts, inner monologues and the lyrics of a popular song. In this way, Leonora's torture, her and her torturer's thoughts and perceptions are interwoven with the lyrics of a song that is played on the radio, creating an intense moment of dramatic presence outside continuous space–time. In addition to the depiction of the brutality of past events, the novel discusses the ambiguity of recollection. Reality becomes highly conflictive especially when Diana finds out that her friend had become a traitor and secretly left the country. In her solitary endeavor to imagine and, if necessary, invent elements of the life of her absent friend, she notes in her diary: "El disparate se mete en la historia" (absurdity enters into history, p. 13). It is in the knowledge of the inevitable ambiguity of historiographic accounts that Heker's fiction unfolds as a true account of the traumatic past.

Only part of Heker's work has been critically explored. The earliest critical text, Marian Smolen's "Liliana Heker: Preserving the Texture of the Text," is a study of the challenges in translating Heker's heterogeneous works, composed of diverse linguistic strata. Ma Victoria García Serrano analyzes affinities to autobiography and "testimonio" (testimonial writing) in Heker's *El fin de la historia*. The novel *Zona de clivaje* has been at the center of various studies: Aída Apter-Cragnolino retraces echoes of Sartrean existential philosophy; Isolda Battistozzi describes different stages in the psychological evolution of the protagonist; and Erica Frouman-Smith reads the novel as a postmodern *Bildungsroman* written from a female perspective; finally; Héctor Mario Cavallari offers a discourse-analytical study on the intrinsic connection of sexuality, power, and writing. Martha Morello-Frosh provides us with an insightful comparison between the presentations of historiographic metafiction in the works of Heker and her compatriot Luisa Valenzuela. While Liliana Heker's novels have been studied to a certain extent, her short stories and essays are still waiting for critical analysis.

ILKA KRESSNER

Selected Works

Los que vieron la zarza. Buenos Aires: Editorial Jorge Álvarez, 1966.
Acuario. Buenos Aires: Centro Editor de América Latina, 1972.
Un resplandor que se apagó en el mundo. Buenos Aires: Editorial Sudamericana, 1977.
Diálogos sobre la vida y la muerte: conversaciones. (Dialogues with Jorge Luis Borges and other writers.) Buenos Aires: Grupo Editor, 1980. (Enlarged edition: Buenos Aires: Aguilar, 2003.)
Las peras del mal. Buenos Aires: Editorial de Belgrano, 1982.
Zona de clivaje. Buenos Aires: Legasa, 1987.
Los bordes de lo real. Buenos Aires: Alfaguara, 1991.
El fin de la historia. Buenos Aires: Alfaguara, 1996.
Las hermanas de Shakespeare. Buenos Aires: Alfaguara, 1999.
La crueldad de la vida. Buenos Aires: Alfaguara, 2001.
Cuentos. Buenos Aires: Suma de Letras Argentinas, 2004 (short fiction).

References and Further Reading

Apter-Cragnolino, Aída. "'Zona de clivaje' de Liliana Heker: discurso explícito y texto inconsciente". *Texto crítico* 4–5 (1997): 145–57.
André, María Claudia. "Entre los bordes de lo real y el desarrollo de la imaginación: Entrevista con Liliana Heker". *Alba de América. Revista Literaria* 33–4 (1999): 419–28.
Battistozzi, Isolda. "Pérdida del paraíso y ejercicio de la libertad en 'Zona de clivaje' de Liliana Heker". *Romance Languages Annual* 8 (1996): 372–6.
Cavallari, Héctor Mario. "Sexualidad, poder, escritura: 'Zona de clivaje', de Liliana Heker". *Alba de América. Revista Literaria* 33–4 (1999): 115–24.
Corpa Vargas, Mirta."Los primeros principios o 'arte poética' de Liliana Heker: Narrativa del proceso, resistencia y reflexiones en un discurso autobiográfico". *América: Revista Literaria* 22–3 (1994): 416–24.
——. "Liliana Heker: La precariedad del orden o esquizofrenia como forma de vida". *Cuadernos de Aleeu* 1 (1995): 185–94.
——. *Los Cuentos de Liliana Heker.* New York: Peter Lang, 1996.
Frouman-Smith, Erica. "Entrevista con Liliana Heker". *Chasqui: Revista de Literatura Latinoamericana* 21(1) (1992): 106–16.
——. "Gender Conflicts in the Fiction of Liliana Heker". *Revista de estudios hispánicos* 53 (1987): 121–34.
——. "Woman on the Verge of a Breakthrough: Liliana Heker's 'Zona de clivaje' as a Female *Bildungsroman*". *Letras Femininas* 19–20 (1993): 100–12.
García Serrano, Ma Victoria. "Autobiografía y testimonio en 'El fin de la historia' de Liliana Heker". In Jesús Pérez Magallón (ed.), *Memorias y olvidos: Autos y biografías (reales, ficticias) en la cultura hispánica.* Valladolid: Universitas Castellae, 2003, pp. 119–27.
Morello-Frosch, Marta. "Entre las palabras: la ficción de la historia: Narradoras y actoras de la ficción histórica argentina reciente: Luisa Valenzuela y Liliana Heker". *Alba de América. Revista Literaria* 33–4 (1999): 299–310.
Smolen, Marian. "Liliana Heker: Preserving the Texture of the Text". *Translation Review* 7 (1981): 41–5.

HENRÍQUEZ UREÑA, CAMILA

Camila Henríquez Ureña (1894–1973) is an important feminist intellectual figure claimed by both the Dominican Republic (the place of her birth and death) and Cuba. Born in Santo Domingo on April 9, 1894, the daughter of Francisco Henríquez Carvajal (one-time president of the Dominican Republic) and Salomé Ureña (Dominican feminist poet), Henríquez Ureña grew up in a home where education was paramount. Her brothers, Pedro and Max Henríquez Ureña are both philologists who are well known in Latin American Studies. Her mother, founder of the first all-girls high school in the Dominican Republic, died when Henríquez Ureña was only 4 years old. In 1904, her father was forced into exile and the family settled in Santiago de Cuba. Henríquez Ureña adopted Cuban citizenship 1926 and lived there most of her remaining years. Her early feminist activism and dedication to teaching have had a profound impact on the development of a generation of writers and scholars in the Caribbean and Latin America.

The basis for her feminist beliefs and professional activities lie in Henríquez Ureña's broad education in literature and pedagogy. She received her undergraduate degree from the Instituto de la Habana (1913). At 22, she finished her doctorate in Philosophy and Literature at the University of Havana (1917). Her father insisted on the importance of studying abroad. Because World War I made it impossible for her to study in Europe, she followed her brother Pedro and completed a master's degree at the University of Minnesota in Romance literatures (1917–21). Upon her return to Cuba, she pursued her study of pedagogy, receiving her degree in 1927 after defending her thesis *Las ideas pedagógicas de Eugenio María de Hostos* [Eugenio María de Hostos' Pedagogical Thought] about the Puerto Rican intellectual with whom Salomé Ureña worked to form her school in the Dominican Republic. During the next two decades she taught in Santiago de Cuba except for a brief period when she traveled to Europe and studied at the Sorbonne University in Paris (1932–34).

Henríquez Ureña's most activist years coincided with the upsurge in political and intellectual activity following the overthrow of the dictator General Gerardo Machado in 1933. She divided her time between Santiago de Cuba and Havana and was incarcerated briefly in the capital city for participating in the welcome celebration for then-communist playwright Clifford Odets in 1936. Most noteworthy, however, is her participation in the strong feminist movement that contributed to the passage of the Equal Rights Amendment (Article 23) of the Constitution of 1940.

Elected to lead the Lyceum Feminine Society, Henríquez Ureña used this forum and its publication *Revista Lyceum* to spread her ideas on feminism and women's culture. She gave her first talk at the Lyceum on Delmira Agustini in 1934. In 1935 she formed the Unión Nacional de Mujeres (National Women's Union) and was elected its vice-president in 1936. Under her leadership, this group organized the 1939 Third National Women's Congress (the first two having been in 1923 and 1925). To promote the event, Henríquez Ureña read her now-famous essay "La mujer y la cultura" (Women and Culture) and gave the inaugural address. She played a crucial role in saving the session from an ideological split when some delegates from the Lyceum, alarmed by the leftist discourse of the opening panels, sought to issue a declaration that would deny the event this most prestigious group's support.

Together with important Cuban intellectuals Fernando Ortiz, Juan Marinello and others, Henríquez-Ureña also promoted the Institución Hispano-Cubana de Cultura (the Hispano-Cuban Cultural Institute). There, on July 25, 1939, she delivered her seminal lecture entitled "Feminismo" (Feminism). Two years later she gave the inaugural address at the American Association of the International Federation of University Women Conference in the United States, where she would soon move to pursue her teaching career.

Due to the hierarchical and polemical nature of academe at that time, Henríquez Ureña was unable to obtain a position as professor at the University of Havana. In keeping with her fundamental ideal of promoting women's education, she chose to teach at Vassar College (1942–59), at that time an all-women's college. She spent her summers either teaching at Middlebury College or continuing her collaboration with Cuban institutions by giving public lectures and summer courses. After the triumph of the Cuban Revolution in 1959, Henríquez Ureña returned to Cuba to participate in the formation of new curricular and publication apparatuses (for the Ministry of Education, as one of the founders of the Consejo de Publicaciones (Editorial Board) of Casa de las Américas, and as a member of the Cuban mission to UNESCO) and finally assumed a position teaching General and Latin American Literature at the University of Havana (1962). She was emeritus professor at the University at the time of her death in Santo Domingo on September 12, 1973.

Theorizing Feminism

Henríquez Ureña's two main treatises on women's oppression and liberation are "Mujer y cultura" and "Feminismo". In both, she celebrates women's difference from men and foresees women's transcendental role in the evolution of society. She calls for the diffusion of culture to women as the necessary route to achieving a feminist consciousness and as essential to realizing social, legal, and economic equality.

"Women and Culture" deals primarily with women's exclusion from dominant culture. In it, Henríquez-Ureña outlines two central issues: first, women's access to culture, and second, the specificities of women's cultural contributions. Women have not had access to Culture (with a capital C), which she defines as the conscious effort through which human intellectual and moral nature is refined and illustrated with the purpose of bettering society. Although she uses a somewhat narrow notion of what is considered today to be elite culture, Henríquez Ureña nevertheless makes a significantly innovative distinction between sex and gender that explicitly denounces relegating women's sphere to the domestic—thereby limiting their access to public culture. "La mujer llega a la cultura cuando empieza a ser un *hombre* (no digo *varón*)" [Woman attains culture when she becomes man (not male)], she says, using the word "man" to mean a free human (*Estudios* p. 451). She calls what she sees as the beginning of women's access to culture as the greatest revolution in the era of revolutions. Exceptional women (Gertrudis Gómez de Avellaneda, María Luisa Dolz) represent women's growth in a vertical sense; but, Henríquez Ureña argues, for women's progress to be collective, culture needs to be spread horizontally through schools, exhibitions, the press, radio, and film. These modes of communication are responsible for much more than simply facilitating the passing of an exam or instilling literary and artistic tastes. And, she argues, women have a transcendental role in transforming cultural communication.

What is that role? Henríquez-Ureña celebrates the essential "feminine" qualities women bring to society: "el sentido maternal de la existencia" [the maternal sense of existence]. Women are more psychological, intuitive, and spiritual than men, and capable of forging the basis for a new morality (*Estudios* p. 454). She notes that it may be centuries before women achieve the moral freedom, satisfying work, and habitual intellectual activity that will create a climate in which a female Shakespeare or the like will be produced. In response to the humanitarian crisis facing society at this time (caused by World War I and with the rising threat of Hitler in the months before World War II), Henríquez Ureña argues, it seems most appropriate that women, to whom the mission of protecting and preserving has always fallen, defend cultural values. Then she challenges those women who know their duty to attend the Women's Conference, where collective action will be discussed.

Four months later, Henríquez Ureña delivered "Feminismo". In it, she gives a historical background to the claims she makes in "Mujer y Cultura". The essay traces the patriarchal parameters of women's identities from primitive tribal organization through the emergence of the bourgeoisie. Moreover, she argues that a feminist (in celebration of the feminine) movement is a natural societal evolution (comparable to, as well as a result of, industrialization). As social organization is evolving, so too is the individual's relationship with the larger whole; because women's roles had changed, naturally a change must come about in the ways women are valued in society. To Henríquez Ureña, women's liberation means solving the problems women experience both as a sex (through ideology), and as social class (through material exploitation).

The evolution of the relationship between men and women that Henríquez Ureña explains in "Feminismo" is based on a Marxist understanding of economic determinism. Her long historical description of early familial organization and other possible roles for women accounts for class differences. For example, when discussing the onset of industrialization and women working outside the home, Henríquez Ureña notes the distinct problems facing working-class women as compared to women from the bourgeois class. Whereas the former lacked legal protection and were exploited without recourse, the latter, claims Henríquez Ureña, realized that along with their inferior legal status, they lacked the knowledge to understand bureaucracy, commerce, and industry.

However, while economic emancipation frames Henríquez Ureña's list of objectives in "Feminismo," it is not exclusive. She outlines other forms of resistance to oppression that mirror the different feminist agendas that evolve during the second and third waves: American (legal/political), English (economic) and French (sexuality, the body). In their entirety, the necessary steps she proposes for improving women's condition reflect a key element in some Latin American feminisms; rather than promoting equality with men, they seek to extend traditionally feminine roles into the public sphere. Henríquez Ureña proposes transforming women's legal status (including laws favoring maternity); obtaining political rights; guaranteeing the right to and the possibility of obtaining a complete education; and, revising the bases on which sexual mores are founded. This last step she sees as the most difficult, as it requires not only a change in law, but in customs and attitudes towards women and their behavior.

"Feminismo" contains an outline of the phallocentrality of woman's existence as correlative to man's (10 years before Simone de Beauvoir's *The Second Sex*!). The consequences of an exclusively male interpretation of the feminine not only leave women few options, Henríquez Ureña argues, but also solidify the prejudicial moral foundation upon which women's behavior is judged. Although she continues to read what is masculine and feminine through a traditional lens, she has clearly set out the difference between sex and gender and the subsequent entrenched sexual mores applied to women.

In both of these essays, Henríquez Ureña celebrates the feminine and feminism as transformative for all of society, not just for women. In "Feminismo," she states, women's two immediate tasks are to break down the barriers to public life while building a strong *vida interior* [interior life/being]. Changing traditional virtues of submission, obedience, silence, separateness and fragility to strong judgment, firmness, serenity, cooperation and community will perhaps contribute to changing the worst masculine characteristics of society: the predominance of violence and brute force, egotism and sensuality.

More importantly, in both essays, Henríquez Ureña recognizes the differences among women and calls for unity. She warns against divisive assumptions that lead women to block their evolution. As "Feminismo" deals primarily with matrimony, she singles out women who believe that laws to loosen divorce requirements or protect illegitimate children constitute a threat to their own security and undermine the sacrifices they have made to remain "virtuous" (*Estudios* p. 566). In "Mujer y cultura," Henríquez Ureña criticizes those women who do not want to become active in the collective transformation of society and who deny feminine culture for religious reasons or "servidumbre tradicional por ignorancia" [traditional subservience caused by ignorance]. Lastly, she accuses some women who believe they are liberated as simply "míseras remedadoras del vicio masculino" [a miserable mimicry of masculine vices] (*Estudios* p. 456).

Henríquez Ureña desired a balance between the divided camps of Cuban feminism. Perhaps a critical view from the twenty-first century would call her an "essentialist". However, her insistence on education and cultural change is found in the basis for current feminist theory on culture and positionality. Her calls for solidarity still ring true: if women have been rivals because their existence was correlative to men's, now women can be sisters in purpose, members of humanity with similar life-problems. Interestingly, Henríquez Ureña's work in Cuba during the revolution did not follow this activist line of thinking. Perhaps she saw the Marxist nature of the new society as synonymous with her fundamental idea of women's access to culture and public life. Rather than espousing these ideas, then, Henríquez Ureña would instead become a successful model through her teaching – promoting culture and its power to produce collective societal transformation.

A Teacher and a Scholar

Camila Henríquez Ureña's scholarly essays read like lectures given by a captivating professor. Her feminist and humanist thematic agenda changed over the years, but was sustained on the underlying notion of the importance of understanding western thought and culture, and its purpose in addressing universal human questions and bettering collective existence. To teach literature, she maintains, is to teach people to read, to discern what is of value, whereas to teach science is to teach a specific knowledge. Therefore, she saw her role as instilling in her students the critical thinking necessary for understanding the evolving nature of human existence.

Her literary studies and lectures on pedagogy were collected and published in *Estudios y conferencias* in 1982. In addition to her meditations about women in society, Henríquez Ureña sought to answer questions about the value of women and the feminine as produced by and as producers of culture. Her readings constitute some of the first feminist literary criticism written in Cuba. Through the praxis of revealing the masculine and feminine as opposites with consequentially assigned values and signs, Henríquez Ureña identifies and celebrates feminine difference in and through literature. For example, she analyses the "masculine" construction of the romantic female ideal in Espronceda's *Estudiante de Salamanca*. Taking the different forms of verse used to portray masculine and feminine characters (the first through concrete octosyllabic verse and the second through hendecasyllabic verses full of metaphor and simile), she suggests that the construction of an unreachable ideal allowed men to continue justifying their misunderstanding of women. Her analysis of the epistle as a "feminine" genre highlights the impassioned (mundane and mystic) correspondence written by Mariana Alcoforado, Sor Juana, Santa Theresa, and Madame de Sevigné. Delmira Agustini's poetry, she suggests, contains a liberating form and content that allows the poet, and women poets to follow, to express feminine passion. Hinting at the erasure of boundaries later to form Cixous' *écriture féminine*, Henríquez Ureña highlights the feminist consciousness she had so avidly promoted during her Lyceum years.

Henríquez Ureña's broad background in Romance literatures is most evident in her papers and her teaching. She seeks out the humanist qualities in the literature of writers from Lope de Vega, to Goethe, to Julián de Casal and Eugene O'Neill. The reciprocal connections between literature, history, and philosophy, for example, are discussed in her writing on the birth of the novel, or the conflicts underlying the Renaissance as seen in texts by Cervantes, Calderón de la Barca and Shakespeare. Always incorporating her vast knowledge into her teaching, she published textbooks in Cuba on *cantares de gesta* (epic poetry), Dante Alighieri, and William Shakespeare in the early 1970s. Many of Cuba's writers and scholars at the end of the twentieth and beginning of the twenty-first century studied under her and continue to seek out connections between the particular and the universal, literature and history, and Western culture's influence over norms and criteria for valuing culture and their own cultural production.

Henríquez Ureña's contributions are well documented and have been celebrated in numerous tributes in the Dominican Republic, Cuba, and the United States, including a fictional portrait of her life in Julia Alvarez's historical novel, *In the Name of Salomé*. Her family roots, feminist activism, and tireless teaching and scholarly labor during Cuba's revolutionary moments make her one of the best-respected female intellectuals of the Hispanic Caribbean in the twentieth century.

BARBARA D. RIESS

Selected Works

Ideas pedagógicas de Eugenio María de Hostos. Dominican Republic: Talleres Gráficos de *La Nación*, 1932.

Origen del hombre. Resumen de los datos de la antropología biológica y la paleontología humana conocidos en la actualidad. La Habana: Universidad EPUH, 1964.

Apreciación literaria. 2nd edn. Havana: Instituto Cubano del Libro, Editorial Pueblo y Educación, 1974.

"Prologue". *Inferno, La divina comedia*. Trans. Bartolomé Mitre. Havana: Editorial Pueblo y Educación, 1977.

Estudios y conferencias. Havana: Editorial Letras Cubanas, 1982.

Invitación a la lectura (Notas sobre la apreciación literaria). Santo Domingo: Editoria Taller, 1985.

Diarios de viaje. Edited with an introduction by Zaida Capote Cruz. Havana: Instituto de literature y Linguística, 1994.

Feminismo y otros temas sobre la mujer en la sociedad. Santo Domingo: Editora Taller, 1994. Excerpt of "Feminism" in *Documents of Dissidence. Selected Writings by Dominican Women*. Ed. and trans. Daisy Cocco De Filippis. New York: The CUNY Dominican Studies Institute, 2000, pp. 63–77.

References and Further Readings

Antuña, Vicentina. "Camila Henríquez Ureña, in memoriam". *Casa de las Américas* 14(84) (1974): 96–105.

Alvarez, Julia. *In the Name of Salomé*. New York: Penguin, 2001.

Davies, Catherine. *A Place in the Sun? Women Writers in Twentieth Century Cuba*. London: Zed Books, 1997.

Mateo, Andrés. *Camila, escritora y maestra*. Santo Domingo: Editora Universal, 2004.

Santos Moray, Mercedes. "Homenaje a Camila Henríquez Ureña: segundo aniversario". *Revolución y Cultura* 38 (1975): 4–7.

Yáñez, Mirta. *Camila y Camila*. Havana: Centro Cultural Pablo de la Torriente Brau, 2003.

HERNÁNDEZ, LUISA JOSEFINA

The Mexican dramatist, novelist, professor and critic, Luisa Josefina Hernández (b. 1928) is a prolific writer. Winner of four national literary awards, her corpus includes some 50 plays and an equal number of novels in diverse styles, almost all produced or published. Like Emilio Carballido, Sergio Magaña, and Jorge Ibargüengoitia, Hernández studied drama under Rodolfo Usigli at the National University of Mexico (UNAM). While she has worked in all genres, her fame derives primarily from her plays, ironic for an artist who calls theater "la maldición de la humanidad" (the curse of humanity) because so much of it is bad. Drama has shaped her personal and professional life. Once married to playwright Hector Mendoza, she taught dramatic theory and composition at UNAM for four decades and followed Usigli as department chair.

Hernández gained recognition early. She won the *Concurso de Primavera* prize (Spring Contest) in 1951 for *Aguardiente de caña* (Sugarcane Fire Water), and in 1954 a literary award from *El Nacional* (a major Mexico City newspaper) for *Botica Modelo* (Corner Pharmacy). The Center of Mexican Writers financed two grant periods: 1952–53, 1955–56. *Los frutos caídos* in 1955 (Fallen Fruit) not only earned her an MA in Literature from UNAM, but also the Fine Arts Dramatic Festival Award from the National Institute of Fine Arts in 1957 (INBA, Spanish acronym). Likewise, *Los huéspedes reales* (1957, Royal Guests) won INBA's Fine Arts Award in 1968; *Huéspedes* and *Frutos* are considered her masterworks. Two novels won awards: the Magda Donato Award for *Nostalgia de Troya* (1971, Nostalgia for Troy), and Xavier Villarrutia Award for *Apocalipsis cum figuris*. Other honors include a Rockefeller Foundation grant to study theater with Eric Bentley at Columbia University in 1955, and a teaching Fulbright at the University of Colorado (1983–84). UNAM named her Professor Emerita in 1991, and in 2002 the Mexican government awarded her its National Prize for Sciences and Arts, their highest distinction.

Despite her success, Hernández laments her career choices. She states in an interview, "El teatro es mi oficio, no mi hobby" (theater is my job, not my hobby), that given another life she would choose a different career (Feliciano 1999: 138). She prefers fiction and writes drama only on commission. She avoids rehearsals allowing directors control over the production. Always passionate about Christian iconography, she nearly completed a doctorate in Art History on the Christian and native motifs that adorn Mexico's colonial churches. Family life intervened. Abandoning her studies, she moved to Cuernavaca where she still lives.

Styles and Themes

A master of dramatic styles, Hernández started with realism but has experimented with didactic theater, miracle plays, and theater of the absurd. Her early plays criticize the stultifying effects of social mores on families and individuals. The protagonists are mainly middle-class women forced to sacrifice happiness to convention, such as Celia in *Los frutos caídos* and Cecilia in *Los huéspedes reales*. Hernández, however, refutes a feminist label because while men inflict much of the pain, they suffer in equal measure. In *Los sordomudos* (1953, Deaf-Mutes), for example, a tyrannical father drives away his children; his solitude symbolic of his alienation from God. A more lyrical style emerges with *La calle de gran ocasión* (1962), created as dialogues for her students; she published a second series in 1985.

Commissioned by the Secretary of Public Education in 1960 to write for adolescents, Hernández plunged into the origins of inequality and injustice in contemporary society, and composed a quintet to create new myths from old stories. Documented incidents ground three plays; two come from Mesoamerican mythology. *La paz ficticia* (1960, False Peace) debunks the slogan of "peace and prosperity" propagated by Porfirio Díaz (1877–1911); *Paz* represents the massacre of Yaqui Indians and theft of their lands. *La historia de un anillo* (1961, History of a Ring) began as a newspaper report: the town's mayor falsely accused an Indian servant of stealing his lover's ring, then destroyed the Indian village. Based on the trial records of a black man accused of malfeasance, *La fiesta del mulato* (1968, The Mulatto's Orgy) decries the decadence of church and state in colonial Guanajuato. The mulatto's true crime was to defy the racial prejudice codified in the caste laws. *Mulato* suggests that the idealized racial harmony posited in "La raza cósmica" (1925, The Cosmic Race), a nationalist essay by José Vasconcelos, remains unrealized.

In contrast, the mythic plays animate exemplary models. *Popul Vuh* (1966) re-enacts the Mayan creation myth, "the Book of Council". The oldest literature of the Americas (scholars date it to the thirteenth century), her version questions how the "men of maize" became so tortured and burned. *Quetzalcóatl* (1967, Feathered Serpent) expresses a similar respect for the "Ancient Words" of the Nahua-Aztec people. The god of duality urges Mexican youth to guard their history for learners yet unborn. By analogy, he emboldens students to take pride in their culture and address the injustices of racism.

Aware of the audience's familiarity with their socio-political problems and mythic heroes, Hernández turned to Brechtian agility to entertain as well as educate. The quintet relies on epic techniques: placards, narrators, allegorical characters, episodic development, and spectacular staging to stimulate Brecht's emotional "distance" and promote critical judgments. Beyond the appeal to political commitment, the scenic images project a textured theatricality, with Christian and native iconography, rich vestments and settings, songs, dances, and lighting.

Hernández's style evolved again in the 1970s; her *autos sacramentales* (miracle plays) imagine a more perfect world. The ritualized development of *Danza del urugallo múltiple* (1971, Dance of the Big Complex Rooster), her most celebrated *auto,* juxtaposes human and divine love in a mystical setting. *Pavana de Aranzazú* (1975, Pavane of Aranzazú), another *auto,* posits a paradise with flexible gender roles, and a young couple about to engender a balanced, healthy society. In *Apocrypha* (1978), the ageless woman who emerges from Brueghal's painting, "The Triumph of Death," is the eternal feminine and mother. In a one-act monologue, she lives backwards as various biblical women to culminate as Eve. In these plays, the supernatural settings and battle between good and evil correspond to the *auto* form; the characters' longing for a cosmic communion recalls the metaphor created by Octavio Paz that Mexicans live in a labyrinth of solitude.

Major Works

Hernández builds upon classical structures to represent the scripted lives of middle-class women trapped in or about to enter flawed marriages in *Los frutos caídos* and *Los huéspedes reales*; irony and fatalism foreshadow the denouement. In *Frutos* Celia, an apparently liberated professional woman with two children by two husbands, returns to her ancestral home to sell her estate. On the verge of another divorce, she dares to consider the seductions of a new suitor. Under pressure from the provincial relatives, she cancels the sale, rejects the suitor, and stays in a loveless marriage for the children, knowing that she will rot like the fruit in the title.

The plot of *Huéspedes* counterposes triangles of forbidden love driven by infamy and incest. Cecilia, a reluctant fiancée, despairs about marrying her true love or the rich lout picked by her mother, while she fantasizes about marrying her father. By nature a good person, Cecilia's hatred demeans her; she delights in her misery and certain defeat. As passions escalate, Cecilia becomes the Greek Electra: loathing her mother, lusting for her father, and failing to recognize her faults. Her best friend counsels moderation, the role of the Greek chorus. Her talk of red carnations at the wedding banquet suggests that the "royal guests" of the title will witness her blood sacrifice. Both *Frutos* and *Huéspedes* denounce honoring unjust traditions such as arranged marriages.

Hernández returned to the realistic portrayal of women and families with *El orden de los factores* (1983, The Order of Factors). María Elena, a female physician, is a new woman. She disregards the sexual hypocrisies of her ex-husband and the recriminations of her mother to transcend the sordidness around her. She dares to love and marry again, and vows to raise her son differently. Marriage becomes an act of solidarity; deference to rigid mores yields to love and companionship.

Emilio Carballido, the most often-produced and celebrated playwright in contemporary Mexico, considers Hernández a pioneer. He identifies *Los duendes* (1960, The Spirits), a farce about a dysfunctional family, a forerunner to the theater of the absurd. He credits her didactic theater with introducing Brechtian techniques to Mexico. He praises the profound and elegant realism of *Los frutos caídos* and *Los huéspedes reales*, and exalts her expressionistic *autos* like *Danza del urugallo múltiple* (1991: 704). Carballido calls Hernández "el talento mayor de nuestra generación (y de varias)". [The greatest talent of our generation (and of several others)] (1991: 706).

Behind Luisa Josefina Hernández's vast corpus and forty years of teaching dramatic construction and analysis, dwells an artist who wants to impose order on the chaos and disparity around her. She experiments with diverse dramatic forms that represent her vision of the struggle between individuals and society. A master technician in both classical or modern forms, her artful use of stagecraft, dance, music, visual and auditory images anchors the characters to a wretched world in need of change. A social system that imposes female abnegation, tolerates sexual hypocrisy and ignores political corruption perverts everyone.

WILMA FELICIANO

Selected Works

Botica Modelo (Corner Pharmacy). Serialized in the newspaper *El Nacional*, Mexico City, 1953.

Los sordomudos (Deaf-Mutes). *América* 69 (March 1954): 133–50.

La hija del rey (The King's Daughter). In Alvaro Arauz (ed.), *Cuarta antología de obras en un acto*. México: Colección de Teatro Mexicano 24 (1965): 7–15.

Los duendes (The Spirits). In Antonio Magaña Esquivel (ed.), *Teatro Mexicano 1963*. México: Aguilar, 1965, pp. 233–305.

Los huéspedes reales (Royal Guests). *Teatro mexicano del siglo XX.* México: Fondo de Cultura Económica, 1970: 81–138.

The Mulatto's Orgy. In William Oliver (ed. and trans.), *Voices of Change in Spanish American Theater.* Austin, TX: University of Texas Press, 1971, pp. 219–55.

Dialogues, Nos. 1, 12 and 15. In Francesca Colecchia and Julio Matas (eds and trans.), *Selected Latin American One Act Plays.* Pittsburgh, PA: University Press, 1973, pp. 125–39.

Apostasía (Apostasy). *Revista de Bellas Artes* 17 (September–October 1974): 48–64.

Pavana de Aranzazú. Tramoya 1 (October–December 1975): 13–37.

Caprichos y Disparates de Goya (Caprices and Nonsense by Goya). Mexico City: UNAM, Coordinación de Humanidades, 1979.

Ciertas cosas (Certain Things). *Tramoya* 18 (January–March 1980): 4–10.

La historia de un anillo (History of a Ring). In *Teatro para obreros*. México: Editores Mexicanos Unidos, 1984, pp. 243–85.

La calle de gran ocasión/diálogos (The Street of Grand Occasion/Dialogues). Mexico City: Editores Mexicanos Unidos, 1985 – includes interview with Espinosa, pp. 11–27.

El orden de los factores (The Order of Factors). *Tramoya* 12/13 (1987).

Danza del urogallo múltiple (The Dance of the Big Complex Rooster). *Dramaturgas latinoamericanas contemporáneas*. Madrid: Verbum, 1991, pp. 199–224; interview 45–50.

Los frutos caídos (Fallen Fruit). *Teatro mexicano contemporáneo, Antología*. México: Fondo de Cultura Económica, 1991: 701–808 (includes prologue by Emilio Carballido).

La paz ficticia (False Peace). México: Editorial Gaceta, 1994; comprises *La paz ficticia*, *Popul Vuh*, *La fiesta del mulato*, and *Quetzalcóatl*.

El galán de ultramar, La amante, Fermento y sueño, Tres perros y un gato: Teatro (The Dandy from Abroad, The Lover, Ferment and Sleep, Three Dogs and a Cat). Xalapa, México: Universidad Veracruzana, 2000.

References and Further Reading

Bisset, Judith. "Luisa Josefina Hernández y Estela Portillo Trambley: La expresión dramática de una voz femenina: Semejante o distinta?" *Ollantay* (1/2) (July 1993): 14–19.

Carballido, Emilio. "Un realismo profundo". In *Teatro mexicano contemporáreo, Antología*. Madrid: Fondo de Cultura Económica, 1991, pp. 703–7.

Cohen, Deb. "Defining and Defying 'Woman' in Four Plays by Luisa Josefina Hernández". *Latin American Theatre Review* 30(2) (Spring 1997): 89–102.

Dauster, Frank. "La forma ritual en *Los huéspedes reales*". In *Ensayos sobre el teatro hispanoamericano*. Mexico: Sepsetentas, 1975, pp. 60–5.

Feliciano, Wilma. "Entrevista a Luisa Josefina Hernández: 'El teatro es mi oficio, no mi hobby.'" *Gestos* (14/28) (November 1999): 135–9.

——. "El nacimiento de México en *Popul Vuh* de Luisa Josefina Hernández". In *Teatro latinoamericano para niños*. Medellín, Col: Universidad de Antioquia, 2002, pp. 285–337; includes text of *Popul Vuh*.

Foster, David W. "Lo incompleto como textura dramática en *Los frutos caídos*". *Estudios sobre el teatro mexicano contemporáneo*. New York: Peter Lang, 1984, pp. 41–51, 143–4.

Knowles, John K. "The Labyrinth of Form: Luisa Josefina Hernández". In Leon F. Lyday and George W. Woodyard (eds), *Dramatists in Revolt*. Austin, TX: University of Texas Press, 1976, pp. 133–45.

Krugh, Janis Lynne. "Solitude and Solidarity: Major Themes and Tecnhiques in the Theater of Luisa Josefina Hernández." Dissertation Abstracts International 47(6) (December 1986): 2174A.

Nigro, Kirsten. "Entrevista a LJH". *Latin American Theatre Review* 18(2) (Spring 85): 101–4.

HERNÁNDEZ-NÚÑEZ, ANGELA

Angela Hernández-Núñez (b. 1954) is a prominent woman author from the Dominican Republic, who has written several works of fiction as well as a number of essays. Born in Jarabacoa, a town located in the central region of the country, Hernández-Núñez was raised in an environment that fostered her academic and intellectual growth. Although this Dominican writer attained a degree in chemical engineering, she is devoted to writing. She also has dedicated considerable time to researching the feminist movement and other social and political events which have influenced her country, her life and her writings. Among these events are the end of the Trujillo era in 1961, the American intervention of 1965, and the weaknesses of the Dominican educational system. In 1985, she published a series of essays entitled *Diez prejuicios sobre el feminismo* (Ten Prejudices against Feminism). One year later, she wrote an essay, *Emergencia del silencio* (Emerging from Silence), published in 1986, which reflects her opinions on education.

Narrative and Poetry

Angela Hernández-Núñez is best known for her collections of short stories, some of them translated into English and Italian. Her first collection, *Las mariposas no les temen a los cactus* (Butterflies Are Not Afraid of Cacti) was published in 1985. It includes eleven stories, one of them, "Carmen quiere vivir", with the title of the collection appearing as one of the last lines in the story. This collection portrays the lives of women suffering because of mistreatment and neglect. These women, in their pursuit for a new horizon in life, have been victims of manipulation and abuse by a man, or men, with whom they have been involved; sometimes the female protagonist becomes a victim of circumstances, dying as a result of common city violence. These women search for a different future, a new life in marriage, an opportunity to see a doctor, a college degree, and they find mockery, hatred, ostracism, or death. These stories depict women trying to succeed in their lives, whichever that direction may be. According to Hernández-Núñez, the stories included in *Las mariposas no les temen a los cactus* were originally published as newspaper articles, based on real life situations.

Alótropos (Allotrope) is the title of a collection of seventeen short stories published in 1989, and one of them has the same title as the collection. The first story, "De comparecer se trata" (It is about Making an Appearance) has an autobiographical tone in which the narrator discusses the meaning of time, and how she has as many stages in life as passions. These stages could last months or years and they are measured by the degree of intensity she is able to interiorize in her inner self. A feature that appears in some of these stories is the unfolding of the main character to represent different voices or several identities. Just as *allotropy* is the representation of an element in many forms, "Alótropos" is a story about a woman and a poet with more than one voice. Two additional stories with a polyphonic style in the narration are "Alí Samán" and "El encuentro" (The Encounter). "Cómo recoger la sombra de las flores" (How to Gather the Shadows of the Flowers) is the story of Faride, a well-educated woman who generates different perceptions in different people; she could appear to be a crazy person as well as a sensible individual. This effect is achieved by using more than one narrative voice in the text. "Amo tres hombres" (I Love Three Men) and "El mejor" (The Best) present the female protagonist as an individual embodying completeness and outstanding qualities. In "Amo tres hombres," the protagonist finds out that the three men can offer her different facets of love that complement each other to provide total happiness. "El mejor" is an entertaining story in which the only female member in a band of terrorists is able to eliminate the best police officer assigned to capture her. The natural wonders of Jarabacoa are reflected in the stories of *Alótropos*.

Piedra de sacrificio (Sacrificial Stone) received the *Premio Nacional de Cuentos* (Short Story National Prize) in 1998, and was published in 2000. Hernández-Núñez includes thirteen stories in this collection, and as with the previous collection, one of the stories has the same title as the collection. In this collection, for instance, in "Cúmulo nimbo" (Cumulonimbus), or "Una gota de sangre" (A Drop of Blood), women appear as a repository of the role of wife and mother, always ready to fulfill the duties society has assigned to them.

Angela Hernández-Núñez is also the author of the novel, *Mudanza de los sentidos* (Change of Senses), which won the *Premio Cole* (The Cole Prize) in 2001 and published that same year. *Mudanza de los sentidos* is narrated in the first person, from the point of view of a young girl, who recounts a series of memories with wonder. The ethnic background of the family reflects a common racial combination in the Dominican Republic, a mix of European and African ancestry. The father dies and the children are cared for by the mother and an aunt, with whom she spends time in different houses. A short time later, the mother, Beba, becomes involved with a man named Demetrio Alonso. This young girl, the main character, has four sisters and a brother named Virgilio. This male character represents a revolutionary who does not like the military; he is a bright individual with significant life experience. He assumes the role of a teacher who motivates his sisters to learn about nature and the world around them. The young child's memories can evoke the degrading changes in the family living arrangements, from a big house with her parents, to a small house without a father, to a tenement house in the capital, rented by Demetrio Alonso, her mother's friend. Hernández-Núñez's novel reveals social differences based mainly on economic success, and it also includes regional vocabulary and popular beliefs in the story. Changes in this novel seem to revolve around the term *adaptación* (adaptation) as a painful way to discover and learn to adjust to a new situation.

Taller de rebeldía (Workshop for Rebellion), published in 1998, is a collection of twenty-eight poems, written in free verse, in a staccato manner. Hernández-Núñez's poetry collection includes narrative and visual poems, with techniques corresponding to contemporary poetry in general. Her poems deal with the subject of identity, and the magic of the landscape of Jarabacoa.

Angela Hernández-Núñez's works are influenced by her closeness to nature while growing up, and her courage and independence. Some of the characters and details in the plot of selected stories show some autobiographical features. As mentioned before, the people of the Dominican Republic are characterized by a racial mixture of European and African descent. Their physical, as well as their social and cultural features are present in Hernández-Núñez's narrative and poetry. In an anthology of Dominican women writers, Daisy Cocco de Filippis classifies the writers in three categories: *combated*, *combative*, and *combatant*. Angela Hernández-Núñez is placed with Julia Alvarez in the latter category, with those who feel more confident and are able to use humor, irony and dialogue in their writings.

CLARA H. BECERRA

Selected Works

Las mariposas no les temen a los cactus. Santo Domingo: Universidad Autónoma de Santo Domingo, Editora Universitaria, 1985.

Alótropos. Santo Domingo, República Dominicana: Editora Grafideas, 1989.

Taller de rebeldía. Santo Domingo, República Dominicana, Editorial Gente, 1998.

Mudanza de los sentidos. Santo Domingo, República Dominicana: Editora Cole, 2001.

Piedra de sacrificio. Santo Domingo, República Dominicana: Editorial Alas, 2000

References and Further Reading

Adams, Clementina R. (ed.) *Rebeldía, denuncia y justicia social: voces enérgicas de autoras hispanoamericanas y españolas*. Miami, FL: Ediciones Universal, 2004.

Fernández Olmos, Margarita and Paravisini-Gebert, Lizabeth (eds) *Remaking a lost harmony: Stories from the Hispanic Caribbean*. Fredonia, NY: White Pine Press, 1995.

González, Carolina. "An Interview with Angela Hernández Núnez." *Callaloo* 23(3) (2000): 999–1010.

Montero, Jenny. *La cuentística dominicana*. Santo Domingo, República Dominicana: Biblioteca Nacional, Colección Orfeo, 1986.

Pérez, Olga Marta, Jiménez, Thelma and Blanco, Andrés D. (eds) *Mujeres como islas: antología de narradoras cubanas, dominicanas y puertorriqueñas*. Santo Domingo, República Dominicana: Ediciones Ferilibro, 2002.

HILST, HILDA

Hilda Hilst (1930–2004) was one of, if not the most, controversial personality in the Brazilian literary scene in the last half of the twentieth century. As poet, playwright and fiction writer, she was a distinct literary personality who incorporated in her unconventional writings an anguished and intricate search for love, lust and metaphysical answers to questions of life. She influenced Brazilian literature through her writings on poetry, theater and fiction. In the latter, she used fragmented sentences, scarce punctuation, a sort of open-ended vocabulary, in a constant search for new meanings for conventional words, revolving themes linked to affection and sensations. In poetry, she applied melodic, lyric expressions and sharp images, imbued of a philosophical intention. For her plays she applied the minimalist style, identifying characters mostly by age ("The Old One"), physical characteristics ("The Hunchback"), or letters ("Nun A", "Nun B"). Hilst's writings expose her reflections about love, personal disappointment, death, friendship, betrayal, solitude, spiritual searches, and mysticism, including God as an unbalanced presence and absent in her life. Her writings' content is paradoxically realistic, metaphysical, subliminal and extroverted, thus the roots of the power of her literary creativity.

Hilda Hilst was born in the town of Jaú, in the state of São Paulo, into a wealthy family. As the daughter of rich landowners, Apolonio de Almeida Prado Hilst and Bedecilda Vaz Cardoso, she enjoyed a privileged way of life, and attended exclusive private boarding schools in the city of São Paulo. Her father, who was a journalist and poet, was diagnosed with schizophrenia early in Hilda Hilst's childhood. Due to his frequent hospitalizations, the tiny family separated, and his wife and their daughter moved out to the city of Santos. Her mother would be diagnosed with similar mental disease later in her life.

At the age of 18, the future author passed the entrance examination at the Law School of the University of São Paulo. At 20, still a student, Hilst presented her first book, *Presságio* (Prophecy), a collection of poems. Weaving tense words and incisive imagery, her lyricism seemed rooted more in a female's passionate feelings and sensuality than in the traditional terminology honored by the romantic literary tradition. For her next books of poems, emphasizing the melodic attribute of poetry, she borrowed terms from the Portuguese medieval poetics such as "baladas" (ballads), "cantos" and "cantares" (songs) as in the books' titles *Baladas de Alzira* (1951, Alzira's Ballads), *Baladas do festival* (1955, Festival's Ballads), *Sete cantos do poeta para o anjo* (1962, Seven Songs from the Poet to the Angel, São Paulo PEN Club Award), *Cantares de perda e predileção* (1980, Songs of Losses and Preferences, Jabuti/Brazilian Chamber of Books Award, and Cassiano Ricardo/Poetry Club of São Paulo Award, 1981), and *Cantares do sem nome e de partidas* (1995, Songs of the Nameless and on Departures).

Graduating in 1952, she did not practice Law, with the exception of a few months right after graduation. Instead, she dedicated her life to reading, writing and publishing. She was an intelligent, attractive, elegant, and rich woman used to courtships, flattery and glamour. As an adolescent and young woman she traveled frequently, mainly to Europe, where she enjoyed parties, luxurious environments and the company of international celebrities.

She brought an end to this way of life in 1965, when she decided to move to a farm that belonged to her mother, near the city of Campinas, in the state of São Paulo, where she built a house that she called *Casa do Sol* (The Sun House). There she lived in semi-seclusion until her death, caring for almost one hundred dogs collected in the streets. In the farm she would regularly receive a handful of visitors, from writers to stage directors to artists in general, cultivating a circle of friends characterized by the participants' congeniality and diversity of talents. She claimed that her decision to change her life style was due to her readings of works by Nikos Kazantzakis (1883–1957), where it is suggested that an artist should live away from the multitudes in order to find the essence of humankind.

In 1968, Hilst married Dante Casarini, a sculptor, with whom she had previously been living. They divorced in 1985, but he continued to keep his studio in the farm, while caring for its administration.

After becoming known as poet and playwright, the author launched her first book of fiction, *Fluxo-Floema* (1970, Flow-Phloem). It consists of five sections that one cannot easily classify as "short stories", or as "chronicles", or as "narratives" either. They present facets of all genders and styles through a gushing of personal emotions, feelings and sensations interspersed with memories, messages, letters and descriptions of isolated incidents that happened to her. She writes, "I know only to write about things that come from my inside, and these things from the inside are very complex, but they are . . . they are the things from the inside" (*Fluxo-Floema*, p. 184).

Claiming that her books were not read by the public at large, she published *A obscena senhora D* (The Obscene Lady D, 1982), with the purpose of startling and eventually attracting readers' attention to her other books. Eight years later she still insisted on bringing an obvious sexual dimension to her literary works with a series of writings that became known as "the trilogy of eroticism": *O caderno rosa de Lori Lamby* (1990, The Pink Notebook of Lori Lamby), *Contos d'escárnio—Textos Grotescos* (1990, Short Stories of Scorn—Grotesque Texts,), and *Cartas de um sedutor* (1991, Letters by a Seducer). The first of them, possibly the most provocative of the three, is a fictional account of an 8-year-old girl who describes in a diary how she submits to sexual acts with adult men. The protagonist's last name, which is part of the story's title, is a play of words in Portuguese: "Lamby" sounds like the first person singular of the past tense of verb *lamber* (to lick). The other two components of the trilogy follow the same pattern of realistic descriptions of sexual acts. Defiant, irreverent, pornographic, scatological, obscene are a few of the epithets sent the author's way by readers and some critics of the series. After the trilogy, Hilst returned to her usual style.

The University of Campinas (Unicamp) acquired Hilst's personal archives in 1995, which is open to the public at the *Centro de Documentação* (Archives Center) Alexandre Eulálio, in the *Instituto de Estudo de Linguagem* (Languages Studies Institute).

In 2002, she received the Moinho Santista Award of Poetry and, in 2003, the *Grande Prêmio da Crítica* (Major Critic's Award) for the re-edition of her complete works.

In January 2004, Hilda Hilst fell in her home and required an operation on her leg as a result of the fall. She died in the hospital of post-surgery complications.

Hilst was known as someone who feared being forgotten. In response to this, immediately after her demise, following the initiative of author José Luiz Mora Fuentes, some of her friends gathered and founded the Hilda Hilst Institute – The Living House of Sun, a non-profit research institution that appeals to the public to continue its cultural mission.

REGINA IGEL

Selected Works

Poetry

Roteiro do Silêncio. São Paulo: Anhambi, 1959.

Trovas de muito amor para um amado senhor. São Paulo: 1959.

Sete cantos do poeta para o anjo. São Paulo: Massao Ohno, 1962. (Illustrations by Wesley Duke Lee.)

Poesia (1959/1967). São Paulo: Livraria Sal, 1967.

Da Morte. Odes mínimas. São Paulo: Massao Ohno, Roswitha Kempf, 1980. (Illustrations by the author.)

Cantares de perda e predileção. São Paulo: Massao Ohno/M. Lídia Pires e Albuquerque Editores, 1980.

Amavisse. São Paulo: Massao Ohno, 1989.

Do desejo. São Paulo: Pontes, 1992.

Cantares do sem nome e de partidas. São Paulo: Massao Ohno, 1995.

Fiction:

Fluxo-Floema. São Paulo: Editora Perspectiva, 1970.

Qadós. São Paulo: Edart, 1973.

Ficções. São Paulo: Quíron, 1977.

A obscena senhora D. São Paulo: Massao Ohno, 1982.

Com meus olhos de cão e outras novelas. São Paulo: Editora Brasiliense, 1986. (Ilustrated by the author.)

O caderno rosa de Lori Lamby. São Paulo: Massao Ohno, 1990. (Ilustrated by Millôr Fernandes.)

Contos d'escárnio/Textos grotescos. São Paulo: Livraria Siciliano, 1990.
Cartas de um sedutor. São Paulo: Paulicéia, 1991.
Do desejo. Campinas: Pontes, 1992.
Rútilo nada. Campinas: Pontes 1993. (Jabuti/Brazilian Chamber of Book Award.)
Do amor. São Paulo: Massao Ohno, 1999.
Obras Reunidas de Hilda Hilst. ed. Alcir Pécora. Rio de Janeiro: Editora Globo, 2004.

Anthologies (Selected)

Pallotini, Renata. "Rútilo nada". Trans. Isabel Meyrelles. In *Anthologie de la poésie brésilienne*. Paris: Chandeigne, 1988, pp. 373–81.
Castro, Sílvio. "Poeti brasiliani contemporanei". Venice: Centro Internazionale della Gráfica di Venezia, 1997, pp. 64–75.
Costa, Flavio Moreira Da. "Agüenta coração". In *Onze em campo e um bando de primeira*. Rio de Janeiro: Relume Dumará, 1998, pp. 39–40.
Moriconi, Ítalo. "Gestalt". In *Os cem melhores contos brasileiros do século*. Rio de Janeiro: Objetiva, 2000, pp. 332–3.

Theater

A Possessa. 1967.
O rato no muro. 1967.
O visitante. 1968.
As aves da noite. 1968.
O verdugo. 1969 (Anchieta/State Council of Culture Award, 1970).
A morte do patriarca. 1969.
Teatro reunido (vol. I: *A empresa, O rato no muro, O visitante, Auto da Barca de Camiri*). Theater Collected, Vol. I. São Paulo: Nankin Editorial, 2000.

Works Translated into English

Glittering Nothing. Trans. David William Foster. In Cristina Ferreira Pinto (ed.), *Urban Voices: Contemporary Short Stories from Brazil*. New York: University Press of America, 1999.
Two Poems. Trans. Eloah F. Giacomelli. *The Antagonist Review*, 20 (October 1975), p. 61.

Works Tranlated into German

Briefe eines Verführers. (Cartas de um sedutor, fragmento). Trans. Mechthild Blumberg Stint. *Zeitschrift für Literatur*, Bremen, 27(15): 28–30, October 2001.
Funkelndes Nichts (Rútilo nada). Trans. Mechthild Blumberg Stint. *Zeitschrift für Literatur*, Bremen, 29(15): 54–66, August 2001.

Works Translated into Spanish

Rútilo nada. Trans. Liza Sabater. *De azur*. New York, pp. 49–59, June/August 1994.

Works Translated into French

Contes sarcastiques – fragments érotiques. Paris: Gallimard, 1994.
L'obscène madame D suivi de Le Chien. Paris: Gallimard, 1997.
Da morte. Odes mínimas / De la mort. Odes minimes. Bilingual edition. São Paulo: Nankin Editorial / Montreal, Le Noroît, 1998

Works Translated into Italian

Il quaderno rosa di Lori Lamby. Rome: Sonzogno, 1992.

References and Further Reading

Arêas, Vilma and Waldman, Berta. *Hilda Hilst – o excesso em dois registros* (The excesses in Two Notes). Rio de Janeiro: *Jornal do Brasil*, October 3, 1989.
Coelho, Nelly Novaes. "*Da Poesia*." *Hilda Hilst-Cadernos de Literatura Brasileira*, 8. São Paulo: Instituto Moreira Salles, October 1999, pp. 66–79.
Pallotini, Renata. "*Do Teatro*". Hilda Hilst, Teatro Reunido. São Paulo: Nankin Editorial, 2000, pp. 165–81.

HUMOR IN CONTEMPORARY FICTION

Si tuviera que escribir mi credo,
empezaría por el humor:
creo en el sentido del humor a ultranza
creo en el humor negro, acérrimo
creo en el absurdo
en el grotesco.

If I had to write out my credo,
I would start with humor:
I believe in humor unto death
I believe in out-and-out black humor.
I believe in the absurd and the grotesque

(Luisa Valenzuela, *Peligrosas palabras*, 2001: 133)

First, a note on terminology: the term humor, and the adjective comic, are used here broadly and generically to refer to a range of discursive strategies meant to provoke an active response from readers who realize the incongruity, double-voicedness, absurdity or hyperbolic nature of the comic articulation, utterance, or situation. Given the noticeably hybrid and permeable nature of the rhetorical strategies adopted by Latin American contemporary women authors, distinctions made by scholars and theorists between humor and "the comic" are not only not useful but counterproductive. The most important aspects of humor in the literature of Latin America, therefore, are how it has been used, and why.

In "The Cultural Overseer and the Tragic Hero. Comedic and Feminist Perspectives on the Hubris of Philosophy," Susan Bordo advances the hypothesis that the comic and the feminine share certain common elements, among the most prominent of which are concreteness and physicality: humor is anchored in particular bodies. According to Bordo, it was the equation of the comic with the feminine, and with the female body in particular, that initially drove Greek philosophers to reject or devaluate the comic as a dramatic genre, and other areas of humor, as worthy subjects of study for thinkers or future statesmen.

Although nineteenth-century Latin American women authors had little encouragement to practice their wit and none to publish it, Clorinda Matto de Turner was said to be a great wit in public, even if no evidence of it appears in her tragic novel *Aves sin nido*. Juana Manuela Gorritti did leave ample proof of her humor, especially in her cooking "texts". One has to wait until the beginning of the twentieth century and the influence of modernism to see a fully-formed gendered wit among Latin American women writers. In *Ifigenia, memorias de una señorita que escribía porque se fastidiaba*, Venezuelan author Teresa de la Parra, adapts Euripedes' tragedy to modern-day Venezuela, only now the sacrifice does not entail a literal but a metaphorical death, through marriage to a moneyed but dull suitor. Written in diary form, and with letters interspersed throughout, the novel reflects María Eugenia's growing disappointment with the society that had allowed her a measure of freedom (through her parents' death and subsequent trip to Paris) only to gradually but brutally take it away from her as she must settle into the expectations of a lucrative but humorless marriage.

Rosario Castellanos, the Mexican writer, poet and journalist whose untimely death in the 1970s ended her career as one of

Mexico's most talented social critics, anchored her fictional and journalistic pieces solidly in concrete bodies found in particular historical or domestic situations, but she did so with the knowledge that the acid force of the ironic humor that was her trademark would begin to work its corrosive properties on the foundations of the vehemently masculinist society in which she lived and wrote. Possessing a more melancholy sense of humor but equally intent on exposing hypocrisy and social injustice through experimentation and satire, Clarice Lispector's work would play a similar role in Brazil. The author's dark satire would soon reverberate well beyond the boundaries of her native country. Although writing for a smaller "target" audience, Silvina Ocampo's surreal verbal wit and often vicious black humor would serve as a powerful model for future Southern Cone writers and poets, just as the lesser known but extraordinarily talented Armonía Somers would keep an entire generation of Uruguayan male writers on the edge of critical red-alarm over what a woman writer's pen could unleash if the woman were as wittily acerbic as she was attentive to detail and well acquainted with the biology of bodies. Castellanos' and Lispector's comic-ironic influence among contemporary women writers can be traced without difficulty on dozens of Latin American women writing in the past two decades as well as to women authors writing today. Ocampo's and Somers' influence, deeply encoded in the poetry and the prose of Alejandra Pizarnik, continues to find powerful echoes in the work of some of today's finest comic-satiric, or "camp" Southern-cone writers like Alicia Borinsky and Ana María Shúa.

Gendered Humor as Embodied Humor

In the superbly ironic *Mujer que sabe latín*, Castellanos noted that laughter is itself an immediate and often involuntary physical response. The title is itself an ironic call to arms. Using only one half of the well known saying "mujer que sabe latín/ no puede tener buen fin"—"a woman who knows Latin/ cannot have a good destiny"—as her title, she proceeds to show that a witty and well-educated woman (in other words, who does know some Latin) might have the last laugh in the end. She proceeds to advocate a campaign of *corrosive laughter* (*la carcajada corrosiva*), one which takes advantage of the embodied mobility of laughter to help disarm the social and cultural clichés that turn women into victims of humorless stereotypes. Like Susan Bordo, Rosario Castellanos was quick to note that the transformative potential of humor, and gendered humor in particular, resided in its physicality. Because the physicality of humor is both diffuse and difficult to articulate, its effects are also difficult to measure. As diffuse semantic and somatic articulations, humor and corporeal expressions of excess are not confined to the same discursive laws as ordinary speech and of more regulated bodily gestures. Herein lie both the unexpected powers of disruption and dislocation of gendered humor and its potential to backfire (or miss its target altogether). Such an example of the power of disruption appears in Clarice Lispector's short story "A menor mulher do mundo" (The smallest woman in the world). Here, the author plays with the social conventions that dictate that a woman will not touch certain parts of her body in public. The smallest woman in the world, black, and pregnant, does just that, to the embarrassment of the white scientist who examines her. The fact is that, indeed, he can never know what she is thinking as she "scratches herself in a place no woman should".

Latin American authors who engage distinct modalities of humor employ diverse comic tactics, engage different moods of the comic spectrum, and point to noticeably distinct ways in which humor can yield different types of de-centering or subversion. Despite some common targets, crucial ideological differences separate the comic-sentimental or comic-erotic effects of Laura Esquivel's *Como agua para chocolate*, Isabel Allende's *Afrodita* or Joyce Cavalccante's *Inimigas Intimas* from the carnivalesque bawdiness of Ana Lydia Vega's stories or Fanny Buitrago's novels. In turn, the Caribbean Rabelaisian punch present in Buitrago's and Vega's works has a distinctly different flavor from the equally physical but more nostalgically compromised comic excess of Zoe Valdés' novels. The skeptical wit and ironic humor of Luisa Valenzuela's stories and novels are marked by both a lighter view towards the sexual adult female body than the devastating black humor of Armonía Somers' *Sólo los elefantes encuentran mandrágora*. The Brazilian Patricia Melo and the exiled Argentine Alicia Borinsky share some interesting common elements in their use of urban black humor, yet the violent satire of Patricia Melo's bloody novels differs significantly from the more entropic *camp* humor of Alicia Borinsky's *Mina cruel* and *Cine continuado*. And there is also the kind of humor that appears in Brazilian writer Lygia Fagundes Telles' short stories, such as "As formigas" (The Ants), which opens with a comic reference to one of Brazil's most revered female characters, the protagonist of *Iracema*, written by José de Alencar in the apogee of the Romantic period. Iracema, the "virgin of honey lips," whose hair was blacker than "the wing of the graúna," in Telles becomes a very strange-looking older woman whose appearance should warn the main characters of the impeding danger. Clarice Lispector, in her turn, has a whole novel that can be read as an extended "philosophical joke": *A paixão segundo G. H.* (Passion According to G.H.) tells the story of a woman who has an "epiphany" while contemplating a cockroach. Social criticism and sharp presentation of the conditions of women as devalued members of a society, *Passion According to G.H.* ends in a note that not even Sartre, whom Lispector read and admired, would expect, but that would, most certainly, elicit laughter.

From Comic Sentimentality to Black Farce Through Carnivalesque Romp

On the more cautious end of the spectrum are narratives that straddle the fence between the wide mass appeal (for a largely female readership) of the sentimental comic and a more daring and offensive use of the comic. Despite significant geographic, cultural and linguistic differences, narratives written by Joyce Cavalccante (Brazil), Carmen Suárez (Colombia), Laura Esquivel and Angeles Mastretta (Mexico), Isabel Allende (Chile), Rosario Ferré (Puerto Rico), or Latina writers Julia Alvarez, Denise Chávez, Ana Castillo and Marta Acosta, frame their narratives in the more or less generically traditional formula of sentimental or domestic romance. Accordingly, the erotic-comic elements in these narratives tend to be muted by the parameters of the genre. Yet the fact that the stories of Mastretta's *Mujeres de ojos grandes*, Suárez's *Un vestido rojo para bailar boleros*, or Chávez's *The Last of the Menu Girls* continue to be read as potentially subversive texts by knowledgeable critics is in part proof that even mildly transgressive bodily humor, when put in practice by women's voices and women's bodies, can threaten to unhinge the frames of the generic frame's more stable social codes. In other words, even at the more cautious end of the gendered-humor spectrum, the combination of the comic with the incontinent or erotic female body can yield disrupting and disorienting results by introducing elements of comic chaos.

If at the mildly transgressive end of the gendered comic spectrum we find incontinent bodies, or bodies bursting with sexual juices, at the opposite end of this spectrum we find bodies exploding with bile and voices whose rage is tuned into the blackest of satirical or farcical outbursts. Appropriating Freudian assumptions about the liberating role of aggression in various kinds of humor, Armonía Somers' *Sólo los elefantes encuentran mandrágora* pitches a chronically ill protagonist against a nation's labor history, a medical and academic establishment, and a culture's maternal obsession with first-born sons. On a symbolic level, the novel's satiric bile is concentrated on the ill protagonist's chances of "infecting" her doctors with her body's own black humor before their experimental treatments finish her off. Her barely controlled fury feeds the narrative's nihilistic rhetoric and its anarchist politics; it also keeps the narrative's cynical wit at the perfect frigid temperature. Some of the same razor-sharp satire appears in Liliana Heker's last novel, *La crueldad de la vida*, but Heker's humor is less punctuated by gendered awareness than is Somer's, or Valenzuela's. Among the cultural clichés that gendered humor targets, especially aggressively dark gendered humor, is the old taboo that declares loud, uncontrollable laughter to be immodest and unattractive in a good woman: in Latin America as elsewhere, only witches and bitches were known to laugh hard and loud. The explanation for this proscription undoubtedly lies in the realization that aggressive laughter is *knowing* laughter—one laughs when one *gets* the joke, or when one is the teller, and not the target, of the joke. In all of Luisa Valenzuela or the late Armonía Somers' narratives, in Borinsky's novels, women not only get the joke—they often get the last laugh, even if the last laugh comes at a high price.

Somewhere in between these two extremes—those of cautious sentimental humor vs. aggressive black humor—one finds the comic irony and ironic or satiric parody of Ana Lydia Vega's stories, where bawdy *femmes fatales* play as hard at games of pleasure as female narrators do at trying to debunk—through irony and humor—the rules will in the end make these vamps pay dearly for their illicit pleasures. In her stories the attitude towards humor is markedly ambivalent. The author behind the narrators relishes her power to make her readers laugh against our own judgment even as she makes us squirm at the guilty pleasure we take in the laughter. Fanny Buitrago's novels, especially *Los amores de Afrodita* and *La señora de la miel*, share with Vega's stories the Rabelaisian sense of jocularity and the celebration of a Caribbean sense of verbal play, but Buitrago is more interested in unmasking her carnivalesque players than in trapping them into a deadly orgy—or a deadly pun—of their own making. The sense of carnivalesque, of excess, is clearly the province of *Señora de la miel*, in which the protagonist's sexual energies, restrained for so long, once released become a once a source of great happiness. Another kind of humor appears in Lygia Fagundes Telles' *As horas nuas* (The Naked Hours), in which one of the main characters is Rahul, a male cat who hears the intimate confidences of the protagonist. Later, when she admits her regret at having had Rahul castrated, the story can be seen as participating in the structure of a joke. The straddling the fence between smart wit and the consequences of being driven witless by cultural clichés that somehow keep resurfacing are Sabina Berman's dramatic characters. Metamorphosing from proper if somewhat predictable ladies to desperate would-be housewives to brave new lovers, these women characters are ultimately saved not by their fortitude or even by their resilience but by the transformative power of their comic wits. On the other hand, we see that in Clarice Lispector's stories, mainly in "A Chicken," the cliché surrounding the maternal body is completely destroyed in a parable that, although comical, reveals the tragic destiny reserved for women. The story depicts the struggle of a chicken who was saved from being cooked because, in the effort to run away from the family that tried to capture her to cook her for the Sunday lunch, she laid an egg, and thus revealed her "goodness," as well as her "maternity". The chicken then becomes "the queen of the house," and lives "between the kitchen and the porch, using her two capacities: apathy and the ability to be easily startled". But she was nothing more than a chicken and so, one day, they "killed her, ate her, and many years went by". What we can see here is some connection between Clarice Lispector and Cristina Peri Rossi, for whom the desired in-between zone for the comic is the space where subtle irony serves up revelation. If the loud laughter that often accompanies one's reading of Vega's stories is a guilty laughter, the half smile that guides one's reading of Peri Rossi's ironic narratives is often melancholy. The humor provoked by the exiled Uruguayan writer's stories and novels is postmodern humor at its most self-conscious—and subdued. In different socio-cultural contexts, the Latina lesbian playwright Cherríe Moraga resorts to deftly handled black humor to explore survival strategies at the crossroads of race and ethnicity.

Regional Comic Inflections and Humor as Social Strategy

Because humor is a social as well as a discursive phenomenon, it bears national, cultural and sometimes regional imprints of the socio-cultural environment in which it is produced or performed. The humor of certain local stereotypes and cultural practices in Laura Esquivel's *Como agua para chocolate* can be appreciated fully only in the context of Mexican history, Mexican cuisine and its crucial role in defining cultural identity, and a certain uniquely Mexican type of popular melodrama. Similarly, the overlapping curves and *cul-de-sac*s of Ana Lydia Vega's comic strategies in her stories are best understood in the context of *choteo* or *guachafita,* a decidedly Caribbean expression of humor, and humorous excess. There are recognizable traces of a distinctly urban *porteño* comic skepticism in Valenzuela's novels and stories. Alicia Borinsky's *Mina cruel* reflects the influence of tango culture (itself a national pastime easily given to parodic imitation). Armonía Somers' bilious humor could be said to bear traces of a specifically *platense* comic-gothic sensibility (the term *platense* comes from the Río de la Plata, the river that separates Montevideo from Buenos Aires).

Art critic Jo Anna Isaak has written extensively about the socially subversive power of gendered parody, black humor and the non-idealized body in contemporary North American and Russian women's art. For Isaak, aesthetic transgressions almost always result in social subversions – although the effect may have a delayed deployment. The critic maintains that by "providing libidinal gratification," laughter provoked by women's transgressive practices of humor can help us imagine new ways of relating "the social and the symbolic" (1996: 5). Isaak is optimistic about the power of comic gendered tactics to effect strategies of resistance not only in symbolic but in actual terms. Not all the humor in the narratives by the authors mentioned in this entry is sufficiently ambivalent, destructive, explosive, or revolutionary to be "Medusan" in Hélène Cixous' sense. Yet all of it threatens to destabilize and derail hegemonic "orders" of various types. Where the ludic tactics and the laughter are truly anarchic, the aesthetic and ethical consequences are left open and uncertain. In other words, in the darker and less festive of the novels studied here, the ludic subversions practiced resist merely turning the tables on the aggressors. Where the practice of humor is most entropic (in farce or camp, for example), the narrative often succeeds in de-centering inherited moral and ethical certainties but resists easy substitutes. It proposes instead an aesthetics of continuous destabilization.

Reflecting on new models of feminocentric discourse in Latin America in her article "Invading Public Space: Transforming Private Space," Jean Franco notes that a growing number of women writers resist direct confrontation with cultural, socio-political or discursive (androcentric) structures and opt, instead, for alternative ways of exposing, questioning or subverting such structures. Among the alternative tactics Franco mentions in this essay are parody, pastiche, an irreverent, iconoclastic approach to generic conventions, and an insistence on re-writing old myths. Without exception, all of these techniques can be subsumed under modalities of humor. Without exception, they are all techniques practiced, to a greater or lesser degree, by the authors mentioned above. Narratives marked by "humored" resistance rely on parodic techniques for exposing social and symbolic structures used to justify gender inequities, resort to pastiche and genre-bending in order to disrupt traditional discursive modes that give cultural credence to those inequities, and rewrite cultural and sociopolitical "myths" with a view to challenging these myths' "authorized" archetypes or foundational (role) models of gendered behavior. The fact that these models of resistance are frequently encoded, or at least experienced, in material female bodies, makes the resistance all the more convincingly concrete, but also more unsuspectingly destabilizing. Fleshed-out and anchored within cultural and historical spaces, the resulting modalities of resistant humor and ludic excess become avenues for challenging hierarchies, de-authorizing dominant models of ideological or actual domination, exploring alternative forms of (female) subjectivity, and celebrating the unexpected power of voices that have learned or are learning how to laugh at all sorts of supposedly serious things, and in all sorts of registers.

DIANNA NIEBYLSKI AND EVA BUENO

References and Further Reading

Acosta, Marta. *Happy Hour at Casa Drácula*. New York: Adobe Reader, 2006.

Allende, Isabel. *Afrodita: Cuentos, Recetas y Otros Afrodisiacos*. New York: Harper Perennial, 1998.

Bordo, Susan. "The Cultural Overseer and the Tragic Hero: Comedic and Feminist Perspectives on the Hubris of Philosophy". *Soundings* 65 (1982): 188–205

Borinsky, Alicia. *Mina cruel*. Buenos Aires: Corregidor, 1989.

——. *Cine continuado*. Buenos Aires: Corregidor, 1997.

Buitrago, Fanny. *Los amores de Afrodita*. Bogotá: Plaza & Janes, 1983.

——. *La señora de la miel*. Bogotá: Arango Editores, 1993.

Campello, Myriam. *São Sebastião Blues*. São Paulo: Editora Brasiliense, 1993.

Castellanos, Rosario. *Mujer que sabe latín*. México, DF: Secretaría de Educación pública, 1973.

Cavalccante, Joyce. *Inimigas íntimas*. São Paulo: Maltese, 1983.

Chávez, Denise. *The Last of the Menu Girls*. Houston, TX: Arte Público Press, 1983.

Cixous, Hélène. "The Laugh of Medusa". Trans. Keith and Paula Cohen. In Elaine Marks and Isabelle de Courtivron (eds), *New French Feminisms*. Brighton: Harvester, 1980, pp. 245–64.

Franco, Jean. "Invadir el espacio público: transformar el espacio privado". *In Marcar diferencias, cruzar fronteras*. Santiago de Chile: Cuarto Propio, 1996, pp. 91–116.

Hekker, Liliana. *La crueldad de la vida*. Buenos Aires: Alfaguara, 2000.

Isaak, Jo Anna. *Feminism and Contemporary Art: The Revolutionary Power of Women's Laughter*. London and New York: Routledge, 1996.

Lispector, Clarice. *Laços de família*. Rio de Janeiro: Francisco Alves, 1960.

——. *A hora da estrela*. Rio de Janeiro: Rocco, 1998.

——. *A paixão segundo G. H.* Rio de Janeiro: Rocco, 1998.

——. *Uma aprendizagem ou o livro dos prazeres*. Rio de Janeiro: Rocco, 1998.

Moraga, Cherríe. *Heroes and Saints and Other Plays: Giving Up the Ghost, Shadow of a Man, Heroes and Saints*. Boston, MA: West End Press, 1994.

Ocampo, Silvina. *La furia*. Buenos Aires: Sur, 1959. Reeditado en Orión, 1976.

——. *Las invitadas*. Buenos Aires: Losada, 1961. Reeditado en Orión, 1979.

——. *El pecado mortal. Antología de relatos*. Buenos Aires, Eudeba: 1966.

——. *Informe del cielo y del infierno*. Prólogo de Edgardo Cozarinsk. Caracas: Monte Avila, 1970.

Peri Rossi, Cristina. *La tarde del dinosaurio*. Barcelona: Plaza & Janes, 1985.

——. *La rebelión de los niños*. Barcelona: Seix Barral, 1988.

——. *El Museo de los esfuerzos inútiles*. 3rd edn. Barcelona: Seix Barral, 1989.

——. *Los museos abandonados*. Barcelona: Lumen, 1992.

——. *La nave de los locos*. 2nd edn. Barcelona: Biblioteca de Bolsillo, 1995.

Shúa, Ana María. *Soy paciente*. Buenos Aires: Ed. Losada, 1980.

——. *Los amores de Laurita*. Buenos Aires: Ed. Sudamericana, 1984.

——. *La sueñera*. Ed. Minotauro, 1984.

——. *El libro de los recuerdos*. Ed. Sudamericana, 1994.

Somers, Armonía. *La mujer desnuda*. Montevideo: Arca, 1950. Reprinted 1990.

——. *Sólo los elefantes encuentran mandrágora*. Buenos Aires: Legasa, 1986.

Súarez, Carmen. *Un vestido rojo para bailar boleros*. Bogotá: Arango, 1996.

Telles, Lygia Fagundes. *Seminário dos ratos*. Rio de Janeiro: Editora Rocco, 1977.

——. *As horas nuas*. 4th edn. Rio de Janeiro: Rocco, 1999.
Valdés, Zoé. *La nada cotidiana*. Salamandra, 2002.
Valenzuela, Luisa. *Cambio de armas*. Hanover, NH: Ediciones del Norte, 1982.
——. *Novela negra con argentinos*. Barcelona: Plaza y Janés, 1990.
——. *Peligrosas palabras*. Buenos Aires: Temas, 2001.
Vega, Ana Lydia. *Encancaranublado y otros cuentos de naufragio*. Rio Piedras, Puerto Rico: Antillana, 1983.
——. *Pasión de historia y otras historias de pasión*. Buenos Aires: Ediciones de la Flor, 1987.
Vega, Ana Lydia and Filippi, Carmen Lugo. *Vírgenes y mártires*. San Juan, Puerto Rico: Editorial Antilla, 1981.

I

IBÁÑEZ, SARA DE

Sara de Ibáñez (1909–71), a highly intellectual, talented and imaginative poet is considered to be an exceptional figure in her native Uruguay. She has been acclaimed by such Nobel Prize laureates as Pablo Neruda and Gabriela Mistral of Chile, Octavio Paz of Mexico and Vicente Aleixandre of Spain. Even though her poetry has been very well received and has been the subject of praise in the academic circles of Latin America, Sara de Ibáñez's poetry remains relatively unknown outside her native country.

Ibáñez, maiden name Sara Iglesias Casadei, was born in the village of Chamberlain, Uruguay. Having spent her childhood in the countryside, she moved to Montevideo with her parents in 1923. Here she was to meet the Uruguayan poet and literary critic Roberto Ibáñez, and they were married in 1928, they set up home together in Montevideo and raised three daughters. All of them followed the literary footsteps of their parents. Ibáñez was a very private person and very little is known about her biography. In 1945, Ibáñez started working in a secondary school in Montevideo where she taught Latin American literature. She continued working there for the next 26 years until her death on April 3, 1971.

A well-recognized poet in her native Uruguay, Ibáñez won many literary awards including the Biennale Prize for Literature, el Premio Unico del Concurso de AIAPE for her "Sonnet to Julio Herrera y Reissig" in 1941, and the Premio del Ministerio de Instrucción Pública for *Pastoral* in 1943. Later *Artigas* was awarded el Premio de la Academia Nacional de Letras in 1952, and *Las estaciones y otros poemas* won the Premio del Ministerio de Instrucción Pública in 1957. She presented papers on her poetry at conferences in London, Jerusalem, Rio de Janeiro, Paris and Mexico City where she received praise for her unusual talent and poetic sensitivity. Ibáñez's poetry was appreciated and understood by other academics.

Among her written work over a 33-year period are eight published books of poetry. Death, despair, and existential anguish are the constant themes of her poems. She was influenced by the avant-garde re-evaluation of seventeenth-century baroque literature (mainly the Spanish author, Francisco de Quevedo, and the Spanish poet, Luis de Góngora) and by avant-garde tendencies such as ultraism, creationism, and surrealism. She followed in the footsteps of the French Symbolists, especially Paul Valéry, Stéphane Mallarmé and Arthur Rimbaud. Of the Latin American poets, it was the Nicaraguan Rubén Darío (the founder of Latin American modernism) who left a mark on her writing. Sara de Ibáñez searches for her own identity and her own voice in the male-dominated literary tradition. She strives for perfection of form in her poetry; her love of symmetry, poetic meter, and rhythm are the landmark of all her poems. Ibáñez writes romances and poems in free verse; she is baroque, surreal, modernist and mystical but her poems are abstract in nature and are, at times, difficult to understand. They appear too hermetic for the majority of readers. In the words of Marci Sternheim: "Ibáñez is a poet's poet; her rigorous baroque form and syntax coupled with her allusive symbolist- and surrealist-inspired imagery are so demanding that they defy the attempts of all but the most serious readers-students of the esoteric poetry or poets themselves" (1990: 55). Ibáñez experiments with rhyme, meter and form. She does not fall into the category of her contemporary well-known Latin American "poetisas" such as Delmira Augustini, Alfonsina Storni, Gabriela Mistral and Juana de Ibarbourou because her works differ in themes and styles.

Major Works and Themes

Sara de Ibáñez wrote her first book *Canto* (Song) in 1940. She wrote her only political poem "El muro" (The Wall) in 1941. It was dedicated to Rafael Alberti and María Teresa León who had to leave Spain when it was under the control of Franco's fascist government. "The Wall" is a symbol of human division after civil war. In 1941, she wrote *Canto a Montevideo* (Song to Montevideo), a patriotic epic which she created in just three days. *Canto* consists of the sonnets "Islas" (Islands), followed by poems consisting of six five-line stanzas, "Liras" (Lyres). These are followed by further sonnets "De los Muertos" (Of the Dead). The book finishes with "Itinerarios" (Itineraries), which are love poems dedicated to her husband. The most prevalent image in *Canto* is the sea. The title is reminiscent of *Canto General* by the Chilean writer Pablo Neruda who wrote the prologue to her first book in which he compared Ibáñez to Sor Juana Inés de la Cruz, the Mexican nun, considered the most outstanding figure in the Hispanic world in the seventeenth century, as well as to the Chilean Nobel Prize winner, Gabriela Mistral.

Hora Ciega (Blind Hour) was written in 1943, and depicts the physical and spiritual condition of people during the Second World War. They lived without light and still remembered atrocities of the recent past. In 1948, she wrote *Pastoral*, a story of an anguished and disoriented man in a world which is divided into three parts: the childhood, youth and maturity of an individual. The main theme of this poem is homage to those poets who influenced Ibáñez's skills as a writer. Tradition, the inheritance of all poets, permits Ibáñez to develop her own style, meter and rhyme. *Artigas*, written in 1952, is based on the life of José Gervasio Artigas, who was one of the major historical figures in the Uruguayan struggle for independence from Spain in the nineteenth century. She dedicates *Estaciones y otros poemas* (1957, Seasons and Other Poems) to the French Symbolist poet Paul Valéry. The poem is divided into four parts, each corresponding to the seasons of the year; spring, summer, autumn and winter. Ibáñez wants to create a perfect rose (the Platonic ideal) but instead she creates the absent shape of an ideal rose. *La página blanca* (The Blank Page) is dedicated to French poet Stéphane Mallarmé, in which Ibáñez experiments with "pure poetry".

Ibánéz won "the battle" of establishing her poetic presence in a male dominated tradition. *La batalla* (1967, The Battle) is an epic poem, a twentieth-century version of *The Iliad* in which Ibáñez explores the myth of a writer who became immortal thanks to his poetic creation. The protagonist of the poem, a solitary warrior lacking free will, undertakes an existential battle to create. He has to remain awake while others are innocently asleep, in constant fear of encountering nothingness; all of nature including the cold wind and darkness are against him. Ibáñez also uses a *fin-de-siècle* image of a sphinx. Part woman, part beast, it represents the warrior's abstract enemies. The Sphinx is an ambiguous creature, of sexual ambivalence, which might be a mother image. However, while the poet-warrior finally dies in battle, of "splendid wounds," he is later resurrected through this poetry. The complicated baroque syntax emphasises the feelings of torment within the warrior. *La Batalla* is written in blank verse of hendecasyllables, a Spanish poetic form that imitates Greco-Latin poetry. Stanzas of four lines are used to express the thought of the author. *La Batalla* is a poem about the battle to create. According to the literary critic Alejandro Paternain, the battle is a process in which both the anguish and the glory of the poetic creation are intertwined.

The apogee of Ibánéz's poetic craft can be seen in *Apocalipsis XX* (Apocalypse XX), written in 1970. This poem, about the destiny of contemporary human beings, consists of 21 "Visiones" (Visions), three "Letanías" (Litanies) of Truth, Liberty and Oblivion, four "Apóstrofes" (Apostrophes) and four "Castigos" (Punishments). Biblical references, the binary oppositions of light and dark, good and evil together with the desolation of the final nuclear explosion are combined in a work of extreme sensitivity and imagination. In *Apocalipsis XX*, Sara de Ibáñez pleads for nuclear disarmament. The powerful images of nature and biblical beauty are contrasted with the nuclear disaster. Harmony between nature and humanity as represented by the farmer before world-wide destruction, evokes rich, powerful and relevant imagery in a twenty-first-century world.

In *Canto Póstumo* (1973, Posthumous Canto) consisting of "Diario de la muerte" (The Diary of Death) and "Baladas y canciones" (Ballads and Songs), Ibáñez reveals her own personal life experiences but the main theme is the passing of time that leads to death. The central theme of "Diario" is the fragility of human life that can only be captured by Symbolic poetry and the third part of the work "Gavilla" (Sheaf of Grain) is dedicated to Rubén Darío, Gabriela Mistral, José Marti, Delmira Augustini and Julio Herrera y Reissig.

The only translation of Ibáñez's poetry into another language is into French by Emilie Noulet, wife of well-known Catalan poet, José Carner. She translated *Pastoral* which appeared in *Cahiers du Sud*, *Le journal des poètes* and *Un demi-siècle de poésie*. Noulet claimed that her desire to translate Sara's poetry stemmed from her desire to enlighten France about her discovery. *Pastoral*, which was written in 1948, focuses on the disoriented position of a man in the world. Emilie Noulet's husband, Carner wrote:

> Nadie maneja hoy la lengua Española con más ciencia, felicidad, facilidad y melodiosa dulzura que Sara de Ibáñez. En ella se combinan, sin esfuerzo y sin imitación, con el sentir y el encanto de Garcilaso, las perfecciones de Góngora.
>
> (*Kañina*, 1985: 46)
>
> [Nobody writes this language with more science, happiness, ability and melodic sweetness than Sara de Ibáñez. In her work, we find without any imitation and force, with the feeling and joy of Garcilaso, the perfection of Góngora. (translation by the author)]

The poetry of Sara de Ibáñez, with its rich metaphorical imagination, love of symmetry and poetic meter and rhythm is not easily accessible to everyone. When asked how she understands poetry, Ibáñez replied that poetry was the exercise of the mystery and an expression of her total commitment to who she was.

On the whole, the existing criticism of Ibáñez's poetry establishes some important groundwork, but it leaves open a myriad of possibilities for future studies.

Anna Hamling

Selected Works

Canto. Buenos Aires: Losada, 1940.
Canto a Montevideo. Montevideo: Impresora Uruguaya, 1941.
Hora ciega. Buenos Aires: Losada, 1943.
Pastoral. México Cita: Cuadernos Americanos, 1948.
Artigas. Montevideo: Impresora Uruguaya, 1952.
Las estaciones y otros poemas. México City: Fondo de la Cultura Económica, 1957.
La batalla. Buenos Aires: Losada, 1967.
Apocalipsis XX. Caracas: Monte Ávila, 1970.
Canto póstumo. Introd. A. Geysse. Buenos Aires: Losada, 1973.
Poemas escogidos: Sara de Ibáñez. México City: Siglo Veintiuno, 1974.

References and Further Reading

Geysse. A. "Introduction". In *Canto póstumo.* By Sara de Ibáñez. Buenos Aires: Losada, 1973, pp. vii–xxvi.

Gómez Mango, Lídice. "Homenaje a Sara de Ibáñez". *Cuadernos de Literatura* 19. Montevideo: Fundación de la Cultura Universitaria, 1971.

Lemaitre León, Monique. "Sara de Ibáñez" In Diane Marting (ed.), *Spanish American Women Writers: A Bio-Bibliographical Source Book*. New York: Greenwood Press, 1990, pp. 254–60.

Neruda, Pablo. *Prologue to Canto by Sara Ibáñez*. Buenos Aires: Losada, 1940, pp. 1–3.

Paternain, Alejando. "Sara de Ibáñez: la esfera cerrada". *Cuadernos Americanos* (1972): 181–208.

Puentes de Oyenard, Sylvia. "Un perfil femenino en la literatura uruguaya: Sara de Ibáñez". *Kañina. Artes y Letras* 9(2) (1985): 43–50.

Ruffinelli, Jorge. "Sínopsis sobre Sara de Ibáñez". *Marcha* 16 March, 1970.

Sternheim, Marci. "Sara de Ibáñez: The Battle to Create". In Noel Valis and Carol Maier (eds), *In the Feminine Mode: Essays on Hispanic Women Writers*. London: Bucknell University Press, 1990, pp. 54–65.

Zapata, Celia de. "Two Poets of America: Juana de Asbaje and Sara de Ibáñez". In *Latin American Women Writers: Yesterday and Today*. Pittsburgh, PA: *Latin American Literary Review*, 1977, pp. 115–26.

IBARBOUROU, JUANA

Juana de Ibarbourou was one of Latin America's first real feminist writers, although her tone was not strident like that of Storni and Agustini. Born in what is now generally considered to have been 1892 (some sources indicate 1895) near the rural town of Melo, Uruguay, on the northeastern border close to Brazil, to Gallician immigrant Vicente Fernández and native-born Valentina Morales, she was the younger of two daughters and originally named Juana Fernández Morales. Because the quality of her formal education was not extensive, she was in many ways self-taught. Throughout her elementary schooling, first at private (Catholic) and then at public schools, she was considered a sensitive, passionate, intuitive and imaginative child, relatively undisciplined, but whose upbringing and surroundings nurtured her aesthetic sensibility. And, although she did not attend university, the culture and background of her parents enabled her artistic spirit to flourish. She was always a great reader and at an early age displayed an affinity for writing, publishing minor poems under a pseudonym in a local paper called *El Deber Cívico* (The Civic Duty). At the age of 17, she published her first prose piece entitled "Derechos femeninos" (Female Rights), demonstrating in an already eloquent style what was to become an ardent interest of hers. In 1915, and still quite young, she married a military captain named Lucas Ibarbourou and bore one child, a boy born in 1917, who was called Julio César Ibarbourou. The year following, the entire family renounced rural life for that of the big city and moved to Montevideo, where Ibarbourou would stay for the rest of her life. Her husband Lucas passed away in 1942 but Juana lived until 1979. In her lifetime, in addition to a number of published works, she won numerous awards and honors, including membership in the National Academy of Letters of Uruguay in 1947 and the National Grand Prize for Literature in 1959. She was named president of the Pen Club in 1941, elected president of the Sociedad Uruguaya de Escritores in 1950 and named "Woman of the Americas" by the American Women's Union of New York in 1953.

Major Works

Her body of poetry consists of a number of works, including the most important of them *Las lenguas de diamante* (The Tongues of Diamond), published in 1919 (in a few places indicated as 1918), under her pseudonym Juana de Ybar, which achieved an immediate success. It was followed by *Raíz salvaje* (Savage Root) in 1922, *La rosa de los vientos* (Rose of the Winds) in 1930, *Perdida* (Lost) in 1950, *Azor* (Hawk) and *Mensaje del escriba* (Message from the Scribe) in 1953, *Oro y tormenta* (Gold and Torment) in 1956, a book of sonnets dominated by biblical themes and references to death and suffering *Romances del destino* (Romances of Destiny) in 1955, *Dualismo* (Dualism), an anthology of her poetry in 1956, and *La pasajera* (The Passenger), *Diario de una isleña* (Diary of an Island Girl) and *Elegía* (Elegy) in 1967. She also published a number of other kinds of works, mostly prose, including *El cántaro fresco* (The Fresh Pitcher) in 1920, works for children which include *Ejemplario* (Exemplary Cases) in 1927 and *Los sueños de Natacha* (The Dreams of Natacha), children's theater based on classical themes, in 1945; *Loores de Nuestra Señora* (Praises of Our Lady) and *Estampas de la Biblia* and (Scenes from the Bible) both in 1934; *Destino* (Destiny), a collection of stories in 1956, and *Juan Soldado* (John the Soldier), another collection of stories in 1971. In 1944, she published her memoirs under the title *Chico Carlo* (Boy Charles), stories from her childhood in autobiographical form with a reference in the title to her first love. Her *Obras completas* (Complete Works) were first published by Aguilar in Madrid in 1953, followed by second and third editions, also by Aguilar, in 1960 and 1968 respectively. Her work has been translated into several languages.

Influence

Ibarbourou is considered one of Latin America's earliest and most powerful women writers and also one of its strongest feminists. She was acclaimed "Juana de América" (Juana of America) in 1929, primarily because she so completely represented, in both her life and art, the ideals to which women of that period aspired. She was an enormously popular figure, as Gustavo San Román affirms: "Juana de Ibarbourou must be the most popular female poet in Uruguayan literature, and one of the most famous literary women in Latin America" (1993: 159). She would never have referred to herself as a feminist, nor was she considered an activist as such, but her works speak for themselves and for women in general, especially in the powerful way that they assert joy in female sexuality and pleasure in open and erotic love. She is often studied together with other more openly feminist poets such as Delmira Agustini (also from Uruguay), Gabriela Mistral (Chile) and Alfonsina Storni (Argentina). The critic Rocío Contreras Romo underscores Ibarbourou's significant place in the development of Latin American women's writing:

> Aunque no fue una participante activa del feminismo, sus versos delinean una poética de claras resonancias intelectuales, voz plena de rebeldía y sensualidad que cantara sin ambages al placer del amor, lo que le valdrá . . . un lugar incuestionable y permanente dentro de la poesía hispanoamericana.
>
> (2003: 2)

Major Poetry Themes

Ibarbourou is best known for her poetry, which can be arranged and analyzed according to the different themes it presents, which in many ways correspond to her chronological development and to the different movements of the times in which she lived. The themes that dominate throughout are love, beauty, nature, maternity, eroticism and sensuality, feminism, and, towards the end, the imminence and inevitability of death. Stylistically and aesthetically, Ibarbourou's poetry evinces the transition of the times from modernism, with its emphasis on new forms and distinct sensibility, to a particular kind of avant-garde representation ("vanguardismo"), to an ultimate serenity and melancholy. Hers is also a poetry that is in many ways and at all levels still "popular," appealing equally to the lower classes and proletariat as well as to the educated upper classes.

In its early phases, especially as exemplified by selections from *Las lenguas de diamante*, her poetry is sensual, erotic and joyful, expressive of Ibarbourou's pleasure in living and vitality. Examples include the lead poem, "Las lenguas de diamante," in which Ibarbourou celebrates the ecstatic fusion of lovers whose passion is expressed silently through the eyes, the metaphoric diamond tongues magically inspired. Another poem which extols the joys of love and eroticism as related to nature is "Como la primavera" (Like the Spring) from *Raíz salvaje*. Here the poet describes herself as physically exuding spring-like fragrances in her love. Nature in all of its beauty and expression of Ibarbourou's love assumes a pantheistic dimension, as evidenced in "Panteísmo" (Pantheism), for the heat of her flesh is transformed into an aroma of roses, lilies and romantic thoughts. "Amor" (Love) also exalts the intertwined beauties of love and nature in an openly sensual manner, since it is love that arrives at her bedside to anoint her flesh with fresh country essences. In fact, her desire for lovemaking is erotic and assertive, as in "La cita" (The Date), wherein she clamors for her lover to envelop her completely. From a passionate and sentimental celebration of love and nature in her earliest works, Ibarbourou begins to develop an outwardly feminist approach, as exemplified in the well-known poem "La higuera" (The Fig Tree) from *Raíz salvaje*. In this poem, Ibarbourou sings the beauty of the fig tree, whose outward harshness belies its inner sensitivity. Her obvious reference is, of course, to women whose beauty is spiritual rather than physical. Maternity is also a recurring theme, as in "La cuna" (The Cradle), from *Las lenguas* or "Ruego por el hijo de veinte años" (I Pray for My Son of Twenty Years), included in her poetic anthology, *Dualismo*.

With the passing of time and advancing age, Ibarbourou's joyful expressiveness gives way to greater serenity and ever-increasing melancholy, as she contemplates the ravages of time, in the form of both illness and death. She herself would suffer from illness as would her husband and parents. "Rebelde" (Rebel), one of Ibarbourou's most famous poems and one that is often anthologized, also forms part of *Las lenguas* and affirms her vitality in life while she fearlessly confronts death. She speaks directly to Charon, Hades' boatman, asserting her defiance in a kind of moral victory, affirming that hers will be the ultimate triumph. Other poems that indicate Ibarbourou's greater recognition and increasing fear of death include "Vida garfio" (Hook Life), "La inquietud fugaz" (The Fleeting Anxiety) and "Carne inmortal" (Immortal Flesh). In the latter, fear begins to overtake her and she admits her "horror a la muerte" or horror of death, hoping to reinforce her own physical immortality. Her fading beauty and declining vitality are especially evident in a poem such as "Perdida" (Lost), in which she links the passing of the seasons to the inevitable aging process. In "Elegía" (Elegy), she adds a melancholy somber note as the final moment has arrived for her, the "Triste mujer del canto" (Sad Woman of Song). Her acceptance of death is presented either with resignation, "Ayer" (Yesterday) or defiance, as in "Rebelde" and "Serenidad" (Serenity), when she finally acknowledges the end, but in a triumphant, joyful tone.

Aesthetics, Stylistics and Technique

In addition to the universal themes of love, nature, beauty and preoccupation with death, often presented from an assertive and feminist standpoint, Ibarbourou was also concerned with the crafting of poetry, and several poems reflect this aesthetic outlook. The fact that she was associated first with the modernist movement, with its attention to renovation of form and art for the sake of beauty, and then with the avant-garde tendencies, which sought to surprise, provoke and to unite extremes, indicates her attention to the importance of both structure and innovation. Many of her poems emphasize the importance of aesthetics and vary from a predominance and reworking of traditional forms, such as the sonnet (see *Oro y Tormenta*), to the frequent use of the 14-syllable alexandrine line, favored by the modernists. In a poem unusual for her, Ibarbourou resorts to a "romance" or ballad to depict her poetic self-portrait in "Autorromance de Juanita Fernández" (Self-Portrait of Juanita Fernández). She also often utilizes the eleven-syllable line (hendecasyllable), imported from Italy during the Renaissance period, as well as a variety of less sophisticated popular verse forms. Technically her work cannot easily be categorized, for it manifests a pleasurable mix of learned forms with more simple songs. Her cultured upbringing is apparent in her verse as is her loyalty to the country life which she found so endearing.

Further Analysis

For the purposes of a better understanding of the nature and importance of Ibarbourou's work, we will focus on several poems specifically, including "Las lenguas de diamante" and "Rebelde" (both from *Las lenguas*), "La rosa de los vientos" (from *La rosa de los vientos*), and "La pasajera" (from *La pasajera*), which together provide a powerful synthesis of the author's style, themes, techniques and influences. In them, Ibarbourou presents a revolutionary approach to her life and work, not so much by what she says but by what she does not say, that is, her use of language to revere silence, silence juxtaposed with erotic expression. Language becomes for Ibarbourou her way of "writing the body" as French feminists define it, that is, of giving verbal form to erotic discourse. Ibarbourou also utilizes language in unconventional ways, employing complicated patterns and classical tropes in a more intellectual approach to the naturally sentimental topics of life, love and death.

In "Las lenguas de diamante," the title poem for her book, Ibarbourou desires verbal silence as a condition for more explicit sexual actions. The poem, written in standard alexandrine lines with consonant rhyme, exalts the power of the physical to express that which remains unspoken verbally, her and her lover's erotic sensations:

Bajo la luna cobre, taciturnos amantes,
Con los ojos gimamos, con los ojos hablemos.
Serán nuestras pupilas dos lenguas de diamantes
Movidas por la magia de diálogos supremos.

(*OC*, 3–4)

Her tone is adamant and unabashed. She is joyful in reaching out to higher powers in her plea for extended silence, which is portrayed metaphorically as a rose in flower: "Silencio en nuestros labios una rosa ha florido". She is, as French feminist critics would say, "writing the body" with her poetry, paradoxically renouncing words to express non-verbal ecstasy through image and metaphor. This is a rather revolutionary stance, given the time period and cultural limitations, yet Ibarbourou is undeterred in her emphatic embrace of her beloved, both physically and poetically. Critic Gustavo San Román centers his approach around Ibarbourou's use of silence as a means to facilitating the expression of supreme erotic pleasure (1993: 165).

The same outlook dominates another well-known poem, "Rebelde," wherein Ibarbourou valiantly addresses Charon in an exclamation of joy in life while she is being transported to death. This poem is also constructed in a series of well-sculpted alexandrine quatrains, one of her preferred literary forms. Again the poet is not intimidated by the idea of confronting death. In fact, she fiercely rebels at the "siniestro patriarca" who attempts to squelch her exultation:

Yo iré como una alondra cantando por el río
Y llevaré a tu barca mi perfume salvaje,
E irradiaré en las ondas del arroyo sombrío
Como una azul linterna que alumbra en el viaje.

(*OC*, 8–9)

Again, it is her language and use of it that enable Ibarbourou to present a feminist stance through creation of a new kind of discourse, blatantly anti-patriarchal and outspoken. Her body becomes her language, as Hélène Cixous would affirm in her definition of "feminine writing" ("The Laugh of the Medusa," in Oliver, *French Feminist Reader*, 2000). Her final words represent the ultimate rebellion, expressed by her physically, thus conjoining the verbal and non-verbal: "Cuando quieras dejarme a la orilla del río / Me bajarán tus brazos cual conquista de vándalo" (*OC*, 8–9).

As her poetry develops, beauty becomes relative for Ibarbourou, true to a feminist approach. As indicated earlier, the well-known poem "La higuera" (*OC*, 108–9) exalts the fig tree for its inner strength and sensibility rather than its outward splendor. Also related is the poem "La rosa de los vientos," very emblematic of what will become Ibarbourou's outlook in her later work. In this complex set of strophes that vary in length and rhythm, Ibarbourou moves from the literal presentation of the rose to an erotic one and, finally, to a spiritual one, the "rosa de los vientos," representing the stage of life at which Ibarbourou finds herself. She insists: "... yo quiero una, solo una, / Celeste y única, / Que has de traerla tú, si me amas" (*OC*, 157–8). That rose symbolizes the journey of life for Ibarbourou, still replete with possibilities despite the ravages of time, here conceptualized and abstract:

Anda, ve a buscarme esa flor sin igual.
La Meteorología es una vieja
Indiferente y sin amor.
Entre mis dedos ágiles de piedad
La rosa de los vientos
Se abrirá como una bendición.

(*OC*, 157–8)

In the final stages of her life and work, Ibarbourou's tone softens and diminishes somewhat, as she approaches aging and death from a more pessimistic frame of mind. Ruth Aponte (1982: 106) refers to Ibarbourou's final book, *La pasajera*, as best representing the poet's descent into the waning years. Here Ibarbourou is forced to acknowledge the inevitable decline of beauty and health, as she does specifically in the book's title poem:

Ah qué triste, qué calma y valerosa
Esta mujer que asciende hasta la noche
Sin un temblor, y sola cual si fuese
La pasajera única e insomne.

(*Antología*, 184–5)

The defiance of word and body that characterized her early work is no longer present. In fact, quite the opposite is true as her physical presence and strength are depleted, exhausted, completely worn out:

Erguida estoy, sin voz y sin sonrisa,
Blanca en la inmensa soledad nocturna,
Con la brasa del verso en la garganta
Y en el pecho la sed de la aventura.

(*Antología*, 184–5)

Finally, then, it is through the verbal "writing of the body" that Ibarbourou has so forcefully and joyously expressed herself throughout the course of her work. Only at the end does she waver and falter, as do the strength in her voice and the spirit of her tongue. So also does her physical prowess decline, as she is ultimately resigned to the final loss of hope and with it her exuberance. The ship that carries her now stands in sad contrast to the one she defied in her youth, for at the end awaits only an "elevada, misteriosa sombra" and her farewell is a tearful one: "Y bajará llorando de la nave / porque no pudo vislumbrar el cielo" (*Antología*, 184–5).

ANNE M. PASERO

Selected Works

Poetry

Las lenguas de diamante. Buenos Aires: Editorial Limitada, 1919.
Raíz salvaje. Montevideo: Maximino García, 1922.
La rosa de los vientos. Montevideo: Palacio del Libro, 1930.
Perdida. Buenos Aires: Losada, 1950.
Obras completas. 1st edn. Madrid: Aguilar, 1953.
Oro y Tormenta. Santiago de Chile: Zigzag, 1956.
Romances del destino. Madrid: Cultura Hispánica, 1955.
Antología poética. Ed. Dora Russell. Madrid: Cultura Hispánica, 1970.

Antología: Poesia y prosa 1919–71. Ed. Jorge Arbeleche. Buenos Aires: Losada, 1972.

Prose

El cántaro fresco. Montevideo: La Editorial Uruguaya, 1920.
Estampas de la Biblia. Montevideo: Barreiro y Ramos, 1934.
Loores de Nuestra Señora. Montevideo: Barreiro y Ramos, 1934.
Chico Carlo. Montevideo: Barreiro y Ramos, 1944.
Juan Soldado. Buenos Aires: Losada, 1971.

References and Further Reading

Aedo, María Teresa. "Hablar y oír-saber y poder: la poesía de Juana de Ibarbourou desde *Las lenguas de diamante* hasta *Mensaje del escriba*". *Revista Chilena de Literatura* 49 (1996): 47–64.

Aponte, Ruth. "La etapa final: Reflexión y búsqueda en la poesía de Juana de Ibarbourou". *Revista/Review Interamericana* 12(1) (1982): 104–9.

Arbeleche, Jorge. *Juana de Ibarbourou*. Montevideo: Arca, 1978.

Contreras Romo, María del Rocío. "El placer de la palabra o la palabra del placer, la poesía de Juana de Ibarbourou". *Espéculo* 22(2002) Nov.–Feb. 2003 (electronic. publication).

Dutra Vieyto, Ethel. *Aproximación a Juana de Ibarbourou*. Montevideo: Ministerio de Educación, 1978.

Feliciano Mendoza, Ester. *Juana de Ibarbourou, Oficio de poesía*. Puerto Rico: UPRED, 1981.

Ianes, Raúl. "Los riesgos del canon: Juana de Ibarbourou y los aspectos literario-ideológicos de una política cultural". *Monographic Review/ Revista Monográfica* 13 (1997): 298–309.

Oliver, Kelly (ed.) *French Feminist Reader*. Lanham, MD: Rowman and Littlefield, 2000, pp. 257–75.

Pickenhayn, Jorge O. *Vida y obra de Juana de Ibarbourou*. Buenos Aires: Plus Ultra, 1980.

San Román, Gustavo. "Expression and Silence in the Poetry of Juana de Ibarbourou and Idea Vilariño". In Catherine Davies (ed.), *Women Writers in Twentieth Century Spain and Spanish America*. Lewiston, NY: Mellen, 1993, pp. 157–75.

IPARRAGUIRRE, SYLVIA

An outspoken human rights advocate, Sylvia Iparraguirre was born in Junín in 1947, in the province of Buenos Aires. In 1966, Iparraguirre entered the Universidad de Buenos Aires to study literature. She later received a doctorate in linguistics with her study of the language transformation of a recently industrialized rural area. While at the Universidad de Buenos Aires in the 1960s, Iparraguirre was a student of Jorge Luis Borges and became acquainted with the prominent writers of the era. Following introductions to Abelardo Castillo she began to write for and edit the legendary journal *El escarabajo de oro*, a literary journal that was instrumental in publishing the works of new Argentine writers of the 1960s. In 1976, a few years after *El escarabajo de oro* ceased publication, Iparraguirre, Castillo and Liliana Heker co-founded the literary journal *El ornitorrinco*. The significance of this journal grew as repression under the military dictatorship increased. During the years of the military junta, 1976–83, *El ornitorrinco* served as a space for cultural resistance against the dictatorship.

As a researcher for the Consejo Nacional de Investigaciones Científicas y Técnicas (CONICET) since 1982, Iparraguirre specializes in sociolinguistics and the work of Mikhail Bakhtin. She is also a journalist and is a contributing writer to *Clarín*, *Página 12*, *Contexto*, *El unicornio*, *Claudia*, *Letras* and *Cuadernos hispanoamericanos*. Her short stories have been featured in anthologies such as *Buenos Aires: Antología de la nueva narrativa argentina* (1991) and *Hand in Hand Alongside the Tracks* (1992). Among other awards, Iparraguirre has won the Primer Premio Municipal de Literatura (1988) for her book of short stories *En el invierno de las ciudades*. In 1999, she also won numerous awards for her novel *La tierra del fuego* including the Premio de la Crítica, the Premio a la Mejor Novela Publicada from the Club de los XIII, and the Premio Sor Juana Inés de la Cruz (México). In 2000, her book of selected texts and interviews entitled *Tierra del Fuego: Una biografía del fin del mundo* (Tierra del Fuego: a Biography of the End of the World) received the Premio Eikon de Comunicación con la Comunidad.

Historical Fiction

Iparraguirre's most critically and popularly acclaimed novel, *La tierra del fuego* (1998), is part of a new generation of historical fiction in Argentina. In *La tierra del fuego*, Iparraguirre takes the reader on a journey to the southern tip of South America, the homeland of the Yámana culture. Taking her cue from some of the great nineteenth-century English novels and injecting the adventurous spirit of an age of colonialism and imperialism, Iparraguirre's novel reflects on the uses of history and asks: *Who* writes history? For *whom* is it written? *What* is written about and *why*? Specifically, Iparraguirre centers her historical narrative on the story of Jemmy Button, or Omoy-Lume, a Yámana teenager who was captured by Captain Robert FitzRoy in the 1830s and taken to England aboard his ship the *Beagle*. Iparraguirre's novel recounts Button's odyssey to England and his return to Tierra del Fuego as well as his frequent encounters with the English in his native land during the following decades. Unlike many nineteenth-century accounts of the indigenous populations of Tierra del Fuego, Iparraguirre does not indulge in stereotypes or images of the "noble savage". Instead she paints a picture of the clash between "civilization" and "barbarism" through the eyes of the colonized instead of the colonizer and thereby inverts the traditional power hierarchy. Through the double vision of the narrator, an Argentine man of the pampas with both English and Argentine heritage who travels as Button's companion across the Atlantic and back, Iparraguirre presents both the side of the indigenous as well as the point of view of the Argentine of the pampas to contrast the scientific and cultural notions regarding the inhabitants of Tierra del Fuego as propagated through the rhetoric of English imperial expansion.

Novels and Short Stories

Iparraguirre's engagement with Patagonia is also evident in her book of short stories *El país del viento* (2003, The Wind Country). In the nine short narratives that make up this book, categorized as young adult fiction, Iparraguirre revalorizes an indigenous past. While these stories invite readers to consider such questions as integration (both racial and cultural), immigration, friendship, and the authority of science versus traditional beliefs, they also suggest that true understanding between two cultures, European and native, and two belief systems, scientific and natural, is nearly impossible because of entrenched power structures.

In contrast to the short stories included in *El país del viento*, the brief texts that form *En el invierno de las ciudades* (1988, In the Winter of the Cities) and *Probables lluvias por la noche* (1993, Probable Rains during the Night) are more closely related to fantastic literature. For example, in the short story "El dueño del fuego," included in *En el invierno de las ciudades*, Iparraguirre shows how a bow and arrow put into the hands of a previously passive city-dwelling Toba Indian can dramatically alter the power dynamics between the observer and the observed. In this way, Iparraguirre implicitly criticizes the treatment of native inhabitants by those intent on studying and categorizing them.

The novel *El parque* (1996, The Park) also blurs the line between reality and fantastic. The adventures played out by the characters that inhabit this amusement park located in a parallel Buenos Aires of the 1950s put one in mind of a puzzle where actions and consequences constantly need to be deciphered according to one's own beliefs and experiences. The characters in this novel weave in and out of each others' lives without realizing that they share an unexpected, common destiny.

Iparraguirre's most recent publication, *Narrativa breve* (2005, Brief Narrative), is a collection of her most noteworthy short stories from *En el invierno de las ciudades*, *Probables lluvias por la noche* and *El país del viento*, as well as ten additional never-before published texts. In "El Packard negro," for example, a simple test drive in this car reveals its potential for intense and disturbing time travel. The reader will also find echoes, not imitations, of Joseph Conrad, Herman Melville, and Robert Louis Stevenson in stories that open a door to the human condition and, with a precise sensibility, reveal the intricacies and subtleties of the heart and mind that motivate us.

The breadth of Iparraguirre's narrative talent is evident in works that range from the historical to the fantastic. From poems to short stories to novels, Iparraguirre demonstrates her skill at moving between genres in order to develop themes, question history, and provoke readers' attention. Although successful in each of these genres, Iparraguirre has received the most critical acclaim for her historical fiction, both the novel, *La tierra del fuego*, and the collection of short stories, *El país del viento*. However, since the publication of *Narrativa breve*, in 2005, critics and scholars have begun to pay more close attention to her contributions as a writer of short fiction.

REBECCA J. ULLAND

Selected Works

En el invierno de las ciudades. Buenos Aires: Galerna, 1988.

Probables lluvias por la noche. Buenos Aires: Emecé, 1993.

El parque. Buenos Aires: Emecé, 1996.

La tierra del fuego. Buenos Aires: Alfaguara, 1998. [*La Tierra del Fuego*. trans. Hardie St. Martin. Willimantic, CT: Curbstone Press, 2000.] Also translated into French, German, Italian, Portuguese, and Dutch.

La tierra del fuego: Una biografía del fin del mundo. Photographs by Florian Von Der Fecht. Buenos Aires: El Ateneo, 2000.

El país del viento. Buenos Aires: Alfaguara, 2003.

Narrativa breve. Buenos Aires: Alfaguara, 2005.

References and Further Reading

Cheadle, Norman. "Rememorando la historia decimonónica desde *La tierra del fuego* (1998) de Sylvia Iparraguirre". In Lady Rojas-Trempe and Catharina Vallejo (eds), *Celebración de la creación literaria de escritoras hispanas en las Américas*. Ottawa: Girol Books, 2000, pp. 81–91.

Neyret, Juan Pablo. "De alguien a nadie. Metáforas de la escritura de la historia en *La tierra del fuego*, de Sylvia Iparraguirre". http://www.ucm.es/info/especulo/numero29/sylviaip.html (30 August 2006).

Roffé, Reina. "Entrevista a Sylvia Iparraguirre". *Cuadernos hispanoamericanos* 603 (Sept. 2000): 99–106.

Sims, Robert L. "Eurocentrismo, marginocentricidad, historia oficial e historia sentida en *La tierra del fuego* de Sylvia Iparraguirre". *Hispanic Journal* 22(2) (Fall 2001): 523–38.

ISTARÚ, ANA

Ana Istarú was born Ana María Soto Marín in San José, Costa Rica in 1960. Her father's influence led her to literature, while her mother's led her to the theater. She published her first poetry at the age of 15. She studied Dramatic Arts with a focus on acting at the University of Costa Rica, graduating in 1981. She has won awards in Costa Rica for her acting, including the National Prize for Young Actress in 1990 and Best Actress in 1997. She has also won awards for her writing. In Costa Rica her awards include the EDUCA prize in 1982 for the poetry of *La estación de fiebre* (The Fever Season), the Áncora Prize for drama in 1999–2000, and in 2005 the Costa Rican equivalent of the Pulitzer Prize, the Aquileo Echeverria National Award for drama for "La loca" (The Madwoman). In Spain, she was awarded the María Teresa León Prize for Dramatic Authors (1995) and the Machado Brothers Theater Award (1999). In 1990, she was awarded a Guggenheim grant for creative writing. The mother of three daughters, she lives and works in San José, Costa Rica.

Poetry

Istarú's poetry is often compared to that of the Nicaraguan poet Gioconda Belli, primarily because the two poets are both feminine and feminist; that is, they are advocates for the equality of women and men, and the right of women to choose their own path while retaining and even celebrating gender differences, including female sensuality and sexuality, and motherhood. Both poets celebrate the body and the erotic. While Pablo Neruda's poems of love extol the beloved as object of his desire, Istarú's poems celebrate the erotic desire and sexual participation of woman as the subject of her own erotic life, in control of her own body.

Istarú's best-known book of poems is *La estación de fiebre*, sometimes subtitled (*canto erótico*). Composed of thirty-three poems numbered with Roman numerals, the collection is an erotic canticle to the stages of passion, beginning with the female subject's approach to the male beloved in Poem I, moving toward the climax in Poem XXVI, the subsequent post-coital reflections, and ending with the physical separation of the final Poem XXXIII, when "este hombre humano / . . . se levanta" [this so human man / gets up]. In Poem VI, she names her lover: "Cuánto ejercer la entrega / . . . para arribar a vos, / César Maurel" [How to practice surrender / ... to arrive at you, César Maurel]. Though the artist-poet Maurel would become her husband and then her ex-husband, in *La estación de fiebre* Istarú has written a passionate, erotic Central American version of *Sonnets from the Portuguese* (Elizabeth Barrett Browning's love poems to her future husband Robert Browning).

But Istarú eulogizes her lover with an explicit language of the body, poeticizing the stark physical vocabulary of "breasts," "vagina," "clitoris," and "penis" while undertaking a critique of patriarchal structures in Central America. In Poem III, a "tratado" or treatise on gender, Istarú notes that both the betrothed and the girl's father are content to find the daughter always "virgen y asexual" [virgin and asexual], but the lyric voice rebels against "esta fálica / omnipotencia" [this phallic / omnipotency]. Istarú celebrates her own sensuality and sexuality, refusing to allow sex and the sex act to be defined by male desire and male initiative. Istarú's woman is a woman of her own desires, but also a woman who refuses to lose herself to those desires, or to pay for them with submissiveness and passivity. Istarú celebrates both the male and female body, male and female desire, but as two lovers conjoin and then separate, the individual—male or female—retains her or his individuality and freedom.

In *Verbo madre* (The Word Mother) Istarú continues the erotic theme, but deals with the role of maternity as well. In "Abrete sexo" (Open Yourself, Sex) she instructs her "sex," that is her vagina, to open to allow a child to be born. In "Al dolor del parto" (To the Pain of Giving Birth), she tells pain that they will be lovers just for today, just until the child's birth. Her approach to traditional women's roles as lovers and mothers is a subversive one, or even transgressive, questioning male dominance from the perspective of a liberated, socially engaged and autonomous woman.

Translations of Istarú's poems by Zoe Anglesey (1941–2003) have appeared in magazines and reviews as well as in a poetry anthology edited by Anglesey (*Ê Ixok Amar Go*: *Central American Women's Poetry for Peace*, 1987).

Plays

Istarú's concerns with the condition or status of women are equally evident in her plays. She has authored six plays, all of which have been performed, and four of which are published. Her earliest plays, *El vuelo de la grulla* (The Flight of the Crane) and *Madre nuestra que estás en la tierra* (Our Mother Who Art on Earth) are dramas while later works are comedies, but all of her plays investigate women's roles and place in Costa Rican and Latin American society.

Dramas

El vuelo de la grulla, a one-act play, presents three conflicting characters living in the same household: an unhappy housewife, an unsympathetic husband, and a domineering mother-in-law. Though the young wife, María Luisa, finally rids herself of both her husband and her mother-in-law, the resolution is not a hopeful one, as she is now alone in a culture in which women "should" be married.

Istarú takes similar elements to her next, more fully developed drama, *Madre nuestra que estás en la tierra*, but here the play ends on a hopeful note. There are no male characters in the play; men—husbands, brothers, fathers, even a lover—exist outside the boundaries of the action, important to the play precisely through their absence. There are four female characters, representing four generations: Eva, the dead grandmother from the family's halcyon days; Amelia, her daughter; Dora, Amelia's daughter and Julia's mother; and Julia. The play takes place over ten years, during three Christmas seasons. In the first, Julia will soon be 15 and in the third she is 24. Each woman is an icon for her generation. Eva was not allowed to be educated as her brothers were, but because she married well she was able to travel. Amelia prayed to the Virgin Mary to stop thinking in order to obey her husband, who refused to let her go to the cinema. Dora's husband died young and left the family unprotected. For Dora, her daughter's goal in life should be to marry, to have the financial security she herself has lacked. But Julia wants more, and much of the tension in the play revolves around the conflict specific to mother and daughter. Dora has fulfilled her role so well that she has failed to live, while Julia has tried to please her mother and failed to please—or even know—herself. The play ends in a hopeful moment of communication and self-awareness, with the clear suggestion that Julia will seek out her own identity, independent of her mother's vision of what she should be or do. Her great grandmother Eva looks on approvingly, the mother "on earth" to guide Julia. *Nuestra madre* is a powerful drama about the human cost of enforcing rigid social roles.

Comedies

Baby Boom en el paraíso (Baby Boom in Paradise) was first performed in 1996 with Istarú herself playing all roles in the one-woman show, tracing the journey of an egg from the Fallopian tubes to its fertilization by a sperm, through pregnancy and birth. The work is self-referential, taking scenes from the birth of one of her daughters, but creating a comic context in which the birth of the child is likened to aiming for a goal in soccer, with the doctor and nurse as rabid fans and supporters. The play has been translated and performed in English by Kirsten F. Nigro and presented as a radio play in German in Germany. For most societies, motherhood is sacred, and mothers idealized, but Istarú deals with the irony that women as a class, despite being mothers, are debased. Though women should be mothers and should take care of their children, as homemakers, women are invisible and powerless members of society. Patriarchal structures are supported by women as well as men; Istarú does not launch an attack on men as a class, but rather on the societal structures that perpetuate male dominance.

Hombres en escabeche (Men in Marinade), originating from the influence of an Italian play, *Dejemos el sexo en paz* (Let's Leave Sex Alone) contains a single female character and a single male actor playing seven roles. The story follows Alicia from youth to maturity, focusing on her relationships with men. The men include the father (the first man a woman must learn to please), the brother, the first boyfriend, the philosopher, the yuppie, the musician, and a stranger, who serve as archetypal male characters. Alicia's interactions with the various permutations of Man reveal the contradictions and ambiguities to which patriarchal societies subject women, denying women their full development, their full sexuality, their full identity.

As a poet, Istarú joins the ranks of her countrywomen Carmen Naranjo and Eunice Odio. Like Gioconda Belli, Istarú writes candidly of the physical and the sensual, with woman as subject and actor of her own erotic life. As a playwright, she writes comedies because dramas appeal less to the contemporary Costa Rican audience, but her comedies have a satirical bite to them, leaving audiences thinking in the midst of their laughter. Istarú is a unique voice in New Wave Costa Rican theater.

LINDA LEDFORD-MILLER

Selected Works

Poetry

La estación de fiebre. San José: Editorial Universitaria Centroamericana, 1983. Translated into French.

La muerte y otros efímeros agravios. San José: Editorial Costa Rica, 1988.

La estación de fiebre (y otros amaneceres). Madrid: Visor, 1991.

Verbo madre. San José: Editorial Mujeres, 1995.

Poesía escogida. San José: Editorial Costa Rica, 2002.

Theater

El vuelo de la grulla. In *Escena* 5(110) (1984): 15–19.

Madre nuestra que estás en la tierra. In *Dramaturgas latinoamericanas contemporáneas: Antología crítica*. Madrid: Editorial Verbum, 1991, pp. 231–59.

Baby Boom en el paraíso; Hombres en escabeche: Teatro. San José: Editorial Costa Rica, 2001.

Unpublished play: "Sexus benedictus," 2003.

La loca. In *Género y géneros: Escritura y Escritoras iberoamericanas*. Vol. 1. Ed. Angeles Encinar, Eva Löfquist and Carmen Valcárcel. Madrid: Colección de Estudios. Ediciones de la Universidad Autónoma de Madrid, 2006, pp. 117–22.

References and Further Reading

Andrade, Ela and Cramsie, Hilde F. (eds) "Ana Istarú (Costa Rica)" and "Ana Istarú; Respuestas al cuestionario". In *Dramaturgas latinoamericanas contemporáneas: Antología crítica*. Madrid: Editorial Verbum, 1991, pp. 50–7, 225–30.

Chen Sham, Jorge. "La insurreción de la mujer y su estrategia liberadora en Ana Istarú: El poema III de *La estación de fiebre*". *South Eastern Latin Americanist* 44(2) (2000): 19–27.

Cramsie, Hilde F. "La marginación lingüística y social de la mujer en dos obras de Ana Istarú". In *Mujer y sociedad en América: VI Simposio Internacional*. Westminster, CA: Instituto Literario y Cultural Hispánico, 1990, pp. 43–58.

Hernández, Consuelo. "Feminidad y feminismo en la poesía de Ana Istarú". *Alba de América* 20 (July 2001): 209–20.

——. "Poetas centroamericanos de fin de siglo: Ana Istarú y Otoniel Guevara: Cuerpo y autoridad". *Ístmica: Revista de la Facultad de Filosofía y Letras* 5–6 (2000): 26–42.

Krugh, Janis L. "La erótica fiebre feminista de Ana Istarú en *La estación de fiebre*". In Oralia Preble-Niemi (ed.), *Afrodita en el trópico: Erotismo y construcción del sujeto femenino en obras de autoras centroamericanas*. Potomac, MD: Scripta Humanistica, 1999, pp. 135–52.

Miller, Elaine Marnell. "Chapter 4: Familiar or Foreign?: Costa Rican Feminist Theatre's Response to National Problems: Migrating Texts: Cross-Cultural Readings of Costa Rican Plays of 1990–2000." Dissertation. University of Maryland, 2003. http://drum.umd.edu/dspace/bitstream/1903/58/1/dissertation.pdf. 2003.

Morera, Ailyn. "Ana Istarú: En pie de lucha". *Informa-Tico*, 76 (Nov. 14, 2005). http://www.informa-tico.com/php/expat.php?id=26–09–0506598

Moyano, Pilar. "Reclamo y recreación del cuerpo y del erotismo femeninos en la poesía de Gioconda Belli y Ana Istarú". In Oralia Preble-Niemi (ed.), *Afrodita en el trópico: Erotismo y construcción del sujeto femenino en obras de autoras centroamericanas*. Potomac, MD: Scripta Humanistica, 1999, pp. 135–52, 198–208.

Rojas, Margarita G. "Transgresiones al discurso poético amoroso: La poesía de Ana Istarú". *Revista Iberoamericana* 53 (Jan.–June 1987): 391–402.

Rojas, Margarita and Ovares, Flores. "Geneología de mujeres: *Madre nuestra que estás en la tierra*". In Carolyn Bell and Patricia Fumero (eds), *Drama contemporáneo costarricense: 1980–2000*. San José: Editorial de la Universidad de Costa Rica, 2000, pp. 307–16.

IZAGUIRRE, ESTER DE

Izaguirre was born in Asunción, Paraguay, in 1923 but has lived in Argentina since she was 4 years old. She considers herself both Paraguayan and Argentinean, and her work displays her spiritual ties to her adoptive country but, also, to her native land and the Guaraní language. She graduated with a degree in Humanities from the Universidad de Buenos Aires. In addition to teaching Literature in several universities in Argentina, the United States (University of California), Spain (Universidad de Granada) and France (the Sorbonne), Izaguirre conducted a popular program in Radio Nacional, *Diálogos con personajes de novela*, in which prominent writers used their characters' personae to chat with the audience. However, one of Izaguirre's most noteworthy activities was the sponsoring of weekly gatherings with Jorge Luis Borges through her institute, Taller Seminario Antígona. During these "tertulias" that lasted over seven years, Borges discussed with Izaguirre the themes that mesmerized him: books, time, knowledge, history, religion, etc. Students, writers and intellectuals, and people of all professions came from different parts of Argentina to listen to the acclaimed author and left with a better knowledge of Izaguirre as well.

Although Izaguirre has written one novel, *Ayer no ha terminado todavía*/ (2001, Yesterday Has Not Happened Yet), and two books of short stories, *Yo soy el tiempo* (1970) and *Ultimo domicilio conocido* (1994), she is mainly known as a poet. She has published eleven poetry books, and selections of her work have been translated into English, French, and Guaraní and have appeared in anthologies such as *Colección Poesía 50*, *Voces femeninas en la poesía paraguaya*, *Poésie Paraguayenne du XX Siècle*, *El ultimo vuelo*, *Un Jardín para Borges*, *Best Friends*, *Women in the Loom of Time*, and *El carnaval cordial de las distancias*, among many others. Enrique Anderson Imbert referred to Izaguirre as a neo-Romantic and an existentialist poet of the "Generación de 1940". Nélida Salvador, on the contrary, says that Izaguirre's inclination for experimenting with different stylistic tendencies like neo-surrealism, inventionism, neo-Romanticism, and neo-humanism, place her closer to the Argentinean innovators of the 1950s. Another critic, Susana Boéchat, finds that Izaguirre's poetry has the tendency to compare opposites. It is neo-Romantic and modern, metaphoric and synthetic, conceptual and transparent, anecdotal and transcendent, subjective and social. Undoubtedly, Izaguirre's work depicts the balance of image and emotion recognized by Anderson Imbert, Salvador and Boéchat, but one notable aspect of her poetry is the continuous dialogue with the entelechies of human knowledge. Like Borges' characters, Izaguirre's poetic subjects rarely lose control, as if they wish to know how to transcend the pain or the disenchantment that besiege them. Desolate and overwhelmed, they never abandon their philosophical inquiring.

In two of her books, *Trémolo* (Startled) (1960) and *El país que llaman vida* (The Kingdom Called Life) (1964), Izaguirre chooses as poetic subjects two female characters of the Christian narrative: Mary and Mary Magdalene. Contrary to the historical interpretations that suppressed their voices, Izaguirre portrays them as discursive figures who want "to tell" their own story. In her elucidation of Mary, for instance, there is no passivity or docility. Izaguirre's Mary is a thinking, independent individual who purposely imagined a new destiny for herself and her child:

> ... mis manos tejen sueños, temerosas
> de despertar a un hoy irrealizado.
> ... Hijo querido, cuando tú naciste
> aniquilé la nada entre mis manos,
> la creación me guareció en su ritmo ...
>
> (T 35–37)

If in most Christian texts St. Paul is suggested as the "author" of Christianity, Izaguirre gives such honor to Mary:

> ... concebí a la humanidad entera,
> ... una estela de luz y de recuerdo
> dejaré en los anales de la tierra,
> si he transformado en cáliz este cuerpo
> al precio de mi sangre medianera.
>
> (T 37)

Izaguirre's Mary Magdalene also is a distant figure from the one represented in the Christian stories as either a corrupt being or a humble woman redeemed from sin. In Izaguirre's portrayal, Mary Magdalene is an outspoken, independent, and analytical individual who intelligently evaluates the reasons for the Pharisees' aggression. She scrutinizes all the possibilities for the attack, rectifying in her interpretation her innocence and the Pharisees' shameful behavior:

> Volví al pasado la mirada
> y vi a aquellos hombres, fariseos,
> que aún seguían echando pedrejones
> a una mujer extraña:
> la mitad de su rostro se encendía
> al suave resplandor de mi conciencia,
> la otra mitad, irremediablemente
> se disipó en las sombras de la tarde.
>
> (EPQV 22)

If it is captivating to observe Mary Magdalene in the process of defining, reflecting, comparing, and rejecting memories, it is also so to learn the memorable moment when she listens to Christ's words. Mary Magdalene is not seduced by the Messiah but by his discourse:

> Entonces pude ver las estrellas
> pensé en el infinito,
> en los pequeños seres que no vemos
> y en los grandes que no consideramos
> ... y amé el dolor porque era dracma noble
> para comprar el olvido.
>
> (EPQV 22)

Erased from the Christian construct of a dishonored woman, Izaguirre's Mary Magdalene is a dignified individual who becomes one of Christ followers not because of her sins but because of her capacity to understand the Messiah's message. Mesmerized by Christ's exceptional language, Mary Magdalene does not enter into the realm of the saved but into the world of abstract knowledge.

It is interesting to note that human love is barely touched upon in Izaguirre's poetry. It is subtly observed in the story of Mary and Joseph in her first book, *Trémolo* (Startled) (1960). In *El país que llaman vida* (The Kingdom Called Being) (1964), *No está vedado el grito* (Screaming is Allowed) (1967), and *Girar en descubierto* (Losing the Masks) (1975), there is no trace of the feeling except as fragmentation or lack. Izaguirre talks about inexistent contacts in a hand, words that silence, a warmth that is not transmitted by a stone. It would not be until 1980, when she published *Qué importa si anochece* (Ignore Darkness), that her vocabulary would shine with an unusual and passionate lexis. The poetic "I" abruptly leaves her secluded solitude to live all the emotions of love:

> ... Desde que no te veo
> está pasando un día que no termina de pasar.
>
> (QISA 25)

> Le pusiste tu nombre a mis orígenes
> y al fin mis ojos se volvieron tierra.
>
> (QISA 34)

The language of love that is revealed in *Qué importa si anochece* (Ignore Darkness), however, is unique to this book. Izaguirre's jubilant words would not be heard again. From *Judas y los demás* (Judas and the Others) (1981) to her latest book, *Morir lo imprescindible* (Relentless Dying) (2007), that recollects poems from all of her previous texts, Izaguirre's poetry is involved in the description of loss and suffering, her yearning for the brief happiness in her native Paraguay, and the analysis of the social and political instability lived in Argentina in the latter years of the twentieth century.

Rosa Tezanos-Pinto

Selected Works

Poetry

Trémolo. Buenos Aires: Editorial La Mandrágora, 1960.

El país que llaman vida. Buenos Aires: Editorial Ismael B. Colombo, 1964.

No está vedado el grito. Buenos Aires: Editorial Ismael B. Colombo, 1967.

Girar en descubierto. Buenos Aires: Editorial Ismael B. Colombo, 1975.

Qué importa si anochece. Buenos Aires: Editorial Ismael B. Colombo, 1980.

Hors Programme. Paris: Bruno Durucher, Ed., 1981.

Judas y los demás. Buenos Aires: Editorial Colombo, 1981.

Y dan un premio a quien lo atrape vivo. Buenos Aires: Ediciones Letras de Buenos Aires, 1986.

Si preguntan por alguien con mi nombre. Asunción: Palabra Gráfica Editora, 1990.

Poemas (1960–1992). Obras Completas. Asunción: Editorial Don Bosco, 1993.

Una extraña certeza nos vigila. Poemas (1960–1992). Obras Completa. Asunción: Editorial Don Bosco, 1993, pp. 243–60.

Morir lo imprescindible. Buenos Aires: Editorial Vinciguerra, 2006.

Narrative

Yo soy el tiempo. Buenos Aires: Editorial Guadalupe, 1970.

Ultimo domicilio conocido. Asunción: Editorial Coraje, 1994.

Ayer no ha terminado todavía. Asunción: Editorial Don Bosco, 2001.

References and Further Reading

Anderson Imbert, Enrique. *Poemas.* Buenos Aires: Ediciones Carrá, 1981.

——. *Antología de Nuevos Poetas Argentinos.* Asunción: Ed. Alcándara, 1986.

Arancibia, Juana. "Diálogos con los personajes de la novela *Ayer no ha terminado todavía* de Ester de Izaguirre". *Alba de América* 21 (2002): 91–5.

Badano, Valeria. "Epopeya del yo. Las construcciones textuales en *Ayer no ha terminado todavía* de Ester de Izaguirre". *Alba de América* 21 (2002): 79–85.

Boéchat, Susana. "Ester de Izaguirre: singularidad de su voz poética". In *SADE.* Buenos Aires: SADE, 1986, pp. 14–21.

Koremblit, Bernardo Ezequiel. *El país que llaman Vida.* Buenos Aires: Editorial Ismael B. Colombo, 1964.

Mazzei, Angel. *Qué importa si anochece.* Buenos Aires: Editorial Colombo, 1980.

Pagés Larraya, Antonio. *No está vedado el grito.* Buenos Aires: Editorial Ismael B. Colombo, 1967.

Tezanos-Pinto, Rosa. "*Ayer no ha terminado todavía* de Ester de Izaguirre". *Alba de América* 21 (2002): 541–6.

——. "Memoria e identidad en el 'texto secreto' de Ester de Izaguirre". *Antípodas, Journal of Hispanic and Galician Studies* XVI (2005a): 177–85.

——. "Metamorfosis del yo en Ester del 'yo poético' en Ester de Izaguirre". In Juana Arancibia (ed.), *La mujer en el mundo hispánico.* Westminister, CA: Instituto Literario y Cultural Hispánico, 2005b, pp. 329–41.

Salvador, Nélida. *La nueva poesía argentina.* Buenos Aires: Nuevos Esquemas, 1969.

Veirave, Alfredo. "La poesía: la generación del cuarenta". In *Historia de la Literatura Argentina.* Buenos Aires: Centro Editor de América Latina, 1968, pp. 76–80.

J

JESUS, CAROLINA MARIA DE

Carolina Maria de Jesus was born in Sacramento (state of Minas Gerais) in 1914, and died in a small town of Parelheiros, in the outskirts of the city of São Paulo, Brazil, in 1977. De Jesus is perhaps the most surprising of all writers, because she did not even attend regular, formal school for more than two years. She is, in fact, a writer who came from the utmost poverty and powerlessness, to write from within her difficult life not just a personal testimonial but a reflection on her historical times in Brazil. Even though De Jesus wrote as an individual, her words can be seen also as a reflection on the fate of poor, colored women everywhere. She wrote by hand, on pieces of paper she picked from the garbage and made into notebooks; she wrote at night, after returning to her shack and three children from a day of difficult and poorly paid work on the streets of São Paulo.

De Jesus was the illegitimate child of Maria Carolina da Silva and João Cândido Veloso, who made a living as an itinerant musician and singer. When João Cândido left Maria Carolina, she had to work as a maid. Soon Carolina Maria—who was nicknamed Bitita—worked alongside her mother cleaning houses. Later her mother started living with the man De Jesus knew as her stepfather. When she was seven years old, she began attending school, in spite of her own mother's disbelief in education. As Levine and Meihy write in *The Life and Death of Carolina Maria de Jesus*, her attendance at school was "the result of the personal philanthropy of Maria Leite, a landowner's wife from the countryside near Sacramento" who "paid the tuition and school expenses of Carolina and several poor black children to the sect-run school as personal penance for her ancestors having owned slaves" (1995: 24).

In spite of her unusual two-year education and her intelligence, early on in her life Carolina Maria learned, first hand, what it meant to be black, illegitimate and poor: she was constantly reminded of "her place". Because she was black, several times she was spurned even by her lighter-skinned relatives, and because she was illegitimate, she was not allowed to enter a Catholic church. When her mother became ill, de Jesus took care of her until the end, and became completely alone in the world at the age of 23. After this time, she made her way to the city of São Paulo, on foot, stopping in towns to work for a while, and always intent on reaching the big city, which at the time was as a magnet for many Brazilians from the poorer parts of the country, who flocked to São Paulo in search of a better life.

Although she worked long hours, Carolina Maria de Jesus continued reading, discussing with people and, in a sense, furthering her education by every means she could find. One of these means was simply writing. When she arrived in São Paulo, she worked as a maid for several important families, but when she got pregnant with her first child, the family fired her, and she did what so many have done in Brazil: she built her own shack in a slum with pieces of wood and metal she found on the streets. The relationship with the father of her first child, João, did not last. She later had another son, José Carlos, and a daughter, Vera Eunice, each with a different white man. She never married any of them.

Quarto de despejo (Child of the Dark)

Carolina Maria de Jesus's best-known work is *Quarto de despejo*, published in 1960. This book consists of entries to her diaries covering events in her life from July 15, 1955 to December 31, 1959. The entries depict not only the repetitious events of the life of a single mother of three who lives in a slum and has to work every day to feed her children; the text also consists of her reflections on the political situation of the country and her thoughts about her neighbors and the overall situation of Brazil. The slum was, in a sense, a patchwork of the whole country, and there she met people not just from the different Brazilian states, but also Portuguese people, and even a Japanese woman.

Quarto starts describing the morning of July 15, 1955, her daughter Vera Eunice's birthday. She wanted to buy the girl a pair of shoes but, she remarks, "the cost of food prevents us from fulfilling our desires ... I found a pair of shoes in the garbage, washed it and fixed it for her to wear" (1960: 9). Indeed, De Jesus worked daily, picking up paper and scrap metal from the streets, then selling these to make a living. Some days mother and children went hungry. Some days she felt sick and could not obtain any help. Some days she had struggles with her neighbors, who wanted to spank her children while she was out, working; she had problems with people on the street who tried to fool and rob her. But she also tried to help others in the *favela*, while keeping a strict moral stance, refraining from drinking, and making sure her children attended school. During all this time, De Jesus kept reading the newspapers she found on the streets, or reading them in the newsstands. She continued discussing politics and thinking about not just her immediate reality, but about the relationship between the *favela* and the wider political scene of the country, as well as about the situation of the poor and the exploitation they suffered on a daily basis.

The history of the making of *Quarto de despejo* is fairly well known: a young journalist, Audálio Dantas, saw a tall black woman threatening to put "in her book" the names of some adults who were using (and almost destroying) a recently opened children's playground close to her *favela*. Dantas became interested in this "book". After many visits to her shack, he gained her confidence, and saw that the "book" consisted of several handwritten notebooks she had picked from the garbage and used to write her diary. De Jesus wanted to interest him in other work she had written, her stories and proverbs, but he preferred to give attention to the diary.

From these initial contacts, Dantas realized he had found something of great value. He writes in the presentation to *Quarto*, that as a young journalist he had gone to the *favela* of Canindé to write the story of the *favela*, but that when he met Carolina, he "gave up writing" it because, he writes, "no journalist, no writer could write that history better (than Carolina)—the vision from within the *favela*" (1993: 3). Dantas started publishing excerpts from the diary in the *Folha da Noite* in 1958. In 1959, more excerpts appeared in the magazine *O Cruzeiro*. Soon afterwards, the edited text appeared in book form under the title of *Quarto de despejo; diário de uma favelada*. The reception was immediate, and the first edition of 9,000 books sold out. José Carlos Sebe Bom Meihy writes that when the diaries were published, Carolina, an "inside out intellectual" was perceived as the result of the ambiguities of the country posed at a historical moment when "progress" was the only form to overcome ties to an unjust past ("A percepção de um brasileiro," 23).

Indeed, the historical context for the appearance of Carolina's first diary is of utmost importance. The "progressist" discourse in Brazil, coupled with the national effort to build Brasília, was contrasted with the social problems in the expanding city of São Paulo, with its multitude of workers who were, for the most part, not very well educated, and most extremely poor. De Jesus's work, then, became a catalyst for all these competing realities of the city and, by extension, of the country itself. It is no surprise that *Quarto de despejo* became an instant success.

But De Jesus does not write only about the situation of her neighbors. In her frank prose, she says that she finds it better to be alone, without a husband, than to have one who would only make her and her children suffer more. She also documents her own life as a sexual being, a woman who had three children from three different fathers, who receives men in her house, and who desires men who come to visit. *Quarto de despejo* is a candid book which shows a woman who does not conform to any pre-set feminine ideal of a pure mother who is only head and feelings. When *Quarto de despejo* was first published, many people hailed its author while not really paying attention to what the book says; however, as time passed, *Quarto* came to be understood not as a critique against the system that makes the *favela*s possible, but as a critique of the *favela* of Canindé, where De Jesus lived. Even though the city of São Paulo had already planned to build a road through Canindé before *Quarto de despejo* was published, the eventual destruction of the slum has sometimes been considered one of the outcomes of De Jesus's book.

Casa de alvenaria: o diário de uma ex-favelada (I Am Going to Have a Little House)

As a result of the publication of *Quarto de despejo*, the royalties enabled De Jesus to make the down-payment for a "real" house in a São Paulo working-class neighborhood and to move there with her children. She was invited to give interviews, and to sign books. The neighborhood was crowded with journalists and tabloid writers; De Jesus became a celebrity. *Quarto de despejo* was published in English, and American magazines like *Time* and *Newsweek* even published news items about her. As De Jesus writes in *Quarto de despejo*, one of her greatest dreams was to be able to publish in other countries, and she sent many of her stories to *Reader's Digest*, only to be rejected every time. Now, with the publication of her diary, this dream became reality, in a certain way.

In the meantime, she continued living her São Paulo reality, one that showed her that simply owning a brick house would not make her happy: she had to contend with the reality of fitting into a different class, strangers constantly asking her for money, journalists writing disparaging things about her every move. She documents the process of owing her brick house in her second diary, *Casa de alvenaria; diário de uma ex-favelada*, written from May 1960 to May 1961, and published in 1961 by Editora P. de Avevedo, of Rio de Janeiro. As this second diary shows, the dream turned sour as soon as she noticed that her children were not well received, and the neighbors looked at her with suspicion. Fernando L. Lara writes that this second book, translated in English as *I'm Going to Have a Little House*, "is a document as astonishing as *Child of the Dark*," because it "shows the process of exclusion in Brazil," and documents the "push and pull factors experienced by poor rural Brazilians during the twentieth century".

Indeed, for De Jesus, as for any other poor migrant who came to live in the outskirts of the huge megalopolis once considered the fastest-growing city in the world, the economical and political forces were formidable. De Jesus, however, instead of being simply crushed by these forces, discussed them while documenting their devastating effect on her life. Thus, these two complex diaries are more than simply one person's recollections of how her life has taken different turns, and include her sharp reflections on how very specific politicians' actions affected everybody's lives. For anyone who knows some of Brazil's history, it is a startling revelation to see how people such as Leonel Brizola (governor of Rio Grande do Sul, 1962, then exiled due to the military *coup d'état* in 1964), Juscelino Kubitscheck (President of the country and the "founder" of Brasília), Adhemar de Barros (the governor of the state of São Paulo), and others, were seen by the common people, through De Jesus's narration.

Fiction and Poetry

Probably coasting on the fame of the first diaries, Carolina Maria de Jesus published the fictional work *Pedaços da fome* (Pieces of Hunger) in 1963, and *Provérbios* (Proverbs) in 1965. Even though to the end of her life she felt that her most important work was her poetry, the sale of none of these books even approximated the success of the diaries, and they were all but forgotten. Besides the fact that it is very difficult to sell poetry and fiction in Brazil, and books are notoriously expensive in that country, there was also an added factor for the commercial failure of *Pedaços da fome* and *Provérbios*: de Jesus tired of being told what to do, and how to appear in public, and what to say. She had lived alone, surviving by her wits, all her life up to that moment, and after the disenchantment with her first discoverer, Audálio Dantas, and with her increasing feeling of being hounded by the Brazilian press that disparaged and patronized her, she became less and less patient with the press and with people coming to ask for money and favors.

It would seem, however, by the unprecedented success of the first book, *Quarto de despejo*, that Carolina Maria de Jesus would have become a successful writer earning a stable income. That did not happen. Instead, Carolina's name disappeared from the public eye, and, in 1964, she was photographed once again picking paper from the streets in São Paulo, although Audálio Dantas insisted that these photos were contrived by de Jesus. In 1970, she moved from the Santana neighborhood to a place in Parelheiros. She and her children built their small house together, and she lived there to the end of her life in 1977. Even her obituary, published in the newspaper *Jornal do Brasil* (and quoted in *The Life and Death of Carolina Maria de Jesus*), was both inexact and unsympathetic, referring to her life as a "failure," and remarking on her "inability to adjust to success" (Levine and Meihy, 1995: 86–7).

Diário de Bitita (Bitita's Diary)

In light of the overwhelming ill-will towards this outspoken, black, and independent woman whose views did not quickly conform with the general Brazilian concepts of a "racial democracy" in her country, it is not surprising that, shortly before she died, De Jesus chose to trust foreigners, and not her fellow countrymen, with the last of her diaries, *Diário de Bitita*, which was published after her death.

The back cover of the Brazilian version of *Diário de Bitita* states that Carolina gave to French journalists the manuscript that compose the book. In the copyright page, it says that the Editora Nova Fronteira acquired the rights to this Portuguese edition from Éditions A. M. Métallié, and published it, in 1986. It is important to note that Editora Nova Fronteira placed the book under the category of "Ficção Brasileira," in flagrant contradiction to the author's own intent, which was to have the text understood as a diary, therefore, not as fiction. Although it is not possible to know with certainty why Carolina decided to trust French journalists with her text, and not to deal directly with Brazilian publishers, it is clear that she no longer trusted Brazilian journalists, or the Brazilian publishing business, or both. Her choice may be explained by what José Carlos Sebe Bom Meihy discusses in his presentation of the unedited version of the first diary (published as *Meu estranho diário* in 1996), when he presents this same problem, from the point of view of the historical moment of the early 1960s: Carolina's book painted a grim picture of Brazil to foreign readers who, then, had just started painting a picture of the country which was, to the Brazilians' chagrin, not just pessimistic, but also static, unchangeable, of a country where racial and class discrimination was rampant.

Diário de Bitita is an important work among De Jesus's diaries, because in it she recalls her family and her childhood in Minas Gerais. In *Diário de Bitita*, we learn, for example, that her maternal grandfather had been a slave, and that his greatest regret in life was that his eight children did not learn how to write. It was probably from this grandfather that de Jesus inherited her great love of learning: "When you go to school," he said, "study with great devotion and diligence to learn" (*Diário de Bitita*, 1986: 57). It was also probably from her grandfather that de Jesus first learned how blacks suffered at the hands of the former owners, even after slavery officially ended in Brazil in 1888.

Carolina Maria de Jesus wrote this *diário* as an adult and, most importantly, as an adult who had already had the experience of writing other diaries, such as *Quarto de despejo* and *Casa de alvenaria; Diário de uma ex-favelada*. It is, however, impossible to say whether all the reflections in *Diário de Bitita* are the product of this adult knowledge, or whether she used to reflect on facts and relationships between the races, relations between men and women, even at an early age. What *Diário de Bitita* undoubtedly reveals is the history of de Jesus' family, a family only one generation removed from slavery.

This fact, in itself, is memorable, because, in the history of Brazilian letters, all writers have been educated, and most of them have belonged at least to the middle class. It is noteworthy that the few other exceptions—Cruz e Souza and Lima Barreto—were respectively black and mulatto, and both had great difficulty obtaining any kind of assistance or recognition during their lifetime. *Diário de Bitita* also explains some of De Jesus's later reactions to people—she had suffered so much rejection and opprobrium for being black and female, that it was very difficult for her to trust others. Not surprisingly, her upbringing finally reveals the source of what can be called her "racism"—or her disparaging comments about blacks: she was raised hearing those comments, she suffered as a result of racism even from her own lighter-skinned relatives, therefore, in spite of her great intelligence and drive to reach her goals, she did not trust blacks and never formed any alliance with them.

One of the most moving aspects in *Diário de Bitita*, however, is De Jesus's attempts to improve herself linguistically. It is important to remember that, unlike all her other counterparts in Brazilian literature, this woman did not attend school for more than two years, and never had any money to buy books, or to attend university lectures. Even though for a period she was greeted among artists, she was, for the most part, considered a freak, and never respected or accepted as an equal.

A Voice Re-discovered

After Carolina Maria de Jesus's death in 1977, her name fell into oblivion in Brazil, but her fame continued to spread abroad. *Quarto de despejo* continued to be translated into many languages. Unfortunately for her and her heirs, the financial gain from these translations has been minimal, because "she had ceded her rights to authorize foreign translations to Editôra Paulo de Azevedo Ltda., a branch of Francisco Alves" (Levine and Meihy, 1995: 84–5). It is important to note, once again, that *Quarto de despejo* is the only Brazilian book that has sold one million copies.

One reason that might help explain why Carolina Maria de Jesus's work disappeared from Brazil for such a long time is given by José Carlos Sebe Bom Meihy, who writes that her work was clearly inserted in a political period between the end of the Estado Novo (1937–45), and the beginning of the military dictatorship (1964) (Meihy, 2006). With the advent of the military dictatorship, especially with the installation of the hard line in 1968, a voice like hers was seen as subversive. The political culture of the time would not allow a strident dissenting voice to report from the margins. There was also the very real dissonance between De Jesus's political views and those of the leftist intellectuals, who had trouble with her politics and openly criticized her. All these factors, combined with her personal disillusion, led her to seek solitude and distance from almost everyone.

Carolina Maria de Jesus's work has recently received more attention from Brazilian and foreign researchers. The efforts of José Carlos Sebe Bom Meihy and Robert Levine to locate De Jesus's family, to arrange for the microfilming of the originals of her manuscripts, and for the publication of the unedited text of her first book are proof of this revival. Even though Brazil of the twenty-first century is very different from the Brazil that De Jesus describes in her diaries, her work is now a document of her struggles, as well as a document of a historical time. Mostly, however, De Jesus's voice stands alone as the voice of an independent black woman who never said she wanted to speak for others and who, to her dying day, wanted to be known as a poet.

EVA PAULINO BUENO

Selected Works

Quarto de despejo. São Paulo: Editora Ática, 1993. Translated in English as *Beyond All Pity*. Trans. David St. Clair. London: Souvenir Press, 1962.

Casa de alvenaria; Diário de uma ex-favelada. Rio de Janeiro: Editora P. De Azevedo, 1961. Translated in English as *I Am Going to Have a Little House*.

Pedaços da fome. São Paulo: Editora Aquila. 1963.

Provérbios. São Paulo: Luzes-Gráfica Editora, 1965.

Diário de Bitita. Rio de Janeiro: Editora Nova Fronteira, 1986.

Meu estranho diário. Ed. José Carlos Sebe Bom Meihy and Robert M. Levine. São Paulo: Xamã, 1996.

Antologia Pessoal. Ed. José Carlos Sebe Bom Meihy. Rio de Janeiro: Editora UFRJ, 1996.

References and Further Reading

Allen, Paula Gunn. *The Sacred Hoop: Recovering the Feminine in American Indian Traditions*. Boston, MA: Beacon Press, 1986.

Anzaldúa, Gloria. *Making Face, Making Soul/Haciendo Caras: Creative and Critical Perspectives by Feminists of Color*. San Francisco, CA: Aunt Lute Foundation Books, 1990.

Bueno, Eva Paulino. "Carolina Maria de Jesus in the Context of Testimonios: Race, Sexuality, and Exclusion". *Criticism* 41(2) (Spring 1999): 257–84.

——. "Race, Gender and the Politics of Reception of Latin American Testimonios". In Amal Amireh and Lisa Suhair Majaj (eds), *Going Global: The Transnational Reception of Third World Women Writers*. New York: Garland Publishing, 2000.

——. "Carolina Maria de Jesus". In Cynthia Margarita Tompkins and David William Foster (eds), *Notable Twentieth-Century Latin American Women: A Biographical Dictionary*. Westport, CT: Greenwood Press, 2001.

Dantas, Audálio. "A atualidade do mundo de Carolina". In Carolina Maria de Jesus, *Quarto de Despejo; diário de uma favelada*. 2nd edn. São Paulo: Editora Ática, 1993.

Dias, Antonio Gonçalves and Lajolo, Marisa. *Nós e os outros: histórias de diferentes culturas*. São Paulo: Editora Ática, 2002.

Dieguez, Maria Luz. *La "Polifonía" como imperativo feminista: Desmistificación, subversión, y creación de nueves narrativas en Esther Tasquets, Paloma Días-Mas, Carolina María de Jesus y Rogoberta Menchú*. Eugene, OR: University of Oregon, 1989.

Fox, Patricia D. "The Diary of Carolina Maria de Jesus: A Paradoxical Ennunciation". In *Proceedings of The Black Image in Latin American Culture*. Slippery Rock, PA: Slippery Rock University, 1989: 241–51.

Joseph, G.M. and Szuchaman, Mark D. *I Saw a City Invincible: Urban Portraits of Latin America*. Wilmington, DL: SR Books, 1995.

Lara, Fernando L. "Review of Carolina Maria de Jesus, *I'm Going to Have a Little House*". H-Urban, H-Net Reviews, May, 1998. URL: htto://www.h-net.msu.edu/reviews/showrev.cgi?path=28393895096838

Levine, Robert M. *The Cautionary Tale of Carolina Maria de Jesus*. Notre Dame, IN: Helen Kellogg Institute for International Studies, University of Notre Dame, 1992.

Levine, Robert M. and Meihy, José Carlos Sebe Bom. *The Life and Death of Carolina Maria de Jesus*. Albuquerque, NM: University of New Mexico Press, 1995.

Meihy, José Carlos Sebe Bom. "Os fios dos desafios: o retrato de Carolina Maria de Jesus no tempo presente". In Vagner Gonçalves da Silva, *Artes do Corpo*. São Paulo: Selo Negro Edições, 2004.

——. "Carolina Maria de Jesus: emblema do silêncio." In Biblioteca Virtual de Direitos Humanos da Universidade de São Paulo. Comissão de Direitos Humanos. http://www.geocities.com/sociedadecultura/meihyusp.html (7–27–2006).

Meihy, José Carlos Sebe Bom and Levine, Robert. M. *Cinderela Negra: A saga de Carolina Maria de Jesus*. Rio de Janeiro: Editora UFRJ, 1994

Vogt, Carlos. "Trabalho, pobreza e trabalho intelectual (*O Quarto de despejo* de Carolina Maria de Jesus)". In Roberto Schwarz (ed.), *Os pobres na literatura brasileira*. São Paulo: Brasiliense, 1983, pp. 204–13.

JÚLIA, FRANCISCA

Francisca Júlia da Silva Munster was born on August 31, 1871, in Xiririca, now Eldorado, in the state of São Paulo, Brazil. When she was eight years old, in order to give her a better education, her parents—the lawyer Miguel Luso da Silva and the teacher Cecília Isabel da Silva—moved to the city of São Paulo.

Francisca Júlia is held to have been one of Brazil's best Parnassian poets, the only one of her sex to have been on a par with the famous Parnassian triad of poets, namely, Olavo

Bilac, Raimundo Correia and Alberto de Oliveira. Péricles da Silva Ramos, a literary researcher of repute considers her "the only one in our milieu who meets all of the conditions of the French Parnassian Poetry" (Ramos 1986: 144).

Francisca Júlia achieved fame during her lifetime. She had her bust sculpted at the Brazilian Academy of Letters and was acclaimed in the newspapers of São Paulo and Rio de Janeiro as the "queen of the sonnet—a writer who produces her poems with the same gusto as a Wagnerian composition," or the one who "achieved ... the highest intellectual representation of her sex in the literature of her country" (Pimenta 1920: XL). At present, her work enjoys a relative prominence and is even known abroad. Her name is included in poetry anthologies and literature dictionaries in France, Spain, Portugal and Italy.

Nevertheless, neither her international renown, nor the fact of her having been considered a poet of superior sensitivity, prevented her from being consigned to oblivion at the universities and publishing houses in Brazil nowadays. She is barely remembered by Brazilian readers. It is somewhat upsetting that very few people in Brazil are able to say who Francisca Júlia was, and even fewer can name just one of her books. Even some students undertaking a literature course at the university do not know who she was. And scarce are those teachers of Brazilian literature who take an interest in her or present any sort of thesis or scientific study on her sonnets, notwithstanding the fact of her having been elected by the most distinguished scholar, Perícles da Silva Ramos, as the only Parnassian poet to succeed in developing a plastic and harmonious art, who professed art for art's sake with remarkable poise, and "who knew the *mot juste*, craved the formal austerity and, above all, prided herself on being impassive—something to which the other Brazilian Parnassian poets did not attach great importance" (Ramos 1986: 144).

In Brazil, little is published about her at present: her work appears in a few literary anthologies, scattered high school textbooks, typewritten texts for students preparing for college entrance exams. A substantial part of said material does, however, present insufficient analyses and interpretations, as well as defective theoretical accuracy, and is far below what the work of the writer in question really deserves.

Francisca Júlia's literary debut took place in the journalistic milieu, around 1891, amidst much controversy and perplexity, owing to the fact that the majority of critics of that time (among them, João Ribeiro, Arthur Azevedo, Araripe Junior, Lúcio de Mendonça) simply did not believe that verses so well written and with such aesthetical elaboration could spring from the mind of a woman. Thus, at the age of 20, Francisca Júlia had her first poem published in the newspaper *O Estado de São Paulo*. This poem—the sonnet "Quadro Incompleto"—was later included in her book *Mármores*. The author went on to contribute to a number of periodicals in São Paulo, including *Correio Paulistano* and *Diário Popular*, and to newspapers in Rio de Janeiro such as *O Álbum* and *A Semana*.

The year 1895 is a major landmark in the career of Francisca Júlia. The author publishes *Mármores*, her first book. She begins to be acclaimed by the critics. Olavo Bilac, known as the prince of Brazilian poets, sees in her poetry "a wondrous shower of novelty and freshness". The severe critic João Ribeiro, one of those who would not believe women could produce Parnassian poems with such high formal accuracy, reviews his former stand by declaring:

> I do not hesitate at present, whatever the consequences of this assertion, to say that, since the generation that we have come to symbolize in the names of such poets as Raimundo Correia, Olavo Bilac and Alberto Oliveira, there has not been a poet who surpassed or even equaled the author of *Mármores*.
>
> (Ribeiro 1895: XVIII)

Most critics consider the poem "Dança das Centauras," included in the book *Mármores*, to be the high point of the poetry of Francisca Júlia. The poem presents a dialogue intertextually with two renowned masters of Parnassian Poetry: the Cuban Jose Maria Heredia and the French Leconte de Lisle. The *centauras*, female centaurs, are singing and laughing dionysiacally, when everything changes dramatically. Hercules, the fierce enemy of the centaurs, makes his appearance, creating panic and terror in their midst. In order to save their lives, they flee, breaking away at a frightful gallop: an intriguing metaphor on the brevity of life and the arrival of unpredictable and infallible death. The beauty of the poem's alexandrine verses and the sonority of its rich rhymes is highlighted when it is read out loud:

Patas dianteiras no ar, bocas livres dos freios,
Nuas, em grita, em ludo, entrecruzando as lanças,
Ei-las, garbosas vêm, na evolução das danças
Rudes, pompeando à luz a brancura dos seios.
A noite escuta, fulge o luar, gemem as franças;
Mil centauras a rir, em lutas e torneios,
Galopam livres, vão e vêm, os peitos cheios
De ar, o cabelo solto ao léu das auras mansas.
Empalidece o luar, a noite cai, madruga ...
A dança hípica pára e logo atroa o espaço
O galope infernal das centauras em fuga:
É que, longe, ao clarão do luar que empalidece,
Enorme, aceso o olhar, bravo, do heróico braço
Pendente a clava argiva, Hércules aparece.

Forefeet raised high, mouths unbridled, naked,
Romping with alacrity, crossing lances,
Behold them, so graceful, in evolutions
Of primitive dance, their white breasts highlighting.
Night listens, moon shines, treetops rustle,
Thousands of female centaurs frolic, joust,
Gallop freely to and fro, their white breasts
In the wind, hair loose in the breeze.
The shining moon wanes, it dawns ...
The equestrian dance suddenly halts and, then,
In the open, the sound of galloping in fright:
It is that far, against the moon's waning light,
Huge, eyes lit, brave, from the stout arm
The Hellenic mace hanging, Hercules surges.

The second book, *Esfinge*, appeared in the bookshops eight years later, in 1903. This is a sort of re-edition of *Mármores* with additional material. Perícles Eugênio da Silva Ramos observes that, at the launch of this book, "Francisca Júlia's reputation was solidly established as Brazil's greatest woman poet and eminent follower of the precepts of the school of

Leconte de Lisle and Heredia" (Ramos 1961: 10). However, many of the sonnets in *Esfinge* do show a change in the author's style. A number of poems are permeated by the musicality, spiritualism and mysticism of the Symbolist Movement, as can be seen in the following stanza of *Noturno*, with a rough translation below:

> Pesa o silêncio sobre a terra. Por extenso
> Caminho, passo a passo, o cortejo funéreo
> Se arrasta em direção ao negro cemitério ...
> À frente, um vulto agita a caçoula do incenso.

> Over the earth, silence hangs. Through
> A long way, step by step, the funereal
> Cortège drags towards the gloomy cemetery ...
> In the lead, a figure stirs the incense burner.

Francisca Júlia assumes her mystical side, accepting invitations to lectures on witchcraft, astral body, mediums and reincarnation.

The author published two more books, both of a didactic nature, meant for children: *Livro da Infância*, in 1899 and *Alma Infantil*, in 1912, the latter with the co-authorship of her brother, Júlio da Silva. In *Alma Infantil*, the author produces a series of pedagogic hymns aimed at teaching children respect for their country, their school, their course of studies, work, their teachers. In *Livro da Infância*, the reader recognizes an author less concerned with issues of a moralizing nature and more interested in skillfully retelling innumerable popular tales from various parts of the world, thus making known to children stories spanning from ancient Greece to Brazilian folklore. Worthy of note are such tales as the story of *Anacreonte*; the German ballad entitled *O Rei Fantasma*; the Scandinavian ballad *O Trovador*; popular Brazilian legends such as *O Aleijadinho* and *O Curandeiro*; and the well-known Brazilian Indian narrative, *A Yara*. It can be said positively that this is an interesting book in that it covers the diversity and plurality of the world's various cultures.

In 1909, aged 37, Francisca Júlia married the engineer Filadelfo Edmundo Munster, devoting herself to home and husband, abandoning her literary career and, as reported by Perícles Eugênio da Silva Ramos, even refusing an offer to join the Academia Paulista de Letras.

Francisca Júlia died on 1 November 1920 in strange circumstances. The day her tuberculosis-stricken husband was buried, she locked herself in her room and, whether deliberately or inadvertently, took an overdose of narcotics that led to her death. According to the newspapers of her time, never at a burial of a writer were there so many people. Thousands of sorrowful admirers were at her funeral. The new generation of poets were all there, including "the future revolutionaries of the Semana da Arte Moderna" (Menezes 1949: 339). In the same year of her death, Victor Brecheret paid her homage: he sculpted her statue for over her tomb, a beautiful work in marble. This sculpture can be seen at the Araçá cemetery, in São Paulo.

The poetry of Francisca Júlia is unlikely ever to be shown on the front page of literary journals. The majority of her readers are no longer alive and her work has long been out of print and not listed in publishers' catalogues. A sad end for one who was honored with a bust at the Academia Brasileira de Letras and acclaimed as the greatest and most fascinating Parnassian woman poet Brazil has ever known.

KENIA MARIA DE ALMEIDA PEREIRA

Selected Works

Mármores. São Paulo: Horácio Belfort Sabino, 1895.
Esfinges. São Paulo: Monteiro Lobato e Cia, 1921.
Poesias. Introduction and notes by Péricles Eugênio da Silva Ramos. São Paulo: Conselho Estadual da Cultura, 1961.

References and Further Reading

Andrade, Mário de. *O empalhador de passarinho*. São Paulo: Livraria Martns S.A, 1955.
Haddad, Jamil Almansur. "Mármores e Esfinges de Francisca Júlia". In *Boletim Bibliográfico*. São Paulo: Biblioteca Municipal de São Paulo, 1945.
Menezes, Raimundo. *Dicionário Literário Brasileiro*. São Paulo: LTS, 1949.
Moisés, Massoud. *História da literatura brasileira*. Vol. 3. São Paulo: Cultrix, 1989.
Moisés, Massoud and Paes, J.P. *Pequeno dicionário de literatura brasileira*. São Paulo: Cultrix, 1987.
Muricy, Andrade. *Panorama do movimento simbolista brasileiro*. Brasília: MES, 1973.
Oliveira, Maria Elvira de Melo. "O ideal de pureza parnasiana: Francisca Júlia". Dissertação de mestrado. Brasília: UNB, 1993.
Picchio, Luciana Stepagno. *La Littérature Brésilienne*. Paris: Presses Universitaires de France, 1981.
Pimenta, Gelásio. "Francisca Júlia". *Jornal a cigarra* (1 Nov. 1920): XL.
Ramos, Péricles Eugênio. "Introdução". In Francisca Júlia, *Poesias*. São Paulo: Conselho Estadual de Cultura, 1961, pp. 5–41.
——. "A renovação parnasiana na poesia". In Faria Coutinho, *A literatura no Brasil*. Vol. 4. Rio de Janeiro: José Olympio/UFF, 1986, pp. 91–173.
Ribeiro, João. *Críticas: poetas parnasianos e simbolistas*. Vol. II. Rio de Janeiro: Academia brasileira de letras, 1957.
Van Thieghem. *Dictionnaire des littératures*. Vol. II. Paris: Presses Universitaires de France, 1968.

JURADO, ALICIA

Alicia Jurado was born in Buenos Aires on May 22, 1922. A writer and essayist, she was also a personal friend of Jorge Luis Borges for over three decades. She received a doctorate in Natural Sciences in the Department of Precise and Natural Sciences at the University of Buenos Aires. An agnostic woman with strong ethical convictions, she always defined herself as a liberal, a republican, and defender of the Alberdi constitution as an instrument of freedom. Of a scientific background and rationalist focus, she offers in her memoirs a crucial testimony to understanding Argentine culture of the latter half of the twentieth century. For Alicia Jurado, the key focus in her life was the ranch where she grew up and spent her summers. This place represented the heart of her domestic intimacy, where she developed an interest in gardening, read countless books, dedicated herself to cooking, sewing, and embroidery, and above all, to enjoying the present with whoever she wanted. Near the end of 1954, she came to know Borges through Estela Canto, a mutual friend, and began a deep friendship of weekly meetings that lasted until her death in 1986. Alicia Jurado in her 1964 essay "The Genius and Figure of Jorge Luis Borges," already offered an important perspective on the author for those who study his work. They also collaborated on a book on Buddhism that was released in 1976 under the title *¿Qué es el budismo?* (What is Buddhism?).

Among her friends also figure Oliverio Girondo, Norah Lange, and Silvina Ocampo. She was also on close terms with Adolfo Bioy Casares, to whom on several occasions she gave manuscripts for him to correct. She also began in 1954 a friendship with Victoria Ocampo who welcomed her into the pages of the magazine *Sur*, along with guiding and counseling her at key points in her career as an investigator. It was Victoria Ocampo who insisted that Alicia Jurado present herself for the Guggenheim Foundation scholarship so that she could do research in the US, and write the biography of William Henry Hudson. Alicia Jurado won the scholarship in the 1966–67 academic year and went to New York. She also had the support of the British Council to go to England in 1967 to gather more material on Hudson. Her essay appeared in publication in 1971 entitled "Vida y obra de W.H. Hudson" (Life and Work of W.H. Hudson) and with this essay she won second prize overall and first prize citywide for an essay in the Juan Bautista Alberdi competition. In 1976, she received a scholarship from the Fulbright Foundation to write Robert Cunninghame Graham's biography. He was an adventurous Scottish noble who spent his youth in Argentina. The biographical essay appeared in 1978 under the title "El escocés errante: R.B. Cunninghame Graham" (The Wandering Scot: R.B. Cunninghame Graham) and in 1983 this essay gained her the National Prize for Literature in the Category of Essay.

Victoria Ocampo supported Alicia Jurado on many occasions, and along with Borges, she was one of the major intellectuals in Alicia Jurado's professional education. The relationship between the two foreshadowed the future, since Alicia Jurado occupied many of the institutional positions previously occupied by Victoria Ocampo. In this manner Alicia Jurado would inherit Victoria Ocampo's role as mentor and friend of the Argentine Association of English Culture, the National Fund for the Arts, the publishing house Sur and even an academic Chair. She was elected as a luminary academic in September 1980, taking the "Juan Bautista Alberdi" Chair which had belonged to Leopoldo Herrera, Ramón J. Cárcano, Ricardo Saenz-Hayes, and her close friend Victoria Ocampo. Her reception speech on 28 May 1981 was entitled "Victoria Ocampo: mi predecesora" (Victoria Ocampo: My Predecessor).

The poet Olga Orozco was another of her good friends. Olga's esoteric, magic, and intense personality inspired one of her characters in her first novel *La cárcel y los hierros* (Jail and Bars), published in 1961 and winner of an Award of Honor by the Argentine Writers' Association. The title of the novel, written in the first person, is inspired by a poem by Santa Teresa. It is a work that clearly reflects a metaphysical stage through which Alicia Jurado passed, immersed in mystic literature. At the time she was searching for what she said very aptly in her memoirs as the desire for transcendence that she believed to be "inherent to the human species," that is to say, she was looking for God. This perspective would change in time into a deep agnostic skepticism.

In 1965, her collection of stories *Leguas de polvo y sueño* (Leagues of Dust and Dream) appeared. The book's title came from a Borges poem written in her ranch guestbook. Of this collection, the story "El regreso" (The Return) is noteworthy. It had appeared earlier in the magazine *Sur* and tells a true story of loss of love with a tragic denouement. In 1967, the romantic novel *En soledad vivía* (I Lived in Solitude) was published, which won the First City Prize for a Novel. Alicia Jurado used a verse from San Juan de la Cruz's "Cántico Espiritual" (Spiritual Hymn) for the title, and the novel became a celebration of beauty. For the author, it was her most important work since in it she portrays her love for nature and her deepest reflections on existential order. In 1968, her second book, *Los rostros del engaño* (Faces of Deception), was published; the title alluded to the poetry of Lope de Vega. This book collects various stories, both unpublished and previously published in the press, that touch on the topic of human couples. Her 1974 novel, *El cuarto mandamiento* (The Fourth Commandment) reflects the story of three mothers and the hardships they face with their teenage children. This was her best-selling novel. In 1981, her novel *El hechicero de la tribu* (The Tribe's Sorceror) came out, building the metaphor of writers as sorcerers of culture. In 2001, a collection of her articles from the newspapers *La Nación* and *La Prensa de Buenos Aires*, along with various other writings and travel notes, were compiled in the book *Revisión del pasado* (Revision of the Past).

1989 saw the publication of *Descubrimiento del mundo* (Discovery of the World), the first volume of her memoirs, which dealt with her childhood and youth. In 1990, *El mundo de la palabra* (The World of the Word) covered twenty years, from 1952 to 1972, and narrated her first experiences with her writer friends, her relationship with Borges and Victoria Ocampo, her scholarships, and also her trips to Europe and Brazil. With the volume *Las despedidas* (Goodbyes) that covered 1972 to 1992, she wanted to close the chapter on her life experiences, recounting her trip to the East, the shock in her family life of her son's death in an accident, and her ideological posture with respect to the dramatic Argentine reality of the military dictatorship.

Alicia Jurado has often been criticized for the distant coldness with which she perceived the excesses of the dictatorship, aligning herself with the perspective of the upper middle class who associated leftist discourse with the end of traditional Argentine culture and society and washing her hands of the repressive reality. Alicia Jurado would write a final memoir entitled *Epílogo* (Epilogue) which covered the period from 1992 to 2002, in which she contemplated old age and the capacity to love. These memoirs, written in the style of an epilogue, offer Alicia Jurado's most refined voice, and she defines herself in this final stage as a woman who perceives death as an absolute end, while also defining her life as a time full of richness and memorable experiences.

ANA MERINO (TRANS. DEREK PETREY)

Selected Works

La cárcel y los hierros. 1961.
"Genio y figura de Jorge Luis Borges". 1964, reprint 1981.
Leguas de polvo y sueño. 1965.
En soledad vivía. 1967.

Los rostros del engaño. 1968.
Vida y obra de W. H. Hudson. Ensayo, 1971.
El cuarto mandamiento. 1974.
¿Qué es el budismo?. with Jorge Luis Borges, 1976.
El escocés errante. R.B. Cunninghame Graham. 1978.
El hechicero de la tribu. 1981.
Descubrimiento del mundo: memorias 1922–1952. 1989.
El mundo de la palabra: memorias 1952–1972. 1990.
Las despedidas: memorias 1972–1992. 1992.
Trenza de cuatro. 1999.
Revisión del pasado. 2001.
Epílogo. 1992–2002. 2003.
Poemas de juventud. 2006.

References and Further Reading

Borges, Jorge Luis. "Alicia Jurado". *Boletín de la Academia Argentina de Letras* 46(179–82) (Jan.–Dec. 1981): 75–9.

——. "Alicia Jurado". *Hispamérica, Revista de Literatura* 17(50) 1988: 69–72.

Pucciarelli, Elsa. "Alicia Jurado, Hechicera de la Tribu". *Revista Sur* 348 (1981): 41–8.

Rosarossa, María Alejandra. "Los hechiceros de la tribu y el cuarto propio según Alicia Jurado y Virginia Woolf". In Daniel Altamiranda (ed.), *Segundas Jornadas Internacionales de Literatura Argentina, Comparatísticas: Actas*. Buenos Aires: Universidad de Buenos Aires, 1997, pp. 382–90.

K

KAMENSZAIN, TAMARA

Born in Buenos Aires, Argentina in 1947, Tamara Kamenszain studied Philosophy at the Universidad de Buenos Aires. Among her many honors are the Premio Konex for poetry, awarded in 2004; the Primer Premio de Ensayo, given by the government of the City of Buenos Aires for her collection *La edad de la poesía* (1996, The Age of Poetry); and a Guggenheim Fellowship for poetry in 1988–89. She has participated in numerous international congresses and has given readings and invited lectures at institutions throughout the United States and Latin America (she lived in Mexico during the 1970s military dictatorship). She has taught courses on literature as well as practical workshops at diverse institutions and served as Director of Extracurricular Activities at the Universidad de Buenos Aires. She has worked as a journalist and has contributed a large number of articles to journals in Argentina and other countries, among them a 2006 issue of *Mal Estar* dedicated to femininity and feminisms, as well as *Clarín*, *La Opinión*, *Vuelta* and *Unomásuno*.

Poetry

The most studied aspect of Kamenszain's poetry has been her preoccupation with images of women, encompassing mythology, folklore, biblical history and other archetypal representations. Frequently noted related themes include maternity, domesticity and interior spaces, and silence. Critics have frequently situated her within the tradition of Jewish storytelling, a motif explored in much of her criticism as well as her creative writing. The "Baroque" quality attributed by many critics to both her poetry and her prose writing coexists with a simple, spare, stripped-down language and a compact structure. Her most important influences – among them José Lezama Lima, Oliverio Girondo and César Vallejo, all of whom are referenced or quoted in the pages of her collections – have been the subjects of essays throughout her prolific career as a critic. Her collections of poetry are generally seen to be woven together around a central theme. Her first book of poetry, *Los no* (1977, The No [Japanese theater]) begins with several pieces that function as extended similes for writing: words are seen as dancers, and expressions used by the writer are musicians. The poems, written in free verse with some instances of assonant rhyme, vary little in form: at 11–13 lines, they are concisely powerful. Later in the collection, the poetic subject expands her exploration of the theatrical with analogies between writing and the *comedias* of the Spanish Golden Age. Poems that frame questions are presented, in italics, at the beginnings of the last three of the four sections introduced by Roman numerals.

La casa grande (1986, The Great House) shares its basic structure with its predecessor: three numbered sections (with an italicized introduction to the first). Parts of a house, and objects contained within, are employed to illustrate the connection between the inhabitants and their individual and collective past. As with *Los no*, the poems are brief (all around twelve lines, with verses of 11–12 syllables), and distinguished by the use of internal rhyme and alliteration. Memory, connections with one's ancestors and with the original language, the importance of names, images of motherhood and of immigration all form part of this collection's interconnected thematic framework. 1991's *Vida de living* (Living Room Life) sees more formal variation, with poems ranging in length from eight lines to two pages. Like *La casa grande*, it is divided into three sections with the third bearing the title of the collection. The tone of this book is more intimate, with the early appearance of the first person singular, uneasy reflections on marriage and children, and more erotic imagery than in previous books. Also similar to *La casa*, the frequent occurrence of doubling serves to reinforce the connection with those who have come before. References to the Beatles, tango, mariachis and various musical instruments and rhythms illustrate the unique power of music to evoke and reflect strong emotions on the part of the poetic voice. Another effective device is the creation of verbs from nouns, or the transitive use of intransitive verbs, to demonstrate the emotional impact of the poetic objects' actions.

The central importance of music is evident in the title of *Tango Bar* (1998), a collection that explores the bonds between women as it questions the *machismo* of the tango tradition. The epigraph (from Delmira Agustini), references to Rubén Darío and Néstor Perlongher, and the incorporation of well-known verses by Pablo Neruda and César Vallejo situate these works between the traditions of modernist and avant-garde Latin American poetry. The increased use of rhyme and plays on words, in addition to the incorporation of tango lyrics, adds to the musicality of these compositions, even as the form becomes longer and more irregular. *El ghetto* (2003, The Ghetto), dedicated to her father, is replete with allusions to the old country, its language and customs, death and mourning, and Jewish history. As in past collections, she honors tradition (represented by ancestors, the immigrant experience and, again, the importance of names) while challenging its limitations. Images of exile and forced conversion coexist with affirmations of solidarity with Christians, portrayed as "doubles" for the poetic subject. *Solos y solas* (2005, [Males] Alone and [Females] Alone) is divided into three sections, again introduced by Roman numerals, that give expression respectively to the subject's experience of loneliness, projections into the future about a first meeting with an as yet unknown poetic object, and the presence of the individual and collective past in the subject's search for a partner.

Prose

Kamenszain's first book, *De este lado del Mediterráneo* (1973, From This Side of the Mediterranean) is a collection of poetic prose pieces loosely grouped around the central theme of a return to origins. These writings are distinguished by themes and devices that were to feature prominently in her poetry: images of God and other Biblical figures; references to the Beatles, her most frequent popular culture allusion; the symbolic use of mirrors and kaleidoscopes; and allusions to the Jewish neighborhoods of the poetic subject's childhood. Woven throughout are images of the poetic subject's grandfather telling and retelling magical stories to his granddaughter. Her critical essays are collected in three volumes: *El texto silencioso. Tradición y vanguardia en la poesía sudamericana* (1983, The Silent Text. Tradition and Vanguard in South American Poetry); *La edad de la poesía*; and *Historias de amor (Y otros ensayos sobre poesía)* (2000; Love Stories [And Other Essays on Poetry]), which includes the previous two texts augmented by a first section dedicated to exploring the connection between poetry and biography in the works of poets including Agustini, Girondo and Alfonsina Storni. Her essay on José Kozer was included in his 2004 collection *In Situ*, and "Musas de vanguardia" is included in Girondo's *Obra completa* (1999, Complete Works). She also contributed the prologue to a 2003 collection of Pablo Neruda's *Cien sonetos de amor* (One Hundred Love Sonnets). The narrative of Sylvia Molloy, whom she has named as a major influence, is the subject of "Espíritu de la anotación" (Spirit of Annotation), published in *Revista Lote*. She has contributed to *Literatura argentina: Perspectivas de fin de siglo* (2002, Argentine Literature: End of the Century Perspectives) and to *Medusario: Muestra de poesia latinoamericana* (1996, Medusiary: Sampling of Latin American Poetry).

STACY HOULT

Selected Works

De este lado del Mediterráneo. Buenos Aires: Ediciones Noé, 1973.
Los no. Buenos Aires: Editorial Sudamericana, 1977.
La casa grande. Buenos Aires: Editorial Sudamericana, 1986.
Vida de living. Buenos Aires: Editorial Sudamericana, 1991.
Tango Bar. Buenos Aires: Editorial Sudamericana, 1998.
Historias de amor (Y otros ensayos sobre poesía). Buenos Aires: Paidós, 2000.
El Ghetto. Buenos Aires: Editorial Sudamericana, 2003.
Solos y solas. Lumen, 2005.

References and Further Reading

Chitarroni, Luis. "El motivo es el poema". *Radar Edición del Domingo*, 30 Oct. 2005 http://www.pagina12.com.ar/diario/suplementos/libros/10-1803-2005-10-30.html (10 July 2006)
Lindstrom, Naomi. "Female Divinities and Story-Telling in the Work of Tamara Kamenszain." *South Central Review* 20(1) (1996): 221–33.
Panesi, Jorge. "Piedra libre: la crítica terminal de Tamara Kamenszain." http://www.beatrizviterbo.com.ar/prensa.asp?vernovedad=214 (accessed 10 July 2006).
Siganevich, Paula. Entrevista: Tamara Kamenszain. *Revista C&p* XI.2 (2004) http://64.233.104/search?q=cache:NP7P_AQ6dzoJ:www.cebela.org.br/imagens/Materia/2004–2%20171–75%20tamara.pdf (accessed 10 July 2006).

KARLIK, SARA

Born in Asunción in 1935, Sara Karlik has lived in Chile since 1962. A writer of novels, short stories and theater, she has also published literary criticism on the fantastic in Paraguayan literature and on the works of the Paraguayan author, Gabriel Casaccia. She has also earned a Diploma in French Language and Literature from the University of Paris. Her short stories have been included in anthologies published in Bulgaria, Chile, Spain and Paraguay, and in translation in Holland and Italy. She has published numerous collections of short stories as well as novels. In 1999, *Nocturno para errantes eternos* (Nocturne for Eternal Wanderers) won the Gabriel Casaccia Award for Novel in Asunción, Paraguay; and *Juicio a la memoria* was nominated for the 1990 Premio Planeta de Novela in Barcelona and the 1994 Premio Herralde de Novela, also in Barcelona, and was a finalist in the 1991 Premio Sésamo de Novela in Madrid. *El lado absurdo de la razón* (The Absurd Side of Reason) was nominated for the 1996 Premio Herralde de Novela in Barcelona.

Themes and Style

A number of themes appear early in Karlik's narrative in works such as *La oscuridad de afuera* (The Darkness Outside) and *Demasiada historia* (Excessive History) and remain constant throughout her short story collections as well as her novels. Among the most striking of these are: challenges and dilemmas facing women in modern times; crises of everyday existence; history and memory; story-telling imagination and fantasy as means of escape, but also as strategies in confronting and assimilating trauma; the seduction, mindscapes, and intricacies of insanity. These last two themes are particularly relevant in *Nocturno para errantes* and *El lado absurdo de la razón*, respectively. Karlik's characters frequently move about in their solitary existence, occasionally colliding, forming alliances, reflecting and repelling each other in constant search for a sense of self, continuously constructing and deconstructing identities within the confines of modern society. The spaces in which characters move typically mark contrasts between claustrophobic interiors with stale air and crowded urban streets, constrictive small towns and busy ports or far-away and longed-for European countries from which persecuted ancestors were forced to flee.

Perhaps the most explored theme in all of Karlik's work is that of her female characters' journeys of self-discovery, an experience that is expressed not only through the perspectives of female protagonists themselves, but also through those closest to them: mothers, daughters, best friends, lovers, and husbands and the professionals they turn to for enlightenment as they fumble about in the lives of women they love but for whom they cannot fulfill every need. *La inquietud de la memoria* (The Anxiety of Memory) is an example of this. The fact that mental illness frequently appears in the lives of these women makes both the theme of insanity and that of the female experience more accessible to readers. Some will identify with the male characters who, in a world in which man as archetypical hero is progressively displaced by man as affectionate companion—useful but in an ancillary way—are often confused, neglected, and thrown into existential crises of their own. Others will identify more with female characters, with their charming yet obsessive eccentricities; insistent and incessant whims; endless, labyrinthine monologues, bold actions of liberation from the restrictive symbols of traditional society; or mysterious, indecipherable, and seductive dream sequences.

The central female characters themselves are not always the ones who experience episodes of mental illness. The theme sometimes tends to haunt them, appearing in other characters, sometimes cyclically as part of manipulation schemes, or chronically and progressively in isolated lives beyond the reach of reality. Almost always, though, the female protagonist finds herself wondering whether or not her own day-to-day encounters with desire, memory, aging, boredom, fantasy, or repressed feelings might be signs that she is unknowingly following the same path.

Karlik's narrative techniques complement her recurring themes through the use of poetic language, imagery, symbols, stream of consciousness, wordplay and ambiguity. Her search for a unique relationship with words and language as a writer is evident in her early works, as characters are flirtatious in their verbal expression, avoiding precision through suggestion and open meaning. This is manifested in longer narrative pieces, where the transition from background and description to dialogue, soliloquy or internal monologue is often almost imperceptible, as the changes in tone between narrator and characters are subtle. In the shorter narrative pieces, a similar effect is achieved through the technique of integrating anecdotes, remarks and gossip of the community depicted into the narrator's discourse. In her more recent works, Karlik's style is more defined; her language consistently manifests poetic imagery, her wordplay is more subtle and sophisticated, and her stream of consciousness and monologue are the most frequent means of expression for her central characters. It is not coincidental that as her style has evolved in these directions, so the general narrative atmosphere has become increasingly existentialist in character.

Nocturno para errantes eternos

One of the more remarkable characteristics of Karlik's writing is the use of memory to personalize history in unique ways. The novel *Nocturno para errantes eternos* can be interpreted as an incursion into the history of an immigrant family as experienced by a young girl growing up in an unspecified city in South America. Poetic language and the intimate first person narrative voice work together with reflections on the mechanism and purposes of memory to create a world in which the impact of history on personal life is clearly emphasized, while the historical moments themselves—Nazi Germany or Stalinist Russia—are only vaguely depicted. This is achieved in part through the point of view of the narrator as a small girl who perceives the effects of historical events on the adults around her though she ignores the facts of the circumstances that forced their immigration. The structure of the text also contributes to the preponderance of memory over historical event, in that the narrative voice periodically emerges from intricately detailed stories from deep in the protagonist's past, and the language becomes momentarily abstract while the psychological relevance of memory for the narrator is described, and then the language of remembering takes over once again as a different event from the past is related. The result of this unique approach to narrating history through memory is an intimacy with the narrator that allows the reader to identify with her recollections as the subjective experience of history distilled in the personal words, tattered facial expressions and silent gestures of its individual survivors.

This narrative technique of implying the universal by identifying with individual experience is also apparent in Karlik's short stories. Combining direct, familiar language with poetic imagery and descriptive precision, these texts delve into a multiplicity of subjective encounters with recent history and postmodern culture. In a number of stories, an evolving and increasingly complex feminine worldview, the irony of alienation in love, and the abuse of power are among the predominant themes explored, in many instances within the paradigm of implying history through narrating memory.

"Puro ocio"

An illustration of this can be found in the story "Puro ocio," from *Preludio con fuga* (Prelude with Fugue), in which the first person narrator describes watching the demolition of a large old house where, it becomes increasingly apparent, she had been imprisoned and tortured while the rest of the city remained blind to the real inhumanity of dictatorship.

The narrative form is stream of consciousness, and the use of language is representative of how Karlik uses poetic imagery and metaphor to penetrate into the imagination of her reader. Although much time has obviously passed since the protagonist's traumatic experience, the episode is metaphorically reenacted through the actions of the construction workers as they slowly bring down the house through the blows and cuts of their hammers, saws, ropes, and machinery. The building that once housed the unmentionable acts of torture enacted upon the narrator, has now become a metaphorical body undergoing its own process of dismemberment. The text itself appears in one- or two-sentence paragraphs that not only are more striking in their presentation of recalled images, sounds, and impressions, but also represent the fragmented self of the victim: the broken narrator speaks though a broken text. The narrator also perceives how she is seen by others—her friends who cannot understand why she is always cold and never wears colorful clothing as before, and strangers who try not to look at her, who feel uncomfortable by her presence. This use of other characters as mirrors, as well as the presence of literal mirrors in all shapes and sizes, is a trademark of Karlik's writing, so rich in experiences of lost, recovered, and mistaken identity and of journeys of self-discovery. In this story, the reflected image of the traumatized protagonist through others, the metaphorical representation of the remembered space as tortured body, and the fragmented self narrating by means of a fragmented text, unite to illustrate how the historical event lies buried beneath the passage of time, while the human scar remains as testimony to the subjective experience.

The narrative world of Sara Karlik posits the fragile existence of the post-modern individual against society's destructive forces in numerous narrative pieces. Her characters struggle through their isolation to make contact, however brief, with the other that reflects and guarantees the existence of the self, or reaches out with love, or kneels down to provide a stepping-off point—or a jumping-off point—into undiscovered spaces. Ironically, through the twists and turns of interior reflections and monologues expressed in a language of poetic images and metaphor, her reader invariably finds a familiar voice within this alienating other reality, and the deeper meanings are revealed in the reality inhabited by all humanity.

AMANDA L. IRWIN

Selected Works

La oscuridad de afuera. Santiago de Chile: Ergo Sum, 1987.

Entre ánimas y sueños. Asunción: Araverá, 1987.

Demasiada historia. Buenos Aires: Grupo Editor Latinoamericano, 1988.

Efectos especiales. Buenos Aires. Grupo Editor Latinoamericano, 1989.

Preludio con fuga. Buenos Aires: Grupo Editor Latinoamericano, 1992.

La mesa larga. Alicante, Spain: Caja de Ahorros del Mediterráneo, 1994.

Presentes anteriores. Santiago de Chile: Red Internacional del Libro, 1996.

Nocturno para errantes eternos. Asunción: El Lector, 1999.

"No hay refugio para todos". In *Teatro paraguayo de ayer y de hoy*, Tomo II. Asunción: Intercontinental Editora, 2001.

El arca de Babel. Buenos Aires: Grupo Editor Latinoamericano, 2002.

El lado absurdo de la razón. Buenos Aires: Grupo Editor Latinoamericano, 2002.

La conciencia indefensa. Buenos Aires: Grupo Editor Latinoamericano, 2004.

La inquietud de la memoria. Buenos Aires: Grupo Editor Latinoamericano, 2005.

References and Further Reading

Méndez-Faith, Teresa. *Breve diccionario de literatura paraguaya*. Asunción: El Lector, 1996.

Peiró Barco, José Vicente. "El cuento femenino paraguayo después de Josefina Plá." *El Cuento en Red* 4 (Fall 2001).

KOCIANCICH, VLADY

Introduction and Early Works

Novelist, literary critic, translator and short-story author, Vlady Kociancich (b. 1941), of Slovene ancestry but born in Buenos Aires, is one of Argentina's most respected contemporary authors. Kociancich wrote her first novel, a mystery, at the age of 9. To date, she has authored six novels, three collections of short stories, a collected volume of literary criticism, and various essays. She has translated Joseph Conrad's fiction into Spanish and contributes regularly to the literary supplements published by newspapers *La Nación* and *Clarín* in Argentina, as well as *Diario 16* in Madrid, Spain.

A graduate of the School of Philosophy and Letters of the University of Buenos Aires, Kociancich studied English with Jorge Luis Borges, with whom she later collaborated on various seminars related to English and American literature. Kociancich frequently participates in literary panels and writing conferences in Argentina and has enjoyed close friendships with such noted authors as Silvina Ocampo, Osvaldo Soriano, and Adolfo Bioy Casares. She has won numerous international awards for her fiction, including Spain's 1990 Gonzalo Torrente Ballester Prize for *Todos los caminos* (All the Roads) and the 1992 Sigfrido Radaelli Award recognizing *Los bajos del temor* (The Sand Banks of Fear) as the best narrative work of the year. *El templo de las mujeres* (The Temple of Women) was a finalist for the prestigious Rómulo Gallegos Award in 1996. In 1998, Kociancich received the Jorge Luis Borges Prize from Argentina's National Foundation for the Arts.

After completing her undergraduate education, Kociancich wrote for Radio Municipal of Buenos Aires and worked as a translator with a special focus on Old English. In 1971, she published her first short story collection, *Coraje* (Bravery), which was dedicated to Borges and included eight works strongly influenced by the mystery genre. From 1972 to 1979, Kociancich worked as managing editor for a tourism magazine, a position that allowed her to further develop her passions for travel and language study. During this period she also co-wrote the screenplay for the respected documentary film *Borges para millones* (Borges for Millions), based on a noted interview conducted with the author in Argentina's National Library. In 1979, Kociancich gave up her magazine position in order to devote herself fully to literature.

Themes and Major Works

Travel, English literature, and the city of Buenos Aires itself are among the most commonly cited themes of Kociancich's writing. Her narrative settings are designed with careful attention not only to the geographic regions being described, but also to the senses of displacement and isolation provoked by the journey. These same experiences of deterritorialization and nostalgia are evident in her representations of her home city. In a 1996 interview with Giselle Casares, the author confirmed, "All of my narratives are either a metaphorical journey or a trip in itself. None of them takes place exclusively in Buenos Aires. There is always a displacement from which one returns with an experience or a new vision" (1996: 6). The author describes her use of the travel motif as a means of evoking a sense of instability or non-existence, her characters with the sense of vague recollection of events that occurred in an unknowable past life. In her conversation with Casares, she highlighted the sense that "no one knows anything about anyone else" as a common thread underlying her fiction; thus, her writing represents the struggle for self-knowledge as a means of gaining access to the realm of the other (1996: 6). The seven short stories in *Cuando leas esta carta* (1998, When You Read This Letter) make frequent use of these dual themes of travel and isolation; often, they offer epiphany attained in the midst of the quotidian. The initial story, "La mujer de Liñares" (Liñares's Wife), for example, heralds the sudden death of her protagonist's love for her cruel, philandering husband, through insomnia, or the death of sleep. Awakened to life, Daisy A. de Liñares leaves her husband and children, and the accompanying pain of the death of their marriage, in Berlin, returning home to Buenos Aires alone and re-awakened. "Idiomas" (Languages) also addresses the senses of dislocation and potential liberation provoked by travel; its protagonist, a translator working in the Balkans and frustrated by her inability to find the right word, "a single shortcut word that would let her express herself fully" loses herself in another couple's love affair, one being conducted in translation. As in the case of Clara, the protagonist of "Ojos negros" (Black Eyes), this female traveler finds herself ultimately unable to move beyond her limits, having lost "the will to language".

Kociancich's first novel, *La octava maravilla* (1982, The Eighth Wonder) was praised by Bioy Casares as a believable foray into the fantasy genre, "an adventure of the philosophic imagination, a story of love, of friendship, of betrayal, an infinite search". Her widely respected second novel, *Últimos días de William Shakespeare* (1984, Last Days of William Shakespeare) was translated into English and Italian and emerged as one of the first fictionalized critiques of Argentina's brutal military dictatorship. Set in an unnamed South American nation, the novel sensitively portrays the atmosphere of terror and confusion provoked by state-sponsored terror through the absurd case of the President Herrero National Theater, a supposedly public site that is nonetheless almost unlocatable and veiled in secrecy. Narrated through the observations of a male author trapped in the Campaign for Cultural Reconstruction and a female diarist employed at the Theater, this novel documents the environment of fear, humiliation, conspiracy, and violence that characterized the Southern Cone during the 1970s and 1980s. The accompanying question of identity construction and unknowability is further explored in the novel *Los bajos del temor* (1992, The Sand Banks of Fear), set in the Delta of the River Plate. As Angela Dellepiane notes in "The Short Stories and Novels of Vlady Kociancich," the work centers on a "mirror game between *real-reality* versus *imaginary-fiction*"; indeed, three texts interact and reverse each other within the novel, "each clarifying the other, 'chatting' with each other, 'mirroring' one another" (1996: 84). As Amy Kaminsky notes in *After Exile: Writing the Latin American Diaspora*, the novel "puts into play the very possibility of establishing identity in the tangles of conflicting and competing levels of representation" (1990: 28).

Kociancich's most recent book, *La raza de los nerviosos* (2006, The Nervous Race), offers the author's personal "cartography" of her favorite books and authors. Primarily a compilation of previously published essays and reviews, this collection offers an insightful critical reading of such authors as Edgar Allan Poe, Joseph Conrad, Anton Chekhov, Bioy Casares, Fyodor Dostoyevsky, Borges, and Julio Cortázar. She offers various essays on genre, including the essay form and epistolary fiction, in addition to a critical analysis of the reading process itself. In addition, Kociancich explores the nature of writing itself, taking her title from Marcel Proust's claim that writers belong to a delinquent, deranged race that is capable of spawning only writers and thieves. For Kociancich, writing is inherently personal and self-revelatory, so that the author's bibliography is essentially his or her biography; thus, the essay form represents a privileged intimate space to which only the most intimate friends of the writer are admitted.

KAREN WOOLEY MARTIN

Selected Works

Coraje. Buenos Aires: Galema, 1971.
Borges para millones. Screenplay co-authored with Ricardo Monti. Directed by Juan Carlos Victorica and Milton Fontaina. Buenos Aires: Distrifilms, 1978.
La octava maravilla. Madrid: Editorial Alianza, 1982.
Últimos días de William Shakespeare. Buenos Aires: Emecé, 1984.
Abisinia. Madrid: Alfaguara, and Buenos Aires: Galema, 1985.
Todos los caminos. Madrid: Espasa-Calpe, 1990.
The Last Days of William Shakespeare. Trans. Margaret Jull Costa. New York: William Morrow & Company, 1991.
Los bajos del temor. Barcelona: Editorial Tusquets, 1992.
El templo de las mujeres. Barcelona: Editorial Tusquets, 1996.
Cuando leas esta carta. Buenos Aires: Seix Barral, 1998.
Amores sicilianos. Buenos Aires: Seix Barral, 2004.
La raza de los nerviosos. Buenos Aires: Seix Barral, 2006.

References and Further Reading

Bedford, David A. "Tiempo, espacio e identidad en *La octava maravilla* de Vlady Kociancich". *Hispania: A Journal Devoted to the Teaching of Spanish and Portuguese* 87(2) (2004): 227–36.
Casares, Giselle. "Viajar por corazones ajenos". *La Nación* 8 Sept. 1996: 6.
Dellepiane, Angela B. "En torno a la narrative de Vlady Kociancich". *La Torre: Revista de la Universidad de Puerto Rico* 7(27–8) (1993): 379–93.
——. "The Short Stories and Novels of Vlady Kociancich". *Letras Femeninas* 22(1–2) (1996): 77–89.
Gargatagli, Ana. "Vlady Kociancich: El amistoso rostro de las viejas fábulas". *Quimera* 123 (1994): 28–9.
Kaminsky, Amy K. *After Exile: Writing the Latin American Diaspora*. Minneapolis, MN: University of Minnesota Press, 1990.
Mahoney, Elizabeth. "Writing So to Speak: The Feminist Dystopia". In Sarah Sceats and Gail Cunningham (eds), *Image and Power: Women in Fiction in the Twentieth Century*. London: Longman Books, 1996, pp. 29–40.

KRAUZE, ETHEL

Ethel Krauze, born in Mexico City in 1954, graduated from the Universidad Nacional Autónoma Mexicana (UNAM) with a degree in Hispanic Language and Literature. She has taught at the Sociedad General de Escritores Mexicanos (SOGEM), is currently the director of the TV program *Cara al Futuro*

(Facing the Future), is well known nationally for her creative writing workshops, and for her collaboration in the publication of literary reviews.

Krauze has published continuously since 1982. Her work includes novels, poetry, short stories, essays, children's books, an autobiographical narrative and a vegetarian cookbook—a genre perhaps representative of her claim that "reading is food". Recently she and Beatriz Espejo have collaborated on three volumes of stories, a project through which a group of the anthologists plan to evaluate the thematic, structural and aesthetic achievements of Mexican women writers in the past half century.

Personal Background

Important childhood experiences have contributed to Krauze's literary interests and personal success. Raised in an environment in which men and women were equal, she saw herself as a person who happened to be born female and unaware of the traditional gender limitations linked to her sex. In such a setting she claims to have been "born into feminism," noting that the first feminist she can recall in those days was her father. Krauze's mother, a philosophy professor, and father were themselves models of intellectual impartiality; her father was known to admire his wife's superior intelligence and found particular pleasure in their stimulating discussions.

The Gender Debate

On account of a supportive and unbiased home environment, Krauze as a young writer never considered whether her work was feminine or masculine. As she describes, she simply wrote as a way of locating herself in the world and relating to others through her own experiences. It was when she began to publish in 1982, in conversation with editors, critics and researchers, that Krauze was faced with the need to articulate her positions on various aspects of the gender debate. It is Krauze's contention that men and women write differently along gender lines. She argues that women writers are more prone to recognize and refer to intimate situations and emotions, the personal or family story, the *petit récit* as a metaphor that encompasses the universal, while male writers tend to narrate the big picture with a comfortable authority that overshadows intimate connections with others. In a larger sense, Krauze concludes that the concept of "human beings" is only an abstraction, given that there are only men and women, separately, in the world.

Themes and Strategies

In contrast to the anti-feminist position typical of many twentieth-century Latin American women writers, Krauze embraces feminist concepts and contributes to their productive evolution through her work. One of her principal concerns is women's need to claim and legitimate portrayals of their sexuality and its relationship to the human creative capacity, a feminist concept that challenges conventional notions of social dynamics. Themes related to this focus include the exploration of women's relationships and women's deconstruction of the existing patriarchal canon. Representative of these concerns are women's (and often men's) disenchantment with their partners, and with general notions of interpersonal issues. Mutual failures to thrive in love contrast sharply with conventional fantasies about marriage, intimacy and family, when frequently infidelity, abuse, and isolation are the outcome of initially good intentions. From within their solitude disillusioned characters explore unconventional relationships that are ultimately unfulfilling for a variety of reasons.

In the current decade, Krauze has taken on new strategies in her exploration of interpersonal communication and individual options. In the 2002 volume of stories, *El instante supremo*, she experiments with what one critic calls an existential "mysticism," or "angeleología," in the form of a spiritual being who metamorphoses from angel to man. The angel's assigned task, somewhat ironically, is to demystify people's fear of vulnerability in relationships, and to demonstrate that the human capacity for uncompromised love does exist. In a similar vein, the narrator in Krauze's recent novel, *El diluvio de un beso* (2004), seeks a return to *el Cielo*, an Edenic space opens for the single couple whose love manages to survive the terrestrial absence of happiness, hope and affection. In these carefully crafted, de-familiarized environments, creativity, openness and faith in the future triumph over the human tendency to destroy happiness.

The desperation–salvation duality of Krauze's recent narratives questions the viability of mundane, or "secular," relationships, proposing the urgent need for individuals to reconnect on the level of each other's humanity. In the context of modern Mexico, where pre-history confronts the twenty-first century in a myriad of both creative and destructive ways, Krauze's insistence on this alternative epistemology is a highly commendable reconsideration of the relationship between gender relations and future hopes for of a humane society.

In seminars, workshops and colloquia Krauze celebrates the many successes of contemporary Mexican women writers. Her own 20-year commitment to the vocation of writing, teaching and encouraging other writers has provided a model for women seeking new ways of relating to the world. Krauze is justifiably proud of her work.

While no writer can reasonably be held responsible for addressing all of society's concerns, it is important to note that Krauze's feminism, and her entire body of work, would be enhanced by a class-based analysis of certain positions she holds. At times, as a Jewish Mexican woman, she discusses her own ties to "minority" issues, while at others she takes the position, as she has done with Chicana writers, that class and ethnic origins interfere in the creation of literature that has universal appeal. In this vein, Krauze has maintained that she has more in common with "Anglos" than Chicanas, in that her writing is more literary than sociological. In light of the limitations that her positions impose on critical thinking, a feminist class-based analysis will highlight important historical connections between Mexican and Mexican-American women writers, and call into question unexamined judgments on aesthetics, reading reception, cultural histories and the qualities that make a text "universal". One likely result of such an analysis is the recognition that both geographical and literary borderlands are easily and productively challenged and crossed.

Within Mexico itself, recognition of the ties between class, ethnicity and women's struggle for a public voice is a move that enhances all women's rights. If ownership of their sexuality and openness to emotions is to be a dynamic to resist the State's mechanisms of normalization, then the knowledge and experience of Mexican working-class and poor women, whose labor makes it possible for educated, rebellious middle- and upper-class women writers to challenge that society, must be recognized, explored and incorporated on all levels of human interaction. Given the breadth of Krauze's humanitarian vision, and her long experience with community-based writing activities, she is well positioned to expand the community of universal voices with the same feminist practices that have already served her well.

JUDITH RICHARDS

Selected Works

Short Stories

Intermedio para mujeres. Mexico: Oceano, 1982.
El lunes te amaré. México: Océano/Instituto Nacional de Bellas Artes (INBA), 1987.
Relámpagos. México: Instituto Coahuilense de Cultura, 1995.
El secreto de la infidelidad. Mexico: Alfaguara, 1998.
El instante suprem. Planeta Pub Corp., June 30, 2004.

With Beatriz Espejo (eds)

Mujeres engañadas. Mexico: Alfaguara, 2003.
Atrapadas en la cama. Mexico: Punto de Lectura, 2005.

Essay

Cómo acercarse a la poesía. México: Consejo Nacional para la Cultura y las Artes (CNCA)/Limusa, 1992.

Autobiography

De cuerpo entero: entre la cruz y la estrella. México: UNAM/Corunda, 1990.

Novels

Donde las cosas vuelan. Mexico: Oceano, 1985.
Infinita. Mexico: Joaquin Mortiz, 1992.
Mujeres en Nueva York. Mexico: Grijalbo, 1993.
El diluvio de un beso. Mexico: Alfaguara, 2004.

Poetry

Un tren de luz (colectivo). México: UNAM, 1982.
Para cantar. México: Oasis, 1984.
Canciones de amor antiguo. México: UAM-Azcapotzalco, Libros del Laberinto, 1988.
Ha venido a buscarte. México: Plaza y Valdés/CNCA, Nigromante, 1989.
Juan. Mexico City: Editorial Aldus, 1994.
Amoreto. Amor en soneto. Plaza y Valdés Editores, 1999.

References and Further Reading

Blanco Cano, Rosana. "Dislocamientos sexuales, genéricos y nacionales en *Infinita*." http://www.lehman.curry.edu/ciberletras/v11/blandocano.html

De Valdés, María Elena. *The Shattered Mirror: Representations of Women in Mexican Literature*. Austin, TX: University of Texas Press, 1998.

Joysmith, Claire. *Las formas de nuestras voces: Chicana and Mexican Writers in Mexico*. Berkeley, CA: Third Woman Press, 1995.

Richards, Judith C. "La búsqueda de una identidad femenina en *Infinita* de Ethel Krauze". *Revista de literatura mexicana contemporánea*. Oct.–Jan. (1996–97): 71–5.

Ruiz, Cristina. "Ethel Krauze y Paloma Villegas: Memoria, imaginación y escritura". *Revista de literatura mexicana contemporánea* VI (1996): 1388–95.

Sasson, Yolanda. file:///Users/jrichards/Desktop/Routledge%20Project/Krauze/Ethel%20Krauze%20interview.webarchive

Schaefer, Claudia. *Textured Lives: Women, Art and Representation in Modern Mexico*. Tucson, AZ: University of Arizona Press, 1992.

L

LABARCA HUBERTSON, AMANDA

Amanda Labarca Hubertson (1886–1975), or Amanda Labarca, as she is more commonly known, is best remembered, along with Gabriela Mistral, as one of very few Chilean women intellectuals to have raised women's consciousness of their position within Chilean society in the first half of the twentieth century.

Amanda Labarca Hubertson was born Amanda Pinto Sepúlveda in a conservative middle-class home in Santiago, Chile, on December 5, 1886, the oldest of thirteen children born to Onofre Pinto and Sabina Sepúlveda. From a very young age, she came to question the social conventions of her time, particularly those that affected women's lives. Frustrated in her early attempts to pursue a medical career, she enrolled in Santiago's Instituto Pedagógico, Chile's premier teaching institute and earned the title of Professor of Spanish in 1905. It was at the Teaching Institute that she met Guillermo Labarca, with whom she eloped in 1904. Due to tensions provoked by her family's obstinate resistance to her independence and relationship with Labarca, Amanda took up residence for a time at Santiago College, a liberal church school founded by the Methodist Mission in 1880. As an expression of her "free love" for Labarca, whom she married in 1906, and of her rupture with oppressive family ties, Amanda Labarca adopted her husband's paternal and maternal last names (Labarca Hubertson).

Early Influences and Political Trajectory

Guillermo Labarca, author, professor at the University of Chile, leader of the Radical Party, and foreign diplomat, was the major influence in Amanda Labarca's career. He not only familiarized her with the literary and social issues of the time, including the expansion of socialism and women's emancipation, but also encouraged her to combine reading and writing with travel. In 1910, Labarca and her husband traveled as foreign diplomats on government scholarship to the United States to attend classes at Columbia University's Teacher's College in New York. Her encounter with reformist educator and pragmatic philosopher John Dewey at Columbia made a profound impression on her, and upon returning to Chile in 1911, she became an active proponent of Dewey's Progressive Education movement in Chile. Dewey's reformist pedagogy clashed, however, with older tensions in Chile between Church and State, hierarchical and democratic society, and with aristocratic fears in the face of an emerging middle class and a more pluralistic society.

In 1915, Labarca founded the Círculo Femenino de Lectura, a Women's Reading Club, the first non-religious women's organization in Chile. In 1919, the Reading Circle fused with the Club de Señoras that would later spawn the National Women's Council that she presided over until 1925. When Labarca was designated Adjunct Professor of Educational Psychology at the Teacher's Institute at the University of Chile in 1922, she became the first Chilean woman to hold a university position. In 1928, for political reasons, Labarca was removed from her teaching post at the University of Chile by the ultraconservative government of Colonel Carlos Ibañez del Campo (1927–31), and exiled to Concepción (south of Santiago) along with her husband. In 1931, with the installment of a more liberal government, she was honored with the title of Director of Secondary Education and later Minister of Education. In 1943, 1946 and 1949 Labarca served as Chilean delegate to the United Nations General Assembly. During these years she also worked untiringly in favor of Chilean women's civic and political rights. Her efforts culminated in 1949 when Chilean women won full voting rights. Between 1949 and 1955, she worked as Director of the Cultural Extension Department at the University of Chile, founding and directing the successful "Seasonal Schools" attached to the University of Chile.

"Amandita," as she was affectionately called, died at home in Santiago, Chile January 2, 1975, at the age of 88, surrounded by her adopted daughter (Yolanda) and close family members.

Pedagogical, Feminist, and Literary Writings

Labarca's numerous educational writings were, in most cases, controversial and ahead of their time. While critical of the Chilean aristocracy and of the regressive educational control of the Catholic Church, Labarca's more polemical works seem to reproduce social practices linked with power and the cultural and social status quo. In *Bases para una política educacional*

(1944), for example, she advocates the *blanqueamiento* (whitening) of the Chilean/Latin American populace to achieve a unified, homogeneous population as well as social progress and uniform prosperity (pp. 200–1). Labarca's educational concerns can be traced back to a consistent principle of bourgeois social theory: the liberal technocratic vision of French sociology recovered from the French Enlightenment, and closer to home, to Argentine writer and statesman Domingo Faustino Sarmiento, who pushed the polarity of civilization vs. barbarism as the basis for building the nation-state in Argentina during the last half of the nineteenth century. Labarca was one of the first Latin American educators to predict education's increasing role in the era of industrialization and technological development, while simultaneously acknowledging the evident contradictions inherent in the modern educational (capitalist) enterprise, which encourages economic gain at the cost of spiritual and ethical enhancement.

In addition to her educational work, Amanda Labarca is the author of innumerable writings dedicated to the study, defense, improvement and theorization of the "profession of being a woman" (*Feminismo contemporáneo*, p. 226). While always reluctant to declare herself a feminist, Labarca foresaw the need for a new transformational discourse for women, the creation of her "own poem" (*Una mujer enjuicia al tiempo*), one that would allow women to speak outside and beyond the models created by men. Labarca saw mothering as the paradigmatic relationship that defined Chilean culture, but she did not always ascribe to the cultural dictates of her time and place. Many of her essays uncover incipient critiques of these same cultural categories, proving that Labarca's political formation and adherence to feminism evolved within a modern international context.

Amanda Labarca's literary, fictional and more private works also spurred controversy, beginning in 1909 with the publication of her first book *Impresiones de Juventud*, which was based on daring literary readings of nineteenth- and early twentieth-century Spanish authors, including the socialist author of erotic novels, Felipe Trigo. Labarca's fictional work was for some time relegated to the margins of intellectual endeavor, particularly by literary and feminist scholars who initially believed that Labarca's non-essayistic work disavowed a feminist consciousness. These more "aberrational" works include a semi-autobiographical novel, *En tierras extrañas* (1915), a short novella, *La lámpara maravillosa* (1921), a collection of short stories, *Cuentos a mi señor* (1921), testimonial *Meditations*, published while in exile in Concepción, often under the pseudonym Juliana Hermil, and mostly reprinted in her journal, *Desvelos en el alba* (1945). These texts, which have begun to receive more serious attention (Boschetto-Sandoval 2004), recast Labarca's feminist identity, including its inherent ambiguities and contradictions, in a new light. They point to the construction of Labarca's inner life as complex, at odds with commonly held assumptions of her time which denied women responsibilities and insisted on the inherent inferiority of the female mind.

Critical Reappraisal

In her almost ninety years, Labarca witnessed significant social and political change in Chile, Latin America and Europe. Between the end of the nineteenth century and the middle of the twentieth that marked her life span, Latin American nations like Chile were struggling to obtain institutional legitimacy and stability, and seeking to reduce social inequalities through expansion of education and legislative action. Labarca's work as author, essayist, women's advocate, and educator reflects the modernist scientific, technological, philosophical, and social upheavals of her time, and the increasing desire of Latin Americans to engage critically with these issues, particularly in Chile which, at the turn of the twentieth century, could still be characterized as a country attempting to lift itself out of feudalism and deep class polarization. Labarca viewed democratic practices as an instrument for creating consensus around an evolutionary model of social change rather than as a channel for the expression of conflicts. In her desire to redefine the nation, promote democracy and justice, progress and modernization, she decided that discipline, order, and respectability were also central to that redefinition. In the field of education Labarca forged an historical perspective on the comprehension of the school as an instrument of social change within a Latin American context. By claiming that it was male irresponsibility, not capitalism, that made women vulnerable, by marshaling a discourse of republican motherhood, Labarca exposed women's direct contributions to national well-being, arguing that women could and should represent themselves politically. Labarca's anticlericalism, along with her persistent struggle to emancipate Chilean women from domestic drudgery, brought her to the forefront of intense pedagogical, religious, and political scrutiny throughout her career. Her views as related to women's status in society are remarkably contemporary for their gender reflection prior to the historical and semantic split between sex and gender (Salas Neumann 1996). This is true of Labarca's recognition of the value of women's private as well as public experiences, and of the importance of friendship between women and men, themes that also reverberate in her more fictional and semi-autobiographical writings.

Other Critical Reflections

Most early readers of Labarca's work focused primarily on her first-wave feminist status, the woman who clamored for equal civil, social and political rights with men. More recent critics (Catherine Manny Paul, Patricia Pinto, Emma Salas Neumann) have turned their attention to examining Labarca's contributions to Chile's educational, literary, and historical legacies, as well as to uncovering her visionary feminist ideas. These critics read Labarca as a woman who was beginning to occupy a space in the public sphere, defiant of the persistent image of woman sanctioned by tradition. Labarca's work has also been used to validate the trajectory of the feminist movement in Chile, to promote solidarity among Chilean women eager to reassert their legitimacy, and identity as women in the wake of the Pinochet dictatorship (Eltit 1994). Other readers have uncovered fissures and gaps of relation between a gender defined by the hegemonic order and a subjectivity that struggles to uncover and express its private as well as public experience (Pinto 1989, 1990; Boschetto-Sandoval 2004).

Sandra M. Boschetto-Sandoval

Selected Works

¿Adónde va la mujer? Santiago de Chile: Ediciones Extra, 1934.

"Chile". In *Educational Yearbook of the International Institute of Teachers College*. New York: Columbia University, 1939, pp. 53–64.

Historia de la enseñanza en Chile. Santiago de Chile: Imprenta Universitaria (Publicaciones de la Universidad de Chile), 1939.

"Educational Development in Latin America". In Charles C. Griffin (ed.), *Concerning Latin American Culture*. New York: Columbia University Press, 1940, pp. 217–34.

Feminismo contemporáneo. Santiago de Chile: Zig-Zag, 1947.

"Women and Education in Chile". In *La femme et l'education*. Paris: UNESCO, 1953, pp. 9–84.

"Influencias norteamericanas en la educación chilena". In *La nueva democracia*. New York: Committee on Cooperation in Latin America (January 1961): 78–81.

Una mujer enjuicia al tiempo. Santiago de Chile: Editorial Andrés Bello (Instituto de Chile. Academia de Ciencias Sociales, Políticas y Morales), 1971.

"About Courage" and "Personal Pages (selections)". In Doris Meyer (ed.), *Rereading the Spanish American Essay: Translations of 19th and 20th Century Women's Essays*. Austin, TX: University of Texas Press, 1995, pp. 135–48.

References and Further Reading

Boschetto-Sandoval, Sandra M. "The Self-Constructing Heroine: Amanda Labarca's Reflections at Dawn". In Doris Meyer (ed.), *Reinterpreting the Spanish American Essay: Women Writers of the 19th and 20th Centuries*. Austin, TX: University of Texas Press, 1995, pp. 90–101.

——. *The Imaginary in the Writing of Latin American Author Amanda Labarca Hubertson (1886–1975): Supplements to a Feminist Critique*. Lewiston, NY: The Edwin Mellen Press, 2004.

——. "(En)Gendering Cultural Formations: The Crossings of Amanda Labarca between Chile and the United States". In Ingrid E. Fey and Karen Racine (eds), *Strange Pilgrimages: Exile, Travel, and National Identity in Latin America, 1800–1990s*. Wilmington, DE: Scholarly Resources, 2000, pp. 113–28.

Eltit, Diamela. "Amanda Labarca: una feminista chilena de principios de siglo". *Revista de crítica cultural* 8 (May 1994): 36–43.

Manny Paul, Catherine. *Amanda Labarca H.: Educator to the Women in Chile (The Work and Writings of Amanda Labarca in the Field of Education in Chile)*. Cuernavaca, Mexico: Centro Intercultural de Documentación, 1968.

Maza, Piedad. "Amanda Labarca: síntesis y ejemplo". *Atenea* 13(135) (September, 1936): 386–9.

Mussa, Moisés. "Amanda Labarca H. (La mujer, la educadora, la pedagoga)". *Occidente* (March–May, 1956): 45–9.

Pinto, Patricia. "Mirada y voz femeninas en la ensayística de Amanda Labarca: Historia de una anticipación chilena". *Nuevo Texto Crítico* 2(4) (1989): 57–67.

——. "El paradigma masculino/femenino en el discurso narrativo de Amanda Labarca". *Acta Literaria* 15 (1990): 133–46.

Salas Neumann, Emma. *Amanda Labarca: dos dimensiones de la personalidad de una visionaria mujer chilena*. Santiago de Chile: Ediciones Mar del Plata, 1996.

LAJOLO, MARISA PHILBERT

Marisa Philbert Lajolo (Brazil) was born in São Paulo, having lived in Santos until she was an adolescent. She graduated in Letters at the Universidade de São Paulo (1967), getting her Masters degree (1975) and her PhD in Literary Theory and Compared Literature (1980), in the same university, under the guidance of Antonio Cândido. She did her post-doctorate at Brown University, and was a visiting researcher at the Biblioteca Nacional de Lisboa, the Biblioteca Saint Genevieve (Paris) and at the John Carter Brown Library. She is currently a professor at the Departamento de Teoria Literária, at Unicamp.

Marisa Lajolo is a writer, an essayist, a researcher and a professor. She is the head of the *Memória da Leitura* (Memory of Reading) project, which collects and makes available documents and materials in order to write the history of reading in Brazil, with the main goal of making available the reading practices in that country. The on-line course she coordinates – "Brasil/Brasis: Literatura e Pluralidade Cultural" (Brazil/Brazils: Literature and Cultural Plurality), is sponsored by Itaú Cultural in partnership with the Universidade Estadual de Campinas (Unicamp), and focuses the cultural plurality according to four topics: Indians, migrants, women and blacks. Their studies are based on texts by Antonio Callado, João Cabral de Melo Neto, Clarice Lispector and Carolina Maria de Jesus.

Used to "work texts by others", in her own words, she is the author of a number of books and essays, outstanding among which are: *A formação da Leitura no Brasil*, *O preço da Leitura*, *Como e Por que Ler o Romance Brasileiro, Monteiro Lobato: um brasileiro sob medida*, *Literatura: leitores & leitura*. Her current research projects deal with literary theory and Brazilian literature, with a focus on the history of reading, literature for children and/or teenagers and Monteiro Lobato. A well-known essayist, Marisa Lajolo's first fiction book was written for children: *Destino em Aberto*. She organized the *Antologia de poesias—Poesia romântica brasileira e Histórias sobre Ética*. She was honored with the Medalha da Ordem do Mérito do Livro 2006, from the Ministério da Cultura/Fundação Biblioteca Nacional (Ministry of Culture/National Library Foundation) and in 2004 with the Jabuti Prize, from the Câmara Brasileira do Livro (Brazilian Book Chamber) for "A leitura na Formação da Literatura Brasileira, de Antonio Cândido", in honor of Antonio Cândido.

In 2004, she published *Como e Por que Ler o Romance Brasileiro,* a history of the Brazilian novel since its beginnings through to present day. In this work, she systematizes the history of literature in the country, emphasizing its main authors and titles, while captivating the reader's interest about the Brazilian novel. It is a didactic and chronological mapping of that genre, approached from a number of perspectives. In the section about the authors, she considers her country based on the writings of José de Alencar, Machado de Assis, Euclides da Cunha, Paulo Setúbal, and Rachel de Queiroz, then moves to analyze the accent of a singular generation of writers in contemporary Brazil, as in the works of Ana Miranda, Luis Ruffato, Bernardo Carvalho and Ferréz, the author of *Capão Pecado* as well as an alert observer of the periphery of São Paulo and an outstanding name of the so-called marginal literature. She also discovered reports that refer to the history and the formation of Brazilian national identity. From the nineteenth century Lajolo rediscovered two unknown woman writers: Ana Luíza de Azevedo Castro (who wrote *Dona Narcisa de Villar* under the pseudonym Indígena do Ypiranga) and Júlia Lopes de Almeida, author of *A Falência* (1901), a novel, presenting an unglamorous Rio de Janeiro.

Literatura: leitores & leitura (2001) includes broad themes related to the work of Lajolo, referring to more recent debates within literary studies. Irreverence and provocation are present. From the provocations one recognizes a debate that began in previous works—and here one should mention the inclusion of an epigraph by the controversial Paulo Coelho, as well as the claim that Brazilian popular music is literature, when the relations between orality and writing are approached. Along such lines she reaffirms: "Literature is what the grumblers like to write with capital letters and is suspicious of everything that is not written, or of everything that adds other codes to the written". Thus, in the continuation of *O que é literatura?*, Marisa Lajolo presents a very full and flexible view of the concept of literature, claiming that there are personal criteria to establish what is and is not literary, attributing to the reader, his/her taste and impressions, the power to characterize the literary. On the other hand, she reflects on globalization, on technology, the techniques of reproduction, the new media, and everything that nowadays favors the multiplication of the text. The concepts of metalanguage and intertextuality are reviewed and related to the notion of the hypertext, so dear to literature and to the users of the virtual universe. Her work shows that the fragmentation of the market favors the visibility of those who were "marginalized" from the literary history (literature for children and teenagers, for women, for blacks, for homosexuals . . .) now with reclaimed identities. This piece of work was awarded the "Selo Altamente recomendável" (Highly Commended Seal) in the essay category, by the Fundação Nacional do Livro Infantil e Juvenil.

In 2000, *Monteiro Lobato: um brasileiro sob medida,* was released. It is the result of years of research, written in a clear style, elegantly colloquial. The biography covers the career of the controversial modernist writer, the product of a world view in conformity with its historical moment. In such a perspective, the profile of the modern writer-publisher points to his efforts to promote the graphic quality of the books. At that time Brazilian publishers had no interest in a book's artistic quality; by hiring graphic artists to illustrate them, Lobato brought modernity, art and called attention to the materiality of the books. A futurist? By estimating the significance of censorship and of scandal as triggering factors in the selling of books, or even by discussing the diversity of interests between writer and publisher—a utilitarian notion of literature that was daring in the 1920s—one can understand a "Brazil that tentatively modernizes itself, and modernizes itself in a capitalist direction". In that same direction, Lajolo reminds us, one should include "the most beautiful creation by Lobato", his books for children—the whole imaginary of the *sítio*—as a great pedagogical project, fit for a modern Brazil. And it is right there, together with language, his raw material, where Lobato once more reaffirms his modernity: in his ability to seduce young readers, weaving his fictional universe with the colloquialism of the narrative voice, an unprecedented resource for Brazilian stories for children. It is worth mentioning that the second reprint (2001) was awarded the Selo Altamente recomendável, by the Fundação Nacional do Livro Infantil e Juvenil.

Written with Regina Zilberman, *A formação da leitura no Brasil* (1996) has its rationale structured as an interaction among three perspectives: historical, analytical and rhetorical. Lajolo and Zilberman offer a long and rich panorama of the cultural history of the formation of a reading public in Brazil, shaped as a reading of the contemporary country, as noted by the authors: "there one finds the aim of this book. As the history of reading is interwoven with distinct configurations of Brazilian society, it gains a welcome political dimension". Such structuring evokes elements that range from author's copyrights, with implications to the incipient Brazilian editorial market, through the late beginning of the press in the country, the lack of an educational project, the universe of textbooks, the faulty background of the teachers and the consequent narrow perspective of the students as readers; in sum, the chronic problems of education that prevent a utopian place for the readers. Accordingly, they relate in an original and fruitful way the areas of sociology, economy and political sciences with their research object—in this case, the modernization carried out in the conditions of inequality characteristic of Brazilian society. This book was awarded the Prêmio Açoreanos 1997, in the Literatura-Ensaios (Literature-Essays) category. It was also a finalist for the Jabuti Prize (1998).

Also in 1996 another book was released, comprising two parts: *Do mundo da Leitura para a Leitura do Mundo* (literally, From the World of Reading to the Reading of the World). The book is organized into two parts, as suggested by the title, with each section subdivided into chapters and each chapter written as a specific essay, with each essay related to the other essays by means of the theme axes of the book: reading, textbook and school. One other element to contribute to the unity of chapters is the expressive language (tangential to the literary) and the constant quotation of poets and writers in order to reaffirm the theoretical stand adopted by the author. It is thus that she tightens the relations between science and art, as if she is trying to say that reading is situated in the confluence between the grave and the leisurely. Fruition and learning, reading depends as much on the reader's knowledge of the world as on the ability of the writer to win over him/her. In that sense, one finds an important issue posited by the book, and which has to do with the performance of the teachers: the imposition of the habit of reading. Her claim is that both the successful teacher and the one who does not reach his/her goals force their students to read. Thus, reading is always a burden for the reader in such an authoritarian way, without fruition or pleasure. The book won the Jabuti Prize that year, in the Literatura-Ensaios category.

In her only fiction book *Destino em Aberto* (2002), Marisa Lajolo tells a story about two antithetical teenagers—one raised in the streets and the other the heir to a fortune. Bilac, the poet, is a street boy who tries to escape from the somber world of crime, drugs and death. The other, young Homero, also wishes to escape from his fate, looking for other possible meanings, beyond the safe world of business. The protagonists, moving against a background of the country's social problems, have a passion in common: music. If the pedagogical character, reaffirming mainstream values, of literature for children and teenagers prevailed throughout the twentieth century, one should note that Bilac (a twenty-first-century character of such literary genre) has no connection with Olavo Bilac, the Parnassian poet; he is only a reference due to his name and his doings (*poiein*), as is Homero, just an echo alluding to classical literature.

Simone Curi

Selected Works

(with R. Zilberman) *Um Brasil para crianças (Para conhecer a literatura infantil brasileira: história, autores e textos)*. São Paulo: Global, 1989.
(with R. Zilberman) *A formação da leitura no Brasil.* São Paulo: Ed. Atica, 1996.
Do mundo da leitura para a leitura do mundo. São Paulo: Ed. Ática, 1996.
Monteiro Lobato: um brasileiro sob medida. São Paulo: Editora Moderna, 2000.
(with R. Zilberman) *O preço da leitura.* São Paulo. Ed. Ática, 2001.
Literatura: leitores e leitura. São Paulo: Ed. Moderna. 2001.
Destino em aberto. São Paulo: Editora Ática, 2002.
Como e por que ler o romance brasileiro. Rio de Janeiro: Editora Objetiva, 2004.
Histórias de quadros e leitores. São Paulo: Editora Moderna, 2006.

Essays

"Ensino, escola apud". In Maria Angela D'Incao and Eloísa Faria Scarabotolo (eds), *Dentro do texto, dentro da vida (Ensaios sobre Antonio Cândido).* São Paulo: Cia das Letras, Instituto Moreira Salles, 1992, pp. 118–26.
"Literatura e história da literatura: senhoras muito intrigantes apud". *História da literatura: ensaios.* Campinas, São Paulo: Editora da UNICAMP, 1994, pp. 19–36.
Historiografia brasileira em perspectiva. 2nd edn. São Paulo: USF/Editora Contexto, 1998, pp. 297–328,
"Leitura, esta dama de tantas faces apud José Luiz Jobim (org.)". In *Literatura e identidades.* Rio de Janeiro: UERJ, 1999, pp. 179–89.
"A crítica literária e as instituições para crianças e jovens". *Revista da FACED* 5 (2001): 127–47.
"Romance epistolar: o voyeurismo e a sedução do leitor". *Matraga,* 9(14) (2002): 61–75.
"Carlos Drummond de Andrade: uma história exemplar de leitura". *Caliban* 6 (2003): 101–10.
"Saudação a Antonio Cândido". *Revista de Crítica Literaria Latinoamericana* 59 (2004): 307–9.
"Y hasta pronto, irmão". *Hispamérica* 34 (2005): 51–60.
"De São Paulo al Aconcágua: una trayectoria latino americana para Monteiro Lobato". *Revista Brasileira de Literatura Comparada* 9(2006): 99–106.

References and Further Reading

Almeida, I. "Eugênio Gomes e a literatura comparada nas décadas de 40 e 50". In *Anais do II Congresso da Associação Brasileira de Literatura Comparada.* Vol. II, Belo Horizonte, 1991.
Behler, Ernst. "Problems of Origin in Modern Literary History". In David Perkins (ed.), *Theoretical Issues in Literary History.* Cambridge, MA: Harvard University Press, 1991.
Iser, Wolfgang. *The Implied Reader. Patterns of Communication in Prose Fiction from Bunyan to Beckett.* Baltimore, MD: The Johns Hopkins University Press, 1974.
Rocha, João Cezar de Castro. "A formação da leitura no Brasil—esboço de releitura de Antonio Candido. Apud JLJS. Fonseca". *Literatura e identidades.* Rio de Janeiro. 1999, pp. 57–70.

LANGE, NORAH

Norah Lange was born Nora Berta Lange Erfjord on October 23, 1906, in Buenos Aires, Argentina. Much of her childhood was spent in Mendoza, where her father, a civil engineer from Norway, had been transferred to work. Upon her father's death in 1915, she returned to Buenos Aires with her family to live on Calle Tronador. Lange began writing poetry at the age of 14 and benefited in her literary education from the cultural salons that her mother hosted at their home. The salons included most of the young intellectuals of the day, including Alfonsina Storni and Jorge Luis Borges.

Lange began publishing her work in Borges' *Prisma* (1922), a one-page publication of poetry and art that he and his friends posted on café walls. She also collaborated with the literary review *Proa* and, with its appearance in 1924, *Martín Fierro,* which championed the new aesthetics of ultraísmo. A literary movement of the Argentine vanguard, "ultraísmo" explored the central importance of image and unusual metaphor in poetry as a means of reinvigorating Argentine culture. The ultraísta movement, associated with the modern Calle Florida in Buenos Aires, engaged in intellectual debate with the Boedo writers whose literature was rooted in the reality of the worker and the need for social change.

As happened with other women poets of her generation—Storni, Juana de Ibarbarou or Gabriela Mistral, for example—Lange's lifestyle and gender often attracted more attention than her actual poetic production. Lange met poet Oliverio Girondo in 1926 and they married in 1943. With Girondo, Lange was at the center of the bohemian cultural life of Buenos Aires, befriending Pablo Neruda and Federico García Lorca. Many critics tend to view her through the lens of her relationships with male writers, particularly Girondo and Borges. With the exception of Lange, the ultraísta movement was made of up solely of men, and, according to her biographer, María Ester de Miguel, Lange was styled as "la musa del ultraísmo", despite the fact that she was an active contributor to the movement from a very young age.

Sylvia Molloy, David Foster and others have noted that of all the writers of the movement, Lange's work most strictly follows the precepts of ultraísmo's attachment to pure image (de Nóbile, 25; my translation). She published three books of poems, *La calle de la tarde* (1925), *Los días y las noches* (1926), and *El rumbo de la rosa* (1929). As Lange said of her poems: "They were pure metaphors, just like ultraísmo dictated" (de Nóbile 25; my translation).

With her first novel, *Voz de vida* (1927), Lange began to explore the possibilities of her narrative voice. Retired from circulation by the author and now largely unavailable, the epistolary novel is a series of letters from the protagonist, Mila, to her absent lover. The novel received much negative criticism, for to its sexual themes—in particular its treatment of an extramarital affair—as well as its limited quality. Lange herself recognized that the book was a flawed exercise in her difficult transition from poetry to prose (De Miguel 1991: 124).

Lange's second novel, *45 días y 30 marineros* (1933), is the semi-autobiographical account of a young woman's journey as the only woman on board a ship bound for Oslo. Although a relatively simple, almost playful book, it nevertheless manages to examine important issues regarding women's sexual situation in male-dominated society. Molloy notes that the protagonist's position aboard the ship echoes that of Lange in the ultraísta movement as the only woman in a "sea" of men who needs to be constantly aware of how to manage them and their sexual interest (in Astutti 2005: 13). Although Lange recognized the limited quality of her first two books, they served as the training ground for her evolving narrative voice (de Nóbile 18).

Lange's most successful and best-known book is *Cuadernos de infancia* (1937), which won the Premio Municipal and the Premio Nacional. The autobiographical work recounts Lange's family life in Mendoza and Buenos Aires, at the age of 14. Molloy notes that this book marks Lange's transition from her poetic work and early narrative exploration into a mature, perfected narrative (2005: 285). The retreat into the small world of the family, the careful remembrance of childhood habits and fears, the moving evocation of beloved people and places connects this work to others such as *Visiones de infancia* by María Flora Yáñez (Chile, 1947), *Memorias de Mamá Blanca* by Teresa de la Parra (Venezuela, 1929) and *Las manos de mamá* by Nellie Campobello (Mexico, 1938). Lange recognized that this kind of writing might be misunderstood by critics:

> No desconozco los riesgos y las limitaciones que puede originar una visión que insiste en ceñirse, voluntariamente, a lo minúsculo, con una persistencia casi llevada hasta la exasperación, como tampoco ignoro los peligros y los reparos que puede ofrecer mi inveterada propensión por lo delicado y lo sentimental.
>
> [I am not unaware of the risks and the limitations that can come out of a vision that insists on clinging, voluntarily, to the minuscule, with a persistence that leads almost to exasperation, nor am I unaware of the dangers and the misgivings that my propensity for the delicate and the sentimental can inspire.]
>
> (quoted in Miguel, 164, my translation)

Cuadernos maintains Lange's fascination with image. Although following a loose chronological development, each memory in the book presents a different image of the protagonist's childhood: her mother's sewing room, the funeral processions that pass by their home, her sister's obsessive self-mutilation. With her concentration on the fears and insecurities of childhood life, Lange's unusual perspective subverts the common idea of a childhood memoir recovering an idyllic lost past. As Molloy states, in this text the quotidian becomes the source of anxiety (in Astutti 2005: 18). *Cuadernos* also serves as a kind of *Küntslerroman*, tracing the roots of the author's preoccupation with words, even those divorced from meaning, such as the forms of English words or the nonsense words she yells from her rooftop in Buenos Aires, and with images: as a child she tries to recreate the shape of adult visitors' faces with her own body.

Three more novels followed: *Antes que mueran* (1944), *Personas en la sala* (1950) and *Los dos retratos* (1956). Nora Domínguez, in her article "Literary Constructions and Gender Performance in the Novels of Norah Lange", argues that Lange's four novels can be read in their totality as one novel of initiation, following the narrator's progression from childhood through adolescence and finally to the adolescent who becomes a writer (1996: 34). Molloy denies the thematic continuity, noting the erasure of the speaker's coherent identity in *Antes que muera,* a book that lacks a story and a protagonist (in Astutti 2005: 23). Common elements in her narratives include melancholy, loss and death filtered through Lange's surrealist vision (Astutti 2005: 26).

Lange received the Gran Premio de Honor, Sociedad de Escritores Argentinos in 1959. After Girondo's death in 1967, she edited a collection of her speeches in a volume entitled *Estimados Congéneres* (1968). Lange died on August 5, 1972.

Alice Edwards

Selected Works

La calle de la tarde. Buenos Aires: Samet Librero Editor, 1925.
Los días y las noches. Buenos Aires: Sociedad de Publicaciones El Inca, 1926.
Voz de vida. Buenos Aires, Proa: 1927.
El rumbo de la rosa. Buenos Aires: Tor, 1930.
Cuarenta y cinco días y treinta marineros. Buenos Aires: Tor, 1933.
Cuadernos de infancia. Buenos Aires: Losada, 1937.
Discursos. Buenos Aires: Losada, 1942.
Antes de que mueran. Buenos Aires, 1944.
Personas en la sala. Buenos Aires: Losada, 1950.
Los dos retratos. Buenos Aires: Losada, 1956.
Obras completas. Vol. I. Adriana Astutti, ed. Rosario, Argentina: Beatriz Viterbo Editora, 2005.

References and Further Reading

De Miguel, María Esther. *Norah Lange: Una biografía*. Buenos Aires: Planeta, 1991.
Domínguez, Nora. "Literary Construction and Gender Performance in the Novels of Norah Lange". In Amy Brooksbank Jones and Catherine Davies (eds), *Latin American Women's Writing: Feminist Readings in Theory and Crisis*. Oxford: Clarendon Press, 1996, pp. 30–45.
Legaz, María Elena. *Escritoras en la sala: Norah Lange: imagen y memoria*. Córdoba: Editorial Alcia, 1999.
López-Luaces, Marta. *Ese extraño territorio: La representación de la infancia en tres escritoras latinomericanas*. Santiago de Chile: Editorial Cuarto Propio, 2001.
Molloy, Sylvia. "Dos proyectos de vida: *Cuadernos de infancia* de Norah Lange y *El archpiélago* de Victoria Ocampo". *Filología* XX(2) (1985): 279–93.
——. "Unatal Norah Lange". In *Obras Completas*. Vol. I. (ed.) Adriana Astutti. Rosario, Argentina: Beatriz Viterbo Editora, 2005.

LARROSA DE ANSALDO, LOLA

Lola Larrosa was born Nueva Palmira, Uruguay, in 1859, into a high-class family impoverished by the political conflicts in the country. She and her family settled in Buenos Aires, where she spent most of her life. Larrosa began to write at an early age. She wrote for *La ondina del Plata* in 1876. Later, she co-edited *La alborada del Plata*, founded by Juana Manuela Gorriti. In 1880, when Larrosa became the sole editor due to the absence of the founder, she changed the title to La *alborada literaria del Plata*. Her first book, a collection of previously published articles, *Suspiros del corazón* (Heart Sighs), appeared in 1878. Later she published a compilation of novellas, *Las obras de misericordia* (1882, Actions of Mercy), and three novels, *¡Hija mía!* (1888 My Daughter!), *El lujo* (1889, Luxury), and *Los esposos* (1893, The Couple). Larrosa married around 1886. Adding her husband's name to hers, she became Lola Larrosa de Ansaldo, the name she is usually known by. Soon after her marriage, her husband became insane, and she had to support him and their only son. She died of tuberculosis at the age of 36 and was buried in La Recoleta, where in February 1896 a group of women writers met to place a commemorative plaque in her honor.

Although she was a journalist and a writer all her adult life, Larrosa's name rarely appears in literary histories, and not a single study is devoted to her work. To the customary silence regarding women writers of her time has to be added the uncomfortable nature, from a modern perspective, of her writings. By today's standards her attitude towards the family and the role of women in society is clearly reactionary. Her novels and novellas are didactic and moralistic, portraying the ideal woman as submissive to male authority and marriage as the ultimate destiny for her. Nevertheless, as Bonnie Frederick has noted, in her stories the patriarchal order is unstable because of changes in society and the traditional family is susceptible to rupture for economic reasons. Larrosa was also, Frederick says, the first author to write on monetary issues from a female perspective. Francine Masiello has analyzed *Los esposos* in terms of the relation of money to both male and female desire.

In fact, in some instances the reality of her time irrupts in her otherwise timeless moralistic tales. On those occasions she directly criticizes the government and denounces abuses against the working class. The clearest example is in *El lujo*, in which Larrosa attacks the oligarchy, which continues to spend incredible amounts of money on charity balls while exploiting the less fortunate social groups in moments of crisis. In this novel Larrosa was not only the first author to condemn the economic and political situation that led to the stock market crash of 1890 in Argentina, but also the only one to show its consequences for the lower classes in a literary work. It is also worth noting that in spite of her conservative position on the role of women as wives and mothers, she also denounces the sexual and economic abuses against women and the lack of appropriate employment for those women who have to support themselves.

There are very few studies devoted to this author and she is rarely included in collective studies. The information on Larrosa's life is scarce, and her literary works still await a more comprehensive analysis.

María T. Ramos Garcia

Selected Works

Suspiros del corazón. (no data available) 1878.
Las obras de misericordia. Buenos Aires: Imprenta Ostvald, 1882.
¡Hija mía! Buenos Aires: Imprenta de Juan Alsina, 1888.
El lujo. Buenos Aires: Imprenta de Juan Alsina, 1889.
Los esposos. Buenos Aires: Compañía Sud-Americana de Billetes de Banco, 1895.

References and Further Reading

Auza, Néstor T. *Periodismo y feminismo en la Argentina (1830–1930)*. Buenos Aires: Emecé Editores, 1988.

Cutolo, Vicente Osvaldo. *Nuevo diccionario biográfico argentino*. Buenos Aires: Editorial Elche, 1968.

Frederick, Bonnie A. "In Their Own Voice: The Women Writers of the Generación del 80 in Argentina". *Hispania* 74(2) (1991): 282–9.

——. *La pluma y la aguja: Las escritoras de la generación del ochenta: antología*. Buenos Aires: Feminaria, 1993.

——. *Wily Modesty: Argentine Women Writers, 1860–1910*. Tempe, AZ: ASU Center for Latin American Studies Press, 1998.

Lichtblau, Myron. *The Argentine Novel in the XIX Century*. New York: Hispanic Institute in the United States, 1959.

Masiello, Francine. *Between Civilization and Barbarism: Women, Nation, and Literary Culture in Modern Argentina*. Lincoln, NB: University of Nebraska Press, 1992.

Ramos-García, María T. "En los límites del melodrama tradicional. Lola Larrosa, de la economía doméstica a la economía nacional". In *Morada de la palabra: homenaje a Luce y Mercedes López-Baralt*. San Juan, PR: Editorial de la Universidad de Puerto Rico, 2002, pp. 1346–53.

LARS, CLAUDIA

Claudia Lars (1899–1974) (pseudonym of Margarita del Carmen Brannon Vega) is unique among twentieth-century Spanish American poets for her background: a maternal grandfather who was 75 percent Indian, a "mestiza" mother, and an Irish-American father. This heritage, which she explained in *Tierra de infancia* (Land of Childhood), a memoir of her youth and adolescence in the department of Sonsonate, El Salvador, contributed greatly to her love of literature and her eclectic themes. Claudia lived in this rural area until a volcanic eruption forced the family to move to the city, but she never forgot the natural beauty of the flora and fauna of the area, as evinced in her poetry.

Claudia's first love was the Nicaraguan poet Salomón de la Selva, who expanded her literary horizons. Allegedly because of her parents' disapproval, she was sent to New York where she met and married her first husband, LeRoy Francis Beers, in 1923, with whom she had one son Roy Beers Brannon. After their divorce she married Carlos Samayoa Chinchilla in 1949, a Guatemalan writer from whom she also separated (1967).

Claudia traveled extensively: Mexico, Cuba, Central America, and various parts of the United States. It was in Santa Barbara, California (1946) that she again saw Gabriela Mistral, whom she had first met in Costa Rica where she was then living with her first husband. She maintained correspondence with the poet laureate from around 1932. In one of these letters Gabriela wrote what is significant for an understanding of Claudia's life and works, namely that her dual heritage, as described above, gave her certain characteristics and a spiritual depth not found in others of her Latin American contemporaries. As a result, Gabriela proposed that Claudia had a special obligation to write and experience life to the fullest. Pursuant to this, two of Claudia's contemporary critics, David Escobar Galindo and Roberto Cea, suggested that Lars' poetry and life were one and the same. In correspondence this contributor received from her son, the latter pointed out another side to his mother, describing her as an extrovert whose dynamic personality contradicted the *persona* revealed in her poetry. He added that a fuller understanding of her life and works was to be found in her diverse interests and journalistic publications. Although his mother had written in a number of Central American periodicals, he specifically cited *La Prensa Gráfica*, San Salvador, where she had a long-running column entitled *Algo Sobre …* (Something About …). An examination of these articles reveals numerous topics showing her spirit of exploration and a mind open to different cultures and philosophies.

Between 1934 and 1973 Claudia Lars wrote numerous collections of poetry and edited one anthology of her own poetry, *Presencia en el tiempo* (1962, Presence in Time). She also edited an anthology of children's poetry, *Girasol* (1962, Sunflower), which includes eleven of her own compositions, a book widely acclaimed and used in schools not only in El Salvador but in much of Central America. *Tierra de infancia*, her memoir, was not written and published until 1958 but has undergone numerous editions and translation into English. Her poetic works are still awaiting translation. They include *Estrellas en el pozo* (1934, Stars in the Well), *Canción redonda* (1942, Full Song), *La casa de vidrio* (1942, House of Glass), *Romances del norte y sur* (1946, Ballads of the North and South), *Sonetos* (1947, Sonnets), *Donde llegan los pasos* (1953, Where Footsteps Fall), *Canciones* (1955, Songs), *Escuela de pájaros* (1955, Bird School), *Fábula de una verdad* (1959, Fable of a Truth), *Sobre el ángel y el hombre* (1962, Over Angels and Men), *Del fino amanecer* (1962, Of the Delicate Dawn), *Nuestro pulsante mundo: apuntes sobre una nueva edad* (1969, Our Pulsating World: Obervations on a New Age) and *Poesía última 1970–1973* (Last Poems), published posthumously in 1975. Several anthologies of her poetic works include: *Claudia Lars: Obras escogidas,* edited by Matilde Elena López (Claudia Lars: Selected Works, 1973–74), *Sus mejores poemas* (1976, Her Best Poems), edited by David Escobar Galindo. There is also an *Obras completas* (Complete Works, 1999–2005) published by Mendoza Enterprises in El Salvador.

Paths to Literary Production

Just as Lars had a dual heritage, so her literary production followed a double path: journalistic and poetic creations. Contrary to many Latin American writers who began in journalism and then switched to fiction or poetry, Claudia pursued both interests throughout her life. Her articles in *La Prensa Gráfica*, particularly from 1966 to 1974, complement the thoughts expressed in her memoir, *Tierra de infancia*, and the thematic interests expressed in her collections of poetry. In these articles her topics included Spanish American culture and history; Irish history, religion and politics; world politics with attention to contemporary events in El Salvador; oriental and western philosophies and religions, world literature (Spanish, Spanish American, French, English, Japanese and Russian); and science and science fiction. Claudia's style in these essays was simple, direct, informative, and personal. In response to certain specialists who criticized some of her articles for superficiality, she responded that she was writing for an audience who had neither the time nor the inclination to read extensively.

The mere enumeration of these topics implies various aspects of her life and works: eclecticism, a consciousness of the world and the time in which she lived, her profound interest in people and their concerns, and an insatiable curiosity. It is through a reading of all of Claudia's creative contributions, both journalistic and poetic, that her audience sees a unity in her work and arrives at a more holistic understanding of the person and her writings.

Gabriela Mistral's advice was not lost on Claudia Lars. Her subsequent poetic endeavors reflected a woman who gloried in life, who synthesized the complexities of modern humankind in her life and art, but did not succumb to pessimism or artificiality in personal and literary goals. Claudia also shares some of the stylistic characteristics of the "Big Four" of the twentieth century: Delmira Agustini (Argentina), Juana de Ibarbourou (Uruguay), Gabriela Mistral (Chile) and Alfonsina Storni (Argentina). Called *posmodernistas*, not to be confused with the postmodernists at the end of that century, their poetry provided a contrast to the *modernista* movement which preceded them. However, Claudia's heritage, her experiences, and eclectic interests gave a dimension to her poetry not found in that of her contemporaries. As a friend and critic, David Escobar Galindo explained in his introduction to *Sus mejores poemas*, a collection of what he considered her best poems, she identified with anything that was new and youthful. The whole universe, he wrote, enchanted her. There is, therefore, in her poetry as well as her articles a universal dimension that defines and permeates her themes.

Completing the Journey

No one collection can totally delineate Claudia Lars' poetry, but *Poesía última, 1970–73* synthesized much of what characterized her life and works. This volume exemplifies Claudia's skill of being straightforward without being prosaic, innovative in her imagery without being hermetic, and concerned about themes both transcendental and mundane without personal exaggeration. As she approached the final days of her life, she also returned thematically to a person who had been a literary muse and apparently the object of undying affection. With regard to this individual, there is an explanatory letter written by Claudia to her friend and critic, David Escobar Galindo. In it readers learn that the poem/letters of "Cartas escritas cuando crece la noche" ("Letters Written as Night Falls") contained in *Poesía última* were sent to an intended recipient whom Claudia thought may not have received them. Escobar Galindo's note explains that they date from the first days of August 1972. They were written in response to three sonnets written from another country by a certain "místico" (mystic) after forty years of silence but who had been her inspiration, especially for two sonnets in *Estrellas en el pozo* ("Stars in the Well), her first collection. *Poesía última* is prefaced by the sonnet "Poeta soy" ("I Am a Poet") from that collection, the earliest indication of her poetic ambitions. Of the twenty-one poems which constitute the volume, including the fifteen brief poetic letters under the title "Cartas escritas cuando crece la noche", all are written in free verse except the final six sonnets. Claudia had also used free verse in *Nuestro pulsante mundo: apuntes sobre una nueva edad* ("Our Pulsating World: Observations on a New Age"). In other works, she used traditional consonantal rhyme.

As Claudia was approaching another new world, the heaven in which she believed, she skillfully presented feelings of nostalgia and unfulfilled love, making the past seem almost palpable in the present. Time became a living entity and appeared again in "Espejo" (Mirror). Rather than being an inanimate object, the mirror becomes a witness to the passage of time. As the poet looks into the mirror, she laments the disappearance of the child of long ago and how the mirror devours both faces and times, leaving in their places a saddened old woman perhaps accompanied by death.

Though a great deal of time has passed, Claudia never forgot her rural upbringing. In the poem "Lenguaje superior" (The Highest Language), the poet laments the excessive chatter of the city, contrasting its sound with the soft murmur of the almond trees from her childhood. Claudia considers Nature her best teacher. Nature provides a symbolic role in "Mi refugio" (My Refuge) and "Gracias Kawabata" (Thank You, Kawabata). The bee's appearance in both these poems also is indicative of Claudia's interest in Middle Eastern philosophies and religions. Utilizing the Moslem concept of the bee as the recipient of a divine message and the Koran as a spiritual drink deriving from bees, the poet contemplates the world with its many problems and what comes after this life. In "Gracias Kawabata", written in honor of the 1913 Japanese Nobel laureate, using this same insect imagery, she contrasts the poet's ability to communicate new worlds amid what she considers the babbling of certain contemporary writers. In other poems, Claudia utilizes the imagery of butterflies; for example, in "Evocación a Gabriela Mistral" (Evoking Gabriela Mistral), she portrays butterflies as wanting to rest on the head of Gabriela as a respite from their restless movement. In this imaginative way, Claudia captures Gabriela's spiritual beauty by her suggestion that others find comfort in the poet's warm and maternal heart.

Just as Claudia had written of the winners of the Nobel Prize for Literature in her newspaper columns, she dedicated three poems to the Latin American laureates Miguel Ángel Asturias (Guatemala) and Gabriela Mistral (Chile) and the already mentioned Yasunara Kawabata. In the first instance, she asked Asturias how he captured the magic of reality in the ordinary. In her poem evoking Mistral, where she reveals their friendship and mutual understanding, Claudia used imagery evocative not only of Gabriela's but her own eclectic religious interests with images both of Buddha and a medieval crucified Christ. In her poem to Kawabata, she alludes to an oriental wisdom which delves into the mysteries of life.

Intensely aware of the value of the individual and the perceived lack of justice in her twentieth-century world, Claudia lamented in the poem "Migajas" (Crumbs) that she had not given enough attention to social problems particularly to rebels who had fought for their causes and individuals unjustly imprisoned. Likewise she captured an aspect of a social concern rarely discussed: a middle class caught between the hunger of the poor and the gluttony of the rich and suffering criticism from both sides.

In *Poesía última* and in other collections, Claudia Lars wrote of particular and universal concerns in a style that drew its strength from her life's experiences, her character, her imaginative mind, and her effective use of symbolism and imagery deriving from all of the above. Her poetry is a testament not only to her desire to write but also to the intensity with which she communicated her thoughts to her readers. Claudia Lars' life was not an easy one but she received various honors including an official statement of gratitude for her cultural contributions by the Salvadoran government in 1973 and the title Doctor honoris causa in 1974. On the occasion of the centenary of her birth, various conferences took place in her honor. Claudia Lars died from cancer at Oschner Clinic in New Orleans, July 22, 1974.

CATHERINE R. PERRICONE

Selected Works

Estrellas en el pozo. San José, Costa Rica: Ediciones de Convivio, 1934.
Canción redonda. San José, Costa Rica: Ediciones del Convivio, 1937.
La casa de vidrio. Santiago, Chile: Zig-Zag, 1942.
Romances del norte y sur. San Salvador: Galería Renacimiento, 1946.
Escuela de pájaros. San Salvador: Ministerio de Cultura, Departamento Editorial, 1947.
Sonetos. El Salvador: Ediciones Estrella, 1947.
Donde llegan los pasos. San Salvador: Ministerio de Cultura, Dirección General de Bellas Artes, 1953.
Tierra de infancia. Prologue by Eduardo Mayora. San Salvador: Ministerio de Educación, Dirección de Publicaciones, 1958. *Land of Childhood*. Trans. Florence Beers Araujo. New York: Universe, 2003.
Fábula de una verdad. San Salvador: Departamento Editorial del Ministerio de Cultura, 1959.
Girasol: antología de poesia infantil. San Salvador: Ministerio de Educación, Dirección de publicaciones, 3rd edn 1975; 1st edn 1962.
Presencia en el tiempo: Antología poética. San Salvador: Dirección General de Publicaciones, 1962.
Sobre el ángel y el hombre. San Salvador: Ministerio de Educación, Dirección General de Publicaciones, 1962.
Del fino amanecer. San Salvador: Ministerio de Educación, Dirección General de Publicaciones, 1967.
Nuestro pulsante mundo: apuntes sobre una nueva edad. Foreword by David Escobar Galindo. El Salvador: Dirección General de Cultura, Dirección de Publicaciones, 1969.
"Algo sobre . . .". *La Prensa Gráfica* (San Salvador) *1967–1972*.
Poesía última (1970–1973). Preliminary Note by David Escobar Galindo. El Salvador: Ministerio de Educación, Dirección de Publicaciones, 1975.
Obras completas de Claudia Lars. Edición del Centenario del natalicio 1899–1974. 2 vols. Compilation and Introduction by Carmen González Huguet. Creativos de El Salvador, Mendoza Enterprises, 1999–2005. http://www.latienda.com (accessed January 4, 2006).

References and Further Reading

Beers, Roy. In the author's possession. 1 March 1977 and 16 August 1983.
Flores, Angel (ed.) *Spanish American Authors: The Twentieth Century*. New York: The H.W. Wilson Co., 1992.
González Huguet, Carmen. "Testimonio de su tiempo: La historia en la poesía de Claudia Lars". *Al pie de la letra*. http://www.pixelescuscatlecos.com/al_pie_de_la_letra_no2.htm. (accessed January 4, 2006).
[González Huguet, Carmen], "Claudia Lars", *Lo mejor de El Salvador*. http://www.chambita.com. (accessed January 4, 2006)
López, Matilde Elena. "Claudia Lars, virtuosa del estilo". A six-part series in *La Prensa Gráfica* (San Salvador) September 1972, 23, 25–26; 27, 29–30.
Nixon, Melody E. "Feminine Bodies That Tell Stories: Narratives by Central American Women Writers". Diss. University of Michigan, 2004. (A discussion of *Tierra de infancia*.) 17–23.
Perricone, Catherine R. "The Poetic Character of Claudia Lars". *Círculo: Revista de Cultura* 10 (1980): 47–55.
Wycoff, Adriann Constantine. "The Life and Works of Claudia Lars". Diss. Northwestern University, Evanston, IL, June 1984.

LEÑERO FRANCO, ESTELA

Estela Leñero Franco is a Mexican playwright, theatre director, theatre critic, journalist and anthropologist.

Leñero was born on November 8, 1960, in Mexico City. Her father is the novelist and playwright Vicente Leñero and her mother Estela Franco is a psychologist. Her personal interest in understanding her world and confronting injustice led her to study social anthropology. After completing her degree in anthropology, Leñero studied theatre at the Centro de Arte Dramático which was directed by Héctor. Leñero's father was also holding theatre workshops which she attended until Jesus González Dávila playfully told her that if she were to continue criticizing and offering her opinions about his work, she would have to write her own so that others could return the favor. Accepting this challenge to write her own work for the theatre, Leñero wrote her first piece, *Casa llena* (Full House) followed by *Las máquinas de coser* (1986, The Sewing Machines).

In her thesis for a Bachelor's degree in Social Anthropology, *El huso y el sexo: la mujer obrera en dos industrias de Tlaxcala* (The Spindle and Sex: The Working Woman in Two Industries in Tlaxcala), Leñero details the oppressive conditions that women textile workers suffer as a consequence of their gender. She would later draw from her research when writing her play *Las máquinas de coser*, in which she presents an exhaustive description of the working conditions of women in the Mexican textile industry at that time. She says that this work proved that "in the theatre I was able to express the entire emotional world and the personal relationships of the workers, something that I was unable to do with my thesis" (personal correspondence).

Leñero has received a number of awards for her work in the theatre. In 1982, *Casa llena* won the "Punto de Partida" award from the *Universidad Nacional Autónoma (UNAM)* in Mexico. Awarded the *Premio Nacional de la Juventud en el área teatro y creación literaria* in 1983, Leñero was able to go abroad to continue her studies of theatre. She studied at the *Centro de Nuevas Tendencias Escénicas* in Madrid in 1984 and 1985. In 1983–84, she received a grant from *Fideicomiso Salvador Novo*, which she used for the writing of *Las máquinas de coser* (1990, honorable mention for the Rodolfo Usigli Prize awarded by the *Universidad Autónoma de Nuevo León*.) In 1987–88, she received another grant from the *Departamento de Literatura del Instituto Nacional de Bellas Artes* (INBA) with whose support she wrote *Habitación en blanco* (Empty Room) (Premio Malcolm Lowry, INBA 1989). Another grant followed for *Jóvenes creadores* and another in 1990–91 from the *Fondo Nacional para la Cultura y las Artes* (FONCA) which allowed her to write *La ciudad en pedazos* (City in Pieces). In 1990, she obtained the support of FONCA for the completion of her work *Paisaje interior* (Internal Landscape) and for the interactive book for children *El mundo del teatro* (The World of Theater). In 1993, she was awarded the *Premio Nacional de Periodismo "Rosario Castellanos"* in the area of print journalism.

From 1993–96, Leñero was the Coordinator for the Promotion of Theatre at the *Centro de Investigación Teatral Rodolfo Usigli* at INBA. In 1997, she became the chair of the Department of Theatre Promotion at UNAM. In recent years she has produced a series of programs for Radio UNAM: *Urbe sonora* (Noisy City) and *Teatro para tus oídos* (Theatre for Your Ears). Since 2000, she has been a member of the *Sistema Nacional de Creadores de Arte de Conaculta* and during this time has written more plays: *Aguasangre* (Bloody Water), *El Codex Romanoff* (Romanoff Codex) (2004, Víctor Hugo Rascón Banda National Drama Award) and *Lejos del corazón* (Far from the Heart) which debuted in November, 2006.

Under her coordination, the interactive show for children, *El mundo del teatro,* was inaugurated at the *Teatro Aguascalientes* in 1997 for the purpose of introducing children to theatre. The show has since traveled to other cities and towns throughout Mexico and is the point of departure for an interactive encyclopedia for children entitled *Asómate al arte* (A Preview to Art).

According to Leñero, she discovered that writing for the theatre allowed many opportunities for expression. She comments that "it seemed marvelous to not have only one voice like that of the narrator but here there is space for many". For her, the theatre is "the ideal means to study human beings given the recreation of real and invented situations, through which we can enjoy ourselves as well as reflect on our own lives and those of others as though looking in a mirror". Leñero also says that "theatre is the very expression of democracy where different points of view come into play through the characters represented in the work. All are given the opportunity for expression and even if the perspective of the author is behind them and it is he who selects the information to present (which gives us subjectivity) the spectator can listen to diverse perspectives on life and either identify with them or reject them" (personal correspondence, October 2006).

In her work, the stage is an intimate one and explores the subconscious of all humans in an attempt to analyze and explain the weaknesses of each individual. As presented in one of her latest plays, the *Codex Romanoff*, the transition between space and emotion have marked the creative process in that time and space participate in the plot of each of her stories. This work is innovative in structure and theme: the search for purpose, for pleasure through food, art and pain, the repression of feelings and friendship between a novice and her Mother Superior. Additionally, *Lejos del corazón* deals with the exile of thousands of Mexicans. Using the theme of the annexation of Mexican territory to the United States and the experiences of Mexican immigrants, this play is a critical look at contemporary Mexican society.

Committed to the theatre for more than 20 years, Leñero claims that writing and criticizing drama are two professions that complement each other and inspire the creative process. So, in addition to her theatrical works, Leñero has worked for over five years as a critic and theatre journalist for the newspapers *Uno más uno, La Jornada Semanal,* and *el Nacional* as well as the magazines *Práctica, Punto de partida* and *Encuentro.* Discussing her role as theatre critic, Leñero says:

> Criticism has allowed me to "professionalize" my position as a spectator. I go to the theatre to have an experience and then write about it. Although at an earlier stage my principal goal was the analysis, research and promotion of works, more recently I have been able to explore more deeply through criticism and analyze more rigorously the works that I am going to see which has allowed me [to have] a greater impact on theatre and allows me to have a voice within Mexican theatre apart form that of a playwright.
>
> (personal correspondence, October 2006)

She has published reviews, feature articles, interviews and reports on contemporary dramatists, in particular the new generation. According to Leñero, the quality of theatre being created and performed in Mexico is equal to that of anywhere else in the world. She goes on to say that the work of documenting theatre is equally as important as that of creating and to that end she has published the book *Voces de teatro en México a fin de milenio* which includes more than thirty interviews conducted over 10 years with key people in Mexican theatre. The book also includes articles about new theatre companies, premieres, and festivals.

Estela Leñero says that she writes about theatre in order to stay current. For Leñero, Mexican theatre is multi-faceted, combining and connecting different generations and is often presented in a comic as well as a dramatic tone presenting not only local themes but those of the global arena.

MARIA R. MATZ AND W. KEITH WOODALL

Selected Works

El huso y el sexo: la mujer obrera en dos industrias de Tlaxcala. México, D.F.: SEP, Cultura, 1984.

Rosario Castellanos, semblanza psicoanalítica: otro modo de ser humano y libre. Mexico: Plaza y Janés, 1985.

Azcarate, Leonor and Leñero Franco, Estela. *La pareja*. Puebla: Universidad Autónoma de Puebla, 1986.

Las maquinas de coser. Azcapotzalco, D.F.: Universidad Autonoma Metropolitana, 1989.

Berman, Sabina and Leñero Franco, Estela. *Muerte súbita*. Madrid: Casa de América, 2000.

Las máquinas de coser: obra en un acto de Estela Leñero Franco. Monterrey, Nuevo León, México: Facultad de Artes Escénicas, UANL, 2001

Paisaje interior norte/sur. México, D.F.: Ediciones el Milagro, Consejo Nacional para la Cultura y las Artes, 2001.

El mundo del teatro. Mexico: CONACULTA, 2003.

Voces de teatro en México a fin de milenio. Consejo Nacional para la Cultura y las Artes, Dirección General de Comunicación Social y Dirección General de Publicaciones: México, 2004.

Leñero Franco, Estela, Zenteno, Sonia and de Teresa, Claudia. *El mundo de la danza*. México, D.F.: Ediciones El Naranjo, 2005.

El codex romanoff. Nuevo León, México: Universidad Autónoma de Nuevo León, Consejo para la Cultura y las Artes de Nuevo León, 2005.

References and Further Reading

Barrera, Reyna. *Escena con otra mirada: antología de dramaturgas*. Col. San Rafael, México, D.F.: Plaza y Valdés Editores, 2003.

Heidrun, Adler and Chabaud, Jaime. *Un viaje sin fin: teatro mexicano hoy*. Madrid: Iberoamericana, 2004.

Larson, Catherine and Vargas, Margarita. *Latin American Women Dramatists: Theater, Texts, and Theories*. Bloomington, IN: Indiana University Press, 1998.

Rascón Banda, Víctor Hugo. *El nuevo teatro*. México, D.F.: Ediciones El Milagro, Consejo Nacional para la Cultura y las Artes, 1997–2000.

LERNER, ELISA

Elisa Lerner's (b. 1932) parents were Russian Jewish immigrants who arrived in Venezuela escaping economic hardship in the early 1930s. Her father was Noich Lerner and her mother Matilde Nagler-Péretz. Elisa Lerner was born in Valencia, Carabobo, Venezuela. The family moved to Caracas when the writer was still a child. Lerner grew up under the regime of Dictator Pérez Jiménez. Scholar Dennis A. Klein has suggested that Lerner is "probably the only female Jewish playwright in the history of the Venezuelan stage" (1997: 335). The writer studied Law at the Universidad Central de Venezuela, receiving her degree in 1959. Lerner is an accomplished attorney, essayist, playwright, and art critic. During the 1980s, Lerner was also cultural attaché at the Venezuelan Embassy in Madrid. In 1999, she won the *Premio Nacional de Literatura* (National Literature Award) as recognition for her dedication to representing Venezuelan cultural life, costumes, and history.

Playwright and Essayist

Elisa Lerner wrote her first piece, the theatrical monologue, *La bella de inteligencia* (1959, The Intelligent Beauty), for the renowned literary magazine *Sardio*. Through the protagonist's incisive and ironic comments about the social and economic situation of the country after Pérez Jiménez's long dictatorship, in this work Lerner celebrates the fall of the tyrant and the advancement of democracy and tolerance in Venezuela. The beautiful protagonist has been interpreted as the embodiment of Venezuela itself; as a country whose citizens start to express themselves, to protest, and to attempt to establish critical dialogue with the emerging democracy that has been slow in introducing the necessary economic and social transformation that the people of the nation need and call for. Concurrently, with this monologue Lerner introduces the most significant leitmotiv of her work: the desolate situation of women in a patriarchal society. In the piece, the beautiful and intelligent protagonist shows awareness that, since she lives in a world that highly esteems the profession "cónyuge" [spouse], societies have little regard for a single intellectual woman writer. Beauty deprecates a society that, due to social demands that limit women's circumstances, views the wedding ring that ties her existence to a man's as more valuable than the protagonist's "anillo de grado" [graduation ring].

In 1961, Lerner's father died and she traveled to New York to study the prevention of juvenile delinquency. In the United States, she wrote *En el vasto silencio de Manhattan* (In the Vast Silence of Manhattan), the life of Rosie Davis, a woman whose life turns into a failure because, failing to fulfill society's expectations, she is not able to marry. This production won the Anna Julia Rojas Award in 1963. In the play Rosie lives with her domineering mother who, afraid that her daughter might remain an unfulfilled old maid, persistently encourages her to go out in the hope that Rosie might find a man who will marry her. But after two unsuccessful relationships, the ironic piece presents how gradually the idea of marriage and men becomes the obsession that rules the existence of these two tormented women who, in their social alienation, longing, loneliness, and frustration, create a distorted view of sexuality and remain trapped in the idea that self-fulfillment, well-being, and social belonging can only be achieved through marriage. In 1962, Lerner wrote the monologue *Jean Harlow* which, through the life of the celebrated and beautiful movie star, exemplarizes an empty life and exposes passivity as an all too human way to escape even the most compelling reality. In 1969, she published the short-essay anthology *Una sonrisa detrás de la metáfora* (A Smile behind the Metaphor) where Lerner, to a large extent, engages with US American pop culture. Lerner, among others, ironically discusses and exposes the human emptiness, and pain of movies like *The Graduate*. In this eclectic volume, the critic also comments on performances by actresses such as Katherine Hepburn, Lotte Lenya, Candice Bergen, Jane Fonda, Joan Crawford, and Greta Garbo. Five more volumes of assorted cultural critical essays and short stories have followed: *Yo amo a Columbo o la pasión dispersa* (1979, I Love Columbo or the Dispersed Passion); *Carriel número cinco: un homenaje al costumbrismo* (1983, Bag Number Five: A Homage to Local Customs); *Crónicas Gineológicas* (1984, Gynecological Chronicles); *Carriel para la fiesta* (2000, Bag for the Party). The latter, to a certain extent, is a revised edition of *Carriel número cinco.* This compilation also includes cultural short essays by Lerner that had appeared in other publications edited by the National Academy of History of Venezuela; the volume is a work of historical memory that records almost fifty years of Venezuelan cultural life from the 1930s until the beginnings of the 1980s. The last anthology, *En el entretanto: catorce textos breves* (2000, In the Meantime: Fourteen Short Accounts), presents cultural essays written from 1986 until 1998. In 2002, Lerner published *Homenaje a la Estrella: tres relatos de Elisa Lerner* (Homage to the Star: Three Short Stories by Elisa Lerner), a compilation of three stories which the author wrote between 1987 and 1991 in Madrid.

In 1975, Lerner wrote her most successful theater piece to date, *Vida con mamá* (Life with Mother). The play has already become a classic of Venezuelan theater. Like *En el vasto silencio de Manhattan*, the work deals with the fear of remaining a spinster; it equally presents a Mother and a Daughter who live together and who similarly remain ensnared in the social demands and expectations imposed on women. The piece is a dialogue between the elderly Mother and the unmarried Daughter of about 40. The Daughter believes that in life there is nothing worse than not being able to marry. Thus she is convinced that because she has not worn "un traje de novia" [a wedding dress], she has had no past, no life, and has no future. The interaction, in which mother and daughter accuse and condemn one another, exposes the passiveness and loneliness of two women whose lives consist of futile communication, uncritical memories, and of waiting for the "right man" to come to give meaning to their lives. The piece has also been interpreted as an allegory of Venezuela's inadequate engagement with its violent history: the mother and daughter represent Venezuelan uncritical confrontation with the past and its subsequent inability to learn from it, to the detriment of the country's development and well-being. Lerner has also written *La envidia o la añoranza de los camareros* (1974, Envy or the Waiters' Yearning) and the monologue *La mujer del periódico de la tarde* (1976, The Woman of the Afternoon Newspaper). This piece engages with the loneliness of a childless woman of about 50 years of age whose main daily activity consists of going to a café to drink tea and read the newspaper.

Themes and Influences

Among her influences Lerner mentions Virginia Woolf, Franz Kafka, Marcel Proust, Simone de Beauvoir, Henrik Ibsen, Samuel Becket, and Teresa de Parra. Lerner's theatrical topics are the alienation and loneliness of women. Her work engages with ironic characters of single, older, childless, menopausal, frustrated, lonely women who, as Susana Rotker explains, often define themselves in terms of "lo que no soy" (1991: 69) [what I am not]. Her work presents women as "cómplices y víctimas" [accomplices and victims] (Castillo 1992: 35). On the one hand, it problematizes the passivity of women who, often subscribing to patriarchal ideology, cannot create meaningful lives without men, children, and marriage. On the other hand, Lerner questions the social tendency to devalue mature women and the sentimental education of women in patriarchal Latin American societies that, at times, has presented marriage and motherhood as the primary factors in a woman's life, thus limiting their options and possibilities.

LUZ ANGÉLICA KIRSCHNER

Selected Works

Theater

En el vasto silencio de Manhattan. In *13 autores del Nuevo Teatro venezolanos*. Edited by Carlos Miguel Suárez Radillo. Caracas: Monte Ávila, 1971, pp. 297–344.

El país odontológico. In *Vida con mamá.* Caracas: Monte Ávila, 1976, pp. 85–92.

La mujer del periódico de la tarde. In *Vida con mamá.* Caracas: Monte Ávila, 1976, pp. 93–102.

Vida con mamá. Caracas: Monte Ávila, 1976, pp. 19–69.

Una entrevista de prensa o la bella de la inteligencia (ensayo para una sátira). In *Vida con mamá.* Caracas: Monte Ávila, 1976, pp. 71–83.

Jean Harlow. In *Las risas de nuestras medusas: teatro venezolano escrito por mujeres.* Ed. Susana Castillo. Caracas: Fundarte, 1992, pp. 61–4.

La envidia o la añoranza de los camareros. In *Los siete pecados capitales: avaricia, gula, lujuria, pereza, envidia, soberbia, ira.* Ed. Manuel Trujillo. Caracas: Monte Ávila, 1992.

Teatro Elisa Lerner. Caracas: Ediciones Angria, 2004.

Nonfiction

Una sonrisa detrás de la metáfora: Crónicas, 1968. Caracas: Monte Ávila, 1969.

Yo amo a Columbo o la pasión dispersa. Caracas: Monte Ávila, 1980.

Carriel número cinco: un homenaje al costumbrismo. Caracas: El Libro Menor, 1983.

Crónicas Gineológicas. Caracas: Linea Editores, 1984.

"La cultura en el ruedo – Culture in the Bullring". In *Así es Valencia—This is Valencia.* Ed. Soledad Mendoza. Bogotá: Talleres Gráficos de Panamericana Formas, 1994.

Carriel para la fiesta. Caracas: Editorial Blanca Pantin, 1997.

En el entretanto: catorce textos breves. Caracas: Monte Ávila, 2000.

Narrative

"Papa's Friends". Trans. Amy Prince. In Ilan Stavans (ed.), *Tropical Synagogues: Short Stories by Jewish-Latin American Writers.* New York: Holmes and Meier, 1994, pp. 141–9.

Homenaje a la Estrella: tres relatos de Elisa Lerner. Caracas: Oscar Todtmann Editores, 2002.

References and Further Reading

Castillo, Susana (ed.) "Sobre el arte de la seducción: la dramaturgia de Elisa Lerner". In *Las risas de nuestras medusas: teatro venezolano escrito por mujeres.* Caracas: Fundarte, 1992, pp. 31–5.

Cordoliani, Silda. "Dos mujeres, un país". In Moisés Pérez Coterillo (ed.), *Teatro venezolano contemporáneo: antología.* Madrid: Fondo de Cultura Económica, 1991, pp. 769–73.

Klein, Denis A. "The Theme of Alienation in the Theater of Elisa Lerner and Isaac Chocrón". *Folio* 17 (1987): 151–66.

——. "Elisa Lerner". In Darrell B. Lockhart (ed.), *Jewish Writers of Latin America: A Dictionary*. New York: Garland, 1997, pp. 335–8.

M. J. "Lerner, Elisa". In Yolanda Patín and Ana Teresa Torres (eds), *El hilo de la voz. Antología crítica de escritoras venezolanas del Siglo XX*. Caracas: Fundación Polar, 2003, pp. 795–9.

Milagros, Socorro "Una atleta de la soledad." http://www.analitica.com/bitblioteca/msocorro/elisa_lerner.asp (acessed 4 June 2006).

Perdomo, Alicia "Monólogos en el vasto silencio del escenario. Personajes en la obra de Elisa Lerner, escritora venezolana." http://www.andes.missouri.edu/Andes/especiales/AP_ElisaLerner.html (accessed 4 June 2006).

Rotker, Susana. *Isaac Chocron y Elisa Lerner: Los transgresores de la literatura venezolana (Reflexiones sobre la identidad judía)*. Caracas: Fundarte, 1991.

Machado, Arlette "Testimonio: Elisa Lerner, hija de barcos." http://noticias.eluniversal.com/verbigracia/testimonios.htm (accessed 4 June 2006).

LESBIAN LITERATURE IN LATIN AMERICA

Latin American critics had, until the 1980s, overlooked the reading of many literary texts as examples of lesbian literature. David William Foster's *Gay and Lesbian Themes in Latin American Writing* (1991) and Elena Martínez' *Lesbian Voices From Latin America* (1996) present groundbreaking approaches to the identification and study of lesbian literature.

One of the determining factors in the study of lesbian writing is the definition of the term. Lesbian literature should not be categorized as such simply because it is written by homosexual writers. Rather, lesbian writing focuses on the development of a lesbian identity and the creation of a new societal/literary consciousness where homosexual issues and sensitivities are explored. The writer's sexual orientation is not a factor. As it is currently understood, lesbian literature creates a space (as the literatures by and about other minorities have done during their inception) which challenges the hegemonic heterosexual tradition within society and within the literary canon.

When does lesbian literature in Latin America begin? According to Foster, the first text to present lesbian acts is *O cortiço* by the Brazilian Aluísio Azevedo in 1890. But the lesbian tradition in Latin America may have its roots in the seventeenth century, with the poetry of Sor Juana Inés de la Cruz, in particular the poems dedicated to the Marquesa de la Laguna. Octavio Paz suggests in his book *Sor Juana Inés de la Cruz o Las trampas de la fe* (1982) that the relationship between Sor Juana and the Marquesa began upon the arrival of the Marquesa in Mexico in 1680. Sor Juana wrote adulatory poems which expressed declarations of exalted love toward her patroness. Paz suggests that any mention of romantic attraction between Sor Juana and the Marquesa may be read as poetry characteristic of the time, but he also points out that Sor Juana's verses were so passionate, that it could only be characterized as an expression of love. They included erotic motifs that echo the rhetoric of the time, but with an added intensity that sets them apart from other poetry of the seventeenth century. Sor Juana's poems are encoded with a lesbian discourse and hint at homoerotic sentiments toward her patroness: "Yo la ceñiré, señora, ... Doyle por ella a tus pies mil besos en recompensa, sin que parezca delito, pues quien da y besa, no peca" [I will hold you tight, my lady ... I will kiss your feet a thousand times as a reward, without it appearing to be a crime, since she who gives and kisses, does not sin] ("Romance" line 23).

After Sor Juana's death in 1695, the lesbian poetic tradition in Latin American literature does not surface until the mid-twentieth century. The Chilean poet Gabriela Mistral (1889–1957) evokes in her poetry motifs and strategies prevalent in lesbian writers. Elena Martínez suggests that the peripheral position of lesbian issues in society is expressed by Mistral's emphasis on themes such as alienation, frustration, denial, and the use of grammatical markers that avoid the identification of gender (1996: 14). Most critics attribute Mistral's stress on love and desolation to the sense of abandonment which she suffered after the death of a male lover. More recent critics have concentrated on Mistral's encoding of a lesbian sensibility and her erotic identification with other women. Like Sor Juana, she expresses in some of her poetry a harsh criticism of men (Sor Juana's "Hombres necios" and Mistral's "Todas íbamos a ser reinas"). Both Sor Juana and Mistral, separated by three centuries, establish a foundation on which to build a lesbian literary tradition, especially in poetry.

Alejandra Pizarnik (Argentina, 1936–72) and Cristina Peri Rossi (Uruguay, 1941) are key figures in the development of a lesbian consciousness and tradition in Latin American letters. Pizarnik's first poems are published in 1951, a time when lesbianism did not have a voice or space in the heterosexist literary order in Argentina. In order to incript in her work a lesbian voice, Pizarnik utilizes a number of different strategies. Like Mistral's verses, Pizarnik's are free of gender markers, which allows her to reveal a level of ambiguity in her often sexually charged poetry. Pizarnik's poems highlight the themes of alienation, death and solitude, and corporal images. Perhaps one of Pizarnik's most candidly lesbian text is *La condesa sangrienta* (1971) which recounts the torture of hundreds of young, virgin girls by the Hungarian Countess Erzébet Bathory in the sixteenth century. This text has been read by some critics as an allegory of Argentina's reign of oppression under a number of dictatorships, but the text may also be read as an example of homoerotic literature. In Frank Graziano's *Alejandra Pizarnik—A Profile*, we read:

> No one was ever able to confirm the truth of the rumors about the countess' homosexuality. We will never know whether she ignored the tendency or, on the contrary, admitted it as a right she accorded herself along with all the other rights. Essentially, she lived submerged in an exclusively feminine universe. Only women populated her nights of crime.
>
> (1987: 100)

Peri Rossi explores in many of her texts the symbiotic relationship between lesbianism and writing. In *Evohé*, images of women, words, the body and sexuality are intertwined to create the text: "La mujer pronunciada y la palabra poseída" [the woman pronounced and the word possessed] (1976: 37). Another writer who explores the relationship between lesbianism and the art of writing is the Argentine critic, novelist and short story writer Sylvia Molloy. Her first novel *En breve cárcel* (1981, Certificate of Absence, 1989) relates the struggle to reconstruct the protagonist's love affair with another woman (the story) and an attempt to heal and restore her body. Both tasks are achieved through the use of pieces and fragments—anecdotes and memories in the case of the story, illnesses and violent acts in the case of her body. *En breve cárcel* generates an inquiry into the literary discourse focusing on the role of the woman's body in the text: " Ella también, ella que escribe, surge como tantos dioses de un juego de palabras y de lo que las palabras . . . muestran y esconden" (150) [She too, she who writes, emerges as do many gods, from a game of words and from what the words . . . show and hide.] The novel is also inhabited by the voices of other women. The protagonist calls upon these women to complete her story: "Yo las convoqué . . . yo quería—madre, hermana, amante—que estuvieran conmigo. Yo no vivo sino por ustedes" (147) [I called upon you . . . I wanted you—mother, sister, lover—to be with me. I live because of you]. As in Peri Rossi and Pizarnik, the text becomes the canvas for a new textual and sexual expression. It confirms and inscribes a lesbian voice, and by so doing, challenges the hegemonic heterosexual model by which we live, read and write.

In a more testimonial tone, the Mexican writer Rosamaría Roffiel presents in *Amora* (1989), the first Mexican lesbian novel, an inquiry into a number of lesbian issues, a perspective on love/sexual relationships among women, and a deconstruction of lesbian stereotypes. Amora focuses on the development of a community of lesbians through the extensive use of dialogue, which allows different voices to share life experiences and their journeys into lesbian selfhood. The novel has a very strong didactic element which explains and attempts to validate lesbianism in modern Mexico.

Another Mexican writer, Sara Levi Calderón, presents in the lesbian Bildungsroman *Dos mujeres* (1992, Two Women) a text of resistance against class, traditional gender roles, and religious parameters. The protagonist, Valeria, abandons her identity as a wife and mother, dutiful daughter and heterosexual woman to be with her lover Genovesa.

The writings of Reina Roffé (Argentina, 1951), Diana Bellessi (Argentina, 1946), Luz María Umpierre (Puerto Rico), Magaly Alabau (Cuba) and Cassandra Ríos (Brazil) incorporate more erotic/sexual elements. Umpierre's *The Margarita Poems* (1987) is a collection of nine poems that relate a journey from "accepted" femininity to lesbianism. It is, as the first poem "Immanence" suggests, a crossing over, a traversing, a transference of the self and a search for her lover, Margarita: "Todo por Margarita / siempre por Margarita / para poder besar, / uno a uno, / los labios de su amarillo sexo" (20) [Everything is for Margarita / always for Margarita / to be able to kiss, / one by one, / the lips of her yellow sex]. Diana Bellessi's *Eroica* (1988), Reina Roffé's *Monte de Venus* (1976), Cassandra Río's fiction *Uma mulher diferente, romance* (1968), *Veneno, romance* (1968), Magaly Alabau's *Electra Clitemnestra* (1986) and Cristina Peri Rossi's *Fantasías eróticas* (1991) explore lesbian eroticism in an explicit manner. The above mentioned texts express physical desires among women and erotic fantasies that may border on the pornographic (Peri Rossi's text is considered by some critics an example of feminine [lesbian] pornography. It includes a notice that states that the book is not recommended for readers under sixteen years of age.) In these texts there is an interplay between sex and art, between lesbianism and the societal and literary constructs which repress it. The interplay is achieved by the constructs of language: the use of feminine markers, the detailed description of the female body, the aggressiveness of the woman's discourse. These writers venture into uncharted waters in Latin American letters and thus create a new space/language to express another reality. They change the predominantly male models of erotic discourse. Latina writers such as Cherríe Moraga (*Loving in the War Years,* 1983) weave into their texts lesbian issues with social and political questions of patriarchy and colonization (as women of color and members of political minorities in the United States).

The work produced by all these writers represents a corpus that challenges the present sexual hegemonic order. This corpus is part of a tradition which seeks the acknowledgment and validation of a lesbian voice in Latin American literature. "Está oscuro y quiero entrar" [It is dark and I want to come in] says Alejandra Pizarnik. These writers have created an opening allowing them to emerge from the darkness into the light; they propose to offer a new vision of the world; they tear the dominant heterosexual fabric of society, offering a new voice.

ADRIANA ROSMAN-ASKOT

References and Further Reading

Alabau, Magaly. *Electra, Clitemnestra*. Chile: Anibal Pinto, 1986.

Bellessi, Diana. *Colibrí ¡lanza relámpagos!* Buenos Aires: Tierra Firme, 1996.

Bergman, Emilie. *¿Entiendes? Queer Readings, Hispanic Writings*. Durham, NC: Duke University Press, 1995.

Berman, Sabina, *El suplicio del placer*. Mexico: Instituto Cultural de Aguascalientes, 1994.

de la Cruz, Sor Juana Inés. *Poesía, teatro y prosa*. México: Editorial Porrua, 1978.

Levi Calderón, Sara. *Dos mujeres*. México: Editorial Diana, 1990.

Foster, David William. *Alternate Voices in the Contemporary Latin American Narrative*. Columbia, MO: University of Missouri Press, 1985.

——. *Gay and Lesbian Themes in Latin American Writing*. Austin, TX: University of Texas Press, 1991.

——. *Latin American Writers on Gay and Lesbian Themes*. Westport, CT: Greenwood Press, 1996.

——. *Sexual Textualities, Essays on Queer/ing Latin American Writing*. Austin, TX: University of Texas Press, 1997.

Foster, David William and Reis, Roberto (eds) *Bodies and Biases Sexualities in Hispanic Cultures and Literatures*. Minneapolis, MN: University of Minnesota Press, 1996.

Graziano, Frank. *Alejandra Pizarnik: A Profile*. Durango, CO: Logbridge-Rhodes, Inc., 1987.

Gregorich, Luis. *Literatura y homosexualidad*. Buenos Aires: Editorial Legasa, 1985.

Leyland, Winston. *Now the Volcano: An Anthology of Latin American Gay Literature*. San Francisco, CA: Gay Sunshine Press, 1979.

——. *My Deep Dark Pain is Love: A Collection of Latin American Gay Fiction*. San Francisco, CA: Gay Sunshine Press, 1983.

Martínez, Elena M. *Lesbian Voices from Latin America*. New York: Garland Publishing, Inc., 1996.

Mistral, Gabriela. *Poesías de Gabriela Mistral*. México: Editores Mexicanos Unidos, 1983.

Molloy, Sylvia. *En breve cárcel*. Barcelona: Editorial Seix Barral, 1981.

——. *Certificate of Absence*. Trans. Daniel Balderston. Austin, TX: University of Texas Press, 1989.

Moraga, Cherríe. *Loving in the War Years*. Cambridge, MA: South End Press, 1989.

Paz, Octavio. *Sor Juana Inés de la Cruz o Las trampas de la fe*. Mexico: Fondo de Cultura Económica, 1982.
Peri Rossi, Cristina. *Fantasías eróticas*. Madrid: Editorial Temas de hoy, 1991.
Pizarnik, Alejandra. *La condesa sangrienta*. Buenos Aires: López Crespo Editor, 1976.
Rios, Cassandra. *Uma mulher diferente, romance*. São Paulo: Editora Terra, 1968.
——. *Veneno, romance*. Preface by Fernando Jorge. São Paulo: Liv. Trio, 1968.
Roffé, Reina. *Monte de Venus*. Buenos Aires: Ediciones Corregidor, 1976.
Roffiel, Rosamaría. *Amora*. Mexico: Editorial Planeta, 1989.
Zimmerman, Bonnie. "Exiting from Patriarchy: The Lesbian Novel of Development". In Elizabeth Abel, Mariane Hirsch and Elizabeth Langland (eds), *The Voyage In*. Hanover, NH: University Press of New England, 1983, pp. 244–57.

LEVINSON, LUISA MERCEDES

Luisa Mercedes Levinson (c. 1914–88) is a notorious woman writer from Buenos Aires, Argentina. Born to a bourgeois family, she lived surrounded by influential people in Argentinian society. Levinson was known for her eccentric personality and her love for cats. Her education reflects what was customary at the beginning of the twentieth century; she received private instruction in art, music and the humanities. Levinson had a natural talent for music and learned how to play the harp very well. Throughout her life she assiduously attended musical and theatre events in the Teatro Colón of Buenos Aires and other prestigious theaters. In her teenage years she enjoyed reading as well as writing. *The Ring of the Nibelung* was one of her favorite books. Her personal life as well as her love for music and German literature is easily seen in her work.

Novels

Levinson's first attempts as a writer appeared in papers and magazines under the pseudonym of Lisa Lenson. It wasn't until she published *La casa de los Felipes* (The House of the Felipes) in 1951 that she used her real name. *La casa de los Felipes* is a story that takes place in a house located on Aromo Street; this house becomes a rather important space in the course of the novel. *La casa de los Felipes* narrates the lives of Felipe and María Felipa del Villar, the grandchildren of José María Felipe del Villar y Terrero. The story of the family develops around the life of María Felipa, a woman unable to bear a child because Roberto, her husband, died before he had the opportunity to father a child. Part of the plot refers to an incestuous relationship between the two siblings, Felipe and Maria Felipa, at the time of adolescence. This relationship was inspired by a sculpture of the nude figure of a young girl gathering fresh water in a fountain located in the house garden. The figure reminds Felipe of Maria Felipa and these feelings are juxtaposed with the image of the Virgin Mary; María Felipa prompts a combination of love and adoration. When María Felipa grows up, she falls in love with Roberto, the son of a former butler. Later in the novel, Felipe metamorphoses into a black dog and follows María Felipa everywhere. In *La casa de los Felipes* there is a mix of living people and ghosts, of reality and fantasy, where chronological time seems not to exist. In the end, when the house is demolished by the passing of time, María Felipa goes out into the open space, the pampas, to welcome the opportunity to have a child. Pedro Luis Barcia offers an interesting study on the meaning of space in this Levinson's novel.

La isla de los organilleros (The Island of the Organ-grinders), published in 1964, is the story of María Soledad Solar de Liviérez who has a husband and a lover, named Dalmacio Robles. When the novel begins, María Soledad leaves her husband and becomes *María Soledad de las islas* (María Soledad from the islands). Upon discovering she is pregnant with Dalmacio Robles' child, María Soledad decides to start a new life, away from the safety of her home in a privileged social class, in a remote island, where she can raise her child and live as an independent woman. She wants Dalmacio, the man she truly loves, to find her and live together a very passionate love story. It is her hope that this relationship will be based on love and not on a sense of duty. Dalmacio comes to the island and stays with María Soledad for a short time because he has to leave to fight for freedom in the Paraná highlands. Unfortunately, his dead body is recovered nearby, in the river. Shortly after, her husband comes looking for her to take his wife home, ignoring everything María Soledad has to say regarding the child she is expecting. The action takes place in three islands: Armuth, the island inhabited by women only, the island of the organ-grinders, and the island where María Soledad lives. María Soledad's main ambition is to find her inner self and to be in charge of her own destiny. The story ends when she leaves with Joaquin Leviérez to go home.

La isla de los organilleros has evoked interesting studies by Rubén Vela and Osvaldo Sabino; Vela has compared the child María Soledad is expecting with an Argentina that wants freedom and a new beginning. On the other hand, Sabino has studied symbolism in *La isla de los organilleros* in three areas: first, related to the earth, the rings, the islands, and the women, which he sees as an expression of the feminine and eternity; another explores the connection between *La isla de los organilleros* and *Der Ring des Nibelungen*; and the final one sees some parallelisms between María Soledad and the Virgin Mary with Dalmacio representing the new Messiah.

A la sombra del búho (In the Shadow of the Owl), published in 1975, is the novel that has received the most critical attention. *A la sombra del búho* starts with an epigraph indicating that Felicitas's destiny is that of moving forward, always walking. The story develops in a chronological manner and is narrated in three sections. The first part of the novel, or "Primer Tiempo" (First Movement), is subtitled "The Eighteen Hundreds". The action starts at La Crucecita where the Monsignor's funeral is being attended by the two sisters, Hermelinda and Esperancita. Soon after Felicitas arrives, they all go to the estancia La Malacara where their cousin Gualterio Mendiburu is the owner. He has a facial deformity and he does not allow anyone to see his face. His nickname is El Malacara, and Felicitas is his niece. After an incestuous relationship develops between Gualterio and Felicitas, Gualterio decides to call on a rustler who resembles him physically to take his place and act exactly like him. The impostor escapes with her to the northern region and tells Felicitas to call him Gualter Lu. Felicitas becomes pregnant and Gualter Lu decides to stay in the area and do some engineering work in that region.

When Felicitas gives birth with the help of the indigenous people, an owl flies over her and spreads its wings above her for a few minutes. This is where the title of the novel comes from; it signals the arrival of the first born. Shortly after, the Jurí takes Felicitas far away to a comfortable house in the mountains to start their life together. There she discovers that Gualterio is alive, confined to a room in the back of the house, old and physically impaired. Felicitas had four boys in the five years she stayed in that house, and after Gualterio passed away, they moved to La Malacara and she had six more children. Finally, the family settles in Buenos Aires where Felicitas becomes a typical Argentinian matron.

The second part of the novel, "Segundo Tiempo" (Second Movement), is called "The Nineteen Seventies" and it takes place in Buenos Aires. It introduces Felisa, whose three husbands have passed away, each one leaving her with a child. Their names are Hermelita, Alterio and Felicitasnena or Phyllis; Felicitasnena is the main character and the men she encounters in her life are named Walter and Gualterio. In this part of the novel, there are references to the owl and its shadow, as well as to cats with the eyes or with the look of an owl, which are related to Felicitasnena and Walter or Gualterio and their destiny.

The last section of the novel, entitled "Tercer Tiempo" (Third Movement), is subtitled "Nineteen ninety-nine". In this part, a character from more recent times is introduced and she bears the name of FelicitasEsperanzaHermelita; her companion is W (Walter) Watson. This time the narration starts with a look at the family photo album; Walter and Gualterio are remembered as two complementary individuals who need each other. A letter from Melita to Felicitasnena links the past with the present, and the novel ends with Monsignor Panchito, Hermelinda, and the old Gualterio, all roaring in laughter. This leaves the reader with the impression of closing a circle in the narration of events.

Ricardo Mosquera Eastman and Perla Giorno offer interesting studies on this novel; Mosquera Eastman compares the structure of *A la sombra del búho* with a kaleidoscope, a prism with three mirrors. He sees recurrent themes in Levinson's works, incest, multiple identities, and the feminine. Giorno, in contrast, researches the significance of the owl in the novel, as part of the Greek mythology.

Short Stories

Luisa Mercedes Levinson also wrote very interesting collections of short stories such as *La pálida rosa de Soho* (The Pale rose of Soho), *Las tejedoras sin hombre* (The Weavers without a Man), *El estigma del tiempo* (The Stigma of Time), *Ursula y el ahorcado* (Ursula and the Hanged Man), and a short story which she co-authored with Jorge Luis Borges, *La hermana de Eloísa* (Eloisa's Sister).

El abra (The Cove) is a story that takes place in an abandoned house in a clear space, in the middle of the jungle of Misiones, and narrated by a *chasque*. Once upon a time a man called Alcibiades lived there with a woman whom he brought one night from a town nearby to live with him. She would spend the day in a hammock outside the house, and at night, he would bring her to his room. Ciro, who helped Alcibiades to take care of the animals and do house chores, was very quiet and a good helper. One day the woman killed a snake, as usual, with a revolver she had in the hammock. Alcibiades decided to reward her by bringing her a blouse upon his return from the fair. Ciro went about his routine in the fields that day and then he approached the hammock, and was tempted to be with this woman. When it happened, a gun shot was heard. Alcibiades had killed Ciro. Alcibiades then tied the hammock ends together, so that she would be trapped inside the net. The woman who was very indifferent before and insensitive, all of a sudden started to feel an increasing amount of hatred towards Alcibiades, and wanted revenge. She managed to call his attention, he approached the hammock and she shot him; Alcibiades fell dead to the ground as well. Unfortunately the woman was not able to free herself completely and died there too. A hammock swinging, full of death, was found by the *chasque*. Levinson reflects the powerful force of nature in this passionate and violent story. *El abra* reminds the reader of Horacio Quiroga's stories and José Eustasio Rivera's novels.

Las tejedoras sin hombre (The Weavers without a Man) is another interesting story. It is part of a collection of fourteen short stories, with the first one bearing the title of the volume. "Las tejedoras sin hombre" is the story of women who work in the mountains of northwestern Argentina making ponchos out of the wool and skin of guanacos and vicunas. They all have seen their men go away to the gold mines of Famatina in search of riches and never have them back home. The narrator inserts stories of men who have died in the mountains, buried by the gold they have collected, as well as a story of a ghost woman, called a "bruja" (witch), who entices men to go to the gold mines. In *Las tejedoras sin hombre* Levinson deals with the topic of women's survival when their male partners leave the area because they feel drawn to a gold mirage and the pleasures money can give them.

La hermana de Eloísa is a story written in collaboration with Jorge Luis Borges. The narrator, an architect, finds himself in a situation where he has the opportunity to see Eloisa after fifteen years of absence. She belongs to the Ferrari family which consists of Don Antonio, the father, and three sisters, Irma, Eloísa and Gladys. Gladys is about to get married and the father is building a chalet for her. The narrator, as a business representative, is in charge of closing the deal for a slighter higher amount of money based on some additions to the basic plan. The narrator's attempts to discuss this with the father are not successful. In the process, the narrator sees Eloísa again bringing back some memories. In the end, he finds out that the decisions really come from Irma, the person in charge of the finances. The narrator will now have to call another office where Irma probably works. The reader can see in this story Levinson's approach to exploring the feminine, and Borges' desire to lead the reader in one direction, to end up with a surprise, leaving the situation unsolved.

El otro amor de Lila Bell (The Other Love of Lila Bell) narrates an episode in Lila's love life, which focuses on her feelings and reactions the entire time she is involved with Kobe. Lila is trying to overcome the painful memories of a previous and very significant relationship when she meets Kobe at a club. Lila is with her friend Lolita, trying to write a letter in Lolita's name to persuade Lolita's boyfriend to come back to her. Lila writes "Dear Carlos, it is said that life is like a piece of fruit; I think it is more like a piece of cheese. We have to nibble it". Then a young man approaches her, as an intermediary, with a photograph showing Lila greeting Borges at a lecture. The interested party claims to have met her at that Borges lecture. Lila lets him, "Kobe" or "the Chinese Buda", a married man, get to know her, and a new relationship develops. She appears to have a carefree attitude about the whole situation. While watching Lolita's boyfriend get involved with another woman, she finds out on her own that Kobe is seeing somebody else. He denies it when Lila confronts him, and the relationship continues gaining strength. In the end, Lila becomes again a victim of deceit; Kobe is taking his new partner to the same place Carlos is taking his. Lila is very disillusioned, makes a couple of trips to Europe, and finds herself one more time with Lolita and some friends at a bar, maybe to begin another episode.

Levinson's novels and short stories are about women's lives, their feelings and their struggle to find their own space in the society they live in.

CLARA H. BECERRA

Selected Works

Obra Completa. Edited with an Introduction by Delfín Leocadio Garasa. Vol. I. Buenos Aires: Ediciones Corregidor, 1986.

"The Boy Who Saw God's Tears". Trans. Elaine Dorough Johnson. *The Secret Weavers: Stories of the Fantastic by Women of Argentina and Chile*. Ed. Marjorie Agosín. Fredonia, NY: White Pine Press, 1991.

The Two Siblings and Other Stories. Trans. Sylvia Ehrlich Lipp. Pittsburgh, PA: Latin American Literary Review Press, 1996.

"The Clearing". Trans. Sarah Arvio. *The Oxford Book of Latin American Short Stories*. Ed. Roberto González Echeverría. Oxford: Oxford University Press, 1997.

Obra Completa. Edited with an Introduction by Leopoldo Brizuela and an Epilogue by Delfín Leocadio Garasa. Vol. II. Buenos Aires: Ediciones Corregidor, 2004.

References and Further Reading

Allen, Paula Smith. *The Metamorphosis and the Emergence of the Feminine: A Motif of "Difference" in Women's Writing*. New York: Peter Lang Publishing, 1999.

Arlt, Mirta. "La fantasía zoológica". In *Luisa Mercedes Levinson: Estudios sobre su obra*. Buenos Aires: Ediciones Corregidor, 1995, pp. 13–19.

Barcia, Pedro Luis. "Constantes en la narrativa de Luisa Mercedes Levinson". In *Luisa Mercedes Levinson: Estudios sobre su obra*. Buenos Aires: Ediciones Corregidor, 1995, pp. 45–63.

Correas de Zapata, Celia. *Ensayos Hispanoámericanos*. Buenos Aires: Ediciones Corregidor, 1978.

Costa Picazo, Rolando. "*A la sombra del búho*: Héroe/antihéroe, mujer y el ciclo de la vida". In *Luisa Mercedes Levinson: Estudios sobre su obra*. Buenos Aires: Ediciones Corregidor, 1995, pp. 37–42.

Giorno, Perla. *Soledad y Búsqueda (Dos novelas latinoamericanas): Rulfo y la nada-México, Levinson y el amor-Argentina*. Buenos Aires: Imprenta Dharma, 1976.

Mosquera Eastman, Ricardo. *Los símbolos en la novela "A la sombra del búho" de Luisa Mercedes Levinson*. Buenos Aires: Universidad Argentina John F. Kennedy, 1975.

Orgambide, Pedro. "Una poética del carnavalismo". In *Luisa Mercedes Levinson: Estudios sobre su obra*. Buenos Aires: Ediciones Corregidor, 1995, pp. 75–9.

Portela, Oscar. "Luisa Mercedes Levinson o las potencias del mito". http://www.triplov.com/oscar_portela/luisa_mercedes/levinson.htm (accessed 10 December 2006).

Sabino, Osvaldo R. *Luisa Mercedes Levinson. Revolución, redención y la madre del nuevo Mesías: alusión mítica y alegoría política en La isla de los organilleros*. Buenos Aires: Ediciones Corregidor, 1993.

Suárez, María del Carmen. "El mito del andrógino o la unión de los contrarios". In *Luisa Mercedes Levinson: Estudios sobre su obra*. Buenos Aires: Ediciones Corregidor, 1995, pp. 29–35.

Vela, Rubén. *La isla de los organilleros de Luisa Mercedes Levinson o una interpretación de la realidad argentina*. Buenos Aires: Ediciones Flor y Truco, 1970.

LISPECTOR, CLARICE

Lispector was born in Tchechelnik, Ukraine, on December 10, 1920. She was the daughter of Pedro Lispector and Marieta Lispector. Her birth took place when her Jewish Russian family were immigrating. They arrived in Brazil, stopping first at Maceió, then moved to Recife, capital of the state of Pernambuco, were they lived till Clarice's adolescence. Her mother, who suffered from progressive paralysis, died in 1929. At the age of 9, Clarice enrolled at the Collegio Hebreo-Idisch-Brasileiro (Hebrew-Yiddish-Brazilian School), where she completed her 3rd grade. In 1934, she moved with her father and her two sisters, Tânia and Elisa, to Rio de Janeiro. In 1939, she entered the Law School Faculdade Nacional de Direito da Universidade do Brasil. In 1943, she married her college colleague Maury Gurgel Valente, who had just begun his diplomatic carrier. Soon after their marriage they moved to Europe, during World War II. In Italy, where they stayed till 1946, Clarice worked as a nurse for Brazilian soldiers. The couple traveled to a number of different countries, where they lived in Naples, Torquay, Bern, and Washington. After her divorce in 1959, she returned to Rio de Janeiro with her two children, Pedro and Paulo. In 1963, she was a lecturer in literature at the University of Texas, at Austin. In 1967 she had a domestic accident, a fire caused by a cigarette end, in which she suffered serious injuries; causing her to undergo a number of operations for plastic surgery. On June 22, 1968, she took part, along with several intellectuals, in a demonstration against the military government: the famous "One Hundred Thousand Demonstration". In 1975, she was invited to the World Witches Congress, in Bogotá, Colombia. On December 9, 1977, she died from cancer.

One of the greatest writers of the twentieth century, Clarice Lispector, together with Guimarães Rosa, is the precursor of a generation that inaugurated a lineage in Brazilian literature, both were outstanding in their experimentation with language and in their themes—the micro, the perceptions of the quotidian and singularity. Internationally known, partly due to her translation and studies of the works by the French feminist Hélène Cixous, her own work has been translated to a number of languages, into English, French, German, Czechoslovakian and Spanish.

Lispector began her literary career as editor and reporter at the *Agência Nacional* (*National News Agency*), a job that would influence her whole trajectory as a journalist, in which she came to know writers such as Antônio Callado, Paulo Mendes Campos, Rubem Braga, Fernando Sabino, Francisco de Assis Barbosa, José Condé, and also Lúcio Cardoso, who came to be an important promoter of her career as a writer. Her literary debut took place on May 25, 1940, in the weekly *Pan*, owned by Tasso da Silveira, with the short story "Triunfo" (Triumph). In October that same year she published another short story, "Eu e Jimmy" (Jimmy and Me), in the magazine *Vamos Ler!*, published by Raymundo Magalhães Júnior. Such works, which were not included in any compilation of her texts, already anticipated some themes dear to the "Claricean" universe. Thus the importance of the opportunities to publish her literary texts in different media, like "Suplemento Letras e Artes" (Letters and Arts Supplement) in the newspaper *A Manhã*, still in the 1940s, anticipating part of her book *Alguns contos* (Some Short Stories) (1952).

Literary and Journalistic Production

Only at the end of the 1950s did she publicly acknowledge being a writer and, *malgré elle-même*, who considered herself just an amateur, turn professional and began to make her living from her writing. From then on, her participation in the cultural industry became intense and undifferentiated. Such a practice meant a guaranteed income, the promotion of her name and work, and functioned as a lab for her writing experiments. She also became known as a newspaper interviewer; some of her interviews can be found in *De corpo inteiro* (1975, In Whole Body).

She translated Poe's (as did Baudelaire) *Amazing Stories* and Jules Verne's *The Mysterious Island*. Her translations are condensed versions, since the readers preferred such versions to the integral texts, which eventually appeared in the Brazilian version of *The Reader's Digest*. Among other texts, she adapted *The Picture of Dorian Grey*, by Oscar Wilde, for teen readers. For the newspaper *Jornal do Brasil* she translated freely fragments by a number of authors, frequently using such fragments as a theme, forgetting to mention where the excerpts came from. In the cultural section of that newspaper from Rio, she used her chronicles to declare her noncompliance to genres.

In 1943, Clarice Lispector published her first book, *Perto do Coração selvagem* (Close to the Wild Heart). Immediately acclaimed by the critics, the book won the prize Graça Aranha, offered by the Academia Brasileira de Letras (Brazilian Academy of Letters). Two years later, she wrote *O lustre* (The Chandelier) in Italy, published in Brazil in 1946. In 1949, *A Cidade sitiada* (The Besieged City) was published. In 1952, from May through October, she was responsible for the column "Entre Mulheres" (Among Women), in the newspaper *Comício*, under the pseudonym Tereza Quadros, as a favor to Rubem Braga, one of the founders of that newspaper. In August 1959, under the pseudonym Helen Palmer, she began a column for the newspaper *Correio da Manhã*, titled "Correio feminino—Feira de utilidades" (Women's Mail—Fair of Furnishings). In 1960, she wrote the column "Só para mulheres" as a ghost-writer for Ilka Soares for the newspaper *Diário da Noite*. In 1954 the first French edition of *Perto do Coração Selvagem*, with the cover by Henri Matisse was published.

In 1960, she published the book of short stories, *Laços de família* (Family Ties), acclaimed by readers and critics and acknowledged as a classic in the genre, winning the Jabuti Prize. In the next year, after years of work, her longest fiction book, *A maçã no escuro* (The Apple in the Dark) was published. Invited by Paulo Francis in 1962, she wrote the column "Children's Corner," in the monthly magazine *Senhor*, where she published a variety of texts, difficult to classify. In 1964, she published *A legião estrangeira* (The Foreign Legion: Stories and Chronicles), a compilation of short texts, and the narrative that the critics came to consider her masterpiece: *A paixão segundo G. H* (The Passion According to G. H.). In August 1967, invited by Alberto Dines, she signed the chronicles in the Caderno B (Culture supplement) of the *Jornal do Brasil*, till 1973, when she was dismissed.

In 1968, she interviewed famous people for the weekly *Manchete*, published by Editora Bloch, for the column "Diálogos possíveis com Clarice Lispector" (Possible Dialogues with Clarice Lispector). In 1969, her novel *Uma aprendizagem ou O livro dos prazeres* (An Apprenticeship, Or, The Book of Delights) won the prize "Golfinho de Ouro". In 1971, the anthology *Felicidade clandestine* (Clandestine Happiness) was published, and in 1973, after three years of work, she published *Água viva* (Stream of Life). In the next year she published *A Via crucis do corpo* (The Stations of the Body), ordered by the editor Álvaro Pacheco. In that same year she published *A Vida íntima de Laura* (The Intimate Life of Laura), for children. The first in her series of books for children was *O Mistério do Coelho Pensante* (1967, The Mystery of the Thinking Rabbit), written in English while living in Washington, and winner of the Calunga prize, offered by the Campanha Nacional da Criança (National Campaign for Children) in that same year. Her other books for children include: *A Mulher que Matou os Peixes* (1968, The Woman Who Killed the Fishes) and, posthumously, *Quase de verdade* (1978, Almost for Real), and *Como nasceram as estrelas: doze lendas brasileiras* (1987: How the Stars Are Born: Twelve Brazilian Legends). The latter, in the form of a calendar, of 1977, was published by the toy maker Estrela. In 1976, she resumed her job as an interviewer, similar to what she had done in the 1960s, for the weekly *Fatos e Fotos/Gente*.

In 1977, she published *A hora da estrela* (Hour of the Star), her last work while she was still alive. Posthumously published: *Um sopro de vida—Pulsações* (Fragments partially compiled by Olga Borelli); *Para não esquecer* (Not to Forget), comprising chronicles already published in 1964, appears in the second part of the book *A legião estrangeira*, in the section titled "Fundo de gaveta" (Bottom of the Drawer). *A hora da estrela* won the Jabuti Prize in the category "Melhor Romance" (best novel) and *A paixão segundo G. H.* was published in France, translated by Claude Farny.

The Critique and the Critics

The critical bibliography on Lispector's work is only shorter than that on Machado de Assis. Since her appearance in 1944, she has been acclaimed by Brazilian critics. From these, the essay "No raiar de Clarice Lispector" (At the Dawn of Clarice Lispector), by Antonio Cândido is noteworthy where he refers to Lispector's style and expression in *Perto do Coração Selvagem*. In his *Diário Crítico* (*Critical Diary*), Sérgio Milliet observes the movement perceived in that first "Claricean" text. About the "heroine", he writes: "with an eye for the smallest, the most subtle movements of life". About her technique: "a simultaneity of chapters assembled disorderly". In his *O romance Brasileiro Contemporâneo* (*The Brazilian Contemporay*

Novel), Álvaro Lins includes the study "A experiência incompleta: Clarisse Lispector [sic]" ("The Incomplete Experience: Clarisse Lispector"), in which he makes two distinct approaches. In the first one, he inaugurates an attachment to feminine fiction, which will later develop as gender studies, with canonical works, among which one can stress those by Hélène Cixous, Marta Peixoto, Lúcia Helena, Rachel de Queiroz, Berta Waldman and Rita Terezinha Schmidt. His second approach refers to her influences, in which he finds technical similarities with Virginia Woolf and James Joyce.

Thus, in a second moment beginning in the 1960s, the critics observe a proximity to the Joycean writing, finding an "epiphanic" dimension in Lispector's text; in a certain way, they canonize revelations, the substrata of consciousness, moments of illumination and the inapprehensible vivid fluidity of the real. Such a concept appears in the studies by Affonso Romano de Sant'Anna and by Olga de Sá. Benedito Nunes analyzes such writing within the context of the philosophy of existence, of the same nature of the Kierkegaardian intuition of the pre-reflexive character, individual and dramatic, of human existence, dealing with problems such as anguish, the void, failure, language, the communication between consciences, which traditional philosophy has ignored or kept in the background.

One other critical trend appears in the 1980s, which begins with the work of her personal friend Olga Borelli—*Clarice Lispector: Esboço para um possível retrato* (Clarice Lispector: Draft for a Possible Portrait)—the first of many biographies that would be written, and which functions as a significant sign of her intellectual trajectory. In 1990, Nadia Battella Gotlib published *Clarice uma vida que se conta* (Clarice, a Life to Be Told). Similarly, in the US, Diane Marting published *Clarice Lispector: a Bio-bibliography* (1993). Such studies are based on the assemblage of fragments, statements, letters, documents and photos. Lispector's most recently published epistolary communication, a specific editorial segment, include *Cartas perto do Coração* (*Letters Close to the Heart*) (2001), letters exchanged with Fernando Sabino, and *Correspondências* (Correspondences) (2002).

Life and writing are elements that concern Claricean literature, and her narratives make evident, to a greater or lesser degree, the problems of language and expression related to existence as a theme. In Lispector, the body's symptoms become language substance, making her close to women writers such as Alejandra Pizarnik, Sylvia Plath, Anne Sexton and Ana Cristina César. Fiction by post-1970s Brazilian women writers has Lispector as its most important and frequent reference, whether for linguistic experiments, or issues of representation. She avoided classification; she defended herself against it with the words: "genre can't catch me anymore".

Thus, Lispector's literature is not one of minorities, since she became a reference from her first debut. After pleasant amazement, she became a landmark in Brazilian letters, well received by the public and in the literary field, the subject of readings, research and the basis of a number of interpretive models. In that sense, her very writing demands a thorough analysis of the internal movements that her own vertiginous production creates.

At the level of language, the movement is created by means of a "foreignness" in relation to the Portuguese language, without forgetting that her social and intellectual biography—considering her heterodox cultural background: her household surroundings, the Jewish neighborhood, her learning to read at the Hebrew school—does not limit her text to an immigrant foreign language. Thus, multilinguism is obtained due to an individual move, which crosses language, mixing it, producing it, translating it, but also through an extra-territorial relationship that she keeps with the literature of her time. She avoids identification with the social problems in Brazil, which marked literature during her literary emergence—regional fiction, the social criticism of the 1930s: Graciliano Ramos, Raquel de Queirós, José Lins do Rego. Moving against a certain political and social "reality," she favors a universe of micro-perceptions, coming closer, aesthetically, to writers such as Guimarães Rosa and João Cabral de Melo Neto.

In Lispector's work, themes are textually repeated, crossing one another, as the itinerant fragments that pervade her whole work. Key themes pervade all her writing, transported: the horse, the chicken, the egg, the child, the old woman, the woman. Also, there are those themes that endure in time and space. They can appear as existential concerns: metaphysical questionings, the limits of the being; or, within the scope of metafiction, as the search for words, for full nomination; or, still, of relations: the *other* and identity issues, untiringly revealed.

As with the themes, the fragments that transit across her textual entirety undermine the notion of a totalizing work. Now in the shorter text, then in others more extensive, whole chapters transformed into newspaper material, press material re-used into noble, literary material. A textual practice transgressing the limits between high and "minor" literature, freely blending categories as arts and entertainment, body and thought, poetry and prose, the self and the "other" denouncing how subtle such limits are, opposing conceptualization in the literature of that time, which recommended the book, the academic essay, the newspaper article as legitimate forms.

Thus, her inter- and intra-textual levels speak of fragments from other sets and contexts, now receiving more superficial changes, then making radical mutations, subtractions or additions: whole paragraphs removed, added, as pieces cut and replaced—modified or not—in a new place. In this way, the most recent composition undergoes a deep transformation in the textual body, sometimes with only the initial raw idea persisting. Such a technique had already been noticed by the first generation of critics, by Sergio Milliet, and in more updated analyses, critics suggest the classification of Claricean literature as postmodern, instead of modern, as seen by Earl Fitz, given its plasticity, self-irony, fragmentation, crisis of genre and gender.

With the publication of *Uma Aprendizagem ou o livro dos Prazeres* (1969), one postmodern trait becomes very visible in her work: the practice of cutting and gluing. In her following books other traits appear such as, for example, the stress on the fragmentary (which will reach its peak in *Água Viva*, 1973), or the prominence given to genre hybridization (in texts difficult to classify, such as *Onde estivestes de Noite* (Where Were You at Night?), 1974), and still the "compliance" with that which is considered less noble (as with the ordered texts, like *A Via Crucis do Corpo*, in the "Explanation" that precedes the short stories, Lispector also claims "the time of garbage").

The unfolding of ideas occurs through certain signs, which animate all her writing: from the animal to the machanical, from the being to the event. About the animals, series that show a very frail body—a *hope* that irrupts at the threshold of the order of the household—crossed by so many others; brute and primitive, bodies that establish a look in itself: the buffalo, a cockroach. Domestic animals, without differentiating species nor kingdoms—wild ones, horses, dogs, chicken, monkeys, rats—invade her texts, confounding their nature with that of the characters. Coordinated, such animals make intense moves across the territory, thus opening new ones, which concern a line of escape that crosses language and thought.

Also with objects one observes an outline that is defined under the perspective of the gaze, anticipating a series in the horizon of the titles, as *luster, city, apple, book, star*. Things that coexist in the world of appearances: pieces, artifacts or machines created for a purpose; utilities with a proper name, objects that designate as words. Object-line that touches the scriptural line so that at this point reflection acquires a wider range: from the name to the thing, from the thing to significance, from significance to the Being.

The movement of the characters is identified at two different levels: in the first, the characters as individuals, concerning displacement, interior/exterior; deterritorialization, experienced by G.H. (*A Paixão segundo G.H*) in her own apartment; by Martim (*A Maçã no escuro*) when he throws himself into a journey from the city to the countryside in Brazil; by Joana (*Perto do Coração selvagem*) in an unrelenting search throughout the narrative, which ends by her taking a ship. They depart in exploratory trips of "the self," as a condition to return to "the world". And on another level, which runs along all of the Claricean territory, in a repetition that reproduces groups, or series, the momentary loss of individual traits: as is the case of the *teacher*, of the *girls* and of the *old woman*, signaled over the textual whole. Such two levels are found in a continuous entanglement, being and series many times confused in one same common fate, crossing each other in the confusing embarkation on a trip.

The constant search for meaning, forgotten and found again within the realm of the quotidian, takes one to the discovery of the significant that is not exhausted in the appearance of the world; the domesticated woman isolated from work outside home, or even reduced to madness (in the texts "Amor" (Love) or "A imitação da rosa" (The Imitation of the Rose), points to the subtleties of language, of existence, but also of writing itself. It suggests distinct stages of displacements that do not lead to truths, but to interrogations through meaning.

Thus, more than a distinction within the literary field, designed from the ideal opposition between hegemony and vanguard, it makes sense to think of Clarice Lispector as someone who abandons literature in order to be able to make it. Obviously, such taking a distance involves in itself a critique, a "political" attitude, and an alternative practice in relation to the literature of her time. To acknowledge a policy as an effect of the Claricean writing is to acknowledge her role in the articulation of the literary field, that is, a machine of the form of expression that avoids the form recommended by the establishment. Involved in a micro-politics that comes from movement, her writing makes a nomadism of means, literature, culture, and thought. Although the text is always created under a dominant system of meanings, the process of singularization is produced from the particular view of that same writing.

SIMONE CURI

Selected Works

O Lustre. 2nd edn. Rio de Janeiro: José Alvaro Editora, 1963.
Água Viva. São Paulo: Círculo do livro, 1973.
Para não Esquecer. São Paulo: Ática, 1978.
A Bela e a Fera. 2nd edn. Rio de Janeiro: Nova Fronteira, 1979.
Perto do Coração Selvagem. São Paulo: Círculo do livro, 1980.
Uma Aprendizagem ou o Livro dos Prazeres. Rio de Janeiro: Francisco Alves, 1980.
A Cidade Sitiada. 6th edn. Rio de Janeiro: Nova Fronteira, 1982.
A Paixão Segundo G.H. 12th edn. Rio de Janeiro: Nova Fronteira, 1986.
Laços de Família. 22nd edn. Rio de Janeiro: Francisco Alves, 1990.
Um Sopro de Vida. 9th edn. Rio de Janeiro: Francisco Alves, 1991.
A Legião Estrangeira. 12th edn. São Paulo: Siciliano, 1992.
A Maçã no Escuro. 8th edn. Rio de Janeiro: Francisco Alves, 1992.
Onde Estivestes de Noite. Rio de Janeiro: Francisco Alves, 1992.
A Descoberta do Mundo. Rio de Janeiro: Francisco Alves, 1992.
De Corpo Inteiro. São Paulo: Siciliano, 1992.
A Via Crucis do Corpo. 5th edn. Rio de Janeiro: Francisco Alves, 1994.
Felicidade Clandestina. Rio de Janeiro: Nova Fronteira, 1994.
A Hora da Estrela. 23rd edn. Rio de Janeiro: Francisco Alves, 1995.

Literature for Children

A Vida Íntima de Laura. Rio de Janeiro: Rocco, 1985.
Como Nasceram as Estrelas: Doze Lendas Brasileiras. Rio de Janeiro: Nova Fronteira, 1987.
A Mulher que Matou os Peixes. Rio de Janeiro: Francisco Alves, 1991.
Mistério do Coelho Pensante. São Paulo: Siciliano, 1993.
Quase de Verdade. 4 ed. São Paulo: Siciliano, 1995.

Translated Works

Family Ties. Trans. Giovanni Pontiero and Richard A. Mazzara. Austin, TX: University of Texas Press, 1984.
The Apple in the Dark (Texas Pan American Series) Trans. Gregory Rabassa. Austin, TX: University of Texas Press, 1986.
An Apprenticeship, Or, the Book of Delights. Trans. Lorri A. Parris and Richard A. Mazzara. Austin, TX: University of Texas Press, 1986.
The Passion According to G.H. Trans. Ronald W. Sousa. Minneapolis, MN: University of Minnesota, 1988.
Soulstorm: Stories. Trans. Alexis Levitin. New York: New Directions, 1989.
The Stream of Life. Trans. Elizabeth Lowe. Minneapolis, MN: University of Minnesota Press, 1989.
Near to the Wild Heart. Trans. Giovanni Pontiero. New York: New Directions Publishing Corporation, 1990–91.
The Foreign Legion: Stories and Chronicles. Trans. Giovanni Pontiero. New York: New Directions Publishing Corporation, 1992.
Discovering the World. Trans. Giovanni Pontiero. Manchester: Carcanet Press Ltd, 1992.
Selected Cronicas. Trans. Giovanni Pontiero. New York: New Directions, 1996.

References and Further Reading

Antelo, Raul. *Objecto Textual*. São Paulo: Fundação Memorial da América Latina, 1997.
Borelli, Olga. *Clarice Lispector: Esboço para um possível retrato*. Rio de Janeiro: Nova Fronteira, 1981.

Candido, Antonio. *Brigada ligeira*. São Paulo: UNESP, 1992.
Castillo, Debra A. *Talking Back: Toward a Latin American Feminist Literary Criticism*. Ithaca, NY: Cornell University Press, 1992.
Cixous, Hélène. *Reading with Clarice Lispector*. Ed. and trans. Verena Andermatt Conley. Minneapolis, MN: University of Minnesota Press, 1990.
Crui, Simone. *A escritura nômade em Clarice Lispector*. Chapecó: Argos editora, 2001.
Fitz, Earl E. *Clarice Lispector*. Boston, MA: Twayne Publishers, 1985.
——. *Sexuality and Being in the Poststructuralist Universe of Clarice Lispector: The Différance of Desire*. Austin, TX: University of Texas Press, 2001.
Gotlib, Nádia B. *Clarice – uma vida que se conta*. São Paulo: Ática, 1995.
Helena, Lúcia. *Nem Musa, nem Medusa. Itinerários da escrita de Clarice Lispector*. Rio de Janeiro: EDUFF, 1997.
Lindstrom, Naomi. *Women's Voice in Latin American Literature*. Boulder, CO: Lynne Rienner, 1989.
Lins, Álvaro. *O Romance Brasileiro Contemporâneo*. Rio de Janeiro: Edições de ouro, 1968.
Marting, Diane. *Clarice Lispector: A Bio-bibliography*. Westport, CT: Greenwood Press, 1993.
Milliet, Sérgio. *Diário Crítico*. São Paulo, 1981, v. 2.
Nunes, Benedito. *Leitura de Clarice Lispector*. São Paulo: Quíron, 1973.
——. *O Drama da Linguagem*. São Paulo: Ática, 1989.
Pazod Alonso, Claudia and Williams, Claire (eds) *Closer to the Wild Heart: Essays on Clarice Lispector*. Oxford: Oxford University Press, 2002.
Peixoto, Marta. *Passionate Fictions: Gender, Narrative, and Violence in Clarice Lispector*. Minneapolis, MN: University of Minnesota Press, 1994.
Pessanha, José Américo Motta. *Arquivo de Clarice Lispector*. Rio de Janeiro: Arquivo – Museu de Literatura da Fundação Casa de Rui Barbosa.
Vasconcellos, Eliane (ed.) *Inventário do Arquivo de Clarice Lispector*. Rio de Janeiro: Fundação Casa de Rui Barbosa/Centro de Memória e Difusão Cultural/Museu de Literatura Brasileira, 1994.
Waldman, Berta. *Clarice Lispector – A paixão segundo C. L.* São Paulo: Escuta, 1992.

LLANA CASTRO, MARÍA ELENA

Born in Villa Clara, Cuba, in 1936, this journalist, short story writer, and poet is known for her use of the fantastic in her short stories. She is one of very few Cuban women writers of narrative fiction to be consistently represented in national and international anthologies, and to have works published during the most important phases of literary production since 1959. Her stories have frequently appeared on syllabi in courses on the fantastic in Latin American Literature in the United States, Latin America, and Europe.

From a relatively wealthy and conservative family, Llana moved from Cienfuegos to Havana when she was just four years old. There, she received two degrees in art and finally a degree in journalism. Although her family had lost some of its assets during the redistribution of wealth in the early years of the Cuban Revolution, Llana saw the ideals of the revolutionary project as parallel to the principles she learned through her Catholic education. She would go on to serve the Revolution as a journalist and/or editor at *Revolución*, *La tarde,* and *Prensa Latina*. Her profession afforded her time abroad as a special cultural envoy to the Soviet Union (1979, 1985), Vietnam, Nicaragua, and Mexico (1992–95), a foreign correspondent in China (1989–92), and as a journalism professor in Angola, Rwanda (1987–88), and Mexico (1995–96). In addition to reporting on literary, art, and film events and administering various international publications (*Prisma Latinoamaericano*, *Cuba Internacional*), Llana has had a long-standing affiliation with the Instituto Cubano de Radio y Televisión (ICRT). There, she polished her craft by writing the minute-long news segments for Radio Reloj, and scripts for radio novels and television shows.

While amply recognized in Cuba for her journalist activity, Llana is better known for her short fiction. She has won awards from the ICRT (1977), the Journalists Union (UPEC, 1983, 1984) but most importantly, the National Critic's Award for her collection of short fiction *Casas del Vedado* (Vedado Homes) in 1984. Her second collection, *Casas* . . . , also brought Llana international attention, and she has since participated on juries for literary competitions in Cuba and abroad. Her stories have been translated into English, French, Portuguese, Russian, Hungarian, German, and Arabic.

Fantastic Short Fiction

Llana's main characters are most frequently Havana's struggling bourgeois families, portrayed through a mixture of the fantastic, irony, and dark humor. Reminiscent of Juan Rulfo's *El llano en llamas* (1953), where the author creates characters that suffer the consequences of what is to them a far-removed social process (the Mexican Revolution), her "in-between" characters, at once ghost-like and of a tangible verisimilitude, offer a compelling perspective on the subjective negotiation of identity amidst the epic construction of a "Revolutionary" Cuba and its literature. Her first two collections, *La Reja* (1965) (The Gate) and *Casas del Vedado* (1984), feature the house as a space of revolutionary and individual struggle. This interior setting is transformed through the trajectory of her short story production. In *Castillos de naipes* (1998) (Playing Card Houses), *Ronda en el malecón* (2004) (Hanging on the Malecón), and *Apenas murmullos* (Murmurs), it becomes a space for slow decay, memory, and, in some stories, into a site for the postmodern performance of identities negotiating the changing winds of post-USSR revolutionary culture.

The structure of Llana's first published collection of short stories, *La reja*, clearly marks her self-conscious positioning as a writer within revolutionary paradigms. Divided into three parts, the collection reflects dominant styles and themes of Cuban narrative fiction during the early years of revolutionary cultural production: the fantastic, ("Divertimientos" (Just for Fun)); the historical ("Narraciones" (Narrations)); and the realist ("Hechos" (The Facts)). Her most popular *divertimiento* is "Nosotras" (The Two of Us). In this Cortázar-like tale, a woman dreams a phone number that rings up her own "self". In "Conócete a ti misma" (Know Thyself), the protagonist keeps tripping over her poor, half-finished personality, as if it were a coffee table. Llana's use of the fantastic represents domestic settings as non-homogeneous or as a site of fragmented identity. Similarly, Llana brings the revolutionary urban struggle against the dictator Fulgencio Batista into the home, disrupting the line between public and private in political struggle. "Nochemala" (Holy Night), for example, posits women as preservers of family values across the generation gap; its ambiguous metaphorical ending imbues agency to the gendered protagonist. Overall, Llana's manipulation of the fantastic and realist literary codes produces a solid collection of hair-raising suspense tales expressed through a female voice.

Her second collection, *Casas del Vedado*, would surface after a twenty-year silence, perhaps due to restrictions put on publishing during the 1970s. As the title suggests, the collection centers all of its texts in the houses found in Havana's Vedado neighborhood. Household objects come alive in such stories as "El gobelino" (The Gobelin Tapestry), "La heredada" (The Heiress), "Reina Ana" (Queen Anne), and "En familia" (In the Family). Llana does not animate these objects in the traditional sense; rather she imbues them with an extraordinary presence that shapes characters' identities, regulates their behavior, or bifurcates time. Llana's manipulation of time, along with its ontological consequences, frames the female protagonist's experience in "La casa vacía" (The Empty House), and "Claudina (Variaciones sobre un viejo tema)" (Claudina, or Variations on an Old Theme), where the reader questions the character's and plot's phenomenological substance. "Un abanico chino" (A Chinese Fan), examines the notion of circular time in identity formation as Llana entraps her protagonist's son, niece, and nephew in a circle of unattainable desire.

The manipulation of the fantastic in the plots and characters in *Casas* ... can be read as a veiled expression of women's identity as still inscribed in traditional roles. Llana's use of stock characters like *la solterona*, the old maid, and the conservative domineering *abuela* [grandmother], suggests a locally feminist discourse that obliquely notes the lack of essential change in Cuban cultural norms where women are concerned. "In the Family," from this collection, is transposed to the *chicana* experience in a PBS video about the culture clash of a young Mexican-American woman in East Los Angeles ("In the Mirror" dir. Carlos Avila, *Fotonovela Series*, 1997).

In *Castillos de naipes*, Llana allows worlds and eras outside the late twentieth-century Havana homes into her stories' settings and textual present. "Alondra pasa" (A Passing Lark), "Cuestión de tiempos" (A Question of Time), and "Ford T" are beautiful tales of loss and love bifurcated in referential time, but occurring in the same time-space of the stories' plots. Other anecdotes take a more explicitly critical view of life in Cuba's so-called Special Period in Times of Peace. In contrast to many of the "dirty-realist" stories and novels that come out of this period, Llana's work maintains a meticulous application of the fantastic and the humorous. For example, "Prefijos" (Prefixes), "Eleggua Sprey" (A Spray for Eleggua), and "Sabor a níspero" (The Flavor of Medlar) integrate amusing *criollo* (Creole) reinterpretations and performances of Afrocuban and Chinese superstitions and rituals. The magical realist element in "Los cuartos" (Rooms) makes the carnivalesque transformation of the narrator's house of residence into an allegory for the island, and "El bumerán" (The Boomerang) subverts time and pokes fun at the sexual double standard in a fantastical deconstruction of male–female relationships. Llana's work published in the twenty-first century also exhibits her particular skill at weaving enjoyable anecdotes and aristocratic airs in a sometimes biting portrait of Cuba's social milieu.

Ronda en el malecón and *Apenas murmullos*, collections of stories Llana wrote in the mid to late 1990s, bring together her particular regionalist mixture of realist, fantastic, and historical narrative forms. "Ronda en el malecón" and "Tríptico actual" (A Contemporary Triptych) criticize both the *performance* the revolution has become and the emigration of young men and women for economic reasons. Llana takes a stronger feminist position through her ubiquitous third person narrator in "En la orilla" (On the Shore), which tells the story of a woman who uses the Mariel boat lift to hide her complicity in the murder of her abusive husband. Similarly, in "Añejo cinco siglos" (A Five-Hundred Year Old Rum), two female protagonists toast across half a century to the departure of their lovers in a retelling of the popular legend of *la giraldilla*, the weathervane in the form of a woman that tops Old Havana's Castillo de la Real Fuerza (Royal Army Castle).

Over the past four decades, Llana's short fiction has consistently, yet implicitly, suggested what many conclude about Cuba's current crisis with the benefit of hindsight: the tenacious hold of colonial and nineteenth-century ideologies surrounding gender and socio-economic conditions in Cuba belies the revolutionary progress celebrated through official channels. Llana is a wordsmith whose work is praised in Cuba and abroad. Her meticulous prose, surprising and inexplicable plots, affable characters, and use of Cuban *choteo* (humor) submerge us in a Havana world at once long gone and everlasting.

BARBARA D. RIESS

Selected Works

La reja. La Habana: Serie de Dragón, 1965.

"The Two of Us". In Sylvia Carranza and María Juana Cazabón (eds), *Cuban Short Stories*. La Habana: Institutodel Libro: 1967.

"Nosotras". In *Cuentos cubanos de lo fantástico y lo extraordinario*. San Sebastian: Equipo Editorial, 1968.

Estatuas de sal: cuentistas cubanas contemporáneas, panorama crítico (1959–1995). Ed. Mirta Yáñez and Marilyn Bobes. La Habana: Ediciones UNION, 1996, pp. 126–32, and in Yates, Donald and Dalbor, John (eds) *Imaginación y fantasía. Cuentos de las Américas*. 4th edn. New York: Holt, Rinehart and Winston, 1983, pp. 49–57.

Casas del Vedado. La Habana: Editorial Letras Cubanas, 1983.

"In the Family". Trans. Beatriz Teleki. In Celia Correas de Zapata (ed.), *Short Stories by Latin American Women: The Magic and the Real*. Houston, TX: Arte Público Press, 1990.

"Baccarat". In Horacio García Brito and Blanca Acosta (eds), *Twentieth Century Cuban Short Stories*. La Habana: Editorial José Martí, 1994.

Castillos de naipes. La Habana: Ediciones UNIÓN, 1998.

"Japanese Daisies". Trans. Dick Cluster and Cindy Schuster. In Mirta Yánez (ed.), *Cubanas, Contemporary Fiction by Cuban Women*. Boston, MA: Beacon Press, 1998, pp. 41–52.

"Añejo cinco siglos". *La Gaceta de Cuba* 3(2001): 35–7.

Apenas murmullos. La Habana: Editorial Letras Cubanas, 2004.

Ronda en el malecón. La Habana: Ediciones Unión, 2004.

"A Five-Hundred Year Old Rum". In *Cuba on the Edge: Stories from the Island*. Nottingham: Critical, Cultural and Communications Press, 2006, pp. 141–50.

"Cuartos". Trans. Barbara Riess. In Mary Berg *et al.* (eds), *Cuba on the Edge: Stories from the Island*. Nottingham: Critical, Cultural and Communications Press, 2006.

References and Further Reading

Bobes, Marilyn. "El esperado homenaje". *Revolución y cultura* 1 (1998): 61–2.

Capote, Zaida. "Cuba, años sesenta. Cuentística femenina y canon literario". *La Gaceta* 1 (2000): 28–31.

Davies, Catherine. *A Place in the Sun? Women Writers in Twentieth Century Cuba*. London: Zed Books, 1997.

Goff, Katrina. "La simetría en tres cuentos cubanos". *Romance Languages Annual* 1 (1989): 455–9.

Redonet, Salvador. *Vivir del cuento*. La Habana: Ediciones Unión, 1994.

Riess, Barbara. Tríptica actual: análisis de tres escritoras cubanas contemporáneas. Dissertation. May, 1999.

Riverón, Rogelio. *Conversación con el búfalo blanco. Selección de cuentos y entrevistas*. La Habana: Editorial Letras Cubanas, 2005, pp. 31–49.

Serafín, Silvana. "Los cuentos fantásticos de María Elena Llana". *Studi de letteratura ispano-americana* 34–5 (2002).

Vázquez Pérez, María Marlene. "Los cuentos de María Elena Llana o la fascinación de la lectura". *El imaginario simbólico femenino en las literaturas cubana y colombiana contemporáneas*. Bogotá: Universidad Distrital Francisco José de Caldas, Centro de Investigaciones y Desarrollo Científico; Santa Clara, Cuba: Universidad Central Marta Abreu de las Villas, Departamento de Literatura, 2001, pp. 211–18.

LOAEZA, GUADALUPE

Loaeza's (b. 1946) career as a bestselling writer began in 1982, when the 36-year-old wife and mother was waiting for the finishing touches on some cushions. The relatively wealthy, French- and English-speaking Loaeza decided to enter the nearby office of the newspaper *Unomásuno* and offer her services, where she successfully pitched the idea of writing about the Mexican upper class in the style of Cristina Pacheco's journalism on the poor. For writing credentials Loaeza had her six-month experience in 1981 with Elena Poniatowska's literary workshop and a resultant short story prize. Loaeza does not possess university-level studies, and she compensates for this lack with a strong work ethic, constant intellectual curiosity, and personal charm. In point of this last fact, the editor who first accepted Loaeza's offer would later become the second of her three husbands. Loaeza maintains a high profile in Mexico through almost daily appearances in mainstream media, including newspapers (most prominently *Reforma* and *La Jornada*), magazines (such as *Paula, Kena*, and *Mira*), television (Televisa and Channel 40), or the radio (Radio Red and Radio Monitor). Despite the place of marginality that Loaeza's work occupies in academic criticism, her books sell tens of thousands of copies. In total, her books have sold more than 500,000 copies and in some cases run through nearly thirty editions. These numbers are extraordinary in the Mexican book market. Common topics in Loaeza's writing include travel, nostalgia, politics, consumerism, women's fashion, and assorted social gatherings, all narrated in terms of Mexican culture.

A Controversial Success

Loaeza's triumph in the Mexican literary market poses the question of what it means to publish in a nation that is often believed to be less interested in reading than in consuming other forms of media, particularly television. The key to Loaeza's success may relate at least partially to Loaeza's attention to narrative surface: her characters self-consciously indulge in superficial pastimes and glib internal monologue, which provides an entertaining if unsubtle read. Generally, Loaeza's texts do not require a second reading. Loaeza cultivates accessibility in her writing through visually fragmenting the page with lists, boxes of information, lengthy quotations from other sources, interviews broken up among questions and answers, short journalistic pieces that function as individual "chapters," and dictionary-style entries. Examples of Loaeza's texts that take their structure from alphabetized lists include the alternately sardonic and sincere manuals of etiquette about the Mexican wealthy, *Manual de la gente bien I y II* (1995, 1996, Manual of 'Nice' People I and II), and the dictionary-like treatment of Mexican political phenomena in *Los grillos y otras grillas* (1988, 'Political Schemers' and Other Plots). Loaeza's short stories were published in the enormously successful *Primero las damas* (1989, Ladies First), launched three narratives on the silver screen: "Mina" and "Besos satánicos" (Satanic Kisses) became short filmic works, while "Miroslava" was adapted by Vicente Leñero as a feature film. None of these cinematic projects equaled the success of Loaeza's published work.

Like her prose, Loaeza's characters sometimes straddle genres. For instance, protagonist and "alter ego," Sofía stars in the autobiographical novel *Las yeguas finas* (2003, The Fine Mares) as well as numerous chronicles of urban Mexican life. It is interesting to note the contrast between Sofía's frivolity and naïveté, and the meaning of her name, "wisdom". Indeed, Loaeza seems to appeal to a paradoxical discourse that takes frivolity seriously. An appeal to what might be considered a feminine world-view appears in Loaeza's biographical vignettes. These basic portraits of historical figures often include details regarding physical appearance and sexual partners in preference to complexities of historical context. For Loaeza, life and love, personality and production overlap in a move that denies the superiority of professional endeavor to domestic and romantic events. A generous reading would also note that Loaeza's frivolity generally engages in pointed social commentary, though newspaper coverage of her career often denigrates her ideas as unreflective and hypocritical.

Besides pointing to the contradiction of producing relentless criticism of the social class to which Loaeza herself belongs, detractors sometimes reject Loaeza's melodramatic politics. In her journalism, Mexico's once official party, the PRI (Institutional Revolutionary Party) tends to receive Loaeza's maximum venom, which produces hilarious though Manichean commentary. Against the traditions of her social class, Loaeza champions the liberal PRD (Party of the Democratic Revolution) and awards unconditional praise to the PRD mayor of Mexico City and presidential candidate, Andrés Manuel López Obrador, and Subcomandante Marcos, the spokesperson for the ELZN (Zapatista Army of National Liberation) involved in the Chiapan struggle for indigenous rights. Loaeza may wear liberal sympathy on her sleeve for the victims of Mexico's social inequities, but that sleeve is—as she might take pains to point out—of designer origin. Perhaps Loaeza tends to simplify social problems through strict separation of the "bad" politicians from her heroes in order to avoid more realistic analysis of what the "Queens of Polanco" (1988, *Las reinas de Polanco*) and their daughters, the "Good Girls" (1987 *Las niñas bien*), might have to give up in order for the *prietos* (dark-skinned people), *nacos* (tacky people), and other *déclassé* Mexicans to enjoy a better life. In concession to the difficulties that accompany social aspirations, texts such as *Debo, luego sufro* (2000, I Owe, thus I Suffer) balance fascination with consumerism with consistent laments regarding the anxiety of paying for luxury items.

Loaeza's insistent defiance of generally accepted literary rules leads to emphatic use of such generally taboo techniques as the diminutive, which is sometimes thought to be effeminate and improper literary language. In the short story, "Las torres de Milán" (1998, The Towers of Milan), three diminutives appear in two sentences: "Little by little (*poquito*) she stuck her head out and suddenly her eyes met those of a little bat (*un murcielaguito*). 'Don't attack me. Pretty please' (*Por favorcito*)" (p. 133). Loaeza's audience may delight in such imitation, or possibly exaggeration, of the language that many Mexican women employ. Additionally, in her chronicles Loaeza often divides words among their syllables with hyphens. This syllabification provokes the impression of emphatic, self-conscious, simultaneously dramatic and frivolous theatricality. Occasionally, the empathically spelled words seem to offer a chant, a call for collective and implicitly female voices to unite for a political cause. Another technique that defies more conventional methods of writing is to argue through insecurity: Loaeza establishes a friendship with her audience by withholding authority or by making the reader a co-participant in a conversation in progress. By drafting paragraph-long lists of questions, Loaeza often manages to convey both an unending doubt and a sense of placement among the question marks. As long as she is questioning, she is involved. This one-degree of removal from active political engagement may simultaneously gain the favor of Loaeza's female readers *and* commit her voice and audience to passive indignation. Loaeza almost never offers concrete suggestions for political action. Such action might, of course, threaten the strict if unrealistic division of good and bad evident in her political views.

Critical Applause

Critical attention to Loaeza's work does not exist in equal proportion to the impressive number of books that Loaeza sells. Even so, Cherie Meacham defends Loaeza through a political argument and reads the collection of chronicles *Sin cuenta* (1996, "Countless") as using Sofía's emotional reactions for comic relief from Loaeza's prevailing plea for mature women's greater political involvement. Loaeza's fictional examination of a group of wealthy Mexican women in *Compro, luego existo* (1992, I Shop, therefore I Am) inspires Cynthia Duncan to read the work through Mikhail Bakhtin's theory of carnival, while Mary K. Long reads the same text through nationalist concerns that show the emptiness of US values. According to Long's reading, the uncritical adoption in Mexico of these values stimulates the need for altered and more cosmopolitan Mexican identity. More criticism of Loaeza's work may arise as her prolific career continues to develop. After all, Loaeza's carefully composed and entertaining first novel promises to be the first of a trilogy.

EMILY HIND

Selected Works

Las niñas bien. Mexico: Océano, 1987.
Las reinas de Polanco. Mexico: Cal y Arena, 1988.
Los grillos y otras grillas. Mexico: Cal y Arena, 1991.
Manual de la gente bien (MGB). Mexico: Plaza y Janés, 1995.
Las yeguas finas. México: Planeta, 2003.

References and Further Reading

Aguilar, Julia VanLoan. "Humor in Crisis: Guadalupe Loaeza's Caricature of the Mexican Bourgeoisie". *Journal of American Culture* 20(2) (1997): 153–8.

Duncan, Cynthia. "Lo carnavalesco y la sociedad de consume en *Compro, luego existo*, de Guadalulpe Loaeza". In Rosaura Hernández Monroy and Manuel F. Medina (eds), *La seducción de la escritura: Los discursos de la cultura hoy*. Mexico: Universidad Autónoma Metropolitana-Azcapotzalco, 1997, pp. 43–9.

Fernández-Levín, R. "Trapped in a Gilded Cage: Guadalupe Loaeza's Unhappy Women". In Juan Cruz Mendizábal and Juan Fernández Jiménez (eds), *Visión de la narrative hispánica: Ensayos*. Indiana, PA: Indiana University of Pennsylvania, 1999, pp. 81–96.

Long, Mary K. "Consumer Society and National Identity in the Work of Salvador Novo and Guadalupe Loaeza". *Chasqui* 30(2) (2001): 116–26.

Meacham, Cherie. "A Woman's Testimony on the Mexican Crisis: Guadalupe Loaeza's *Sin cuenta*". *Letras femeninas* 26(1)–2 (2000): 111–24.

Ortiz, Verónica. "Interview with Guadalupe Loaeza". In *Mujeres de palabra: Rosa Beltrán, Fabienne Bradu, Laura Esquivel, Eladia González, Mónica Lavín, Guadalupe Loaeza, Silvia Molina y Rosa Nissán*. Prologue by Elena Poniatowska. Mexico: Joaquín Mortiz, 2005, pp. 86–108.

Peña, Luis H. "La nostalgia del milagro: Guadalupe Loaeza y la crónica como crítica cultural". *Letras femeninas* 1 (1974): 131–7.

Schaefer-Rodríguez, Claudia. "Embedded Agendas: The Literary Journalism of Cristina Pacheco and Guadalupe Loaeza." *Latin American Literary Review* 19(38) (1991): 62–76.

LOBO, LUIZA

Luiza Lobo (b. 1948) (Luiza Leite Bruno Lobo), at the age of 19, began her career as a literary critic, a writer and a translator and an English teacher as well. Later she became a university professor. She graduated in Philosophy (1970) and English (1968) and took her post-graduate and post-doctoral degrees in Comparative Literature in the United States (1978; 1985) and Germany (1995). She was a Visiting Researcher at the Center for Brazilian Studies of the University of Oxford (2000) and at the University of Nantes (2001). She has taught, lectured and published extensively, in Brazil and abroad. Her work encompasses essays, book editing, short stories, translation and poetry.

As a creative writer, Lobo published five books of short stories and some poems, in Brazil and Portugal. She has translated more than thirty works of fiction, by authors such as Woolf, Austen, Burgess, Golding, Poe and Burns (the first and only translation in Portuguese). She is currently engaged in the publication of the second editions of several of her books. She has signed a contract for 2007 with Rocco Publishers from Rio de Janeiro to deliver her first novel, for which she has been collecting material for a decade.

Luiza Lobo's imaginary style is made up of humor and word puns. Her narrator is a feminist voice which questions cultural tradition and the literary canon by means of an anti-logocentric and anti-patriarchal misreading of society.

Her first book of short stories, *Por trás dos muros, arte-fábulas* (1976, Behind the Walls, Fable Art Crafts), employs a dreamlike style related to Surrealism and the unconscious. It centers on experimental language rather than on plot or description. Humor is present in her story "Mestre Radin e seu falso cadafalso" (Master Radin and his False Scaffold) and in "De como me transformei em repasto de morcegos malvados" (On how I Became the Repast of Very Wicked Bats), which was included in the *Antología de contistas novos* (1971, Anthology of New Authors). There are echoes of several authors' voices in this first phase, such as Clarice Lispector, Guimarães Rosa, Virginia Woolf, Kafka and Dostoevsky.

Lobo's second collection, *Vôo Livre* (1982, Free Flight), as well as *Behind the Walls*, breaks with the logic of discourse, as was often practiced in the literary scene of the 1970s. Its main theme is existence, craziness and death, as in "Manuscrito de um homem só" (Manuscript by a Lonely Man.) Its atmosphere is pervaded by dream and fantasy, as in the title story "Free Flight," which narrates the end of the world as lived by a surviving couple.

A maçã mordida (1982, The Bitten Apple) shows a livelier tone. The title story plunges into the everyday scene of postmodern life in New York City, where Luiza Lobo lived in 1985 during her post-doctoral research in New York University. The half-eaten apple hints at New York's deterioration in the postmodern era and is one among several cannibalistic images that Lobo develops, especially in the stories of her fourth collection, *Sexameron. Novelas sobre casamentos* (1997, Sexameron: Stories about Marriages). Like the previous anthology, its style also resembles a film script. Sex, death and the end of the world are again the prevailing themes. Sex relates to contemporary life and is seen from a critical and humorous standpoint. Its title draws a humorous pun with the word sex and six in Greek, and the book is a parody of Boccaccio's *Decameron*. The setting is also a castle, but in Rio de Janeiro, where a group of six young men and women take refuge against AIDS, the new plague of the twentieth century. They call one another by classical names, as in Boccaccio, and each of them narrates a tale on the decadent era that comes to its close together with the century. As in Boccaccio's one-hundred *novellas*, a small introduction precedes each story. As a follow-up to intertextuality, the book pretends to be presented by the Renaissance French writer Marguerite of Navarre's *Heptameron*. Some of the intertextual references of these postmodern stories are the pre-Raphaelite David Millet's painting of a drowning Ophelia and the Decadent writing of Oscar Wilde. These Brazilian novellas, a genre hardly exercised in Brazil, are not devoid of lechery, debauchery and the exploitation of pleasure, as in Boccaccio's counterpart. The book conveys disgust with present civilization and AIDS, its "flower of evil". Loneliness, indifference, melancholy and obsession with artificial paradises haunt the imagination of the characters, marking the crumbling of rational utopias, only to shape a new mannerist geography in postmodernism. Particularly in this book, Lobo practices a sort of cannibalization of several canonical styles through a decentered, intertextual and boundless look (Fontes 2000: 27–36). This remapping of cognitive-cultural knowledge of reality builds a new cartography of transgression. The author's look at cosmopolitan centers, such as Rio de Janeiro, New York and London, in her several stories, leads to a double conquest, that of a feminist independent identity and that of a path to the lively media writing of the 1990s.

Luiza Lobo's fifth and latest book of short stories, *Estranha aparição* (2000, Strange Apparition), aims to capture the flimsy aspects of everyday life, as in Woolf's and Lispector's stream of consciousness. Its fantastic-surrealist style approaches fiction to its modern counterpart, cinema. However, it is less immersed in the unconscious, delirium and fantasy than are her previous works, especially *Behind the Walls*, 1976. *Strange Apparition* represents a turning point in Lobo's writing, since it shifts from psychological motivation and language experimentation to a more cinema-like action, plot and character development. The stories vary from an intertextual rereading of the canon to a cultural discussion of the foundation of human relationships and behavior. In brief, these new stories show a change of focus from the "word" to the "world".

The title story is a humorous rendering of a grotesque love affair which parodies Mary Shelley's Gothic novel *Frankenstein* and Edgar Allan Poe's "The Fall of the House of Usher," a short story Lobo translated in 1970. "Guerra dos Orixás" (Battle of Orixas) experiments with a hybrid genre that merges essay and fiction. Lobo derives its topic from a research on Afro-Brazilian literature she did for Ford Foundation (1986). It confronts the Brazilian Yoruba gods with the traditional Greek Pantheon in a humorous battle that reaches its climax on the beaches of Rio de Janeiro at New Year's Eve.

Lobo's critical work includes the publication of 120 articles, in Brazil and abroad, five books of essays and five edited books of essays. Among these books, *Épica e modernidade em Sousândrade* (1986, 2nd edn 2005, Sousandrade: a Forerunner of Modernism in an Epic Frame), originally her Ph.D. dissertation (1978), presents the Romantic poet's main work *O Guesa* (1884, The Guesa), in a comparative literature perspective. Lobo's preoccupation with post-metaphysical logic is reflected in *O haikai e a crise da metafísica* (1993, Haiku and the Crisis of Metaphysics). *Crítica sem juízo* (1993, 2nd edn 2006, Criticism Without Judgment) collects twenty-five years of literary criticism. It is divided into three parts: Women Writers, Humor in literature and Afro-Brazilian literature. It includes Lobo's first literary article (*O Globo*, Rio de Janeiro, 1968), which was on Virginia Woolf, whose *To the Lighthouse* she translated in 1968. *Teorias poéticas do Romantismo* (1987, Romantic Theories on Poetics), is a reader of the seminal texts by the European Romantic writers on poetics. It has been widely used in universities of Brazil and Portugal.

Her activities in the cultural and literary scene show her to be an engaged professional who researches new modes of literary expression and searches for new roles for women in Western society.

MARIA APARECIDA RODRIGUES FONTES

Selected Works

Por trás dos muros / arte-fábulas. Rio de Janeiro: Brasília, 1976.

Vôo livre. Rio de Janeiro: Cátedra/INL, 1982.

A maçã mordida. Rio de Janeiro: Numen, 1992.

Sexameron. Novelas sobre casamentos. Rio de Janeiro: Relume-Dumará, 1997. (The story "La guerra de los orichas" was translated and appeared in *Revolución y Cultura*, La Habana, n. 4, July–August 2000, pp. 40–4).

Estranha aparição. Rio de Janeiro: Rocco, 2000.

References and Further Reading

Coelho, Nelly Novaes. *Dicionário crítico de escritoras brasileiras (1711–2001)*. São Paulo: Escrituras, 2002.

Coutinho, Afrânio and de Sousa, J. Galante (eds) *Enciclopédia de Literatura Brasileira*. Rio de Janeiro: MEC-Fename-FAE, 1990. 2 vols. 2nd edn. Rio de Janeiro, São Paulo: Global, BN, ABL, 2001.

Fontes, Maria Aparecida Rodrigues. "*Sexameron*: antropofagia e identidade cultural na pós-modernidade". *Ipotesi: Revista de Estudos Literários* 4(1) (2000): 27–36.

Hollanda, Heloísa Buarque de and Araújo, Lúcia Nascimento. *Ensaístas brasileiras. Mulheres que escreveram sobre literatura e artes de 1860 a 1991*. Rio de Janeiro: Rocco, 1993, pp. 176–7.

Lopes, Maria Angélica. "Lobo, Luiza. A maçã mordida: contos". In Library of Congress (ed.), *Handbook of Latin American Studies*. Austin, TX: University of Texas Press, vol. 54, 1995.

——. "Lobo, Luiza. Estranha aparição". In Library of Congress (ed.), *Handbook of Latin American Studies*. Austin, TX: Univeristy of Texas Press, Vol. 60, 2003.

Wanderley, Marcia Cavendish. "Prosa/rosa: presença feminina na literatura brasileira pós-64". In *Gênero*. Niterói: UFF, Cadernos do NUTEG (Núcleo Interdisciplinar de Estudos de Gênero), Vol. 1, 2000. pp. 21–7.

LOJO, MARÍA ROSA

Novelist, poet, storyteller, and researcher, María Rosa Lojo was born in Buenos Aires in 1954, the daughter of Spanish immigrants. Although born in Buenos Aires, Lojo spent most of her childhood in Castelar, a suburb approximately 20 kilometers from Buenos Aires free from skyscrapers and factories, and she still lives there. Lojo received a doctorate in philosophy and literature at the Universidad de Buenos Aires where she now works as a researcher for the Consejo Nacional de Investigaciones Científicas y Técnicas (CONICET) in the Instituto de literatura argentina Ricardo Rojas. She is also a professor at the Universidad del Salvador where she is director of two research projects and also leads seminars in the doctorate program. She has been a conference participant and visiting professor in many universities, both in Argentina and abroad. She is a cultural journalist and writes articles for *Clarín* and is a permanent collaborator for the Literary Supplement of *La Nación*. Lojo has won numerous awards, including the Primer Premio de Poesía at the Feria del Libro de Buenos Aires in 1984 for *Visiones*; the Premio del Fondo Nacional de las Artes in 1985 for her collection of short stories, *Marginales*, and in 1986 for her novel, *Canción perdida en Buenos Aires al Oeste*; the Primer Premio de Poesía "Alfredo A. Roggiano" in 1990, for her book of prose-poems *Forma oculta del mundo*; the Segundo Premio Municipal de Poesía de Buenos Aires for the biennial 1990/91 also for *Forma oculta del mundo*; the Primer Premio Municipal de Buenos Aires "Eduardo Mallea" in 1996 for *La pasión de los nómades*; the Premio del Instituto Literario y Cultural Hispánico de California in 1999 for her literary trajectory; the Premio Kónex for her narrative works from 1994 to 2003; and the Premio Nacional "Esteban Echeverría" for the sum total of her narrative works up to 2004.

Lojo's fiction is influenced by two complementary geographical locations: Galicia and the Argentine pampas. Although born and raised in Argentina, Lojo's father, a republican from Galicia who fled Spain during the Civil War, often spoke of his homeland. His nostalgia for Galicia and his descriptions of his birthplace deeply affected Lojo and her writing. At the same time, as a youth in Castelar, Lojo formed a strong connection with nature and became fascinated with the sparsely populated interior of the country. For many Argentine writers the pampas represent the barbaric, virgin, unexplored, and unknown land. However, Lojo's works do not perpetuate simplistic and unquestioned representations of the pampas, rather she explores these same ideas from the perspective of the margin, or the outsider, in order to show that these lands were never barbaric, virgin, unexplored, or unknown, but rather civilized by indigenous cultures whose cosmic vision of the universe was never fully understood or valorized.

Historical Fiction

Her fascination with the past as a means to view the present is the impetus behind Lojo's re-writing and re-evaluation of Argentine history through historical fiction. Her novels *La pasión de los nómades* (1994), *La princesa federal* (1998), *Una mujer de fin de siglo* (1999), *Las libres del Sur: Una novela sobre Victoria Ocampo* (2004), and *Finisterre* (2005) are set in nineteenth- and twentieth-century Argentina and the stories included in *Historias ocultas en la Recoleta* (2000) and *Amores insólitos de nuestra historia* (2001) recreate the lives of famous and infamous men and women of Argentina's history. Throughout these novels and stories Lojo subverts the traditional civilization versus barbarism dichotomy propagated by Domingo F. Sarmiento's *Facundo: Civilización y barbarie* (1845) and other popular nineteenth-century texts. In order to portray the lives and realities of some of the less prominent players in Argentina's history, Lojo's main characters are often revealed through the eyes of an outsider. Most significantly, Lojo always approaches her novels and short stories from the point of literature. That is, while her fiction may be based on historical events or people, it maintains the imagination, rhythm, complexity, and style necessary for critically-acclaimed fiction.

In *La pasión de los nómades*, Lojo utilizes gothic, carnivalesque, and mythical elements in order to reconstruct and re-evaluate the journey to the land of the Ranquel Indians undertaken by Lieutenant Colonel Lucio Victorio Mansilla (nephew of General Juan Manuel de Rosas) and narrated in his *Una excursión a los indios ranqueles* (1870). Perhaps the most unique characteristic of this text is Lojo's hybridization of various genres. That is, not only does she mix fiction and history, but also *lo maravilloso* and *lo real*. Through the parodic and lyrical intervention of mythical and legendary characters, Mansilla is able to "return" to the present day and undertake a second trip to the pampas. Through this intertextual approach, Lojo juxtaposes the events of the late twentieth century with the narration of Mansilla's travels. By intertwining fiction and history, she blurs the division between lived experiences and narrativized reality and succeeds in questioning historical truth claims.

Both *La princesa federal* and *Una mujer de fin de siglo* insert women into history and show them not as passive citizens but rather as actors during important post-independence and nation-building stages of the nineteenth century. *La princesa federal* intertwines fictional diary entries from Manuela Rosas's teacher and confidante with her own "memories" of her father's regime as remembered from her exile in London. Lojo's depiction of this woman complicates the myth, founded and perpetuated mostly by José Mármol, of her as chaste and merciful, in contrast to her father's demoniacal nature. While elements of the myth still exist in this historical novel, Lojo shows that Manuelita was not simply the angel to her father's devil, but rather a key advisor to her father with political power in her own right. *Una mujer de fin de siglo* also addresses the role of women through the figure of the writer Eduarda Mansilla de García, niece of General Rosas. The novel is divided into three sections that show the intellectual and authorial development of Mansilla from the perspective of three different characters. Just like the earlier novel, this work paints a picture of Argentine women as active in the social and cultural life of the era.

While Lojo's earlier historical novels focus on the nineteenth century, *Las libres del Sur* is set during the early twentieth century and weaves in and out of the life of Victoria Ocampo. Similar to much of her historical fiction, Lojo utilizes a fictional outsider who is witness to both Ocampo's world as well as to people and places that the main character cannot access. In this case, the Galician Carmen Brey Moure travels to Argentina as the interpreter for Rabindranath Tagore who has been invited by Ocampo to visit the country. While Carmen's professional dealings take the reader into the intimate circle of Victoria Ocampo, Carmen's private quest to find her brother leads her and the reader outside the metropolis. Carmen, assisted by Jorge Luis Borges and Leopoldo Marechal, discovers that her brother is living with a group of indigenous people.

Finisterre, while considered a historical novel, is less constrained by this category since it is not a biographical historical novel. That is, the main plotline does not revolve around a central historical figure; rather, some of the characters in the novel are historical but the main characters are not. The events of this novel unfold through a series of letters written by the middle-aged Rosalind, daughter of an Irishman and a Galician, to the young Elizabeth, born in Argentina to a wealthy English father who refuses to talk about her mother. Through these letters Rosalind keeps her promise to Elizabeth by revealing the link between the two women and breaking the silence imposed by Elizabeth's father about her own birth in Argentina. Historical personages of the nineteenth century, including Manuelita Rosas, Manuel Baigorria, and Oscar Wilde, also weave in and out of the story. *Finisterre* invokes the inner search for identity in the face of secrets and prohibitions.

By utilizing various narrative strategies in her historical novels, Lojo's texts criticize the repression of the recent dictatorship (1976–83). Her novels link the omissions and limitations of the nineteenth century to the political and social climate of the 1970s and 1980s that allowed the existence of the dictatorship. In fact, Lojo links the problems of gender and ethnicity in the nineteenth century with the recent dictatorship by focusing on minority perspectives, utilizing fantastic elements to contrast with the horror of a government's actions against its own citizens, revealing the way in which the recent repressive regime ensured the loyalty of future citizens, and questioning official governmental policies and doctrines that naturalize gender roles.

Similarly, Lojo's collections of short stories, *Historias ocultas en la Recoleta* and *Amores insólitos de nuestra historia*, re-envision times, places, and people that are linked either by their place of burial or their tumultuous passions. Lojo does not simply recreate legends or myths, but rather attempts to uncover the hidden story behind the figures of Argentine history by utilizing first and third person narrators who do not always realize their singular roles as witnesses to historical events. Since it is clear that the characters who inhabit *Historias ocultas en la Recoleta* are linked by death, these stories delve into the course of destiny that lead all these people to a shared resting place. Meanwhile, instead of focusing on traditional themes of historical research such as wars and the men who fought them, the stories in *Amores insólitos de nuestra historia* utilize the theme of love as a means by which historical memory is reproduced. By focusing on unusual passions, Lojo consciously centers her narration on marginalized perspectives: female, indigenous, and mestizo.

Poet

As a poet, Lojo questions and then redefines the very poetic language she utilizes. Some of her prose poetry, like her historical novels and stories, re-elaborates myths and legends to produce a new, unexpected perspective on such things as vampires ("Fragilidad de los Vampiros," *Esperan la mañana verde*) and the man in the moon ("Hombre de la luna," *Forma oculta del mundo*). Her poetry also often takes up the theme of dreams and their relationship with reality and human destiny. Overall, there is a strong sense of mystery in the world around us that Lojo attempts to communicate to readers in order to give them a sense of the grandiose while at the same time conveying a sense of intimacy.

A precise and agile poet and prose writer, María Rosa Lojo succeeds in opening the door to the hearts and minds of a variety of famous and infamous figures of Argentine history. Her critically acclaimed historical fiction offers outstanding examples of the integration of historical research with a variety of narrative strategies while her poems often experiment with language and meaning as Lojo stretches the boundaries of poetic expression.

REBECCA J. ULLAND

Selected Works

Visiones. Buenos Aires: Exposición Feria Internacional, 1984.

Marginales. Buenos Aires: Epsilon, 1985.

Canción perdida en Buenos Aires al Oeste. Buenos Aires: Torres Agüero, 1987.

Forma oculta del mundo. Buenos Aires: Ediciones Último Reino, 1991.

"A quinientos años, desde el país del monte". *Alba de América* 10(18–19) (July 1992): 81–92.

"Mirar desde espacios imaginarios". *Alba de América* 11(20–1) (July 1993): 41–52.

La "barbarie" en la narrativa argentina: siglo XIX. Buenos Aires: Corregidor, 1994.

La pasión de los nómades. Buenos Aires: Atlántida, 1994.

Cuentistas argentinos de fin de siglo. Buenos Aires: Vinciguerra, 1997.

"Una nueva excursión a los indios ranqueles". *Ciencia Hoy: Revista de divulgación científica y tecnológica de la Asociación Ciencia Hoy* 6(36) (1997): 41–50.

Sábato; en busca del original perdido. Buenos Aires: Corregidor, 1997.

El símbolo: poéticas, teorías, metatextos. México, D.F.: Universidad Autónoma de México, 1997.

Esperan la mañana verde. Buenos Aires: El Francotirador Ediciones, 1998.

La princesa federal. Buenos Aires: Planeta, 1998.

Una mujer de fin de siglo. Buenos Aires: Planeta, 1999.

Lojo, María Rosa and Elissalde, Roberto (historical research). *Historias ocultas en la Recoleta.* Buenos Aires: Alfaguara, 2000.

Amores insólitos de nuestra historia. Buenos Aires: Alfaguara, 2001.

Las libres del Sur: Una novela sobre Victoria Ocampo. Buenos Aires: Sudamericana, 2004.

Finisterre. Buenos Aires: Sudamericana, 2005 (translated into Gallego).

References and Further Reading

Arán, Pampa O. "De la Argentina y sus fantasmas". *Letterature d'America. Rivista Trimestrale. Ispanoamericana* XXII (90) (2002): 39–57.

——. "María Rosa Lojo: espacios de rehistorización". *Umbrales y catástrofes: literatura argentina de los '90.* Ed. Pampa O. Arán, *et al.* Córdoba: Epoké, 2003, pp. 143–59.

Cebrelli, Alejandra. "La ficción de los límites: A propósito de la narrativa de María Rosa Lojo". *Confluencia: Revista Hispánica de Cultura y Literatura* 14(2) (1999 Spring): 34–44.

Crivello, Victorina M. "*La pasión de los nómades*, María Rosa Lojo. El espacio autobiográfico ficcional en el entrecruzamiento genérico". In Stella Benvenuti (ed.), *Auto (bio) grafías. La densidad de la memoria en nuevas novelas históricas argentinas de fin de siglo.* Córdoba: Ediciones del Boulevard, 2004, pp. 54–108.

Da Cunha-Giabbai, Gloria. "Re-visión de la identidad argentina en los cuentos históricos de María Rosa Lojo". *Alba de América* 25(47–8) (July 2006): 177–86.

Filer, Malva. "Imaginación histórica y memoria colectiva en la obra de María Rosa Lojo". XXIV Simposio Internacional de Literatura, Instituto Literario y Cultural Hispánico, California, Buenos Aires 9 al 14 de agosto de 2004. *Alba de América* 19(45–6) (July 2005): 347–57.

Flawiá de Fernández, Nilda. "Mujeres, hombres; pasado y presente en dos novelas de María Rosa Lojo". In *Itinerarios literarios. Construcciones y reconstrucciones identitarias.* Madrid and Frankfurt: Iberoamericana and Vervuert, 2001, pp. 83–94.

Lehman, Kathryn. "Navegando en la narrativa histórica para encauzar el futuro: deseo romántico y sujeto nacional en la narrativa de María Rosa Lojo". *Alba de América* 19(45–6) (July 2005): 359–71.

——. "The New Historical Novel and Domestic Politics under *Rosismo*". *Monographic Review/Revista Monográfica* XIX (2003): 180–95.

——. "Women, Subalternity and the Historical Novel of María Rosa Lojo". *Studies in Twentieth and Twenty-First Century Literature* 29(1) (2005): 82–98.

Tacconi de Gómez, María del Carmen. "La elaboración literaria del discurso narrativo de María Rosa Lojo". In Juana A. Arancibia (ed.), *La mujer en la literatura del mundo hispánico.* Vol. VI. Westminster, CA: Instituto Literario y Cultural Hispánico, 2005, pp. 161–9.

Zelaya de Nader, Honoria. "Estatutos del discurso en *Una mujer de fin de siglo*, de María Rosa Lojo". In María del Carmen Tacconi de Gómez (ed.), *Ficción y Discurso.* Tucumán: Universidad Nacional de Tucumán, Facultad de Filosofía y Letras, Instituto de Investigaciones Lingüísticas y Literarias Hispanoamericanas, 1999, pp. 47–67.

LOPES CANÇADO, MAURA

Maura Lopes Cançado (1930–93) is one of the most important modern Brazilian writers. Her relevance is not due to her fame in the Brazilian literary field – for she is an unknown writer for the general public – but is instead due to her singular talent and sensibility, along with her distinct thematic contribution and unique narrative. Her own mental illness was the launching point for her texts. She was inspired by a long trajectory of mental illness and treatment in psychiatric hospitals, presenting an autobiographical work of two major titles: *Hospício é Deus* (Asylum is God), written between 1959 and 1960 and published in 1965, and *O Sofredor do Ver* (1968, The Sufferer of Seeing).

Hospício é Deus is a journal, written while Lopes Cançado was an inmate in a public asylum for the mentally ill in Rio de Janeiro. *O Sofredor do Ver* is a collection of short stories, most of them already published in the *Suplemento Dominical do Jornal do Brasil* (The Sunday Literary Supplement of the Journal of Brazil) during the 1950s and 1960s, in which Lopes Cançado appeared together with such prominent writers as José Louzeiro, Reinaldo Jardim, and Margarida Autran. This group, supported by Oliveira Bastos, Mario Faustino and Amilcar de Castro, were defenders of the concretism of Ferreira Gullar. At this time Lopes Cançado was acclaimed as one of the most talented young Brazilian writers of her generation by critics such as Assis Brasil and Ferreira Gullar.

In the 1960s, Brazil was stepping into modernity with important cultural movements such as Bossa Nova, and the promise of economic and social progress. Because this period was favorable to the emergence of alternative popular expressions, Maura's work, and texts such as the diary *Quarto de despejo*, written by Carolina Maria de Jesus (1960), expressed the emerging political-social context of the country. These texts marked a turn towards self-referential narrative, for biographies and testimonies written by authors belonging to subalterns' social classes. These narratives, however, if received with great enthusiasm in the beginning, were also quickly forgotten. As José Meihy (1998), remarked, their success was superficial, transforming their authors into totems representing the subaltern classes. Instead of inaugurating an authentic space for the expression of marginalized voices, the movement failed to develop the rich possibilities of these discourses.

Lopes Cançado, herself a victim of this "culture of difference", as Baudrillard (2004) would put it, denounced this "subtle and immoral" mechanism, criticizing an artificial procedure of "accepting" differences that, in fact, patronized and marginalized:

> Dona Dalmatie (a nurse at the psychiatric hospital) called me by the window where she stores her work materials and introduced me to the two ladies: Dr. Maria Tereza, doctor. And Aline Paim, writer and wife of the Hospital's director. They stared at me with curiosity and spoke with excessive politeness and friendliness – completely dispensable, even immoral. I said goodbye feeling sick in my stomach about their smiling faces – only later I started feeling better again.
>
> (p. 100)

Lopes Cançado was born in the interior of Minas Gerais, and at the age of 14, she married a young pilot, four years her senior. At 15, she found herself divorced, and the mother of a son. As a result she experienced the social contradictions and prejudices that came with not corresponding to traditional expectations for a woman of her social status. Indeed, she posed a threat to those traditional expectations. She was cast as crazy, mad; and, in an attempt to be accepted by society, she played that role, setting off on her journey through clinics and psychiatric asylums. If in the beginning the asylum offered her a role to play, a way of being in a world that rejected her, it soon became yet another site for radical alienation, another place for her to be the stranger who doesn't belong. She could not identify with her colleagues/inmates, and lived in constant conflict with them. As she wrote:

> Sometimes I am terribly depressed, the external things hurt hard on me, and in my intimacy a pale suffering, an anxiety, an almost desire to reveal myself. No: a profound tiredness. Complete lack of pain or happiness. A difficult and slow existence, the heart dark as a secret. The certainty, the sureness, that I am alone. And as loud as I scream, nobody will listen ... They [the interns] have a place to go, and I don't. Because even here, I am still an outsider.
>
> (p.79)

And that suggests the underlying theme, the recurrent struggle in her writing: whether to surrender to the determination of labels, of the social codes; or to refuse this surrender, thereby making something valuable of her singularity and alterity.

> I am one more number. A humble prefix stamped on a uniform. When I speak, my voice gets lost in this uniformity that confuses us. Nonetheless, I still speak ... Nothing surrounds me. Nothing is a still river of lost sight. I don't believe, but if I believed it would be nice. I don't believe and I have Nothing – and the madhouse.
>
> (p. 60)

But she also reveals: "I like this uniform. I like to see myself dressed as many others. What brings me close to other people, even if only in appearance, comforts me" (p. 128).

Lopes Cançado's courageous struggle to reveal herself, with all her multiple facets and complexities, gives brilliance to her work. In narrating her life and daily activities in a public asylum, she does not pretend to narrate the story of a successful person, and woman. The author presents herself as somebody who struggles to overcome her own difficulties and defects but also someone who surrenders to them at times. Her texts reveal the anguish and suffering of someone with an acute vision of the world, of someone who "suffers in seeing", as in the title of her collection of short stories.

Lopes Cançado disturbs us, for example in her analysis of the silent, subtle and cruel social process in the production of madness, observed in the day-to-day life and social interactions, that are apparently naive and neutral, but in fact deadly to the psyche. She also obliges us to reevaluate the psychiatric orthodoxies when she describes her suffering in facing the coldness of a psychiatric science. She reveals this feeling in a beautiful metaphor found in *Hospício é Deus* (1979): the suitcase covered with baggage claim tags and destination labels. In her words:

> I will end up this life like these suitcases, in which the travelers visit many countries and in every hotel they go they stamp a label: Paris, Rome, Berlin, Oklahoma. And I: Paranoia, Schizophrenia, Epilepsy, Psychosis, Manic-Depressive, etc. My own personality will be suffocated by clinical scientific labels.
>
> (p. 44)

In this excerpt, Cançado sees her own personality suffocated by scientific concepts but she is able to become a detached observer of this very technical labeling in her relationship with her doctors. She suffers the alientation that comes with reducing her singularity to the abstract labels of psychiatric theory, but she is able to detach herself enough to reflect on her experience.

When she writes that "the painter for whom I posed gave up the lines, abandoned the paint: my portrait is a white canvas" (p. 143), she reveals the impoverished viewpoint of the doctors; in the portrait drawn according to the medical code, her individuality disappears into the white of a blank canvas. Not finding anybody she could pose for, no one who could see outside the narrow perspective of psychiatry and cultural convention, Lopes Cançado portrayed herself with all the lines and colors she was able to reach.

Even though she was a writer who narrated her own journey, Cançado stepped beyond her own existence and her own pain, in meditating about the quality of contemporary human interactions and the social production of culture, while creating a singular critique of modernity. Her body of work, full of beauty and sensibility, transcends a strictly fictional character and is located in a philosophical dimension of thought. She transcended her own real surroundings to imaginatively reflect on the possibilities of being human. Because she reported as a woman facing the enormous difficulty of confronting gender roles in a traditional and patriarchal society, creating a unique literary account, Lopes Cançado's books are among the finest in the Portuguese language, and in spite of her disappearance from the literary scene, she is still well remembered by prominent writers and critics of her generation such as Nelson Oliveira, José Louzeiro and Margarida Autran as a woman with great intelligence and learning, uniquely reporting from inside a mental health institution in Brazil.

Maura died in Rio de Janeiro in 1993. She was poor, had lost sight in both of her eyes, and stood accused of murdering another inmate, a pregnant woman who, according to Maura's testimony, asked her to do it.

SONIA RONCADOR AND LUCIANA CASTRO

Selected Works

O Sofredor do Ver. Rio de Janeiro: José Alvaro Editor, 1968.
Hospício é Deus: Diário I. Rio de Janeiro: Record, 1979.

References and Further Reading

Brasil, Assis. "O Sofredor do Ver". *Suplemento Literário de Minas Gerais* IV(130) (1969): 7–8.

Cony, Carlos Heitor. " A Arte de Falar Mal" in *O Tudo e o Nada*. São Paulo: PubliFolha, 2004.

Louzeiro, José. "Da Razão e da Loucura". *Jornal Estado de Minas*, April 7, sec. Feminino & Masculino. 2002.

Oliveira, Nelson. *Verdades Provisórias*. São Paulo: Escrituras, 2003.

Roncador, S. "A Lição de Maura: entre a Alteridade da Loucura e a Normatização dos Códigos." Master's Diss. UCB, Brasilia, 2006.

Saraiva, Paulo. "Do Que Também Devia Tratar a Psicologia". In *Suplemento Literário de Minas Gerais* III(101) (1968): 5–6.

Scliar, Moacyr. "O Hospício não é Deus" Homepage: http://www2.uol.com.br/vivermente/conteudo/editorial/editorial_2.html (September 2004).

LÓPEZ GONZÁLEZ, ARALIA

Born in Havana in 1938, Aralia López González left Cuba in 1965. Originally a psychiatrist and psychotherapist, she settled in Mexico. Literature was a pleasure for her since childhood yet she never considered it as a career until, while completing her Master's degree at the University of Puerto Rico (1972), she realized that literature was her vocation. At this time she also became a feminist. Her later analytical and academic work would revolve around developing feminist literary theory and Women's Studies in Mexico, where she received her doctorate from Colegio de México in 1976. There, López González would teach and participate in the formation of the Programa Interdisciplinario del Estudio de la Mujer (PIEM), inaugurated in 1983. She is a professor at the Universidad Autónoma de México, Iztapalapa, where she participated in establishing the institution's first graduate program in Literary Theory.

López González's collaboration with the PIEM has resulted in the publication of materials that are essential resources for reading Latin American women's fiction. After founding the Taller de la narrativa femenina mexicana (Workshop on Mexican Women's Narrative Fiction) in 1984 with Ana Rosa Domenella, López González wrote the oft-cited introduction to the collection of essays *Sin imágenes falsas, sin falsos espejos* (Without False Images and Untrue Mirrors). In the meantime, the PIEM branched out and organized two colloquia at the Colegio de la Frontera Norte in 1987 and 1988 called "Mujer y literatura mexicana y chicana: culturas en contacto" (Women and Mexican and Chicana Literature: Cultures in Contact). López González helped coordinate these events and wrote the introductions for the two volumes of collected essays that resulted. Her collaborative teaching and creative and critical work place López González in the avant-garde of intellectuals whose probing dialogues about culture influence the conceptualization and study of Latin American women's fiction.

Feminist Theory and Literary Criticism

López González's work in developing a praxis of feminist literary criticism follows a trajectory frequently found in feminist studies in other fields. Her first work, *De la intimidad a la acción: la narrativa de escritores latinoamericanas y su desarrollo* (1985, The Development of Latin American Women's Prose Fiction: From Intimate to Active) surveys early Latin American women novelists in a comparative study with their male counterparts, and proposes their insertion into the Latin American literary canon. In López González's next work, *Espiral parece un círculo* (Spirals Look Like Circles) she overcomes issues of the canon. Instead, she conceptualizes a theoretical bridge between structuralist and feminist literary theory (combining Tzvetan Todorov and Julia Kristeva) that she calls the *visión del mundo* (world-vision), and applies it to her analysis of Rosario Castellanos' prose. Later, in her syntheses of the essays generated from the conferences on Chicana and Mexican women's literature, we begin to see a common theme in her interpretive framework—that of historicizing female subjectivity as a method for reading women's literature. The results of her development of a Latin American feminist literary critical apparatus are most clearly expressed in her introduction to the PIEM's collection *Sin imágenes falsas* ... (1995).

López González develops her theory and applies it to the *corpus* of Mexican women's narrative fiction in the essay "Justificación teórica: fundamentos feministas para la crítica literaria" (Theoretical Justification: The Feminist Fundamentals of Literary Criticism). In it, López González links the central element of her former analytical model for feminist writing, the *visión del mundo*, and female subjectivity's transition towards an awareness of its historically constructed gendered identity. In addition, she provides a panorama of women's consciousness-raising historical texts, proclaiming Rosario Castellanos' *La cultura femenina* (Feminine Culture) as the protofeminist Mexican work.

Using the concept of positionality, López González argues for feminist literary criticism's goals of teasing out underlying tensions between the discourses that result from women's different historico-cultural positions: discourses of femininity, and feminine and feminist discourses. Most notably, she cites other Latin American feminist studies (by Marcela Lagarde, Mabel Burin, Linda Alcoff) in addition to looking towards European interpretive modes and those generated in the US. She adapts the latter to the particular Mexican context reworking, for example, Elaine Showalter's categorization of women's writing (that of canonical imitation, protest and denunciation, and the search for self-expression). Using the terminology *colonizado* [colonized], *panfletario* [cheaply demagogic], and *auténtico* [autonomous], López González attempts to distinguish Mexican women writers' doubly marginal position due to their nation's colonial experience and search for independence.

Her well-structured and documented argument has provided many feminist literary scholars with essential tools for analysis since the book's publication. The essay was written during a period of profound change in the study of literature and culture. Poststructural and postcolonial theory, replacing the neo-Marxist criticism most popular in the Latin American academy, took hold among critics suspicious of Western postmodernism as the fall of the Berlin Wall popularized the notion of the end of history's grand narratives and the crisis of the Cartesian subject. While López González's earlier work was criticized for privileging this "theoretical moment" over a concrete poetic analysis of literary work (Perus), her attempts to employ a new logic in theorizing feminine subjectivity and feminist literary expression reflect a broader interdisciplinary trend in the study of Latin American culture. For example, in tackling the problematic relationship between texts and their contexts (fiction vs. "reality") in order to incorporate feminism's political commitment to a feminist literary criticism, López González's work parallels that of the Chileans Nelly Richard and Lucía Guerra-Cunningham, who also turn to history, philosophy, and social theory in their search for a legitimized voice for women and their literature.

López González's exploration of the relationship between theory and writing, highly important to defining and legitimizing women's literature, is the hallmark of her contributions to Latin American culture. It underlies a fundamental conviction articulated in her work: that writing (about) women's literature creates a body of knowledge. Indeed, the typology she has developed for women's narrative fiction in Mexico transformed the country's literary historiography. Centered on the construction, representation, and specific location of different female protagonists in Mexican novels written by women, her categorization has been used as a structural apparatus for more extensive cultural studies on the historical construction of feminine subjectivity in Mexico (see Meza Márquez 2000, for example). In addition, her interpretations have been debated and used as a point of departure for further study (see essays in Domenella 2001 and Ibsen 1997). Moreover, her creative writing adds to the body of contemporary Latin American fiction that incorporates many different discursive forms (popular, scientific, theoretical) shaping, in many ways, our subsequent study of its evolution and meaning.

Creative Writing

López González has written both poetry and fiction. Her early prose was not well received by critics in Mexico, perhaps due to the fact that it was an oddity—published much before the "boom" of Mexican women writers and feminist criticism in the mid to late 1980s. Her first novel, *Novela para una carta* (1975, A Novel for a Letter) is just that: a novel written so that López González could communicate with her children to whom she was denied access for some years. The narrative voice's stream of consciousness prevails, indicating that her thoughts take precedence over elements of plot or setting. Instead, the narrator sends us to a series of appendices (one being the legal discourse surrounding her divorce and battle for her children) that "clarify" the narrative material. Embedded in the very middle of the book (Chapter 10 out of the twenty short vignettes), are two letters from the narrator's children and the narrator's response. This formal and stylistic experiment is the creative manifestation of the multiple discourses López González would conceptualize theoretically fifteen years later.

Her second novel, *Sema o las voces* (1987, Sema or the Voices) is another experimental novel. In it, López González parodies form—from genre as form to the most minimal element of linguistic form, the morpheme. Through the narrator's non-chronological stream of conscious discourse, the protagonist Sema searches for her identity. The title suggests the ambivalent relationship between meaning (the Greek root "sema," sign, of semantics) and discourse, or the voices that manipulate the signs from which we gain understanding of our identities. The protagonist's search coincides with the narrator's simultaneous deconstruction of ideological, sociological, and psychoanalytic discourses that attempt to explain human identity, as well as the very same narratological discourses that form her protagonist's identity. Deserving of further scholarly analysis is the author's creative use of a wide range of the most important theoretical discourses that attempt to explain twentieth-century human behavior and literary creation. Published before the surge of postmodern theory and critical analysis, López González's second novel can be considered not only a precursor to the recent boom of women's writing in Mexico, but also as forming part of Mexican postmodern prose.

El agua en estas telas (1996, The Water through these Cloths), López González's most mature collection of poems, can be read as a poetic self-portrait. The book is separated into three parts. The first, consisting of fifteen numbered poems, contains different themes in the poetic voice's experience such as love, loss, and language's (in)capacity to express illegible silences. The second, ". . . Y en el pretil de un puente" (And on the Bridge's Parapet), juxtaposes the image of the world on the edge with those of poetic contemplation, while the third, "Cicatrices" (Scars), explores the relationship between the simultaneous presence and absence of metaphorical wounds. López González's poetry is frequently dedicated to César Vallejo and the idea of pushing language beyond images in order to create a universe of expression.

López González's key role in feminist literary studies in Mexico is relatively well known. Her creative work, rich in formal experimentation, remains to be more fully explored. It mirrors her critical objective of deconstructing the historically gendered and engendering discourses establishing female identity. Her body of work will only grow in importance as the convergence between literature and theory becomes fundamental to the advancement of Latin American cultural studies.

BARBARA D. RIESS

Selected Works

Novela para una carta. México: Ediciones El Tucán de Virginia, 1975.

De la intimidad a la acción: la narrativa de escritores latinoamericanas y su desarrollo. México, D.F.: Universidad Autónoma Metropolitana, Unidad Iztapalapa, Dirección de Ciencias Sociales y Humanidades, Departamento de Filosofía, Area de Literatura y Lingüística, 1985.

Sema o las voces. México: Ediciones El Tucán de Virginia, 1987.

La espiral parece un círculo: la narrativa de Rosario Castellanos. Análisis de *Oficio de tinieblas y Album de familia*. México, D.F.: Universidad Autónoma Metropolitana, Unidad Iztapalapa, División de Ciencias Sociales y Humanidades, 1991.

"Nuevas formas de ser mujer en la narrativa contemporánea de escritoras mexicanas". *Casa de las Américas* 31:183 (1991): 3–8.

Mujer y literatura mexicana y chicana: culturas en contacto. Edited by Aralia López- González, Amelia Malagamba, and Elena Urrutia. Mexico City: Colegio de México, Programa Interdisciplinario de Estudios de la Mujer. Tijuana, B.C., México: Colegio de la Frontera Norte, 1988. Vol. 2, 1991.

"Quebrantos, búsquedas y azares de una pasión nacional: Dos décadas de narrativa mexicana: 1970–90". *Revista iberoamericana* 59(164–5) (1993): 659–85.

Sin imágenes falsas, sin falsos espejos: narradoras mexicanas del siglo XX. Ed. Aralia López González. México, D.F.: Colegio de México, Programa Interdisciplinario de Estudios de la Mujer, 1995.

El agua en estas telas. México: Editorial Praxis, 1996.

Cercanías y barcos. Colección: La hoja murmurante, Separata de Arte Libertario, 262. México: La tinta del Alcatraz, 1997.

Un país sin invierno. México: Editorial Praxis, 1998.

References and Further Reading

Bradu, Fabienne. "Algunas reflexiones sobre la crítica feminista". *Literatura mexicana* 2(2) (1991): 471–80.

Domenella, Ana Rosa (ed.) *Territorio de leonas. Cartografía de narradoras mexicanas en los noventa.* Mexico: UAM, Iztapalapa, 2001.

Ibsen, Kristine (ed.) *The Other Mirror. Women's Narrative in Mexico, 1980–1995.* Westport, CT: Greenwood Press, 1997.

Meza Márquez, Consuelo. *La utopia feminista. Quehacher literario de cuatro narradoras mexicanas contemporáneas.* Mexico: Universidad Autónoma de Aguascalientes, 2000.

Perus, Franciose. "Sobre la narrativa de Rosario Castellanos y *La espiral parece un círculo* de A. López". *Nueva Revista Filológica Hispánica* 39(2) (1991): 1083–95.

LUFT, LYA

Lya Luft was born in the southern Brazilian state of Rio Grande do Sul in 1938. She is primarily of German heritage and was raised in a predominantly German community. Luft's early writings were poems and short stories. Her academic background is in letters and she was a professor of literature for a time. Her fiction career really began after a near fatal car crash in 1979. After recovering from this terrifying accident, she decided to be bold in her writing and to take on subjects that she had ignored or avoided previously.

The literature of Brazilian writer Lya Luft epitomizes the search for the feminine self. Her works also reveal an understanding of the patriarchal culture and the role of dominant women within that paradigm. With her newfound feminine voice, Luft began creating female protagonists who are generally involved in a quest for a sense of identity, independent from the constraints placed upon them by the symbolic order. The author portrays the conflicts and sense of enclosure the woman suffers as she searches for her female identity and her feminine voice. Susan Canty Quinlan has explained that Luft's characters construct identities that are inextricably linked one to another. Each female protagonist is somehow tied to the others ("Mutatis Mundis," pp. 168–9).

Fear and unhappiness force Luft's protagonists into a world controlled by suspicion and self-doubt. They become concerned with their quest for happiness, which to them involves love, security, and overcoming their self-hatred. The women in Luft's novels seek stronger and self-reliant identities. They feel an overwhelming need for an identity that will give them worth and freedom in their lives. Quinlan says that they are constantly forced to face ghosts from their pasts. This contributes to the sense of mystical realism that one gets from Luft's narratives ("Mutatis Mundis," p. 169).

Because the Brazilian woman as a whole is locked into the patriarchal structure, she is often looked upon and described as a psychologically fragmented being. The feminine is viewed as unstable and is denied by patriarchal society, which insists upon stability and certainties. Luft's version of feminine identity is unstable because of its multiplicity, which is defined by a constant process of becoming. Luft's protagonists resist or question pre-established notions of an essential nature or a stable, fixed identity for themselves. Each character is afflicted by multiplicity and self-contradiction because of different self-representations of gender, race, class and culture.

For example, in *A asa esquerda do anjo* (1981, The Left Wing of the Angel), the protagonist Gisela feels herself divided between two countries, Germany and Brazil. This is noted in the confusion surrounding the pronunciation of her name: "Am I Guisela or Gisela? My mother pronounced it Gisela, but the rest of the family said Guisela, the German way, which I hated" (p. 21). She finds herself torn between the two cultures, often thinking that she is not a part of either. This internal division becomes an obstructive force in her quest for her own separate identity and for true happiness in her life.

Luft's female protagonists rarely have a strong, positive, feminine presence in their lives. It is often difficult for them to bestow tenderness and affection on others. For example, a domineering matriarchal character appears in *A asa esquerda do anjo*. She is the grandmother of Gisela and is described as having many strong masculine and dominating character traits. The grandmother's name is Frau Wolf and she is of German descent. Frau Wolf tries her best to maintain complete control of her immediate family's lives: "Frau Wolf controlled the entire family" (p. 18). The grandmother would have Sunday dinners where everyone was required to speak only in German. With the exception of the grandmother, everyone else in the family was Brazilian. The use of the German language was her means of control: "They were family get-togethers, but always under the direction of Frau Wolf, who controlled everyone with a certain look and gave her opinion on everything and no one could argue with her" (p. 19).

In Luft's texts, the dominating figure presents itself in the form of the father, mother, husband, lover or son. The patriarchal figure causes the female protagonist to take on situations that push her to her limits. An example of this is found in *Exílio* (1994, The Red House), when the Doutora describes her constant turmoil and pain caused by a past filled with loss, and a husband and his infidelities. She is driven to abandon her own home and only child because of her husband's constant unfaithfulness. Yet at the end of the novel, she forces herself to return home. She sees her return to the strictures of marriage as the only way to participate in the raising of her son. Whatever the origin of the constraint or entrapment, it is shown to be inevitable due to the limited alternatives available to the female in the patriarchal society. Giovanni Pontiero explains in the Translator's Note that the work is "a claustrophobic limbo of decadence and degradation where the female protagonist feels herself being drained and contaminated".

Another example of the imposition of the patriarchal order is from *A asa esquerda do anjo* (The Left Wing of the Angel) and is found in a creature described as a kind of "worm" to which the protagonist gives birth. Gisela exhausts all of her strength in giving birth to this parasite. The image of this internalized worm is shown to be responsible for Gisela's major problems in life. She feels that once she has rid herself of this filthy creature that has been living inside of her for so many years, she can define a purpose for her life. Gisela feels that she must free herself of the parasite before she is able to establish her own identity.

Luft's protagonists even mirror the author's personal experience. In *O quarto fechado* (The Island of the Dead), McClendon and Craige explain in the Translator's Note that Ella, "who because of an accident that paralyzed her long ago has rotted in the closed room for thirty years as a huge mass of flesh, unable to speak, attended by Mother". Ella is locked in a small room and ignored by everyone around her, except her mother who cares for her as one might care for a caged pet. Luft's use of the accident victim is largely autobiographical.

Luft's personal experience in a near fatal car accident is what spawned her literary genius and allowed her to experiment with her thought processes and writing style.

Because of Luft's tragic female protagonists, her works have been popular subjects of psychological study. Pontiero explains in the Translator's Note to *The Red House*, "Morbid realities and humiliating discoveries are expressed with disarming honesty and vigor. Lya Luft's perceptions about existence and its traumas are articulated with chilling frankness".

Several of Luft's works are available in English translation and a number have been translated into German and Italian. Luft was the recipient of the best novel award from the Associação de Críticos de Arte de São Paulo in 1996 for *O rio do meio*.

BRYAN L. KENNEDY AND LOIDA PEREIRA PETERSON

Selected Works

Poetry

Canções de limiar. Porto Alegre: Instituto Estadual do Livro, Divisão de Cultura, Secretaria de Educação e Cultura, 1967.
Flauta doce. Porto Alegre: Sulina, 1972.
Mulher no palco: poemas. Rio de Janeiro: Salamandra, 1984.
Secreta mirada. São Paulo: Editora Mandarim, 1997.
Histórias do tempo. São Paulo: Editora Mandarim, 2000.

Novels and short stories

Matéria de cotidiano. Porto Alegre: GRAFOSUL/IEL, 1978.
As parceiras. Rio de Janeiro: Editora Nova Fronteira, 1980.
A asa esquerda do anjo. Rio de Janeiro: Nova Fronteira, 1981.
Reunião da família. Rio de Janeiro: Nova Fronteira, 1982.
O quarto fechado. Rio de Janeiro: Nova Fronteira, 1984.
The Left Wing of the Angel. (1985) limited printing, out of print and rare (translation of *A asa esquerda do anjo*).
The Island of the Dead. Trans. Carmen Chaves McClendon and Betty Jean Craige. Athens, GA: Georgia University Press, 1986 (translation of *O quarto fechado*).
Exílio. Rio de Janeiro: Editora Guanabara, 1987.
Lado fatal. Rio de Janeiro: Rocco, 1988.
Sentinela. São Paulo: Editora Siciliano, 1994.
The Red House. Giovanni Pontiero. Manchester: Carcanet, 1994 (translation of *Exílio*).
O rio do meio. São Paulo: Editora Mandarim, 1996.
O ponto cego. Rio de Janeiro: Record, 1999.
Mar de dentro. Rio de Janeiro: Record, 2000.
Perdas e ganhos. Rio de Janeiro: Record, 2003.
Pensar é transgredir. Rio de Janeiro: Record, 2004.
Para não dizer adeus. Rio de Janeiro: Record, 2005.

Children's literature

Histórias de bruxa boa. Rio de Janeiro: Record, 2004.

References and Further Reading

Bueno, Eva Paulino. "Maternidade, mito e ideologia na ficção de Lya Luft". *Revista Iberoamericana* 66(192) (July–Sept. 2000): 601–16.
Costa, Maria Osana de Medeiros. *A mulher, o lúdico e o grotesco em Lya Luft*. Rio de Janeiro: Annablume, 1996.
Duarte, Constância Lima. "Lya Luft e a identidade feminine". In Sylvia Maria von Atzingen Venturoli Auad (ed.), *Mulher: Cinco Séculos de Desenvolvimento na América: Capítulo Brasil*. Belo Horizonte: Federação Internacional de Mulheres da Carreira Jurídica, 1999, pp. 391–6.
Payne, Judith A. "Lya Luft: Fiction and the Possible Selves". *Brasil/Brazil: Revista de Literatura Brasileira/A Journal of Brazilian Literature* 5(4) (1991): 104–14.
Peterson, Loida Pereira. "The Feminine Condition in the Prose of Lya Luft". MA Thesis. University of North Carolina Chapel Hill, 1996.
Quinlan, Susan C. *The Female Voice in Contemporary Brazilian Narrative*. New York: Peter Lang, 1991.
——. "Mutatis Mundis: a evolução da obra de Lya Luft". In Peggy Sharpe (ed.), *Entre Resistir e Identificar-se: Para uma Teoria da Prática da Narrativa Brasileira de Autoria Feminina*. Goiânia: UFG, 1997, pp. 167–83.
Sadlier, Darlene (ed.) *One Hundred Years After Tomorrow: Brazilian Women's Fiction in the 20th Century*. Bloomington, IN: Indiana University Press, 1992, pp. 215–27.

LUGO FILIPPI, CARMEN

Carmen Lugo Filippi (b. 1940) spent her childhood and teenage years in Ponce, Puerto Rico, her hometown. At a very young age she became acquainted with Peninsular and Latin American literature. She started exploring the field of writing short romantic stories in her teen-years after reading writers such as Benito Pérez Galdós, Armando Palacio Valdés, Julio Verne, Victor Hugo and Flaubert. She graduated from the University of Puerto Rico at Río Piedras with a degree in French Literature. Afterward she obtained her Masters degree in French from the University of Columbia. Subsequent to her graduation she moved back to Puerto Rico where she taught French for several years at the University of Puerto Rico before traveling to France to study for her Ph.D. at the University of Toulouse. She received her doctoral degree in 1976. Her dissertation is a comparative work between the Experimental French Novel and the New Latin American Novel.

Carmen Lugo Filippi belongs to the so-called generation of the 1970s in Puerto Rico. Her literary work as well as the works by Puerto Rican authors such as Luis Rafael Sánchez (1936–), Ana Lydia Vega (1946–), Magali García Ramis (1946–), Manuel Ramos Otero (1948–), Rosario Ferré (1938–) among others, innovate with new literary devices, themes and humor. The generation of the 1970s starts using inter-textuality and mixes foreign, local and regional vocabulary. They proclaim themselves to be against the patriarchal narrative of the previous writers and become more independent with their writings. It is relevant to note that most of the writers of this generation are women. Lugo Filippi as well as her compatriots Rosario Ferré, Ana Lydia Vega, and Magali García Ramis start portraying women in a different way from how they were portrayed by previous generations, mainly by male writers.

As a member of this generation, Lugo Filippi, in her narrative, re-appropriates women's roles to revalorize them. For instance, in two of her short stories "Recetario de incautos" and "Pilar tus rizos" published in the book *Vírgenes and mártires*, she presents the idea of the re-creation of the female character to raise the intensity of women's reflections on their role. The protagonists, who represent any woman trapped in the house, change their environment through their imagination to rebel against the traditional stereotypes created by the patriarchy in Puerto Rican society. Her female characters think and react in a revolutionary way. Therefore her themes embrace a feminism that supports the destruction of the patriarchy in Puerto Rican society. In the short stories "Milagros, calle Mercurio" and "Con llave digo basta," Lugo Filippi presents the idea of transcending the stereotypes of the submissive woman. The characters act in response to their oppression caused by the patriarchal traditions for women and take action to find their own way of surviving.

With her first publication, "Pilar, tus rizos," she won an award from the literary magazine *Sin Nombre* in 1976. In 1977, she published "Recetario de incautos" and in 1979 with the short story "Adiestrados ya los pies en la carrera," she won honorary mention in the contest for satirical literature organized by the newspaper *Claridad*. In 1981, her first book of short stories "*Vírgenes and mártires*" was published. "*Vírgenes and mártires*" is a book that she worked on with another famous female Puerto Rican writer, Ana Lydia Vega. In the 1980s she published her first essays in the newspaper *Claridad*. These essays were recompiled and published in *El tramo al ancla* by the University of Puerto Rico in 1988. A study on Latin American short stories by several Puerto Rican female writers, *Los cuentistas y el cuento: encuesta entre cultivadores* was published in 1991 and it was reprinted and updated as a second edition in 1997. Her first novel, *Narromaniando con Mirta o, no me platiques más* was published in 1999 by Isla Negra. This novel embraces the idea of reviving the *bolero caribeño*. The lyrics of this kind of song help to create an environment of love and mystery. Regarding the translation of her work, some of her short stories such as "Milagros, calle Mercurio" and "Recetario de incautos" have been translated into English as well as in French. Other stories such as "Pilar, tus rizos" and "Tic-tac" have been translated into English.

Lugo Filippi's literature, in general, reveals topics related to the lives of women. She creates stories of loving, abandoned and abused women. Her female characters, in order to transform their oppressive lives, develop, throughout her stories, a feminist conscience. Her work is full of autobiographical details that show characteristics of Caribbean life of past decades when *boleros* were in style and everybody used to dance and sing them. Her narrative tries hard to stay close to the reality of the Puerto Ricans of her times. Her work criticizes the male-oriented society and shows her didactic interests. She parodies the trouble of racism and the bourgeoisie in Puerto Rico. She attempts to motivate her readers to change the traditional patterns that oppress underprivileged groups, most frequently women. The labor of studying her literature is not that of reducing her work to a just one matter in Puerto Rican society but rather to recognize and to learn about several aspects that define it. Her narrative offers an analytical interpretation of the constructive process of searching for an identity.

As a number of studies have shown, Lugo Filippi's discourse proposes an appreciation of Puerto Rican culture. It points out the development of cultural awareness. Her work on old *boleros*, or typical food from Puerto Rico, for example, is not an act of just missing the old times but it aims to restore all the necessary pieces to preserve the uniqueness of Puerto Rican Society in past decades. On the other hand, critics have agreed that Lugo Filippi parodies Puerto Rican life from different perspectives; she combines the power of eroticism with humor to suggest that entering the world through women's imagination is a way of breaking the established rules in society for women. However, neither in theory nor in practice is her intention to preserve the old-fashioned way of being of Puerto Rican society. Her work only teaches us to think and to affirm that a society must always keep what constructs their own space and voice for marginalized individuals.

In addition to her literary work and her teaching of French and literature at the University of Puerto Rico, Lugo Filippi has studied the literary work by the Puerto Rican writer Ramón Emeterio Betances, known as the father of the Puerto Rican independence movement. She has translated several of Betance's short stories and poetry.

Nowadays Carmen Lugo Filippi lives in Puerto Rico with her husband, the writer Pedro Juan Soto. She has been retired from the University of Puerto Rico since 1996. However, she continues writing and teaching and always has something relevant to share with her students as well as her readers.

DOLORES FLORES-SILVA

References and Further Reading

González-Hernández, Miriam M. "Conciencia y revalorización neofeminista de la cuentística de Carmen Lugo Filippi y Ana Lydia Vega". *Dissertation Abstracts Internacional* 55(8) (1995 Feb), 2413A.

Horno-Delgado, Asunción. "Voyerismo, peinetas y otros rizos paródicos: La narrativa de Carmen Lugo Filippi". *Explicación de Textos Literarios* 24(1–2) (1995–96): 81–90.

Nuñez-Miranda, Armando. "Carmen Lugo Filippi o las fronteras de la plenitud". *Detrás de la mirada.* San Juan: Ediciones Callejón, 2000.

Rodríguez-Luis, Julio. "De Puerto Rico a Nueva Cork: Protagonistas femeninas en busca de un espacio propio". *La Torre: Revista de la Universidad de Puerto Rico* 7(27–8) (1993): 577–94.

Santiago-Stommes, Ivelisse. "Entre el humor y la crítica social: Cultura popular e ironía en un relato de Ana Lydia Vega y Carmen Lugo Filippi". *Diáspora: Journal of the Annual Afro-Hispanic Literature and Culture Conference* 11 (2001): 45–51.

Santos Silva, Loreina. "Cuatro selecciones por una peseta: Patrones del sexismo machista". *Revista/Review Interamericana* 12(4) (1982–83 Winter): 515–20.

Torres, Víctor Federico. "Carmen Lugo Filippi." Narradores Puertorriqueños del 70. Puerto Rico: Editorial Plaza Mayor, 2001.

Umpierre, Luz María. "Incitaciones lesbianas en 'Milagros, calle Mercurio' de Carmen Lugo Filippi". *Revista Iberoamericana* 59(162–3) (1993): 309–16.

Wallace, Jeanne C. "Social Criticism in the Contemporary Short Story of Selected Puerto Rican Women Writers". *MACLAS: Latin American Essays* 3 (1989): 113–23.

LYNCH, MARTA

Marta Lynch (1925–85), born in Buenos Aires, Argentina (original name Mirta Lía Frigerio de Lynch), was one of the most important and talented Argentinian writers in the second half of the twentieth century.

A novelist, short story writer, journalist and television personality, Lynch also wrote newspaper articles for *La Nación*, *Clarín* and *Gente y Claudia* in which she presented her political and feminist ideas to Argentinian readers.

Lynch married Juan Manuel Lynch, a middle-class lawyer ten years her senior when she was only 17 years old. They had three children together. She enrolled at the University of Buenos Aires in 1952 where she studied liberal arts. Lynch became a member of the political party La Unión Civil Intransigente and claimed to be a socialist. She also belonged to a group of writers called "parricidals" formed during Juan

Perón's government. This group, all of whom wrote in neorealist style, focused on the conflicts of generations of their time as well as restrictive gender roles in a variety of social and political domains. The theme of Lynch's literary work reflects the new vision of the world presented by "parricidals" filtered through the internal reality of their characters. Lynch hoped for the return of Perón but also supported Raúl Alfonsín, subsequently the Argentinean president until 1989. Her critics accused her of political vacillation because Lynch did not condemn either the armed forces or the leftists. However, she searched for the middle ground in Argentina, what she called "esa tercera posición que en realidad es la posición de la justicia y libertad" [that third position which really is the position of truth and liberty].

Marta Lynch wrote thirteen novels and collections of short stories; they were translated into Croatian, French, Italian, English, German, Norwegian, Portuguese, Russian and Swedish. She travelled extensively in Europe and the United States of America, received numerous invitations to lecture in Chile, Peru and Germany and lived in Lima, Peru for five–six months on several occasions. In *Apuntes para un libro de viajes* (1978, Notes for a Travel Book), a reminiscence of her travels, Lynch hoped to capture the spirit of the people and the essence of the culture of the countries she had lived in.

Lynch admitted that Ernesto Sábato, David Viñas, Ernest Hemingway, F. Scott Fitzgerald, William Faulkner, John Dos Passos, Virginia Woolf and Alfonsina Storni all had an influence on her novelistic techniques including flashbacks, interior monologues and the use of colloquial expressions in her novels.

One of the most notable facts in Lynch's life was her preoccupation with aging. She would never reveal her date of birth or her age; her fear of aging, her fear of losing the power to attract men and be at the centre of attention ended tragically when she committed suicide just as her last novel *No te duermas, no me dejes* (1985, Don't Go to Sleep, Don't Leave Me) became a best-seller in Argentina. Her obituary appeared on the front pages of *La Nación*, the most influential newspaper in Buenos Aires, in *El País* in Spain which also published an article about her life. Her photograph appeared on the cover of the periodicals *Somos*, *Fama* and *Gente*. After her death her husband revealed that Marta had been under psychiatric care for years and she had talked about committing suicide on numerous occasions in the last eight years of her life.

Lynch has been recognized for her innovative ability to make fiction "her best vehicle to express the condition of the Argentine woman in the world dominated by male power and fantasy". In her narrative, Lynch pinpoints the oppressive dimensions of the roles historically assigned to women. She considers herself a feminist and states that the emancipation of women depends upon external factors (cultural, social and historical) as well as the interior freedom of women. Lynch also admitted that everything she wrote had the social and political reality of Argentina as its backdrop.

She refused to publish *La luz sobre el espejo* (Light above the Mirror) and *Después del verano* (After the Summer) as she considered them "superfluous". In her novels, Lynch fuses the social and political issues of her time. *La alfombra roja* (1954, The Red Carpet) won her the Fabril Prize in 1962. *El vencedor* (1965, To the Victor) and *Los cuentos tristes* (1967, Sad Stories) won her El Primer Premio Municipal.

In *El cruce del río* (1972, Crossing the River), *Un árbol lleno de manzanas* (1973, A Tree Laden with Apples), events are seen through the eyes of the male protagonists. Lynch captures the spirit of the male world of politics where power and prestige are the desired goal. Lynch also wrote three articles about the condition of women: "La mujer y su mundo" (A Woman and her World), "La mujer y los hombres" (A Woman and Men), and "La mujer y el hijo adolescente" (A Woman and her Adolescent Son), all published in *Claudia* in 1974.

Major Works

Lynch considered her novel *Un árbol lleno de manzanas* to be her best work. She said that she became a writer, found her own language, her own style and way of expression writing this novel. However, it was *La señora Ordóñez* (1967, Mrs Ordóñez) that brought Lynch her well-deserved fame and success. Five editions were published in 1967 alone and it was also edited for television in 1984. The narrative presents the female character Bianca Maggi at the age of 20, then the experiences that influence her formative process until she reaches 40 years of age. Her life is a struggle with gender and the molding of a woman by Argentinian society. Bianca Ordóñez deals with the problems of middle age and her middle-class environment. The novel has a circular action and the reader is led by the interwoven threads of different phases of Bianca's past life: her childhood, her first marriage and her second marriage to urologist Raúl Ordóñez. The author uses the present tense when referring to the recent past of Bianca's realization that her affair with her young lover, Rocky, is over. Half of the novel is narrated in the first person, thereby revealing Bianca's private and political views while the other half, narrated in the third person, completes the story. Sra Ordóñez is obsessed with aging; mirrors show her physical deterioration and, in turn, show the deteriorating state of Argentina. Bianca believes that marriage is the only solution to her solitude and financial insecurity. Sra Ordónez' fears of aging stem from the importance that society gives to a woman's physical attractiveness (very often associated with power). Lynch uses historical background to emphasize the exclusion of women from the public sphere.

Critics of the author's works claim that *La señora Ordóñez* conceals autobiographical elements from Marta Lynch's life. However, Lynch claimed that Sra Ordóñez was a fictional character. Despite the haunting presence of Perón in the narrative, the reader is sympathetic to the universal, existential yearning of a middle-aged, alienated woman who wants to alter her identity but is subordinated to the social canons of her age. Amy Kaminsky concludes that by exploring Bianca's motivations, her needs, her solitude, Lynch has performed a revolutionary act in literature. Naomi Linstrom provides a valuable analysis of construction of gender and determining gender roles as depicted in "Señora".

La Penúltima Versión de la Colorada Villanueva (1978, The Penultimate Version of Colorada Villanueva) was well received, even by the most persistent critics of Lynch's narrative. The relationships between personal and political spheres in the characters' lives, and the relationships between mothers and daughters are explored in depth and with a great sophistication in the character of Colorada. While Señora Ordóñez was not able to love and share, Colorada gives too much of herself to her children and to her husband. It is Fernando (obsessed with growing old), who abandons all his responsibilities when he leaves Argentina for political reasons. Colorada pretends that her marriage is still alive. Her life revolves around daydreams of their past and of their future, and is enhanced by the romantic letters she still receives from Fernando. Upon receiving a letter from her husband asking her for a permanent separation, Colorada finds a lover, Alejandro, who mirrors Fernando's lack of commitment and responsibility. Colorada eventually gives up hope of rejoining her husband and finally becomes aware of her life alone. In discussing the reversed roles and the treatment of the male characters in *La Colorada*, Gwendolyn Díaz noted that both masculine characters are assigned traditionally female qualities in the novel: beauty and passivity. In addition, in *La Colorada*, the prevailing political situation causes the weak family structure to disintegrate completely.

In *Informe bajo llave* (1983, Report under Lock and Key), the protagonist, Adela, lives in her obsessive world of preserving youth, of beauty and of men. On the advice of her psychiatrist, she writes a diary and records her encounter with Vargas, who became her obsession even though he is not attractive physically or in any other way. Adela does not love him, but her sexual obsession leads her to neglect her 11-year-old son. She is only 28 years old but she fears aging and eventually she disappears and is proclaimed to be "desaparecida" (one of the disappeared). Lynch states that her novel is an allegory about a country under a dictatorship.

Lynch's last work *No te duermas, no me dejes* (1985, Don't Go to Sleep, Don't Leave Me) also focuses on love but it celebrates married life and fidelity lasting a lifetime. In this sense, it differs from the rest of Lynch's short stories that include the dark side of our existence. Alfonsina Storni, whom Lynch admired, sent a poem to *La Nación* with a similar title *Voy a dormir* (I am going to sleep). Just like Lynch, she also committed suicide in 1985 at the peak of her career.

According to literary critic Ernest Lewald, the male–female relationships in Lynch's works are a reflection of Argentine cultural identity where men cannot approach women on anything other than a sexual basis, equating sex with virility and love with weakness. Lewald has also drawn attention to the strong component of sex role analysis in Lynch's works.

Marta Lynch is one of the most successful writers in Argentina. She is an innovative author of love themes (eroticism, maternity, beauty); her female characters, although placed in the political and social reality of Buenos Aires, have universal significance in their existential solitude. However, her novels have not yet received the acclaim they deserve in other countries.

ANNA HAMLING

Selected Works

La alfombra roja. Buenos Aires: Fabril, 1962.
El vencedor. Buenos Aires: Losada, 1965.
Crónicas de la burguesía. Buenos Aires: J. Alvárez, 1965.
Los cuentos tristes. Buenos Aires: Centro Editor de América Latina, 1967.
La señora Ordoñez. Buenos Aires: Jorge Alvárez, 1968.
Cuentos de colores. Buenos Aires: Sudamericana, 1970.
El cruce del río. Buenos Aires: Sudamericana, 1972.
Un árbol lleno de manzanas. Buenos Aires: Sudamericana, 1973.
Los dedos de la mano. Buenos Aires: Sudamericana, 1976.
La penúltima versión de la Colorada Villanueva. Buenos Aires: Sudamericana, 1978.
Los años de fuego. Buenos Aires: Sudamericana, 1980.
Toda la función. Buenos Aires: Editorial Abril, 1982.
Informe bajo llave. Buenos Aires: Sudamericana, 1983.
Páginas de Marta Lynch seleccionadas por la autora. Buenos Aires: Celtia, 1983.
Apuntes para un libro de viajes. Buenos Aires: Cástor y Póllux, 1978.
No te duermas, no me dejes. Buenos Aires: Sudamericana, 1985.

References and Further Reading

Bennet, Bernice Lynne. "Narrative structure in the Novels of Marta Lynch". PhD diss. University of California, 1981 (DAI 42 [1981]: 1169A).
Birkemoe, Diane S. "The Virile Voice of Marta Lynch". *Revista de Estudios Hispánicos* 16(2) (1982): 191–211.
Díaz, Gwendolyn Jossie. "Images of Heroine: Development of the Female Character in the Novels of Beatriz Guido, Marta Lynch, Sylvia Poletti". PhD diss. University of Texas, 1981 (DAI 42 [1981]:3174A).
Foster, David William. "Raping Argentina: Marta Lynch's *Informe bajo llave* de Marta Lynch". *The Centennial Review* 35–7 (1991): 663–80.
Kaminsky, Amy. "The Real Circle of Iron". *Latin American Literary Review* 9 (1976): 77–86.
Lambright, Anne. "History, Gender and Unsuccessful Revolutions in Mara Lynch's *La Señora Ordónez*". *Hispanofila* 134 (2002): 105–38.
Layera, Ramón. "Marta Lynch: *La penúltima versión de la Colorada Villanueva*". *Revista de la Crítica Literaria Latinoamericana* 13 (1981): 142–6.
Lindstrom, Naomi. "The Literary Feminism of Marta Lynch". *Critique: Studies in Modern Fiction* 20 (1978): 49–58.
Lewald, Ernest H. "Aspects of the Modern Argentine Woman". *Chasqui* 5(3) (1976) 24–30.
Manuel, Alberto, trans. "Latin Lover". In Alberto Manuel (ed.), *Other Fires: Short Fiction by Latin American Women*. New York: Clarkson Potter, 1986, pp. 32–41.
Paley de Francescato, Martha. "Entrevista a Marta Lynch". *Hispanoamérica* 10 (1975): 33–44
Vance, Brigitta, "Nice Guy". *Shenandoah* 32(2) (1981): 105–11.
——. (trans.) "Hotel Taormina". In Doris Meyer and Margarite Fernández Olmos (eds), *Contemporary Women Authors of Latin America: New Translations*. Brooklyn, NY: Brooklyn College Press, 1983, pp. 194–204.
——. "Marta Lynch". In Diane E. Marting (ed.), *Spanish American Women Writers: A Bio-Bibliographical Source Book*. New York: Greenwood Press, 1990, pp. 292–302.

M

MACHADO, GILKA DA COSTA MELLO

Gilka da Costa Mello (1893–1980) is considered the precursor of erotic women's poetry in Brazil. She was born on March 12, 1893, in Rio de Janeiro, not long after the abolition of slavery (1888) and the proclamation of the republic in Brazil (1889). Her family lived in the neighborhood of Estácio de Sá, the heart of the small middle class, and all her relatives belonged to the world of art: her grandmother was a singer; her grandfather was a violinist; her mother was an actress in radio theater; and her father was a journalist and poet. She began to compose verses in school and at the age of 13 she made news by taking the three first places in a poetry contest promoted by the Rio de Janeiro newspaper, *A Imprensa*. The poems had erotic overtones very much beyond what one might imagine a young person to produce. In 1910, she married the journalist, art critic and poet Rodolpho Machado, and began signing her name as Gilka Machado. Two children were born into this marriage, Hélios and Heros Volúsia. In 1915, she published her first book. Others followed in 1917, 1918 and 1922. The first, *Cristais Partidos* (Broken Crystals), carries in its title an allusion to the book *Mármores* (Marble) by Francisca Júlia, who, at the time, was a model of women's poetry. The remaining books' suggestive titles border on the scandalous: *Estados de Alma* (States of the Soul), *Poesias* (Poems), a compilation of the first two volumes, and *Mulher Nua* (Nude Woman). At the same time, her work was also published in a number of magazines and newspapers in town. In 1923, Rodolpho Machado died, leaving her with no resources. In order to support her family, Gilka Machado opened an inn where, most of the time, she herself was the cook. At this inn, located in downtown Rio de Janeiro, which at the time was the nation's capital, politicians and poets alike frequently dined, among whom were Andrade Muricy and Tasso da Silveira. In an atmosphere in which slavery was not a very distant memory, where manual labor was considered nearly servile, and in which culinary terms were often employed to designate sexual commerce, one can comprehend the difficulties that she encountered in continuing to write and publish. In any case, through her work, Gilka Machado managed to educate her children: Hélios graduated in Law and went on to take a position as Juridical Assistant for the State of Guanabara; Heros Volúsia became a dancer, and later was appointed teacher of the National Theater Service of the Ministry of Education and Health. Under the name Eros Volúsia, she was known throughout Brazil and abroad as the creator of the *Brazilian Ballet*, based on the folklore of Brazil. In 1927, Gilka Machado was linked to the symbolist group "Festa", publishing in the magazine of the same name. The following year, she published *Meu glorioso pecado* and *O grande amor* (My Glorious Sin and Great Love), as well as *Poemas* (Poems), a compilation of these two books. In 1931, she published *Carne e Alma: Poemas escolhidos* (Flesh and Soul: Selected Poems). In 1933, in a contest promoted by the Rio de Janeiro magazine *O Malho*, she was chosen as the best poet of Brazil. In 1938, at 45 years of age, with a daughter whose dance career was at its peak, for the first time she presented a social poem, publishing *Sublimação* (Sublimation), her last book to be entirely composed of previously unpublished poems. In 1941, she accompanied her daughter on tour to the United States. As the country entered the war, Gilka Machado demanded to be repatriated, together with Eros Volúsia. In 1947, she published the anthology, *Meu rosto* (My Face), and from this moment forward abandoned the poetry scene, dedicating herself to accompanying her daughter, with whom she travelled to Europe in 1948. She only reemerged on the literary scene in 1965 with the publication of *Velha poesia* (Old Poetry), a selection of her poems followed by other previously unpublished works. Even if at this time she was little known to the larger public, Gilka Machado always maintained a certain prestige among her peers. In 1977, when the Brazilian Academy of Letters modified its statutes to allow the entrance of women, she was invited by Jorge Amado to apply for a seat that had opened, but she refused. In 1978, her *Poesias Completas* (Complete Poems) were published and in the following year, once again at the instigation of Jorge Amado, she received the Machado de Assis award from the Brazilian Academy of Letters for her lifetime work. Gilka Machado died in Rio de Janeiro on December 11, 1980. A new edition of her *Poesias Completas* was prepared by her daughter Eros Volúsia Machado and published in 1992, in commemoration of a hundred years since her birth.

Critical Looks

Considered overall, appreciation for her work was always ambiguous. In general, her first books received praise from the critics of the time. However, the erotic nature and claim for women's rights did not fail to surprise the society of Rio de Janeiro, especially as it came from a woman recognized as beautiful and allowed to publish with the consent of her husband. In their assessments of her poetry, the critics of the time wavered between poetic judgement, moral critique and the "condescending look" (Silvia Paixão, 1991) with which the work was read, and the criticism was not completely free of misogyny nor class prejudices. In the 1930s, the critics were less interested in Gilka Machado, who was only cited as part of a panel for the analysis of other authors. The reassessment of her work is due to the advent of studies on women's literary production in Brazil. In 1978, at the same time as her *Complete Poems* were published, accompanied by a beautiful critique by Fernando Py, a publication that followed the Machado de Assis award from the Brazilian Academy of Letters, Nádia Batella Gotlib and Ilma Ribeiro interviewed the poet in her Rio de Janeiro home and Pedro Lyra compared her to the Portuguese Florbela Espanca. In 1986, with the creation of the Work Group "Women and Literature" at the National Association of Postgraduate Studies and Research in Letters and Linguistics (ANPOLL), new studies emerged on the poet, for whom the hundred years since her birth was commemorated at the 5th National Seminar on "Women and Literature", held at the Universidade Federal do Rio Grande do Norte, under the coordination of Constância Lima Duarte.

Themes and Modes

The work of Gilka Machado can be divided into two phases: the first, from 1915 to 1931, contains her first five books; the second, from 1938 to 1965, groups *Sublimation*, the anthologies *My Face* and *Old Poetry*, which also contains previously unpublished poems, and *Complete Poems*.

The first phase displays the best of her poetry, the peak of which is found in the books from 1928, *My Glorious Sin* and *Great Love.* Her fundamental themes are love, liberty and the constitution of identity – themes that prove to be inextricable, for, in the poetry of Gilka Machado, the lyrical self is only aware of its characteristics and possibilities through being propelled toward the Other by its own erotic longing: "Beijas-me e todo o corpo meu gorjeia / e toda me sonho uma árvore alta / cantando aos céus, de passarinhos cheia". ("Beijas-me tanto", in OGA) [You kiss me and my entire body sings in delight, / and I imagine myself a tall tree / singing to the heavens, filled with birds]. Poetry of the senses, in her work, involves sensations that provoke feelings:

> No vestido que trago / há um macio debrum, debrum de arminho; / este vestido, em qualquer parte, / faz-me sentir-te, faz-me gozar-te / roçando-me a garganta, de mansinho, / de um modo quase etéreo, muito vago.
>
> ("Página esquecida" in MN)
>
> [In the dress I wear / there is a soft lining, lining of ermine; / this dress, in any part, / makes me feel you, makes me enjoy you / tugging at my throat, softly, / in a nearly ethereal manner, very vague]

In the second phase, with the book *Sublimation,* the poet nourishes the spirit of the rediscovery of Brazil, characteristic of the 1930s, in which her daughter Eros Volúsia develops her art. Gilka Machado turns toward the world and her desire is now sublimated, directed toward the social Other, singing about the Brazilian people, its myths, its idols, its dances and beliefs, its problems. In these poems, there are emotions and not political ideas; sentiments and not reflections; and the sensibility of the poet, free from partisan political commitments, avoids literary-political platitudes. As an example, one can cite "Alerta, Miseráveis" (Warning, Miserable Ones), which refuses paternalism and denounces the political opportunism of acute contemporaneity. In *Old Poetry,* among the previously unpublished poems presides the tone of final revision, in which bitterness and serenity alternate. The poems of this collection are simpler, not only in the motifs, vocabulary and meter, but also with regard to the sentiments they display, revealing a decanting process through which the poetry of the author has passed. In this second phase, there is the sense of bidding farewell to the body, all the more poignant when considered in the set of poetry, which in its larger and better part, precisely exalts the body and its passions: "Toda minha faceirice / e minha vaidade toda/ estão na sonora face"("O retrato fiel" in VP) [All my ostentation / and all my vanity /are in the sonorous face].

Gilka Machado emerged on the poetic scene at the crossroads of the Parnassian and symbolist esthetics, at a time that was conventionally known as pre-modernism, later adding to her work procedures of the modernist matrix. In her libertarian, non-conformist poetry, she used various poetic forms that go from the sonnet to free verse without ever straying from the cultured norms of the Portuguese language. Such stylistic choices will have certainly contributed toward the non-central place that she occupied on the Brazilian poetry scene. Indeed, in face of the pre-modernists, above all proponents of the sonnet, she was presented as "too new" due to her themes; starting in 1922, among those who from then on instituted a new poetic canon in Brazil, she appeared, because of her preferentially utilized forms and meters, as "epigonal". Later, the valuation of the erotic content of her verses was also at times hampered an overall interpretation of her work, which still awaits a just evaluation.

ELIANA BUENO-RIBEIRO

Selected Works

Cristais Partidos. Rio de Janeiro: Revista dos Tribunais, 1915.

A Revelação dos Perfumes. Rio de Janeiro: Associação dos Empregados do Comércio, 1916.

Estado de Alma. Rio de Janeiro: Revista dos Tribunais, 1917.

Poesias 1915–1917. Rio de Janeiro: Jacinto Ribeiro dos Santos, 1918, 3rd edn 1929.

Mulher Nua. Rio de Janeiro: Jacinto Ribeiro dos Santos, 1922.

O Grande Amor; amores que mentiram, que passaram. Rio de Janeiro: Livraria Azevedo-Erbas de Almeida e Cia, 1928.

Carne e Alma (poemas escolhidos). Rio de Janeiro: Civilização Brasileira, col. Benjamin Costallat, 1931.

Sonetos y Poemas de Gilka Machado. Trans. Gregorin Reynolds. Cochabamba, 1932.

Sublimação. Rio de Janeiro: Tipografia Batista de Sousa, 1938.
Meu rosto. Rio de Janeiro: Irmãos Pongetti, 1947.
Velha poesia. Rio de Janeiro: Tipografia B. de Sousa. 1965.
Poesias Completas. Rio de Janeiro: Cátedra/INL, 1978.
Poesias Completas: Gilka Machado. Rio de Janeiro: Léo Christiano Editorial/FUNARJ, 1991.
Carne e Alma. Rio de Janeiro: Civilazão Brasileira, s.d.

Participation in Collected Works

Andrade, M. de, Bandeira, M., Carvalho, R. and Machado, G. *9 Poetas Nuevos de Brasil*. Trans. Henrique Bustamante y Ballivián, 1930.

References and Further Reading

Barros, Jaime de. *Poetas do Brasil*. Rio de Janeiro: José Olympio, 1944.
Bueno-Ribeiro, E. "Gilka Machado, une poétesse". in J.-Y. Casanova, C. Dumas, and R. Forgues (eds), *Femmes en poésie. Représentations et récritures de la tradition*. Université de Pau et des Pays de l'Adour, 2002, pp. 15–26.
Campos, Humberto de. *Crítica*. 2nd series. Rio de Janeiro: Marisa Ed., 1933.
——. *Diário Secreto*. Vol. I. Rio de Janeiro: O Cruzeiro, 1954.
Carvalho Da Silva, D. *Vozes femininas da poesia brasileira*. São Paulo: Conselho Estadual de Cultura, 1959.
Castello Branco, L. "As incuráveis feridas da natureza feminina". In L. Castello Branco and R. S. Brandão (eds), *A mulher escrita*. Rio: Casa Maria Editorial, Livros Técnicos e Científicos, 1989, pp. 87–109.
Coelho, N.N. "Eros e Tanatos: a poesia feminina na Î metade do século X". In *Anais do V Seminário Nacional Mulher & Literatura*. Natal: FAPERJ/URRN, 1995.
Ferreira-Pinto, C. "La mujer y el canon poético en Brasil a principios del siglo XX: hacia una reevaluación de la poesía de Gilka Machado". Puerto Rico: La Torre 34 (April–June), pp. 221–41.
Gotlib, N. B. " Com Dona Gilka Machado, Eros pede a palavra (poesia erótica feminina brasileira nos inícios do século XX)" In *Polímica*. S. Paulo: Associação Polímica de Crítica e Criação, 4, 1982, pp. 23–47.
——. "Gilka Machado: a mulher e a poesia". In *Anais do V Seminário Nacional Mulher & Literatura*. Natal: FAPERJ/URRN, 1995.
Grieco, A. "As poetisas do segundo parnasianismo". In *Evolução da poesia brasileira. Obras completas*, 2. Rio de Janeiro: José Olympio, 1947.
Linhares, M. *Poetas esquecidos*. Rio de Janeiro: Irmãos Pongetti, 1938.
Lyra, Pedro. "Sensual, espiritual, sensual". *Jornal do Brasil, Livro* (7 April 1979): 3.
Medeiros E. Albuquerque, J.J. CC. "Gilka da Costa Machado – *Estados de Alma*." In *Páginas de crítica*. Rio de Janeiro: Leite Ribeiro & Maurillo, 1920.
Miller, Beth. "Uma reavaliação do canon poético". *Brasil/Brazil*, 1988, pp. 54–64.
Muricy, A. *Panorama do movimento simbolista brasileiro*. Rio de Janeiro: Ministério da Educação e Cultura, Departamento de Imprensa Nacional, 1952, 2 vols.
Paixao, Sílvia P. *A fala a-menos. Repressão do desejo na poesia feminina*. Rio de Janeiro: Numen, 1991.
——. "Reencontro: Gilka Machado. A fala de Eros". In *Poesia sempre*. Rio de Janeiro: Fundação Biblioteca Nacional, 1 (2), July. 1993.
——. "Mulheres em revista: a participação feminina no projeto modernista do Rio de Janeiro, anos 20". In S.B. Funck (ed.), *Trocando idéias sobre Mulher e Literatura*. Florianópolis: UFSC, 1994, pp. 421–40.
——. "Gilka Machado e a esfera pública". In *Anais do V Seminário Nacional Mulher & Literatura*. Natal: FAPERJ/URRN, 1995a.
——. "Gilka Machado e as contradições de seu tempo". In *Convergência lusíada* no. 12. Rio de Janeiro: Real Gabinete Português de Leitura, 1995b.
Py, F. "Prefácio". In G. Machado, *Poesias completas*. Rio de Janeiro: Cátedra/MEC, 1978, pp. xix–xxviii.
Queiroz, V. *Crítica literária e estratégias de gênero*. Niterói: EDUFF, 1997.
——. "Eros, o filho dileto de Gilka Machado". In *Pactos do Viver e do Escrever*. Fortaleza: 7Sóis, Editora, 2004, pp. 80–95.
Soares, A. "Presença feminina no erotismo do poema hoje". *Revista Tempo Brasileiro* 80, Rio de Janeiro: Tempo Brasileiro, 1985, pp. 31–41.
——. "A vigência de Eros no poema de autoria feminina". In A. Soares *et al.* (eds), *Perspectivas 3. Modernidades. Ensaios de teoria e crítica*. Rio de Janeiro: Faculdade de Letras da UFRJ, 1988, pp. 199–214.
——. "A consciência erótica do literário no poema de autoria feminina". In A Soares *et al.*, *Poesia, Crítica e Autocrítica*. Curitiba: Scientia et Labor, 1989, pp. 1–18.
Soffiati, A. "Gilka e Mário: dois centenários". In *Poesia Sempre* 1(2) (July 1993), Rio de Janeiro: Fundação Biblioteca Nacional.

MACHADO, MARIA CLARA

Actress, director, teacher, Maria Clara Machado (1921–2001) is considered the most important playwright for young audiences in Brazil. Children's theater emerged in Brazil in the late 1940s with the staging of Lúcia Benedetti's *O casaco encantado* (The Enchanted Overcoat) in 1948. But the true landmark came with pioneer Machado, who became a reference for the standards and expectations of children's theater in Brazil. Since 1955, with her play *Pluft, o fantasminha* (Pluft, the Little Ghost), Machado has achieved national recognition. *Pluft* has become a children's classic, staged all over the world.

Machado was born in Belo Horizonte, Minas Gerais. She was 4 years old when her parents moved to Rio de Janeiro. At the early age of 9, Machado experienced the death of her mother. In an autobiographical text Machado stated that the death of her mother haunted her throughout her life and that she was only able to "exorcise the ghost of loss" with twenty years of psychoanalysis and through her writing, especially through the plays *Pluft, o fantasminha* and *Cavalinho azul* (The Little Blue Horse). Machado's father, who had remarried his sister-in-law, was the short-story writer Aníbal Machado (1894–1964), author of *João Ternura* (Tenderness John). Machado grew up involved with her father's intellectual friends: artists, writers, and painters (including poets Pablo Neruda, Manuel Bandeira, Carlos Drummond de Andrade, and Vinícius de Moraes; writers Rubem Braga, Clarice Lispector; painter Di Cavalcanti; and French actor-director Jean-Louis Barrault). Aníbal Machado was a contradictory liberal-minded Marxist who wanted his five daughters to attend a girls-only Catholic school and to be raised in the traditional old-fashioned style of Minas Gerais. According to Maria Clara Machado, "there was a general hypocrisy in receiving a Victorian education in a house visited by Pagu [Patrícia Galvão] and Oswald de Andrade; where the subjects were existentialist, surrealist, modern, free, but family life was ruled by strict Catholic principles" (Machado 1991). Aníbal Machado, "a father concerned with the morals of his troublesome daughter," seems to have been a larger-than-life image for Maria Clara Machado who was eager for his acceptance and recognition but refused to fulfill the roles expected of a woman from a traditional family.

Machado's interest in theater emerged early on. As a member of the Federação de Bandeirantes do Brasil – the Brazilian branch of the World Association of Girl Guides and Girl Scouts – she started experimenting with marionettes, and in the 1940s she founded a puppeteer group which she directed for five years. During these formative years Machado wrote plays to be staged by her group and also her first book: *Como fazer teatrinho de bonecos* (How to Make a Marionette Theater). At 29, unmarried and in what she defined as a "search for balance," Machado realized the need to distance herself from her family. With a scholarship from the French government, she went to Paris to study theater; from there she traveled to London with another scholarship awarded by UNESCO.

Returning to Brazil in 1951, Machado founded an amateur theater group that became her enduring legacy to Brazilian theater and culture: the school-theater Tablado ("Stage"). In the first issue of *Cadernos de teatro* (Theatre Notebooks), a newsletter published by the Tablado, the mission of the group was defined as follows: "In a country without a theater tradition, we need to search for our path in the lessons of our ancestors, in our own experience and in imported experience. Brazilian theater is being formed from a mixture of these experiences" (1956). The main purpose of the newsletter was to teach basic theater techniques to new theater groups that were being formed throughout the countryside of Brazil, hence their motto "Remember Amapá," coined in English, expressing the international resources available to theater groups in the metropolitan centers of southern Brazil and the isolation of counterpart groups in remote areas such as a state located at the mouth of the River Amazon. In the first ten years of Tablado, Machado staged roles in plays by García Lorca, Chekhov, and Thornton Wilder but eventually she dedicated herself primarily to playwriting and directing. The Tablado, which was initially an adult theater group, developed into the most innovative center for children's plays in Brazil.

In 1963, the year of the death of her father, Machado met the ballerina and choreographer Tatiana Leskova. Leskova was a catalyst for the emergence of feelings and fantasies Machado had previously repressed. Machado describes the encounter as the coming out from a well-behaved repressed world to a new world of freedom (Machado 1991). It was during that time that she wrote *A menina e o vento* (The Girl and the Wind), a play in which the main character encounters a dangerous yet desired world.

Machado's plays introduced a performative interaction between young audiences and staged texts. She used to say that a theater play was not an instrument to be used to preach to children who are not prepared to hear and assimilate "the convulsions of the human condition". She wanted children to conquer their inner fears and to be able to use their conquered freedom. In *Cavalinho azul* (The Little Blue Horse), a play that Machado would claim as her favorite, we have a hero in search of a dream in a disenchanted world without transcendence. In his lonely search and frequent disillusionment, the hero succeeds in finding his lost blue horse. The success of his mission is something that takes place despite the world. The story is narrated by the omnipresent (but not omniscient) character João de Deus who symbolizes a god destitute of powers. As has already been pointed out, the theme of the play is the search in itself as a meditation of the anguish and lack of understanding characteristic of children's experience. The character most immediately associated with Machado herself is that of Pluft, the little ghost who is afraid of people. Struggling with the fear of growing up and facing the world outside the safe boundaries of the home, Pluft transcends the fears of abandonment, rejection, and the unknown. "Mommy, do people really exist?" Pluft asks his mother. In discovering the "other," Pluft defines his own "ghost identity". As Denise Moreira de Souza has analysed, even the name of the character is significant, hinting at something that explodes, that bursts open, and becomes exposed to the world.

The heroes that emerge in Machado's children's plays are interconnected and tap precisely into what was not only a central theme in her personal life, but also a common theme in the lives of children in general. We can perhaps think of Machado's plays as lullabies. In the same way that lullabies prepare children for separation, for the temporary departure from the known world ruled, protected, and restrained by adults, Machado's heroes (and her protagonists are always children) plunge into the world without a safety net, relying on their desire and intuition as they follow their search for what has up until then been denied them. Machado's villains are rounded characters with a human, sympathetic dimension, and adults are often comic characters who lead their lives in restrained and disproportionate seriousness depicted as absurd and laughable. As Machado once stated: "perhaps the make-believe, the fantasy, relieves me from all that is mediocre in life and the seriousness with which we are supposed to live it".

Isis McElroy

Selected Works

Children's Plays

O boi e o burro no caminho de Belém. 1953.
O rapto das cebolinhas. 1954.
Pluft, o fantasminha. 1955.
O chapeuzinho vermelho. 1956.
O embarque de Noé. 1957.
A bruxinha que era boa. 1958.
A volta do camaleão Alface. 1959.
O cavalinho azul. 1960.
Marroquinhas fru-fru. 1961.
A gata borralheira. 1962.
A menina e o vento. 1963.
A volta do camaleão Alface. 1965.
O diamante do grão-mogol. 1967.
Maria minhoca. 1968.
Aprendiz de feiticeiro. 1968.
Camaleão na lua. 1969.
Tribobó city. 1971.
A cigarra e a formiga. 1974.
O patinho feio. 1976.
Camaleão e as batatas mágicas. 1977.
Quem matou o leão? 1978.
João e Maria. 1980.
O dragão verde. 1984.
O gato de botas. 1987.
Passo a passo no paço imperial (co-authored with Cacá Mourthé) 1993.
A coruja Sofia. 1994.
A bela adormecida. 1996.
Jonas e a baleia (co-authored with Cacá Mourthé) 2000.

Adult Plays

Referência 345. 1963.
Miss Brasil. 1964.
As interferências. 1965.
Os embrulhos. 1969.
Um tango argentino. 1972.

Published Children's Plays

Teatro Infantil I (Pluft, o fantasminha; A bruxinha que era boa; O rapto das cebolinhas; Chapeuzinho vermelho; O boi e o burro no caminho de Belém). Rio de Janeiro: Agir, 1957.
Teatro Infantil II (A volta do camaleão Alface; Camaleão na lua; O embarque de Noé; O cavalinho azul). Rio de Janeiro: Agir, 1960.
Teatro Infantil III (A menina e o vento; Marroquinhas fru-fru; A gata borralheira; Maria minhoca). Rio de Janeiro: Agir, 1968.
Teatro Infantil IV (O diamante do grão-mogol; Aprendiz de feiticeiro; Tribobó city; O gato de botas). Rio de Janeiro: Agir, 1972.
Teatro Infantil V (As cigarras e as formigas; Quem matou o leão?; O patinho feio; Camaleão e as batatas mágicas). Rio de Janeiro: Agir, 1979.
Teatro Infantil VI (João e Maria; Um tango argentino; O dragão verde; A coruja Sofia; A bela adormecida). Rio de Janeiro: Agir, 1986.

Published Translations

Plouf, le petit fantôme ... Un Prologue et un acte ... Trans. Michel Simon. Paris: L'Avant-scène, 1960.
La niña y el viento. Pluft, el fantasmita. El caballito azul. Trans. Maria Julieta Drummond de Andrade. Buenos Aires: Ediciones Losange, 1966.
Teatro infantil de Maria Clara Machado: Pluft, el fantasmita; El rapto de las cebollitas; La caperucita roja.—El caballito azul. Trans. Carlos Miguel Suárez Radillo. Madrid: Escelicer, 1971.

Children's Stories

A menina e o vento. Rio de Janeiro: Agir, 1967.
O cavalinho azul. Rio de Janeiro: Bruguera, 1969.
A viagem de clarinha. Rio de Janeiro: Editora Nova Fronteira, 1972.
Clarinha na ilha. Rio de Janeiro: José Olympio, 1979.
O dragão verde. Rio de Janeiro: Agir, 1989.

Other Primary Sources

Como fazer teatrinho de bonecos. Collaboration Virginia Valli. Rio de Janeiro: Melhoramentos, 1965.
100 Jogos dramáticos: improvisação. Co-authored Marta Rosman. Rio de Janeiro: Indústrias de Artes Gráficas Atlan, 1971.
A aventura do teatro. Rio de Janeiro: José Olympio, 1985.
Maria Clara Machado: eu e o teatro. Rio de Janeiro: AGIR, 1991.
Exercício de palco. Rio de Janeiro: Agir, 1994.

References and Further Reading

Campos, Cláudia de Arruda. *Maria Clara Machado.* (Artistas Brasileiros, 10). São Paulo: Editora da Universidade de São Paulo, 1998.
Cunha, Maria Antonieta Antunes. *A comicidade em Maria Clara Machado.* Belo Horizonte: Editora Bernardo Álvares, 1971.
Souza, Denise Moreira de. *Pluft: O avesso poético de um fantasma.* Rio de Janeiro: INACEN, 1986.

Website

http://www.otablado.com.br

MADRID, ANTONIETA

Antonieta Madrid (b. 1939) was born in Valera, a medium-sized city in Trujillo State in Venezuela, where she shared her interest in American and Russian literature with her relatives. In 1963, she moved to Caracas to pursue her undergraduate studies focusing on Education until 1968, when she obtained her college degree and an invitation from the University of Iowa to enroll in the International Writing Program of the School of Letters as a resident writer for two years. However, the global agitation during the 1960s in universities also reached Venezuela's public universities, forcing Universidad Simón Bolivar to stay closed for periods. This conflict provided a time frame for the young student to visit Paris, Berkeley and Gainesville in Florida, while becoming aware of current political flows. Later, it can be said that Madrid's professional life was divided into three areas: writing, teaching and public service as a diplomatic. Accordingly, Madrid, after her experience in Iowa, began to complete relevant pieces such as *Nomenclatura Cotidiana* and "Psicodelia". After this, Madrid won several prizes for her Spanish and bilingual contributions. Madrid not only worked for Venezuela's embassies in cities such as Buenos Aires, Athens, Beijing, Varsovia and Barbados, but also served as ministerial advisor in the Chancellery of the Venezuelan Internal Service. Madrid developed a career devoted to teaching in well-known universities like Taller de Narrativa CELARG (Venezuela), Universidad Católica Andrés Bello (Venezuela), and University of The West Indies (Barbados). Madrid received her Master's degree in Contemporary Latinamerican Literature from Universidad Simón Bolivar in 1989 and her doctorate from FACES/UCV during the 1980s.

The 1960s Experience and Beyond

Nomenclatura cotidiana (1971, Daily Nomenclature) resulted from her work in the United States. In this piece Madrid combines a sensitive dialogue regarding the distance and solitude with memories that emerge from materiality, including the physical surroundings and the human body. Here mere things and everyday routines are considered part of a liberation process of anxieties after the loved one is no longer around. *Reliquias de trapo* (1972, Rag Relics), a short story collection, was well received by readers and critics who one year earlier had awarded "Psicodelia" the First Prize in the Interamerican Short Story Contest INCIBA. The university during the 1960s provided Madrid with a unique setting to explore several political discourses assumed within schools. In this way, one finds characters using parody to question social and political roles that change from Marxists, Socialists to capitalists. Critics paid special attention to these texts due to the author's ability to express the dreams and delusions of Venezuelans during the crisis of 1968 and the violent consequences derived from it. *No es tiempo para rosas rojas* (1975, It Is Not Time for Red Roses), Madrid's first published novel, introduces perhaps the key concepts within her work from now on: love, language, and gender relations. This novel uses the vibrant context of the 1960s in which identity and political revolution affect society, provoking confrontations between the individual and social interests. *No es tiempo* belongs to the corpus of Literature of Violence in which subject commitment plays a substantial part, based on the general desire to change the social realities of those days that later resulted in frustration. Madrid provokes, through the use of a modern language, several simultaneous layers of acts that invite the readers to discover cinematographic elements inside the novel and, at the same time, to get pleasure from an erotic vocabulary. *Ojo de pez* (1990, Fish Eye) is structured into a complex narration in which the protagonist incorporates family pictures to revisit intimate memories after experiencing an abortion. Thus, Vanessa, the main character, decides to approach her painful incident through the act of writing multiple fragments on women in her family, including three generations of women. Critics point out the self-reflexive spirit condensed by Madrid in this novel, regarding not just the subject performance, but the way in which language becomes a point of reference to rethink the limits of representation. *Ojo* comprehends the visual and literary languages, according to Liduvina Carrera, who finds a close relationship between *No es tiempo* and *Ojo*, since both combine a cinematic perspective supported by the implementation of the camera's technique. Distance, height and angle provoke in this sense a game in which the writer / photographer projects a darker side that needs to come into view. Similar to the former novel, *De raposas y de lobos* (2001, On Foxes and Wolves) explores the relationships based on love. However, the delirium suffered by a patient in a mental institution and her proximity to one of the doctors present contemporary trends to insert academic and medical bureaucracy. In short, Madrid underscores how far women and men are from satisfying their wish to love and to be loved.

Postmodern Aesthetics: Territories and Fictions

At this point, Madrid has been able to depict a postmodern society including characters that collapse conventional personalities in order to set up real doubts about what is understood as mental disorders and modern domination. To accomplish this, the author permits the unity of the novel to fall apart in segments which are linguistically dynamic and divergent. The novel creates a visual atmosphere that restructures for the reader/spectator frames that melt the images of objective and insane memories. In 2004, Madrid published *Al filo de la vida* (To the Thread of Life), the last compilation of short stories, divided into three parts entitled: Passions, Pulsations and Visions. The whole work is both realistic and nostalgic regarding personal relationships. It is realistic, because it listens to everyday love narrations in which something is always missing. Romantic disappointments flow here toward a universe where shared lives are not necessarily the best way to secure happiness. Doubts and local memories set a geographic point of reference, according to Krina Ber, who sees in those narrations something that is clearly part of the character of Venezuelans. This conclusion is based on female characters who pass through many cities of the world where none of them feel alien while most of them recognize the essence of belonging to a particular context frame by time and space in Venezuela.

In addition to her fictional texts, Madrid has also produced a series of essays that draw attention to the act of writing itself, such as *El duende que dicta* (1998, The Dictating Gnome). At the same time, *Novela Nostra* (1991, Our Novel) takes an academic approach to the contemporary Latin American novel, taking fundamentally the psychological trauma in relation to the questions of identity and language. "Del arte de novelar" (On the Art of Making Novels) is a particular essay in which Madrid most concisely and brilliantly puts together her own perspective about writing fiction. The author highlights irony as an instrument to escape autobiographical impulses but also recalls parody, imitation, mimicry, simulacrum and representation as a platform of an alternative everyday life composed of unfolded, experimental and fictional characters. Imagination and memory for Madrid facilitate the encounter of the writer within her labyrinth with the power of creation. However, it is necessary to note that Antonieta Madrid's approach to creative work does not present a path which readers can easily follow to access the society in which she has decided to participate, since her references are not restricted to personal experience and the memories of it. Moreover, Madrid brings to her writing more than the story; she introduces her interest in reading and researching about the context in which the novel she is writing is located. In the same way, Madrid talks in an interview by Mara L. García about the indispensable role of the essay for the contemporary novel. In other words, the novel for Madrid must provide in a single text different perspectives such as annotations, thoughts, and at last but no less important, history.

Contextual readings

Earlier remarks regarding Madrid's understanding of the novel may be interpreted according to key publications on Latin American Women Writers such as *A Dream of Light and Shadow: Portrait of Latin Women Writers* (1995), edited by the Chilean poet Margorie Agosín, and *Reinterpreting the Spanish American Essay: Women Writers of the 19th and 20th Centuries* (1995), edited by Doris Meyer. On one hand, Agosín notes the importance of understanding women's contributions to literature as the feminine way of reading their societies within the cultural landscape of the Americas rather than as intimate phenomena. In this sense, Madrid may share with other women writers analyzed in that volume what Agosín calls a "tradition" that connects inner sensibilities with other perspectives through reading and writing about personal and social issues, identity, consciousness, social reform, and language. On the other hand, Madrid, by incorporating the essay within her corpus, opens the debate concerning the irrelevance of the genre of pedagogic segmentation, but more notably the discussion related to the canon in the rubric of Latin American Essay where women have been relegated, as Doris Meyer stated. In this way, Madrid's work establishes connections with this preceding body of essays in which the interest seems to be alike. For instance, topics addressed by both parties such as patriarchal institutions, family roles, city landscapes, cultural identity, gender issues, and reflections on writing situate Madrid's texts within the scope of a corpus that must be revisited in order to shape heterogeneous thoughts beyond the "male monologue" evident in the current Latin American Essay canon.

Own Words and Other Interpretations

Criticism on Antonieta Madrid is as rare as it is conventional in its observations. It mainly follows three streams: (1) the role of history in the fictional work of Madrid; (2) women's participation within social dynamics; and (3) analysis of the postmodern key concepts. Paradoxically it is the interview and its format that provide the intimate links between the creative work and the personal sphere. Madrid explains to García in a volume dedicated to contemporary Venezuelan women writers that her feminine characters are all contained within her. She considers the act of writing almost as a cathartic process in which her experiences and others of her close friends, together with her reading of universal literature, give her female characters the ability to be invented by themselves while occupying their own creator, the writer. In the same text, Madrid states that women's writing emerges from their own inner self where attachments to private spaces are basic. In addition, Madrid explains, cited by García, how she introduces through her literature strong and rebellious feminine characters who break down the traditional cultural structures by giving intimate release to hegemonic views. In this sense, women not only find liberation, taking into consideration external agents such as madness, frustration or suicide, but they also may assemble internal paths to avoid men's schemes. From this perspective, Antonieta Madrid's fictional work finds echoes in the corpus of other literatures of Latin America in which women are depicted within the geography of the private spaces, as was the case previously in the last centuries, and simultaneously in current political and work spaces shared with men. In other words, Madrid amalgamates a feminine intimate literary tradition with postmodern currents that allow her to forsake the flow of conciseness to adopt a challenge with the reading experience. In Madrid's work, gender issues go beyond the debate between women and men. Instead, she addresses the problematic abyss shaped by the exercise of socially constructed gender attitudes of women and men regarding normative behavior. Her previous statement is reflected by the personal relationships in several works, but more explicit in *De raposas* where internal issues touch gender and identity questioning. Consequently, Madrid has contributed to disarticulating male-oriented discourses, and at the same time radical feminist activists and critics who found in men and their economic structures the image of machinery dedicated to promoting passive roles. Thus, Madrid, by using parody and irony in her texts, distorts grand narratives in order to bring to literature the complexity of the human subject and the heterogeneity derived from it. Love is perhaps one of those narrative elements that confer upon Madrid's writing the possibility of exploring different landscapes where negotiation among genders, identities, individualities, and relationships is a crucial micro-political laboratory composed of multilayered historical references. In short, Madrid's creativity emphasizes women's agency since there are fictional characters who find their paths to engage a metaphorical journey to the interior and exterior conditions of the subject in which nothing seems to be easily accessible or ideal.

Hegemonic Discourse: Politics of the Text and the Image

In conclusion, Madrid brings to literature a delicate prose shaped through a cosmopolitan life and her experience as a professor and diplomat. The 1960s was, then, a point of departure for establishing a socially and politically committed perspective, mainly assumed by students who provided Madrid's social and geographical location with a global interest in the crisis of 1968. In this sense, it is possible to understand the author's concern to keep Caracas and its surroundings present in her work despite the fact that the characters engage universal questions about feelings and subject identities. However, the traditional structures are revisited in order to grasp from an innovative feminine point of view the gender relations where women are no longer alienated from productive spheres and male-oriented schemas. On the contrary, women find complex realities in which they have to use their political participation and changes. Madrid's commitment to creative work proposes creativity as a subversive tool since it allows the arrangement of fictional exits and spaces to break away from hegemonic power. More to the point, institutions like universities and hospitals are some of the physical limits for Madrid to dig inside the psychology of characters that exceed common-sense and conventional readings of everyday reality. In this way, a postmodern attitude is evident in her recent corpus since fictional worlds are considered alternatives to escape boredom and frustration arising from contemporary sentimental relationships. Thus, Madrid makes use of irony and parody to go beyond the chronicle through a complex structure composed of simultaneous layers and, enriched with photographic and filmic elements.

Madrid's incorporation of visual resources within her work matches what Jesús Martín Barbero has called "Visual Thinking" in relation to the process of Latin American cultural appropriation of audiovisual imaginary instead of written languages. This displacement of the written word from the center of culture takes Latin Americans beyond the traditional hegemonies in which popular and alternative cultural production begin to be valued in the same way. Nevertheless, the new symbolic character that mediates between the frontiers of languages brings with it the challenge to connect literary and visual perception to heterogeneity and difference in which a context is no longer understood as hybrid as it used to be. In an article entitled "La historia como pretexto: La obra de Carmen Boullosa, Antonieta Madrid y Alicia Kozameh" published by Erna Pfeiffer in *Confluencia*, Pfeiffer states how Antonieta Madrid's literature underlies the way in which the hegemonic discourses from the political left met, during the 1960s, others coming from the right wing of the legitimate Venezuelan status quo of those days. In other words, the guerrillas groups, according to this critic, repeated a unique social model provided by the empowered segments of the society regarding gender issues. Specifically this approach follows *No es tiempo para rosas rojas* in the irrelevance given to women's participation within political dynamics, since those women's relationships with power were addressed from the perspective of capitalistic and bourgeois people who already held social, economical, and political authority. In this sense, paraphrasing Pfeiffer's text, the protagonist seems to adopt a disruptive attitude in relation to the traditional social institutions while accepting personal concessions with the guerilla and hippy movements. However, this dislocation from the normative feminine roles never took her away from the oppression performed in the patriarchal spectrum even within those dissident currents mentioned earlier. Then, what this anonymous woman encountered was a repetition of most of the fixed hierarchy in which she found at the same time disillusionment and perhaps in the end, self-punishment because of her socially detached feelings. Seven years earlier Alicia Perdomo had written a book with particular interest to Antonieta Madrid's work. In that contribution Perdomo explains the way Madrid interrupts everyday reality to embrace through her narratives the diffuse limits of the fantastic. Accordingly, this critic states that Madrid builds two narrative layers in her literature: one realistic and another supernatural, where there is no chronological use of time and space. Feminine characters understood, in this perspective, how several stages of the human experience come together as a single feeling. For instance, love and hate emerge blended for these women portrayed by Madrid since they realize throughout biological developments, as maternity may be in the most basic sense, how complex the subject's relationships with others around or within her can become. Thus, the body occupies a point of departure for Perdomo to figure out how Madrid regards her feminine subject's identities based on some conceptual figures such as the mirror, transmigration, fragmentation, and the labyrinth. Thus, Antonieta Madrid's work represents more or less forty years of transition within Venezuelan women's literature from a committed perspective to a postmodern attitude in which the intimate constellations of women renew their understanding of subject relationships. Love and frustration address erotic narratives that blur everyday life within the fictional world where there is no secure spot to occupy within conventional values. In this way, Madrid through a reflexive sensibility, locates not only a new social criticism, but also individual labyrinths to invite the readers to ask questions to themselves.

MAURICIO DUARTE

Selected Works

Naming day by day. Trans. Bill Dickerson, Ray Kril and Sydney Smith. New York: Art and Poetry, 1971.

Nomenclatura cotidiana. New York: Art and Poetry, 1971.

Reliquias de trapo. Caracas: Monte Ávila, 1972.

No es tiempo para rosas rojas. Caracas: Monte Avila, 1975.

Feeling. Caracas: CADAFE and Caja Redonda, 1983.

Lo Bello/lo Feo. Caracas: Academia Nacional de la Historia, Col. El libro Menor No. 43, 1983.

La Última de las Islas. Caracas: Monte Ávila Editores, 1988.

Ojo de pez. Caracas: Editorial Planeta, 1990.

Novela nostra. Caracas: FUNDARTE. Alcaldía del Municipio Libertador, 1991.

De raposas y de lobos. Caracas: Alfaguara, 2001.

Al filo de la vida. Caracas: Bid & Co, 2004.

References and Further Reading

Carrera, Liduvina. "La evolución estilística en dos novelas de Antonieta Madrid". Centro de investigaciones literarias. http://www.ucab.edu.ve/ucabnuevo/index.php?load=laev2.htm&seccion=143 (accessed July 25 2006).

Cunha-Giabbai, Gloria da. "La problemática de la mujer hispanoamericana como reflejo del conflicto social: *No es tiempo para rosas* de Antonieta Madrid". *Inti* 37–8 (1993): 145–53.

Dietz-Hertrich, Dagmar "*Reliquias de Trapo* de Antonieta Madrid". *INTERLIT* 3 (1993): n.p.

García, Mara L. "Antonieta Madrid". In *Escritoras venezolanas de hoy*. Mexico: Universidad Autonoma de Tlaxcala, 2005, pp. 49–59.

Martín Barbero, Jesús. "Comunicación: el descentramiento de la modernidad". *Analisi* 19 (1996): 79–94.

Perdomo H, Alicia. *La ritualidad del poder femenino: parodia, fantasía e ironía en Antonieta Madrid*. Caracas: Fundarte, 1991a.

——. *Ritualidad Del Poder Femenino: Parodia, Fantasía e Ironía en Antonieta Madrid*. Caracas: Fundarte, 1991b.

Pfeiffer, Erna. "La historia como pre-texto: la obra de Carmen Boullosa, Antonieta Madrid y Alicia Kozameh". *Confluencia* 13.2 (1998): 145–55.

MANSILLA DE GARCÍA, EDUARDA

Eduarda Mansilla (c. 1834–1892) was an Argentine writer whose works were known and respected in her own lifetime; today, she is one of the most studied Argentine women writers of the 1800s. In Argentina, she was one of the first female novelists; she wrote the first collection of children's stories; she pioneered women's travel narratives; she was among the first women composers; and she helped break barriers for women journalists. In all these activities, her novels have most frequently captured the attention of today's scholars.

Mansilla was born into a wealthy and powerful family; her uncle was Juan Manuel Rosas. She received an unusually good education for a woman at that time; she particularly took pride in serving as French interpreter for her uncle. Mansilla's marriage to Manuel García, of a prominent anti-Rosas family, was regarded as a Romeo and Juliet match. She traveled with her husband to his diplomatic postings in Paris and Washington, holding literary and musical salons wherever she lived. After her husband's death, she returned to Buenos Aires, where she lived until her death in 1892.

Novels

Beginning in 1860, Eduarda Mansilla published three influential novels. The first was *Lucía*, a version of the Lucía Miranda legend, published under the pseudonym of "Daniel"; in 1882, it was republished as *Lucía Miranda*, under Mansilla's name. The second was *El médico de San Luis* (1860), influenced by Oliver Goldsmith's *Vicar of Wakefield*. The third, *Pablo ou la vie dans les Pampas*, was first published in Paris in 1869, but her brother, Lucio, translated it into Spanish for *La Tribuna* the following year. (Subsequent translations omit his deliberate deformations of the text.)

Lucía Miranda draws on the legend first reported in Ruy Díaz's *La Argentina* (1612). According to Díaz, Lucía and her husband, Sebastián, sailed to Argentina in 1532 as colonists. Two indigenous men, Siripo and Mangoré (in Mansilla's version, Marangoré), fall in love with the beautiful Lucía. She speaks of friendship's love, which the Indians hear as romantic love. When Lucía rejects their advances, they attack the fort and take the Mirandas captive. To save Sebastian's life, Lucía agrees to become Siripo's wife. However, the Spanish couple cannot disguise their love for each other, and Siripo orders their death. Díaz describes their end in the language and imagery of traditional saints' tales. In Mansilla's novel, the events taking place in Argentina occupy only the final third of the text; the first two-thirds are an exploration of Lucía

Miranda's construction of the self. Through reading, travel, debate, and finally courtship, she becomes a model of womanhood in the European style; in the context of Argentina, however, her attributes turn fatal. When the Mirandas' European "civilization" clashes with the Timbús' American "barbarism," barbarism triumphs.

Barbarism also triumphs in *Pablo o la vida en las pampas*. The institutions charged with bringing peace, order, and civilization to the countryside (such as the army and the judicial system) are presented in this novel as violent and corrupt. Unlike the cultivated Lucía Miranda, the women in *Pablo* are uneducated and unable to influence their surroundings. The elite women of the countryside, such as Dolores, Pablo's love interest, have only their wealth and their race to separate them from the women of the lower classes. As in *Lucía Miranda*, the lovers find death rather than their destiny of happiness: Pablo is hanged for desertion from the army, and Indians kill Dolores during a raid.

El médico de San Luis seems at first glance to be a very different novel from the violent ones described above. In this work, there is an ideal family that is able to exercise a civilizing influence on their surroundings. And unlike the other two novels, that take place in the open spaces of indigenous Argentina, this one is located within domestic, even cosy, spaces. Yet here too, there is a clash between civilization and barbarism. In this case, the civilizing forces are represented by the English doctor of the title and English, Protestant values. The opposing barbarism is represented by the families of Spanish, Catholic heritage. The key difference between the two heritages, according to the novel, is in the status of the mother. The Argentine mother in *El médico* is degraded, uneducated, and lacking in rights; as a result, she, unlike the respected and enlightened English mother, cannot fulfill her destiny of civilizing the nation.

Short Stories

Eduarda Mansilla was one of the first Argentine women writers to explore the short story genre, which she knew well from French and English literature. Her *Cuentos* (1880) is considered the first work of children's literature to be written in Argentina; the stories are clearly influenced by British tales from the Victorian era, i.e., many of the child heroes die as proof of a moral teaching.

In contrast, the stories in Mansilla's *Creaciones* (1883) are for adults, and as such, they are more ambiguous in their treatment of matters such as marital unhappiness ("Sombras"). Perhaps the most striking of these stories is "El ramito de romero" in which a medical student has a vision of the future: despots replace rulers, the traditional family is destroyed, and materialism triumphs, before humankind finally reaches a shining new state of being. Not all of Mansilla's stories are published in this collection; "Un amor," for example, was published on its own.

Travel Memoirs

Travel narratives were a popular new form of writing among the male authors of the Generation of 1880; few women, however, ventured into a genre that required a first-person narrator willing to reveal many personal details. While Eduarda Mansilla dared to write about herself at a time when women were supposed to be self-effacing, she did not dare to imply anything but the most upright of behavior, unlike her brother Lucio, whose memoirs are full of bohemian adventures as a wealthy man-about-town. Besides, Lucio traveled as if he were a bachelor (he left his wife behind in Buenos Aires), while Eduarda traveled with husband and children. As a result, Eduarda Mansilla's travel memoirs are genuinely about traveling; they lack the sensationalist aspects that made Lucio's memoirs sell well. Nevertheless, Mansilla's *Recuerdos de viaje* offers many perceptive observations, particularly about the lives of women in the United States. She clearly envies their access to being reporters, for example.

Essays

In spite of having many advantages—wealth, family connections, education, servants to provide leisure to write—not enjoyed by many of her contemporaries, Eduarda Mansilla faced similar barriers to publishing in periodicals. All the genres described above could be published with one's own money; periodical publication, however, depended on the willingness of editors to allow women into spheres dominated by men. Domingo Sarmiento, in an article in 1885, described Mansilla's ten-year fight for the right to be a journalist. In light of such obstacles, then, it is not surprising that many of Mansilla's essays were written under male pseudonyms or anonymously. Nevertheless, her output of essays was prolific, covering most of the subjects permitted to women.

Modern Interpretations

The majority of today's many scholarly studies of Eduarda Mansilla's works focus on her novels. Other women novelists contemporary with Mansilla generally focus on the marriage plot; their narratives, while interesting on their own terms, usually lack the national implications that Mansilla posited in her novels. Mansilla's short stories also tend to deal with questions of romance (with the exception of "El ramito de romero"); readers interested in disillusionment with traditional notions of love will find interesting material there. Of Mansilla's other works, her travel memoirs have attracted recent attention among researchers. Her children's stories and dramas, however, are usually mentioned only for their historical value. Mansilla's essays have not received extensive critical attention; they often demonstrate the disconcerting limitation of class blindness, as when she states that seamstresses earn a good living. Historians of feminism have been disappointed to find that Mansilla denies being pro-emancipationist in her essays (although her short stories contain hints of contradictions of this stance).

In her novels, however, Mansilla questions established notions of national identity and reveals the weaknesses of traditional patriarchal culture. As Francine Masiello points out, Mansilla often uses female characters to suggest ways to address national problems, while male characters take the path of violence, abuse of authority, or ineffectiveness. In particular, *Pablo* has been studied as a counterpoint to Sarmiento's *Facundo*. Both novels are concerned with questions of civilization and barbarism, but they often depart from each other in their handling of these questions. Mansilla's *Lucía Miranda* is the subject of several studies, such as the ones by Hanway and Lehman. Mansilla, like Rosa Guerra, goes back to the Miranda legend to question Argentina's creation mythology; both writers reject a version of history that does not take women's participation into account.

BONNIE FREDERICK

Selected Works

Lucía Miranda. Buenos Aires: Alsina, 1882. First published in 1860, the full text is available online.

El médico de San Luis. Buenos Aires: La Paz, 1860. The full text is available online.

Pablo ou la vie dans les Pampas. Paris: E. Lachaud, 1869.

Cuentos. Buenos Aires: Imprenta de la "República", 1880.

Recuerdos de viaje. Buenos Aires: Alsina, 1882.

Creaciones. Buenos Aires: Imprenta de la "República", 1883.

References and Further Reading

Davies, Catherine. "Spanish-American Interiors: Spatial Metaphors, Gender and Modernity". *Romance Studies* 22(1) (2004): 27–39.

Frederick, Bonnie. *Wily Modesty: Argentine Women Writers, 1860–1910*. Tempe, AZ: ASU Center for Latin American Studies Press, Arizona State University, 1998.

Guerrero, César H. *Mujeres de Sarmiento*. Buenos Aires: n.p., 1960.

Hanway, Nancy. *Embodying Argentina: Body, Space and Nation in 19th Century Narrative*. Jefferson, NC: McFarland, 2003.

Lehman, Kathryn. "Naturaleza y cuerpo femenino en dos narrativas argentinas de origen nacional". *Revista Iberoamericana* 70(206) (2004): 117–24.

Masiello, Francine. *Between Civilization and Barbarism: Women, Nation, and Literary Culture in Modern Argentina*. Lincoln, NB: University of Nebraska Press, 1992.

Monder, Samuel. "De la seducción y otras miradas. La institución del flirt en los *Recuerdos de viaje* de Eduarda Mansilla". *Revista Iberoamericana* 71(210) (2005): 105–17.

Szurmuk, Mónica. *Women in Argentina: Early Travel Narratives*. Gainesville, FL: University Press of Florida, 2001.

Veniard, Juan María. *Los García, los Mansilla y la música*. Buenos Aires: Instituto Nacional de Musicología "Carlos Vega", 1986.

MANSO, JUANA

Most Argentine women writers of the 1800s spoke carefully of their hopes for greater women's rights, so as not to offend or provoke personal attacks. This was not the case with Juana Manso (1819–75) for she, in articulate and unmistakable terms, boldly demanded fundamental changes in women's status. Most of all, she dedicated herself to the cause of education, which she viewed as the key to revolutionizing Argentina. Vilified in her day, Manso is today considered a leading figure in Argentine history.

Born in 1819, Juana Manso dedicated herself to teaching and educational reform as a young woman. Along with thousands of other Argentines, Manso and her family fled the dictatorship of Rosas in 1840, moving first to Uruguay, then Brazil, then back to Uruguay. She gave up her teaching career for marriage to a musician, and she accompanied him on tours of the United States, Cuba, and Brazil. He abandoned her and their two daughters the same year that Rosas was defeated (1852). Manso then moved back to Argentina, spending the rest of her life in Buenos Aires. She formed a life-long friendship with Domingo Sarmiento, and together they set about revolutionizing the educational system, starting with Argentina's first coeducational school, which Manso directed. Audiences at her lectures were often unreceptive; at times, they threw stones and objects at her. Manso further offended some Argentines by becoming an Anglican; on her deathbed, a Catholic priest tried to convince her to recant, to no avail. When she was denied burial at the municipal cemeteries, the British ambassador stepped in and allowed her to be buried in the British cemetery. Later, however, public sentiment changed, and her remains were transferred to the Pantheon of Teachers at Chacarita cemetery. In 1967, a stamp was issued in her honor. A street in Buenos Aires, a prize in Rosario, and many schools are named after her.

Manso's pedagogical publications are numerous indeed; this discussion will focus only on her novels, a drama, and her feminist newspaper.

Novelist and Dramatist

In 1846, Manso wrote *Los misterios del Plata: Episodios históricos de la Epoca de Rosas*, which later, after the defeat of Rosas, was published as a book in Argentina. It fictionalizes the horrors of the political murders during the Rosas era, focusing on the tribulations of a noble unitarian family at the hands of barbaric, bloodthirsty federalists. Various characters are killed, most notably the heroic gaucho Miguel. In two pivotal chapters, Manso describes Rosas's house as an image of the nation as a whole; just as barbarism reigns in his household, so it reigns in his country. The women of his family are presented as ignorant and vicious, in contrast to the noble and refined wife of the unitarian prisoner. When the novel was published, the Argentine public was seeking stories of the recently ended Rosas era, especially ones that denounced the *mazorca* death squads. Like *Amalia*, which was published in Uruguay a few years after *Los misterios*, Manso's novel was well received, going through many editions. (Some editions available today were edited by Ricardo Isidro López Múñiz, who "completed" Manso's novel by adding a happier ending, with a lesser role for the women characters.)

Manso began publishing an anti-slavery novel, *La familia del Comendador*, in 1854 as a serial in her *Album de Señoritas*, but the newspaper soon folded; the novel was then published as a book that same year. In it, Juan das Neves, oldest son of a wealthy Brazilian family, is happy among his English friends, the Smiths, but when his father dies, his mother insists on his return to Brazil. Seeing his family's plantation after an absence of many years, he is shocked by the violence and oppression directed at the slaves. When he protests, his own mother orders him to be whipped by the slavemaster. Juan loses his sanity, is cared for by a slave, and has two children by her, whom his mother baptizes as slaves. Meanwhile, Juan's mother and brother scheme to marry him off to his niece, in order to keep the family money within the family. Many plot complications later, Juan's mother dies, her slaves are freed, and the various generations of couples—white, black, and mulatto—are paired off happily. In *La familia*, Manso denounces slavery, the Catholic Church, and forced marriages; she defends the rights of both the free and slave women; and she weaves a complicated sexual web among the races. Unlike the popular *Los misterios del Plata*, this abolitionist novel did not find a receptive audience (slavery in Buenos Aires was not outlawed until 1861), and exists only in its first edition.

In 1864, Manso published *La Revolución de Mayo, 1810*, a drama focusing on the heroes of Argentine Independence. The male political figures—such as Belgrano, Moreno, and Rodríguez Peña—speak and act according to the official version of Independence history that the intended audience would know well. In this sense, *La Revolución de Mayo* is an ordinary historical drama, perhaps suitable for teaching schoolchildren. But Juana Manso did not write works with all-male casts. She created a central character, Lola Bargas, who is a fiery revolutionary. She speaks in a political voice, or at least within the political margins permitted to women. Bargas chooses to become a nun as a symbolic virgin sacrifice for the new nation. Two other female characters, Cecilia and Susana, speak from the viewpoint of women's traditional realm: Cecilia loves Belgrano from afar. The two women discuss their enforced passivity; they are not allowed by respectable society to initiate the actions that would bring about their destiny as women, that is, marriage and motherhood.

Editor and Essayist

Manso successfully edited various pedagogical periodicals, but her women's newspaper, *Album de Señoritas*, lasted barely two months. In the first number, Manso declares her intention: to emancipate Argentine women. She denounces male domination, the degradation of motherhood to mere perpetuation of the race, and the frivolous activities that uneducated women use to fill their unhappy lives. The starting point for social revolution, according to Manso, is education for women, who, once enlightened themselves, can raise their children to be enlightened citizens who will rectify the inequities imposed on women. Apparently, Argentine readers were not ready for such blunt talk, and the newspaper folded for lack of subscribers.

Modern Interpretations

For scholars today, Juana Manso is considered important for a variety of reasons: (1) she is remembered for being Argentina's first militant feminist. Manso's ideas, particularly those expressed in *Album de Señoritas*, are scrutinized for their pioneering analyses of the structures of male domination. She was not just a reformist, satisfied with slow steps toward a brighter future. Instead, she was a revolutionary, who envisioned a fundamental restructuring of Argentine society. (2) Manso's feminism is reflected in her literary works, which focus on the roles of women, revealing the barbarism of the uneducated women and the civilizing potential of the enlightened ones. Her female characters are active participants, not mere observers or prizes for the male characters. However, they often lament the societal restrictions on their actions and opportunities. (3) During Manso's lifetime, she was one of the few Argentines who employed gender to critique national issues. She was able to see the connection between the microcosm of the family and the macrocosm of the nation; her description of the Rosas house and family in *Los misterios del Plata* is an example of her ability to see that (in a phrase from the next century) the personal is political.

Manso's literary works are usually studied for their themes rather than their aesthetic qualities, and they vary in their interest to researchers. For example, although *Los misterios del Plata* was Manso's most popular work, it has often been overshadowed by other anti-Rosas works that it resembles, such as *Amalia* and "El matadero". Other researchers have explored Manso's rewriting of official versions of Argentine history to include issues of gender and race. Kathryn Lehman, for instance, focuses on Manso's revisionism in *La Revolución de Mayo*. Manso's pedagogical works often propose revisionist histories; one example is *Compendio de la historia de las Provincias Unidas del Río del Plata* (1859, with many subsequent editions).

La familia del Comendador is an original work in many ways. There are few abolitionist works in Argentina; given Rosas's treatment of the Afro-Argentine population, it is not surprising that works that were sympathetic to the plight of slaves were not well received by the reading public. Manso presents many ideas about race that would have been shocking to her audience then, such as a white woman falling in love with a mulatto man (the novel implies that they marry or at least live together, without saying so explicitly). The complicated gender and race issues in the novel have intrigued several of today's scholars, such as Lea Fletcher.

BONNIE FREDERICK

Selected Works

Los misterios del Plata. Buenos Aires: Imprenta Americana, 1846. The second edition (1855) is available online.

Album de Señoritas. January 1–February 17, 1854. Available at the Benson Library, University of Texas at Austin.

La familia del Comendador. Buenos Aires: J.A. Bernheim, 1854.

La Revolución de Mayo, 1810. Buenos Aires: Imprenta de Mayo, 1864.

References and Further Reading

Area, Lelia. *Juana Manso. Periodismo y frustración para un proyecto doméstico de fundar una nación.* Buenos Aires: Feminaria, 2005. http://www.feminaria.com.ar/colecciones/archivos/archivos.asp

Fletcher, Lea. "Patriarchy, Medicine, and Women Writers in Nineteenth-Century Argentina". In Bruce Clarke and Wendell Aycock (eds), *The Body and the Text: Comparative Essays in Literature and Medicine.* Lubbock, TX: Texas Tech University Press, 1990, pp. 91–101.

——. "Juana Manso: una voz en el desierto". In Lea Fletcher (ed.), *Mujeres y cultura en la Argentina del siglo XIX.* Buenos Aires: Feminaria, 1994, pp. 108–20.

Forcinito, Ana. "La cita del romance nacional argentino: Performatividad e inestabilidades en Mansilla, Manso y Gorriti". *Crítica Hispánica* 24(1–2) (2002): 223–38.

Frederick, Bonnie. *Wily Modesty: Argentine Women Writers, 1860–1910.* Tempe, AZ: ASU Center for Latin American Studies Press, Arizona State University, 1998.

Guerrero, César H. *Mujeres de Sarmiento.* Buenos Aires: n.p., 1960.

Lehman, Kathryn. "Entre Eros y Polis. El engendramiento de la Madre Patria". In Lea Fletcher (ed.), *Mujeres y cultura en la Argentina del siglo XIX.* Buenos Aires: Feminaria, 1994, pp. 176–84.

Lewkowicz, Lidia F. *Juana Paula Manso (1819–1875): una mujer del siglo XXI*. Buenos Aires: Corregidor, 2000.
Masiello, Francine. *Between Civilization and Barbarism: Women, Nation, and Literary Culture in Modern Argentina*. Lincoln, NB: University of Nebraska Press, 1992.
Mizraje, Maria Gabriela. *Argentinas de Rosas a Perón*. Buenos Aires: Biblos, 1999.

MARÍN DEL SOLAR, MERCEDES

Born in Santiago on September 11, c. 1804, Mercedes was the daughter of José Gaspar Marín, First Secretary of the First "Junta Nacional de Gobierno" (First Government of Chile) and Luisa Recabarren. Because of the nature of her father's work, and an epidemic that developed in Santiago, Chile, she was raised and educated by a guardian, Mercedes Guerra, who dedicated her time to satisfying Mercedes Marín's intellectual curiosity. One of the problems that Mercedes Guerra had to solve in order to give a complete education to her pupil was the lack of books, since the government of Spain had banned the importation of all types of books to the colonies. For this reason, Mercedes Guerra was forced to borrow books from various private libraries and convents. These obstacles she came across in pursuing an education would later encourage Marin to promote laws to protect women's right to education. Under the direction of her guardian, Marin read novels and poetry, learned several languages, and studied music. Marin lived with Mrs Guerra until the death of the latter, at which point she moved to the family house. As a child, Mercedes learned quickly and by the age of 12 she already spoke French, among other languages. French was the language that established a very strong connection between Mercedes and her father. A close relationship based on knowledge of literature and languages existed between them, and she was raised in an atmosphere saturated with intellectual discourse about the value of education, and specifically the education of women. This father–daughter bond provided her with protection, security, and self-confidence. The cultural changes that the new nation was undergoing after independence led to women's increased involvement in activities related to the arts and politics. Thus, Mercedes Marin, unmarried until the age of 26, when she was already old according to the standards of her time, took leadership roles in the new society. No substantial research exists related to the relationship between her father's progressive educational ideas and his persistent efforts to instruct her in appropriate feminine behavior in line with his educational philosophies. Marín wrote a telling book about her father as one of the fathers of the new Chile, where he appears as an intellectual stimulating and open-minded person. Later in her life, by virtue of her friendship with Andrés Bello and the politician Ventura Blanco Encalada, she would develop a more audacious attitude towards her position as a woman in the new Chilean society.

Poet and Politics

Four poetic lines can be recognized in her works, each of which possesses a voice that mirrors Marin's self-image. While Marín was engaged in her work, Chile was entering into the problem of nation-building. This issue constitutes one of the first topics of her poetry. The creation of a poetic related to the idea of the images not only designates specific geographical areas, but also imaginary spaces, concretizing the ideal of the Chilean citizens. It is in this frame that Mercedes started to develop her poetics, according to the political movement in the country. For most of the nineteenth century, sexism forced women writers to assume male names. This was not her case. Mercedes did not fear society. On the contrary, she was the voice of a new femininity, or more accurately, she gave voice to the femininity of the new nation. It was in this context that she wrote about the powerlessness of the women around her, something that was due to the lack of educational opportunities not only for women, but for all Chilean people. Seeking rationalization of a new citizenship, she outgrew that plight in search of new roles for Chilean women as the way to strengthen the idea of Chile as a unified nation. In that same vein, she wrote her most famous work: *Canto Fúnebre a la Muerte de Don Diego Portales* (Funereal Song on the Death of Mr. Diego Portales). This poem, endowed with an elegiac structure, immerses the reader in a world where the dichotomy "civilization and barbarism" goes hand in hand, portraying the nation as a gross spectacle. For this reason Marín compared the death of Diego Portales to an old tragedy of the barbarian, who bursts into the city from nowhere, destroying civilized places and creating chaos.

The second theme of her poetics is that of the woman as an intellectual body, and a body with awareness that it pertains to society. As Michael Foucault argues, while the rise of a democratic ideology created the birth of a new understanding of personal political liberty, a new agency, it also marked a new era of harsh discipline toward the human body (Foucault 1977: 227). In this conception women did not escape new ways of discipline. Thus, as a way of collaborating with the new government, Marín developed not only poems dedicated to women in which she praised the talents that she thought were distinctive of women, but also the performance of a woman's body in relation to a Chilean citizenship. Some examples of this are poems dedicated to Andrés Bello's wife "Soneto a doña Rosario Reyes de Bello" (Sonnet to Rosario Reyes de Bello), "A la distinguida cantante doña Teressa Rossi" (To the Distinguished Singer Teressa Rossi), "A la señorita Angela Caamaño, una poetisa de Guayaquil" (Miss Angela Caamaño, a Poetess from Guayaquil) and the poem "A la distinguida poetisa doña Jertrudis Gómez de Avellaneda" (To the Distinguished Poetess Jertrudis Gómez de Avellaneda), to name just a few. In these poems the division between Romantic and Classic aesthetics is visible. In one way she never seems to have thought for a moment about the real physical qualities, except for those characteristics that show the work of women. The reader can see the classic style in her descriptions of hands, voices, eyes, and foreheads. In another way, in these same poems, what she finds praiseworthy is goodness, which shines out from the "poetic character" features so that everyone rejoices in it, while sweetness fills the heart. For her, the supreme quality in a woman is that her beauty resides both inside and outside. A woman who was graced with love, education, faith and courteous gentleness had the possibility to become a model of patriotism. Along these lines she wrote an article published in the magazine *La República Literaria* about the lack of opportunities for women to meet and have intellectual conversation. In Chile, in the first quarter of the nineteenth century, the cultural movement was centered on "tertulias" (*soirées*), where members of the political and intellectual community met to discuss art, literature and philosophy. Mercedes Marín was the hostess of many of these. Her home was where Domingo Faustino Sarmiento was introduced to Andrés Bello, and painters like Raymond Monvoisin and Johann Moritz Rugendas found space to exchange different cultural views.

The third line of Mercedes Marín's work relates to the Chilean community. Marín did not see the gift of participation in an intellectual way of life as a license for domination. Instead Marin used her intellectual privilege to engage in creative work in a double sense, both as a writer and later as a teacher. She thought that she had a responsibility to build a Chilean society that integrally included girls. Marín advocated gender equality including education for both boys and girls.

Fourth, in defense of women's rights, Mercedes Marín continued considering marriage as an innate destiny of women, which is why she did eventually marry, though later than most women of her class. But when a woman becomes a mother, this changes the scenario. It was supposed to be the supreme experience for a woman. Marín created a feminine discourse focused on the experience of motherhood, which helped her to consolidate a nationalist discourse, where she substituted the idea of Nation for the idea of Motherland. This can be seen, for example, in the following poems: "A mi hermana después de la muerte de su amado esposo" (To my Sister after the Death of Her Beloved Husband), "La Patria" (The Motherland), "Defensa" (Defense), "A la muerte de la joven y virtuosa señora doña Adela Solar de Aldunate" (On the Death of the Young and Virtuous Madam Adela Solar de Aldunate), "A mi amada hija" (To my Beloved Daughter), "A mi amiga Mercedes Recasen de Zegers" (To my Friend Mercedes Recasen de Zegers). Marín creates a new image: the Chilean woman. The images highlighted women's primary responsibilities as mothers and as citizens. She incorporated both concepts by using the religious symbol of the Virgin Mary. The Virgin who sacrificed her position as mother and woman and became *the motherland* of all human beings.

Modern Interpretations

Most of the critiques of Mercedes Marín praise or question some fundamental aspects of her intellectual constructs. All the literary analyses are based on the tradition. Most of them celebrate the religious presumptions of a woman in the nineteenth century and assumed that Marín's feminine nature inspired her. Other critical readings, to greater and lesser extents, highlight the social role that Marín played in the creation of a nation. One of the common views of her works has been the ways that she contributed to the patriarchal discourse. Most of these readings do not take into account the social and historical situation of Marín and repeat stock analyses based on romantic figures and themes. Few critics emphasize that Mercedes Marín del Solar worked within a male-centered and dominated circle in Chilean society at a pivotal moment of gendered nation-building, a major defining aspect of her life and works. Mercedes Marín del Solar died in 1866.

ANA FIGUEROA

Selected Works

Discurso fúnebre pronunciado en las exequias a los tres hermanos Carrera. Santiago de Chile: Impr. de Nuestro Ambrosy, 1828.

Canto Fúnebre de Homenaje de gratitud a la memoria del benemérito Ministro Don Diego Portales. Santiago de Chile: Impr. de la Opinión, 1837.

Elojio histórico del Ilustrísimo señor don Manuel Vicuña, primer arzobispo de esta Santa Iglesia Metropolitana de Santiago de Chile. Santiago de Chile: Impr. de La Opinión, 1843.

La caridad: ofrenda dedicada a la señora, doña Antonia Salas, Presidenta de la Sociedad de Beneficencia. Santiago de Chile: Impr. Nacional, 1855.

Canto fúnebre a la memoria del ciudadano José Romero: Drama Chileno. Santiago de Chile: Impr. del Conservador, 1858.

Al indulto del 14 de octubre: Discurso. *La Semana*. Año 1, No. 25. November 5, 1859.

Escepticismo i fe: Leyenda religiosa. Completed by Enrique del Solar. Santiago de Chile: Impr. del Independiente, 1867.

La tumba de Errazuriz: Leyenda. Valparaíso: Impr. de la Patria, 1869.

Poesías de la señora Doña. Mercedes Marín de Solar. Edited by Enrique del Solar. Santiago de Chile: Impr. Andres Bello, 1874.

La novia i la carta: leyenda. Santiago de Chile: Impr. La Estrella de Chile, 1874.

References and Further Reading

A. P. "La poesía femenina en Chile desde 1837 hasta 1914". *La Mañana*, Chillán. November 21, 1984: 4.

Baticuore, Graciela. *La mujer romántica. Lectoras, autoras y escritores en la Argentina: 1830–1870*. Buenos Aires: Edhasa, 2005.

Burgos, Camila. "Desafíos de las pioneras". *El Mercurio*. Santiago. July 25, 1993: 1–8.

C. A. Z. "Doña Mercedes Marín del Solar, poetisa y pionera". *El Diario de Aysen*. April 11, 1994: 2.

Fuente, Darío de la. "La Primera poetisa de Chile". *La Prensa*. Curicó. June 15, 1996: 6.

——. "Mercedes Marín del Solar". *La Región*. San Fernando. February 1, 1995: 3.

Figueroa, Pedro Pablo. *Diccionario biográfico de Chile*. Vols I–IV. Santiago de Chile: Imprenta y Encuadernación Barcelona, 1897.

Fletcher, Lea. *Mujeres y Cultura en la Argentina del siglo XIX*. Buenos Aires: Feminaria Editora, 1994, pp. 60, 68.

Foucault, M. *Discipline and Punish: The Birth of the Prison*. New York, Pantheon: 1977.

Gallardo, Andrés. "1941, Año de aniversarios". *El Sur*. Concepción, August 3, 2004: A23.

González Colville, Juan Carlos, "Dos mujeres notables: Mercedes Marín del Solar y Úrsula Suárez". *El Heraldo*. Talca. September 9, 1994: 3.

Milla, Luis A. "Mercedes Marín del Solar". *Negro en el Blanco*. February 22, 1988: 8.

Morgado, Benjamín. "Poetisa nacida con la independencia". *La Nación*. September 19, 1983: 14.

Muñoz-Hjelm, Ruth. "El Invisible castigo del silencio". In Silvia Elguea Véjar (ed.), *La otredad: Los discursos de la cultura hoy*. Mexico City: Universidad Autónoma Metropolitana, 1997, pp. 133–42.

Peralta Herrera, Galvarino. "Mercedes Marín del Solar, poetisa en su vida y en su obra". *El Día*. La Serena. April 30, 2006: 18.

Rodríguez Trujillo, Carlos. "Mercedes Marín, poetisa y madre respetable". *El Ovallino*. Ovalle. May 13, 1990: 8–9.

Simpson Trostel, Adolfo. "Portales, y su corazón". *El Mercurio*. Valparaíso. June 15, 1993: A3.

Valenzuela Solis de Ovando, Carlos. *Mujeres de Chile*. Santiago de Chile: Editorial Andújar, 1995

MASTRETTA, ÁNGELES

Ángeles Mastretta was born in the state of Puebla in Mexico in 1949 where she spent most of her early years. Following the death of her father Carlos Mastretta in 1971, she moved to Mexico City. Mastretta graduated in journalism at the Universidad Autónoma de México and later contributed to newspapers and magazines such as *Excelsior* and *Unomásuno*. She had a regular column (*Del absurdo Cotidiano*) in the cultural review, *Ovaciones*, to which she contributed articles on politics and feminism. Following the award of a scholarship from the Centro Mexicano de Escritores in 1974, she published *La pájara pinta* (1975), her only collection of poetry. For three years, from 1975 to 1977, Mastretta was director of both *Difusión Cultural* of the ENEP-Acatlán and from 1982 to 1985 she formed part of the editorial council of the feminist magazine *Fem* to which she also contributed several articles. Mastretta currently sits on the editorial board of *Nexos*, edited by her partner, the writer and essayist, Héctor Aguilar Camín, from 1983 to 1995.

In Mexico, Mastretta is a well-known and popular figure, enjoying a worldwide reputation as a leading feminist writer. Mastretta's major works have been translated into English as well as into many other international languages. Her first book *Arráncame la vida*, 1985 (winner of the *Premio Mazatlán*) has been translated into ten different languages. Set in the 1930s and 1940s, this referential testimonial narrative tells the story of Catalina Guzmán, the wife of a powerful and corrupt politician who becomes the governor of Puebla. Catalina's first person narrative conveys the concrete daily reality of patriarchal repression. The novel offers much more than the traditional story of an unequal marriage, since it traces Catalina's struggle to define her own sense of identity in a male and politically oppressive society. In its exploration of alternative representations of female sexuality, motherhood and womanhood, *Arráncame la vida* can be situated within the broad category of feminist resistance writing which challenges traditional gender roles. The work also provides discerning comment on post-revolutionary Mexico and represents an important contribution to the existing corpus of Latin American testimonial narrative. For Mastretta, testimonial writing is an attempt to challenge the official version of history and to speak of *lo no dicho*, that is, the other side of history where the marginalized and silenced Other moves to centre stage.

At three generations removed from the contemporary reader, the world of *Mujeres de ojos grandes* (1990) is populated by a series of aunts who appear to follow the expected social roles they should fulfil as wives and mothers but are in fact sexually subversive. In 1997, Mastretta became the first woman to win the prestigious *Premio Rómulo Gallegos* for *Mal de amores* (1996). The time frame of Mastretta's most accomplished work overlaps the nineteenth and twentieth centuries, extending from the last years of Porfirio Diáz's presidency to the outbreak of the Revolution of 1911 and beyond. But the novel is not merely—or even mainly—historical, since the plot centres on personal passion and disillusionment in the revolutionary period. The protagonist is Emilia Sauri, and her upbringing prepares her for her positive feminist contribution to the revolutionary struggle. The plot also traces her relationships with two men, Daniel Cuenca and Antonio Zavalza. Like *Arráncame la vida, Mal de amores* can be aligned with the contemporary woman's novel of education which traces women's physical and metaphysical journeys in history. Both these novels conform to Bakhtin's definition of the *Bildungsroman*, in which the protagonist's individual coming of being is closely linked to historical emergence. Thus, in both novels the development of both female protagonists coincides with the socio-political awakening of a nation and its gradual disillusionment with a corrupt government. This interrelation between the private and public reflects Mastretta's feminist stance on her own writing: "Yo creo que soy una feminista en tanto que sí acepto y promuevo . . . que lo privado es público y lo personal es político" (Lavery 2001b: 364).

Mal de amores is very much written in the style of nineteenth-century realist novels and, like *Arráncame la vida*, has a close affinity with the novelists of the Mexican (post) Revolution such as Martín Luis Guzmán, Nellie Campobello, Elena Garro and Rosario Castellanos. By writing from a feminist perspective, Mastretta revises the history of the Mexican Revolution and its aftermath, questioning patriarchal ideologies, offering a critique of the mystification of the institutional revolution through state propaganda and icon manipulation. By focusing on women's direct contribution to the Mexican Revolution and their experiences of the upheaval in *Mal de amores*, Mastretta is giving a voice to those sectors of society which have been silenced or ignored by official historical texts. Women, such as the *soldaderas* (female soldiers), played a vital role in the Revolution. Female doctors, who were not in the front line, also contributed indirectly, proving themselves to be as strong as any man, although their crucial role has been almost entirely overlooked in the historical and photographic record. Emilia from *Mal de amores* contributes to the revolutionary cause through her work as a doctor working alongside *soldaderas*. Her contribution to the struggle often overshadows that of her revolutionary lover, Daniel. The mythical, the magical and the carnivalesque (also prevalent in *Arráncame la vida*) are frequently used in *Mal de amores* to subvert and reinstate authoritative historical and patriarchal discourses. Finally, throughout *Mal de amores* there is an important interplay between magic, the indigenous, popular medical practices and the mythic, on the one hand, and science, orthodox medicine and officialdom on the other.

Throughout her works, Mastretta questions the Mexican feminine stereotypes as outlined in Octavio Paz's *Laberinto de la soledad* (1950) and seeks to redress the gender imbalance. Mastretta portrays female characters who, in an attempt to construct self-defined images in a male environment which frequently suppresses such endeavours, appear stronger than men themselves. Mastretta's desire to speak of the silenced voices of women by portraying diverse, complex and often ambiguous images of womanhood puts her works in direct line with post-Boom Spanish American female writers such as Marta Traba, Isabel Allende, Elena Poniatowska and Carmen Peri Rossi. *Arráncame la vida*, *Mujeres de ojos grandes* and *Mal de amores* all share broadly commonly voiced themes such as the corporeal, female sexuality, masturbation and orgasm. Such a focus may be understood as Mastretta's desire to break with sexual taboos and to repudiate the belief that sex is a "dirty" activity whose legitimacy is restricted to reproductive purpose.

Other works by Ángeles Mastretta's which have also enjoyed popular success include: *Puerto libre* (1993), a collection of short stories and essays, literary and journalistic vignettes, biographical and non-biographical writing, memoirs and anecdotes all reflecting today's festive postmodern world of multiple surfaces. *El mundo iluminado* (1998) is also a collection of short stories and essays, which reflects more closely than *Puerto libre* Mastretta's own personality and literary priorities. In 1999, Mastretta published *Ninguna eternidad como la mía*, a short story which centres on the frustrated love of a ballet dancer Isabel Arango. Mastretta's latest publications include *Cuentos de Encuentros* y *Desencuentros Amorosos* (2003) and *El cielo de los leones* (2003). *Cuentos de encuentros y desencuentros amorosos* comprises a collection of thirteen short stories by various authors which centre on individual passion and romance, loyalty and friendship, unrequited love and loss, frequently arousing in the various characters an array of contradictory emotions. The prologue, written by Mastretta, describes these zealous texts as a celebration of life and love. Mastretta's essayistic works – *Puerto libre*, *El mundo iluminado* and *El cielo de los leones* – deal with topical issues such as feminism, politics, environmental pollution, consumerism, the role of writing, writer's block, love and death, but the serious messages connected with such issues are often lost in what appears to be a mere exercise in frivolity where obsessive self-indulgence and individualism prevail.

Despite the commercial and critical success of her best-selling works, Mastretta is still considered a popular writer whose literary credentials remain unproven. Mastretta's reliance on conventional story lines and on "light" entertainment such as romantic intrigue, together with her scarce interest in formal experimentation, has led critics to pigeonhole her as a popular writer. Aralia López González, for example, finds little to commend *Arráncame la vida*: "here everything is linear: the life, the story, and the course of events. There is no surprise or poetry, no original character or situation" (García 1994: 67).

Notwithstanding some of the negative criticism attributed to Mastretta's *œuvre*, critical interest in Mastretta has increased in recent years. But much academic research still remains to be done. Critical work on Mastretta is to be found in the form of articles and PhD theses, most of which relate to her first novel *Arráncame la vida*. Kay García's book *Broken Bars: New Perspectives From Mexican Women Writers* (1994) includes an interview with Mastretta and a chapter on *Arráncame la vida* which explores the implicit intertextual relationship between Mastretta's account and the official record of Mexican history. Mastretta's other works, notably *Mal de amores*, have received relatively little attention. Jane Lavery's *Ángeles Mastretta: Textual Multiplicity* (2005) is the first major study to be published on the fiction and essayistic works of this author, demonstrating the rich complexity and range of Mastretta's narratives. The monograph includes two chapters devoted almost exclusively to *Mal de amores*.

The strength of Matretta's work lies precisely in the way she eludes rigid categorization. Her postmodern narrative frequently oscillates ambiguously yet compellingly between the private and the public domains, interweaving the biographical, the fictional and the historical. Furthermore, Mastretta has developed a unique style defined by its diversity, ranging from plain literary description typical of the realist novel, to a colourful narrative peppered with the colloquial and the obscene, typical of popular discourse. Mastretta is a versatile writer who makes use of a wide variety of discourses (literary, journalistic, historical, colloquial) and narrative techniques such as humour and irony. While she may provide the reader with ample entertainment, by drawing on a variety of popular sources and rhetorical devices, her work is simultaneously underpinned by serious intent, fulfilling social and documentary functions, by showing particular sensitivity towards the position of women.

JANE LAVERY

Selected Works

La pájara pinta. Mexico City: Altiplano, 1975.
Arráncame la vida. Mexico City: Océano, 1985.
Mexican Bolero. Trans. A. Wright. México: Oceano, 1985.
Mujeres de ojos grandes. Mexico City: Cal y Arena, 1990.
Puerto libre. Mexico City: Cal y Arena, 1993.
Mal de amores. Mexico City: Alfaguara, 1996.
Lovesick. Trans. Margaret Sayers Peden. New York: Riverhead, 1997.
El Mundo iluminado. Mexico City: Cal y Arena, 1998.
Ninguna eternidad como la mía. Mexico City: Cal y Arena, 1999.
El Cielo de los Leones. Mexico City: Editorial Seix Barral, 2003.
Cuentos de encuentros y desencuentros amorosos. Mexico City: Alfaguara Ediciones: 2003.
Women with Big Eyes. Trans. Amy Schildhouse Greenberg. New York: Riverhead Books, 2003.

Other Articles

"El albañil de los ojos oscuros". *Fem* 16 (1980), 69–70.
"Rosa Luz Alegría: ¿Triunfo feminista?" *Fem* 15 (1980), 83–4.
"Un amante con lengua de cometa". *Fem* 49 (1987), 61–2.
"Laura Díaz y Carlos Fuentes: La edad de sus tiempos". *Nexos Virtual* July 1999: 259, *http://www.nexos.com.mx*, (accessed: 11 Dec. 2004).

References and Further Reading

Braun, Diane. "Silence and Dream as Textual Strategies in Selected Works of Sor Juana Inés de la Cruz, María Luisa Bombal and Ángeles Mastretta". Unpublished doctoral dissertation, State University of Florida, 1994. Dissertation Abstracts, 1995. 9502800.
García, Kay S. *Broken Bars: New Perspectives from Mexican Women Writers*. Albuquerque, NM: University of New Mexico Press, 1994.
González, Aralia López. "La huella de lo reprimido: fisuras y suturas". *Signos: Anuario de humanidades* 5(1) (1991): 239–48.
Ibsen, Kristine. *The Other Mirror: Women's Narrative in Mexico 1980–1995*. Contributions to the Study of World Literature, 80. Westport, CT: Greenwood Press, 1997.
Lavery, Jane, "The Physical and Textual Body in the Works of Ángeles Mastretta and Elena Poniatowska". *Romance Studies* 19(2) (2001a): 173–86.
——. "Entrevista a Ángeles Mastretta: La escritura como juego erótico y multiplicidad textual". *Anales de literatura hispanoamericana* 30 (2001b): 293–319.
——. *Ángeles Mastretta: Textual Multiplicity*. London: Tamesis, 2005.
Rivera Villegas, Carmen M. "Las mujeres y la Revolución Mexicana en *Mal de amores* de Angeles Mastretta". *Letras femeninas* 24(1–2) (Spring–Fall 1998): 37–48.

MATTO DE TURNER, CLORINDA

Clorinda Matto was born Grimanesa Martina Mato Usandivaras in Cuzco, Peru, in 1852. She grew up on her family's ranch and there learned to speak both Quechua and Spanish. The nature of her childhood allowed her to become familiar with indigenous Peruvian culture, a closeness which would manifest itself in a large majority of Matto's writings. Matto attended one of the best-known schools for girls in Cuzco. In 1871, she married Englishman José Turner. The two lived in a town called Tinta, near Cuzco, the city in which Matto's intense literary activity began. Turner died in 1881. Matto continued her prolific writing career and social activism in Peru, campaigning in both realms for a more enhanced understanding of Indian life and white treatment of indigenous culture and for improved education for women.

Besides producing a significant amount of prose, Matto also founded one weekly newsmagazine (*El Recreo*) in 1876, and in 1883 began to edit a daily newspaper in Arequipa (*La Bolsa*). In 1886, Matto moved to Lima and came into contact with Manuel González Prada, who would become her mentor. Matto was a key figure in Lima literary circles, including the well-known group established by the Argentine writer Juana Manuela Gorriti. Within these circles, Matto often met other important Peruvian writers and thinkers, such as Mercedes Cabello de Carbonera, Ricardo Palma, and Manuel González Prada, the famous Indianist reformer to whom Matto dedicated her 1889 novel, *Aves sin nido*.

In 1889, she began to edit and direct the Lima literary periodical (*El Perú Ilustrado*), and founded La Imprenta Equitativa in Lima in 1892. Only women worked on La Equitativa, thus revealing Matto's desire to create educational and professional realms in which women had the opportunity to work, write, and make decisions. After much debate over the publication in *El Perú Ilustrado* of a supposedly heretical story by Brazilian writer Henrique Coelho Netto, Matto de Turner was both spurned by her fellow citizens and excommunicated from the Catholic Church. Later, when fighting broke out in the capital in 1895, Matto was forced to leave Peru due to her sympathy for the political leader Andrés Cáceres. Matto de Turner first went to Chile and then lived the rest of her life in Argentina, where she founded and wrote for the journal *Búcaro Americano*. The Peruvian author died in Buenos Aires in 1909.

Journalist

Clorinda Matto de Turner proved to be a powerful force in nineteenth-century journalism, as she served formally as director and editor of several journals over three decades, wrote prolifically on a variety of topics, and participated actively in the literary circles of Peru and Argentina. Matto's extensive journalistic production provides a fascinating view of nascent nineteenth-century feminism in Peru and, more broadly, in Latin America.

Matto's directorship of the weekly *El Recreo de Cuzco*, which began in 1876, provided a forum for Matto to establish platforms for social reform, especially in the realm of education. It is particularly remarkable that Matto served as editor of the *Market News* (*La Bolsa*), a major daily newspaper of Arequipa. In that role, Matto wrote articles on two of the themes that would form the axes of her literary world view—improving the lives of indigenous Andean peoples and improving education for all. In addition, she contributed pieces on the state of Peru, commerce, agriculture, and immigration (Berg, "Matto de Turner: periodista y crítica").

Journalism continued to serve as Matto's primary field, even as she became extremely well-known by 1889 for her novel *Aves sin nido*. By 1889, Matto had become the director of *El Perú Ilustrado*, which Berg (1997) cites as "Lima's most important literary journal of the era". In this publication, Matto wrote resolutely in favor of "celebrating the Incan past and recognizing the philological importance of Quechua in the realization of the nation" (Ward 2002: 405). Contributors to the journal included Manuel González Prada and Rubén Darío. This was the journal that in 1890 published the aforementioned anticlerical article by Henrique Coelho Netto, which caused a storm surrounding the journal and its editor, Matto de Turner. By 1891, the banned journal was back in business, but Matto had resigned as its editor and director.

In February of 1892, Matto founded *La Equitativa*, which was billed as a feminist press, one that worked with and for women writers. It was with this press that Matto published her book *Leyendas y recortes* (1893). An exemplary essay among the articles included in *Leyendas y recortes* is one in which Matto advocates knowledgeably and convincingly for broader study of Quechua across Peru. She states unequivocally that a Peruvian cannot know her or his country—intellectually, topographically, or socially—until she or he has learned and understood the Quechua language upon which so much of the nation was built.

As soon as Matto de Turner moved to Buenos Aires in 1895, she began writing for several different Argentine papers and literary reviews, including, *La Nación*, *La Prensa*, *La Razón*, and *El Tiempo*. Once again, Matto founded and edited a social and literary magazine. This Argentine publication, which ran from 1896 to 1909, was called *Búcaro Americano*, and in it appear many of Matto de Turner's later articles.

Textbook Author

True to her vocation as educational reformer and teacher, Matto de Turner produced two textbooks designed for high-school students. The first of the two, *Elementos de literatura según el reglamento de instrucción pública para uso del bello sexo*, was published in 1884 and contained a series of literary pieces to instruct young women on how to become capable citizens who think about "justice, equal rights, and power" (Berg, 1997) and who appreciate well-written works of literature. Berg aptly points out that the textbook, although seemingly softly humanistic in nature, uses three female role models—Santa Teresa de Jesús, Mme. de Staël, and Cecilia Bohl de Faber—who are "not female role models famous for their docility and passivity". Berg summarizes the complex nature of the textbook: "This is a manual of feminist revolution, camouflaged as Fray Luis' 'perfecta casada' (the perfect married woman)".

The second high school text written by Matto was her *Analogía. Segundo año de gramática castellana en las escuelas normales, según el programa oficial*, published in Buenos Aires in 1897.

Short Fiction Writer and Novelist

Matto de Turner's short fiction and novels reveal in fictional form the political platforms proposed in her essays and articles. Throughout the 1880s, Matto de Turner continued Ricardo Palma's *costumbrista* tradition, creating brief portrayals of typical events of daily life in Cuzco. Palma, in fact, wrote the prologue to Matto's 1884 publication of the first volume of *Perú: Tradiciones cuzqueñas*. The second volume of the collection was published the following year. These collections of sketches attempt to move readers away from a Eurocentric view of Peru and towards a more complete view of Peruvian culture, one that includes the culture of Quechua.

In 1889, Matto completed her polemical novel *Aves sin nido* (Birds Without a Nest). This work, Matto's first of three novels, is widely considered the beginning of the "Indianist" tradition in South American literature, an approach to writing that would promote awareness of the political and social realities of Peru and would take into serious consideration the accurate portrayal of indigenous concerns within the larger context of the nation. In addition, Matto would exert a powerful influence on Indianist novels that gave face, name, and character to the indigenous peoples who populated the works. In the same year of the publication of *Aves sin nido*, Matto also wrote and published a book of biographical sketches entitled *Bocetos*.

Critics agree that the most significant contribution to South American literature from Matto's corpus is her 1889 "Indianist" novel *Aves sin nido*. The author displays her motives at the beginning of her Preface:

> If history is the mirror wherein generations to come shall contemplate the image of generations that went before, the novel must be the photograph that records the vices and virtues of a people, along with a moral prescription for the former and an admiring homage to the latter.
>
> (p. 1)

The work is remarkable for two reasons: its sincere and non-cartoonish portrayal of indigenous culture and its layered depiction of Peruvian women. In this novel, the author portrays a loving and sensitive couple who adopt two Indian sisters after their parents have been brutally murdered. As the novel unfolds, the reader observes the social mores of Kíllac, a small Peruvian village. Matto de Turner succeeds in portraying the corruption of the town's political and religious leaders, the struggle against racial and social injustices of the Andean Indians, and the intelligence and sensitivity of the female characters. Naomi Lindstrom, in her Preface to the 1996 revised translation of *Aves sin nido*, states that "language and culture of Andean Indians are represented in *Birds Without a Nest* with a thoroughness truly unusual for its time" (p. xv) and that "her [Matto's] concept of companionship marriage (illustrated by Fernando and Lucía), her advocacy of women's education, and her beliefs about women's distinctive character reveal to today's readers the outlook of a nineteenth-century Spanish American feminist and progressive" (ibid., p. xix).

Indole, Matto's second novel, was published two years later. Like *Aves sin nido*, *Indole* met with mixed reviews, as many readers were taken by surprise by the debate about clerical celibacy. The novel foregrounds the theme of clerical corruption and promotes the concept of permitting priests to marry. In 1895, Matto completed her last full-length novel, *Herencia*, which reveals a strongly naturalist bent, what Bautista Gutiérrez labels "almost prototypical of Latin American realism-naturalism held in check by the concept of bourgeois morality" (1996, p. 109). In the novel, Matto de Turner continues her platform against the abuse of power, especially in the religious and political arenas. Arambel-Guiñazú and Martin attribute real innovation to Matto's novels for the author's frank examination of the life of women and women's expression of emotions and sexuality (2001, p. 181).

Playwright

Hima-Sumac, the first and only play written by Clorinda Matto de Turner, debuted on October 16, 1884, in Arequipa, Peru. It had its Lima debut four years later in 1888. Berg (1997) sees the drama as being representative of its era, that is, as a reflection of Peru's struggle for identity in the face of the brutal War of the Pacific and the Chilean occupation of the country. A combination of Túpac Amaru I and II, heroes of indigenous uprisings in Peru, is cast as the fiancé of the central character, Hima-Sumac, the "Peruvian princess" of the play. The concept of the realization of a "Peruvian spirit" is the principal impulse, as the characters struggle for independence and recognition for Andean peoples. The play is a musical that contains many different lyric elements: individual instruments and voices, choral singing, national anthems. Berg comments upon the critics' response to the play, which, generally, was to "omit all discussion of the play's pro-indigenous fervor" (1999, p. 44), but at the same time to appreciate its patriotic thrust.

Themes and Influences

Clorinda Matto de Turner's lifelong vision was one of social and political reform, a vision greatly influenced by Matto's upbringing, her contact with people from around the world, and her movement within the literary circles of Lima and Buenos Aires. Her main areas of concern encompassed the clergy, the judicial and executive branches of government, the rights of indigenous peoples, education and access to the professions, particularly for women (Miller 1977: 25). John C. Miller says of Matto that "a dichotomy of thought exists in the life and works of Clorinda Matto de Turner—a representative of traditional conservative moral values and a revolutionary in a new sociopolitical awakening" (ibid., p. 28).

Thomas Ward observes the strong emphasis in the works of Matto de Turner on the concept of a "clearly Peruvian spirit," which must be linked to "creating harmony" in a nation coming to terms with its own identity (2001, p. 404). Matto de Turner's tireless literary and oratory work established a solid platform to help Peruvian citizens to consider and to battle against corruption in state and religion, to advocate for recognition of contributions and needs of indigenous peoples, and to lobby for improved education for all, and particularly for women of all races, religions, and colors. Her feminism was one always influenced by the concept of race and, therefore, her advocacy for women was more complex than that of feminists of her time from many other Western nations. In particular, her depiction of women as full human beings with intellectual thoughts, emotions, and physical desires advances the movements of Latin American feminism through the early twentieth century.

Modern Interpretations

It is clear that Clorinda Matto de Turner stirred the public conscience through her writings and speeches. Her tireless, intelligent, and impassioned advocacy for Indian peoples and for women, very much shaped by her condition as educated woman of a privileged class, produced intense social and political debates. Catherine Davies examines from a gender perspective the negative response to Matto de Turner at the turn of the century:

> What strikes us today is the especially virulent, sexist nature of the attacks waged against Matto, targeting not her writings as such but that the novelist was a woman. In 1910, a year after her death, Ventura García Calderón, a respected author in his own right, referred to her as 'the literary seamstress, genius of vulgarity, who patched up domestic prose in letters, novels—novels like those written by each and every English governess—until death broke the spool of thread and stopped the machine'.
>
> (2005, p. 186)

The sewing/weaving metaphor, used pejoratively by García Calderón, is one that is recuperated with great admiration by feminist critics of the twentieth century. It is likely that García Calderón, and other detractors like him, lacks distance in time and perspective to be able to examine objectively the life and works of Matto de Turner.

Contemporary critic Ismael Márquez sees Matto's portrait of Indians as "external and stereotypical," but is able to see the significant contribution of her work to the larger canon:

> Matto de Turner's portrayal of the Andean people, however, is external and stereotypical and represents the Indian as an individual dispossessed of any vestiges of cultural or ethnic identity. At the same time, *Aves sin nido* is the first significant effort to bring to light the appalling condition of the Peruvian Indian in a novel. It will be up to a later generation of writers who steered away from Romantic sentimentalism and Modernist exoticism to place the plight of the Indian in its proper economic and cultural context.
>
> (2005, p. 145)

Catherine Bryan examines Matto's role as a woman writing from a privileged class in nineteenth-century Latin America and views her position as eminently complex:

> At the same time, Matto, as a writing woman in nineteenth-century Peru, articulates a counterlanguage to male-centered narratives of national foundation. Matto's double-consciousness as *woman* of the dominant class, both inside and outside of official systems of power, is further problematized by her novelistic introduction of subaltern women marked by race and class.
>
> (1996, p. 118)

Although some scholars believe that Matto's style lacks sophistication, Gloria Bautista Gutiérrez says of her literary style: "It is humanistic, her locutions formal and intentioned, enriched with delicate images that are expressed naturally, but also in a correct and conceptual way" (1996, p. 108). In general, many Matto de Turner scholars view her as a prolific progressive whose literary works and non-fiction essays delve profoundly and sensitively in the social and political questions of her day, even as they are marked by the author's own social class and race.

In the Epilogue to *The Cambridge Companion to the Latin American Novel*, Efraín Kristal recognizes the international importance of Matto de Turner's *Aves sin nido*. The novel was one of the first Latin American novels translated to English (in 1904), under the title *Birds Without a Nest: A Story of Indian Life and Priestly Oppression in Peru*. The English title reveals the political bent and the weight of the polemic surrounding the novel. Its translation at a time when few Latin American works were being translated demonstrates the extent of international attention garnered by *Aves sin nido*. The novel, especially via the 1996 Lindstrom edition, has become an important part of the literary canon of Latin American letters.

Matto de Turner has been widely hailed as an important thinker and writer who contributed to shaping egalitarian thought in late nineteenth- and early twentieth-century Latin America. Contemporary critics view her as an author who both adopted the rhetoric of a woman of her era—particularly in terms of women's training to become good wives and mothers—and vociferously campaigned for equal access to education for all, equal rights for indigenous groups, and improved platforms for all women's advancement. Lindstrom cites Matto scholar Mary G. Berg in order to capture the essence of Matto's importance: "Burned in effigy, excommunicated, the presses of her feminist print shop smashed and her manuscripts burned by mobs just before her hasty flight from Lima in 1895, Clorinda Matto de Turner may have been the most controversial woman writer of nineteenth-century Latin America" (*The Cambridge Companion*, p. 39).

Much critical work remains to be completed on Clorinda Matto de Turner's non-fiction and literary corpus. Matto's work begs a more detailed examination of the author's life, of the political and social framework of turn-of-the-century Peru and Argentina, of the form and foundation of the works themselves, and of their influence on other works produced in the twentieth century.

ELLEN MAYOCK

Selected Works

Drama

Hima-Sumac: Drama en tres actos y en prosa. Lima: Imp. "La Equitativa," 1892.

Essays and Articles

"La mujer y la ciencia". *Búcaro Americano*, 1 January 1898.

"Ahorrar es virtud". *Búcaro Americano*, 15 June 1906.

Cuatro conferencias sobre América del Sur. Buenos Aires: Juan A. Alsina, 1909.

Viaje de recreo: España, Francia, Inglaterra, Italia, Suiza, Alemania. Valencia: F. Sempere, 1909.

Stories

Aves sin nido (1889) (translated as *Birds Without a Nest: A Story of Indian Life and Priestly Oppression in Peru*. Trans. J. G. Hudson. London: Charles J. Thynne, 1904.) See also the 1996 Lindstrom edition, University of Texas Press.

Indole. Lima: Bacigalupi, 1891.

Leyendas y recortes. Lima: La Equitativa, 1893.
Herencia. Lima: Masías, 1895.
Boreales, miniaturas y porcelanas. Buenos Aires: Juan A. Alsina, 1902.
Tradiciones cuzqueñas completas. Lima: Peisa, 1976.

References and Further Reading

Arambel-Guiñazú, María Cristina and Martin, Claire Emilie. "La prensa no tiene seso". In *Las mujeres toman la palabra: escritura femenina del siglo XIX*. 2 vols. Madrid: Iberoamericana, 2001a, vol. I, pp. 45–76.

——. "Del romanticismo al realismo. Novelistas peruanas de fin de siglo". *Las mujeres toman la palabra: escritura femenina del siglo XIX*. 2 vols. Madrid: Iberoamericana, 2001b, vol. II, pp. 179–96.

Bautista Gutiérrez, Gloria. *Voces femeninas de Hispanoamérica. Antología*. Pittsburgh, PA: University of Pittsburgh Press, 1996, pp. 107–15.

Berg, Mary G. "Clorinda Matto de Turner". In Diane E. Marting (ed.), *Spanish-American Women Writers*. Westport, CT: Greenwood Press, 1990, pp. 303–15.

——. "Writing for Her Life: The Essays of Clorinda Matto de Turner". *Reinterpreting the Spanish American Essay: Women Writers of the 19th and 20th Centuries*. Austin, TX: University of Texas Press, 1995, pp. 80–9.

——. "Clorinda Matto de Turner: periodista y crítica (Perú, 1852–1909)". In Betty Osorio and María Mercedes Jaramillo (eds), *Las desobedientes: Mujeres de nuestra América*. Bogotá: Panamericana, 1997, pp. 147–59. http://www.evergreen.loyola.edu/~tward/Mujeres/critica/berg-matto.htm (accessed 21 June 2006).

——. "Contexts of Clorinda Matto de Turner's *Hima-Sumac*". *La Chispa* (1999): 37–47.

——. "Presencia y ausencia de Clorinda Matto de Turner en el panorama literario y editorial peruano". In Ignacio Arellano and José Antonio Mazotti (eds), *Edición e interpretación de textos andinos*. Navarra: Universidad de Navarra, 2000, pp. 211–29. http://www.evergreen.loyola.edu/~tward/Mujeres/critica/berg-matto-presencia.htm (accessed 21 June 2006).

Bryan, Catherine M. "Making National Citizens: Gender, Race, and Class in Two Works by Clorinda Matto de Turner". *Cincinnati Romance Review*. Cincinnati, OH: 1996, pp. 113–18.

Davies, Catherine. "Gender Studies". In Efraín Kristal (ed.), *The Cambridge Companion to the Latin American Novel*. Cambridge: Cambridge University Press, 2005, pp. 183–99.

Lindstrom, Naomi. Forward to *Birds Without a Nest. A Story of Indian Life and Priestly Oppression in Peru*. Trans. J.G.H. (1904). Austin, TX: University of Texas Press, 1996.

——. *Early Spanish American Narrativity*. Austin, TX: University of Texas Press, 2004.

——. "The Nineteenth-century Latin American Novel". In Efraín Kristal (ed.), *The Cambridge Companion to the Latin American Novel*. Cambridge: Cambridge University Press, 2005, pp. 23–43.

Márquez, Ismael. "The Andean Novel". In Efraín Kristal (ed.), *The Cambridge Companion to the Latin American Novel*. Cambridge: Cambridge University Press, 2005, pp. 142–61.

Miller, John C. "Clorinda Matto de Turner and Mercedes Cabello de Carbonera: Societal Criticism and Morality". In Yvette E. Miller and Charles M. Tatum (eds), *Latin American Women Writers: Yesterday and Today*. Pittsburgh, PA: Latin American Literary Review, 1977, pp. 25–32.

Ward, Thomas. "La ideología nacional de Clorinda Matto de Turner". *Neophilologus* 86 (2002): 401–15.

Zanetti, Susana E. "*Búcaro Americano*: Clorinda Matto de Turner en la escena femenina porteña". In *Mujeres y cultura en la Argentina del siglo XIX*. Buenos Aires: Feminaria, 1994, pp. 264–75.

MATURANA, ANDREA

The Chilean critics started acknowledging Andrea Maturana's (b. 1969) work at a time when the country was leaving behind Augusto Pinochet's dictatorship, and the nation was full of expectation concerning a new democracy. In 1991, she was invited to participate in the anthology *Cuentos eróticos*, and she presented a sensual short story that surprised the readers. The critics were even more astonished to discover that Maturana was barely 22 years old. The following year, she published her volume *(Des) Encuentros (Des) Esperados*, defined by the critics as a series of masterly written erotic stories, though they might be better understood as intimate stories. This novel writer soon became the new promise of the so-called new Chilean narrative.

Maturana comes from a family of artists, psychologists, scientists, and intellectuals. She took a degree in Biology, avoiding the formal study of literature, to prevent the academy from constraining her relationship with Letters. She started writing as a girl, illustrating her first stories, and as a teenager she decided to explore her ability to write literature. When she finished high school, she attended the workshop of the well-known writer Pía Barros (who is considered one of her major literary influences), and later on, those of Antonio Skármeta and Marco Antonio de la Parra. Since then, literature has been present in her life at different periods, with different intensities.

Maturana and the New Chilean Narrative

During the 1990s, Chilean critics started to define the literature of young writers, aged 20–40, as the new Chilean narrative. These authors wanted to differentiate their writing from those of the generation of the 1950s (Violeta Parra, Flora Yáñez, José Donoso, Jorge Edwards) and the group of 1972 or *novísimos* (Antonio Skármeta, Ariel Dorfman, and later on, Diamela Eltit, Lucía Guerra-Cunningham).

Although this new narrative should not be defined as representative of a homogeneous group, this writing presents some trends compared to previous literary movements. Most of these young writers—born in or after 1955—represent a society which was influenced by dictatorship. Writers are profoundly individualistic if not skeptical of the validity of literary groups and movements. Since their vital experience has been marked out by dictatorship, topics, such as exile, violence, loneliness, as well as the loss of community, disintegration of the universe, and transition to democracy characterize their literature. They also want to distance themselves from magical realism, labels and exotic portrayals of Latin American culture. Essentially, they are *revising* the act of literary writing and creation.

Maturana, considered the youngest writer of this group, adopted the intimate as a medium to discuss solitude and lack of communication in contemporary society. In fact, she speaks about the body in its materiality. At the beginning of the 1990s, critics were not used to studying eroticism, since this topic was considered taboo in traditional Chilean society. By introducing a woman's sexuality and physical body as part of the feminine experience, Maturana was contributing to the renewal of the cultural debate of a post-dictatorial Chile.

At 17 years old, she won her first award in the *Bata* literary contest (1986), and later on in the *Juegos Literarios Gabriela Mistral* contest (1989). She also won a second recognition at the Encuentro Nacional de Arte in 1990. By the end of the 1980s, she had been included in a number of Chilean anthologies: *Cuentos de mi país* (Santiago: Antártica 1986), *26 Cuentos ilustrados 'Ensacados'* (Santiago: Ergo Sum 1987), *25 cuentos* (Santiago: Ergo Sum 1988), *El cuento feminista latinoamericano* (Santiago: Ilet, 988), *Machismo se escribe con M de mamá* (Santiago: Ergo Sum 1989), *Cuando no se puede vivir del cuento* (Santiago: Ergo Sum 1989), *Brevísima relación del cuento breve de Chile* (Santiago: Lar, 1989).

Maturana started taking her own literary workshops, and was a columnist for *Revista Ya*, a magazine affiliated to the newspaper *El Mercurio* (1993–95). Later on, she also became a translator for Andrés Bello Publishers in Chile.

After *(Des) Encuentros (Des) Esperados* (1992)—her first book of short stories—Maturana was well known enough to be called "the promise of the new Chilean literature;" however, this sort of excessive expectation caused problems for someone who does not like exposure or public exhibition. By the end of the 1990s, her public appearances were rare.

Andrea Maturana doesn't feel the pressure to publish in order to become a popular writer, her production is associated with erratic writing. She took her time between *(Des) Encuentros* (1992), and the novel *El daño* (1997) (translated into Dutch in 1999). Then she published two books for children: *La isla de las langostas* (1997), and *Eva y su Tan* (2005). There was a silence until 2006, when she presented the collection of short stories *No decir*. In this literary corpus, readers can identify an evolution in her writing style.

Style and Themes

No magical realism, no flowers, nor butterflies are to be found in Maturana's work. She is precise and concise. Her methodology is to write when she has an idea, and then get straight to the point. Time will pass until she feels the need to write something new; therefore, she tends to write less than more.

Maturana's work is a narrative of intimacy, avoiding long discourses. Her literature can be described as a whisper in the ear, unveiling wounds and secrets of Chilean society instead of confronting those traumas in the public arena. The erotic loneliness in *(Des) Encuentros (Des) Esperados* (1992) shows the emptiness of life in contemporary urban space. "Verde en el borde" (in *Los pecados capitales*, 1993) examines anorexia nervosa, and "Yo a la mujeres me las imaginaba bonitas" (in *17 narradoras latinoamericanas*) relates to a girl's experience of menstruation. Her literary voices adopt a calm and serious tone which talks about and criticizes the fears, hypocrisy, and cultural repression of society.

Her narrative is a dialogue between the body and contemporary Chilean society. Kaempfer (2000) analyzes the search for private pleasure in *Desencuentros* (1992) as a form of resistance to constraining mechanisms produced by society. Lopez Cotín (2002) also views this book as a conversation among the private body, perception of time, and public urban space which results in a contest between the individual and the alienating collectivity.

In sum, the concept of the feminine body allows Maturana to shape an alternative point of view of women's agency (Lagos 1997; Maiz Peña 2002); sometimes turning the representation of the material body into an anti-discourse that explores trauma as a tool to overcome a society defined by oppressive patriarchy (Promis 1997). Therefore Maturana's narrative is about more than intimacy; it is an account of women's political resistance, and as an extension, of everyone's resistance to repression.

In *El daño* (1997), Maturana explores the trauma of incest as a family secret, associated with repressed memories within Chilean history. The novel also presents the topic of the spoken word—or a spoken truth—as a dual effect of healing and hurting at the same time.

In the story, two friends travel to the north of Chile in search of memory and emotional healing. One was abused by her father as a child, and the other has recently been abandoned by her lover. The dialogue between the characters and their exploration of bodily sensations liberates one and anguishes the other. Crosby (2004) reads the novel as the wound of Chilean history as a result of dictatorship.

No decir (2006) is a continuation of the theme proposed in *El daño*: unresolved historical negations, silences, unnamed truth, and hypocrisies latent in any Chilean family, and in middle-class society. Once again, spoken words become channels to liberate repressed experiences.

Although there is a change of themes from *(Des) Encuentros* to *No decir* (from the search–loss of the couple to the revelation of those hidden family secrets), Maturana's literature can be read from a transversal perspective as a problem of communication. Language—its presence or absence—is a metatextual topic in Andrea Maturana's stories. In fact, this is a powerful literature written with the appearance of simplicity and transparency.

Literature, Motherhood and Place

After being "the young erotic writer", living in Santiago and Buenos Aires, publishing a number of books before the age of 30 and becoming the mother of two girls, Andrea Maturana moved to a small Chilean town, by the sea. Instead of dealing with large urban places, she prefers to be by the sea, and is indifferent to public exhibition. Once in a while, she returns to the city to direct literature workshops.

Vania Barraza Toledo

Selected Works

(Des) Encuentros (Des) Esperados. Santiago de Chile: Editorial Los Andes, 1992.

El daño. Santiago de Chile: Alfaguara, 1997.

La Isla de las Langostas: México, D.F.: CIDCLI: Consejo Nacional para la Cultura y las Artes, 1997.

"Cradle Song" and "Out of Silence". *Cruel Fictions, Cruel Realities: Short Stories by Latin American Women Writers*. Ed. Kathy S. Leonard. Pittsburgh, PA: Latin American Literary Review Press, 1997.

Eva y su Tan. Santiago de Chile: Aguilar Chilena de Ediciones, 2005.

No decir. Santiago de Chile: Alfaguara, 2006.

References and Further Reading

Crosby, Margaret. "La traición paterna y el incesto en *El daño* de Andrea Maturana". Edited with an Introduction by Jorge Chen Sham and Isela Chiu-Olivares. In *De márgenes y adiciones: Novelistas latinoamericanas de los 90*. San José, Costa Rica: Perro Azul. 2004.

Flores, Arturo C. "Escritura y experiencia femenina: *(Des) Encuentros (Des)Esperados* de Andrea Maturana". *Revista Chilena de Literatura* 47 (1995): 129–35.

Kaempfer, Álvaro. "La fuga es el mensaje: Andrea Maturana y las citas imposibles de una escritura en transición". *Alpha: Revista de Artes, Letras y Filosofía* 16 (2000): 73–90.

Lagos, María Inés. "Cuerpo y subjetividad en narraciones de Andrea Maturana, Ana María del Río y Diamela Eltit". *Revista Chilena de Literatura* 50 (1997): 97–109.

López Cotín, Olga. "Andrea Maturana o la erótica del paisaje urbano". *Anales de Literatura Chilena* 3 (2002): 107–20.

Maiz-Peña, Magdalena. "Los apetitos de la ansiedad: Cuerpo-texto de Andrea Maturana". *Texto Crítico* 5(10) (2002): 179–86.

Mateo del Pino, Ángeles. "Cuando lo que (des)une no es el amor sino el espanto (El discurso de la modernidad en la narrativa chilena actual: Andrea Maturana)". *Texto Crítico* 5(10) (2002): 187–202.

Muñoz, Willy O. *Polifonía de la marginalidad: la narrativa de escritoras latinoamericanas*. Santiago de Chile: Editorial Cuarto Propio, 1999.

Olea, Raquel. *Lengua víbora*. Producciones de lo femenino en la escritura de mujeres chilenas. Santiago de Chile: Cuarto Propio / Corporación de Desarrollo de la Mujer La Morada, 1998.

Promis, José. "Heridas invisibles". *Revista Hoy* 1063 (1997): 58.

Silvy, Claudia. "Las identidades fluctuantes en *El daño* de Andrea Maturana y Beatriz y los cuerpos celestes de Lucía Etxebarria". MA thesis, Bowling Green State University, OH, 2003.

Villalobos, Daniel. "(Des) encuentros (des) esperados de Andrea Maturana, La ciudad que vigila". In Priscilla Gac-Artigas (ed.), Vol. 2 of *Reflexiones; ensayos sobre escritoras hispanoamericanas contemporáneas*. New Jersey: Ediciones Nuevo Espacio, 20 (2002). 101–7.

MELÉNDEZ, CONCHA

Concepción Leticia Meléndez Ramirez (1895–1983) was born in Caguas, Puerto Rico, the youngest daughter of nine children; eight girls and one boy who died young. Her parents were Jose Meléndez Valero from Ceiba and Carmen Ramirez Munoz from Hato Grande. Her family moved to Rio Piedras when Meléndez was 7 years old. Being near the sea for the first time would mark a turning point for the future writer. Meléndez would find inspiration in the mountains and sea that surrounded her from this point on as Rio Piedras lays between the radiant and turquoise-colored Atlantic Ocean and the mist-covered Yunque Mountain in the Caribbean National Rainforest. In her literary criticism work she often uses mountains and waves metaphorically as she reviews a writer's or poet's work.

Her education included a teaching certificate (1921) and Bachelor's degree from the University of Puerto Rico (1922), a course in the Madrid Center of Historic Studies (1924), a Master's Degree from Columbia University in New York (1926), and a Doctorate in Philosophy and Letters from the University of Mexico (1932), the first woman to be so awarded. In addition, since 1942 she was a fellow at the Kenyon School of English in Indiana, forming a part of a special group of literary experts.

Meléndez is one of the most honored Puerto Rican writers. Her numerous awards and honors include: the Eugenio Maria de Hostos Medal from El Mundo (1938), the Cultural Institute of Puerto Rico honors Meléndez for her literary work (1963), the Puerto Rico State Department honors Meléndez as an example of Americanism (1963), the Institute of Puerto Rican Culture awards a Gold Medal of Honor to Meléndez on its 10th Year Anniversary (1965), the Society of the Family of Man awards Meléndez the Gold Medal for Excellence in Education (1966), the Venezuelan government inducts Meléndez into the Order of Andres Bello (1971). In addition, the Concha Meléndez lecture Hall was created at the Central University of Bayamon (1978) and the Institute of Puerto Rican Culture has a special Concha Meléndez Library in Santurce, Puerto Rico.

Meléndez was a prolific writer and researcher. Her complete works have been compiled into a five-volume set by the Institute of Puerto Rican Culture. Her first publication was a small volume of poems entitled *Psiquis doliente* (1923, Bereaved Pyschic). She was inspired by the poet Jose de Diego, who in 1916 wrote a poem about Meléndez foretelling her success in the literary field. He would serve as a spiritual father and literary mentor, culminating in Meléndez's book, *Jose de Diego: From My Memory* (1967), based on a presentation she gave at a conference celebrating the 100th year of Diego's birth (1966). Although Meléndez would leave poetry aside after this one effort, her poetic tendencies continued to be evident in all her writings, infusing them with rhythm and eloquence. She has also been criticized for not being able to control the conflict between Meléndez the poet and Meléndez the researcher.

Meléndez is considered one of the pillars of Latin American Literary studies because of her uncompromising dedication to scholarly research in a field she developed with a belief that Latin America could be united through education and the self-understanding of its own cultures. In fact, Meléndez would spend an inordinate amount of time traveling around Latin America, including Mexico, Venezuela, Argentina, Uruguay, Brazil, Panama, Colombia, Ecuador and Peru, collecting native language books and other cultural materials that she integrated into her courses in Puerto Rico. She believed that the direct experience of the psychology of the cultures was the only way to illuminate the true essence of the culture itself – everything was dependent on the "person". These trips also helped her to understand the cultures more intimately and this would give her much more insight for her literary criticism work.

These travels helped Meléndez to develop a profile of Latin America for contemplation and meditation while she worked. She wrote based on her memories of her travels, what she experienced in the different countries and how she felt while experiencing it. Meléndez then wrote with a poet's heart, if not with a poet's form. The travels helped her in her literary artistry. For example, in her dedication in *Entrance into Peru* (1941) she writes, "I have written these pages more to keep alive my memories, than to share my experiences". When she writes about the poet *Amado Nervo* (1926), she states poetically "he accented in my spirit the love of mystery". The reader never forgets that Meléndez began as a poet, even though she abandoned that form to embrace the essay as her best medium of expression.

Some examples of how these experiences influenced her work can be found in: *The Indian Novel in Hispanic-America*, doctoral thesis (1934); *Signs from Iberoamerica*, eleven essays of different Latin-American writers (1936); *Entrance in Peru*, travel diary (1941); *Asomante*, collection of articles, essays and conference papers about Hispanic-American studies, her travels and book reviews (1943); the *Art of the Puerto Rican Story* (1961); and the annual *Handbook of Latin American Studies* for the University of Puerto Rico, from 1935 throughout her tenure.

Meléndez is known for her precision of her language and her solid knowledge base of her subject-matter. Her work has been described as dedicated, intellectually wise and spiritual, sometimes even severe, although the true sense is that Meléndez does not add words for their own sake. She feels a sense of responsibility in the use of language and does so consciously. She is generous when she evaluates another writer's work but is not shy in stating where she differs in their thoughts or when she feels their form did not measure up to her high standards. Through her work Meléndez emphasizes that writers and artists have a role to play in creating the opinions and consciousness of society and thus should endeavor to educate the collective thought to inspire individuals about art, civics and esthetics. She states that the salvation of Latin America is in education and the internationalization of Latin American cultures, which is what as a writer, researcher and educator, she devoted her life to. Meléndez's travels and work recognized outside of Puerto Rico were the starting point for creating nexus among the Latin American countries. Her most urgent message was for her students and readers to challenge their imaginations.

Themes in her work include ethnic and esthetic art, including the connection between art and literature; and Latin American literature, including writers and poets. Her work shows a propensity to focus on indigenism; the American drama; man and nature; Latin American solidarity; and the act of creation (artistic and literary).

For example, her first work in *Asomante* is "The Indian Art of Matilde Perez". Before describing and evaluating Perez's work, Meléndez offers an overview of the use of archeology and poetry in Latin America contrasting it with the history so beloved by Europeans. "There [in Europe] archeology is a complement to history. Here [in Latin America] it is history itself. We need to read our history in our monuments, in the accessible residues of our cultures" since the ancient civilizations of Latin-American did not leave us a written language.

DEBORAH GONZALEZ

Selected Works

Psiquis Doliente. San Juan, PR: privately published, 1923.
Amado Nervo. New York: Hispanic Institute, 1926.
The Indian Novel in Hispanic-America, doctoral thesis, Spain: Hernando, 1934.
Signs from Iberoamerica. Mexico: Sanchez, 1936.
Entrance in Peru. Cuba: Verónica, 1941.
Asomante. San Juan: Cordillera, 1943.
The Art of the Short Story in Puerto Rico. New York: Las Americas, 1961.
Jose de Diego, as I Remember Him. San Juan, PR: Instituto Cultural de Puerto Rico, 1966.
Hispanic-American Literature. San Juan, PR: Cordillera, 1967.
People and Books. San Juan, PR: Cordillera, 1970.
Diverse Hispanic-American Poets. San Juan, PR: Cordillera, 1971.
Fiction of Puerto Rico: Story and Novel. San Juan, PR: Cordillera, 1971.
The Poetry of Alfonso Reyes. San Juan, PR: Cordillera, 1973.
Hispanic-American Stories: Tradition and Notes. Mexico: Orion, 1978.

References and Further Reading

Arnaldi de Olmeda, Cecilia. *Concha Meléndez: Vida y Obra*. San Juan, PR: University of Puerto Rico, 1972.
Fabre, Mariano Feliciano. *Antología y Cartas de sus Amigos*. San Juan, PR: Cordillera, 1995.
Gale, Thomson. *Contemporary Authors*. Amazon.com, 2004.

MENDOZA, MARÍA LUISA "CHINA"

Mendoza (b. 1930), nicknamed la "China," [girl] was born in Guanajuato, Mexico, to a large Catholic family. Due to multiple ailments, such as eczema, as a child Mendoza spent much of her time indoors reading. The social ambience of Guanajuato remains a staple in Mendoza's prose, and she often examines hypocritical attitudes taken to be characteristic of *provincia* (Mexican territory outside its national capital). Mendoza does not have children, and she likes to narrate her life as one of self-reliance, solitude, and independence even when married. Her love of Mexico finds its balance in statements that she is an outsider and that she is overlooked on the Mexican literary landscape. Despite the financial pressures that Mendoza recalls from her adolescence after her father's death, she studied three advanced degrees: interior design at the Universidad Femenina de México (Mexican Feminine University), stage design at the Instituto Nacional de Bellas Artes (National Institute of Fine Arts), and Spanish literature at the Universidad Nacional Autónoma de México (National Autonomous University of Mexico). Mendoza settled on journalism as her most profitable job.

Pioneering Style

Unlike some other female reporters of the time, Mendoza published in newspapers sections outside the social column. In 1962, she co-founded the newspaper *El Día*, and she helped establish the women-oriented magazines *Mujeres* and *Mujer de Hoy*. Eventually, she wrote for such mainstream newspapers as *Novedades*, *El Universal*, *El Sol de México*, and *Excélsior*. She won the first of two National Journalism Prizes in 1972 for a story about Chile. At its most innovative, Mendoza's journalistic style tends toward a fragmented impressionism and generally favors horizontal development that skims the surface of perception, moving among spontaneous impressions in a proliferation of horizontally-associated details. The achievement of exploring the world through horizontally arranged association rather than more vertical structures of deeper, detained reflection owes much to Mendoza's extraordinary vocabulary, which encompasses popular expressions, learned terms, and a good number of neologisms. The resultant journalistic prose is a celebration of baroque style that flourishes in ever greater complexity in Mendoza's fiction. Notwithstanding this creatively autonomous language, Mendoza sometimes grumbles about contemporary slang and degradation of the Spanish language (see *Confrontaciones* [1985; Confrontations], p. 11).

A Rewarding Public Life

Mendoza exercises a public voice through multiple disciplines. In the mid-1970s Mendoza was a radio commentator, and from 1972 to the late 1980s she articulated her opinions on Mexican television, including the programs *24 horas*, *La Hora 25* and *TV Debate*. She won her second National Journalism Prize in 1984 for her television program *Un Día un Escritor* (One Day, One Writer) (later renamed "Un Día un Mexicano" [One day one Mexican]). In an interview, Mendoza claims that she was a pioneer on the small screen as the first woman in Mexico to speak about literature on television (Sánchez Ambriz 2001: 22).

Following a family political vocation, Mendoza became one of Mexico's female political pioneers by representing the state of Guanajuato in federal Congress from 1985 to 1988. This political service with the ruling party, the PRI (Institutional Revolutionary Party), does not seem to have been lucrative, as Mendoza is the first to complain about her financial situation. Mendoza consistently articulates the belief that she ekes out a subsistence living from daily writing and other forms of service. Her perception of financial precariousness may lessen in future interviews, as she received federal funding as an artist in the Sistema Nacional de Creadores (National System of Creators) from 1997–99 and 1999–2001.

Earlier in her career, she received a grant from the Centro Mexicano de Escritores in 1968–69 that allowed her to draft her first and most famous novel, *Con Él, conmigo, con nosotros tres* (1971; With Him, with Me, with Us Three). This politically motivated, innovative text examines the 1968 assassination of unarmed citizens in the Plaza de las Tres Culturas (Plaza of Three Cultures) in Mexico City by sharpshooters acting with governmental complicity. Mendoza subtitles the work "*Cronovela*," a neologism that combines the words "chronicle" and "novel" and indicates her interest in experimental literature. The text uses a leitmotif of blood and considers the historical legacy of one family over the centuries in Mexico whose bloodline ends with the childless female protagonist. From the first edition, the novel sold well and won the Magda Donato award in 1971. Some critics reject the classification of the work as a novel. Dolly and William Young view Mendoza's work as pertaining to New Journalism, including *Con Él, conmigo, con nostoros tres* and *El perro de la escribana* (1982, The Scribe's Dog). This last title is sometimes described as Mendoza's most mature text and reflects her awareness of domestic realms, perhaps inspired by her experience with interior and stage design. *El perro de la escribana* organizes chapters according to shifts in domestic scenery, and so elements that in other texts might function as background detail come to occupy the foreground in much of Mendoza's fiction, in complement to her baroque style that cultivates surface detail.

Against the spontaneity and straightforwardness characteristic of journalism, Mendoza's fiction often seems to witness an elaborate process of rewriting that creates distanced narratives that express nostalgia. Mendoza describes complex relationships among characters that tend to develop through more or less static portraits, given that the relationships tend to be worked out in advance and narrated from a distance. Even Mendoza's short stories, published in *Ojos de papel volando* (1985, Eyes of Flying Paper) manage to distance the narration of the central anecdote from the impression of immediate action, despite the reduced number of pages a short story allows to accomplish this distancing. Her fiction richly employs epigraphs, in particular quotations from poets Sor Juana Inés de la Cruz and José Carlos Becerra. For this awareness of the literary tradition and for her stylistic intricacy, Mendoza perhaps is most accurately classified as a fiction writer's writer. Her introspective narrations supply aesthetic innovation in the near absence of suspenseful action and dialogue.

An Ambivalent Success

Though she laments her invisibility as a writer in Mexico, Mendoza's works are nearly ubiquitous in what is otherwise a fickle literary market. New and used bookstores stock her texts, and such prestigious labels as Joaquín Mortiz promote her work. As recently as 2001, Mendoza won the José Rubén Romero Novel Prize for *De amor y lujo*, subsequently published by the well-distributed Tusquets house. This novel compares generations (a grandmother and granddaughter) and cultures (the Russian Revolution of 1917 and the 1911 Mexican Revolution). In 2005, Mendoza notes in an interview that *De Ausencia* (1974, About Ausencia) was in its fifteenth reprint. The contradiction between the successes of Mendoza's prolific career and her self-perception of literary marginality is typical of Mendoza's contradictory, complex habits of thought. For example, she seems to vacillate between aspects of conservative, nationalist ideology and radical defiance of that conservatism through skeptical social criticism. Thus, Mendoza displays a strong faith that coexists with constant irreverence.

Mendoza expressly rejects the label of "feminist" and considers herself sympathetic to women in an interesting contradiction that proposes a tension with the erotic content of her writing. Consequently, the historical-erotic novel, *De Ausencia* explores the *lack* of liberty that sexual explorer Ausencia Bautista actually comes to enjoy, as articles by David William Foster and Aralia López González observe. Mendoza also writes erotic literature in texts that uphold religious faith. In *Fuimos es mucha gente* (1998, 'We' Does Not Include You), Mendoza employs the concept of guardian angels who interact with characters, even as this faith in the divine coincides with the elaboration of the elderly female protagonist's sexual history and returns to the scene of a young girl's molestation at the hands of her cousin. A similar scene of incest among cousins appears in the earlier novel, *El perro de la escribana* and proposes the possible rewards available to the critic who would contemplate Mendoza's work in its entirety. Mendoza's contradictory, yet carefully crafted fiction offers a challenging read, which perhaps explains why her œuvre has yet to be examined as thoroughly as Mendoza might wish.

EMILY HIND

Selected Works

Chronicles

La O por lo redondo. Mexico: Grijalbo, 1971.
Crónica de Chile. Mexico: Diana, 1972.

¡Oiga usted! Mexico: Samo, 1973.
Raaa Reee Riii R: Rusia (URSS). Mexico: FCE, 1974.
Las cosas. Mexico: Joaquín Mortiz, 1976.
Trompo a la uña. Villahermosa: Gobierno del Estado de Tabasco, 1989.

Autobiography

Confrontaciones. Azcapotzalco, Mexico: UAM, 1985.
De cuerpo entero. Mexico: Corunda, UNAM, 1991. Reprinted in *Mujeres que cuentan: Siete escritoras mexicanas de su puño y letra.* Mexico: Ariadne, 2000, pp. 17–54.

Short Story

Ojos de papel volando. Mexico: Joaquín Mortiz, 1985.

Novels

Con Él, conmigo, con nosotros tres: Cronovela. Mexico: Joaquín Mortiz, 1971.
De ausencia. Mexico: Joaquín Mortiz, 1974.
El perro de la escribana o Las piedecasas. Mexico: Joaquín Mortiz, 1982.
Fuimos es mucha gente. 1998. Mexico: Alfaguara, 1999.
De amor y lujo. Mexico: Tusquets, CONACULTA, INBA, 2002.

References and Further Reading

Bearse, Grace M. "Entrevista con María Luisa Mendoza". *Hispania* 64(3) (1981): 459.
Foster, David William. "Espejismos eróticos: *De Ausencia*, de María Luisa Mendoza". *Revista Iberoamericana* 51(132–3) (1985): 657–63.
López González, Aralia. "Nuevas formas de ser mujer en la narrativa contemporánea de escritoras mexicanas". *Casa de las Américas* 31(183) (1991): 3–8. Reprinted as "Dos tendencias en la evolución de la narrativa contemporánea de escritoras mexicanas". In Aralia López González, Amelia Malagamba, and Elena Urrutia (eds), *Mujer y literatura mexicana y chicana: Culturas en contacto.* Mexico: Colegio de México, Colegio de la Frontera del Norte, 1990, pp. 21–4.
Maíz, Magdalena and Peña, Luis H. "María Luisa Mendoza". Trans. Owen Williams. In Diane E. Marting (ed.), *Spanish American Women Writers: A Bio-Bibliographical Source Book.* New York: Greenwood Press, 1990, pp. 329–16.
Parada, Andrea. "Subjetividad femenina y alienación en 'Me olvido de olvidarte' de María Luisa Mendoza". *Chasqui* 28(2) (1999): 3–13.
Robles, Martha. "María Luisa Mendoza". In *La sombra fugitiva: Escritoras en la cultura nacional.* Vol. 1. Mexico: Diana, 1999, pp. 325–41.
Sánchez Ambriz, Mary Carmen. "Recuerdos de una escribana". *Bucareli* 8(213) (Sept. 10 2001): 22.
Young, Dolly J. and Young, William D. "The New Journalism in Mexico: Two Women Writers". *Chasqui* 12(2–3) (1983): 72–80.

MERCADER, MARTHA

Martha Mercader's (b. 1926) writing includes a wide range of themes and techniques but she is best known for the fictional rewriting of history through the use of intertextuality, polyphony, and dialogic structure. Her historical novels destabilize, question, and offer new alternatives to historical knowledge. In *Juana Manuela, mucha mujer* (1980) *Belisario en son de Guerra* (1984) and *Vos sabrás* (2001), her three historical novels, Mercader re-creates a militaristic, male-centered history, questioning its premises and rejecting patriarchal authority. Her historical novels displace the figure of the hero with the histories of spouses, sisters, daughters or marginal women, the true victims of wars.

In an interview published in the Argentine newspaper, *Página 12*, on December 14, 2004, Martha Mercader affirmed that political commitment has been and integral part of her life. Mercader has been an uncompromising defender of social justice, free public education for all, and sexual equality.

Martha Mercader was born in 1926 in La Plata, the city capital of the province of Buenos Aires, Argentina, in a highly educated, middle-class family which, as she has noted, always placed political ideals and civic responsibilities above their own well-being. Her father was a lawyer. Her mother left her profession as a teacher to look after her family. Mercader obtained a degree in English language and Literature at the University of Buenos Aires in 1949 and pursued graduate studies in London through a scholarship from the British Council. In 1952, she married Nicolas Sánchez Albornoz, a Spanish exile of the Franco dictatorship who became a well-known historian. They divorced several years later. From 1963 to 1966 and again from 1984 to 1989, Mercader held the position of Director of Culture in the Government of the Province of Buenos Aires and from 1993 to 1997 she was a Representative for the Union Cívica Radical in the National House of Representatives. Mercader was co-author of the screenplay of a very successful television program *Cosa juzgada* which ran from 1969 to 1971, the scriptwriter of the movie *Solamente ella* (1975) and co-author of the script of the movie *La Raulito* (1975).

Mercader's autobiography, *Para ser una mujer* (1992) is an insightful essay that illustrates her ideas about "woman" and women's lives, as well as an account of her political viewpoints. The title of the book is the title of a *bolero* (a trendy romantic song of the 1940s and 1950s in Latin America). As in much of her writing, Mercader makes use in *Para ser una mujer* of the lyrics of boleros, tangos, popular poetry and colloquial language expressions to allude to the discourses that constructed the model for women's behavior in her youth.

Her most successful work, *Juana Manuela, mucha mujer* (1980) was very favorably received by critics and the public, and in 1981 the book won the literary prize awarded by the Municipality of Buenos Aires. The novel examines the life of Juana Manuela Gorriti, the nineteenth-century Argentine fiction writer. Martha Mercader writes the biography of Gorriti as an open dialogue with her protagonist creating a palimpsest text in which the biography of a nineteenth-century writer becomes a reflection on the author's present. The violence, the dictatorships and the civil wars the protagonist endured during her life time allude to and parallel Mercader's present that of life under the military dictatorship that ruled Argentina from 1976 to 1983. That dialogue recognizes the interference of time and the input of ideology on the language by which history is read. In an intertextuality conscientiously assumed, the text quotes, but does not name, the influential writer Jorge Luis Borges who illustrated in his short stories the constructed nature of our reading of reality. Gorriti's life story reincarnates in a complex narration that recognizes the ambiguous character of interpretation and the impossibility of a linear reading of history. The documents of historical research; texts themselves that have interpreted the facts are (re)ordered (re)interpreted and (re)read from divergent perspectives. Like many other versions of women's biographies written mainly after the 1970s in Europe and in the United

States, *Juana Manuela, mucha mujer* emphasizes alternative life options and the search of women for spaces of power as expressed in the protagonist's decisions. Thus, Mercader evokes Juana Manuela Gorriti as an exemplar woman who, by confronting difficult choices, becomes a role model for our present.

In *Belisario en son de Guerra* (1984), Mercader explores the biography of Belisario Blumengarten, the pseudonym of a man that existed but is not named. Belisario is a military man who participates in the civil wars of nineteenth-century Argentina, the period of conflict the country endured before becoming a unified nation. When Argentina seems to overcome the turmoil of the post-independence years, Belisario enlists in the Union Army of the United States and later joins Benito Juárez's struggle to liberate Mexico from French occupation. Thus, Mercader brings into light the violence that afflicted not only post-independence Argentina but also the conflicts that followed independence from the colonial powers in the rest of the American continent.

Unlike *Juana Manuela, mucha mujer* and her last historical novel, *Vos sabrás*, in *Belisario en son de Guerra*, Mercader does not delve into literary tradition but rather resorts to historical investigation of documents and letters to back up the protagonist's history. Through the protagonist's life history, Mercader recreates Argentina's historical configuration: the fratricide conflicts, the violence exercised by those in power, and the persistence of poverty in the heart of a country growing richer day by day. Mercader demystifies the heroic and denounces the misery and hardship that war brings to ordinary people while greatly benefiting landowners and big business. Belisario's biography synthesizes, on the other hand, the prototypical features of a militaristic and male centered culture: "A military man should be vain and a womanizer," claims Belisario. He fathers several children, indiscriminately with upper-class ladies or with servants, with black or white women, considering all of them as little fungible "things" that can be taken or being left. The narration's axis is later displaced from Belisario to the women that are part of his life, mainly his sister Candela. Candela hides in the bathroom to read Georges Sand and has the boldness to buy and read a newspaper. She writes the memories of her family and tries to elucidate the meaning of words like "fatherland" or the motto "civilization or barbarism", the language that justifies war: Candela supports her impoverished family by making and selling candy, a trade she has to keep secret because it does not correspond with her social status. At the end of the novel, the withdrawn Candela grows into a rebellious female. When Belisario, in one of his scarce visits home, attempts "to put things in their place" by forbidding his sister to visit the public library, Candela confronts him and imposes her will: "In this household I am the only one that puts things in its place" (p. 184)—she cries out—not referring to arranging the closets, which she also does, but taking charge of her own life. The novel ends in 1930 when a military coup brought down Argentina's first constitutionally elected president, Hipólito Irigoyen. Nevertheless, the narrator declares her hope that some day things will improve and therefore—she assures the reader—this novel does not end but "continues".

In Martha Mercader's last historical novel, *Vos sabrás* (2001), the narrator, Carolina Pérez, an aging woman disillusioned with her historical present, embarks on a quest for her own identity. She begins by tracing the life of her Spanish great-grandfather, Juan José Pérez, who joins a revolutionary movement against the Spanish monarchy at the beginning of the nineteenth century. As a consequence of his actions Juan José Pérez has to go into exile and lands in Brazil after a shipwreck. His descendants, following in his path, enlist in the battles for an ongoing quest for freedom and justice that spans three generations and three countries, Brazil, Uruguay and Argentina. Instead of narrating the deeds of historical icons, the novel focuses on ordinary people as the very name of the main protagonist, Juan José Pérez (a Spanish equivalent of John Smith) reveals. The narrator engages in a dialogic relationship with the writing of history and with literary tradition and declares that her intention is to construct a story based on the different beliefs of those people and the "colors of their passions". Consequently literature is upheld as a link to the past because literature is able to transmit the feelings and passions of its characters. Carolina writes her personal history and that of her ancestors by means of vague testimonies and her own memories filtered by references to Spanish, Latin American and world literature. Her history connects to a past that transcends national borders creating a bond among cultures. Carolina presents herself as a reader of oral and written texts that include literary references, rewritten or transformed, but seldom acknowledged. Through these texts the narrator tries to define the different meanings of "freedom and justice" in each historical period. Her account acquires a mirror-like quality through the deeds of four generations in their quest of similar ideals. At the end, Carolina Pérez's connection with the values of her ancestors, which constitutes the center of the search of her identity, extends into the future through her grandson, Rafael. Rafael brings hope and joy to his disillusioned aging grandmother when he announces that his rock music group "Los vos sabrás" will perform to support unemployed fishermen, workers of the meat packing companies and the homeless.

Other novels by Mercader are *Los que viven por sus manos* (1973) and *Solamente ella* (1981). *Los que viven por sus manos* denounces the corrupting influence of American businessmen on Argentinian society through the story of the dealings of a young American lawyer living in Argentina. *Solamente ella* was originally the script for a movie. The novel quotes tango lyrics as a collective unconscious that punctuates the protagonist's thoughts and feelings. In her journey through the show business world and her search for a fulfilling love, the protagonist encounters a male-dominated landscape in conflict with her need to be herself. Mercader also wrote several short story books on a vast variety of themes. Most of these stories reclaim woman's right to define her life choices, control her body and enjoy her sexuality, free from the trappings of the patriarchal symbolic.

Critical interpretations on Mercader's work have concentrated on her historical novels, mainly on *Juana Manuela, mucha mujer*. Several critics, among them Clara Agustina Suarez Cruz, affirm that the "feminine condition" becomes a structural element of her historical novels and Mercader rewrites history to reveal the omissions of a history based on patriarchal discourse. Works on Martha Mercader have also pointed out the post-modern nature of Mercader's historical fiction which questions traditional concepts of history and representation. Post-modern theorists assert that the different narrative styles chosen by historians (Hayden White, in *Metahistory,* calls those narrative styles "modes of emplotment"), render alternative forms of apprehending the past. On the other hand, the Argentinean writer Jorge Luis Borges had denied through his short stories the possibility of ascertaining reality. Daniel Balderston asserts that the New Historical Novel in Latin America, including *Juana Manuela, mucha mujer,* owes much to Borges' protagonist in his short story "Pierre Menard, autor del Quijote" in which he ascertains that "history is not what happened but that which we judge that happened". Beatriz Urraca indicates that in *Vos sabrás*, Mercader deconstructs the "finality of the printed text" which characterized conventional history and constructs her text through literary tradition. Mercader deliberately emphasizes that her novel is mostly based on invention and therefore suggests that more than lived experience, a text is the result of textual organization of experience.

Whether rewriting the history of Juana Manuela Gorriti, or creating rebellious characters like Candela Blumengarten, the revolutionary Juan José Pérez and the women who populate her short stories, Martha Mercader defies the prevailing order convinced that women (and men) have the power to generate new discourses, a new language, which will enable them to be liberated from the architecture of the overwhelmingly dominant society.

AIDA APTER-CRAGNOLINO

Selected Works

Novels

Los que viven por sus manos. Buenos Aires: Sudamericana, 1973.
Solamente ella. Buenos Aires: Plus Ultra, 1976.
Juana Manuela, mucha mujer. Buenos Aires: Sudamericana, 1980.
Belisario en son de guerra. Buenos Aires: Sudamericana, 1984.
Vos sabrás. Buenos Aires: Grupo Editorial Norma, 2001.

Short Stories

Octubre en el espejo. Buenos Aires: Sudamericana, 1966.
De mil amores. Buenos Aires: Sudamericana, 1982.
La chuña de los huevos de oro. Buenos Aires: Legasa, 1982.
Decir que no. Buenos Aires: Brughera, 1983.
El hambre de mi corazón. Bueno Aires: Sudamericana, 1989.

Essays

"El difícil matrimonio de la literatura y la política". In *Cuadernos Americanos. Nueva Época.* 2(4) (July–Aug., 1988): 170–9.
Para ser una mujer. Buenos Aires: Planeta, 1992.

References and Further Reading

Balderston, Daniel *et al.* (eds) *The Historical Novel in Latin America.* Baltimore, MD: Hispamérica, 1986.

Battaglia, Diana. "La escritura como espejo de otra escritura en *Juana Manuela, mucha mujer* de Martha Mercader". In Juana A. Arancibia (ed.), *Literatura como intertextualidad: IX Simposio Internacional de Literatura.* Buenos Aires: Instituto de Literatura y Cultura Hispánica, 1993, pp. 338–45.

Morello-Frosh, Martha. "Autorrepressentaciones de lo femenino en tres escritoras de la literatura latinoamericana". In Juana A. Arancibia, Yolanda Rosas and María Rosa Lojo (eds), *La nueva mujer en la escritura de autoras hispánicas: Ensayos críticos.* Montevideo: Instituto de Literatura y Cultura Hispánica, 1995, pp. 143–54.

Moreno, María. "Adiós al invierno". Interview. In "La mirada de las mujeres". Buenos Aires: *Página 12.* "Cultura," December 14, 2004.

Sisson-Guerrero, Elizabeth. "Conversación de un siglo". In *Chasqui: Revista de literatura latinoamericana* 31(2) (Nov. 1997); 3–14.

Suarez Cruz, Clara Agustina. "El espacio femenino en la nueva novela hispanoamericana-una lectura de *Juana Manuela, mucha mujer* de Martha Mercader". São Paulo: Congreso Brasilerio de Hispanistas 2 (2002).

Urraca, Beatriz. "Una vida de novela. Martha Mercader and the Contemporary Argentine Historical Novel". *Ciberletras* 14 (2006).

MERCADO, TUNUNA

Tununa Mercado (b. 1939) is one of the most outstanding contemporary women writers in Argentine literature, as well as a journalist and literary scholar. Born in 1939 in Cordoba Argentina into a well-educated middle-class family, Mercado spent much of her childhood between her home town and Buenos Aires. Her father was a renowned lawyer and her mother a writer, which contributed to her prompt familiarization with the world of letters and writing. In 1958, Mercado entered the Faculty of Philosophy and Letters at the Universidad Nacional de Cordoba to pursue a degree in humanities. Three years later, she married Noé Jitrik, a prolific Argentine literary critic who was at that time a professor at the Universidad Nacional. The family lived in Buenos Aires from 1964 until 1966, when Jitrik was offered a position in France. Mercado's first collection of short stories *Celebrar a la mujer como a una pascua* appeared in 1967 and received an honorable mention in the contest of the Casa de las Américas in Cuba. Nobody knew she was working on a literary project until Jitrik discovered the news during a periodic visit to the island. During their stay in the south of France, Mercado dedicated her time to the study of French and to the teaching of Latin American history and civilization. Back to Buenos Aires in 1970, she worked for the journal *La Opinión* whose ideology was focused on raising social consciousness, and it served as grassroots for the intellectual and progressive cultural sectors. Since the Chilean military *coup d'état* in 1973, both Mercado and her husband have been involved in solidarity commissions with many Latin American countries against political corruption and totalitarian governments. In September 1974, Jitrik was invited to teach in Mexico for six months. Mercado's intention was to join him with their two children during the summer of the following year, but due to phone threats she received from the Triple A—Alianza Anticomunista Argentina—they were forced to leave their home country earlier. Mexico was hosting at that time a mass of exiled Argentines—together with exiles and immigrants from other places—shaken by social and political upheavals in the Southern Cone country. As a consequence of this migration, Mercado organized very frequently a cine-forum that became the meeeting place to strengthen bonds of affection among the community; it was a recreation of the native home, a small colony founded on the exiles' experiences in the foreign country.

Mercado's family lived in Mexico until 1987 when they returned to Argentina—four years after the collapse of the Argentine dictatorship referred as the Proceso de Reorganizacion Nacional of 1976–83. In Mexico, she worked as a freelance journalist, an editor of the feminist magazine *Femme,* and she wrote *Canon de alcoba*, a collection of short stories published in 1988. She won the Boris Vian Prize for *Canon de alcoba* awarded by a group of Argentine writers. The relevance of this prize lies in the fact that it originated as a counter-prize to the official mentions during the dictatorship and therefore *Canon de alcoba* reflects a move against patriarchy and governmental cultural precepts. She has lived in Buenos Aires since 1987 working as a translator of French and collaborating in local journals fostering political activism and the voice of women. She has continued to dedicate her life to creative writing and has published subsequent works of international impact. The turn of the century welcomed a prolific female writer read across continents. *En estado de memoria* (1990), one of the most important post-dictatorship novels in South American of the fin-de-siècle, has preceded other works such as the collection of essays *La letra de lo mínimo* (1994), the novel *La madriguera* (1996), a book of essays *Narrar después* (2003) and her recent novel *Yo nunca te prometí la eternidad* (2005). In 1998, she received the Guggenheim fellowship to work in her last project. That same year, her book *En estado de memoria* was reedited by Alción Editora, from Cordoba. In 2004, she was awarded the Konex Diploma al Mérito Prize under the rubrics: "Cuento: quinquenio 1999–2003".

Major Themes

From her personal experience, exile becomes the fundamental condition in her life and in her writing. But exile is not only the consequence of a geographical and physical displacement. Being a woman already locates her on the margins of culture. Moreover, women's absence in the public space is an intrinsic element of Latin American cultures, where their role has been historically restricted to motherhood and domesticity. Therefore, Mercado undergoes a double exile followed by the difficulties of finding a "room of her own" in a foreign country—France and Mexico. Writing at the limits of culture allows her to rethink and rework traditional notions of home, nation, memory and exile from a particular female perspective. In this fashion, Mercado shares a social and political commitment with other neighboring writers such as Chilean Diamela Eltit, Argentine Luisa Valenzuela or Uruguayan Cristina Peri Rossi, among others. As its main focus of analysis, this group of writers who have suffered rejection in one way or another and have undergone the effects of political dictatorships evinces the presence of women as cultural agents. Mercado, Diamela Eltit, Luisa Valenzuela and Cristina Peri Rossi provide a space for the female subject from where to destabilize hegemony and patriarchal constraints. Topics that include the experience of exile, women's testimony, homosexuality and other excluded identity categories are central in their writing. If literary content presents new cultural contentions, there is also a stylistic experimentation. In this specific case, Mercado condenses creative writing with literary theory, philosophical references and a variety of literary genres that favor a spatio-temporal fragmentation. Thus, an aesthetic and content revolution shapes her works. Together with these practices, this group of writers promotes alternative voices within the literary canon and history, questioning monolithic and andro-centric cultural structures. Their writing and criticism expose as well a counter-hegemonic political position crucial for social engagement. In this vein, Mercado's collection of short stories *Canon de alcoba* establishes new alternatives of re/inscribing eroticism, desire and sex at the limits of patriarchal hierarchies. Mercado defies the cultural canon proposing a conceptualization of a "bedroom canon" which includes modes of understanding female sexuality that are socially immoral and lack decorum. In it, not only does she destabilize gender ideologies but she also interweaves literary genres combining essays with fiction, theory and vignettes.

The aftermath and post-traumatic effects of the Argentine dictatorship become the point of reflection for Mercado Mercado once she returned to Buenos Aires. And this anxiety to mourn the past and reinterpret silenced histories organizes many literary works of the post-dictatorship Argentine canon. Along with Mercado, writers such as Ricardo Piglia or Marta Traba are involved in projects that uncover the histories of the traumatic events and tortured bodies that took place during the years of the Proceso de Reorganizacion Nacional. And it is the task of writing itself that endows these authors with the ability to deconstruct static assumptions of culture, history, and the subject. Writing the body and printing one's own textuality through language is the most effective way to overcome the trauma, a trauma that has to be accepted and assimilated through that same writing experience.

Emerging at the interstices between autobiography, memoir, and fiction, Mercado's *En estado de memoria* (1990) opens up multiple spaces to contend with static and fix notions of subjectivity, history, home, memory, nation and exile. Narrated in the first person, the protagonist presents herself as an errant body constantly crossing geopolitical borders, a diversity of homes, and different languages. Mercado explores the psychological and physical effects of the narrator's transition into a life in exile: the intricacies of incorporating herself into a host culture, her physical illness, and the haunting memories of her past and the loved ones she left behind. In exile the narrator is confronted with the remembrance of the *desaparecidos* (disappeared) through daily practices like wearing secondhand clothes or buying secondhand furniture. The last part of the novel shows how difficult it is to recognize the city she left years before, and how complex it is to attach memories to particular places. This feeling might project a universal experience of the painful process any exiled subject goes through. By means of flashbacks, recollections, and short narratives, this story powerfully communicates a woman's experience of exile that goes beyond the individuality towards a collective solidarity.

Influenced by postmodern trends, Mercado introduces techniques of fragmentation, the split of identity and the impossibility of historical narration. These are topics recurrent in her last novel *Yo nunca te prometí la eternidad* which is structured once more through memory and exile. But this time, Mercado abandons the Argentine landscape in order to set her novel in Europe during the Second World War. Geographical and psychological mobility shapes the protagonists of the novel who move between Berlin, Paris, Israel and Mexico and who suffer the painful experiences of personal and national loss. Again, the task of writing serves as a therapeutic treatment for the mourning trauma.

Because of Mercado's literary techniques and her challenges to male domination and heteronormativity, her works are gaining a lot of attention from critics. Specialists in Argentinean and Latin American contemporary literature underscore Mercado's accurate ability to re/conceptualize traditional and androcentric notions on exile. She allows her female characters to narrate their experiences of exile and memory, thus situating women as cultural agents and subjects of their own bodies and desires. Most of Mercado's criticism has focused on those specific aspects, plus her capacity to reinterpret eroticism at the interstices of conventional gender and sexual hierarchies.

IRUNE DEL RIO GABIOLA

Selected Works

Celebrar a la mujer como a una pascua. Buenos Aires: Jorge Álvarez, 1967.
Canon de alcoba. Buenos Aires: Ada Korn, 1988.
En estado de memoria. Rosario: Beatriz Viterbo, 1990.
La letra de lo mínimo. Rosario: Beatriz Viterbo, 1994.
La madriguera. Buenos Aires: Tusquets, 1996.
"Escritura a ciegas". *Celehis: Revista del Centro de Letras Hispanoamericanas* 11(14) (2002): 339–46.
Narrar después. Rosario: Beatriz Viterbo, 2003.
Yo nunca te prometí la eternidad. Buenos Aires: Planeta, 2005.

References and Further Reading

Avelar, Idelber. "Restitution and Mourning in Latin American Post-dictatorship". *Boundary 2: An International Journal of Literature and Culture* 26(3) (1999): 201–24.

Buchanan, Rhonda Dahl. "Eros and Writing in Tununa Mercado's *Canon de alcoba*". *Chasqui: Revista de Literatura Latinoamericana* 25(1) (1996): 52–61.

García-Calderón, Myrna. "La escritura erótica y el poder en *Canon de Alcoba* de Tununa Mercado". *Revista Iberoamericana* 65(187) (1999): 373–82.

Logan, Joy. "A Study on Exile and Subjectivity: Locating the Self in Tununa Mercado's *En estado de memoria*". *Revista Hispánica Moderna* 50(2) (1997): 391–402.

O'Connell, Patrick L. "Homecoming and Identity in the Autobiographical Narrative of Tununa Mercado". *Chasqui: Revista de Literatura Latinoamericana* 27(2) (1998): 106–15.

Ostrov, Andrea. "*Canon de alcoba*: una pornografía de la diferencia". *Hispamerica: Revista de Literatura* 22, no. 66 (1993): 99–108.

Tompkins, Cynthia. "La palabra, el deseo, y el cuerpo o la expansión del imaginario femenino: *Canon de alcoba* de Tununa Mercado". *Confluencia: Revista Hispánica de Cultura y Literatura* 7(2) (1992): 137–40.

MEREILES, CECÍLIA

Cecília Benevides de Carvalho Mereiles (1901–64) was a Brazilian journalist, a poet and teacher, who can be considered one of the most important poets of the second phase of the Brazilian Modernism. She is praised as the outstanding female poetic voice of Brazil writing in Portuguese. In her poetry, she deals with topics such as the ephemeral and eternal components of life focusing on silence and isolation. Meireles traveled extensively and her traveling inspired her literary production. As a teacher she was very interested in promoting educational reforms, and founded the first children's library in Rio de Janeiro in 1934.

She was born in Rio de Janeiro, Brazil, on November 7, 1901, where she also died on November 9, 1964, a victim of cancer. Her father, Carlos Alberto de Carvalho, died three months before her birth. Mathilde Benevides, her mother, was an elementary school teacher and died when Cecília was only 3 years old. Cecília Mereiles was raised by her Portuguese grandmother, Jacinta Garcia Benevides, who was born on the Azores. From her early childhood she was aware of the meaning of death, silence and loneliness. She used to listen to her grandmother's stories from the Azores, relating to her oceanic and Iberian imagery which later inspired her poetic work.

Since her childhood Cecília Meireles had been very interested in studying languages and literature. She started to compose poems at the age of 9. In 1917, she completed her teacher's training at the *Escola Normal* (Normal School) in Rio de Janeiro, a modern school founded by the American philosopher John Dewey, whose main objective was the teaching of democratic principles, laicism, co-education of both sexes in a public school without nepotism and influence of the Catholic Church. It was at that time that she started her career as a schoolteacher in several elementary schools. She also studied violin and took voice lessons at the *Conservatório Nacional de Música* (National Conservatory of Music). Moreover she continued to study literature, foreign languages, educational theory, music, and folklore.

Meireles made her literary debut at the age of 18, with her first volume of poetry *Espectros* (1919, Spectra), a collection of symbolist sonnets, which was the starting point for her career as a poet. Her early poetry has been described as "an airy and vague poetry, languid and fluid, set in an atmosphere of shadows and dreams". Two literary and spiritual currents influenced her early work: Neo-Symbolism whose famous representative was the Brazilian poet Cruz e Sousa (1861–98) and the movement of the so-called *espiritualistas* (Spiritualists). The Brazilian Neo-Symbolism characterizes the transition period between *parnasianismo/simbolismo* (Parnassianism / Symbolism) and *modernismo* (Modernism).

The *espiritualistas,* with whom Mereiles had been in contact since 1922, was a group of Catholic authors who in their publications went in for the renovation of literature based on religion and philosophy. They had a universal concept of literature in opposition to the Modernist movement of São Paulo, which emphasized national trends in art and culture.

Between 1919 and 1927 she joined a group of Catholic writers who published their poetry and prose writings in the magazines *Árvore Nova* (New Tree) and *Terra do Sol* (Land of the Sun). The spiritual and transcendental magazine *Festa* (Feast) started to publish her poems from 1922 on. The *Festa* magazine supported more traditional expression and universality than the futurists and avant-garde writers of São Paulo, whose *Semana de Arte Moderna* (Modern Art Week) in 1922 caused much controversy.

Much modernist writing after World War I was symbolist in spirit. Although her next collections included lyrics in free verse, she also kept to traditional verse forms. The decade of the 1920s was a revolutionary one in Brazilian literature. Meireles' poetry, however, showed very little affinity with the Modernist tendency of free verse and colloquial style in poetry. Meireles always retained symbolist traits in her poetry.

In 1922, she married the Portuguese painter Fernando Correia Dias, who had settled in Brazil before World War I. It was through him that she became acquainted with the

Portuguese poetry of the beginning of the twentieth century, especially with Fernando Pessoa's outstanding poetic work. Since the publication of *Nunca mais e poema dos poemas* (1923, Never Again and Poem of Poems), it was her husband who illustrated her books of poetry. They had three daughters, one of whom became a famous actress. But their family life was not an easy one because of economic and social reasons.

Her topics at that time were of biblical and historical origin, and characters like Anthony and Cleopatra, Samson and Delila, among others, pervaded her poetry. In her collections of poems *Nunca mais e poema dos poemas* (1923), and *Baladas para El-Rey* (1925, Ballads for the King), there was still a strong influence of Symbolism. The themes are mystic longing, disillusionment and nostalgic strife.

Her early poetry maintains a strong connection with the European and in particular the Portuguese poetic sources. It was especially the Portuguese medieval poetry and poets of the *Decadentismo/Simbolismo* such as Antônio Nobre, Camilo Pessanha, Eugênio de Castro, among others, who were appreciated very much by Brazilian intellectuals. The identification of Meireles with the Portuguese tradition of poetry is remarkable. Nevertheless she gradually developed her own concept of stylistic and formal devices. *Baladas para El-Rey* expresses the anxious strife of being a Christian facing the concept of life being limited, full of obstacles, frustration and suffering. She also points out the difficulties in achieving a link to a spiritual life. This is connected with *El-Rey*, which is a metaphor from the Middle Ages, symbolizing the almighty and inaccessible God, who can only be reached by faith, dreams or death.

In 1929, Cecília Meireles presented her masters thesis *O espírito vitorioso* (The Victorious Spirit) at the Department of Literature at the *Escola Normal do Distrito Federal* (Normal School of the Federal District). Although the defense of her thesis was brilliant, she did not succeed in getting the vacant position as a professor of Brazilian literature there because she openly demonstrated her ideas on individual freedom of thought in society, which did not fit in the ideological pattern of a high representative of the *Liga Eleitoral Católica* (Catholic Election League), which was decisive in the designing of a new Constitution in 1934.

There followed a period for Cecília Meireles of both being not accepted as a poet and being persecuted rather for ideological and political more than for artistic reasons. As an alternative she got work as an education editor, writing a daily page on education in the *Diário de Notícias* (News Diary). In this "Página de Educação" (Education Page), she wrote 960 articles fighting for the right of education for every individual and for the implementation of a democratic constitution in Brazil.

In 1934, she was authorized by the *Secretaria de Educação* (Office of Education) to found the first library for children and be director of the *Centro Infantil* (Children's Center). Her husband decorated the new centre and transformed it into a kind of enchanted city where children could do a great deal of different educational and leisure activities. She also wrote several children's books.

In this same year Cecília Meireles traveled to Portugal on the invitation of the Portuguese government, to give lectures and courses on Brazilian Literature at various Portuguese universities. She was supposed to meet Fernando Pessoa in Lisbon, but he did not turn up, leaving her a message, which said that his horoscope did not allow him to meet her but he left for her a book just being published. It was *Mensagem* (1934, Message), the only book he published during his lifetime. That means that Cecília Meireles was the first in Brazil to read this book.

In the following year, her husband, who was suffering from acute depression, committed suicide. As a widow with three daughters to support, her life became even more difficult. In order to survive, she took various jobs: In 1936, she had become a professor of Brazilian and Portuguese literature at various universities in Brazil and outside the country. In addition, she taught *Técnica e Crítica Literária* (Literary Technique and Criticism) at the *Universidade Distrito Federal do Rio de Janeiro* (Federal District University of Rio de Janeiro) from 1936–38.

At this time she also wrote *crônicas* (very short stories reflecting situations of everyday life) and articles on folklore, education and literature in various newspapers and worked at the *Departamento de Imprensa e Propaganda* (Department of Press and Propaganda).

After fourteen years of silence as a poet, Cecília Meireles published one of her major works, *Viagem* (1939, Travel), which marked her poetic maturity in handling poetic devices. She won the Poetry Prize from the *Academia Brasileira de Letras* (Brazilian Academy of Letters) for this lyric collection. The title refers to a spiritual journey where life and poetry are connected. The poems in this and her subsequent works demonstrate a completely individual style but still without any impact of the Brazilian *modernismo* (Modernism), which even in the 1930s followed a nationalist and anecdotal kind of lyrical style. With *Viagem*, Mereiles documents her concepts of life and philosophy. Her style is spontaneous and at the same time very disciplined, profoundly emotional but dominated by intellectual lucidity, which results in a poetry of timeless expression and validity. In this poetic work she achieves a highly refined artistic accomplishment. From the topical point of view she questions human existence, which oscillates between the exaltation of life and discouragement, facing the inevitable end of it. It is poetry, which reveals the secret structure of life:

> Eu canto porque o instante existe / e a minha vida está completa. / Não sou alegre nem sou triste: / sou poeta / Irmão das coisas fugidias. . . . Sei que canto. E a canção é tudo. / Tem sangue eterno na asa ritmada. / E um dia sei que estarei mudo: / e mais nada.
>
> (*Obra Completa*: 2002, p. 227)

> I sing because the moment does exist / and my life is complete. / I am neither happy nor sad: / I am a poet / Brother of the transitory. . . . I know that I sing. The song is everything. / There is eternal blood on the rhythmic wing. / One day I know I will be mute: / and nothing else.

This profound identification with the singing of life symbolizes the vitality and high degree of creativity in her poetry. For her, poetry is something that has much to do with music and rhythm – it is flowing in a permanent process of creativity. This very authentic style is also maintained in her later works such as *Vaga Música* (1942, Vague Music); *Mar absoluto*

(1945, Absolute Sea); *Retrato natural* (1949, Natural Picture); *Doze noturnos da Holanda y O aeronauta* (1952, Twelve Nocturnes from Holland and the Aeronaut).

Five years after her husband's death, Heitor Vinícius da Silveira Grillo, professor and agricultural engineer, became her second husband. In the 1940s, Cecília Meireles traveled widely, for instance to the United States of America and México. On one of these travels she gave a course on Brazilian literature and culture at the University of Texas, Austin, in 1940. In this period her life became more balanced and her career as a poet gained more stability and strength. During this time the sea became an important image in her poetry. *Mar Absoluto* is a poetic work dealing with the sea with the quality of "pure poetry".

In 1951, she visited different countries in Europe and India, often participating in various congresses and symposia throughout these countries. In 1953, she took part in a symposium on the work of Gandhi and was honored by the title Doctor honoris causa from the University of Delhi. She had taught herself both Hindi and Sanskrit. As a consequence of her Indian experiences and impressions she wrote *Poemas escritos na Índia* (1951, Poems Written in India) as a reflection of a cultural background she had been studying for many years. On her way back to Europe she stayed in Italy for a while composing *Poemas Italianos* (1968, Italian Poems), which was published only in 1968.

In her later work she increasingly deals with historical celebrities and topics, and adopts the simple forms and style of the fifteenth-century Spanish romances like in her *Romanceiro da Inconfidência* (1953, Romance of Inconfidência), a cycle of ballads on the tragically failed rebellion of 1789 in Minas Gerais. The work reflects the first colonial attempt of Brazilian Independence from the Portuguese empire, centering on its revolutionary leader and martyr Joaquim José da Silva Xavier, who was hailed later as a liberator and hero.

Another work in this series is the *vita* of a saint, *O Pequeno Oratório de Santa Clara* (1955, The Little Oratory of Saint Claire) as well as the lyrical meditations on the history of Rio de Janeiro, *Crônica Trovada da Cidade de São Sebatião* (1965, Chronicle in Rhymes of the City of Saint Sebastian. In colonial times Rio de Janeiro was called *Cidade de São Sebastião do Rio de Janeiro*).

The climax of her poetic life was the complete edition of her work, *Obra poética,* in 1958, from which the neo-symbolist collection *Nunca mais e poema dos poemas* and *Baladas para El-Rei* were omitted. It was Mereiles' own decision to dissociate herself from these early works.

At the age of 63, in full maturity, and creative activity, she died after a short illness. She is buried in Rio de Janeiro. *Solombra* (1963) was the last book published during her lifetime. There we can find her poetic universe completed:

> Falar contigo. / ... / Dizer com claridade o que existe em segredo. / Ir falando contigo e não ver mundo ou gente. / E nem sequer te ver – mas ver eterno o instante. / No mar da vida ser coral do pensamento.
>
> (Obra Completa, 2002, p. 1265)

> Talking to you. / ... / To express clearly what exists secretly. / Talking to you and not to see the world and its people. / And not even see you – but the eternal moment. / In the sea of life to be the coral of thought.

Journalist and Interpreter

Cecília Meireles broke many taboos of Brazilian politics and education in the 1930s. In her articles in various Brazilian journals and magazines on politics, education, and culture, Meireles shows us a completely different side of her character, contrasting the image of a fragile, sensitive and spiritual poet. For the poet Sérgio Millet, she was a synonym for the island of isolation. For the critic Mário da Silva Brito, she was a writer whose poetry was not inserted in the collective drama of her generation. In her career as a journalist and editor she was very keen to defend the universal ideas of democracy at a time when many young Brazilian intellectuals were passionately involved in the upcoming authoritarian structures and ideology of the *Estado Novo* (The New State).

She translated diverse writers such as Maurice Maeterlinck, García Lorca, Jean Anouilh, Henrik Ibsen, Rabindranath Tagore, Rainer-Maria Rilke, Virginia Woolf, and Alexander Pushkin into Brazilian Portuguese. On the other hand, Meireles' work was translated into various languages such as English, Spanish, Italian, German, Hungarian, Hindi and Urdu.

Characteristic Traits in Meireles' Poetry

Cecília Meireles is always reflecting the transitory character of life, the inevitable reality of death and the meaning of poetry. In this respect she is a very authentic representative of her time mirroring the crucial spiritual crisis at the beginning of the twentieth century. Her poetry does not only express the diversity of formal and topical traits of poetry in the first half of the twentieth century but also the difficult approach to find an individual style and expression in poetry in the midst of fragmentation and decomposition of traditional values and paradigms.

In Cecília Meireles' work, different poetic characteristics may be distinguished. An eminent feature is the intention to perceive and interpret the world not only through analytic reason but all her senses. Doing so she is not lost in emotion or exaltation, quite the contrary, her art never loses the reference to reality. Her poetry was often categorized as being neo-symbolist, which is not really an adequate classification. Her poems deal with the painful experience of human guilt, limitation, and ignorance. For Mereiles, life is a permanent reinvention (*reinvenção*). This explains a view of life, which looks to the past but lacks any sterile sentimentality and never loses control of a reflective mind in spite of the intense and nostalgic atmosphere in her poem.

According to John Nist (1962): "Cecília Meireles was a Catholic Platonist whose poetry 'sings' and ... she is distinguished from other major figures of Brazilian modernism by the universality of her concerns".

Manuel Bandeira, the eminent Modernist poet and contemporary of Cecília Meireles, characterized her in his poem "Improviso," published in his book *Belo Belo*:

"Cecília, és tão forte e tão frágil. Como a onda ao termo da luta. Mas a onda é água que afoga: Tu não, és enxuta" [Cecilia, you are so strong and so fragile. Like the wave at the time of struggle. But the wave is water that drowns: You aren't, you are dry] (Bandeira, 1967).

He also pointed out Meireles' affinity with music and claim to stylistic perfection in her poetry. In his opinion, you can feel that Meireles has always tried to achieve a perfect poetic style applying both traditional and modern stylistic devices. In her major works of poetry you can find the classical transparence, the refined style of *gongorismo* (Gongorism; a seventeenth-century refined Spanish style of poetry), the clarity of the Parnassian verse meters, rhymes, and sound patterns, the vagueness of the syntax and the musical texture of the Symbolists, the unexpected approach towards surrealism. A fine mixture of different styles still based on an individual one, which is sure of itself and of its writing.

Cecília Meireles was honored by and won several prizes after her death: the most outstanding is the "Machado de Assis Prize" offered by the Brazilian Academy of Letters, an award for her *Complete Works*.

GERHILD REISNER

Selected Works

Poetry

Espectros. Rio de Janeiro: Leite Ribeiro & Murillo, 1919.
Viagem. Lisboa: Ocidente, 1939.
Mar Absoluto e outros poemas. Porto Alegre: Globo, 1945.
Doze Noturnos da Holanda & O aeronauta. Rio de Janeiro: Livros de Portugal, 1952.
Romanceiro da Inconfidência. Rio de Janeiro: Livros de Portugal, 1953.
Poemas escritos na India. Rio de Janeiro: São José, 1961.

Prose

Escolha o seu sonho: crônicas. Prefácio de Carlos Drummond de Andrade. Rio de Janeiro: Record, 1964.

Complete Editions

Obra Poética. Rio de Janeiro: Aguilar, 1958.
Obra Poética. 3rd edn. Rio de Janeiro: Nova Aguilar, 1972.
Poesia Completa. Rio de Janeiro: Nova Fronteira, 1997, 4 vols.
Antologia poética. 3rd edn. Rio de Janeiro: Nova Fronteira, 2001.
Poesia Completa. Secchin, Antônio Carlos, org. Rio de Janeiro: Nova Fronteira, 2002, 2 vols.

Poems in English Translation

Poems in Translation. Washington, DC: Brazilian-American Cultural Institute, 1977.
Bishop, Elizabeth and Brasil, Emanuel (eds) *Anthology of Twentieth-century Brazilian Poetry.* Middletown, CT: Wesleyan University Press, 1972, vol. II.

References and Further Reading

Andrade, Carlos Drummond de. *Reunião.* 9th edn. Rio de Janeiro: José Olympio, 1978
Bandeira, Manuel. "Modernistas". In *Modernistas. Apresentação da poesia brasileira: seguida de uma antologia de poetas brasileiros.* Rio de Janeiro: Ediouro, n.d.
——. "Improviso". In *Poesia Completa and Prosa.* Biblioteca Luso-Brasileira. Rio de Janeiro: José Aguilar Editora, 1958.
Brito, Mário da Silva. *Poesia do Modernismo.* Rio de Janeiro: Civilização Brasileira, 1968.
Carpeaux, Otto Maria. *Ensaios reunidos.* Rio de Janeiro: Topbooks, 1999, vol. I.
Coelho, Nelly Novaes. "O eterno instante na poesia de Cecília Meireles". In *A literatura feminina no Brasil Contemporâneo.* São Paulo: Siciliano, 1993, pp. 35–55.
——. *Dicionário Crítico de Escritoras Brasileiras (1711–2001).* São Paulo: escrituras, 2002.
Coutinho, Afrânio (ed.) *A literatura no Brasil.* 3rd edn. Rio de Janeiro: José Olympio, 1986, vol. III.
Lamego, Valéria. *A farpa na Líra – Cecília Meireles na revolução de 30.* Rio de Janeiro: Record, 1996.
Lins, Álvaro. "Consciência artística e beleza formal em Cecília Meireles". In *Os mortos de sobrecasaca.* Rio de Janeiro: Civilização Brasileira, 1963.
Nist, John. *Modern Brazilian Poetry.* Bloomington, IN: Indiana University Press, 1962.
Peixoto, M. "'Caminhante do Vazio': Voyages and Disconnection in Cecília Mereiles". *DL*, I (1984), 2, 267–76.
Sadlier, D.J. *Imagery and Theme in the Poetry of Cecília Mereiles: A Study of «Mar Absoluto».* Madrid: J. Porrúa Turanzas, 1983.
Silveira, Jorge Fernandes de. "*Romanceiro da Inconfidência* escrever Portugal no Brasil?" In Arnaldo Saraiva (ed.), *Literatura brasileira em questão.* Porto: Faculdade de Letras, 2000.
Stackhouse, K.A., *The Sea in the Poetry of Cecília Mereiles. LBR*, 18 (1981), I, 183–95.
Zilberman, R. *A Leitura e o Ensino da Literatura.* São Paulo: Contexto, 1989.

MERUANE, LINA

Journalist and writer Lina Meruane (b. 1970) was born in Santiago, Chile. She belongs to the younger generation of contemporary writers who grew up during the dictatorship (1973–89). She is a regular columnist for the newspaper *El Mercurio* where she writes on literary and cultural issues. She currently lives in New York City where she is completing a PhD in Latin American literature under the direction of Comparative Literature scholar and writer, Sylvia Molloy.

Lina Meruane's literature has privileged childhood and adolescence and their subverting development within the institution of the family. Her narrative, as several critics have pointed out, also tends to show the mechanisms of the writing process and a reflection on literary genres. This last feature is in line with what Diamela Eltit's literary work inaugurated in contemporary Chilean literature.

Meruane's first book, *Las Infantas* (1998), is a collection of short stories that focuses on childhood and transgression. The protagonist is a young girl in most cases, a curious and rebellious figure who is on the threshold of cultural norms, free to explore a wide range of possibilities. This literary character has been underrepresented in Chilean literature and has been almost absent from contemporary literature. In this sense, Meruane's short stories in particular have contributed to opening up new avenues of female identities and subjectivity stretching cultural and representational limits. In this narrative, the young girl displays great freedom from the established order and its dominant values, endowing childhood with the potential to subvert binary oppositions and morality. Meruane's daring and rebellious young girls are most of the time sexually ambiguous and unbound by cultural mandates and restrictions. In this repertoire, girls are wandering and fugitive beings who pursue imagination and knowledge, sexual knowledge in particular, against the regimentation and prohibitions of the adult world, family members and school officials. They transgress the seclusion imposed on women of the older generation and leave the house in search of their desire. The collection *Las Infantas* also rewrites children's tales by inverting them and transforming princesses and queens into beggars or assailants who suddenly take ambiguous positions that dislocate the traditional victim/dominator opposition.

Meruane has also published two novels: *Cercada* (2000) and *Póstuma* (2000). The first work is narrated as a thriller that unfolds in the middle of a sociopolitical turmoil where the abuse of political power marks the lives of the characters. In this novel, writing is characterized by the disruption of logical and linear structures resonating with the literary works of other women writers in Chile today. Critic Juan Armando Epple has argued that recent female literature in Chile is characterized by the absence of the nation and a fractured and dysfunctional family, and that Meruane presents this same perspective. The novel combines genres and multiple points of view while privileging space and performance as sites of identity. The written word problematizes the relationship between truth and discourse in a cultural and social context determined by dictatorial rule. *Cercada* is also the writer's attempt to come to terms with recent Chilean history from the perspective of the children of the dictatorship—that is the children of the disappeared and the military who inherited from their parents today's society. The narrative structure resembles a film script in which commands and repetitions shape a context of treasons and violence within a present that leaves grim possibilities for political and social reconciliation. In the midst of this ideologically charged scenario a romantic triangle develops between Lucía and two brothers, Ramiro and Manuel. The three inherit their parents' stories, memories and values while struggling to make sense of their own postmemory and life. The impossibility of love shows the unresolved conflict that shapes Chilean culture, its institutions and subjectivities. The characters are ultimately trapped within a dictatorial social order and discourse that has fragmented the sense of community as well as the possibility of a collective history. Discourses about the past have made the three characters suspicious and the only thing they are left with is the performance of their own representations, as the end reveals. Here the crisis of the subject is linked to the crisis of epistemological paradigms in a postmodern society that was inaugurated with the dictatorship.

Póstuma, on the other hand, is a novel that revisits a fractured family order and links it to memory. The novel interrogates writing and its conventions through the senses, opening meanings that counter a logocentric rationale. Female imagination in the story appears to be in revolt against a binary logic that has been handed down from the patriarchal family structure and its phallic tradition. Two narrations contrast and weave the structure of the novel: one belongs to Renata, who writes her story after the announcement of her grandmother's imminent death, and the other is by an external voice who narrates the present and the ways Renata spends her day caring for her younger sister. Eros and death are central to the narrative discourse in which writing becomes a space to test and expand limits.

In 2004, Meruane won the Guggenheim award for *Fruta podrida*, an in-progress novel. Many of her texts have appeared in anthologies featuring contemporary Chilean short stories—*Salidas de Madre* (1996), *Relatos y Resacas* (1997), *Voces de Eros* (1997), *Cien Microcuentos Chilenos* (2002) among others—and several others have been adapted to the theater and TV. The story "Engranajes de pureza" was adapted by film director, Paola Castillo, who made it into a short film. "Bolsa de huesos" was produced by Productora Nueva Imagen and shown in the TV show, *Cine Video*. "Función triple" which appeared in the anthology *Salidas de Madre* was staged and performed at the Goethe Institute in 2005. Meruane has also been invited to read and discuss her work in several universities in the USA, thus extending her reach beyond Chilean borders. Meruane's incursions into the short story places her in the group of younger writers who continue Pía Barros's *microcuento* tradition, a very brief narration that tends to have a sudden and unexpected end.

Lina Meruane's subversive stories of youngsters and her rewriting of children's tales expose cultural taboos such as incest, rape and cannibalism, re-editing them in a language that evokes not only the fears of childhood and adulthood but also their most hidden desires. In this way, her writing is provocative in its attempt to blur the cultural and moral boundaries that have been created to found social orders. Meruane returns to young girls the power to turn the world of rules and prohibitions upside down and subvert the established social order. She explores female identity right before it becomes a mimicry of the hegemonic model of Latin American femininity.

BERNARDITA LLANOS

Selected Works

Novels

Póstuma. Santiago de Chile: Editorial Planeta, 2000.
Póstuma. Trans. Henrique Tavares. Lisbon: Oficina do Livro, 2001.
Cercada. Santiago de Chile: Editorial Cuarto Propio, 2000.
Fruta Podrida. Unpublished novel.

Short Stories Collection

Las Infantas. Santiago de Chile: Editorial Planeta, 1998.

Short Stories in Anthologies

"Función Triple". In *Salidas de Madre*. Santiago de Chile: Editorial Planeta, 1996, pp. 125–35.
"Cuerpos de papel". *Relatos & Resaca*. Santiago de Chile: Editorial Planeta, 1997, pp. 175–81.
"Café Obola". In *Voces de Eros*. Ed. Mariano Aguirre. Santiago de Chile: Editorial Grijalbo–Mondadori, 1997, pp. 123–39.
"Cuencas Vacías". In *Relatos de Mujeres*. Santiago de Chile: Caras, 1998, pp. 59–65.
"Madrugada con Titi". In *Cuentos de Primavera*. Santiago de Chile: Caras, 1999, pp. 43–55.
"Tijeretazos". In Alberto Fuguet and Edmundo Paz Soldán (eds), *Se Habla Español*. Miami, FL: Editorial Alfaguara, 2000, pp. 337–44.
"Sangre de narices". In *Con Pasión*. Santiago de Chile: Editorial Planeta, 2000, pp. 123–35.
"La huesera". In *Cuentos chilenos contemporáneos*. Santiago de Chile: LOM, 2000, pp. 175–86.
"Pajarete". In *Seis Cuentos de Amor*. Santiago de Chile: Caras, 2001, pp. 79–94.
"Linternas en el túnel," "Apagar las farolas" and "Mascarada". In Juan Epple (ed.), *Cien microcuentos chilenos*. Santiago de Chile: Editorial Cuarto Propio, 2002, pp. 115–18.
"Reina de Piques". *Pequeñas resistencias III*. Madrid: Páginas de espuma, 2005, pp. 163–6.
"Dientes de leche". In *MicroQuijote*. Barcelona: Thule Ediciones, 2005, pp. 77–8.
"Hojas de afeitar". In *Cuentos eróticos. Revista Caras*. Santiago de Chile, 2006, pp. 27–33.
"Razor Blades". Trans. Lina Meruane and Ronald Chris. *Two Lines* 14 (March, 2007). Forthcoming www.twolines.com

Short Stories in Magazines and Newspapers

"Obturado/Shuttered". *Hoja–lata. Bilingual Cultural Review.* 3 (Jan. 1995): 21.

"Reina de Piques". *Revista de Critica Cultural* 10 (May 1995): 46.

"Cáscaras". *La noche* II(8) (1996): 28.

"Función Triple". *Lucero. Journal of Iberian and Latin American Studies* 10 (Spring, 1999): 85–90.

"Jeringas desechables (fragment)". *Cuentos de Navidad.* Revista Ya, *El Mercurio.* 899 (12 Dec. 2000): 22.

"Platos sucios". *Plagio* 8 (2003): 44–7.

Adaptations to Other Media

"Salidas de Madre". Compañía Retratos, Sala Nuval, November, 1997.

"Engranajes". Short film directed by the documentalist, Paola Castillo. Productora Nueva Imagen. Shown in the TV Program *El Show de los libros* conducted by the writer Antonio Skármeta in Televisión Nacional de Chile, 1998.

"La bolsa de huesos". Short Film. Productora Nueva Imagen. Emitido en el Programa *Cine Video.* Televisión Nacional de Chile, 1999.

"Cercada (fragments)". Productora Nueva Imagen. Shown in the TV Program *El Show de los libros* conducted by the writer Antonio Skármeta in Televisión Nacional de Chile. 2000.

"Función Triple". Sala Goethe. Santiago de Chile, 2005.

References and Further Readings

Andonie Dracos, Carolina. "En medio de la vorágine. Entrevista a Lina Meruane". *Letras.s5.com*

Cánovas, Rodrigo. "*Las Infantas* de Lina Meruane". *El Mercurio.* 25 Nov. 1998.

Edwards, Javier. "Meruane en breve". *Letras.s5.com*

Epple, Juan Armando. "De piel a piel: el erotismo como escritura en la nueva narrativa femenina de Chile". *Revista Iberoamericana* 187 (1999): 383–94.

——. "Nueva narrativa chilena". In Guillermo García-Corales and Cecilia Ojeda (eds), *Imaginarios de la decepción.* New York: Mellen, 2004, pp. i–viii.

——. "La nación ausente en la nueva narrativa femenina chilena". In Mabel Moraña and Javier Campos (eds), *Ideologías y literatura. Homenaje a Hernán Vidal.* Pittsburgh, PA: IILI-Biblioteca de América, 2006, pp. 107–14.

Franz, Carlos. "Presentación de *Las Infantas*". Plaza Mulato Gil, Santiago de Chile, October 22, 1998.

Hozven, Roberto. "Trama y argumento de *Póstuma*, novela de Lina Meruane". *Taller de Letras* 29 (2001): 271–6.

Iñiguez, Ignacio. "Infancia, literatura y perversidad". *Rocinante* 11 (2000): 10–11.

Mena, Catalina. "El fracaso de la lección moral". *Revista de Crítica Cultural* 17 (Dec. 1998): 75.

——. "Presentación de *Póstuma*". Biblioteca Nacional, Santiago de Chile, July 17, 2000.

MIGUEL, MARÍA ESTHER DE

María Esther de Miguel was born in 1929, in Larroque, Entre Ríos, in Argentina and died in 2003. De Miguel was the daughter of a Spanish immigrant to Argentina and a Jewish mother. As a teenager, she began to question the idea of God's existence and in her spiritual quest she entered a Pauline convent. During her time at the convent she studied philosophy and literature at the University of Buenos Aires and earned a scholarship to study contemporary Italian literature in Rome. She also taught at rural schools and worked as a journalist then. After ten years of soul searching, De Miguel left the convent and dedicated herself to literature completely. In the late 1960s she met and then married Andrés Alfonso Bravo. She said that she never wanted to have children and that when she was young she wanted to have a lover and write a book, and that is exactly what she did.

De Miguel made her literary debut at the precocious age of 9 when she sent an essay entitled "The Malvina Islands are Argentinian" to the magazine *Figuritas* without her teacher's authorization. From that moment, De Miguel showed a special affinity for historical and political themes especially in such bestsellers as *El general, el pintor y la dama* (Premio Planeta 1996), *El amante del restaurador* (1993) and *Las batallas secretas de Belgrano* (1995).

De Miguel's literary career was not only long and prolific, but it was characterized by a variety of literary and cultural roles. She served as Director of the National Arts Foundation and on the council for the Book Foundation in Argentina. She also was literary critic for the newspaper *La nación* and the literary magazine *Señales.*

Her writing also earned her acclaim through a variety of awards including the Emecé Award in 1961, for her novel *La hora undécima*; an award from the Fondo Nacional de las Artes y Municipal in 1965, for *Los que comimos a Solís*; the Primer Premio Municipal and the Premio de Cultura de la Provincia de Entre Ríos in 1980 for *Espejos y Daguerrotipos*; the award from *Feria del Libro* in 1994; the Silvina Bullrich Prize in 1995; the National Prize in Literature in 1997, for *La amante del Restaurador*; and the Planeta Prize in 1996, for *El general, el pintor y la dama*. In addition, she has received the Palma de Plata from Pen Club, and the platinum from the Konex Foundation for her short stories.

De Miguel's love of the written word and cultural endeavors was best expressed when she donated her house in Entre Ríos and converted it into a cultural center. She decided to donate her house after reflecting upon the fact that she had no children and she frequented Larroque less and less. She then decided to donate her house to the city even though it made her sad at first. All of her books were there, but in Entre Ríos the books would be happy. They would now have an amphitheater in the garden and there would be boarding rooms for writers and artists. Her only condition for the donation of her house was that it was not to be used by officials.

De Miguel has often been asked if feminine literature exists. De Miguel quotes Virginia Woolf when trying to explain the role of a writer. For Woolf and De Miguel, the writer is a sort of hermaphrodite. It is often the case that the author has to take on the roles of both men and women. Thus, the author has to seamlessly transition when writing about a male character or a female character. In that sense, feminine literature does not exist because the author, whether male or female, has to imagine him or herself in those roles. De Miguel's literature deals with fast paced topics such as the life of warriors in battles, a very masculine sort of writing. Yet it can nonetheless be said that De Miguel created these characters from a female perspective.

It is also interesting to point out that De Miguel's general writing trajectory has moved from purely fiction to historical fiction. In this shift, De Miguel encountered a lot of resistance.

Critics felt this was a bad move, but she considered the fictional novel to be basically the same as the historical novel. The only difference for her was that in historical novels, the characters came from reality rather than from inside her imagination. After a while, her writing found acceptance among her readership, as it seemed to agree with the popular taste at the time. De Miguel believes that the historical novel grants access to history for the masses. She notes that the novel had the advantage of teaching, but for her the protagonist needs to be more or less part of the popular imagination as well as part of the historical archive. She indicated in various interviews that she was aware of the new trend in which history was being rewritten, but she felt that it was important to not do what other historical novelists had done.

One such example is the novel *Un dandy en la corte del Rey Alfonso* with the protagonist Fabían Gómez y Anchoren, a man who has the opportunity to experience utmost happiness and the most awful tragedies in nineteenth-century Argentina. De Miguel consulted many sources and historical documents about the people and places of this period in order to create a believable and loved fictional work that allowed the reader to suffer with as much intensity as she experiences joy. One of the themes of the novel deals with the immigration waves that occurred during the nineteenth century in Argentina. In addition, Buenos Aires is also a character, as she shows the city as a contradictory and complex factor, complete with poor neighborhoods, cramped and crammed with immigrants from all over the world. This characterization demonstrates her interest in history and the dynamic events that shaped Argentina without changing or rewriting history. She simply used the historical as the basis for her fictional narratives.

SYLVIA MORIN

Selected Works

La hora undécima. Buenos Aires: Emecé Editores, 1961.
Pueblamérica. Buenos Aires: Editora Pleamar, 1974.
Espejos y daguerrotipos. Buenos Aires: Emecé Editores, 1978.
Jaque a Paysandú. Buenos Aires: Bruguera, 1984.
Dos para arriba, uno para abajo. Buenos Aires: Editorial Pleamar, 1986.
Norah Lange: una biografía. Buenos Aires: Plantea, 1991.
La Amante del Restaurador. Buenos Aires: Planeta, 1993.
Las batallas secretas de Belgrano. Buenos Aires: Seix Barral, 1995.
El general, el pintor y la dama. Buenos Aires: Planeta, 1996.
En el otro lado del tablero. Buenos Aires: Planeta, 1997.
Un dandy en la corte del Rey Alfonso. Buenos Aires: Planeta, 1998.

References and Further Reading

Batticuore, Graciela. *Mujeres argentinas: el lado femenino de nuestra historia.* Buenos Aires: Alfaguara, 1998.

Brotherston, Gordon. *The Emergence of the Latin American Novel.* Cambridge: Cambridge University Press, 1977.

Collette, Marianella. *Conversación al sur: entrevistas con escritoras argentinas.* Buenos Aires: Ediciones Simurg, 2003.

De García, Mansilla and Siscar, Cristina. *Violencia II: visiones femeninas.* Buenos Aires: Ediciones Instituto Movilizador de Fondos Cooperativos, 1993.

Giuffre, Mercedes and Castelli, Jorge. *En busca de una identidad: la novela histórica en Argentina.* Buenos Aires: Ediciones del Signo, 2004.

Fares, Gustavo and Hermann, Eliana Cazaubon (eds) *Contemporary Argentinean Women Writers: A Critical Anthology.* Trans. Linda Britt. Gainesville, FL: University Press of Florida, 1998.

Mucci, Cristina and Aguinis, Marcos. *Voces de la cultura argentina.* Buenos Aires: El Ateneo, 1997.

Tacconi de Gómez, María del Carmen. *Ficción y discurso.* San Miguel de Tucumán, Argentina: Universidad Nacional de Tucumán, Facultad de Filosofía y Letras, Instituto de Investigaciones Lingüísticas y Literarias Hispanoamericanas, 1999.

Web sites

"María Esther de Miguel". In *Literatura Argentina Contemporánea.* October 1999. http://www.literatura.org/deMiguel/index.html

"Murió María Esther de Miguel, una de las escritoras más leídas". In Clarín.com. July 28, 2003. http://www.clarin.com/diario/2003/07/28/s-02801.htm

MINAYA BELLIARD, LIGIA

Ligia Minaya Belliard was born in Moca, Dominican Republic, on January 11, 1941. She has been a lawyer, attorney, judge, and a university professor of Criminal Studies at the Pontificia Universidad Católica Madre y Maestra in Santo Domingo, where she subsequently became Director of the Department of Criminal Studies. Additionally, she speaks on behalf of academia and the Dominican Republic in general. In part due to the economic crisis in her country, she retired to Denver, Colorado, in January 2004.

Minaya started her literary career as a newspaper columnist in the 1990s, when she began writing a social column for the women's magazine *Mujer Única* in Santo Domingo and for the newspapers *Última Hora* and *Diario Libre.* In 1997, she compiled all the articles she had written for these columns and published them in a comprehensive work entitled *Palabras de Mujer.*

Staying true to her journalistic roots and that style, Ligia Minaya is primarily a short story writer. Her first short stories appeared in the "Concurso de Cuentos de Casa de Teatro" in 1995 ("No lo hice por maldad") and in 1997 ("El fuego sagrado del hogar"), both of which received honourable mentions. In 1998, she was awarded First and Second prizes for "Un abuelo impropio" and "Llanto de cactus en la noche interminable". These short stories have been translated into Italian by Tiziana Gibilisco in the anthology *Onde, Farfalla E Aroma Di Café. (Storie di donne dominicane)* (Alessandria: Edizionni Estemporanee, 2005). In 1999, she published *El Callejón de las Flores*, a collection of twelve erotic short stories, which was awarded the National Literary Prize in the Dominican Republic in 2000. Also in 2000, she was awarded the National Short Story Prize. Apart from her national success in literary circles, she has also received significant international attention. In particular, Rita de Maeseneer, a Belgian professor of Latin American literature, has published a significant analysis of her work.

Of her many significant contributions, *El Callejón de las Flores* (1999) remains her major literary achievement as it redefined Hispanic erotica. Even though Ligia Minaya was the first Dominican woman to write erotic literature in her country, she has been described by the Dominican male critic, José Rafael Lantigua, who wrote the prologue to her book, as the first author to have spoken about sexuality in Dominican literature (p. 14).

Ligia Minaya's short stories contain a heavy sexual content yet are thought-provoking. Her stories frequently tackle delicate issues such as paedophilia, incest, female infidelity, and adultery. The stories with the most controversial content are perhaps the three narratives about authoritative religious figures, which discuss their secret sexual encounters. These stories are included with the story that shares the same title as the compilation, "El Callejón de las Flores". In this story, the life of a prostitute is portrayed, who, after losing her husband in a tragic accident, repents by becoming a deeply religious and moral person.

The twelve short stories in "El Callejón de las Flores" deal centrally with human relationships and a common feature of them all is that they are narrated by female characters who are usually the main protagonists and, more significantly, sexually liberated women. Their sexual autonomy is rewarded through their role as narrator. None of these female characters is repressed or oppressed by their male counterpart. Through the use of both male and female protagonists, Minaya demonstrates their equality and never positions them as one superior to the other. The twelve *intimate* voices of *El Callejón de las Flores* speak not just of sexual relations but also, and more profoundly, of the very intimate personal matters of human relations. Although broadly erotic and about love and sex, these stories are also about life and living. Ligia Minaya has a knack for including in her stories the sense of monotony of everyday life as well as the subversive.

Minaya's skill in constructing these powerful texts is derived from her ability to present erotic experiences. The way in which she constructs the experiences forces the reader to focus more on the complexity of the main characters' relationship instead of the sexual act itself. Emotional truth and highly charged prose are present in her work in such a way that subverts the usual conventions of erotic literature. By doing this, Minaya uses erotica as a form of transgression, to undermine literary and social conventions. She makes the sexual act less relevant by proliferating the language, characters, situations, settings, and the forbidden relationships of her works with eroticism, thus making the erotic common.

Minaya uses erotica to gain access to and explore the substance and implications of subversive content and often ignored figures. She gives voices to the marginalised groups, for instance, she subverts the stereotypical model of the prostitute in "El Callejón de las Flores" with the juxtaposition of the new morally sound figure who takes her place. Minaya's intentions and the reactions these themes provoke are by no means only sexual in nature. In *El Callejón de las Flores*, her language to make the sensuousness of the mundane is at the foreground. This is done not primarily to sexually arouse the reader but to elicit from the reader an aesthetic heightening of perceiving the world anew.

Minaya's first novel, *Cuando me asalta el recuerdo de ti* (2003), is about a woman who reflects upon her life as an upper-class married woman with children and a lover. Although to her family and friends she seems to be happy, upon further inspection, she realizes she is not. This realization begins a process of naming and putting into effect what makes her happy. Once again, the major themes in Minaya's writing are present in this sensual novel.

Minaya's intentions with her writing are related to the very origin of Latin American literature, which was born from dissidence. According to Donald Shaw's *Nueva Narrativa Hispanoamericana* (2003), the essential role of the Latin American writer was and still is to raise the consciousness of the reader by using literature "as a weapon against oppression and injustice" (p. 251). Minaya's writing belongs to this tradition of *littérature engagée*. Her commitment is to defend the poor and fight for a more humane society through her literature, as we see in her journalistic book, *Palabras de Mujer* (1997).

Minaya's socio-cultural background places her among the pioneers of the sexual revolution of the 1960s and her literature seeks to accomplish a second sexual liberation. Minaya's erotic tales bring about decidedly original perspectives on sexual mores. Within a Dominican context, Minaya belongs to the group of notable women writers such as Carmen Imbert Brugal, Ida Hernández Caamaño, Emelda Ramos and Aurora Arias.

ENRIQUE ÁVILA LÓPEZ

Selected Works

Palabras de Mujer. Santo Domingo: Editora de Colores, 1997.

El Callejón de las Flores. Santo Domingo: Cocolo Editorial y Editora Manatí, 1999.

References and Further Reading

Bahr, Aida (ed.) *Palabras de espuma (Selección de narrativa)*, Santiago de Cuba: Editorial Oriente, 2001.

Corniel, Zaida. "La pornografía es una mecánica y el erotismo es un sentimiento (Entrevista a Ligia Minaya)". *Listín Diario*, 20 May, 2000: 15C.

Manera, Danilo. *Non L'ho fatto con malizia, Il sacro fuoco della famiglia, Dove crescono le guayabe.* Rome: Editore Feltrinelli, 2000.

——. (ed.) *Cuentos dominicanos (una antología)*, Madrid: Siruela, 2002a.

——. *Mujeres Como Isla. Antología de narradoras cubanas, dominicanas y puertorriqueñas.* Santo Domingo: Ediciones FERILIBRO, 2002b.

——. *Cuando me asalta el recuerdo de ti.* Santo Domingo: Editora Cole, 2003.

Señales de Voces. Antología de Cuentos Dominicanos. Santo Domingo: Grupo Editorial Norma, 2004.

Fornerín, Miguel Ángel. "El Callejón de las Flores de Ligia Belliard". *Listín Diario*, 6 May 2000: 20C.

Gibilisco, Tiziana. *Onde, Farfalla e Aroma Di Café. (Storie di donne dominicane).* Alessandria: Edizioni Estemporanee, 2005.

Maeseneer, Rita De. "La sombra de la Masacre en Ligia Minaya y Marcio Veloz Maggiolo (1)". *Confluencia: Revista Hispánica de Cultura y Literatura.* Thomson Gale, September 22, 2005.

Miller, Jeannette. "Sobre Ligia Minaya y su particular forma de recordar. (Cuando me asalta el recuerdo de ti)". *Confluencia: Revista Hispánica de Cultura y Literatura.* Thomson Gale, September 22, 2003.

Jiménez, Vivian. "Palabras de mujer. Palabras de Ligia Minaya". *Última Hora*, 10 August 1999: 33.

——. "El Callejón de las Flores: otro parto literario de Ligia Minaya". *Última Hora*, 27 October 1999: 37.

Lantigua, José Rafael. "Palabras de mujer: para que tú igual las sigas sollozando". *Última Hora* 24 August 1997: 36.

——. "Palabra henchida de dureza y desagravio". *Última Hora* 24 August 1997: 37.

——. "Escándalo en la vía pública: los cuentos eróticos de Ligia Minaya". *Última Hora* 24 October 1999: 28.

——. "Ligia Minaya, una mujer libre para contar el sexo". *Última Hora* [Biblioteca] 24 de octubre de 1999: 30.

Mella, Cesar. "El erotismo de lo excelso no es pornografía ni obscenidad". *Última Hora*, 31 October 1999: 11.

Parra, Isabel. "Ligia Minaya Belliard, complacida de escribir cuentos eróticos". *Última Hora*, 31 October 1999: 8–9.

Valdez, Pedro Antonio. "El festín de los cuerpos". http://www.monoadivino.org/valdez.html

MIRANDA, ANA

Ana Miranda was born in Fortaleza, Ceará, in Northeast Brazil, in 1951. At the age of 5, she and her family went to live in Rio de Janeiro. Her father, an engineer, was hired to assist in the construction of Brazil's modernist capital city, Brasília, and she and her family moved there in the late 1950s. She returned to Rio de Janeiro in 1969. After settling back into life in Rio, she began her studies in the arts. Since 1999, Ana Miranda has lived in the city of São Paulo.

History as a Backdrop for Her Fiction

Although Ana Miranda began her writing career as a poet in the late 1970s and early 1980s with the publication of *Anjos e Demônios* (1978, Angels and Demons), and *Celebração do Outro* (1983, Celebration of the Other), she is best known as an accomplished writer of historical fiction. Miranda is celebrated in particular for works that highlight the lives of notable literary figures in Brazil. Since the late 1980s, she has published three novels which richly portray a canonical figure in Brazilian literature. Seventeenth-century poet Gregório de Matos is featured in *A Boca do Inferno* (1989, The Mouth of Hell), a best-selling novel that presents a colorful rendering of Colonial Bahia. In addition to its fictionalized portrait of Gregório de Matos, *A Boca do Inferno* contrasts the poet's popular, earthy verses with the enlightening sermons of another figure in Brazilian literary history, Jesuit priest Antonio Vieira. The city of Rio de Janeiro during the Belle Époque is the backdrop to *A Última Quimera* (1995, The Last Chimera), a novel centered on early twentieth-century poet Augusto dos Anjos and his metaphysical meditations. Finally, nineteenth-century Romantic poet Gonçalves Dias is the subject of *Dias e Dias*, of 2002 (the title, literally meaning Days and Days, is a play on the poet's last name). Of these three novels, two—*A Boca do Inferno* and *Dias e Dias*—have won Brazil's top literary prize, the Jabuti. The latter also received a prestigious prize in the category of novel by Brazil's Academy of Arts and Letters in 2003.

Ana Miranda has dedicated three additional novels, supported by the assiduous research that accompanies all of her work, to representing distinct periods in Brazilian history. The eighteenth-century opulence of Brazil's Golden Age, or Baroque period, is richly depicted in *O Retrato do Rei* (1991, The Portrait of the King), the rough formation of the sixteenth-century Brazilian colony is represented in *Desmundo* (literally, Un-world, 1996); and Lebanese immigration to São Paulo at the end of the nineteenth century is the subject of *Amrik* (a corruption of America, by Lebanese immigrants), of 1997. In each of these novels, the author not only meticulously reconstructs a period in Brazilian history, she also expertly appropriates the language of the time, weaving it into her own stylistic approach. Her novel *Desmundo* was subsequently made into a feature film directed by Alain Fresnot in 2003.

Brazil Seen from a Female Vantage Point

Although Ana Miranda's historical novels have focused on the lives of male protagonists, she frequently articulates the role that women have played in the shaping of Brazil as a nation. It is often through the perspective of a female character that her works of fiction unfold. This narrative approach expertly permits an extensive period in history to be articulated through a personal, intimate, feminine voice. In *Desmundo*, for instance, the young colony—in all its foundational awkwardness and coarseness—is seen through the eyes of a Portuguese orphan named Oribela, who is transported by royal decree to sixteenth-century Brazil, much against her will. Written in page-long chapters and in the intricate Portuguese language of the period, the novel recounts the difficulties a young woman faced in adapting to a hemisphere, a life, and a marriage not of her own choosing. Along the way Oribela learns from the disparate human beings who populate a young, rugged nation, especially the indigenous women who serve her husband's household:

> Nesse tempo se deu de minha amizade se encantar por uma natural, de cor muito baça, bons dentes brancos e miúdos, alegre rosto, pés pequenos, cabelo aparado e que me falava a língua, com a rudeza dos matos e modos de animais silvestres. [It so happened during this period, that my friendship was captivated by a natural girl, very brown in color, with dainty, well-appointed white teeth, cheerful face, small feet, trimmed hair, who spoke the language to me with the roughness of the woodlands and the manners of wild beasts.]

Oribela's life in the New World is fraught with emotional conflict; her loyalties are divided between her Portuguese-born husband and the Moor with whom she falls in love. She experiences the birth of her son, only to confront his subsequent kidnapping by her husband (in a scene vaguely reminiscent of the concluding pages of *Iracema*, José de Alencar's masterpiece of Brazilian Romanticism, father and son depart on a ship bound for Europe). Faced with various forms of material loss at the novel's end, Oribela seemingly begins to lose her sanity, even as she questions her place as a woman in such a society. In the concluding sentences, however, Oribela's fate remains restoratively open-ended by means of a lasting vision of renewal.

Similarly, in Ana Miranda's novel *Amrik*, the story of Middle Eastern immigration to Brazil is told through the transgressive voice of its narrator, a sensual Lebanese belly-dancer named Amina, who leaves the security of her homeland at the turn of the twentieth century and passes briefly through New York before settling in São Paulo, Brazil. According to Cristiane Costa's review of *Amrik* in the *Jornal do Brasil*, the novel is written in homage to Miranda's husband, Emir Sader, of Lebanese descent. It includes a list of bibliographical sources with references to Borges, Flaubert, Rimbaud, and others who depicted the Orient through the eyes of a Westerner.

In *Sem Pecado* (Without Sin)—its subject matter might loosely be compared to that of Clarice Lispector's classic novella *A Hora da Estrela* (The Hour of the Star) of 1977—contemporary, urban Brazil provides the backdrop for the sexual experiences of Bambi, an adolescent migrant from the

Northern state of Maranhão. The novel, which some critics consider Miranda's most radical work, begins with its protagonist stepping off the bus in Rio de Janeiro, her head filled with idealistic dreams of becoming an actress. The journey south literally symbolizes her passage into womanhood. Written as a first-person narrative from the young woman's point of view, and frequently told in retrospect, the novel represents an individual's response to the multifarious perils and sins of society.

In Miranda's 1996 novella *Clarice*, biographical details about Brazil's venerated writer Clarice Lispector—here represented as a protagonist—are woven into a fictional narrative that draws from Lispector's own prose. *Noturnos* (Nocturnes), Ana Miranda's first book of short stories, was published in 1999. Its title is evocative of Chopin's mood-filled musical compositions, and it includes eighty-one distinct narratives written from the perspective of a solitary, melancholic woman confined to her high-rise apartment. The page-long narratives offer a contemplative perspective on the search for love and meaning in life, as well as the laboring suffering that accompanies it. Although the short stories are presented in a determined, static sequence, the thematic fluidity of the individual stories allows the reader to approach the short pieces in random order. As a technique, the latter lends the book an air of memoir.

In the acclaimed *Dias e Dias,* Ana Miranda constructs a novel centered on Gonçalves Dias' life. The text progresses through the first-person narration of Feliciana, a woman of modest means who grew up alongside the young poet and subsequently became devotedly enamored of him and his poetry. In the author's customary style of short chapters and female narration, Feliciana's own life unfolds as an embodiment of the spirit of Romanticism, complete with the suspense created by lost love letters and culminating in a tragic shipwreck. As in other examples of her skill with historical fiction, Ana Miranda accurately encapsulates in atmospheric terms both the life of Gonçalves Dias and his notable work.

Ana Miranda has recently returned to the writing of poetry, evident in the publication of *Prece a uma aldeia perdida* (2004, Invocation to a Lost Village), which is written as a long poem in two voices: one from within the village, and the other from an outside perspective. Also in 2004 she published a book of children's literature entitled *Flor do Cerrado* (Prairie Flower), a memoir centered on the construction of Brasília. Told from the point of view of a young girl and her father, this book evokes the author's own childhood experience.

Other Contributions

Ana Miranda has contributed short stories for anthologies and numerous articles for newspapers and magazines. In 1998, Dantes Editora published an anthology of erotic poetry from the seventeenth and eighteenth centuries entitled *Que Seja em Segredo* (That It Be in Secret), which Ana Miranda both edited and introduced. An anthology of dreams that Miranda recorded as a young woman in her early twenties was published in 2000, under the title *Caderno de Sonhos* (Notebook of Dreams). She has contributed essays to *Caros Amigos* since 1998 and to *Correio Braziliense* since 2004. Her collected essays from *Caros Amigos* were published in *Deus Dará* in 2003.

Several of Ana Miranda's books have appeared in translation, including the award-winning novel *A Boca do Inferno*, which was published in an English version translated by Giovanni Pontiero, entitled *Bay of All Saints and Every Conceivable Sin* (New York: Viking, 1991). Her works have appeared in translations published in a variety of countries, including Spain, France, Italy, Germany, England, the Netherlands, Denmark, Norway, Sweden, and Argentina.

MARGUERITE ITAMAR HARRISON

Selected Works

A Boca do Inferno. São Paulo: Companhia das Letras, 1989.
O Retrato do Rei. São Paulo: Companhia das Letras, 1991.
Sem Pecado. São Paulo: Companhia das Letras, 1993.
A Última Quimera. São Paulo: Companhia das Letras, 1995.
Desmundo: Romance. São Paulo: Companhia das Letras, 1996.
Clarice: Novela. São Paulo: Companhia das Letras, 1996.
Amrik: Romance. São Paulo: Companhia das Letras, 1997.
Noturnos: Contos. São Paulo: Companhia das Letras, 1999.
Dias e Dias. São Paulo: Companhia das Letras, 2002.
Deus Dará: Crônicas. São Paulo: Casa Amarela, 2003.
Prece a uma aldeia perdida: Poesia. Rio de Janeiro: Record, 2004.
Flor do Cerrado: Brasília. São Paulo: Companhia das Letrinhas, 2004.

Website

For a biographical introduction to the author, complete with individual descriptions of her literary works, as well as brief reviews of her fiction, access the following website: www.anamirandaliteratura.hpgvip.ig.com.br

References and Further Reading

Costa, Cristiane. "A dança da transgressão". Review of Ana Miranda's *Amrik*. *Jornal do Brasil* (23 Sept. 1997), Caderno B.
Cruz, Maria de Santa. "Heróis sem nenhum caráter". *Colóquio: Letras* 134 (Oct.–Dec. 1994): 131–8.
Faria, Álvaro Alves de. *Palavra de Mulher: Entrevistas*. São Paulo: Senac Editora, 2003.
Lehnen, Leila. "Questionable Genealogy: History and Nation in Ana Miranda's *Desmundo*". *Chasqui: Revista de Literatura Latinoamericana* 34(2) (Nov. 2005): 48–61.

MISTRAL, GABRIELA

Chilean Nobel Laureate Gabriela Mistral (1889–1957) was born Lucila Godoy y Alcayaga in 1889 in the Andean village of Vicuña. From such a humble beginning, one that may have only included a primary school education, Godoy made herself into a schoolteacher, head of a succession of schools, an international expert on education and culture, a seasoned diplomat, a prolific essayist, and a poet—and she re-christened herself "Gabriela Mistral". Mistral the poet is best known for her affectionate and yearning poems of mother-love and children and for her emphasis on the fragility of life. She won the Nobel Prize for Literature in 1945, the first awarded to a Latin American writer. Mistral's poetry found coherence in her political causes, and Mistral earned international recognition for her passionate defense of children, women, and indigenous people in the face of casual and bureaucratic indifference. She worked to promote public education programs and cultural understanding across the Americas and around the world. She was committed to simplicity and truth in her daily life as in her poetry and was a lay member of a Franciscan order. In Chile, Mistral's literary and public reputation among social and religious conservatives has been affected by broader public awareness of her lesbian relationships.

Early Life and Poetic Inspiration

Mistral's birthplace in the Andes sits on the Elqui River "in a valley where the sweetest grapes grow". Of indigenous and Basque-Spanish heritage, Lucila Godoy y Alcayaga was reared by her mother and then by an older sister after her father, Juan Gerónimo Godoy Villanueva, deserted the family when Mistral was 3. At 15 or 16, in 1909 or 1910, she became a teacher's aide and later passed the teacher exams in order to support herself and her mother. At the same time, Mistral began writing poetry and newspaper articles, activities that she continued throughout her life, along with her teaching. A number of events in Mistral's life are considered formative for her poetic voice and perspective. She wrote a number of poems supposedly dedicated to Romelio Ureta, a young railroad employee with whom she is said to have fallen in love during her regular visits to the railway station to pick up mail, and who committed suicide in 1909 after being convicted of embezzlement

Shortly after of Ureta's death, Mistral, who was working as an assistant teacher, passed the necessary exams, and she became a teacher in her own right in Santiago in 1912. In the succeeding years, she worked as a teacher or head of school in a number of Chilean communities, and was made head of a school in Punta Arenas in 1918. She published on education topics extensively and became known to the Latin American educated public for her essays. In 1921, she became head of Santiago de Chile's national secondary school for girls, a crowning appointment for her teaching career, but she soon left Chile for international appointments as consultant, cultural diplomat, poet, and university teacher. She returned to Chile only rarely, but for the remainder of her life continued to involve herself in matters of children's welfare and education, taking advisory roles in international and national culture and education policy. She worked on the reform of Mexico's education system and its public libraries with José Vasconcelos from July 1922 to April 1924 (see Schneider 1996).

With the League of Nations (1925–34), Mistral furthered the cause of culture as a member of the League of Intellectual Cooperation. She served as Chile's delegate to the United Nations and served on the Subcommittee on the Legal and Social Status of Women. Mistral was instrumental in forming UNICEF, the United Nations Children's Fund. Mistral worked in the United Nations and in other venues for a peaceful world community and a unified hemisphere. She took up appointments as a teacher of literature in American colleges and universities such as Columbia, Middlebury, and Vassar and served Chile in cultural diplomatic posts in Spain, Italy, Brazil, Portugal, and in the United States (Los Angeles). From 1922 onward, she made her homes in France, Italy, Brazil, Mexico, and the United States and returned to Chile only for brief periods.

Mistral never married, though she apparently had several committed relationships with men and, later, with women. She adopted and reared Juan Miguel "Yin-Yin" Godoy, her nephew, when he was an infant, and he died unexpectedly at the age of 17 in 1943 when Mistral was Chilean consul in Brazil. The police ruled the death a suicide.

During her extended residence in New York, Mistral was taken ill late in 1956, and after a brief illness, she died of cancer at the age of 67 on January 10, 1957, in Long Island, New York. She is buried in Chile, and Yin Yin's remains were transferred from Brazil to be interred near Mistral's tomb.

Literary Career

Mistral's early writing was published in Chilean newspapers, around 1904 and 1905, the years when she began to seek a career in teaching, applying to the Normal School for teacher training and taking a position as an assistant teacher. Goic reports that she began using her pen name, Gabriela Mistral, with minor spelling variants in 1908 and that she had her work published in the Chilean literary magazine *Penumbras* (Shadows) in 1909. American poet Langston Hughes writes in the introduction to his translation of selected Mistral poems that she adopted the pen name because she feared that she would lose her teaching position if it became known that she was the author of "such emotionally outspoken verse" (1957, p. 9).

In 1914, Mistral won Chile's *Premio Juegos Florales*, a national poetry prize, for *Sonetos de la muerte* (Sonnets of Death), a small group of poems which she signed with her pen name. Between 1914 and 1922, Mistral continued to publish poetry and essays in Chilean literary magazines such as *Revista de educación* and *Primrose* and contributed fifty-five pieces of poetry and prose to a series of textbooks, *Libro de lectura* (Readings) (Goic 1989: 678). Regarding her penname, some accounts claim that Mistral adopted the surname of Frédéric Mistral, a French Provençal scholar and poet who had won the Nobel Prize for Literature in 1904 (sharing the prize with Spaniard José de Echegaray); and that for her given-name, she feminized and hispanicized the baptismal name of Gabriele D'Annunzio, Italian patriot, poet, dramatist, and fiction writer. Dinamarca, following Figueroa (1958, p. 217), however, writes that the pen name has nothing to do with the poet Mistral, but that she took it from the name of the cold, dry north wind known as the *mistral* in the Mediterranean (1958, p. 48). Hughes concurs that she took the surname from "the sea wind" and adds that she took the baptismal name from "the archangel Gabriel" (1957, p. 9).

Gabriela Mistral published only five books of poetry in her lifetime, according to most accounts, but Dinamarca stipulates that her work may be found in three books (1958, p. 49), not counting *Sonetos de la muerte* (1914) or *Ternura* (1924, Tenderness). The collection *Desolación* (Desolation) did not appear until 1922, eight years after Mistral won the national prize for *Sonetos*, and it was published in New York through the good auspices of Columbia University professor Federico de Onís and other professors living in the United States. Two Chilean editions of *Desolación* appeared soon after the first, and the second, "corrected and enlarged," was released in 1926 (Dinamarca 1958: 49). The definitive version is found in the Margaret Bates *Complete Works* text. The contents of these editions vary significantly. In 1924, *Ternura: Canciones de niños* (Tenderness: Children's Songs) was published, and included the "Canciones de cuna" ("Cradle Songs") of *Desolación*. *Tala* (Destruction or Felling [Trees]) was published in Mexico in 1938 through the efforts of Victoria Ocampo, Argentine publisher and critic. *Tala*'s poems are personal reflections on death and loss, both experienced and anticipated; in these poems, Mistral records her life in Spain at the beginning of the Spanish Civil War in view of the fascist presence in Spain, Italy, and Germany. Goic describes *Tala*, interestingly, as lacking "the marked subjectivity" of previous work and adopting "a poetry of objective representation" (see Goic's extended discussion of semantics and "New Worldism" in regard to *Tala*, 1958, pp. 681–2).

In spite of the sadness and longing in many of *Tala*'s poems, Mistral affirms her orthodox faith in Christ and in the life to come and, in a subdued way, celebrates the gift of memory to reclaim the past and animate the future. Mistral assigned her rights and the proceeds from *Tala* to the cause of children orphaned by the Spanish Civil War. During the war years, Mistral continued to publish in periodicals such as *Repertorio americano* and in capital city daily papers such as *El Mercurio* in Chile and *La Nación* in Argentina.

Following the war, *Lagar* (Wine Press) was published in 1954 in Chile, and in the same year, *Desolación* was released in its "definitive" edition in Chile. This new edition of *Desolación* and the publication of *Lagar* are the last poetic works published in Mistral's lifetime, and *Lagar* was the only new book of poetry she published after winning the Nobel Prize. According to Pedro Pablo Zegers, *Lagar* was originally intended to be one large volume, but Mistral was persuaded to divide the work into two parts. *Lagar* (I) contained "setenta poemas distribuidos en trece secciones más un prólogo y un epílogo" (seventy poems divided into thirteen sections with a prologue and epilogue). *Lagar II* (1991) contains fifty-eight poems in twelve sections, and omits two additional untitled sections from the original manuscript (on microfilm), which is typed with corrections to the text by Mistral and Doris Dana, Mistral's American secretary and the executrix of her estate. Dana supervised publication of Mistral's last work, *Poema de Chile* (Chilean Poem or Poem of Chile), in its unfinished form, after Mistral's death in 1957.

Critical Reception

Mistral's reputation as the childless poet of simple and sentimental verse celebrating motherhood and children grew by means of twentieth-century editorial choices that governed which of her poems were chosen as reading selections and translations in texts and anthologies. Certainly those kinds of poems and the romanticized image of Mistral have had wide exposure. Stephen Tapscott explains this popular reverence for Mistral: "In an important sense, she won the Nobel Prize in 1945 because after the Spanish War and World War II, the world seemed to need an icon of healing, devout, even oddly virginal 'maternity'" ("Translator's Remarks"). Recent critical examination has nuanced this "iconic" view of Mistral's work, as critical assessment has been better informed through Mistral's essays in literary criticism, religion, philosophy, and biography, and her large correspondence, which has been edited and published in the years since her death.

Mistral's poetry is characterized by its vital passion and fearless intimacy and, as has often been said, by the poet's conscious rejection of modernism. She employed a variety of forms, from the traditional metrics of the Alexandrine sonnet, to the "free verse" of her *recados* (messages). Mistral's use of Chilean and indigenous language, naming, and expression gives her work a characteristic richness and rhythm that speak of her native Andes. Her subjects are most often nature, love, death, children, and the search for truth and authenticity. She explores man's place within nature and in the cosmos and seeks truth—social and political or religious and philosophical—above all. Her most frequently anthologized works are the "cradle songs," which, though beautiful in the well-wrought brevity and images, do not indicate the range of interests and tones in the poet's work. Indeed, Mistral wrote poetry about the darker side of humanity as well. Her poems of mothers and children generally imply vulnerability, suggesting an immediate threat to the safety and security of the tender image. Some of Mistral's poems about children suggest a sinister and disturbing underside of violence, evil, or indifference juxtaposed with images of beauty and tenderness.

"Piececitos" ("Little Feet"), frequently anthologized, is much more than a sentimental view of endearing, neglected children, and it is meant to do more than break the reader's heart. Mistral paints an image of suffering, and like a filmmaker, repeatedly places it before the reader, each time from slightly different angle. One sees—and even "feels"—the open cuts and sores on the filthy, bleeding bare feet of children who are impoverished and neglected by society, and who have no other choice than to make their way over sharp rocks and mud- and filth-laden tracks in order to live another day in their miserable condition. She places the reader, like the "hombres ciegos" (blind men) whom the speaker directly addresses, in the position of "seeing" and failing to see, and in the end, of failing to intervene. The poem is a mirror of her witness and a mirror of the reader's inaction—for whatever reason. Published at the end of World War II, the poem evokes a disturbing image of the effects of war, as well as of the public policy of neglect in peace time. The poem continues to speak to a public well-versed in images of war, famine, and other ills that have their greatest effect on children.

One of Mistral's darkest poems is the seldom reprinted, "Caperucita Roja" ("Little Red Riding Hood"). Mistral versifies the initial elements of the tale, adding poignant descriptors in a seemingly innocent trail of detail, that, like the child's trail to grandmother's house and the wolf's answers, lead to unexpected danger and ultimately to violence. In this poem, there is no hunter to save the day, as there is in the folktale, and both grandmother and child have their flesh and bones crushed between the wolf's jaws.

Even the most familiar of Mistral's compact lines, concise metaphors, and frequent short stanzas with their images of mothers and children and scenes of nature and ordinary life reflect the poet's habits of care and constant revision. Much of Mistral's work is, as has often been claimed, inspired by personal suffering, and in this poetry, she poetizes that process of mediation in concrete as well as emotional terms, coming to modes of understanding and ways of seeing through the process of textual revision. In this spirit, Mistral's poetry was never "finished" during her lifetime. Goic records the many "transformations" and re-orderings of her collections (1958, pp. 680–1). Preston (1964) and Daydí-Tolson (1989) note the extent of her revisions, and both argue against carelessness or casualness in Mistral's habits of composition. Tolson notes that Mistral would compose several lines for the same position in the poem and deliberate at length over which might be best. An early editor of her work, Raúl Silva Castro, writes that in Mistral's published work—not considering any notes or papers of the author—the variants are notable (quoted by Preston 1964, p. 195). Inspired by Silva Castro's suggestion that these differences warranted further examination, Preston's detailed study of variants in the extant redactions of Mistral's work notes all sorts of authorial revisions—minor, extensive, and substantive—based on the poet's aims of style, meter, clarity of image, and the possibility of the reader's making an inaccurate interpretation of meaning.

Throughout her life, which was mostly spent outside Chile, Mistral remained conscious of her role as a representative of Chile, as well as of her Spanish heritage. In her Nobel Prize banquet speech in Stockholm, she spoke of heritage and responsibility: "I am the direct voice of the poets of my race and the indirect voice for the noble Spanish and Portuguese tongues". In her final work, *Poema del Chile*, published posthumously, she creates a minutely realized recollection of her agrarian childhood in the Andes. Critic Daydí-Tolson finds Mistral committed, in *Poema del Chile*, to the nationalist spirit and showing her great passion for all things Chilean, both natural and man-made. Her determination to defend children, indigenous people, and natural resources—the innocent essence of Chile—from exploitation and neglect through her poetry remains constant. (See Chapters 2, 4, and 5, especially, of Daydí-Tolson's study.)

Recent Biographical and Literary Criticism

Mistral biographies abound and are often repetitive; even the Nobel Prize Committee adopted at surprising length the more tragic and romantic aspects of her biography for her formal presentation in Stockholm, with the theme that these events had created the poet. It is likely that some of these matters will be clarified in the future by more careful documentary research. Recently, Mistral's secretary Doris Dana has asserted publicly that Yin-Yin was Mistral's natural child; this "news" and newer treatments of Mistral's biography, like Pedro Pablo Zeger's discussion of the discouragement, abandonment, and injustice that Mistral suffered during her childhood, point toward re-evaluating Mistral's fairly standardized biography and its relationship to her work as a poet—often a strongly autobiographical poet. In 2003, Tapscott's closing essay on his work as a translator of Mistral suggested that certain standard biographical elements may be embroidered.

In 2001, the British rock singer Sting was awarded the Gabriela Mistral medal for his song "They Dance Alone," which honors the courage of Chilean mothers whose children were among the *desaparecidos* (the missing, or "disappeared ones") during the Pinochet regime. The lines recall the haunting images as well as the emotionally-charged images of Mistral's political poems:

> Why are these women here, dancing on their own?
> Why is there this sadness in their eyes?
> Why are the soldiers here, their faces fixed like stone?
> I can't see what it is that they despise.

Mistral's "holograph manuscripts of poetry and prose, working papers, drafts, and correspondence" (1912–57) archived at the Library of Congress were arranged and indexed by Doris Dana and Gastón von dem Bussche for the Organization of American States (OAS) in Washington, DC, and microfilmed in four series (I–IV). Manuscript papers, including notebooks and loose leaves "con intrincadas correcciones y tachaduras" (with involved corrections and deletions), according to Mistral's habits of revision, are archived at the Archivo del Escritor de la Biblioteca Nacional (Writer's Archive in the National Library) in Santiago de Chile (Zegers 1969: 18).

ELIZABETH MOORE WILLINGHAM

Selected Works

Antología: Selección de la autora. Ismael Edwards Matte, "Introduction". Santiago de Chile: Zag-Zag. 1940, 1946, 4th edn 1955.

Selected Poems of Gabriela Mistral. Trans. Langston Hughes. Bloomington, IN: Indiana University Press, 1957.

Poesías completas, Margaret Bates, 3rd edn. Madrid, 1966, 1st edn 1958.

Lecturas para mujeres. Mexico: Porrúa, 1974.

Lagar. Santiago de Chile: Andrés Bello, 1989.

Lagar II. Santiago de Chile: Biblioteca Nacional, 1991.

Desolación. Barcelona: Andrés Bello, 2000.

Selected Prose and Prose-poems of Gabriela Mistral. Trans. Stephen Tapscott. Austin, TX: University of Texas Press, 2003.

Further Reading

Agosín, Marjorie (ed.) *Gabriela Mistral: The Audacious Traveler*. Athens, OH: Ohio University Press, 2003.

Concha, Jaime. "Tejer y tranzar: aspectos del trabajo en la Mistral." Ed. Gastón Lillo. Ottawa, 1969, pp. 97–118.

Daydí-Tolson, Santiago. *El último viaje de Gabriela Mistral*. Chile: Aconcagua, 1989.

Dinamarca, Salvador. "Gabriela Mistral y su obra poética". *Hispania* 41(1) (1958): 48–9.

Goic, Cedomil. "Gabriela Mistral". Trans. Irene and Nicolás Goic. In Carlos A. Solé (ed.), *Latin American Writers*. 2 vols. New York: Scribner's, 1989.

Horan, Elizabeth. *This America of Ours: The Letters of Gabriela Mistral and Victoria Ocampo*. Austin, TX: University of Texas Press, 2003.

Horst, Frenz (ed.) *Nobel Lectures, Literature 1901–1967*. Amsterdam: Elsevier, 1969.

Lillo, Gastón and Rebart, Guillermo. *Re-leer hoy a Gabriela Mistral: Mujer, historia y sociedad en America Latina*. Simposio de Ottawa. Ottawa: University of Ottawa Press, 1997.

Nobel Prize Committee. "Gabriela Mistral." http://nobelprize.org/literature/laureates/1945/mistral-bio.html (accessed 15 November 2006).

Preston, Sister Mary Charles Ann. *A Study of Significant Variants in the Poetry of Gabriela Mistral*. Washington, DC: Catholic University of America Press, 1964.

Schneider, Mario. "Gabriela Mistral en México: una devota de misionerismo vasconcelista." Ed. Gastón Lillo. Ottawa, 1969, pp. 147–58.

Silva Castro, Raúl. "Producción de Gabriela Mistral de 1912–18". *Anales de la Universidad de Chile* 106 (1957): 195–249.

Zegers, Pedro Pablo. "Infancia y Valle de Elqui en Gabriela Mistral." Ed. Gastón Lillo. Ottawa, 1969, pp. 127–45.

MOLLOY, SYLVIA

The academic work of Sylvia Molloy (b. 1938), Albert Schweitzer Professor of the Humanities at New York University, has firmly established her as an important and vital critic of Latin American literature and culture. Born in Buenos Aires, Argentina, to a family of French and English background, she traveled to France at the age of 20 to study at the Sorbonne. After she received her *Doctorat d'Université* (Ph.D.) in 1967 in Comparative Literature, Molloy pursued her professional career in the United States. Here she held academic positions at Princeton and Yale, and received honors such as the Guggenheim Fellowship, a National Endowment for the Humanities Fellowship, the Presidency of the Modern Language Association, the Achievement Award for Outstanding Service to La Herencia Latina and the Latino Community, among others. Molloy travels regularly to Argentina where she lectures at the University of Buenos Aires and other universities in the country. Although Molloy is well known as a critic, her novels have carved her a space as a fiction writer as well.

Literary Critic

Sylvia Molloy has published numerous articles and essays in academic journals and anthologies on twentieth-century Latin American literature and culture, gender issues and women writers, which exhibit the breadth and depth of her knowledge of the region. In her dissertation on *La Diffusion de la Littérature Hispano-Américaine en France au XXe Siècle* (1972, The Growth of Interest of Spanish American Literature in France in the Twentieth Century), she discusses the reception of Spanish American literature in the Gallic country and the French impact on Spanish American authors such as Darío, Güiraldes, Huidobro, and Victoria Ocampo, as well as the influences on French authors of Spanish America. Here Molloy begins her research on the Argentinian fiction writer Jorge Luis Borges by devoting a section of her book to his work.

Molloy's attention to Borges will come to fruition in her next critical study *Las letras de Borges* (1979, Signs of Borges). In this influential analysis of the work of the Argentinian writer, Molloy develops a new critical approach by focusing on the intertextuality of Borges' work, the fragmented world he composes, and the tension language creates between the real and the uncanny. In the revised edition of the *Signs of Borges* (1999), Molloy acknowledges that although she never met Borges, he introduced her to writing, reading, and thinking by the process of interpreting his works.

Her next critical work was an anthology edited with Luis Fernández Cifuentes, *Essays on Hispanic Literature in Honor of Edmund L. King*. In this collection Molloy published the essay *Ser / decir: tácticas de un autorretrato* (1983, To Be / To Tell: Strategies of a Self-Portrait). Here she discusses the difficulties of expressing the self in poetry as seen in Rubén Darío's work. Her interest in biographical and autobiographical literature and the authors' desire to express their personal voices through their work culminates in her critical study *At Face Value: Autobiographical Writing in Spanish America* (1991). Molloy focuses on nineteenth- and twentieth-century authors to argue that autobiographical writing has been marginalized in Spanish American letters. Molloy remarks on the literary strategies to construct the autobiographical "I", the relationship this self establishes with the reader by sharing personal memories, events and rituals, and pays special attention to the obstacles the subject must defy representing itself and gaining a place in Spanish-speaking literature. This study includes the work by female writers, such as Victoria Ocampo and Norah Lange, who had received little critical attention because their writing did not conform to the heroic and civic qualities expected of autobiographical texts.

Molloy continues her critical contribution to the literature of marginalized communities developing theoretical frames that explain and rescue texts and authors who have been critically forgotten because of their inability to accept tradition or the literary norms. In 1991, she edited an anthology with Sara Castro-Klarén and Beatriz Sarlo, *Women's Writing in Latin America* where translations into English of an extensive sample of the works of women writers from Spanish America and Brazil were made available for the first time to the English-speaking public. In the introductory essay to the second part, *Female Textual Identities: The Strategies of Self-Figuration*, Molloy showed her particular preoccupation with the female self and its bodily inscription in the text.

Molloy's last collection, *Hispanisms and Homosexualities*, was edited with Robert McKee Irwin in 1998. Here the editors set out to question the notion of definitiveness and of canonicity through the collected essays on Hispanic literatures. This compilation features *The Politics of Posing*, in which Molloy conducts a cultural and literary comparative analysis of the concept of posing as defined during Oscar Wilde's trial and its influences on and the reactions to Spanish American writers such as Darío and José Ingenieros. Molloy sees the act of posing of the queer as a political resistance. The decadent or deviant during this period is a conflictive and unpatriotic image that questioned a male-defined national identity. Thus it had to be repressed or destroyed.

Fiction Writer

Sylvia Molloy has written two novels and an anthology of short stories in which she explores issues that are of importance in her critical work such as the autobiographical narrative, the articulation of the "I", language, minority cultures and displacement, and gender and sex issues. These works of fiction are important testimony to her success in crossing from academic to fiction writing.

Molloy's first novel, *En breve cárcel* (1981, *Certificate of Absence*) has received wide acclaim and has been the subject of many academic articles and doctoral dissertations. The novel is a meditation on the act of writing, and an exploration of lesbian sexuality and identity. Written in the third person, it depicts the difficulty of language to create and destroy memory through a fragmented narrative that continually displaces expectations of voice and point of view and captures the disjointed self of the lesbian narrator. This is a complex novel that crosses genres, as it is not completely autobiographical, but is constructed as a fictional autobiography. The female narrator, who is writing in a small room specifically rented for the purpose of writing her story, reminds us of Virginia Woolf's call for the importance of a woman to have a room of her own. The narrator and writer reconstructs her past and her family's, bringing up memories of incest and violence while waiting for the arrival of her lover, Renata. In doing so, she reflects on the power of love and of retelling experience to gain a sense of self, intimacy and meaning. In the end the narrator remains alone, with the certainty that her alienated self and body cannot be inscribed in a text with words, but that in the act of trying she has accomplished the articulation of herself as a subject, that absence to which the title refers.

Molloy's second novel *El común olvido* (2002, The Common Forgetfulness) contrasts deeply with her first. While *Certificate of Absence* is claustrophobic in its setting, *The Common Forgetfulness* is full of movement as Daniel, the main character and narrator, walks and visits friends and relatives and the different landmarks of Buenos Aires where he has returned to scatter his mother's ashes. Daniel's ability to speak Spanish and English, to navigate two different cultures, and his homosexuality perhaps reflect Molloy's own life. In this novel Molloy deals with the issues of displacement and exile, the difficulty or impossibility of language to firmly establish what is real, and to recover the past. There are many levels on which we can read *The Common Forgetfulness.* One can read it as a sort of detective fiction in which Daniel is searching for his mother's story and his own identity, discovering in the process many secrets. At another level, the novel is the account of exiles and their voyage back to a place, both physical and psychological, which no longer exists. Another possible interpretation is that *The Common Forgetfulness* is a form of historical novel, which merges real and fictive characters, depicting the intellectuals that encircled the famous Argentinean magazine *Sur* (South).

Her third work of fiction is the collection of short stories, *Varia imaginación* (2003, Various Imagination). The common thread of memory connects these short stories. Through each account, the first person female narrator recovers scenes of the past, trying to recover pieces of a puzzle that in the end will present a whole picture of fragmented selves through language and through the questioning of patriarchal norms.

There are several recurrent themes in Molloy's writings which demonstrate that she has maintained integrity of thought and commitment on questions that are dear to her, both as an academic and a fiction writer. To understand Molloy's work in an encompassing manner, the critic must grapple with feminist issues regarding gender construction and the role writing and language play in it. Molloy's characters and narrators constantly problematize the act of remembering, inscribing and exercising control over narrative to fix the female subject. This effort, however, proves elusive because, as the characters find, the female self is fragmented, multiple, and contradictory; not a monolithic construct that can be framed through language.

Students of Molloy's work will also be confronted with the relevance of autobiographical efforts and the constant struggle of the feminine "I" in the making. Her critical studies on autobiography and the determining conditioning of gender on the enunciator have led Molloy to discuss the relevance of female texts in literature and the reasons for their continuous marginalization. Furthermore, she has not limited her studies to women writers but has discovered that for homosexuals to gain power over their texts and move out of the private space that has imprisoned them, they must develop strategies that complicate their messages, allowing them to obviate censorship and exclusion from the public space.

Molloy's work as a critic and fiction writer has broken new paths in feminist and queer theory and literature. In her task as a critic she has relentlessly pursued the recovery of absent voices from the canon, those of women and gay writers; and, as a writer herself, she has recreated her own voice and self, affirming her presence in the space of academia and literature.

PATRICIA VARAS

Selected Works

La Diffusion de la Littérature Hispano-Américaine en France au XXe Siècle. Paris: Presses Universitaires de France, 1972.

Las letras de Borges. Buenos Aires: Editorial Sudamericana, 1979. Translated as *Signs of Borges.* Trans. Sylvia Molloy and Oscar Montero. Durham, NC: Duke University Press, 1994.

En breve cárcel. Barcelona: Seix Barral, 1981. Translated as *Certificate of Absence.* Trans. Daniel Balderston. Austin, TX: Texas University Press, 1989.

Molloy, Sylvia and Cifuentes, Luis Fernández (eds). *Essays on Hispanic Literature in Honor of Edmund L. King.* London: Tamesis, 1983.

At Face Value: Autobiographical Writing in Spanish America. New York: Cambridge UP, 1991. (Translated as *Acto de presencia: la escritura autobiográfica en Hispanoamérica.* Trans. José Esteban Calderón. Mexico: El Colegio de Mexico, 1996.)

Molloy, Sylvia, Castro-Klarén, Sara and Sarlo, Beatriz (eds). *Women's Writing in Latin America.* Boulder, CO: Westview Press, 1991.

Molloy, Sylvia and McKee Irwin, Robert (eds). *Hispanisms and Homosexualities.* Durham, NC: Duke University Press, 1998.

El común olvido. Buenos Aires: Grupo Editorial Norma, 2002.

Varia imaginación. Rosario: Beatriz Viterbo, 2003.

References and Further Reading

Badano, Valeria. "Arquetipos rotos. Sobre *Varia imaginación* de Sylvia Molloy". In Juana Alcira Arancibia (ed.), *La mujer en la literatura del mundo hispánico.* Buenos Aires: Instituto Literario y Cultural Hispánico, 2005.

Boling, Becky. "The Gaze, the Body and the Text in Sylvia Molloy's *En breve cárcel.*" *Hispanofila* 123 (1998): 73–89.

García Pinto, Magdalena. "La escritura de la pasión y la pasión de la escritura: *En breve cárcel*, de Sylvia Molloy". *Revista Iberoamericana* 51(132–3) (1985): 687–96.

——. "Entrevista con Sylvia Molloy en su departamento en Nueva York en noviembre de 1982". In Magdalena García Pinto (ed.), *Historias íntimas. Conversaciones con diez escritoras latinoamericanas.* Hanover, NH: Ediciones del Norte, 1988, pp. 123–47.

Godsland, Shelley. *Writing Reflection, Reflecting on Writing. Female Identity and Lacan's Mirror in Helena Parente Cunha and Sylvia Molloy.* Valladolid: Universitas Castellae, 2006.

González Echeverría, Roberto. "The Criticism of Latin American Literature Today: Adorno, Molloy, Magnarelli". *Profession* 87 (1987): 10–13.

Haydu, Susana. "Molloy, Sylvia. *El común olvido*". http://www.lehman.cuny.edu/ciberletras/v09/haydu.htm (accessed 23 March 2006).

Masiello, Francine. "*En breve cárcel*: La producción del sujeto". *Hispamérica* 14(41) (1985): 103–12.

Montero, Oscar. "*En breve cárcel*: La Diana, la violencia y la mujer que escribe". In Patricia Elena González and Eliana Ortega (eds), *La sartén por el mango: Encuentro de escritoras latinoamericanas.* Puerto Rico: Ediciones Huracán, 1985, pp. 111–18.

Norat, Gisela. "Textual/Sexual Inscription of Lesbian Identity in Sylvia Molloy's *En breve cárcel*". *Monographic Review/Revista Monográfica* 11 (1995): 291–301.

MONTERO, MAYRA

Mayra Montero was born in Havana, Cuba, in 1952, and has lived in Puerto Rico since 1972. She holds a degree in literature from the University of Puerto Rico and studied journalism in Mexico. For many years, Montero worked as a correspondent in Central America and the Caribbean. She is a highly acclaimed journalist in Puerto Rico; she writes stories about musical spectacles and a regular weekly column "Antes que llegue el lunes" (Before Monday Arrives) in the Puerto Rican newspaper, *El Nuevo Día*. Montero has compiled and published many of the columns that have appeared in newspapers in *Aguaceros dispersos*. Her journalistic endeavors also include collaborations with various sources of communications in Spain and the Dominican Republic, and translations of her columns have appeared in *The New York Times*.

Montero has written all her fiction in Spanish and is well received in Europe and Latin America. Her first book was a collection of short stories, *Veintitrés y una tortuga* (Twenty-Three and a Turtle). The second book, a novel entitled *La trenza de la hermosa luna* (The Braid of the Beautiful Moon), was a finalist for the Herralde award, one of Europe's most prestigious literary awards. Her fame, however, came with *La última noche que pasé contigo* (The Last Night I Spent with You), finalist for La Sonrisa Vertical award in 1991. She won her next award, Premio Liberaturpreis, in 1995 for *Tú, la oscuridad* (In the Palm of Darkness), a work that was critically acclaimed. In 2000, she won La Sonrisa Vertical award for her erotic novel *Púrpura profundo* (Deep Purple), a work that has earned critical accolades. Her books have been published in the United States in English translations by Edith Grossman, as well as in several European countries. Some of her works are also available in several other languages including French, German, Czech and Polish. Her nonfiction work appears frequently in scholarly and literary publications throughout the world.

Themes and Influences

Mayra Montero is notable for her multilayered fiction with intricately woven historical background (particularly events of the 1950s) packed with lyrical intensity and mystery, eroticism and social/cultural insights inviting the reader to form part of a subversive Caribbean world. Through her novels and essays she explores the Caribbean music, flora and fauna, ethnicity, and travel narratives contributing to the theorizations of a Caribbean experience that acknowledges and recognizes the black Caribbean experience. Her works show that deciphering the national identity quite often results in an unavoidable clash of cultures, and with her incredible ability to draw in the reader's curiosity, Montero brings to life a place and people from a subversive world, unfamiliar to many. The depicted tales of culturally diverse individuals from different walks of life invite the reader to see the other side and to share their longings and desires, their explorations of the interrelated fantasies of passion and destruction, their often predictable lives, the tormented existence of some, and the courage to survive of others.

The presence of music and the exploration of the cultural and religious aspects of the natives of the Caribbean also situate Montero's novels within a tradition in the Hispanic Caribbean started by the prominent Dominican writer Alejo Carpentier and other intellectuals in the mid-1900s. Many of Carpentier's narratives are based on musicology and the importance of religious practices such as voodoo, and there is an attempt to foreground and revalorize an Afro-Caribbean experience. Similarly, Montero's *In the Palm of Darkness* presents a compelling multilayered story that reads like a murder mystery about an American biologist and his native Haitian guide as they search for an endangered amphibian. The intention is to present another way of understanding the world, an Afro-Caribbean perspective at odds with the reason and logic of western science. In *Del rojo de su sombra* (The Red of His Shadow), Montero persuades the reader to look closely at the mysterious practice of voodoo by immersing the reader in the Haitian culture and its potent smells, colors, sounds, and surroundings to show that, despite the deplorable and impoverished conditions of the Haitian society, people have managed to preserve their spiritual strength, and in the midst of all the negative forces they are able to find beauty, dignity and love. *El capitán de los dormidos* (The Captain of the Sleepers) is an erotic allegory that centers on the intricate relationship between the United States and Puerto Rico, often highlighting the clash of cultures between these two countries. As in her other works, Montero's aim is not to reproduce history but to rediscover it through her fiction. In this case the author chooses the failed 1950s Nationalistic Insurrection in Puerto Rico to invite the reader to embark on a historical yet metaphorical journey through the eyes of a narrator whose memories of the past still haunt him in the present. In *Son de Almendra* (Dancing to Almendra), Montero presents a passionate story that can be read as a detective story or a historical novel that explores the Cuban mafia corruption of the 1950s and portrays the effects of the revolution and the subsequent political repression on the people. The story portrays the life of individuals who live despite not having any control over their lives—lives marked by failed possibilities, the pain of an impossible love, and the injustice that surrounds them.

In the study of contemporary narrative, many critics affirm that to speak of the contemporary Latin American subject one must trace its origins and its transformations through the social and ideological forces confronted throughout history. Such an endeavor brings forth individuals who are displaced, often within their own country, and are searching for an identity. In the search for an identity within the Caribbean culture, Montero's characters undergo a journey into the past, allowing each individual to somehow come to terms with the past, an endeavor that promotes an understanding of the present and future. Each one of Montero's texts inscribes in its own way a journey in search of origins, a way to understand the past and the hybrid Caribbean cultural makeup while providing an opportunity for self-exploration. Such a journey also leads to the recognition of a trans-cultural origin portrayed by those who identify with the natives—the conquered—and those who identify with the Europeans—the conquerors. The award-winning *Deep Purple* presents a less serious tale about a classical music critic addicted to seducing the virtuosos, regardless of sex. Later he writes about it in a San Juan newspaper. Montero has structured the text to resemble that of a piece of music with erotic elements. Its vignettes meticulously resemble the movements of a musical piece in length and tone and the story includes a number of peculiar sex-charged scenes.

Mayra Montero's works are a viable example of what critics refer to as *la nueva narrativa latinoamericana* or the (neo)narrative of Latin America. This trend is characterized by the inclusion of the previously marginalized literary or cultural manifestations, fragmented narrative and the presence of other voices. Furthermore, the traditional form of the novel and its place within the established canon are challenged by the creation of texts that are an amalgamation of diverse genres that defy classification.

MARISA HERRERA POSTLEWATE

Selected Works

"Ya no estaremos a las seis veinticinco. Delma". In Emilio Díaz Valcárcel and Edgardo Sanabria Santaliz (eds), *17 del taller: antología de cuentos y relatos*. San Juan, P.R.: Instituto de Cultura Puertorriqueña, 1978.

Veintitrés y una tortuga. San Juan, P.R.: Instituto de Cultura Puertorriqueña, 1981.

La trenza de la hermosa luna. Barcelona: Editorial Anagrama, 1987.

Prólogo. In *El día que me dieron el premio*. Puerto Rico: Editorial Grafito, 1991.

La última noche que pasé contigo. Barcelona: Tusquets, 1991. Translated by Edith Grossman as *The Last Night I Spent With You*. New York: HarperCollins Publishers, 2000.

Del rojo de su sombra. Barcelona: Tusquets, 1992. Translated by Edith Grossman as *The Red of His Shadow*. New York: HarperCollins, 2001.

Tú, la oscuridad. Barcelona: Tusquets, 1995. Translated by Edith Grossman as *In The Palm of Darkness*. New York: HarperCollins, 1997.

Corinne, amiable girl. In Margarite Fernández Olmos and Lizabeth Paravisini-Gebert (eds), *Remaking a Lost Harmony: Stories from the Hispanic Caribbean*. Fredonia, NY: White Pine Press, 1995.

"Como el arrollo de palmas ... el discurso autobiográfico de las mujeres del Caribe". *Quaderni Ibero-Americani: Attualita Culturale della Penisola Iberica e América Latina* 78 (1995): 87–9.

Aguaceros dispersos. Barcelona: Tusquets, 1996.

"Cuentas para el caimón y otras lágrimas de cocodrilos madur-os".*Encuentro de la Cultura Cubana* 1 (1996): 102–6.

Como un mensajero tuyo. Barcelona: Tusquets, 1998. Translated by Edith Grossman as *The messenger*. New York: Harper Flamingo, 1999.

"Dorso de diamante". In Mercedes Abad and Ana Estevan (eds), *Cuentos eróticos de Navidad*. Barcelona: Tusquets, 1999.

"El hombre Pollack". In Bradford Morrow and Walter Abish (eds), *American Fiction: States of the Art*. Annandale-on-Hudson, NY: Bard College, 2000.

Prologue. In *Pedir de boca*. Barcelona: Casiopea, 2000.

Púrpura profundo. Barcelona: Tusquets, 2000. Translated by Edith Grossman as *Deep Purple*. New York: HarperCollins, 2003.

Como un mensajero tuyo (fragmento). In Aida Bähr (ed.), *Palabras de espuma: selección de narrativa*. Santiago de Cuba: Editorial Oriente, 2001.

"'My work is Obeah': an interview with poet/painter LeRoy Clarke". In Margarite Fernández Olmos and Lizabeth Paravisini-Gebert (eds), *Healing Cultures Art and Religion as Curative Practices in the Caribbean and its Diaspora*. New York: Palgrave, 2001.

"That man, Pollack". In Thomas Colchie (ed.), *A Whistler in the Nightworld: Short Fiction from the Latin Americas*. New York: Plume, 2002.

El capitán de los dormidos. Tusquets, 2002. Translated by Edith Grossman as *Captain of the Sleepers*. New York: Farrar, Straus and Giroux, 2005

Vana ilusión: las memorias noveladas de Narciso Figueroa. San Juan, PR: Ediciones Callejón, 2003

"Desnudos en la niebla". In *Granta en español*. Barcelona: Planeta, 2004.

Son de almendra. Guaynabo, PR: Alfaguara, 2005. Translated by Edith Grossman as *Dancing to Almendra*. New York: Farrar, Straus and Giroux, 2007.

References and Further Reading

Fernández Olmos, Margarite. "Trans-Caribbean identity and the fictional world of Mayra Montero". In Margarite Fernández Olmos and Lizabeth Paravisini-Gebert (eds), *Sacred Possessions: Vodou, Santería, Obeah, and the Caribbean*. New Brunswick, NJ: Rutgers University Press, 1997.

Fuente, José Luís de la. "Las novelas de Mayra Montero: Hacia una nueva magia". *Horizontes: Revista de la Universidad Católica de Puerto Rico* 45(89) (2003): 87–126.

Lauer, A. Robert. "El (homo)erotismo musical en la narrativa caribeña de Mayra Montero: *Púrpura profundo*". *Chasqui: Revista de Literatura Latinoamericana* 34(1) (2005): 42–50.

León-Vera, Antonio. "Mayra Montero: Las islas del deseo". *Torre: Revista de la Universidad de Puerto Rico* 10(38) (1996): 183–201.

López, Irma Margarita. "*La última noche que pasé contigo*: el crucero hacia el placer y el autoconocimiento". *Latin American Literary Review Press* 33 (2005): 133–44.

Morell, Hortensia. "Presencia de Cortázar en *La última noche que pasé contigo*: Mayra Montero y su isla caribeña a mediodía". *Caribe: Revista de Cultura y Literatura* 4–5(2–1) (2001–2): 8–21.

Pérez Torres, Yazmin. "Regresando a la Guinea: Historia, religión y mito en las novelas caribeñas de Mayra Montero". *Revista Iberoamericana* 65(186) (1999): 103–16.

Piña, Cristina. "Mayra Montero y los topoi de la erótica masculina revisitados por una mujer". *Cuadernos Hispanoamericanos* 659 (2005): 7–15.

Rivera, Angel A. "Etica y estética de la compasión en Mayra Montero: *Aguaceros dispersos*". *Atenea* (2003) 23.2: 39–51.

Rivera Villegas, Carmen M. "Viajes y revelaciones en el Haití de Mayra Montero". In Priscilla Gac-Artigas (ed.), *Reflexiones: Ensayos sobre escritoras hispanoamericanas contemporáneas*. Fair Haven, NJ: Nuevo Espacio, 2002, pp. 111–23.

Rosario-Vélez, Jorge. "Somos un sueño imposible: ¿Clandestinidad sexual del bolero en *La última noche que pasé contigo* de Mayra Montero?" *Revista Iberoamericana* 68(198) (2002): 67–77.

Rosell, Sara: "El embarque y el desborde: Navegando el Caribe junto a Mayra Montero y Ana Lydia Vega". *South Eastern Latin Americanist* 44(1) (2000): 47–59.

MOREJÓN, NANCY

Nancy Morejón (b. 1944) is a major Cuban as well as Caribbean poet of the contemporary era. Critics state that as an Afro-Cuban and female poet Morejón has no predecessors; in fact, she is one of few internationally acclaimed women poets of the Spanish-speaking world, and perhaps the only well-known Caribbean poet of African heritage. Caribbean women writers play a vital role in the creation of a postmodern poetics, decentering the ideological nature of literature and launching a female literary tradition (Dash 1998: 108–9).

Born on August 7, 1944, and raised in the working-class, historic Havana neighborhood of Los sitios, Morejón enjoyed little material resources but an environment rich in love and attention. Her mother had been raised in an orphanage; she worked in the tobacco harvest and as a seamstress before her marriage. The poem with which Morejón opens each poetry reading is *Madre* or "Mother," in which she admires a woman who had nothing in terms of material possessions, but who imparted the treasures of song and her hands, as she cared for others. Her father was a former merchant marine who enriched his time while docked at various ports by traveling and discovering cities such as New Orleans, New York and San Francisco. After his daughter's birth he worked as a longshoreman at the Havana docks. Although theirs was a humble household, Morejón's parents were self-educated, and instilled in her a love of reading and learning. She attended a private grade school, where she was one of few black children; she remembers being aware of her minority appearance, which contributed to her introverted feelings. She recalls discovering new worlds through reading. Morejón excelled and received outstanding grades. By age 15, she had earned enough credentials to become an English teacher. She was a teenager when her nation obtained the autonomy it had sought since José Martí and Antonio Maceo fought for its independence from Spain. For this to occur at the moment in her life that Morejón embarked on adult life was meaningful: "All of a sudden the social barriers were gone that prohibited access for blacks to many public spaces, including beaches and restaurants".

She arrived at the university in 1962, and thrived on the new freedom and rich intellectual environment where people arrived from various countries to talk about erasing class and racial distinctions, a theme that would influence her early poetry. Barriers against women, however, had not disappeared, which surprised Morejón because of her father's positive influence. He had allowed her the freedom to choose her path, her own hours, and the issues she chose to be involved in. Morejón graduated with honors from the Universidad de la Habana, where she studied European, Caribbean and Cuban literature, specializing in French literature. She began working as professor and critic, but her poetry would always be her primary focus.

Morejón had begun composing poems at age 13; she published her first book of poetry (*Mutismos*) in 1962, when she was only 18 years old. Her early work reveals a unique poetic voice and constant images of eyes, sea, mirrors, birds, and the city. The poetic voice is solitary, observing and contemplating influences on society, demonstrating the fusion of two major cultures, Spanish and African, into one Cuban heritage. For Morejón, African heritage is an integrating, not isolating element of national and hemispheric culture. Her poetry evaluates history and Caribbean ethos, but she also paints light, often humorous evaluations of her people, demonstrating typical Antillean humor.

Themes and Influences

Morejón's poems represent the discourse of the Cuban community in a Caribbean or Latin American ethos. According to Amy Kaminsky, consciousness-raising—a strategy of twentieth-century Latin American writers—is part of the process of making a people known. Such a transformative, collective process toward self-definition, which delineates "the communal nature of the self—the way in which that fallen, disappeared, invisible one is present in the continued action of others" (1993, p. 25), is evident in Morejón's body of work. Her community, her forebears, the impact of her neighborhood, and the woman as a changing force of society, are each prevalent.

Morejón's childhood was spent among white, *mulato* and black people who gathered in each other's homes or in the central street for celebrations. A strong sense of folklore permeated the neighborhood lifestyle, and this imbues her poetry. Her neighbors included some of the world's greatest *rumba* players, as well as the musical genius Richard Egües, who inspired her collection *Richard trajo su flauta y otros argumentos* (1967, Richard Brought His Flute and Other Arguments). Here Morejón merges European music—Mozart's music for flute—with the sounds of the "drumbeats rising from the same fire". The book-length poem depicts the discovery and celebration of Africanity, restoring Black independence heroes, African gods such as *Eleggua*, and popular music such as *sones* and *rumbas* which incorporate African and European influences. The *orishas* (spirits) encircle the house where Richard plays his flute, and vibrate around the musician's fingers, affecting the rhythm as he plays.

Morejón's poetry is highly lyrical, at times intimate, spiritual or erotic, on other occasions strongly ideological in historical contexts. She often centers and articulates the Afro-Cuban "nation" through foremothers, who bestow strength and faith, as in the poem "Madre" (Mother):

> My mother had the song and the handkerchief
> to cradle my heart's faith
> to lift her head of a queen, ignored,
> and to leave us her hands, like precious stones,
> *before the cold remains of the enemy.*
>
> (*Looking Within* p. 211)

In "La cena" (Supper), a title evoking a Western religious connotation of spiritual communion, the mother is the important figure sought for safety and continued existence: *urgently yearning for my mother's gaze / like our daily water* ("pidiendo con urgencia los ojos de mi madre / como el agua de todos los días" (*Looking Within* p. 214)). Upon arriving home, the child-voice in the poem searches her mother's eyes and finds an attentive and sad gaze resulting from certainty that war may break out at any minute. Still, the mother figure provides the ritual of everyday life and breaks the bread inaugurating nightfall. This act of daily communion (communal activity) sustains the family (Hampton 1999: 174) and the poet's vision. The mother figure provides inspiration and strength for creative nourishment.

Morejón celebrates her father's mother as a powerful, creating force in the short and powerful poem, "Presente Brígida Noyola" (Brígida Noyola lives):

> You are seed and volcano
> divine quartz wide
> a vast blur in the rain
> your long black hair
> sprouts from your dark forehead
> and comes down to your mouth
> diminutive in spirit
> voracious black woman
> you are cannon charcoal quartered flesh

pitiful soft coal of night
you grow like the ear.

(Hampton 1999, p. 175)

The progenitor in this verse is associated with seed and volcano (each of which each instills new life), and quartz, which, although one of the commonest minerals of the earth, represents the contrasting elements of fire and water. This unification of opposites, spirit and matter, produces neither one nor the other but a reflection of each. As a symbol of light, purity and clarity (the formal splendor of the mineral world), the crystal quartz stimulates the imagination. The poem suggests balance and harmony produced by this acknowledgment, and projective energy connected to the grandmother, who remains present in her community even after she has passed on. She is the earth, the creative energy, and the community that now accompanies the poetic voice to relate the history, politics and existence of her community.

Morejón affirms Cuban and Caribbean identity in her poetry through the living experience of the Black woman. In *Mujer negra* (Black Woman), her most frequently quoted and anthologized poem, the poetic "I" is a collective representation of the Caribbean mindset, not a mere victim of colonial history. Here she adapts a keen understanding of Cuban history, emphasizing the slave's point of view in order to demonstrate the influence of ideological freedom found in the Cuban Revolution. The lyrical voice connects several generations discussing immigration, slavery, poverty, rebellion, the independence movement (from Spain), and the long-sought affirmation of the Afro-Cuban as a true member of society. It emphasizes the point of view of the slave, later disenfranchised citizen. The women of her community are examined under a capitalist, patriarchal gaze, but they are also the subjects of their own lives and the driving force of their families. The female subject assumes actions, takes up the charge, and thus, exists. The racial together with feminist dimensions of Cuban nationalism are underscored by making the Black Woman the central figure and speaking voice for the Caribbean citizen in the contemporary era, as she relates her history:

This is the land where I suffered mouth-in-the-dust and the lash.
I rode the length of all its rivers.
Under its sun I planted seeds, brought in the crops,
but never ate those harvests.
A slave barracks was my house,
built with stones that I hauled myself,
while I sang to the pure beat of native birds.

(*Looking Within* p. 201)

Afro-Cuban history is relayed—through voyage, slavery, freedom from slavery, the 19th century independence movement, and the Cuban revolution. The lyrical voice assumes action, takes up the charge, and exists. Thus, "Mujer negra" is not about the individual woman so much as her nation, and the continuous existence of her community. "Now I exist: only today do we own, do we create" (203). The poet's nation and the Cuban and/or Caribbean people cohere because of its collective vision.

Nicolás Guillén once stated that Nancy's poetry was as black as her skin when you looked at its intimate, sonambulistic essence, and that it was also Cuban, "with roots so deep they emerge on the other side of the planet".

Poet, Critic, Artist and Translator

Morejón is fluent in three languages, Spanish, English and French. She has taught French language and literature at a prestigious Cuban academy, worked for Cuba's Ministry of the Interior, as an editor for the Writers/Artists Union, and for the Pablo Milanés Foundation (which aided Black artists). She is a theater critic and journalist, an avid translator, and has published numerous critical texts, including three book-length studies on Nicolás Guillén ((1902–89), the first Cuban poet to embody black consciousness in his poetry in the 1930s). She has translated into Spanish the works of prominent French and French-Caribbean authors, and is currently Director of the Center for Caribbean Studies at Casa de las Américas. A prominent critic, she has suggested that Guillén's poetic voice is not an "I" but a "we," both cultural and epic; the same could now be said of her own work. She creates artistic depictions which grace several her books of poetry, while her prolific poetry is often informed by her critical work.

Morejón's work is neither apolitical nor overtly political. She highlights both Cuba and the US in discussions of slavery, lynching and inhumane treatment, but her poems focusing history inspire outrage in a cool, measured tone. One of her strongest poems is on the slave's response to sexual servitude: "Amo a mi amo" (I Love my Master), elicits a natural human reaction to love, followed by compromise, intellectual awareness and rebellion during the colonial era (Howe 1998: 165). The master's concubine in this poem rebels against him in a dream—portraying the near impossibility of escape: I love my master, but every night . . . / I see myself knife in hand, / flaying him like an innocent animal (*Looking Within* p. 198). The speaking voice here did not get to choose her lot, her "love," and in her dream the slave woman uses her sex to subjugate the master. Because she holds him in her sexual power she can dream she overpowers and kills him. Morejón's poem retells history without allowing the slave to be a victim, providing a subjectivity ignored by Western society. The historical figure finds her place in the spiritual subconscious of the contemporary Afro-Cuban.

A superficial reading interprets participatory enjoyment and complicity with the master, in terms of the sexual liaison. A more complicated understanding comes with further readings, the complicity of interaction with life, and the strength of the mind and will in describing one's history. Conjugated to first person, the verb for *love* in Spanish, *amo*, is spelled the same as the word for master. Thus any "love" the lyrical voice assumes to have found is instead servitude to a master. The realization of her social condition changes the "love" to making love. Once the lyrical voice is aware of differences, and her powerlessness, she desires to kill the master, to take action for her own and others' sakes. She has overheard the conversation of the black overseers, and learns of the whippings that her master (or lover) gives the workers. In her dream she takes a step as an individual, but her resolve is the resolve of all slaves—as the poem ends she hears bewitching drumbeats drowning his cries, and the bells of the sugar-mill calling to action, perhaps to revolt. This powerful poem, like much of

Morejón's work with double-intention, elicits subtle commentary. Self-definition for this poet is the act of portraying her community as thinking actor. In a less-anthologized poem, "Cocinera" (Cook), the slave woman begins work at 5 a.m., greeting and serving her master's breakfast "against her will". She is required to eat from a can, outdoors, while she must serve the master's dogs in the dining room.

In a very different, earlier poem, Morejón weaves sensuality into female subjectivity, taking the reins as such, in lovemaking. In "A un muchacho" (To a Boy), the lyrical voice takes possession sexually of the boy:

I had his black eyes, like grasses,
among the brown shells of the Pacific.
I had his delicate lips
like a salt heated on the sands.
I had, in short, his sweet-smelling chin
under the sun.

(*Looking Within* p. 151)

The lovemaking source, the "boy," is objectified, in a warm and loving ecstasy which the lyrical voice controls, and into which she releases her spirit and will:

In his strong arms, I live.
In his strong arms I wished to die
like a wet bird

(ibid., pp. 150–1)

Nancy Morejón affirms Cuban and Caribbean identity through the living experience of the Black woman. The women in her community are resistant to a capitalist, patriarchal gaze, but they are also the subjects of their own lives and the driving force of their families. Her discourse may appear *feminist* to First-World criticism, but it is more an act of consciousness-raising, of empowering her community, and by means of it, a Caribbean / Latin American ethos.

Modern Interpretations

Morejón received the prominent Cuban *Premio de la crítica* for her book *Piedra Pulida* in 1986, and her nation's National Prize in Literature in 2001, marking the first time a Black woman has been awarded Cuba's most prestigious literary prize, and equally, the first time for a Black Woman throughout Latin America. Her international status was confirmed in 2006 when she was awarded the Sturga lifetime achievement award for poets, a prestigious international honor bestowed by the Republic of Macedonia, and sponsored by UNESCO. Morejón is the only woman (and second person of color) to have ever received this tribute. Earlier recipients include W.H. Auden (1971), Allen Ginsburg (1986) and Joseph Brodsky (1991) from the US, and only one Latin American, Pablo Neruda (1972).

Her poetry has been translated to French, Portuguese, Italian, Russian, German, Polish and Dutch, as well as English, and her poems have appeared in numerous books and anthologies. Her work has surprisingly found its way into English-language anthologies and critical surveys more quickly than those in Spanish language. The first collection to appear in English was *Granada Notebook* in 1984, and the first commercial anthology of her poetry in English, *Where the Island Sleeps Like a Wing*, was published the next year. The bilingual presentation of the latter book served as a biographical review of her body of work. The *San Francisco Chronicle* called it one of ten best books of poetry that year. An extensive critical text on her poetry, *Singular Like a Bird: The Art of Nancy Morejón*, was released in 1999 (which also includes several of her artistic drawings). New bilingual collections were published in 2001 in London, *Black Woman and Other Poems*, and in 2003, *Looking Within/Mirar adentro*.

Now with more than fifty books published, between poetry, criticism and translation, Morejón's work transcends gender, ethnicity, race and nationalistic borders. Her lyrical assessments of history and community, vivid in details about humans living and being aware of each other, helps breach an understanding that there are not separate Euro-Caribbean and Afro-Caribbean cultures, but one complex hybrid culture that is neither of their origins. As Juanamaría Cordones-Cook states, Morejón creates objective poetry that is at the service of society, reflective but situated in the warm, loving environments of family home, neighborhood, city and people who take care of each other, carrying along in its flow the history of the Cuban people.

ELIZABETH COONROD MARTÍNEZ

Selected Works

Mutismos. La Habana: Ediciones El Puente, 1962.

Amor, ciudad atribuída, poemas. La Habana: Ediciones El Puente, 1964.

Richard trajo su flauta y otros argumentos. La Habana: Unión de Escritores y Artistas de Cuba, 1967.

Lengua de pájaro. With Carmen Gonce. La Habana: Instituto Cubano del Libro, 1971.

Recopilación de textos sobre Nicolás Guillén, ed. La Habana: Casa de las Américas, 1974.

Parajes de una época. La Habana: Editorial Letras Cubanas, 1979.

Poemas. Mexico City: Universidad Autónoma de México, 1980.

Elogio de la danza. Mexico City: La Universidad Nacional Autónoma de México, 1982.

"A un muchacho," "Niña que lee en Estelí," "Soldado y yo" (monograph). Toulouse: Caravelle, 1982.

Nación y mestizaje en Nicolás Guillén. La Habana: Ediciones Unión, 1982.

Octubre imprescindible. La Habana: Ediciones Unión, 1982.

Nancy Morejón. New York: Center for Cuban Studies, 1983.

Grenada Notebook/Cuaderno de Granada. Trans. Lisa Davis. New York: Círuculo de Cultura Cubana, 1984.

Cuaderno de Granada. La Habana: Casa de las Américas, 1984.

Where the Island Sleeps Like a Wing. Trans. Kathleen Weaver. San Francisco, CA: The Black Scholar Press, 1985.

Piedra pulida. La Habana: Editorial Letras Cubanas, 1986.

Poetas del mundo latino en Tlaxcala. Tlaxcala, Mexico: Universidad Autónoma de Tlaxcala, 1988.

Fundación de la imagen. La Habana: Editorial Letras Cubanas, 1988.

Dos poemas de Nancy Morejón. Drawings and design by Rolando Estévez. Matanzas, Cuba: Ediciones Vigía, 1989.

Baladas para un sueño. La Habana: Unión de Escritores y Artistas de Cuba, 1989.

Ours the Earth. Trans. J.R. Pereira. Mona, Jamaica: Institute of Caribbean Studies, 1990.

Poemas de amor y de muerte. Toulouse: Caravelle, 1993.

Paisaje célebre. Caracas: Fundarte, Alcaldía de Caracas, 1993.

Le Chaînon Poétique. Trans. Sandra Monet-Descombey. Champigny-sur-Marne, France: Edition L. C. J., 1994.

Elogio y paisaje. La Habana: Ediciones Unión, 1996.

El río de Martín Pérez y otros poemas. Drawings and design by Rolando Estévez. Matanzas, Cuba: Ediciones Vigía, 1996.

Black Woman and Other Poems. London: Mango Publishing, 2001.

Looking Within/Mirar Adentro, Selected Poems/Poemas escogidos, 1954–2000 (bilingual edition, African American Life Series). Ed. Juana María Cordones Cook. Detroit, MI: Wayne State University Press, 2003.

Poética de los altares. La Habana, 2006.

References and Further Reading

Afro-Hispanic Review 15 (Spring 1996, issue dedicated to Nancy Morejón).

Callaloo 28.4 (2005, issue dedicated to Nancy Morejón).

Chíchester, Ana García. "Nancy Morejón". In María A. Salgado (ed.), *Dictionary of Literary Biography*, volume 283: *Modern Spanish American Poets, First Series*. Chapel Hill, NC: University of North Carolina (Gale Group), 1998: 231–41.

Cordones-Cook, Juanamaría (ed.) *Looking Within/Mirar Adentro, Selected Poems/Poemas escogidos, 1954–2000*. Detroit, MI: Wayne State University Press, 2003, pp. 18–63.

Dash, Michael J. *The Other America: Caribbean Literature in a New World Context*. Charlottesville, VA: University Press of Virginia, 1998.

Davies, Catherine. "Nancy Morejón". In Verity Smith (ed.), *Encyclopedia of Latin American Literature*. Chicago, IL: Fitzroy Dearborn, 1997.

DeCosta-Willis, Miriam. *Singular Like a Bird: The Art of Nancy Morejón*. Washington, DC: Howard University Press, 1999.

Feracho, Lesley. "Arrivals and Farewells: The Dynamics of Cuban Homespace through African Mythology in Two Eleggua Poems by Nancy Morejón". *Hispania* 83(1) (March 2000): 51–7.

González Mandri, Flora María. *Guarding Cultural Memory: Afro-Cuban Women in Literature and the Arts (New World Series)*. Richmond, VA: University Press of Virginia, 2006.

Hampton, Janet J. "Black Woman Empowered: Portraits of the Black Woman in the Poetry of Nancy Morejón". In Miriam DeCosta-Willis (ed.), *Singular Like a Bird: The Art of Nancy Morejon*. Washington, DC: Howard University Press, 1999, pp. 169–86.

Howe, Linda S. "Nancy Morejón's Womanism". In Miriam DeCosta-Willis (ed.), *Singular Like a Bird: The Art of Nancy Morejon*. Washington, DC: Howard University Press, 1999, pp. 153–68.

Kaminsky, Amy K. *The Body Politic: Feminist Criticism and Latin American Women Writers*. Minneapolis, MN: University of Minnesota Press, 1993.

Luis, William. "The Politics of Aesthetics in the Poetry of Nancy Morejón". *Afro-Hispanic Review* 15(1) (Spring 1996): 35–43.

Maloof, Judy. "Entrevistas: Nancy Morejón". *Hispamérica* 25(73) (April 1996): 47–58.

Martínez, Elizabeth Coonrod. "A Remarkable Woman and Poet: Nancy Morejón". *Hispanic Outlook in Higher Education* 17(2) (23 October 2006): 36–8.

Phaf, Ineke. "El 'Cuaderno' de Nancy Morejón: La Habana 1967–93". *Revista Iberoamericana* 65(188–9) (July–Dec 1999): 535–51.

Rosario-Sievert, Heather. "Nancy Morejón's Eye/I: Social and Aesthetic Perception in the Work of Nancy Morejón". *Afro-Hispanic Review* 15(1) (Spring 1996): 44–9.

Tillis, Antonio D. "Nancy Morejón's 'Mujer Negra': An Africana Womanist Reading". *Hispanic Journal* 22(2) (Fall 2001): 483–94.

Weaver, Kathleen. "The World of Nancy Morejón". In *Where the Island Sleeps Like a Wing*. San Francisco, CA: The Black Scholar Press, 1985, pp. xiii–xvii.

West, Alan. "Nancy Morejón: Poet of Cultural Crossroads". In *Tropics of History: Cuba Imagined*. Westport, CT: Bergin & Garvey, 1997, pp. 13–34.

Williams, Lorna V. "The Revolutionary Feminism of Nancy Morejón". *CLA Journal* 39 (June 1996): 432–53.

MORENO, MARVEL

Marvel Luz Moreno (1939–95) is considered one of the most important Colombian writers of the late twentieth century. Though her work did not receive the widespread attention and recognition it deserved throughout her lifetime, it has been celebrated by critics and followers with fervent admiration and is rapidly gaining wider acceptance. Her literary production exemplifies her times, caught between strict conventions and changing ways.

Rebel and Author

Moreno was born on September 23, 1939, in Barranquilla, Colombia, the daughter of a lawyer from Cartagena and a mother who belonged to the local bourgeoisie. Her maternal grandmother was a key influence during her early years, instilling a great appreciation for personal independence. As a child and teenager, she attended two Catholic schools, Lourdes and La Enseñanza; she was expelled from the latter as a result of her defense of Darwin's theory of evolution. Moreno was then transferred to a Marxist-oriented public school for working-class boys and eventually dropped out at age 16. After a brief stint as nurse and assistant at a relative's clinic, Moreno deferred to class obligations: in 1956, she made her social debut. Under pressure from her mother, she participated in beauty pageants and served as the local carnival's queen in 1959, gaining public renown.

In the early 1960s, Moreno renewed her studies and read copiously (Cervantes, Faulkner, McCullers). She also befriended local artists and intellectuals like Alejandro Obregón and Álvaro Cepeda Samudio. In 1962, with Cepeda Samudio and his wife as best man and maid of honor, she married Plinio Mendoza, a journalist and writer from the interior of the country. The couple socialized with members of Barranquilla's literary scene, including Gabriel García Marquez, at La Cueva, a local bar. In 1963, Carla, her first child, was born. In 1964, she became the first woman to enroll in the economics program of a local university, eventually opening a marketing consultancy and an advertising firm, which she managed till 1969. In 1966, she named Camila, her second child, after priest Camilo Torres, whom she met through her husband. A year later, she befriended art critic Marta Traba.

In 1969, Moreno published her first short story, "El muñeco," in *Eco*, an important literary magazine, and shortly afterwards, in the prestigious literary magazine of *El Espectador*, a national daily. That same year, after an initial marriage crisis, she traveled to Paris. Almost immediately, given financial constraints, she moved to Deya, Mallorca, where she met and befriended British poet Robert Graves. In September 1971, she returned to Paris, where she lived for the rest of her life.

Life in Paris was, like for most Latin American immigrants, a mixed bag of joys and misfortunes. Moreno participated actively in *Libre*, the Latin American literary journal, and became a staple of the Latin American émigré community, befriending authors like Carlos Fuentes and Severo Sarduy. Eventually, she distanced herself from leftist circles, rejecting dogmas and ideologies. Moreno only stayed in touch with a few acquaintances, like Catalan writer Juan Goytisolo. In late 1972, after a second marriage crisis, with two children to raise, she fell seriously ill. A year later, destitute and penniless, she was treated at a hospital and diagnosed with lupus, a chronic disease. Between 1973 and 1974, she received psychological treatment and was almost committed to an asylum, after being declared insane. Moreno then returned to live with Mendoza until 1980. In 1975, *Eco* published a second short story, "Oriane, tía Oriane". During this time of seclusion, her limited social circle included Venezuelan anthropologist Elizabeth Burgos and filmmaker Fina Torres, and Colombian painters Luis Caballero and Darío Morales. Through this period, while working as a language teacher, she wrote feverishly, finishing her first short-story collection, *Algo tan feo en la vida de una señora bien* (1980), and a novel, *En diciembre llegaban las brisas* (1987). In 1980, Moreno met French engineer Jacques Fourrier, whom she married two years later. In 1983, scholar Jacques Gilard, who eventually became the guardian of her literary production, translated her short stories into French.

By 1985, thanks to Torres's film adaptation of one of her short stories, which received the Camera d'Or at Cannes, Moreno gained greater exposure. As a result, her novel was translated into Italian and, thanks to the success of this edition, Moreno won the Grinzane Cavour award in 1989. The following year, the novel was translated into French. In 1990, when she began to write a second novel, Moreno was diagnosed with pulmonary emphysema. Two years later, Moreno published a second collection of short stories, *El encuentro y otros relatos*. Between 1993 and 1994, Moreno worked on two different versions of the second novel, titled *El tiempo de las amazonas*, and a final short-story collection, *Las fiebres del Miramar*. On June 5, 1995, after years of battling ailments, Moreno passed away. In 2001, Gilard and Fabio Rodríguez Amaya, another champion of her work, edited and published a compilation of short stories titled *Cuentos completos*.

Literary Production

Moreno's responses to the political, religious, and social concerns of her time are, doubtless, formed by her own experiences as a woman in provincial Colombia, as well as by her times in the effervescent Paris of 1970s. Her first book, *Algo tan feo en la vida de una señora bien*, was published in Bogotá by a barely known press, with a foreword by Goytisolo, an introduction by Gilard, and a cover image by Obregón, a combination that underscores the high regard of her work. Though well received by a few critics, the volume had scant circulation. Unfortunately, a story titled "Autocrítica," which alluded to the Padilla affair—the cause of substantial disenchantment with the Cuban revolution among international left-wing circles in 1971—was removed from the collection. Subsequently, the short-story collection was translated and published in France in 1982, with a prologue by Monique Lange, Goytisolo's lifetime companion. The posthumous compilation of Moreno's short stories includes "Autocrítica," and, following her wishes, the title of this first collection was changed to *Oriane, tía Oriane*. Moreno's first set of short stories contains the novella "La noche feliz de Madame Yvonne," with cues to her forthcoming novel, including the introduction of Lina, the author's alter ego. It is a compilation of nine stories written during many years, some of which had previously appeared in magazines. The common theme of these stories is, as the name suggests, the persistence of a past where unknown truths lurk, as well as the search for freedom, away from social constraints, hypocrisies, and secrets. They are tales of incest, assassination, and jilted lovers, revealing the intimacies of pretentious circles: in short, the ghosts of her adolescence cloaked in a web of monologues and parallel discourses.

Moreno's first novel, *En diciembre llegaban las brisas*, represents a novelty in the Colombian literary scene. Written between 1977 and 1984, Moreno and her circle of friends playfully nicknamed it "Barranquilla's Bible," given the large size of the manuscript. It is, quite evidently, one of the most important Colombian novels of the twentieth century. The novel rejects magic realism and narrates the story of three generations of women (Dora, Catalina, and Beatriz) along the Colombian Caribbean, illustrating a reality that had been, until then, depicted unilaterally. Amidst biblical quotations, proverbs, and nostalgia, Moreno portrays a conformist world where the fate of women is determined by a sexist, racist milieu. The book is organized sequentially, contrasting the experiences of the three younger protagonists with those of their grandmothers and aunts. Making little explicit reference to the physical setting—though the allusion to her hometown is unmistakable—Moreno reveals these characters as paradigms for succeeding generations. Overall, the action is witnessed and narrated by Lina, Moreno's double, who closes the literary account. The book, which the author dedicated to her two daughters, shares a sense of responsibility and caution towards the intricacies of cultural and societal heritage, through the memorable illustration of the world the author left behind. Like most of Moreno's work, the book displays a propensity for the multiplicity of characters, with a number of stories that interweave and collide. The text shows an author perfectly at ease with and conscious of her narrative style, with scarce dialogue and a proclivity for triptychs.

El encuentro y otros relatos, her second short-story collection, reflects a more deliberate acceptance of her role as an author. Although they share her novel's festive disclosure of eroticism, the resolutions and arguments are more direct and pragmatic, revealing maturity and intentionality in the work. As the title proclaims, the book contains eleven stories that narrate a series of encounters, meetings that lead to moments of discovery, catharsis, and, at times, epiphanies. The accounts revolve around sexuality, the intricacies of mother-daughter relationships, and the repressive role of institutions like religion and marriage. Though most stories are centered on women, there is a certain reconciliation with the male figure, as it supports a more comfortable embracement of sexuality. Ultimately, *El encuentro* also alludes to the author's renewed sense of self-discovery thanks to a more relaxed association with the act of writing.

Moreno's final collection of short stories, *Las fiebres del Miramar*, on which she was working at the time of her death, includes accounts like "La hora del gato," which, though finished at a much earlier date, were not included in previous volumes, as they did not fit in well thematically. Four of the stories deal with the Caribbean in a more evenhanded manner. They show the author coming to term with her cultural legacy with more patience and resolve. The other three stories pertain to Moreno's Parisian world and propose a more critical, less utopian depiction of her French experience. In all, they evince an author's efforts to bring a sense of balance and proportion to her previous assessment.

Her unpublished novel, *El tiempo de las amazonas*, represents by all accounts a radical departure from her previous work. Having mastered a style in *En diciembre* . . . , Moreno explored a different voice and method. While the manuscript preserves the narrative structure, with a story centered on three main characters, Isabel, Virginia, and Gaby, the language approach is drastically different. The text is difficult to classify, as it combines aspects of novel, chronicle, and even essay. Though its publication has been predicted repeatedly, obstacles have hindered this possibility.

Moreno's finest contribution is the substantiation of a representative alternative for the Colombian Caribbean. Her writing, which exhibits the influence of Southern writers like Carson McCullers, distanced itself tenaciously from magic realism. Her lengthy, rhythmical sentences, which she always cultivated in longhand, recall the seductive verbosity of nineteenth-century diaries and letters. In the short time since her death, two key conferences—one in France, the other in Colombia—have been dedicated to her work, demonstrating the growing interest for a life and production of myth-like proportions.

HÉCTOR D. FERNÁNDEZ L'HOESTE

Selected Works

Algo tan feo en la vida de una señora bien. Bogotá: Editorial Pluma, 1980. Translated by Jacques Gilard as *Cette tache dans la vie d'une femme comme il faut*, Paris: Ed. Des Femmes, 1983. Translated by Monica Molteni and Anna Roberto as *Qualcosa di brutto nella vita di una signora perbene*, Milan: Jaca Book/Università di Bergamo, 1997.

En diciembre llegaban las brisas. Barcelona: Plaza & Janés, 1987. Translated by Monica Molteni as *In dicembre tornavano le brezze*, Florence: Giunti, 1988, 2002. Translated by Eduardo Jiménez as *Les dammes de Barranquilla*, Paris: Robert Laffont, 1990.

El encuentro y otros relatos. Bogotá: El Ancora Editores, 1992.

Cuentos completos. Edited by Jacques Gilard and Fabio Rodríguez Amaya. Bogotá: Editorial Norma, 2001.

References and Further Reading

Abdala Mesa, Yohainna. *El devenir de la creación. Marvel Moreno: escritura, memoria, tiempo, Beca Nacional de Investigación en Literatura 2004*. Bogotá: Ministerio de Cultura, 2005.

Angel, Miguel Arnulfo. "Barranquilla en las líneas apretadas de *En diciembre llegaban las brisas*". *La Palabra y el Hombre: Revista de la Universidad Veracruzana* 93 (1995): 157–65.

Araújo, Helena. "Siete novelistas colombianas". *Manual de literatura colombiana*. Bogotá: Planeta, 1988: 409–62.

——. "Marvel Moreno's Caribbean novel, *En diciembre llegaban las brisas*". *Latin American Literary Review* 17 (1989): 118–20.

Burgos Cantor, Roberto. "A *Señorita* at the Piano". *Caravelle: Cahiers du Monde Hispanique et Luso-Bresilien* 66 (1996): 129–30.

Cobo Borda, Juan Gustavo. "La costa colombiana con ojos de mujer: Marvel Moreno". *Quimera: Revista de Literatura* 123 (1994): 40–1.

Ferrer Franco, Yury. "Marvel Moreno: el encuentro con la claridad y la magia". In Luz Mery Giraldo (ed.), *Fin de siglo: Narrativa colombiana*. Cali: Editorial Facultad de Humanidades, 1995, pp. 275–95.

Garavito, Carmen Lucía. "Ideología y estrategias narrativas en *Algo tan feo en la vida de una señora bien* de Marvel Moreno". In María Mercedes Jaramillo (ed.), *Literatura y diferencia: Escritoras colombianas del siglo XX*, 2 vols. Bogotá: Uniandes, 1995, pp. 399–421.

Gilard, Jacques. "Ser escritora en Colombia: Cuatro casos en la costa atlantica". In *Femmes des Amériques*. Toulouse: Université de Toulouse-Le Mirail, 1986, pp. 209–30.

Gilard, Jacques, and Amaya, Fabio Rodríguez (eds) *La obra de Marvel Moreno*. Viareggio: Mauro Baroni Editore, 1997.

Gonzalez Keelan de Mojica, Sarah. "*En diciembre llegan las brisas*, de Marvel Moreno: Una escritura feminista". In María Mercedes Jaramillo (ed.), *Literatura y diferencia: Escritoras colombianas del siglo XX*, 2 vols. Bogotá: Uniandes, 1995, pp. 3–15.

Goytisolo, Juan. "A Sketch of Marvel Moreno". *Caravelle: Cahiers du Monde Hispanique et Luso-Bresilien* 66 (1996): 137–38.

Olaciregui, Julio. "That Marvel Luz Lives". *Caravelle: Cahiers du Monde Hispanique et Luso-Bresilien* 66 (1996): 137–8.

Ordoñez Vila, Monserrat. "Cien años de escritura oculta: Soledad Acosta, Elisa Mujica y Marvel Moreno". In Luz Mery Giraldo (ed.), *Fin de siglo: Narrativa colombiana*. Cali: Editorial Facultad de Humanidades, 1995, pp. 323–38.

——. "With Marvel Moreno". *Caravelle: Cahiers du Monde Hispanique et Luso-Bresilien* 66 (1996): 140–1.

Ortega, José. "La alienación femenina en los cuentos de Marvel Moreno". *Monographic Review* 4 (1988): 43–50.

Various authors. *Memorias del Encuentro de Escritoras Colombianas "Ellas cuentan". Homenaje a Marvel Moreno*. Bogotá: Consejería Presidencial para la Equidad de la Mujer, 2005.

MOSCOVICH, CÍNTIA

Born in Porto Alegre, Rio Grande do Sul, Brazil, on March, 15, 1958, today Cíntia Moscovich is a well-known name in contemporary Brazilian fiction. With a Master's degree in Literary Theory from the Pontifícia Universidade Católica do Rio Grande do Sul, as a journalist she has also edited books for the *Zero Hora* newspaper. She has worked as translator, critic and literary consultant, and also as journalist on several periodicals throughout the country.

Literature and a taste for reading have always played a special role in Cíntia Moscovich's life due to the fact that she grew up among the books in her family's private library. She is a member of a Jewish family in an area characterized by its cultural diversity. This melting pot is due in part to the asylum sought by several nationalities at the beginning of the twentieth century, such as the Italians, Germans, Poles, Arabs, Jews, and Japanese. Moreover, this area is near the border of Argentina and Uruguay, which provided additional opportunities for exposure to literature, particularly Hispanic. Her writing skills, therefore, have traces of many cultural traditions which, specifically in the literary field, present and complete themselves, often conflicting with each other, but always in an insightful way where further understanding is reached in the end.

Aesthetic Commitment

Moscovich's first appearance in literary circles took place in 1996 with the publication of her book *O reino das cebolas* (The Kingdom of the Onions), a selection of seemingly simple short stories, which, upon deeper reading, reveals a careful formal work that would in the years to come serve as an important indication of her writing talent and style. Her first work was nominated for the Jabuti Prize, one of the most important awards in Brazilian Literature. *O reino das cebolas* is a mature text, in which Moscovich deals very well with language and at the same time offers her readers a glance at her attachment to a classical literary tradition, demonstrating a vital dynamism in the narrative genre that is far from equaled.[1] She also addresses the "here and now" with multiple voices that accurately reflect and confront the contemporary socio-cultural mosaic of today.

The group of fifteen short stories within *O reino das cebolas* brings a strict composition rarely found in the writings of first-time writers. This aesthetic commitment, however, only shows how sensitive Moscovich is to the multiplicity of the human experience, as it is always intertwined with the self's disappointment and achievement in routine life and how, although small, this marks the human desire to overcome our flaws in order to become an extraordinary condition of a unique experience in time and space and of the self.

Two years after the release of her book, Moscovich published the novel *Duas iguais: manual de amores e equívocos assemelhados* (The Equal Two: Manual of Similar Loves and Mistakes), which narrates the lives of two teenage girls, Clara and Ana, as they enter adulthood. This, however, is a very challenging topic, one that demands from a writer the skill of observation and a memory capable of recalling the awkwardness that often we all experience when confronted with sudden transformations, discoveries, and experiences with our first contact with what will define the rest of our lives. It is deep within Moscovich's universe that she reveals a homosexual love that binds the two adolescents. The writer does not simply dictate this dynamic to the reader, but instead narrates this connection through the prejudice that, so many times, ends up suffocating the beauty and nature of the love itself. In Clara and Ana's environment—a traditional Jewish neighborhood in Porto Alegre, that could be anywhere in the world—*Duas iguais* shows, with no stereotypes, the battles and hostility that reside within social relationships, politics, religion, culture and affection.

The writer's return to short narrative stories took place in 2000 with the first edition of *Anotações durante o incêndio* (Notes during the Fire), which consists of eleven short stories that have the same concise language which marked her previous work in addition, poetry of everyday life is included. ("Amor, corte e costura" (Love, Cutting and Sewing); "A paixão e a ratoeira" (Passion and the Mousetrap), "A fome e a vontade de comer" (Hunger and the Desire to Eat). Topics of family life, unwanted love, solitude, and exile are the focus of this collection, bringing to life Jewish culture, which is not only its chosen theme, but one that is balanced through the use of irony, loneliness and a certain melancholic tune. This collection overflows towards embedded texts on Judaism and, at the same time, questions it, not for its naïve and inconsequent rebel expression but for its own and irrefutable real life ambiguity.

In *Arquitetura do arco-íris* (The Architecture of the Rainbow), released in 2004, Cíntia Moscovich explores several narrative voices sharing with the reader equally disparate realities. Despite the nature of each experience revealed, the ten short stories in this book depict the flow of something intrinsic to the human condition, its desires, insecurities, its emotions, and often its contradictions. It is with this work that Moscovich established a productive dialogue within the modern literary tradition and in which, behind the allusion of a legendary character from Yiddish literature (Sholem Aleykhem's *Tevye the Dairyman*), in "O telhado e o violinista" (The Roof and the Violinist), she makes an intriguing homage to the well-known Brazilian writer Clarice Lispector and an explicit reference to Jorge Luis Borges, in "O tempo e a memória" (Time and Memory).

Awards

Cíntia Moscovich's works had received, even before the release of *O reino das cebolas*, many nominations for national and international awards. This alone demonstrates the recognition of this writer who has developed a symbiotic relationship with one of the most rigid literary traditions of our time, therefore enabling herself to be considered the equal of unique authors such as Jorge Luis Borges, Italo Calvino and Isaac Bashevis Singer, or in Brazil, Machado de Assis, Clarice Lispector, Moacyr Scliar and Lya Luft. Recognition not only comes from professional critics, but also from renowned writers and readers, making this young writer one of the most highly regarded names of her generation.

Moscovich's writings have won other awards such as the Concurso de Contos Guimarães Rosa in 1995 and the Radio France Internationale in Paris, which followed her nomination for the Jabuti Prize in 1996 with *O reino das cebolas*. In 1998, she won the Açorianos prize, in the long narrative category with *Duas iguais: manual de amores e equívocos assemelhados*, and one more in 2000 with *Anotações durante o incêndio*, in the short stories category. In 2005, *Arquitetura do arco-íris* won the Portugal Telecom and Jabuti Prizes.

The inclusion of her short stories in countless anthologies is another example of recognition she has received. Many of her texts have been translated into English, Spanish, and Italian; *Anotações durante o incêndio* is being translated into Italian, and from this book a short story, "A fome e a vontade de comer", has been adapted for TV by RBS TV.

VÍVIEN GONZAGA E SILVA

Selected Works

O reino das cebolas. Porto Alegre: L&PM, 1996.

Duas iguais: manual de amores e equívocos assemelhados. Porto Alegre: L&PM, 1998.

Anotações durante o incêndio. Porto Alegre: L&PM, 2000.

Arquitetura do arco-íris. Rio de Janeiro: Record, 2004.

References and Further Reading

Di Malta, Patrizia (ed.). *Sex'n'bossa*. Milano: Mondadori, 2005.

Freire, Marcelino (ed.). *Os cem menores contos brasileiros do século*. São Paulo: Ateliê Editorial, 2004.

Garcia-Roza, Lívia (ed.). *Ficções fraternas*. Rio de Janeiro: Record, 2003.

Mosovich, Cíntia. "Ouro e pano". In Abrão Slavutzky (ed.), *O dever da memória. O levante do gueto de Varsóvia*. Porto Alegre: AGE / Federação Israelita do Rio Grande do Sul, 2003.

Oliveira, Nelson de (ed.). *Geração 90: manuscritos de computador*. Porto Alegre: Boitempo Editorial, 2001.

Putas: novo conto português e brasileiro. Several Authors. Vila Nova da Famalicão; Portugal: Quasi Edições, 2002.

Ruffato, Luiz (ed.) *25 mulheres que estão fazendo a nova literatura brasileira*. Rio de Janeiro: Record, 2004.
Sztraus, Rosa Amanda (ed.) *13 dos melhores contos de amor da literatura brasileira*. Rio de Janeiro: Ediouro, 2003.
Zilberman, Regina and Bernd, Zilá (eds) *O viajante transcultural: leituras da obra de Moacyr Scliar*. Porto Alegre: Edipucrs, 2004.

MOSQUERA, BEATRIZ

Beatriz Mosquera was born in Buenos Aires on March 10, 1940. A story writer, literary critic, pedagogue, and most importantly, playwright, she studied philosophy and education in La Plata. At the age of nineteen she published a collection of short stories compiled under the name *Cuentos porque sí . . .* (Stories, Just Because . . .). A decade later, she started her dramatic production with a children's play, *Tolón y Tolina* (1968). Since then, she has been one of the most prolific playwrights in Argentina, having written more than twenty plays.

In addition to her writing, teaching, and participation in festivals – both national and international – she has also been actively involved with the academic theatrical programs in Buenos Aires. She served as rector in the *Escuela Nacional de Arte Dramático* (National School of Drama), and broadened its academic curriculum by co-founding, along with Raúl Serrano, the field of theatrical pedagogy. Currently, she is president of the board of directors of *Argentores*, the national playwright guild, as she continues writing both drama and fiction.

Style, Language, and Dramatic Action

Structurally, most of Mosquera's plays observe the unities of time, place and action. There is a preference for closed spaces, but even when the action takes place in an open space, the tension among characters transmits the sensation of entrapment. With regard to dramatic action, most of her plays open by presenting a well-planned action conveying considerable information about the character's inner life and present condition. As her plays progress, characters tend to deliver a short explanation of the motives for their previous actions. In *La luna en la taza* (The Moon in the Cup), for example, the audience is immediately confronted with an image that captures by itself the protagonist's internal and external conflicts. Alba, a housewife and successful college student, abandons her studies to raise her two children, since her husband's low income is insufficient to hire a nanny. The character's frustration is represented in the first scene, which shows Alba tired of picking up her children's toys. In vain, she tries to assemble one of them when it falls completely apart, causing great frustration for the character. This opening action is important in that it captures the character's attempt to reconcile or hold together all the components of her identity as a woman, wife, mother, and college student.

In terms of dramatic language, Mosquera practices a linguistic economy, a constant feature since her early production which is also reflected in her short fiction, *Cuentos porque sí . . .* (Stories, Just Because . . .). She reproduces the speech styles of working and middle-class people. Characters' speech is colloquial and direct. In this sense, language is transparent, and rarely draws attention to itself.

Characters and Themes

The majority of Mosquera's characters belong to urban working and middle-class families. They represent a wide range of occupations and professions, and include doctors, intellectuals, factory workers, prostitutes, and former soldiers, among others. What remains a constant across this entire spectrum of characters is that Mosquera is interested in depicting how the political and economic situation permeates theirs lives, greatly impacting their relationships, friendships, self-esteem and sexual encounters.

There are also many couples in her plays, and through them the playwright explores the intimacy of married life. Consequently love, infidelity, routine, companionship, and motherhood are subthemes that appear in many of the plays; only in a few cases is marriage a happy experience. Teresa and Pedro from *Primer Domingo* (First Sunday) are among the few couples happily married in her fictional universe.

In general, the frustration experienced in marriage is explored from the female character's point of view. In Mosquera's plays, women are more than capable of scrutinizing the failure in their relationships, but this does not necessary mean that they have the desire to act upon it and change their present situation. In some cases, women struggle to combine marriage, motherhood and career, like Alba in *La luna en la taza* (The Moon in the Cup). Other times, they simply prefer to stay with their husbands because of the economic security and lifestyle provided by their partners, like Viviana in *Primer Domingo* (First Sunday).

Although marriage, love, interpersonal relations, and the feminine universe are recurrent themes in Mosquera's dramatic production, not all of her plays are limited to these aspects of life. She is also concerned with current social issues, such as unemployment, injustice, authoritarianism and political violence, among others. When exploring these topics, Mosquera is more likely to depart from the realistic style she frequently practices. Instead she writes in allegorical mode, resulting in more intriguing plays such as *En nuestro propio nombre* (In Our Own Name) or *La soga* (The Rope). In this later one, she depicts the present situation of a former soldier of the Falkland War (1982), who desperately tries to enter the workforce. In a broad sense, the play contrasts those who question the given condition with those who would rather follow the rules. Unlike with other works, in *La soga* Mosquera deliberately cultivates an ambiguity regarding the meanings of this omnipresent rope. It is present throughout the play, and ultimately divides the characters, causing the death of one of them.

As Mosquera's dramatic production continues to expand, her old works are being restaged and the recent ones produced, getting great receptions from theater critics and audiences. However, in spite of that, her entire corpus has not yet received the critical attention it deserves, with the exception of the studies written by Marta Lena Paz and Magda Castellví deMoor. These literary critics have focused mainly on the plays known under the name "trilogy of the moon", which refers to *La luna en la taza* (The Moon in the Cup), *Otra vez la luna* (Once Again, The Moon) and *Eclipse*.

In her essay, Lena Paz states that Mosquera explores the daily encounters of a group of friends whose different reactions to an authoritarian regime gradually set them apart. Through a close reading of the subtext of *La luna en la taza*, Lena Paz analyses the four characters to argue that by creating multi-layered characters Mosquera avoids the duet victim-victimizer, a frequent set of protagonists employed in plays written under or about the last military dictatorship (1976–83). Although this critic refuses to establish analogies between Mosquera's dramatic production and other contemporary playwrights, she does ultimately suggest that Mosquera's work be studied alongside that of another famous Argentine dramatist, Griselda Gambaro.

Castellví deMoor also enriches the reading of Mosquera's trilogy by analyzing how the main characters come to terms with the political violence of the past once democracy has been restored. Concentrating on *Eclipse*, Castelví deMoor emphasizes the role of memory in the play during the times of societal forgetting. In addition, she has approached Mosquera's work from a feminist perspective in her recent book *Dramaturgas argentinas: Teatro, política y género* (2003), where she has included an interview with the playwright. In sum, it could be said that while a comprehensive study of Mosquera's drama has yet to come, these critics have helped shed light on her most known plays.

MÓNICA B. BOTTA

Selected Works

Cuentos porque sí. . . . Buenos Aires: Editorial Stilcograf, 1959.
Teatro de Beatriz Mosquera. Volumen 1. Buenos Aires: Torres Agüero Editor, 1992.
Cuando Crezca. Buenos Aires: Editorial El Francotirador, 1993.
Teatro de Beatriz Mosquera. Buenos Aires: Editorial Tierra Firme, 1999.
Eclipse. Obras argentinas premiadas en Nueva York. Buenos Aires: Fundación Argentores, 2001.
Pintura fresca. Obras breves. Santa Fé: Centro de Publicaciones, 2003.

References and Further Reading

Castelví deMoor, Magda. "Entrevista a Beatriz Mosquera: A través de las máscaras". *Latin American Theatre Review* 30(1) (1996): 105–10.
——. "Visión esperpéntica del poder: *La irredenta*". In *Dramaturgas argentinas. Teatro, política y género.* Mendoza: Universidad Nacional de Cuyo, 2003, pp. 71–82.
——. "Teatro de resistencia y trasgresión: *Eclipse* de Beatriz Mosquera". In Juana Arancibia (ed.), *La mujer en la literatura del mundo hispánico.* Buenos Aires: Instituto Literario y Cultural Hispánico, 2005, pp. 177–85.
Paz, Marta Lena. "*La luna en la taza*: la fragmentación de la esperanza". In Juana Aranncibia and Zulema Mirkin (eds), *Teatro argentino durante el proceso (1976–1983).* Buenos Aires: Editorial Vinciguerra, 1992, pp. 113–22.
Zayas de Lima, Perla. "Mosquera, Beatriz". In *Diccionario de autores teatrales argentinos, 1950–1980.* Buenos Aires: Editorial Rodolfo Alonso, 1981, pp. 121–2.

MOTHER IMAGES

The concepts of mother and mothering vary from one culture to another, even from one generation to the next. Consequently, several studies have revealed that the image of the good or bad mother has been determined by economic, social and political interests over the centuries. Currently, owing to the influence of psychoanalysis, Western culture has constructed the image of the empathetic and all-powerful mother whose behavior and even thoughts towards her child during pregnancy and its first years of rearing will determine his/her development. She has been attributed tremendous power over the life of her offspring despite the economic and social powerlessness that actually characterizes Latin American women.

Mothers and Daughters

The conflictive nature of the mother as a constructed image and motherhood as a reality has led to a seemingly open matrophobia, or hate, towards mothers in literature. As a general rule, women who are mothers are not portrayed as individuals. Instead, they are judged and declared a failure in their fulfillment of the maternal role in most cases. Surprisingly, the factor that most contributes to the dehumanization of mothers is the pervasive daughter-centrism—that is to say, the prevalence of the daughter's perspective or point of view in the narrative—that we find in many of the novels that deal with mother/daughter relationships. Furthermore, even those female characters who are mothers themselves adopt the perspective of the daughter and see themselves as helpless victims of their mothers.

Few human relationships are as conflictive as the mother–daughter relationship in which feelings such as love and admiration, dependence and rejection, obsession and indifference go hand in hand. However, this issue hardly appeared in Latin American women's writing until very recently. Indeed, most novels present a female protagonist who is orphaned or whose mother is a blurred character with no importance in the development of the plot. Several critics have agreed that this absence of mothers in Latin American literature written by women may be well due to a certain self-censorship whose purpose is to avoid portraying a negative mother figure.

The phenomenon of daughter-centrism refers to the predominance of the daughter's voice and perspective and the absence of those of the mother. In the narrative, daughters create a maternal image based on their perception of their mothers' behavior and response to their needs. However, the mother's voice is not only silenced but rejected, revealing the fact that society assumes their experience to be inferior and unworthy in comparison to that of the father figure. It is as if daughters need to silence their mothers in order to be able to acquire their own personal voices and grow. Emotional distance from the mother and closeness with the father seem to be a prerequisite in order to become independent. Clarice Lispector's (Brazil) short story "Laços de família" (1965, Family Ties) shows the complicity that exists between the daughter and her father and the contempt she feels towards her mother. She experiences a mixture of compassion and repugnance towards her mother. Mother and daughter feel as they have nothing in common, but at the same time, they struggle with feelings of guilt and anguish towards each other for the emptiness of their relationship.

Motherless daughters

Until recently, it was unusual to find mothers playing major roles as literary characters. Many female protagonists were orphaned before the narrative began or their mothers were left in the background. Significantly, only dead mothers were depicted as potentially having a positive influence on their daughters. Gabriela Mistral's (Chile) poems dedicated to her dead mother, specially the poem entitled "Madre mía" (My Mother) and Claudia Lars' (El Salvador) poem "Canción del recuerdo" (Remembrance's Song) included in *Estrellas en el pozo* (1934, Stars in the Well) are good examples of the mystification of the absent mother. The absence of the mother becomes a symbol for the lack of support and direction in the life of her daughter. In *As Três Marias* (1939, Three Marias) by Rachel de Queirós (Brazil) Maria Augusta, the main character, believes that not having a mother is the same as not having a family at all. *Ifigenia* (1924) by Teresa de la Parra (Venezuela) and *Perto do Coração Selvagem* (1944, Close to the Savage Hearth) by Clarice Lispector (Brazil) are two coming-of-age novels in which the main character grows up isolated and helpless in a patriarchal world whose rules she does not understand. The main cause of the alienation she feels is the lack of a mother figure with which to identify, to mirror herself. Consequently, underlying the plot there is the search for a substitute mother, a maternal figure who can help her reconcile with her feeling of displacement and who will guide her until she finds her place in the world.

Mothers and Female Oppression

Nonetheless, in those novels in which the mother is alive and is constructed as a strong presence, her image is usually distorted. The mother figure does not represent support or guidance. On the contrary, it is characterized as a mad woman too blind or selfish to perceive her daughters' needs or care for them. In "La flor de lis" (1988, The "Fleur de Lis") Elena Poniatowska (Mexico) portrays a mother so distant that her daughter feels deprived of her love and longs for a connection that never happens. Some mothers are portrayed as mere caricatures, ridiculous stereotypes. Others are depicted as oppressive figures, a burden whose purpose is to prevent the development of the protagonist. In most cases, the mother figure becomes a rigid stereotype of a social class and, in that sense, she symbolizes the values and traditions the daughter refuses to accept. The protagonists of Gioconda Belli's (Nicaragua) *La mujer habitada* (1992, The Inhabited Woman), Rosario Castellanos's (Mexico) *Balún-Canán* (1957), Marta Lynch's (Argentina) *La señora Ordóñez* (1968, Mrs. Ordonez), Albalucía Angel's (Colombia) *Estaba la pájara pinta sentada en el verde limón* (1975, The Spotted Bird was Sitting in the Lemon Tree), and Marta Brunet's (Chile) short novel *La mampara* (1946, The Screen) portray their mothers not as individuals but as social caricatures. These daughters blame their mothers for not behaving as the constructed image of the ideal mother, meanwhile rejecting that part of their mothers' personality which conformed to the maternal role of reproducing patriarchal values from one generation to the next. This blaming does not mean that daughters feel no attachment or love towards their mothers. Quite the opposite, as underlying every anecdote that dehumanizes the mother figure lies the daughter's reproach of not being loved enough.

Furthermore, some daughters implicitly accuse their mothers of showing a clear preference in their affections for their son/s. As in Castellanos' and Angel's novels mentioned above, Mexican American Lucha Corpi's *Delia's Song* (1989) closely intertwines a profound love for her mother with a hidden rancor because she believes that her existence matters less to her mother in comparison to that of her sons. Lucha Corpi's protagonist Delia feels that her mother would never recover from the death of her two sons, and likewise her mother's constant pain deprives her of her love and connection. Delia ponders that for a mother losing a son means losing the world, however, losing a daughter does not change anything; it means nothing. This preference of males over females shows how the mother figure in these narratives has completely internalized patriarchal values to the detriment of her sex.

Thus, as the maternal figure embodies the social pressure put upon the daughters to become little more than the repetition of a role, many characters feel trapped and even suffocated by the mere presence of their mothers. This feeling of entrapment and alienation is portrayed in works such as Marta Brunet's (Chile) short story "La raíz del sueño" (1949, The Root of a Dream) as well as in Laura Esquivel's *Como agua para chocolate* (1989, Like Water for Chocolate). In these works the mother becomes a sinister character, half-nurturing, half-monster, who is capable of devouring her own daughter by exerting complete control over her life, as if she were still in her womb. The enclosed spaces that characterize this type of narrative are metaphors for the mother's will to keep her daughters from leading an independent life of their own and to make them accept their subordinate role in society. The anguish that daughters feel living in this claustrophobic environment is symbolized by different somatophobia, that is, physical discomfort, medical symptoms or even actual illness. It is as if their body lets out the pain they feel inside.

The rejection many female protagonists feel towards their mothers is closely related to the fear of becoming one's own mother, that is to say, the horror of repeating what patriarchal culture has determined to be women's position in society. Nevertheless, this rejection does not liberate women from fighting similar struggles and repeating the same errors as their foremothers, as Maria Alice Barroso (Brazil) depicts in *História de um Casamento* (1960, History of a Marriage) and *Um Nome Para Matar* (1967, A Name to Kill), and Karym Taylhardat Garcés (Venezuela) illustrates with a mixture of humor and irony in her short story "Con la red perforada" (1991, With the Broken Net). Funnily enough, there are stories such as "Aguas abajo" (1930, Waters Below) by Marta Brunet, that describe a daughter's maneuvers to take over her mother's role in the family in order to acquire what she perceives as power and control over her rural environment.

The dehumanization of the mother by turning her into a stereotype or a role shows two conflicting sides. Together with matrophobia there is the mystified image of a perfect mother, a self-sacrificing silenced entity with apparently no needs of her own. This personification of the perfect mother can be found in Nellie Campobello's (Mexico) *Las manos de mamá* (1937, Mom's Hands). The mystification of women as mothers, as well as their degradation, is closely intertwined. Both of them rise from the cultural construction which establishes that when a woman becomes a mother she loses her individuality. Supposedly, this process in which women acquire a different identity is an innate trait that develops as soon as they become pregnant. Women's failure or success at adjusting to the constructed image of the ideal mother will be closely linked to the degree to which she erases herself as a person and adopts the standardized behavior presented by patriarchal culture as natural. When a woman does not conform to the ideal mother figure she is rejected by her offspring, as Marcela Serrano (Chile) portrays in *Para que no me olvides* (1993, So That You Will Not Forget Me). Rosario Castellanos (Mexico) in her essay "La abnegación es una virtud loca" (Abnegation Is a Crazy Virtue), criticizes the Mexican idealization of maternity and denounces the actual discrimination that this mystification masks in Mexican culture and society.

Maternity

Few female protagonists are involved in the very experience of motherhood itself. In most cases the narrative ends with the young female shortly before getting married, but hardly ever deals with the ensuing marriage and the rearing of children. In a sense, this is somewhat surprising because these two events are part of what patriarchal society has promised to be the climax in every woman's life. However, there are some examples which not only depict women experiencing motherhood but subvert the whole concept by associating maternity with themes until now silenced and excluded from literature. Rosario Castellano's poem "Hablando de Gabriel" (Talking about Gabriel) explores the experience of pregnancy in relation to the changes in a woman's body and her feelings of otherness. Marta Lynch (Argentina) describes two opposing views to the childbirth experience in *La señora Ordóñez* (1968, Mrs. Ordonez) y *El cruce del río* (1970, River Crossing). In the first novel childbirth is perceived as degrading and alienating, while in the second it is described as a mystical experience. Pregnancy as a result of rape is depicted by Isabel Allende (Chile) in *La casa de los espíritus* (1982, The House of the Spirits), Rosario Ferré (Puerto Rico) in her short story "La bella durmiente" (1976, Sleeping Beauty) and Sara Gallardo (Argentina) in *Enero* (1958; January). Abortion as a choice appears in *La nave de los locos* (1984, Fool's Ship) by Cristina Peri Rossi (Uruguay), Ana Castillo's *The Mixquiahuala Letters* and in *El lugar donde crece la hierba* (1959, The Place Where the Grass Grows) by Luisa Josefina Hernández (México). In the last two novels, the female protagonist opts for an abortion against the wishes of her partner. In both cases, this fact prompts the distancing of the couple. Fanny Buitrago's (Colombia) main character reveals with strong infanticide feelings in her short story "Los espectros de la Calle Cantarrana" (1973, The Ghost of Cantarrana St.). Laura Esquivel's *La ley del amor* (1995, The Law of Love) and Magda Portal's (Peru) short story "Círculos violetas" (Violet Circles) included in *El derecho de matar* (1927, The Right to Kill) deal with an actual infanticide. Portal's short story depicts a woman who decides to kill her newborn baby in order to free him from the life of poverty and misery she is enduring, while Esquivel's deals with this subject within the frame of a science fiction narrative.

Finally, motherhood as a choice, not as a biological mandate, appears in some recent texts. In her testimonial book *Me llamo Rigoberta Menchú y así me nació la conciencia* (1985, My Name is Rigoberta Menchú), Menchú explains her conscious decision of never to have children in order to be able to dedicate her entire life to her career as a political activist in favor of the indigenous communities in Guatemala.

Some novels question the myth of the maternal instinct which depicts mothers as essentially nurturing, while childless women are presented as bitter and resentful. They do so by portraying the latter behaving in a much more nurturing fashion than actual mothers, as is the case of Maria Alice Barroso's (Brazil) *Um Simples Afeto Recíproco* (1960, A Simple Reciprocal Love).

Usually the representation of the mother figure by Afro-Hispanic or indigenous women writers offer a positive image of a woman. Mothers are depicted as victims of oppression but, at the same time, strong enough to endure the suffering and to offer hope to her children. Afro-Uruguayan Virgina Brindis de Salas praises the endurance and vitality of a mother in her poem "Marimorena" while Guatemalan Caly Domitila Cane'k's poem "Ellos destruyeron la casa de mi madre" (They Destroyed my Mother's Home), written in Caqchiquel, describes her mother's desolation at witnessing the assassination of her children and her hope for a better future. The same positive attitude toward her mother can be found in Rigoberta Menchú's books of memories. Bolivian Domitila Barrios de Chungara's testimony as a woman and mother can be found in *Si me permiten hablar* ... and *Aquí también, Domitila*. The wife of a Bolivian miner and the mother of seven children, Barrios narrates her experience as a political activist and her travels in Europe and America in order to denounce human rights violations in Bolivia.

Mothers as Protagonists

There are few novels in which mothers are granted a voice that enables them to express their love, guilt, frustration, their contradictory feelings of love and rejection towards their own children, and their struggle against becoming a role and losing their own individuality. One of the earliest works that grant voice to women who are mothers is Chilean María Luisa Bombal's novel *La amortajada* (1938, The Shrouded Woman). However, the appropriation of a voice by the protagonist is achieved only when she is already dead and is reflecting on her past during her own wake. Likewise, in both *Mañana digo basta* (1968, Tomorrow I'll say, Enough) by Silvina Bullrich (Argentina) and Clarice Lispector's short story "Amor" (1965, Love), the reader is confronted with the feelings of uselessness, impotence and emptiness in the life of a housewife. Lispector's protagonist, although content at having achieved what is perceived by society as a woman's destiny by marrying and becoming a mother, one day discovers with fear that she has chosen to live this uneventful and passive life in order to escape from the danger of living a more intense or productive life. On the other hand, Bullrich's main character is a mature woman who tries to escape the role of motherhood when she becomes a grandmother. According to her, this role only allows her to feel anguish for the safety of her daughters when they are not around and impatience at having to control her anger at their constant criticism and contempt for her when they are together.

Brazilian author Lya Luft's novels can be seen as focusing on what she calls "closed family relationships". In these highly dramatic novels, Luft repeatedly subverts the myth of motherhood by portraying this experience not as a rewarding climax but as a stressful, confusing and often empty period of a woman's life. In *Exilio* (1987, The Red House) the protagonist deals with the anger and pain caused by both the memories of her drunken, suicidal mother and her perceived failure in her own role as a mother. Funnily enough, in this novel both male characters, the husband and the lover, never abandon their own children, even when this choice will mean the end of the relationship with the female protagonist. *O Quarto Fechado* (1980, The Island of the Dead) depicts a mother, Renata, who gives up her career as a pianist to be a better mother; however, her sacrifice does not lead to happiness nor prevent her only son's suicide and her daughter's descent into madness. Moreover, motherhood brought tension and feelings of inadequacy to her marriage. She believes that children do not create ties, but bring separation in a couple's life because they always become problems themselves. Marta Brunet's "Piedra callada" (1943, Silent Rock) also portrays children as a terrible challenge for the survival of women living in poverty. This short story depicts a mother's unsuccessful efforts to prevent her daughter from becoming a slave to her husband. After a life of hard work to maintain her pride and self-sufficiency, she finds herself having to rear her grandchildren and becoming a replacement of her daughter in her abusive marriage.

In a more humorous manner, Angélica Gorodischer's (Argentina) *Floreros de alabastro y alfombras de Bokhara* (1985, Alabaster Vases and Bokhara Carpets) and Marcela Serrano's (Chile) *Antigua vida mía* (1995, Antigua and My Life Before) portray several women dealing with the pain and guilt of trying to maintain their individuality and the conflict that this attitude rises in their relationship with their children. *Un aire de familia* (1995, A Family Resemblance) by Silvia Italiano (Argentina) subverts the pervasive daughter-centrism in Latin American literature written by women by allowing Amanda, her protagonist, to construct a monstrous portrayal of her mother during most of her novel. Only at the end of the novel is the mother allowed to speak for a few pages. Those pages deconstruct her daughter's perception of reality and denounce the suppression of the mother's voice as a requirement for the reproduction of patriarchal ideology. In a similar way, Claribel Alegría's (Nicaragua/El Salvador) *Cenizas de Izalco* (1982, Izalco's Ashes) allows the mother's voice to appear through the pages of an old lover's diary which she gave to her daughter upon her death. By reading this diary, Carmen learns that her mother was a different woman from the one whom she remembered, from the image she had constructed of her in her own mind, opening the possibility of an understanding and reconciliation between them, even after death.

Mothers' voices can also be heard in the political testimony of Salvadoran Claribel Alegría's *No me agarran viva* (1983, They Will Not Get Me Alive) and in narratives such as *Conversación al sur* (1981, Conversation in the South) by Argentinian-Colombian Marta Traba and *The Little School: Tales of Disappearance and Survival in Argentina* by Argentinian Alicia Partnoy. These texts have allowed women who have been silenced both by patriarchal society and by political repression to express their experiences and feelings as mothers. In these works, women recount the horror they have gone through and the piercing pain of living with the loss or the fear of the disappearance of their sons and daughters. *Conversación al sur* introduces a long conversation among the three main characters, three mothers who are dealing with the horror of the military repression in Uruguay, Argentina, and Chile. Dolores lost her unborn baby girl during a police beating in Montevideo, Elena joined the "crazy mothers of La Plaza de Mayo" after the disappearance of her daughter and, finally, Irene waits for news of her son after the military coup in Chile. Alicia Partnoy describes her own experience at a concentration camp: her anguish at the unknown fate of her one-year-old baby, the stealing of newborn babies from female prisoners and the subtle ways she found to be able to cope with torture and degradation.

Matriarchal Families

The lack of communication between generations is one of the main problems that women have endured for centuries. This silence is due to the lack of respect for female knowledge based on the assumption that only the masculine understanding of the world is the sensible interpretation of reality, or at least, the only rational interpretation. Hence, an interesting development in Latin American women's narrative during the last decades is the proliferation of novels that deal with the search for matrilineal roots. There are several Latin American women authors concerned with this issue. In their works, different generations of women struggle through life without the benefit of the experience and knowledge of their female predecessors. In *Dreaming in Cuban* (1992) by Cuban-American Cristina García, *Antigua vida mía* (1994, Antigua and My Life Before) by Marcela Serrano and *La casa de los espíritus* (1982, The House of Spirits) by Chilean Isabel Allende, grandmothers, mothers and daughters exhibit unique personalities not inhibited by the impositions of any patriarchal roles or stereotypes. These works stress the significance of an alternative knowledge of reality that is not based upon rationality and manages to connect several generations of women. Even though these women struggle alone, the novels suggest some hope. The fact that the youngest of the female characters, Alba, in the novel by Allende, and Pilar in *Dreaming in Cuban*, search for the memories of their female predecessors and in so doing raise the question of the need to unearth mothers' stories in order to learn from them and, above all, to reconsider and construct new gender roles.

A matriarchal genealogy in which a new kind of knowledge is transmitted from mother to daughter is fully achieved in works such as Teresa de la Parra's (Venezuela) *Memorias de mamá Blanca* (1929, Mama Blanca's Souvenirs), Claribel Alegría's (Nicaragua-El Salvador) *Cenizas de Izalco*, Isabel Allende's *Paula* (1994) or Cristina Peri Rossi's (Uruguay) short story "Primer amor" (1996, First Love). In these works the female characters do not play the patriarchal game of mother-trashing, but rather they manage to unravel the women buried by the myth of the "good mother" and love her by learning from her own life's struggle.

Many of the novels mentioned above emphasize the belief that our patriarchal society uses women in their role as mothers to reproduce the ideological system that will guarantee its survival. Hispanic mothers were supposed to teach conservative moral values to their children by becoming a model of self-denial and self-sacrifice. The young generation rebelled against those values and against the mother who personified them. Stories about mothers and daughters teach us how women need to differentiate between their mothers as individuals and the role they learned to represent which had turned them into victims, powerless and voiceless. Only by breaking the reproduction of women's victimization will they manage to reconcile and repair the mother–daughter love ties. Latin American women writers rewrite and analyze the role of motherhood in order to offer new models for a different family relationship that allows women to maintain their own individuality while trying to support and educate their children in the best possible way.

MIRYAM CRIADO

References and Further Reading

Alegría, Isabel. *Cenizas de Izalco*. San José, PR: Editorial Universitaria Centroamericana, 1982.

Allende, Isabel. *La casa de los espíritus*. Barcelona: Plaza y Janés, 1982.

Badinter, Elizabeth. *The Myth of Motherhood: An Historical View of the Maternal Instinct*. London: Souvenir Press, 1981.

Barroso, Alice. *História de um casamento*. Rio de Janeiro: Edições GRD, 1960.

——. *Um simples afeto recíproco*. Rio de Janeiro: Edições GRD, 1963.

——. *Um nome para matar*. Rio de Janeiro: Edições GRD, 1967.

Belli, Gioconda. *La mujer habitada*. Barcelona: Emecé, 1992.

Bombal, María Luisa. *La amortajada*. Buenos Aires: Editorial "Sur", 1938.

Bullrich, Silvina. *Mañana digo basta*. Buenos Aires: Editorial Sudamericana, 1968.

Burk, Frances. *Mothers Talking: Sharing the Secret*. New York: Saint Martin's Press, 1986.

Cahill, Susan. *Motherhood: A Reader for Men and Women*. New York: Avon, 1982.

Caplan, Susan. *Don't Blame Mother: Mending the Mother-Daughter Relationship*. New York: Cornell University Press, 1992.

Castellanos, Rosario. *Balún Canán*. Mexico: Fondo de Cultura Económica, 1957.

Castillo, Debra. *Talking Back: Toward a Latin American Feminist Literary Criticism*. New York: Cornell University Press, 1992.

Chodorow, Nancy. *The Reproduction of Mothering: Psychoanalysis and the Sociology of Gender*. Berkeley, CA: University of California Press, 1978.

Dally, Ann. *Inventing Motherhood: The Consequences of an Ideal*. New York: Schocken, 1983.

Davidson, Cathy. *The Lost Tradition: Mothers and Daughters in Literature*. New York: Frederick Ungar, 1980.

Esquivel, Laura. *Como agua para chocolate. Novela de entregas mensuales con recetas, amores y remedios caseros*. Mexico: Planeta, 1989.

Friday, Nancy. *My Mother/My Self: The Daughter's Search for Identity*. New York: Dela corte, 1977.

Garro, Elena. *Los recuerdos del porvenir*. Mexico: Joaquin Mortiz, 1963

Gorodischer, Angélica. *Floreros de alabastro y alfombras de Bokhara*. Buenos Aires: Emecé, 1985.

Italiano, Silvia. *Un aire de familia*. Barcelona: Seix Barral, 1995.

Lars, Claudia. *Estrellas en el pozo*. San José, PR: Convivo, 1934.

Leonard, Linda Schierce. *Meeting the Madwoman*. New York: Bantam, 1993.

Lispector, Clarice. *Perto do coração selvagen* (1944) Rio de Janeiro: José Olympio, 1974.

——. *Laços de família; contos*. Rio de Janeiro: Editôra do Autor, 1965.

Luft, Lya. *The Island of the Dead*. Trans. Carmen Chaves and Betty Craige. Athens, GA: University of Georgia Press, 1986.

Lynch, Marta. *El cruce del río*. Buenos Aires: Editorial Sudamericana, 1972.

Mistral, Gabriela. *Poesías completas*. Madrid: Aguilar, 1968.

Parra, Teresa de la. *Memorias de mamá Blanca*. Paris: Le Livre Libre, 1929.

Partnoy, Alicia. *The Little School: Tales of Disappearance and Survival*. Trans. Alicia Partnoy with Lois Athey and Sandra Braunstein. Pittsburg, PA: Cleis, 1986.

Peri Rossi, Cristina. "Primer amor". In *Madres e hijas*. Barcelona: Anagrama, 1996.

Portal, Magda. *El derecho de matar*. La Paz: S.E., 1926.

Rich, Adrienne. *Of Woman Born: Motherhood as Experience and Institution*. New York: Norton, 1976.

Serrano, Marcela. *Antigua vida mía*. Mexico: Alfaguara, 1995.

Traba, Marta. *Conversación al sur*. Mexico: Siglo XXI, 1981.

MUÑIZ-HUBERMAN, ANGELINA

The Jewish-Mexican writer Angelina Muñiz-Huberman (b. 1936) was born in Hyères, Provence, southern France, where her parents, exiled Republican Spaniards, were in provisional refuge from the Spanish Civil War. Her mother was the Madrilenian Carmen Sacristán, an early feminist. Her father, Alfredo Muñiz, was a journalist and theater critic for *El Heraldo de Madrid* (Madrid Herald). In 1938, her only sibling and elder brother died in Paris. In 1939, the family, desperate both with the tragic loss and the political situation in Spain and the rest of Europe, decided to leave France in order to move to La Habana, Cuba. During the next three years the Muñiz-Sacristán family lived in the Guajiro town, Caimito del Guayabal, before finally moving and settling down in México, D. F., in March 1942. As a young girl, Muñiz-Huberman learned about her *converso* (convert) Jewish ancestry when her mother revealed it to her. Her ancestors had remained in Spain after the decree of expulsion in 1492, but, throughout the ages, the family had managed to keep words in Hispanicized Hebrew that identified them as Jews. Later on, the writer would learn that the Christian sounding name Sacristán was just the translation of the Hebrew *Shamash* (synagogue custodian). After the revelation about her spiritual roots, Muñiz-Huberman started to engage in the study of Judaism and her Jewish heritage. Eventually, she underwent a formal conversion to Judaism and became a Jewish writer. At the university she met Alberto Huberman, who would later become her husband. Currently, Muñiz-Huberman is professor in the faculty of Philosophy and Letters at the National Autonomous University of Mexico.

Writer and Poet

Muñiz-Huberman, of Sephardic ancestry, senses herself to be multipally marginalized: as a woman, as an exiled Spaniard, and as a Jew. The novelist, poet, essayist, translator, interpreter of literary and philosophical texts of the Sephardic tradition, literary critic, editor, short-story writer, and professor of Spanish Renaissance literature and Comparative Literature has engaged in revealing the crypto-Jewish heritage in Mexican culture and Hispanic civilization. In 1989, she compiled *La lengua florida: antología sefardí* (The Blossoming Language: Sephardic Anthology); in 1993, she published *Las raíces y las ramas: Fuentes y derivaciones de la Cábala hispanohebrea* (The

Roots and the Branches: Sources and Derivations of the Hispanohebraic Kabbalah). The accumulation of her Spanish, French, Cuban, Mexican, and Israeli descents and experiences makes it difficult to situate Muñiz-Huberman artistically, nationally, thematically; she belongs to the Hispanomexican literati, but also to the Jewish-Mexican, the Sephardic, and the Mexican "Generación de Medio Siglo" [mid-century generation] (Zamudio Rodríguez 2003: 17). Muñiz-Huberman does not identify herself with any one literary genre. In fact, she calls her open-ended works transmutations; taking great liberty as her literary style is eclectic, paying little attention to traditional genre conventions. In her evocative, lyrical prose she moves freely in time, space, form, characters, genres, invention, reflections. Muñiz-Huberman views the genre transgression and the uncertainty present in her works as direct effects of her experience of exile which has pushed her to seek new forms of expression in her attempt to rename reality; to create new physical and spiritual worlds of her own. As a person who has had to cross cultural and religious boundaries all her life, in her work she attempts to present intricate worldviews; to construct worlds that are not necessarily nationalistic in nature but ambiguous "mundos sin fronteras" [worlds without frontiers] (Payne 1997: 432). And yet, because language can create and destroy realities, for Muñiz-Huberman it has a sacred dimension. Influenced by the Cabalists, she understands that in her occupation as a writer, she has the duty to use language responsibly and to attempt perfection. As she explains in her autobiographical work *De cuerpo entero* (1991, Entire Body), her aesthetic is "una ética de lenguaje" [an ethics of language]. Thus, in her use of words, she leaves nothing to chance; her language is concise, precise, and carefully honed. In her pursuit of linguistic excellence, Hispanomexican Muñiz-Huberman also likes to generate "new words or revitalize archaic ones; to change the use of verbs, nouns, adjectives; to cut phrases; to punctuate in an unconventional manner" in a language of her own that is neither Mexican nor Spanish (Sullivan 1996: 12).

Themes and Influences

Muñiz-Huberman's literary works witness her multiple cultural traditions and her exceptional erudition. Her subject matters are inward looking, alchemical, philosophical, and mystical. As the translator of Muñiz-Huberman's *Huerto cerrado, huerto sellado*, 1985 (1988, Enclosed Garden), Lois Parkinson Zamora, suggests in the preface to her translation, Muñiz-Huberman's accounts expose "[a]n acute intuition of history gone wrong". The most predominant topic in her work is exile. In fact, Muñiz-Huberman sees herself as an embodiment that links the Sephardic exile of 1492 and the Spanish Republican exile of 1936–39 as she expresses through her poem "Yo, sefardí de 1942 y de 1939" (I, Sephardim from 1492 and 1939) in her work *La sal en el rostro* (1989, Salt on the Face). Though her works sometimes display an ambivalent relationship to exile, at the personal level, as a writer, she views the exile experience as an enriching one that has broaden her consciousness. Muñiz-Huberman also writes about obsession with childhood memories, life and death, loneliness, silence, trauma, the workings of memory, religious questions, the fragile construction of identity, the ambiguity of emotions, hidden passions, the Spanish Civil War, World War II, historical characters, and the position of the Jew in the New World. Her inter-textual stories often allude to the history of the twelfth century in Spain, and to the succeeding period of cultural renaissance, the *Siglo de Oro* or "Golden Age". Spanish and Latin American historical characters like Sor Juana Inés de la Cruz, Saint Teresa de Ávila, and Bartolomé de las Casas often appear in her creations. Among her literary influences, besides Louisa May Alcott, the Brontë sisters, Marcel Proust, Azorín, Jorge Luis Borges, Rosario Castellanos, Franz Kafka, Rabbi Nahman of Bratslav, Inés Arredondo, Gershom Sholem, María Zambrano, the Odyssey, the Iliad, the Bible, and the Kabbalah, she counts the literary productions of the Golden Age as the greatest: Miguel de Cervantes Saavedra, the theatre, the mystique, and the picaresque.

The prolific Muñiz-Huberman, who has published some thirty books and whose poetry and narratives have frequently been anthologized, has been awarded numerous recognitions. Her works have been translated into English, French, Hebrew, and Italian. She is considered one of the best contemporary Mexican women writers; she is also one of the most distinguished and most creative Jewish and Spanish refugee writers. Though her works may sometimes be removed in place and time from present-day realities, her topics are of contemporary relevance. For instance, in her first book, *Morada interior* (Internal Abode), for which the writer won the Magda Donato literary award 1972, Muñiz-Huberman engages with the life of Santa Teresa de Cepeda. In the work, the religious crisis that the saint undergoes in her search for identity as a converted Jew whose Jewish past cannot be completely deleted by a Christian identity, Santa Teresa becomes a representative of the cultural and religious negotiations and the conflicts of loyalty that, in the time of transnationalism, many women and men experience. Scholar Judith Payne expresses that the novel in itself is a transgression since Muñiz-Huberman's treatment of Santa Teresa as a *conversa* (convert) was made at a time when "the *converso* origin of St. Teresa was not widely acknowledged" (1997a: 438). Or *La guerra del unicornio* (1983, The War of the Unicorn), though on the surface a lyrical historical account set in the Middle Ages, engages with the desire for power and disloyalty; the brutality and irrationality of war, specifically the Spanish Civil War. But Muñiz-Huberman's work is also subversive in the way she approaches common-sense knowledge about women. In her short story "La madre" (1963, The Mother) included in *El libro de Miriam y Primicias* (1990, Miriam's and Primicias' Book), the writer complicates ideas that propagate the alleged extraordinariness of the experience of motherhood for women and the naturalness of motherly love. The short account presents a woman who has given birth to a son and who, against common social expectations, declares that she is not happy with the baby since the boy is a stranger to her, and that she does not view the act of giving birth to a child as something exceptional. Expressing her discomfort with having to display satisfied motherhood to the outside world, she decries that she is now required to forget that she is a woman in order to become Mother. Muñiz-Huberman's versatility is further displayed in *Dulcinea encanta* (1992, Enchanted Dulcinea), a work that was awarded the Sor Juana Inés de la Cruz Award in 1993, and which gives voice to displaced children by approaching exile from the point of view of a child of Spanish Republican refugees. The work engages with the widespread predicament of Hispanomexican children whose parents, expecting a quick return to Spain, resisted promoting the Mexican identity of their children, even after several decades of residency in the country, and instead insisted on fostering the culture of an imaginary country that the children only knew from the tales of their parents. The novel presents the misfortune of the young protagonist Dulcinea, a girl who has additionally been an exile of the Spanish Civil War and has thus been a Russian refugee for many years before coming to Mexico. The narration depicts Dulcinea's breaks with reality after she arrives to Mexico to be reunited with her parents and finds out that, after so many years, she is no longer able to recognize them.

The literary critic Luz Elena Zamudio Rodríguez has completed a comprehensive study on Angelina Muñiz-Huberman's literary work. Zamudio Rodríguez's work is a valuable bibliographic resource for scholars who might like to engage with the work by a woman writer who in her writing displays extraordinary sensitivity and vast sophistication in literature, philosophy, and religion.

LUZ ANGÉLICA KIRSCHNER

Selected Works

Creative Writing

Morada interior. México: J. Mortiz, 1972.
Tierra adentro. México: J. Mortiz, 1977.
Vilano al viento: Poemas del amor y del exilio. México: UNAM, 1982.
La guerra del unicornio. México: Artífice, 1983.
Huerto cerrado, huerto sellado. México: Editorial Oasis, 1985. (Translated by Lois Parkinson Zamora as *Enclosed Gardens*. Pennsylvania: Latin American Literary Review, 1988.)
El libro de Míriam y Primicias. México: UAM, 1990.
Primicias. In *El libro de Míriam*. México: UAM, 1990.
De cuerpo entero: Angelina Muñiz-Huberman. México: Coordinación de Difusión Cultural, Dirección de Literatura, UNAM: Ediciones Corunda, 1991.
Serpientes y escaleras. México: Coordinación de Difusión Cultural, Dirección de Literatura, UNAM, 1991.
Dulcinea encantada. México: J. Moritz, 1992.
El ojo de la creación. México: Universidad Nacional Autónoma de México, 1992.
Narrativa relativa: antología personal. México: Consejo Nacional para la Cultura y las Artes, 1992.
Castillos en la tierra (Seudomemorias). México: Consejo Nacional para la Cultura y las Artes: Ediciones del Equilibrista, 1995.
La memoria del aire. México: Facultad de Filosofía y Letras, Coordinación de Humanidades, UNAM, 1995.
De magias y prodigios: transmutaciones. México: Fondo de Cultura Económica, 1997.
El trazo y el vuelo: Poemas. Salta: Editorial Biblioteca de Textos Universitarios, 1997.
Las confidentes. México: Tusquets, 1997.
El mercader de Tudela. México: Fondo de Cultura Económica, 1998.
La sal en el rostro. México: UAM, 1998.
Conato de extranjería. México: Trilce Ediciones, 1999.
Trotsky en Coyoacán y otros sucesos. México: Biblioteca del ISSTE, 2000.
Molinos sin viento: (Seudomemorias). México: Aldus, 2001.
Aréusa en los conciertos. México: Alfaguara, 2002.
La tregua de la inocencia. México: Consejo Nacional para la Cultura y las Artes, 2003.
Cantos treinta de otoño. México: Verdehalago, 2005.
El sefardí romántico: la azarosa vida de Mateo Alemán II. México: Plaza y Janés, 2005.

Nonfiction

Notas de investigación sobre la literatura comparada. México: Facultad de Filosofía y Letras, UNAM, 1989.
Las raíces y las ramas: Fuentes y derivaciones de la Cábala hispanohebrea. México: Fondo de Cultura Económica, 1993.
Las voces de la mística en Ramón Xirau. México: Facultad de Filosofía y Letras, UNAM, 1995.
El canto del peregrino: Hacia una poética del exilio. Sant Cugat del Valles: Cop d'Idees, 1999.
El siglo del desencanto. México: FCE, 2002.

Chapters in Books

"The Shepardic Legacy". Trans. Miriam Huberman. In Marjorie Agosín (ed.), *Memory, Oblivion, and Jewish Culture in Latin America*. Austin, TX: University of Texas Press, 2005, pp. 15–29.

References and Further Reading

Baer Barr, Lois. "Muñiz-Huberman, Angelina". In Darrell B. Lockhart (ed.), *Jewish Writers of Latin America: A Dictionary*. New York: Garland, 1997, pp. 365–70.
Filer, Malva E. "The Integration of a Fragmented Self in the Works of Angelina Muñiz-Huberman". *Studies in Twentieth Century Literature* 27(2) (2003): 263–77.
Hind, Emily. "Entrevista con Angelina Muñiz-Huberman". In *Entrevistas con quince autoras mexicanas*. Frankfurt: Vervuert, 2003, pp. 119–31.
McInnes, Judy. "Arthurian Material in Angelina Muñiz-Huberman's *La guerra del unicornio*". *Hispanic Journal* 22(1) (2001): 217–25.
Payne, Judith. "Writing and Reconciling Exile: The Novels of Angelina Muñiz-Huberman". *Bulletin of Hispanic Studies* 74(40 (1997a): 431–59.
——. "A World of her Own: Exilic Metafiction in Angelina Muñiz-Huberman's *Morada Interior* and *Dulcinea encantada*". *Revista Canadiense de Estudios Hispanicos* 22(1) (1997b): 45–63.
Parkinson Zamora, Lois. "Fragmentary Fictions: Angelina Muñiz Huberman, *Dulcinea Encantada*; Sandra Cisneros, *Woman Hollering Creek*". In *The Usable Past*. New York: Cambridge University Press, 1997, pp. 156–77.
Sullivan, Rosemary. "Language is the Only Country: An Interview with Angelina Muñiz-Huberman". *Paragraph: The Fiction Magazine* 18(2) (1996): 10–15.
Zamudio Rodríguez, Luz Elena. *El exilio de Dulcinea encantada. Angelina Muñiz-Huberman escritora de dos mundos*. México: Universidad Autónoma Metropolitana, 2003.

N

NAJLIS, MICHÈLE

Of French and Jewish heritage, the poet, essayist, mystic, revolutionary, and feminist Michèle Najlis was born in Granada, Nicaragua in 1946 and was educated by Catholic nuns at the *La Asunción* College in Managua. She later received a degree in Education from the Universidad Nacional Autónoma de Nicaragua (UNAN).

From 1962–72, Najlis taught literature in various secondary schools in Managua. Later, she was a professor of literature and, at various times, directed poetry workshops at the UNAN, as well as at the University of Costa Rica between 1972 and 1997. She held the post of Director of Culture for the Universidad Centroamericana in Managua from 1991–97.

In 1963, at the age of 17, Michèle Najlis was one of the instigators of the clandestine women's group, Patriotic Alliance of Nicaraguan Women, a predecessor to the Nicaraguan women's movement with which she would be involved subsequently in different ways (and still is). This participation stemmed from her staunch commitment in favour of the Sandinista movement in Nicaragua through the *Frente Sandinista de Liberación Nacional* (FSLN). Najlis was active early on in her adolescence in the then clandestine faction and remained a loyal collaborator until 1990.

With the end of the Somoza era and the new FSLN government created in 1979, Najlis was employed as a public servant in the administration until 1981. Arising from the theme of her studies, she was entrusted with the creation of new educational materials for national primary and high school programs from 1982–90 for the Ministry of Education. This was a key position because of the dramatic increase in literacy rates brought about by Sandinistas policies in Nicaragua. Still in the cultural field, Najlis wrote a regular cultural column for the newspaper *El Nuevo Diario* (in Managua) until 1989, and in the same period was involved in the selection of appropriate cultural programming for Nicaraguan public television broadcasts.

Written in 1969 and published in Guatemala two years later, before the Sandinista Revolution, Najlis' collection of poetry, *El viento armado* (The Armed Wind) is one of the first collections of revolutionary poetry to emerge from the intellectual questioning of the members of the then-nascent Sandinista movement. Along with some humble considerations, the thirty-three poems confirm an obvious bias in favour of the Sandinistas struggle in Nicaragua, a theme that the author will later distance herself from despite more than 25 years of revolutionary activism. The poems of this neophyte astonish due to the simplicity and sincerity of the language used to convey a message of solidarity as is illustrated in the minimalist poem titled "Icarus": "Icarus / also / had wings".

It is not until 1980—a year after the Sandinistas' victory—that she published her second collection of poetry entitled *Augurios* (Augurs). Although it also includes poems that contain revolutionary metaphors and messages, this second book is much more personal, with poems dedicated to the births of Najlis' children as well as a "Self-portrait".

In 1988, the author published *Ars Combinatoria*, borrowing the title from Leibniz' theories. It is a markedly experimental prose poetry collection in which she (often humorously) approaches the theme of machismo throughout the ages in prose poems such as "The true story of the Trojan War" with Helen as the protagonist. It is also in these poems that she shows a patent determination to distance herself from the exteriorist (read realist) poetic style propagated nationally by Ernesto Cardenal, the Nicaraguan poet and Minister of Culture at the time. For Mantero (2003), the poem "Non-Euclidean Geometry" attempts to dialogue—and possibly subvert—Cardenal's canonical norms. Through the use of scientific and mathematical language and the questioning of laws, Najlis defies imposed rigidity.

In 1990, Najlis released a compilation of newspaper articles previously published between 1982 and 1987 in *El Nuevo Diario*, under the title *Caminos de la Estrella Polar* (Roads to the North Star). In these articles, and owing to her poet's vision, she details the lives of the common (and exceptional) people she came across as she travelled in Sandinista Nicaragua during key moments of the struggle. She also includes personal observations such as that published after the death of her long-time Sandinista companion Julio Cortázar.

With the publication of *Cantos de Ifigenia* (Iphigenia's Songs), Najlis returns to the poetic voice in 1991. This collection was translated into German and published in a bilingual edition in 1997 by Verag Drava. Although the poems primarily speak to the theme of earthly love and its conversion through mystical and existential speculations into a divine worship, Najlis continues her previously initiated disengagement from the Sandinista ideals. Both A. Kaminsky (1995) and J.M. Mantero (2003) consider this collection to be the substantiation of the author's spiritual doubts. Mantero (2003) states that the collection exemplifies post-Sandinista literature because of its existential contemplations.

Although the author chooses to avoid concrete mentions of political involvement, A. Kaminsky (1995) finds that by creating a text riddled with intertextuality, Najlis is in effect consciously including herself in the universal legacy of poetic defiance. However, in the wake of Najlis' revolutionary participation, Kaminsky questions the apparent message of voluntary self-sacrifice it contains as a possible "capitulation to a tired masculinist, Christian ideology". Mantero (1999) illustrates the argument that the key to resolving the poet's (and, by extension, women's) existentialist struggle lies in the revelation of amorous and erotic themes he detects in Najlis' collection.

Due to her involvement with the FSLN from the early 1960s, first in the clandestine organization and then in the government, Najlis was a self-proclaimed Marxist atheist throughout the 1970s. The shock of the electoral defeat and disillusionment caused the author much personal anguish and led to her rupture (as with many Nicaraguan intellectuals such as Ernesto Cardenal and Gioconda Belli) with the FSLN led by Daniel Ortega in the 1990s.

In the process of finding a new direction to her life, Najlis (re)turned to the Catholicism she had been subjected to in her childhood, all the while remaining an unfaltering Marxist. The author does not consider the two terms at all contradictory, despite the ostracism that she has been subjected to for her ideals from both the left and the religious community in the years since the Sandinistas' defeat (Najlis in Martin).

Najlis studied theology in various seminaries and schools in Managua and as of 2005 was employed by the Antonio Valdivieso Ecumenical Centre as director of Theology and editor of the ecumenical journal called *Xilotl*: *Revista Nicaragüense de Teología*, in which she regularly publishes articles on contemporary Christian questions of faith. This new spiritual field of study has also influenced her most recent poems with the writing of *La soledad sonora* (The Loud Solitude) in 2005 (unpublished).

Since its founding in 2000, Najlis has held various roles in the Asociación Nicaragüense de Escritoras (ANIDE) of which she is currently President (2007). ANIDE, which has its own editorial board and publishes a literary journal *Revista Anide*, promotes the writing of Nicaraguan women of all generations.

SOPHIE M. LAVOIE

Selected Works

El Viento Armado. Guatemala: Universidad de San Carlos, 1971.
Augurios. San José, Costa Rica: Edit. Costa Rica, 1981.
Ars Combinatoria. Managua: Editorial Nueva Nicaragua, 1988.
Caminos de la Estrella Polar. Managua: Editorial Vanguardia, 1990.
Cantos de Ifigenia. Managua: Editorial Vanguardia, 1991.

References and Further Reading

Kaminsky, Amy K. "The Poet After the Revolution: Intertextuality and Defiance in Michele Najlis's *Cantos de Ifigenia*." *Latin American Literary Review* 23(460 (July–Dec. 1995): 48–65.

Mantero, José María. "Michèle Najlis y la demolición de la poesía sandinista". *Revista Salina* Facultat de Lletres, Universitat Rovira i Virgili, Tarragona, Spain, 17 (Nov. 2003): 187–92.

——. "Esta mujer que explora los espejos: El desdoblamiento erótico en *Cantos de Ifigenia* de Michele Najlis". In Oralia Preble-Niemi (ed.), *Afrodita en el trópico: amor y erotismo en las obras de escritoras centroamericanas*. Potomac, MD: Scripta Humanistica, 1999, pp. 169–82.

Martin, Victoria. "The Perils of Trailblazing: Contemporary Mystic Michele Najlis". In *International Poetry Review*, University of North Carolina, Greensboro, NC, Fall 1999.

Randall, Margaret. *Sandino's Daughter Revisited: Feminism in Nicaragua*. Chapel Hill, NC: Rutgers University Press, 1994.

NARANJO, CARMEN

Carmen Naranjo (b. 1928), a prolific novelist, short story writer and a poet is considered one of the most prominent women writers in Costa Rica. She has presented her political and feminist ideas to a large number of readers in all the Spanish American countries. Several of her short stories have been translated into English, Greek and Hebrew.

Carmen Naranjo was born in Cartago, Costa Rica, and currently resides in Alajuela, near San José, the capital of Costa Rica. Her father, Sebastián Naranjo Prida, came from the Canary Islands while her mother, Caridad Coto Troyo, was from a family of Sephardic origin which had immigrated to Costa Rica in the sixteenth century. Carmen was the youngest of four children and her father introduced her and her brothers to the works of Spanish writers such as Lope de Vega, Cervantes, Calderón de la Barca and Miguel de Unamuno when they were only teenagers.

Alter graduating from Colegio Superior de Señoritas in San José, Naranjo enrolled at the University of Costa Rica and was awarded her degree in Spanish philology. She pursued her postgraduate studies at La Universidad Autónoma de México in Mexico City and spent a year at the University of Iowa with the International writing Program. Naranjo was one of the first women in Costa Rica to hold important positions in public administration at both a national and international level. She served as an assistant to the Administrative Director of Social Security in Costa Rica and an assistant to the Director of the Costa Rica Institute of Electricity. She was the Ambassador to Israel from 1972 to 1974 and then to India from 1974 to 1976. She was the Director of Central American University Press and a Director of the Costa Rican Museum of Arts. She was Minister of Culture, Youth and Sport between 1978–82 when she established the National Theatre Company, the National Symphonic Orchestra, the Publishing House of Costa Rica and the College of Costa Rica. She was a managing director of Central American University Publishing House (EDUCA) and served as Costa Rica's UNICEF representative in Guatemala, El Salvador, Dominican Republic and Mexico. Currently she is a member of the Costa Rican Academy of Language.

Although Naranjo has written seven books of poetry, she is better known for her technically innovative prose. Since 1962 she has published four books containing thirty-seven short stories, eight novels, four books of essays, and has written over two hundred journalistic articles. Naranjo writes on diverse subjects covering the spectrum of literature, art, women's issues, political problems, mass communication, tourism, and social and economic problems. She has been the recipient of literary awards in Costa Rica including el Premio Nacional Magón de la Cultura (1986); for *Ondina* (Premio EDUCA in 1982) even before the story was published in 1985; for *Diario de una multitud* (Premio EDUCA in 1974), for her short story *Hoy es un largo día* (El Premio Editorial Costa Rica in1973), for *Los perros no ladraron* (Premio de Aquileo J. Echeverría in 1966).The University of Santo Domingo in the Dominican Republic awarded Naranjo the degree of doctor honoris causa in 1991 and in 1996 the Chilean government presented her with the Gabriela Mistral medal awarded in honour of the Chilean Nobel Prize winner.

Major Themes in Naranjo's Essays

In her essays Naranjo writes about the importance of the understanding of culture and about human concerns. She aims at promoting gender equality and social liberation. Naranjo's style is simple, direct and accessible. In *Mujer y cultura* (1989, Woman and Culture), Naranjo published approximately forty essays divided into four groups: "Cultural Myths about Women," "Women and Circumstance," "Famous Women," and "Feminism and Liberation". In them she analyzes the lives and values of the mythological and literary figures from the Western world; she encourages women in Costa Rica to obtain a better education and to develop their potential as human beings. She also supplies practical information on a variety of everyday topics such as health, housing, family, domestic violence and the services available to women. Naranjo is part of the literary feminist awakening in Costa Rica and defines feminism as a consciousness-raising and humanistic endeavour, emphasizing the eradication of inequality and discrimination for all people. She states that an awareness of woman's real value as "provider of life, peace and justice" must replace the perception of her as pure, weak, incapable, a second-class citizen whose value is measured by her capacity to serve.

Major Themes in her Short Stories

In three volumes of short stories *Hoy es un largo día* (1974, Today is a Long Day) *Ondina* (1983) and *Nunca hubo alguna vez* (1984, Once upon Never), for Naranjo, marginality is a recurring topic. The first woman protagonist appears in *Hoy es un largo día* where she is excluded from political, social and economic decisions, which in turn marginalize her from society. *Nunca hubo una vez*, a story from which her third collection derives its name, is narrated from the perspective of children who live joyfully for the moment, unaware that tomorrow may bring different experiences, and the pre-adolescents who begin to understand the complexity of life when "behind one reality there can be another".

Major Novels and Poetry

Naranjo's major themes as explored both in her novels and her poetic works are the expression of three elements: her knowledge of bureaucracy, corruption in public service and her compassion for humanity. She also writes about human isolation and frustration in a materialistic and consumer driven society while experimenting with narrative perspective: for example, one work is based on a dialogue between several indefinable first person narrators (as in a film), another on anonymous voices that create a collective stream of consciousness, representatives of individuals that make up society, and yet another is written with a pointillist technique borrowed from impressionist painting.

In Naranjo's first novel *Los perros no ladraron* (1966, The Dogs Didn't Bark), her character, the nameless bureaucrat subservient to the system leads an uneventful everyday life. The monotony of his daily routine unfolds before the reader's eyes like a film. His companions at work are selfish individuals who have no qualms about destroying their colleagues' lives for their own self-advancement and achievements. His awakening to the awareness of being trapped in the system highlights the helplessness of the individual. *Dario de una multitud* (1974, Diary of a Multitude) consists of the voices of many, a collage of voices, absorbed by the voices of the crowd who are without any motivation to live, are passive in their existence and are the spokesmen for today's humanity. There are also fragments that represent the dominant attitudes of men. Women are dependent upon men who use them as sexual objects or as vehicles to achieve their own means. The writer strongly criticizes the middle class which behaves in an irresponsible way and receives easy money without recognizing the needs of the less privileged.

In *Camino al mediodía* (1968, On the Way to Noon), the past is revealed from the perspective of the present. The unnamed narrator reminisces after hearing about the death of his friend Eduardo Campos Arguello, who became a millionaire through the continuation of the immoral practices of his father, his rich wife and her family ties. He "buys" lovers and lives a meaningless existence. However, when Arguello becomes bankrupt and is abandoned by his family, he commits suicide. The novel centres on his funeral and the funeral procession that arrives at the cemetery at noon, hence the title. The readers learn about the monotony, hypocrisy and lack of goals in Arguello's life. The boundaries between time (past/present) and space (real/unreal) are blurred and signify the condition of each and everyone's life.

Naranjo wrote the novel *Memorias de un hombre palabras* (Memories of a Wordsmith) in 1968. The protagonist, an anonymous individual, reminisces about his life. He was born into the middle class but his father left his family when he was a child; his mother did not show him affection or love and eventually rejected him; as a result, he is socially degraded, passive and does not possess a will to change his destiny. However, when he "hits the bottom" he discovers solidarity, human bonds with other human beings belonging to the marginal community that he is now part of.

In a lyrical novel, *Responso por el niño Juan Manuel* (1971, Requiem for a Child Juan Manuel), Naranjo again uses an unnamed narrator who seeks to verify the existence of a 15-year-old boy who died in an accident. Through the conversations of four friends, the reader realizes that the boy is in fact the result of the imagination of one of the speakers. Furthermore, the fictional Juan Manuel has himself created an imaginary friend. At his young age he experienced love but also loneliness and helplessness.

In *Sobrepunto* (1985, Overpoint), Naranjo's only longer work with a female protagonist, Olga is the focus of attention in the memory and diary of her male friend—Yo (I). The narrator develops the story of Olga, who represents the voice of all women in Latin America expected to play a role determined by male values and rules. Olga's mother was excluded from the upper middle class she belonged to, because she became an alcoholic and prostitute. Olga rejects the norms of the society in which she lives. Her marriage fails; she loses her children, is driven to the world of drugs and ultimately commits suicide. The "machista" attitude of Latin American men deprives Olga of her freedom and rights.

In *Homenaje a Don Nadie* (1981, Homage to Mr. Nobody), a book of poems, Naranjo rejects the distinction between gender constructions; Don Nadie is the synonym of any universal human being, powerless, ignored, forgotten by the middle and ruling classes, denied any dignity. Naranjo suggests that all human beings suffer and belong to the category of Don Nadie.

The notion of the essential equality of all human beings, often ignored in Latin America, prevails in Naranjo's prose. Her characters try to reach out to others but they fail as they are all unable to determine their own identity. According to *Misa*, God is insensitive to human suffering. All human beings suffer pain and isolation, the commonality of human experience. They are orphans as they walk towards nothingness because "the great creator is asleep" in *Misa a oscuras* (1967, Mass in the Dark).

Naranjo continues writing; her last novel *Más allá del Parismina* (Beyond Parismina) which was written in 2004, is a symbolic name for the search of the meaning of life. The violent river in Costa Rica that flows through the village of Parismina is like an encounter with death.

Carmen Naranjo remains one of the most successful writers in Costa Rica and she has received a degree of international acclaim, mostly in the United States of America. All the critical literature on Naranjo places her works firmly in the context of Costa Rican women's literature

Among the most comprehensive works on Naranjo's fiction are critical studies by Alfonso Chase, Luz Martínez, Evelyn Picón Garfield, Janet Gold, Linda Britt, Patricia Rubio, Arlene Schrade and Nelson Ardis.

ANNA HAMLING

Selected Works

Canción de la ternura. San José: Ediciones Elite de Lilia Ramos, 1964.
Los perros no ladraron. San José: Editorial Costa Rica, 1966.
Misa a oscuras. San José: Editorial Costa Rica, 1967.
Camino al mediodía. San José: Editorial Costa Rica, 1968.
Memorias de un hombre palabras. San José: Editorial Costa Rica, 1968.
Responso por el niño Juan Manuel. San José: Editorial Conciencia Nueva, 1971.
Idioma de invierno. San José: Editorial Conciencia Nuevo, 1971.
Diario de una multitud. San José: Editorial Universitaria Centroamericana, 1974.
Hoy es un largo día. San José: Editorial de Costa Rica, 1974.
Homenaje a don Nadie. San José: Editorial Costa Rica, 1981.
Mi guerrilla. San José: Editorial Universitaria Centroamericana, 1984
Nunca hubo alguna vez. San José: Editorial Universidad Estatal a Distancia, 1984.
Sobrepunto. San José: Editorial Universitaria Centroamericana, 1985
Otro rumbo para la rumba. San José: Editorial Universitaria Centroamericana, 1989
El caso 117,720. San José: Editorial de Costa Rica, 1989.
Ventanas y asombros. San José: Editorial Universitaria Centroamericana, 1990.
En partes. San José: Farben Grupo Editorial Norma, 1994.
Los poetas también se mueren. San José: Editorial Tecnológica de Costa Rica, 1994.
Esta tierra redonda y plana. Madrid: Ediciones Torremozas, 2001.
Los girasoles perdidos. Editorial Osada, 2003.
Más allá del Parismina. San José: Uruk Editores, 2004.

Translations of Naranjo's Works

Britt, Linda. *Nunco hubo alguna vez* (There never was a Once upon a Time) Pittsburgh, PA: Latin American Literary Review Press, 1989.
"Listen". *Mundos Artium* 7(1) (1975): 87.
Mathieu, Corina. "The Flowery Trick;" "The Journey of Journeys;" trans. Marie J. Panico; "Inventory of a Recluse," trans. Mary Sue Listerman. *Five Women Writers of Costa Rica*. Ed. Victoria Urbano. Beaumont, TX: Asociación de Literatura Femenina Hispánica, 1976, pp. 3–18.
Santos, Rosario. *And we sold the rain: Contemporary Fiction from Central America*. New York: Seven Stories Press, 1996.

References and Further Reading

Chase, Alfonso. *Narrativa contemporánea de Costa Rica*. San José: Ministerio de Cultura, Juventud y Deportes, 1975, pp. 124–5, 127–8.
Helmuth, Charlene. "Carmen Naranjo". *Hispamérica: Revista de la Literatura* 25(74) 1996: 47–56
Lagos, Ramiro. "Mujeres poetas de Hispanoamérica: Movimiento, surgencia e insurgencia". Bogotá: Ediciones Tercer Mundo, 1986, pp. 83–4.
Martínez, Luz Ivette. *Carmen Naranjo y la narrativa femenina en Costa Rica*. San José: Editorial Costarricense, 1987.
Miranda Hevia, Alicia. "Introducción a la obra novelesca de Carmen Naranjo". *Cahiers du Monde de Hispanique et Luso-Bresilien* 36 (1981): 121–9.
Minc, Rose and Méndez-Faith, Teresa. "Conversando con Carmen Naranjo". *Revista Iberoamericana* 132–3 (June–Dec. 1985): 507–10.
Nelson, Adris L. "Carmen Naranjo and Costa Rican culture". In Doris Meyer (ed.), *Reinterpreting the Spanish American Essay: Women Writers of the 19th and 20th Centuries*. Austin, TX: University of Texas Press, 1995, pp. 177–87.
Picón Garfield, Evelyn. "La luminosa cegura de sus días: los cuentos 'humanos' de Carmen Naranjo". *Revista Iberoamericana* 138–9 (Jan.–June 1987): 287–301.
Rubio, Patricia. "Carmen Naranjo". In Diane E. Marting (ed.), *Spanish American Women Writers. A Bio-Bibliographical Source* Book. New York: Greenwood Press, 1990, pp. 350–60.
Russotto, Márgara. "Propuestas de la cultura: Visiones de Costa Rica en las escritoras de la modernidad centroamericana (Yolanda Oreamuno, Eunice Odio, Carmen Naranjo)". *Revista Iberoamericana* (71–210) (2005): 177–88.
Sandoval de Fonseca, Virginia. *Resumen de la literatura costarricense*. San José, PR: Editorial Costa Rica, 1978, pp. 39–52.
Vargas, Aura R. "*Los perros no ladraron*: una novedad técnica en la novelística Costarricense". *Kāñina* (July–Dec, 1977): 33–6.

NAVA Y SAAVEDRA, JERÓNIMA

Although not a renowned Colonial Spanish American cloistered woman from the New Kingdom of Granada like her counterpart Sor Francisca Josefa de Castillo y Guevara, Jerónima Nava y Saavedra (1669–1727), her worldly name, wrote a spiritual autobiography as well. For a long time, this manuscript was kept at the Biblioteca Nacional de Colombia in the Rare Books section while another faithful copy of this manuscript, but in a different version, is stored at the Convent of Poor Clares in Bogotá. According to Don Juan de Olmos y Zapiaín, her confessor and priest of the Metropolitan Saint Church in Bogotá, Nava y Saavedra was born in Tocaima, near Bogotá, Colombia, on April 25, 1669. She was the legitimate daughter of Juan de Nava and Doña Juana de Saavedra, who passed away after having given birth to her. Along with her sister, she was raised by her father and three aunts until Juan de Nava had to leave the city. At the age of 16, she entered the convent and took the profession of faith as Jerónima del Espíritu Santo in 1683 at the Monastery of the Poor Clares. At the convent she had different positions, from a lowly convent gate attendant to a groceries manager and on to nurse, choir vicar, and finally Abbess. For ten years, she suffered from anguish. Don Juan de Olmos praises her as an experienced woman, with a high intellect, who scrutinized theology very profoundly. From Don Juan de Olmos we learn that Nava y Saavedra passed away at the age of 58 on May 29, 1727. An artist's presentation of her face, which remained peaceful and calm even in death was kept and revered.

Jerónima Nava y Saavedra as a Writer

She wrote a spiritual autobiography which encompasses twenty years of her religious life and this record, recently published by the Colombian literary critic Ángela Inés Robledo, is an important contribution to the feminine convent literature which, despite its historical importance, remained in relative obscurity until quite recently. Nineteenth-century writers and literary critics such as José María Vergara y Vergara and Antonio Gómez Restrepo have cited Nava y Saavedra's spiritual account, and yet her autobiography remained inexplicably unexplored until now. Like many other spiritual autobiographies written by women, *Autobiografía de una monja venerable. Jerónima Nava y Saavedra (1669–1727)* proves that feminine convent writing was a unique way for a woman to speak out in a public arena normally allowed only to the male priesthood. In her confession, Jerónima del Espíritu Santo employs rhetorical and discursive strategies as she reveals her desires, dreams, visions, and inner conflicts. Expressions of self-deprecation, self-humiliation, and rapture are found all over her spiritual autobiography and by using a style of spontaneity and loving tendency, Nava y Saavedra establishes her own view and thoughts. Situated outside of the traditional discourse of the dominant male religious figure, she sought to establish a feminine voice of authority by characterizing her writing as a flow of discursive negotiations between her confessor and herself.

Hermeneutics of Her Work: the Body

By assigning a strong visionary perspective to her work, Jerónima del Espíritu's writing allows her access to power. Even though she possesses a strong biblical and theological foundation, the nun utilizes an abstract and symbolic language which subverts the male hierarchy. As Betty Osorio has indicated, Nava y Saavedra's subversion is established in the assessment of the colonial subject, projected first in the imagination, fulfilled through the body and last remembered in the act of writing (2001: 78). Within these complex spaces, Jerónima del Espíritu Santo discovers new ways of ritualizing the subversion so that it penetrates the discourse surreptitiously through expressions of self-deprecation and self-humiliation. Images of her own crucified and fragmented body are reminiscent of the passion and crucifixion of Christ. Both Jerónima Nava y Saavedra and Christ become one, and from this oneness, she evokes and expresses the realization of her vindication, emotions, and feelings. The fragmentation of her body marks the point of departure from the Christ analogy, with Jerónima's body being cursed by illness, sin, and despair. Since the reader can interpret Jerónima's body as the recipient of the enemy's wrath (allowed by God as in the Book of Job), she takes advantage of the opportunity to present herself as the suffering servant of God united in and within him. By swallowing the Eucharist, she feels as if Christ were inside her body—as Ibsen points out—and thereby creates a sacred Oneness. Despite the male priesthood's rejection of her as a Servant of God, she demonstrates her search for inner identity inscribed into a love discourse as explained by Robledo. Nava y Saavedra's self-images of being nursed by the Virgin Mary and her kinship with Jesus bring her nearer to God's embrace.

On the other hand, love discourse is also reflected in the irrationality of her being loved by and offering love to Jesus. Jerónima Nava y Saavedra shows herself as a loving and tender person to Jesus the man. Jesus descended into her thoughts, life and intellect; transforming himself for her, from the divine to the human. The latter reaffirms the close relationship of love held by a colonial Spanish American nun and her lover, Jesus.

Literary Hermeneutics of Her Work: Visions and Imaginary World.

Innocent sheep, fierce bears, poisonous snakes, ferocious wolves, among other wild animals make up part of this colonial nun's imaginary world. On the same visionary level, handsome youths, erotic imagery, damned people, and demons characterize the spiritual contemplation and visionary world influenced by the New Kingdom of Granada's historical context. The *Autobiografía de una monja venerable. Jerónima Nava y Saavedra (1669–1727)* can be described as an emblematic colonial text. The innumerable visions and dreams demonstrate Nava y Saavedra's main interests as her discourse presented as offered to her confessor, unfolds. Through her visionary world, this woman writer affirms a discourse that echoes the post-tridentine creed seeking a sexual identity denied by the Catholic Orthodoxy. Unlike the sexual violence experienced by her counterpart Mother Castillo, also from the New Kingdom of Granada, Jerónima del Espíritu Santo in her dreams and visions enjoyed the erotic bonding with young men, one of whom was Jesus. Since hers is a "discourse of love" as Robledo states, this divine and sexual affection could only be felt, without moral conflict, in Christ's arms. By having erotic bonding with the figure of Christ, Jerónima Nava y Saavedra remained pure and immaculate. This closeness to

Christ permits Jerónima to enjoy his favors, as she presents her discourse on self-importance and—as Ibsen has indicated—on self-assurance.

Through Jerónima Nava y Saavedra's writings the reader can grasp the intellectual movements in the late Spanish American Colonial period in the New Kingdom of Granada in which writing was understood as a religious process where the faith was in an ongoing conflict with the individual and vice versa. Rationality was no longer the reality, but a mixture of imagery and visions deeply influenced by the historical events shaping her society. The New Kingdom of Granada, one of the most important viceroyalties in the Americas, is presented, though Jerónima's startling view, as a world of sensations, emotions, and love.

ALEXANDER STEFFANELL

Selected Works

Autobiografía de una monja venerable: Jerónima Nava y Saavedra (1669–1727). Ed. Ángela Inés Robledo. Cali: Universidad del Valle, 1994.

References and Further Reading

Ibsen, Kristine. *Women's Spiritual Autobiography in Colonial Spanish America*. Gainesville, FL: University of Florida Press, 1999.

McKnight, Kathryn Joy. *The Mystic of Tunja: The Writings of Madre Castillo, 1671–1742*. Amherst, MA: University of Massachusetts Press, 1997.

Osorio, Betty. "La escritura religiosa de Jerónima Nava y Saavedra: juego entre afirmación y obediencia". *Cuadernos de literatura* 6(12) (2001): 71–81.

Robledo, Ángela Inés (ed.) *Autobiografía de una monja venerable: Jerónima Nava y Saavedra (1669–1727)*. Cali: Universidad del Valle, 1994.

——. "La autobiografía espiritual de Jerónima Nava y Saavedra: historia de un yo fragmentado". *Cuadernos de literatura* 6(12) (2001): 81–90.

NAVAU, FLAVIA COMPANY

Flavia Company Navau was born in Buenos Aires, Argentina in 1963. She currently lives in Spain, where she has resided since she was 10 years old. She obtained a degree in Hispanic Philology in 1986. Navau is best known for her fictional work, but she also translates, publishes book reviews, and has written weekly columns for newspapers such as *El Periódico de Cataluña*.

Some of her most acclaimed novels include *Dame placer* (1999), *Melalcor* (2000), and *Género de punto* (2002). Her most recent works include *L'illa animal* (2002) and *El missatge secret* (2004), both of which were written in Catalan and her latest novel is *Negoci rodó*, which was published in 2005. Her earlier fictional work includes: *Querida Nélida* (1988); *Fuga y contrapuntos* (1989); *Círculos en acíbar* (1992); and *Saurios en asfalto* (1997). Her literary activity, however, is not limited to writing books or articles. Navau actively participates in conferences and in public forums, and she contributes to various journals such as *La Vanguardia, Nou Diari, Diario 16, Diari de Tarragona,* Ayui, and *Quimera*.

In her first novel, *Querida Nélida*, Navau explores universal themes such as freedom, memory, love, passion, and the paradigm that characterizes everyday life. She focuses on a series of problems and anxieties in this text that surface in her later work.

The novel, *Luz de Hielo* (1998) narrates the story of a double obsession. This duality is demonstrated through the often difficult conflicts people face when they confront their past and how this relates to the realities of the present. In the text, this confrontation results in an obsessive, passionate relationship between a man and a woman that borders on both pleasure and pain, love and hate, and death and an unbearable life. These two characters, however, never see, touch, or find each other, and in the end only share in the desiring of the idea of the other. Their confessions, told through monologues, construct deep psychological conflict in which their thoughts, dreams, and words anticipate tragedy. *Luz de Hielo* creates a claustrophobic situation where both main characters, hungry for love, are trapped and thus reduced to a state of madness because they lack the tools of communication, allowing loneliness to permeate their lives and the rest of the narrative.

In *Melalcor*, Navau deals with love without sex and sex without love. She playfully surprises the reader with memories and various reflections that seem to appear in the future; however, they are left ambiguous. A famous proverb states that one knows someone by the company one keeps. For Navau, and this novel, this is especially true in relation to sex and which of the two sexes one finds to be attractive. Through this book she asks the reader, is it only men or women that they find attractive, or both? She also offers the idea of attraction to that which is neither masculine nor feminine, man nor woman, and instead, proposes attraction to androgynous beings.

It is because of these reasons that *Melalcor* has been very successful. The novel focuses on sexless, winged beings that exist without the need to cover or hide the physical features that define their sexuality. *Melalcor* uses the techniques of magical realism in conjunction with the dream-like influences of Julio Cortázar. The reader is never quite sure if the narrative is a "true story" or if it is simply imagined. One reading of the text can be interpreted to be something that really happens, or the text could be read to be a desire that the protagonist of the novel projects. For instance, the protagonist states that Mel misses him/her. While this may be true, Navau structures this language so that the reader could interpret it to be a feeling this winged being wants to experience because of his/her loss. With Mel gone, the protagonist can state that Mel misses him/her as Mel is not there to verify or correct that statement.

After the surprising success of *Melalcor* and *Dame Placer*, which explores feminine homosexuality, Navau chose to write on other topics. Her concern was focused on demonstrating the exterior body as unimportant. She did this by highlighting the soul, the interior of the person as what really matters more than the physical self. Furthermore, through the way in which her stories are narrated, she is able to introduce discussions on various subjects including gender and its intersection with sexuality. The sex scenes in *Melalcor* are just as edgy as those that some critics thought are too explicit in *Dame Placer*, where some scenes border on the pornographic. Regardless of this possibly offensive material, many readers identified with the text because, as the author noted, of the similarity between the sexuality of men and women.

Género de punto, published in 2002, is a collection of short stories that resembles one of Company's earlier collections, *Viajes subterráneos*. The more recent collection differs from the earlier work in a fundamental way. Following each of the nineteen narratives is a letter that comments, contradicts, or completes the content of the story. In these, some characters describe their impressions of certain events that have happened in their lives while others write as a way to appeal to the reader, meanwhile some letters function as a way of providing the reader with a clue to some key aspect of another story within the collection. In addition to the movement between the real and fictional, *Género de punto* offers a variety of characters and themes that give depth to the narrative. Men and women of different social classes populate the text's pages. Among other differences between these figures are the various levels of education, which is a noticeable difference between characters.

Navau's work investigates the physical as well as the non-physical aspects such as gender, sexuality, the inner self, which appeal to her readers as these are topics in need of genuine investigation. She does not simply write about these topics because they are interesting, instead it is evident through her writing that she is actively working with and defining the unique issues these topics present. While Navau works to resolve these issues for herself and on her own terms she does not restrain her readers' conclusions by including her own; instead, her narratives are open to interpretation, allowing multiple readings.

SYLVIA VERONICA MORIN

Selected Works

Querida Nélida. Barcelona: Montesinos Editor, S.A., 1987.
Fuga y contrapuntos. Barcelona: Montesinos Editor, S.A., 1989.
Círculos en acíbar. Barcelona: Montesinos Editor, S.A., 1992.
Viatges subterranis. Tarragona: El Mèdol, Edicions, 1993.
Retrat de la Ràpita. Tarragona: Ayuntamiento de Sant Carles de la Ràpita, 1996.
Saurios en el asfalto. Barcelona: Muchnik Editores, S.A., 1997.
Viajes subterráneos. Vitoria: Bassarai Ediciones, 1997.
Luz de hielo. Vitoria: Bassarai Ediciones, 1998.
Ni tu, ni jo, ni ningú. Barcelona: Península. Edicions 62, 1998.
Dame Placer. Barcelona: Emecé Editores España, S.A., 1999.
Melalcor. Barcelona: Edicions 62 S.A., 2000.
El llibre màgic. Barcelona: Cruïlla, 2001.
Género de punto. Barcelona: El Aleph, 2002.
L'illa animal. Barcelona: Cruïlla, 2002.
El missatge secret. Barcelona: Cruïlla, 2004.

Further Reading

Díaz-Diocaretz, Myriam and Zavala, Iris M. *Breve historia de la literature española en lengua castellana*. Madrid: Anthropos, 1993.

Cuevas García, Cristóbal, Enrique, Baena and Torres, Ana María Gómez (eds) *Escribir mujer, narradoras españolas hoy*. Málaga: Publicaciones del Congreso de Literatura Española Contemporánea, 2000.

"Flavia Company". In escritoras.com [en línea]. 1 Jan. 1970 (accessed: 17 Nov. 2006). http://www.escritoras.com/escritoras/escritora.php?i=161

Glenn, Kathleen Mary. *Women's Narrative and Film in 20th Century Spain*. New York: Routledge, 2002.

Martin Gaite, Carmen. *Desde la ventana: enfoque femenino de la literature española*. Madrid: Espasa Calpe, 1987.

Nichols, Geraldine Cleary. *Des/cifrar la diferencia: narrativa femenina de la España contemporánea*. Madrid: Siglo Veintiuno de España Editores, 1992.

Scarlett, Elizabeth A. *Under Construction: The Body in Spanish novels*. Charlottesville, VA: University Press of Virginia, 1994.

Vollendor, Lisa. *Literatura y feminismo en España, S. XV-XXI*. Barcelona: Icaria Editoria, 2005.

NEGRONI, MARÍA

Born in Rosario, Argentina in 1951, María Negroni is a writer, poet, essayist, translator and professor. After studying in Argentina, she enrolled at Columbia University and received her Master of Arts in Latin American Literature in 1987. Professor Negroni was awarded the degree of Doctor of Philosophy in 1994 after having written a dissertation entitled, "El testigo lúcido. Estudio sobre los textos en prosa de Alejandra Pizarnik". Since 1998, she has divided her time between her teaching duties as professor of Latin American Literature and Creative Writing at Sarah Lawrence College in New York, and Buenos Aires, where she participates in the Instituto de Literatura Hispanoamericana.

In addition to her academic duties, Maria Negroni is the editor of various journals. She is the director of *Abyssinia*, a poetry magazine published in Buenos Aires. She is also on the editorial board of *Auna*, an electronic poetry magazine, as well as spearheading *Globalnet de mujeres*, a monthly electronic publication which focuses on the activities and initiatives for women worldwide. Negroni is a member of the Fundación Proyecto al Sur, which is a group of psychoanalysts, critics, artists and academicians who collaborate to produce their works.

Works

Her work contains both creative and critical writings. Creatively she has published eight books of poetry, three of which have been translated into English and one into French, and one novel. Critically, she has written two books of essays and over fifty articles. *Cuidad gótica*, Negroni's first book of essays, is divided into two sections. The first focuses on a variety of concerns among them the writer's desire to create poetry, life in New York City, pop culture, and preconceived notions about Latin America. The second section includes essays written about twentieth-century North American poets. In *Museo negro*, the critical essays explore different topics pertaining to Gothic literature from the figure of the mythical vampire to frequently used metaphors. She has translated the poetry of Louise Labé, Charles Simic, H.D., and Elizabeth Bishop among others. Negroni has also translated a series of children's books into Spanish such as *Amos y Boris* by William Steig, *La verdadera historia de los tres cerditos* by Jon Scieszka, *El tesoro* by Uri Shulevitz, and *Tontimundo y el barco volador* by Arthur Ransome.

Once, Negroni described her writing process as a result of personal experience:

> Since I started writing poetry, I seemed to be searching for a density, for condensation. It was not until a few

> years ago that I connected my rejection of the loose and anecdotal mode with the fact that my mother has always suffered from asthma. The possibility for long speech is reduced when you don't have enough air. Was I repeating ... her voice? ... There is also the literary tradition in my country. An extreme consciousness of language, a certain mistrust of rhetoric and a parsimonious intensity of meaning have imbued (for obvious political reasons) the poetry written by the generation of poets who began to write during the military dictatorship that governed Argentina from 1976 to 1983.
>
> ("Working Notes". www.scc.rutgers.edu/however/print_archive/mn2notes.html)

Various critics have pointed to Pizarnik and Borges as writers who have had an influence on this poet's literary production. One cannot underestimate the impulse that being exiled has provided this poet as it seems to be the source of her emotive outpouring. Chavez-Silverman feels that the leitmotif that is frequently present in Negroni's writing is sadness, which constitutes the impulse of the poetic creation (2001: 53). One of the persistent metaphors in Negroni's work is that of the voyage, since the poet views it as an experience which resembles the creative process (Dreyfus 2004: 133).

In her initial poetic works, *De tanto desolar, Per/Canta,* and *La jaula bajo el trapo,* her brief poems hold dense meaning and reveal the preoccupations that will become central to her later poetry. In these works, Negroni tries to engage the reader to go beyond easily identifiable topics and rote linguistic combinations. Hers is a poetry filled with ellipses, pauses, disjunctions, topographical dislocations, and at times surrealistic images that are difficult to understand for a reader expecting typical poetic convention. *Night Journey* consists of sixty-two poems composed in her dense lyric prose. The voyage begins with the oneiric experience which adopts surrealistic tones achieved through the displacement of objects. Ultimately the quest leads to the realization that the act of writing is intimately linked to love and memories. *Islandia* is a collection of sixty-two poems which narrate dreams of tenth-century Scandinavian heroes who rebel against the oppressive forces that have exiled them. Metaphorically, this exile could parallel the poet's own exile and the feelings of solitude which she has been sublimating. In *Islandia* and the works that follow, Negroni's prosified poetry shows maturity in more developed and cohesive imagery and themes. The flowing prose of her only novel, *El sueño de Ursula* reveals a poetic influence as well as revisiting many of the preoccupations found in her poetry.

Awards and Honors

The high regard in which Negroni's works are held has led to many awards and distinctions. She has received several scholarships to participate in various creative writing workshops in France, Italy and Argentina. She has been invited to give conferences on poetry in Canada, Holland, Ireland and England. She was the writer in residence at the *Espace Van Gogh* in Arles, France in 1999, and at the American Academy in Rome in 2001. In 1994, she won the prestigious John Simon Guggenheim Foundation Fellowship for poetry and a Rockefeller Foundation Fellowship in 1998 and the Octavio Paz Poetry Fellowship 2001–2. Several of her poetry books have won prizes including: *Islandia* PEN Award for Best translation 2002, second prize in the Concurso Internacional de Poesía Qunito Centenario Murcia España, 1992, and finalist in the Premio International de Poesía Pérez Bonalde, Cara Rómulo Gallegos, Caracas 1995; *El viaje de la noche* received a special mention in the Premios Nacionales 1993–96 by the Secretaria de Cultura de la Nación; *Per/canta* second place in the Richard Wilbur Translation Prize in 1987 and second prize in the New York Institute of Latin American Writers in 1991. Her book of essays *Cuidad gótica* received a special mention in the Premios Nacionales 1995–98 by the Secretaría de Cultura de la Nación, and her novel *El sueño de Ursula* was a first runner-up in the Premio Planeta 1997.

VICKI KETZ

Selected Works

De tanto desolar. Buenos Aires: Libros de Tierra Firme, 1985.
Per/canta. Buenos Aires: Libros de Tierra Firme, 1989.
La jaula bajo el trapo. Buenos Aires: Libros de Tierra Firme, 1991. (2nd edition Santiago de Chile: Editorial Cuarto Propio, 1999).
Ciudad gótica. Buenos Aires: Ediciones bajo la Luna Nueva, 1994.
Islandia. Caracas: Monte Avila Editores, 1994. (trans. Anne Twitty, Station Hill Press, 2001).
El viaje de la noche. Barcelona: Editorial Lumen, 1994. (Trans. Anne Twitty. Princeton, NJ: Princeton University Press, 2002).
Translator. *Helena en Egipto* by H.D. Caracas: Ediciones Angria, 1994.
Translator. *Hierba a la luna y otros poemas* by Valentine Penrose. Caracas: Ediciones Angria, 1995.
Translator. *Lo ancangélico* by Georges Bataille. Caracas: Fundarte, 1995.
El sueño de Ursula. Buenos Aires: Seix-Barral Bibiloteca Breve, 1998.
Translator. *Sonetos* by Louise Labé. Barcelona: Editorial Lumen, 1998.
Museo Negro. Buenos Aires: Grupo Editorial Norma, 1999.
Translator. *Totemismo y otros poemas* by Charles Simic. Córdoba: Alción, 2000.
Diario extranjero. Caracas: La Pequeña Venecia, 2001. (Translated into French by François Garnier. St Nazaire: Maison des Ecrivains Etrangers, 2001.)
Co-editor. *Morada imposible* by Susana Thénon. Buenos Aires: Ediciones Corregidor, 2001.
Camera delle Meraviglie. Italia: Quaderni della Valle, 2002.
La ineptitud. Córdoba: Editorial Alción, 2002.
Co-editor. *Maldad de escribir: 9 poetas latinamericanas del siglo XX*. Montblanc, Tarragona: Igitur Ediciones, 2003.

Articles

"Estanterías derruidas". *Diario de Poesía*. Buenos Aires, 1986.
"Carmen Ollé: los besos de la cintura para abajo". *Revista Viva* Lima, 1987.
"Cultura latinoamericana en Nueva York: un castigo del cielo". *Diario de Poesía*. Buenos Aires, 1987, p. 31.
"New York: poesía y efectos especiales". *Diario de Poesía*. Buenos Aires, 1987.
"Galway Kinnell, un poeta en la adversidad". *Periódico de Poesía*. México, 1989.
"David Ignatow: una desobediencia a dos puntas". *Periódico de Poesía*. México: 1989.
"Laurie Anderson: la mise en scene de otro splendor". *Imagen*. Caracas, 1990.
"Cordiality and Conversation". *Belles Lettres – A Review of Books of Women*. Washington, DC, 1990.

"Judith, la hermana de Shakespeare". *Diario de Poesía.* Buenos Aires, 1990.
"Elizabeth Bishop: La pasión del exilio". *Feminaria.* Buenos Aires, 1991.
"Cage, el mundanal". *Diario de Poesía.* Buenos Aires, 1992.
"La ambición del suicidio". *Página 12.* Buenos Aires, 1992.
"Adrienne Rich: la ensayística de la passion". México: Milenio, 1992.
"H.D.: El prestigio de la épica". *Hora de Poesía.* Barcelona, 1992.
"Orfeo o el corazón de la noche". *Imagen.* Caracas,1992.
"Nota sobre Marianne Moore". *Hora de Poesía.* Barcelona, 1992.
"Sylvia Plath: Los bosques de mármol". *La Jornada Semanal.* 1993: 3–5.
"La dama de estas ruinas". *Feminaria.* Buenos Aires, 1993.
"Robert Duncan y el canto circular". *Página 12.* Buenos Aires, 1994.
"Valentine Penrose, la hermosa alucinada". *Imagen Latinoamericana.* Caracas, 1994.
"Adrienne Rich, Atlas de un mundo difícil". *Entorno.* Juárez: Universidad Autónoma de Ciudad Juárez, 1994: 12–17.
"Una esperanza llamada beats". *Imagen Latinoamericana.* Caracas, 1994; 28–9.
"Espectros de la gran manzana". *Primer Plano, Página 12.* Buenos Aires, 1994: 8.
"El caso Sexton". *La Jornada Semanal.* México, 1994: 4–5.
"Robert Duncan: El canto circular". *Primer Plano, Página 12.* Buenos Aires, 1994.
"Georges Bataille: Abjurar del lirismo". *Fundarte.* Caracas, 1995: 7–11
"Circulaciones del canto". *Revista Atlántica.* Cádiz, 1995: 51–9.
"Alejandra Pizarnik: Escritura de lo siniestro". *La Condición del Autor.* Buenos Aires, 1995.
"La Condesa Sangrienta: Notas sobre un problema musical". *Hispamérica.* Maryland, 1995.
"Georges Bataille: la poética del hereje". *Página 12.* Buenos Aires, 1995.
"La poeta en su salon". *Revista Atlántica.* 1996.
"El fantasma de la Opera: Memorias del subsuelo". *Espacios.* Buenos Aires, 1996.
"El castillo de Sabato". *El Cronista Cultural.* Buenos Aires, 1996.
"Un error sobre Paul Celan". *Diario Clarín.* Buenos Aires, 1996.
"Vlad". *Primer Plano, Página 12.* Buenos Aires, 1996.
"¿A quién le tema Victor Frankenstein?" *Magazín Literario.* n. 5, Buenos Aires, 1997.
"Un mundo difícil: las poetas norteamericanas de este siglo". *Magazín Literario.* Buenos Aires 1997.
"Ann Radcliffe: El monstruo femenino". *El desierto.* Buenos Aires, 1997.
"H.D., épica y prestigio". *Poesía y Poética.* México D.F.: Universidad Autónoma de México, 1997: 123–7.
"Charles Simic y Joseph Cornell: El arte del ladrón". *Tokonoma.* Buenos Aires, 1997.
"El testigo lúcido: gótica y melancolía en Alejandra Pizarnik". *Tokonoma.* Buenos Aires, 1997.
"Ann Radcliffe en La ciudad vampire". *Magazín Literario.* n. 4, Buenos Aires, 1997.
"La leyenda de Elizabeth Siddal". *Radar.* Buenos Aires, 1998.
"Baudelaire, Dracula y las flores del mal". *Abyssinia.* Buenos Aires, 1999.
"Primer plano de un infierno musical". *Abyssinia.* Buenos Aires, 1999.
"La invención del desierto". *Quimera.* Barcelona, 2000.
"Las cosas que digo son ciertas". *Quimera.* Barcelona, 2000.
"Jean Cocteau y el 'viaje de la luz.'" *Hablar de poesía.* Buenos Aires, 2001.
"La música vidente de Amelia Biagioni". *Abyssinia.* Buenos Aires, 2001.
"Los instrumentos filosóficos de Julia Margaret Cameron". *Abyssinia.* Buenos Aires, 2001.

References and Further Reading

Chavez-Silverman, Susana. "El género de la tristeza: dos poetas argentines en el después". *Latin American Literary Review* 29(57) (January/June 2001): 52–70.
Dreyfus, Mariela. "Mariela Dreyfus Interviews María Negroni". *Review: Literature and Arts of the Americas* 37(1) (2004): 132–8.
Reisz, Susana. *Voces sexuadas: género y poesía en Hispanoamérica.* Madrid: Asociación Española de Estudios Literarios Hispanoamericanos, 1996.

NISSÁN, ROSA

Rosa Nissán (b. 1939) is representative of a new generation of late twentieth-century Mexican women writers portraying the overlooked female perspective in contemporary society. Her three novels, two works of non-fiction (a combination of travel journalism and cultural assessment), and a book of short stories and essays, launched her into the limelight a few years before her sixtieth birthday. She had spent more than twenty years as wife, mother and homemaker before valiantly embarking on her own career in writing and videography. A woman of Sephardic Jewish heritage, she unveiled the lives and voices of this minority group in her semi-autobiographical novels, which quickly gained attention and soaring sales. Her first novel was immediately released as a major full-length film, with the same title as her novel, *Novia que te vea* (May I Soon See You as a Bride).

Nissán was born in 1939 in Mexico City, but her parents—who arrived as child immigrants—were born in Turkey and Persia. Their arrival in this hemisphere coincided with that of many other Jewish-heritage immigrants seeking stability and safety after the First World War. In Mexico, they clustered in small communities in Guadalajara, Monterrey, and Mexico City, creating their own schools and running shops or small businesses. Nissán grew up in such a sheltered environment, married young as her tradition requires, and squelched her creative desires until much later in life, once her five children were well on their way in school.

Novelist, Photographer and Essayist

At the age of 40, Nissán signed up for a writer's workshop, taught by the eminent Mexican writer Elena Poniatowska. Her stories and essays were based on her home life and the small world she knew, but she was unsure about publishing them. Nissán also started doing photography projects, home weddings and commemorative occasions, from which she created a business of creative audiovisuals. When she got divorced and struck out independently, she earned her living from her photography and videography projects. She credits Poniatowska with prodding her to finally release her writing in the form of semi-autobiographical novels. The first, *Novia que te vea*, is a classic coming-of-age story following the childhood and educational experience of a girl who is the oldest child of six siblings, who wants to be a journalist, while tradition requires that she marry by age 15. She stubbornly resists, but is finally married at age 17, and the novel ends with her honeymoon. The second novel, *Hisho que te nazca* (a Jewish saying for "May a son be born to you"), follows the same young woman through marriage, raising children, and observations of women around her, until she finds her way to a writing career.

Her narratives are fun to read, with humor, unique observations of her society, criticisms of mores and restrictions for women, and a loving tribute to Jewish heritage while also espousing Mexican nationalism. Her innovative writing strategy—memories, anecdotes, historical record (the 1940s, 1950s and 1960s) and social criticism—included dialogue by characters who speak in the Sephardic *Ladino* language, the Judeo-Spanish archaic tongue passed down for generations since the Jewish expulsion from Spain in 1492. Critic Ilán Stávans, who is also Jewish-Mexican, noted that it was the first time the Sephardic tongue had become an essential part of a Mexican novel. Nissán's protagonist gratefully acknowledges her mother's role in preserving this tongue, and other customs, while simultaneously criticizing a tradition that foresees for daughters only the role of wife and mother.

The latter premise, demonstrated by the frustration and resistance put up by the protagonist, surely contributed to Nissán's first two novels' popularity, because a patriarchal tradition rings true for all Mexican women—Jewish or not—who surely saw themselves in Nissan's protagonist/narrator. The release of the film based in part on the first novel, with Nissán's involvement in the screenplay, also brought attention to her work and some financial success. During the 1990s and into the new century, Nissán's commentaries and observations on urban Mexican society appeared regularly in newspaper and magazines.

Themes and Influences

As a published author, Nissán decided to travel and get to know a world outside her experience. She created a travel account from her first trip to Israel, where she openly criticizes the Jewish custom of segregating women, whether at weddings or in the temple, furthering her arguments on gender roles. Her travel around Mexico and a trip to India contribute to her subsequent books: another new travel account and cultural overview; and a delightful novel that furthers her creative strategies of humor, societal criticism, and use of contemporary Mexican lingo.

The novel, *Los viajes de mi cuerpo*, alternates the stories of two large women in their forties as they spend leisure time together, getting a meal, doing to dance clubs, or making day and overnight trips outside of Mexico City. The larger woman helps the protagonist over her shyness and shame about her size; the former is interested only in younger men, which surprises Lola, the main character, and even more so when she decides to marry a younger man by the end of the novel. Lola learns to feel respect for herself, but in the process analyzes the prejudice that her own friends and relatives exhibit in regard to her *mulato* boyfriend. This novel is one of the first to examine racism and prejudice in Mexican society, and it furthers Nissán's reputation as a solid, versatile writer. Nissán has written a movie script from this novel, and is working to arrange filming.

Modern Interpretations

As Yael Halevi-Wise has noted, Nissán's early characters construct their own Jewish reality in relation to a greater Mexican reality, and according to Darrell Lockhart, her use of Ladino as well as her depiction of Sephardic customs enriches Mexican society by demonstrating greater ethnic diversity. Dual cultural heritage is as significant for Mexican society as that symbolized by the fusion of the indigenous and Spanish in Mexican culture, as Manuel F. Medina has put it.

While she joins other contemporary Mexican women writers—both in her novels and travel accounts—in depicting gender roles and the lack of privilege for the female, Nissán reveals this status for Jewish as well as Mexican tradition. The legacy of her work is that it makes the Mexican and/or Sephardic woman no longer the "other" of this society, an image with no voice, but instead, an intelligent creature and integral member of Mexican life.

The only English translation of Nissán's work released so far is *Like a Bride and Like a Mother*, a combination of her first two novels in one volume. Although it loses the inclusion of Sephardic language (archaic Spanish), the book depicts for those who do not read Spanish the unique experience of this aspect of Mexican society.

Nissán now conducts her own writing workshops, often three or four per week, coaching and teaching the skills she so carefully developed. She is currently compiling a collection of her articles and commentaries published in newspapers and magazines over the past two decades, for a new book.

ELIZABETH COONROD MARTÍNEZ

Selected Works

Novia que te vea. México: Editorial Planeta, 1992.
Hisho que te nazca. México: Plaza y Janés, 1996.
Las Tierras Prometidas: Crónica de un viaje a Israel. México: Plaza y Janés, 1997.
No sólo para dormir es la noche. México: Nueva Imagen, 1999.
Like a Bride and Like a Mother (English translation of first two novels). Trans. Dick Gerdes. Albuquerque, NM: University of New Mexico Press, 2002.
Los viajes de mi cuerpo. México: Plaza y Janés, 2003.
Horizontes sagrados: Diarios de viaje. México: Nueva Imagen, 2003 (reissue of *Viaje a Israel*, with a second section *Viaje a la India*).
Novia que te vea. 35mm film. 104 min. Dir. Guita Schyfter. México: Conaculta-Imcine, 1993 (script by Nissán and Hugo Hiriart).

References and Further Reading

Ferreira, César. "Una nueva versión de la infancia en México: *Novia que te vea* de Rosa Nissán". *Revista de Literatura Mexicana Contemporánea* 4.9 (Oct. 1998–Jan. 1999): 66–70.
Gardner, Nathanial Eli. "'Como te ven, te tratan': The Projection of the Subaltern Character in Three Contemporary Mexican Novels". *Neophilologus* 87(1) (2003 Jan): 63–78.
Halevi-Wise, Yael. "Puente entre dos naciones: idioma e identidad sefardí en *Novia que te vea* e *Hisho que te nazca* de Rosa Nissán". *Hispania* 81(2) (1998 May): 269–77.
Lockhart, Darrell B. "Growing up Jewish in Mexico: Sabina Berman's *La bobe* and Rosa Nissán's *Novia que te vea*". In Kristine Ibsen (ed.), *The Other Mirror: Women's Narrative in Mexico, 1980–1995*. Westport, CT: Greenwood Press, 1997, pp. 159–73.
Loyola, Beatriz. "Género, etnicidad y nación en la narrativa judía-mexicana de Angelina Muñiz-Huberman, Rosa Nissán y Sara Levi Calderón." DAI Section A: the Humanities and Social Sciences 65.2 (2004 Aug) 534, University of Colorado, Boulder, DA3123262.

Maiz-Peña, Magdalena, Trans. Wendy G. "Mapping the Jewish Female Voice in Contemporary Mexican Narrative". In *Passion, Memory and Identity: Twentieth Century Latin American Jewish Women Writers*. Albuquerque, NM: University of New Mexico Press, 1999, pp. 17–33.

Martínez, Elizabeth Coonrod. "Turning the Page on Mexican Women". *Américas* 56(6) (2005 Nov.–Dec. 1999): 48–53.

——. "Rosa Nissán: Cultural Memory and the Mexican Sephardic Woman". *MOSAIC* 37(1) (March 2004): 101–18.

Medina, Manuel F. "Imagining a Space in Between: Writing the Gap between Jewish and Mexican Identities in Rosa Nissán's Narrative". *Studies in the Literary Imagination* 33(1) (2000 Spring): 93–106.

Mennell, D. Jan. "Memoria, midrash y metamorfosis en *Novia que te vea* de Guita Schyfter, Un diálogo texual-visual". *Chasqui* 29(1) (2000 May): 50–63.

Schneider, Judith Morganroth. "Rosa Nissán's Representation of Diasporic Consciousness, Reflections on Genealogy, Geography and Gender in *Las Tierras Prometidas*". *Yiddish* 12(4) (2001): 65–83.

Scott, Renée. "*Novia que te vea* y *Sagrada Memoria*: Dos infancias judías en Latinoamérica". *Revista Iberoamericana de Bibliografía* 45(4) (1995): 605–12.

——. "La experiencia sefardí en Latinoamérica: Tres novelas de Teresa Porzencanski y Rosa Nissán". *Sefarad: Revista de Estudios Hebraicos y de Oriente Próximo* 48(2) (1998): 387–99.

Stávans, Ilán. "On Separate Ground". In Marjorie Agosín (ed.), *Passion, Memory and Identity: Twentieth-Century Latin American Jewish Women Writers*. Albuquerque, NM: University of New Mexico Press, 1999, pp. 1–16.

NOLLA, OLGA

Olga Nolla (1938–2001), a member of the Generation of the 1970s in Puerto Rican literature, was born into a distinguished and privileged family of poets and politicians in Mayaguez, Puerto Rico. She completed her primary and secondary education in Puerto Rico, and then came to the United States where she was awarded a Bachelor of Science degree at Manhattanville College in Purchase, New York. Later, she studied at the University of Puerto Rico with her cousin, another internationally recognized writer, Rosario Ferré, where she was awarded a Master of Arts degree in Hispanic Studies. It was at the University of Puerto Rico where her literary vocation was forged after studying with Latin American luminaries, such as Angel Rama and Mario Vargas Llosa. These literary giants encouraged Olga Nolla and Rosario Ferré to found one of the most important literary magazines of the island: *Zona de carga y descarga* (Loading and Unloading Zone). *Zona* made an important contribution to Puerto Rican letters in promoting new talent: the writers who would come to be known as the Generation of the 1970s in Puerto Rican literature. It also explored groundbreaking issues of the time, such as feminism in Puerto Rico, the status of women, homosexuality and the colonial status of the island nation.

Nolla contributed to a number of newspapers and journals in Puerto Rico, such as *El Nuevo Dia*, *Prensa Libre*, *El mundo*, *Claridad*, *Cariban* and *Sin nombre*. She also worked as a screenwriter, developing scripts for Distance Education projects for the Puerto Rican university system, where she was a professor at the Universidad Metropolitana for twenty years, a time during which she wrote the majority of her literary production. As an editor of *Palabra de mujer*, the magazine of la Federación de Mujeres Puertorriquenas and *Cupey*, the literary magazine of the Universidad Metropolitana, she promoted Puerto Rican literature and culture and gave voice to many younger writers who were able to publish and disseminate their works. In 2000, she was awarded el Premio Internacional de Poesia Jaime Sabines (the Jaime Sabines International Poetry Award) in Mexico for her work *Unicamente mio* (Only Mine).

Poetry and Stories

It was in *Zona de carga y descarga* that Nolla constructed the foundation for what would become a lifelong passion for literature. Encouraged by faculty mentors, she and Rosario Ferré co-founded the journal, which was published from 1972–75. It was conceived as a student-directed literary journal that would publish young Puerto Rican authors and create a forum that would give voice to the social, political, and cultural concerns of the day. Many of her poems and short stories were first published in *Zona*.

Her collections of poetry are often out of print and only a few poems have been translated and made accessible to an English audience. Her novels have not been translated into English. The poet and literary critic Marjorie Agosín calls her "one of the most original and daring voices of the Caribbean" for the characteristic defiance, rebellion and eroticism in her poetry. In *El sombrero de plata* (The Silver Hat) and *Dafne en el mes de marzo* (Daphne in the Month of March), Nolla explores feminine desire and sexuality from the perspective of a powerful woman, unwilling to compromise with the patriarchy and subverting images from the classics of both Greco-Roman and Spanish Literature, of Medusa, Ulysses, San Juan de la Cruz, Calixto and Hippolytus.

Nolla has published six books of poetry and then, in the 1990s her interest turned to the narrative. Beginning in 1990, she published a collection of short stories, *Porque nos queremos tanto* (Why We Are So In Love), where she continued the exploration of themes of female sexuality that had appeared earlier in her poetry.

Her collection of short stories is followed by a trilogy of novels: *La segunda hija* (1992, The Second Daughter), *El castillo de la memoria* (1996, The Castle of Memory), and *El manuscrito de Miramar* (1998, The Miramar Manuscript). These novels helped Nolla gain an international following and *La segunda hija* was awarded the prize for best novel by the Pen Club of Puerto Rico in 1994.

Themes

Nolla combined a refinement in her command of poetic language coupled with a willingness to express an uncensored female sexuality. Her poetry, especially, is characterized by the exploration of female eroticism and a rejection of sexual stereotypes. Her novels combine the sexual and sentimental themes of her earlier poetry with the historical legacy of colonial Puerto Rico, migration, and class segregation. In the first novel of the trilogy, *La segunda hija*, Nolla studies the class implications when an upper middle-class Puerto Rican family moves to the United States. This novel was censured in Puerto Rico because of its sexual content. *El castillo de la memoria* used the theme of the search for the Fountain of Youth by Juan

Ponce de Leon and inverted the tale when Ponce de Leon searches for the antidote for eternal youth. *El manuscrito de Miramar* explores themes of female infidelity and sexuality, mother/daughter relationships and historical and political identity of Puerto Rico. *El manuscrito de Miramar* is a powerful, mature novel that is probably the author's most important work. The manuscript is a narrative found during the demolition of the family home, and through it Sonia Sabater de Gómez (mother) reveals her innermost passions and desires to her daughter, who reads it as a grandmother. The author, without a "room of her own" serves as inspiration to her daughter, who first destroys the manuscript, then restores it by re-writing it. The daughter must confront and reconcile her image of her mother with her mother's words. The feminism inherent in the text leaves the reader with a positive notion of reconciliation between generations and lifestyles. Her last novel *Rosas de papel* (2002, Paper Roses), was published posthumously.

ANTONIA GARCIA-RODRIGUEZ

Selected Works

De lo familiar. Buenos Aires: Dead Weight, 1973.

El ojo de la tormenta. San Juan, PR: Palabra de mujer, 1976.

El sombrero de plata. San Juan, PR: Palabra de mujer, 1976.

Clave de sol. San Juan, PR: Instituto de Cultura Puertorriquena, 1979.

Dafne en el mes de marzo. Madrid: Editorial Playor, 1989.

Porque nos queremos tanto. Buenos Aires: Ediciones de la Flor, 1989.

Green Cane Juicy Flotsam: Short Stories by Caribbean Women. Ed. Carmen C. Esteves and Lizabeth Paravisini-Gebert. New Brunswick, NJ: Rutgers University Press, 1991.

La segunda hija. San Juan, PR: Editorial de la Universidad de Puerto Rico, 1992.

Dulce hombre prohibido. San Juan, PR: Editorial Cultural, 1994.

These Are Not Sweet Girls: Poetry by Latin American Women. Ed. Marjorie Agosín. New York: White Pine Press, 1994.

Il castillo de la memoria. New York: Vintage, 1996.

El manuscrito de Miramar. Mexico City: Alfaguara, 1998.

El caballero del yip colorado. San Juan, PR: Editorial Cultura, 2000.

References and Further Reading

Acosta-Cruz, Maria I. "Historia y escritura femenina en Olga Nolla, Magali Garcia Ramis, Rosario Ferre y Ana Lydia Vega". *Revista Iberoamericana* January–June (1993): 62–163.

Esquilin, Mary Ann Gesser. "Rosario Ferré y Olga Nolla, reconceptualizando la nación?" *Confluencia: Revista Hispánica de Cultura y Literatura* 19(2) (1999): 58.

Hintz, Suzanne S. "Olga Nolla's *La segunda hija*: The Real, the Imaginary, the Physical, and the Emotional". *Monographic Review.* 12 (1996): 406–15.

Paravisini-Gebert, Lizabeth. "Unchained Tales: Women Prose Writers from the Hispanic Caribbean in the 1990s". *Bulletin of Latin American Research* 22(2) (2003): 445–63.

Torres, Victor Federico. "Conversaciones con Olga Nolla". *Exegesis: Revista de la Universidad de Puerto Rico en Humacao* 18(52) (2005): 60–3.

O

OCAMPO, SILVINA

The work of Silvina Ocampo (1903–93), which includes poetry, narrative, plays, and translations, extends across fifty years of Argentine literature. A reserved and somewhat eccentric woman, Ocampo is considered one of the best Argentine women storytellers of the twentieth century. She was the sister of Victoria Ocampo, founder of the literary magazine *Sur*, to which Silvina was an assiduous collaborator, although always on the margins. When younger, she spent long periods in Europe, where she studied painting with Giorgio de Chirico and Fernand Léger.

She soon established a friendship with Jorge Luis Borges and, in 1940, she married Adolfo Bioy Casares. As a consequence of her relationship with these two writers, she was in a position to participate in a representative way that attempted to move the realistic novel toward a modality of fantastic literature. But she distinguished herself from them mainly in the use of the banal and daily in her rejection of pseudoscientific explanations and mythological and learned references.

Her work has been collected in the volumes of *Poesía completa* (2001, two volumes) (Complete Poetry) and *Cuentos Inedicor* (2006, two vols) (Complete short stories). There is also a volume of *Poesía inédita y dispersa* (2001) (Unpublished and scattered poetry), with a prologue by Noemí Ulla, and numerous anthologies of her work have been published in recent years. Silvina Ocampo wrote several books of fairytales, among them, *El cofre volante* (1974, The Flying Chest), *El edicor* (1974, The Slide), *El caballo alado* (1976, The Winged Horse), and *La naranja maravillosa* (1977, The Wonderful Orange); she also wrote a book of poetry for children, *Canto escolar* (1979, School Song).

In 1946, she published *Los que aman, odian* (1946, Those who Love, Hate), a semi-detective novel written in collaboration with her husband. Deploying a mainly ironic tone, the authors recreate the situation of a group of individuals isolated in a secluded hotel by the sea, where a homeopathic physician, Humberto Huberman, offers a chronicle of his mistakes and hasty conclusions in solving a mysterious murder. Ocampo also wrote a verse drama in collaboration with Juan Rodolfo Wilcock concerning life in ancient Rome, *Los traidores* (1956, The Traitors).

Along with Borges and Bioy Casares, Ocampo worked on the *Antología de la Inedicor de fantástica* (1940, The Book of Fantasy), in which she had scant participation, and the *Antología poética argentina* (1941, Argentine Poetic Anthology). She also translated the works of John Donne, Alexander Pope, Gérard de Nerval, Charles Baudelaire, Paul Verlaine, among others, and more recently of Emily Dickinson.

Ocampo won numerous prizes for her literary activity. In 1945, the book of poetry *Espacios métricos* (Metric Spaces) won the Municipal Prize for Poetry. In 1953, she won the second Argentine National Prize for *Los nombres* (The Names) and in 1962 the National Prize for *Lo amargo por dulce* (That which is Bitter but Sweet). Ocampo was denied the National Prize for Fiction in 1979 for stories described by the judges as "too cruel". Nevertheless, in 1988, she received the Club of XIII Prize for *Cornelia frente al espejo* (Cornelia in the Mirror) and, finally, the PEN Club Gold Pen.

Poetic Work

A member of the Argentine generation of the 40, Ocampo's poetry is of a spiritualist and reflective tendency, characterized by a clear workmanly quality, with and without rhyme. Her verse work consists of several poem books. The first is *Enumeración de la patria y otros poemas* (1942, Enumeration of the Nation and Other Poems), where she practices a type of descriptive and enumerative poetry to give an account of the love for the mother country and where the emotion felt comes from the memory of a fragmented and minimum landscape, from whose totality the meaning of the country arises. *Espacios métricos* (1945, Metric Spaces) has a traditional form, with sonnets of classic perfection, quartets and rhyming couplets, with a few texts without rhyme. In *Poemas de amor desesperado* (1949, Poems of Desperate Love), the cultural reference is to Pablo Neruda. In *Lo amargo por dulce* (1962), oxymoronic patterns are particularly prominent. Later on, she published *Amarillo celeste* (1972, Sky yellow), *Árboles de Buenos Aires* (1979, Trees of Buenos Aires), and *Breve santoral* (1984, Short Book of Saints).

Her poetry, as a whole, is based on paradoxical metaphors, oppositions, and unexpected assertions. In her best work,

Ocampo achieves the expression of the subtle mechanism of the feminine conscience in the face of the issues of reality. For Ocampo, literature must have the place that her very language promotes: the place of the myth and the rhetoric, a place where the time would not have to exist. Nevertheless, although her poetry is important, it is in the short stories where the conventional practices of reading are provoked and destabilized.

Short Stories

Ocampo emerges in her stories as a transgressor in themes and in her ironic stance, making use of a suggestive and poetic language, which allows her to develop common situations suddenly transformed by the irruption of the strange. In her work, she uses inner monologue and stream of consciousness. Another characteristic is the construction of an original, independent, and completely verisimilar world imaginary: a space full of paradoxes, references, and multiple details. In many cases, it is a cruel, sadistic, and shady world, in which children and infantile women abound. Crimes, betrayals, and tragedies occur in the context of an invariably indifferent and ingenuous perspective.

Her first story book is *Viaje olvidado* (1937, Forgotten Journey). Here, the referential world is constituted by plants and gardens, the interior of mansions with typical décor and furniture, humble houses where simple, even marginal, people live, scrutinized from a narrative stance that erases or denatures the objects, transforming them poetically. Thus, for instance, in "Los funámbulos" (The funambulists), the strange occurs in an ordinary world, in which the extraordinary becomes normal. The two children of an ironing woman, after visiting a circus, throw themselves from a third floor in a glorious leap, with the result that they end up smashed on flagstones of the patio. In *Viaje olvidado*, four fantastic stories are included, three of which are written with a horror-story approach: "La cabeza pegada el vidrio" (The Head Stuck to the Glass), "El Edicor ancho de sol" (The Wide Sun Corridor), "La familia Linio Milagro" (The Linio Milagro Family), plus one that constitutes the most lasting contribution of the author to the genre, "La enemistad de las cosas" (Enmity of Things).

In her second collection, *Autobiografía de Irene* (1948, The Autobiography of Irene), Ocampo combines her interest in the world of children with the development of fantasy. In "La red" (The Net), the narrator yields the word to her friend, Kêng-Su, to whom after having killed a butterfly with a pin there appears a book marked with small dots, that includes her name: "Kêng-Su, what will you gain from your dark crime?" Finally the young girl paints an amulet that she carries everyplace with her. On one occasion, when she is swimming in the sea, she is attacked by the ghost of the butterfly and dies. What we have is a story within a story. In this collection, we also confront a narrative with multiple optional endings ("Epitafio romano" Roman Epitaph), the story-within-a-story ("El impostor" The Imposter), and a circular structure ("Autobiografía de Irene").

The following collection, *La furia* (1959, The Fury), contains stories that are both violent and strange. They maintain Ocampo's interest in the child's perspective and the recurring themes of magic objects and prediction of the future. For example, in "Las fotografías" (The Photographs), the narrator is one of the guests at the birthday party of Adriana, a paralytic girl who dies that same day. Humberta, who stays in the same house, is considered to be a miserable human being.

The narrator tells of her preference for the good girl and her disdain for the other one. In "La boda" (The Wedding), a child narrator forms a relationship with a young woman, Roberta, who feels threatened by the latter's impending marriage. When the wedding takes place, the child places a spider in the older woman's hair bun and she dies from a poisonous bite. Despite the child's confession, no one believes her. The ending of the story is unsettling because the narrator concludes with the observation that Roberta holds a grudge against her. In "La paciente y el médico" (The Patient and the Doctor), two differing worlds intersect via the interior monologues of the protagonists. There is, first of all, the woman patient, who is madly in love with the doctor. She decides to commit suicide to get his attention. Nevertheless, the doctor, who cannot stand her, goes to see her but makes her walk so she will die. Throughout the monologues, there is the mention of the small objects the woman gives the doctor in the belief that he likes to receive them. Additionally, the theme of the double is frequent in Ocampo's short stories, as it is seen in "La casa de azúcar" (The House of Sugar), "El vástago" (The Descendant) and "Nosotros" (We).

Alongside irony, several stories, like "Mimoso," "La sibila" (The Sybil), "El vestido de terciopelo" (The Velvet Dress), and "Voz en el teléfono" (Voice on the Telephone), reveal a broad humorous intent. In "Mimoso," for example, a couple decide to embalm their dog when he dies. They are warned that the only risk they might run is if they eat the dog, because he has been treated with poisonous substances. What is strange is that the wife decides to kill a guest, whom she accuses of sending an anonymous letter, and she carries her plan out by serving him a meal made from the dog.

Ocampo went on to publish the short stories, *La furia* (The Fury), *Las invitadas* (1961, The Guests) and *Los días de la noche* (1970, The Days at Night), which have a caustic edge to them: their humor is grotesque, intensely sarcastic, or even dark. For example, in "La raza inextinguible" (The Invincible Race), there is a reversal in that children must go to work, while adults carry out children's activities. Another example is in "La revelación" (Revelation), where a mentally deficient child can see things others fail to perceive: a photograph he has taken captures something that when subjected to close scrutiny, turns out to be the image of a woman.

Most recently, she published *Y así sucesivamente* (1987, And So On), where the story "El automóvil" (The Automobile) deserves mention, and *Cornelia frente al espejo* (1988), which includes "La nave" (The Ship), one of the most successful and impressive stories Ocampo has ever written.

Many of Ocampo's texts adopt the epistolary form to structure the stories that they narrate. For Ocampo, the letter is suitable as a genre, because the interlocutors recognize the facts that are spoken and do not need to have an explanation for everything. Such is the case with "Carta perdida en un cajón" (Lost Letter in a Drawer) or "La recreación" (The Recreation), from *La furia*, or "Carta bajo la cama" (Letter under the Bed), or "Carta de despedida" (Letter of Goodbye) from *Las invitadas*. Certain objects appear with regularity, such as black velvet dresses in "El vestido de terciopelo" and "La casa de azúcar," both of *La furia*, and in "Las vestiduras peligrosas" (The Dangerous Clothes), from *Los días de la noche*.

Poetry and Aestheticism

Literary criticism on the work of Silvina Ocampo arose, in the first place, from the members of the group *Sur*, among others Rosa Chacel, Mario Lancelotti and Ezequiel Martínez Estrada. They cleared a way to the considerations of Jorge Luis Borges and Alejandra Pizarnik, for whom Silvina belonged to the poetics of pure poetry, symbolism and metaphysical poetry. A new perspective on her literature, represented by Enrique Pezzoni, Sylvia Molloy and Julio Cortázar, points out the transgressive attitude towards the canon, one that places her writing in terms of her inscription in different sets of textuality: the problems of the fantasy, of the bad taste, etc.

Several recent attempts have been made to define the poetic narrative of Silvina Ocampo. Noemí Ulla defines "La continuación" (The Continuation), story of *La furia*, as a possible axis of reading to describe the aesthetic clues of the author. After emphasizing the form of the letter that supposedly a woman writes to a man whom she wishes to leave, it operates through the imaginary possibility of the reader who will construct an interpretation from the data that the narrator offers. Via the writing, Ocampo "pretends" that the letter "communicates," and the quotes from a novel that are inserted in the narrative tell the story poetically. Thus, from the beginning of the text the narrative obsession to disappear, to lose identity becomes evident. This is a game of Chinese boxes in which the voice of the feminine narrator adopts the masculine form. The value of the story resides in its metaliterary effectiveness, that is to say, the narration acts like a center from which to explain the totality of Silvina Ocampo's narrative. This position as explanatory reading of the work as a totality has been objected to, although the value that it has to define a perspective, a plurality of forces that constitutes the literature of the author is not rejected.

For Graciela Tomassini, the central element of cohesion in Ocampo's texts, from *Viaje olvidado* to *Cornelia frente al espejo*, is the predominance of the inner action and the practice of a nonconventional vision of the narrated world. Thus, the apparent nonmeaning of her narrations demands the collaboration of the reader to fulfill the sense of her writing.

Turning to a different text, "Informe del Cielo y del Infierno" (Report on Heaven and Hell), David Lagmanovich analyzes the effect produced by the chaotic enumeration that can be seen in this story and in others like "Visiones" (Visions), of *Las invitadas*, in "Autobiografía de Irene," or even in "Anamnesis"; such chaotic enumeration is characteristic of modern poetry and deployed in prose by the author. Lagmanovich detects two fundamental influences, Franz Kafka and the dramatists of the theater of the absurd. A third influence is added: the generic blending between essay and short story that had been described by Borges and that Ocampo puts into operation.

DANIEL ALTAMIRANDA

Selected Works

Leopoldina's Dream. Trans. Daniel Balderston. Ontario: Penguin Books, 1988.

Los que aman, odian. With Adolfo Bioy Casares. Buenos Aires: Emecé, 1996.

Poesía completa. Buenos Aires: Emecé, 2002.

Cuentos completos. 2 vols. Buenos Aires: Emecé, 2006.

References and Further Reading

Clark, Marcia B. "Feminization as an Experience of Limits: Shifting Gender Roles in the Fantastic Narrative of Silvina Ocampo and Cristina Perry Rossi". *Inti: Revista de Literatura Hispánica* 40–1 (1994): 249–68.

Klinenberg, Patricia N. *Fantasies of the Feminine: The short stories of Silvina Ocampo*. Lewisburg, VA: Bucknell University Press, 1999.

Lagmanovich, David. "Un relato de Silvina Ocampo". *Espéculo: Revista de Estudios Literarios* 29 (2005): (no pagination).

Lockert, Lucía Fox. "Silvina Ocampo's Fantastic Short Stories". *Monographic Review/Revista Monografica* 4 (1988): 221–9.

Mancini, Adriana. *Silvina Ocampo. Escalas de pasión*. Buenos Aires: Norma, 2003.

Percas, Helena. "La original expresión poética de Silvina Ocampo". *Revista Iberoamericana* 19 (1955): 283–98.

Pezzoni, Enrique. "Silvina Ocampo". *El texto y sus voces*. Buenos Aires: Sudamericana, 1986, 187–216.

Tomassini, Graciela. *El espejo de Cornelia: La obra cuentística de Silvina Ocampo*. Buenos Aires: Plus Ultra, 1995.

Ulla, Noemí. *Invenciones a dos voces: ficción y poesía en Silvina Ocampo*. Buenos Aires: Torres Agüero, 1992.

Zapata, Mónica. "Modalidades de lo fantástico en *La Furia y otros cuentos*, de Silvina Ocampo". *Co-Textes* 33 (1997): 91–106.

OCAMPO, VICTORIA

Victoria Ocampo (1890–1979) was born in Buenos Aires and educated in French by her governess, learning to write in this language well before Spanish. Her life reflects the tastes and lifestyle of the privileged class she belonged to and the contradictions of her era. At the same time that Ocampo considered herself a liberal "universal American", she explicitly promoted the idea that the American educated elites had the social responsibility of becoming the guiding force behind opening, renewing and blending the cultural production of the region with the European. It has been argued that this vision "was founded on a moral imperative particular to an educated elite of their generation whose intellectual consciousness was matched by a sense of social responsibility" (Meyer 2000), a responsibility that shaped Ocampo's identity.

Although when very young she excelled in music and literature, she was not allowed to pursue a formal education like most women at the turn of the century. She traveled to Europe many times since she was a child. In 1908, she was permitted to attend some lectures at the Sorbonne, properly chaperoned. The European intellectuals of the period made a great impact on her. She was drawn to the theatre after reading Racine in France and taking lessons from Marguerite Moreno, but she was never able to pursue her love of acting, an activity that her father considered below her social class. However, her theatrical talent was put to use in the many literary events she created, such as the one described by Majstorovic, in which some of Borges' short stories printed in Buenos Aires in French translation were scattered from a plane over Paris at Ocampo's expense.

In 1912, she married Bernardo de Estrada, although relations between the two rapidly deteriorated and she separated from him in 1920 and began a thirteen-year relationship with his cousin Julián Martínez. Her life, however, was anchored in the intellectual relationships she forged across the continents.

Her many visits to Europe and later to USA—which she ended up preferring in her later years—were planned around expanding her literary and artistic circles. She met prominent figures such as George Bernard Shaw, Igor Stravinsky, Graham Greene, H.G. Wells, Keyserling, Anna de Noailles, Gisèle Freund, Paul Valéry, Pierre Drieu La Rochelle, Jean Cocteau, Lacan, Ramón Gómez de la Serna, Leo Ferrero, Le Corbusier, Virginia Woolf, Malraux, Indira Gandhi. Many of them accepted Ocampo's hospitality in her elegant residence in San Isidro and were her inspiration and human resource for her renowned literary magazine *Sur*.

Funded by Ocampo in 1931, during the Depression years and shortly after the turmoil of the "semana trágica" in Buenos Aires, *Sur* came to represent one of the most prestigious, controversial and internationally connected literary magazines of her time. Inspired in a conversation with Waldo Frank—who initiated Ocampo in the discovery of North American values and culture—and named with the telephonic assistance of Ortega y Gasset, the magazine was launched with the support of Ocampo's sister, Silvina Ocampo, and the prestigious literary figure Jorge Luis Borges. This was the international flavor that *Sur* had since its foundation. Its explicit aim was to initiate a liberal dialogue between American (North and South) and European literature. Among the writers published in her magazine were Enrique Anderson Imbert, José Bianco, Adolfo Bioy Casares, Jorge Luis Borges, Julio Cortázar, Albert Camus, Santiago Davobe, Ezequiel Martínez Estrada, Pierre Drieu La Rochelle, Waldo Frank, Eduardo Mallea, Silvina Ocampo, José Ortega y Gasset, Manuel Peyrou, Alfonso Reyes, Ernesto Sábato and Enrique Pezzoni. The magazine also published translations of Gide, Kerouac, Pound, Joyce, Faulkner, Mann, Miller, T.S. Eliot, and Woolf, among others. Being a prolific translator from French and English, Ocampo contributed greatly to the promotion of European literature in Latin America. Oblivious to her privileged upbringing, she believed that her own cosmopolitan ideals and translation abilities were part and parcel of being an Argentinean.

To be able to sustain the journal, she founded an editorial of the same name, *Sur*, which published authors like Federico García Lorca, Eduardo Mallea, Juan Carlos Onetti, Alfonso Reyes, Horacio Quiroga, Bioy Casares, Alfred Huxley, C.G. Jung, Virginia Woolf, Sartre, Kerouac and Camus. Ocampo published most of her own work in *Sur*.

Her writing centers on the testimony of her life and her times, from her own personal viewpoint. Her literary achievements are best represented in her *Autobiografía*, begun in 1952 and her multi-volume *Testimonios* which included her collected correspondence. As a writer she is best known for these works. Her critics range from admiration to refusal to give any literary acknowledgement to her writings. Some believe Ocampo just writes gossip informed by her privileged bourgeois contacts (Viñas) while others praise her writing as a cross-pollination between memoir, essay and epistle, believing that her memoirs are illustrated by her personal connection to cultural works (novels, music, theatre) that illuminate her own sense of herself (Meyer). Ocampo admitted her own incapacity to write creative literature, novels or poems, although she declared she could see the poetry in every person. Julio Cortázar said that Ocampo never feared the first person because she was so passionately attentive to and fascinated by the others, from whom she drew her inspiration and energy.

Major influences on Ocampo include Rabindranath Tagore, whose *Gitanjali* (in Gide's French translation) she first read in 1914, and whom she met and looked after on his visit to Argentina in 1924, becoming one of his muses; José Ortega y Gasset, whom she met in 1916 and who became a major influence on her career publishing her early book *De Francesca a Beatrice* (written in 1921) in his *Revista de Occidente* in 1924 (a significant step for Ocampo, although she had already published her first article "Babel" in 1920); and Virginia Woolf, whose *A Room of One's Own* she read in Paris in 1929, and with whom she later had a (somewhat one-sided) correspondence. Ocampo was perceived by different people as charismatic, flamboyant, controversial, "malhablada", willful and even at times racist but indeed somebody not to be forgotten.

She won awards and PhDs honoris causa from the governments of France, England, Italy, The French Academy, the Argentinean Writers Society, Harvard University and University Visva Bharati in India and in 1977 took her seat in the Academia Argentina de Letras, an honor she had previously refused as she did not consider herself suitably qualified for the role. She finally accepted this honor in order to pave the way for other women to enter the Academia. Ocampo was renowned as a feminist as well as a mentor of other writer's talents.

She was at the centre of political controversy during Perón's years whose government she considered non-democratic. In 1951, she was considered a dissident, an alarming experience that motivated her to send her library and collected papers away for safekeeping. In 1954, Ocampo was arrested as a political prisoner and the offices of *Sur* were broken into. She was eventually released after the intercession of several internationally renowned figures including Gabriela Mistral and Jawaharlal Nehru. Her political position remained controversial with criticisms surrounding her membership of the wealthy upper class as well as her role as a promoter of foreign culture, anti-Peronist and pro-military. Her political comments were at times naïve and even banal, having declared that she would have been a Communist is she did not like so much the "beautiful clean things, luxury (ah! J'aime le luxe . . .)" in one of her letters to Angélica. Ocampo's social position gave her a blind spot in many political and social issues.

Without a doubt, however, Ocampo is best remembered for her contributions to Argentina's literary culture and as an international literary figure through her work as an editor and publisher of *Sur*. Even if this magazine has been accused of not reporting on the main Latin American literary developments of her time (Narayanan 1992) due to Ocampo's selective vision, it is also true that it greatly contributed to the promotion of European culture and arts in Latin America and in a lesser but equally selective way to the promotion of Latin American and especially Argentine letters in Europe. Nationally, *Sur* has been assessed as a "forum for the most significant literary debates in Argentina during the first half of this century and a model for future literary publications", where the faith in authorial subjectivity was established as a strong basis of literary analysis in future journals (Masiello 1985). Even one of her most acid critics (Viñas 1998) recognizes that Ocampo managed to beat the market forces that shape cultural production by using *Sur* "to work for pleasure". Octavio Paz commented that "Victoria is something above and beyond: she is the founder of a spiritual space. Because *Sur* is not merely a publication or an institution: it is a tradition of the spirit". A tradition that ceased to exist in 1971, forty years after its birth.

Her legacy is embodied in the Villa Ocampo property in San Isidro, her welcoming home and meeting place for so many national and international figures, which was donated by Ocampo to UNESCO in 1973 for use as a cultural centre.

ESTELA VALVERDE

Selected Works

Testimonios

Testimonios, 1TM serie. Madrid: Revista de Occidente, 1935.
Testimonios, 2TM serie. Buenos Aires: Sur, 1941.
Testimonios, 3TM serie. Buenos Aires: Sudamericana, 1950.
Soledad Sonora (Testimonios, 4TM serie). Buenos Aires: Sudamericana, 1950.
Testimonios, 5TM serie. Buenos Aires: Sur, 1954.
Testimonios, 6TM serie. Buenos Aires: Sur, 1962.
Testimonios, 7TM serie. Buenos Aires: Sur, 1967.
Testimonios, 8TM serie. Buenos Aires: Sur, 1971.
Testimonios, 9TM serie. Buenos Aires: Sur, 1975.
Testimonios, 10TM serie. Buenos Aires: Sur, 1977.

Autobiographies

Autobiografía I: El archipiélago. Buenos Aires: Sur, 1979.
Autobiografía II: El imperio insular. Buenos Aires: Sur, 1980.
Autobiografía III: La rama de Salzburgo. Buenos Aires: Sur, 1981.
Autobiografía IV: Viraje. Buenos Aires: Sur, 1982.
Autobiografía V: Figuras simbólicas. Medida de Francia. Buenos Aires: Sur, 1983.
Autobiografía VI: Sur y Cía. Buenos Aires: Sur, 1984.

Other Selected Works

La laguna de los nenúfares. Madrid: Revista de Occidente, 1926.
Domingos en Hyde Park. Buenos Aires: Sur, 1936.

Websites

http://www.villaocampo.org/index.htm (Villa Ocampo.)
http://www.parabaas.com/rabindranath/articles/pKetaki1.html (Ocampo's relationship with Rabindranath Tagore.)

References and Further Reading

Abella, Encarnación. "Victoria Ocampo: Historia de una vocación literaria". In Hernández de López and Ana María (eds), *Narrativa hispanoamericana contemporánea: Entre la vanguardia y el posboom.* Madrid: Pliegos, 1996, pp. 17–29.

Foster, David William. "Bibliography of Writings by and about Victoria Ocampo (1890–1979)". *Revista Interamericana de Bibliografía: Órgano de Estudios Humanísticos/Inter-American Review of Bibliography: Journal of Humanistic Studies* 30 (1980): 51–8.

Gallo, Marta. "Las crónicas de Victoria Ocampo: Versatilidad y fidelidad de un género". *Revista Iberoamericana (RI)* 51(132–3) (July–Dec. 1985): 679–86.

Kaminsky, Amy. "Essay, Gender, and Mestizaje: Victoria Ocampo and Gabriela Mistral". In Ruth-Ellen Joeres Boetcher and Elizabeth Mittman (eds), *The Politics of the Essay: Feminist Perspectives.* Bloomington, IN: Indiana University Press, 1993, pp. 113–30.

Majstorovic, Gorica. "Cosmopolitanism and the Nation: Reading Asymmetries of Power in Victoria Ocampo's 'Babel'". *Contra corriente* 3(3) (Spring 2000): 47–64.

Masiello, Francine. "Argentine Literary Journalism: The Production of a Critical Discourse". *Latin American Research Review* (2091) (1985): 27–60.

Meyer, Doris. *Victoria Ocampo: Contra viento y marea.* Buenos Aires: Sudamericana, 1979. Transl. *Victoria Ocampo: Against the Wind and the Tide.* Austin, TX: University of Texas Press, 1990.

——. "Victoria Ocampo and Alfonso Reyes: Ulysses's Malady". *Studies in Twentieth Century Literature* 24(2) (Summer 2000): 307–24.

Narayanan, R. "Victoria Ocampo: Prophetess of her Country?" In *Victoria Ocampo: An Exercise in Indo-Argentine Relationship.* Buenos Aires: Publishing Corporation, 1992, 107–28.

Pezzoni, Enrique. "Ocampo, Victoria". In Pedro Orgambide and Roberto Yahni (eds), *Enciclopedia de la Literatura Argentina.* Buenos Aires: Editorial Sudamericana, 1970, pp. 477–80.

Vázquez, María Esther. *Victoria Ocampo. El mundo como destino.* Buenos Aires: Seix Barral, 2002.

Viñas, David. "Victoria Ocampo, el Gran Gatsby y los pobres negros", 219–22; "Victoria Ocampo, vegetarianismo, Krishnamurti y la ecología", 245–46; "Victoria Ocampo y Frank Sinatra", 257–58; "Victoria Ocampo y Rita Hayworth", 268–69; "Victoria y Waldo Frank; mecenas, *Sur* y los viajes sucesivos", 273–78; "Bioy Casares, su cuñada y Nueva York", 283–87; "La Ocampo y la Mistral; Perón, tiempos y los *boyfriends*", 295–96; "Penúltima victoria", 310–12; "Victoria en despedida", 315–18. In *De Sarmiento a Dios. Viajeros argentinos a USA.* Buenos Aires: Editorial Sudamericana, 1998.

ODIO, EUNICE

Eunice Odio (1922–74) was one of the most intrepid and free-spirited Spanish American women artists of the twentieth century. Born in San José, Costa Rica, her childhood and youth were marked by two traumatic incidents. At the age of 11, Odio suffered the death of her beloved mother. It was her mother who had taught her to read (according to Rima de Vallbona, Odio learned to read in only two days) and who had introduced her to literature. The second trauma occurred as a result of her arranged marriage at the age of 16, which ended in divorce only three years later.

After leaving her husband, she became engaged with literary circles in San José and started to publish her first poems in literary journals and anthologies. In 1947, she moved to Guatemala, where she published her first book of poems, *Los elementos terrestres* (Terrestrial Elements). This work won the prestigious "Premio Centro-americano 15 de septiembre" (Central American Prize 15th of September). In her new home country, the poet and autodidact also began to lecture on various literary topics in academic circles. In addition to her writing, recitation of poetry, and lectures, Odio became a political activist and ardent supporter of socialist concerns. In 1949, she served as secretary for the Editorial Center of the Ministry of Public Education and as spokesperson for several leftist groups. Many of her publications from that period were in left-wing literary and political journals. From 1948 to 1953, Odio wrote her second book, *Zona en territorio del alba* (Zona in the Territory of Dawn), which was published in

Argentina in 1953. In 1948, she began work on her lyrical sequence *El tránsito de fuego* (The Fire's Journey), which later critics have considered her most important contribution (Laureano Albán, Luis Jiménez). Completed in 1954, it was eventually published in San Salvador in 1957, where Odio had acquired new citizenship in 1954. In 1956, she moved to Mexico, where she succeeded again in establishing herself in local poetry circles and among leftist groups. She met and was fascinated by the Cuban exile Fidel Castro.

In the period after 1959, Odio gradually distanced herself from her earlier leftist militancy. Following two stays in the United States, she returned to Mexico City in 1962 and became a Mexican citizen. This time, she was to remain for the rest of her life. In order to alleviate her financial difficulties, she worked as a translator and journalist. During these years, she became increasingly fascinated with mysterious phenomena and spiritual practices. According to Luis A. Jiménez, this period saw the awakening of Odio's curiosity for "mystery, paranormal experiences, the cabbala, and the Rosicrucian Order" (2003, p. 274). Despite her economic difficulties and serious health problems, she continued to write prose and published in several Latin American journals, among them the prestigious Venezuelan *Zona franca* (Free Zone), until her suicide in 1974.

The biographical adventures and misfortunes that were endured by this restless traveler are reflected in her lyrical works. Odio was a woman who, according to the critic Laureano Alban, "vivió a contrapelo de los paradigmas existenciales y sociales que su época le asignaba a su rol de 'mujer de bien'" (1987, p. 327, "lived against the grain of the existential and social paradigms that her time assigned to her role as a 'respectable woman"). A salient example of her unconventionality and daringness, particularly in Latin America at the time, is echoed in the opening of the introductory poem of her first collection, where the poetic voice invites the (male) beloved to an erotic adventure:

Ven
Amado
Te probaré con alegría.

(*Los elementos terrestres* p. 11)

(Come / Beloved / With joy, I will try you).

Another important theme in Odio's work is the precariousness of home, as well as the recurrent thematization of soil and earth. Many poems are constructed around the figure of the mother. Odio's early "Recuerdo de mi infancia privada" from 1946 describes a candid childhood scene, where the lyrical instance invokes a moment of unadulterated joy, which occurs as the little girl plays hide and seek with her mother. The poem recalls the simple words, sounds, and repetitions characteristic of a child's perception:

Mi madre . . .
ciñéndose el perfil,
la trenza,
la memoria . . .
y yo corría,
corría
con mis piernas de niña
para ser hallada
con la voz
en la tarde.

(*Twentieth-Century Latin American Poetry*, p. 284)

(My mother . . . / girding her profile, / the braid, / the memory // and I ran, // ran // with my little girl's legs / to be found // with the voice / in the afternoon.)

Alongside the invocation of an erotic encounter or a poem that features the intimate surroundings of a child's world, Odio's lyrical voice may equally portray a desolate self facing a shifting ontological reality. Her poetry reworks biblical and mythological themes, often in ways that highlight the characters' feelings of loneliness and uncertainty in their surroundings. Many of her lyrical texts present isolated subjects who are lost among fragments of disjoined realities. These fragments do not create a logical universe but an atmosphere, a mood transported by the lyrical voice. A poem from "Proyecto de mí mismo" (Project of Myself), the title of the first part of the long lyrical sequence *El tránsito de fuego*, offers an example of this lyrical practice. In alluding to the book of Genesis, Odio engenders an aura that transforms biblical images: Rather than being the subject matter of creation, a woman creates herself through the projection of her own thought; Adam's rib is supplanted by Eve's hip; and the fateful utterance through which this projection springs into being does not rely on divine grace but engenders itself by the strength of the lyrical instance:

Me pienso, me proyecto en cavidad de sombra,
del más alto contorno de sangre,
a la cadera próxima,
de la piel a la luz entrando por la aurora,
de la sombra a los labios
trepando por la sílaba.

(p, 78)

(I think myself, I project myself in the cavity of the shadow, / from the highest form of blood, / to the proximate hip, // from the skin to the light entering at dawn, / from the shadow to the lips, / rising with the syllable).

Odio's poetry has received relatively little critical attention. In this respect, the publication of the collection of essays *La palabra innumerable: Eunice Odio ante la crítica* (The Innumerable Word: Eunice Odio in the Face of the Critique) in 2001, edited by Jorge Chen Sham and Rima de Vallbona, serves as a cornerstone for further studies on her poetry and also on her prose works and essays.

Signs of Odio's literary creativity and a passion that was bound in words also manifest themselves in her epistolary. In a letter to Carlos Pellicer from June 29, 1971, Odio describes her love to the addressee in inventive words, which are reminiscent of the language of Federico García Lorca. The list of gifts she is presenting to the beloved may be read as a prose poem of sparkling images:

Hoy, voy a regalarle . . . : una gota del Sol; un azul que encontré en la calle, la segunda parte de una golondrina . . . el fondo de una perla dinosaurio que es donde vamos a vivir y morir usted y yo . . . le regalo la sonrisa de una bisabuela suya que usted no conoció porque era ángela y árbola y se fue a la eternidad en un segundo . . . Se me había olvidado regalarle todo el horizonte y sus consecuencias. ¿Los acepta? ¿Verdad que sí porque los sintió en los ojos desde antes que en su infancia apareciera la primera Luna redonda de marzo? (p. 290)

(Today, I'm offering you . . .: a drop of sun; a blue I found on the street, half of a swallow . . . the depth of the dinosaur pearl where you and I will live and die . . . I offer you the smile of a great-grandmother you never knew because she was an angel and a tree and she went off to eternity in a flash . . . I forgot to offer you the horizon and all its effects? Do you accept these things? Is that because you felt them in your eyes even before the first round moon of March appeared in your infancy?)

While Odio's extensive correspondence with Juan Liscano, the editor of *Zona Franca*, has been published after her death in 1975 (*Antología: Rescate de un gran poeta*, Anthology: Rescue of a Great Poet), there remain many more poetic and metapoetic letters that have not yet been appropriated by critics to their full extent, much less translated into English.

ILKA KRESSNER

Selected Works

Los elementos terrestres. Guatemala City: El Libro de Guatemala, 1948.

Zona en territorio del alba: Poesía 1946–1948. Mendoza, Argentina: Brígadas Líricas, 1953.

El tránsito de fuego. San Salvador: Ministerio de Cultura, 1957.

El rastro de la mariposa. Mexico City: Finisterre, c. 1960–69. Translated as *The Trace of the Butterfly* in Victoria Urbano (ed.), *Five Women Writers of Costa Rica*, trans. Catherine G. Bellver. Beaumont, TX: Lamar University Press, 1978.

En defensa del castellano. Mexico City: Gráficas de Méhir, 1972.

References and Further Reading

Albán, Laureano. "Eunice Odio: Una mujer contra las máscaras: 'Los elementos terrestres' ante 'Máscaras mexicanas.'" *Revista Iberoamericana* 53(138–9) (1987): 325–30.

Araya, Seidy and Zavala, Magda. "Frida Kahlo y Eunice Odio. El surrealismo latino-americano, imágenes pictóricas y verbales". *Letras: Revista de la Escuela de Literatura y Ciencias del Lenguaje*, 35 (2003): 103–15.

Chen Sham, Jorge and Vallbona, Rima de (eds) *La palabra innumerable: Eunice Odio ante la crítica*. San José: Editorial de la Universidad de Costa Rica, 2001.

Cruz Burdiel, de las Heras and Leda, María. "La poesía bíblica y Eunice Odio". *Foro Literario: Revista de Literatura y Lenguaje* 10(10) (1987): 42–50.

Esquivel, Mario A. *Eunice Odio en Guatemala*. San José: Instituto del Libro, 1983.

Jiménez, Luis A. "Eunice Odio" in *Dictionary of Literary Bibliography*. Vol. 283: *Modern American Poets, First Series*. Ed and intro. María A. Salgado. Detroit, MI: Gale, 2003, pp. 272–5.

Tapscott, Stephen (ed.) *Twentieth-Century Latin American Poetry. A Bilingual Anthology*. Austin, TX: University of Texas Press, 1996, pp. 282–90.

Vallbona de, Rima. *La obra en prosa de Eunice Odio*. San José: Editorial de Costa Rica, 1980.

——. "Eunice Odio: Rescate de un poeta". *Revista Interamericana de Bibliografía / Inter-American Review of Bibliography* 31 (1981): 199–214.

OLLÉ, CARMEN

Carmen Ollé (b. 1947) is one of Peru's most innovative and provocative contemporary writers. A member of the "Generation of 1970", she has published poetry, short fiction, novels and many pieces of journalism. Ollé attended the *Universidad Nacional Mayor de San Marcos*, in Lima, and between 1967 and 1980 she lived in Spain and France, where she discovered the writings of Georges Bataille and came into contact with the Feminist Movement. By then, her poetic vocation was taking its first steps. Ollé's writing marked a milestone in the founding of what would be the boom of women poets of the 1980s in Peru. Her first collection of poems, *Noches de adrenalina* (1981, Nights of Adrenaline), revealed some of the most important topics in her writing: time as an enemy of feminine youth and beauty, physical and inner exile, and a pessimistic conception of destiny. At times, *Noches de adrenalina* has been read as a provocative stand against a chauvinist society. Overall, however, it stands out for the bitter irony with which it juxtaposes sex, physiology, and bodily discourse. Its language is direct, and stripped of all romanticism. In many verses she examines the decadence of the body, physical misery, and the female condition. For example, in a dismantling of the stereotypes of feminine beauty, the genitals have no metaphorical value in the lyrics, serving only to illustrate the specific condition of the woman. In the final instance, the recurrence of erotic and physiological elements attempts to underscore the existence of a complex, turbulent feminine world, expressing many metaphysical and social concerns.

Ollé's verse is free and of varying length, with a very evident experimental and oral quality. Often she uses calligrams or inserts verses in French in her writing, and even includes a mini-drama of sorts entitled "Damas al dominó" ("Ladies at Dominoes"), a long poem with the formal appearance of a theatrical piece. It features a dialogue between two women, one smoking a cigarette and another chewing gum at a park. At the same time, there are men grouped in front of a television set watching a soccer game. The two scenes establish a marked contrast between men and women: while the female protagonists display a liveliness of spirit with their enigmatic, baroque phrases, and their fantastic imagery, the men appear to be alienated by their fanaticism for soccer, here portrayed as a quintessential aspect of Peruvian chauvinism. Moreover, in contrast to the intimate and personal dialogue that the women display, the men do not communicate among themselves; they only yell as a group when a goal is scored.

Todo orgullo humea la noche (1988, All Pride Makes for a Steamy Night) reaffirms many of the themes of Ollé's first book. This time, however, along with poetry, Ollé also includes a number of short stories and prose texts. From these brief narrative pieces emerges another interesting feature of her work: a portrayal of Lima's complex urban character. Such is the case in stories like "Arrabal" ("Slum"), "Mujer con sayonaras celestes" ("Woman with Light Blue Sandals"), and "Lince y el último verano" ("Lince and the Last Summer"), all of which show the clash of the individual – complex, contradictory, and sexualized – with its urban world. Feminine identity is expressed with an unusual severity, loaded with skepticism and bitterness, as well as irony and sarcasm.

Ollé's next book, *¿Por qué hacen tanto ruido?* (1992, Why Do They Make So Much Noise?), is again an atypical text, best described as a volume that mixes poetic prose and a novella. The novella's plot is simple: the progressive growing apart of the marriage of two writers, Sarah and Ignacio, and their final breakup, which is the pretext for setting out the female protagonist's reflections regarding the poetic vocation and her roles as a university professor, wife, and mother. The physiological language of *Noches de adrenalina* does not appear here. However, the narrative uses a stream of consciousness to examine Sarah's complex personality and multifaceted inner world.

Ollé would continue similar explorations in her next book, *Las dos caras del deseo* (1994, The Two Faces of Desire), arguably her most important novel. It tells the story of Ada, whose stagnant life as a middle-class university professor has reached a dead end. Eventually, social and political violence in Peru force Ada into exile in a small town in New Jersey, where she comes into contact with working-class women, many of whom are immigrants like herself, as well as with the trials and tribulations of surviving in a foreign culture. Ada is one of Ollé's richest and most complex characters, a woman of many masks. The plot is complemented by a narrative that juxtaposes a tender and aggressive tone in order to render a novel that is ultimately a meditation about interior and exterior exile, including the exploration of feminine homosexuality and cultural identity.

Pista falsa (1999, False Clue) tells the story of Irene, who leads a boring and solitary life in Lima. Irene sets out to find the facts about the mysterious death of Tessa, a friend from her adolescent days. In so doing, she discovers the existence of a secret cult linked to Tessa's family, made up of a number of extravagant characters that include Nadia, a Jewish ballerina who once danced for Hitler; Joaquín, a Bolivian detective who is also a playwright; Rafael, an eccentric poet; and Melania, an opera singer and former lover of a Peruvian president. Diary writing and detective fiction are at the core of this psychologically charged narrative, filled with surreal and grotesque situations, where Lima is portrayed as a city filled with hidden mysteries of romantic tradition and a false sense of modernity.

Ollé returns to the topic of exile in *Una muchacha bajo su paraguas* (2002, Young Woman Under Her Umbrella). The novel reflects on the myth of Paris as a haven for aspiring Latin American writers and artists. A first-person narrative, it is an intimate portrait of the French capital as seen through the eyes of an educated Peruvian woman, who is forced to make a living as a servant in a French family's home. The aspiration of finding literary fame and fortune in Paris is complemented by the seduction of an intense bohemian lifestyle for many Peruvian characters, who not only share stories of solidarity and survival in a marginal existence, but also of infidelity and amorous disappointment. This novel is an attempt to underscore the false glamour of Paris for Latin Americans, as well as the many myths the city has created through literature and the arts.

Ollé's writing emerges from a conflicted vision of the relationship between man and woman, the exploration of the female's interior world, and a certain tone of skepticism and disillusionment. Her works can be credited for addressing a number of taboo subjects for women in contemporary Peruvian society, ranging from sexual identity to social inequalities. Moreover, Ollé's hybrid texts defy the traditional classification of genre, both in poetry and prose. In many ways, her literary world is complex and often times controversial, but it is slowly receiving critical attention in international circles. Overall, Ollé's works address the need for a new sense of protagonism for women in Latin America, vindicating gender equality through artistic renewal.

César Ferreira

Selected Works

Noches de adrenalina. Lima: Cuadernos del Hipocampo, 1981.
Todo orgullo humea la noche. Lima: Lluvia Editores, 1988.
¿Por qué hacen tanto ruido? Lima: Universidad Nacional Mayor de San Marcos, 1992.
Las dos caras del deseo. Lima: Peisa, 1994.
Noches de adrenalina/Nights of Adrenaline. Trans. Anne Archer. Encino, CA: Floricanto Press, 1997.
Pista falsa. Lima: El Santo Oficio, 1999.
Una muchacha bajo su paraguas. Lima: El Santo Oficio, 2002.

References and Further Reading

Borsò, Vittoria. "La poesía del eco en la escritura de los años 80: Blanca Varela, Giovanna Pollarolo y Carmen Ollé". In Karl Kohut, José Morales Saravia, and Sonia V. Rose (eds), *Literatura peruana hoy: Crisis y creación*. Frankfurt: Vervuert – Iberoamericana, 1998, pp. 196–217.
Forgues, Roland. *Plumas de Afrodita: Una mirada a la poeta peruana del siglo XX*. Lima: Editorial San Marcos, 2004.
Hart, Stephen M. "Three Tropes of Postmodernism in Contemporary Peruvian Poetry". *Neophilologus* 89(4) (2005): 575–85.
Minardi, Giovanna. "Carmen Ollé". *Hispamérica* 28(83) (1999): 55–9.
——. "Entrevista a Carmen Ollé, escritora peruana". *Alba de América* 19(35–6) (2000): 505–10.
Ollé, Carmen. "Poetas peruanas: ¿Es lacerante la ironía?" In Karl Kohut, José Morales Saravia, and Sonia V. Rose (eds), *Literatura peruana hoy: Crisis y creación*. Frankfurt: Vervuert – Iberoamericana, 1998, pp. 187–95.
Rojas-Trempe, Lady. "Carmen Ollé y el des/en/mascaramiento de los géneros en *Las dos caras del deseo*". In Priscilla Gac-Artigas (ed.), *Reflexiones: Ensayos sobre escritoras hispanoamericanas contemporáneas II*. Fair Haven, NJ: Ediciones Nuevo Espacio, 2002, pp. 142–53.
Rowe, William. "The Subversive Languages of Carmen Ollé". *Poets of Contemporary Latin America: History and the Inner Life*. Oxford: Oxford University Press, 2000, pp. 327–51.
Vilanova, Núria. *Social Change and Literature in Peru (1970–1990)*. Lewiston, PA: The Edwin Mellen Press, 1999.
Zapata, Miguel-Angel. "Carmen Ollé y la fisiología de la pasión". *Confluencia* 12(2) (1997): 181–5.

OREAMUNO, YOLANDA

Yolanda Oreamuno (1916–56), novelist, short story writer and essayist, is known in her native Costa Rica for her experimental use of language as well as for her controversial life style and beliefs. In her fiction, Oreamuno effectively combines feminist concerns with the social problems of Costa Rica. As one of the leading feminist writers in her country, she focused her work on the role of women in a patriarchal society.

Yolanda Oreamuno was born on 8 April, 1916, in San José, Costa Rica. Her father, Carlos Oreamuno Pacheco, died when

Yolanda was only nine months old. She was raised in part by her mother Margarita Unger Salazar and in part by her maternal grandmother. While still a student at Colegio Superior de Señoritas, 16-year-old Oreamuno wrote a well-received essay "¿Qué hora es?" (What Time is It?) about the importance of education in women's lives. In 1932, Oreamuno continued her education by undertaking secretarial studies in the hope of learning skills that would support her writing. She also worked for a time in the Ministry of Education in 1935.

Oreamuno's short, albeit productive life was marked by series of tragedies that had a profound influence on her literary work. Her first husband, Jorge Molina Wood (a Chilean diplomat) committed suicide a year after their wedding in 1936. She married Oscar Barahona Streber in Costa Rica in 1937. He was an economist and supporter of Communist groups. Oreamuno divorced him in 1945 when her only son Sergio Siméon Barahona was 3 years old. The custody of Sergio was granted to her husband. Unhappy and lonely, Oreamuno moved to Guatemala in 1947 where she found appreciation and recognition as a person and as a writer, but an emotional relationship with Antonio Morales Nadjler caused her further pain and psychological turmoil.

Oreamuno suffered from kidney and heart problems. When her health deteriorated, she travelled to the United States of America for surgery, paid for with financial help from the Costa Rican poet Eunice Odio and the prize money awarded in 1948 for her novel *La ruta de su evasión* (The Path of their Evasion). She became very ill – a charity actually bought a coffin for her – while in Washington, DC. However, Oreamuno survived and travelled to Mexico in 1951 where she lived until her death on July 8, 1956, at the home of Eunice Odio. Five years after her death, Oreamuno's friends had her remains brought back to Costa Rica. She was buried in the General Cemetery in San José where stone 7–363 marks her grave.

Major Works

According to García Carillo, who studied the content of the writer's letters, Oreamuno wrote many essays, short stories, poems and five novels: *Por tierra firme* (1940, For the Native Land), *Dos tormentos y una aurora* (1944, Two Tempests and a Dawn), *Casta sombría* (1944, Dark Race), *Nuestro silencio* (1947, Our Silence) later renamed *De ahora en adelante* (From Now On), *La ruta de su evasión* (1948, The Path of their Evasion) (originally scheduled to be published by Editorial Leyenda de México in 1945). Only La *ruta de su evasión* (also called *La poseída* (The Possessed)) was published and it received the "Premio Centroamericano 15 de Setiembre" award in Guatemala in 1948. Oreamuno's essays and short articles were published in *A lo largo del corto* camino (1961, Along the Short Road) in Costa Rica and in *Relatos escojidos* (1977, Selected Stories).

Her novel *Por tierra Firme* together with two other novels by Fabián Dobles and by José Marín Cañas were all awarded joint first prize by the Congress of Spanish American Writers sponsored by Farrar & Rinehart in 1940. However, *Por tierra Firme* was never published and this award-winning novel by Oreamuno was subsequently lost.

Oreamuno's stories were published in *Repertorio Americano* edited by Joaquín García Monge, who became her mentor and friend. Among them: *18 de Setiembre* (the 18th of September), *Vela Urbana* (Urban Vigil), *and Misa de Ocho* (Eight o'clock Mass), *40° sobre Cero* (40°C above Zero), *Insomnio* (Insomnia), *El Espíritu de mi Tierra* (The Spirit of my Land), *El Negro, Sentido de la Alegría* (The Black, Filled with Happiness) which appeared in 1937.

Repertorio Americano published her article "El ambiente tico y los mitos tropicales" (The Costa Rican Environment and Tropical Myths) in 1939 in which Oreamuno criticizes the passive spirit of the people of Costa Rica.

In 1944, while in Bogotá, Colombia, Oreamuno wrote "Apología del limón dulce y el paisaje" (A Defense of the Sweet Lime and the Countryside) describing the beauty of nature. In the same year she wrote "México es mío" (Mexico is Mine) in which she presents the poverty of Mexico City in contrast with the rich splendour of its parks and historical monuments.

Oreamuno also wrote "Protesta contra el folkore" (A Protest against Folklore) in 1944 in which she encourages writers to portray the reality of urban life with the isolation of its people. Oreamuno postulates abandoning writing the regional narratives which was the prevailing literary style of that time in Costa Rica.

She wrote the short story *Valle alto* (High Valley) in 1946 using innovative, experimental techniques that preceded the literary movement of magical realism. In this story, two strangers, a female and a male, are stranded in a storm; they make love in rhythm with the wind but upon awakening the following morning, the woman is alone with only her memory of the previous night. There is no one to interfere with her thoughts so the notion of reality and fantasy is blurred.

In 1949, Oreamuno wrote *Harry Campbell Pall*, a satire on the historical construction of a character who lives in the country and constantly searches for his own historical identity.

Major Themes and Influences

Oreamuno began writing when "costumbrismo" (a literary style stressing local rural customs) was predominant in Costa Rica. She rejected folklore and any form of decadent literature and wrote literature penetrating the human soul and transcending the regional. Oreamuno was the first writer in Costa Rica to use new writing techniques: a polyphonic narrative voice and a non-linear time with unmarked dialogue that required active participation on the part of the readers. In this sense, she opened "a new way" for the Costa Rican literature. She claimed that the role of an artist was to convey a new message, interpret a transcendent moment, paint the essence of the country and respond to its vital necessity. In her search for originality, Oreamuno studied the poetry of Spanish twentieth-century avant-garde poets such as Lorca, Alberti, and Guillén. Even though her work is associated with Surrealism, her foremost influence was Proust and his analysis of the human soul. Marcel Proust's influence on Yolanda began when she was only 16 years old. In her own words, she learned to suffer with Proust who also taught her to search for the truth, not in the words of others but in the lack of them.

Oreamuno read and admired *Miau* by Galdós, *The Magic Mountain* by Thomas Mann and *La bahía de silencio* (The Bay of Silence) by Eduardo Mallea. Like these writers, Oreamuno wrote in her prose about the agony of existence, solitude, the forces of nature and the search for eternal youth. According to Costa Rican critic, Victoria Urbano, the prevailing theme in all of Oreamuno's texts is Yo/Yolanda Oreamuno (I-Yolanda Oreamuno).

Oreamuno was searching for form, for her own identity and for the identity of Latin America. She used a complex stream of consciousness technique, interior monologue revealing the subjective thoughts of her characters and abandoned all conventions of plot. Abelardo Bonilla noted that technical innovations in her narrative indicated the influence of James Joyce on Oreamuno's works. However, she stated in her letters that she had never read any works by Joyce, María Luisa Bombal or Jean Paul Sartre, the writers to whom she had been compared by her critics.

In the most important and best-known of her novels, *La ruta de su evasión*, Oreamuno uses an interior monologue technique through which the conscious thoughts of the characters are explored; the prevailing themes are of solitude and the recurrent cycles of life. In addition, conventional notions of time, place, matter, identity, or logical cause and effect are also challenged. A very complex text, based on the introspective memories of the moribund Teresa.

It is the story of the Vasco family, with their three sons, their wives and lovers. The despotic father, don Vasco, is the true dictator of the family. Feminine characters, Elena, Aurora and Teresa, reveal their thoughts, their motives and their sexual behaviour through conscious thoughts but also through the free interpretation of their dreams and memories. This novel, written in present and past tenses, includes the social scene of Costa Rica, the past being revealed through the device of memories and mental analysis. Urban life is reflected in the social scene and external descriptions. *La ruta* also reveals the conflict of generations, the submission of women to men, family violence and the spiritual emptiness of people. The leitmotif of the novel resides in the contrast between man and woman: woman—the victim of the man. A well-known literary critic, Alfonso Chase considers *La ruta* to be a significant literary achievement regarding the observation of the feminine character and the technique of introspection. Ofélia Ferrán studies Oreamuno's concept of feminine writing through the theories of Hélène Cixous. She concentrates on the revolutionary role of Oreamuno in the authorization of a disobedient female's sexuality while at the same time situating her in the tradition which proceeds and follows her. Ferrán looks at how Oreamuno incorporates Hélène Cixous' concept of feminine writings to make it distinctly her own and distinctly Latin American.

In 1961, Editorial Costa Rica published *A lo largo del corto camino* which contained most of Oreamuno's published work: four chapters of *La ruta de su evasión*, some critical commentaries, some letters and her short biography. In 1977, Editorial Costa Rica also published *Relatos escojidos: Yolanda Oreamuno*, a collection of her fiction with a commentary by Alfonso Chase, who was one of the editors.

Yolanda Oreamuno, an imaginative, original author, has not yet been adequately recognized in Costa Rica or in wider Latin America. Her work has been subjected to intense scrutiny by scholars of all descriptions, maybe because she was female, a supporter of Marxism, experimental, rebellious and one of the most beautiful women in the country. Oreamuno's works were analyzed in great detail by three Costa Rican academics: Rima de Vallbona, Victoria Chase and Victoria Urbano. The close circle of her friends preserved most of her works and her letters. Among them, there was a letter to Joaquín García Monge in which Oreamuno writes: "I am mature enough to produce the best work of my generation in Latin America, *José de la Cruz recoge su muerte* (José de la Cruz Suspends his Death). It will be a book full of magic without any useful thing". Sadly, we do not know if she merely dreamed about writing "her best work" or whether the dream ever reached fruition.

ANNA HAMLING

Selected Works

"La lagartija de la panza blanca". *Repertorio Americano* 32(24) (1936): 373.

"Para Revenar' No para Max Jiménez". *Repertorio Americano* 32(24) (1936): 339.

"40° sobre cero" (en Panamá). *Repertorio Americano* 33(1) (1937): 5.

"18 de septiembre". *Repertorio Americano* 33(8) (1937): 11.

"Misa de ocho".*Repertorio Americano* 33(5) (1937): 66.

"Vela urbana".*Repertorio Americano* 33(8–9) (1937): 136.

"Insomnio". *Repertorio Americano* 33(12) (1937): 187.

"El negro, sentido de la alegría". *Repertorio Americano* 33(18) (1937): 282.

"El espíritu de mi tierra". *Repertitorio Americano* 34(9) (1937): 137.

"Medios que usted sugiere al colegio para librar a la mujer costarricense de la frivolidad ambiente". *Repertorio americano* 36(2) (1938): 21–2, 30.

"El ambiente tico y los mitos tropicales". *Repertorio Americano* 36(11) (1939): 169–70.

"El último Max Jiménez ante la indiferencia nacional". *Repertorio Americano* 36(18) (1939): 281, 283.

"La vuelta a los lugares comunes". *Repertorio Americano* 37(1) (1940): 8–12.

"Protesta contra el folklore".*Repertorio Americano* 40(6) (1944): 84.

"Pasajeros al norte". *Repertorio Americano* 41(12) (1944): 182–3.

"México es mío". *Repertorio Americano* 41(15) (1944): 236.

"Valle alto". *Repertorio Americano* 42(14) (1946): 216–21.

"Max Jiménez y los que están". *Repertorio Americano* 43(4) (1947): 53–5.

La ruta de su evasión. Guatemala: Editorial del Ministerio de Educación Pública, 1949. San José, Costa Rica: Editorial EDUCA, 1971.

A lo largo del corto camino. San José: Editorial Costa Rica, 1961.

Relatos escojidos: Yolanda Oreamuno. Ed. Alfonso Chase. San José: Editorial Costa Rica, 1977.

Translations of Works

Bellver, Catherine G. (trans.) "The Tide Returns at Night". In *Five Women Writers of Costa Rica: Naranjo, Odio, Urbano, Valbona, Oreamuno*. Beaumont, TX: Asociación de la Literatura Femenina Hispánica, 1978.

O'Nan, Martha (trans.) "High Valley". In *Five Women Writers of Costa Rica: Naranjo, Odio, Urbano, Vallbona, Oreamuno*. Beaumont, TX: Asociación de la Literatura Feminina Hispánica, 1978.

References and Further Reading

Bonilla, Abelardo. *Historia de la literatura costarricense*. San José: Editorial Universitaria, 1957.

Chase, Alfonso. "La firme evasión de Yolanda Oreamuno". *La República* (June 7, 1964): 23.

——. "Yolanda Oreamuno y Marcel Proust". *La República* (Aug.13, 1970): 9.

Ferrán, Ofelia. "Pero quisite más ... Yolanda Oreamuno o la sexualidad desobediente". In Betty Osorio (ed.), *Las desobedientes*. Bogotá: Panamericana, 1997.

García Carillo, Eugenio. "Cartas íntimas de una dama de la literatura". *La República* (30 April 1970): 90.

Gold, Janet N. "Yolanda Oreamuno: The Art of Passionate Engagement". In Doris Meyer (ed.), *Reinterpreting the Spanish American Essay: Women Writers of the 19th and 20th Centuries*. Austin, TX: University of Texas, 1995, pp. 157–66.

Ramos, Lilia. "Sin noviciado, Yolanda Oreamuno escribe libros psicoanalíticos". *Repetitorio Americano* 44(12) (1950): 185–8.

Schrade, Arlene. "Yolanda Oreamuno". In Diane E. Marting (ed.), *Spanish American Women Writers A Bio-Bibliographical Source Book*. New York: Greenwood Press, 1990, pp. 394–414.

Urbano, Victoria. *Una escritora costarricense. Yolanda Oreamuno*. Madrid: Ediciones Castilla de Oro, 1968

Vallbona, Rima de. "*La ruta de su evasión* de Yolanda Oreamuno. Escritura proustiana suplementada". *Revista Iberoamericana* 53 (1999): 138–9.

OROZCO, OLGA

Olga Orozco (1920–99) is considered one of the most important women poets in twentieth-century Argentina. She was born on March 17, 1920, in the little town of Toay (province of La Pampa, Argentina) where her father, of Sicilian origin, owned some lands. In fact, it was her father who first introduced Orozco to the classical heritage and poetry of Dante and Petrarch. Orozco spent the first eight years of her life in Toay, and the town is a recurrent motif in her work. In 1928, the family moved to Bahía Blanca and in 1936 to Buenos Aires, where Orozco graduated with a teaching degree a year later.

She worked in a radio station and collaborated on such journals as *Correo Literario*, *La Nación* and *Sur*. She was also a translator from French and Italian into Spanish. Throughout her life, Orozco traveled to South America, Europe and Africa, trips that broadened her vision and experience and therefore enriched her poetry, making her a more cosmopolitan writer. She married twice: first to Miguel Ángel Gómez and then to Valerio Peluffo. She had no children in either marriage. Among her friends should be mentioned Norah Lange, Oliverio Girondo and Alberto Girri.

Historically, her writings coincide with *peronismo*, the 1976 coup, the dictatorship and the "Dirty War", not to mention other events that were taking place farther away, such as the Second World War (1939–45) and the Spanish Civil War (1936–39), which had cultural consequences in her own country. Although the connections between Orozco's poetry and her historical context are not immediately visible, and she seems to be detached from a historical context, the fact is that this apparent disengagement from the political circumstances of her time only shows her introspectiveness. She questions the world through the search of the self.

Olga Orozco died in Buenos Aires on August 15, 1999.

Influences

Although Orozco is often considered a member of the Generación del 40, due to her introspectiveness and subjectivity, this classification should be used carefully and considered mostly chronological, since Olga Orozco's poetry is made of such uniqueness that resists easy classification. Writers who were part of this generation include Enrique Molina, César Fernández Moreno, Juan Rodolfo Wilcock, Daniel Devoto, Julio Marsagot and Miguel Ángel Gómez, all associated with the origin of the journal *Canto*. They have been called neo-romantics and their poetry has shown an elegiac note.

Surrealism has been said to be one of the greatest influences on Olga Orozco's work, because of the extended use of oneiric images and the emphasis on the imaginary. Orozco herself admitted her use of surrealist techniques such as the subconscious search, the imagery and the oneiric, but she did not consider herself an orthodox surrealist. The coherent structure of her symbolic images brings her closer to the Symbolists, as does her concept of the poet as a visionary, an intermediary who deals with the immediate, transforming it in search of knowledge.

Her use of fragmented dreams, childhood recollections and search of the metaphysical, make her poetry eclectic and difficult to classify. Orozco herself has mentioned on numerous occasions her indebtedness to authors such as San Juan de la Cruz, Rimbaud, Baudelaire and Rilke, but she has also insisted on the fact that their influence on her was more as a reader than as a writer.

Themes

Olga Orozco has been mainly acknowledged for her poetry, as several literary prizes at national and international level prove, among which stand out the Gran Premio del Fondo Nacional de las Artes (Great Prize from the Nacional Arts Fund) in 1980, Primer Premio Nacional de Poesía (First Nacional Poetry Prize) in 1988, Premio Interamericano de Cultura "Gabriela Mistral" (Interamerican Cultural "Gabriela Mistral" Prize) in 1994 and Premio Juan Rulfo (Juan Rulfo Prize) in 1998.

Despite her nine volumes of poetry, Orozco also wrote two works in prose, full of autobiographical references; *La oscuridad es otro sol* (1967, Darkness is Another Sun) and *También la luz es un abismo* (1995, Light Also Is an Abyss), where in both the main character is a little girl, Lía, the alter ego of the writer. She also wrote a play: *Y el humo de tu incendio está subiendo* (And the Smoke of Your Fire is Rising), which won a municipal Drama Prize in 1972.

Her first book of poems was published in 1946, *Desde lejos* (From Afar). She looks nostalgically to the past, recollecting places and family members who have already died: "La abuela" (The Grandmother), her brother: "Para Emilio en su cielo" (For Emilio in his Heaven) and "Cuando alguien se nos muere" (When One of Us Dies), as well as "1889 Una casa que fue" (1889 A House That Once Was). Orozco reflects on the passage of time and transitoriness of life, and surrounds her poems with a metaphysical aura that continues throughout her poetic production.

Her second book, *Las muertes* (1952, The Deaths), is also dedicated to those who died, but in this case, it is fictional characters from Faulkner, Rilke, the Comte de Lautréamont, Dickens and Melville. The book, composed of seventeen poems, includes one, "Olga Orozco", dedicated to herself, in which the poet envisions her own death. It is important to realize that the poet was only 32 years old when the book was published and she decided to write about her own death, which was yet far off. This is not the only aspect which gives complexity to the poem: her combination of first, second and third person in the poem and the juxtaposition of present, past and future tenses demonstrate that her neoromantic leaning is not as clear as it seems, and although present in her first book, will diminish progressively throughout the rest of her work.

In 1962, she published *Los juegos peligrosos* (Dangerous Games), probably her most symbolic and methaphorical book, in which oneiric images abound. For this reason, it has been considered her closest book to surrealism. References to the esoteric "Para hacer tu talisman" (To Make Your Talisman) and the search of herself "Para ser otra" (To Be Another One) are common also.

Her next book was *Museo salvaje* (1974, Wild Museum). Orozco's poetry is in constant search for unity and self-explanation. This book, more than any other, reflects such a search. From a more objective point of view, the book concentrates on the components of the body and the puzzlement Orozco feels at how the body as a representation of herself, feels at the same time alien to her true self. Orozco accepts that the body is the only element to represent herself, but she also realizes its inability to truly define who she is.

In 1977, she published *Cantos a Berenice* (Songs to Berenice). This book is addressed to her deceased cat, Berenice, following authors such as Kipling, Mallarmé, Carroll, Eliot, Baudelaire and Rilke, all ardent admirers of felines.

Mutaciones de la realidad (1979, Mutations of Reality) is a confrontation with reality from a different perspective, playing with time and space. Orozco returns to the concept of poetry as search. She reflects on the role of the poet and asks herself many questions which only reveal frustration with regard to the impossibility of achieving unity, as the title of one of her poems suggests: "Densos velos te cubren, Poesía" (Thick Veils Cover You, Poetry). To this book belongs the poem dedicated to Alejandra Pizarnik: "Pavana para una infanta difunta" (Pavane for a Deceased Infanta).

Final Works

La noche a la deriva (1983, Night Adrift) constitutes a new shift in her poetry. There is a sense of resignation and understanding of the poet's role. This resignation brings her to a reconciliation with herself. There is also an increasing number of visual images and constant references to painters and their works.

Her next book was published in 1987, *En el revés del cielo* (On the Other Side of the Sky). As Olga Orozco approaches her final works, there is a sense of recollection. Images of not only the end of her own work but also her own death are common again. Poems such as "El resto era silencio" (The Rest Was Silence), "El retoque final" (The Last Touch) and "En el final era el verbo" (At the End It Was the Verb) revolve around these recurrent themes.

Con esta boca en este mundo (1992, With This Mouth, In This World), the last of her books, is composed of seventeen poems that are a compilation of the previously mentioned themes and poems and focus particularly on poetry. The mouth from the title constitutes the link between the body and poetry, since it is the part of the body through which poetry is projected.

For an author so well received and recognized in her time, the critical work on her poetry is not as abundant as expected, probably due to its complex nature. As Melanie Nicholson and Thorpe Running have pointed out, critics have limited themselves to questioning the nature of Orozco's poetry and the influences on her work. In general, her complex poetry has divided critics between those who underline the emotional and lyrical aspects of her poetry, concentrating in its subjectivity, and those who emphasize the metaphysical search the poet undertakes throughout her work, focusing on its intellectuality.

However, there is one aspect of Orozco's work that all critics agree on, and that is Orozco's individualism. Her poetry is characterized by a subtle combination of the ordinary and the fantastic, that is, reality and fiction. For Orozco, life and death are intertwined and she likes to go beyond the surface of life to see what is on the other side. There is no question that she is a woman of profound spirituality and her interest in the magic and the esoteric is a constant in her work. Her work has been translated into several languages including English, French, Italian, Portuguese, German and Japanese.

ELENA GONZÁLEZ-MUNTANER

Selected Works

Páginas de Olga Orozco. Selections by the author with an introduction by Cristina Piña. Buenos Aires: Editorial Celta, 1984.

También la luz es un abismo. Buenos Aires: Emecé Editores, 1995.

Relámpagos de lo invisible: Antología. Buenos Aires: Fondo de Cultura Económica, 1998.

Obra poética. Olga Orozco. 5th edn. Buenos Aires: Ediciones Corregidor, 2000.

Engravings Torn from Insomnia: poems by Olga Orozco. Trans. Mary Crow. Rochester, NY: BOA Editions, 2002.

La voz de Olga Orozco. Madrid: Publicaciones de la Residencia de Estudiantes, 2003.

References and Further Reading

Brú, José (ed.) *Acercamientos a Olga Orozco.* Guadalajara, Mexico: Universidad de Guadalajara, 1998.

Escaja, Tina. "'La posible aproximación a lo indecible': metafísica del deseo en la poesía de Olga Orozco". *Hispanic Journal* 19(1) (1998): 33–47.

Fagundo, Ana María. "La poesía de Olga Orozco o la aproximación a lo indecible". In *Literatura femenina de España y las Américas.* Madrid: Editorial Fundamentos, 1995, pp. 209–19.

Kuhnheim, Jill S. *Gender, Politics, and Poetry in Twentieth-Century Argentina.* Gainesville, FL: University Press of Florida, 1996.

Martín López, Sarah. "Olga Orozco, metafísica de los sentidos". In *La literatura hispanoamericana con los cinco sentidos: Actas del V Congreso Internacional de la AEELH.* Ed. Eva Valcárcel. A Coruña: Universidade da Coruña, 2002.

Nicholson, Melanie. "Olga Orozco and the Poetics of Gnosticism". *Revista de Estudios Hispánicos* 35(1) (2001): 73–90.

——. *Evil, Madness and the Occult in Argentine Poetry.* Gainesville, FL: University Press of Florida, 2002.

Requeni, Antonio. *Travesías.* Buenos Aires: Editorial Sudamericana, 1997.

Running, Thorpe. "Imagen y creación en la poesía de Olga Orozco". *Letras femeninas* 13, no.1–2 (1987): 12–20.

Torres de Peralta, Elba. *La poética de Olga Orozco: desdoblamiento de Dios en máscara de todos.* Madrid: Editorial Playor, 1987.

Zonana, Víctor Gustavo. "Imágenes de la memoria en la obra de Olga Orozco". *Boletín de la Academia Argentina de Letras* 67(265–6) (2002): 327–45.

ORPHÉE, ELVIRA

Elvira Orphée was born in San Miguel de Tucumán, Argentina, on May 29, 1930. She studied literature at the University of Buenos Aires and at the Sorbonne in Paris. She resided in France, Italy, Spain, Venezuela and Argentina. She married to Miguel Ocampo, an artist and a diplomat with whom she had three daughters. She was awarded Honorable Mention for her novel *Uno* in 1961, Second Prize in the Municipality of Buenos Aires for *Aire tan dulce*, 1967, First Prize for *En el fondo* in 1969, the Regional Prize for *La muerte y los desencuentros*, and Honorable Mention in the 1970 short story contest sponsored by *Imagen*. She has published short stories and articles in *Sur, Ficción, Cuadernos, Asomante, El Tiempo, Razón, Revista de Occidente, Zona Franca* and others.

The themes and the atmosphere of Orphée's novels reflect the characteristics of the literary group often called "the patricidals". Representing the Generation of 1955 in Argentina, this group includes authors such as Marco Denevi, Marta Lynch, Beatriz Guido and Alicia Jurado, all of whom wrote in the neorealistic style. This group rebelled against the aestheticism of their literary predecessors and, instead of writing escapist stories within refined settings, they rendered their own vision of the world filtered through an internal reality. "The patricidals" often depicted their protagonists in adolescence, focusing on generational conflicts within the framework of the Perón Regime. Another popular motif was the plight of women, a subject which allowed them to question restrictive taboos and the false double standard of gender roles in a variety of social milieus, thus revealing their frustration and rebellion against the status quo. Orphée herself favors first-person narration, often from the point of view of her different characters. She uses a lyrical style, applying elliptical dialogue, lyrical introspection, and often analepsis instead of chronological linking.

As do the protagonists of her fiction, Elvira Orphée considers herself a loner and a fatalist. Having spent her sickly childhood in the Argentine hinterland, she sets most of her works in a doomed provincial environment, where "everything was imbued with mystery, diseases, apparitions, guilt from afar" (Picón Garfield 1988: 104). Existential malaise and the presence of tainted and condemned characters typify this zone. Even the corporeal is a hindrance and a curse because, as Orphée argues "the very fact that we possess a body mutilates our freedom" (Picón Garfield 1988, p. 108). Pain and sorrow are essential steps in achieving self-control ("You can never be happy, but you can feel as if you have conquered your fears" (Picón Garfield 1988: 110), but nothing can help Orphée's doomed characters attain supreme bliss or love because they are unachievable goals.

Her tainted, unloved, and ostracized protagonists perform within the parameters of an incessant struggle against mundane limitations. Men who feel humiliated and impotent before an implacable destiny adopt extreme forms of behavior, such as cruelty and crime. For instance, both Sexto Rivera, the protagonist of *Dos veranos* (1956), and Félix Gauna, one of the narrators in *Aire tan dulce* (1966), feel mortified by their low economic status and strive in vain to attain a better position through violence and murder. On the other hand, Orphée's female characters, with the exception of Atala from *Aire tan dulce*, tend to escape into a world of fantasy and delusion, envisioning death as the final liberator. They suffer from mental and physical illnesses often unnamed and unusually painful. This condition restricts their lives, subjecting them to the confinement of four walls and an overpowering depression, isolating them even further from the rest of society. Orphée populates her fiction with female characters whose bodies are ill or deformed and whose minds are incessantly tortured: Sexto's foster mother in *Dos veranos* is paralyzed by arthritis; Margarita, one of the characters in *Uno* (1961), a novel depicting Buenos Aires during the Perón era of the 1950s, suffers from an unnamed psychological and physical illness; the heroine of *En el fondo* (1969) becomes ill just like her paralytic mother, and Atala from *Aire tan dulce* lives stigmatized by an unknown malady. Also, the characters of *La última conquista de El Angel* (1977) suffer agonizing bodily afflictions in the form of the physical torture wrought upon them by victimizers, who perceive their actions as a sacred duty to cleanse society of a sociopolitical cancer. Living under such signs of exclusion, as Flori determines, "Orphée's characters are generally social misfits (outcasts, orphans, and criminals) or those who are psychologically dysfunctional (unfeeling, unloved, and humiliated), unsuccessfully seeking to vindicate themselves" (1995, p. 60). Set against a background of primordial passions that transcend the triviality of existence, they struggle in vain to go beyond the limiting conditions imposed on them by an implacable fatalism. Some of them signify exemption from original sin, while others represent fallen angels cursed and eternally exiled from paradise.

Dos veranos deals with two summers in the life of the picaresque adolescent Sixto Riera. Blinded by his feelings of inadequacy, Sixto craves power over others at all costs. During the course of his turbulent youth, he turns to hatred and violence, which lead to crimes, murder, and his eventual incarceration. *Uno*, Orphee's second novel, takes place in Buenos Aires in the 1950s. The work explores how political events (and Peronism) change the lives of a dozen characters during the course of one year. *En el fondo* tells a story of a woman who returns with her family to the idealized region of her childhood, only to experience a disappointment which makes her retreat to an inner world of illness and insanity. *La última conquista de El Angel* is perhaps Orphée's most famous novel. Here, the unnamed protagonist develops into a sadistic torturer, a man who dedicates himself to destroying others with passion and utter devotion. He admires and learns to emulate his boss, Winkel, a man whose sole purpose in life is to serve his homeland by executing the most brutal yet soberly calculated torture. The novel distances itself from torture's unspeakable effect, by referring to it with objective and technical knowledge. Such an approach—devoid of any passion or even attention towards the victims—makes Orphée's work even more disquieting. The victim and his/her body—tied, gagged and blindfolded—becomes the state's voiceless property, an expendable entity whose personal qualities are irreversibly wiped out. Since torture is clearly the state's primary method of keeping order, its widespread infusion is overpowering in its magnitude. Despite the fact that Orphée never alluded to Argentina's infamous era of "El Proceso," it is not difficult to understand why the novel was banned in Argentina until recently. Its testimonial character is clearly reminiscent of Argentina's "Dirty War," making the text a grim and compelling document of Argentina's darkest times. *Las viejas fantasiosas* is a collection of short stories narrating episodes from provincial life. The novel *La muerte y los desencuentros* (1990) depicts once again a politically volatile country, to which the main character returns after many years. When the protagonist's father disappears and her husband begins to ignore her, she withdraws into the world of literature and the imagination. *Ciego del cielo* (1991) is a collection of short stories which deal with various aspects of crime, punishment, justice, and moral responsibility.

The protagonist Atala Pons of *Aire tan dulce* stands out by marking a path very different from that of Orphée's "typically" subdued and quieted heroines. Placed within repressive surroundings of a small town, Atala chooses to live dangerously, manipulating mesmerized men and playing games with death. She provides the readers with an example of a strong, disabled but de-victimized woman who represents a striking exception to the typical marginalization of women because she follows in the steps of the writer's male protagonists by quenching her sexual curiosity and spreading destruction in her community.

Orphée, who denies being a "militant feminist," consciously focuses on women's experiences, believing that enough has been written about the lives of men. Most of her male characters are mere fillers, whereas women, weak and strong, infirm or healthy, are the focus of her unique prose. Presented in symbolic settings, Orphée's novels contemplate primordial human passions, conveying, nevertheless, the suffocating atmosphere of the Argentine province, as well as the terror of the "Proceso" era.

ALDONA BIALOWAS POBUTSKY

Selected Works

Novels

Dos veranos. Buenos Aires: Sudamericana, 1956.
Uno. Buenos Aires: Fabril Editora, 1961.
Aire tan dulce. Buenos Aires: Sudamericana, 1966.
En el fondo. Buenos Aires: Emecé Editores, 1969.
Su demonio preferido. Buenos Aires: Emecé Editores, 1973.
La última conquista de El Ángel. Caracas: Monte Avila, 1977.
Las viejas fantasiosas. Buenos Aires: Emecé Editores, 1981.
La muerte y los desencuentros. Buenos Aires: Fraterna, 1999.
Ciego del cielo. Buenos Aires: Emecé Editores, 1991.
Basura y luna. Buenos Aires: Planeta, 1996.

Short Fiction

"Las casas". *Sur* 198 (1950): 44–51.
"La calle Mate de Luna". *Sur* 262 (1960): 43–50.
"La pequeña Ning". *Sur* 306 (1967): 39–44.
"¡Ay, Enrique!" *La Opinión*, 27 November 1977.
"Nunca la compasión". In *Recontres. Ecrivains et artistes de l'Argentine et du Québec/ Encuentros: Escritores y artistas de la Argentina y Quebec*, ed. Gilles Pellerin and Oscar Hermes Villordo. Québec: Les Editions Sans Nom, 1989, 209–16.

Critical Article

"La realidad y las normas del cuento". *La Nación*, 27 July 1985.

Works Available in Translation

El Angel's Last Conquest. Trans. Magda Bogin. New York: Ballantine, 1986.
"Angel's Last Conquest". Trans. Evelyn Picón Garfield. In Evelyn Picón Garfield (ed.), *Women's Fiction from Latin America: Selections from Twelve Contemporary Authors*. Detroit, MI: Wayne State University Press, 1988, pp. 162–77.
"The Silken Whale". Trans. Evelyn Picón Garfield. In Evelyn Picón Garfield (ed.), *Women's Fiction from Latin America: Selections from Twelve Contemporary Authors*. Detroit, MI: Wayne State University Press, 1988, pp. 178–86.
"The Beguiling Ladies". Trans. Christopher Leland. In Marjorie Agosín (ed.), *Landscapes of a New Land: Short Fiction by Latin American Women*. New York: White Pine Press, 1989, pp. 173–81.
"Do Not Mistake Eternities". Trans. Oscar Montero. In Sara Castro-Klarén, Sylvia Molloy and Beatriz Sarlo (eds), *Women's Writing in Latin America*. Boulder, CO: Westview Press, 1991, pp. 180–1.
"Silences". Trans. Oscar Montero. In Sara Castro-Klarén, Sylvia Molloy and Beatriz Sarlo (eds), *Women's Writing in Latin America*. Boulder, CO: Westview Press, 1991, pp. 178–9.
"Voices That Grew Old". Trans. Oscar Montero. In Sara Castro-Klarén, Sylvia Molloy and Beatriz Sarlo (eds), *Women's Writing in Latin America*. Boulder, CO: Westview Press, 1991, pp. 181–5.
"An Eternal Fear". Trans. Janice Molloy. In Marjorie Agosín (ed.), *Secret Weavers: Stories of the Fantastic by Women of Argentina and Chile*. New York: White Pine Press, 1992, pp. 93–9.
"How the Little Crocodiles Cry". Trans. Janice Molloy. In Marjorie Agosín (ed.), *Secret Weavers: Stories of the Fantastic by Women of Argentina and Chile*. New York: White Pine Press, 1992, pp. 104–7.
"I Will Return, Mommy". Trans. Janice Molloy. In Marjorie Agosín (ed.), *Secret Weavers: Stories of the Fantastic by Women of Argentina and Chile*. New York: White Pine Press, 1992, pp. 100–3.

References and Further Reading

Agosín, Marjorie. "So We Will Not Forget: Literature and Human Rights in Latin America". *Human Rights Quarterly* 10(2) (1988): 177–92.
Collette, Marianella. *Conversación al Sur: Entrevistas con escritoras argentinas*. Buenos Aires: Simung, 2003.
Flori, Mónica. *Streams of Silver: Six Contemporary Women Writers from Argentina*. Lewisburg, PA: Associated University Press, 1995.
Pinto, Magdalena García. *Historias íntimas: Conversaciones con diez escritoras Latinoamericanas*. Hanover, NH: Ediciones del Norte, 1988.
Pobutsky, Aldona Bialowas. "From the Bottom of My Pain: Living Dangerously in Elvira Orphée's *Aire tan dulce*". *Letras Femeninas*. 18(2) (2002): 137–57.
Tompkins, Cynthia. "El poder del horror: Abyección en la narrativa de Griselda Gambaro y de Elvira Orphée". *Revista Hispánica Moderna* 46(1) (1993): 179–92.

P

PACHECO, CRISTINA

Cristina Pacheco (b. 1941) is one of Mexico's most dedicated chroniclers of the twentieth- and the twenty-first-century urban experience. As both a journalist and a writer of fiction, her focus is the metropolis of Mexico City and the myriad stories of its inhabitants. While her interviews reflect a cross-section of Mexican society, her fictionalized stories tend to depict its marginalized segments more; yet, in both cases, she expresses a combination of respectful inquiry, harsh honesty, grotesque reality, and unending tenderness. Mexican cultural critic Carlos Monsiváis says of her, "Cristina desatiende los prejuicios, y se ocupa en lo que quiere y consigue: un panorama diversificado y elocuente donde los protagonistas se expresan sin trabas" [Cristina ignores prejudices, and concerns herself with that which she loves and can attain: a diversified and eloquent panorama wherein protagonists express themselves freely] (in Pacheco, *La luz de México*, p. 13).

Although her career places her within the public realm, she remains protective of her personal life. Pacheco was born on September 13, 1941, in San Felipe, Guanajuato, Mexico. During her youth, her family sustained itself through farming and cattle-raising in this central area north of Mexico City known for its rich mines and fertile farmlands. In 1946, due to the increased difficulty of farming, her family relocated to Mexico City, where she still lives. While the move from a rural to an urban existence is substantial, she also sees it as an experience that continues to connect her with her subject-matter. It also provided her with increased educational opportunities, which eventually led her to study Spanish literature at La Universidad Nacional Autónoma de México. In 1962, she married noted Mexican poet José Emilio Pacheco (Mexico, 1939–), to whom she has dedicated some of her manuscripts.

Journalist

Pacheco began her writing career in the 1960s as a journalist publishing in no less than five Mexico City newspapers. During the 1960s and 1970s, she was also the director of three women's magazines. In the 1980s and 1990s, she hosted the weekday radio call-in program *Aquí y ahora* (Here and Now) and the investigative television program *Aquí nos tocó vivir* (This is Where We Happen to Live) for which she received the "Best Community Service Program" award from the Asociación Nacional de Periodistas (1986). She won awards, too, for her interviews, such as the Premio Nacional de Periodismo (1975, 1985) and the Premio Manuel Buendía (1992).

Pacheco has published several books of interviews that provide insights into Mexican art and popular culture. They range from a homage to famous muralist José Clemente Orozco (Mexico, 1883–1949), to an examination of forty Mexican artists and photographers, to an exploration of thirty-two people from the world of popular entertainment (including, for example, singers, wrestlers, actors, dancers), to collaborative collections of interviews with writers. These interview subjects represent the breadth of Mexican society and, through its variety, one can note Pacheco's aim of humanizing these individuals and make them accountable to and approachable by the general public.

A Mixture of Journalism and Fiction

Pacheco's strong journalistic formation is still noted in the use of question/answer interviews and testimonial text segments in some of her other publications, for example *Zona de desastre* (1986, Disaster Zone), *La rueda de la fortuna* (1993, The Wheel of Fortune), *Imágenes: Renovación Habitacional Popular* (1987, Images: Popular Housing Renovations), and *Oficios de México* (1993, Mexican Crafts). Yet, a hybrid genre is evident in such texts in that Pacheco blends the more traditional journalistic elements with fictionalized narrations and, in the case of the latter two, photographs taken by Guillermo Soto Curiel and Ricardo Kirchner, respectively. While these blended texts share a similar format, their topics are varied: from relating the 1985 earthquake that struck Mexico City, to documenting Mexico's economic collapse during the 1970s–1990s, to presenting Mexico's traditional craftspeople and their crafts.

Fiction

The diversity of topics noted in her journalistic pieces and her journalism/fiction blends is also seen in Pacheco's purely fictional works, which are her most relevant contributions to the field of Latin American literature. Although the majority of these fictionalized short stories originally appeared as part of her "Mar de historias" (Ocean of Stories) column in the Sunday edition of the Mexico City newspaper *La Jornada*, many of them have been republished as collections.

While the specific subject matter of each of Pacheco's many compilations varies greatly, format and overall theme unite them. Each collection consists of an average of thirty-five stories, all of which are brief, which creates an almost *media res* (in the middle) urgency that immediately immerses the reader in the context and the characters. This connection is further cemented by Pacheco's use of first person and second person narration, names or nicknames, and dialog. The use of vernacular speech also establishes verisimilitude. Each separate story, nevertheless, portrays its own individual characters and there is no cross-referencing among the stories, even though there is an abundance of them, such as: an elementary school janitor longing to learn to read, a single mother supporting two children, a prostitute killed by police, a starry-eyed youth immigrating to Mexico City to become a musician, a wife selling herself to have water delivered to her home, a couple having communication issues in their relationship, a family celebrating a wedding anniversary.

This multiplicity of situations and characters, however, also serves as the uniting force of all of Pacheco's writing: life in Mexico City. The parallel is clear: just as Mexico City is one of the world's largest cities in terms of size and population (which is estimated to be over twenty million inhabitants), so too do Pacheco's stories offer a seemingly unending sampling of narrative opportunities.

Critical Overview

In spite of the fact that during her most productive years, her weekly stories in *La Jornada* reached millions of readers, she received relatively little critical acclaim for them. This may be due to the very nature of her stories and their relationship with the genre of the chronicle, which within a post-modernist context is a hybrid and liminal genre that crisscrosses through traditionally defined categories.

Nevertheless, and apart from the generally positive reviews of Pacheco's narrative collections, it would seem that the majority of the literary critiques of her work focus on the portrayal of the feminist voice, especially as contextualized within realistic settings. Ironically, critics find her work to be both pro-feminist (due to the representation of a vast array of female characters and situations) and anti-feminist (due to a perceived hopelessness of those same characters and situations).

Other critics, however, note that such a division is limiting and a disservice to the larger context of Pacheco's short stories. Her fictionalized chronicles do portray female perspectives, but they also express the immigrant experience, with a special focus on urban migration, issues of physical and mental illness (such as Alzheimer's disease), loneliness and isolation, economic constraints of underemployment, and ethnic, social, linguistic, class, and gender prejudices. While these topics are serious, and potentially depressing, a careful examination of them within their context leads to the realization that in spite of the stark realities covered, there are positive over-riding themes, such as the force of the family unit (allowing that family may be defined in multiple ways) and the resilience of individuals. "Tú, yo, la casa" (You, Me, The House) from *Sopita de fideo* (1984, Noodle Soup) exemplifies this in that a group of people have struggled to build their own homes only to learn later that their deeds are fake. The absentee landowner wants them off the land, thus, their homes are razed by bulldozers. Faced with this physical and emotional destruction, however, one woman defies the ruin by writing her family's names and address on a piece of cardboard, which she then places on top of the rubble that once was their home. Within a few hours, everyone has done so. In spite of the situation, survival and hope remain strong.

Whether through Cristina Pacheco's dedication to journalism or literature, her contributions as a writer are substantial. The messages of crisis and comfort, criticism and praise, poverty and promise that she conveys in her works are fundamental. By humanizing public and famous figures through her interviews and by highlighting in a personalized manner the unfortunate situations of the marginalized through her fictional narrations, she draws attention to the underlining humanity of those involved, which forms a connection with the reader, and therefore, the potential for progress.

Dawn Slack

Selected Works

Aquí nos tocó vivir: testimonios de la vida en México con imágenes y palabras. Instituto Politécnico Nacional. Channel 11, Mexico City, 1980s–1990s.

Orozco: iconografía personal. Mexico City: Fondo de Cultura Económica, 1983.

Para vivir aquí. Mexico City: Editorial Grijalbo, 1983.

Sopita de fideo. Mexico City: Ediciones Océano, 1984.

Testimonios y conversaciones. Mexico City: Fondo de Cultura Económica, 1984.

Cuarto de azotea. Mexico City: SEP, Ediciones Gernika, 1986.

Zona de desastre. Mexico City: Ediciones Océano, 1986.

Imágenes: Renovación Habitacional Popular. Photographs by Guillermo Soto Curiel. Mexico City: Renovacion Habitacional Popular, 1987.

La última noche del "Tigre". Mexico City: Ediciones Océano, 1987.

La luz de México: entrevistas con pintores y fotógrafos. Guanajuato: Gobierno del Estado de Guanajuato, 1988.

El corazón de la noche. Mexico City: Ediciones El Caballito, 1989.

Para mirar a lo lejos. Mexico City: Instituto de Cultura de Trabajos, 1989.

Los dueños de la noche. Mexico City: Planeta, 1990.

Aquí y ahora: nuestras realidades vistas a través de los comentarios de una periodista de toda la vida, Cristina Pacheco. XEUU, Radio 900, Mexico City, 1990s.

Oficios de México. Photographs by Ricardo Kirchner. Mexico City: Nacional Financiera, S.N.C., 1993.

"La dimensión de un hombre" y otros dos. Mexico City: Plaza y Valdés, 1993.

La rueda de fortuna. Mexico City: Ediciones Era, 1993.

Amores y desamores. Mexico City: Selector: Colección Aura, 1996.

Los trabajos perdidos. Mexico City: Océano de México, 1998.

Boystown: La zona de tolerancia. With Dave Hickey and Keith Carter. Ed. William D. Wittliff. New York: Aperture Foundation, 2000.

Al pie de la letra: entrevistas con escritores. With Mauricio José Sanders. Mexico City: Fondo de Cultura Económica, 2002.

Limpios de todo amor. Mexico City: Océano de México, 2002.

La chistera maravillosa. Mexico City: Planeta, 2004.

El oro del desierto. Mexico City: Random House Mondadori, 2005.

References and Further Reading

Charles, Mercedes. "Navegando por el 'Mar de historias.'" 11(56) *FEM* (Aug. 1987): 38–9.

Egan, Linda. "Entrevistas con periodistas mujeres sobre la prensa mexicana". *Mexican Studies/Estudios mexicanos* 9(2) (Summer: 1993): 275–94.

——. "The Sound of Silence: Voices of the Marginalized in Cristina Pacheco's Narrative". In Kristine Ibsen (ed.), *The Other Mirror: Women's Narrative in Mexico, 1980–1995*. Westport, CT: Greenwood Press, 1997, pp. 133–46.

Espinosa Rugarcia, Amparo. "Con el sexo a cuestas". In Amparo Espinosa Rugarcia, Marcela Ruiz de Velasco and Gloria M. Prado Garduño (eds), *Palabras de mujer*. Mexico City: Editorial Diana, 1989 pp. 123–33.

Ferman, Claudia. *Política y posmodernidad: hacia una lectura de la anti-modernidad en Latinoamérica*. Buenos Aires: Editorial Almagesto, 1994.

Prado Garduño, Gloria M. "Cuando la injusticia encuentra su voz". In Amparo Espinosa Rugarcia, Marcela Ruiz de Velasco and Gloria M. Prado Garduño (eds), *Palabras de mujer*. Mexico City: Editorial Diana, 1989, pp. 115–22.

"El registro de lo cotidiano". *Gaceta UNAM* 24 Aug. 1987. Reprinted in *Pido la palabra: cuarto nivel,* by Carolina Cordero, Cecilia González, Mónica de Neymet, and Silvia Peña Alfaro, 184. Mexico City: Universidad Nacional Autónoma de México, 1991.

Schaefer-Rodríguez, Claudia. "Embedded Agendas: The Literary Journalism of Cristina Pacheco and Guadalupe Loaeza". *Latin American Literary Review* 19(38) (July–Dec. 1991): 62–76.

Slack, Dawn. *The Writing of Cristina Pacheco: Narrating the Mexican Urban Experience*. Ann Arbor, MI: UMI Dissertation Services, 1998.

——. "Cristina Pacheco's Narratives: Multimedia Chronicles". In Ignacio Corona and Beth E. Jörgensen (eds), *The Contemporary Mexican Chronicle: Theoretical Perspectives on the Liminal Genre*. Albany, NY: State University of New York Press, 2002 pp. 221–39.

Valdés, María Elena de. "Feminist Testimonial Literature: Cristina Pacheco, Witness to Women". *Monographic Review* 4 (1988): 150–62.

PALACIOS, ANTONIA

Antonia Palacios (1904–2001) overcame a difficult childhood and lack of formal education to become one of the most important novelists and mentors of young writers in Venezuela of the second portion of the twentieth century.

Life and Literary Formation

Born and raised in Caracas, Palacios' childhood was a difficult time. Her mother was a kind woman, but her father was an epileptic who created an atmosphere in the home that was at once repressive and capricious. In interviews, Palacios would later recount that her method of escape was to go lie on the roof and dream.

The family, while of the bourgeoisie, passed through difficult economic times during Palacios' early years. Due to this situation, Palacios was unable to continue her education past the fourth grade. She has described to interviewers how her father's illness required all members of the family to bring work into the home and let domestic help go in order to maintain appearances.

Her desire to write came as a result of her need to exorcise what she described as the "ghosts" of her childhood. These ghosts were produced by the suffering and pressure of living in the childhood home she describes in many of her works. Indeed she has portrayed the process of writing as similar to the process of a séance, with herself as a "medium of myself".

In the 1920s, however, due to the family connections, Palacios had the chance to meet the important Venzuelan authors Miguel Otero Silva, Arturo Uslar Pietri, Pablo Rojas Guardia and María Teresa Castillo. These intellectuals encouraged the young woman's literary aspirations. In 1932, Palacios married the author and publicist Carlos Eduardo Frías, who was also supportive of his wife's desire to write.

Palacios' marriage gave her the opportunity to travel, and when Frías was appointed to the National Delegation to France in 1936, she met Pablo Neruda and César Vallejo. This time with the great poets would be foundational in her literary career. After this point, she began a period of great activity, publishing articles and papers in magazines and newspapers across Europe, and beginning to write novels.

Upon the couple's return to Venezuela, between 1939 and 1945 Palacios served actively in the women's cultural movement serving as an officer on various national committees. In 1945, she traveled to Havana and met with Alejo Carpentier. She continued to write novels during this time, including her most famous work, *Ana Isabel una niña decente* (Ana Isabel, a Decent Girl).

In 1975, Palacios became the first woman to receive the Venezuelan National Literature Prize (the nation's highest honor for literature) for her collection of short stories *El largo día ya seguro* (The Now Sure Long Day). One year later she was appointed to the jury of the prestigious International Novel Prize "Rómulo Gallegos".

Beginning in 1978, Palacios began directing a literature workshop at the literature center CELARG in Caracas. This workshop quickly became the most prestigious and productive place for young writers in the capital to hone their craft. The CELARG workshop then evolved into a literary group called *Calicanto* (Lime and Song) that met at Palacios' home. This group met until 1980, and is generally considered to be both emblematic and foundational in the formation of the writers of the generation of the 1980's in Venezuela. The *Calicanto* workshop produced its own journal called *Hojas de Calicanto* (Pages from *Calicanto*) edited by Palacios. Palacios has been hailed by authors including Yolanda Pantin, Elizabeth Schön and Elisa Lerner for her generosity to young authors. She is considered a true leader in the education of the next generation of writers in Venezuela.

Work: Prose

Palacios' work is divided into two periods: the prose production of the years from 1939 to the 1970s, and the poetic prose of the 1970s to 1990s. Her first important works were short stories in the realist or *costumbrista* style, presenting vignettes of life in Venezuela as experienced by the author and presented through various voices in the texts.

This style of narration is best represented by Palacios' most famous novel, *Ana Isabel una niña decente*, a somewhat autobiographical tale which tells the story of an 8-year-old girl in the slowly urbanizing Caracas of the 1920s. Through Ana Isabel's eyes the reader receives a faithful depiction of the

Venezuela of the day, the customs and the family practices. The reader is invited into the key spaces of a young Venezuelan woman of the middle class: the home, the school and the church, and invited to see how the connections between these spaces, like the rules that go with them, trap the young girl.

One key technique that makes the novel stand out is how Palacios uses the protagonist's innocence and awakening consciousness to explore the inequities and social problems of the period. Ana Isabel explores such questions as: what makes a girl "decent"? and why is there such pressure to be a "decent girl"? The reader is invited into the text, to laugh and cry for the young girl as she struggles to understand the mystifying rules. It is this connection that the novel forges with its readers that has made it so popular for so long.

Poetry

After a long period of writing prose, in the 1970s and 1980s and early 1990s, Palacios also dedicated herself to a type of poetic prose sometimes called "story-poems". These poems have a strong interior focus, seeking to speak to and describe the "ghosts" of the bourgeoisie feminine existence. These poems are an attempt to construct the feminine identity through language. The images and spaces in the poems are fluid and many times seem to flit just beyond the grasp of the reader.

All of Palacios' work sees an emphasis on the transitory nature and fragility of life. Themes of lost innocence and youth resound throughout the work. This is particularly true in the poetry which was written in Palacios' later years. Especially in the last collections of poems, the reader finds a poetic voice aware of impending death. The fluidity of imagery and language in these poems shows how not only language, but life itself, slips away from an individual. Despite this feeling of life slipping away, however, the poems in these collections show an image of death that continues identity beyond this life, with consciousness as an infinite light leading others forward.

Criticism

Palacios is highly regarded for the faithfulness with which she paints the nation, the home and the family in her early prose work. Critics repeatedly use the words "sensitivity" and "sensibility" to describe how Palacios uses young and impressionable protagonists and narrators to present the world with fresh and innocent eyes. Especially in her novel *Ana Isabel*, critics note how this technique functions to represent the family dynamics and formation of a young girl. Critics also note how her use of melancholy tone suggests the domination of the dictator José Vicente Gómez without needing to overtly refer to the difficult situation posed for the nation at the time.

While critics note that much of the charm of the early prose work of Palacios lies in the recognizable space of the home and the environs of Caracas, the language used to describe her poetry ranges from "evanescent" to "absent". This, note critics, is both a reflection of the threat of the "nothingness" of the bourgeois feminine existence and a reflection of the end of Palacios' own life.

ELIZABETH GACKSTETTER NICHOLS

Selected Works

Novel

Ana Isabel una niña decente. Buenos Aires: Losada, 1949.

Essays

París y tres recuerdos. Caracas: Suma, 1944.
Viaje al frailejón. Carcas: Monte Avila, 1973.

Short Stories

Crónica de las horas. Caracas: Ateneo de Caracas, 1964.
Los insulares. Caracas: Monte Avila, 1972.
El largo día ya seguro. Caracas: Monte Avila, 1975.
Una plaza ocupando un espacio desconcertante: Relatos 1974–1977. Caracas: Monte Avila, 1981.

Poetry

Textos del desalojo. Caracas: Arte, 1973.
Multipicada sombra. Caracas: Editorial Oasis, 1983.
La piedra y el espejo. Caracas: Ediciones Maeca, 1985.
Ese oscuro animal del sueño. Caracas: Monte Avila, 1991.

References and Further Reading

Araujo, Orlando. *Narrativa venezolana contemporánea.* Caracas: Nuevo Tiempo, 1972, pp. 238–86.
Liscano, Juan. "La infancia de los hijos o *Ana Isabel una niña decente.*" *Caminos de la prosa: comentarios.* Caracas: Ediciones El Pensamiento, 1953, pp. 25–39.
Milani, Domingo. "Trilogía de artífices: Isaac J. Pardo, Antonia Palacios, Arturo Uslar Pietri". *Cuadernos Americanos* 60 (1996): 201–16.
Orozco Vera, María Jesús. "Imagen y realidad de la mujer venezolana en las novelas de Teresa de la Parra y Antonia Palacios". *Diversidad sociocultural en la literatura hispanoamericana (Siglo XX).* Sevilla: Universidad de Sevilla, 1995, pp. 129–43.
Pantin, Yolanda and Torres, Ana Teresa. *El Hilo de la voz: Antología crítica de escritoras Venezolanas del siglo xx.* Caracas: Fundación Polar, 2003, pp. 81–2, 822–3.
Picón Salas, Mariano. *Estudios de literatura venezolana.* Caracas and Madrid: Edime, 1973, pp. 166–7.
Rodríguez-Arenas, Flor María. "'Reflexiones' del yo en Ana Isabel, una niña decente de Antonia Palacios". *Venezuela: Fin de siglo.* Caracas: Casa de Bello, 1993, pp. 159–69.
——. "Búsqueda de la identidad en Ana Isabel, una niña decente de Antonia Palacios". *Imagen: Artes, Letras, Espectáculos* March (1992): 24–6.
Stolk, Gloria. *37 Apuntes de crítica literaria.* Caracas and Madrid: Edime, 1955, pp. 173–7.

PANTÍN, YOLANDA

Yolanda Pantín is one of the most influential contemporary poets in Venezuela today. Her position as an author, editor, scholar, mentor and teacher cannot be underestimated in the Venezuelan context.

Life and Literary Formation

Pantín was born in 1954, in a suburb of Caracas, Venezuela to a middle-class family. She spent her childhood going between a city home and her family's farm in Aragua. After early studies in the visual arts, in 1972 she enrolled in the Universidad Católica Andrés Bello and there began to participate in what would become, for her, the first of a series of poetry groups. It was as part of this group of young poets, who called themselves *Rastros* (Leavings) that she began to seriously write poetry. These first works, written in the hyper-aesthetic tradition of the French Symbolists favored by the Venezuelan poets of the day, earned her admission first into one of the government-sponsored poetry workshops at the *CELARG* (Center for Latin American Studies "Rómulo Gallegos"), and then in 1981 the poetry workshop *Calicanto* run by the respected poet, Antonia Palacios.

During the *Calicanto* workshop Pantín met several other young poets: Igor Barreto, Miguel Márquez, Armando Rojas Guardia and Rafael Castillo Zapata. During this time Pantín began to explore others avenues of poetry, and began to bring to the workshop poems that broke with the traditional interiorist aesthetic promoted therein. Rojas Guardia, Barreto and others felt a great affinity with what Pantín was trying to accomplish with her exploration of everyday language and inclusion of the mundane details of the world around her. While some of the older poets of the group were shocked by this radical break with the metaphysical poetic tradition, the younger poets saw in it a call to reject the symbolist attempts to purify language.

In 1980, Pantín published an essay criticizing the old guard of Venezuelan poets, accusing them of repeating a tired aesthetic that had displayed no new ideas since 1958. Soon after, Pantín, along with Barreto, Márquez, Rojas Guardia and Castillo Zapata left *Calicanto* and formed the poetry group *Tráfico*. The group's objective was to re-imagine both the role of the poet and the role of poetry. They wanted to bring poetry back to the streets, back to the common people, and to rediscover "the language of the tribe". To achieve this goal, the poets wrote verse that included everyday language and scenes from everyday life. They group read poetry on street corners, on television and in public parks, sometimes drawing a live audience of 2,000 people and a television audience of thousands more.

Pantín's association with *Tráfico* lasted until 1983, when she was the first member of the group to leave. She felt that the militant social message was beginning to overshadow the production of poetry, and that the pressure to write poetry to fit the group's manifestoes was stifling her creativity. She had, in fact, come to see value in some elements of the previous generation's poetic production.

In 1989, Pantín, in conjunction with Veronica Jaffé and Blanca Strepponi, founded an editorial house dedicated to poetry: *Pequeña Venecia* (Little Venice). In 1991 she became a member of the executive committee of the *Casa de la Poesía "Pérez Bonalde"* and directed the poetry workshops of the *CELARG* from 1995 to 1996. In 1999, she received with Ana Teresa Torres a Bellagio Center Residential Grant from the Rockefeller Foundation to live in the Bellagio Study Center in Bellagio, Italy. There, she and Torres wrote and edited a chronological, critical anthology of Venezuelan women writers in the twentieth century.

Pantín continues to write poetry, but also writes political commentary, literary criticism, prose, theater, and children's literature.

Work: Themes and Form

Pantín's poetic production can be profitably divided into three periods. The first includes her production prior to, and as part of her participation in the literary workshop *Calicanto*. During this time, she composed a collection of intellectual poetry that follow the poetic tradition of poets such as Vicente Gerbasi and Antonio Silvia Estrada. These poems are characterized by interior themes exploring the speaker's consciousness. Many of the poems represent an idyllic or mythic view of childhood. The language of the poetry of this time period is highly stylized, minimalist and often difficult. Indeed, the majority of the texts that appear in these first works are prose poems which present fragments of scenes or ideas without sentiment. Communication is not the explicit object of this early work.

The second phase of Pantín's work is the product of her participation with the poetry group *Tráfico*. These poems are radically different in theme and tone, as they strive to capture everyday reality in communicative language. Of all the texts produced by the members of *Tráfico*, Pantín's *Correo del corazón* (Letters from the Heart) may be the work that most clearly captures the spirit of that group in its desire to write a type of poetry that communicated effectively both about and to a wide audience. This collection treats urban themes and everyday reality with room for sentimental and emotional content. The work is particularly interested in the urban reality of women, their feelings of enclosure and entrapment in the home. The poems describe the repetitive nature of daily living, and the isolation of individual women in apartments of the city. Instead of celebrating marriage and family, the poetry focuses on the banality of the everyday life of a housewife. Instead of the minimalist language of the earlier works, these scenes of quiet desperation are presented in conversational and easily accessible style that was meant to be read by a wide audience and spoken aloud in poetry readings.

The third period of Pantín's production shows a retreat from some of the more radical ideas of *Tráfico* and achieves a new type of expression, mixing the experiences of her first two works. The poetry of Pantín's later collections remains more grounded in external reality than her first collection, but allows the poetic voice to turn to more interior and abstract themes. Two common threads can be perceived in later collections: a return to the consideration of the idyllic realm of childhood, and an extended consideration of the figure of the vampire.

The vampire, both as physical and metaphysical construct, has provided Pantín in recent years with a profitable symbolic avenue for the exploration of love, danger, life and death both in her poetry as well as in drama and prose. Pantín's work shows a particular interest in the figure of the psychic vampire, who drains not the blood, but the vital force and energies of its victim. The poetry suggests that unhealthy love relationships are like that of vampire and victim. Conversely, however, the main character of Pantín's most popular children's book is a playful bat named "vampire".

Taken as a whole, Pantín's work continues that of early poets such as Enriqueta Arvelo Larriva in the project of opening areas of discursive and descriptive space in Venezuela. Her participation in the world of publishing as well as writing strengthens the position of women in Venezuela's literary establishment. At the same time, Pantín's poetry describes previously unrecognized and disregarded experience and opens small spaces of dialog where that experience can be examined.

ELIZABETH GACKSTETTER NICHOLS

Selected Works

Poems

Casa o lobo. Caracas: Monte Avila, 1981.
Correo del corazón. Caracas: Fundarte, 1983.
La canción fría. Caracas: Angria Ediciones, 1989.
Poemas del escritor. Caracas: Fundarte, 1989.
El cielo de París. Caracas: Pequeña Venecia, 1990.
Les bas sentiments. Paris: Editions Fourbis, 1992.
Los bajos sentimientos. Caracas: Monte Avila, 1993.
La quietud. Caracas: Pequeña Venecia, 1998.
Enemiga mía: Selección poética 1981–1997. Frankfurt: Americana Eystettensia, 1998.
La épica del padre. Caracas: Fondo Editorial La nave va, 2002.
El hueso pélvico. Caracas: Grupo Editorial Eclepsidra, 2002.
Poemas huérfanos. Maracay: La Liebre Libre, 2002.

Prose

Paya. Maracaibo: Ediciones Clandestinas, 1991.

Theater

La otredad y el vampiro. Caracas: Fundarte, 1992.

Children's Literature

Ratón y vampiro se conocen. Caracas: Monte Avila, 1992.
Ratón y vampiro en el castillo. Caracas: Monte Avila, 1994.
Splash. Caracas: Editorial Playdeco, 2000.

Literary Criticism

El hilo de la voz: Antología crítica de escritoras venezolanas del siglo xx. (with Ana Teresa Torres) Caracas: Fundación Polar, 2003.

References and Further Reading

Castillo Zapata, Rafael. "Palabras recuperadas, la poesía venezolana de los ochenta: Rescate y transformación de las palabras de la tribu. El caso 'Tráfico'". *Inti Revista de Literatura Hispánica* 37–8 (1993): 197–205.

Liscano, Juan. "Yolanda Pantín". In *Panorama de la literatura venezolana actual*. Caracas: Alfadil, 1996, pp. 324–5.

Miranda, Julio. *Poesía en el espejo: Estudio y Antología de la nueva lírica femenina venezolana (1970–1994)*. Caracas: Fundarte, 1995.

Nichols, Elizabeth Gackstetter. *Rediscovering the Language of the Tribe in Modern Venezuelan Poetry*. Lewiston, NY: The Edwin Mellen Press, 2000

Reisz, Susana. *Voces sexuadas: Género y poesía en Hispanoamérica*. Lleida: Ediciones de la Universitat de Lleida, 1996.

Rodríguez Ortiz, Oscar. "Las nuevas promociones literarias tienen la palabra". *Zona Franca: Revista de Literatura* 23 (1981): 4–27.

Zambrano, Gregory. "Yolanda Pantín: El poema como rendición". In *Los verbos plurales*. Mérida: Ediciones Solar, Colección Ensayo, 1993, pp. 93–126.

PARRA, TERESA DE LA

Teresa de la Parra (1889–1936) was born Ana Teresa Parra Sanojo on October 5, 1889, in Paris to Venezuelan parents. She was the third child and the first daughter in the Parra Sanojo family. Her father, Rafael Parra Hernáiz, was the Venezuelan consul in Paris at the time of her birth. When she was two years old, her family returned to Venezuela where she spent her early childhood in Tazón, a small town outside of Caracas. Both her parents belonged to Venezuela's prestigious founding families, dating back to the Spanish Conquest. In *Mujer Ingeniosa*, Lemaître explains Teresa's family history, starting with the arrival of the first Parra (Juan de la Parra) in Venezuela in 1539, one of the founders of the city of Caracas. In addition, her father's side of the family was related to Simón Bolívar. Her mother's side of the family—the Sanojos—also belonged to one of the oldest aristocratic families of Venezuela. They were part of a wealthy sector of the colonial society which declined during the struggle for Independence. Although the Parra family had a prestigious name, Teresa did not grow up in affluence. When she was 9 years old, her father died, and her mother along with her five siblings, moved to Valencia, Spain, to be closer to her mother's family still residing in Spain. De la Parra and her sisters studied at the Sacred Heart School in Godella, Spain, where they received a strict Catholic upbringing. At 18, Teresa returned to Venezuela, to find that Caracas had undergone immense changes. Juan Vicente Gómez was in power and his government was implementing political reforms that were driving the country to be more open to the world and to modernization. In 1923, Teresa de la Parra moved to Paris, published *Ifigenia,* her first novel, and never went back to live in Venezuela again. In 1930, she became ill with tuberculosis and began a long and painful odyssey through several European hospitals. She died in 1936 in Madrid with her mother and her great friend Lidia Cabrera at her side. Her remains were exhumed and taken to Caracas in 1947. On the 100th anniversary of her death (1998), her remains were moved to the Panteón Nacional where she rests with some of the most important figures of Venezuelan history.

Teresa de la Parra conducted her private life in a very discreet manner, making it very difficult for literary critics who attempted to write about her personal life. For this reason many writers have interpreted her novels as biographical reflections of her life, causing them to elaborate a speculative personal history based on her novels. Among the few facts we know, Teresa de la Parra never married or had children. She also established a close friendship with two women: Emilia Ibarra de Barrios and Lidia Cabrera. The importance of these two women throughout her life is recorded in her correspondence, which is documented in an extensive collection.

Emilia Ibarra de Barrios was the sister-in-law of Venezuela's ex-president, Guzmán Blanco, and was an older, widowed and childless woman whom Teresa met because she lived very close to the Barrios-Parejo family in Caracas with her mother and sisters. A very close friendship developed between Teresa de la Parra and Emilia de Barrios that lasted until Emilia's death in 1924. As a consequence of this friendship, the writer gained social and financial independence because Emilia left Teresa a substantial inheritance that afforded her a comfortable life. Uslar Pietri writes that Emilia de Barrios, in her will, left Teresa her whole fortune, while she remained unwed (Uslar Pietri in Bosch, *Iconografía*, p. 48). Teresa's letters shortly following her friend's death plainly portray the severe impact of Emilia's demise on her.

In 1929, Teresa began her long and close relationship with Lidia Cabrera, the other woman who occupied an important place in the author's life. Lidia Cabrera was a renowned anthropologist and Cuban folklorist. She was the daughter of the famous Cuban historian Raimundo Cabrera, was related to Batista, and was the sister-in-law of Fernando Ortiz, and thus belonged to the Cuban oligarchy. In an interview she explains how she met Teresa de la Parra for the first time. It was in

1925 on a ship that was heading to Venezuela where a Spanish priest who was also a poet—whose name Cabrera claims to have forgotten—introduced them after dinner. In this same interview she says that when they exchanged visiting cards she wrote on the one she gave to Teresa "Favor de no olvidarme" (Please do not forget me). It was not until 1927 when Cabrera visited Paris with her mother that she met Teresa again in a chance encounter while dining at the Hotel Vernet. After Cabrera introduced herself, a remarkable friendship flourished between the two that lasted until Teresa's death in 1936. Lidia remembers that Teresa de la Parra showed her the visiting card where she had jotted down the phrase "Favor de no olvidarme" (Please do not forget me) at that second encounter. There are various biographical similarities between the two: they belonged to the ruling class of their native countries, they were related to important intellectual and historical figures and both maintained a certain mystery in their personal lives. After 1929, the two women were in permanent contact and lived on and off together for almost seven years until Teresa's death.

Literary Prose

Teresa de la Parra's work is not very extensive. It consists of two novels, *Ifigenia: diario de una señorita que escribió porque se fastidiaba* (1924) and *Memorias de mamá Blanca* (1929). Her published work also includes her correspondence and diary, which constitute revealing sources for a better understanding of her fiction; three lectures read in Bogotá and published under the title "La influencia de las mujeres en la formación del alma americana" (1930), and some short stories. Even though Teresa de la Parra lived a great part of her life in Europe, her work is marked by her experiences in Venezuela. Her country of origin is always present in her novels, but her texts avoid falling into a brand of *criollismo*, or the picturesque Venezuelan literature of the time. In her first novel, *Ifigenia: diario de una señorita que escribió porque se fastidiaba*—in which the author denounces the situation of women in Caracas in the 1920s—she recreates her return to Venezuela when she was only 18 years old. Her second novel *Memorias de Mamá Blanca* is based on her early childhood, spent in fin-de-siècle Venezuela in the rural atmosphere of the family farm in Tazón. Her first works were short stories, which are now considered by her critics as preparation for her novels, published in the newspaper *El Universal* under the pseudonyme "Fru Fru". Her short stories "El genio del pesacartas" and "La historia de la señorita grano de polvo" were her only works that followed the style of the time known as modernism. Her "Diario de una caraqueña en el lejano Oriente" published in the magazine *Actualidades*, was based on a collection of letters that her sister sent her from a trip to the Middle East. Also, de la Parra's story "Mama X" earned first prize in a contest held in a provincial Venezuelan city. This story and her "Diario de una señorita que escribió porque se fastidiaba" (which was published in the magazine *La Lectura Semanal*) were the inspiration and constitute the beginning of her first novel.

Ifigenia: diario de una señorita que escribió porque se fastidiaba is an amazingly lucid vision of the few options that women in early twentieth-century Latin America were offered. Her ideas in this novel are very innovative not only for Latin American women but also for European and American women as well. The novel is so radical that for years critics have misunderstood the meaning of her work and underestimated the power of her discourse. *Ifigenia* can be seen as the first satiric reformulation of the fairy tale in which a poor girl marries a rich prince. From this perspective, *Ifigenia* functions for Latin American's satiric literature much as *Don Quijote* does in Peninsular literature in the same genre. If *Don Quijote* is a satirical reformulation of the chivalric romance novels in which a modern anti-hero is created, *Ifigenia: diario de una señorita que escribió porque se fastidiaba* is the first novel written by a Latin American woman which is a satiric reformulation of the traditional fairy tale told to young girls and young women in western cultures for centuries. *Ifigenia* won the annual award that carried a prize of 10,000 French francs funded by Casa Editora Franco-Ibero-Americana in Paris in 1924, which finally made it possible for Teresa de la Parra to publish her first novel *Ifigenia,* which became a success among Parisian critics and readers and was soon translated into French.

Two years later de la Parra began her second major work *Memorias de mamá Blanca*. The Tazón small farm atmosphere pervades her second novel where she describes, in a sweet and sharp way, the daily life of six young girls on a sugar cane farm. She describes their conflicts and their joys with a style characterized by indulgence, irony, and humor. If in *Ifigenia* we find a radical criticism of society and the status of women, conversely, *Memorias* offers a positive re-evaluation of a traditional conservative female space and the colonial past. This change in style may be in response to criticism written about her first novel. It seems as if *Memorias de mamá Blanca* was a creative effort towards a reconciliation between her later self and some of the colonial values that were considered conservative in her time, which shows a defensive stance regarding an obscure past based on a divisive social caste system. Teresa de la Parra may have perceived this style of writing about the situation of women as a more acceptable way to criticize society.

In 1929, Teresa de la Parra was invited to present her lecture, "La influencia de la mujer en la formación del alma americana" in Bogotá, Colombia. The lecture was composed of three parts which, as her title announces, were an exploration of the influence and role of women in three different historic periods: the Conquest, the Colony and post-Independence. Even though the lecture was written to be read aloud, María Parra Bunimovich, de la Parra's sister, edited and published it in 1961. While writing lectures for conferences, Teresa de la Parra began outlining another novel. She wanted to write the history of Simón Bolivar from a different perspective than the official one. In her version, she wanted to emphasize not the heroic side of Bolivar's life, but his personal life, his loves, his dreams.

The historical perspective in Teresa de la Parra is quite unique, since she always finds a humorous angle, exploring the minute details that lead the reader to experience history from a much more intuitive perspective than the one proposed by the traditional historical narrative which tries to be as accurate as possible while detailing events, and giving precise dates and names. The novel about Bolivar's life was never written, because de la Parra became ill. Part of the preparation for this novel can be found both in the third lecture read in Bogotá and in her correspondence. In her letters, de la Parra alludes frequently to the less felicitous events in the life of the "libertador de América," and to his relationship with his mistress Manuela Saenz. The correspondence from the years of her illness (1932–36), as well as her diaries provide a very intimate look at how she prepared materials for her novels.

Criticism and Interpretations of her Work

Of the critical writings about Teresa de la Parra, most concentrate solely on her novels. Her letters, diary and conferences have been used in critical studies only as references, even though all of them have a high aesthetic value. Before the 1980s, critical works on de la Parra have oscillated between a literal reading of her fiction and an autobiographical reading of her work. Neither view takes into consideration the irony that underlies her writing. In addition, de la Parra's work cannot be easily placed within any of the literary movements of her time. The themes in her work always relate to Venezuela and to the time she spent in this country; however, her life in Europe as well as her extensive readings give a more cosmopolitan flair to her work. Currently younger scholars commonly accept that there are two important themes in her work: her vision of women's position in society, and the introduction of modernity to Venezuela at the beginning of the twentieth century. The first theme has engendered a number of critical studies which contend that there are enormous contradictions between her published writings and her diaries and commentaries (Garrels 1986; Sommer 1988). The fact that she denounces the situation of women through irony but does not propose solutions, while simultaneously idealizing the colonial times, has led some critics to consider her conservative (Garrels). However, it is very clear that in her work, especially in *Ifigenia*, she denounces and criticizes what she sees as an unjust situation for women in the Venezuela of the beginning of the twentieth century. As far as her understanding of the effects of modernity is concerned, it is possible to see some nostalgia for a more prosperous past, when the social class to which she belonged had more privileges. *Memorias de mamá Blanca*, which describes life on the farm Piedra Azul in the middle of the nineteenth century, presenting it as a lost paradise, offers a good example of a certain dichotomy in her work. In this novel, Teresa de la Parra's position oscillates between that of a conservatism characteristic of the interests of a decadent aristocracy and an attempt to claim a better position for women in Venezuelan society.

Her work, more than a feminist or conservative position, shows lack of conformity with the social organization of the nation and tries to deconstruct patriarchal patterns and construct new patterns, based on an exploration of "otherness" in general: women, servants, peasants, and children. Furthermore, Sylvia Molloy's article (1995) has opened a new line of study of her work. Prior to Molloy, critics read her work as either a feminist, or a conservative production. Even though this article does not intend to be a detailed biography of de la Parra, it proposes a new interpretation of her work. Molloy states that the mystery of de la Parra's private life and her consideration of love as a cultural product of capitalism; her passionate rejection of the physicality of love and its replacement with tenderness, and most importantly, her repudiation of Latin American's position on heterosexuality as expressed in her writings (1995, pp. 245, 246) aim at a different recreation of the feminine in which it is possible to see an unwritten sexuality, that of the lesbian author "waiting to be named" (ibid., p. 253), while unwittingly building her rightful place. This interpretation of her work may account for the difficulties faced by critics in categorizing and judging her work. If she was obviously trying to write about and denounce the status of women of her time, it was from the perspective of a woman who rejected heterosexual relationships as the foundation of human society by depicting the contradictions in a world built on strong social and gender hierarchies. Her work in this sense gives a new dimension to the literature of her time because she explored and questioned the representation of masculine authority even though she did it within the scope of themes and discourse allowed to a woman writer in the 1920s. In her novel *Ifigenia,* she presents a young lady who questions the social rules imposed on her by a decadent society, and unsuccessfully tries to change them. In *Memorias,* an idyllic colonial world is surreptitiously governed by women, peasants, children, cowboys, servants and any other figure rather than the strong father of the house. He is allowed to think that he rules the sugar plantation, thus exposing some of the weaknesses of the patriarchal system. Her series of lectures entitled "Influencia de la mujer en la formación del alma americana" are an idyllic re-creation of a Colonial past where a new culture separated from Europe offered more freedom for Latin American women than the perceived freedom started during the Independence period. This colonial way of living is considered by the author a kind of utopian space for women because of the freedoms they enjoyed in their private and anonymous lives (Molloy 1995).

Her own intuitive preference for an oral, conversational and delightfully spontaneous style of writing makes her one of the most underestimated and most original Latin American writers of the 1920s and an important precursor—however reluctant—of the great emancipatory wave in Latin American women's writing half a century later.

Ana María Caula

Selected Works

Cartas a Rafael Carias. España: Talleres penitenciarios de Alcalá de Henares, 1957.

Obras completas de Teresa de la Parra. Caracas: Editorial Arte, 1966.

Obra (Narrativa-Ensayo-Cartas). Caracas: Biblioteca Ayacucho, 1982.

Las Memorias de mamá Blanca. Barcelona: Colección Archivos, 1988.

Obras Escogidas. Caracas: Monte Ávila Editores / Fondo de Cultura Económica, 1992.

References and Further Reading

Bosch, Velia. "Esta pobre lengua viva". *Teresa de la Parra ante la crítica*. Caracas: Monte Ávila Editores, 1980.

Garrels, Elizabeth. *Las grietas de la ternura. Nueva lectura de Teresa de la Parra*. Caracas: Monte Ávila Editores, 1986.

Molloy, Sylvia. "Disappearing Acts: Reading Lesbian in Teresa de la Parra". In Emilie Bergmann and Paul Smith (eds), *¿Entiendes? Queer Readings, Hispanic Writings*. Durham, NC: Duke University Press, 1995.

Palacios, María Fernanda. *Mitología de la doncella criolla*. Caracas: Ediciones Angria, 2001.

Sommer, P. "'It's Wrong to Be Right' Mama Blanca on Writing Like a Woman" in *Las Memorias de mamá Blanca,* Barcelona: Colección Archivos, 1988.

Varios. *Lengua viva de Teresa de la Parra*. Caracas: Pomaire, 1983.

PARRA, VIOLETA

Violeta Parra (1917–68) is known as a poet and songwriter, composer, folklorist, ceramist, tapestry weaver, sculptor, and painter. Having achieved an almost iconic stature in Chile, her native country, she is widely celebrated for the poetic pieces she composed and her work as a collector of folk songs. Recognized throughout Latin America as a precursor of the Chilean New Song that flourished in the 1960s and 1970s, she paved the way for the kind of socially and politically committed music still performed by Angel and Isabel Parra, two of her children, among many others.

Much of what we know about Parra is taken from testimonies of relatives and friends collected in various anthologies as well as letters from her correspondence that her family kept. Another source of information is her autobiography written in verses in 1958 at the urging of her older brother Nicanor, who played a major role in Violeta's life, and published posthumously in 1970. Although some of the dates and details contained in these diverse sources are at times vague and even contradictory, there are largely undisputable facts we can learn from them.

Humble Beginnings

Parra was born on October 4, 1917, in San Carlos de Ñuble, a small town near the city of Chillán in Southern Chile. Her father, Nicanor Parra, an elementary school teacher and musician, lost his job during the Ibáñez administration (1927–31) and died in 1930, leaving his family in poverty. Her mother, Clara Sandoval, a seamstress, had no choice but to use her wits to raise Parra and her nine siblings by herself. Although very young at the time of their father's death, Violeta and her sister Hilda contributed to the family's survival by singing in public on makeshift stages at train stations, outdoor markets, and town plazas. For a time, they also worked as circus performers. In the early 1930s Parra left the countryside for Santiago, the capital, to join her brother Nicanor (named after their father), a renowned poet in Latin America and the only one of the siblings who had received a formal education. There, Violeta Parra attended school at the insistence of her brother, but only for a short time. Parra met her first husband, Luis Cereceda, at a bar frequented by railroad workers and they were married in 1937. Isabel and Angel, her older children, were born in 1939 and 1941. The marriage lasted about ten years, after which Cereceda left Parra reportedly because of her refusal to conform to the role of traditional wife and mother. In 1949, she married Luis Arce, and a year later her daughter Carmen Luisa was born. In the early 1950s, they had another daughter, Rosita Clara, who died at a young age while Parra, after having attended a Youth Festival in Poland in 1954, was living in Paris. This sad incident inspired Parra's song "Rosita se fue a los cielos" (Rosita Went to Heaven) as well as guilt-laden pages in her autobiography, whose last two sections are devoted to this loss.

A Tragic and Sorrowful Ending

After her return to Chile in 1956, Parra spent two years in Concepción managing a museum of popular art and conducting further research on folklore. In 1958, she returned to Santiago, where she took up pottery and painting. A year later she spent time in the Northern provinces as well as in Chiloé collecting folklore. In 1960, she was bed-ridden due to hepatitis and, unable to remain inactive, took up a unique popular form of weaving known as *arpilleras* in Chile. The following year, she traveled to Buenos Aires, Finland, the Soviet Union, Germany, Italy, and France, finally settling in Paris, where she gave a number of recitals. Also in 1960, she met Gilbert Favre, a Swiss musical anthropologist and musician who, even though many years her junior, would become Violeta Parra's companion and lover. The break-up with Favre several years later caused Parra a great deal of despair and is said to have in part led her to take her life. In April 1964, the Louvre Museum organized an exhibition of her weavings, oil paintings, and sculptures. In 1965, her book on Andean popular poetry was published in a bilingual edition by Maspero, the prestigious French publisher. She returned to Chile permanently in 1965 and began to sing at La peña de los Parra (the Parras' *peña*) with Angel and Isabel Parra. The *peñas*, quaint public places where protest and folk songs were performed and wine and *empanadas* (meat pies) served, thrived throughout Latin America in the 1960s and 1970s and some still exist today. In 1966, Parra managed to get a plot of land in a neighborhood called La Comuna de la Reina outside Santiago. There, she put up a huge tent with the intention of opening a *peña*, which she did, and an arts center, for which she did not receive enough official support. She recorded an album called *Las últimas composiciones de Violeta Parra* (Violeta Parra's Latest—or Last—Compositions). After two unsuccessful suicide attempts in the mid-1960s, Parra shot herself on February 5, 1968. Although she left a suicide note that her brother Nicanor Parra has kept, it has not been made public.

Parra's Remarkable Work as a Folklorist

Violeta Parra's profound interest in music began at an early age. Given the absence of formal training, she did not master the art of reading music, relying instead on pentagrams she made up and only she could interpret. In the 1940s, she joined a Spanish dance company and later sang conventional forms of Spanish music at a night club. Spanish music was popular in Argentina and Chile at the time and there was a large public for the better-known Spanish rhythms. Although Chilean folk music was also performed, it was not as warmly embraced, and it appears that in a majority of the cases, it was a sanitized, stylized form of folk music that was staged. It was not until 1952 or 1953 that Parra began to collect folk songs in rural Chile. Those who knew her or worked with her collecting this invaluable material have noted Parra's remarkable ability to get informants to collaborate as well as her keen interest to recreate the circumstances surrounding the performances. She also reconstructed lyrics that had been partially lost over time. Those interested in "hearing" the voice of the informants should review *Cuentos folklóricos chilenos* (Chilean Folk Tales), in which the dialogues she held with some of her informers are transcribed. When Parra was invited to do radio programes in 1953, she attempted to convey the music as well as the context that gave rise to it. At times, she brought in her elderly informants for interviews, prodding them tactfully and affectionately whenever their memory faltered. Parra's radio program, *Canta Violeta Parra* (Violeta Parra Sings), gained a large following from among common folk, who saw their lives and surroundings reflected in the music. While she was far from being the only Chilean folk singer to gain wide, albeit unofficial recognition, her class and rural origins gave Parra a unique insight into popular forms of artistic expression. She only had to tap into her childhood memories to make them come alive. Parra is said to have collected nearly three thousand folk songs.

As she grew older, Parra's interest turned toward songwriting. The lyrical quality of her songs is so remarkable that many are considered poems and have been analyzed as such.

The Many Faces of Parra

Violeta Parra's poetry deals with love, politics, society, and religion. Among her favorite and most accomplished pieces are her renowned compositions "Gracias a la vida" (Thanks to Life) and "Volver a los diecisiete" (To Be Seventeen All over Again), both written toward the end of her life. The former is a hymn to life that celebrates our senses and feelings as a means of valuing what is noble in life, including love. The song conveys a deep appreciation for simple, unadorned things. The latter uses figurative language effectively to communicate that being in love makes one feel young at heart no matter the age. That feeling of fulfillment, joy, and vibrancy associated with one's first love can be relived over and over. On the other hand, Parra was also capable of finding fault with life, as reflected in another one of her last compositions, "Maldigo del alto cielo" (Damn the High Heavens). In this composition, the poet's hurt prevents her from seeing anything pleasant around her; nature, which in the previous songs was a source of pleasure, is now a threat. Her soul is in mourning. Therefore the stars, the ocean, the mountains, the seasons, the entire universe, and even the passage of time, are to be put down, denigrated. These lyrics make Parra's suicide seem almost inevitable. They provide a marked contrast not only to her numerous love poems, but to others where she writes differently: rebellious and nonconformist, as in "Me gustan los estudiantes" (I Like Students), "Yo canto a la diferencia" (I Sing to Difference), and "Arauco tiene una pena" (Arauco is Deeply Sad); thoughtful and wise, as in "Cantores que reflexionan" (Singers Who Reflect) and "Ayúdame Valentina" (Help me, Valentina); humorous and festive, as in "Mazúrquica Mayórquica" (Major Mazurka—in jargon); and religious and a believer, as in "Rin del angelito" (Song for the Little Angel). In all, Isabel Parra lists one hundred and ten songs composed by her mother, who cultivated folk themes and forms to create her art.

Parra used the *décima*, a popular meter composed of stanzas of ten lines of eight syllables each, as well as Chilean vernacular language to write her autobiography. It has been said that this work is one of the first autobiographies written in Latin America that deals with gender and social marginality head-on. Parra denounces the poverty and inequality she sees all around her, preferring to highlight the vulnerability of children and women. Although some sections focus on Parra's success as a poet/songwriter, it would seem that she easily fell back on hard times.

Both Nicanor Parra and Pablo Neruda wrote poems praising Violeta Parra, and the great Peruvian novelist José María Arguedas spoke highly of her work. It was not until recently, however, that part of the Chilean's multifaceted art production was seen in her native country. In May 2006, an exhibition of thirteen *arpilleras*, twenty-five oil paintings, and nine works in papier-mâché opened at the recently-created La Moneda Cultural Center. This stands, at long last, as an overdue official recognition of Parra's worth.

IRAIDA H. LÓPEZ

Selected Works

Cantos folklóricos chilenos. Santiago de Chile: Ed. Nascimiento, 1979.

21 son los dolores. Antología amorosa. Introducción, selección y notas de Juan Andrés Piña. 4th edn. Santiago de Chile: Ed. Aconcagua, 1981.

Décimas. Autobiografía en verso. 2nd edn. Buenos Aires: Editorial Sudamericana, 1998.

References and Further Reading

Agosín, Marjorie and Dolz-Blackburn, Inés. *Violeta Parra: Santa de pura greda. Un estudio sobre su obra poética*. Santiago de Chile: Ed. Planeta Chilena, 1988.

Dolz-Blackburn, Inés and Agosín, Marjorie. *Violeta Parra o la expresión inefable. Un análisis crítico de su poesía, prosa y pintura*. Santiago de Chile: Ed. Planeta Chilena, 1992.

González, Juan Pablo and Rolle, Claudio. *Historia social de la música popular en Chile, 1890–1950*. Santiago de Chile: Ed. Universidad Católica de Chile, 2005.

Manns, Patricio. *Violeta Parra*. Madrid: Ed. Júcar, 1977.

Morales T., Leónidas. *Violeta Parra: la última canción*. Santiago de Chile: Ed. Cuarto Propio, 2003.

Parra, Isabel. *El libro mayor de Violeta Parra*. Madrid: Ediciones Michay, 1985.

Subercaseaux, Bernardo, Stambuk, Patricia and Londoño, Jaime. *Gracias a la vida. Violeta Parra, testimonio*. Santiago de Chile: Editorial Granizo/CENECA, 1982.

PARTNOY, ALICIA

Born in Bahía Blanca, Argentina, Alicia Partnoy (b. 1955) is a writer of poetry, fiction, and essays, a professor, and a human rights activist. She was married in 1974 to Carlos Samuel Sanabria and in 1975 they had a daughter, Ruth. Partnoy and her husband were activists in the Juventud Universitaria Peronista at the Universidad Nacional del Sur (Bahía Blanca) where they both studied. After the military coup of 1976, military forces began to illegally detain, arrest, torture, and murder anyone critical of the regime. Many of these people *disappeared*: i.e. held clandestinely by the military, without due process, leaving their loved ones with absolutely no information as to their whereabouts and condition. On January 12, 1977, both Partnoy and her husband disappeared, taken by the Argentine army where they were imprisoned at "The Little School". During this period they had no knowledge of what happened to their daughter, who had been with them when they were abducted. After three and a half months during which Partnoy was detained and tortured, she and her husband were transferred to the prison of Villa Floresta (located in Bahía Blanca) where they were kept for two more months. Later they were transferred to other jails. Near the end of 1979, they were forced into exile and they traveled to the United States where the family was reunited by the end of that year. Partnoy returned to Argentina in 1984 to appear before the Commission for the Investigation of Disappeared Persons. She has also testified before the United Nations, the Organization of American States, and Amnesty International. Once again living in the United States, Partnoy returned to her studies and received her doctorate in Latin American literature. In an effort to bring the voices of victims of state-directed violence to public attention, she launched *Proyecto VOS* (Voices of Survivors), an organization that brings survivors of human rights abuses to lecture at colleges in the United States. She is currently married to Antonio Leiva and they have two daughters, Evita and Anahi. She lives in Los Angeles and teaches at Loyola Marymount University.

A Prison Poetics of Solidarity

While imprisoned during Argentina's "Dirty War" (1976–83), Partnoy secretly composed poetry and stories that were smuggled out as messages to loved ones and for anonymous publication in newspapers and magazines associated with human rights organizations. During her time at "The Little School," Partnoy struggled to survive and was unable to write, but five months after her detention when she ceased to be a disappeared person, she began to write. Many of her poems from this period are collected in *Revenge of the Apple* (1992), a bilingual edition of poetry that includes a Foreword by the author. Partnoy explains that these poems were crafted as a means of survival and of communicating with fellow prisoners. Partnoy's poems became birthday presents, tokens of camaraderie, and gestures of comfort during her years in prison. Her poems gave her solace and strength and they worked to build a bridge of solidarity with the other prisoners. Growing from her direct knowledge of the way that poetry facilitates human connections among prisoners and between prisoners and the outside world, Partnoy later analyzed the theme of prison poetry and solidarity in her dissertation and in various critical essays.

The Little School

Upon her arrival in the United States, she began lecturing on her experiences in conjunction with Amnesty International, religious organizations, and by invitation at many universities. She also provided testimony about her experience at various official venues. Her 1984 testimony before the Argentina Commission charged with investigating the cases of arrest and torture appears in *Nunca Más* (Never Again) – a compilation of testimonials by the Argentine Commission for the Investigation of the Disappeared. Her active commitment to denouncing the abuses of the Argentine dictatorship via the discourse of testimony and truth was combined with her dedication to using literature and poetry to evoke the pain and anguish of torture and repression. This tactic of mixing the language of testimony with the language of fiction in order to more intensely and accurately portray the experience of human suffering at the hands of the state is evident throughout her work, but it would be her first collection of short stories, *The Little School* (1986), that would establish this mode of writing for Partnoy. *The Little School* is a collection of short stories that narrate the experience of life in a concentration camp from a variety of viewpoints, combining anguish with wit, and mixing her story with those of her fellow captives. In keeping with her desire to merge narrative with political activism the text also includes an appendix with specific information on her place of imprisonment, on other prisoners, and on the men who acted as guards and torturers. This text had a widespread influence on the political acknowledgment of women's experiences in prison and it has served as a model for other such writing. Her narrative account of life in a clandestine prison cut off from her family, especially her daughter, is a raw and touching expression of torture and survival.

The Poetics of Fire/The Poetics of Defeat

In 1988, Partnoy united a series of voices in the volume, *You Can't Drown the Fire: Latin American Women Writing in Exile,* an anthology of women's writing dealing with gender issues during periods of severe political repression. This anthology includes the work of thirty-five Latin American women who wrote while in exile and it is broken down by genre into sections of testimonial, narrative, essay, poetry, and letters. Partnoy explains her motivations in creating the text: to build cultural bridges, to destroy stereotypes about Latin American women, and to publicly denounce political repression in the region. Most importantly, though, Partnoy's work helped to gain visibility for many Latin American women who were virtually unknown in the Untied States. The texts in the volume denounce repression through strength and fiery spirit.

Partnoy's next literary project was the volume, *Volando bajito/Little Low Flying* (2005), her second bilingual edition of poetry. While the poems that comprise the volume denounce the repression of the Argentine dictatorship, the Introduction, written by poet and translator Gail Wronsky, builds comparisons between Partnoy's experience of torture and the news of torture during the US war on terror in Iraq, thereby casting Partnoy as a trans-American writer whose work represents themes related to both Latin America and North America. The volume's subtitle is the "Poetics of Defeat" ("Poéticas de la Derrota"), but what is meant by "defeat" is actually quite complex. On the one hand, the volume attempts to describe what it means to write poetry from a position of defeat, from a position of loss. On the other hand, that position of loss requires that the poet develop communicative subtlety and creativity that then turns the poetry of defeat into a poetry of power. This idea is conveyed in the volume's title since "little low flying" means to "fly under the radar," a practice that suggests that the poet must use great skill. That skill allows the poet to go unnoticed during moments of danger and to find power in art in moments of denunciation. The poems in this collection are both sensual and raw, beautiful and disturbing.

In sum, Partnoy's writing reveals a poetics of solidarity and protest that draws on the themes of camaraderie, resistance, fiery spirit, and the strength of the defeated. It is important to note that Partnoy has used a variety of media to transmit her message. In addition to her short stories, essays, poetry, and public lectures, she has worked with music and the fine arts, often collaborating with her mother, Raquel Partnoy, who has illustrated many of Partnoy's books, and with her daughter Ruth Sanabria, who is a poet.

SOPHIA A. MCCLENNEN

Selected Works

The Little School: Tales of Disappearance & Survival in Argentina. Pittsburgh, PA: Cleis, 1986.

Ed. *You Can't Drown the Fire: Latin American Women Writing in Exile*. London: Virago, 1989.

Venganza de la manzana /Revenge of the apple. Pittsburgh, PA: Cleis, 1992.

"Poetry as a Strategy for Resistance in the Holocaust and the Southern Cone Genocides". In Kristin Ruggiero (ed.), *The Jewish Diaspora in Latin America and the Caribbean: Fragments of a Memory*. Portland, OR: Sussex Academic Press, 2005, pp. 234–46.

Volando Bajito. Trans. and Introduction Gail Wronsky. Granada Hills, CA: Red Hen Press, 2005.

References and Further Reading

Bermúdez-Gallegos, Marta. "*The Little School* por Alicia Partnoy: El testimonio en la Argentina". *Revista Iberoamericana*. 151 (April–June 1990).

Detwiler, Louise A. "The Blindfolded (Eye)witness in Alicia Partnoy's *The Little School*". *The Journal of the MMLA* 33(3) (Fall 2000): 60–72.

Franco, Jean. "Gender, Death, and Resistance. Facing the Ethical Vacuum". In Corradi, Weiss Fagen, and Garretón (eds), *Fear at the Edge: State Terror and Resistance in Latin America*. Berkeley, CA: University of California Press, 1992, pp. 104–18.

Kaminsky, Amy. "Body/Politics: Alicia Partnoy's *The Little School*". In *Reading the Body-Politic: Feminist Criticism and Latin American Women Writers*. Minneapolis, MN: University of Minnesota Press, 1993.

Manzor-Coats, Lillian. "The Reconstructed Subject: Women's Testimonials as Voices of Resistance". In Lucía Guerra Cunningham (ed.), *Splintering Darkness: Latin American Women Writers in Search of Themselves*. Pittsburgh, PA: Latin American Literary Review, 1990, pp. 157–71.

Millet, Kate. "The Little School". in *The Politics of Cruelty: An Essay on the Literature of Political Imprisonment*. New York: W.W. Norton & Co., 1994, pp. 225–52.

Pinet, Carolyn. "Retrieving the Disappeared Text: Women, Chaos and Change in Argentina and Chile after the Dirty Wars". *Hispanic-Journal* 18(1) 1997: 89–108.

Taylor, Diana. "Writing Torture: Alicia Partnoy Talks/Writes Back". In *Disappearing Acts: Spectacles of Gender and Nationalism in Argentina's "Dirty War"*. Durham, NC: Duke University Press, 1997, pp. 157–72.

Treacy, Mary Jane. "Double Binds: Latin American Women's Prison Memories". *Hypatia* 11(4) (1996): 130–45.

PAZ PAREDES, MARGARITA

Poet Margarita Paz Paredes (born Margarita Camacho Baquedano) was born in San Felipe Torres Mochas, Guanajuato, Mexico on March 30, 1922. When Paz Paredes was very young, her family relocated to Mexico City where she completed middle and high school. She earned both a Bachelor's and a Master's Degree in Letters from the *Universidad Nacional Autónoma de México* (National Autonomous University of Mexico). Additionally, she pursued and a degree in journalism from the *Universidad Obrera de México* (Worker's University of Mexico). Paz Paredes' passion for poetry is evidenced by her first book, *Sonaja* (Little Bell) published in 1922 when she was merely 20 years old. In addition to her literary career, Paz Paredes was also a Professor of Spanish and World Literature at the *Universidad de Toluca* (University of Toluca) and the *Escuela Normal Superior de México* (Superior Teachers School of Mexico).

Throughout her life, Paz Paredes remained active both in publishing and as an educator. She published over 15 volumes of poetry in four decades. She was married to Mexican novelist Emilio Abreu Gómez. Paz Paredes was well regarded by her contemporary writers and poets. Her friend, compatriot, and colleague Efraín Huerta wrote introductions to several of her books. She traveled extensively presenting her work in multiple poetry recitals. She died in Mexico City on May 22, 1980.

Voz de la tierra

Despite moving to Mexico City, her small town is echoed in many of Margarita Paz Paredes' works. The poet's native San Felipe is at the heart of her work in *Voz de la tierra* (1946, Voice of the Homeland). She looks to the Mexican province to write poems that evoke the ways of traditional Mexico. Through her poems in this collection, a sincere admiration for the customs left behind, when she moved to the city at a young age, is evident. Moreover, the poet reflects not only on rural customs but also on the everyday people. Her poems speak of rural young women, of peasant young men, and of people working for her own family. In "Muchacha," for example, Paz Paredes speaks to small-town young women. She praises the simplicity of their life as a valuable asset while showing awareness of her own positionality as a writer: the poet recognizes that she is not the young woman whose simplicity she admires, but a cosmopolitan young woman who creates art. Throughout the entire collection, Paz Paredes demonstrates an awareness of her privileged position in her community, going so far as to offer apologies to the people who worked for her family.

Presagio en el viento

In 1955, the *Organización de Estados Centroamericanos* (Organization of Central American States) commissioned Paz Paredes to edit an anthology of Central American poetry. Her *Presagio en el viento* (Premonition in the Wind) was also published that year in San Salvador. The book is a series of heart-felt poems dedicated to prominent El Salvadorian poets such as Serafín Quiteño, Adalberto Ordoñez Argüello, Luis Mejía Vides, and Oswaldo Escobar Velado, among others. The poems in this collection explore the complexity of romantic relationships while, at the same time, looking at the Central American landscape and establishing a connection to her own country.

La imagen y su espejo

The poet reflects on the intimate relationship between nature and human beings in *La imagen y su espejo* (The Image and Its Mirror). Paz Paredes places natural elements such as water, light, and rain in opposition to humans to create poems that speak of human dependence on nature. As a result, the poems demonstrate a search for balance in life. Each poem in *La imagen y su espejo* shows great admiration and respect for Mother Earth. In "Imagen y semejanza de la tierra" (Image and Resemblance of Earth), for instance, Paz Paredes directly equates humans to the Earth by establishing how life is shaped in the same manner as the Earth. Moreover, the poet pays homage to Mother Earth when she acknowledges the fact that death will return humans to the source. Her own connection to nature comes in the form of "Yamilé", a poem named after her daughter. In this poem, Paz Paredes gives her daughter characteristics of natural elements such as wind, fire, water, and earth while she reflects on the role she plays in her daughter's present and the future life. Finally, her passion for poetry is manifested in "A la poesía" (To Poetry) where the poet praises its power as she reveals, metaphorically, how she found it.

Lumbre cautiva

Lumbre cautiva (Captive Fire) constitutes a passionate collection of poems where love and desire are the main characters. In Paz Paredes' poem, Adam and Eve gain entrance to "another Paradise" when they are asked to leave the original Paradise for giving in to their carnal desires. In their newly found paradise Adam and Eve transform their surroundings with beautiful things created by them. The poet praises their love as she suggests that their love resulted in the creation of lives in harmony with nature. Romantic relationships and the feelings associated with them – happiness, excitement, sadness, and sorrow – are all at the heart of this collection.

Memorias de hospital/Presagio

Paz Paredes' *Memorias de hospital/Presagio* (1979, Hospital Memoirs/Premonition) was published posthumously in 1980. The two long poems in the book manifest the poet's maturity as she reflects about life and death. Her being admitted to the hospital results in a sincere long poem ("Memorias de hospital") that shows her love for life and her fears surrounding her death. In the ten sections of the poem, the writer reflects about sickness, losing control, being near death, and realizing that she will continue living. Moreover, while in the hospital, the poet observes the ongoing fight for life that both children and adults experience. In the poem, Paz Paredes speaks of the feelings of fear and sadness, not only of the patients in a hospital, but also of their relatives. Five months before her death (December, 1979), Paz Paredes wrote "Presagio" (Premonition) in which she talks about her own imminent death.

Distinguished Daughter

A contemporary of Guadalupe (Pita) Amor, Margarita Michelena, and Rosario Castellanos, Paz Paredes is one of the first female poets of the twentieth century to embrace topics as varied as class, nation, and social justice. She is considered one of the precursors of feminine poetry in twentieth-century Mexico. Although a prolific poet, Margarita Paz Paredes' work remains relatively unknown to a wide audience of readers. A collection of her most important poems was published in an anthology entitled *Litoral del tiempo*. The anthology was first published by the Guanajuato government. A second edition was published by the Campeche government, and a third edition was published by the *Secretaría de Educación Publica* (Public Education Secretariat). Margarita Paz Paredes continues to be lovingly remembered in Mexico, and specifically in her native state of Guanajuato where schools and streets are named after her and where her work has been recognized in official ceremonies. Her native San Felipe recognizes her contribution to the Mexican letters and culture by listing her as one of its most distinguished personalities.

BRENCI PATIÑO

Selected Works

Voz de la tierra: Poemas. México: Firmamento, 1946.

Presagio en el viento. San Salvador: Ministerio de Cultura, Departamento Editorial, 1955.

La imagen y su espejo. México: B. Costa-Amic, 1962.

Lumbre cautiva. México: Ediciones Oasis, 1968.

Litoral del tiempo: Antología poética. México: Ediciones del Gobierno del Estado de Guanajuato, 1978.

Memorias de hospital/Presagio. México: Miguel Angel Porrúa, 1983.

References and Further Reading

Calvillo Madrigal, Salvador. "Poetisas Mexicanas: Margarita Paz Paredes". *Nivel* 195 (1979).

Lucotti, Claudia. "De traductores y de fronteras: la importancia de traducir a P.K. Page en México". *Revista Mexicana de Estudios Canadienses*. 5 (2002). http://www.amec.com.mx/revista/num_5_2002/Lucotti_Claudia.htm

Mead, Jr., Robert G. "The Mexican Literary Scene in 1956". *Hispania* 4(10 (1957): 37–43.

Nohemí, Sosa Reyna. "Margarita Paz Paredes: sus palabras fluyen inevitables como un caudal." http://nohemisosatextos.bitacoraglobal.com.ar/index.php/827 (accessed 17 July 2005).

Pardo García, German. "Memorias de Hospital: Poemas de Margarita Paz Paredes". *Nivel* 200 (1979).

Vergara, Gloria. "Miradas que se cruzan: construcción de la identidad en las poetas mexicanas del siglo XX". *Estudios sobre las culturas contemporáneas* XI(22) (2005): 291–304.

Walsh, Donald Devenish. "Spanish American Literature in 1946". *Hispania* 30(1) (1947): 20–6.

PELLIZA DE SAGASTA, JOSEFINA

Josefina Pelliza de Sagasta (1848–88) was an Argentine essayist, poet, and novelist who defended women's right to a literary career and protection under the law, but also upheld the traditional roles of wives and mothers. Born under a wagon during her parents' flight from the dictator Rosas, Pelliza was raised in Concordia but returned to Buenos Aires as a young woman. Sometimes using the pseudonyms of Figarillo and Judith, she published prolifically, and, in 1878, edited *La Alborada del Plata,* the women's newspaper founded by Juana Manuela Gorriti.

Essayist and Polemicist

Throughout the 1870s and until her death, Josefina Pelliza regularly published essays in the periodicals of the day. Unlike many of her contemporaries, who advocated reforming the patriarchal family, Pelliza vigorously supported it, opposing proposals that would fundamentally change women's domestic status, such as paid work outside the home. But she just as vigorously attacked those who took advantage of traditional ideas to belittle motherhood, thwart women's creative impulses, and prevent women from having legal custody of their children and control over their own finances. She supported education for women to the extent that a mother should raise her children to be enlightened citizens and also express her creative instincts with the pen. However, she opposed the sort of education that would lead women to neglect their children, teach "unladylike" subjects such as astronomy, and provide training that would lead to non-domestic employment.

Josefina Pelliza's boldly stated opinions drew her into debates on several occasions, of which two are of interest to today's scholars. The first occurred in 1876, when Pelliza exchanged views with María Eugenia Echenique on the subject of women's emancipation. Pelliza presented the arguments in favor of traditional womanhood, while Echenique argued for abandoning that model in favor of a more "progressive" womanhood suitable for the nineteenth century. The second debate was sparked by attacks on women writers by "Da Freito" (Antonio Argerich). For Pelliza, a writing career did not interfere with being a good wife and mother, because it could be carried out with modesty at home. Argerich scoffed at such notions. He was not the genteel opponent that Echenique was, and the debate took on uglier tones than the previous one. Both debates were widely read and commented on in the press.

These experiences, along with others that put Pelliza on the defensive, produced an embittered tone in her *Conferencias: El libro de las madres* (1885) that had not been present in her earlier works. This work is really two short books published together: *El libro de las madres* is a manual for new mothers, and is of interest to historians of maternal issues, such as the hiring of wet nurses. *Conferencias*, on the other hand, is a long essay that sums up Pelliza's ideas about women's roles in the national identity and the difficulties of being a woman writer in Argentina. She advocates legal reform to protect the rights of mothers and their children, saying that current law gives mothers no more rights "than a dog"; defends the nobility of motherhood, calling Catholicism's view of Eve as a sinner "a ridiculous fable"; laments the marginal role of women writers in Argentina, saying that a woman must be "heroic" to dare try to enter into a realm jealously guarded by men; and reaffirms her opposition to women's participation in "impure" politics. Like many women who placed their hopes in nineteenth-century concepts of progress, Pelliza imagines a brighter future in the impending twentieth century.

Poet and Novelist

Josefina Pelliza began publishing poetry in various periodicals while still a teenager, a practice she continued throughout her life. Her sentiments—love, appreciation for nature (especially flowers and birds), and the marvels of progress in the nineteenth century—and imagery are conventional ones for that era. During the 1870s, her poetry was praised by the leading writers of the day. With the arrival of Modernism in Argentina in the 1880s, however, appreciation for poetry such as Pelliza's began to wane, and her critics grew increasingly harsh. Her novels in the 1880s met a similar fate. One critic in 1881 suggested that she stop writing altogether.

However, Josefina Pelliza's first novel, *Margarita*, published in 1875, was a best-seller, and was praised on the front page of *La Nación*. The heroine, Margarita, flees the advances of Luis, her supposed father. To her lover Plácido, however, she puts up no "ridiculous resistance" and is soon pregnant. Luis sends a hired killer after her; she survives, but the assassin takes her baby. Despairing, Margarita temporarily loses her sanity. Plácido manages to kill Luis, then he tracks down Margarita. Meanwhile, a kindly couple who have adopted Margarita's lost son turn out to be her real parents. Margarita and Plácido are married by her father, since she considers Catholic marriage to be a "stupid social formula". The novel is surprising for its sexual gusto and its dismissal of institutional religion. Readers who knew Pelliza's sometimes extreme defense of motherhood in her essays would know that they were supposed to interpret Margarita's sexuality in an approving way, since it produced a child. To Pelliza's way of thinking, motherhood was an even higher calling than religion or conventional morality.

Josefina Pelliza saw her approaching death due to kidney failure, and wrote her last poem, "¡Muerta!," just eight days before she died on August 10, 1888. Her friend, Juana Manuela Gorriti, mourned her loss in *Lo íntimo*. One of Pelliza's sons donated her papers to the library in Concordia. In 1982, a memorial plaque was placed on the house where she lived in Buenos Aires.

Modern Interpretations

After her death, Josefina Pelliza was largely forgotten; Gorriti speculated that Pelliza's admirers appreciated her beauty and charm more than her writings. When she was remembered, it usually was in connection with her friendship with Domingo Sarmiento. The memory of Pelliza the writer was recovered when feminist scholars such as Lily Sosa de Newton and Lea Fletcher began to rewrite Argentine literary history to include women's contributions. Pelliza now routinely appears in lists of writers who were active in the 1870s and 1880s.

Pelliza's significance to today's scholars is based on: (1) her anti-emancipation ideas, which form an important counterpoint to Argentina's nascent feminism; (2) her defense of crusading motherhood, which anticipates the roles of the Madres de la Plaza de Mayo; and (3) her defense of women's right to write. Francine Masiello, for example, examines Pelliza's ideas alongside those of her pro-emancipation contemporaries, revealing the ways in which their opinions differed and coincided. Bonnie Frederick places Pelliza in the context of other women writers of the time, showing how she was both conventional and unconventional in her beliefs and literary works.

BONNIE FREDERICK

Selected Works

Margarita. Buenos Aires: El Orden, 1875.

"La emancipación de la mujer" (Debate with Echenique). *La Ondina del Plata*. May 7, 1876–September 10, 1876. English translation: Palouse Translation Project. "The Emancipation of Women: Argentina 1876". *The Journal of Women's History* 7 (1995): 102–26.

"La mujer literata en la República Argentina" (Debate with Argerich). *El Album del Hogar.* November 24, 1878–January 5, 1879.
Conferencias: El libro de las madres. Buenos Aires: Jeneral Lavalle, 1885.

References and Further Reading

Fletcher, Lea. "Poesía femenina argentina del siglo XIX." http://www.elarcadigital.com.ar/papi.asp?archivo=/57/suplementos.asp
Frederick, Bonnie. *Wily Modesty: Argentine Women Writers, 1860–1910.* Tempe, AZ: ASU Center for Latin American Studies Press, Arizona State University, 1998.
——. "Harriet Beecher Stowe and the Virtuous Mother: Argentina, 1852–1910". *Journal of Women's History* 18(1) (2006): 101–20.
Guerrero, César H. *Mujeres de Sarmiento.* Buenos Aires: n.p., 1960.
Masiello, Francine. *Between Civilization and Barbarism: Women, Nation, and Literary Culture in Modern Argentina.* Lincoln, NB: University of Nebraska Press, 1992.
Maubé, J. and Capdevielle, A. (eds). *Antología de la poesía femenina argentina.* Buenos Aires: Ferrari, 1930.
Sosa de Newton, Lily. *Diccionario biográfico de mujeres argentinas.* Buenos Aires: Plus Ultra, 1986.

PERI ROSSI, CRISTINA

Cristina Peri Rossi was born in Montevideo, Uruguay, on 12 November 1941. Like many Uruguayans, her parents' families were nineteenth-century immigrants. Her mother's side of the family is Italian and her father's is Basque and Canarian. In 1947, at the age of 6, she began her studies at José Enrique Rodó, a public school named after a famous Uruguayan essayist. At university, she studied music and biology, gaining her degree in Comparative Literature at the Instituto de Profesores Artigas in 1964. At this same time she began teaching at university and writing for the leftist magazine *Marcha.*

Her early writing was provocative and political and her first collection of stories, *Indicios Pánicos* (1970, Panic Signs), foreshadowed the repressive state that was to govern her country and force her into exile. The Uruguayan government was threatened by socialism in the early 1970s at a time when the country was suffering economic decline. In response, the government moved progressively toward a repressive military state, which officially took power in 1973. Peri Rossi's political writing made connections between bourgeois values and authoritarianism, linking the compulsive social norms of the bourgeoisie with state repression and ideological authoritarianism. Given that Peri Rossi's early work was openly political, her notoriety as a writer would have been enough to lead to her exile. Nevertheless, it was only after personal loss that Peri Rossi decided to flee her country. In March of 1972, Peri Rossi gave refuge to a young student, Ana Luisa Valdés, who was being pursued by the secret police. On the one day that Ana decided to venture out of the house she was picked up by the secret police and never heard from again. It was then that Peri Rossi began to realize how dangerous the dictatorship had become and she made plans to leave Uruguay, arriving by boat in Barcelona in October of 1972. In 1974, the military government in Uruguay withdrew her citizenship. She left for Paris and later returned to Barcelona as a Spanish citizen where she continues to live.

Peri Rossi has an extensive body of work, she has published poetry, stories, novels, and books of essays and she has received numerous awards and prizes, including a John Simon Guggenheim grant in 1994. Her writing can be divided roughly into two periods: her work preceding and during exile and that following. In her early fiction of *Viviendo, Los museos abandonados, El libro de mis primos, Indicios pánicos* and *Evohé* Peri Rossi explores many of the themes which would persist in her work post-exile: the erotic, the political, and the function of art. From the outset Peri Rossi's literary style was unique in its combination of the fantastic, the poetic, the political, and the highly literary. Multifaceted in all of its fictive forms, Peri Rossi's writing has remained inaccessible to many readers who generally focus on only one of the many aspects that drive her literature. Her work can be categorized as exile literature, lesbian writing, feminist, fantastic, post-boom, allegorical, erotic, anti-bourgeois, psychoanalytic to name only the primary ways in which her work has been studied. Her identity as a lesbian exile committed to highlighting the world of marginalized existence has also affected her work's reception inasmuch as it challenges all of the essential premises of Western society: heterosexuality, patriarchy, capitalism and religion. Her work has been awarded some of the highest honors beginning with her first publication *Viviendo,* a collection of short stories, and her work has received multiple literary honors within Latin America. Peri Rossi's writing is a rich exploration of the social, sexual, and political world of those members of society who challenge the prevailing system. An appreciation of her work requires that all the issues represented in her writing be understood as intertwined and complimentary aspects of her literary accomplishments.

Before and During Exile

Her first work was *Evohé,* a collection of sensual lesbian poetry that describes lesbian love as a threat to Christian society. The sexual identity of lesbians is the main focus. The social system is also the object of her critique in *Indicios pánicos* where a man is faced with the difficult decision of denouncing his lover. Throughout the text Peri Rossi makes reference to the role of fascism in Latin America and indicts the region's practice of authoritarian rule. This text can now be read as foreshadowing the military junta which would rule Uruguay starting in 1973, the year after she fled to Spain in exile.

In exile, Peri Rossi continued to explore these issues from a style that revealed distrust for high modernist forms of literary expression. In her exile writing, Peri Rossi investigated the relationship between language and power and these works often attempt to unravel these structures by using a fragmented narrative voice and by calling attention to the inability of language to adequately express experience. One of the ways that she focuses on these dilemmas is through the use of children narrators. Peri Rossi's children question the rules and structures of society in ways that facilitate her critique of how adults acquiesce to authority and authoritarianism. In stories from *La tarde del dinosaurio,* for instance, children rebel against the way that adults control language. One girl changes her name, another questions her father's explanation of why they need to change their watches when they travel, and a young boy wonders what he should write about for an essay on his "padres" because the word could refer to his father and stepfather or to his mother and his two fathers or to his mother and father. In this way Peri Rossi's children ask simple, yet disturbing, questions about how language structures the way people think and thereby prepares them to submit to other forms of control.

In addition to the themes present in her early work, after exile, Peri Rossi demonstrated an obsession with classical, modern, and contemporary representations of travel and its effect on the self. Beginning with her novel, *La nave de los locos* and her collection of poetry *Descripción de un naufragio*, ships, water, islands, foreign cities, linguistic displacement and the anguish of wandering become narrative interests consistent throughout her work.

La nave de los locos may well be one of her most internationally read works and it narrates the travels of Ecks (X), an exile and social outcast. The novel, while political and critical of social norms, questions its own degree of efficacy as a messenger of change. In fact, the ability of language, especially literary, to relate to the existence of others is consistently questioned. At a certain level the rise of the city, capitalism, and modern ideology are conceived of as homogenizing and normalizing, leaving only the fringes of society available for those who do not conform. This point is made in the comparison between the Island on which the exiles and outcasts reside and the City which they occasionally must visit. Ecks feels great panic in the city and its inhabitants are described as automatons who spend their entire lives looking at their belly-buttons refusing to recognize the world in which they live. Both hopeful and pessimistic, celebratory and critical, this novel is full of contradictions and fragments, all of which revolve around the central dilemma of how modernity is predicated on ostracizing those who do not conform.

After Exile

Much of her post-exile work, such as *Babel Bárbara*, *La última noche de Dostoievsky*, and *Cosmoagonías,* continues to pursue themes of identity and social repression. The end of authoritarian rule in Uruguay freed her, however, to consider these issues within a broader context. Her interest in how language shapes identity also continues in this period with increased attention to poststructural and postmodern theories that suggest that resistance to social control requires destabilizing the master narratives that script identity and drawing attention to the multiple meanings repressed by official discourse. In her novel, *La última noche de Dostoievsky*, the influence of Roland Barthes's notion of the "pleasure of the text" is emphasized: writing and reading are erotic acts similar to the adventurous and manipulating behavior of the protagonist, who is addicted to gambling and in love with his therapist. The short stories in *Cosmoagonías* reflect the role of the writer within an era of multinational capitalism. As before, the city is represented as the home for capitalist ideology but the difference is that the texts in this collection wonder whether any place can be safe from the reach of such ideology. In *El amor es una droga dura*, Peri Rossi displays postmodern sensibilities of mediation and mass media by having her narrator observe the world through his camera lens.

The exploration of erotics and desire in *El amor es una droga dura* also appears in her collection of poetry, *Estrategias del deseo*. The collection explores the enigma of the other, the desire for what can never be known, the twists and turns of the memory of desire, the links between nostalgia and desire. In another recent collection of poetry, *Estado del exilio* Peri Rossi continues to consider how spatial displacement affects identity. The poems alternate between treating the condition of exile as one of loss, lament and nostalgia and engaging with exile from a perspective which is ironic, sarcastic, and ludic. Similar to her work during exile, these poems indicate a series of dialectic tensions in her literary investigations of identity. Whether identity is explored through desire or through the displacement of exile, Peri Rossi's work always provides multivalent critical angles on social dilemmas.

Power and Pleasure: Eroticism, Social Transgression, and Authoritarianism

Passion, desire, and the erotic flow throughout Peri Rossi's works. From the beginning of her career to her most recent published works, the erotic has been central to her writing. While it is possible to mark shifts in her literature, certain common themes run throughout her literary presentation of sexual desire and passion: Peri Rossi is especially interested in producing literature that breaks down traditional gender categories and her writing challenges the hegemony of patriarchal, heterosexual society. Another common theme is the association of woman's body with language and of writing with sex.

Peri Rossi often uses multiply gendered narrative voices to destabilize gender identities. She also frequently writes her poetry and short stories from ambiguous gender positions that allow the reader to imagine either a male or a female speaker. Since her poetry clearly has the female body as an object of desire, this ambiguous gender identity of the poetic voice allows the reader to receive the poem as an example of either heterosexual or lesbian love. Peri Rossi rarely specifies the narrative or poetic voice as female and it is noteworthy that she often adopts a male voice. Such a practice could be disturbing since it could suggest her avoidance of openly lesbian literary representation. Alternatively, one could argue that the reader is always aware that the author is a woman. According to this position, Peri Rossi's adoption of a male voice is transgressive because it destabilizes pre-established notions of gender identity.

One further way that Peri Rossi's literature challenges traditional gender relations is through the depiction of impotent and/or anti-patriarchal male characters. In her novel *La nave de los locos* (The Ship of Fools), the protagonist, Ecks (X) is an exile as well as a symbol for all marginalized segments of society. The novel critiques the master narratives of authoritarianism, patriarchal society, Christian ideology, and heterosexism. Each of these is intertwined within the novel suggesting that to address only one of these axes of oppression is insufficient. Ultimately, the novel suggests that social change depends on ending male domination and phallocentric control of the symbolic order. Ecks, the marginalized and impotent male narrator, dreams that the way in which patriarchy can be destroyed is through men's renunciation of virility as an act of love. If all men gave the women they loved their virility, then patriarchy would be destroyed. In a similar vein *Solitario de amor* (Solitaire of Love) has an unnamed protagonist who, while capable of sexual intercourse with the woman he loves, is effectively impotent. He tells the reader that he is a man without a "key" (p. 109). Like Ecks, he is nameless and marginalized. His only identity is his obsession with a woman who has rejected him.

Just as Peri Rossi eschews a stable subject position and critiques patriarchy, she also refuses fixed categories of desire. Desire and identity are fluid and interconnected. Peri Rossi draws attention to the fact that fixing identity and containing desire are ways of controlling and repressing society. Her multiple narrative and poetic voices are combined with myriad forms of sexual desire. Peri Rossi also describes passion and desire as feelings that resist narrow definitions. For instance, her collection of short stories *Una pasión prohibida* (A Forbidden Passion) includes many different descriptions of human desire. The theme throughout the collection is that identity and desire are inseparable and that social forces have always tried to limit and control desires. Many of the stories focus on the ways that desires have been brutally restricted, causing great suffering. Alternatively, other stories focus on the ways that when desire is coupled with power it often results in the marginalization and oppression of others. Peri Rossi emphasizes that desire almost always relates to issues of power. While her writing tries to free those whose desires have been repressed, she also challenges the use of power to forcefully control desire. For instance, she often describes lesbian love as a social transgression and she even refers to the love between women as wonderfully incestual. *Lingüística General* (General Linguistics) ends with two clearly lesbian poems that are celebratory and playful. In contrast to her celebration of lesbian desire, Peri Rossi associates military dictatorships and authoritarianism with rape and the violation of humanity's freedom to desire. Three of her collections of poetry written during exile, *Descripción de un naufragio* (Description of a Shipwreck), *Diáspora* (Diaspora) and *Europa después de la lluvia* (Europe after the Rain), narrate desire as loss and they represent fear at the inability to connect and love. In these collections Eros implies power and it can lead to corruption, objectification, and alienation. Yet in other texts, Eros also is about adoration, celebration, pleasure, and harmony. Peri Rossi describes an eroticism unbound and examines the dark as well as the beautiful aspects of desire.

The Female Body and Language

The images of women that reappear in her poetry and prose are often similar to traditional icons of women. She associates the female body with a utopic refuge (focusing on the womb) and women are connected to nature, especially water. Contrasted to these traditional images where woman's body occupies the center of desire and is celebrated as a source of passion and pleasure, Peri Rossi also depicts the female body as violated and vulnerable. These images are especially recurrent in her novel *La nave de los locos* (The Ship of Fools). The novel describes the clitoral castration of women and the experiments performed on Jewish women during the Holocaust. The main character (Ecks) watches a movie where a woman is raped by a machine, he befriends an ageing prostitute, and he also falls in love with a woman who has a clandestine, painful abortion. In addition to these images, Peri Rossi's literature depicts women who are resistant and who refuse to submit to the system and to be victims of the desires of others. In *Solitario de amor* (Solitary of Love), for example, the protagonist is desperately in love with a woman named Aída. She is alternatively described as a welcoming, nurturing figure and as a strong and self-sufficient woman who steadfastly rejects the protagonist.

Focusing on language and desire, Peri Rossi equates writing with sex and language with women. In this way she links the aesthetic with language. These themes are particularly noteworthy in her poetry. Her first collection of poetry, *Evohé,* caused a scandal when it was published in Uruguay in 1971. Beginning with a quote from Sappho, the collection is a passionate, sensual series of poems about the female body, at times equating the female body with a temple and love with prayer. Peri Rossi draws on the tie between the collection's title, which comes from Euripedes' play, *The Bacchae*, in her exploration of passion unbound. The Bacchae were the female followers of Bacchus (Dionysus) and "Evohé" was the cry uttered at the end of their celebration of freedom from civilization. Consistent with her critique of Christianity and of confining systems of social organization, this text demonstrates the way in which lesbian love challenges the prevailing system of belief. Woman and word are equal symbols and the poet / lover interacts with women through words and through the sensuality of language. In *Babel bárbara* (Barbarous Babel), Peri Rossi continues to work with sensual, lesbian-oriented poetry. In this collection the concept of "woman" is likened to the Tower of Babel where the multiplicity of meaning in language and in the female body are equated. The result is a highly ambiguous fusion and confusion of sex and language. In *Otra vez eros* (Eros Again), she continues to explore sensuality, language, pleasure and the female body. The title, again, refers to Sappho's poetry where she describes the untying of desire. The collection continues to exalt lesbian love, passion for the female body and the ties between sensuality and language, but Peri Rossi also includes relatively newer themes like the effects of science, technology, and AIDS on contemporary passions.

SOPHIA A. MCCLENNEN

Selected Works

Viviendo: relatos. Montevideo: Alfa, 1963.
Indicios pánicos. Montevideo: Nuestra América, 1970.
Evohe: poemas eróticos. Montevideo: Girón, 1970.
Descripción de un naufragio. Barcelona: Lumen, 1975.
Diáspora. Barcelona: Lumen, 1976.
El Libro de mis primos. 2nd edn. Barcelona: Plaza & James, 1976.
Lingüística general: poemas. Valencia: Prometeo, 1979.
"Génesis de Europa después de la lluvia". *Studi di Letteratura Ispano-Americana* 13–14 (1983): 63–78.
La Tarde del dinosaurio. Barcelona: Plaza y Janes, 1985.
Europa después de la lluvia. Madrid: Fundación Banco Exterior de España, 1987.
Una Pasión prohibida. 2nd edn. Barcelona: Seix Barral, 1987.
La Rebelión de los niños. Barcelona: Seix Barral, 1988.
El Museo de los esfuerzos inútiles. 3rd edn. Barcelona: Seix Barral, 1989.
Babel bárbara. Caracas: Angria, 1990.
Solitario de amor. México: Grijalbo, 1990.
Fantasías eróticas. Madrid: Temas de Hoy, 1991.
La Ultima noche de Dostoievski. Madrid: Grijalbo Mondadori, 1992.
Los Museos abandonados. Barcelona: Lumen, 1992.
La Ciudad de Luzbel. Montevideo: Trilce, 1993.

Cosmoagonías. Barcelona: Juventud, 1994.
Otra vez Eros. Barcelona: Lumen, 1994.
Papeles críticos. 2nd edn. Montevideo: Linardi Risso, 1995.
La Nave de los locos. 2nd edn. Barcelona: Biblioteca de Bolsillo, 1995.
Aquella noche. Barcelona: Lumen, 1996.
Desastres íntimos. Barcelona: Lumen, 1997.
Inmovilidad de los barcos. Vitoria-Gasteiz, Spain: Bassarai, 1997.
Poemas de amor y desamor. Barcelona: Plaza y Janés, 1998.
El amor es una droga dura. Barcelona: Seix Barral, 1999.
Las musas inquietantes. Barcelona: Lumen S.A., 1999.
Cuando fumar era un placer. Barcelona: Lumen S.A., 2003.
Estado de exilio. Madrid: Visor Libros S.L., 2003.
Estrategias del deseo. Barcelona: Lumen S.A., 2004.
Por fin solos. Barcelona: Lumen S.A., 2004.

References and Further Reading

Basualdo, Ana. "Cristina Peri Rossi: Apocalipsis y paraíso". *El viejo topo* 56 (1981): 47–9.

Camps, Susana. "La pasión desde la pasión: entrevista con Cristina Peri-Rossi". *Quimera* 81 (1988): 40–9.

Dejbord, Parizad Tamara. *Cristina Peri Rossi: Escritora del exilio*. Buenos Aires: Editorial Galerna, 1998.

Deredita, John F. "Desde la diáspora: entrevista con Cristina Peri Rossi". *Texto Crítico* 9 (1978): 131–42.

Feal, Rosemary G. "Cristina Peri Rossi and the Erotic Imagination". In Doris Meyer (ed.), *Reinterpreting the Spanish American Essay: Women Writers of the 19th and 20th Century*. Austin, TX: University of Texas Press, 1995, pp. 215–26.

Golano, Elena. "Sonar para seducir: entrevista con Cristina Peri Rossi". *Quimera* 25 (1982): 47–50.

Guerra-Cunningham, Lucía. "La referencialiadad como negación del paraíso: exilio y excentrismo en *La nave de los locos* de Cristina Peri Rossi". *Revista de Estudios Hispanicos* 23(2) (1989): 63–74.

Invernizzi-Santa Cruz, Lucía. "Entre el tapiz de la expulsión del paraíso y el tapiz de la creación: multiples sentidos del viaje a bordo de *La nave de los locos* de Cristina Peri Rossi". *Revista Chilena de Literatura* 30 (1987): 29–53.

Kaminsky, Amy. "Gender and Exile in Cristina Peri Rossi: Selected Papers from Wichita State University Conference on Foreign Literature, 1984–85". In Ginette Adamson and Eunice Myers (eds), *Continental, Latin-American and Francophone Women Writers*. Lanham, MD: University Press of America, 1987, pp. 149–59.

Kantaris, Elia. "The Politics of Desire: Alienation and Identity in the Work of Marta Traba and Cristina Peri Rossi". *Forum for Modern Language Studies* 25(3) (1989): 248–64.

Mántaras, Graciela. "Cristina Peri Rossi en la literatura erótica uruguaya". In Rómulo Cosse (ed.), *Cristina Peri Rossi: Papeles críticos*. Montevideo: Librería Linardi y Risso, 1995, pp. 31–45.

McClennen, Sophia A. *The Dialectics of Exile: Nation, Time, Language and Space in Hispanic Literatures*. Detroit, MI: Purdue University Press, 2004.

Morana, Mabel. "*La nave de los locos* de Cristina Peri Rossi". *Texto Crítico* 12(34–5) (1986): 204–13.

Narvaez, Carlos Raul. "Eros y Thanatos en *Solitario de amor* de Cristina Peri-Rossi". *Alba de América* 10(18–19) (1992): 245–50.

——. "La poética del texto sin fronteras: *Descripción de un naufragio*, *Diáspora*, *Lingüística general*, de Cristina Peri Rossi". *Inti* 28 (1988): 75–88.

Olivera-Williams, María Rosa. "*La última noche de Dostoievski*: la escritura del deseo o el deseo de la escritura". *Hispamerica* 24(71) (1995): 97–106.

Pertusa, Immaculada. "Revolución e identidad en los poemas lesbianos de Cristina Peri Rossi". *Monographic Review/Revista Monografica* 7 (1991): 236–50.

Rowinsky, Mercedes. *Imagen y discurso: Estudio de las imágenes en la obra de Cristina Peri Rossi*. Barcelona: Editorial Trilce, 1997.

San Roman, Gustavo. "Fantastic Political Allegory in the Early Work of Cristina Peri Rossi". *Bulletin of Hispanic Studies* 67(2) (1990): 151–64.

Schmidt, Cynthia A. "A Satiric Perspective on the Experience of Exile in the Short Fiction of Cristina Peri Rossi". *The Americas Review* 18(3–4) (1990): 218–26.

Sosnowski, Saul. "Los museos abandonados". *Revista Sur* 349 (1981): 147–55.

Verani, Hugo J. "Una experiencia de límites: la narrativa de Cristina Peri Rossi". *Revista Iberoamericana* 48(118–19) (1982): 303–16.

——. "La historia como metáfora: *La nave de los locos* de Cristina Peri Rossi". *La Torre* 4(13) (1990): 79–92.

——. "La rebelión del cuerpo y el lenguaje". In Rómulo Cosse (ed.), *Cristina Peri Rossi: Papeles críticos*. Montevideo: Librería Linardi y Risso, 1995, pp. 9–21.

Zeitz, Eileen. "Cristina Peri Rossi: El desafío de la alegoría" (Interview.) *Chasqui* 9(1) (1979): 79–101.

PETIT, MAGDALENA

Born in Santiago in 1900 to a medical doctor and his wife, Magdalena Petit forms part of Chile's literary "Generation of 1927" which sought narrative inspiration in national historical episodes and rejected themes and styles imported from Europe. Although hailing from the centre of the country, Petit was greatly attracted to the south of Chile. This area was the source of a great number of themes and ideas for much of her writing and she made it her "spiritual" home and, temporarily, her place of residence. Although her considerable output has received scant attention from modern critics, those scholars who have directed attention to her work have offered a feminist view of the female protagonist of her best-known work, *La Quintrala* (1932), for which she was awarded *La Nación* prize. Having submitted the manuscript to the selection panel for the prize under a pseudonym, the jurors declared themselves surprised that it should have been written by a woman when they eventually discovered the identity of the author. Nonetheless, its warm reception by the critic Alone ensured recognition for Petit as a novelist of merit.

The story of Doña Catalina de los Ríos, the novel is based on the popular Chilean legend that grew up around the historical figure, infamous during the colonial period for her brutality and association with devil worship. Petit's tale presents a figure in torment who tries to reconcile her compulsion for association with black magic encouraged by indigenous servants and her desire for Christian redemption. The text is largely sympathetic to La Quintrala's efforts to lead a pious life and offers no moral comment on her many crimes. The work is of interest from a feminist perspective precisely because Petit fails to condemn a character who transgressed every rule governing female behaviour in colonial Latin America. Through the medium of La Quintrala, the novelist explores the link perceived by society to exist between devil worship and unrestrained female sexuality, ultimately indicating that such an equation is invalid. Significantly, her protagonist has sufficient strength of character to remain unconcerned with the gossip that ensues from her sexual liaisons, and is revealed to suffer no morally imposed fate as a result of her actions. Petit gently points out, too, that the male partner in such a relationship is not devoid of blame, either: although La Quintrala's mother seduced a priest, he lacked the moral strength to deny her. Gendered behaviours are also scrutinised, and analysis of them ultimately reveals that they are social constructs and the product of patriarchal colonial society. Not only is La Quintrala sexually liberated, she is also violent, cruel and exhibits murderous traits traditionally associated with the male in the context of Spanish colonial expansion. She thus defies all the norms for womanhood within the context of her social space and historical time.

Figures and events from Chile's past, and the geography of her homeland, furnished Petit with material for further works. *Don Diego Portales* (1937), based, like *La Quintrala* on an historical biography by Vicuña Mackenna, presents a detailed vista of nineteenth-century Santiago. Her next novel, *Los Pincheira* (1939), portrays the historical reality of Chile's southern cities and focuses on the immensity of a natural environment protagonised by the Andes and the southern lakes, and on the violence and banditry with which the region's inhabitants had to contend. This work also offers a discussion of indigenous issues, a theme introduced in *La Quintrala*. Petit's beloved southern Chile would provide a backdrop for yet another of her works, *Caleuche* (1946). The tale of a ghost ship, it conveys the author's fascination with the island of Chiloé and, combining folklore and fiction, highlights the mystery and magic interwoven with the traditions of the area. The novel won the *Premio Municipal* in 1946, and the dramatised version of it was awarded the only prize in the *Concurso del Teatro Municipal Condon D'Evieri*.

Magdalena Petit died in Chile in 1968.

SHELLEY GODSLAND

Selected Works

Novels

La Quintrala. Santiago de Chile: Zig-Zag, 1932.
Don Diego Portales. Santiago de Chile: Zig-Zag, 1937.
Los Pincheira. Santiago de Chile: Zig-Zag, 1939.
Caleuche. Santiago de Chile: publisher unknown, 1946.
El patriota Manuel Rodríguez. Santiago de Chile: Zig-Zag, 1951.
Un hombre en el universo. Santiago de Chile: Zig-Zag, 1951.
Una llave y un camino. Santiago de Chile: Zig-Zag, 1955.

Theatre

La Quintrala. Santiago de Chile: publisher unknown,1935.
Kimeraland. *Escelsior*, 25, 1936.
Caleuche. Unpublished, 1941.
Un autor en busca de representación (undated). In *Atenea*, 133.
Teatro infantil (Comprising: "Pulgarcito", "El cumpleaños de Rosita", "El desencantamiento de los juguetes".) Santiago de Chile: Zig-Zag, 1937.

Other Works

Gabriela Mistral. Santiago de Chile: Zig-Zag, 1946.
"Rosa Manheim". *Nosotros*, 239.
"Fidelidad". *Revista Atenea*, 87,
"Tormenta". *Atenea*, 101.
"Del arte en la crítica". *Atenea*, 106.
"Pablo Neruda". *Atenea*, 99.

References and Further Reading

Agosín, Marjorie. "Una bruja novelada: *La Quintrala* de Magdalena Petit". *Chasqui* 12(1) (1982): 3–13.
Araya, Juan Gabriel. "Magdalena Petit Marfan (1903–68)". In *Escritoras chilenas, III: Novela y cuento*. Santiago de Chile: Cuarto Propio, 1999.
Llanos, Bernardita. "Tradición e historia en la narrativa femenina: Petit y Valdivieso frente a La Quintrala". *Revista Iberoamericana* 60(8) (1994): 1025–37.
Montes, Hugo and Orlandi, Julio. *Historia y Antología de la Literatura Chilena*. Santiago de Chile: Zig-Zag, 1955, pp. 134–5.

PIÑÓN, NÉLIDA

Nélida Piñón was born in Rio de Janeiro, Brazil, on May 3, 1937. Her parents, Lino Piñón Muiño and Olivia Cuiñas Piñón, were Galician immigrants who arrived in Brazil in the 1920s. The name Nélida, an anagram of her grandfather Daniel's first name, seems to signal, from the very beginning of the writer's life, that she would be seriously interested in family matters, cultural heritage, and how a writer resolves these matters in more than one national reality.

But before she became a published writer, Piñón formed her taste and her literary referents by being an avid reader of the books that her parents gave her. She was also, as we can see from her subsequent work, an observant traveler: when she was 10 years old, she returned to Galicia, where she lived for two years. This period was crucial for the future writer's understanding of her own identity and to her attachment to both Brazil and Galicia. And it was also in her own childhood that, as the writer says in "The Territory of my Imagination" that she began inventing the books that she did not have at hand. Piñón developed her sense of the craft of literature by reading not only the Brazilian masters such as Machado de Assis and Monteiro Lobato, but also, from other cultures and times, Homer, Shakespeare, Proust, and Dostoyevsky who, she writes, "showed [her] the darkness that keeps humans prisoners of desire" ("The Territory of My Imagination"). From outside of literature, she fine-tuned her moral and ethical sensibilities by reading history, theology and philosophy.

Piñón's professional life has always been related to writing: after graduating in journalism from the Catholic University of Rio de Janeiro, she worked in several magazines. In 1965, she was awarded a "Leader Grant," which enabled her to travel widely in the United States. Upon her return to Brazil, Piñón worked as assistant editor of *Cadernos Brasileiros* from 1966 to 1967, and since then she has participated in several consulting and editorial capacities in Brazilian magazines such as *Tempo Brasileiro* (1976–93), *Impressões* (1997), and *Cadernos Pedagógicos e Culturais* (1993). She was also member of the editorial board of the Venezuelan magazine *Imagem Latinoamericana* in 1993, and has been on the editorial board of *Review: Latin American Literature and Arts* since 1995. In addition, Piñón has written a weekly column for the Rio de Janeiro newspaper *O Dia* since 1995.

Besides her writing engagements, Piñón has also been a teacher in several institutions in Brazil and abroad. One of her most important accomplishments, early in her teaching career, was the establishment of the course on literary creation at the Federal University of Rio de Janeiro in 1970. Later, she taught courses and gave lectures in institutions such as The City University of New York, Columbia University, Johns Hopkins University, The Catholic University in Lima, Peru, the Sorbonne in Paris, and the Universidad Complutense de Madrid. She currently teaches every spring at the University of Miami.

Piñón has received several literary awards, including the Walmap Award in 1970, the Mário de Andrade Award in 1973 (for the novel *The House of Passion*), the Award given by the Paulista Association of Art Critics and the Pen Clube Award for Fiction in 1985 for her novel *The Republic of Dreams*; the Award José Geraldo Vieira, from the Brazilian Writers' Union in 1987 for her novel *Caetana's Sweet Song*, the Bi-Annual Nestlé Prize in 1991, the International Juan Rulfo Award in 1995, and the Menéndez Pelayo Award, given by the Universidad Menéndez Pelayo in 2003. In 2004 she received the Puterbaugh Fellowship. She has also been awarded the Prince of Asturias Award in Spain in 2005.

In 1989, Piñón was elected for the Chair number 30 of the Brazilian Academy of Letters, and became a full participant since her official reception in 1990. At the Academy, after holding several offices, she was elected president in 1996. Piñón is the first woman to preside over the Brazilian Academy of Letters, an institution which, it must be stressed, did not accept female members until 1977 when Rachel de Queiroz was—some say reluctantly—accepted.

Reviewing Myths, Revisiting the Past

Piñón's first novel, *Guia-mapa de Gabriel Arcanjo* (1961, Guide-Map of the Archangel Gabriel) deals with the matter of sin, and of how it is forgiven through a dialogue between the female protagonist Mariella and her guardian angel Gabriel. The new writer's exquisite sense of the Portuguese language and her sense of how it can be renewed relate her to another great writer of a previous generation, João Guimarães Rosa, and the intense interrogations about good and evil as fundamental questions in human life align Piñón's fiction with the work of her friend and celebrated writer Clarice Lispector.

It is with her novel *Fundador* (1972, The Founder), that Piñón first deals with a subject that has since been an even more crucial aspect of her work: the matter of how a family develops in time, through different experiences and permutations. *The Founder* already sets the basis upon which she will build other novels, using fictional characters alongside historical ones.

In 1973, Piñón published a short story collection, *Sala de armas* (Weapons Room), containing some stories which more strongly discuss the matter of women's role in society. In the story "I love my husband," the female narrator reviews her life and her relationship with her husband, in comparable terms to what Rosario Castellanos does in "Lección de cocina" (Cooking Lesson). In "I love my husband," however, there is no comedy. The trajectory of the woman from her first days with the husband, her growing awareness of her caged situation under the rule of a cold and demanding man is not told in chronological order. Even though the narrator knows that her individuality is being crushed, her intelligence mocked, and even her own sexuality dismissed, she cannot break the chains, and pronounces, at the end, that she does love her husband.

In *A casa da paixão* (The House of Passion), published in 1977, the theme is sexual awakening, and how it can change the characters' lives and ways of seeing the world. Here, Piñón presents the complex matters expressed by contradictory forces through the traps of traditional religious mores set against the seductions of eroticism. Through her use of characters that can be seen as archetypal, Piñón presents the human situation as fractured by taboos and interdictions, laws and coercions. A limited number of characters (the young Marta, the housekeeper Antonia, her unnamed widowed father, and Jerônimo, the suitor) open up the space for a discussion of how the traditional values represented by the Father thinly disguise his incestuous desire for his own daughter. Over against this edifice of prohibitions, there stands Nature, which, in this novel, also has its own laws and appears as an almost separate character.

Another important work of the 1977 is *A força do destino* (The Force of Destiny), which, according to the author's own words, was inspired by Giuseppi Verdi's opera. This is a story in which a woman, Lenora, decides to break with the romantic tradition that dictates a woman should die of love. Instead, Lenora chooses to live her love in all forms and with all her senses. The novel has proved to be so compelling that in 2006 a group of artists in Rio de Janeiro used it as the basis of a play, adapting freely from the plot of the novel and including, among its characters, the writer herself.

Her next novel, *A república dos sonhos* (1984, The Republic of Dreams) is probably Piñón's most celebrated novel and her first work translated into English (in 1989). It was received with wide acclaim. For example, *Publishers Weekly* praises "the Amazonian plenitude of Piñón's imagination" which "puts her in the category of genius". *The Republic of Dreams*, based in part on the experience of the Piñón family, tells the story of a family from the Spanish province of Galicia who move to Brazil. Even though the financial fortunes of the family increase throughout the years, it seems that the spiritual and cultural stock diminishes. The patriarch Madruga, responsible for the emigration as well as for the initial wealth upon which the family members built, feels deeply disappointed in his descendants, who are all, except one, cold and uninspired people.

The solution, for Madruga, is to take the only person in his family with whom he has a deeper relationship, his young granddaughter Breta, back to Galicia. This trip, their encounter with the green Galicia, and Breta's subsequent understanding of the travails and losses caused by her family's immigration, are the seeds that the grandfather entrusts her with. The result is the book about the family's experience. Of course, the fact that Piñón herself returned to Galicia when she was 10 years old, and that she published *Republic of Dreams*, seems to have constituted the realization of that fictional grandfather's, as well as Piñón's own family's, dream of having their history told. Once again, narrative becomes the narrative of a family.

This novel was followed by *A doce canção de Caetana* (1987, Caetana's Sweet Song). Set in the 1970s, the story takes place in Trindade, a small backward town where the wealthy middle-aged cattle baron, Polidoro Alves, waits for the return of the love of his youth, the itinerant artist Caetana. He hopes to reignite their passion and their love affair. But Caetana, like him now middle-aged, returns with different ideas: she wants to offer the town ART in the form of a performance of *La Traviata*. In the process, she herself wants to have the experience of singing like Maria Callas. The story is set in the grim 1970s, when Brazilians were taking refuge inside their homes in order not to see what the dictators were doing with the people.

As some critics have pointed out, *Caetana's Sweet Song* is a tale of dreams and their destruction. Reality—or, small daily disillusions—is the obstacle that prevents the characters from doing what they set themselves to do. Caetana, for example, cannot sing like Maria Callas, simply because she cannot sing; instead, she has to lip sinc. The town does not have actresses, just old prostitutes; and yet, they become actresses for a short while. In *Caetana's Sweet Song*, Piñón presents us a very carefully crafted novel in which Art, however imperfect, is, if not the antidote, at least the contrasting force, to both the political apathy and the incipient consumerism that helped anesthesize people's consciousness of their own political repression. It is interesting to observe that, whereas in *Republic of Dreams* Piñón is passionate about the history of a family, in *Caetana's Sweet Song*, even though it seems that her story is based exclusively in the small Trindade village, the novel can be seen as a complex allegory of the situation of Brazil under the military dictatorship.

In the 1990s, Piñón published a novel (*Até amanhã, outra vez*) (1999, See You Tomorrow, Again); a novel for young readers (*A roda do vento*) (1996, The Wheel of the Wind), and *O pão de cada dia* (1994, Our Daily Bread, fragments, short stories).

In the new century, she published a book of short stories, *Cortejo do Divino e outros contos escolhidos* (2001, The Procession of the Divine and Other Selected Stories), and a collection of her speeches, *O presumível coração da América* (2002, The Alleged Heart of America). In 2004, she published the novel *Vozes do deserto* (Voices of the Desert) which has been hailed as a masterpiece.

Even though Brazilian writers are often tired of setting their stories anywhere but in Brazil, for fear of being considered unpatriotic, Piñón chose as her setting the Baghdad of the tenth century of the Abassid Dynasty. In "The Territory of My Imagination," Piñón herself says of *Voices of the Desert*, "Whereas in *The Republic of Dreams* I tried to come to terms with Brazil of the last two hundred years, in *Vozes do Deserto* . . . I traversed the territory of the imagination itself and explored human nature".

To write this book, Piñón conducted extensive research on the history and culture of the Islamic world of one thousand years ago and read the Koran. However, what makes *Voices of the Desert* such a compelling book is the way in which Piñón uses the central figure of *Arabian Nights*, the story-telling Scheherazade, in an unusual way which emphasizes female resilience throughout the ordeal of telling stories to keep herself alive, as well to gain the freedom for other women. Nélida Galovic Norris writes

> Piñón revisits Scheherazade's personal odyssey sustained by an authorial disposition to venture further into a given artistic source and, as in the case of this novel, to stage unique and enticing alternatives to the prescribed limitations imposed in the traditional rendition of the celebrated stories [of the *Arabian Nights*].

Even though Nélida Piñón has created many remarkable female characters in her fiction, she has said that she sees herself as a storyteller more than an advocate. Suzanne Ruta quotes her as saying, "I want my night porter to tell me his secrets. That is my mission". And this mission continues, reaching ever more distant places, as more of Piñón's books continue being translated into different languages.

EVA PAULINO BUENO

Selected Works

Guia-mapa de Gabriel Arcanjo. Rio de Janeiro: Ediçoes G.D.R., 1961.
Madeira feita cruz. Rio de Janeiro: Edições G. D. R., 1963.
Tempo das frutas. Rio de Janeiro: J. Alvaro, 1966.
Fundador. (1969) Rio de Janeiro: Editorial Labor do Brasil, 1976. 2nd edn.
A casa da paixão. (1977) Rio de Janeiro: Nova Fronteira, 1982.
Sala de armas. Rio de Janeiro: Sabiá, 1973.
Tebas do meu coração. Rio de Janeiro: J. Olympio, 1974.
A força do destino. Rio de Janeiro: Editora Record, 1977.
O calor das coisas. Rio de Janeiro: Nova Fronteira, 1980.
A república dos sonhos. (1984) Rio de Janeiro: Francisco Alves, 1987, 3rd edn.
The Republic of Dreams. Trans. Helen Lane. Austin, TX: University of Texas Press, 1991.
A doce canção de Caetana. Rio de Janeiro: Editora Guanabara, 1987.
Caetana's Sweet Song. Trans. Helen Lane. New York: Alfred A. Knopf. 1992.
O pão de cada dia. Rio de Janeiro: Editora Nova Fronteira, 1994.
A roda do vento. (1996) São Paulo: Editora Ática, 1998, 2nd edn.
Até amanhã, outra vez. Rio de Janeiro: Editora Record, 1999.
Cortejo do Divino e outros contos escolhidos. Porto Alegre: L & P.M. 2001.
O presumível coração da América, discursos. Rio de Janeiro: Academia Brasileira de Letras: Topbooks, 2002.
Vozes do deserto. São Paulo: Editora Record, 2004.

References and Further Reading

Beard, Laura J. "Transgressive Textualities, Transgressive Sexualities: Nélida Piñon's *A Força do Destino*". *Brasil/Brazil: Revista de Literatura Brasileira/A Journal of Brazilian Literature* 21(12) (1999).

——. "Consuming Passions in *A Doce Canção de Caetana*". *Monographic Review/Revista Monográfica* 21 (2005): 104–16.

Espadas, Elizabeth. "Destination Brazil: Immigration in Works of Nélida Piñón and Karen Tei Yamashita." *MACLAS: Latin American Essays* 12 (1998): 51–61.

Fiori, Elizabet. "Intimismo, Feminismo e Metalinguagem em 'Colheita'". *Estudos Lingüísticos* 27 (1998): 656–9.

Fuentes, Carlos. "Tras la república de los sueños". Suplemento Literario *La Nación* (Buenos Aires) (April 7 1996): 1–2.

Latorre, Carolina. "El cuerpo como espacio de aprendizaje: Transcendencia de lo corporal en 'Colheita' de Nélida Piñón y *Uma aprendizagem ou o livro dos prazeres* de Clarice Lispector". *RLA: Romance Languages Annual* 9 (1997): 555–60.

Marting, Diane E. "Female Sexuality in *A casa da paixão* de Nélida Piñon: A Ritual Wedding Song in Narrative". In Alun Kenwood (ed.), *Love, Sex, and Eroticism in Contemporary Latin American Literature*. Madrid: Vox Hispana, 1993, pp. 143–52.

Moniz, Naomi Hoki. "*A casa da paixão*: Ética, Estética e a Condição Feminina". *Revista Iberoamericana* 126 (Jan.–Mar. 1984): 129–40.

——. "Nélida Piñon: A Questão da História em Sua Obra". In Peggy Sharpe (ed.), *Entre Resistir e Identificar-se: Para uma Teoria da Prática da Narrativa Brasileira de Autoria Feminina*. Florianópolis, 1997.

Norris, Nélida Galovic. "Nélida Piñón's *Desert Voices*". *World Literature Today* (April–January 2005): 17.

Piñón, Nélida. "The Territory of My Imagination". *World Literature Today* (January–April 2005): 11.

Quinlan, Susan Canty. "History Revisited: Nélida Piñón's *A república dos sonhos*". *Literatura de vanguarda luso-brasileira. Hispanic Studies Series* 4 (1989): 164–9.

Ruta, Suzanne. "A Village of Quixotes". *The New York Times*, May 24, 1992.

Sobral, Patricia. "Nélida Piñón: Imaginário e Arte na *República dos Sonhos* e na Academia". *Brasil/Brazil: Revista de Literatura Brasileira/A Journal of Brazilian Literature* 18 (1997): 83–105.

——. "Entre Fronteiras: A Condição do Migrante n'*A República dos Sonhos*". *Portuguese Literary and Cultural Studies* 1 (1998 Fall).

Teixeira, Vera Regina. "Nélida, The Dreamweaver". *World Literature Today: A Literary Quarterly of the University of Oklahoma* 79(1) (Jan–Feb 2005): 22–6.

Tosar, Luís González. "Nélida Piñón ou a paixón de contar". *Grial: Revista Galega de Cultura* 28(105) (Jan.–Mar. 1990): 85–95.

Vieira, Nelson Harry. "Saudade, 'Morriña' e Analepse: O Elemento Galego na Ficção Memorialista de Nélida Piñón". In A. Carreño (ed.), *Actas do 2 Congreso de Estudios Galegos*. Vigo: Editorial Galáxia, 1991, pp. 327–36.

Zolin, Lúcia Osana. "A Construção do Feminino nas Literaturas Portuguesa e Brasileira Contemporâneas: Miguel Torga e Nélida Piñón". *Acta Scientiarum* 21(1) (Mar. 1999): 27–35.

PINTO, JULIETA

Julieta Pinto was born in San José, Costa Rica in 1922. She spent her childhood on a farm in San Rafael de Alajuela. Her experiences at San Rafael would create the affinity she portrays in her works for the working farmer and the marginal classes.

Pinto attended an all-girls high school and obtained a degree in Philology from the University of Costa Rica. It was at the university that two of her professors discovered her literary promise and encouraged her to pursue this path. Pinto then traveled to Paris, to take a course in the Sociology of Literature. When she returned to Costa Rica, she founded and directed the School of Literature and Language Sciences at the National University in Heredia. During the early part of her life, Pinto held a number of public administration posts in social institutions, each one offering her more insights into the corruption and crisis of Costa Rica, fodder she would use again and again in her works.

Pinto was honored in Costa Rica for her various works in novels and stories. She was awarded the National Aquileo J. Echevarría Prize for Best Novel in 1969 and 1994. She won the National Aquileo J. Echevarría Prize for Best Short Story in 1970 and 1993. The Cultural Ministry awarded her the National Prize for Cultural Contribution – the Magón – in 1996, making her the fifth woman to be so honored.

Theme: Social Criticism

Pinto is among a minority group of Costa Rican writers denouncing a society in social crisis and pleading for social progress. At a time when Costa Rican literature was turning to lighter fare in novel form, Pinto continued her theme of class struggle with wisdom and subtlety, with a style that was simple but enriched with layers of experience and meaning. Her *The Echo of the Steps* (1979), a novel about the 1948 Costa Rican civil war, is a great example of her style.

Pinto describes her work in her own words as works of "denouncement and creation". She wants to "open the eyes of those who are ignorant or comfortable and refuse to see the grave problems of their country". Pinto believes that all Costa Ricans are responsible for the current situation in their country.

After exploring other themes, Pinto returns to social commentary with a collection of short stories in *Open Your Eyes* (2004). The stories describe dramatic social conditions of Costa Rica and focus on the marginal sectors of the Costa Rican population as they search for dignity and hope for a better future. Pinto's smooth personality and authenticity is evident in her writings and is one of the reasons her work has been well received in her native land.

Theme: Peasant Life and Strife

Pinto's first book was *Stories of the Land* (1963) a collection of short stories focusing on the lives of *campesinos*, i.e. farmhands. She followed this with a steady production of social critical work including: *If You Could Hear the Silence* (1967); *The Season that Follows the Summer* (1969); *The Marginalized* (1970); and *Around the Corner* (1975), a collection of stories of everyday people. *The Station* and *The Marginalized* won her the National Prizes for Novel and Short Story in both 1969 and 1970. In 1993, her *Land of Mirages* (*Espejismos*) would again win her the National Prize for Short Story.

Two of Pinto's stories have been selected in academic collections for Latin American Literature studies and unlike her other works, are readily available for readers outside of Costa Rica. The first, "The Old Housewife," appears in *Album, Stories from the Hispanic World* (1993). The second, "The Gift," forms part of *The Short Story: Art and Analysis* (2002). "The Gift" is a wonderful example of Pinto's connection with the poor and unfortunate. She makes no judgment as she tells the story of Hilda, who is left in the care of an abusive neighbor when her mother dies and her siblings are taken into better homes. It is a coming-of-age story, from ugly duckling to a blossoming youth so eager for affection that Hilda succumbs to a series of married men. In the end she finds a miracle – a friend and wants to give a gift to her friend. But all she has is her blond-haired, blue-eyed youngest son. It is through the actions of the characters that we understand Pinto's world. It is a world of reality, not idealism. Simple people trying to survive.

Theme: Philosophy of Life and Death/Pinto's Personal Story

In 1994, Pinto's *The Awakening of Lazaro* was published. This novel is a break from her traditional style as she uses the literary technique of interior monologue to explore the philosophy of life and death psychologically. This worked to her advantage as she won the National Aquileo J. Echevarría Prize for Best Novel.

It is at this time that Pinto's literary work takes a turn inward. *Behind the Mirror* (2000) is a book of personal reflections of the author through poetry and correspondence. In *The Language of Rain* (2001), Pinto looks back to her childhood, focusing on her father and the natural Costa Rican countryside she was raised in. As she crosses time and space, she also speaks about her first great love.

Pinto's latest work is *Tata Pinto* (2005), a semi-biographical novel about one of her ancestors and a key Costa Rican historical figure, the Portuguese mariner, Antonio Pinto. Told through inner reflections via interior monologue of the main character and diary entries of his wife Rosario, it is a mix of an adventure story and a love story. Told with tenderness and a certain delicate handling, the story weaves its web of nostalgia as we begin to care for the main character Pinto, and his anguish over his leadership duties (he must send a prisoner to his death) as well as rejoice in a female character as independent and self-reflecting as Rosario.

Pinto also reached out to a younger audience when it came to her expression of her philosophy. In 2002, she ventured into children's literature with *The Boy Who Lives in Two Houses*. In this hope-filled story, Pinto plants the ideals of humanitarian values and Latin-American solidarity as a way to understand and relate to the larger world.

Theme: Costa Rica

Pinto's work in extending connections between Costa Rica and the outside world includes a short story translated into English by Angela McEwan entitled "The Blue Fish". This story forms a part of the anthology *We Have Brought You the Sea: Costa Rica, a Traveler's Literary Companion* (1993). Unlike the other contributions to this book celebrating Costa Rica, Pinto gives us a story of an unnamed boy who travels to a small Costa Rican island and becomes obsessed with a magical blue fish who refuses to be caught. As we watch the interactions of the boy on his travels and his quest for the fish, we are witnesses to his obsession and to the immense beauty of the Costa Rican landscape. Pinto creates a mythological setting that would entice any tourist to visit her beloved country.

DEBORAH GONZALEZ

Selected Works

Stories of the Land. San Jose: Editorial Costa Rica, 1963.
If You Could Hear the Silence. San Jose: Editorial Costa Rica, 1967.
The Season that Follows the Summer. San Jose: Lehmann, 1969.
The Marginalized. San Jose: Editorial Conciencia Nueva, 1970.
Around the Corner. Heredia: Editorial Universidad Nacional, 1975.
The Echo of the Steps. San Jose: Mesen Editores, 1979.
Between the Sun and Dusk. San Jose: Editorial Costa Rica, 1987.
Land of Mirages. San Jose: Editorial Universidad Estatal a Distancia, 1991.
"The Blue Fish". In Barbara Ras (ed.), *Costa Rica: A Traveler's Literary Companion*. San Francisco, CA: Whereabout Press, 1993.
The Awakening of Lazaro. San Jose: REI Centroamerica, 1994.
Behind the Mirror. Heredia: Editorial Universidad Nacional, 2000.
The Language of the Rain. San Jose: Editorial Costa Rica, 2001.
"The Gift". In Edward Friedman (ed.), *The Story: Art and Analysis*. New Jersey: Prentice Hall, 2003.
Open Your Eyes. Heredia: Editorial Universidad Nacional, 2004.
Tata Pinto. San Jose: EUNED, 2005.

References and Further Reading

Chase, Alfonso, "Review of Tata Pinto," Club de Libros, 2005. http://www.clubdelibros.com/repotatapinto.htm
Pinto, Julieta, "Interview for Magón Prize," Ministry of Culture, 1996. http://www.mcjdcr.go.cr/magon/julieta_pinto_1996.html

PITA, JUANA ROSA

A poet and editor born in Havana, Juana Rosa Pita (b. 1939) left Cuba in 1961. Since then she has resided in Madrid, Washington, DC, Caracas, Miami, Boston, and New Orleans, where she was a Visiting Professor of Spanish at Tulane University from 1989 to 1992. Pita earned a B.A. and a M.A. from George Mason University, Virginia, 1973–75, and a Ph.D. in Latin American literature in 1984 from the Catholic University of America, Washington, DC. With the Argentinean poet David Lagmanovich, she co-founded and co-directed Ediciones de Poesía Solar from 1976–86. She is the author of twenty-three collections of poetry and her poems have been published in literary magazines in Latin America, Spain, the United States, Germany, Greece, Italy and Portugal. Pita writes in Spanish and often collaborates with her son Mario Alejandro Pita in the translations of her poetry into English. Known primarily as a poet, Pita has also published a considerable number of essays about art, music, literature, philosophy and travel in *Vuelta and Pauta* (Mexico), *La Prensa Literaria* (Nicaragua), *Cielo Abierto* (Peru), *El Nuevo Herald* (US), *Cuadernos del Matemático* and *Alhucena* (Spain), *Revista del Pensamiento Centroamericano* (Costa Rica), and *Spiritualità e Letteratura* (Italy). As a literary critic she has shown particular interest in the work of Cuban novelist, essayist, and journalist Enrique Labrador Ruiz (1902–91), editing his epistolary *Cartas à la carte* (Miami: Ediciones Universal, 1991). She is also a recognized translator of Italian poetry.

Pita won the First Prize for Poetry of Latin America at the Instituto de Cultura Hispánica, Málaga, Spain, in 1975. She was finalist for the poetry prize in the First Biennal of Editorial Ámbito Literario, Barcelona, 1979, for her book *Manual de magia* (Manual of Magic). Some of her other awards include: (Finalist) of the "Premio Juan Boscán" in Barcelona, 1980 for her work *Florencia nuestra*; the Eighth "Premio Internazionale Ultimo Novecento," in the category Poets of the World, in Pisa, Italy, 1985; the Premio Alghero "La cultura per la pace" in Sardegna, Italy, 1987; and the prize "Letras de Oro 1993" for her book *Una estación en tren/ Vivace legatissimo* (A Season in the Train). In 1989, Pita was finalist for the prize "Letras de Oro" for her collection of poems "Metamor". Presently, she continues work on her poetry in Boston.

Beneath the apparent starkness of Pita's sparse, unadorned verse lies an intimate lyricism, rich in innovative imagery, with a well-balanced tonality. An outstanding feature is Pita's ear for the unusual word. Her poetry has included sonnets, but is usually characterized by free verse and lines of variable length.

Pita sees the Spanish-speaking world as her linguistic soil, and Cuban culture as an unfinished sculpture whose face she must help form. The major themes of Pita's poetry are love and exile. With clear universal language and subtle symbolism, she converts lyric poetry into an epic of being that goes beyond all set boundaries. In creating her own mythology, she forges an insular mythology. The intimate and the collective merge in her work. Pita considers that the most important person in her life is the mailman, but she credits César Vallejo, Pedro Salinas, Jorge Guillén, Pablo Antonio Cuadra, Octavio Paz, and Roberto Juarroz for helping her to grow as a poet. She also feels as much at home with ancient Egyptian poets as with the French philosopher, Simone Weil.

Pablo Antonio Cuadra has described her poetry as having the capacity to revive emotion and transform it into myth within herself. For him, Pita is one of the most important exiled Cuban poets. Galvarino Plaza states that her poetry has a mastery of tone that moves from the intimate to the collective, meaning that from the starting point of personal experiences, it opens up to a commitment of broad emotional margins. Raúl Gustavo Aguirre writes that the essential characteristics of her work are its direct language and its intimacy of tone.

Her first book, *Pan de sol* (1976, Bread of Sun), already showed her to be a master of her craft. Love makes its presence known in a world with room only for "you" and "I". In this collection one perceives her affinity for the Spanish poet Pedro Salinas. *Las cartas y las horas* (1977, Letters and Hours) is a poetic speculation about the nature of time. Pita's premise is that the world is saved by the exchange of letters. Five of these poems were published in *New Directions* 49 (1985, New York, translated by Donald D. Walsh). Published in 1978, although written earlier, *El arca de los sueños* (The Ark of Dreams) is a profound reflection on the nature of poetry itself. In *Mar entre rejas* (1977, Sea Behind Bars), Pita explores the mysterious ways in which poetry responds to history.

Among Pita's most important books are two collections where the author identifies herself with a female mythological figure in a personal and spiritual quest. Pita presents her female heroes (and herself) transcending the traditional limitations of intellectual freedom imposed upon women. In *Eurídice en la fuente* (1979, Euridice at the Fountain), the poet sees herself as the wife of Orpheus, but unlike the original Eurydice, she escapes from Hades. Eurydice, through her risk-taking, manages to unite the fragments of her world. The second book that offers powerful images for the female quest is *Viajes de Penélope* (1980, Penelope's Journeys). It occupies a pivotal position in Pita's works. Reinaldo Arenas describes this book as a new Odyssey, a voyage through the infinity of a woman's inner adventures. Penelope's journey takes places inside herself. Instead of confronting and battling monsters, the quester learns to embody mythic powers within herself and with love as her most powerful weapon, she conquers time. The language in these poems flows with self-assured playfulness and a celebrating sensuality.

Crónicas del Caribe (1983, Caribbean Chronicles) continues to deal with the spiritual quest depicted in the previous books. The Caribbean Sea is the protagonist of these poems, and from it emerges the Island (Cuba) which triggers the poet's voyage of rediscovery. *Grumo d'alba / Grumo de alba* (1985, Clot of Dawn) is esentially a selection of poems from her previous books and included some unpublished poems.

The attempt to reach a complete understanding of her inner poetic vision and historical time is further illustrated in *Aires etruscos/ Arie etrusche* (1987, Etruscan Airs). This time the Mediterranean is the setting of the journey. History and myth are intertwined with the present reality, and the poet transform exile into a zest for reaching the Other: a major adventure through writing that she continues in her books *Plaza sitiada* (1987, Besieged Plaza), *Sorbos de luz/Sips of Light* (1990), *Florencia nuestra* (1992, Our Florence), *Transfiguración de la armonía* (1993, Transfiguration of Harmony), *Una estación en tren* (1994, A Season in the Train), *Tela de concierto* (1999, Concert's Canvas), *Cadenze* (2000), and *Pensamiento del tiempo* (2005, Thought of Time). Her work is included in the anthologies *Doscientos años de poesía cubana/ 1770–1990/ Cien poemas antológicos* (La Habana: Casa Editora Abril, 1999), *Voces viajeras* (Madrid: Torremozas, 2002) and *Poesía cubana del siglo XX* (Mexico D.F.: Fondo de Cultura Económica, 2002).

Pita's notion of poetry as the discovery of new dimensions in which different times and spaces are interrelated can be summarized in the following verses: "Poetry is the height of letters:/inside are the powers/destined by love/for endless communion". (*Las cartas y las horas*, p. 35).

CARLOTA CAULFIELD

Selected Works

Pan de sol.Washington, DC: Solar, 1976.
Las cartas y las horas. Washington, DC: Solar, 1977.
Mar entre rejas. Washington, DC: Solar, 1977.
El arca de los sueños. Washington, DC: Solar, 1978.
Manual de magia. Barcelona: Ámbito Literario, 1979.
Eurídice en la fuente. Miami, FL: Solar, 1979.
Viajes de Penélope. Preface by Reinaldo Arenas. Miami, FL: Solar, 1980.
Crónicas del Caribe. Miami, FL: Solar, 1983.
Grumo d'alba. Bilingual edition, Spanish-Italian. Trans. Renata Giambene. Pisa: Giardini Editore, 1985.
El sol tatuado. Boston, MA: Solar, 1986.
Aires etruscos/Arie etrusche. Bilingual edition, Spanish-Italian. Trans. Pietro Civitareale. Cagliari: GIA Editrice, 1987.
Plaza sitiada. San José de Costa Rica: Libro Libre, 1987.
Sorbos de luz/Sips of Light. Bilingual edition. Trans. Mario de Salvatierra in collaboration with the author. San Francisco, CA: Eboli Poetry Series, 1990.
Proyecto de infinito. New Orleans, LO: Edizione di Amatori, 1991.
Florencia nuestra (Biografía poemática). Miami, FL and Valencia: Editorial Arcos, 1992.
Sorbos venecianos/Sorsi veneziani/Venetian Sips, (hand-made edition of 48 copies numbered and signed). Miami, FL: author's edition, 1992.
Transfiguración de la armonía. Coral Gables, FL: La Torre de Papel, 1993.
Una estación en tren. Coral Gables, FL: Instituto de Estudios Ibéricos, 1994.
Infancia del pan nuestro. Somerville, MA: Poetry Planting, 1995.
Tela de concierto. Preface by Jesús J. Barquet. Miami, FL: El Zunzún Viajero, 1999.
Cadenze/ Poesie. Preface by Pietro Civitareale. Collana di Poesia Il Capricornio. Foggia: Bastogi Editrice Italiana, 2000.
Cantar de Isla. Selection and Introduction by Virgilio López Lemus. La Habana: Letras Cubanas, Poesia, 2003.
Cartas y cantigas. Madrid: Betania, Col. Separatas – 4, 2003.
Pensamiento del tiempo. Miami, FL: Amatori, 2005.

References and Further Reading

Aguirre, Raúl Gustavo. "Juana Rosa Pita. *El arca de los sueños*". Review. *La Gaceta* (15 Oct. 1978): 2.
Arenas, Reinaldo. "Los viajes revelantes de Juana Rosa Pita". Preface to *Viajes de Penélope.* Miami, FL: Solar, 1980, pp. 9–11.
Barquet, Jesús J. "Juana Rosa Pita o Penélope reescribe *La Odisea*." In *Escrituras poéticas de una nación: Dulce María Loynaz, Juana Rosa Pita y Carlota Caulfield.* La Habana: Ediciones Unión, 1999, pp. 55–78.
Caulfield, Carlota. "Ruptura, irreverencia y memoria en la obra de Juana Rosa Pita". *Alba de América* 15(28–9) (1997): 154–64.
Civitareale, Pietro. "La magica scrittura di Juana Rosa". *Il Cagliaritano* 16(2) (1988): 58–9.
Cuadra, Pablo Antonio. "Poetas de América: Juana Rosa Pita". *La Prensa Literaria* 12 (Dec. 1982): 6–7.

Plaza, Galvarino. "Juana Rosa Pita. *Las cartas y las horas*". Review. *Cuadernos Hispanoamericanos* 326–7 (1977): 538–9.

Pérez Heredia, Alexander. "Las estancias del ser en la poesía de Juana Rosa Pita". *Cuadernos del Matemático* 35 (Dec. 2005): 99–101.

PIZARNIK, FLORA ALEJANDRA

A poet and painter, Flora Alejandra Pizarnik (1936–72) (known as Alejandra Pizarnik) was born in Buenos Aires Argentina into a family of Russian Jews who immigrated to Argentina. In 1954, she attended the University of Buenos Aires where she studied philosophy and from 1955 to 1957, literature. She studied painting under the tutelage of surrealist painter Juan Battle Planas (1911–66) well known in Argentine art circles for his deeply personal art, combining Zen Buddhism with psychoanalysis.

In 1960, she left for France where she lived for the next four years and worked as a freelance proofreader and translator, writing poetry and criticism for Latin American, Spanish and French literary magazines. She worked on the staff of the journal *Cuadernos* and joined the editorial board of *Les Lettres Nouvelles*. She translated from French to Spanish authors such as André Breton, Paul Eluard, Yves Bonnefoy, Marguerite Duras, Henri Michaux, and Aimé Césaire. This period of fertile literary and human experiences shaped her life and her literary production. In Paris, she came in contact with André Pieyre de Mandiargues, Francisco Farreras Valentí, Julio Cortázar, Octavio Paz, and other leading twentieth-century European and Latin American artists and writers. An avid reader, she continued her studies of contemporary and avant-garde literature, taking courses in contemporary French literature and the history of religion at the Sorbonne.

Back in Buenos Aires after her artistically successful and economically miserable Parisian years, she continued her intense literary activity and her epistolary passion in order to keep herself intellectually connected to artists and writers from all around the world. She wrote reviews and essays on many Latin American and French writers such as Julio Cortázar, Alberto Girri, Ricardo Molinari, Silvina Ocampo, Octavio Paz and André Pieyre de Mandiargues. She conducted interviews with Jorge Luis Borges, Roberto Juarroz, and Victoria Ocampo. Some of her literary essays, as well as her own poems, were published in the literary reviews *Cuadernos*, *Mundo Nuevo*, *Sur*, *Papeles de Son Armadans*, *Zona Franca*, *Poesía Buenos Aires*, Imagen, and *La estafeta literaria*, among others. She contributed to the literary sections of newspapers such as *La Gaceta* and *La Nación*.

In 1965, her book *Los trabajos y las noches* (Works and Nights) was named the best book of poetry by the Argentine Foundation of Arts. She was awarded a Guggenheim Fellowship in 1969 and in 1971 a Fulbright. She died in Buenos Aires on September 25, 1972, of a self-induced overdose of Seconal.

Pizarnik is undoubtedly one of the most important poets in modern Latin American literature. What is known about her life seems important for the understanding of her work. The suicide, for example, is the expression of her enduring obsession with death, one of the central motifs of her poetry. Her prose poem "Tangible Absence" is a good example of the poet's awareness of life lost to literature: "Life, my life. What have you done with my life?" (Graziano 1987: 84). Reflexive self-questioning of this kind is recurrent in her work. She is the subject-matter of her writings in one way or another. She wrote poetry full to bursting with movement and visions, and many of her poems carry a shock effect. Through her poems we find key words (absence, childhood, fear, mirror, garden, forest, earth, water, solitude, silence, sound, wind, rift, night) that she usually set out in a series of binary oppositions. She uses the three symbolic colors of red, white, and black, interlaced with green and lilac. Her poetry appeals directly to the senses like a painting. She herself a painter was "attracted to the absence of mythomania in the language of painting. Working with words, or, more specifically, seeking my words, implies a tension that does not exist in painting" ("Some Keys to Alejandra Pizarnik," p. 97). Most of Pizarnik's poems are written with extreme word-condensation. Pizarnik's work is obsessed with language and silence. She experienced language as the shape of her true inner inexpressible self and silence as a more authentic domain, but also terrifying.

Critics associate her work with existentialism, and in particular with surrealism. The dreamlike flow of images in her poems and their collaged nature indicate a compositional method similar to automatic writing. Pizarnik also shared with the surrealists a preoccupation with violence, perversity, and death. Affinities with the "poètes maudits," in particular with the French Symbolist Arthur Rimbaud have also been noted in Pizarnik's search for the Absolute against trivial existence, and in the representation – and living – of transgression.

Pizarnik's obsession with the craft of writing can be seen through her poetry. In her fourth book, *Árbol de Diana* (1962, Diana's Tree) her concern with language and poetic expression is expressed in very brief poems of disconcerting images. Many of these poems reveal the poet's dissatisfaction with reality and her constant search for something beyond words. Published by the prestigious Sur publishing house, and with an introduction by Octavio Paz, this book indicates that she was already well known in Latin America.

In spite of her constant preoccupation with intellectual concerns and philosophical reflections, in some poems of *Los trabajos y las noches* (1965, Works and Nights), there is a brief moment where love is celebrated in lyrical poems. But poems of oblivion and death overshadow the celebration of the senses in favor of ashes, as when the poet confesses in "Falling": "Never again the hope / in a coming and going / of names, of figures. / Someone dreamed very badly, / by mistake someone used up/the forgotten distances" (Graziano 1987: 47).

Notable in Pizarnik's work is *Extracción de la piedra de locura* (1968, Extraction of the Stone of Folly) and *El infierno musical* (1971, The Musical Hell). In these two collections of prose poems the images accumulate, overlap and repeat as they do in dreams, creating a reality that rearranges the conventional logical order. The new arrangement that Pizarnik seems to propose in her poems is subject, as with the surrealists, only to desire, dreams and poetry. It is expressed in a poetic discourse dominated by plasticity, a collage of images, such as can be seen in "Nocturnal Singer," the opening poem of *Extraction of the Stone of Folly*: "She who has died of her blue dress sings. Imbued with death she sings to the sun of her drunkenness. Inside her song there is a blue dress, there is a white horse, there is a green heart tattooed with echoes of her dead heart's beat . . ." (Graziano 1987: 51).

In these prose poems we find Pizarnik's constant preoccupation with language and silence. In *The Musical Hell* she refers constantly to the nature of her writing and asks herself "Where does this writing lead," and she answers, "To blackness, to the sterile, to the fragmented" (ibid., p. 67). The fragmentation of the self is another recurrent theme of these books. Many of the poems seem to be reconstructions of dreams conceived to provide access to the subconscious. The poetic voice doubles back constantly, obsessed with remembrances of childhood, ghosts and hallucinations. For example, in the poem "Extraction of the Stone of Folly," the dialogue of the fragmented self is marked by a bitter humor that is both intellectual game and ingenious paradox. The poet makes use of the popular Dutch saying which is found in the painting by Hieronymous Bosch with the same name "Master take out the stone now / they call me crazy" which is the equivalent of "extirpate the madness," and she writes, "I don't know the names. Who will you tell that you don't know? You want yourself another. The other that you are wants herself another" (Graziano 1987: 57).

A major theme of her work is, precisely, the *doppelgänger* or double. The repetition-compulsion in the act of seeing oneself as other is expressed in her writings as a love for mirrors where as the poet herself states she sees, "The other who I am (Actually I have a certain fear of mirrors). Sometimes we reunite. It almost happens when I write" ("Some Keys to Alejandra Pizarnik," p. 100). Taking the ego as object is a libidinal assumption, an erotic process that is clearly manifest in *La condesa sangrienta* (1971, The Bloody Countess), her last published text before her suicide. Pizarnik's text is based on *Erzébet Bathory: La Comtesse Sanglante* by Valentine Penrose, published in Paris in 1963. Penrose was an exceptional poet whose work was filled with strange and beautiful imagery, eroticism, exoticism, legends and magic. She became part of the Surrealist movement during the 1920s. Penrose's *The Bloody Countess* (trans. by Alexander Trocchi) is a disturbing lyrical account of the life of Erszébet (Elizabeth) Báthory, the historical sixteenth-century bloody Hungarian Countess. Descended from one of the most ancient aristocratic families of Europe, the Countess was a very unusual character and a female psychopath. She indulged in sadistic erotic fantasies, where only the spilling of young women's blood could satisfy her urges, torturing and murdering more than six hundred virgins. Her castles had torture chambers with a throne where she sat observing her servants acting out their atrocities and where she had her youth-giving ritual: the bath of blood. Legends that surrounded her behaviour are also believed to be the source of many vampire myths. According to Graziano, "'the convulsive beauty' of the Countess' sexual perversion and dementia is what piqued the intrigue of both Penrose and Pizarnik, the latter opening her *The Bloody Countess* with Sastre's epigraph 'The criminal does not make beauty; he himself is authentic beauty" (Graziano 1987: 98).

In the story, Pizarnik identifies (as a narrator) with the Countess. Pizarnik's fascination with Báthory's lack of restraint is essential to understand the poet's desire to free herself from the order expressed by reason. Always regarding herself as an outsider, Pizarnik wanted to transcend the limitations of the human condition. This is one of her most transgressive works that some critics read as a lesbian text, opening new possibilities for the understanding of the theme of cultural displacement that is a central motif of her writing. Among the critics who examined Pizarnik's interpretations of the lesbian dimensions of Báthory's rituals are David William Foster, Stephen Gregory and Alexandra Fitts.

Her poem "In this Night, in this World," included in *Textos de sombra y últimos poemas* (Texts of Shadow and Last Poems), a posthumous volume of her previously unpublished works, dating between 1963 and 1972, is a good example of her dualism, when she states, "(everything that can be said is a lie) / the rest is silence / except silence doesn't exist" and she adds, "no / words / don't make love / they make absence / if I say *water*, am I drinking? / if I say *bread*, am I eating?". For Pizarnik, the dialectic of the poetic process was both her damnation and the method of attaining harmony and self-completion. In this book, edited by Olga Orozco and Ana Becciú, we find texts of extraordinary biting humor, puns, profanity, verbal violence and senseless alliterations which occupy a pivotal position in the development of Pizarnik's experimentation with language. As Cristina Piña observes, "There were never any obscene texts signed by women until Pizarnik's work appeared" ("La palabra obscena," p. 17).

Alejandra Pizarnik was an exceptional correspondent, whatever the subject, whatever the mood. She wrote letters full of lively perception, offering fascinating insights not only into her own personality, but also into the process of her creativity. Her letters display her insight, the forcefulness of her language, and humorous use of wordplay and puns, giving us a much more intimate portrait than any biographer could achieve. She wrote many intimate literary and personal letters to artists, critics and writers of the stature of Anna Balakian, Antonio Beneyto, Arturo Carrera, Julio Cortázar, Ivonne Bordelois, Pierre de Mandiargues, Enrique Molina, Sylvia Molloy, Silvina Ocampo, Olga Orozco, Octavio Paz, Antonio Requeni, Osias Stutman, and Luisa Sofovich, among others.

Always informative and interesting, we learn from these letters about her literary friends, what influenced her, which authors she preferred and how she reacted to them, in what way the works of other artists, poets and writers appealed to her. She was very interested in the intellectual scene of her times. The letters give, in many instances, a running commentary on Pizarnik's work in progress and of her struggle with the ambiguity of words and the artificiality of fixed meanings. They are lively and spontaneous. In many of them she shows her wit, her pleasure in playing with words, and her fear of losing her sense of humor. For example, in a letter to the Spanish editor-writer-painter Antonio Beneyto, dated November 8, 1969, she writes,

> Your words referring to "knowing things about me" moved me because of the friendship they imply. Also, because of a text by Hölderlin which speaks of "telling each other about themselves" because "that is what language is for". Well, I can't tell you very much "about myself," at least not now . . . Please, let's stop talking about my problems. I would like to tell you more about myself when I recover my humor (don't you think that it's a kind of Savior or Mender. I am referring to "the

blessed gift of humor"). Anyway, little by little I will reveal myself, as we send letters and drawings.

(Caulfield 200, p. 41)

Many of her letters seem written in a kind of explosive way, with all the senses. Her handwriting had a nervous and pictorial quality. In her typed letters there is always a handwritten note. She filled her letters with marks, lines, French words and expressions, many brackets and ellipses as her own type of punctuation. Pizarnik choose unusual letterhead or stationery for her letters. She often sent to her best friends her naïve and colorful drawings as a token of friendship. Very concerned about her artistic sensitivity, her letters are a supremely eloquent record of the ways in which her art and life interacted with one another. In a letter dated September 26, 1969 she wrote: "I am crazy about beautiful printing and, more than anything, high-grade paper . . . Yes, I also draw and paint, although I don't hold exhibitions of my work, since I draw and paint exactly like the savages—those savages without tradition or art training who learn by inheritance". (Ibid., p. 35).

From the time she was very young, Alejandra Pizarnik was an avid reader of other writers journals, in particular those of Katherine Mansfield, Virginia Woolf and Frank Kafka. Pizarnik's copy of Kafka's journal in Spanish (published in Argentina in 1953) was her bedside companion. She purchased it in 1955 and through the years filled it with marks and annotations, underlining numerous passages.

Pizarnik can be considered one of the first Latin American poets who kept a journal as an essential part of her literary work. Ana Becciú, in the introduction of Pizarnik's *Diarios*, observes that for the poet her journals were her place for learning and improving her writing and her style, not a place to write her "life" in conventional terms. From 1960 on, in particular during her stay in Paris, Pizarnik began writing her thoughts about what she was reading and also about her feelings and emotional state. (Becciú 2003, pp. 7–11).

Upon her return to Buenos Aires from Paris in 1964, Pizarnik began to edit her Parisian journals and published some journal entries dated 1960–61 in the Colombian literary magazine *Mito* (Numbers 39–40, 1962). Pizarnik's journals were selected and edited by Ana Becciú from among twenty notebooks belonging to the poet. Becciú, as Pizarnik herself wanted, made a rigorous chronological selection that covers from 1954 to 1971 and chose to publish entries that deal in particular with Pizarnik's creative writing.

In spite of Pizarnik's aversion to all forms of political involvement, her concerns with the problem of women's power and powerlessness in her writings makes her also a feminist writer. Her talent was recognized at the time of her death. Since then she has come to be considered one of the greatest of Latin American women poets. Her work has served as a model for succeeding generations of women writers.

Among the most noteworthy essays about Pizarnik's work are Francisco Lasarte's "Alejandra Pizarnik and Poetic Exile" (*Bulletin of Hispanic Studies* 67 (1990): 71–76) where he studies how Pizarnik uses in her poems the image of the exile or expatriate with striking frequency. And in doing so, the poet joins many poets who, from Romanticism onwards, have seen in the figure of the exile an emblem for the artist's alienation from self and society; Suzanne Chávez Silverman's "The Discourse of Madness in the Poetry of Alejandra Pizarnik" (*Revista Monográfica/Monographic Review* 6 (1990): 274–81), a discussion of the theme of madness in Pizarnik's poetic discourse using Shoshana Felman's *Writings and Madness* and Michel Foucault's *Madness and Civilization* as two of the major theoretical and critical works on the subject, examining how Pizarnik's discourse participates fully in the dichotomy between *Outside* and *Inside*, or the discourse of reason vs. that of madness; and David William Foster's "The Representation of the Body in the Poetry of Alejandra Pizarnik" (*Hispanic Review* 62 (1994): 319–47), a detailed study of Pizarnik's literary strategies for the representation of the female body/her body, which discusses the poet's vocabulary and in particular her language in "Poema para el padre" (Poem for my Father) and "Tragedia" (Tragedy), two essential Pizarnik poems. Foster observes that Pizarnik's biographers and critics have been unwilling to deal with the poet's sexual identity, in particular with the lesbian dimension of her personal experience.

The corpus of Pizarnik's writing translated into English has expanded in the last eighteen years, in particular thanks to Frank Graziano's edition *Alejandra Pizarnik. A Profile* (1987), Susan Basnett's *Exchanging Lives: Poems and Translations* (2002) and Carlota Caulfield's *From the Forbidden Garden. Letters from Alejandra Pizarnik to Antonio Beneyto* (2003).

CARLOTA CAULFIELD

Selected Works

La tierra más ajena. Buenos Aires: Botella al Mar, 1955.

La última inocencia. Buenos Aires: Ediciones Poesía Buenos Aires, 1956.

Las aventuras perdidas. Buenos Aires: Altamar, 1958.

Árbol de Diana. Buenos Aires: Sur, 1962.

Los trabajos y las noches. Buenos Aires: Sudamericana, 1965.

Extracción de la piedra de locura. Buenos Aires: Sudamericana, 1968. Buenos Aires: Centro Editor de América Latina, 1988; Madrid: Visor Libros, 1993.

Nombres y figuras. Barcelona: Colección La Esquina, 1969.

La condesa sangrienta. Buenos Aires: Acuarius, 1971.

El infierno musical. Buenos Aires: Siglo XXI Argentina, 1971.

Los pequeños cantos. Caracas: Árbol de Fuego, 1971.

El deseo de la palabra. "Palabras iniciales" by Octavio Paz. Edited by Antonio Beneyto and Marta Moia. Barcelona: OCNOS/Barral Editores, 1975.

Antología poética. Edited by Miguel Angel Flores. México, DF: Serie Poesía Moderna 93, Universidad Nacional Autónoma de México, 1980.

Zona prohibida Xalapa, Veracruz: Ediciones Papel de envolver/Colección Luna Hiena, 1982.

Poemas. Buenos Aires: Centro Editor de América Latina, Colección Capítulo, 1982.

Textos de sombra y últimos poemas. Buenos Aires: Sudamericana, 1982 and 1986.

L'autre rive. Toulon: Editions Unes, 1983.

Poemas. Medellín: Editorial Unicornio, 1985.

Poemas Ed. Gustavo Zuluaga. Medellín: Editorial Endymion, 1986.

Poemas. Buenos Aires: Centro Editor de América Latina, 1987.

Prosa Poética. Medellín: Editorial Endymion, 1987.

Diario 1960–1961. Alejandra Pizarnik 1936–1972. Colombia: Museo Rayo, 1988.

Alejandra Pizarnik: A Profile. Ed. Frank Graziano. Durango, CO: Logbridge-Rhodes, 1987.

Alejandra Pizarnik. Ed. Cristina Piña. Buenos Aires: Centro Editor de América Latina, Colección Los grandes poetas, 1988.

Antología poética. Ed. Orietta Lozano. Cali, Bogotá: Editorial Tiempo Presente, 1990.

Poesía y prosas. Buenos Aires: Corregidor, 1990.

Antología breve. Caracas: Fondo Editorial Pequeña Venecia, Series 13, 1991 and 1994.

Semblanza. Ed. Frank Graziano. México, D.F.: Fondo de Cultura Económica, 1992.

Obras escogidas. Edited by Gustavo Zuluaga. Medellín: Ediciones Hölderlin, 1992.

Obras completas: poesía completa y prosa selecta. Ed. Cristina Piña. Buenos Aires: Corregidor, 1993 and 1998.

Correspondencia Pizarnik. 2nd edn. Ed. Ivonne Bordelois. Buenos Aires: Seix Barral, 1998.

Alejandra Pizarnik. Textos selectos. Ed. Cristina Piña. Buenos Aires: Corregidor, 1999.

Alejandra Pizarnik. Poesía completa. Ed. Ana Becciú. Barcelona: Editorial Lumen, 2000.

Alejandra Pizarnik. Prosa completa. Ed. Ana Becciú. Barcelona: Editorial Lumen, 2002.

Exchanging Lives: Poems and Translations. Susan Bassnett; Alejandra Pizarnik. Ed. Susan Bassnett. Leeds: Peepal Tree, 2002.

From the Forbidden Garden. Letters from Alejandra Pizarnik to Antonio Beneyto. Ed. Carlota Caulfield. Lewisburg, PA: Bucknell University Press; London: Associated University Presses, 2003.

Alejandra Pizarnik. Diarios. Ed. Ana Becciú. Barcelona: Editorial Lumen, 2003.

References and Further Reading

Bassnett, Susan. "Speaking with Many Voices: The Poems of Alejandra Pizarnik". In Susan Bassnett (ed.), *Knives and Angels: Women Writers in Latin America*. London: Zed Books, 1990, pp. 36–51.

Caulfield, Carlota. "Entre la poesía y la pintura: elementos surrealistas en *Extracción de la piedra de locura* y *El infierno musical* de Alejandra Pizarnik". *Chasqui* 21(1) (1992): 3–10.

Chávez Silverman, Suzanne. "The Look that Kills: The 'Unacceptable Beauty' of Alejandra Pizarnik's *La condesa sangrienta*". In Emilie L. Bergmann and Paul Julian Smith (eds), *¿Entiendes? Queer Readings, Hispanic Writings*. Durham, NC: Duke University Press, 1995, pp. 281–305.

DiAntonio, Robert E. "On Seeing Things Darkly in the Poetry of Alejandra Pizarnik: Confessional Poetics or Aesthetic Metaphor?" *Confluencia* 2(2) (1987): 47–52.

Fitts, Alexandra. "Alejandra Pizarnik's *La condesa sangrienta* and the Lure of the Absolute". *Letras Femeninas* 24(1–2) (1998): 23–35.

Foster, David William. "Of Power and Virgins: Alejandra Pizarnik's *La condesa sangrienta*". In Terry J. Peavler and Peter Standish (eds), *Structures of Power: Essays on Twentieth-Century Spanish-American Fiction*. Albany, NY: State University of New York, 1996, pp. 145–58.

Gregory, Stephen. "Through the Looking-Glass of Sadism to a Utopia of Narcissism: Alejandra Pizarnik's *La condesa sangrienta*". *Bulletin of Hispanic Studies* 74(30 (1997): 293–309.

Lasarte, Francisco. "Más allá del surrealismo: la poesía de Alejandra Pizarnik". *Revista Iberoamericana* 125 (1983): 867–77.

Moia, Martha I. "Algunas claves de Alejandra Pizarnik". Entrevista. *Plural* 18 (1973): 8–9. Trans. Susan Pensak as "Some Keys to Alejandra Pizarnik". Interview. *Sulfur* 8 (1983): 97–101.

Leighton, Marianne. "El jardín vedado: el espacio de la pintura en Alejandra Pizarnik". *Taller de Letras* 29 (2001): 177–90.

Parra, Jaime D. "El amor de Alejandra Pizarnik". *Turia* 55–6 (2001): 7–21.

Piña, Cristina. "La palabra obscena". *Cuadernos Hispanoamericanos*. Los Complementarios 5 (May 1990): 17–38.

——. *Poesía y experiencia del límite: leer a Alejandra Pizarnik*. Buenos Aires: Botella al Mar, 1999.

PLA, JOSEFINA

Josefina Pla (1903–99) is a quiet, albeit prolific writer whose vast bibliography evidences her literary dexterity and scholastic achievement. Her life spans the European and the American continents and almost the entire twentieth century. Her legacy to the rigorous documentation of Paraguayan history (artistic, literary, and sociological) is as immense as her personal contribution of poems, short stories, and dramas to the Hispanic canon. In spite of her versatility and productivity, she remains unknown to most recognized experts in the field. Few critics categorize her as anything more than a minor figure; ironically, some of the "major" writers who eclipse her—such as Augusto Roa Bastos—are themselves among Pla's most devoted admirers. Asunción publishing houses strove to compile her creative works, thus facilitating the recovery of Paraguayan letters' most preeminent adopted female representative. Yet mystery surrounds even some elementary aspects of her biography, specifically the correct spelling of her last name (Pla or Plá) or the year of her birth (official documents corroborate both the 1903 and 1909 dates). Her nomination to the Premio Cervantes in 1989 and 1994, although neither resulted in the coveted prize, demonstrates the pristine quality of her voice as well as the esteem with which her readers—few but ardent—hold this enigmatic artist.

Although recognized as a Paraguayan writer, Pla originally came from the Spanish territory Isla de los Lobos. The daughter of a Spanish civil servant, she lived throughout the peninsula and the Canary Islands before meeting her husband, the Paraguayan ceramic artist Andrés Campos Cervera, better known by his artistic pseudonym Julián de la Herreria. Given the generational gap between the couple, Pla's family objected to the marriage; this did not stop intrepid newlywed in 1926 from following her husband to his native Paraguay. The couple only shared a brief decade of wedded bliss before Herreria's passing shortly after the conclusion of the Spanish Civil War. Pla scraped together whatever funds she could to return to the country she preferred to call home and on whose cultural landscape she ultimately made an indelible mark.

Scholar and Artist

Once settled in Asunción, Pla threw herself into the capital's avant-garde scene. Her critical essays and creative poems appear in the nation's chief journals, and she is one of the few women members of what becomes known as the "Generación del 40". This movement grounds its aesthetic ideal in Modernist search for innovative purity yet also searches to go beyond the superficial trappings of the Symbolist and Decadent branches; thus, they become known as Postmodernists. Pla complements her writing with forays into the ceramic arts. Mainly she is remembered for the vigor and breadth of her intellectual and artistic labor. Her enthusiasm reaches beyond simply producing great works, for she also stimulates other fresh voices through her participation in theatrical groups like *El Galpón* and magazines like *Juventud* and *Alcor*.

Josefina Pla distinguishes herself among the male voices of generation (including Heriberto Fernández, Battilana de Gásperi, Pedro Herrero Céspedes, José Concepción Ortíz, Vicente Lamas, Hérib Campos Cervera, Augusto Roa Bastos, and Gastón Chevalier París) because of her gender; however, she is far from a token figure. The superior quality of her creation matches its abundant quantity. Her first book is a collection of poems entitled *El precio de los sueños* (The Price of Dreams); published in 1934, this debut is credited with marking the definitive break with the excesses of Modernism and ushering in the stripped-down transparency and intimacy of the Postmodernist epoch. Pla does not follow up her auspicious inauguration immediately; consequent poetic tomes do not appear until almost three decades later, although many of the texts are written in the preceding decades, a period when she begins garnering acclaim for her narrative and theatrical efforts.

Creative Inspiration

Josefina Pla's artistic vision remains unchanged throughout the seven decades of her creative production. Timeless imagery, existential preoccupation, and metaphors complex in their simplicity characterize her poetry, in which meditations on the enduring themes of death, love, and the passage of time are expressed in a dense, evocative idiom. The abstract oppositions of day and night, body and spirit, heavens and earth symbolize the universal human experience. Pla also respects the poetic tradition through honing august forms such as the sonnet and the romance. Whereas her poems conceptually announce a new, humble approach to the word, her poetic persona is cognizant of aligning itself with a great literary ancestry.

Pla explores a different aspect of her expressive dexterity in her prose and theatrical pieces. Her realistic approach to capturing Paraguay's regional characteristics puts her in the company of the slice-of-life storytellers of her day. Linguistically she faithfully depicts indigenous dialects such as the guaraní native tongue or its Castilian tinged variant yopará. Her observant social commentaries delve into taboo subjects like illegitimacy, marital infidelity, and ethnic discrimination. Pla's curious vantage point as an Old World immigrant recently arrived on American soil leads her on a distinct search for cultural identity. This desire to compensate for the sins of the Conquest inspires the story "La mano en la tierra," in which a Spanish male protagonist seeks to undo the damage to the American territory and people. Pla's main theatrical piece, "Historia de un número," follows a similar trajectory; the stock-type characters represent varying groups of societal stratum; these generic persons are identified only by all-encompassing pronouns or reductive adjectives. Thus a detached, third-person narrator bears witness in Pla's fiction and drama to a multicultural community in search of understanding the social prejudices that limit its evolution.

Intellectual Contribution

Josefina Pla's commitment to her own creative writing never takes her away from her serious academic endeavors. She painstakingly rescues Paraguayan literary, linguistic, social and artistic history from oblivion. Encyclopedic in their scope, her studies prove not only her worth as a scholar but also her love for the people and customs of her oft-ignored sentimental homeland. Her passion for research and reputation as an investigator earned her a doctora honoris causa from the Universidad Nacional de Asunción and membership into the Real Academia Española de la Lengua. Though monumental, these honors, cannot make up for the fact that Pla's creative output is as far-reaching and worthy of recognition as her scholastic achievements, yet critics more often highlight her educational merits despite her more than forty literary collections.

Lasting Legacy

Pla's humility could be to blame for her virtual obscurity. Numerous acquaintances comment on her shyness, remembering more about her constant feline companions and extensive library than about the conversations exchanged with the elusive writer. Clearly Pla preferred that the spotlight be on others. Her detached poetic speaker and certain biographical coincidences between her creations and her life provide faint sketches of her personality. Paradoxically, her objective documentation of the Paraguayan experience left little room for recording her personal reality. Future scholars of her creative work must rely on the artistic clues embedded in the texts themselves if this exceptional woman who recovered a practically disappeared tradition does not become lost to history herself.

JANA F. GUTIÉRREZ

Selected Works

La poesía paraguaya. Caracas: Lírica Hispana, 1963.
"Antología de la poesía paraguaya (Recuento de una lírica ignorada)". *Cuadernos Hispanoamericanos* 68 (1966): 281–7.
El teatro en el Paraguay: De la fundación a 1870. Asunción: Escuela Salesiana, 1967.
Hermano negro: la esclavitud en Paraguay. Madrid: Paraninfo, 1972.
"Teatro religioso medieval: Su brote en Paraguay". *Cuadernos Hispanoamericanos* 291 (1974): 666–80.
El barroco hispano-guaraní. Asunción: Editorial del Centenario, 1975.
Obra y aporte femeninos en la literatura nacional. Asunción: Centro Paraguayo de Estudios Sociológicos, 1976.
Teatro paraguayo en la colonia (1537–1811). New York: Senda Nueva de Estudios y Ensayos: 1981.
La cerámica popular paraguaya. Asunción: Museo del Barrio, 1994.
"Cómo me veo". *Alba de América* 13(24–5) (1995): 39–46.
Poesías completas. Asunción: Editorial El Lector, 1996.
Cuentos completos. Asunción: Editorial El Lector, 1996.
Teatro escogido. Asunción: Editorial El Lector, 1996.
Obra selecta: Poesía y prosa. Santa Cruz de Tenerife: Idea, 2003.

References and Further Reading

Calbarro, Juan Luis (ed.) *Oficio de mujer: Homenaje a Josefina Pla en el centenario de su nacimiento*. Fuerteventura: Servicio de Publicaciones del Ayuntamiento de La Oliva, 2003.
De Izaguirre, Ester. "Con Josefina Plá en Asunción del Paraguay". *Alba de América* 14(26–7) (1996): 547–9.
Mateo del Pino, Ángeles. "En la piel de la mujer: Un recorrido por la cuentística de Josefina Plá". *Philologica Canariensia* (1994): 281–97.
Minardi, Giovanna. "Josefina Plá: Una voz a recuperar". *Letras femeninas* 24(1)–2 (1998): 157–72.
Roa Bastos, Augusto. "La poesía de Josefina Pla". *Revista Hispánica Moderna* 32 (1966): 56–61.

Rodríguez-Alcalá, Hugo. "Josefina Pla, española de América, y la poesía". *Cuadernos Americanos* 159 (1968): 73–101.
——. "El vanguardismo en el Paraguay". *Revista Iberamericana* 48(118–19) (1982): 241–55.
Solórzano, Carlos (ed.) *Teatro breve hispanoamericano contemporáneo.* Madrid: Aguilar, 1970.

PLAGER, SILVIA

Silvia Plager (b. 1942) was born in Buenos Aires, Argentina. She was raised in the heart of Once, the traditionally Jewish neighborhood of Buenos Aires. The urban Jewish cultural milieu of her native city is often at the center of her fiction, particularly her most recent works. She lived for several years in Israel, but her permanent home is Buenos Aires. Plager is a prolific author, not only in the sense that she has written over a dozen books, but also because her books showcase her talent as novelist, short story writer, essayist, and humorist. Her work has earned her recognition in the form of several important literary awards. In addition to her fiction, she often writes articles and columns for several of the leading newspapers in Buenos Aires and she conducts literary workshops on a regular basis.

Women's Issues

Plager began publishing her fiction in the early 1980s and less than ten years later she had five books in print. These early volumes—*Amigas* (Girlfriends; 1982), *Prohibido despertar* (Forbidden Awakening; 1983), *Boca de tormenta* (Mouth of Torment; 1984), *A las escondidas* (In Secret; 1986), *Alguien está mirando* (Some One Is Watching; 1991)—have in common the author's clear intent to portray the lives of Argentine women from a variety of perspectives. All the above-mentioned texts are novels save *Boca de tormenta*, which is a collection of short stories. Plager reveals a close personal relationship with many of her characters, as they appear in more than one novel. This is the case with *Amigas* and *Prohibido despertar* as the reader follows the story of a group of friends as they experience different challenges, life changes, relationship problems, and family strife against the backdrop of the sociopolitical reality of Argentina. In *A las escondidas* and *Alguien está mirando* Plager presents her focus on the women character in relation to the men in their lives. There is an emphasis on the perceived safety that the middle-class provides for the women, even though they are neither happy nor fulfilled with the lives that they have. The twenty-six short stories that comprise *Boca de tormenta* adhere closely to Plager's narrative project as she presents glimpses into women's lives in varying states of disarray. Again, middle-class values are scrutinized as ultimately harmful to these characters as they try to negotiate personal desires and social responsibilities, juggle relationships, and deal with tragedies or dark pasts. The stories are almost overwhelmingly bleak in their outlook and exploration of the murky waters of self-realization, regret, and the sinister side of people's intimate lives.

Jewish Issues

While Plager has included Jewishness in her works from the onset, in her early works—or what one may call her first phase as an author—it remained secondary to the examination of feminine/feminist issues. The stories "El silbato" (The Whistle) and "La vereda de enfrente" (The Sidewalk Out Front) in *Boca de tormenta*, for example, bring specifically Jewish themes (generational discord in immigrant families, and the Holocaust) to the fore. It is in *Alguien está mirando* that Plager inserts Jewish identity into the story as an integral component to the plot and development of the characters. Nonetheless, it is with the publication of *Mujeres pudorosas* (1993, Modest Women) that the author sets the foundation for a new direction in her narrative in which she begins to explore Jewish issues in depth, while at the same time maintaining her commitment to women's concerns. *Mujeres pudorosas* tells the story of the relationship between two women in an innovative way. Graciela is a writer and Clara is the protagonist of the novel she is writing. Through her character, Graciela begins to sort out many of the unresolved issues in her own life and undergoes an examination of her self identity. While she cannot quite break free from her own ties, Graciela finds freedom in writing the story of Clara and living vicariously through her fictional alter ego. Many aspects of Jewish identity are explored in the novel, which takes place in Israel, not Argentina. For example, the weight of Jewish history and women's role in Judaism is quite prevalent throughout the novel, as well as the topics of Jewish exile and wandering. By the end of the novel, both the writer and the character manage—at least to a certain extent—to free themselves from the past and begin to live in the present, outside the limits of history and identity.

Plager's next books differ quite radically from anything she had previously published. Deviating from a rather somber strain of narrative, she enters the domain of humor with great success and astounding results. Her 1994 novel *Como papas para varenikes* is a parody of the Mexican writer Laura Esquivel's hugely popular *Como agua para chocolate* (*Like Water for Chocolate*; 1989) that uses recipes for Jewish dishes (latkes, borsht, kreplaj, knishes, varenikes, gefilte fish) interwoven into the hilarious tale of a middle-aged caterer in Buenos Aires. The book was very successful in Argentina and in 2004 Plager published a revised and expanded version of the novel with additional chapters. In addition to humor, Plager began to explore mattes of sexuality more openly and lightheartedly in this novel. By contrast to Esquivel's novel set in rural Mexico, Plager's novel takes place in modern-day urban Buenos Aires as a locus of postmodern cultural hybridity. Furthermore, Plager makes Jewish culture dominant while her Hispanic-Catholic assistant represent the margins and strives to assimilate through such efforts as adopting Yiddish expressions. As is the case in much of contemporary Argentine writing, there is a good deal of mocking of the so-called magical realist style. In *Como papas para varenikes* food is inextricably linked to the insatiable erotic desires of Cathy Goldsmith de Rosenfeld and her suitor-lover Saúl Steinberg. Both characters are widowed and middle-aged, which breaks with convention with regard to erotic literature. The novel's plot develops around the rivalry between Cathy and her arch-nemesis Sara Rastropovich, who is also a caterer. The novel ends with a "Kama Sutra para golosos" (Kama Sutra for Sweet-tooths) in which sexual positions are intended to recreate the form of a given Jewish food or symbol (a bagel, a kishke, a Star of David, a menorah).

Questions of sexuality are examined at great length, specifically in relation to Jewish tradition. Plager's novel is a truly original work that combines parody, popular culture, and serious social issues in way that is both effective and greatly entertaining.

The same year that *Como papas para varenikes* was released, Plager also published a humorous book entitled *Al mal sexo buena cara* (Putting on a Good Face for Bad Sex). It is easily the best Jewish humor book to come out of Argentina. Plager's talent as a humorist is highlighted in this ingenious collection of disparate texts on the idiosyncrasies of the Argentine Jewish community. She covers such topics as religion, marriage, social attitudes, Jewish mother, and sexuality. Furthermore, there is a Jewish horoscope, a fictionalized sex manual, and a collection of sayings that express popular Jewish wisdom. Plager's observations are not only very witty, but they are also at times scathing in their perspective or charmingly endearing.

Plager's novel *La rabina* (2006, The Female Rabbi) is a crowning achievement in her career. The novel represents the author's return to a more solemn vein of writing. It recounts the story of a young Argentine woman who wants to become a rabbi and the many obstacles she must overcome in order to reach her goal. The novel takes place in the United States, Israel, and Germany. Esther Fainberg's journey from wife of a prominent attorney to rabbi provides a fascinating look into feminist aspects of Judaism and Jewish tradition. In *La rabina*, Plager manages an excellent fusion of her two primary themes, Jewish and women's issues.

Other Works and Criticism

In addition to her main corpus of work, Plager has written a book on women and aging titled *Nosotras y la edad* (2001, We Women and Aging) and she has co-authored two historical novels based on nineteenth-century figures of Argentina, *Nostalgia de Malvinas: María Vernet, la última gobernadora* (1999, Nostalgia for the Falklands: María Vernet, the Last Governor) and *Vernet, caballero de las islas* (2005, Vernet, the Gentleman of the Islands). Both books were written in conjunction with her longtime friend and fellow author Elsa Fraga Vidal.

To date, Silvia Plager's work has not received the critical attention it is worthy of. Nevertheless, there are several excellent studies on a selection of her works.

DARRELL B. LOCKHART

Selected Works

Amigas. Buenos Aires: Galerna, 1982.
Prohibido despertar. Buenos Aires: Galerna, 1983.
Boca de tormenta. Buenos Aires: Galerna, 1984.
A las escondidas. Buenos Aires: Galerna, 1986.
Alguien está mirando. Buenos Aires: Planeta, 1991.
Mujeres pudorosas. Buenos Aires: Atlántida, 1993.
Al mal sexo buena cara. Buenos Aires: Planeta, 1994.
Como papas para varenikes. Buenos Aires: Beas Ediciones, 1994.
La baronesa de Fiuggi. Buenos Aires: Simurg, 1998.
Nostalgia de Malvinas: María Vernet, la última gobernadora. Co-authored with Elsa Fraga Vidal. Buenos Aires: Ediciones B / Javier Vergara Editor, 1999.
Nosotras y la edad. Buenos Aires: Ediciones B / Vergara, 2001.
Como papas para varenikes. Buenos Aires: Ediciones B / Vergara, 2004. (Revised and expanded second edition)
Vernet, caballero de las islas. Co-authored with Elsa Fraga Vidal. Buenos Aires: Sudamericana, 2005.
La rabina. Buenos Aires: Planeta, 2006.

References and Further Reading

Gimbernat González, Ester. "El subversivo territorio del deseo: *Prohibido despertar*". In Ester Gimbernat González (ed.), *Aventuras del desacuerdo: novelistas argentinas de los 80*. Buenos Aires: Danilo Albero Vergara, 1992, pp. 99–103.
Goldberg, Florinda F. "Pudor y poder: femeneidad, identidad judía y escritura en *Mujeres pudorosas* de Silvia Plager". In Judit Bokser Liwerant and Alicia Gojman de Backal (eds), *Encuentro y alteridad: vida y cultura judía en América Latina*. México, D.F.: Fondo de Cultura Económica, 1999, pp. 613–24.
Lockhart, Darrell B. "*Al mal sexo buena cara*: Silvia Plager y la cultura popular judía". In Ricardo Feierstein and Stephen A. Sadow (eds), *Recreando la cultura judeoargentina/2. Literatura y artes plásticas*. 2 vols. Buenos Aires: Editorial Milá, 2004. Vol. 1, pp. 198–208.

POLETTI, SYRIA

Syria Poletti (1922–91) was born in Pieve di Cadore, El Véneto, in Northern Italy, and graduated from the Instituto Superior del Magisterio in Venice in 1943 as Professor of Pedagogy. In 1945, Poletti emigrated to Argentina, which she adopted as a second home. Poletti attained a remarkable mastery of the Spanish language and wrote fiction exclusively in her second language. In the late 1940s she earned her second degree, in Italian and Spanish pedagogy, from the University of Córdoba, Argentina. Shortly after completing her education, she relocated to Buenos Aires.

Born into a family of limited financial means, Poletti began working as a child. She sold embroidery and taught classes in cooking and sewing to finance her secondary and post-secondary education. From childhood the author had a passion for math and science, two areas she later considered vital to her formation as a writer. As she claimed in several interviews, writers must be capable of intuiting exact laws; thus, her early studies strengthened the logical, intuitive, and sequential elements of her writing, particularly her detective fiction. Despite her self-described obsession with writing, until early adulthood, Poletti's financial circumstances convinced her that a literary career was out-of-reach, a privilege reserved for the affluent.

Immediately after emigrating from Italy, Poletti taught her native language at the Dante Alighieri School in Argentina. During the 1940s she began writing for newspapers, magazines, and radio programs. Although literary critics would later condemn the advice columns she wrote for women's magazines as superficial and frivolous, throughout her career Poletti defended such texts as a rich, vital part of South American women's history. In her view, such writing represented archival work, and the epistolary form offered women a means of overcoming the isolation suffered by Latin American housewives. Additionally, Poletti viewed these letters as her greatest source of insight into the realities of mid-century female life; in fact, she later described them as a primary research base for her fiction.

Poletti's first published fiction was an autobiographical short story that appeared in 1951 in Buenos Aires's newspaper *La Nación*. During the 1950s, she published several short stories and children's stories in magazines and anthologies in Buenos Aires. Her first novel, *Gente conmigo* (People with Me), was a best-seller and won publisher Losada's international novel competition in 1961. This novel was later translated to various languages, including German, Italian, English, and Czech, adapted for film in Argentina, and selected by Alan Williams Publishing in New York as one of the ten best South American novels. In 1964, Poletti's first short-story collection, *Línea de fuego* (Line of Fire), also became a commercial success, and several of its stories were adapted for television and radio. Later that year her short story "Rojo en la salina" ("Red in the Salt Pit") was included in the *Cuentos de crimen y misterio* (Stories of Crime and Mystery) anthology edited by Jorge Alvárez. This collection placed Poletti alongside such internationally respected Argentinian authors as Jorge Luis Borges, Adolfo Bioy Casares, and María Angélica Bosco. Poletti's third book, the crime-story collection *Historias en rojo* (Stories in Red), was awarded the prestigious Municipal Prize in Buenos Aires in 1969. In 1971, her second novel, *Extraño oficio* (Strange Calling) was nominated for Argentina's National Literature Award, and the following year Poletti published the respected children's story collection, *Reportajes supersónicos* (Supersonic Broadcasts).

As Poletti's international renown increased, she used her literary credentials to increase opportunities for other authors. In 1973, she co-founded the Club of XIII, a group of respected authors who award an annual narrative prize in Argentina. Poletti also directed the Leonor Alonso Workshop in Buenos Aires, a program that allowed fledgling writers, particularly women, the space and time to devote themselves to writing. Poletti's prologue to *Cuentos desde el taller* (Stories from the Workshop) highlights her commitment to women's writing: "Woman wants to be herself as a thinking being; she doesn't defend the right to write as a male. She wants to write as a woman ... with the same right to her self-conception ... to contribute the product of her thoughts, filtered through her own talent and experiences" (p. 8). Poletti also participated frequently in various literary panels throughout Europe and the Americas dedicated to women's literature, Italo-Argentine cultural understanding, and contemporary narrative.

Two of Poletti's preferred literary genres were detective fiction and juvenile fiction. She defended these fields against marginalization, frequently asserting that quality of writing rather than literary tradition should be the primary standard against which fiction of any genre is evaluated. For Poletti, crime fiction and children's literature were united in their focus on human reality and the human heart. In *Taller de imaginería* (Workshop of Imagination) she pointed out that both forms offered "excellent exercises in narrative technique" and that her writing's common denominator, regardless of genre, is the presence of the child witness (p. 159).

Poletti's fiction consistently privileges the child or adolescent's point of view. Each of her works is dedicated to her grandmother, "la vieja del extraño oficio" ("the woman with the strange calling"), whom she credited with giving her physical and spiritual life. This granddaughter–grandmother relationship, often strengthened as a result of the child's maternal abandonment, drives the plots of much of Poletti's fiction. For example, "El tren de medianoche" ("The Midnight Train"), selected by the author as her best short story and originally published in *Línea de fuego*, narrates a child's nightly treks with her grandmother to watch the Berlin–Rome train race past them. The train, presented as both alluring and menacing, offers the women voyeuristic access to the worlds forbidden to them but occupied by those who have abandoned them: the child's mother, who left on the train to be with her husband and son; and the older woman's son, a musician who used the train to escape his humble origins. The train's movement inspires a nightly sense of floating between memories and the "absurd hope" of reunion; its speed parallels the intensification of the women's sense of stagnation and abandonment (p. 70). These themes of abandonment and stagnation are also key to the tales of Lilín-Sin-Patio (Lilin No-Patio) in *Reportajes supersónicos*. Lilín is a lonely city girl who dreams of a having her own tree-laden patio filled with animals and fascinating visitors. Her supersonic tape recorder allows Lilín to imagine a limitless patio for herself, the setting for her interviews with a series of visible and invisible guests.

As Gianna Martella points out in "Pioneers: Spanish American Women Writers of Detective Fiction," Poletti's mystery writing is ground-breaking; it differs from the male-authored tradition rooted in piecing together clues in order to solve a crime. Instead, her integration of love stories as key plot elements, her focus on the role of woman as investigator, and her inclusion of children's intuition as a means of solving mysteries created new options for female detective authors. "Rojo en la salina" ("Red in the Salt Pit"), included in *Historias en rojo*, incorporates these traits and also foreshadows later pivotal themes of Latin American literature. As Martella points out, this story "deals with issues that will become predominant in the Spanish American literature of the next two decades: social and political unrest, the rise of left-wing movements, and confrontations between unionists and the defenders of the status quo" (2002, p. 33).

KAREN W. MARTIN

Selected Works

Gente conmigo. Buenos Aires: Editorial Losada, 1962.

Extraño oficio (Crónicas de una obsesión). Buenos Aires: Editorial Losada, 1971.

Historias en rojo. Buenos Aires: Editorial Losada, 1973.

Taller de imaginería. Buenos Aires: Editorial Losada, 1977.

Reportajes supersónicos. Buenos Aires: Editorial Losada, 1979.

Cuentos desde el taller. Buenos Aires: Plus Ultra, 1983.

References and Further Reading

Castelli, Eugenio. "La palabra-mito en las novelas de Syria Poletti". *Sur* 348 (1981): 101–7.

——. "Para una evaluación crítica de la novelística de Syria Poletti". *Káñina: Revista de Artes y Letras de la Universidad de Costa Rica* 9(2) (1985): 51–6.

Gardini, Walter. *Syria Poletti: Mujer de dos mundos*. Buenos Aires: Asociación Dante Alighieri, 1994.

Martella, Gianna M. "Pioneers: Spanish American Women Writers of Detective Fiction". *Letras Femeninas* 28(1) (2002): 31–44.

Martínez, Victoria. "Symbols of Oppression: Eliminating the Patriarca in Alonso Sastre's *La mordaza* and Syria Poletti's 'Pisadas de caballo.'" *Hispanic Journal* 18(1) (1997): 67–78.

Mathieu, Corina S. "Syria Poletti: Intérprete de la realidad argentina". *Sin Nombre* 13(3) (1983): 87–93.

Schiminovich, Flora H. "Two Argentine Female Writers Perfect the Art of Detection: Maria Angélica Bosco and Syria Poletti". *Review: Latin American Literature and Arts* 42 (June 1, 1990): 16–20.

Titiev, Janice. "Structure as a Feminist Statement in the Fiction of Syria Poletti". *Letras Femeninas* 15(1–2) (1989): 48–58.

PONIATOWSKA, ELENA

Elena Poniatowska is one of Mexico's most distinguished writers, famous for her innovative testimonial novels, her testimonial documentary works, and, increasingly, for her fiction. She was born Helène Elizabeth Louise Amelie Paula Dolores Poniatowska Amor on May 19, 1932, in Paris (or 1933; she herself has given two different dates in interviews). Her father, Jean (Juan) Joseph Evremont Poniatowski Sperry, was a French citizen of Polish heritage, descended from the last king of Poland. Her mother, María de los Dolores (Paula) Amor Iturbide, was born in France of Mexican parents who had lost their hacienda and lands during the Mexican Revolution and the subsequent agrarian reforms carried out by the Lázaro Cárdenas administration in the late 1930s.

Paula Amor took Elena and her sister Kitzia (born Sophia) to Mexico in 1942 to escape the war in Europe. (Poniatowska's father fought with the French military and later joined them in Mexico.) They lived with Paula's mother and the girls attended a British school. They later attended the Liceo Franco-Americano, and Poniatowska finished her high school education by attending a convent school in Philadelphia, Pennsylvania. She briefly attended Manhattanville College. Poniatowska spoke French as her first, and native, language, was schooled in French and in English, and learned Spanish without any formal study at all, though interaction with her nanny, household staff, and on the streets. Nevertheless, her writing has been almost entirely in Spanish.

After returning from the United States she worked briefly as a tri-lingual secretary, a job not to her liking. At a cocktail party with her mother in 1953, Poniatowska managed to interview the newly arrived ambassador from the United States. It was the first interview she had ever done; after it was published in *El Excelsior* she took a job writing social columns, but quickly moving to interviews of artists, writers, musicians and other cultural figures. She produced 365 interviews, one per day, in her year at *El Excelsior*, and then moved to *Novedades* in 1954. She has written for *La Jornada* since 1985. Her first novel, *Lilus Kikus*, a series of semi-autobiographical vignettes, was published in 1954.

In 1968, Poniatowska married the astronomer Guillermo Haro (1913–88); the couple had three children. Poniatowska became a naturalized Mexican citizen in 1969. She also published the novel that would first bring her notoriety, *Hasta no verte Jesús mío* (translated into English, French, German, and Polish), for which she won the 1970 Premio Mazatlán de Literatura.

Early Writings

Hasta no verte Jesús mío is based on a series of interviews conducted over a year's time with a poor, uneducated washerwoman. Poniatowska transformed the real-life Josefina Bórquez into Jesusa Palancares and created what has been called a testimonial novel. As Poniatowska tells Jesusa's story from childhood to old age, she also tells the story of the Mexico of the time, particularly of the difficulties and sufferings of the popular classes. Jesusa marries Pedro at only 15 years of age, and her husband, like her father, has many lovers. But he beats her as well, so when he is killed in front of her just two years later, she refuses to ever consider marrying again. Jesusa witnesses the Mexican Revolution, following the troops and even leading them after Pedro's death. And she witnesses the growth of an increasingly impersonal Mexico City, living in various tenements over the next decades. A stubborn, often unlikeable character, Jesusa raises issues that will be central to Poniatowska's work henceforth, such as class differences, the machismo so deeply rooted in Mexican society, and perhaps above all, the importance of listening. Poniatowska has often been credited with giving voice to the voiceless, but she has also refused to be so credited, countering that she has simply listened to the voices around her.

Though she has written dozens of books and innumerable essays, Poniatowska remains best known for *Hasta no verte, Jesús mío* and her second book, published just two years later, *La noche de Tlatelolco: testimonios de historia oral* (translated into English and Japanese). In the summer of 1968, just months before the Olympic Games scheduled to take place in Mexico City, student activism threatened to undermine the image the government hoped to present to the world. On October 2, 1968, while students demonstrated peacefully on the Plaza de las Tres Culturas near the Tlateloco neighborhood, the army opened fire on them, wounding and killing not only demonstrators, but observers and local inhabitants, including some children. Poniatowska was at home during the event, and when friends told her about it she had to see for herself. She visited the Plaza, saw the bullet holes and bloodstains, and then began talking to witnesses. Unable to get any of her articles published in the Mexican press, she kept them and gathered them into what is her most famous work of investigative reporting. Mexican newspapers reported that twenty or thirty had been killed; the foreign press estimates ranged up to 325 or even 400. *La noche de Tlatelolco* counters the official story with the testimony of many voices and many texts, including excerpts from poems, slogans from banners, photographs, and even reproductions of pamphlets from the movement. Ironically, Poniatowska was awarded the Premio Xavier Villaurrutia in 1971 by the very government that had tried to silence her; she rejected the award in protest at the government's repressive actions. She was awarded the Premio Nacional de Periodismo (National Journalism Award) in 1978, the first woman to win it.

Other Non-fiction

Poniatowska has published several other important works of non-fction. *Fuerte es el silencio* ("Strong is the Silence"; translated into German) contains five chronicles, including essays on the massive migration from rural areas to the megalopolis of Mexico City and another on the student protest of 1968. Poniatowska chronicles the results of and reactions to the devastating earthquake in Mexico City of September, 1985, in

Nada, nadie: las voces del temblor (Nothing, Nobody: The Voices of the Mexico City Earthquake), which began as a series of articles published in *La Jornada* after *El Excelsior* refused to publish them. (Poniatowska moved to *La Jornada* as a result.) Like *La noche de Tlatelolco*, the narrative weaves together the testimony of many, and presents an alternative vision to the official one, but *Nada, Nadie* is the work of eighteen writers—a work by a small collective on the lives of the larger collective.

In 1990, she began to publish *Todo México* ("All of Mexico"), a series of volumes collecting her many interviews with Mexican cultural and political figures from 1953 to 2000. Planned as a series of fourteen volumes, by 2003, she had published eight.

In 2000, she published *Las siete cabritas* ("The Seven Little Goats"; translated into Czech), a series of seven essays on seven essential female figures in Mexican arts and letters, including the artists Frida Kahlo and María Izquierdo and the writers Elena Garro and Rosario Castellanos among them. Poniatowska has said that she is a "natural feminist". She has long contended that women writers and artists are commonly relegated to second place, at best, or completely invisible at worst, in a male-dominated society where women's artistic production is considered a hobby. She has made special efforts to promote the work of women when possible. She helped found Mexico's first feminist magazine, *fem*, in 1976, which has featured many women writers. Poniatowska continues to write for *fem*, as well as writing prefaces and introductions to book that promote women artists and preserve Mexican history and culture—often an alternative history. She wrote the text to accompany the photographs of women soldiers (like the Jesusa of *Hasta no verte, Jesús mío*) in *Las Soldaderas* (Las Soldaderas: Women in the Mexican Revolution); she introduces the photographs of the great Mexican photographers such as Graciela Iturbide (*Juchitán de las mujeres* [1989; "The Juchitán of Women"]), Manuel Alvarez Bravo (*Manuel Alvarez Bravo: el artista, su obra, sus tiempos* [1991, "Manuel Alvarez Bravo: The Artist, His Work, and His Times"]), and Mariana Yampolsky (*La raíz y el camino* [1985, "The Root and the Path"]). Poniatowska works tirelessly to promote, document, and preserve those aspects of Mexican culture and the arts that might otherwise be marginalized.

Fiction

Though Poniatowska has often said in interviews that she considers herself a journalist more than a "writer," and she continues to work as a journalist, she has also occasionally lamented the lack of time to dedicate to writing, especially fiction, in her busy life as the wife of an important scientist (until her husband's death in 1988) and the mother to three children. She has increasingly dedicated herself to writing fiction. In addition to her early, "young" novel, *Lilus Kikus*, she has published two collections of short stories (*Los cuentos de Lilus Kikus* (1967, [*Lilus Kikus and Other Stories*, 2005]) and *De noche vienes* (1979, "You Come by Night"; translated into French), a novella (*Querido Diego, te abraza Quiela*) and five novels.

In 1978, Poniatowska published the epistolary novella, *Querido Diego, te abraza Quiela* (*Dear Diego*; translated into French, German, and Polish), based on the letters to the Mexican muralist, Diego Rivera, from his Russian common-law wife, Angelina Beloff, a painter. They lived together in Paris for ten years; the couple had a son who died in infancy. In 1921, Rivera returned to Mexico, telling Beloff that he would send her the money to join him. The novella is based in part on a biography of Rivera by the historian Bertram Wolfe (*The Fabulous Life of Diego Rivera* [1963]). Poniatowska's novella, titled like the opening and closing lines of a letter, is composed of twelve letters written over a nine-month period, all fictionalized except the final letter, dated July 22, 1922, which comes from Wolfe's text. In the final letter Beloff recognizes that the relationship is over and alludes to Rivera's "Mexican love". Though Rivera did send small amounts of money to Beloff in Paris, he never took steps to bring her to Mexico. Thirteen years later, when she passed him on a Mexican street, Rivera did not recognize her. In this slim book, Poniatowska foregrounds an artistic woman who might otherwise have been little more than a footnote of Mexican art history.

Published ten years later, the novel *La flor de lis* (Fleur de lis), is semi-autobiographical like Poniatowska's early first novel and her early short stories. *La flor de lis* narrates the childhood of the protagonist, Mariana, who, like Poniatowska, was born in France and moved to Mexico during World War II. Set primarily in the Mexico of the 1940s, Mariana, like Poniatowska, attends private schools, including two years at a convent high school in the United States. The novel is divided into two parts, the first on Mariana's early years and her devotion to her mother and the second when Mariana is an adolescent and has a crucial encounter with a priest, Father Jacques Teufel, who incites a transformation in the young woman previously so acquiescent and conformist. The title "Fleur de lis" suggests French nobility. (One of Poniatowska's critics, Beth Jörgensen, refers to these fictions of a young girl's development as "fictions of privilege".) Poniatowska and her protagonist Mariana descended from noble lines, and both reject that heritage in favor of a newly constructed identity in an adopted country.

Poniatowska spent ten years researching her next novel, *Tinísima* ("Very, Very Tina"; translated into Dutch, English, and German), for which she won the Premio Mazatlán in 1993. *Tinísima* is a lengthy novel (nearly seven hundred pages; cut almost in half in the English translation) about the notorious Italian photographer and dedicated Communist activist, Tina Modotti (1896–1942), whose friendships and liaisons included the photographer Edward Weston, the painter Xavier Guerrero, the muralist Diego Rivera (for whom she modeled), and the Cuban revolutionary Julio Antonio Mella, assassinated in Mexico City on January 10, 1929, while walking home with Modotti. After Mella's death, Modotti began a liaison with Vittorio Vidali, a Stalinist assassin who may have been involved in Mella's death. Modotti was accused of involvement in Mella's death, tried, convicted, and imprisoned. She was released soon after and asked to leave the country. Her trial was serialized in Mexican papers. Poniatowska reimagines Modotti's life, using true historical events, Modotti's own photographs, newspaper clippings, and quotations from actual letters. She weaves in Modotti's early life in the United States and her life in Europe and the Soviet Union after she left Mexico, essentially expelled. She and Vidali worked in Spain on the Republican side during the Spanish Civil War, and returned to Mexico in 1939, where she died in 1942 under an assumed name. *Tinísima*, with its multiple sources, texts, and voices, has been called a "polyphonic" novel. It has also been criticized for being overly archival. Yet *Tinísma* brings a new perspective to a period of utopian left-wing activity in Mexico, the feminine perspective.

Poniatowska received a Guggenheim grant in 1994. Two years later she published *Paseo de la reforma*. The title refers to a famous broad avenue lined by impressive examples of high society such as fine architecture, shops, and museums. But it may also mean something like "passage to reform," as one of the main characters, Ashby Egbert, undergoes a metamorphosis of sorts. A member of the upper class, Ashby finds himself unexpectedly interned in a public, government hospital after an accident. There he confronts a Mexico never before encountered, the Mexico of the poor and dispossessed. He enters into a passionate love affair with Amaya Chacal, a contradictory, untameable woman who dies in a political uprising. Her loss releases him to a new life, but a more informed life than he previously led.

In 2001, Poniatowska won the Mexican National Award for literature as well as the Premio Alfaguaga for the novel published that same year, *La piel del cielo* (The Skin of the Sky; translated into Chinese and Portuguese). The novel competed anonymously with 592 manuscripts for the award, sponsored by one of Spain's most prestigious publishers. *La piel del cielo* is inspired by Poniatowska's husband, Guillermo Haro, a gifted astronomer. The protagonist, Lorenzo de Tena, is born in 1930s Mexico, the illegitimate son of a peasant woman and a businessman. After his mother's death, the father takes him and his siblings to live in Mexico City, where, like many of his class, Lorenzo studies law—the typical first step to public office. Unhappy in his studies and his life, the young Lorenzo hides himself in the study of the stars. Educated at Harvard, Lorenzo returns to Mexico, where he finds it difficult to pursue research under the impoverished conditions of his native country. In his dedication to improve Mexico's scientific capabilities, de Tena ignores his personal life and undervalues the women in it. The novel is considered historical fiction, and incorporates many historical figures and moments, such as the inauguration of the new telescope in 1942, the amateur astonomer Luis Enrique Erro, the observatories of Tonantzintla and Tacubaya, and the writer José Revueltas. The novel has been criticized for an excess of historical detail. It has also been called an "unusual valentine" to her husband, for whom an observatory in Sonora is named. *La piel del cielo* recalls Haro's life, but it also contributes to the history of the science of astronomy in Mexico.

In 2004, Poniatowska was given France's Legion of Honor award. In 2005, she published her most recent work, the novel *El tren pasa primero* ("The Train Passes First"), based on the 1959 railroad strike led by Demetrio Vallejo, whom she interviewed several times along with other jailed railroad workers in 1959. The novel begins with the struggles of railroad leader Trinidad Pineda Chiñas, who leads a strike that paralyses the country. Trinidad is followed day and night by secret agents, and soon imprisoned. Though Trinidad is the main character, the novel brims with strong female characters as well, including Trinidad's niece, Barbara, who is expecting his child at the end of the novel.

Poniatowska won the Lifetime Achievement Award from the International Women's Media Foundation, in 2006, given to honor a woman journalist with a pioneering spirit, who has consistently demonstrated commitment to freedom of the press, and through her work and example paved the way for future generations of women in the media. In her acceptance speech, Poniatowska noted that she has always listened to the voices of others, beginning in 1959 with jailed striking railroad workers, then in 1968, to the voices of those in the student massacre, then again in 1985 with those affected by a devastating earthquake. She also states that "although the population of Mexico is 52 percent female, women have always been the forgotten ones" (Acceptance Speech at http://www.iwmf.org/press/9533).

Poniatowska's work is sometimes considered difficult to classify, existing on the border of journalism and literature, between criticism and creation. One of Mexico's most prolific and most respected writers, much of her work remains untranslated. Elena Poniatowska has, despite her disclaimers, indeed given voice to the otherwise ignored, whether the women *soldaderas*, the invisible members of the popular classes, or the neglected histories of her beloved Mexico.

LINDA LEDFORD-MILLER

Selected Works

Fiction

Hasta no verte Jesús mío. Mexico: Era, 1969. Trans. Deanna Heikkinen as *Here's to You, Jesusa!* New York: Farrar, Straus, Giroux, 2001.

Querido Diego, te abraza Quiela. Mexico: Era, 1978. Trans. Katherine Silver as *Dear Diego*. New York: Pantheon, 1986.

La flor de lis. Mexico: Era, 1988.

Tinísima. Mexico: Era, 1992. Trans. Katherine Silver as *Tinisima*. New York: Farrar, Straus and Giroux, 1996.

Paseo de la reforma. Barcelona: Plaza y Janés, 1996.

La piel del cielo. Mexico: Alfaguara, 2001. Trans. Deanna Heikkinen as *The Skin of the Sky*. New York: Farrar, Straus and Giroux, 2004.

El tren pasa primero. Mexico: Alfaguara, 2005.

Nonfiction

La noche de Tlatelolco: testimonios de historia oral. Mexico: Era, 1971. Translated by Helen R. Lane as *Massacre in Mexico*. New York: Viking Press, 1975.

Fuerte es el silencio. Mexico: Era, 1980.

Nada, nadie: las voces del temblor. Mexico: Era, 1988. Trans. Aurora Camacho de Schmidt and Arthur Schmidt as *Nothing, Nobody: The Voices of the Mexico City Earthquake*. Philadelphia, PA: Temple University Press, 1995.

Las Soldaderas. Mexico: Era, 1999. Trans. David Dorado Romo as *Las Soldaderas: Women in the Mexican Revolution*. El Paso: Cinco Puntos Press, 2006.

Las siete cabritas. Mexico: Era, 2000.

Todo México. Mexico: Editorial Diana, 1990–2003. Eight vols.

References and Further Reading

Gardner, Nathaniel. *Through Their Eyes: Marginality in the Works of Elena Poniatowska, Silvia Molina and Rosa Nissán*. New York: Peter Lang, 2007.

Jörgensen, Beth E. *The Writing of Elena Poniatowska: Engaging Dialogues*. Austin, TX: University of Texas Press, 1994.

Kerr, Lucille. "Gestures of Authorship: Lying to Tell the Truth in Elena Poniatowska's *Hasta no verte Jesús mío*". In *Reclaiming the*

Author: Figures and Fictions from Spanish America. Durham, NC: Duke University Press, 1992.

Maier, Linda S. and Dulfano, Isabel. (eds) *Woman as Witness: Essays on Testimonial Literature by Latin American Women*. New York: Peter Lang, 2004.

Maloof, Judy. "The Construction of a Collective Voice: New Journalistic Techniques in Elena Poniatowska's Testimonial: *Nada, Nadie: Las voces del temblor*". *Hispanófila*, 135 (May 2002): 137–51.

Medeiros-Leichem, María Teresa. *Reading the Feminine Voice in Latin American Women's Fiction from Teresa de la Parra to Elena Poniatowska and Luisa Valenzuela*. New York: Peter Lang, 2002.

Morell, Hortensia R. "Crossed Words between the Lines: The Confusion of Voices in the Love Soliloquy of Elena Poniatowska's *Querido Diego, te abraza Quiela*". *Journal of Modern Literature* 25, no. 1 (Fall 2001): 35–51.

Perilli, Carmen. "Identidades, arte y revolución en *Tinísima* de Elena Poniatowska". *Ciberletras* 12 (January 2005). *http://www.lehman.cuny.edu/ciberletras/*

Schuessler, Michael K. *Elenísima: Ingenio y figura de Elena Poniatowska*. Mexico City: Editorial Diana, 2003. Translated as *Elena Poniatowska: An Intimate Biography*. Tucson, AZ: University of Arizona Press, 2007.

Snook, Margaret L. "Elena Poniatowska's *La piel del cielo*: Mexican History Written on the Female Body". *Hispania: A Journal Devoted to the Teaching of Spanish and Portuguese* 89(2) (May 2006): 259–67.

Sommer, Doris. "Taking a Life: Hot Pursuit and Cold Rewards in a Mexican Testimonial Novel". *Signs* 20(4) (Summer 1995): 913–40.

Valdés, María Elena de. "Identity and the Other as Myself: Elena Poniatowska". In *The Shattered Mirror: Representations of Women in Mexican Literature*. Austin, TX: University of Texas Press, 1998, pp. 114–43.

PORTAL, MAGDA

A Leftist Ideology

Magda Portal (1900–89) is one of the major Peruvian revolutionary thinkers of the twentieth century. She began working as a poet and encouraged political action that came from a leftist ideology. She sought the transformation and participation of women in society. Portal was committed by her fighting woman's character, aware of the painful Peruvian reality that goes beyond what is problematic to women. She was a well-known dissident and denounced the relationship between official institutions and society as a cause of social inequity.

Portal was receptive to the ideologies of her time. She believed that socialism created potential and supported the anti-imperialist ideas that came out of the Mexican Revolution's agenda. On the other hand, she argued against the international promulgation of American capitalism. The principles of agrarian reform advocated by revolutionaries were a motive for the foundation of several political movements in Latin America in which the defense of the proletariat was Portal's and other participants' dream. She clearly opposed the bourgeois and fascist systems because she believed the symbiotic relationship of both factions had laid the groundwork for the world wars in Europe. She was not indifferent to historical catastrophes. Therefore, she pointed out the necessity of reforms based on the political battle. She stated that resistance and criticism were forms of political action that enhanced social transformation. Her main intention was to challenge the leading sectors of the government, not only the political parties but also the coercive State apparatus. In this sense, Portal denounced the absence and invisibility of women in Peru as a type of social injustice. She looked for a voice that came from the struggle of women between the end of the nineteenth century and the beginning of the twentieth. Such a voice emerges in her prose, poetry and political speech confronting history and the treatment of the patriarchal establishment in which she promoted women's needs through confronting injustice. Her approach was diametrically opposed to the male perspective that dominated all political arenas and ideological references in Latin America by this time. In this sense, she explained the nonexistent participation of women in politics by the fact that their education was controlled by the alliance of conservative political parties and authoritarian religious institutions. Regarding this historical apathy, she understood the process of women's liberation and the acquisition of civil rights as an innovative system wherein women create their own education and learning process.

Political Involvement

In 1924, she organized a political party in Peru called the Alianza Popular Americana Revolucionaria (APRA). Her first step in putting her ideas into practice was when, in a symbolic act, she threw the pages of the poetry collection "Ánima absorta" (Absorbed Soul) and "Delirios de amor" (Deliriums of Love) into the Rimac River in order to emphasize her new focus on politics. In the same year she was forced into exile in Mexico after she rejected an award granted by Universidad Mayor de San Marcos.

According to Daniel Reedy, she is the only woman who participated in the ideological formation of the international movement of the APRA. She reached a powerful position when she was elected as a member of the National Executive Committee of Peruvian Aprista Party in 1928. During the 1930s and 1940s as a national leader, Magda Portal developed and promoted the doctrine of the APRA and wrote the documents that oriented the propagandistic and cultural platform for women. In 1946, Portal organized the First Convention of Women of the APRA, with the direct participation of women who requested the right to be considered independent party members. The Executive Committee denied this right and replied with the enormous abusive power of masculine members over female requests. Later on, she decided to retire from the APRA. According to Roland Forgues, her disagreements with the party ended with Portal's accusation that Haya de la Torre, one of the APRA founders, had betrayed the ethics of the party.

Some of her official biographers underscore her ability to realize her ideological dreams. Recently, post-feminist critics have revisited her as a role model for intellectual and activist women. She assumed culture was a human element that transformed the spiritual gesture of society. In effect, this writer recognized with sadness that people could not advance when only assisted by the economy; rather they also need to contribute to society as citizens. Furthermore, intellectual freedom facilitates the capacity to learn and to live more democratically.

Women's Advocate

Magda Portal's poetry and prose, full of anger, reflected her denunciation as a nonconformist. Her life covered eight decades in which she experienced both the restrictions of patriarchal society and the price of taking her dissidence too far from the traditional guidelines. She suffered imprisonment and exile because of her political militancy. In other words, the establishment attacked her through repressive practices, censorship, and the brutal structural paradigm of coercion leading to the suppression of her critical insurgency. Cecilia Bustamante, a Peruvian writer, declared in Ottawa University during the III Interamerican Women Writers Conference in 1978 entitled "Perspectives on the social, economic and political role of women in Latin America", that Portal, and other intellectual and political women of Mariátegui's generation, were characterized by their militant language that challenged official messages and called for direct action. The short story collection *El derecho a matar* (Right to Kill) by Magda Portal is an example of this kind of strong approach in which the right to fight is invocated not only in the title, but also when it legitimizes women's militancy. Moreover, the destiny of racial minorities, the labor sector, and women requires historical changes that define their new condition by real confrontation on several levels. In the same way, Roland Forgues states that Magda Portal constitutes an example of the Peruvian social path whose writing reveals the compromise with her time and contemporary history. She contended that the act of writing served as a weapon against patriarchal and capitalist systems that marginalize and oppress females. From this angle Portal's work endorsed the initiative of a new aesthetic and social space for women.

Her Literary Works

Una esperanza y el mar (1927, One Hope and the Sea) confirmed the historical sensitivity and lyricism of this author. "El poema de la Cárcel" (Prison Poem), "La sonrisa de Cristo" (Christ's Smile) and "Círculos violeta" (Violet Circles) are poems of this volume in which passion and tenderness are important elements of Magda's verses. In her first verses, Portal feels emotion as a human being and in some verses her lyricism and humanity are recognized indeed within phases like: "Pequeña soy . . .!" [I am so small!]. Her poetry gives a pure version of herself; it is not mystified, nor idealized. Her poetry is the truth of her soul. She does not offer an image; her art and pure lyricism reduce the proportion of artifice that needs to be considered art, especially in the vanguard period where human action is pivotal ("El Amauta y el arte de la vanguardia" (The Amauta and the Art of the Avant-Garde). According to Cecilia Bustamante, there is a perennial resistance between two principles: life and death which govern not only the world but what her poetry says.

She wrote a famous essay "Flora Tristán, la precursora" (1946, Flora Tristán, the Precursor). Portal in that study admired Tristán because she decided to cross the Atlantic to claim her inheritance and the rights of her mother. Tristán affirmed her feminist voice against status quo. Portal understood her own life while studying Tristan's life. Curiously, both have been labeled "Mujer-Mesias" [Messiah Woman] by critics. Furthermore Reedy, with a feminist and historical literary perspective established that Portal's poetry was a continued test in her battle to improve conditions for women in Peru and her persistent search for political and literary strategies to eradicate the causes of oppression. In the same way, Lady Rojas-Trempe stated that Portal is better recognized for her militancy in politics than for her literary works. However, she demonstrated that the twentieth century in Peru had important individuals working and fighting for the vindication of the proletarian class and for gender equality.

It is important to mention her relationship with the popular Peruvian writer José Carlos Mariátegui. He was an intellectual and political leader admired by Portal because of his faith and integrity in the spread of socialist ideology throughout Perú. She affirmed that José Carlos taught her to see the world and people in a different light (II 386). Reedy points out in his book that Portal was one of José Carlos Mariátegui's closest friends who even refers to her poetry in his own work. Now Magda Portal belongs to the corpus of Latin American Literature in which there are significant references to contemporary theory and criticism. In addition, in the Latin American Short Stories competition Magda Portal is part of the literary agenda for writers in search of publishing opportunities.

ÁNGELA MARÍA GONZÁLEZ ECHEVERRY

Selected Works

El nuevo poema y su orientación hacia una estética económica. México: APRA, 1928.

"Dos poemas proletarios para los compañeros de Vitarte". *Amauta* 25 (July–Aug. 1929): 18–23.

Frente al imperialismo y defensa de la Revolución Mexicana. Lima: Editorial Cahuide, 1931.

Hacia la mujer nueva. Lima: Editorial Cooperativa Aprista Atahualpa, 1933.

Costa Sur. Santiago de Chile: Imprenta Nueva, 1945.

Flora Tristán, La precursora. Lima: Ediciones Páginas Libres, 1946.

Constancia del ser. Lima: Talleres Gráficos P. L. Villanueva, S. A. 1965.

La mujer en el Partido del Pueblo. Lima: El Cóndor, 1948.

Flora Tristán, Precursora. Lima: Editorial La Equidad, 1983.

References and Further Reading

Busse, Erika. *El símbolo Flora Tristán en el feminismo peruano*. Lima: Ediciones Flora Tristán, 2003.

Bustamante, Cecilia. "Magda Portal y sus poderes". *Ciberayllu*, 17 Nov. 2003.

Forgues, Roland. "Magda Portal, Nací para luchar". *Palabra viva las poetas se desnudan*. Lima: El Quijote, 1991, pp. 51–62.

Mariátegui, José Carlos. "(1928) Magda Portal". *7 Ensayos de interpretación de la realidad peruan*. Lima: Biblioteca Amauta, 1959, pp. 280–5.

Reedy, Daniel R. "Aspects of the Feminist Movement in Peruvian Letters and Politics". *SECOLAS Annals*. v.VI. Ed. Eugene R. Huck. Georgia: Kennesaw Junior College, March, 1975: 53–64.

——. "Magda Portal (1903–89) Perú". In *Spanish-American Women Writers: A Bio-Bibliographical Source Book*. Westport, CT: Greenwood Press, 1990, pp. 483–92.

——. *Magda Portal. La Pasionaria peruana. Biografía Intelectual*. Lima: Centro de la Mujer Peruana Flora Tristán, 2000.

Roland, Morgues. *Plumas de Afrodita. Una mirada a la poeta peruana del siglo XX*. Lima: San Marcos, 2004.

http://www.andes.missouri.edu/andes/Cronicas/CB_MagdaPortal.html (accessed 13 July 2006).

PORTELA, ENA LUCÍA

No doubt one of the most talented contemporary Cuban fiction writers, Ena Lucía Portela was born in Havana on

December 19, 1972. The daughter of a professional translator and a copy editor, Portela pursued her undergraduate studies at the University of Havana, where she majored in Classical Languages and Literature. She has been the recipient of several awards for her published work so far—three novels and a collection of short stories. Portela's first novel, *El pájaro: pincel y tinta china* (The Bird: Brush and Chinese Ink), was awarded the 1997 Cirilo Villaverde Prize of the Cuban Writers and Artists Union (UNEAC). It was published in 1999 by both Ediciones Unión, in Havana, Cuba, and Editorial Casiopea, in Barcelona, Spain. *Una extraña entre las piedras* (An Unknown among the Stones), a collection of short stories, appeared also in Havana in 1999. That same year Portela's short story "El viejo, el asesino y yo" (The Old Man, the Assassin and I) received the renowned Juan Rulfo Prize of Radio France International and was subsequently published in 2000 by Editorial Letras Cubanas. A second novel, *La sombra del caminante* (The Walker's Shadow), came out a year later, in 2001. A third novel, *Cien botellas en una pared* (One Hundred Bottles on a Wall), obtained in 2002 the Jaén Award for novel granted by Granada's Caja de Ahorros in Spain. It came out that same year, published by Debate, in Madrid, and a year later by Ediciones Unión, in Havana, and Editions Du Seuil, in Paris. In 2003 this novel was the recipient of the Dos Océanos-Grinzane Cavour prize that French critics award to the best Latin American novel appearing in France every two years. Following this warm reception, the novel was also published in translation in Portugal, Holland, and Poland, and further plans for publication have been announced in Greece, Turkey, and Italy. To have a novel written in highly colloquial Cuban slang translated into seven languages is quite an accomplishment for a writer of Portela's age, an achievement she attributes to a combination of hard work, talent, and luck, as well as the benefits of globalization. Portela is also the author of essays, testimonies, and criticism, which have been included in several anthologies, in addition to journals and periodicals in Cuba and abroad.

Portela's Generation in Cuban Literature

Even though Portela objects to being identified with a movement or generation, her name is usually mentioned alongside *los novísimos* (the newest ones), a group of Cuban writers known for their rupture with revolutionary aesthetics. While a majority of writers who came before the *novísimos* generally observed the parameters of Cuban-style social realism, which upheld the revolutionary ideals of the Cuban people since the coming to power of the socialist regime in 1959, those born between the end of the fifties and the beginning of the 1970s sought to disengage literature from any extraneous obligations, including the dictates of exalted nationalism. Instead of an ongoing emphasis on the utopian transformation of Cuban society, there was a shift toward experimenting with literary form. These writers also experimented with parody, intertextuality, the mix of "high" and popular culture, and narrative technique. Furthermore, they explored marginalization and otherness, especially the one stemming from sexual orientation.

After the fall of the Berlin Wall in 1989 and the subsequent collapse of the Soviet bloc, this generation of writers experienced the worst economic crisis faced by Cubans in recent times, which for a while prevented them from having their work appearing in print. The effects of the so-called Special Period, a euphemism for the ensuing shortages of every kind and the dubious moral standards these shortages sadly brought about, became in many instances the subject matter of the fiction these writers produced. Many chose to leave the island in search of better conditions to write and publish. Portela, however, chose to stay in Cuba for personal reasons, where she has since published all her work. She shares with the rest of the *novísimos* an interest in narrative experimentation, in her case, tied to a fascination with the darker side of the human being, including violence and criminality, all presented in a carefree, even humorous tone. One critic has said that Portela seeks to both "tingle and amuse". The absence of angst is a noteworthy feature of her work, as well as her eminently critical perspective. Portela keeps all ideologies and master narratives, including nationalism and feminism, at arm's length, claiming that they keep people from thinking independently. She goes beyond critiquing the Cuban political system to make a radical call for human liberation from all systems of thought she deems constraining. Although her work has never been censured, she has been denied the perks attached to official recognition, such as frequent travel and national major awards.

A Flair for the Frenzy of Violence

Portela's early stories as well as her first novel, *El pájaro: pincel y tinta china* (1999), contain some of the elements that would continue to turn up in her later narrative, such as the blurring of reality and fiction, the use of Cuban vernacular, the emphasis on writing and creative techniques, the reappearance of characters and allusions to incidents across the various texts, erotic desire in gay and lesbian relationships, the absence of family ties, and a myriad of cultural references that range from Shakespeare, Julia Kristeva and Polanski to figures closer to Cuban and Hispanic culture like Lourdes Casal and Federico García Lorca. Some also depict her penchant for the frenzy of violence.

La sombra del caminante (2001) is a dystopian novel that begins with a homicide and ends with the imminent death by suicide of the perpetrator. This is perhaps the only deference to justice found in a dense and sometimes inscrutable plot that piles one violent incident on top of another. Portela depicts a world where there is no certainty except for gratuitous violence and abuse. There is no certainty even with regard to the gender of the criminal protagonist, who alternates between Gabriela and Lorenzo. Although disturbing at the level of plot, the novel casts a spell on the reader, who keeps looking in vain for the rational causes of so much evil. Contributing to the spell is the dazzling writing displayed by this young, gifted novelist in command of her craft. The novel is set in contemporary Havana, a city that seems to offer no way out of an oppressive human landscape.

The built environment is just as dreary in Portela's third and most accessible novel, *Cien botellas en una pared* (2002), which takes place also in Havana during the critical 1990s. Zeta, the female protagonist of the novel, lives in a mansion located in the once stately neighborhood of El Vedado. The mansion, however, is far from offering any kind of refuge since it now houses over forty families whose needs for privacy and quiet are anything but met. Zeta has been abandoned by her father, a homosexual who left Cuba at the onset of the Special Period. The young woman gets involved with an older man who abuses her, but against her best friend's advice, does nothing to get rid of her lover; as a masochist, she actually derives pleasure from the abuse. The reader is introduced to marginal sectors of Cuban society made up of gays and lesbians, *jineteras* or prostitutes, and punks. Doing their best to survive under the circumstances, they all function semi-legally in quasi-autonomous communities that sometimes come face to face with the mainstream, with dire consequences. But even in this eccentric world there are selfless acts of kindness and thanks to one of these the novel ends on a positive note—a ray of hope uncommon in Portela's work and one that might signal an opening for optimism in her future writings.

Portela's still unpublished work includes a second collection of short stories, *Alguna enfermedad muy grave* (An Illness so Grave), and a new novel, *Djuna y Daniel* (Djuna and Daniel), about the life of Djuna Barnes in Paris, both of which are scheduled to appear in 2006–7. The novel was a challenge to write, since it required the use of standard Spanish. It also marks the first time that Portela has dipped into a non-Cuban subject.

This young writer is poised to become one of the most celebrated Cuban fiction writers of the beginning of the twenty-first century—no small feat in a country that has produced many prominent women poets but few outstanding novelists. Portela is a clever, audacious, cultured, and prolific writer who deserves broad recognition.

IRAIDA H. LÓPEZ

Selected Works

El pájaro: pincel y tinta china. La Habana: Ediciones Unión, 1999.
Una extraña entre las piedras. La Habana: Editorial Letras Cubanas, 1999.
"El viejo, el asesino y yo". *Revolución y cultura* 1, Época IV (Jan.–Feb. 2000): 46–52.
La sombra del caminante. La Habana: Ediciones Unión, 2001.
Cien botellas en una pared. Barcelona: Random House Mondadori, 2002.

References and Further Reading

Álvarez Oquendo, Saylín. "Negro sobre blanco: Blanco sobre negro . . . y no hace falta Malévich". *Encuentro* 39 (Winter 2005–6): 77–85.
Araújo, Nara. "The Sea, the Sea, Once and Again: *Lo cubano* and the Literature of the *Novísimas*." In Damián J. Fernández and Madeline Cámara Betancourt (eds), *Cuba, the Elusive Nation: Interpretations of National Identity*. Gainesville, FL: University Press of Florida, 2000, pp. 224–39.
——. "Erizar y divertir: La poética de Ena Lucía Portela". *Cuban Studies/Estudios cubanos* 32 (2001): 55–73.
Camacho, Jorge. "¿Quién le teme a Ena Lucía Portela?" May 15, 2006. http://habanaelegante.com/SpringSummer2006/Angel.html
Cámara, Madeline. "Antropofagia de los sexos como 'metáfora de incorporación' en 'La urna y el nombre (cuento jovial)' de Ena Lucía Portela". *Torre de papel* 7(3) (1997): 167–83.
Casamayor Cisneros, Odette. "¿Cómo vivir las ruinas habaneras de los años noventa? Respuestas disímiles desde la isla en las obras de Abilio Estévez, Pedro Juan Gutiérrez y Ena Lucía Portela". *Caribbean Studies* 32(2) (2004): 63–103.
Estévez, Abilio. "Ena Lucía Portela: un 'frisson nouveau'". Prologue to Ena Lucía Portela, *El pájaro: pincel y tinta china*. Barcelona: Editorial Casiopea, 1998, pp. 9–14.
López, Iraida H. Personal correspondence with the author.
Lys Valdés, Sandra. "¿Género y nación? en *El Pájaro: pincel y tinta china*, de Ena Lucía Portela". *La Gaceta de Cuba* 4 (July–Aug. 2000): 44–7.

PORZECANSKI, TERESA

Teresa Porzecanski was born in 1945, in Montevideo, Uruguay, to a family of Jewish immigrants who came from the Baltic on her father's side, while her mother's family were from Syria, and of Sephardic origin. In addition to being one of Uruguay's most prolific literary authors, Porzecanski's formal training is in social work and cultural anthropology with a specialization in ethnography. Her work has earned her several important literary prizes, including the Montevideo Municipal Prize (1986), a Fulbright award (1988), a Guggenheim Foundation fellowship (1992), and the Premio de la Crítica Bartolomé Hidalgo (Bartolomé Hidalgo Criticism Prize (1995)). Her fiction has been included in a wide variety of anthologies and her work has been translated into English, Dutch, German, and French.

Jewish Identities

Teresa Porzecanski approaches the matter of Jewish identity in her work—both fiction and nonfiction alike—from at least two distinct perspectives. Being from a family of both Ashkenazi (Eastern European) and Sephardic (Iberian) origins, the finds in these two Jewish traditions fertile ground for storytelling. In her nonfiction studies that reveal her education as a cultural anthropologist, *Historias de vida de inmigrantes judíos al Uruguay* and *El universo cultural del idisch* (1992), Porzecanski mixes ethnography, history, testimony, and social analysis to chronicle the saga of immigration to Uruguay. Both books are important documents for the information that she painstakingly collected in order to detail the Jewish experience in her native country. In her fiction, Porzecanski is able to delve into this experience more freely. While Jewishness has formed a component of her writing from the beginning, it is in her more recent works that it comprises the main focus of the narrative. For example, in the novel *Mesías en Montevideo* (1989, Messiah in Montevideo) the fragmented plot provides parallel narrative threads that explore similarities between a leftist guerilla leader and Shabbtai Tzevi as (false) messianic figures while contrasting seventeenth-century pogroms with the turbulent violence of 1960s Uruguay. Representations of the Sephardic past seemingly opened up avenues that Porzecanski takes up in subsequent books beginning with *Perfumes de cartago* (1994, Perfumes of Carthage), for which she was awarded the Guggenheim fellowship. Like *Mesías*, in this novel, the social reality of Uruguay in the 1930s is juxtaposed with that of Sephardic history. In this case, Porzecanski obviously draws on her maternal ancestry and her own family's story of having to abandon Syria and emigrate to Uruguay. In *La piel del alma* (1996, The Soul's Skin), the narrative format is similar and takes place a generation later in the 1950s. Again, the unfolding sociopolitical circumstances of Uruguay converge with fifteenth-century Toledo, Spain—the site of Jewish persecution and suffering. Jewishness melds with Uruguayan and broader social realities in a much more experimental way in *La invención de los soles* (1979, Sun Inventions), one of her early novels. The main character of the novel is the daughter of Jewish immigrants who narrates a disjointed tale told by piecing fragments of stories together. Family history and human holocausts come together in the form of pogroms, Auschwitz, Hiroshima, and disappearances carried out by military regimes. Style and form take precedence over plot and theme in this fragmented tale in which chronological time has little meaning, language unravels, and narrative conventions fall apart. These elements in the novel have led to the study of *La invención de los soles* as a prime example of experimental, postmodernist literature by critics (Payne; Barr). Lois Barr examines Porzecanski's fiction mainly from a Jewish studies approach, but in general finds it to be characteristically subversive in the way that it systematically seeks to undermine patriarchal authority.

Other Fictions

Porzecanski is the author of several short story collections. Principal among them are *El acertijo y otros cuentos* (1967, The Riddle and Other Stories), *Historias para mi abuela* (1970, Stories for My Grandmother), *Construcciones* (1979, Constructions), and *La respiración es una fragua* (1989, Breath Is a Forge). Her stories often focus on simple settings, common occurrences, and the stuff of everyday life with an almost dirty realist attention to the grungy details but often with a twist reminiscent of the fantastic so common in River Plate literature. One of Porzecanski's more intriguing novels is the 1986 *Una novela erótica* (An Erotic Novel) for the way in which she inverts the patriarchal paradigm of eroticism as a male domain. In a plot line that is somewhat suggestive of Mario Vargas Llosa's *La tía Julia y el escribidor* (*Aunt Julia and the Scriptwriter*; 1977), the main character writes and broadcasts radio melodramas around which most of the action develops. The novel is written with a good deal of humor and irony. For example, the narrator searches for romantic stories in unusual places, such as tale about a sperm and an egg. Likewise, she returns to beginnings with stories of Adam and Eve as well as pre-historic man. Once again, Porzecanski's training as an anthropologist seeps into the text, not only in the form of one of the characters, but more significantly in the manner in which love and eroticism is scrutinized as relating to cultural and gender-specific values. Porzecanski's text avoids explicit sexual narrative by representing a system of erotics that relies on language to create unique metaphors and symbols for the expressive of sexual desire. Indeed, language is key to the novel's development of a decidedly feminocentric erotic agenda. Much of Porzecanski's fiction can be identified with an overt preoccupation to represent female agency and empowerment in opposition to patriarchal control over their lives and individuality. In addition to *Una novela erótica*, the 2002 novel *Felicidades fugaces* (Fleeting Happiness) is an excellent example of just such a narrative program. Returning to the Montevideo of the 1950s, Porzecanski creates an environment populated by female characters who all live in the same building and who go about constructing their lives largely without the influence of male intervention.

In sum, Porzecanski's writing is unique and multifaceted in its approach. Her literature tends to meld fantasy with reality, draw parallels between different historical events and periods, and address issues of identity while experimenting with form and language.

DARRELL B. LOCKHART

Selected Works

El acertijo y otros cuentos. Montevideo: Editorial Arca, 1967.
Historias para mi abuela. Montevideo: Letras, 1970.
Esta manzana roja. Montevideo: Letras, 1972.
Intacto el corazón. Montevideo: Banda Oriental, 1976.
Construcciones: Montevideo: Editorial Arca, 1979.
La invención de los soles. Stockholm: Nordan, 1979.
Ciudad impune. Montevideo: Monte Sexto, 1986.
Una novela erótica. Montevideo: Margen, 1986.
Historias de vida de inmigrantes judíos al Uruguay. Montevideo: Comunidad Israelita de Montevideo, 1988.
Mesías en Montevideo. Montevideo: Signos, 1989.
La respiración es una fragua. Montevideo: Trilce, 1989.
El universo cultural del idisch. Montevideo: Kehila—Comunidad Israelita del Uruguay, 1992.
Perfumes de Cartago. Montevideo: Trilce: 1994.
La piel del alma. Montevideo: Seix Barral / Planeta, 1996.
Sun Inventions and Perfumes of Carthage: Two Novellas. Trans. Johnny Payne and Phyllis Silverstein. Albuquerque, NM: University of New Mexico Press, 2000.
Felicidades fugaces. Montevideo: Planeta, 2002.

References and Further Reading

Barr, Lois Baer. "Recreating the Code: Teresa Porzecanski". In Lois Baer Barr (ed.), *Isaac Unbound: Patriarchal Traditions in the Latin American Jewish Novel*. Tempe, AZ: ASU Center for Latin American Studies, 1995, pp. 159–82.
Flori, Mónica. "De almíbares, perfumes y sedas: La recuperación histórico-biográfica en *Perfumes de Cartago* de Teresa Porzecanski". *Alba de América* 17(32) (1999): 235–43.
Horan, Elizabeth Rosa. "Emigrant Memory: Jewish Women Writers in Chile and Uruguay". In Marjorie Agosín (ed.), *Passion, Memory, and Identity: Twentieth-Century Latin American Jewish Women Writers*. Albuquerque, NM: University of New Mexico Press, 1999, pp. 115–60.
Payne, Johnny. "Cutting Up History: The Uses of Aleatory Fiction in Teresa Porzecanski and Harry Matthews". In Johnny Payne, *Conquest of the New Word: Experimental Fiction and Translation in the Americas*. Austin, TX: University of Texas Press, 1993, pp. 76–98.
Scott, Renée. "La experiencia sefardí en Latinoamérica: Tres novelas de Teresa Porzecanski y Rosa Nissán". *Sefarad: Revista de Estudios Hebraicos, Sefardíes y de Oriente Próximo* 58(2) (1998): 387–99.
Valverde, Estela. *Banquetes eróticos y perfumes letales: los mundos de Teresa Porzecanski*. Montevideo: Linardi y Risso, 2005.

PRADO, ADÉLIA

Adélia Luzia Prado de Freitas was born on 13 December 1935, in Divinópolis, in the state of Minas Gerais, Brazil, where she has lived ever since. The memories of her childhood in this peaceful and essentially religious place are a constant presence in her works, always imbued with a colorful tone of yearning for a past of material poverty mingled with the riches of affectionate relationships.

Divinópolis, with approximately 200,000 souls at the beginning of this century, owed its development to activities connected with ore mining and its Catholic traditions, a condition similar to that of a large portion of the state of Minas Gerais in the southwest of Brazil. Mining brought with it the railway, where Adélia's father, João do Prado Filho, worked. Her mother, Ana Clotildes Correa, divided her time between household chores and religious devotion. Suffering from a heart condition made worse by pregnancy, she died in childbirth aged 35, leaving four children, Adélia, her eldest aged 15, at the time.

Adélia Prado acknowledges the relationship with her family and their traditions, and the influence her parents had on her, when she declares:

> I know exactly what their tribute is, his contribution and her contribution. Hers—a melancholia, a taste for poignant, ejaculatory prayers. His—faith in life, in resurrection, in the meaning of life. That is a portrait of a psychological nature: that is my spiritual heritage.
>
> (Prado 1996)

Although writing from her childhood and adolescence, and having counted on her family's support for her educational successes in the area of letters, it was in the situations of loss and mourning that her poetry rose and began to be acknowledged. Her mother's death was what led her to write that which she believes to be her first poem, when she was undergoing her last year in secondary school. The loss of her mother is present in a number of passages in her works. In the book *Quero minha mãe* (I Want My Mother), of 2005, the character's experience, written in poetic prose, coincides with the author's autobiographical notes:

> . . . Poor mother, she might have been in that state of anguish the day she hit me: "Worthless shit". She certainly did not stand the idea, the burden of having to handle and put up with those greasy clothes of my father's, with that murky liquid in the basin, reeking of black soap, and her looking forward to having a spare time to read, even if for the thousandth time, my school handbook, the ADOREMUS, the REVISTA DE SANTO ANTONIO. Mother, what a tough and short life, your life. She forbade my wearing a small wrist watch, but was not able to forbid my staying atop the bank in the late afternoon watching the workers leaving the plant, she knew I would fathom the reason. Two women, we communicated with each other. Are you happy, mother? You don't mind staying home, do you? Can I go to the park with Dorita? Are you going to call aunt Ceição to come over and chat with you? Not even to the school party, neither to the parade to see me bearing the flag, did she go. It wouldn't do going with a "ladies' coat". Because it was daylight, and hot and sunny. It took me fifty years to understand.
>
> (p. 41)

As can be seen, even after thirty years from the time of her first published works, the author's historical, geographical and cultural context bears a strong presence in her work.

Religion is one of the issues most discussed when the subject is Adélia Prado, and it is she who says

> This religion, which was part of my development, my inner view, my feeling of the world, is something that shows up unequivocally in my work. My work has this religious register, both in poetry and in prose. However, along with that, it is not only that. It is really something vital for me.

And she further reasserts: "a poetic experience is, in its ultimate and first nature, a religious experience" (Prado 1996).

Adélia Prado's name cannot go unmentioned when mention is made of authors who relate poetic experience to a religious one. To her, the expression of beauty, transcendence, the sublime, all is closely related to the quest for contact with the Divine. This aspect of the author's work is the theme for the works of critics Moliterno (2002), Huamán (1999), La Rosa (1995), Olivieri (1994), in addition to innumerable texts in literary sections of newspapers and periodicals.

In the opinion of Frei Betto, the poetry of Adélia Prado "is profanely religious" (20000, p. 121) because in it there is nothing that will not want for God's presence: the sensory experiences, the body, the sex, the rapture, the inner life surface or the depths of the human soul. Religion to her is an experience, not just a doctrine. Experience unutterable otherwise, other than in poetic language: "God does not exist in a manner thinkable" (Poem "Não blasfemo"—"I don't blaspheme", from *A faca no peito,* The Knife in the Heart, 1988).

In her work, this can be easily seen, as in the following poem from *Oráculo de Maio* (1999):

> **Human rights**
> I know God lives in me
> as his best house.
> I am his panoramic view,
> his alchemic retort
> and to his joy
> his two eyes.
> But this lyric is mine.

Associated with the issue of a substantially Catholic religiosity, it is possible to observe the idea that suffering is inherent in the human condition as is the quest for overcoming this condition.

> In fact, we are in a vale of tears; with no way to escape (. . .) the human condition is sheer pain. I can say pain or sin; to me it is the same thing. (. . .) Joy is quest, aim. And this joy, what is it? It could be the union with God, the triumph over the human condition.
>
> (Instituto Moreira Salles 2000, p. 22)

In face of the suffering inherent in the human condition, Adélia Prado brings together the religious experience and the artistic expression as a way to triumph and to proximity to God. "It arises out of art, a new path for the soul" (Prado 1996), she asserts. For her, then, the poet has a mystic role, serving as herald and translator, who, with a poetic language, shapes experience's transcendent aspects. "Das tripas coração"—"From your innards you make a heart"—is a popular expression she makes a poetic use of to define Art ("Arte", *Oráculo de Maio*, 1999, The Oracle of May), and can be translated into: out of the visceral sensibility that makes personal the pain in the world, come feeling, the meaning of life and beauty. A psychological study of the author and her creative process can be found in Melo (2002).

Suffering, which once vanquished turns into glory, and the possibility of coloring pain with beauty, can also been seen in her verses: "When I was fifteen years old, my mother died. / It was suffering most beautiful, / the green life such a beautiful pasture. I yelped beautifully, / a calf without her mother, simply that" ("Impropérios," in *O coração disparado*, The Headlong Heart, 1978).

The tendency to mobilize in situations involving suffering points to the fact that, similarly to the first poem that came out following her mother's death, it was only in 1972, when her father died, that she turned to a truly and admittedly literary production that led to the publication of her first book.

Prior to this, she was educated at state-owned schools, graduating as a school teacher. In 1958, she married José Assunção de Freitas, a clerk in Banco do Brasil, with whom she has had five children. Working as a teacher both before and after getting married and having children, she was encouraged to quit the classroom by her husband, who had sensed her lack of satisfaction with teaching (Prado 1996).

She graduated in Philosophy in 1973, having enrolled on this course together with her husband in 1965. About this, she wrote: "I took a course in Philosophy to brush up my mind, / it did not pay" ("Tabaréu," in *Bagagem,* 1976, Luggage).

Her literary background is broad. As a child she used to read enthusiastically religious themes: from the Bible to the orthodox Russian religion passing through such Catholic mystics as St John of the Cross and St Teresa of Ávila and many others. In her adolescence, her contact with the work of romantic and pre-modernist authors was markedly important, leading her to write in imitation of authors such as Olavo Bilac and Augusto dos Anjos in her moralistic sonnets (Prado 1996).

In special, in the realm of Brazilian literature, she acknowledges João Guimarães Rosa, Clarice Lispector and Carlos Drummond de Andrade to be those with whom she identified, with a feeling of ownership, when she decided she was a writer. She was in quest of her own diction. When her first book was published, she gained confidence and eventually discovered her true vocation. João Guimarães Rosa was also a native of Minas Gerais, and had a regional style rife with neologisms arising from colloquial language and popular speech; Clarice Lispector was a writer whose woman's voice is specially remarkable for its psychological depth, and Carlos Drummond de Andrade is considered by many the greatest Brazilian poet of all times, and regarded as being Adélia Prado's "godfather" for having presented her to the public on a chronicle published in *Jornal do Brasil* (Andrade 1975).

Adélia Prado's first book, *Bagagem* (Luggage), of 1976 is, as the name attests, evidence of what she carries with her and can show. The book begins with "Com licença poética" (With a Poetic License), a poem in which she offers her perception of her mission as a woman and a writer, and her faith in her ability of success: ". . . what I feel, I write, I fulfill my destiny. / I inaugurate language, I establish kingdoms / – pain is not bitterness. / My sorrow has no pedigree, / yet my craving for happiness, / its roots reaches my thousandth grandfather./ To be lame in life, it is a curse to man. / Woman is unfoldable. I am".

The above poem attests to the importance of Drummond in Adélia Prado's art organization, as both an influence and an interlocutor. In it, one can see a clear intertextuality with the verses of his "Poema de sete faces" (Poem of Seven Faces), a fact that attracted marked attention due to the courage and boldness of the then novice writer. It can be observed that while Drummond assumes the tough male look, the "lame angel" and the "curse", as negative signs associated with his being born as a man, Prado claims "a graceful angel, / out of those who blow the trumpet", and being "unfoldable", among other qualities associated to her condition of being a woman. Silva (1984) offers a detailed study of the opposing nature of the two poems.

When Affonso Romano de Sant'Anna, a renowned Brazilian writer, sent Drummond a few poems by Adélia Prado, Drummond had already been sent by Adélia herself the originals of her first book. Sant'Anna at that time was writing reviews for an important periodical of national circulation, and would write the preface for Prado's second book (*O coração disparado,* 1978). Apparently, it was thanks to Drummond and Sant'Anna that Adélia Prado was made visible and attracted the attention of publisher Pedro Paulo de Sena Madureira, who published her work for the first time with the seal of Imago publishing house, of Rio de Janeiro.

It is worth mentioning that when her talent was made known, Adélia Prado was already a mature woman. It is around 1976, at the age of 40, that what she considers to be her literary beginning.

Her rise, however, was not free from criticism. Formal disengagement, daily life themes, liturgical fervor, or a pretense to populism, were the most frequent allegations for attacks. Examples of that can be found in Proença Filho (1983) and Lucas (1982).

In order to understand this resistance to her work, it is worth noting that the author rose in Brazil of the 1970s, under military dictatorship. Brazil relied on art in order to survive the strict censorship imposed to all types of cultural manifestation. Many of those who criticized Prado seemed to expect that, amid so much violence, all who had a voice (authors, for instance) would use it to protest and to raise public awareness. But that was not Prado's point.

References to the Brazilian political situation appear at times, for instance in the poem she wrote when President Juscelino Kubitscheck died: "The president dies: it is a good reason. / I take this opportunity and cry the Brazilian people" ("Um bom motivo," in *Coração disparado*, 1978). In "O falsete" (The Falsetto), Prado mentions the torture, the silence imposed and the despair of mothers whose children were killed by the military dictatorship, and in *Terra de Santa Cruz* (Land of the Holy Cross), she pays homage to Frei Tito, who committed suicide in Paris after being victimized by torture in Brazil.

The two last poems mentioned above are in the book *Terra de Santa Cruz*, of 1981, a reference to the second name given to Brazil by the Portuguese around the time of the discovery. The intention for the book's title seems clear: the cross imposed on Christ symbolizes the sacrifice and the suffering imposed on the Brazilian people.

Hohlfedt explains the initial criticisms to the author as being related to the context of her emergence:

> In fact, Adélia Prado rises amid a productive literary movement then prevailing in Minas Gerais . . . And

> what is more, Brazilian poetry was undergoing a certain dichotomy: on the one hand, the varied formal experimentalisms arising out of the concretism and the tropicalism from the fifities onwards and, on the other hand, the quest—starting in the 1960s and following the military coup of 1964—for the retaking of the politico-ideological poetry. Adélia Prado's poetry, however, will be neither the one nor the other.
>
> (2000, p. 72)

Another consideration is that her themes did not follow the vanguard and feminist movements of the time. A literature in which the condition of women is a target for a close and intimate reflection rather than ideological reflection, would hardly find doors open in the political and cultural framework of Brazil in the seventies.

Often a character in her own work, Adélia Prado speaks up on behalf of women: "... but (also) not against the sweetness or the household condition of women, to which greatness and dignity is given" (Miranda 2000: 131).

Although in the beginning readers were not able to identify how, Prado showed, from the moment she debuted in poetry writing, that she in her own way was against patriarchy. However, it is in her prose texts, coming to light in 1979, that she definitely clarifies her ideas on the feminine and on the relationship between the sexes, such themes having generated many studies among which those by Carlson-Leavitt (1989), Guerra (1992), Puzzo (1997), Kirk (2004) all of which in the form of thesis. In addition, Camargo (1989), Hollanda (1994) and Soares (1999) wrote essays and articles in books.

One example of Prado's peculiar look at women and marriage, without any feminist or submission claims, is clearly shown in the poem "Casamento" (Marriage) (in *Terra de Santa Cruz*, of 1981):

> Marriage
> There are women who say:
> My husband, if he wishes to go fishing, let him,
> but he must clean the fish.
> Not me. At night, any time, I get up,
> help scale, open, slice and salt.
> It is so good, just us alone in the kitchen,
> our elbows rubbing together at times,
> he says things like "this one was tough"
> "shaking its silvery tail-fin in the air"
> And he gestures with his hand.
> The silence of the time we first saw each other
> goes through the kitchen like a deep river.
> At last, the fish in the platter,
> we go to bed.
> Silvery things suddenly appear:
> we are bride and groom.

Similarly to what is in the above poem, there is evidence in both her poetry and her prose the disguise that hints at her own self: the "unfolding" of the character Adélia. Her experiences are her harvests, and the taste for thinking the everyday routine is explicit: sounds, smells, flavors, shapes, colors, sensations, all permeate her work in a clear, experimental tendency, as Carneiro sets out in his thesis for a master's degree in Literature and Culture Diversity, 2004.

Following the publication of her first works, the commentaries by critics and literates begin to show a better understanding of her purpose, as is shown in the commentaries of poet Ferreira Gullar "the religious view, in her, is perfectly integrated in her life proper, as a way of being ... A complacent God who is not against the need in the animal body for pleasure and whose kindness is not questioned by human misery either" (1984, p. 10).

Like all other sensations, the body and sexuality are sources of inspiration for Prado. Miranda on this, writes: "Adélia Prado is a writer and a powerful woman, with her literary personality, without renouncing her true nature, she prizes the feminine way of thinking, with enhanced feelings, love, sensuality" (2000, p. 131). Feminine sexuality and desire are, also, recurrent themes in her work and the object of theoretical and critical studies, as seen in Soares (1999; 2005) and Bahia (1994).

Sensuality meets religiosity in Adélia Prado in the character shown for the first time in *O coração disparado* (1979): Eliud Jonathan, a heteronym for Jesus. This character appears more frequently in the book *O pelicano* (1987, The Pelican), simply as Jonathan.

> Weeping to move Jonathan
> Diamonds, are they indestructible?
> More is my love.
> The sea, is it vast?
> My love is vaster,
> more beautiful, without ornaments,
> than a field with flowers.
> More sorrowful than death
> more hopeless
> than the wave breaking against the rocks,
> more tenacious than the rock.
> It loves, and not even knows what it loves.

And then, in the page following, in the poem "O sacrifício" – "the Sacrifice", the confirmation of what was assumed: "Jonathan is Jesus".

It is in *O pelicano* that Adélia Prado shows, explicitly, the nature of her religious convictions and the link that exists, to her, between experience, God and poetic language: "When you see and wonder, you face a poetic phenomenon which, deep inside, is religious, you are beholding the nature of things that leads to the being par excellence that is God" (Prado 1996).

"God is the Logos and the son of God is the Word" (Instituto Moreira Sales 2000: 24). Thus, her passion for Jonathan-Jesus-Word-Poetry is also her passion for life, for experience and for the feeling of rejoicing that is associated with the creative act.

Prado composes free, unrhymed verses, though many of her poems are cadenced and sonorous. Free is also her poetic prose, which publishers and publishing houses find difficult to classify, now and then categorizing it as chronicle or tale.

On the whole, one major characteristic of her work is the fact that her books are split into blocks which are interrelated. Many of these open with epigraphs she adapts using biblical sayings to serve her purposes. A few other books open with epigraphs using the words of Guimarães Rosa. In addition, Prado usually begins her works with longer blocks and closes them with one block containing one single poem. Hohlfeldt

(2000) gives in his essay a detailed description and the interpretations likely to be made of this habit of Adélia Prado, showing her intentionality in every one of her works.

In addition to producing books, Prado directed an amateur theater group in 1980. Her love of the theater and the rhythm and cadence of her poetry soon caught the attention of producers, actors and other people involved in the world of the arts: she participated, together with Fernanda Montenegro, a renowned Brazilian actress, in the adaptation for the theater of a few of her poems, for the play *Dona Doida: um interlúdio* (Crazy Woman: an Interlude), performed under the direction of Naum Alves de Souza, in 1987, at Teatro Delfim, in São Paulo.

Another play, *Duas horas da tarde no Brasil* (Two p.m. in Brazil), was an adaptation of Adélia Prado's work, by her daughter Ana Beatriz Prado and Kalluh Araújo, staged at Teatro Sesi Minas, in Belo Horizonte in 1996. A dance show on her work, created by Teresa Ricco with music by Marku Ribas and directed by Rui Moreira, was staged at Teatro Clara Nunes, in Belo Horizonte, in 1999. In 2000, based on *Manuscrito de Felipa* (Felipa's Manuscript), José Rubens Siqueira adapted the monologue *Dona de casa* (Housewife), staged by Georgette Fadel.

Prado also delivers lectures and gives interviews not only to those interested in literature but also to, among others, journalists, philosophers, theologians, psychologists, as well as to different types of social and educative institutions in Brazil and abroad.

SANDRA AUGUSTA DE MELO

Selected Works

Poetic Work

Bagagem. Rio de Janeiro: Imago, 1976.
O coração disparado. Rio de Janeiro: Nova Fronteira, 1978.
Terra de Santa Cruz. Rio de Janeiro: Nova Fronteira, 1981.
O pelicano. Rio de Janeiro: Nova Fronteira, 1987.
Faca no peito. Rio de Janeiro: Rocco, 1988.
Oráculos de maio. São Paulo: Siciliano, 1999.
Poesia reunida. São Paulo: Siciliano, 1999.
Vida doida. Porto Alegre: Alegoria, 2006.

Stories

Solte os cachorros. Rio de Janeiro: Nova Fronteira, 1979.
Cacos para um vitral. Rio de Janeiro: Nova Fronteira, 1980.
Os componentes da banda. Rio de Janeiro: Nova Fronteira, 1984.
O homem da mão seca. São Paulo: Siciliano, 1994.
Manuscritos de Felipa. São Paulo: Siciliano, 1999.
Filandras. São Paulo: Record, 2001.
Quero minha mãe. São Paulo: Record, 2005.

Co-authored Stories

with Lázaro Barreto. *A lapinha de Jesus*. São Paulo: Vozes, 1969.
with Lya Luft, Frei Betto, and others. *Caminhos de solidariedade*. São Paulo: Gente, 2001.

Children's Literature

2006 *Quando eu era pequena*. São Paulo: Record. Ilustrations by Elisabeth Teixeira.

Participation in Anthologies

Prado, Adélia *et al. Contos mineiros*. São Paulo: Ática, 1984.
Hortas, Maria de Lurdes (ed.) *Palavra de mulher*. Rio de Janeiro: Fontoura, 1989.
Embaixada do Brasil em Pequim. (1) *Antologia da poesia brasileira*. Trans. Zhao Deming. Pequim/China. Departamento Nacional do livro / Fundação Biblioteca Nacional, 1994.
Brasil, Assis (ed.) *A poesia mineira no século XX*. Rio de Janeiro: Imago, 1998.

Translated into English

"Thirteen poems". Trans. Ellen Watson. *The American Post's Supplement*. Jan/Feb. 1984.
The Headlong Heart. Trans. Ellen Watson. New York: Livingston University Press, 1988.
The Alphabet in the Park. Trans. Ellen Watson. Middletown, CT: Wesleyan University Press, 1990.

Translated into Spanish

1994 *El corazón disparado*. Trans. Cláudia Schwartz and Fernando Roy. Buenos Aires: Leviatan.
(to be published). *Bagagem*. Trans. José Francisco Navarro Huamán. México: Universidade Ibero-Americana.

Lectures on DVD

The human condition according to Adélia Prado: class administered at the Course of Graduation in Clinical Psychology at USP. São Paulo: Livraria Resposta, May 4. Digital media (DVD). 2005.

Website

http://virtualbooks.terra.com.br/padregabriel/adeliaprado/links_adelia.htm

References and Further Reading

Andrade, Carlos Drummond de. "De animais, santo e gente". *Jornal do Brasil*. 9 (October 1975).
Bahia, Mariza F. "Entre o corpo e a palavra: a poética de sedução, paixão e fé de Adélia Prado". Master's Diss. Rio de Janeiro, Universidade Federal do Rio de Janeiro, 1994.
Betto, Frei. "Adélia nos prados do Senhor". In Instituto Moreira Salles *Cadernos de Literatura Brasileira* 9 (June 2000).
Camargo, Ana M. de (ed.) *Feminino singular: a participação da mulher na literatura brasileira contemporânea*. São Paulo and Rio Claro: Edições GRD and Arquivo Municipal de Rio Claro, 1989.
Carneiro, Claudilis da S.O. "Epifanias do real: o olhar lírico de Adélia Prado". Diss. Feira de Santana / B.A. Universidade Estadual de Feira de Santana.2004.
Carlson-Leavitt, Joyce-Anne. "Gilka Machado and Adélia Prado: Two Brazilian Women Poets. Vision of the Female Experience". Diss. Albuquerque, University of New México, 1989
Guerra, Valéria Ribeiro. "A vertigem e os cacos: o feminino e a prosa de Adélia Prado". Diss. Rio de Janeiro, Pontifícia Universidade Católica, 1992.
Gullar, Ferreira. "Uma poesia brasileira". Belo Horizonte, *Suplemento Literário de Minas Gerais* 925 (23 June 1984): 10.
Hohlfeldt, Antônio. "A epifania da condição feminina". In Instituto Moreira Salles, *Cadernos de Literatura Brasileira* 9 (2000).
Hollanda, Heloísa Buarque de (ed.) *Tendências e impasses – o feminino como crítica da cultura*. Rio de Janeiro: Rocco, 1994.
Huamán, José Francisco Navarro. "La poesia, la más ínfima, es serva de la esperanza. La mística de la vida cotidiana en la poesia de Adélia Prado". Diss. Cidade do México. Universidad Iberoamericana, 1999.
Instituto Moreira Salles. *Cadernos de Literatura Brasileira* 9 (2000).
Kirk, Stephanie L. "'Eu sou filha de Deus': some observations on religion and gender in Adélia Prado's Bagagem". *Luso-Brazilian Review*. University of Wisconsin, 41(2) (2004): 42–55.
La Rosa, Gisela Campos Álamo de. "A experiência mística na prosa de Adélia Prado". Diss. Rio de Janeiro: Pontifícia Universidade Católica, 1995.

Lucas, Fábio. "O escritor e a literatura na sociedade brasileira". In Lucas Fábio (ed.), *Razão e emoção literária*. São Paulo: Livraria Duas Cidades, 1982.

Melo, Sandra Augusta de. *Duas vezes Adélia: a transfiguração criativa da realidade*. Rio de Janeiro: Sotese, 2002.

Miranda, Ana. "Um rosto marcado pela História das mulheres". In Instituto Moreira Salles, *Cadernos de Literatura Brasileira* 9 (2000).

Moliterno, Isabel de Andrade. "A poesia e o sagrado: traços do estilo de Adélia Prado". São Paulo: Universidade de São Paulo, 2002.

Olivieri, Rita de Cássia da Silva. "Mística e erotismo na poesia de Adélia Prado". Thesis. São Paulo: Universidade de São Paulo, 1994.

Prado, Adélia. "Entrevista concedida a Sandra Augusta de Melo". *Divinópolis*, MG (17 June 1996).

Proença Filho, Domício. *O livro do seminário*. São Paulo: LR Editora / Bienal Nestlé de Literatura de 1982, 1983.

Puzzo, Miriam Bauab. "A condição feminina na literatura brasileira: Cecília Meirelles e Adélia Prado". Diss. São Paulo: Universidade de São Paulo, 1997.

Silva, Irene Vieira da. "Bagagem de Adélia Prado: uma poética do desdobramento". Diss. SP. Universidade Estadual Paulista, Assis/SP, 1984.

Soares, Angélica M. S. *A paixão emancipatória: vozes femininas da liberação do erotismo na poesia brasileira*. Rio de Janeiro: DIFEL, 1999.

——. "Extensões erótico-religiosas nas 'Fantasias do céu', de Adélia Prado". *Poesia sempre* 20 (2005): 53–64.

PUGA, MARÍA LUISA

María Luisa Puga (1944–2004) was born in Mexico City. After the death of her mother, 9-year-old María Luisa and her three siblings went to live with their maternal grandmother in Acapulco. Following her father's second marriage, the family moved to Mazatlán where she completed her university studies. When Puga was 24, she went to London where she worked for the newspaper *The Economist*. After spending a number of years in Europe, she moved to Nairobi, Kenya, with her then husband who worked for the United Nations. After an absence that lasted ten years, she returned to Mexico in 1978 and in August of 1984, she settled in a cabin that she and her longtime companion designed in the woods of the small tranquil town of Zirahuén, Michoacán. The serenity of Lake Zirahuén, the woods surrounding it, and the enormous tree (that she named Esteban) viewed from the window of her studio provided Puga with a setting that distanced her from the cultural agglomeration of city life yet allowed her to remain in contact with the Mexican people and culture.

Puga began keeping a diary when she was 9 years old, in an attempt to understand her mother's death and to fill the void, accumulating about two hundred notebooks during her lifetime. Unlike many of her contemporaries, her only desire was to write and her only profession was that of a writer. She was a dedicated and very versatile writer, and her works include novels, volumes of short stories, such as *Inmóvil sol secreto* and *Intentos*, and children books, such as *El tornado* and *Los tenis acatarrados*. Likewise, Puga wrote very diverse texts such as *Cuando rinde el horno* and *La cerámica de Hugo X. Velázquez*, where storytelling and the interview come together, and *La crónica*, where she illustrates an itinerary of words. Some of her works have been translated into English and French and have appeared in various magazines and are included in several anthologies. In addition to writing, she was active in the academic world coordinating literary and writing workshops, and participating in national and international conferences. She organized literary workshops in Pátzcuaro and Morelia, Michoacán, until her health no longer permitted it. Some of the magazines and journals with which she collaborated include *Revista de la Universidad de México, Revista de Bellas Artes, La Jornada, La Plaza, Nexus, El Universal* and *Unomásuno.*

She won several awards, including the Xavier Villarrutia Award for *Pánico o peligro* in 1983 and the Juan Ruiz de Alarcón National Award in 1996 for her literary contribution. In December 2003, she was honored in Morelia by the Michoacan Institute of Culture for her role as a writer and for her endless contributions to workshops for children and adults. Puga continued to write until her death because it was the only way she knew how to deal with the physical pain, the insomnia and the desperation caused by a series of ailments. At the time of her death, she was working on a novel and left two unpublished novels that may be published posthumously.

Themes and Influences

In spite of the relatively few published studies, critics have recognized the value of María Luisa Puga's literary output, and her work is included among the leading Mexican literature of the last decades of the twentieth century. Some critics situate Puga's works within a new, yet to be officially named, period of realism because of the use of simple language and the apparent simple storytelling technique. This writing style allows the exploration of the socio-psychological makeup of the self in a specific context. In addition to the search for an identity, the writing process, which includes the blending of genres, and history are common themes in Puga's works, providing a unifying thread to her literary output. Critics attest that Puga examines the social aspects of Mexico from 1968 to present by telling a personal story and by demonstrating how the history of the time affects the protagonists in their search for an identity, thus giving her works an autobiographical tone. The narrative also highlights the author's concern about the ongoing Mexican societal problems, which include poverty, corruption, the conflict between men and women, the generational gap and the struggle for self-realization. As a narrator, Puga has an innate ability to truly know the characters and allow them to be the ones expressing their innermost thoughts, feelings, and conflicts. Similarly she engages the reader in the various levels of the narrative, including the creative process.

Puga's first novel, *Las posibilidades del odio* (1978) narrates the diverse identities and life styles originating with colonialism, and it exposes the injustice and corruption experienced daily from the point of view of a young white man of British descent living in Nairobi. In the final story of the six that compose the novel, the reader experiences the injustice from the perspective of Nyambura, a young African girl who becomes a minority representative when she is sent to study in Rome, and comes to realize that only in her native Kenya can she reaffirm her own identity. This novel generated a great deal of critical attention because of its rather exotic topic, the narrative style and the author's skillful technique of presenting Mexico's problematic situation as a developing country by paralleling the story of Kenya's seventy-year struggle for a better future. The award-winning *Pánico o peligro* (1983) is often seen as representative of Puga's work and is her most studied novel to date. This novel narrates the constant effort to find meaning to everyday rituals that provide security in contrast with the violence that is embedded in city life. It reads like the personal diary of three middle-class girlfriends as they walk through Avenida Insurgentes in Mexico City. At the same time, the notebooks that the protagonist, Susana, writes represent her life and transformation from an insecure and dependent young girl to a mature, independent and satisfied woman. The protagonist's preoccupation with the creative process and her need to write in an attempt to search for her identity and her own space mirror the author's own preoccupations and goals. The need to reaffirm one's identity continues with *Antonia* (1989), a first person account of the relationship between two childhood friends and their trips through Mazatlán and London. Such a trajectory ultimately represents the shortened lifespan of Antonia, a relatively young and vital woman who dies of breast cancer. *La forma del silencio* (1987) presents a contrast of cultures: the city versus the country and the Mexican culture versus that of the United States, placing emphasis on the importance of silence in a contemporary society that is in constant crisis. In the course of the story, its anonymous female narrators search for their identity. Furthermore, as is often the case in Puga's works, the reader finds an analysis of the development of the creative process alongside the narrated story. In this case, the narrator/writer engages in a dialogue with the characters and defines what a novel is and how it is created. *La viuda* (1994) presents the problematic situation of a submissive woman who finds a new life and freedom after the death of her husband, when she no longer has to fulfill the roles of wife and mother assigned to her by a patriarchal society. The novelty of this text resides in the presence of a 68-year-old woman who, in spite of her age and contrary to stereotypes, is not willing to consider her life to be over and is determined to leave behind her married life of fifty years to (re)examine her present identity and embark on a new life with an old friend. Where Puga's contemporaries present much younger characters searching for an identity, *La viuda* shows that this search is endless and it can take place at different stages of a woman's life. *Inventar ciudades* (1998) is a story of an older couple from a small town who take in an 8-year-old city girl after she loses both parents. In spite of the presence of an omniscient narrator, the monologue and the play of narrative voices dominate, and the use of dialogue is much more frequent than in her other works. *Nueve madrugadas y media* (2003) is an autobiographical account that presents an extensive dialogue between a young man and a mature female writer about the creative process while also narrating incidents from the author's life. Puga's last work, *Diario del dolor*, is a collection of short fragments that puts forward the writer's relationship with her interlocutor, Dolor (Pain). This is the author's attempt to deal with the rheumatoid arthritis and the pain she endured during her last years. Puga also wrote a brief autobiography, *De cuerpo entero* (1990), in which she details her development as a writer, her search for a space to call her own and her need to distance herself from the world to better observe it and ultimately record it in her writings.

Most of the female characters in Puga's narrative are strong or have the potential of being strong and independent individuals. It is of interest to note that the author presents women of all ages, young, middle-aged and old, a rarity in contemporary Mexican literature in particular and Hispanic literature as a whole. While the style, location and plot vary from text to text, the unifying thread is the author's ability to totally immerse the reader in the story allowing him/her to get to know the characters, feel their pains and witness their particular journey and development (at a given stage in life) as independent human beings that are in control of their lives and how they live them.

Much like in contemporary society, Puga's texts reflect the need to redefine boundaries—whether they be generic, social, cultural or racial—to create a blend that better represents the hybridity experienced in Mexico, as well as in the rest of Latin America, at the end of the twentieth century and into the twenty first century.

MARISA HERRERA POSTLEWATE

Selected Works

Las posibilidades del odio. México, D.F.: Siglo XXI, 1978.

Inmóvil sol secreto. México, D.F.: La máquina de escribir, 1979.

Cuando el aire es azul. México, D.F.: Siglo XXI, 1980.

"Literatura y sociedad". *Revista mexicana de ciencias políticas y sociales* 102 (1980): 103–9.

Cómo muere la otra mitad del mundo: las verdaderas razones del hambre. México, D.F.: Siglo Veintiuno Editores, 1980.

Accidentes. México, D.F.: Martín Casillas, 1981.

Pánico o peligro. México, D.F.: Siglo XXI, 1983.

La cerámica de Hugo X. Velázquez: cuando rinde el horno. México, D.F.: Martín Casillas, 1983.

Obras completas de Alejo Carpentier Vol. 5, El siglo de las luces. México, D.F.: Siglo Veintiuno Editores, 1984.

El tornado. México, D.F.: CIDCLI, 1985.

La forma del silencio. México, D.F.: Siglo XXI, 1987.

Intentos. México, D.F.: Grijalbo, 1987.

"El lenguaje oculto de la realidad". *Tinta* (1987) 5: 63–67.

Antonia. México, D.F.: Grijalbo, 1989.

Las razones del lago. México, D.F.: Grijalbo, 1990.

De cuerpo entero. México, D.F.: UNAM/ECO, 1990.

Ruptura y diversidad. México, D.F.: Coordinación de Difusión Cultural, Dirección de Literatura, UNAM, 1990.

Lo que le pasa al lector. México, D.F.: Grijalbo, 1991.

Los tenis acatarrados. México, D.F.: Ediciones Corunda, 1991.

La viuda. México, D.F.: Grijalbo, 1994.

La ceremonia de iniciación. Travesías, 1994.

"El solapado realismo de la novela mexicana". In *Literatura mexicana hoy: Del 68 al ocaso de la revolución*. Karl Kohut, ed. Frankfurt, Germany and Madrid, Spain: Vervuert and Iberoamericana, 1995. 167–75.

Crónicas de una oriunda del kilómetro X en Michoacán. México, D.F.: Consejo Nacional para la Cultura y las Artes, 1995.

La reina. México, D.F.: Planeta Mexicana, 1995.

Crónica de una oriunda del kilómetro X en Michoacán. México, D.F.: Consejo Nacional para la Cultura y las Artes, 1995.

"Mi hermano mayor". In Mónica Lavín and Mario Luis Fuentes (eds), *Todos los niños: antología de cuentos*. Monterrey, México: Ediciones Castillo, 1997.

Inventar ciudades. México, D.F.: Alfaguara, 1998.

De intentos y accidentes. México, D.F.: Instituto de Seguridad y Servicios Sociales de los Trabajadores del Estado, 2000.

Nueve madrugadas y media. México D.F.: Alfaguara, 2003.
Translator, *La forma del cine*. México D.F.: Siglo XXI, 2003.
Diario del dolor. México D.F.: Alfaguara, 2004.

References and Further Reading

De Beer, Gabriella. *Contemporary Mexican Women Writers: Five Voices*. Austin, TX: University of Texas Press, 1996.

López, Irma M. *Historia, escritura e identidad: la novelística de María Luisa Puga*. New York: Peter Lang, 1996.

——. "En trance continuo de autodefinición: Hispanoamérica examinada por dos de sus escritoras". *Hispanic Journal* 21(1) (2000): 91–100.

——. and Spanos, Tony. "*Antonia* y *Demasiado amor*: El bildungsroman: Su estrategia y definición en la experiencia mexicana femenina". *Confluencia: Revista Hispánica de Cultura y Literatura* 13(1) (1997): 120–30.

Moorhead-Rosenberg, Florence. "A Language to Call My Own: Utopian Space in María Luisa Puga's *Pánico o peligro*" *Intertexts* 1)(1) (1997): 78–91.

Pellicer, Juan. "*La viuda*: Una femineidad utópica". *Revista Iberoamericana* 63 (181) (1997): 689–96.

Pfeiffer, Erna. "El enfoque tercermundista en *Las posibilidades del odio* de María Luisa Puga". In Juana Alcira Arancibia (ed.), *Literatura del mundo hispánico: VIII Simposio Internacional de Literatura*. Westminster, CA: Inst. Literario y Cultural Hispánico, 1992, pp. 181–8.

Smith, Susan M. "María Luisa Puga: Reflexiones sobre la identidad en *Las posibilidades del odio*". *Chasqui: Revista de Literatura Latinoamericana* 23(1) (1994): 75–82.

Unruh, Vicky. "Puga's Fictions of Equivalence: The Tasks of the Novelist As Translator". In Daniel Balderston and Marcy Schwartz (eds), *Voice-Overs: Translation and Latin American Literature*. Albany, NY: State University of New York Press, 2002, pp. 194–203.

Urrutia, Carlos. "María Luisa Puga: Heroine of Writing". *Voices of Mexico* 73 (2005): 65–72.

Valdés, María Elena de. *The Shattered Mirrors: Representations of Women in Mexican Literature* Austin, TX: University of Texas Press, 1998.

Q

QUEIROZ, MARIA JOSÉ DE

Maria José de Queiroz was born in Belo Horizonte, Minas Gerais, on May 29, 1936. She has a Ph.D. in Neolatin Letters by the Federal University of Minas Gerais, and lectured in Spanish Language and Literature at the latter. In 1961, she published *A poesia de Juana de Ibarbourou,* her doctoral thesis, and in the following year, *Do indianismo ao indigenismo nas letras hispano-americanas.* From these first essays onward, Queiroz's works have been marked by a critical-literary project engaged in the reflection on Brazilian literature and culture, and their relationship to the Spanish America and universal culture.

A poesia de Juana de Ibarbourou discloses a concern, under the title "Paralelos", with the Uruguayan author's affiliation, seeking influences and sources. The entwining of the analysed texts and authors takes place when the mirroring between life and art is proven, and how this relationship manifests itself in a given period of time within the intellectual production process of Ibarbourou. In the set of essays entitled *Do indianismo ao indigenismo nas letras hispano-americanas,* Queiroz points to a certain indigenous "quest for an expression of their own" within the Spanish-American and Brazilian literature. The writer states that, as two literary practices, Indianism and Indigenism reveal two different ways of looking at the Indian figure; as the good savage, the national hero, or capturing its image through a more realistic and less idealized perspective.

In *César Vallejo: ser e existência* (1971), Queiroz analyses the autobiographical traces in the work of the Peruvian writer. The long-suffering nature of the poet's work would be defined, according to the writer, by the real outlines of the poet's life. Withdrawing from the concept of the "lyrical I", the essayist ponders on the poet as an author, and hence defines his "poetics of pain". In *Vallejo,* the essayist analyses the value of details – the horizons of the house, of the wardrobe, of the drawers and of the closets – the secret intimacy of the things that assure the subject's consciousness. The details, finely drawn in her essay, are then incorporated into her own writings, thence functioning as a peculiar profile in her work.

Under the title *Presença da literatura hispano-americana,* the essayist published, in 1971, a series of essays whose literary course – already announced by the title – points out and denounces the Spanish-speaking American people's disavowal of each other. Queiroz also shows that the Brazilians, disavowing their ancestral colonizers, reveal a loss of notion of kinship: "we renounce Spain, common peninsular origin, and confound, in this renouncement, the whole continental offspring that works hard and suffers on our side . . . Also it, the Spanish America, pays us back in the same currency". In 1971, Queiroz published *A literatura encarcerada,* a thematic essay on authors and their literary productions in prison. In this project, the writer analyses authors and works that, in "bodily prisons", take charge of creating "evasions of freedom" through language.

The author's first production as a poet took place with the publication of *Exercício de levitação* (1971), *Exercício de gravitação* (1972) and, after the book of short stories book, namely *Como me contaram . . . fábulas historiais* (1973), she launched *Exercício de fiandeira,* in 1974. Her poetry, noteworthy for the intertextual references to other poets, also discloses her accuracy and method regarding the poetic word and the selection of the right word. In *Como me contaram . . . fábulas historiais,* the writer retrieves part of the cultural and historical memory of Minas Gerais through fiction, but without the traditional historiographical rigor. With the oral narratives, included in the text, which was not subject to the imprisonment of dates, facts and precise documentation, she composed a mosaic of cities and texts that deconstructed the unity of a monolithic and centered Minas Gerais. The factual data are deconstructed by the short stories' narrator who, disguised as a familiar chronicler, apparently devoid of any historical intention, registers cases and recollections from the past, as well as from the cultural imaginary of Minas Gerais.

Based in Latin, Maria José de Queiroz redefines the word "love" and its etymological relations to feelings and life in *Resgate do real: amor e morte:* amor, amoris, in 1978. The narrative invention and the distance between the feeling and the telling reach their peak in the plot of *Invenção a duas vozes,* a novel dated 1978. Locked during Carnival in a tiny bathroom of a mansion at Pampulha, a couple reflects on life and social representations. In *Homem de sete partidas* (1980), Bernardo searches for his missing uncle in order to disclose his life and adventures. On this pretext, the writer draws a map of Latin

American territory, whose lines try to guide narrator and reader to a fictional voyage throughout the wanderings of a vagrant character. The 1987 novel, *Joaquina, filha do Tiradentes* presents a refined plot between fiction and history. Placed at the end of the Inconfidência (Insurgence) stage, the narrative recreates details of life in the eighteenth-century Minas Gerais State, through the invention of the daughter of Tiradentes, the hero and martyr of the Minas Gerais' Insurgence.

What follows is the novel *Sobre os rios que vão* (1990), in which Queiroz, through a narrative pervaded by Judaic metaphors, unfolds the verses "Babel e Sião" by Camões, that point to the biblical intertext and the rewriting practice. In this novel, she engages in the construction of a text that causes signs such as the exile, the duplicity of the proper name and the foreigner condition of the Sephardites to circle in order to fictionally reinvent, in a contemporary context, the life of the Jewish immigrants in Brazil. The work, *A literatura alucinada: do êxtase das drogas à vertigem da loucura* (1990), deals with literature and the relationship among writing, drugs and madness. In *A literatura e o gozo impuro da comida* (1994), the writer unveils, in the delirious kitchen of literature, the table and its relationship to art, from Homer to Pedro Nava, via Eça de Queirós and Machado de Assis. These essays, together with *A comida e a cozinha: iniciação à arte de comer* (1988), which preceded them, show an aesthetical concern that seeks to portray the table in the universal literature as an aspect inseparable from culture.

In *A América: a nossa e as outras* (1992), in an outstanding essay from the standpoint of the colonizing nations regarding America, Queiroz ponders on the Old World's point of view that sees our continent as "a patchwork America", composed of several cloths, with apparently loose cuts, in an outsized exoticism. In 1998, Maria José de Queiroz published *Os males da ausência ou A literatura do exílio*. A reference work for literary studies and the history of exile, this book is an important reflection on the condition of exile and its consequences upon the writings of the exiled. Beginning with the expulsion from Eden to Egypt, and undergoing the Babylonian exile, Queiroz muses on the pursuit of the Jews up to the contemporary times and writers. Expelled from their motherland and language, like Hannah Arendt and Walter Benjamin, these thinkers made a portable country out of writing, whose universal appeal is indisputable. Throughout the reflections on America, ours and the others, the essays on food and culture, besides the studies on exile, prison and drugs in their relationships to literature, Maria José de Queiroz builds a unique fictional and poetical work in contemporary Brazilian literature. Choosing Brazilian lands as scenery, be it inside the eighteenth-century Ouro Preto, or in the Amazonian forests, Queiroz's characters always disclose the human condition of the subject in search of knowledge, of themselves, of others, of life.

LYSLEI NACIMENTO

Selected Works

Essays

A poesia de Juana de Ibarbourou. Belo Horizonte: Imprensa da UFMG, 1961.

Presença da literatura hispano-americana. Belo Horizonte: Imprensa da UFMG, 1971.

A literatura encarcerada. Rio de Janeiro: Civilização Brasileira, 1971.

A comida e a cozinha: iniciação à arte de comer. Rio de Janeiro: Forense, 1988.

A literatura alucinada. Rio de Janeiro: Atheneu Cultura, 1990.

A América: a nossa e as outras. Rio de Janeiro: Agir, 1992.

A literatura e o gozo impuro da comida. Rio de Janeiro: Topbooks, 1994.

Refrações no tempo: tempo histórico, tempo literário. Rio de Janeiro: Topbooks, 1996.

A América sem nome. Rio de Janeiro: Agir, 1997.

Os males do exílio ou a literatura do exílio. Rio de Janeiro: Topbooks, 1998.

Poetry

Exercício de levitação. Coimbra: Atlântida, 1971.

Exercício de gravitação. Coimbra: Atlântida, 1972.

Exercício de fiandeira. Coimbra: Coimbra, 1974.

Resgate do real: amor e morte. Coimbra: Coimbra, 1978.

Para que serve um arco-íris? Belo Horizonte: Imprensa da UFMG, 1982.

Novels

Ano novo, vida nova. Rio de Janeiro: Civilização Brasileira, 1978.

Invenção a duas vozes. Rio de Janeiro: Civilização Brasileira, 1978.

Homem de sete partidas. Rio de Janeiro: Civilização Brasileira, 1980.

Joaquina, filha do Tiradentes. São Paulo: Marco Zero, 1987.

Sobre os rios que vão. Rio de Janeiro: Atheneu Cultura, 1990.

Joaquina, filha do Tiradentes. Edição integral com pósfacio da autora. Rio de Janeiro: Topbooks, 1997.

Homem de sete partidas. 2nd edn. Rio de Janeiro: Record, 1999.

Vladslav Ostrov: príncipe do Juruena. Rio de Janeiro: Record, 1999.

Short Stories

Como me contaram ... fábulas historiais. Belo Horizonte: Imprensa/Publicações, 1973.

Amor cruel, amor vingador. Rio de Janeiro: Record, 1996.

References and Further Reading

Almeida, Carlos Heli. "Vida e lógica num romance". *Estado de Minas* (24 April 1979): 4.

——. "Uma viagem pela história". *Tribuna da Imprensa*, 28 Nov. 1987, p. 3.

Araujo, Zilah Corrêa de. "Maria José de Queiroz, uma visita". *Minas Gerais*, Suplemento Literário 221 (21 Nov. 1970): 10.

Bichara, Ivan. "*Joaquina, filha do Tiradentes*, numa história de amor e desamor. "*Minas Gerais*, Suplemento Literário 1107 (17 Nov., 1988).

Castro, Moacir Werneck de. "Um cardápio continental". *Jornal do Brasil*, 9 Jan. 1993, p. 12.

Carvalho, Gilberto Vilar de. "Prisioneira da História". *O Globo*, 8 Nov. 1987.

Clemente, José. "O maior pleito a Afonso Pena Júnior". *Estado de Minas*, 29 Sept. 1968, p. 10.

——. "Presença da ausente Maria José de Queiroz". *Estado de Minas*, 2 June 1971, p. 6.

——. "Maria José de Queiroz, também romancista". *Estado de Minas*, 1972, p. 1.

——. "Como me contaram". *Estado de Minas*, 17 July 1973, p. 1.

Duarte, José Afrânio. *De conversa em conversa*. São Paulo: Editora do Escritor, 1976, pp. 96–9.

——. "Ficção histórica". *Estado de Minas*, 14 April 1988, p. 5.

Figueiredo, Guilherme. "Sobre Dráculas e Tiradentes". *O Globo*, Rio de Janeiro, 26 Mar. 1993, p. 3.

Fleury, Beth. "Maria José, escrevendo a literatura dos encarcerados". *Jornal de Casa*, 5 July 1981, pp. 1–3.

França, Eurico Nogueira. "Maria José de Queiroz: *Joaquina, filha do Tiradentes*". *Colóquio/Letras* 107 (Jan./Feb. 1989).

Frieiro, Eduardo. "Sobre Juana de América". *Estado de Minas*, 22 Oct. 1961, p. 3.

——. "Indigenismo e revolução". *Estado de Minas*, 7 Oct. 1962, p. 3.
——. "Literatura indigenista". *Estado de Minas*, 30 Sept. 1962, p. 3.
Gazolla, Lúcia Helena. "A história secreta de Tiradentes". *Jornal do Brasil*, 21 Dec. 1987.
Gomes, Danilo. "Presença da Literatura Hispano-americana". *Estado de Minas*, 18 Feb. 1971, p. 7.
——. "Maria José de Queiroz, poetisa". *Estado de Minas*, 25 Sept. 1973, p. 4.
——. "Prosadores e poetas". *Estado de Minas*, 3 Mar. 1975, p. 4.
——. "A imortalidade de Maria José". *Estado de Minas*, 25 Sept. 1978, p. 5.
Hohlfeldt, Antonio. "Relembrando a bastarda". *Minas Gerais*, 7 Nov. 1988, Suplemento Literário, n. 1112.
Laporte, Silvia Helena. "História do homem através da mesa". *Estado de Minas*, 18 Dec. 1994, p. 12.
Lucas, Fábio. "O Tiradentes de cada um". *Leitura*, 8 Jul. 1989, p. 13.
Mendes, Oscar. "Exercício de fiandeira". *Estado de Minas*, 23 July 1975, p. 6.
——. "Três romances". *Estado de Minas*, 9 May. 1981, p. 8.
Mengozzi, Federico. "Um nome para esquecer: Joaquina". *Jornal de Letras*, 16 July 1989, p. 2.
Miraglia, Sylvio. "Romance à margem da História". *Estado de Minas*, 17 Jan. 1988, p. 2.
Nascimento, Lyslei. "Exercício de fiandeira: uma análise do romance *Joaquina, filha do Tiradentes*, de Maria José de Queiroz". Master's diss. Faculdade de Letras, Belo Horizonte, 1993.
——. "O Tempo, violência, memória". *Hoje em Dia*, 31 March, 1993, p. 4.
——. "O romancista-historiador e a melancolia em *Joaquina, filha do Tiradentes*, de Maria José de Queiroz". In: *Anais do II Congresso de Ciência Humanas Letras e Artes das Universidades Federais de Minas Gerais*. Uberlândia: Zardo, 1995, p. 58.
——. "América Latina: um nome a ser resgatado". *Hoje em Dia*, 4 May, 1997, p. 4.
——. "Exercício de Fiandeira: *Joaquina, filha do Tiradentes*, de Maria José de Queiroz". In *Em tese*. Belo Horizonte: Pós-Lit, 1997, pp. 141–7.
——. "Nos Bastidores da Inconfidência Mineira". *Hoje em Dia*, 29 June, 1997, p. 3.
——. "História ocidental do exílio tem inventário". *O Tempo*, 18 April, 1998, p. 5.
——. "Os males da ausência de Maria José de Queiroz". *Anais do IX Congresso Nacional Mulher & Literatura* 2(1), Belo Horizonte: Programa de Pós-Graduação em Letras: Estudos Literários da FALE/ UFMG, 2001, pp. 242–5.
——. "Como me contaram ... fábulas historiais". *Aula Magna: Revista de Cultura Universitária* 1(1) (2002): 17–21.
Oliveira, Maria do Carmo Gaspar. "*Joaquina, filha do Tiradentes* pela mão de Maria José de Queiroz". *Jornal do Brasil*, 1988.
Pignataro, Iolanda. "As duas vozes de Maria José de Queiroz". *Estado de Minas*, Belo Horizonte, 20 Oct. 1979, p. 5.
——. "Maria José de Queiroz e o seu Homem de sete partidas". *Estado de Minas*, Belo Horizonte, 27 Nov. 1980, p. 1.
Silva, Zina Bellodi. "O conflito que a história esqueceu". *Afinal*. 31 May 1986, no. 196, p. 23.
——. "*Joaquina, a filha de Tiradentes*. Inconfidência Mineira". *Leitura*, 8 Nov. 1988.
Villas-Boas, Luciana. "Obra injustiçada". *Jornal do Brasil*, 17 Sept. 1994, p. 2.

QUEIROZ, RACHEL DE

Rachel de Queiroz (1910–2003), one of Brazil's most famous women writers and a contributor to *regionalismo* (regional literature), was born on November 17, 1910, in Fortaleza, Ceará. She was related to the famous romantic writer of *O Guarani*, José de Alencar (1829–77). Queiroz incorporates her childhood experiences of the droughts of the *sertão* "dry land in Northeastern Brazil" as a setting for her novels including her most famous *O quinze*, published in 1930. *O quinze* (Fifteen) refers to the year 1915 when the *sertão* experienced a particularly severe drought. From the publication of her first novel, Rachel de Queiroz became a pivotal part of Brazilian culture and literature. In 1964, she was chosen to be Brazil's representative to the United Nations and in 1977, she became the first woman to be voted into the Brazilian Academy of Letters. At the age of 93, Queiroz died at her home in Rio de Janeiro on November 4, 2003. Her last work was *Visões: Maurício Albano e Rachel de Queiroz*, a collection of photographs of her native Ceará for which she wrote the text to accompany the images taken by Albano.

To appreciate Queiroz's work and her contribution to Brazilian literature of the twentieth century, it is necessary to define the *sertão* and literary milieu of Brazil in the 1930s. As mentioned previously, the *sertão* is a region of Northeastern Brazil, home to several famous writers including João Guimarães Rosa (1892–1953), Graciliano Ramos (1908–67), and José Lins do Rego (1901–57). The natives of the *sertão* lived close to the land and relied on what the land provided for their existence. The close bond with nature made the *sertão* synonymous with the identity of the inhabitants. An example of the closeness between natives of the *sertão* and the land comes from *O quinze* when the *vaqueros* (cowboys) are ordered by the landowners to free the cattle from the corrals because there were no longer sufficient amounts of water or feed to give to the animals. Vicente, one of the *vaqueros*, chooses not to abandon the cattle and continues to care for the cows. The author describes how the animals would approach Vicente and other people of the *fazenda* (farm) as if to bid farewell. The livestock are representative of the few possessions that remain for the impoverished inhabitants of the *sertão*.

The presence of the *sertão* continues as we see in the case of *Dôra Doralina*, published in 1975. In the final section of the novel entitled, "Livro do Comandante" (Captain's Book), Dôra speaks of the relief she experiences upon returning home after a failed marriage:

> Sozinha no mundo, eu sabia, sozinha mais que sozinha—como aquele bando de velhos inúteis ás minhas costas—mas pelo menos não me via no meio de estranhos como nos últimos meses do Rio, ah meu Deus, os últimos meses do Rio. De manhã tinha a tigela de leite tirada da minha vaca, o resto do feijão do meu paiol para o almoço, o frango, o ovo, o peixe do açude; comendo da minha pobreza, mas comendo do que é meu.
>
> (p. 237)

> [Alone in the world, I knew, more than alone, like that group of useless old people at my side but at least I did not see myself among strangers like the lasts months in Rio, oh God, the last months in Rio. In the morning I had milk drawn from my cow, the rest of the beans from my storage for lunch, chicken, eggs, fish from the pond, eating from my poverty, but eating from what is mine.]

Dôra, narrator of the novel, finds comfort in the food that she obtains from the animals on her *fazenda*. It soothes her to be surrounded by the familiar of the country which is a consolation after living among strangers in Rio de Janeiro.

What distinguishes Rachel de Queiroz's viewpoint and experience of the *sertão* from other writers of *regionalismo* (João Guimarães Rosa, Graciliano Ramos, and José Lins do Rego) is the unique perspective she takes from her female characters (Conceição from *O quinze*, Guta from *A três Marias*, Dôra from *Dôra Doralina*). Born in a region that suffers poverty and drought, women are twice marginalized for their gender in addition to their economic status. Queiroz gives voice to female characters to underscore female experience in relationship to education, sexuality, and class. As an author Rachel de Queiroz becomes an advocate for the marginalized people of her native Brazil. This essay investigates Queiroz's treatment of women's experience in three of her most distinguished works: *O quinze* (1930), *As três Marias* (1939), *Dôra Doralina* (1975).

O quinze (1930)

O quinze marked the author's first contribution to the narrative of Northeastern Brazil commonly referred to as *regionalismo*. Writers like Rachel de Queiroz broke away from a preoccupation with abstract avant-garde language and focused on how inhabitants of the *sertão* genuinely spoke. What follows is an example of the colloquial conversation of Rachel de Queiroz's first work *O quinze*, when Vicente, one of the *vaqueros*, asks his aunt for some feed for his cattle, "Eu vim aqui para lhe pedir um favor. Soube que a senhora tinha carrapaticida e queria que me cedesse um bocado; o meu gado anda em tempo de cair" [I came here to ask a favor. I found out that *senhora* has some tick medicine and I wanted to ask if she could give me some; my cattle are about to fall over] (p. 11). Vicente places more importance on the welfare of the livestock than on his own basic needs. Rachel de Queiroz creates a tender bond between man and animal in a time of crisis when many inhabitants of the *sertão* decide to leave to find a more suitable place to live. *O quinze* captures what is intrinsic to Brazil and simultaneously reflects universal concerns for survival and humanity.

O quinze narrates the experience of two distinct groups: the upper-class landowners of the *fazenda* and the lower-class farmhands. The short novel begins with a dialogue between Conceição and Mãe Nácia that exhibits a contrast between the two main female characters of the novel. Conceição is young and spirited, in contrast to the practical and traditional Mãe Nácia. Mãe Nácia is the matriarch of the *fazenda* which they must leave behind because of the impending drought.

De Queiroz's first novel also narrates the experience of Chico Bento, Cordulina, and their children; all are workers who suffer greatly due to the annual drought of the *sertão*. The culmination of Chico Bento and his family's suffering results in the death of two children. Chico Bento and Cordulina lose their first child, who is poisoned by eating rancid sugar, and later their other son dies of starvation. As Chico Bento and his family travel on foot to a refugee camp, he notices a goat and quickly kills it. Immediately the owner of the goat screams accusing Chico Bento of stealing. The argument quickly ceases because Chico Bento and the other travelers are so hungry that they immediately devour the animal.

It is immediately obvious to the reader that the experience of Conceição and Mãe Nácia is very different from that of Vicente, Chico Bento, and the other land workers. A precise example is the conclusion of Chapter 5 and the beginning of Chapter 6, early in the novel, when both the owners of the *fazenda* and the farmhands must decide how they will escape the drought. The last sentences of Chapter 5 express the frustration of Chico Bento and his wife Cordulina, who expects her husband to obtain train tickets for them to leave the *sertão*. This is a tense moment because Chico Bento feels the anxiety and desperation of failing to meet the expectations of his family. In contrast, Chapter 6 begins with the tranquil state of Conceição and Mãe Nácia as they make their way on train to a more hospitable area.

Conceição realizes she is different from other women of the *sertão* who prefer to concentrate on their domestic duties. Mãe Nácia criticizes Conceição for having *idéias* (ideas). Conceição's "ideas" are a metaphor of her interests that rest outside of the *fazenda* and the traditional life as a wife and mother. Mãe Nácia says that Conceição must have a disability or problem because she does not want to marry, "a avó encolhia os obros e sentenciava que mulher que não casa é um aleijão" [grandmother shrugged her shoulders and stated that a woman who doesn't marry is a deformity] (p. 7). Mãe Nácia's words encapsulate the popular opinion of the time that did not recognize that women could possibly have an existence outside of marriage. Later Mãe Nácia makes another telling comment when Conceição becomes disillusioned when she learns that Don Vicente has become involved with another woman. Mãe Nácia once again makes a statement that captures a predominant attitude towards women's experiences, "Minha filha, a vida é assim mesmo" [My daughter, life is like that]. Mãe Nácia's comment reflects that women should not expect nor question the quality of their surroundings.

In two later novels, *As três Marias* and *Dôra, Doralina*, the female characters Guta and Dôra will make strides in redefining their lives and thus dismiss an attitude of indifference towards life that contrasts with Mãe Nácia's words "a vida é assim mesmo". Unlike Conceição, who has "ideas" but does not actively work towards realizing her ambitions, Rachel de Queiroz's later characters act upon their desires to live independently and explore alternative futures.

As três Marias (1939)

The novel *As três Marias* (The Three Marias) takes its name from three female characters of the text Maria Augusta (Guta), Maria José, and Maria da Glória (Glória). Rachel de Queiroz continues to focus on women's experiences in her native country and utilizes the characters' lives to demonstrate the challenges women faced in the first part of the twentieth century in Brazil. Each of the Marias represents a distinct personality and aspect of character. Maria Augusta, the narrator, is reserved and timid, but eventually leaves the confines of boarding school to seek a new life away from antiquated traditions of family and church. Maria José differs from Maria Augusta because she maintains her religious beliefs and seeks out an acceptable profession for a woman of her day, and therefore becomes a teacher. Maria da Glória is an orphan and seeks the other only suitable destiny for women, marriage. The three Marias become close friends while attending boarding school and decide to confirm their friendship by giving themselves tattoos. Each of them makes a tattoo of three stars to represent the bond the three girls share. The young Marias substitute the loneliness they feel at boarding school with the affection they find in each other. At the end of the novel Guta looks up at the sky and is reminded by the stars of the pleasant times she once shared with Maria José and Maria da Glória. Guta's memories serve to boost her confidence as she is forced to face an uncertain future.

As narrator, Guta not only guides the storyline but breaks with the traditions of patriarchal Brazil. Through Guta's observations and experiences de Queiroz questions the irony of sending young girls off to boarding school, *"Para que sair do Colégio para que ser a final uma mulher se a vida continuava a mesma e o crescimento não me libertava da infância?"* (p. 68). [Why bother leaving school if life remained the same and growing up did not liberate me from childhood?] Guta is acutely aware, more than any of her peers, of the world that awaits beyond the walls of the school. Education for women functions to reinforce patriarchal norms that Maria José and Maria da Glória accept. Conversely, Guta chooses to become a secretary after graduation in the city of Fortaleza. Guta meets Isaac, a Jewish immigrant, in Rio de Janeiro. Unlike Glória, who is passionately in love with her husband, Guta is aware of the lack of communication between her and her lover Isaac. This is Queiroz's commentary of patriarchal gender roles where the woman is expected to be demure and submissive to her husband. Although not married, Guta sees that she and Isaac repeat certain behavior patterns. As Guta narrates her experience with Isaac, she becomes aware that she speaks more about him than about herself. She also realizes that Isaac is selfish and only considers his own sexual pleasure, and does not consider Guta's needs. Later Isaac leaves her and Guta discovers she is pregnant. The novel ends in an unfortunate manner, but Guta is resilient and looks back on the friendship she shared with Maria José and Maria da Glória as a source of strength.

In addition to a critique of the limited possibilities for women, being an orphan and the loss of a parent are repeated in Queiroz's fiction. *A três Marias* begins with Guta's loss of her mother at the age of 12. Guta describes her life as having two distinct parts, before and after her mother died, "antes e depois". The loss of a maternal figure is never healed, and the nuns at the boarding school are stern and unsympathetic. Guta shares a bond with Glória, who suffered the loss of her father before being sent off to boarding school. In *O quinze* and as we will see in *Dôra Doralina*, there is a lack of positive maternal role models. Likewise there is a lack of encouraging examples of happy or enduring marriages. Guta's father marries a woman whom she refers to simply as *Madrinha* (godmother) and describes her as formal and virtuous. Maria José's mother was left by her husband for a younger woman. The isolation and loneliness that the three girls feel encourage them to seek love and support in each other.

Guta lends a sympathetic eye to other lonely students at the boarding school, particularly Jandira, who is an illegitimate child as a result of the adultery committed by her parents. Jandira's character introduces the topic of class, which is a recurrent theme in de Queiroz's work. Jandira, the daughter of a prostitute, arrives at the *Colégio* (boarding school) frustrated by the poor treatment she receives from her aunts who tell her "conheça o seu lugar" (know your place). Jandira, similarly to Conceição in *O quinze*, is reminded by her elders that she cannot expect much out of life. Guta says that injustice was familiar for the girls of the *Colégio*, having all experienced some hardship. Due to Jandira's status as an illegitimate child, there is a debate in the school regarding what would be a suitable future for her. Some classmates say that because Jandira was not born to married parents she should go to the convent. Others think that a convent is not the appropriate environment for someone of her background. Guta explains that Jandira's plan was to marry in order to relieve herself of the prejudice of not coming from a "proper" family. Jandira complies with the often seen fate of orphans found in romance novels. Guta reminds the reader that in such stories a poor young girl is swept away by a rich man, rescuing her from an unfortunate fate. Jandira is one of the first girls of the *Colégio* to marry; however, she finds herself destitute by the end of the novel. Once again Rachel de Queiroz makes a social commentary on women's experiences and demonstrates that society's prescribed behavior does not assure well-being.

Rachel de Queiroz creates female characters who face the crisis of limited freedom in a patriarchal society. Their conflicts elicit the question of whether or not novels such as *O quinze*, *Dôra, Doralina*, and *As três Marias* can be considered *Bildungsromane*. The term *Bildungsroman* comes from the German: *Bildung* means "portrait" and *Roman* means "book". Often such a term is used to classify canonical texts including Charles Dickens' *David Copperfield* (1850) or Johann Wolfgang Goethe's *The Sorrows of Young Werther* (1774). When some critics use the term *Bildungsroman* they often refer to books with male protagonists who face challenges in society but are ultimately accepted into the community and are then integrated. The novels discussed here do not contain protagonists who are male and nor are they accepted into society. *As três Marias* serves as just one example of the lack of resolution for the female protagonist at the conclusion of the novel. We see that the protagonist Maria must begin her life again where the novel ends. There is no sense of completion in *O quinze*, *Dôra, Doralina*, and *As três Marias* that is found in a traditional *Bildungsroman*. Therefore, it would be remiss to label Queiroz's works as *Bildungsromane* without addressing the differences between the traditional *Bildungsroman* and the unique experience of female characters in Queiroz's novels. Due to their gender women remain second rate citizens in a patriarchal society.

Dôra, Doralina (1975)

The novel *Dôra, Doralina* is the most recent of the three novels analyzed here. The title refers to the protagonist who is called Maria de Dores by her mother, but Doralina by her father. This novel is a psychological study because the point of departure of the book comes from Dôra's inner world. The three parts of the novel indicate three very important periods in Dôra's life: "Livro de Senhora" (Senhora's Book) is the first section that examines Dôra's life from childhood to her marriage. The second section "Livro da Companhia" (The

Company's Book) marks Dôra's exit from the *sertão* to fulfill her dreams of becoming an actress. The third and last chapter "Livro do Comandante" (The Capitain's Book) narrates Dôra's marriage to her second husband and her return to the *fazenda*.

Life, according to Rachel de Queiroz, is a cycle, because Dôra leaves the *sertão* but later returns to take over her mother's place as matriarch of the *fazenda*. As Dôra matures, what most satisfies her is returning to her native land rather than following her childhood dream to become an actress. After losing her second husband, Dôra finds comfort in very simple things: drinking milk from her own cows and eating eggs from her own hens. Dôra left the *sertão* but ultimately returns to it because her identity is intrinsically tied to the land.

Dôra's journey is also metaphorical because it is necessary for her to leave her home to be able to return to it and take on the role as head of the household. Dôra's rejection of her mother is symbolic because *Senhora* is a voice of the patriarchy, reinforcing tradition and order. Using the name *Senhora* to refer to her mother instead of *mãe* (mother) symbolizes the emotional distance between mother and child. Dôra learns that her world is the *sertão*, although she has traveled and visited many places and met many people unlike herself.

Although there are several critical analyses of Rachel de Queiroz's writing, a lot of research still remains to be done. This short review of three of Queiroz's novels should serve as an invitation for others to further examine her remarkable novels, short-stories and other fiction.

DEBRA OCHOA

Selected Works

O quinze. Fortaleza, Brazil: Establecimiento Gráfico Urânia, 1930.
João Miguel. Rio de Janeiro: José Olypio, 1937.
Caminho de pedras. Rio de Janeiro: José Olypio, 1937.
As três Marias. Rio de Janeiro: José Olympio, 1939.
The Three Marias. Trans. Fred P. Ellison. Austin, TX: University of Texas Press, 1963.
Lampião: drama em 5 quadros. Rio de Janeiro: José Olympio, 1953.
A beata Maria do Egito: peça em 3 atos e 4 quadros. Rio de Janeiro: José Olympio, 1958.
Dôra, Doralina. Rio de Janeiro: Jose Olympio, 1975.
Dora, Doralina. Translated by Dorothy Scott Loos. New York: Avon, 1984.
Memorial de Maria Moura. São Paulo: Siciliano, 1992.

References and Further Reading

Barbosa, Maria de Lourdes Dias Leite. *Protagonistas de Rachel de Queiroz: Caminhos e descaminhos*. São Paolo: Campinas, 1999.

Courteau, Joanna. "Dôra, Doralina: the Sexual Configuration of Discourse". *Chasqui* 20(1) (1991): 3–9.

Coqueiro, Wilma dos Santos. "A Decadência Espacial no Romance 'Dôra, Doralina'/ The Space Decadence in the Novel 'Dora, Doralina'". *Estudios Lingüísticos* 31 (2002).

Ellison, Fred P. *Brazil's New Novel: Four Northeastern Masters*. Berkeley, CA: University of California Press, 1954.

Gotlib, Nádia Batella. "Las mujeres y 'el otro': Tres narradoras brasileñas". *Escritura: Revista de Teoria y Crítica Literarias* 16(31–2) (1991): 123–36.

Karpa-Wilson, Sabrina. "Contemporary Brazilian Women's Autobiography and the Forgotten Case of Adalgisa Nery". *Portuguese Literary and Cultural Studies* 4–5 (2000): 189–95.

Oliveira, Emanuelle K.F. "La República y las Letras: Literatura y carácter nacional en Brasil y Venezuela". *Mester* 24(2) (1995): 81–114.

Rosas Lopátegui, Patricia. "A Tradição Oral en Rachel de Queiroz". *Hispanic Journal* 17(1) (1996): 17–29.

Rueda-Acedo, Alicia. "La doble crónica de un Bildungsroman: As três Marias de Rachel de Queiroz". In María Luisa Collins, Gustavo Nanclares, and Alicia Rueda-Acedo (eds), *Selected Proceedings of the Fifth Annual Graduate Student Conference on Lusophone and Hispanic Literature and Culture*. Santa Barbara, CA: University of California, 2004, pp 49–61.

Wasserman, Renata R. "A Woman's Place: Rachel de Queiroz's Dora, Doralina". *Brasil/Brazil: Revista de Literatura Brasileira/A Journal of Brazilian Literature*, 2 (1989): 46–58.

R

RAZNOVICH, DIANA

Diana Raznovich was born in Buenos Aires, Argentina on May 12, 1945. Her father, Marcos Raznovich, was a pediatrician, and her mother, Bertha, a dentist. Both her maternal and paternal grandparents sought exile in Argentina, escaping from the anti-Semitic persecution of the Czar in Russia. Her great-grandmother, the baroness of Rothschild, was a patient of Sigmund Freud and a friend of Gustav Mahler, and her grandfather, a wealthy aristocrat who survived the Nazi persecution in Vienna before the war.

She first published *Tiempo de amar y otros poemas* (1963, Time to Love and Other Poems), *Caminata en tu sombra* (1964, Walking in Your Shadow), and *Parte del Todo* (1968, Part of the Whole), a collection of nihilist poems mostly inspired by the iconic figures of the times: Samuel Beckett, Ernesto "Che" Guevara, Simone de Beauvoir, Jorge Luis Borges, and Julio Cortázar.

Her interest in drama and theatrical performance sparkled while studying literature and modern languages at the University of Filosofía y Letras in Buenos Aires. At the age of 22, Raznovich received the First Municipal Prize for Best Unpublished Play for *Buscapies* (1968, The Squib), an allegorical representation of mediocrity and conformism in modern society. In her first play, Raznovich already uses humor and satire as powerful mechanisms with which to represent not only the ups and downs of human relationships, but also to expose the hypocrisy behind traditional perspectives on sexuality and gender.

Raznovich's unconventional style manifests itself most eloquently in her second play, *Plaza hay una sola* (1969, There is Only One Plaza), an eight one-act piece originally staged outdoors at the Teatro al aire libre in the Plaza Roberto Art in Buenos Aires. *Las ciudades son las plazas de los edificios* (Cities are the Building's Plazas), *El globo azul* (The Blue Balloon), *Alicia en el país* (Alice in the Land), *Del orden de las prensoras, de la familia de las psitácidas* (From the Order of the Psittaciformes, from the Psittacine Family), *Mi hijo el pintor* (My Son, the Painter), *Comunicación* (Communication), *La rebellion de los padres* (Parents' Rebellion), and *Los reyes* (The Kings), all expand the boundaries of more traditional dramatic interpretations of Argentina's socio-political instability by bringing the theatre into the street. Passing pedestrians and passive viewers are invited to witness microcosmic representations of their own phobias, insecurities, and fears.

Soon after *El Guardagente* (1970, The People Keeper), *Contratiempo* (1971, Setback), and a children's musical, *Texas en Carretilla* (1971, Texas in a Wheelbarrow), Raznovich wrote *Marcelo el mecánico* (Marcelo The Mechanic), play originally staged in 1975 in Buenos Aires, and later re-written and performed in Madrid's Teatro Rex under the title *Jardín de Otoño* (1977, Autumn Garden). The play demystifies mass media, television and consumerism through the transformation, and final empowerment, of Rosalía and Griselda, two spinsters who reside in an old mansion property of Rosalía's family. Their lives revolve around "Marcelo el mecánico," a soap opera in which Mariano Rivas, their favorite actor, stars as the leading character. Moved by passion and admiration for the actor, Griselda and Rosalía make plans to kidnap Marcelo/Mariano, bring him to their house, and then force him to perform love scenes with them.

In the second act, already in the house, and dressed up as a mechanic, the spinsters coerce the actor into performing the same passionate kisses as seen on the TV. Confused and fearing that his fans might kill him, the man tries to play along and to perform as directed; however, when he is unable satisfy the spinsters' sexual demands, the women begin to humiliate him. Finally, the disappointed fans kick him out of the house and immediately return to admire the character as seen on television. Since its premiere, *Jardín de Otoño* has been one of Argentina's best-known plays. It has also been staged in Chile, the United States, Italy, and Germany, where it has been re-adapted by a variety of theatrical performers and directors.

Pressed by political threats under the military dictatorial regime in Argentina (1976–83), Raznovich sought exile in Madrid, where she published her first novel, *Para que se cumplan todos tus deseos* (1989, So That Your Dreams May Come True). In 1980, Raznovich participated in the Festival de Teatro Latinoamericano in Stuttgart in Germany organized by Theater-und-Mediengesellschaft Lateinamerika, thus becoming one of the founding members of this theatre company. The following year, the playwright returned to Argentina for the inauguration of Teatro Abierto (Open Theatre Festival), where she joined other four women invited to participate among a group of twenty-one male authors. For this festival, the author readapted and staged *Fyodor y Nastenka,* based on Fyodor Dostoyevski's novel *White Nights,* and *El desconcierto* (translated as *Disconcerted*, 1989), an extensive monologue in which, the pianist, Irene della Porta addresses her audience to explain that her manager has muted her instrument so as to avoid censorship. The play's political innuendoes not only make a clear allusion to Argentina's years of repression—when most public performances were heavily censored by the military regime—but also comment on the oppressive and repressive mechanisms behind fascist ideology.

In 1984, Raznovich traveled to Sydney, Australia for the premiere of *Objetos personales* (*Personal Belongings*), a play based on the author's experience as an exile. The monologue's protagonist is Casalia Belprop, a woman locked up in the luggage deposit of an international airport. Surrounded by bags and parcels, she desperately searches for her own missing luggage. Throughout the monologue, the woman also tries to figure out where she is, and if she is arriving or departing. Unable to find the answers, she searches through other people's personal belongings coming across a variety of weird objects, such as human bones (that she is able to recognize as the remains of her friends and family), and even Leonardo da Vinci's *Gioconda*, recently stolen from the Louvre Museum in Paris. Unable to find the answers she is looking for, Casalia Beltrop gets into a piece of luggage never to come out. *Objetos personales* is a clear reflection of our existential quest and the paradox of our inability to understand the meaning or the reason behind our existence.

In 1985, Raznovich traveled to Italy for the opening of *Casa matriz* (*Dial-a-Mom*), at the Teatro Studio di Roma. Casa Matriz Incorporated, a rental agency of substitute mothers, provides mothering services for anyone who wishes to create their own "ideal" mother. Bárbara, a 30-year-old woman facing a personal crisis, hires the professional service of one of Casa Matriz's employees to comply with specific and previously instructed demands. For example, in one scene, the drug addict rocker daughter argues with a submissive mother, while in the next, the despotic mother argues with a repressed daughter. The display of mothers and mothering skills ranges from the overly protective to the emancipated, the intellectual to the frivolous, the repressive to the indulgent, etc. The idea behind the plot is to show how bipolar roles are part of everyday relationships and how these structured roles are basically sustained though life. Frustration, anger, fear, irony, and a heavy dose of irony are the main elements of this theatrical game in which emotions and feelings are manipulated for the thrill of an affluent consumer.

In her constant search for new codes of representation, Raznovich's work reflects upon the influence of consumerism in modern society, where everything, even maternal love and care, may be bought or hired as easily as any other service (maids, dog walkers, prostitutes, etc.). Transforming every discourse of power into an irreverent parody, the playwright not only raises the spectator's awareness of the consumerist vein of modern culture, but also mirrors the perpetual acting and role-playing required to fulfill the expectations or demands within our own existence.

In 1992, her two novels, *Oliverio Pan, Magier* and *Mater erótica* were edited and presented respectively at Frankfurt and Barcelona's Book Fairs, and in 1993, Raznovich wrote *De la cintura para abajo* (From the Waist Down), *De atrás para adelante* (Rear Entry), and *Fast Food a la velocidad de la muerte* (Fast Food to the Speed of Death); this last play, based on *Alice in Wonderland,* mocks the relation between the audience and the mass media. Alicia, a famous diva, intends to sell her suicide rights to Monina Monet, a renowned television reporter who wants to raise her ratings. As seen in contemporary reality television shows, the audience is able to follow Alicia's emotional downfalls and scaling depression, which lead her to think that suicide is the only alternative for her instability. Ex-lovers, family members, and even people from the entertainment world chat with the protagonist on screen so as to provide pathos and emotion to the pre-staged suicide. Even though *Fast Food* clearly mirrors the frivolity and skepticism of an Argentine middle upper class, the play's theme is universal in its representation of cultural relations and dynamics of any institutionalized society ruled by consumerism.

A year after receiving the John Simon Guggenheim Award for her outstanding career as a playwright and director, Raznovich's *Máquinas divinas* (1995, Divine Machines) premiered in the Sala ETC at the Centro Cultural San Martín in Buenos Aires. This two-act surrealist play takes place in the future in Buenos Aires, approximately in the year 2050, right after an unexpected hecatomb. A completely different play to the previous ones in *Máquinas divinas,* the author recreates a surreal utopian world where the poetics of love and joy make out of nothingness a more breathable space for all.

Back in Latin America, Raznovich lectured at the Encuentro Latinoamericano Mujer y Creatividad in Santiago de Chile; conducted a three-month seminar on literature and humor at Florida's Atlantic University (1995); participated in the Congreso de Teatro Iberoamericano y Argentino organized by GETEA (Gente de Teatro) in the Teatro Nacional Cervantes in Buenos Aires (1996–98); and exhibited her art work at La Morada art gallery in Santiago de Chile (1996) as well as the Centro Cultural Recoleta in Buenos Aires (1997). Moreover, Raznovich's poems were performed in *Klezmer y Klezmer* (1998), a show of popular Jewish songs staged at the Hebraica Argentina and the Centro Cultural Marc Chagall in Buenos Aires. Also in 1998, several translations of her work were published in German by Fischer Verlag Editors.

Diana Raznovich is an innovative playwright, cartoonist, novelist, poet, and essayist whose futuristic vision of drama has gained her fame and recognition worldwide. Her plays have been translated and staged in Germany, Italy, Sweden, Norway, Denmark, United States, Australia, Brazil, Ecuador, Colombia, and Chile.

MARIA CLAUDIA ANDRÉ

Selected Works

Tiempo de amar y otros poemas. Buenos Aires: Ediciones Nuevo Día, 1963.

Caminata en tus sombra. Buenos Aires: Editorial Stilcograf, 1964.

Parte del Todo. Buenos Aires: Editorial Mares del Sur, 1968.

Plumas blancas. Buenos Aires: Ediciones Dédalos, 1974.

Jardín de otoño. Buenos Aires: Subsecretaría de Cultura, Dirección Provincia de Buenos Aires, 1985.

Cables Pelados. Buenos Aires: Editorial Lúdica, 1987.
"*Casa matriz*," *Salirse de madre*. Ed. Hilda Rais. Buenos Aires: Ediciones Croquiñol, 1988, pp. 163–86.
Para que se cumplan todos tus deseos. Madrid: Exadra de Ediciones, 1988.
Indira Gandhi, el imposible término medio. Madrid: Exadra de Ediciones, 1989.
Oliverio Pan, Magier. St. Gallen: Edition dia, 1992.
Mater erótica. Barcelona: Robin Books, 1992.
Teatro completo de Diana Raznovich. Buenos Aires: Ediciones Dédalos, 1994.

Translations

El Desconcierto, trans. Vicky Martínez as "Disconcerted," *The Literary Review* 32(4) (Summer 1989): 568–72.
Argentine Jewish Theatre: A Critical Anthology (Lewisburg: Bucknell University Press, 1996), includes "Objetos personales," trans. and ed. Nora Glickman and Gloria Waldman as "Lost Belongings".
Women Writing Women: An Anthology of Spanish-American Theater of the 1980s (Albany, NY: SUNY Press, 1997), includes "Casa matriz" trans. and ed. Teresa Cajiao Salas and Margarita Vargas as "Dial-a-Mom".
Taylor, Diana and Martínez, Victoria. *Defiant Acts: Four plays by Diana Raznovich/Actos desafiantes: Cuatro obras de Diana Raznovich*. London: Bucknell University Press, 2000.

References and Further Reading

Castillejos, Manuel. "El valor del sonido en *Buscapies* de Diana Raznovich". In Alcira Arancibia (ed.), *Mujer y sociedad en America: IV Simposio Internacional*. Vol. 1. Buenos Aires: Vinciguerra Editorial, 1988, pp. 233–40.
Foster, David William. "Recent Argentine Women Writers of Jewish Descent". In Marjorie Agosín (ed.), *Passion, Memory, and Identity: Twentieth-Century Latin American Jewish Women Writers*. Albuquerque, NM: New Mexico Press, 1999, pp. 35–57.
Glickman, Nora. "Paradojas y mitos judaicos en dos obras de Diana Raznovich". *Noaj* 9 (1993): 83–7.
——. "Parodia y desmitificación del rol femenino en el teatro de Diana Raznovich". *Latin American Theatre Review* 28(1) (Fall 1994): 89–100.
López, Liliana. "Diana Raznovich: una cazadora de mitos". In Halima Tahan (ed.), *Drama de mujeres*. Buenos Aires: Ciudad Argentina, 1998.
——. "Fighting Fire with Frivolity: Diana Raznovich' Defiant Acts". In Keidrun Adler and Kati Rottger (eds), *Performance, pathos, política de los sexos: Teatro postcolonial de autoras latinoamericanas*. Madrid: Iberoamericana, 1999, pp. 69–81.

RESTREPO, LAURA

Laura Restrepo (b. 1950) is the most renowned Colombian woman writer of her generation. In recent years, her works have been translated into a number of languages (English, French, Italian, Dutch, Polish) and have earned her a number of prestigious literary awards. In her books, Restrepo combines an interest for her two main passions, politics and literature, amid a narrative greatly influenced by her experience as a journalist. Considered a member of the post-boom generation, her success heightens the profile of women authors in the Colombian context, habitually shaped by the overwhelming presence of Gabriel García Márquez.

Activist and Novelist

She was born on January 1, 1950, in Bogotá, Colombia to a prominent family of the Colombian bourgeoisie. As a child, Restrepo was influenced greatly by her family's penchant for traveling, as well as her father's love of reading and disdain for pedagogic institutionalism. In the 1970s, while attending the Universidad de los Andes, where she studied philosophy and literature as an undergrad and political science at the graduate level, Restrepo joined a radical group of socialist leanings. At the time, her writings were limited to political propaganda, but her talent was evident, so she was sent to Brussels and, subsequently, to Spain, as part of an international political network. In Madrid, she witnessed Spain's remarkable return to democracy. Afterwards, Restrepo traveled to Argentina, where, despite military persecution, she joined the locals in their political militancy. At the time, her clandestine lover, and the father of her son Pedro, was a leading member of Argentine Trotskyism, whose name she only discovered thanks to a utility bill. After the baby was diagnosed with toxoplasmosis, Restrepo fled to a working-class neighborhood in Cordoba, her last stop in Argentina. Eventually, given the degree of risk from military repression, the situation became untenable. Having donated a substantial portion of her inheritance to her Argentine colleagues, Restrepo returned to her upper-class milieu in Bogotá, where she joined the staff of an established newsweekly magazine and gained credentials as journalist. In the early 1980s, she was chosen by then president Belisario Betancur as part of a commission to supervise the ongoing peace process with two guerrilla organizations, the M-19 and the EPL, a bitter experience that would feed her early literary efforts. At the same time, as part of her work as political editor for the magazine, Restrepo published weekly columns covering the development of the peace proceedings. In the end, due to the disruption of the truce and its eventual failure, Restrepo grew disenchanted with the government's actions and became a harsh critic of its policies. Her first major literary work, *Historia de una traición* (1986), subsequently renamed *Historia de un entusiasmo*, is an account of the string of events that led to the demise of the process.

Restrepo's relationship with a guerrilla leader led to exile in Mexico, where given the ample time at hand, she began considering writing seriously. Thanks to a stroke of luck—legend has it that the author discovered a roll of bills in a Mexican supermarket—she traveled around the country, researching her first novel thoroughly and establishing a literary method based on her experience as journalist. Deciding to pursue a literary career, Restrepo then returned to Colombia, eager to embrace new projects. Soon after, her relationship with a member of the Liberal Party who had been appointed to a diplomatic post in Rome led to more time abroad. While in Italy, Restrepo shunned official engagements, preferring to read avidly, browse through old Latin manuscripts, and engage in research that, in due course, would feed her following novels, which narrate feuds between two drug-running clans of the Colombian Caribbean and the appearance of an angel in an impoverished neighborhood of Bogotá.

Thanks to her third novel, *Dulce compañía*, Restrepo's international profile began to rise. By the time she returned to Bogotá, where the new left-wing administration of Mayor Luis Garzón named her the head of the Instituto Distrital de Cultura y Turismo, she was well known abroad. Most recently, after the obligations resulting from receiving the Alfaguara Prize became evident—which involved touring a number of countries in a massive promotional campaign—she resigned. In 2006, following Colombian authors like Álvaro Mutis and Marvel Moreno, Restrepo won the Grinzane Cavour award in Italy.

Restrepo has taught literature at the Universidad Nacional de Colombia and the Universidad del Rosario. Though she travels frantically, given her literary obligations, Restrepo currently lives and works in Bogotá, where she reads and writes in a disciplined manner. In recent years, thanks to the English translation of her novels, she has become a staple of the US Latino literary scene. Hollywood has recently acquired the rights for two of her novels, *El leopardo al sol* and *Dulce compañía*, kindling the possibility that her work will reach the big screen.

Literary Production

Restrepo has participated in politics for thirty years; in contrast, her literary career only spans the last twenty years of her life. Given her journalistic roots and political commitment, Restrepo has successfully collaborated with other well-known, socially active Latin American journalists, like Roberto Bardini and Miguel Bonasso. She has frequently contributed to collective projects, such as *Operación Príncipe* (1988), a chronicle of the kidnapping of a Chilean military officer by the group responsible for the assassination attempt on dictator Augusto Pinochet. She has also co-authored or contributed to texts covering Colombia's protracted conflict, such *Once ensayos sobre la violencia* (1985), *En qué momento se jodió Medellín* (1991), *Del amor y del fuego* (1991), and *Otros niños* (1993). At other times, Restrepo has worked on books for children, like *Las vacas comen espaguetis* (1989) and *Olor a rosas invisibles* (2002).

Though lending primacy to imagination, Restrepo's literary production is anchored solidly on journalistic rigor, combining exhaustive documentation and convincing fictionalization of the yield of her investigative efforts. Without a doubt, novels make up the backbone of her hard-earned prestige. During her time in Mexico, she carefully documented a fascinating, forgotten episode of Mexican history. *La isla de la pasión* (1989) is the saga of a young military officer and his family, who, forgotten by the establishment as a result of the Revolution, live long, hazardous years on Clipperton, an island in the Pacific Ocean, in a theoretical defense of national sovereignty. Restrepo has defended the text as a metaphor for exile, inspired by her years as political refugee in Mexico.

Next, upon her return to Colombia, Restrepo painstakingly detailed the feud between two clans in the Colombian Caribbean involved in the marihuana trade of the 1970s and caught in a fratricide war that marks the beginning of the violence prompted by the trade. Originally, Restrepo had planned a script for a television series, but she was soon approached by representatives of the families alluded, who asked her to abandon the audiovisual formula and opt instead for a literary text. The book, *El leopardo al sol* (1993), serves as an early balance of the impact of drug cartels on Colombian life. Although the author consistently upheld her journalistic bent, stylistically, this work exhibits the influence of García Márquez. The book is also marked by Restrepo's residence in Italy, where she gained precious information on the customs of the local underworld.

Her third novel, *Dulce compañía* (1995), shows a more developed, independent voice. It was a major literary success, earning the Sor Juana Inés de la Cruz award in Mexico and the Prix France Culture in Europe. Set amidst the chaos and poverty of a slum in the Colombian capital, Restrepo writes the story of a modern archangel, who seduces the protagonist, a journalist, and then spurs a failed revolt. The religious overtones of the book are an effective literary device, as Restrepo appropriates a mythical tone and mixes it with her customary descriptive bent. In a sort of whimsical, feminist twist of fate, in the story, hypothetically divine contact—the main character's dalliance with the supposed angel—gives rise to a female lineage, in contrast to the strict patriarchal order of conventional Judeo-Christian manuscripts.

The following title, *La novia oscura* (1999), combines melodrama and social criticism more thoroughly. It chronicles the lives of Colombian prostitutes at the site of an oil refinery by the Magdalena River, in a zone of the country particularly prone to violence and conflict. The name of the book alludes to an image by Leo Matiz, a renowned Colombian photographer, which Restrepo pasted to her computer. Eventually, the portrait of the young mestizo girl, used for the cover of the novel's first edition, took hold of Restrepo's imagination, engendered a narrative, and became a vehicle to tackle the level of injustice in this part of Colombia. The main thread of the story is straightforward: Sayonara, the main character, makes the mistake of falling in love, even though she works as a prostitute. The portrayal of the world of brothels in the river port is striking, but Restrepo's goal is patent. Besides the accounts of love, lust, and betrayal, the novel focuses on relevant social issues about the rights of workers, the nearly total absence of public health, and the harsh implications of corporate duplicity.

In her next study, *La multitud errante* (2001), Restrepo returns to the same setting, though the general quality of the place could describe any location in rural Colombia. The main theme of the story is the plight of millions of Colombians displaced from their households as a result of war in the country. To address this situation, Restrepo relies, as usual, on a tale of passion. The book narrates the story of Three Sevens, a man desperate to find Matilde Lina, the woman who rescued and raised him until he was separated from her in the middle of violence. The narrator falls for Three Sevens and must compete with the character's feverish fascination for Matilde Lina, in a slight nod to Freudian theories. The yarn leads to a succinct but emblematic love story, a mix of modern-day fairy tale and pop psychology. In the end, Restrepo ornaments her political sensibilities with specks of magical realism. While it engages an almost apocalyptic scene, fraught with violence and despair, it preserves a nostalgic, lyrical charm.

Restrepo's most recent novel, *Delirio*, tells the story of a man's attempt to unravel the mystery of his wife's mental breakdown during his brief absence from home. Unlike her previous novels, which earned awards after publication, *Delirio* was submitted as an unpublished manuscript, earning the Alfaguara Prize. Nobel laureate José Saramago, a member of the jury, praised the novel as an outstanding achievement. The novel explores the psychological impact of extreme realities, such as Colombia's, and paints a wide canvas of Bogotá, the national capital.

Most critical work on Restrepo's novels emphasizes the fact that her literary production is born largely from a figurative tension between her love for Colombia and its capital, and the harsh realities evident in both locations. In a sense, her work emerges from a dichotomy: the disparity between the imagined nation, that which many Colombians would like to experience—a place to celebrate difference—with the lettered city as its most pristine incarnation, and the obvious limitations of the Colombian state, which have resulted in an unfair, limited national project, leading to inner strife and prolonged conflict. In first instance, novels like *La isla de la pasión* and *El leopardo al sol* center on the lack of government presence at the margins of the nation, and the consequences this might imply for the future of a country. While *La isla* takes place in Mexico—or, for that matter, in a place that would like to think of itself as part of Mexico—it shares many aspects with Restrepo's second novel. Like the marooned protagonists of the Mexican tale, the mobsters in *El leopardo* demonstrate how the fabric of the nation begins to unravel from its very edges, echoing the excesses of a culture that, altogether ignored in the late 1970s and early 1980s, clearly threatens societal status quo by the early 1990s. Along this same vein, *La novia oscura* and *La multitud errante* propose more inclusive versions of nationality—or, at the very least, an enhanced understanding of *colombianidad*—shedding light on marginalized groups, conveniently ignored and demonized by the political establishment. *Dulce compañía*, on the other hand, stands almost as a love letter to the Colombian capital city, a place besieged by social violence and class inequity, but all the more fascinating for its imperfections. *Delirio* brings both tendencies together; its critique of the violent national environment finds roots in the hypocrisies of Bogotá's upper crust, which lives with its back to the rest of society. Critics like Monserrat Ordoñez and Claire Lindsay have pointed out these aspects clearly in their analyses of Restrepo's work. Her concern for memory and history, they argue, hopes to address the injustices of Colombian society from a literary viewpoint.

Stylistically, Restrepo's literature has gradually developed an idiosyncratic style, based on the author's customary graceful and lyrical prose. While the weight of García Márquez and magic realism is evident in some titles—particularly, in portions of *El leopardo al sol*, *Dulce compañía*, and *La multitud errante*—his influence has attenuated swiftly. Most of Restrepo's literature is based on a well-documented formula, which stands at the heart of her literary production: she persistently relies on a love story as a narrative springboard. With a romantic premise at hand—be it Monita and the angel, Sayonara and El Payanés, Three Sevens and Matilde Lina, or Aguilar and Augustina—Restrepo then turns to the surroundings, which habitually embody the inequities and fallacies common to Colombian reality. Yet, what gives her production a high degree of distinctiveness is, undoubtedly, the beautifully detailed spirit of her language, an apparent by-product of her years as journalist, during which she mastered a method that combines meticulous research and fiction, social criticism and humor.

HÉCTOR D. FERNÁNDEZ L'HOESTE

Selected Works

Historia de una traición. Bogotá: Plaza & Janés, 1986; published later as *Historia de un entusiasmo*, Bogotá: Norma, 1999.

La isla de la pasión. Bogotá: Planeta Colombiana, 1993; trans. Dolores M. Koch as *Isle of Passion: A Novel*, New York: Ecco, 2005.

Dulce compañía. Bogotá: Editorial Norma, 1995; trans. Dolores M. Koch as *The Angel of Galilea*, New York: Crown, 1997; trans. Dolores M. Koch as *If an Angel . . .*, New York: HarperCollins, 1998; trans. Françoise Prebois as *Douce compagnie*, Paris: Payot et Rivages, 1998.

El leopardo al sol. Bogotá: Editorial Norma, 1996; trans. Stephen Lytle as *Leopard in the Sun*, New York: Vintage International, 2000.

La novia oscura. Barcelona: Grupo Editorial Norma, 1999; trans. Stephen Lytle as *The Dark Bride*, New York: HarperCollins, 2001.

La multitud errante. Bogotá: Planeta Colombiana, 2001; trans. Dolores M. Koch as *A Tale of the Dispossessed*, New York: Ecco, 2003.

Olor a rosas invisibles. Buenos Aires: Editorial Sudamericana, 2002.

Delirio. Bogotá: Alfaguara, 2004; trans. Natasha Wimmer as *Delirium*, New York: Nan A. Talese/Doubleday, 2007.

Co-works

Various authors. *Once ensayos sobre la violencia*. Bogotá: Fondo Editorial CEREC, 1985.

with Roberto Bardini and Miguel Bonasso. *Operación Príncipe*. Mexico, D.F.: Planeta, 1988.

with Carmen Restrepo. *Las vacas comen espaguetis*. Bogotá: Carlos Valencia Editores, 1989.

with Roberto Burgos Cantor *et al*. *Del amor y del fuego*. Bogotá: Tercer Mundo Editores, 1991.

with Juan Gómez Martínez *et al*. *En qué momento se jodió Medellín*. Bogotá: Editorial Oveja Negra, 1991.

with Azriel Bibliowicz *et al*. *Otros niños: testimonios de la infancia colombiana*. Bogotá: El Áncora Editores, 1993.

References and Further Reading

Cruz Calvo, Mery. "La construcción del personaje femenino en *Dulce compañía*". *Estudios de Literatura Colombiana* 13 (July–Dec. 2003): 84–96.

Lindsay, Claire. "'Clear and Present Danger': Trauma, Memory, and Laura Restrepo's *La Novia Oscura*". *Hispanic Research Journal* 14(1) (February 2003): 41–58.

Melis, Daniela. "Una entrevista con Laura Restrepo". *Chasqui* 34(1) (May 2005): 114–30.

Mejía, Gustavo. "Fragmentación del discurso histórico: Individuo y multitud en *La multitud errante* de Laura Restrepo". *Revista de Crítica Literaria Latinoamericana*30 (59) (2004): 297–304.

Ordóñez, Montserrat. "Ángeles y prostitutas: Dos novelas de Laura Restrepo". In Lady Rojas-Trempe and Catharina Vallejo (eds), *Celebración de la creación literaria de escritoras hispanas en las Américas*. Ottawa, ON; Montreal, QC: GIROL; Enana Blanca, 2000, pp. 93–102.

Rueda, María Helena. "Escritura del desplazamiento. Los sentidos del desarraigo en la narrativa colombiana reciente". *Revista Iberoamericana* 70(207) (Apr.–June 2004): 391–408.

RHEDA, REGINA

The fictional universe of this author is fully contemporary, built upon late twentieth-century and early twenty first-century experience. Her works maintain a primarily urban focus but visit revealing rural sites as well, involving throughout significant transcontinental movement of persons of various stripes. Whether in brief stories set in the megalopolis of São Paulo or novels whose characters cross oceans, Rheda writes with acumen and humor about people, places and variegated relationships.

Regina Rheda (b. 1957) was born in Santa Cruz do Rio Pardo, in the State of São Paulo, Brazil. Still at grammar school, she moved with her family to the ever-burgeoning state capital of São Paulo. She studied in the school of arts and communication at the University of São Paulo (USP), taking a Bachelor of Arts degree in Cinema Studies. From the early 1980s through the mid-1990s, she wrote and directed short films, videos and television programs produced by public organizations, such as the USP, the Department of Culture of the State of São Paulo, and Embrafilme, the national film-production company. Rheda's carnivalesque cinematic works won awards at the most important Brazilian film and video festivals. These short films—which could be described as *neo-chanchadas*, reliving in compact form Brazil's *sui generis* light musical comedies of the 1930s–1950s—were shown in movie theaters throughout the country. From 1982 to 1984, she was singer-songwriter for the irreverent rock band Esquadrilha da Fumaça (Smoke Squadron). Rheda's debut as a writer came in 1994 with the collection of short stories, *Arca sem Noé—Histórias do Edifício Copan* (Noahless Ark: Stories from the Copan Building), including "O mau vizinho" (The Neighbor from Hell), for which she received the Lusophone fiction award from the Parisian Maison de l'Amérique Latine. The volume garnered a Prêmio Jabuti, a national book award in Brazil, in the category of short fiction. The author's first novel, *Pau-de-arara Classe Turística* (First World Third Class), appeared in 1996. Her third book, *Amor sem-vergonha* (Dirty love), is a collection of postfeminist erotic short stories, originally commissioned. In mid-1998, Rheda was writer in residence at the Ledig House International Writers' Colony (Ghent, New York). She worked as editorial assistant for educational books at Editora Saraiva in São Paulo through 1998, after which she relocated to the United States. Her creative and professional experience to this point earned her a description as "expert in multimedia and editorship" (Coelho). Rheda's second novel *Livro que vende* (Book that Sells), published in 2003, took an intensely ironic look at aspects of the publishing industry. Several stories of hers appeared in thematic anthologies, including "O santuário" (The Sanctuary), in a collection of stories involving immigration and emigration, and "Dona Carminda e o príncipe" (Miss Carminda and the Prince), in a volume about school-day experiences. "A frente" (The Front) was a segment in a collection of new women's literature. A university-press volume of Rheda's works in translation includes the Copan stories, the first novel, and a trio of stories with particularly significant international elements.

Rheda writes about city life, turn-of-the-millennium malaise, and global movement. Her incisive wit can serve both to create amusing situations and to question historical conjunctures. Her literary generation was the first to emerge following the demise of the authoritarian military regime that marked all facets of society in Brazil for two decades (1964–85). Rheda grew up during the consolidation of the Brazilian media industries, now among the world's most prominent. As a young critic aptly observes in an introduction to her work in English translation, given the author's background in film, "there is a palpable cinematic quality to her narrative style replete with jump cuts, close-ups, and intensely visual descriptions". In terms of formative influences, the "languages of cinema and television are the most salient," but it is useful to note "affinities with an earlier generation of Brazilian women writers like Sonia Coutinho and Márcia Denser, who explored issues of female sexuality and changing gender roles in the 1970s" (Dunn 2005: xiii–xiv). Rheda herself has referred to such historical literary influences as the principal Portuguese novelist of the nineteenth century, the acerbic Eça de Queiroz (1845–1900); the celebrated Brazilian prose-fiction writer, Graciliano Ramos (1892–1953); the São Paulo regionalist, children's literature master and pioneer publisher, Monteiro Lobato (1882–1948); and the "pope" of Brazilian Modernism, Mário de Andrade (1893–1945).

The setting of the interconnected stories of Rheda's first book is the unevenly modernized cosmopolis of São Paulo, symbolized and embodied in an architectonic habitational monument designed by Brazil's famed architect Oscar Niemeyer. The physical elements of the Copan narratives recall the crossing patterns characteristic of film director Robert Altman. If taken as a whole, the stories are almost like a location-specific "novel of space," in the terms of the venerable German critic Wolfgang Kayser. The Copan building itself was a grand project of prestige in the 1950s, but it became somewhat debased and decadent by the 1990s. The edifice embodies a sort of national allegory in Rheda's opening story, which alludes to the demise of Brazil's democratic modernity with the imposition of military control. The story's protagonist is an unkempt and malodorous dramatist, former victim of dictatorial repression, who aggravates his elderly neighbor, a fastidious widow who looks back on the rule of the generals as an epoch of prosperity when transgressors got due punishment. In the rest of the tales, the Copan building can be seen to operate as a microcosm of urban Brazil, as a diversified array of characters from various walks of life confront each other and difficult situations. *Stories from the Copan Building* is marked by Rheda's well-placed quips and sensitivity to vehicles of pathos and eros alike.

The novel *First World Third Class* follows an adventurous protagonist from her native São Paulo to London, Italy, and back, in an exploration of changing times and values. The imaginary literary sphere, though not necessarily originally composed with a world audience in mind, speaks with universal energy and attitude to current shared interests in urbanization, sexuality, new women's roles, relocation, transnational identities in transition, and globalization *qua* cultural phenomena. In what has been interpreted as a "female-centered traveler's tale," there is an "inevitable clash between callous first-world determinism and not-so-innocent third-world ingenuity and opportunism," and as events develop, the first world's "upper hand ... exploits and exoticizes its entrapped third-world prey" (Harrison 2006). The social and cultural observation, far from ponderous, is cased in a sprightly prose, often engaged to narrate comical circumstances. The narration is punctuated with epistolary flair, a series of letters from the protagonist to friends back home.

The first novel might be regarded as a kind of *Bildungsroman* (novel of education / formation) for a generation of disillusioned middle-class youth. In contrast, the second novel, *Livro que vende*, is much more hybrid and "postmodern". It seems designed to tickle common notions of the novel in its weaving of narrative genres, drawing on all manner of sources, including children's lore, thrillers, romance, cubist script, and broadside ballad. The second part, and last third, of the book, in fact, is composed in folk septains and printed on brown paper to simulate *literatura de cordel* ("stories on a string"), folk literature sold at markets since the nineteenth century or earlier. The title of the extended addendum to Rheda's novel is *Rockordel*, which combines the international pop culture of rock music and Brazil's renowned practice of traditional verse-making and story-telling. As a whole, the novel serves to "dismantle schemes of hypocrisy and ideology" (Amâncio). What Rheda accomplishes in her works of imagination, most especially in the mixed undertaking of *Livro que vende*, aligns with what the Russian theorist Bakhtin called *carnivalization*, a tendency with manifestations throughout the course of literate Western civilization, ever since the Greeks and the Mennipean satire of Luciano: high culture becomes low, low culture ascends to high, rich mixes with poor, virtue is phony, euphemism gives way to salubrious profanity, all in an exorcizing and revitalizing fest.

Indeed, Rheda's fiction contrasts social classes, levels of development (both of nations and diversely defined communities), geographical locations, and narrative currencies. In a variety of ways, the stories, long and short alike, communicate a fundamental generic interplay of parts, aspects of internationalization, and peopled interfaces. With respect to better known international signposts of Brazilian literature, Rheda's 1990s' prose is decidedly post-Jorge Amado, who is known for exotic essentialism, and post-Clarice Lispector, who excelled at abstract expressionism. Rheda's stories in the twenty-first century explore new territory and moral dilemmas. "The Front" deals with matters of ecology, work environments, and gender politics in a small but significant village in the crucial Amazon region. In this tale, Rheda's Brazil is certainly globalized. "The Sanctuary" is set in the United States. Brazilian immigration to the USA increased dramatically since c. 1990, which has generated new inquiries, implicit or explicit, with respect to national identity, notably *vis-à-vis* other Latinos. The precarious, subaltern conditions of transnational migrants in general share the stage in this story with animal rights, also the impetus for "Dona Carminda" and chief concern of Rheda's most recent novel, whose title is taken from a poem by Percy Bysshe Shelley (1792–1822) in which he advocates a vegetarian (without animal product) diet.

CHARLES A. PERRONE

Selected Works

Arca sem Noé—Histórias do Edifício Copan. São Paulo: Paulicéia, 1994. 2nd rev. edn Rio de Janeiro: Booklink, 2002.

Pau-de-arara Classe Turística. Rio de Janeiro: Record, 1996.

Amor sem-vergonha. Rio de Janeiro: Record, 1997.

"O santuário". In Silviano Santiago *et al*. *Pátria estranha*. São Paulo: Nova Alexandria, 2002.

"Dona Carminda e o príncipe". In Moacyr Scliar *et al*. *Histórias dos tempos de escola*. São Paulo: Nova Alexandria, 2002.

Livro que vende. São Paulo: Altana, 2003.

"Miss Carminda and the Prince", trans. Lydia Billon. In *Meridians: Feminism, Race and Transnationalism* (Fall 2004).

"A frente". In Luiz Ruffato (ed.), *Mais trinta mulheres que estão fazendo a nova literatura brasileira*. Rio de Janeiro: Record, 2005.

First World Third Class and Other Tales of the Global Mix. Austin, TX: University of Texas Press, 2005.

Humana Festa (forthcoming).

References and Further Reading

Amâncio, Moacir. "Review of *Livro que vende*". *O Estado de São Paulo*. 7 March 2004, p. D7.

Coelho, Nelly Novaes. "Regina Rheda". In *Dicionário crítico de escritoras brasileiras 1711–2001*. São Paulo: Escrituras, 2002, p. 559.

Dunn, Christopher. "On the Ground in the Global Mix." In *First World Third Class and Other Tales of the Global Mix*. Austin, TX: University of Texas Press, 2005, pp. xiii–xviii.

Foster, David William. "Days and Nights at the Copan: Regina Rheda's *Arca sem Noé*". In *Essays in Honor of Claude Hulet*. Los Angeles, CA: UCLA Department of Spanish and Portuguese, in press.

Harrison, Marguerite Itamar. "Brazil Beyond the Borders". *Women's Review of Books* 25(2) (2006): 27–8.

RIBEIRO TAVARES, ZULMIRA

Zulmira Ribeiro Tavares was born in 1930, in São Paulo, the city that serves as the backdrop to her works of fiction. After being taught at home, she enrolled in a cinema course at the Museum of Art of São Paulo (MASP) in 1952. Her first experience as a writer was as a film critic. In response to an overall interest in the arts, particularly cinema, Tavares has also been an active participant in and supporter of Brazil's national film institute, the Cinemateca Brasileira. In 1955, she published a collection of poems entitled *Campos de Dezembro* (December Fields). Her prize-winning work *Termos de Comparação* (Terms of Comparison), published in 1974, is divided into two parts: a fictional section including poetry and prose, and a more analytical section of essayistic reflection. Subsequently, her short works of prose have often been described as a crossover between short stories and essays.

Fictional Displays of Human Frailties

In her works of fiction, Zulmira Ribeiro Tavares focuses the reader's attention on "universal" concerns, while at the same time concentrating thematically on the mundane, even microscopic (or myopic), details of the lives of middle-class *paulistas*, the inhabitants of São Paulo. She cleverly, and often humorously, uncovers—as if with the aid of a zoom lens—the perilous assumptions and underlying prejudices that lurk beneath the surface of interpersonal relationships. For example, lifelong friends argue incessantly over the ethnicity of a neighbor in the short story "O Japonês dos Olhos Redondos" (The Round-Eyed Japanese) and racial tension simmers amongst members of the Pompeu family in the novel *O Nome do Bispo* (1985, The Name of the Bishop), winner of the Mercedes Benz Prize in Literature. The latter tells the story of 50-year-old Heládio Marcondes Pompeu—named after a distinguished bishop who met Pope Pius XII in 1940—a promising member of an upper-class family who fails to live up to the prominence of his name. Set against the backdrop of the military dictatorship, the novel alternates between remembrances, moments of delirium, and wakeful clarity as it relates the point of view of the main character who, hospital-bound, is undergoing surgery for an intestinal ailment. The novel's ironic wit serves as biting commentary on the fate of an elite family resistant to change, as well as on the state of a nation in turmoil.

Zulmira Ribeiro Tavares' fictional works serve to highlight major themes that encompass the broader scope of human weaknesses, particularly the biases and narrow-mindedness of twentieth-century bourgeois society in São Paulo. The richness of Tavares' fictional language enlivens the banality of her subject matter. *Café Pequeno*—the term itself means trivial minutiae—is a fictional rendering of 1930s São Paulo, written in 1995. The novel is composed of peculiar juxtapositions that together comment critically upon observed reality. Bulls unexpectedly stampede through downtown streets; a public commemoration of the anniversary of the French Revolution is suppressed by the police; a private birthday party is held: all occur on the same day—July 14th—and bring into focus and mock, by way of dark humor and satire, a society deaf to the early indications of Getúlio Vargas' despotic rule. In terms of style, Tavares' prose is finely sculpted from her precise grasp of language. As Luiz Fernando Valente has underscored, her fiction consistently relies on a third-person, omniscient narrator whose overarching point of view intentionally casts a critical eye over all characters and subject matter.

Published in 1990, *Jóias de Família* (Family Jewels) is Zulmira Ribeiro Tavares' fictional jewel, winner of the prestigious national literary prize, the Jabuti. By presenting a protagonist, Maria Bráulia, who is represented as a deceitful, prejudiced upper-class woman, the novel forces the reader to confront the hierarchical structure of a twisted patriarchal legacy. Indeed, the short novel blurs temporal (past and present) and spatial (public and private) distinctions to emphasize the perpetuation of rigid social structures and society's artificial rules. The novel is a compelling portrayal of intrigue and duplicity, revolving around a central question: is the multifaceted jewel Maria Bráulia was given by her late husband real or fake? This dilemma frames the novel's main exposition on the true nature of human beings and their behavioral interactions with each other. Moreover, the concise, well-crafted narrative reveals the double-role of the protagonist as both victim and victimizer. *Jóias de Família* reflects upon opposing concepts of conduct, such as loyalty and betrayal, decorum and deceit, while also underscoring privileged society's biases based on class and race. Well trained in servitude, for instance, the family maid, Maria Preta (literally, Black Mary) remains loyal to her mistress's inherited power. By contrast, this legacy is questioned only by Maria Preta's young niece, Benedita, who alone attempts to subvert the familial hierarchy through access to education.

Short Fiction in Snapshot Form

Zulmira Ribeiro Tavares' 1998 publication *Cortejo em abril* (April Procession) is a collection of 26 separate fictional narratives of varying lengths which—like previous works such as *O Mandril* (The Mandrill), published ten years earlier—focus simultaneously on the universalizing aspects of the human condition (matters of life and death, ambition and loss, among others) and the peculiarities of private relationships. Despite the volume's misleadingly slim stature, the overall effect is of weight and substance, conveyed by way of its wide-ranging thematic sections: meditative reflections on the subject of the sea and belonging in "A praia, o mar" (The Beach, the Sea), for instance, contrast with voyeuristic sketches focused on sex, captured in "Encontros reservados" (Private Encounters), and the media in "Televisão, Televisores" (TV, Television Sets).

In the novella that lends its title to the collection, two male characters with very different life experiences—an architect and a handyman—meet on a historic day of national public mourning for the death of Brazilian President-elect Tancredo Neves. Whereas the funeral procession interrupts the day's routine, it also serves to create an unexpected bond between these two men, who uncharacteristically wind up comparing notes (and revealing secrets) regarding the particular racial characteristics of the women they love.

Other characters are brought to the surface of these fictional pieces in snapshot form, at times revealing different levels of eccentricity. The story "Uma Senhora" (A Lady), for instance, highlights a lady's choice of lingerie for a visit to the cemetery, where she rescues a runaway dog. The mere fact, revealed by another woman, that her underwear is showing brings her inner character into view. In other stories, trivial events are highlighted, such as that presented in "No Motel Tique-Taque" (In the Tic-Toc Motel). Here the story concentrates on a middle-aged woman in an amorous encounter with her lover in a cheap motel. Her feelings of insecurity, as well as her acute consciousness of the irregularity of the situation, give the story a bittersweet flavor that underscores both the woman's position in society and her willingness to "take the best she can" of her illicit affair. This story contrasts with others such as "Doutor em Filosofia e a Manicure de Doutores" (The Philosophy Doctor and the Manicurist of Doctors) which presents women as sexual pawns, manipulated by men.

Maturity and experience also come to the fore in these fictional stories. The tightly written and highly poetic piece "Pequena Mulher a Caminho" (Small Woman on the Road) touches tenderly upon the trajectory of a fragile woman who nevertheless proves competently tough against the rugged, rural landscape:

> Os dias do calendário não são os dias do meu futuro nem foram os dias do meu passado. Os meus dias chegam pelo ar, tão pouco firmes como aquelas férias no campo, da gente da cidade que me dá serviço. Adiante está o mata-burro; mais adiante o sítio, ora com neblina, ora com sol, ora com negrume. No mata-burro me equilibro com o feixe de lenha na cabeça e sigo em frente, a pé; sem ajuda de menino ou motor. Mas, se quebrar as canelas como um burro, sei folgar no meio do caminho e me ajeitar, mesmo com os pés no cativeiro, entre os bichos pequenos da terra que se alegram na minha companhia.
>
> [The calendar days are not my future, nor were they my past. My days blow in, just as breezy as holidays in the countryside taken by city folks who give me work. The cattle-guard is up ahead; beyond is the ranch: sometimes in fog, sometimes in sunlight, sometimes in darkness. At the cattle-guard I balance myself with the bundle of firewood on my head, and I continue forward, on foot, without the aid of man or machine. But, if I should break my ankles like a mule, I know how to be still in the middle of the road, and straighten myself out, even with hobbled feet. I am one with nature's small critters who revel in my company.]

Another paragraph-long piece, entitled "Um Assassino" (An Assassin) is a meditation on aging by the then 68-year-old author, in which Tavares presents in abridged form the "murderous" effects of the passage of time upon a once youthful woman now grown old. The final story in *Cortejo em abril* entitled "Abandono" (Abandonment) takes aging a step farther to depict a world—frightening to those, like the author, whose craft is writing—in which vanishing words witness the tragic loss of memory.

Works in Translation

In addition to translations of *O Nome do Bispo* into German and *Jóias de Família* into German and Italian, Zulmira Ribeiro Tavares' short works of fiction have appeared in translation in English and French in *Brasil/Brazil: A Journal of Brazilian Literature*, *Metamorphoses* and *La Revue Meet*.

MARGUERITE ITAMAR HARRISON

Selected Works

Termos de Comparação. Rio de Janeiro: Perspectiva, 1974.
O Japonês dos Olhos Redondos. Rio de Janeiro: Paz e Terra, 1982.
O Nome do Bispo: Prosa de Ficção. São Paulo: Brasiliense, 1985. New edition: São Paulo: Companhia das Letras, 2004.
O Mandril. São Paulo: Brasiliense, 1988.
Jóias de Família. São Paulo: Brasiliense, 1990.
Café Pequeno. São Paulo: Companhia das Letras, 1995.
Cortejo em Abril: Ficções. São Paulo: Companhia das Letras, 1998.

References and Further Reading

Brandão, Luis Alberto. *Grafias da Identidade: Literatura Contemporânea e Imaginário Nacional*. Rio de Janeiro and Belo Horizonte: Lamparina Editora and Fale, 2005.
Faria, Álvaro Alves de. *Palavra de Mulher: Entrevistas*. São Paulo: Senac Editora, 2003.
Harrison, Marguerite Itamar. "Between Duplicity and Decorum: Memory as Transgressed Reality in Zulmira Ribeiro Tavares' *Jóias de Família*". *Latin-American Literary Review* 33(66) (July–December 2005): 65–76.
Louyot, Anne. *São Paulo en mouvement: Des innovateurs dans la ville*. Paris: Autrement, 2005.
Passos, Cleusa Rios. "*Jóias de Família*: O Prazer da Encenação". *Revista da USP* 13 (1992): 179–82.
Sanches Neto, Miguel. "Identidades para Quatro Paredes". *Travessia* 25 (1992): 118–28.
Valente, Luiz F. "Onisciência e Controle em *O Nome do Bispo*". *Brasil/Brazil* 2 (1989): 28–45.
Waldman, Berta. "Cara e Coroa". *Remate de Males* 7 (1987): 109–14.

RIVAS MERCADO, ANTONIETA

Born into a wealthy family accustomed to the benefits of friendship with the turn-of-the-century Mexican dictator Porfirio Díaz, Antonieta Rivas Mercado (1900–931) received a privileged education. She grew up among notable artists, who were friends of her architect father, and she spent significant portions of her childhood in Europe, where she studied dance and perfected her French. Rivas Mercado's father's wealth and support allowed her to participate actively in an artistic realm typically proscribed for women at the time. However, in 1931, years after her divorce from a US-born husband and her father's death, Rivas Mercado wearied before the unaccustomed challenges of financial difficulty; she renounced a projected novel and a custody fight with her ex-husband for their son, and committed suicide in Notre Dame cathedral in Paris.

An Artistic Life

In the years preceding her unhappy end, Antonieta used her inheritance to sponsor artists in Mexico. She helped found the Mexican Symphonic Orchestra, she published novels such as *Dama de corazones* (1928, Queen of Hearts) by Xavier Villaurrutia and *Novela como nube* (1928, Novel Like a Cloud) by Gilberto Owen, and in 1928 she collaborated in the establishment of the experimental theatre company, *Teatro de Ulises* (Ulysses Theatre). The theatre project produced six works and brought together the central figures of the Mexican literary and artistic group, the *Contemporáneos*. Kristen Pessola's dissertation indicates the exclusive nature of the Ulysses Theatre by noting that for the first performances, the group sometimes played to by-invitation-only audiences of 50 guests (2001, p. 43). Rivas Mercado belonged to an elite group, notwithstanding her influential innovations in Mexican art. Despite her participation as performer and all-round participant in the experimental theatre, to date, Rivas Mercado's name is only loosely associated with the *Contemporáneos* and their cosmopolitan artistic vision, perhaps due to sexism in the critical vision.

Rivas Mercado's love letters to the homosexual painter Miguel Rodríguez Lozano, dated from 1927 until 1931, are available under the title *87 cartas de amor* (1975, Eighty-seven Love Letters). The frustration of loving a man unable to fulfil her sexual interest seems to have galvanized Rivas Mercado to seek other outlets for her intense blend of artistic and amorous passion. In 1929, Rivas Mercado teamed up with José Vasconcelos and supported his ultimately unsuccessful bid for president of Mexico. Rivas Mercado received little for her investment in Vasconelos, as his financial backer, political collaborator, and lover. Even so, after leaving Vasconcelos in 1929 for a move to New York and then France, in 1930, Rivas Mercado penned an account of the campaign, *La campaña* (The Campaign), that idealizes Vasconcelos's character and his role as national savior. In 1931, Vasconcelos published the story, along with two dramas by Rivas Mercado, in the magazine *La antorcha* and later he included *La campaña* in his memoirs. Rivas Mercado's original text was not published in its entirety until 1975 in Luis Mario Schneider's edition.

Rivas Mercado's complex romantic affairs perhaps motivated a temporary collective amnesia regarding her life and work. In the 1980s and 1990s, however, international interest in Rivas Mercado was rekindled with the publication of her letters in 1975 and her complete works in 1981. Rivas Mercado wrote four short stories, four chapters and a detailed outline for the novel, two plays, and a brief diary. Pessola notes that the short stories, which tend to focus on gender issues, may have enjoyed only Rodríguez Lozano as an audience ("Antonieta," 2001, p. 131). The incomplete novel, "El que huía" (The One who Fled) was intended to examine themes of travel, Mexican national identity, and gender. The plays select political topics. The one-act "Episodio electoral" (Electoral Episode) considers the experience of a political prisoner and examines the military's manipulation of public opinion. The longer, though incomplete "Un drama" (A Drama) represents the experiences of prisoner José de León Toral, the assassin of ex-president Álvaro Obregón in 1928, as Toral and his advisor, the nun Madre Conchita make a bid for morally superior status against a corrupt Mexican political machine.

Criticism of the Artistic Life

Given the intimate relationship between Rivas Mercado's personal and artistic life, it comes as no surprise that contemporary critics analyze the artist through concepts of performance. Vicky Unruh examines how Rivas Mercado might be seen to "dress and undress" with ideas. In an article entitled "Una equívoca Eva" (An Equivocal Eve), Unruh parallels Rivas Mercado's self-consciously created public persona with her theatrical characters' development of social masks. Unruh expands this analysis in a chapter from her book *Performing Women*. There, Unruh examines the process of performance as a cognitive tool that values rehearsal over finished product. Unruh identifies Rivas Mercado's central artistic concern from 1929 to 1931 as the question of "how to combine a life of intellectual reflection with critical engagement in the world", a topic that is intersected with gender tensions (2006, p. 128). The concept of performance allows Unruh to reconceptualize the same problem that other critics find—namely, Rivas Mercado's small literary production and complex life, through terms that do not center on the romantic discourse often used to understand Rivas Mercado. An example of this latter tendency appears in Martha Robles's analysis of Rivas Mercado as suffering from an intelligence that was superior to her capacity to love. Fabienne Bradu writes a readable biography of Rivas Mercado that portrays the artist as spoiled and unable to establish discipline and measured maturity over her romantic or artistic passions. Contrary to the tendency to view Rivas Mercado through her romantic troubles is Kathryn Skidmore Blair's English-language novel, *In the Shadow of the Angel* (1995). Blair drafts 570 pages of her realistic, carefully researched, mechanical prose perhaps in tribute to her husband, Rivas Mercado's only son. Only on page 419 does Rivas Mercado meet Rodríguez Lozano, and not until page 458 does the possibility of meeting presidential candidate Vasconcelos arise.

The most recent and provocative criticism on Rivas Mercado appears in an article by Kristen Pessola, entitled "Forgeries of a Failed Hero," where she argues persuasively that Vasconcelos forged Rivas Mercado's suicide letter in his autobiography *La flama* (1959, The Flame) and thus created a fictitious ending to their story, an ending that absolved Vasconcelos of responsibility for Rivas Mercado's suicide and cleared him of being abandoned by his lover, since according to the letter, he had declared to her that he needed no one but God. Pessola bases her conclusions on the similarity in style between the letter and Vasconcelos's writing and the fact that none of the supposed entries that Vasconcelos quotes appear in the version of the *Diario de Burdeos* (Diary from Burdeos) we have today. This argument casts new light on previous criticism, since as Pessola notes, the suicide confession tends to function as an explanatory element for Rivas Mercado's biography.

Thus, when read through Pessola's argument, Jean Franco seems to misunderstand Rivas Mercado by arguing that her suicide note and last acts "indicate that she was unable to live a freedom she found impoverished without love" (1989, p. 122). Nevertheless, Franco's argument that Rivas Mercado acts with male logic by shooting herself with Vasconcelos's pistol captures an aspect of Rivas Mercado's vacillations between recommending traditional feminine roles in her writing and attempting to alter them in her life. For example, an ambivalent view of the United States and its supposedly liberated conditions for women surfaces in Rivas Mercado's essay "La mujer mexicana" (The Mexican Woman) when she argues that Mexican women must assume power through the moral education of their husbands and sons. A discourse of love gives Rivas Mercado the authority to comment on the public sphere and thus she recommends a stronger, though domestic, role for Mexican women.

Tensions and Contradictions

Rivas Mercado's privileged upbringing perhaps encouraged her appreciation of Catholic values and women's domestic roles. This appreciation endured even as she transgressed these principles throughout her adult life. Rivas Mercado seems caught between attractions that are not necessarily opposites, but that somehow impede a coherently unified discourse: she trades private love letters to a homosexual for public, political panegyric to a heterosexual macho. She vacillates between the ultimately unsuccessful voice in love with Rodríguez Lozano or Vasconcelos and the voice that tells others how to love. She wavers between her desire for rebellious experimentation that claims authority by disdaining it and the desire to establish personal authority as a stable, Mexican, conservative model. In sum, Rivas Mercado lives and writes in an incongruous yet fascinating manner.

Rather than overtly examine these contradictions, Rivas Mercado seems to search for narrative formulas that support clear-cut distinctions that impede recognition of her ambivalence. Rivas Mercado may employ this Manichean view as an expedient method to assert publicly her own correctness. In other words, she may have found it easiest to consider herself correct by insisting on clear distinction between right and wrong positions. Even her unfinished novel brings into play these melodramatic aspects, with names such as "Malo" (Bad) for a character. As such binaries may imply, Rivas Mercado does not write with a well-developed sense of humor. This seriousness may expose another bid for authority. A more humorous technique would trust the reader to understand the joke, and Rivas Mercado does not trust her audience. Her efforts to control texts as an unambiguous allegory encourage her to establish the rules and follow them with devotion otherwise inexplicable in such an iconoclastic artist.

EMILY HIND

Selected Works

Cartas a Manuel Rodríguez Lozano. Ed. Isaac Rojas Rosillo. Mexico: Secretaría de Educación Pública, 1975. Enlarged edition(s) published as *87 cartas de amor y otros papeles*. Xalapa: Universidad Veracruzana, 1981.

Obras completas de María Antonieta Rivas Mercado. Ed. Luis Mario Schneider. Mexico: Secretaría de Educación Pública, Editorial Oasis, 1981.

La campaña de Vasconcelos. Prol. Luis Mario Schneider. Mexico: Oasis, 1981.

Correspondencia. Ed. Fabienne Bradu. Xalapa: Universidad Veracruzana, 2005.

References and Further Reading

Blair, Kathryn Skidmore. *A la sombra del ángel*. 1995. Trans. Leonor Tejada. México D.F.: Grupo Patria Cultural, Nueva Imagen, 2000. Trans. as *In the Shadow of the Angel*. S.I.: 1st Books, 2005.

Bradu, Fabienne. *Antonieta (1900–1931)*. México D.F.: Fondo de Cultura Económica, 1991.

Domínguez Michael, Christopher. "Crimen en el altar". In *Tiros en el concierto: Literatura mexicana del siglo V.* 2nd edn. México D.F.: Ediciones Era, 1999, pp. 124–56.

Franco, Jean. "Body and Soul: Women and Postrevolutionary Messianism". In *Plotting Women: Gender and Representation in Mexico*. New York: Columbia University Press, 1989, pp. 102–28.

Pesola, Kristin. "Antonieta Rivas Mercado: Power, Culture, and Sexuality in Post-Revolutionary Mexico." Diss. Duke University, 2001.

——. "Forgeries of a Failed Hero: Antonieta Rivas Mercado in the Hands of José Vasconcelos". *Latin American Literary Review* 33(66) (2005): 95–114.

——. "Gendering the Melodrama of Legitmacy: Antonieta Rivas Mercado and José Vasconcelos Write the Campaign of 1929". *Revista de Estudios Hispánicos* 38(3) (2004): 487–508.

Unruh, Vicky. "Una equívoca Eva moderna: *Performance* y pesquisa en el proyecto cultural de Antonieta Rivas Mercado". *Revista de Crítica Literaria Latinoamericana* 24(48) (1998): 61–84.

——. "'Dressing and Undressing the Mind': Antonieta Rivas Mercado's Unfinished Performance". In *Performing Women and Modern Literary Culture in Latin America*. Austin, TX: University of Texas Press, 2006, pp. 115–34.

ROBLES, MARTHA

The third oldest of seven brothers and sisters, Martha Robles (b. 1948) grew up in Guadalajara, Jalisco, Mexico, where she freely sampled books from her paternal grandfather's library. As a young woman, Robles overcame her family's lack of enthusiasm regarding her education and graduated with honors in 1973 with a degree in sociology. She received the Gabino Barreda award from the National Autonomous University of Mexico (UNAM) for her Master's degree in literature in Spanish. She also obtained a Master's degree in social urban development from the Institute of Social Studies in Holland. Robles's personal life follows the trajectory of many of her protagonists: she divorced her first husband, a Norwegian architect, when her daughter Sofía was less than a year old. Later, she married and eventually divorced journalist and historian Gustavo García Cantú. From 1976 until the mid-1980s, Robles worked as a professor at the Center for Political Studies in the UNAM. In 1989, she entered the National System of Researchers. Martha Robles has lived for several decades in a privileged southern zone of Mexico City, from where she exercises the ferocious discipline that makes her one of the most prolific women intellectuals in Mexico. During various and occasionally overlapping periods, Robles has participated in Mexican public life through weekly radio programs, weekly publications in the newspaper *Excélsior*, and the publication of biographies, poetry, and novels.

Clandestine Biographies

Despite Robles's long bibliography, critics rarely comment on her work. Her series of four novels, collectively titled *Biografías clandestinas* (Clandestine Biographies) provides a good starting point for explaining this lack of critical attention. Robles wrote the first installment of the series when she was 21 years old with the help of a grant from the Mexican Center for Writers from 1978–79. The novel *Memorias de la libertad* (1979, Memories of Liberty) shows Robles's strength as a critical, political thinker and takes up the difficult years surrounding the student clash with the violently oppressive Mexican government in 1968. The autobiographical elements of the novel examine the protagonist's dissatisfaction with marital life, pregnancy, and divorce, as well as her renewed search for independence and intellectual integrity. This search leads to travel and study in Europe and the United States. *Memorias de la libertad* anticipates two aspects of Robles's style that will intensify with the later novels: hermeticism and a lack of immediate narrated action.

The second novel in the series, *Los octubres de otoño* (1982, The Octobers of Autumn) depends more heavily on dialogue than the first. The first novel's protagonist, Mariana, is transformed into the second novel's Natalia, a brainy, rebelliously independent and hypercritical, yet conservative 23-year-old who divorces her husband, has a young child, and returns to school. Additional similarities to the first novel involve the focus in *Los octubres de otoño* on Mexico over the same difficult period surrounding the year 1968. Fernando Alegría gives a glowing review to this second novel and finds the prose poetic, sensual, and combative, among other adjectives.

The last two novels in the series of *Clandestine Biographies* increasingly retreat from accessible techniques in favor of hermetic musings on failed relationships. *La condena* (1996, The Sentence) also meditates the idea of the Nation, while *La ley del Padre* (1998, The Law of the Father) takes up the topic of God. These last two novels also display Robles's autobiographical tendencies and her desire to be taken seriously as an erudite, profound thinker concerned with the nature of human existence. Robles's characters suffer philosophical restlessness expressed in lengthy interior monologues that showcase thorny though lucid prose and learned quotations. The novels' endings tend to articulate a declaration of liberty and rupture with the past. Thus, each novel ends with at least the promise of a new beginning.

Poetry and Nonfiction: Trials and Ideals

Across genres, Robles appears a largely humorless and confident authority who almost never asks a question unless she already has an answer. Despite Robles's self-characterization as a non-believer, her poetry reveals constant religious inquiry. Her cerebral poetry often jumps from indigenous themes from Mesoamerican religious beliefs to ancient European thought to personal reminiscence and fears. In her nonfiction writing, Robles seems enamored of abstract notions of justice, truth, rationality, and liberty. From her early studies of education in Mexico (1977) and the related study of José Vasconcelos (1989), Robles proves herself a careful though idealistic academic. Both these early nonfiction texts favor fact collection and vehement argument rather than meditative questioning and the posing of original and provocative hypotheses. As her career progresses, Robles begins to publish biographies that eschew careful detailing of bibliographical sources and seem paradoxically couched in stiff language and aimed at a non-specialized, general public. Robles's concern with classical studies and especially with ancient Greece appears in many of her texts. In *Los pasos del héroe* (1998, The Hero's Steps), Robles studies the life of Alejandro the Great, and this interest may stem from her admiration of Alfonso Reyes, whom she defends in an introduction to his work as a great critic and historian. In later texts, Robles transfers this admiration to her second husband, Gastón García Cantú, whom she sometimes cites as a historical authority on such topics as José Vasconcelos. It appears that García Cantú wielded considerable influence over Robles's interest in these fields.

In 1985, Robles began her career as a journalist, mostly drafting op-ed pieces for *Excélsior*. Her journalism strikes a tone of self-assured authority, and often champions feminist precepts. Thus, Robles's journalism worries about the quality of life for the Mexican poor, sometimes singling out the problems of poor women, and despairs over a national government that seems uninterested in controlling the rate of population growth and limiting corruption. The conservative thrust of this criticism surfaces when Robles offers negative generalizations concerning the Mexican people. For example, her pessimistic view of education in Mexico, earlier expressed in her book-length study of the subject, reappears in her journalistic pieces for *Excélsior* anthologized in *La metáfora del poder* (1993, The Metaphor of Power), where Robles decries the lazy multitudes at the UNAM that devolve instead of progressing (p. 35). In a second anthology of her journalism, *Nosotras y el sistema* (1995, We Women and the System), Robles states than less than 10 percent of the half million students at the national university are academically salvageable (p. 105). In this same collection, Robles expresses characteristic frustration with what she identifies as passivity and a lack of gentility in the Mexican populace (p. 265). Against the implication in the title, the reader is never sure if Robles belongs to the "we" and her heated generalizations about Mexicans. Perhaps Robles's viewpoint stems not only from conservatism but also from idealism: she seems to criticize Mexican national events from a cherished notion of what the nation ought to be. This unbending and perhaps unrealistic ideal may encourage a criticism that seems rigid and more abstract than practical.

The Authoritative Feminist

Robles's nonfiction exhibits a tense relationship with feminism. Beginning with her first novel and its relentlessly negative portrayal of the dominating, selfish mother figure, Robles consistently isolates her women protagonists from nurturing relationships with other females and concentrates on failed heterosexual romance. In her essays, she often acts as a relentless critic of other Mexican women writers and bemoans what she perceives to be the women writers' lack of academic rigor. Even as Robles rescues women writers in her valuable two volume collection of criticism on Mexican women writers, *La sombra fugitiva: Escritoras en la cultura nacional* (1989, The Fugitive Shadow: Women Writers in the National Culture), Robles seems to prefer to express herself in an ungendered, authoritative voice perhaps modeled after the self-assured and erudite prose of her preferred twentieth-century male subjects of study: José Vasconcelos, Alfonso Reyes, Octavio Paz, and José Ortega y Gasset. In fact, Robles's typically ruthless critical reading of women's texts becomes all-forgiving when she analyzes the work of her ex-husband García Cantú, Vasconcelos, and her other intellectual heroes. In sum, Robles's work alternates between high points of critical lucidity, cold rationality, stylistic grace, erudition, and intuitive illumination, and low points of imitative, unoriginal, tedious, overwritten, self-indulgent, and overgeneralized "universalizing" texts. Over the course of her prolific career, Martha Robles may provide an excellent case study in the difficulties of exercising intellectual ambition in a sexist context that discourages truly autonomous women thinkers.

EMILY HIND

Selected Works

Novels from the Cycle Biografías clandestinas

Memorias de la libertad. México: CIA General de Ediciones, 1979.
Los octubres de otoño. Mexico: Océano, 1982.
La condena. Mexico: FCE, 1996.
La ley del Padre. Mexico: FCE, 1998.

Poetry

Deslumbramientos. Mexico: Tiempo Extra, 1992.
Evocación de goces. Illustrations by Héctor Xavier. Mexico: Gottdiener, 1996.

Cultural and Literary Criticism

Educación y sociedad en la historia de México. Mexico: Siglo Veintiuno, 1977.
Entre el poder y las letras: Vasconcelos en sus memorias. México D.F.: Fondo de Cultura Económica, 1989.
La sombra fugitiva: Escritoras en la Cultura Nacional. Vols I and II. Mexico: Diana, 1989.
La metáfora del poder. Mexico: Porrúa, 1993.
Memoria de la antigüedad. Mexico D.F.: CONACULTA, 1994.
Nosotros y el sistema. Mexico: Planeta, 1995.
Mujeres, mitos y diosas. México D.F.: FCE, CONACULTA, 1996.
Los pasos del héroe. Mexico: CONACULTA, FCE, 1998.
Mujeres del siglo XX. Mexico: Fondo de Cultura Económica, 2002.

Prologues

Reyes, Alfonso. *Posición de América*. Mexico: Ceestem, Nueva Imagen, 1982.
García Cantú, Gastón. *Idea de México*. Puebla: Gobierno del Estado de Puebla, Secretaría de Cultura, 1988.

References and Further Reading

Alegría, Fernando. "Review of *Los octubres de otoño*". In *Nueva historia de la novela hispanoamericana*. Hanover, NH: Ediciones del Norte, 1986, pp. 428–30.
Hind, Emily. "Entrevista con Martha Robles". In *Entrevistas con quince autoras mexicanas*. Madrid: Iberoamericana; Frankfurt: Verveurt, 2003, pp. 199–210.

Joffroy, Michelle. "Engendering a Revolution: Crisis, Feminine Subjects, and the Fictionalization of 1968 in Three Contemporary Mexican Novels by Women." Diss. University of Arizona, 1999.

Jozef, Bella. Interview with Martha Robles. In *Diálogos Oblíquos*. Rio de Janeiro: Francisco Alves, 1999, pp. 57–62.

Sisson-Guerrero, Elisabeth. "Martha Robles: Enfrentamiento con su México." Interview. *Dactylus* 15 (1996): 121–33.

Valencia, Tita. "Las biografías clandestinas". *Revista de literatura mexicana contemporánea* 4(9) (1998): 75–81.

RODRÍGUEZ DE TIÓ, LOLA

Lola Rodríguez de Tió (1843–1924) is hailed as one of the greatest Puerto Rican poets, activists, and expatriates of the nineteenth century. She is known for composing the lyrics to the original version of today's Puerto Rican national anthem, and for coining the phrase "Cuba and Puerto Rico / are two wings of one bird". Scholarship on Rodríguez Tió reveals many discrepancies; further study is necessary to arrive at a definitive version of her life and works.

Patriotism and Exile

Lola (née María de los Dolores) was born in San Germán, Puerto Rico on September 14, 1843, to María del Carmen Ponce de León y Martínez Mariño and the founder of the island's first law bar, Sebastián Rodríguez de Astudillo y Ramírez del Postigo. At a young age Lola showed signs of a sharp intellect and a talent for writing verse. According to a family source, Lola's father had her attend a school for boys but chose to tutor her himself when she claimed that she "already knew more than the teacher".

In 1865, Lola married Bonocio Tió Segarra, a journalist and businessman educated in Barcelona's reformist circles. In a willful riposte to a teasing comment about her tresses during her courtship, Lola had them cut and began to sport her androgynous "man's haircut". From 1866 to 1871, they settled in San Germán, where Lola gave birth to a daughter, María Dolores Elena Patricia (also known as Patria). The couple hosted a literary salon frequented by reformists from all over the island. Lola's revolutionary anthem is said to have been composed at their salon shortly before the failed attempt at a separatist insurrection in the nearby town of Lares in 1868.

In 1871, the couple settled in the city of Mayagüez, where Lola published her first book of poems, *Mis cantares* (My Songs), in 1876. In the Preface, her husband criticized the failure of the Spanish regime to bring education and culture in the island. Soon after, the regime made them relocate to Caracas, Venezuela, where Rodríguez de Tió worked as a journalist and befriended the exiled Puerto Rican revolutionary and intellectual Eugenio María de Hostos (1839–1903).

In 1878, the Tió-Rodríguez family returned to Mayagüez to work in journalism and in the founding of the city's first *casino* (cultural center). In 1881, they launched the women's journal *La Almojábana*, whose title refers to a typical cornbread dish. Six years later, when a number of secret societies, often made up by *autonomistas,* orchestrated a successful boycott against Spanish merchants, the Governor Romualdo Palacios imprisoned Autonomist Party founders and terrorized sympathizers in the *compontes* ("corrective" torture sessions). Through her contacts in Madrid's official circles and liberal press, Rodríguez de Tió successfully petitioned for Palacios's freedom. Later she personally persuaded the new Spanish governor, José Contreras, to free the fourteen imprisoned *autonomista* leaders. Historians celebrate Rodríguez de Tío's interventions during the *compontes* as her greatest accomplishment in political activism.

The Tió-Rodríguez family was again forced to leave the island in 1889. They settled in Havana, where Lola collaborated in newspapers such as *El Figaro* (The Figaro) and *La Habana Elegante* (Elegant Havana) under the pseudonym of Hipatia. She collected her patriotic poetry about Antillean "siblinghood" in *Mi libro de Cuba* (1893, My Book of Cuba). In 1896, Lola and Patria left Cuba to join Bonocio in New York, as the Spanish reaction against the war of independence launched in eastern Cuba in 1895 began to marginalize political activists in Havana. In New York, Rodríguez de Tió subscribed to the Cuban revolutionary cause by serving as an official in fund-raising clubs and participating regularly in recitals commemorating heroes and events of the first Cuban War of Independence. After the war ended with the US intervention of 1898 the family returned to settle permanently in Cuba.

Rodríguez de Tió's ongoing nostalgia for Puerto Rico is manifest in the poetry she wrote in Cuba. In 1915 she toured her homeland in her first public visit after a 23-year absence. She was honored at various cultural centers, including the Ateneo Puertorriqueño. At the Ateneo celebration, her comments about the "civilizing" effect US rule had brought to the island were reproved in the press by Union Party independence advocates. She would visit the island twice before her death in 1924 at the age of 81 in Havana.

Early Feminist Advocacy

Education was a lifelong passion of Rodríguez de Tió. In 1875, she published in *El Eco de las Lomas* (The Echo of the Hills) the essay "La influencia de la mujer en la civilización" (The Influence of Women on Civilization), in which she lobbies for women's education. At a time when modernization and progress were key national concerns, she emphasized higher education for women as a way of fomenting national development. In 1884, she gave the speech "La educación de la mujer" (Women's Education; published in 1885), to mark the opening of a school for young women in Mayagüez. Her advocacy for women's rights continued throughout her life. In 1907, she published the essay "El feminismo" (Feminism) calling for full suffrage and greater equality for women.

Poetry and Prose

Rodríguez de Tió is considered a major figure of Puerto Rican romantic poetry. Her verses are intimate and lyrical, with epic tones in her patriotic poems. Her primary themes are abstract ideas such as love, liberty, family, Antillean sovereignty, patriotic nostalgia, and, in her later verses, existential themes that explore the meaning of life. Literary influences observed in her poetry include the Spanish romantic poet Gustavo Adolfo Bécquer and the Spanish mystic poet Fray Luis de León (1527–91). Although her published poetry dates from 1876 to 1924, scholarly studies generally note that her work never subscribed to the esthetic agenda of the *modernismo* movement in vogue among Latin American writers from the 1880s. Instead, Rodríguez de Tió relied on romantic themes and styles to engineer new modes of civic discourse in poems written to be performed live in public forums rather than read privately.

Mis cantares marked the beginning of a rich literary career. Other major works published during her lifetime were *Claros y Nieblas* (1886, Clearings and Fog) and *Mi libro de Cuba*. Rodríguez de Tió's full collection of verses are published in her *Obras completas* (Complete Works).

Rodríguez de Tió's prose, in the form of articles, editorials, literary criticism, and her private letters, is still being rediscovered and made available to scholars. An edition of her New York epistolary to her niece Laura Nazario (*Cartas a Laura;* Letters to Laura; 1896–99) is forthcoming. The fourth volume of the *Obras completas* contains a selection of her speeches, journalistic articles, cultural commentaries, and literary criticism. Many of her articles and much of her correspondence has not been published in recent editions; Aileen Schmidt notes that Rodríguez de Tió's articles appeared in the periodicals *La crónica* (Caracas, 1877–78), *El Eco de Las Lomas* (San Germán, 1880), *La Patria* (New York, 1898), *La Provincia* (Havana, 1900). Carlos F. Mendoza Tió has edited three volumes of miscellanea regarding Rodríguez de Tió's literary career under the series *Investigaciones literarias* (Literary Investigations). These mixed writings include various verses dedicated to the poet, announcements of events and speeches read in her honor, and some of her own verses.

Lola Rodríguez de Tió is a key figure in the national literature of Puerto Rico and Cuba for her prolific, intelligent, and moving verses that speak to the human experience and for her tenacious and passionate efforts to realize a sovereign Puerto Rico.

NANCY LAGRECA AND CÉSAR SALGADO

Selected Works

Obras completas. 4 vols. San Juan, Puerto Rico: Instituto de Cultura Puertorriqueña, 1968.

Diecisiete cartas inéditas con otras editadas cambiadas con doña Lola Rodríguez de Tió (1894–1907). Edited by Luis Alberto Sánchez.

References and Further Reading

Birmingham-Pokorny, Elba. "Del centro a la periferia: en el discurso de Lola Rodríguez de Tió". In Luis Jiménez (ed.), *La voz de la mujer en la literatura hispanoamericana fin de siglo*. San José, Costa Rica: Editorial de la Universidad de Costa Rica. 1999.

Cancel, Mario R. "Imágenes de una poeta; un asomo a la bibliografía de Lola Rodríguez de Tió". In *Anti-figuraciones: bocetos puertorriqueños*. San Juan, Puerto Rico: Isla Negra, 2003, pp. 51–9.

Leila Cuevas, Carmen. *Lola de América*. San Germán, Puerto Rico: Editorial Cultural, 1969.

Meléndez, Concha. "Nuevo verdor florece: Homenaje a Lola Rodríguez de Tió". In *Obras completas*. Vol. 2. San Juan, Puerto Rico: Instituto de Cultura Puertorriqueña, 1970.

Mendoza Tió, Carlos F. *Investigaciones literarias: Lola Rodríguez de Tió*. 3 vols. San Juan, Puerto Rico: Carlos F. Mendoza de Tió, 1975–78.

——. "Apuntes para una biografía: Lola Rodríguez de Tió". *Al Margen: Revista de las Artes* 1 (1979): 3–42.

Rosario Vélez, Jorge. "Registros de la patria y la nostalgia en Gertrudis Gómez de Avellaneda y Lola Rodríguez de Tió". *Revista de Estudios Hispánicos* 31(1) (2004): 83–103.

Ruiz, Vicki L. and Korrol, Virginia Sánchez (eds) *Latina Legacies: Identity, Biography, and Community*. New York: Oxford University Press, 2005.

Santos Silva, Loreina. "Mujeres poetas puertorriqueñas del siglo xix". In Luisa Campuzano (ed.), *Mujeres latinoamericanas: Historia y cultura siglos XVI al XIX*. Vol. 2. Havana: Casa de las Américas, 1997, pp. 279–86.

Schmidt, Aileen. "Travels and Identities in the Chronicles of Three Nineteenth-Century Caribbean Women". Trans. Lizabeth Paravisini-Gebert. In Lizabeth Paravisini-Gebert and Ivette Romero-Cesareo (eds), *Women at Sea: Travel Writing and the Margins of Caribbean Discourse*. New York: Palgrave, 2001, pp. 203–23.

Toledo, Josefina. *Lola Rodríguez de Tió: Contribución para un estudio integral*. San Juan, Puerto Rico: Editorial LEA, Ateneo Puertorriqueño, 2002.

ROFFÉ, REINA

Reina Roffé (b. 1951), of Sephardic Jewish ancestry, was born in Buenos Aires, Argentina. She studied journalism, public relations, and literature in Buenos Aires. Roffé views herself as a feminist. Besides being a recognized writer, she has made a successful career as a literary critic and a columnist. Roffé has written for magazines and newspapers in Argentina, the United States, and Spain. She has contributed to magazines such as *Latinoamericana, Siete días*, *Marie Claire*, *Cambio 16*; and newspapers such as *Página 12*, *La Opinión*, *Chicago Sun Times*, and *El Tiempo Argentino*. In 1981, she was awarded a Fulbright Fellowship at the University of Iowa International Writing Program and stayed for almost four years in the United States. In 1985, she returned to Argentina. In 1988, for economic reasons, she went to live in Madrid where she now resides and works as a journalist. Despite the long absence from her native land, Roffé feels deeply attached to Argentina.

Writer

Reina Roffé published her first autobiographical novel, *Llamado al puf* (A Call to Puf) in 1969. In this work, young Celia looks back on her life in order to make sense of her desolate present situation. She tells about her conflicts growing up in a bourgeois, repressive, middle-class Buenos Aires immigrant family. Despite the despair conveyed in the account, however, it suggests a hopeful end when Celia is finally able to leave her oppressive family to start a life outside her home. The novel was acclaimed by the critics and won the Sixto Pondal Ríos Award in Buenos Aires for the best novel by a younger writer. Nevertheless, the narrative was also criticized for allegedly offering too much personal content and for lacking social conscience. In 1973, she published the non-fictional work about the Mexican writer Juan Rulfo called *Juan Rulfo: autobiografía armada* (Juan Rulfo: An Assembled Autobiography). Her second fictional narrative with the provocative title *Monte de Venus* (1976, Mons Veneris) takes place in a women's evening school. It makes reference to other authoritarian regimes in Argentinean history and criticizes the political climate of the country. The realist account also presents straightforward lesbian identities and relationships. The narrative portrays an aggressive "masculine" lesbian identity that, by parodying traditional gender roles, makes a mockery of them and a devastating critique of patriarchal Argentinean society. The book was banned by the Videla dictatorship on charges of immorality and was subsequently ignored in Argentina.

In 1985, during her stay in the United States, Roffé published *Espejo de escritores* (Mirror of Writers), a compilation of interviews with renowned Latin American writers such as Jorge Luis Borges, Carlos Fuentes, Juan Carlos Onetti, Juan Manuel Puig, and Julio Vargas Llosa. In 1987, after eleven years of relative literary silence and already in Spain, the writer published her third novel *La rompiente* (The Breaking Surf), an experimental exile narrative that immediately received critical appraisal. The complex work, that requires a savvy reader, has been widely studied. The book was awarded Spain's International Prize for Short Novel and was published simultaneously in Buenos Aires and in México. The narrative, which explores repression and paralyzing self-repression, has been categorized as a "novela del Proceso" (Martínez de Richter) (Process' novel) and takes place in the period of tyranny and silence between 1976 and 1983 in Argentina. The novel's subject matter is the need to break the silence, tell, and name. In fact, the account has been considered Roffé's "novela de ruptura" (Szurmuk 2000: 124) (novel of rupture) in which she parts with everything that she had written before. In it, Roffé transgresses genre boundaries; breaks with the demands of literary critics; collapses binaries; experiments with space and time; and disrupts nationalist and authoritarian discourse in an effort to find a "voz propia" (p. 127) (voice of her own). That is, a subjectivity that can simultaneously document the repression of the dictatorship; and the social devaluation and subjugation of women. In 1996, her fourth novel *El cielo dividido* (The Divided Sky), which is situated in the late 1980s, was published in Buenos Aires. In this work, Roffé presents the main protagonist from *La rompiente* returning from her long period of exile in the United States to Buenos Aires. Through Eleonora's diary, her letters, and the stories of other women, the work suggests that as a part of Argentina's healing process after the terror regime, it is necessary to bring together forgotten fragments of collective memory and non-canonical narratives in order to work through and rewrite Argentine history. In 2002, her second collection of interviews with Latin American authors was published in Spain. It contains some of the interviews published in the first volume, *Espejo de escritores*, but unlike the first collection, the present anthology does not include *boom* writers. Among the new authors included are Adolfo Bioy Casares, Giselda Gambaro, Elena Poniatowska, Alfredo Bryce Echenique, Ricardo Piglia, and Ángeles Mastretta. In 2004, her second and expanded non-fictional work on the hermetic Mexican writer Juan Rulfo, *Juan Rulfo: Las mañas del zorro* (Juan Rulfo: The Tricks of the Fox), was published in Spain. Aimed at throwing light on the reasons for Rulfo's literary silence after the publication of his masterpieces *El llano en llamas* in 1953, and *Pedro Páramo* in 1955, Roffé's biography offers an analysis of the historical and cultural contexts of Rulfo's life that might have contributed to his creative silence. Her short-story collection, *Aves Exóticas: cinco cuentos con mujeres raras* (2004, Exotic Birds: Five Short Stories about Strange Women), was published in Argentina. With the story "Aves Exóticas" in this volume, Roffé, like in *La rompiente*, connects with her Jewish identity by once again evoking her Sephardic grandmother who was born in Spanish Morocco. Some of the narratives of this new collection have been translated into English in anthologies in the United States and Europe. Other short stories by Roffé have been translated into English and German.

Themes and Influences

A central theme of her novels is the demythologization of traditional stereotypes of sexuality and gender. However, due to the overwhelming sociopolitical realities in Argentina, politics is also a constitutive element of her work. Reina Roffé belongs with, among others, Cecilia Absatz and Alicia Steimberg to a generation of independent Argentinean young writers that published in the 1970s and that critics have called "marginal to the literary establishment in terms of lifestyle, values, and writing" (Flori 1995: 216). Roffé started to write at a very young age; she wrote her first novel *Llamado al puf* when she was only 17. And though the author cannot tell the reasons that induced her to write or why she writes, she mentions the impact that the narrative *The Broken Woman*, by Simone de Beauvoir, had on her. Beauvoir's work made Roffé aware not only of her desire to be a writer but also of the power a writer can have "to provoke 'something' in others". Her most significant influence has been Jorge Luis Borges; but Roffé has additionally mentioned the impact of writers such as Virginia Woolf, Roberto Arl, Katherine Mansfield, Juan Rulfo, Colette, Djuna Barnes, Alejandra Pizarnik, Manuel Puig, Iris Murdoch, Silvina Ocampo, Alfonsina Storni, José Blanco, Marguerite Yourcenar, Marguerite Duras and Flannery O'Connor.

LUZ ANGÉLICA KIRSCHNER

Selected Works

Llamado al puf. Buenos Aires: Pleamar, 1973.

Monte de Venus. Buenos Aires: Corregidor, 1976.

La rompiente. Buenos Aires: Puntosur, 1987.

El cielo dividido. Buenos Aires: Editorial Sudamericana, 1996.

Aves Exóticas: cinco cuentos con mujeres raras. Buenos Aires: Editorial Leviatán, 2004.

"Convertir el desierto". In Birgit Merz-Baumgartner and Erna Pfeiffer (eds), *Aves de paso: autores latinoamericanos entre exilio y transculturación 1970–2002.* Frankfurt: Vervuert, 2005, pp. 47–51.

"Exotic Birds". Trans. Margaret Stanton. In Thomas Nolden and Frances Malino (eds), *Voices of the Diaspora: Jewish Women Writing in Contemporary Europe.* Evaston, IL: Northwestern University Press, 2005, pp. 13–20.

Nonfiction

Juan Rulfo: autobiografía armada. Buenos Aires: Corregidor, 1973.

Espejo de escritores: entrevistas con Borges, Cortázar, Fuentes, Goytisolo, Onetti, Puig, Rama, Rulfo, Sánchez, Vargas Llosa. Hanover, NH: Ediciones del Norte, 1985.

Conversaciones americanas. Madrid: Páginas de Espuma, 2001.

Juan Rulfo: Las mañas del zorro. Madrid: Espasa, 2003.

"El enigma femenino". *Cuadernos Hispanoamericanos* 64 (2003): 13–20.

References and Further Reading

Flori, Mónica. "Reina Roffé". In *Streams of Silver: Six Contemporary Women Writers from Argentina.* Lewisburg, PA: Bucknell University Press, 1995, pp. 215–45.

Locklin, Blake Seana. "'Qué triste ser mujer': The Chinese Microcosm of Reina Roffé's *Monte de Venus*". *Revista de Estudios Hispánicos* 33(3) (1999): 473–94.

Morello-Frosch, Marta. "Las tretas de la memoria: Libertad Demitrópulos, Reina Roffé y Matilde Sánchez". In Adriana J. Bergero and Fernando Reati (eds), *Memoria colectiva y políticas de olvido: Argentina y Uruguay, 1970–1990.* Rosario, Argentina: Beatriz Viterbo, 1996, pp. 185–208.

Pereyra, Marisa. "Recordar la historia desde la censura: el modo utópico como estrategia de la nostalgia en Reina Roffé y Alina Diaconú". *Ciberletras* 9 (2003): no pagination.

Pfeiffer, Edna (ed.) "La escritura: un puente válido para romper el silencio". In *Exiliadas, emigrantes, viajeras: encuentros con diez escritoras latinoamericanas.* Madrid: Vervuert, 1995, pp. 158–76.

——. (ed.) "Existencias dislocadas: la temática del exilio en los textos de Cristina Peri Rossi, Reina Roffé y Alicia Kozameh". In Birgit Mertz-Baumgartner (ed.), *Aves de paso: autores latinoamericanos entre exilio y transculturación 1970–2002.* Frankfurt: Vervuert, 2005, pp. 105–15.

Szumuk, Mónica. "Entre mujeres: sexo, pasión y escritura en *El cielo dividido* de Reina Roffé". In Daniel Balderston (ed.), *Sexualidad y nación.* Pittsburg, PA: IILI, 2000, pp. 271–82.

ROFFIEL, ROSAMARÍA

Rosamaría Roffiel was born in 1945 in Veracruz, Mexico, and has worked as a journalist for the Mexican newspaper *Excelsior* and the political magazine *Proceso*. She has also served on the editorial board for the feminist magazine *fem* and has co-authored a book on the fundamentalist revolution in Iran. She currently gives Eckankar workshops on spiritual fulfillment in Mexico, the United States, and Spain.

Roffiel did not receive formal training in creative writing or literary studies at the university level because she never had the opportunity to attend college. However, because her grandmother spent many hours reading to her as a child, she became fascinated with literature and read extensively on her own.

In 1979, after reading the autobiography of Simone de Beauvoir, Roffiel began to believe that she too could write creatively. Following this inspiration, she spent a year in Nicaragua covering the Sandinista Revolution. It was in Nicaragua, a country of poets, where she began keeping a diary and writing poetry. After returning to Mexico, her production of poems increased, and various radio programs invited her to share some of her writings and her opinions on poetry with their audiences. She published a selection of the many poems she wrote in a collection in her first book *Corramos libres ahora* (1986, 1994), which is divided into six sections. The theme of solidarity with other women in general is certainly present, but the majority of the poems deal primarily with lesbian pride, dignity, and love. Also, based on information from her diary, she published her personal experiences in the testimonial *¡Ay Nicaragua, Nicaragüita!* (1986), the style of which is a mixture of journalism and poetry. In this book, Roffiel conveys her solidarity with the Nicaraguan people and her respect and admiration for them, especially the women and children who were so committed to revolution. She admits, however, that she was disillusioned by the machismo of the male revolutionaries.

This book serves as a transition from journalistic writing to creative narrative writing and provided the motivation for her to finish her first novel *Amora* (1989), which she had begun in 1983. This work is considered to be the first Mexican lesbian novel (Foster 1991: 115). Seeking a therapeutic outlet, she narrated a recent break-up in this novel. Even though the text deals with delicate issues like lesbianism and rape, and that some parts have a didactic quality to it, the text was written with a great sense of humor and a positive approach to life. Her primary goal was to transmit in a practical and familiar way what she had learned as a feminist and as a lesbian. She also wanted to provide potential readers who might not have been knowledgeable about or supportive of homosexuality an alternate view about lesbians and lesbian relationships. The novel is composed of short chapters; its central story revolves around a romantic relationship between two women, Guadalupe/Amora and Claudia, and includes peripheral stories that narrate heterosexual relationships as well as women who work in a rape crisis center in Mexico City.

Her most recent work, *El para siempre dura una noche* (1999, 2003) is a collection of short stories that she wrote from 1982 to 1994. This text includes a story she wrote in 1997 as four years had passed before her book was published. Roffiel's intention with this collection of twelve stories was to help create a higher level of consciousness for the reader by demonstrating how all humans are worthy of love and of have the right to their own voice. These marginalized, misunderstood humans include among others: lesbians, an exiled female politician, a man dying of AIDS, a transgendered person, a rape victim, a female urban Argentine guerrilla, and a child born through artificial insemination to two lesbian mothers.

Roffiel plans to write another novel in which she will address the sexual abuse she suffered as a child and how she overcame it. She is anxious to explain how she was able to transform this negative experience into one that is a source of strength and creativity. She also intends to finish writing a film script, the topic of which centers around a lesbian relationship.

In summary, Rosamaría Roffiel's work is written from the perspective that love is the transforming source for everything. Her work invites readers to respect different beliefs and preferences and alternate ways of living. By reading her work, the reader is invited to "enter into a bigger room with bigger windows and bigger doors" (Loisel 2002: 106), allowing a more profound awareness of not only himself/herself but also of all fellow human beings.

Rosamaría Roffiel currently resides in Mexico City.

CLARY LOISEL

Selected Works

Corramos libres ahora. Mexico City: Ediciones Femsol, 1986; Taller de Impresión Norma Flores, 1994.

¡Ah, Nicaragua, Nicaragüita! Mexico City: Claves Latinoamericanas, 1986; Rome: Edizioni Associate, 1987.

Amora. Mexico City: Planeta, 1989; Madrid: horas y HORAS, 1997; Hoja Casa Editorial, 1999.

El para siempre dura una noche. Mexico City: Hoja Casa Editorial, 1999.

References and Further Reading

Aburto Guzmán, Claudia. "Rosamaría Roffiel desde Bates College". Online Posting. 16 de noviembre de 1998. Grafemas: publicación de la asociación de literatura femenina hispánica. Vol. IV, no. 2

(accessed 18 June 2002). http://mocl.tamu.edu/~grafemas/v4n2.html#ROFFIEL

Ayala. "Amora, femenino de amor". Online posting. 11 Dec. 2001. Amazonas (accessed 18 June 2002). http://www.angelfire.com/ego/leslibros/amora.txt

Carroll, Amy Sara. "Influential Border-Crossings: Chicana Queer and Mexican Lesbian Feminist Cultural Production". Online posting. 18 June 2002. http://epsilon3.georgetown.edu/~coventrm/asa2000/panel6/carroll.html

Fernández Olmos, Margarite and Paravisini-Gebert, Lizabeth. *Pleasure in the Word: Erotic Writings by Latin American Women*. Fredonia, NY: White Pine Press, 1993, pp. 213–26.

Foster, David William. *Gay and Lesbian Themes in Latin American Writing*. Austin, TX: University of Texas Press, 1991, pp. 114–18.

Lailson, Silvia. "Aún con resistencias y prejuicios, las editoriales empiezan a publicar literatura lésbica: la mayoría de las obras circula marginalmente; fue Amora, de Rosamaría Roffiel, la primera novela lésbica en México; el temor y el prejuicio dificultan la distribución de las publicaciones". Online posting. 14 Jan. 2003. http:www.jornada.UNAM.mx/2000/oct00/001002/lesbianismo3.html

Loisel, Clary. "Entrevista con Rosamaría Roffiel". *Revista de Literatura Mexicana Contemporánea*. 16(8) (2002): 101–7.

Martínez, Elena. "A Review of *Dos mujeres* (Sara Levi Calderón) and *Amora* (Rosamaría Roffiel)". *Letras feminas* 18(1–2) (1992): 175–9.

Martínez, Pablo Salvador, "Atracción fatal". *La jornadad semanal* 19 (Oct. 1989): 13.

Molina, Arturo. "La Obsesión de una Feminista en la Literatura Mexicana". *La Voz de Michoacán*, Nov. 1, 1989.

Rojas Cárdenas, Luis. "Militancia feminista". Sat. suppl. To *Unomásuno*, Oct. 28, 1989, p. 13.

Rosman-Askot, Adriana. "Lesbian Literature en Latin America". Online posting. 4 Aug. 2002. http:www.hope.edu/latinamerican/Lesbian%20Literature.html

Schaefer-Rodríguez, Claudia. "Roffiel, Rosamaría (Mexico; 1945)". In David William Foster (ed.), *Latin American Writers on Gay and Lesbian Themes: A Bio-Critical Sourcebook*. Westwood, CT: Greenwood Press, 1994, pp. 382–5.

Vega, Patricia. "Alebrijes. Amora". Online posting. 16 Aug. 2000. http://www.jornada.unam.gmx/2000/ago00/000816/04aa2clt.html (accessed 18 June 2002).

Villalobos, José P. "La novela lésbica en México: *Amora* de Rosamaría Roffiel and *Dos mujeres* de Sara Levi Calderón". *Historia, Literatura e Identidad: Los Discursos de la Cultura de Hoy, 1994* (1996): 103–7.

Zimmerman, B. Del estudio "The safe sea of women". "El rincón literario". Online posting. Amazonas (accessed 18 June 2002). http://www.angelfire.com/hi/docprim/liter.html

ROJAS, TERESA MARÍA

Teresa María Rojas was born in 1938 in Havana, Cuba. Poet and actor. While her interest in poetry began earlier in life, the passion for theater developed during her studies at the University of Havana. Rojas went into exile in 1960 and worked as an actor in Venezuela, Mexico, Dominican Republic, Ecuador and the United States, where she currently lives. Through the years, she has played leading roles such as *Blanche du Bois*, by Tennessee Williams, *Antigona*, by Jean Anouilh, *Ester*, by Jean Cocteau, *Luz Marina* and *Clitemenestra*, by Virgilio Piñera. Rojas graduated with a degree in Psychology but teaches drama and directs plays at the Miami-Dade Community College in Florida. In addition to drama, poetry provides an outlet for her creative skills and self-expression.

Poet

The thematic nucleus in Teresa María Rojas' poetry is the recognition of the female voice as subject of the discourse. Her literary work concurs with postulates of feminist *difference* and marks a synthesis between the female body and the textual body to address her origins, her family structure, and her confrontation with daily life. The objective of her poems is to transcend apparently immediate anecdotes by inciting her readers to consciously and actively reflect about loneliness and solitude, the enigma of poetic creativity, and the vindication of the female voice in culture and society. In addition, Rojas continuously experiments with language to craft an effective background of irony and humor that is complemented with an ambivalent tone of frolic and criticism.

The first of her collections, *Señal en el agua* (Sign in the Water), depicts a search for self-identity and the need to effectively communicate feelings. Water, a symbol of life, fertility and fluidity, delineates the female realm of poetic creativity and defines a transforming essence that integrates the child, the woman, and the Proteic lover who changes with versatility to accommodate moods and circumstances. The result is a challenge of traditional and cultural concepts prevalent in society. Rojas describes her poetry as restless, like the wind on a scarf, a poetry coming from the streets which "is searching in the clouds, sea and valleys / for the blue crack where the sky is born". With this premise, the poet evokes her grandparents, mother, father, and her childhood with a patina of sorrow and nostalgia: "Teresa is a smile / for which I cry everyday". In other compositions like "Walt," paying homage to Walt Whitman, Rojas defends the naturalness and anguish of her verses inspired by the palm, sugar and smoke of distant Cuba. Realizing the impossibility of returning to her country, the poet immerses herself in daily activities, seeks originality in her expression, gloomily conforms to social gatherings and finds a refuge against routine in the confines of her home.

A sentiment of sadness, innocence and disappointment dominates parts of her collections *La casa de agua* (The Water House), *Campo oscuro* (Obscure Field) and *Capilla ardiente* (Wake). This feeling provokes introspection and the unfolding of differing personalities which facilitate the recognition of the woman through time and the revelation of her passion for freedom in a society dominated by stereotypes. In her quest for the inward self, the true self, Rojas entrenches herself in the mystery of solitude and poetic creation to subvert religious, social and love roles by using continuous and playful language deviations, especially very suggestive paronomasias, metaphors, riddles that convey a subtle irony and that, sometimes, portray a world upside down. Mary Seale states that Teresa Rojas' discourse alternates between frailty and force, that her poetry possesses "a gift for surprise that permits Teresa María to capture what is fugitive, what is chance, but that she captures it not to concretize it but to share it, as you share a secret, or warmth – or fear".

Childhood represents in Rojas' poetry the recovery of genuine innocence, naturalness, and surprise; the children's world also functions as a resource for creative imagination. The poet looks for the little prince created by Saint-Exupéry and, not finding him, she leaves her address in one of the stars symbolizing that innocence and illusions are defining traits of her existence. The simple tone and ambience of amazement found in fairy tales capture the poet's willful work to recreate a realm in which everything is a subject of poetic endeavor: the glorification of small objects, such as her boots or her beeper, the stylization of plain anecdotes, the meaning of the days of the week, the confrontation between appearance and authenticity, and her longing for Cuba. The poet returns imaginatively to her native land to walk again the streets and parks, to relive Pedro Luis Boitel's imprisonment and death, to reencounter her father, and to show her absolute love for her country, although her fading memories prevent her from remembering the name of the street where she once lived.

Throughout Rojas' poetry, the woman claims her active role in love and proclaims its genuineness and spontaneity in opposition to the trivial sexual act or the cult of money and superficiality in social gatherings. Rojas finds the space for flirting and playfulness in a delicious and sensual blazon of the female body portrayed in her poem "Tour" and also a domain for eroticism and passionate love encounters, a realm of physicality that must complement a seduction of the mind and spirit in "8/27/70": "Neither cerebral nor Sapphic: / love must be made to her spirit".

Rojas' last volume, *Hierba dura* (Hard Grass), includes a selection of poems from all her published poetic work and also the new books *Brasilendas, El diablo mirándose en tu espejo* (The Devil Looking at Himself in Your Mirror), *Tiros de Gracia* (Coups de Grâce) and *El horizonte volador* (The Flying Horizon). These collections depict instinct emerging as a force restrained by traditionalism, a "devil" who calls for physical authenticity. Rojas will affirm frequently in her poetry that she is a woman who will not abide by conventionalism, a sort of recurring criminal record which illustrates her sense of identity: "And here it is expressed / that she is prepared to challenge everything / to take the apple from the tree". Characteristic of her confronting discourse is the use of double meaning which allows Rojas to censure hypocrisy, to denounce abortion or the tragic accidents of those fleeing Cuba, to subvert conventional understandings and practices of religion and to reflect about orphanhood, God, and life: "Life is a needle / that sometimes forgets to sew God's cuts".

The articulation of her writing is also a constant theme in Rojas' work. With sincerity and anguish, the poet struggles to materialize words that would express her emotions by penetrating through "a half-open iron gate / somewhere in a wing". This metapoetic awareness coexists with the realization that the voice in the discourse is a superposition of the biographical person, a different entity: "These things are written with another name / on top of my name". With the fairy tale of Little Red Riding Hood in the background, the poet becomes *Caperucita Rojas*, a symbiotic figure who faces a wolf-poem "who looks at me so I can see, / who listens to me so I can hear, / and devours me so I can die". Poet and poem conform, then, a realm of interaction to acknowledge a subversion of roles and conventions with sincerity, anguish, playfulness and irony seeking to vindicate the space of the feminine voice throughout Rojas's poetic discourse.

FRANCISCO J. PEÑAS-BERMEJO

Selected Works

Señal en el agua. Poemas 1956–1968. Costa Rica: Imp. Borrase, 1968.
Raíz en el desierto. Barcelona, 1971.
La casa de agua. Poemas (1968–1972). Madrid: Playor, 1973.
Campo oscuro. Miami: Ediciones Universal, 1977.
Capilla ardiente. Miami: Ediciones Isimir, 1980.
Hierba dura. Antología (1956–1995). Contiene los libros inéditos *Brasilendas, El diablo mirándose en tu espejo, Tiros de gracia* y *El horizonte volador.* Coral Gables: La Torre de Papel, 1996.

References and Further Reading

Aparicio Laurencio, Ángel (ed.). *Cinco poetisas cubanas, 1935–1969: Mercedes García Tuduri, Pura del Prado, Teresa María Rojas, Rita Geada, Ana Rosa Núñez.* Miami, FL: Ediciones Universal, 1970.
Baeza Flores, Alberto. "Señal en la vida". En *La casa de agua. Poemas (1968–1972).* Madrid: Playor, 1973.
González Montes, Yara and Huidobro, Matías Montes. *Bibliografía crítica de la poesía cubana (exilio: 1959–1971).* Madrid: Plaza Mayor, 1973.
March, Susana. "Papel Literario". *El Nacional* (25 Aug. 1968).
Meyer, Doris and Olmos, Margarite Fernández (eds) *Contemporary Women Authors of Latin America.* Brooklyn, NY: Brooklyn College Press, 1983.
Peñas-Bermejo, Francisco J. (ed.). "Teresa María Rojas". *Poetas cubanos marginados.* El Ferrol: S.C.V-I., 1998, pp. 28–9, 169–89.
Perricones, Catherine R. (ed.). *Alma y corazón. Antología de las poetisas hispanoamericanas.* Miami, FL: Ediciones Universal, 1977.
Seale, Mary. "Nota preliminar". In *Campo oscuro.* Miami, FL: Ediciones Universal, 1977, pp. 7–8.
Unduraga, Antonio de (ed.). *Poesía en mesa redonda: antología latinoamericana 1948–1968.* Tegucigalpa: Eds. de la Revista "Caballo de Fuego," 1969.
Vásquez, Mary S. "La inocencia poética de Teresa María Rojas: artificio y trasfondo". *Monographic Review. Revista monográfica* VI (1990): 316–22

ROQUÉ DE DUPREY, ANA

Ana Roqué de Duprey (1853–1933) was best known as a fervent suffragist, early feminist, and writer. Roqué's diverse œuvre earned her awards and recognition. A respected member of Puerto Rico's intellectual circles, she became the first female member of the Ateneo Puertorriqueño (Puerto Rican Athenæum), the most prestigious intellectual center on the island. To recognize Roqué's numerous civic and literary accomplishments, the University of Puerto Rico awarded her an honorary doctorate in 1932.

Ana Roqué was born in Aguadilla, Puerto Rico on April 18, 1853, and was the daughter of businessman Ricardo Roqué and Cristina Géigel de Roqué. As a child she studied a broad range of subjects, including advanced mathematics, a subject usually reserved for boys. Roqué graduated from her secondary studies and founded a school at the age of thirteen after passing the examination to become a primary schoolteacher. In 1872, she married the landowner Luis Duprey, with whom she had three children, and later earned the degree necessary to become a secondary schoolteacher. Illustrious Puerto Rican writers and intellectuals including Alejandro Tapia y Rivera; the novelist Carmela Eulate Sanjurjo; the well-known doctor, politician, and novelist Manuel Zeno Gandía;

Dr. Pedro Jerónimo Goyco; and Dr. Gabriel Ferrer Hernández often gathered in Roqué's San Juan home for literary and scholarly discussions. Her friendships with doctors likely owed to her interest in the natural sciences. Her best-known novel, *Luz y sombra*, reflects her fascination with the natural world in its vivid descriptions of tropical weather and flora.

An active journalist, Roqué wrote for periodicals under the pseudonyms "Flora del Valle" and "Aguenora". She was a contributor to *La Ilustración Puertorriqueña*, *El Buscapié*, *Puerto Rico Ilustrado*, *El mundo*, and others. She also edited and founded the periodicals *La mujer* (discussed below), *La Evolución* (1902), *La Mujer del Siglo XX* (1917), *El Album Puertorriqueño* (1918), and *El Heraldo de la Mujer* (1920). These publications were important and rare venues for debates on women's education and suffrage.

Roqué was a dedicated educator and scholar whose intellectual interests ranged from the sciences to the history of ideas. She studied meteorology, philosophy, astronomy, and, as a member of the Astronomy Society of Paris, held star-gazing seminars at her home. Her non-fiction books include *Elementos de geografía universal* (1888, Elements of Universal Geography), *Explicaciones de gramática castellana* (1889, Explanations of Castilian Grammar), *Explicaciones de pedagogía* (1894, Explanations of Pedagogy), *La botánica en las indias occidentales* (The Botany of the West Indies; date not available), and the essay "Estudio sobre la flora puertorriqueña" (1908, Study on Puerto Rican Flora). The sum total of her life's work, however, shows that most of her achievements aimed to advance women's education and suffrage.

Early Feminist Activism

Since a teenager, Roqué had pursued her dream of improving women's education. She founded several schools and established scholarship funds for women's academic and vocational studies in order to provide women with the necessary skills and knowledge to support themselves. As part of her feminist project, she started the journal *La Mujer* (scholars list the date as 1893 or 1894), the first periodical of its kind in Puerto Rico owned and edited by a woman. Its mission was to improve women's culture and professional options. As evidence of her resourcefulness in achieving this goal, Roqué used the periodical's print shop to train her female students in the printing process. *La mujer* encouraged solidarity among educated women and provided a place for them to exchange ideas.

Roqué knew and was familiar with the projects of the Puerto Rican feminist and workers' rights advocate Luisa Capetillo (1879–1922). However, like many of her bourgeois contemporaries, Roqué disagreed with Capetillo's thoughts on women's rights to free love. Although Roqué did not subscribe to the abolition of marriage, she does make an unambiguous defense of female sexual desire and the right to sexual fulfillment within marriage in her best-known novel *Luz y sombra*. Roqué founded the women's rights organizations Liga Femínea (League of Women; 1917) and the Asociación Puertorriqueña de Mujeres Sufragistas (Puerto Rican Association of Women Suffragists; 1924). She lived to witness the approval of limited suffrage, when the vote was given to literate women in 1932, shortly before her death.

Luz y sombra and Other Prose

Luz y sombra (1903, Light and Shadow) is Roqué's only novel to receive critical attention in recent years. A realist novel, it shows a strong influence of naturalism, a literary movement begun by the French writer Emile Zola in 1880 that emphasized the role of the environment and heredity in social problems. The epistolary structure of *Luz y sombra*, however, creates a more intimate tone than the third-person narration of naturalism. The first- and second-person narrative style reveals to the reader the innermost thoughts and feelings concerning two women's loves, sorrows, and close friendship.

Luz y sombra is a coming-of-age story of two schoolmates, Julia and Matilde. The plot focuses on Julia's illicit flirtation with the young officer Rafael. Although the affair is never consummated, Julia's husband Sevastel catches the lovers in a compromising position and kills Rafael in a duel, leaving Julia in misery. *Luz y sombra* has been read as a didactic morality tale that denounces the sinful and materialistic Julia and exalts Matilde's simple rural life. However, the dynamics of morality are complex. For example, Julia's guilt is mitigated when several characters cite Sevastel's frigidity as the cause of Julia's temptation, while Sevastel also declares himself guilty of spousal neglect and forgives his wife. As mentioned above, a striking feature of the novel is its defense of Julia's sexual desire, a taboo subject in turn-of-the-century Puerto Rico.

Roqué's other prose fiction, ripe for rediscovery, is available in specialized archives but has not been re-edited since the original printings. *Un ruso en Puerto Rico* (1919, A Russian in Puerto Rico) is a short adventure novel that recalls the style of the Spanish Golden Age comedy, with Puerto Rican settings and types. *Un ruso* narrates the adventures of Pedro, a Russian visiting his father's homeland, and his sidekick Antoñito. The mischievous pair's flirtations with beautiful Puerto Rican *jíbaras* (country women) cause chaos in the small towns they visit. *Un ruso* depicts regional customs and employs the vocabulary and accent of Puerto Rican *jíbaros*. The story satirically highlights the privileged and arrogant attitude of foreigners who unthinkingly exploit those around them.

Sara la obrera y otros cuentos (Sara, the Working Woman and Other Stories) is a collection of realist prose and fantasy fiction. The short realist novel *Sara la obrera* is a tragic story of a *mulata* seamstress, Sara, who is drugged and raped by her best friend's husband, a man of European descent. Most devastating is her friend's participation in this crime, as she is too fearful of her husband's temper to resist him (a scenario that reminds the reader of Manuel Zeno Gandía's heartbreaking depictions of incest and rape in the 1889 novel *La charca*). *Un ruso* and *Sara* both contain critiques of the sexual and economic domination of white men over Puerto Ricans of African and racially mixed heritage. The fantastical stories "Andina" and "La hada del Sorata" (The Fairy of Sorata) reveal the influence of Latin American *modernismo* in their escapist and mystical content, which includes fairies and a sumptuous palace of solid gold. Several of the stories in *Sara* depict the beauty of Latin America and speculate about its future, a common preoccupation of artists and intellectuals of the turn of the century. *Pasatiempos* (1894, Pastimes) is a collection of stories in the style of social realism; it includes "El rey del mundo" (The King of the World), "El secreto de una soltera"

(A Single Woman's Secret), and "La fiesta de reyes" (The Kings' Celebration).

Ana Roqué's indefatigable efforts to achieve suffrage, her early feminist influence in Puerto Rico's intellectual circles, and her bold critiques of male dominance have earned her a place among the most important early feminist figures in Latin America.

NANCY LAGRECA

Selected Works

Pasatiempos. Humacao, Puerto Rico, 1894.
Novelas y cuentos. Ponce, Puerto Rico, 1895.
Sara la obrera y otros cuentos. Ponce, Puerto Rico: Imprenta Manuel López, 1895.
Luz y Sombra. Ed. Lizabeth Paravisini-Gebert. 1903. Río Piedras, Puerto Rico: Universidad de Puerto Rico, 1994.
Un ruso en Puerto Rico. Ponce, Puerto Rico: Imprenta Manuel López, 1919.

References and Further Reading

Acevedo Loubriel, Suzette. "Nuevas propuestas sobre la domesticidad: Emilia Pardo Bazán y Ana Roqué". *Cuadernos de Aldeeu* 20(1) (2004): 64–74.
"Ana Roqué de Duprey". http://www.duprey.cps.k12.il.us/Biography.htm (accessed June 26, 2006).
Azize Vargas, Yamila. *La mujer en la lucha*. San Juan: Editorial Cultural, 1985.
——. (ed.) *La mujer en Puerto Rico: Ensayos de investigación*. Río Piedras: Ediciones Huracán, 1987.
Chen Sham, Jorge. "Sanción moral y castigo: Contradicciones ideológicas en la narrativa de Ana Roqué". In Luis Jiménez (ed.), *La voz de la mujer en la literatura hispanoamericana fin-de-siglo*. San José, Costa Rica: Universidad de Costa Rica, 1999, pp. 167–80.
Delgado Votaw, Carmen. *Puerto Rican Women / Mujeres puertorriqueñas*. Washington, DC: Lisboa, 1995.
Feliú Matilla, Fernando (ed.) *200 años de literatura y periodismo, 1803–2003*. San Juan, Puerto Rico: Ediciones Huracán, 2004.
Matos Rodríguez, Félix V and Delgado, Linda C. (eds) *Puerto Rican Women's History: New Perspectives*. Armonk, NY: M.E. Sharpe Publishers, 1998.
Paravisini-Gebert, Lizabeth. "Introducción" and "Esquema biográfico". In *Luz y sombra* by Ana Roqué. Río Piedras, Puerto Rico: Universidad de Puerto Rico, 1994, pp. 1–21.
——. "Las novelistas puertorriqueñas inexistentes". *Cupey* 6(1–2) (1989): 91–113.
Rivera de Alvarez, Josefina. *La gran encyclopedia de Puerto Rico: Tomo 5 Novela. La novela puertorriqueña desde sus orígenes hasta el presente*. Madrid: Ediciones R, 1976.
Suárez Findlay, Eileen J. *Imposing Decency: The Politics of Sexuality and Race in Puerto Rico, 1870–1920*. Durham, NC: Duke University Press, 1999.

ROSENBERG, MIRTA

Mirta Rosenberg was born in 1951, in Rosario, Santa Fe Province, Argentina. She graduated in literary studies from the UNL, and has a degree in translation from the Instituto Lenguas Vivas. She has worked professionally as an English and French translator since 1978. Rosenberg is the author of *Pasajes* (1984), *Madam* (1988), *Teoría Sentimental* (1994, Sentimental Theory), *El arte de perder* (1998, The Art of Losing), and *Poemas* (2001, Poems). She has translated and published the works of Katherine Mansfield, William Blake, Walt Whitman, Emily Dickinson, Harold Bloom, Anne Sexton, W.H. Auden, Anne Talvaz, and Marianne Moore, among others. The anthology *El árbol de las palabras* (The Tree of Words), published in 2006, collects all of her poems to date as well as some inedited poetry. It also includes a selection of Rosenberg's literary translations. Since 1986, she has been the editor and director of the quarterly publication *Diario de Poesía*. In 1990, Rosenberg founded Bajo la Luna Nueva publishing house where she still works as a consultant, and which has already published over fifty titles in poetry, essay, translation and narrative of Argentine authors. Rosenberg works as the editor of the poetry section and translation of foreign literature of the Sunday magazine of the newspaper *La Nación*. In addition, she is a consultant editor for the Casa de Poesía of City of Buenos Aires as well as the coordinator of "Los Traidores," a workshop on poetic translation. In 2003, she was awarded the Beca Guggenheim and in 2004, she received the Konex award for her excellency in translation.

Along with Diana Bellessi, Tamara Kamenzain and María Negroni, Rosenberg is one of the most recognized contemporary female poets of Argentina. Her poetry, as Olvido García Valdés points out in the introduction to *El árbol de las palabras,* may be defined by her distinctive and easily identifiable writing style, style characterized by the musicality and the rhythm of words. In a personal interview, the author notes that she was attracted by the sound of words and the rhythm language at a very early age. Because rhythm is everything, it is the generating force of the poetic voice. *El árbol de las palabras* includes several translations by the author. In its introduction, Rosenberg writes that the inclusion of translations in books of poetry has a longstanding tradition within Argentine literature. In fact, according to the author, Alberto Girri was the first poet to merge both genres into the text, thus placing translation at the same level of poetry. As Rosenberg points out, all the translations published in *El árbol de las palabras,* were chosen in response to a certain impulse, and to the paths they opened in her own literary production at different times and for different reasons. This selection includes poetry by Marianne Moore, James Laughlin, Sharon Olds, and Ruth Fainlight.

Rosenberg recognizes two major influences in her development as a poet: her formation as a translator and Argentine fellow poet Hugo Padeletti. According the author, translation is a crucial influence in her poetry because it has allowed her to expand and explore the limits of the Spanish language. English expressions that are not translatable into Spanish, such as: "no soy del todo misma," "I am not quite myself," for example, have enhanced her own relationship with the language. It was with Padeletti, though, that she started reading the poetry of Marianne Moore and gaining an appreciation for the complex mechanisms behind the poetic construction, rhyme and style.

Another strong influence in Rosenberg's poetry is Zen Buddhism. After reading three books by Zen Buddhist author Suzuki at the age of 18, Rosenberg felt a strong attraction to Buddhist religion and its freedom of interpretation towards divinity and God. This vision is most evident in *El arte de perder,* collection in which readers are able to perceive, on one hand, Rosenberg's compromise towards language and, on the other, her insightful interpretation of life and death, loss and survival, and the constant challenge of being alive. Poems such as "Revelados," "Una elegía," "Lo seco y lo mojado" and "Retrato terminado" deal with the author's feelings and memories about her childhood, her parents and coping with her mother's death. All of these poems blend beauty, truth and wisdom, and are an affirmation that poetry is not only the means to unravel the essence of language, but also a means to transcend our own physical and emotional limitations. Rosenberg's metaphysical imagery and insightful metaphors unwrap a world rich in imagery, in which nature, creativity, and spirituality share a common relationship. Along with fellow poets Tamara Kamenzain, Diana Bellessi and María Negroni, Rosenberg is one the major figures in Argentine poetry today.

MARÍA CLAUDIA ANDRÉ

Selected Works

Pasajes. Buenos Aires: Trocadero, 1984.

Madam. Buenos Aires: Libros de Tierra Firme, 1988.

Teoría sentimental. Buenos Aires: Libros de Tierra Firme, 1994.

Poemas. Badajoz, España: Asociación de escritores extremeños, 2001.

El árbol de palabras: Obra reunida 1984 – 2005. Buenos Aires: Bajo la luna nueva, 2006.

References and Further Reading

André, María Claudia. *Antología de escritoras argentinas contemporáneas*. Buenos Aires: Ed. Biblos, 2004.

Aguirre, Osvaldo. "Recortes de un diario íntimo". *Página 12/Radar Libros*. December 10, 2006. http://www.bajolaluna.com/bajo%20la%20luna%202/el%20%87rbol%20prensa.html.

Kuhnheim, Jill. *Gender, Politics and Poetry in Twentieth-Century Argentina*. Gainesville, FL: University Press of Florida, 1996.

ROSSI, ANACRISTINA

Anacristina Rossi (b. 1952) is a prominent Costa Rican writer, feminist, and environmentalist well known for her courageous ethical stands. Rossi grew up in the countryside of Costa Rica, amid remote rainforests and the hues of the Caribbean Sea. As a child she lived in Turrialba, a small town nestled in the mountains, and, later, in the plains of Matina. Her grandparents, who along with other family members usually presented her with books on nature as gifts, owned a farm in the central valley that she visited frequently. From an early age, Rossi devoured the books of Spanish author Elena Fortín, collections of fairy tales from around the world, the massive collection of Zane Grey novels, and tales of the wild by Jack London. As a young adult, she began her studies at the University of Costa Rica but soon decided to leave for London and Paris in order to study linguistics, literature and psychoanalysis. She soon completed a Master's degree in Women and Development at the Institute of Social Studies in La Haya, Holland. While having authored several poems during this period, Rossi confesses to having solemnly burned them all while on a patio behind Cornwall Gardens. Two years later she began to write her first novel and, with its publication, returned to Costa Rica. Today, Rossi divides her time between Limón, where she culls the archives for a trilogy in progress, and San José, where she lives with her husband and two daughters.

María la noche (Mary, the Night), Rossi's first novel, narrates the sensual memories of Antonio, an economist finishing his doctorate in London; Maristela, a young Central American woman whose father abandoned her in Europe; and Octavia, who becomes their lover. In interviews, Rossi has revealed that this surreal account of erotic pursuit and the ghosts of the imagination expose the sexual and cultural taboos prevalent in Costa Rican society. Published in 1985, this novel quickly captured the attention of critics and won the Aquileo J. Echeverría Prize (Costa Rica's National Literary Award for the best novel) that same year and the Ancora Prize (granted by Costa Rica's major newspaper *La Nación* to a literary work every two years) the next. Although Rossi had expected to publish this work in her native country, she had found it very difficult to find a press willing to take on the novel. She therefore opted to publish *María la noche* in Spain. Subsequent editions of this intriguing linguistic and literary experiment, however, have all been published in Costa Rica.

The Ecofeminist Novel

La loca de Gandoca (Mad About Gandoca), Rossi's second novel, engaged the emotional aspects of environmental crisis and healing. As an extremely biodiverse region, Costa Rica possesses at least 10 percent of all the world's species and serves as a biological bridge for species to the north and south. Yet despite Costa Rica's environment friendly policies, activists working for sustainable alternatives have sometimes found themselves under fire. As she wrote this novel, Rossi was no exception. According to the author, the act of writing—and the attention her novel received—helped save her life. Fusing fiction and reality, *La loca de Gandoca* generated such debate in Costa Rica that it would take a Supreme Court decision to rule on the future of the very wildlife refuge the author sought to protect with its publication. This best-selling novel—having sold over 150,000 copies—documents the ecological disaster that ensued when government officials in Costa Rica united with foreign investors to initiate a large-scale tourist development project for the Caribbean coast. Public outrage over the illegal development schemes uncovered by this novel most likely forced Hernán Bravo Trejos, the Costa Rican Minister of the Natural Resources, Energy and Mining, as well as former head of Coca-Cola in Costa Rica, to resign from his government post. Sections of the novel describe with suspense the labyrinth of bureaucracy that accompanied the struggle to save protected lands and wildlife, government policies that marginalized Afro-Caribbean and indigenous peoples, and the poetic vigor of nature and its relative human relationships.

Throughout the novel, government bureaucrats and developers in the act of taking control over the Gandoca-Manzanillo ecological refuge also disparage the voice of Daniela Zermat, the novel's female protagonist who identifies herself as just one biota residing in the rainforest and near the sea. Such tension is certainly evident when a policeman handcuffs Daniela after she turns in a French neighbor who has illegally opened beach cabins and routed their sewage to the sea. "Don't place obstacles in front of foreign investment," she is told, "woman, come on, let's go". Furthermore, any actions taken against commercial development are suspect. In one case, the assistant to the Minister of the Environment tersely ends a discussion with a biologist who feels that the plan to create a "Miami of the Jungle" complete with a "green" McDonald's, JC Penney's, and ice skating rink, could never be sustainable. "Well, sir, your objections seem awfully suspicious to me," the assistant tells the biologist. "Are you a communist?" In the aftermath of the Cold War, nature becomes yet another commodity that official discourse deems subservient to the needs and desires of humans.

In 2007, an unauthorized English translation of *La loca de Gandoca* was published in the United States, leading Rossi to seek legal action for copyright infringement. The Costa Rican Ministry of Foreign Affairs and the Department of Exterior Commerce quickly offered Rossi their support, and used this example of the foreign appropriation of a national treasure to emphasize the government's position on intellectual property rights during negotiations for the Central American Free Trade Agreement.

Literature as Public Memory

While Rossi believes that literature cannot provide the "collective fright" necessary to create a cultural shift towards ecologically oriented policies and ways of life, her fiction has certainly driven readers to the verge. In 1993, Rossi found herself at the center of a fierce struggle to preserve the historical section and wooded area of downtown San José. Her compilation of short stories, *Situaciones conyugales* (Conjugal Situations) responded through fiction to the actual polemic and emerged victorious. One of the stories narrates a female protagonist's rise to consciousness—and final protest—that ultimately halts the construction of an American-style bypass in the Costa Rican capital.

In recent years, Rossi has worked extensively with archival materials to compile a historically based trilogy on racial relations in Limón, Costa Rica. *Limón Blues* is the first in the trilogy and winner of both the Aquileo L. Echeverría and Ancora prizes. This work highlights the travails of Orlandus, one of the many Afro-Caribbean immigrants who arrive in Limón, Costa Rica, at the turn of the twentieth century to work in the banana plantations and on railroad construction projects. The passions and relationships that emerge from social turmoil are narrated with only odd-numbered chapters as if to imply that the divisions prevalent in Costa Rican society—with references to Minor Keith's exploitative banana plantations and the arrival of Marcus Garvey and his Black Star Line that promised to liberate the Afro-Caribbean peoples of the region—still haunt this Central American nation. It is, after all, still a history in the making. The second part of the trilogy, the recently completed *Limón Reggae*, introduces a Palestinian female protagonist who becomes involved with the Black Panther movement of Costa Rica. She later moves on to El Salvador, facing the violence of civil war and the emergence of gang violence, yet never forgetting the utopian ideals of the Rastafarians and reggae songs of Limón. The final part of the trilogy, still a work in progress, focuses on the crimes and passions that erupt in the battle to conserve the natural wonders surrounding this ethnically diverse port city.

Beyond the merit of several national literary prizes, Anacristina Rossi has received the 2004 Pablo Neruda Medal from the government of Chile and the 2004 José María Arguedas Prize granted by the Casa de las Américas to a distinguished Latin American novelist annually. While some of Rossi's works have been translated into other languages, several projects underway promise to expand her international readership.

New Directions

Scholars have focused their attention on the autobiographical tensions and gender dynamics at play in the search for justice—environmental and social—in several of Rossi's novels. With the Costa Rican Ministry of Education having initiated a regional tour of a musical based on Rossi's autobiography in 2004, such emphasis is not surprising. Yet despite Rossi's prominent role in Costa Rican culture and the international recognition of her work, critics have been slow to link her writing on local issues to the forces of globalization at work in the region. A few critics, like Sofía Kearns and Laura Barbas Rhoden, point to the significance of Rossi's feminist commitment to local peoples and marginal spaces within the shifting frames of globalization. Scholars have yet to profile this author's journalistic essays—with topics ranging from the violence of the *piropo* (a flirtatious remark made by men to women in public) to the earth rights movement. Throughout her career, she has served as a columnist and writer for Costa Rican newspapers *Universidad*, *La Prensa Libre*, *La Nación* and *El Financiero* and the magazines *Rumbo* and *Vieja Lilita* of Argentina. In recent years, Rossi has written less in the mainstream press as she has professedly tired of the censorship and ensuing political battles, persecutions, and threats. Given Rossi's impressive stature in Costa Rican letters, further studies on the fiction, essays and research of this exciting author are still needed in order to link her work more effectively to the realm of contemporary environmental writing and Latin American letters at large.

Regina A. Root

Selected Works

María la noche. Barcelona: Lumen Tusquets, 1985.

La loca de Gandoca. San José, Costa Rica: Editorial Universitaria Centroamericana (EDUCA), 1991. For an English translation of the first chapter of *Mad About Gandoca*, see *ISLE. Interdisciplinary Studies in Literature and Environment*, trans. Regina A. Root, forthcoming.

Situaciones conyugales. San José, Costa Rica: Red Editorial Iberoamericana (REI), 1993.

Limón Blues. San José, Costa Rica: Alfaguara, 2002.

References and Further Reading

Barbas Rhoden, Laura. "Greening Central American Literature". *ISLE. Interdisciplinary Studies in Literature and Environment* 12(1) (Winter 2005): 1–17.

Kearns, Sofía. "Otra cara de Costa Rica a través de un testimonio ecofeminista". *Hispanic Journal* 19(2) (Fall 1998): 313–39.

Molina-Jiménez, Iván. "*Limón Blues*: una novela de Anacristina Rossi". *Istmo. Revista virtual de estudios literarios y culturales centroamericanos* 5 (Jan.–June 2003). http://www.denison.edu/collaborations/istmo/n05/resenas/limon.html

Perera de Moore, Mónica. "Un discurso femenino ecológico hispanoamericano: *La loca de Gandoca*". *Letralia. Tierra de letras* 10(124) (May 23, 2005): http://www.letralia.com/124/articulo05.htm

RUBINSTEIN, BECKY

Becky Rubinstein (b. 1948) is widely known as a writer of children's literature. Yet, her œuvre covers fiction, and poetry in the field of children's literature, as well as essays, translations, and critical works on other topics. Some of her works outside of juvenilia deal with Mexican-Jewish literature, Mexican culture, and other wide-ranging topics such as Mexican recipes, and folk tales from different regions of the country. Even though her interests are wide-ranging, she is most widely recognized within the field of children's literature.

Rubinstein was born in Mexico City, on December 8, 1948. She received a Bachelor degree in Hispanic Language and Literature and a Master's degree in Spanish Literature, from the National Autonomous University of Mexico (UNAM). Later she studied Hebrew and Children's Psychology in the Seminar Hakibbutzim, Israel. Finally, Rubinstein was given an honorary degree in Colonial Art, Literature and History from the Ibero-American University (UIA).

Rubinstein belongs to a group of children's literature writers, the Cultura Infantil Como Alternativa (CUICA) (Children's Culture as an Alternative). This group encourages children's writers and poets, and supports juvenilia in the culture. She is a Professor of Medieval Sephardic literature, at the Department of Philosophy and Letters at UNAM. Some of her work, essays, poems, fiction have been published in the following periodicals: *Hojas de sal*, *Nuevas Horizontes*, *Revista Fenix*, *Foro*, *Wizo*, *de Ovaciones*, *El Universal*, *El Sol de Mexico*, *Casa del Tiempo*, *Alejandria*, *Cocolitos*, *El Cocodrilo Poeta*, *Alejandria y Tiempo de Niños*, and *Tribuna Infantil*, among others.

Rubinstein has been the recipient of many honors including: Medalla Gabina Barreda al Merito Universitario, 1980; Premio Cuento Brevisimo, of the journal El Cuento, 1986; Premio Nacional de Cuento Infantil Juan de la Cabada, Instituto Nacional de Bellas Artes (INBA) from the government of the state of Campeche, 1988 for her novel *Un Árbol Gatológico* (The Catological Tree). Finally, she received a bronze Sor Juana Inés de la Cruz medal, in 1990 and in 1997 a mention of honor in the Premio Mondial de Literatura José Martí, de la Fundación Iberoamericana de Creación para Ninos y Jovenes José Martí in Costa Rica.

Máscaras Para La Luna

In 1986, Rubinstein published her first collection of poems, *Máscaras Para La Luna* (Masks for the Moon). The collection deals with characters from the Italian commedia dell'arte, improvised drama, from the seventeenth century. The approach the author takes to the stock characters, Pierrot and Colombina, is modernist. These characters have been made famous in twentieth-century ballet and painting, namely Cubist works by Joan Miró and Picasso, and the Ballet Russe of Diaghilev. The theme of the masquerade and moonlight has many antecedents one of which is Arnold Schoenberg's musical work, *Pierrot in the Moonlight*. Although Rubinstein's work does not have a heightened musicality or the visual rhetoric of Cubism it is reminiscent of Marcel Carné's 1945 French film, *Children of Paradise* and Jean-Luc Godard's *Pierrot Le Fou* of 1965. The choice of topic betrays a fascination with the unreal and the inauthentic; yet the dolls have many human characteristics, they suffer, love, and enjoy existence. The collection is divided into four sections, two of which deal with Colombina, the laughing doll and Pierrot, the sad clown character. In constructing her work, the author leaves out the Harlequin, who usually makes up the third in the trio. For many reasons the collection complements her work as a children's writer, the symbolism of dolls that experience human emotions are reminiscent of Rubinstein's juvenilia.

All the poems in the collection are dreamy, magical, and highly figurative. The first section of the collection is entitled, "Like Colombina Before the Mirror". Colombina is both before a mirror and at once looking at a self-portrait; she is interested in masks, counterfeit, and make-up. At the same time Colombina enjoys life, and is in love with the freedom of the ocean and the heat of the sun which reflect her beauty. The laughing Colombina loves only herself, and never Pierrot. The third division of the text is called "At the Tomb of Pierrot" in the index, and "At the Dream of Pierrot" in the actual title headings; both seem appropriate. This chapter is the reflection of Pierrot's melancholic character, whose destiny it is to always feel unrequited love. The poems in the Pierrot cycle are laced with traces of obsession, aggression, anger, and a longing for revenge. Given the author's interest in Mexican Jewish literature, it is possible that the poems are highly symbolic of the plight of Jews in Mexico. One of the quotes which Rubinstein uses to introduce the second chapter is authored by Jewish Spaniards from Tetuan.

Autores Judeoconversos en la Ciudad de Mexico

In collaboration with Herlinda Dabbah Mustri, Rubinstein wrote *Autores Judeoconversos en la Ciudad de Mexico* (Converted Jewish Authors in Mexico City) on converted Jews in Mexico City. The work deals with the converted Jews of the seventeenth century whose parents had escaped the Inquisition by converting to Christianity and emigrating to the New Spain. This work was published in 2002 by Galileo Ediciones. The first chapter situates the work in the history of Sephardic Jews, who had lived a relatively free existence in Spain until the thirteenth century, when prosecutions of non-believers began. Dabbah Mustri and Rubinstein begin the work by weaving the tale of the peoples who were forced to choose between expulsion from an adopted homeland or a forced conversion. The first chapter explains the exodus of Jews into Portugal, Northern Africa and Europe. It points to the cruel fate that met those expelled to Portugal, where in the fifteenth century the expelled were forced to convert or face death with no second choice of expulsion allowed to them. The authors explain that the converts in New Spain were divided into two groups, the secret converts who maintained their Judaism, and those who took the new faith seriously. It then delves into the history of the persecutions in the New World, where the watchful eyes of the Inquisition monitored the converts for signs of secret Judaic practices.

The rest of the work deals specifically with each of the converted Jewish writers, including: Fray Bartolomé de las Casas, Fray Bernardino de Sahagún, Juan Bautista Corvera, a historian called Fray Diego Durán, Mateo Rosas de Oquendo, Luis de Carvajal, Tomás Trevino de Sobremonte, Mateo Alemán, Carlos de Sigüenza y Góngora, and Juan Ruiz de Alarcón. Finally, the work makes a case for Sor Juana Inés de la Cruz's origins based on her obsession with the Kabbalah and her embrace of humanism. The important conclusion that the authors arrive at in the end of the text is the inherent value in situating these writers in their proper religious and ethnic contexts. Except for a footnote from Marcos Raul Pesah Misha, the conclusion fails to address the recent rediscovery of a whole group of Mexican Jewish converts through DNA tests.

Toro Aciago

For her collection of poems, *Toro Aciago* (Fateful Bull), published in 1999, Rubinstein received the honor of the 8th Premio Nacional de Poesia given by the Tintanueva Editions. In an interview in the 27 Feria Internacional del Libro del Palacio de Mineria, the author notes that the work is about an all-encompassing passion that can prove disastrous to the participants. In writing about this subject she searched for a metaphor that would most accurately describe this feeling. She finally settled on the bull and the bullfighter, as two of the most potent symbols of obsession, destruction, and the violence of passion.

ANNA KATSNELSON

Selected Works

Que se rompe la luna. México: Editorial Selet, 1982.
La casamentera: cuentos y relatos. México: Editorial Selet, 1983.
Sapos y espantajos. México: Naroga, 1984.
El circo. México: Edición de la Rubinstein B., 1984.
Brujitas, Magos y fantasmones de la mochila de mochildreta. Amecameca, México: Amaquemecan, 1985.
Los servidores públicos. México: Quinto Sol, 1985.
Mi libro de Navidad. México: Sitesa, 1986.
Amigos intergalácticos. México: CUICA, 1986.
Máscaras para luna. Tacuba, México, D.F.: SEI, 1986.
Yo quiero un verso, yo quiero dos. México: CUICA, 1987.
Invéntame un cuento. Mexico, D.F.: SITESA, 1987.
Un arbol gatologico. Amecameca, México: Instituto Nacional de Bellas Artes: Editorial Amaquemecan, 1988.
Senderos de cuatro licores. México, D.F.: Claves Latinoamericanas, 1988.
La fórmula secreta de la tatarabruja. México, D.F.: Trillas, 1989.
Todas se llamaban Isabel. México: Amaquemecan, 1990.
Un Cuento más de las abuelas. México: Trillas, 1990–94.
Hadas y ensal-hadas. México: Del Rey Momo, 1990s.
De nubes. México: CUICA, 1991.
Paseo de amigas. México: CUICA, 1991.
¿Dónde está mi mascota? México: Trillas, 1992.
La bruja bailarina, Los Cuentos de la Tatarabruja. México: Trillas, 1992.
El tianguis de Juan Juguetero. México: Amaquemecan, 1993.
Caballero de polvoso azul y El vientre de Pandora, El Bifronte. México: Del Rey Momo, 1993.
El único unicornio. México: Del ReyMomo, 1993.
Vitrales. Toluca de Lerdo, Estado de México: Coordinación General de Comunicación Social: Tinta del Alcatraz, 1993.
Coro de encajes. México: Edición de la Rubinstein B., 1993.
Lentejuelas negras. México: B. Rubinstein, 1994.
Lindilis y Maximino, o, El desenlace enlazado. México: Instituto Mexiquense de Cultura, 1994.
Hijas de la Rueca. México, D.F.: Nautilium, 1994.
El conejo y sus relojes. México: ECO: Consejo Nacional para la Cultura y las Artes, 1995.
Una Sonrisa de aljofar. México: Del ReyMomo: FONCA, 1996.
Cuéntame una de vaqueros. México: Tintanueva, 1999.
Toro Aciago. México, Tintanuevo, 1999.
Un tía para Héctor. México, D.F.: Alfaguara, 2000.
¿De quién es tu voluntad? México: Tintanueva, 2000.
Cantar de cantar. México: Fundación Cultural Trabajadores de Pascual y del Arte, 2002.
Entre la piel de una manzana. México, D.F.: Editorial Letras Vivas, 2003.
Teatro de Sombras. Ciudad de México: CEIDSA, 2003.
Una Bruja en mi cachucha. México: Selector. 2005.

Co-authored Books

Berline, Y., Glantz, Y. and Rubinstein, B. *Tres Caminos: el germen de la literature judia en Mexico*. Mexico: Ediciones El Tucán de Virginia, 1997.
Rubinstein, B. and Dabbah Mustri, H. *Autores Judeoconversos en la Ciudad de Mexico.* Ciudad de México: Servicios de Edición e Información Galileo: Secretaría de Cultura del Gobierno del Distrito Federal, 2002.
Suárez, I., Rubinstein, B., Remolina, T., Gonzalez Obregon, L., and de Valle-Arizpe, A. *Leyendas de la provincial mexicana, zona centro*. México, D.F.: Selector, 2002.
Remolina, T. and Rubinstein, B. *Leyendas de la Provincia mexicana: zona costera*. México, D.F.: Selector, 2002.
Remolina Lopez, M.T., Rubinstein Wolojviansky, B. and Suarez de la Prida, M.L.I. *El Refranero Mexicano*. México: Selector S.A., 2004.
Remolina Lopez, M.T., Rubinstein Wolojviansky, B. and Suarez de la Prida, M.L.I. *Tradiciones de Mexico*. México, D.F.: Selector S.A., 2004.
Remolina, T., Rubinstein, B., and Suárez de la Prida, M.L.I. *Leyendas de la Provincia mexicana, Zona Altiplano*. México, D.F.: Selector, 2004.
Rubinstein, B., Martinez Chalamanch, R. and Rodriquez, E. *Un Mercadito de Cuentos*. México: CONACULTA, 2004.

References and Further Reading

Rubinstein, B. "Becky Rubinstein". *Publicación Feminista Mensual* 16(110) (April 1992): 44.

S

SALDAÑA, EXCILIA

Cuba

Celebrated in Cuba as a poet, essayist, translator, editor and professor, the multifaceted writer Excilia Saldaña (1946–99) was born in Havana, Cuba. Of Afro-Cuban descent, Saldaña was from a middle-class black family and grew up in the home of her grandparents. She studied Spanish and Literature at the Instituto Superior Pedagógico in Havana and worked as a high school teacher in the 1960s. First noticed and encouraged by the Casa de las Américas Prize Jury with an honorable mention in 1967 for her first book of poetry called *Enlloró* (unpublished), Saldaña's first poems were translated for the French magazine *Les Lettres Nouvelles* the same year. She worked as an editor in various cultural organizations in Cuba including Casa de las Américas (1971), *El Caimán Barbudo* (1972), and Editorial Gente Nueva (from 1975). Since that time Saldaña's production has been prolific and she has always strived to present Afro-Cuban traditions in order to preserve them, especially the female figure that she considers indispensable to the transmission of Afro-Cuban culture, a responsibility that she has explicitly espoused.

During her lifetime, Excilia Saldaña published a number of books of poetry for children including *Cantos para un mayito y una paloma* (Songs for Mayito and a Dove) written in 1979 (also adapted for theatre), *Soñando y viajando* (1980, Dreaming and Travelling), and *La noche* (1989, The Night), for which she won the Rosa Blanca Prize, for the third consecutive year. In 1979, she had already won the National Ismaelillo Prize (bestowed by the National Union of Cuban Writers and Artists, UNEAC) and the Golden Age Prize for her children's literature, as well as the Rosa Blanca Prize in 1984. Along with teaching children's literature at various universities, she has translated children's stories from English, Russian, German, Hungarian and Czech. Saldaña was awarded the prominent Nicolás Guillén Award for Distinction in Poetry in 1998 (UNEAC).

In 1987, Excilia Saldaña published a compilation of five Afro-Cuban myths (known as *patakines*) in *Kele kele* (Softly Quietly). The main characters of these tales are based on the deities of the Yoruba culture of West Africa, the largest group brought to the island of Cuba at the time of slavery. Throughout the centuries, the adaptation by Afro-Cubans of these beliefs has come to be known as *santería*, an intermingling of ancient tribal beliefs and Christian saints. Through these stories, important information on traditions and values is kept alive. In her decision to convert these folktales from the oral tradition to the written word, Saldaña is explicitly passing on these stories for future generations in Cuba, as they have through their recounting from Saldaña's grandmother (and namesake) to Saldaña and again to Saldaña's own son. However, the author not only recounts the stories but also, according to Gabriel Abudu's meticulous study of *Kele Kele*, skillfully adapts these by means of her prosaic style. Various theatrical adaptations have been made of this text and a script was made for a cartoon television program.

Perhaps Saldaña's most renowned poem is *Monólogo de la Esposa* (The Bride's Monologue), first published by Casa de las Américas in 1985 and translated into English (with the Saldaña's assistance) in *In the Vortex of the Cyclone* (2002). This lengthy poem tells of the discovery of the weight of the patriarchal society and the rebellion of the woman who, in these circumstances, takes on the empowering role of a priestess—a figure that is distinct, but not entirely, from the Bride. Saldaña writes in this poem: "... I am the Wife / and I only have open questions / and a lead key / that does not open, but closes". The role of priestess, associated with the Afro-Cuban folklore and Saldaña's family tradition, allows Saldaña to address the questions that she cannot answer. The poem calls upon numerous other texts and literary characters—including, but not limited to, Greek myths, classical English texts and modern Spanish poetry—in order to create a erudite union that makes for fertile interpretation.

In the lengthy autobiographical poem *Mi nombre: antielegía familiar* (My Name: A Family Anti-Elegy), published in 1991, Saldaña questions her identity, celebrates her grandmother and melds together past, present and future. She scrutinizes her place in the family unit and subverts the patriarchal bourgeois family constructs, as demonstrated by Catherine Davies' analysis of the work (2000). Saldaña delves into a poetic space that is often erotic as it celebrates the Afro-Cuban woman's body in all its minutiae. The text occasionally resembles (and provokes) profound philosophical meditations: "... Perhaps it was before or after. / Time is an acrobat / without a trapeze / to grasp, / nor a net / to let him repeat the nimble leap, his own or another's. / What does it matter if the tent disintegrates? ..." The repetitive nature of the circus imagery and its parallel with time is not lost in this existential fragment of the poem. In a direct association with contemporary alienation, Saldaña again develops imagery from Cuban and Caribbean history throughout the poem, for instance in her mention of the plight of the Maroons.

Other books by Excilia Saldaña, include the book of essays called *Un testigo de la historia* (A Witness of History), from 1979 and a collection of refrains from the Havana neighborhood of La Víbora entitled *El refranero de la Víbora*, from 1989. She is also the author of a scholarly study on mystery and horror films, *Cine de horror y misterio: Ensayo* (Films of Horror and Mystery: Essays) published in 1978 and on women in the work of José Martí called *Flor para amar* (A Flower to Love), published in 1980. Finally, Saldaña composed a text on Bulgaria entitled *Bulgaria, el país de las rosas* (Bulgaria, the Country of the Roses) in 1987.

Most of her work has appeared exclusively in Spanish in Cuba with only scattered translations, including the following (among others): "From My Name (A Family Anti-Elegy)" in Ruth Behar's *Bridges to Cuba/Puentes a Cuba* (1995) and the short story "Ofumelli" in Pedro Pérez Sarduy and Jean Stubbs' *Afro-Cuba: An Anthology of Cuban Writing on Race, Politics, and Culture* 1994). A bilingual (Spanish-Italian) selection of her work was published in 2002, edited by Valeria Manca: *Cuando una mujer no duerme—poesie di Cuba al femminile* (When a Woman Doesn't Sleep—Feminine Poetry from Cuba). Her poems and stories have been translated into Russian, French, Portuguese, German, Serbo-Croatian and Arabic, among others.

Although the author had begun to collaborate in the English version of her works, translators Flora González Mandri and Rosamond Rosenmeier only published the collection entitled *In the Vortex of the Cyclone* posthumously in the United States. Having suffered from asthma for most of her life, Excilia Saldaña passed away from complications due to an acute attack on July 20, 1999. In Cuba, several of her books have now been published and/or are being republished posthumously.

SOPHIE M. LAVOIE

Selected Works

"C'est l'heure des râles du soleil". Trans. Claire Staub. In *Les Lettres Nouvelles*, Paris, France, December 1967–January 1968.

Kele kele. Havana: Letras Cubanas, 1987.

In the Vortex of the Cyclone. Eds. and trans. Flora González Mandri and Rosamond Rosenmeier. Gainesville, FL: University Press of Florida, 2002.

La noche. Havana: Gente Nueva Editorial, 2002.

Mi nombre. Havana: Unión, 2003.

References and Further Readings

Abudu, Gabriel A. "African Oral Arts in Excilia Saldaña's *Kele Kele*." *Afro Hispanic Review* 21(1/2) (Spring 2002): 134–43.

Behar, Ruth. *Bridges to Cuba/Puentes a Cuba*. Ann Arbor, MI: University of Michigan Press, 1995.

Davies, Catherine *A Place in the Sun? Women Writers in Twentieth-Century Cuba*. London: Zed Books, 1998.

——. "Hybrid Texts: Family, State and Empire in a Poem by Black Cuban Poet Excilia Saldana." In Ashok Bery and Patricia Murray (eds), *Comparing Postcolonial Literatures*. New York: St. Martin's Press, 2000, pp. 205–18.

DeCosta-Willis, Miriam (ed.) *Daughters of the Diaspora: Afra-Hispanic Writers*. Kingston, Jamaica: Ian Randle Publishers, 2003.

González Mandri, Flora. *Guarding Cultural Memory*. Charlottesville, VA: University of Virginia Press, 2006.

Manca, Valeria (ed.) *Cuando una mujer no duerme – Poesie di Cuba al femminile*. Rome: Datanews Editrice, 2002.

Pérez Sarduy, Pedro and Stubbs, Jean. *Afro-Cuba: An Anthology of Cuban Writing on Race, Politics, and Culture*. Melbourne: Ocean Press/The Center for Cuban Studies, Australia, 1994.

SANTA CRUZ, GUADALUPE

Chilean writer and visual artist, Guadalupe Santa Cruz (b. 1952), was born in Orange in the United States. She lived in Mexico as a youngster to finally settle in Chile where she studied Philosophy at the Universidad Católica. After being detained by the military regime in 1974, Santa Cruz left Chile and went into exile to live in Belgium. In the Belgian city of Lieja, she studied engraving and Adult Continuing Education. Together with other exiles she created the Latin American Cultural Association of Lieja and became the editor of its journal.

Today, back in Chile, she teaches at the Universidad de Arte y Ciencias Sociales, ARCIS, in Santiago, in the School of Architecture and the School of Philosophy. She also leads literary workshops and speech workshops for union leaders and women. Santa Cruz has published numerous cultural essays on literature, art and urban culture. She has also worked as interpreter (French/Spanish) and has translated into Spanish the main works of important contemporary thinkers such as Julia Kristeva, Cornelius Castoriadis, Jacques Derrida, and Félix Guattari.

Santa Cruz has written five novels: *Salir (la balsa)* (1989, Leave (the Raft)), *Cita capital* (1992, Main Meeting), *El contagio* (1997, The Infection), *Los conversos* (2001, The Converted) and *Plasma* (2005). This last novel won the prestigious Premio Atenea for the best literary work of 2005. It also won the Premio del Consejo Nacional del Libro for the best unpublished novel in 2004. In 1992, the R.T. B. (Belgium Radio and Television) made a documentary on her literary work that was directed by Andre Romus and entitled *Guadalupe Santa Cruz*. In 1998, she was awarded a John Guggenheim Foundation Fellowship. In 1998–99, she received a grant from FONDART (Fondo de Apoyo a las Artes y la Cultura) from the Ministery of Education in Chile. In 2006, Le College International de Philosophie invited Santa Cruz to a dialogue centered on the novel *El contagio* which took place at the Latin American Cultural Center in Paris, Maison d'Amérique Latine.

In 2004, she was awarded a grant from the Fundación Andes to carry out a literary and visual arts project that came to fruition in her book entitled *Quebradas. Las cordilleras en andas* (Rough Terrain, The Mountain Ranges on Foot), which combines text and visual images and stories of the inhabitants of the Northern region. This text is forthcoming in Santiago and will be published by Francisco Zegers Editor.

Chronologically, her literary production could be situated within what Carlos Olivares turned "la nueva narrativa chilena" from the 1980s. However, aesthetically Santa Cruz's literature presents coincidences with the younger generation of female writers, such as Lina Meruane, Andrea Jeftanovich and Nona Fernández. Guadalupe Santa Cruz's singular writing constructs memory in the condensed trope of the *spectrum*. Her work explores the experience of exile as the displacement of body, psyche and landscape where memory and language are the instruments of reconstitution for the subject and the citizen after the dictatorship. This is a migrating narrative that travels through diverse geographies and cities presenting the reader with speeches and images that attempt to find a new place and space to inhabit after catastrophic loss.

In the novel *Salir (la balsa),* language provides a way to reconstruct a sense of place and meaning when the past has been destroyed. Exile and the dictatorial heritage constitute an experience of displacement and marginalization that leave the protagonist with a sense of vulnerability and homelessness. Thus, home here is a place of absence and mourning that forces a journey into other locations and meanings. The author herself asserted in an interview that her writing followed the word and the confrontation between bodies and spaces that confine them. In her exploration she traces the ways social subjects transcend power relations through language.

In Santa Cruz's second novel, *Cita capital*, the city is traveled and revisited through an urban cartography that delineates its cultural and social stratifications. Her concern here lies in the ways cities are constructed, the places that characters have in it according to a job, discipline or gaze. Santiago, in this novel, is the city portrayed and reconstructed in a new map in ways that parallel what the characters to with their bodies. The text also contrast the North and the South as well as a male and female vision that does not fit in with a North–South binary perspective. Thus, the novel is a reflection of a way of thinking is which time and space have been dislocated, creating a new cartography of the capital city.

In the novel, *El contagio,* speech and food converge in the ambivalent treatment of the sick body within the closed and sanitized space of the hospital. Here the city operates inside the hospital in the social hierarchies, laws and movements of the people within, echoing those that might be found outside its walls. The hospital also becomes a metaphor for a nation obsessed with destroying moral and cultural contamination, recalling the public discourse of the dictatorship and its enforcement of cleanliness and health for the fatherland. The experience of migration is developed in *Los conversos* through the imposition of conversion and the memories left and passed onto the next generations. In 2000–1, Santa Cruz's art exhibit entitled *Crujía I* interrogated the relationship between immigration and memory. Her visual exploration of *Los conversos* and migration continued in the art show *Crujía II*, *Coloquio Suelo Americano*, which opened at the School of Architecture in the Universidad Arcis, blurring the boundaries between the visual and written discourse.

In her last novel, *Plasma,* the image of the journey reappears in a criminal investigation led by a detective named Bruno, who travels across Chile's Northern landscape pursuing Rita, his female suspect and object of desire. Letter writing and orality cross over to unfold the construction of history and story-telling in a detective plot. Bruno chases Rita, a presumed drug dealer, through canyons, valleys, *pampas* and deserts, places where his rational and urban discourse is confronted with the ambiguity and the heterogeneity of a rural culture he hardly knows. Social themes such as water rights, seasonal and part-times workers' rights, and micro drug-trafficking intertwined with the characters' lives within a rampant neoliberal economy whose legal system condemns Rita for Bruno's death.

Santa Cruz's writing reveals her interest in language and the reconfiguration of the fractured political and social memory left by the dictatorship. Through avant-garde techniques and different narrative perspectives, her novels dwell on experiences that have been largely absent from public discourse, calling attention to the configuration of new subjectivities in postmodern urban spaces and cultures.

BERNARDITA LLANOS

Selected Works

Novels

Salir (la balsa). Santiago de Chile: Editorial Cuarto Propio, 1989.
Cita capital. Santiago de Chile: Editorial Cuarto Propio, 1992.
El contagio. Santiago de Chile: Editorial Cuarto Propio, 1997.
Los conversos. Santiago de Chile: LOM, 2001.
Plasma. Santiago de Chile: LOM, 2005.

Nonfiction

Quebradas. Las montañas en andas. Santiago de Chile: Francisco Zegers Editor, 2006.

References and Further Reading

Chávez, Loreto. "El territorio del texto. Las novelas de Guadalupe Santa Cruz". *Nomadías feminista. Pulsiones estéticas: Escritura de mujeres en Chile.* Santiago de Chile: Universidad de Chile, Gobierno de Chile, Cuarto Propio, 2004, pp. 213–23.

Espinosa, Patricia. "Imaginación transgresora". *Revista Rocinante* 43 (May 2002): 15.

Ferreira, Carolina. "Contra la gramática". *Perfiles Semanales* (21 May 2000): 14–15.

Gelpí, Juan. "La seducción de la diferencia. Entrevista con Guadalupe Santa Cruz". *Nómada* 4 (1999): 55–61.

Lombardo, Francesca. "De grafías e incisions: dos novelas de Guadalupe Santa Cruz". In Kemy Oyarzún (ed.), *Pulsiones estéticas: Escritura de mujeres en Chile. Nomadías* 7. Santiago de Chile: Filosofía y Humanidades, Universidad de Chile and Cuarto Propio, 2004: 217–23.

Moscoso, Patricia. "Entrevista con Guadalupe Santa Cruz". *Revista Pausa (Revista del Consejo Nacional de la Cultura y las Artes)* 3 (Marzo, 2005): 84–7.

Ojeda, L. Cecilia. "Recuperando el sujeto femenino exiliado: *Salir (la balsa)* de Guadalupe Santa Cruz". *Acta Literaria* N. 24 (1999): 93–105.

——. "La grabación del duelo y el goce en la narrativa de Santa Cruz". *Alba de América.* Vol. 19, n. 35–36 (Julio, 2000): 539–53.

Olea, Raquel. "Los territorios de la escritura. La narrativa de Guadalupe Santa Cruz". In *Lengua Víbora. Producciones de los femenino en la escritura de mujeres chilenas.* Santiago de Chile: Cuarto Propio/La Morada, 1998, pp. 83–100.

Ortega, Julio. "Guadalupe Santa Cruz". In *Caja de Herramientas. Prácticas culturales para el Nuevo siglo chileno.* Santiago de Chile: LOM, 2000, pp. 81–6.

Oyarzún, Kemy. "Los fuegos de la memoria: *Los conversos* de Guadalupe Santa Cruz". *Revista de Crítica Cultural* 23 (Nov. 2001): 68–9.

Sánchez, Cecilia. "Economías del traspaso: Presentación de la novela de Guadalupe Santa Cruz *Los conversos*". In *Escenas del cuerpo escindido. Ensayos cruzados de filosofía, literatura y arte*. Santiago de Chile: Universidad ARCIS/Cuarto Propio, 2005: 291–8.

SANTOS FEBRES, MAYRA

Mayra Santos Febres (b. 1966) is one of the most critically acclaimed writers currently living and writing in Puerto Rico. She was born in Santurce, Puerto Rico, the daughter of educators. In an interview in the Barcelona Review, she recounts that she began to write at the age of 5 because she was restricted from participating from much physical activity because she suffered from asthma. In this same interview, she credits her asthma with giving her a literary voice. She developed a love for literature and the craft of writing at a very young age. Santos Febres attended school in Puerto Rico until finishing her B.A. At that point, she came to the United States, where she studied for an M.A., and Ph.D. from Cornell University. She has taught as a Visiting Professor in the United States at Harvard University and Cornell University, and in Latin America and Europe. Currently, she is a Professor at the University of Puerto Rico, Rio Piedras Campus. Her first literary publications were poems, although now she is known mostly for her novels, short stories, and literary criticism. Her main works have been translated into many languages.

Poet, Novelist and Literary Critic

Her first publications were poetry collections, *El orden escapado* (The Escaped Order) and *Anamu y Managua*, both in 1991. From 1991 also is her doctoral dissertation "The Translocal Papers: Gender and Nation in Contemporary Puerto Rican Literature," a critically acclaimed study of gender, sexuality, race and class in such contemporary Puerto Rican writers as Luz Maria Umpierre, Ana Lydia Vega, and Manuel Ramos Otero. She has published poetry and literary criticism for years in magazines and journals. More recently, she has gained fame as a talented prose writer. Over the past several years she has garnered a host of awards, among them the 1994 Letras de Oro Prize from the University of Miami for her first collection of short stories, *Pez de vidrio* (Glass Fish) and the 1996 Juan Rulfo Prize for short stories awarded by Radio Internationale in Paris for her short story "Oso blanco" (White Bear) from her second collection of short stories *El cuerpo correcto* (Urban Oracles). She was a finalist in a number of awards, including the Romulo Gallegos Prize for the best novel for 2001 for *Sirena, Selena, Vestida de Pena* and recently for the Espasa Calpe award in Madrid for *Nuestra Señora de la Noche* (Our Lady of the Night) from 2006.

But it was the critics' reaction to her second novel *Sirena, Serena* that established her as an important voice in Puerto Rican letters, and a gifted prose writer. The novel *Sirena, Serena* is the story of a young drag queen, Sirena and her aging mentor, Martha Divine, who travel to the Dominican Republic to attempt to launch the career of Sirena as a performer of drag and singer of boleros. Since US labor laws prohibited the underage Sirena from working in her home country of Puerto Rico, they decided to go to the neighboring island to try their luck. A parallel story develops describing two young Dominican boys who work in a local gay bar catering to tourists. There is also a constant allusion to two universal myths: the Homeric sirens who lured sailors to their deaths with their seductive song, and that of the Little Mermaid by Anderson who fell in love with a prince and lost her voice when she became human. Sirena is part innocent young girl and part street-smart boy. This is also the story of Martha Divine, searching for a unified gender for herself, hoping that the success of Sirena will give her enough money to undergo a sex change operation to attain wholeness. The boleros are a source of comfort for Sirena, who sang them to comfort herself while she walked the streets of Puerto Rico, working as a prostitute. The novel is a fascinating study of sexual ambiguity, the construction of sexual identity, and the world of the transvestite, written with sensitivity, sensuality and erotic expression.

In 2002, she published *Any Wednesday I'm Yours* and changed her focus, In this novel, Santos Febres uses sensuality and eroticism to develop the character of Julian Castrodad, a writer and ex-reporter who has lost his way and finds a job working the night shift at a run-down motel. He discovers the urban underworld of drugs and money and corrupt police that answer to a different set of laws.

Her latest novel, of 2006, *Nuestra senora de la noche*, recounts the story of Isabel Luberza Oppenheimer, also known as "Isabel la Negra" in Puerto Rico. Isabel Luberza is a legendary figure in Puerto Rican history, a woman who rose from abject poverty to wealth and privilege through her own will to survive. She has appeared in Puerto Rican fiction previously in the works of writers such as Manuel Ramos Otero and Rosario Ferré.

Themes and Influences

What sets Santos Febres apart from many other writers is her unabashed portrayal of homoerotic themes. While she shares an interest in the study of Puerto Rican identity, Caribbean urban life and colonization with many other Puerto Rican writers, both male and female, it is in the area of the portrayal of desire and sexuality that she is probably most unique. In her works, convention is defied while she examines transgression, erotic expression and transvestism. She has a particularly keen interest in the popular music of the Caribbean, especially the bolero, and utilizes the rhythm and cadences of poetry in her narration.

Santos Febres' works are refreshing in their unabashed portrayal of characters breaking out of rigid gendered and sexual constructs and struggling to live an honest life in a repressive and often hostile society. *La guaracha del Macho Camacho* and *La importancia de llamarse Daniel Santos* by Luis Rafael Sanchez, and much of the work of Ana Lydia Vega and Manual Ramos Otero share with Santos Febres an attempt to overcome a repressive society using humor, the carnavalesque, popular culture, and Caribbean music to redefine sexual and constructed gendered identity.

ANTONIA GARCIA-RODRIGUEZ

Selected Works

Anamu y manigua. Río Pedras: La Iguana Dorada, 1991.
El orden escapado. Puerto Rico: Editorial Triptico, 1991.
Pez de vidrio. Florida: Letras de Oro, 1995.

Mal hablar: antologia de nueva literatura puertorriquena. Puerto Rican Humanities Foundation, 1997.
El cuerpo correcto. San Juan: R & R Editores, 1998. Trans. as *Urban Oracles*. Trans. N. Bydoff and L. Plason Lazaro. Cambridge: Lumen.
Tercer mundo. Trilce, 2000.
Sirena Serena vestida de pena. Barcelona: Mondadori, 2000. Translated as *Sirena Selena: A Novel*. Trans. Stephen Lytle. New York: Picador USA.
Cualquier miercoles soy tuya. Barcelona: Mondadori, 2002. Trans. as *Any Wednesday I'm Yours*. Trans. James Graham. New York; Riverhead Books.
Nuestra senora de la noche. Madrid: Espasa Calpe. 2006.

References and Further Reading

Barradas, Efrain. "*Sirena Selena vestida de pena* o el Caribe como travesty". Centro: *Journal of the Center for Puerto Rican Studies* XV(2) (Fall 2003): 53–65.
Castillo, Debra A. "She Sings Boleros: Santos-Febres' Sirena Selena". *Latin American Literary Review* 29(57) (Jan.–Jun. 2001): 13–25.
Cuadra, Ivonne. "Quién canta? Bolero y ambiguedad en *Sirena Selena vestida de pena* de Mayra Santos-Febres". *Revista de Estudios Hispánicos* XXX (2003): 153–63.
Morgado, Marcia. "Literatura para curar el asma: Una entrevista con Mayra Santos Febres". *Barcelona Review* (Mar.–Apr.2000). http://www.barcelonareview.com17/s_ent_msf.htm
Paravisini-Gebert, Lizabeth. "Women Prose Writers from the Hispanic Caribbean in the 1990s". *Bulletin of Latin American Research* 22(4) (2003): 445–64.
Van Haesendonck, Kristian. "El arte de bregar en dos novelas puertorriquenas contemporaneas: *Sirena Selena vestida de pena* y Sol de medianoche." *Revista de Estudios Hispánicos* XXX(1) (2003a): 141–63.
——. "*Sirena Selena vestida de pena* de Mayra Santos Febres: transgresiones de espacio o espacio de transgresiones?" *Centro: Journal of the Center for Puerto Rican Studies* XV(2) (Fall 2003b): 79–96.

SANTOS SILVA, LOREINA

Loreina Santos Silva, one of the most innovative twentieth-century Hispanic American writers, was born in 1933 in Hato Rey, Puerto Rico. She has lived mainly in Mayagüez and San Juan, but her graduate studies were completed outside the Island. She has a B.A. from the University of Puerto Rico, a Special Degree in the Teaching of English as a Foreign Language from the University of Michigan at Ann Arbor, an M.A. and a Ph.D. in Hispanic Literature from the University of California at Berkeley and Brown University, respectively. For many years, Santos Silva enjoyed an international reputation as an essayist, critic, and academic. It was not until 1973 that she published her first book of poetry, *Incertidumbre primera* (First Uncertainty) and since then, she has written 15 more. Her narrative work appeared in the last decade of the twentieth century. Her book of memoirs, *Este ojo que me mira* (1996, This Eye that Looks at Me) was then followed by two short stories: *Cuentos para perturbar el alma* (2000, Stories to Perturb the Soul), *Cuentos de Alas* (2006, Bird Stories), and two novels: *La bestia* (2003, The Beast) and *La Panteonera* (2005, The Grave Sentinel).

Poetry

Even though Santos Silva's literary career began in the 1970s, Josefina Rivera de Alvarez places Santos Silva as a member of "Generación Puertorriqueña de 1960," a group acknowledged for its opposing styles: traditional or radical. Rivera de Alvarez points out that Halmar Fax and José Luis Vega, for instance, looked for unusual metaphors in amorous poetry or dealt with the simple occurrences of daily life while Angela María Dávila remained under the *vanguardista* model. Rivera de Alvarez considers Olga Nolla, Olga Mattei, and Loreina Santos Silva the innovators preferring experimental, feminist, and erotic poetry (Rivera de Alvarez 1983: 727–8). Santos Silva, however, is the most distinguished member of her generation not only because of her versatile style expressed in eclogues or pastoral poems, ballads, songs, poems of *arte mayor* (a poem with verses of more than nine syllables) and poems of *arte menor* (a poem with verses of two up to eight syllables), sonnets, lullabies, haikus, and free verse, but because her work recurrently examines juxtaposed discourses: metaphysical, scientific, religious, social, and political.

In the Forewords to *Incertidumbre Primera/ First Uncertainty* and *Del Onto/On Ontology*, Adelaide Lugo-Guernelli points out that Santos Silva's poetry is a combination of various periods: *culteranismo*, modernism, and romanticism, and that because of this array of tendencies, her images search for contradictions and sensations. (Lugo-Guernelli 1980: 12, 17). In addition to the synesthesic language noticed by Lugo-Guernelli, Santos Silva's poetry pursues something essential and intangible that could complete the dialogue that her poetic subjects have with their inner self—issues that seem to be beyond the subject's control. It could be the absence of love as seen in the secluded world of the fishermen in *Vocero del mar / Chronicler of the Ocean* (1982); the lack of exhilaration in the lullabies of *ABC, rimas para los niños puertorriqueños* (1990, ABC, Rhymes for the Puerto Rican Children); or the need for freedom as stated in *El reclamo de las rocas* (1997, The Rocks' Request). All of Santos Silva's work is a multi-perspectival study on how to understand these deficiencies. Where language hinders the possibility to do so, Santos Silva invents a new lexis. This is evident in her descriptions of unexplored universes in *Del Onto / About Ontology* (1978) where neologisms such as *allases, acases, solalba, soliluna, polifurco*, and *tierraluna* proliferate. Verbs are transformed in *Umbral de soledad* (1987, Prelude to Solitude) as well: *se galaxia, se planeta, se criatura, se fantasma, me arrecifo*, etc., and even words that imply loneliness are assumed in foreign terms: *soledumbre, brisales, sequedales, soledosa*. In *Como puñales* (1993, Like Daggers), there is a profusion of new expressions: *energigonía, citroso, torolumbre, tardenoche, astrogónico, extraplaneta, erogonías, polifórmicas, vaciedumbre* and unheard verbs like *fantasman* and *sintagman*.

Each of Santos Silva's poetic texts has its own complex argument and configuration, but all of them are related in the common quest of equating discernment with the appalling limits set by time and death. In *Del Onto* (1978, About Ontology), for instance, she encompasses a hypothesis on the role of electro-magnetic energy with the quandaries of human time. Santos Silva refers to the mutations of Astarte, Adonis, Cybele, Hermaphrodite, Venus, and Narcissus and relates them to her vision of an "unbounded" time. Santos Silva examines the same question in poems about evolution and the liaison between humankind and cosmos that, sometimes, converge to the theories pondered by Einstein, Friedman and Oppenheimer. In *Del Onto* (1978), *Mi Ría* (1981, My Ría),

Motor Mutable (1984, Mutating Engine), *Amor, Amor una veleta* (1990, Love, Love, a Wind Vane), *Como Puñales* (1993) and *El Reclamo de las rocas* (1997). In the latter part of the twentieth century when her poetry becomes solemn and severe, her imagined time appears vanquished by grief and the certainty of death.

Equally important practices in Santos Silva's poetry are her defiant revisions of historical and religious books like the Judeo-Christian ones in which she eliminates the commonly known sanctified male characters and substitutes them with female characters. Santos Silva's women are interpreters of life, awaited saviors of mankind, and creators of a new genesis. In *Amor, Amor, una veleta* (1990), she states that the first breath of humanity took place when a female ancestor descended from a tree and changed from animal into woman: "el mito de la chispa/ me erecciona el contacto ... Desaparece el rabo/—eslabón del enigma sosteniendo el atraso" [the myth, the sparkle arises me at contact ... The tail disappears/ – chain of the enigma holding the backwardness] (42). Santos Silva's feminism is also obvious in her observations about the right of women to exercise ownership over their bodies and minds. In *Rikelme/ Rikelme* (1974), and years before Hélène Cixous, Luce Irigaray, or Judith Butler would establish their postulates, Santos Silva explored the body as a discourse. She displayed without any censorship the desires of the feminine Eros and dealt with crucial women's issues such as equality between the sexes and the entitlement to discuss and enjoy the pleasures of sex freely.

Two of Santos Silva's poetry books, *Poemas para la madre ausente* (1995, Poems for the Missing Mother) and *Salmos a la gran madre* (2005, Psalms for the Great Mother), are entirely dedicated to the mother figure—although she has inserted poetic meditations about her in most of her texts. These ruminations imitate the intricacies of recapturing the ideal image of her mother and her premature death. Santos Silva's poems do not release the poetic "I" from her mourning, as she does not want an elucidation of pain, but a constant regression to the moment when the physical and irrevocable separation from her mother occurred. Santos Silva expresses superbly a disquieting, repetitive, and unending sorrow.

If Santos Silva's poetry constantly looks at pioneering approaches, it also shows a careful planned structure where tone and rhythm contrast with dissimilar poetic articulations. In *Brevialias/ Brevity*, poems of a few syllables imitative of Basho's haikus, Santos Silva's lyric stanzas highlight the splendid flora and fauna of the Island while a parallel language expresses her country's claim for independence. In *Vocero del mar/ Chronicler of the Sea* (1982), a text that summarizes a ten-year long cycle of interviews with Puerto Rican fishermen, Santos Silva skillfully illustrates the secluded and self-absorbed world of fishermen and transforms their memoirs into a multi-leveled discourse that defines Puerto Rico in allegorical, mythical, historical, and testimonial terms. This testimony—perhaps one of Santos Silva's most relevant poetic accomplishments—would antecede her future testimonial narrative of the 1990s.

Prose

At the end of the twentieth century, Santos Silva transferred her insightful study of self and nation displayed in her poetry to the narrative genre. Her book of memoirs, *Este ojo que me mira* (1996, This Eye that Looks at Me) is a revealing story of Puerto Rico before and after the political repressions of the 1930s and the massive migrations of the 1950s and 1960s. The official data and recollections from her past are narrated through a variety of cinematic techniques that imitate a visual discourse. As Rojas-Tempre well says, Santos Silva creates "un carrusel de diapositivas en proceso de montaje en donde la diégesis de las múltiples miradas detiene la pantalla en una sola diapositiva ... De esta manera limita el enfoque parcial a un acto infantil mágico o perverso" [a carousel of slides imitating a montage process in which the diegesis of the multiple gazes stops the camera on a single slide. In this way, [Santos Silva] limits the partial focal point into a magical or cunning moment of her childhood] (Rojas Tempre 1997: 141–2).

Santos Silva's narrative is devised in a double structure of cinematic and testimonial languages. Her visual discourse appears as the only alternative when words are corrupted by a disintegrating society. This is clearly exposed in her novel, *La Bestia* (2003). In *Cuentos para perturbar el alma* (2000), Santos Silva formulates a similar anguished view but, in this case, of the political predicaments of Puerto Rico. Her short-stories book, *Cuentos de Alas* and her novel, *La Panteonera* (2006) are suggestive allegories of the traditional stories and native myths of Puerto Rico that nonetheless encompass a national preoccupation.

As observed, Loreina Santos Silva's cleverly crafted poetic and narrative work has been characterized by a multiplicity of voices, styles, and themes. Angel M. Aguirre, Miriam González, and Roberto Fernández Valledor, Julia Rivera de Alvarez, and Lady Rojas Tempre point out to the erudite character of her work that nevertheless refers to emotion with such complexity and lyricism. Doris Ponce and Rafael Gomensoro emphasize Santos Silva's poetry as a study on desire—a human passion or an ontological need for the Absolute. Linda Rodríguez, for her part, underlines Santos Silva's construal of Puerto Rico as a country in a distressed search for a national identity. This mixture of views articulate that Loreina Santos Silva's poetry and narrative are brilliantly conceived universes of speculation. She might stage her metaphysical, social, and political concerns in the enthralling world of metaphors or in the dramatic events of her narrative, but all of her production confers the same significance to human vulnerability and justice.

ROSA TEZANOS-PINTO

Selected Works

Poetry

Incertidumbre primera. San Juan: Juan Ponce de León, 1973.
Rikelme. Río Piedras: Edil, 1974.
Del Onto. San Juan: Instituto de Cultura Puertorriqueña, 1978.
Mi Ría. Madrid: Repografía Alvarellos, 1981.
Vocero del mar. Mayagüez: Sea Grant, UPRM, 1982.
Motor Mutable. Río Piedras: Editorial Cultural, 1984.
Umbral de soledad. San Juan: Instituto de Cultura Puertorriqueño, 1987.
Amor, amor, una veleta. Santo Domingo: Ediciones Alfa y Omega, 1990.
ABC, rimas para los niños puertorriqueños. Hato Rey: Yuquiyú, 1990.
Como puñales. Mayagüez: Impresos RUM, 1993.

Poemas para la madre ausente. Mayagüez: Impresos RUM, 1995.
El reclamo de las rocas. Mayagüez: Impresos RUM, 1997.
Hijos apócrifos. Mayagüez: Antillian Press, 2001.
Brevialias. Mayagüez: UPR RUM, 2001.
Nanas del zodiaco. Mayagüez: UPRM, 2005.
Salmos a la Gran Madre. Mayagüez: UPRM, 2005.

Prose

Este ojo que me mira. San Juan: Editorial de la Universidad de Puerto Rico, 1996.
Cuentos para perturbar el alma. San Juan: Instituto de Cultura de Puerto Rico, 2000.
La Bestia. Mayagüez: Antillian Press, 2003.
Cuentos de Alas. Mayagüez: UPRM, 2006.
La Panteonera. San Juan: Publicaciones Puertorriqueñas, 2006.

Scholarly Articles

"*El Josco*, una fábula política". In *Por los Caminos de lo Otro*. New Delhi: Consejo Indio de Relaciones Culturales, 1997, pp. 237–44.
"El simbolismo de las aves en la obra de José de Diego". *Revista de la Academia de artes y ciencias de Puerto Rico* 6 (1993–94): 26–35.
"Los romances de Emilio Prados: Dos compromisos". In *Estudios del folklore dedicados a Mercedes Díaz Roig*. México: Colegio de México, 1992.
"Descarnando el parto. Proceso creativo de Metalepsis". *Letras Femeninas* December (1990).
"Zoe o la angustia interespacial". *Alba de América* July (1986): 189–94.
"Loor del espacio de Francisco Matos Paoli: una mística materialista". *Cuadernos Americanos* Nov.–Dec. 12 (1978): 240–2.
"Lo cómico en *Torquemada*". *Papeles de Son Armadans* March (1977): 239–54.

References and Further Reading

Aguirre, Angel M. "*Amor, amor, una veleta*". *Atenea* 13 (1993): 27–39.
Canellos, Nicolás (ed.) *Biographical Dictionary of Hispanic Literature in the United States*. New York: Greenwood Press, 1990, pp. 283–4.
Fernández Valledor, Roberto. "*Como puñales*: síntesis vital y poética de Loreina Santos Silva". *El Cuervo* 15 (2003): 25–37.
Gomensoro, Rafael. "*Motor Mutable*: energía y erotismo. El camino de las rías". *Mairena* XI (1989): 119–28.
González, Miriam. "La figura femenina y su antagónico masculino en *Este ojo que me Mira*". *Horizontes* 39 (1997): 109–14.
Lugo Guernelli, Adelaida. "*Mi ría*, poemario de Loreina Santos Silva". *Mairena* 5 (1980): 55–62.
Ponce, Doris. *El erotismo y sus claves en Rikelme de Loreina Santos Silva y Dulce* hombre prohibido de Olga Nolla. Mayagüez: RUM, 2004.
Rivera de Alvarez, Julia. *Literatura Puertorriqueña. Su proceso en el tiempo*. Madrid: Ediciones Partanón, 1983.
Rodríguez, Linda. "*Este ojo que me mira*: fragmentación y reconstrucción de una identidad caribeña". *El Cuervo* 20 (1998): 46–51.
Rojas Tempre, Lady. "Lectura Bajtiana de *Este ojo que me mira* de Loreina Santos Silva". *Letras Femeninas* 23 (1997): 139–48.
Tezanos-Pinto Rosa. "El lenguaje polifónico en la poesía de Loreina Santos Silva". *El Cuervo* 26 (2002): 43–50.
——. Descodificación de los diálogos discursivos en Ester de Izaguirre y Loreina Santos Silva/). Ann Arbor, MI: University of Michigan Press, 2003.
——. "*Cuentos de Alas*: fábulas de reencuentro con la armonía y la equidad". *Opinión Hispana*, Melbourne, Australia 20 (November 2004): 26–7.
——. *Redimiendo la infancia en la estructura poética. Análisis crítico de los textos de Ester de Izaguirre y Loreina Santos Silva*. Buenos Aires: Editorial Nueva Generación, 2005.

SARLO, BEATRIZ

A significant intellectual figure in Argentinean and Latin American culture, Beatriz Sarlo (b. 1942) has produced a substantial body of work. Born in Buenos Aires, this university professor and internationally known speaker is also an essayist, literary historian and critic. She has worked actively to promote culture through compiling anthologies, founding and directing what is considered the journal of cultural resistance during the dictatorship – *Punto de vista* (1978, Point of View) – and publishing extensively in national newspapers (*Página 12*, *Clarín*, *La Nación*). Through her ideas and her consistent visibility in the cultural sphere, Sarlo takes a prominent stand as a scholar committed to understanding her times and to contributing to the field of Latin American Studies.

In 1966, Sarlo received her degree from the University of Buenos Aires. She was a literature professor there for twenty years until 2003. During that time, numerous institutions recognized her academic work internationally. She has been a fellow of the Guggenheim Foundation and the Wilson Center, a member of the Wissenschaftskolleg in Berlin, and the "Simón Bolívar Professor of Latin American Studies" at the University of Cambridge. Her work has garnered her many awards: the Premio Trayectoria from the Fondo Nacional de las Artes in Buenos Aires (1998), the Ezequiel Martínez Estrada Essay Prize from Casa de las Américas in Havana (2000), the Premio Iberoamericano de las Letras José Donoso in Santiago de Chile (2002) and the Premio Platino from the Fundación Konex in Buenos Aires (2004). She continues to be active publishing in specialized literary journals and in newspapers (on topics from rock music, shopping malls, and soccer, to AIDS), while maintaining her position directing *Punto de vista*, a key forum for cultural discussion. Some of her texts have been translated into English, German, Portuguese and Italian.

Foundations

Sarlo was trained in traditional literary criticism. Her work on canonical Argentinean literature spans the nineteenth (Sarmiento and Echeverría) and twentieth (Borges and Cortázar) centuries. She then turns to the evolving notion of what constitutes literature. The boundaries defining literature and its contents have changed significantly with the influence of new technologies and mass culture on literary discourse. Sarlo extended her field of inquiry to cultural production outside the canon through which she continues to develop important contributions to Cultural Studies in and about Latin America from her intimate perspective on the Argentine experience.

In addition to the history of literature and culture from a social and aesthetic perspective, Sarlo's work since the 1970s has taken up the widespread concern related to the intellectual's role in peripheral countries. Her outstanding contribution to the writing on these subjects is found in her collaborative books with Carlos Altamirano: *Conceptos de sociología literaria* (1980, Concepts in Literary Sociology), *Literatura/sociedad* (1983, Literature/Society), and *Ensayos argentinos. De Sarmiento a la vanguardia* (1983, 1997, Argentine Essays from Sarmiento to the Avant-garde). These works examine the history of literature, its readers and writers through a social theory of literary praxis. They also study the problems surrounding cultural/literary analysis and the suitable instruments for analyzing the circulation and consumption of culture as symbolic goods belonging to spheres of representation and meaning, with the idea that culture and society are inseparable.

The sociological discourse defining culture is explicitly marked in Sarlo's work. She pulls from the Frankfurt School, in particular Walter Benjamín, and the Birmingham Cultural Studies group, especially Raymond Williams. She also examines the idea surrounding what makes up cultural taste or pleasure (in its broadest sense) and the configuration of the intellectual field a stage for the struggle for power (Pierre Bourdieu), as well as Roland Barthes' semiology of daily life.

In *El imperio de los sentimientos* (1985, The Rule of Feeling) Sarlo deals with weekly serial fiction between 1917 and 1927, a medium for sentimental narratives and a feminine imagination. She studies their edition, authors and reading public through a socio-historic perspective. And through a textual perspective, the texts' systematic codification of the body, the gaze, and the resulting semantic value of the model for happiness they purport (p. 11). In *Una modernidad periférica: Buenos Aires 1920 y 1930* (1988, A Periphery of Modernity) she relates textual analysis with the analysis of cultural practice and diverse discursive expressions. A "*mezcla*" (mixture), the book combines Sarlo's treatment of this relationship with her attraction to critics who develop "disrespectful readings" (Schorske/Freud, Berman/Marx) (p. 9).

Interrelated discourses, the expansion of symbolic registers, and textual "mixtures" are the repeated themes in two books Sarlo writes about twentieth-century Argentinean culture. In *La máquina cultural. Maestras, traductores y vanguardistas* (1998, The Cultural Machine) and *La pasión y la excepción* (2003, Passion and the Exceptional) she builds an analytic framework that enables her to place different voices and cultural registers in dialogue with each other through a three-part structure. In the first, her analysis of a teacher's, translator's (none other than Victoria Ocampo) and young film-maker's experiences suggest the construction of a "cultural machine" that produces ideas, practices, institutions, and the characters and plots that make up the different patterns for reconfiguring lived experience. In the second, Sarlo's examination of two exceptional and passionate historical events (the Eva Perón phenomenon and a political kidnapping) and one narrative episode (a story by Jorge Luis Borges), shows the confluence of two forces that have nourished Argentina's—and consequently Sarlo's—political and cultural scene: Peronism and Borge's œuvre.

Sarlo often places herself at the center of her ruminations. In this way, while she is describing the processes for articulating a "structure of feeling," she makes the course of her personal understanding an object for study. She takes on each book as a stage in her own intellectual development, an ethical stance she also exhibits by explicitly recognizing from whom she borrows and with whom she is affiliated.

A Polemical Critic(que)

Innovative and controversial, Sarlo's cultural criticism is characterized by her interest in change and rupture, in modernization and the avant-garde, as well as in technology's impact on urban culture. While her work forms part of the field of cultural studies developed in the second half of the twentieth century, it also reminds us of the pitfalls such studies carry with them. She insists on recovering "aesthetic value," lost with the discursive homogenization brought on by market forces and a postmodern "anything goes" attitude ("Los estudios culturales en la encrucijada valorativa" *Revista de crítica cultural*, 1997, An Assessment of Cultural Studies). For example she questions, in some of her other work, contemporary critics' repeated idea of the cosmopolitan in Borges, and the overused notion of the question of power in reading Walter Benjamín.

Late twentieth-century culture and the cultural phenomena that mark the quotidian are the subjects of Sarlo's inquiry in *Escenas de la vida posmoderna: intelectuales, arte y videocultura en la Argentina* (1994, Scenes from Postmodern Life) and its follow-up *Instantáneas. Medios, ciudad y costumbres en el fin de siglo* (1996, Snapshots). In them, she attempts to comprehend what she views as the consummate changes that the media and computer technology have introduced into cultural practice and daily life. She assumes an acutely aware intellectual position vis-à-vis the lure of the market in order to maintain a critical distance from her postmodern landscape.

If in *Tiempo presente. Notas sobre el cambio de una cultura* (2001, Present Times. Notes on a Changing Culture) she reveals the connections between the market and the state, her most recent book *Tiempo pasado. Cultura de la memoria y giro subjetivo* (2005, Times Past. The Culture of Memory and the Subjective Spin) questions the way in which the political history of Argentina in the sixties and seventies has been narrated. As she does, for example, in *La máquina cultural* ... with the teacher's memoir, Sarlo brings to the fore a discussion of the ideological and cultural causes behind what is considered historical fact. She proposes that this period not only be remembered, but understood. Her theoretical reflection seeks to relate actions and ideology to the larger socio-cultural system. In taking on the testimonial, Sarlo questions the value, in a political and cultural context, of the subjective "I" much in the same way, as she maintains, literary theory has done with autobiography, psychoanalysis with subjectivity, and philosophy with truth. To subject the historical first person to this discussion implies a critique of the testimonial narrative so highly valued in the Latin American cultural context. It questions the witness's "truth". Not doing so, she maintains, risks everything remaining a melodramatic and Manichean tale that, in this specific case, would absolve almost all Argentineans (*Debate*, March 2006).

In the broader discussion of the dictatorship in Argentina, these controversial statements are heretical. Nonetheless, in these times of ephemeral images and virtual discourses, Sarlo defends the valuable role of the intellectual in the search for an epistemology that contributes to a concrete discussion of historical truth. Consequently, Sarlo's work surpasses the questions asked by Latin American Studies to resonate on a universal level.

NARA ARAÚJO

Selected Works

El imperio de los sentimientos. Narraciones de circulación periódica en la argentina (1917–1927). Buenos Aires: Catálogo editora, 1985.

Una modernidad periférica: Buenos Aires 1920 y 1930. Buenos Aires: Ediciones Nueva Visión, 1988.
La imaginación técnica, sueños modernos de la cultura argentina. Buenos Aires: Nueva Visión, 1992.
Escenas de la vida posmoderna: intelectuales, arte y videocultura en la Argentina. Buenos Aires: Ariel, 1994.
Borges: a Writer on the Edge. London: Verso, 1993.
Borges, un escritor en las orillas. Buenos Aires: Ariel, 1995.
Instantáneas. Medios, ciudad, y costumbres en el fin de siglo. Buenos Aires: Ariel, 1996.
La máquina cultural. Maestras, traductores y vanguardistas. Buenos Aires: Ariel, 1998.
Siete ensayos sobre Walter Benjamin. Buenos Aires: FCE, 2000.
Scenes from Postmodern Life. Trans. Jon Beasley-Murray. Minneapolis, MN: University of Minnesota Press, 2001.
Tiempo presente. Notas sobre el cambio de una cultura. Buenos Aires: Siglo XXI, 2001.
La pasión y la excepción. Buenos Aires: Siglo XXI, 2003.
Tiempo pasado. Cultura de la memoria y giro subjetivo. Una discusión. Buenos Aires: Siglo XXI, 2005.

Anthologies

El cuento argentino contemporáneo. Jorge Luis Borges, Julio Cortázar y otros. Buenos Aires: Centro Editor de América Latina, 1977.
Evaristo Carriego y otros poetas. Buenos Aires: Centro Editor de América Latina, 1980.
Conceptos de sociología literaria. Buenos Aires: Centro Editor de América Latina, 1980.
Ensayos argentinos. De Sarmiento a la vanguardia. Buenos Aires: Centro Editor de América Latina, 1983.
Literatura/sociedad. Buenos Aires: Hachette, 1983.
Martín Fierro y su crítica. Buenos Aires: Centro Editor de América Latina, 1994. In collaboration with Carlos Altamirano.

References and Further Readings

Balderston, Daniel, González, Mike and López, Ana M. (eds) *Encyclopedia of Contemporary Latin American and Caribbean Cultures*. New York: Routledge, 2000.
Corbatta, Jorgelina. "Veinte años después: Beatriz Sarlo y la cultura de la resistencia en la Argentina durante la guerra sucia." Ar/libros/LASA 98/Corbatta.
D'Allemand, Patricia. "Hacia una crítica literaria latinoamericana. Nacionalismo y cultura en el discurso de Beatriz Sarlo". *Estudios* 1(2) (1993): 27–40.
King, John "Introduction". In *Jorge Luis Borges: A Writer on the Edge. Beatriz Sarlo*. London: Verso, 1993, pp. vii–xvii.

SAVARY, OLGA AUGUSTA MARIA

Olga Savary (b. 1933) has made a prolific contribution to Brazil's intellectual life as poet, novelist, short-story writer, anthologist, literary journalist and editor throughout a career spanning fifty years. She was born in the city of Belém in the Northern state of Pará, Brazil, on 21 May 1933, the only daughter of a Russian father, Bruno Savary, and a Brazilian mother, Célia Nobre de Almeida, descended from a family of Portuguese immigrants. Savary also has a native Indian great-grandmother, and has claimed this, and her mixed ancestry in general, as a crucial element in her life and work. Savary's childhood was somewhat unsettled; partly due to her parent's separation when Savary was six years old, and also her father's work as an engineer, which took his family at several points in Savary's childhood to the interior of Pará state, and to the city of Fortaleza in the northern coastal state of Ceará. Savary also lived briefly in the city of Rio de Janeiro, where she discovered Japanese culture through exposure to her uncle's library. The physical landscapes, stories, folklore and legends of the Amazon and North-east of Brazil were to have a crucial formative influence on Savary's work in her later years; although she has resided in Rio de Janeiro throughout her adult life, she has proudly asserted her eclectic heritage and her roots in the North and North-east of Brazil. Savary's literary talent manifested itself at an early age; she produced her first work at the age of 10, and published poems under the pen-name of Olenka in journals and newspapers in Rio, Belém and Minas Gerais. Yet the author was discouraged from pursuing a literary career by her parents, especially her mother, from whom Savary was estranged for many years, and who appears as a Medusa figure at several points in her work. Thus it was only in 1970, at the age of 37, that Savary's first collection of poems, *Espelho Provisório*, was published.

Brazilian Author and Poet

Although Savary has been prolific in many genres, it is as a poet that she attained fame on a national level, and esteem from her peers. As a writer she has followed a somewhat independent path, and has eschewed adherence or affiliation with any one of the numerous literary schools or movements which have proliferated in Brazil throughout her career; she is not actively engaged in a political sense either. Yet her contribution to almost every aspect of Brazilian cultural and literary life has been considerable. Besides her twenty collections of poetry, she has contributed in various capacities to more than five hundred books published in Brazil. Her work as an anthologist and organizer of other people's work must be particularly noted: the first major collection of erotic works written by Brazilian poets, *Carne Viva—Antologia Brasileira de Poesia Erótica* (1984) was a project undertaken at her own instigation, and a collection, *Antologia da nova poesia brasileira* (1992) organized and edited by herself, presents the work of three hundred and thirty-four poets born after 1945 and active since the advent of the military dictatorship. Her contribution to Latin American letters is principally as a translator: she has translated fifty works by the most canonized Latin American authors: Júlio Cortázar, Mário Vargas Llosa, Pablo Neruda, among many others. This tireless literary activity in so many fields has won her a reputation as one of the pre-eminent figures in contemporary Brazilian literary and cultural life, to the extent of having been awarded more than thirty-six national literary prizes; she has been extensively honoured in other ways, with tributes from representatives of the other creative arts, and has represented Brazil on an international level. Her work has also been translated and anthologized in countries in Europe, North America and the Far East.

Themes and Influences

Olga Savary has maintained an independent stance and orientation in all her work, and in her poetry in particular. The poetry for which she is principally known, composed in unmetered blank verse, and much of it written in the first person, is avowedly confessional: according to the poet's own account, her poems are about herself, of what she lives and observes from day to day, the nature of unconditional love, and, in their erotic aspect, profoundly affirmative. But her poetry also treats themes of absence and loss, that which she has not experienced, inchoate emotions and the inexpressible which is sublimated through literature. Yet although she is not overtly "nationalist" in orientation, Olga Savary expresses a strong, almost umbilical affinity with her heritage and homeland of Brazil, and weaves elements from the geographical and human landscape of Brazil into her work, including many drawn from her childhood impressions of her native Pará, the Amazon and the North-east of Brazil. In her work. Savary achieves a vividness and depth of statement through concision and a unique appropriation, or the juxtaposition of common and unexpected lyrical imagery, drawn in large part from sources of the natural landscape and diverse mythologies, from Judeo-Christian, Greek, indigenous Brazilian and Japanese traditions. Proud in particular of the indigenous heritage of her great-grandmother, her assertion of the syncretic heritage of Brazil is expressed, not only on a thematic, but also on a linguistic level; interwoven in her poems are words derived from and related to Tupi, the language spoken by the indigenous population along the litoral of Brazil. One example is the collection entitled *Rudá*, (1994) meaning "love" in Tupi. The poet also affirmed her link to the "Indianist" tradition in Brazilian literature by reworking and publishing a poem she had begun at a very early age, "Morte de Moema" (1986, Death of Moema) named after a female Indian protagonist in the eighteenth-century Indianist epic *Camarumu* by the poet Santa Rita Durão. This work also illustrates her constant predilection to renovate and bring something new to an established tradition.

Critical Interpretations

Savary affirms that her work is not overtly intellectual or abstract in nature, but informed by the concrete sensorial reality of the elements and the numerous phenomena in nature that they produce. The poet thus creates landscapes composed of the four elements of fire, water, wind and earth, highly allusive, and hinting at some transformative power or metaphysical principle beyond and above the physical world. With regard to poetic language, her poetry deals with a theme prevalent in much contemporary Brazilian poetry: the relationship between the word and the signified. There is a constant meditation on the dilemma worked through her poems, whether words are the pure essence of the thing, or whether they point to some other ideal beyond themselves, or if they do indeed hold some transforming or transformative power. As the title of one of her volumes, *Éden Hades* (1994), reveals, the poetry also illustrates Savary's need to recover some primal unity behind ostensible opposites, or things that appear to be opposites, and also to reveal that each spiritual or metaphysical principle bears its opposite within itself.

Her work, in its concision and lyrical density, has a natural affinity with Japanese haiku, its insistence on meditation and harmony with nature, and Savary herself has adapted the traditional haiku form, written many haikus herself, and published a collection devoted to the genre, *100 Haikais* (1986, 100 Haikus). Yet of all the physical and natural elements in her work, water is a principal and informing motif, and, as the title of two of her volumes, *Altaonda* (1979, High Wave) and *Linha d'água* (1987, Line of water) illustrate. Water and oceanic imagery suffuses her work, as a symbol, a philosophical principle, and the primordial origin from which life and creation originate. It represents psychical and spiritual change, movement and metamorphosis: both the tension of the poet's inner psychic and emotional states, and the perceived flux in the outer world of nature. In particular, this trope is linked to the female erotic, another informing and central theme in Savary's work: she traces the liminality of female eros and language through water, liquid and the ocean. Eros, in this context, is not to be interpreted in a narrowly sexual sense; Savary states that the erotic is "the great triangle between man, woman and God" and can be celebrated also in, for example, the act of breast feeding, in the upbringing of children, in conviviality and communion with friends. Thus Olga Savary also defines herself as a feminist, although, again, she is not affiliated to any specific movement or organization. Nonetheless, her work in general is oriented towards the liberation of women, their right to greater freedom of expression and self-expression; she asserts that the focus of a woman's life need not be exclusively focused on the other or the family. This theme is most fully realised in her short stories, in particular the collection *O olhar dourado do abismo* (1997, The Golden Look of the Abyss), which features strong and rebellious female protagonists. Olga Savary continues to innovate and affirm many currents in Brazilian life and literature, while remaining true to her personal and individual vision.

MARGARET ANNE CLARKE

Selected Works

Poetry

Espelho Provisório. Rio de Janeiro: Livraria José Olympio Editora, 1970.
Sumidouro. São Paulo:Massao Ohno/João Farkas Editores, 1977.
Altaonda. São Paulo:Edições Macunaíma/ Masao Ohno Editor, 1979.
Magma. São Paulo: Massao Ohno/Hipocampo Editores, 1982.
Natureza viva: Uma seleta dos melhores poems de Olga Savary. Recife: Edições Pirata, 1982.
100 Haikais. São Paulo: Roswitha Kempf-Editores, 1986.
Linha-d'água. São Paulo: Massao Ohno/Hipocampo Editores, 1987.
Retratos. São Paulo: Massao Ohno Editor, 1989.
Rudá. Rio de Janeiro:Universidade Estadual de Rio de Janeiro, 1994.
Éden Hades. São Paulo: Massao Ohno Editor, 1994.
Morte de Moema. Rio de Janeiro: Impressões do Brasil, 1996.
Anima animalis – Voz de Bichos Brasileiros. São Paulo: Massao Ohno Editor, 1998.
Repertório selvagem – obra poética reunida (12 collections of poetry in one volume). Rio de Janeiro: Fundação Biblioteca Nacional/Universidade de Mogi das Cruzes/ MultiMais Editorial, 1998.

Short stories

O Olhar Dourado do Abismo. Rio de Janeiro: Impressões do Brasil, 1997.

Anthologies compiled by Olga Savary

Carne Viva: Antologia brasileira de poesia erótica. Rio de Janeiro: Editora Ânima, 1984.

Antologia da nova poesia brasleira. Rio de Janeiro: Fundação RioArte/ Secretária Municipal de Culturar/Prefeitura da Cidade do Rio de Janeiro/Editora Hipocampo, 1992.

References and Further Reading

Coelho, Joaquim-Francisco. "Olga Savary – Sumidouro". *Colóquio-Letras* May 1979.

Coelho, Nelly Novaes. "Tempo/Espaço/Poesia na palavra de Olga Savary". *Anuário das Artes*. São Paulo: Edição APCA, 1978.

——. *A Literatura Feminina no Brasil Contemporâneo*. São Paulo: Siciliano, 1993.

Lobo Filho, Blanca. *World Literature Today*. Norman, OK, October 1980.

Marcondes, Marleine Paula and Toledo, Ferreira de. *A voz das águas. Uma interpretação do universo poético de Olga Savary*. São Paulo: Edições Colibri, 1999.

——. *Olga Savary: Trajetória em verso e prosa*. São Paulo: Ateliê, 2006.

Merquior, José Guilherme. "Musa Morena Moça: notas sobre a nova poesia brasileira". *O fantasma romântico e outros ensaios*. São Paulo: Editora Vozes.

Ricciardi, Giovanni. *Auto-retratos*. São Paulo: Martins Fontes, 1991.

Soares, Angélica. *A paixão emancipatória: vozes femininas da liberação do erotismo na poesia brasileira*. Rio de Janeiro: DIFEL, 1999.

Valle, Gerson. "Olga Savary, toda poesia". *Poiésis: Literatura, Pensamento e Arte*. http://www.jornalpoiesis.com/mambo/index (accessed 11 May 2006).

SEFCHOVICH, SARA

Sociologist, novelist, political commentator, translator, and researcher at the UNAM for almost three decades, Sara Sefchovich Wasongarz (b. 1949) is one of the most versatile, provocative, and prolific writers in Mexico today. As a lifelong resident of the nation's capital, Sefchovich has been a thoughtful conversant on Mexican politics and on women's role in the public sphere. She has contributed articles to a wide variety of publications, among them *El Universal* and *La Jornada*, the magazines *Fem*, *Revista de la Universidad de México*, and *Revista Mexicana de Sociología*; she also comments on radio. She has used her regular opinion column at El Universal as a vehicle for exploring human rights polemics such as the US government's treatment of Mexican immigrants and Guantánamo Bay detainees. Sefchovich holds a Master's degree in sociology and a Ph.D. in Mexican history from the UNAM, and has taught courses in history, culture and sociology both in Mexico and the United States.

As a sociologist, Sefchovich has worked to define a sociology of Mexican literature and of Mexican feminism. Her works *México: país de ideas, país de novelas* and her two volumes entitled *Mujeres en espejo* chart a history of Mexican writers and Latin American women writers respectively, and the social conditions that shaped their education, styles, subject matter, ability to publish, and reception. She asserts an interest in tracing a history of Mexican and of feminist thought and its expression in literature, but as a pragmatist who eschews the type of highbrow literary criticism that consists of "frases lapidarias, adjetivos, sentencias de muerte, o profecías de éxito" (*México: país de ideas*, p. 6). She is widely respected for her three works of fiction and has been honored with many awards, among them a Guggenheim Fellowship and the Agustín Yáñez Award in 1990 for her first novel *Demasiado amor*. The novel has been made into a movie with the same title and *La señora de los sueños*, her second novel, is in cinematic production. In addition to her professional titles, the author defines herself as a militant feminist, a voracious reader, and a devoted wife and mother.

Sefchovich acknowledges a lifelong fascination with biography, and the overriding question that guides much of her corpus of writing is, "What does it mean to fully live?" It is this question that shapes her three novels as explorations of the realities of—and the possibilities for—women's lives in Mexico. Her narrative work is a testament to her strongly held belief that fiction can deeply enhance women's lives by offering them a variety of interesting answers to this question, and thus her fictional characters lead lives that provide readers with both entertainment and insight.

Sefchovich's literary maternal lineage can be traced directly to Rosario Castellanos, mother of an entire generation of Mexican writers and feminists. In her essays and novels, Sefchovich continues Castellanos's work of exposing double standards and ridiculous stereotypes for women in Mexican society, and consequently her protagonists share with those of Castellanos lives that contain a certain amount of absurdity and irony. Sefchovich's characters, however, have clearly heard Castellanos' call for the need to invent oneself as a woman, and they seek to free themselves of the pessimism, studied passivity, and repressed sexuality that characterized the lives of a previous generation of women in poems such as "Kinsey Report" and stories such as "Lección de cocina". Sefchovich's protagonists are not afraid to break with societal expectations to seek a full life of self-determination and to model a new definition of femininity.

Sefchovich's Fiction

Sefchovich's first novel, *Demasiado amor* (1990), is organized as a series of alternating letters dedicated to the protagonist's sister and to her former lover. In letters to her sister, the unnamed young woman imagines a life for herself with her sibling in Italy, and in diary entries addressed to a past lover, she reconstructs time spent with him exploring Mexico. Balanced between past and future lives are the present adventures of the protagonist, who narrates to sister and reader her gradual and largely pleasurable drift into prostitution, a profession that allows her windows into the lives of a multiplicity of men. Sefchovich's portrait of her protagonist defies the stereotype of the prostitute as only having one possible narrative in Mexican society, that of the alluring but unfortunate woman forced into a miserable life that leaves her morally destitute, a social outcast to be pitied and scorned. On the contrary, this young Mexican woman is a strong, generous, happy woman who lives a full life assisting lonely men in discovering their own happiness and sensuality; in so doing, she claims that she gives them life. The narrative of this ordinary woman convinces readers that women don't lead stereotypical lives in Mexico, even though popular storytelling would have us believe otherwise. In a metafictional moment, the protagonist refutes her sister's epistolary claim that she is living life like a character in a novel in loving so many men, by replying that her 79 kilos, short stature, thick hips and legs, and lack of makeup and adornment defy the possibility of her being a fictional character in a novel of lies. She is a real woman who embodies what men truly want—eyes to contemplate men, ears to listen to them, and a heart to accept them; she is not a femme fatale who scorns and teases, and nor is she a flat character from historical Mexican fiction who exists only to service men from the sidelines of narrative action.

The protagonist and her lover jointly explore the wealth of people, food, places, culture, and history that is Mexico, traveling from one extreme of the country to another on weekends; she creates running lists in her journal of the abundance of experiences, sounds, smells, and sights that comprise a varied yet uniquely Mexican life, one that all Mexican women share. Her developing love affair both with Mexico and with her partner help her realize that she has discovered life and what it means to truly live it happily. This nameless "everywoman" who is everywhere in Mexico represents the millions of Mexican women with the power to shape their own happiness and design their own *Bildungsroman*.

Sefchovich's novel ends on a decidedly feminist note, as the protagonist reaffirms that she is an ordinary woman who has lived an extraordinary life of love and exploration of her own choosing. Sefchovich's protagonist is one of the few well-rounded, fully realized, happy women in Mexican fiction; and if a prostitute can be happy, a reader can just imagine the possibilities for her own life. Sefchovich's prostitute joins the ranks of female characters like Emilia in Angeles Mastretta's *Mal de amores* and Teresa in Brianda Domecq's *La insólita historia de la Santa de Cabora* who offer positive roles to an increasing female readership in Mexico hungry for tales of strong women who live interesting and unusual lives.

The author's second novel, *La señora de los sueños*, introduces the reader to the voices of a family of four who are struggling in therapy with the mother's unhappiness and increasing absorption into a world of fiction. Ana Fernández, mother and wife in question, takes up reading to assuage her hours of boredom as a full-time housewife, and to answer her own question, "What must other women's lives be like?" Much to her surprise, the seven novels she reads about the lives of seven women cause her to reconsider and reshape her own life and to seek an alternate narrative for her existence than the one she has let society shape for her. Her story becomes the unifying thread for a "chain of pearls", a series of highly polished tales that begins in Arabic Spain, where the storytelling tradition began, and ends in Gandhi's India. In each tale a female protagonist faces unexpected challenges with bravery and aplomb and narrates her self-realization as a woman. Sefchovich is a consummate storyteller in this collection, and deftly combines aspects of postmodern narrative such as a constantly changing perspective with those of classic storytelling, such as the use of the framed tale. In the end, her protagonist chooses to enhance her life as a mother and wife by opening her own business, inspired by the different women's roles she has vicariously "tried on" in her travels outside the home in the world of literature.

Sefchovich's latest novel, *Vivir la vida*, presents a protagonist who is the antithesis of the sexually fulfilled and happy prostitute in *Demasiado amor*. Susana Martínez is an unfortunate woman whose life reads like a running catalog of the many challenges to women's equality in Mexico. Susana suffers repeated abuses when patriarchal ideology is allowed to control decisions regarding her life and her body, among them: Susana's father marries her off to a gay man who wants to spend her money but leave her virginity intact; she is gang-raped by strangers; she is forcibly admitted to a psychiatric home for not acting suitably domestic; and her breasts are removed and she undergoes chemotherapy from a doctor who collects his money, only to learn later that the spots on the X-ray were not cancer at all. In spite of these repeated assaults on her person, Susana resists the messages she receives throughout her life that women's role is "Limpie la casa, prepare la comida, planche la ropa, que para eso se casó" (p. 27). Susana decides to walk away from domestic life and her disinterested newlywed husband and claims, "Yo misma me hice mujer" (p. 28). Her journey of no apparent destination leads to herself, as she walks away from a lifeless existence in the home time and again to seek a life worth living, one in which she could exercise control over her own destiny. In the end, she inscribes a space of freedom for herself in a textual representation of her life that she leaves behind as a lesson and a reward for the next generation of women. *Vivir la vida* questions patriarchal master narratives by an inversion of romantic intrigue, as traditional romantic linear storylines are aborted as soon as they begin, and by using parody to demonstrate the severe disjuncture between societal expectations for male and female behavior under patriarchy and the need of generations of Mexican women to live life in ways that are more congruous with their desires.

Sefchovich's Political Writings

Sefchovich's non-fictional writings have centered on presidential politics and on presidential wives. In *La suerte de la consorte*, Sefchovich attempts to recuperate the stories of women left out of Mexican history books in spite of their pivotal and public roles as political consorts. Her series of biographies begins with a general history of the female partners of Mexican leaders through five hundred years of history and continues with a series of closer examinations of individual women's lives.

According to Sefchovich, the role of women in Mexican society has not fundamentally changed since the Conquest; the family has been a unit resistant to change and woman is a repository for the values of hearth and home. For the most part, presidential women have had neither political power nor influence in spite of their intimate connection to heads of state. They themselves were not elected, and have had no official handbook to dictate their roles in government, no place in history, and no choice but to accept the destiny accorded them by their husbands. After a few brief years in the public eye, regardless of their ability to inspire legions of women in the country, these Mexican consorts return to anonymity and the limited sphere of their private homes.

At the end of the study, Sefchovich posits an intriguing question, whether a first lady should have a specific role defined by society along with a salary and assistants to accomplish the tasks assigned her. She claims that Mexican society could use a public female figure to assist with its many challenges in a modern age, one free from a slavery of forced smiles and photo-ops. It could be an important step towards women's equality if the most visible woman in the country had a role other than simply being her husband's consort figure.

It is interesting to note that when a woman finally does claim power for herself within the political sphere of the presidency, Sefchovich criticizes her attempt. Her most recent book is an extended mock interview in which she poses and answers her own questions about the political activities of Marta Traba, wife of President Vicente Fox. Entitled *Veinte preguntas ciudadanas a la mitad más visible de la pareja presidencial*, the book probes the rights, responsibilities, and actions of Mexico's first lady.

Sefchovich's main complaint is that Traba intervenes in government affairs and public life without any mandate from the people. Her acts impact Mexican society yet this society has no control over her actions, as they did not elect her. Sefchovich returns to her initial suggestion that the Mexican people delineate a specific role for its first ladies, a move that would focus and limit Ms. Traba's actions in the political realm.

Veinte preguntas is a political book but one written in a highly original fashion, in a Talmudic style that juxtaposes a variety of complementary academic, periodical, and popular commentary. The panoply of facts and opinions are threaded together by Sefchovich's terse diagnoses of Mexico's ills that run along the top of the page, and all point to a larger truth, that power is created and maintained vertically in Mexico by a political mechanism that must be reformed to operate more horizontally and to better serve its people.

In another explicitly political text, *Las Prielecciones: historia y caricatura del dedazo*, Sefchovich collaborates with the well-known political caricaturist Magú (Bulmaro Castellanos) to reflect upon the absurdity of the selection of political ascendancy in Mexico by way of the "dedazo" or "finger-pointing" of the incumbent. The PRI has historically allowed its president to hand-pick his successor, defeating the democratic process. Unabashedly critical, published shortly before Vicente Fox changed Mexican history in 2000, Sefchovich's book is written from the point of view of a frustrated citizen tired of the pretext of democracy. It notes that elections cost a great deal, are full of the same recycled empty promises made by unscrupulous politicians, and are to a large extent predetermined—yet remain a national obsession for a people swayed into believing that they are in control of the "democratic" process. Sefchovich's narration of the history behind Magú's sequence of cartoons is as tongue-in-cheek as Magú's depictions of presidential corruption, excesses, and incompetence. Sefchovich offers a history of the Mexican presidency followed by a collaboration of her commentary and Magú's drawings critiquing the electoral system in Mexico, beginning with the election of José López Portillo in 1976. As with all of Sefchovich's political treatises, it is publicly didactic, written with the intent of informing a Mexican citizenry and encouraging it to take democracy into its own hands to shape its country's political future.

Sara Sefchovich is clearly an activist who uses her talents in both fiction and non-fiction writing to express her concern for women's equality, human rights, democratic freedom, and the future of Mexico. She has sought ways to insert women into both historical and literary discourse and to offer alternative narratives for women's lives; given her thirty years of effort, Sefchovich can be considered a leading feminist writer and scholar in contemporary Mexican letters.

ANNE C. GEBELEIN

Selected Works

Fiction

Demasiado amor. Mexico City: Editorial Planeta Mexicana, 1990.
La señora de los sueños. Mexico City: Grupo Editorial Planeta, 1993.
Vivir la vida. Mexico City: Alfaguara, 2000.

Nonfiction

Las primeras damas. Secretaría de Educación Pública-Martín Casillas, Mexico, 1982. (Distribution censured and suppressed by the same).
Mujeres en espejo, I. Mexico City: Folios Ediciones, 1983.
Mujeres en espejo, II. Mexico City: Folios Ediciones, 1985.
Ideología y ficción en la obra de Luis Spota. Mexico City: Grijalbo, 1985.
México: País de ideas, país de novelas. Una sociología de la literatura mexicana. Mexico City: Editorial Grijalbo, 1987.
Gabriela Mistral en fuego y agua. Mexico City: UNAM, Coordinación de Difusión Cultural, Serie El Estudio, 1997.
La suerte de la consorte. Las esposas de los gobernantes de México: Historia de un olvido y relato de un fracaso. Mexico City: Océano, 1999.
Las Prielecciones: historia y caricatura del dedazo. Mexico City: Plaza Janés, 2000.
Veinte preguntas ciudadanas a la mitad más visible de la pareja presidencial. Mexico City: Océano, 2004.

References and Further Reading

Arreguín Bermúdez, Antonio. "La intertextualidad en la novelística de Sara Sefchovich y Luis Spota: Los escritores crean a su precursor, Dante." Dissertation Abstracts International, Section A: The Humanities and Social Sciences (DAIA) 2002 Nov; 63 (5): 1823. U of Arizona, 2002. Abstract no: DA3053888.

Bird, Rosa Julia. "Ausencia y arquetipos en tres novelas mexicanas contemporáneas." *Revista de Literatura Mexicana Contemporánea* 4(10) (Apr.–July 1999): 15–19.

Del Campo, Alicia. "Reterritorializando lo mexicano desde lo femenino en el contexto neoliberal: *Demasiado amor* de Sara Sefchovich." *New Novel Review: Nueva Novela/Nouveau Roman Review* 2(2) (Apr. 1995): 60–75.

Duncan, Cynthia. "Mad Love: The Problematization of Gendered Identity and Desire in Recent Mexican Women's Novels." *Studies in the Literary Imagination (SLitI)* 33(1) (2000): 37–49.

Durán, Javier. "Narrar la nación: (Des)Construyendo el imaginario nacional en *Demasiado amor* de Sara Sefchovich." In Rosaura Hernández Monroy and Manuel F. Medina (eds), *La seducción de la escritura: Los discursos de la cultura hoy*, Mexico City: n.p. 1996, pp. 355–63.

Fahey, Felicia. "(Un)Romancing Mexico: New Sexual Landscapes in Sara Sefchovich's *Demasiado amor.*" *Inti: Revista de Literatura Hispánica* 54 (2001): 99–120.

López, Irma and Spanos, Tony. "Antonia y Demasiado amor: El bildungsroman: Su estrategia y definición en la experiencia mexicana femenina." *Confluencia: Revista Hispánica de Cultura y Literatura* 13(1) (1997): 120–30.

Pelayo, Rubén. "Cosmopolitismo, erotismo, y feminismo en México." *Texto Crítico* 7(13) (2003a): 21–9.

——. "La estructura novelística en la narrativa de Sara Sefchovich." *Revista de Literatura Mexicana Contemporánea* 20(9) (2003b): 37–52.

——. "Mujeres en el espejo: Susana, la peor de todas." *Latin American Studies Association Papers* March 28, (2003c).

Rivera Villegas, Carmen. "Autodeterminación y reconciliación en *La señora de los sueños* de Sara Sefchovich." *Revista de Literatura Mexicana Contemporánea* 5(11) (Sept.–Dec. 1999): 44–9.

Sánchez-Blake, Elvira. "Mujer y patria: La inscripción del cuerpo femenino en *Demasiado amor* de Sara Sefchovich". *Confluencia: Revista Hispánica de Cultura y Literatura* 13(2) (1998): 105–13.

Snow, Penny. "Sara Sefchovich's *La señora de los sueños*: Evolving Realities, Evolving Forms." Thesis, Southern Connecticut State University, 2001.

SEIBEL, BEATRIZ

As a scholar Beatriz Seibel has been an active researcher of Argentinean drama from its origins to the early twentieth century. She subscribes to the line of cultural studies with special attention dedicated to the area of popular manifestations of performances. In particular, she has done pioneer work in the study of the role the spectacle of *"circo criollo"*, an early form of popular theater placed in the genesis of the genre in Argentina. In addition, she is especially interested in the participation of female players in the origins of Argentinean theater. As mentioned by Margot Milleret in *Latin American Women On/In Stage* regarding her study, *De ninfas a capitanas* of 1990:

> Beatriz Seibel has documented the monumental gap between real historical women, those from the conquest and colonial periods, who could have provided exciting material for the stage, and the female characters in the early days of Latin American theater who were portrayed as subordinate to the tutelage of husbands and priests.
> (p. 2)

De ninfas a capitanas starts with an introduction to theater regarded as a religious ceremony placed in the geographical confinements of Argentina. These origins are connected to the rite of *"hain"*, considered the first theatrical ritual text of the Argentinean territory. *Hain* shows the process of transformation of a matriarchal to a patriarchal society. According to Seibel, already in *Romance sobre su vida* (1624) by Luis de Tejeda, believed to be the first local drama author, the representation of women's role is presented as typical: the father figure has the power to decide who marries whom and the only options left to women besides marriage are the convent or death. Seibel mentions a play by Cristóbal de Aguilar in *Venció el desprecio al desdén*, from the 1700s in which the central character, Doña Rufina del Olmo, considers matrimony a negative option for her freedom until the disdain of the male character entices her into marriage.

Seibel refers to the presence of women actresses starting in 1783, when the first theater hall (Teatro de la Ranchería) is established. She provides a history of the role of women in marriage and as property holders, takes into account issues related to female education, their presence in theater as part of the audience and their roles as actresses portraying idolized roles as Greek deities. Seibel points out that mythical figures, such as Lucía de Miranda, a faithful wife who rejects the possibility of saving herself from a life in captivity to honor the marriage bond, and La Maldonada, who chooses to live as a captive are not subjects in dramas of the period. On the topic of women actresses, Seibel mentions the relatively good salaries they received during the period, particularly in the popular Teatro de la Ranchería, due in part to audience's requests and also to their scarce number in the profession. Seibel also makes references to moral issues regarding actresses of good reputation, and the presence of black and enslaved women during the 1790s. As in many of Seibel's studies, this one includes excerpts of famous pieces such as *El amor de la estanciera*. She introduces fragments of many unpublished plays, which provide an important source of research for scholars.

Her most important work regarding the history of Argentinean theater is *Historia del teatro argentino*. In it the author revises and enriches the information presented in some of her previous work. Her contribution resides in her approach to the interpretation of the meaning of theater, which includes the idea of performance, which Seibel calls *"teatralidad"*. This concept comprises gestures and signs produced in religious ceremonies and celebrations of Carnival and it incorporates characters and performers from the circus, Afro-American cultural and religious celebrations, radio soap operas and activities related to community and political organizations. From Seibel's perspective the stage is placed within the society, marking the inseparable connection between the historical and the dramatic.

Seibel's interest in the early twentieth-century historic moments in Argentina is further proved in her study of the events surrounding the so-called *Semana trágica*, which took place in Buenos Aires in 1919. Seibel interprets the riots and repression of this "Tragic Week" as a confrontation between the oligarchy, workers and militants, which excluded the participation of the middle class. Seibel considers this the first occasion in which the National Army was called in to repress a workers movement in Argentina.

In addition to the publication of more that 170 articles in journals and newspapers in her native Argentina, Beatriz Seibel has published various essays in the United States, in renowned Journals such as *Latin American Theater Review*, *Gestos*, *Diógenes*, and *Nuevo Texto Crítico*, as well as in periodicals in Venezuela, Cuba, Chile, Brasil, Mexico, England, Germany and Spain.

Playwright

Beatriz Seibel started out as an author of children's theater. During the 1960s Seibel presented her plays in different theaters of Buenos Aires, Mar del Plata and Necochea. Some of the titles include: *De gatos y lunas* (1965–1966), and *Retablillo para tres* (1968–69). Different versions of these plays also were presented on TV: *Teatrillos de magos y lunas* (1966), *Si todos los niños del mundo* (1970), and *Show de gatos y lunas* (1966).

For adult audiences she wrote *Aquí Federico*, on the life of Federico García Lorca performed in 1977, *Canto latinoamericano* staged in 1987 with the participation of the famous actor Pepe Soriano and *Azucena* on the life of the tango singer Azucena Maizani produced in 1991.

In 1980, she published *7 veces Eva*, translated into English in 1987. This single act play combines Seibel's interest in history and drama. The text presents a series of female characters, some historical, some fictional and legendary, introduced by a small-town chronicler, La Mosquetera. She brings in women from different eras and social strata. At the beginning and the end of this list we hear from Violante, the Conquistador's daughter, who faithfully waits for her husband, and from Paloma, a twentieth-century salesperson turned actress, who confronts her stage fright to face a public with whom she would try "to play a game and tame it until it becomes my friend". Juana Manuela Gorriti, the second woman in this gallery, is not deterred by men's negative opinions. Presented all by herself, like the other women characters in the play, she remains convinced of her value as a writer and school founder. Seibel's inclusion of characters such as Teresa Guzmám, the local sex worker, refers to the tango sung by Azucena Maizani, and some fictional characters created by the famous actress and comedian Niní Marshall, point to her preoccupation for the class struggles performed in the society and reflected on the stage.

Honors

Beatriz Seibel has won several honors and awards, which testify to the recognition her creative and scholarly work has obtained over the years. Among them, she won the Premio Nacional de las Artes de Fomento a la Producción Literaria Nacional in 1999 for her book *De ninfas a capitanas*; the Premio del Senado de la Nación in 2000, the Premio Teatro del Mundo en Ensayística, VII Jornadas Nacionales de Teatro Comparado, Centro Cultural Ricardo Rojas, Universidad de Buenos Aires, in 2002 and the National Fellowship from the Fondo Nacional de las Artes in 2006.

GRACIELA MICHELOTTI

Selected Works

Los artistas trashumantes. Testimonios de circo criollo y radioteatro. Buenos Aires: Ediciones de la Pluma, 1985.

El teatro bárbaro del interior. Testimonios de circo criollo y radioteatro. Buenos Aires: Ediciones de la Pluma, 1985.

De ninfas a capitanas. Mujer, teatro y sociedad desde los rituales hasta la independencia. Buenos Aires: Editorial Legasa, 1990.

Siete veces Eva. Translated as *7 Times Eve*. In Teresa Cajiao Salas and Margarita Vargas (eds), *Women Writing Women: An Anthology of Spanish American Theater of the 1980's*. New York: State University Press, 1997, pp. 311–36.

El cantar del payador. Historia y antología de versos payadorescos. 4th edn. Buenos Aires: Ediciones Del Sol, 1999.

Crónicas de la Semana Trágica. Enero de 1919. Buenos Aires: Ediciones Corregidor, 1999.

Teatro e Identidad Nacional: La revelación de nosotros mismos. Buenos Aires: Ediciones Faiga, 2001.

Historia del Teatro Argentino. Desde los rituales hasta 1930. Buenos Aires: Ediciones Corregidor, 2002.

Historia del circo. 2nd edn. Buenos Aires: Ediciones del Sol, 2005.

Staged Plays, Selected List

Nací o me hice. Café-Concert Bar Sur, El Vitral, Bar del Puerto (Punta del Este, Uruguay), El Trovador (Martínez, Buenos Aires), Los Teatros de San Telmo, Teatro Opera de La Plata y gira. 1971–72.

Crónicas de mi gente. Teatro Payró. 1972–73.

El amor. Teatro El Vitral, 1970. Los Teatros de San Telmo, La Cebolla Café Concert. 1972.

Aquí Federico. Teatro Altos de San Telmo. 1977.

Canto latinoamericano. Teatro Municipal San Martin, Sala Casacuberta. 1985.

Azucena. Co-authored with Estela Dos Santos. Konzert La Plaza. 1991.

References and Further Reading

Azor, Ileana. "Review. *Beatriz Seibel. De Ninfas a Capitanas. Mujer, teatro y sociedad. España: Fundación Municipal de Cultura. Excmo. Ayuntamiento de Cádiz, 1990*". *Gestos* 18 (Nov. 1994): 192–4.

Figari, María Rosa. "Review. *Beatriz Siebel. Historia del circo. Buenos Aires.: Ediciones del Sol, 1993*. *Gestos* 21 (April 1996): 206–7.

Mazziotti, Nora. "Review. *Beatriz Seibel. El teatro 'bárbaro' del interior. Testimonios de circo criollo y radioteatro. Buenos Aires, Ediciones de la Pluma. Col. Teatro popular, tomo I, 1985,* and *Los artistas trashumantes. Testimonios de circo criollo y radioteatro. Buenos Aires, Ediciones de la Pluma. Col. Teatro popular, tomo II, 1985*". *Gestos* 2 (1986): 124–6.

Proaño-Gómez, Lola. "Review. *Historia del teatro argentino. Desde los rituals hasta 1930. Buenos Aires. Corregidor, 2002*". *Gestos* 37 (April 2004): 192–3

Vargas, Margarita. "From Body to Voice: Self-Realization through Art in 'Siete veces Eva' by Beatriz Seibel". *Romance Languages Annual 1991* 3 (1992): 617–21.

SELIGSON, ESTHER

Critics sometimes associate Esther Seligson (b. 1941) with the Generation of 1950, a group of Mexican writers interested in experimental literature. Nevertheless, her work resists easy classification. The daughter of immigrant orthodox Jews, Seligson is an inveterate traveler whose texts often inspire critics to read her work through the theme of Jewish exile. Indeed, Seligson's travels reach beyond tourism: as a young woman, she lived and studied for two years in Jerusalem and then traveled to the south of India for a five-month stay. The writer earned her undergraduate degree in Spanish and French literature from the National Autonomous University of Mexico (UNAM). Also in Mexico, she completed advanced studies in Art History. Beginning in 1968, she taught theatre with various schools, including the University Center of Theatre with the UNAM where she worked for more than twenty-five years. Over the course of her teaching career, which spans an impressive number of university-level institutions, she has lectured on the history of theatre, culture, ideas, Jewish thought, Medieval art, and comparative religion. Though not well-known in international circles, Seligson's small audience has not dampened her enthusiasm for writing. Since 1965, Esther Seligson has regularly published novels, short stories, poetry, and cultural essays, as well as accessible literary criticism, including theatre reviews. Her work has appeared in the Mexican cultural supplements of newspapers such as *Excélsior* and *La Jornada*, and literary magazines in Mexico, including *Vuelta* and *Proceso*. In 1970, Seligson won a grant from the Mexican Writers' Center. In 2005, she was accepted into the grant funding available through the National System of Creators of Art in Mexico. Today, she leaves in Jerusalem.

Three Novels

With the recent exception of anthologies issued by major publishing houses in Mexico, Seligson has tended to publish in small presses. The small editions have not impeded recognition among her Mexican peers, and Seligson's early honors include the Xavier Villarrutia award in 1973 for the novel *Otros son los sueños* (Others are the Dreams). In 1979, Seligson's collection of short fiction *Luz de dos* (Light of Two) won the Magda Donato prize. The novels *Otros son los sueños*, *La morada en el tiempo* (A Home in Time), and *Sed de mar* (Thirst for Sea) have attracted the most attention in the criticism. *Otros son los sueños*, according to Mary Ann Stuckert, involves an unfulfilled, unresolved trip that is metaphorical and mystical. This novel has in common with *Sed de mar* the theme of a journey, which for the female protagonist of *Otros son los sueños* and for Penelope in *Sed de mar*, seems a metaphorical journey, an impossible one that involves an unresolved search and unstable identity. Carlos Von Son views *Sed de mar* as an example of parody due to the reworking of *The Odyssey*: in Seligson's version, Penelope becomes the focus and when Odysseus returns to take her place, she travels beyond known experience. In her criticism, Mariana Solares points out that Penelope's voice cannot become wholly transformed because the original version of *The Odyssey* remains in the reader's mind. Von Son does not explore this issue, which leaves him free to celebrate a successfully achieved ironic, epistolary novel. The third central text of Seligson's oeuvre, *La morada en el tiempo*, borrows Biblical figures in an experimental style that is heavy-going for the casual reader. As Daniela Schuvaks notes, the novel challenges the literary market because it posses no main character or determined sequences.

Main Themes and Influences

Across genres, Seligson's work insistently and overtly contemplates the meaning of life. In addition to her religious and mystical interests, Seligson reveals an influence from her early interest in existentialism. As a young woman in Paris, Seligson studied Jewish culture and eventually made the acquaintance of pessimistic philosopher E.M. Cioran, whose work she translated from French to Spanish. Seligson has commented that from 1966 to 1986 she was "enamored" of Cioran, though after working through that period of nihilism in her life she moved away from his cynicism. Seligson is also known for her translations of Edmond Jabés, a Jewish poet. Despite her efforts with opening up meaning through translation, Seligson's own literary work privileges opaque narrative. In the introduction to the writer's anthology *Tríptico* (Tryptich), critic José María Espinasa describes Seligson's reader as entering the cadence of her prose with the sensation of being "un elegido" (a chosen one). Espinasa specifies the emotional charge of being a chosen reader as someone who gains access to the initiatory, secret meaning of Seligson's texts and consequently finds renewed meaning in themes of life, friendship, pain, and death.

It can be added that Seligson's work recalls Borges's inquiries on similar themes for their shared interest in "universalist" literary references. Yet, Seligson abandons plot in many of her texts in a move that to some extent defies Borges's approach. Perhaps her lack of interest in plot motivates the use of mythological figures predominantly drawn from the classical Greek tradition; reference to mythology allows Seligson an echo of a pre-established plot and frees her text for abstract, metaphorical contemplation couched in an exploration of the possibilities of language. Seligson's narrative voice often addresses a mysterious second person. True to traditional Spanish poetic forms, it is often unclear whether the "you" connotes an erotic relationship with a human lover or mystic relationship with a deity. Also reminiscent of Spanish poetic tradition, Seligson shows deep concern with the fleeting nature of experience. Consequently, her literature serves to create an alternative space apt for lingering over fundamental themes, such as the point of life. Seligson once again differs from Borges when these alternative worlds are not so much posed in ways that encourage paranoid, modernist readings that take into account the resonant symbolism of each detail, but rather in sustained vague prose that may require a reading as abstract and nebulous as the original text.

Complexity

Seligson's colloquial, humorous oral style in interviews contrasts with her lyrical, complex prose that often favors bewilderingly yet beautifully arranged sentences. In fact, Seligson sometimes writes sentences that extend for paragraphs and even pages. The density of her prose contrasts with the brevity of her texts, which at their pithiest favor adages, character sketches, and philosophical meditation. In interviews, Seligson reveals an interest in astrology, destiny, and reincarnation. In personal conversation, the writer exhibits an impressively broad knowledge of literature and tends to insert references to indigenous Mexican religions, Hinduism, and Cabbalistic belief. Thus, Seligson is nothing if not obtusely complex in her work and profoundly hybrid in her personal philosophy. To offer another example of this hybridism, in an interview published in 1996 with Miguel Angel Quemain, Seligson notes that she denied her Jewish background for twenty years, until the movements of Saturn obliged her return to that influence. Also while chatting with Quemain, Seligson rejects categorization of her work as Jewish and proudly defends her language as Mexican Spanish. The Mexican theme that Seligson defends is perhaps most evident in later works, especially *Isomorfismos* (Isomorphisms). It could be theorized that Seligson drains Judaism of politics and is left with spirituality, which is why she may state that she is not a Jewish writer and yet she may produce texts that become legible through Jewish-influenced spiritual readings.

Prose Poetry/Nonfiction

Martha Robles describes Seligson's melodic prose style as privileging rhythm over meaning and relying on instinct, intimacy, self-absorption, sensuality, and repetitive metaphors. Good examples of this style surface in the lyrical *Diálogos con el cuerpo* (Dialogues with the body), which assumes an ungendered body and celebrates Seligson's characteristic, fluidly intelligent prose. The best approach to describing this style is to offer an selection from *Diálogos con el cuerpo*:

> The gaze, on exploding, becomes name, generator dance of vowels and consonants, whirlwind that will model with invisible hands a body, chiseling a face until pausing in that presence that the gaze made explode, naming it, creating it through the word, word-spiral, gaze-spiral, until the dialogue is now a body, a heat that one enjoys radiating desire, happiness of touch that burns and by itself names, dialogues, articulates syllables, those tepid nooks that together compose a body, untranslatable phrase, and nevertheless decipherable, open, more opened while more gazed, touched, spoken: a body is the birth of voice.
>
> (my translation, In *Toda la luz*, p. 177)

By contrast to this dense, lyrical prose comes Seligson's accessible popular journalism that reviews the work of well-known writers. Early journalism appears under the title *La fugacidad como método de escritura* (Fugacity as a Method of Writing). More recent journalism with a less concentrated focus on revered writers and with an interest in topics beyond the literary appears in *Escritura y el enigma de la otredad* (Writing and the Enigma of Otherness). A personal tragedy, the suicide of one of Seligson's two sons, inspires *Simiente* (Seed), the highly personal collection of notes, drawings, and poems that celebrates the son's life even as it grieves for him.

Criticism

Most of the scant criticism regarding Seligson's work employs some sort of feminist perspective or a hypothesis about perceptions of time and exile in relation to Jewish experience. Critics who study Seligson as a Jewish-Mexican writer include Ilan Stavans, Daniela Schuvaks, and Angelina Muñiz-Huberman. Stavans complains about the lack of attention devoted to Seligson's work and identifies *La morada en el tiempo* as Seligson's best work, though he concludes his study with the recognition that the writer remains a mystery to him. Muñiz-Huberman places Seligson in the intriguing current of "neo-mysticism in Jewish literature" (2001: 91).

EMILY HIND

Selected Work

La morada en el tiempo. Mexico: Artífice, 1981.

Anthologies: Fiction and Nonfiction

Toda la luz. [includes *Diálogos con el cuerpo* (1981), *Luz de dos* (1978), *Por el monte hacia la mar* (1978), *La invisible hora* (1988), *Las quimeras* (1988), *Sed de mar* (1986).] Mexico: Ediciones Sin Nombre, 2002.

Jardín de infancia. [includes *Otros son los sueños* (1973), *Hebras* (1996), *Travesías, Jardín de infancia, Isomorfismos* (1991).] Mexico: Ediciones Sin Nombre, 2004.

Toda la luz. [includes the contents of the previous anthologies *Jardín de infancia* and *Toda la luz*.] Mexico: Fondo de Cultura Económica, 2006.

A campo traviesa. [includes essays from the nonfiction collections *La fugacidad como método de escritura* (1988), *El teatro, festín efímero (reflexiones y testimonios)* (1989), *Escritura y el enigma de la otredad* (2000), *Apuntes sobre E.M. Cioran* (2003).] Mexico: Fondo de Cultura Económica, 2006.

Translations

"The Invisible Hour". In Ilan Stavans (ed.), *Tropical Synagogues: Short Stories by Jewish-Latin American Writers*. New York and London: Holmes & Meier, 1994.

References and Further Reading

Muñiz-Huberman, Angelina. "Exile and Memory in Latin American Jewish Literature." *Yiddish* 12(4) (2001): 84–96.

Quemain, Miguel Ángel. "Esther Seligson". *Reverso de la palabra*. Mexico: El Nacional, 1996, pp. 291–8.

Robles, Martha. "Esther Seligson". *La sombra fugitiva: Escritoras en la cultura nacional*. Vol. II. Mexico: Diana, 1989, pp. 279–97.

Schuvaks, Daniela. "Esther Seligson and Angelina Muñiz-Huberman: Jewish Mexican Memory and the Exile to the Darkest Tunnels of the Past". In David Sheinin and Lois Baer Barr (eds), *The Jewish Diaspora in Latin America: New Studies on History and Literature*. New York and London: Garland, 1996, pp. 75–88.

Solares, Mariana. "Undermining the Space of the Hero: Esther Seligson's *Sed de mar*". *Letras Femeninas* 31.2 (2005): 139–52.

Stavans, Ilan. "Visions of Esther Seligson". In Robert DiAntonio and Nora Glickman (eds), *Tradition and Innovation: Reflections on Latin American Jewish Writing*. Albany, NY: State University of New York Press, 1993, pp. 193–9.

Stuckert, Mary Ann. "Esther Seligson y los espacios imaginarios". In Silvia Elguea Véjar (ed.), *La otredad: Los discursos de la cultura hoy: 1995*. Mexico: UAM, Centro de Cultura Casa Lamm; Louisville: University of Kentucky, 1997, pp. 239–45.

Von Son, Carlos. "Parodia como estrategia narrativa de subversión: La otra voz en *Sed de mar*". *Deconstructing Myths: Parody and Irony in Mexican Literature*. New Orleans, LO: University Press of the South, 2002, pp. 111–36.

SEPÚLVEDA-PULVIRENTI, EMMA

Emma Sepúlveda was born in 1950, in Argentina and lived in Chile from the age of six until her senior year at the university, pursuing a degree in history. Since 1974, she has lived in the United States, where she earned her Doctorate from the University of California, Davis. She taught at the University of Nevada at Reno for more than twenty years before becoming a full professor in 2001. During the last two decades, she has tirelessly defended human rights in both Chile and in Nevada, where she has been working closely with Latinoamerican and Latino communities. Twenty years after the Chilean coup, her political activism, and her academic and humanitarian callings inspired her to collect visual and oral testimonies, capturing the voices of the mothers of the detained and the disappeared during the Pinochet dictatorship (1973–90). She compiled their autobiographical accounts in *We, Chile: Personal Testimonies of the Chilean Arpilleristas* (1996). Sepúlveda-Pulvirenti has written poetry books, critical essays, an epistolary work, and a political manifesto-chronicle entitled *From Border Crossings to Campaign Trail: Chronicle of a Latina in* Politics (1998). She is also an editor of testimonies and critical monographs, a photographer and an illustrator, as well as a writer of the editorial page for the *Reno Gazette Journal*. In 1994, she was a Democratic candidate for the Nevada Senate, and an advisor to the US-Hispanic Task Force of the U.S. Senate. Her artistic, social, and political activism, and her passionate commitment to serve the Latino community of Nevada motivated her to be cofounder of the organization "Latinos for Political Education," as well as to assume a leadership position in Nevada Hispanic Services.

In 1984, Emma Sepúlveda won the first prize in the International Polaroid Competition, and since then has contributed with illustrations and photographs from her critical and artistic lenses to various books. She also received the Peabody Award in 1993 as a result of her consultant work on a documentary about the Chilean tapestries entitled "Tapestries of Hope, Threads of Love: The Arpillera Movement in Chile 1974–94," in conjunction with Marjorie Agosín. She was the well-deserved winner of the "Caroline Kizer Foreign Language and Translations Prize" in 1993, and was recognized with the Thornton Peace Prize in 1994. Sepúlveda was also the recipient of the "Woman of the Year Award" in 1998, the "GEMS International Television Network" in 1997, the "Educator of the Year Award" in 1998, and the "Nevada Silver Pen Award" in 2000. In 2003, she won the "Foundation Professor Award," and more recently the "Governor's Arts Award," in recognition of her outstanding contributions to the Arts at the State level.

Poetic Production

Emma Sepúlveda restores the buried voices of interior landscapes by naming the face of silence, death, and the horrors of the dictatorship. In her poetic works, she touches the borders of silence and words, and inscribes moments in her memory. Sepúlveda takes the pulse of the power of the word and interrogates the borders of language by capturing experiences that are traces of her personal and political memory. Her critical meditations on rebellious silence contest memory, draw the reader and the critic, to her profound experience before her exile, denouncing the pains, sorrows, and fractures of her beloved Chile during the Pinochet dictatorship. Her poems "A la prisión de Carmen," "Me pregunto a solas," "No," and "La loca de la casa," included in the anthology *Writing Toward Hope* (2006), edited by Marjorie Agosín, illustrate her powerful and incisive poetic testimonial voice, denouncing, remembering, denunciating, and touching the bodies, souls, and narratives of those voices in her heart that lead her fight for Human Rights in Latin America.

Critical Works

In *We, Chile: Personal Testimonies of the Chilean Arpilleristas* (1996), her political commitment, her passion for social justice, and the denunciation of oppression motivate her to compile a series of essays of historic, cultural, and gender-based significance. Photographs, life stories, and oral testimonies of eight mothers, sisters, and family members of the detained and the disappeared under the dictatorship of Pinochet accompany this collection. From her courageous text, she creates a deposit of personal stories that reveal the culture of terror under the dictatorship, allowing the reader a glimpse into a mutilated country populated by dead and absent citizens. In *El testimonio femenino como escritura contestataria* (1995), Sepúlveda edits along with Joy Logan selected critical articles related to Latin American engendered testimonials, subaltern subjects, representation, and decolonization. Her collection of essays about Rigoberta Menchú, the Mothers of the Plaza de Mayo, Alicia Partnoy, Luisa Futoransky, and Elena Poniatowska's protagonist Jesusa Palancares provides her audience a unique socio-feminist theoretical frame. This scholarly work also includes testimonies from Central American refugee mothers, life-lines of Chilean arpilleristas, memoirs of exile by Mapuche women, as well as a study of the Argentine film "The Official Story".

Auto/biographical Body

In *Amigas: Letters of Friendship and Exile* (2001), Sepúlveda traces her own life lines from the profile of a young woman whose sensibility, critical wit, intelligence, and personal loyalty motivate her to exchange epistolary correspondence with Marjorie Agosín, a young Jewish-Chilean woman born in the United States but educated in Chile. With her close friend, she shares a common history marked by Pinochet's coup, the migration to a new country, and the untiring fight for human rights advocacy. This epistolary narrative describes two lives that entwine through a calling to the commitment, dedication, and beloved passion for a Nerudian Chile that inhabits their memories and weaves throughout the letters an embracing dialogue that solidifies a 35-year friendship. *Amigas* was adapted to the stage by the Nevada Shakespeare Company, and presented at the Nevada Museum of Art.

In *From Border Crossings to Campaign Trail* (1998), she interweaves a personal, familial, social, and political chronicle about her Chilean life, her experiences as an immigrant and Latina citizen from the State of Nevada, and as a university professor, and community activist. This personal meditation, that could be considered a political manifesto, describes the awakening of her social awareness in Chile, her university years under the socialist government of Salvador Allende (1970–73), her feelings about the catastrophic day of the *coup d'état* on the 11th of September 1973, and her abandonment of the country. Her memories take the narrator back to her Chilean roots, to her privileged Catholic upbringing, to her personal suffering derived from an authoritarian family culture, to her mother's voice, source of strength, integrity, and dignity, to the beginning of her life in a new country. As a Latina, she assumes in her memoirs with pride, strength, intelligence, and determination, her conviction to fight for social justice, and to continue her struggle for human rights, and equality.

Her essay "The Dream of Nunca Más: Healing the Wounds" included in *Women Writing Resistance: Essays on Latin America and the Caribbean* (2003), represents a unique synthesis of her poetic thoughts as Sepúlveda-Pulvirenti writes about a testimonial commentary about her journey to Vietnam: "The fruit of memory has planted the seeds of hope and has taught the lesson of beginning to forgive without forgetting" (pp. 63–64).

Passion for Images

In her study about poetic discourse entitled *Los límites del lenguaje: Un acercamiento a la poética del silencio* (1999), Emma Sepúlveda proposes a theory about the sound of silence, reading it as an act of resistance. In *Memorial de una escritura; aproximaciones a la obra de Marjorie Agosín* (2002), Sepulveda edits and creates a unique perspective of the poetic body, aesthetics, and cultural production of the Chilean, Latina-Jewish defender of human rights Marjorie Agosín. Her passion for the poetic and visual image inspired her to collaborate with the writer on diverse artistic projects. These include the feminist essay *Otro modo de ser: poesía hispánica de mujeres* (1994), her photographs in "Tapestries of Hope, Threads of Love" (1996), and the colorful engravings of American fruits in *Generous journeys: travesías generosas* (1992). The provocative critical study on her photographic works by Bruce Williams focuses the politics of the feminine body, the edges of exile, desolation and alienation, as well as on the scars of the tortured body.

MAGDALENA MAIZ-PEÑA; TRANS. TRINITY PRATT

Selected Works

Tiempo cómplice del tiempo. Madrid: Ediciones Torremozas, Serie Prímula, 1989.

We, Chile; Personal Testimonies of the Chilean Arpilleristas. Falls Church, VA: Azul Editions, 1996. Trans. Bridget M. Morgan.

Death to Silence/Muerte al Silencio. Houston, TX: Arte Público, 1997. Trans. Shaun T. Griffin.

From Border Crossings to Campaign Trail; Chronicle of a Latina in Politics. Falls Church, VA: Azul Editions, 1998.

Los límites del lenguaje: Un acercamiento a la poética del silencio. Madrid: Ediciones Torremozas, 1999.

Co-authored Works

Sepúlveda, Emma and Agosín, Marjorie. *Otro modo de ser; Poesía Hispánica de Mujeres*. San Juan Puerto Rico: Ediciones Mairena, 1994.

——. *Amigas: Letters of Friendship and Exile*. Austin, TX: University of Texas at Austin, 2001. Trans. Bridget M. Morgan.

——. *Memorial de una escritura; aproximaciones a la obra de Marjorie Agosín*. Santiago de Chile: Cuarto Propio, 2002.

——. "The Dream of Nunca Más: Healing the Wounds". In Jennifer Bowdy de Hernandez (ed.), *Women Writing Resistances: Essays on Latin America and the Caribbean*. Cambridge: South End Press, 2003, pp. 61–8.

——. "A la prisión de Carmen," "Me pregunto a solas," "No," and "La loca de la casa". In Marjorie Agosín (ed.), *Writing Toward Hope*. New Haven, CT: Yale University Press, 2006, pp. 5–8.

Sepúlveda, Emma and Logan, Joy (eds) *El testimonio femenino como escritura contestataria*. Santiago de Chile: Asterión, Colección Tierras Altas, 1995.

Illustrations and Photography

Generous Journeys/Travesías generosas. Trans. Cola Franzen. Reno, NV: The Black Rock Press, University of Nevada, 1992.

with Marjorie Agosín. *Tapestries of Hope, Threads of Love; The Arpillera Movement in Chile 1974–1994*. Albuquerque, NM: University of New Mexico Press, 1996.

Bilingual Poetry Included

Desert Wood: An Anthology of Nevada Poets. Lincoln, NB: University of Nevada Press, 1991.

References and Further Reading

Williams, Bruce. "In the silence of the tortured image: Emma Sepúlveda-Pulvirenti." In Marjorie Agosín (ed.), *A Woman's Gaze*. Fredonia, NY: White Pine Press, 1998, pp. 145–61.

SERRANO, MARCELA

Marcela Serrano was born in Santiago de Chile in 1951. She graduated from La Universidad Católica with a degree in Engraving. She has worked as visual arts specialist, university professor and writer. After living in Mexico for several years, she returned to Chile.

Marcela Serrano is one of the most successful Chilean authors. She has been described by Carlos Fuentes as today's Sheherezade for her impressive skills as a storyteller. All her novels have become best-sellers around the Spanish-speaking world. Her books have been translated into several languages, and she has been very well received in the European book market. In fact, several of her novels turned out to be best-sellers in Italy. Her popularity has increased even more after two of her novels became movies. However, her popular success has proven to be a challenge in her literary career. Some literary critics attribute her popularity to the fact that her novels are about women and that Serrano's readers are mainly women. Therefore they do not consider her a serious writer. Despite this fact, Marcela Serrano has never showed much concern over this, and in several interviews has declared her determination to keep on writing about women's feelings and women's struggles to find a new identity in our rapidly changing world.

Novels

Marcela Serrano's first three novels make up a trilogy that reflects on the impact that Pinochet's dictatorship had on the lives of women in Chile. *Nosotras que nos queremos tanto* (1991, We Love Each Other So Much), which received the "Sor Juana Inés de la Cruz" award to the best Spanish American novel written by a woman, portray four adult women – Ana, Sara, María, and Isabel – who get together in a country house. Through the narration and their conversations, the reader learns not only about the characters' past but also those of their sisters, mothers and female friends. Their memories go from their childhood and their first sexual encounters to the impression that Chile's socialist years under Salvador Allende and the subsequent military repression left on their lives. Their experiences show how political ideals and compromise do not always go together with sexual or female liberation. In the final analysis these women realize that speaking up, sharing the guilt, the joy and the pain they feel with other women is the only road to liberation. On the other hand, *Para que no me olvides* (1993, So That You Will Not Forget Me), which won Santiago's "Municipal de Literatura" award – the most prestigious prize for short stories in Chile – stresses the need to remember the past to build a strong future. Blanca, the main character, has lost her speech due to a blood clot in her brain. However, her silent memories give voice to several silenced voices of the tortured and forever-traumatized families of the disappeared. Serrano's novel urges the reader to remember the past and learn from the silenced voices of the marginalized and the disappeared to be able to build a real democracy in Chile. The last novel in this trilogy, *Antigua vida mía* (1995, Antigua and My Life Before), depicts a democratic Chile that has lost the strength of the revolutionary ideals of the previous decades. Josefa Ferrer, a famous folk singer, searches for the memories of her friendship with Violeta Dasinski after her mysterious disappearance. Josefa's reading of Violeta's diary becomes intertwined with her own story, as in a colorful quilt or "huipil", that exposes the beauty and contrast of these women's lives and choices: from fame to rape, from adultery to spousal abuse, and from the anxiety of a longed-for maternity to the frustrations of motherhood. However different the lives of both women are, they learn that the only thing that will save them in this confusing world is their friendship and their inner strength.

Her next two novels, *El albergue de las mujeres tristes* (1997, The Sad Women's Hotel) and *Nuestra Señora de la Soledad* (1999, Our Lady of Solitude) depart from her previous work. In *El albergue de las mujeres tristes*, for the first time a man's voice—Flavián's—, a local family physician, joins those of her female characters. The plot is set in a lodging designed to welcome women who are in distress. During their stay they tell their stories, and by doing so learn how to deal with their pain. The setting of the novel, a faraway little village with hardly any contact with the rest of Chile, serves to isolate the stories of the women and make their experiences and concerns universal. On the other hand, *Nuestra Señora de la Soledad* explores the detective genre. Rosa Alvallay is a failed lawyer-turned private investigator who has been assigned the case of C.L. Ávila. Carmen L. Ávila, a popular author of detective narratives who, after attending a conference in Miami, has disappeared, leaving no trace. Through interviews with different characters and fragments of Ávila's novels, Rosa Alvallay and the reader complete the puzzle of the writer's life and discover the motives behind her wish to leave everything behind. The unexpected final decision of Rosa Alvallay at the end of the narrative serves to reinforce the idea of the need for women's solidarity with each other in order to survive in a hostile world. Comically, Marcela Serrano's first collection of short stories entitled *Un mundo raro* (2001, A Weird World) is the actual title of one of the books published by her fictional character C. L. Ávila.

Lo que está en mi corazón (2001, What Is Inside My Heart), which was finalist for the prestigious literary award Premio Planeta, reflects a return to the social and political concerns that appeared in her first three novels. Marcela Serrano explained in one interview that this novel originated after her visit to the Chiapas region in order to learn about the Zapatist movement. The people she met, especially a woman who belonged to this revolutionary movement, as well as the fact that she got to see first-hand the repression of the government affecting the indigenous people of Chiapas, led her to write *Lo que está en mi corazón*. The title makes reference to the way indigenous people traditionally tell their stories. Usually they finish their accounts using those words "What I have just said is what is inside my heart". Camila is a newspaper woman who is suffering a long depression after the death of her only son. She has been assigned to travel to Chiapas to report on the Zapatist movement. During her investigation several women will make a difference in Camila's life: Paulina, an indigenous women involved in the Zapatist guerrilla; Ninotshka, a Nazi concentration camp survivor; Reina, a failed revolutionary and, finally, her own mother, who supported Allende's government and was detained and tortured during Pinochet's dictatorship. Camila learns for herself what it really means to get involved in the revolutionary struggle of the people.

Marcela Serrano's next novel *Hasta siempre, mujercitas* (2004, So Long, Little Women) plays with the concept of intertextuality. It portrays the lives of four cousins: Nieves, Ada, Luz and Lola, whose personalities and choices closely resemble those of the four sisters of Louise May Alcott's *Little Women* (Meg, Jo, Beth, and Amy). The similarity of the characters in both narratives is reinforced by the inclusion of a quote from one of the characters of Alcott's novel at the beginning of every chapter. Nieves is a devoted wife who struggles to hide her dissatisfaction; Ada is single and has just discovered her vocation for writing; Luz is absent, though letters shed light into the cousins' past and Lola is a beautiful women with a successful life that feels empty. They revisit their past and their darkest and most hidden memories in order to understand their present lives. The attack on the New York World Trade Center and the invasion of Afghanistan serve as a background for the complex story of the four cousins. We learn how small mistakes or decisions made in the spur of the moment affected the lives of innocent people as if the events that took place on a large scale involving people, in several continents were duplicated on the tiny scale of a small rural village in Chile.

El cristal del Miedos (2006) is Marcela Serrano's latest novel.

Themes

Marcela Serrano's novels have a common denominator: women and friendship. Her novels reveal women's experiences and the sisterhood they find in sharing and getting to know each other. However, this sisterhood is not defined by the similarity in women's feelings and experiences; her objective is far from essentializing women. In her works Serrano challenges monolithic views of female experience by depicting not only the differences among women but also the contradictions they feel in themselves. She portrays conflictive responses to maternity, sexuality, love, men, politics, etc. with amazing directness and sincerity. Marcela Serrano's characters show that women's strength lies not in their similarities but in their differences, as well as in their ability to accept, love and support one another.

The layering of different women's experiences helps recreate an open and fluid new feminine identity that does not meet the traditional criteria conveyed in the roles of daughter, spouse and mother. Women struggle with feelings of lack of adjustment, of feeling unnatural and of not fitting in until they help each realize that these traditional roles that they have been trying to fulfill unsuccessfully are the masks that disguise their real identity. Most of her characters, women in their forties and fifties, reevaluate their lives and choices and take the determination to start a new path that will allow them enough space to develop their individuality as women.

Nevertheless, in order for this revelation to take place and to achieve enough strength to start anew, these women need to leave behind their homes, cities and sometimes even their own country. In some sense, Serrano's characters need a space of their own such, as Virginia Woolf defended in "A Room of One's Own". However, Serrano does not advocate a personal space inside the home. Her novels show the need for a new space, rural or foreign, far away from home, which allows women to distance themselves from their lives, their responsibilities, their families and their jobs. This physical distance grants women the possibility of analyzing their choices and judging their weaknesses. It is a necessary first step to abandon a life of misery and dependency and reach for self-esteem and independence.

Miryam Criado

Selected Works

Antigua vida mía. Mexico D.F.: Alfaguara, 1995
Nosotras que nos queremos tanto. Mexico D.F.: Alfaguara, 1996.
Para que no me olvides. Mexico D.F.: Alfaguara, 1997.
El albergue de las mujeres tristes. Mexico D.F.: Alfaguara, 1997.
Nuestra Señora de la Soledad. Madrid: Alfaguara, 1999.
Lo que está en mi corazón. Barcelona: Editorial Planeta, 2001.
Antigua and My Life Before. Trans. Margaret Sayers Peden. New York: Anchor, 2001.
Cuentos de mujeres solas. Madrid: Alfaguara, 2003.
Hasta siempre, mujercitas. Barcelona: Editorial Planeta, 2004.
El cristal del Miedos. Barcelona: Ediciones B, 2006.

References and Further Reading

Agosín, Marjorie. "Travesía de la memoria: Para que no me olvides de Marcela Serrano". *Revista Iberoamericana de Bibliografía* 44(4) (1994): 637–42.

Foresti, Carlos. *"Lo que está en mi corazón* de Marcela Serrano: Chiapas y las huérfanas de la Apocalipsis". *Moderna Spray* 6(2) (2002): 214–20.

García-Corales, Guillermo. "Nostalgia versus modernidad: Entrevista a Marcela Serrano". *Confluencia.* 13.1 (1997): 228–34.

Jurewiez, Liliana. *"Nosotras que nos queremos tanto*: ¿novela o tratado de ayuda personal y otros enseres?". *Selected Proceedings of the Pennsylvania Foreign Language Conference.* (2005): 75–83.

O'Connell, Patrick. "The Voice of Silence in Marcela Serrano's *Para que no me olvides." Monographic Review* 16 (2000): 336–44.

Pereyra, Marisa. "Sobre orfandad y utopías: Entrevista a Marcela Serrano". *Hispanic Journal* 24 (2003): 223–33.

Pinto, Patricia. "La sororidad en Para que no me olvides, de Marcela Serrano". *Acta literaria.* 19 (1994): 10–15.

SHÚA, ANA MARÍA

Ana María Shua (b. 1951) is among the few authors whose texts have received both extensive popular acclaim and rigorous scholarly attention. The exhaustive bibliography to date numbers 33 works (many of them have been re-edited and translated), in addition to the extensive list of critical analysis, prove the impact of her writings in her home country, Argentina, and abroad.

Born in Buenos Aires in 1951, Shua received her doctorate in literature at the National University in Buenos Aires. She has worked as a journalist, editor, script writer and creative writer of slogans for print media, radio and television commercials. Rhonda Dahl Buchanan, in the introduction of the thorough collection of critical articles, *El río de los sueños: Aproximaciones críticas a la obra de Ana María Shua*, describes her compellingly as an "escritora-camelelón" [chameleon writer] (2001, p. 5). As a result of the different themes Shua works on and genres she explores, she is above all a prolific and versatile "fabuladora", a story teller and writer, who would doubtlessly live much longer than the critical 1001 nights, if she were in the situation of the fabulous princess Sheherazade.

Shua published her first collection of poetry *El sol y yo* (The Sun and Me) at age 16. This volume received the "Faja de Honor de la Sociedad Argentina de Autores" (Honor Strip of the Society of Argentinean Authors). Her second publication, the novel *Soy paciente* (Patient, translated into English and Italian, two further editions, 1980), won the International contest of fiction, organized by the publishing house Losada. In 1981, Shua published *Los días de pesca* (Fishing Days), her first collection of short stories that had initially appeared under a pseudonym in several women's magazines. 1984 saw the publication of her second novel, *Los amores de Laurita* (Laurita's Loves, adapted to the screen, translated into German), and *La sueñera* (Sleepy Mood, 1984, two further editions), and her first collection of micro-fiction, a genre she pioneered in Argentina. After the publications of several more collections of short stories, the author presented *El marido argentino promedio* (The Average Argentinian Husband, three further editions, 1991), a humorous guide of possible and impossible relationships. The next year Shua published the children's short story *La puerta para salir del mundo* (The Gate To Exit the World, 1992, five further editions) and her second collection of micro-fiction, *Casa de Geishas* (The House of the Geishas, 1992). Next, *Risas y emociones de la cocina judía* (Laughter and Emotions of the Jewish Kitchen, 1993) is composed of Jewish recipes and folklore. With *El libro de los recuerdos* (1994, The Book of Memories), for which she received a Guggenheim Fellowship, Shua presents a partially autobiographical novel on the odyssey of emigration of a family of Eastern European Jews and their lives in Argentina during the second half of the twentieth century. In the following years, she published several anthologies of popular texts, among them are a collection of traditional Jewish folklore and humor, a compilation of popular coplas, and a collection of presentations of women in popular literature and folklore. *Botánica del caos* (2000, Botany of Chaos), is another inventive collection of very short fiction. With *Libros prohibidos* (2003, Prohibited Books) and *Historias verdaderas* (2004, True Stories), Shua presents two collections of chronicles and essays on repression and book censorship during the Argentinean dictatorships from 1969–73 and 1976–83. So far the last entry in the author's impressive list of publication is the anthology *El libro de las mujeres* (The Book of Women) of 2005.

Ana María Shua's texts are difficult to classify. Her cookbooks, for example, also include creative re-writings of biblical, talmudic, and folkloric tales; her anthologies also portray creative re-writings and sequences of the tales. Furthermore, the author explores rare genres such as poetry for children and very short fiction for adult readers. "¡Huyamos!" (Let's Run Away) from *Casa de Geishas*, is probably one of the shortest stories ever written in the Spanish Language: The entire account of a literally fatal ending is: "¡Huyamos, los cazadores de letras están aquí!" (114, Let's run away, the letter-hunters have arrived!). Her short texts even seem to escape a generic labeling. Critics are proposing different names to capture the very short phenomena, and describe Shua's texts alternating as collections of "microrelatos" [micro-stories] (Noguerol Jiménez 2001: 195), "cuentos brevísimos" (Buchanan 2001: 5), "microcuentos [or] microensayos" (Brasca, 220, 222, micro-short stories or micro-essays) or as "fractal series" (Zavalo 2001: 177–8). A common characteristic of all these diminutive texts is their comical and ironic tone. *La sueñera* presents 250 dream-like snippets of minimal epiphanies. Text number 108 states: "Yo contra los huevos fritos no tengo nada. Son ellos los que me miran con asombro, con terror, desorbitados" (I have nothing against fried eggs. It's them that are staring at me, wide-eyed, with fear and terror, p. 52). *Casa de Geishas* offers postmodern versions of fairy tales, where a desperate Cinderella waits for her prince to rescue her, not knowing that he is a fetishist and simply prefers her beautiful and slender shoe for his erotic pleasures (p. 74).

Humor is a vital feature in all of Shua's writings. Even horror stories such as the children stories in *Fábrica del terror I-II*, "maintain [a basic] humor" (Manier 2001: 290). Also, many of Shua's longer writings display a strong element of distancing slapstick or sarcasm. An example for this is *Soy paciente*, the novel of a nameless man, who is hospitalized and even operated on without ever getting diagnosed and who suffers a series of absurd and abusive situations in the hospital from where he will never again be able to break out. This allegory of the "época del miedo" (Flores de Molinillo 2001: 21), with the submissive patient in the country converted into a nightmarish hospital, nevertheless contains strong undertones of black humor. In one situation, the patient is frightened when he sees an enormous red stain on a medical assistant's overalls, but learns that the blood is not from another patient, but from a laboratory animal. A pig, which unfortunately has not survived a heart surgery, is at that moment being roasted to serve as a delicious lunch for the principal surgeon and his team. Humor here has a double purpose: on the one hand it highlights the patients' subjugation to the sadistic system; in this respect, the novel echoes a Kafkaesque world. On the other hand, beyond all atrocity, humor also conveys a deep optimism and jubilation for language as an expression of human life, and celebrates the witty puns and sarcastic turns as ways to subvert a discourse of power.

Shua's writings have received much critical attention. A main topic that has been discussed, most concisely by Beth Pollack and Mariano Siskind, is the presentation of the Argentine-Jewish experience in several novels and anthologies. Siskind underlines the importance of the act of story-telling as a main trait of Jewish tradition (2001: 96), whereas Pollack discusses the ways the texts present resettlement and immigration in Argentina (1994: 119). Another major theme in critical approaches to the author's œuvre is the description of women, and especially the female perception of the body. Laura Beard discusses the transgressive act of writing about the pregnant female body in *Los amores de Laurita* as a breaking of the taboo of erotic pleasure during pregnancy (2001: 35–48). Elsa Ducaroff highlights sexuality as a privileged way of knowledge, where the body, strange and incomprehensible, is conceived as the protagonist of joy and pleasure. Alongside a large number of critical articles, Rhonda Dahl Buchanan's edition *El río de los sueños: Aproximaciones críticas a la obra de Ana María Shua* is to date the most accurate collection of critical writing and an invaluable point of reference for any study of the works of the "fabuladora" Ana María Shua.

ILKA KRESSNER

Selected Works

El sol y yo. Buenos Aires: Ediciones Pro, 1967.
Soy paciente. Buenos Aires: Losada, 1980.
Los días de pesca. Buenos Aires: Corregidor, 1981.
Los amores de Laurita. Buenos Aires: Sudamericana, 1984.
La sueñera. Buenos Aires: Minotauro, 1984.
Viajando se conoce gente. Buenos Aires: Sudamericana, 1988.
La batalla entre los elefantes y los cocodrilos. Buenos Aires: Sudamericana, 1988.
Expedición al Amazonas. Buenos Aires: Sudamericana, 1988.
La fábrica del terror. Buenos Aires: Sudamericana, 1990.
El marido argentino promedio. Buenos Aires: Sudamericana, 1991.
La puerta para salir del mundo. Buenos Aires: Sudamericana, 1992.
Casa de geishas. Buenos Aires: Sudamericana, 1992.
Risas y emociones de la cocina judía. Buenos Aires: Grupo Editorial Shalom, 1993.
Cuentos judíos con fantasmas y demonios. Buenos Aires: Grupo Editorial Shalom, 1994.
El libro de los recuerdos. Buenos Aires: Sudamericana, 1994.
El pueblo de los tontos. Humor tradicional judío. Buenos Aires: Alfaguara, 1995.
El tigre gente. Buenos Aires: Sudamericana, 1995. [Re-edited as *Miedo en el sur: El tigre gente y otros cuentos*.]
Ani salva a la perra Laika. Buenos Aires: Sudamericana, 1996.
La muerte como efecto secundario. Buenos Aires: Sudamericana, 1997.
Sabiduría popular judía. Buenos Aires: Ameghino, 1997.
Historia de un cuento. Buenos Aires: Sudamericana, 1998.
Como agua del manantial: Antología de la copla popular. Buenos Aires: Ameghino, 1998.
La fábrica del terror II. Buenos Aires: Sudamericana, 1998.
Las cosas que odio y otras exageraciones. Buenos Aires: Alfaguara, 1998.
Cabras, mujeres y mulas: antología del odio/miedo a la mujer en la literatura popular. Buenos Aires: Sudamericana, 1998.
Cuentos con magia. Buenos Aires: Ameghino, 1999.
Cuentos con magia II. Buenos Aires: Ameghino, 1999.
El valiente y la bella: Cuentos de amor y aventura. Buenos Aires: Alfaguara, 1999.
Botánica del caos. Buenos Aires: Sudamericana, 2000.
El libro de los pecados, los vicios y las virtudes. Buenos Aires: Alfaguara, 2002.
Libros prohibidos. Buenos Aires: Sudamericana, 2003.
Historias verdaderas. Buenos Aires: Sudamericana, 2004.
El libro de las mujeres. Buenos Aires: Alfaguara, 2005.

References and Further Reading

Agosín, Marjorie. "Ana María Shua, Marisa Di Giorgio y Liliana Heker". In Marjorie Agosín (ed.), *Literatura fantástica del Cono Sur*. San José, Costa Rica: Editorial universitaria centroamericana, 1992, pp. 149–60.
Beard, Laura "Celebrating Female Sexuality from Adolescence to Maternity in Ana María Shua's 'Los amores de Laurita.'" *El río de los sueños: Aproximaciones críticas a la obra de Ana María Shua*. Washington, DC: Organización de los Estados Americanos, 2001, pp. 35–48.
Brescia, Pablo. "De cómo escribir la pareja y reírse en el intento". *Del humor en la literatura: Compilación*. Monterrey: Consejo para la Cultura y las Artes de Nuevo León, 2001, pp.134–41.
Buchanan, Rhonda Dahl "Narrating Argentina's 'Epoca del Miedo' in Ana María Shúa's 'El libro de los recuerdos.'" *Confluencia: Revista Hispánica de Cultura y Literatura* 13(2) (1998): 84–91.
——. "El género rebelde en la literatura: El cuento brevísimo en 'Casa de geishas' de Ana María Shua". *Cuento en Red. Estudios Sobre la Ficción Breve* 2 (2000a): [no pag.].
——. "Visiones apocalípticas en una novela argentina: 'La muerte como efecto secundario' de Ana María Shua". *Revista Iberoamericana* 66(192) (2000b): 545–55.
——. (ed.) *El río de los sueños: Aproximaciones críticas a la obra de Ana María Shua*. Washington, DC: Organización de los Estados Americanos, 2001.
Corbatta, Jorgelina. "Ficción e historia: presencia de la 'Guerra Sucia' en 'Soy paciente' de Ana María Shua". In Rhonda Dahl Buchanan (ed.), *El río de los sueños: Aproximaciones críticas a la obra de Ana María Shua*. Washington, DC: Organización de los Estados Americanos, 2001, pp. 7–18.
Drucaroff, Elsa. "La lección de anatomía: Narración de los cuerpos en la obra de Ana María Shua". *Enfocarte.com: Revista de Arte y Cultura* 5(25) (2005): [no pag.].
Flores de Molinillo, Eugenia. "'Soy paciente': La metáfora hospitalaria". In Rhonda Dahl Buchanan (ed.), *El río de los sueños: Aproximaciones críticas a la obra de Ana María Shua*. Washington, DC: Organización de los Estados Americanos, 2001, pp. 19–34.
Foster, David William. "Ana María Shua". In Marjorie Agosín (ed.), *Pasión, identidad y memoria*. Albuquerque, NM: University of New Mexico Press, 1999, pp. 40–5.

Gimbernat González, Esther: *Novelistas argentinas de los '80: Aventuras del desacuerdo.* Buenos Aires: Danilo Albero Vergara, 1992.

Huberman, Ariana. "Threading Layers of Memory into Family Trees: Family Collective Memory and Jewish Memory by Two Contemporary Latin American Writers". *Cincinnati Romance Review* 23 (2004): 117–30.

Lagmanovich, David. "El microrelato en Ana María Shua". *El relato breve en las letras hispánicas actuales.* Ed. Patrick Rollard. Amsterdam: Ediciones Rodopi B.V., 1997, pp. 11–22.

Manier, Martha. "Ana María Shua's Short Stories for Children 1988–98: Tradition and Innovation in Fantasy". In Rhonda Dahl Buchanan (ed.), *El río de los sueños: Aproximaciones críticas a la obra de Ana María Shua.* Ed. Washington, DC: Organización de los Estados Americanos, 2001, 283–93.

Noguerol Jiménez, Francisca. "Para leer con los brazos en alto: Ana María Shua y sus 'versiones' de los cuentos de hadas". *El río de los sueños: Aproximaciones críticas a la obra de Ana María Shua.* Ed. Rhonda Dahl Buchanan. Washington, DC: Organización de los Estados Americanos, 2001, 195–204.

O'Connell, Patrick L."The Recuperation of Immigrant Identity: Remembering with a Purpose in Argentina". *Revista Hispánica Moderna* 54(2) (2001): 499–509.

——. "Historical Memory, Parody, and the Use of Photography in Ana María Shua's *El Libro de los Recuerdos*". *World Literature Today* 73(1) (1999): 77–87.

Oviedo, José Miguel. "Una novela sobre la muerte". *Cuadernos Hispanoamericanos* 571 (1998): 153–7.

Plotnik, Viviana. "Sexualidad y maternidad en la obra de Ana María Shúa". *Monographic Review/Revista Monográfica* 17 (2001): 252–67.

Pollack, Beth. "Ana Maria Shúa". *Hispamerica: Revista de Literatura* 23:69 (1994): 45–54.

Siskind, Mariano. "Tradición y reescritura: La construcción de una identidad judía en algunos textos de Ana María Shua". In Rhonda Dahl Buchanan (ed.), *El río de los sueños: Aproximaciones críticas a la obra de Ana María Shua.* Washington, DC: Organización de los Estados Americanos, 2001, pp. 89–102.

Zavalo, Lauro. "Estrategias literarias. Hibridación y metaficción en 'la sueñera' de Ana María Shua". In Rhonda Dahl Buchanan (ed.), *El río de los sueños: Aproximaciones críticas a la obra de Ana María Shua.* Washington, DC: Organización de los Estados Americanos, 2001, pp. 177–88.

SILVA, CLARA

Clara Silva was born in Montevideo, Uruguay in 1905. In her teens she married Alberto Zum Felde who was almost twenty years older than her. She did not go to college, but she was a voracious reader. She started publishing poetry in 1945. Her first poetry book was *La Cabellera Oscura-Dark Hair.* She continued writing poetry and obtained several national awards. Her poetry requires a good understanding of her constant dichotomy between soul and body. Her prose helps to understand Clara Silva's agonic intensity; *La Sobreviviente* and *El alma y los perros* are considered by many to be her best novels.

In 1951, she started writing novels. Her first novels were *La Sobreviviente* (The Survivor), followed by *El Alma y los Perros* (1962, The Soul and the Dogs), *Aviso a la Poblacin* (Warning to the People) in 1964, and *Habitación Testigo* (A Witness Room) in 1967. Her work is very original and explores the social and psychological traps that women suffer. Her poetry expresses the anguish facing the sexual act. She, as a poet and fiction writer, would like to transcend the sexual demands of the male and find her own purpose in her spiritual search.

La Sobreviviente is a novel that presents the world as it is seen by the lone protagonist, Laura Medina, a young Latin American girl who passes through some of the great cities of the world: Florence, Paris, and a Latin American capital, possibly Montevideo in the 1940s. At twenty, her purpose in life is to seek her vital relationships with the people and things that surround her. Without a linear plot, the novel presents chapters with titles such as "The room as witness," "Morning," "Purple," "The Body," "I am Laura Medina," "A Boy of Solids," "Separation," and "City". The protagonist vacillates between God and nothing, sensuality and spirituality, poverty and wealth, love and indifference, masculinity and femininity. Daily problems fill the novel and cause the protagonist to abandon her position as spectator and became a participant in the anonymous, collective unit. This requires her to compromise herself, submerge herself with the masses. In several of her recollections she appears as an only child, so alone that she invents her own friend to accompany her. At times la Otra, "the Other One" appears. She is a facet of her personality with whom she carries on a dialogue. Frequently, "the Other One" reproaches her for not acting: "If they have allowed me to be as I wished, I would have made of your life, which is already my life, a long process of pleasure". (p. 144). To Laura's question "Why do we not have any brothers?" the answer is that perhaps it was necessary that there were no other children, with the implication that it was a premeditated act. Her mother is "the woman of the tresses" and appears with an image of the Virgin above her bed. She is a violent woman and causes terrible scenes with her husband, she spits on the Virgin and exclaims, "Take that, God" (p. 102). The author is rather vague about her family which appears surrealistically in the form of visits and reunions that her mother calls bitter family problems. Moreover, there are other people present in these after-dinner chats, the Dead: "Yes the dead, they are never lost? Their tears, desires, take the form of dripping wax. It is like walking through the silence of torment" (p. 149).

The girl also remembers an absent father, who comes from time to time late at night accompanied by the sounds of chains and squeaking doors. She describes her return to her childhood home many years later as "an enormous black breast of a wet nurse, full of heavy milk and warm with fear" (p. 149).

This novel is very precise in the description of the rich and the poor. Laura, the protagonist, is poor and earns a miserable salary at the Medical Institute, yet she has attended university and could be called an intellectual. Although she despises the bourgeoisie, she wonders what her life would have been if she had been one of those rich women who are so empty and superficial. She comes to the conclusion that it is not merely a question of having been born here or there, she has had to confront her problems with sensitivity, everything that has "made her what she is" (p. 109). She cannot avoid being a spectator, spying on the rich. Once, she is invited by a lawyer, a former friend from secondary school, to a reception he is giving for a poet whom she greatly admires, and who is probably Pablo Neruda. She describes the confrontation between the world of the rich and the world of the poor, and she realizies that she is poised between these two worlds.

Through her reading of Nietzsche, Baudelaire, Gide, Huxley, and many others, she belongs to the exquisite world of the "elite", but at the same time she harbours the seeds of non-conformity. Her literary studies go beyond intellectual stimulation and come to a basic idea: her desperate search for a theological position when faced with the injustice of God and her own lack of faith. "Is the source of some people's faith and other's lack of it to be found in heavenly hierarchies or is it in God's injustice? She sees this spiritual exile that transcends even social relations among men. Thus throughout the novel there is a dilemma between two systems, one with faith in a Christian God, and one Communistic, omitting God entirely. She herself vacillates between two extremes. Laura uses three symbols of spirituality which she has seen attacked and destroyed: the saint of peace, Gandhi, who was assassinated, the persecuted poet Neruda, and the lonely, tormented girl. This last symbol is very significant since it applies not only to her own reality, but also to women without economic, social or family protection, who become victims of masculine exploitation since the male is in a dominant position when the woman works for him. The men try to force sexual favors from the woman by promises of work or better positions. She uses the visual comparison of a compass at whose center we find the man and on the outside the women, like so many points and without autonomy. This novel shows us the misery that exists in the streets and the houses and at the Institute where she works. In this novel we are given a careful detailed dissection of Laura's sexuality. She suffers from a duality that causes her to constantly separate sensuality and spirituality.

After making love, her lover asks,"Do you love me?" and she answers, "Perhaps I love myself" (p. 29). The explanation for this reaction of disgust is that she considers that during the "terrible and miserable" act she has left her soul behind, like a careless angel. In other words, her spirit and body were separated, even during the sex act. She also tries to interpret her lover's attitude:

> He had already demanded the maximum submission from a woman. Now he looked at her with his desire satisfied. And Laura felt that from his irritating pedestal he looked at her with a calm assurance that she, without him, was nothing more that a thing, an empty force, a sterile jewel.
>
> (p. 58)

If she perceives this male pride in him, it is because she herself feels inferior. Something that has been taught to her through what the Church literature reveals about the condition of womankind. Using many Biblical quotations, she shows how the Church Fathers sustain dogma against women, and in one instance she gives the example of King David who could take any woman as if she were a slave. But it is her personal experience that has caused her loathing of sex and the sexual act and that causes her disgust. The most objective case that illustrates her resentment is that of her friend Mariusa, a beautiful and very feminine girl. She is seduced and used by her lover:

> He had only the hint of a soul. He was empty. His worldliness was evident in a sea of vanity. She did not want only his body, she also wanted to reach his soul. But he constantly rejected her.
>
> (p. 126)

Pregnant and alone, Mariusa has an abortion and afterwards she feels dirty, broken, sacrificed, ready to die.

> 'Let's go to bed,' that phrase, that cry persisted, followed her . . . Woman's fate. With her mouth, breasts, belly, from the beginning she brought her own destiny. Her designation: matter, carrier of sin. The virus of sin extended in the savage miasma of matter. Ah!
>
> (p. 126).

Thus, for Laura Medina, the sexual act always leaves her full of frustration, and she even doubts that she knows herself. "I seem to be two strangers, thrown apart from themselves" (p. 59). She tells her lover that instead of feeling happy, she always feels alienated, anguished, and not calm. "The Other One" accuses her of being frigid, "Last night, while you gave yourself, dispassionately, analyzing the very act, I, like a beggar in the shadows, in your shadow, fought to act, to leave. But you suffocated me, drowned me. It was horrible. With him, you were alone" (p. 143). Laura cannot accept the accusations that she is hard and egotistical because she indeed loves, but she is not capable of a "gross, brutal, careless life" (p. 144).

In a world where sex by itself does not create bonds between two people, the author wants to know if there is still the possibility "to be happy in such a harsh, sad, miserable reality" (p. 158). What could she hope to find in a world without faith in God? And, if she herself does not believe, what other alternative is there, but to organize love like a socio-political system? Is there any hope that a woman might at last find her place and sexual justice in a system that is not economically exploitative? She seems to have drowned in desperation, but there is something that keeps her afloat: the belief in her responsibility to be a human being. She believes that the intellectual people protect themselves with books, that they have forgotten how to live outside of themselves, of their own dreams. What is needed then is to give oneself, not to a man but to a cause. When she chooses a cause, she does not do so for intellectual reasons, and it doesn't matter what the cause is. The real thing is the act of commitment. She believes that she has been poisoned with the drug of egotism. From her anguish, her confusion of body and spirit, a new woman will be able to face life. Silva expresses this gesture that combines commitment and rebellion, the impetus of the soul to find a destiny for the earthly body, and the search for universal value that transcends the egotism of individual instinct. She will unite with those who suffer:

> In the morning I was once again innocent and intact as the first. I will be happy. Will I be happy? I will become part of the great army of the world, taken to the collective whole. I will give myself. To whom? Why? It doesn't matter. It is necessary. I will commit myself. I will step down or up to others. I will unite with their wounds.
>
> (p. 161)

In *El Alma y los Perros* published in 1960, the protagonist feels that she is sexually abused by her husband, a man of great prestige, a college professor, a man much older than herself. She is an ignorant girl, but she is eager to learn. However, she only receives sarcastic remarks which cause her to lose what little confidence she has. It is not only her husband, but her whole society than confirm that a woman alone is worth nothing. Once she overhears a conversation in the office where she works:

> They say that a girl needs a man in order to grow up, that a woman is nothing without a man, that to be a woman is a disgrace, unclean with that that happens to them every month, a burden, etc. The man who is at her office, her desk companion, says that when a man and a woman take off their clothes, then the woman is no longer an object, she becomes a person.
>
> (p. 109)

In her novels Clara Silva shows that many women carry over attitudes of their strict upbringing. Under the stress of the prejudices retained from early family life, communication between husband and wife breaks down. The women begin to feel like strangers in their own marriage. Clara Silva's protagonists are disgusted by the sex act and are full of anguish because they are searching for something more, something transcendental that does not come to them with or because of men. In *La Sobreviviente*, she carries on a dialogue supposedly with Christ, and she writes a short poem: "Tie me to your heart/ Don't let me fall to earth? With a darkened mirror in my hands and blind at night ? I harass myself? Looking at me surviving my body, / That went to look for your crown in the dark dust" (p. 372).

In 1976, Clara Silva died. Her death forced me to clarify many questions about her biography. Martha Restuccia her closest friend wrote me a letter. She says:

> As for the information you ask me, I can help you. For example, she did not travel before she was married. She met Alberto Zum Felde when she was almost a child. There was a great age difference between them. He was an eminent critic from our country, a national glory. That he was more than very intelligent, as you stated, and the marriage between him and the extraordinary personality of Clara Silva had nothing to do with anything relatively ordinary. As for the anguish revealed in her novels, Clara was an extremely sensitive woman and it is not at all strange that she felt the trials of other women in her own flesh. I think that the work of a great genius does not have to be autobiographical.

Clara Silva's novels have left us a very vivid portrait of women that live the dichotomy between body and soul. I should add that although her poetry presented the same dichotomy, her fiction offered a frank view of the struggle.

In "Protagonists of Latin American Women Writers" (*Michigan Academician,* 1992.) I wrote:

> The themes of alienation, victimization, and madness are explored with many perspectives. Society, imposing roles and oppressing women y positive or negative categorization, has inhibited the cohesive development of Latin American women.
>
> (p. 65)

LUCIA FOX-LOCKERT

Selected Works

La Cabellera Oscura. Montevideo, 1945.
Memoria de la Nada. Editorial Nova, 1948.
La Sobreviviente. Montevideo: Editorial Arca, 1951.
Los Delirios. Montevideo: Ediciones Salamanca, 1954.
Preludio Indiano y Otros Poemas. Caracas: Editorial Lírica Hispana, 1960.
Las Bodas. Montevideo: Editorial Atenea, 1960.
El Alma y los Perros. Montevideo: Editorial Alfa: 1962.
Aviso a la Población. Montevideo: Editorial Alfa, 1964.
Habitación Testigo. Montevideo: Editorial Alfa, 1967.
Prohibido Pasar. Buenos Aires: Editorial Losada, 1969.

References and Further Reading

Bordoll, Domingo Luis. *Antología de la poesía uruguaya contemporánea–Anthology of Uruguayan Contemporary Poetry*. Montevideo: Departamento de Publicaciones, 1966.
Conde, Carmen. *Once Grandes poetisas Américo-hispanas*. Madrid: Ediciones de Cultura Hispánica, 1967.
Fox Lockert, Lucia. *Women Writers of Spanish America*. New York: Greenwood Press, 1987.
Gilbert de Pereda, Isabel. "Clara Silva". *Escritura*, 7, 1969.
Paganini, Alberto. *Cien Autores del Uruguay*. Montevideo: Editorial Latina, 1969.
Rama, Angel. *La Generación crítica* (1939–69). Montevideo: Arca, 1972.
Rela, Walter. *Diccionario de Escritores Uruguayos*. Montevideo: Editorial de la Plaza, 1986.
Renfrew, Ileana. *Letter to Lucia Fox*. September, 1978.
Restuccia, Marta. *Letter to Lucia Fox*. Montevideo, 1978.

SOMERS, ARMONÍA

Born in Montevideo, Uruguay, Armonía Somers (1914–94), whose pseudonym was Armonía Etchepare de Henestrosa, was a twentieth-century Uruguayan novelist and short story writer. She also wrote a number of pedagogical studies. While employed as a school teacher and educator, and in retirement, she wrote five novels and six collections of short stories. Her literary work can broadly be classified within the tradition of women's writing focusing on psychological disturbance, the abject and bodily experience, although there is a strong political undercurrent in her major novel, *Sólo los elefantes encuentran mandrágora* (1986, Only Elephants Will Find the Mandrake Root).

As Armonía Etchepare, she obtained her professional title in the Instituto Normal de Montevideo in 1938, after which she worked in primary education as well as in the elaboration of educational policy. Her pedagogical studies, published in Mexico, include *Educación de la adolescencia* (which won a Uruguayan pedagogical prize in 1957), *El adolescente de novela y su valor testimonial*, and *Ana Sullivan Macy, la forja en noche plena*. Her pedagogical career culminated in her being appointed Director of the National Pedagogical Museum (*Museo Pedagógico Nacional*) in 1960, acting as editor of the museum's journal, and subsequently becoming Director of the National Centre for Educational Documentation and Dissemination (*Centro Nacional de Documentación y Divulgación Pedagógicas*) from 1962 to 1971. She also edited the *Enciclopedia de educación* (1967–71). However, from 1972 she abandoned her career in education to dedicate herself to her less public career as a writer of fiction under the pseudonym Armonía Somers.

Somers' first major literary work was a novel, *La mujer desnuda* (The Naked Woman), which originally appeared as a double edition of the magazine *Clima* in 1950. Its publication caused a literary scandal, immediately projecting Somers into notoriety as the "Steppenwolf" of Uruguayan letters, in the words of one anonymous review, while the identity of its author was the subject of much speculation. Like her later collections of short stories, *El derrumbamiento* (1953), *La calle del viento norte* (1963) and the short novel *De miedo en miedo* (1965), this text deals frankly and disturbingly with desire, sexuality, death, and fear, in particular feminine sexuality symbolized in surrealist manner by a decapitated naked woman, Rebeca Linke, wandering around an oneiric landscape. Given the controversial nature of her subject matter and the sensitivity of her profession as an educator, the author maintained a shroud of secrecy surrounding her true identity, and her writing was variously attributed to a learned foreign author writing under a pseudonym, a male Uruguayan writer, a homosexual male writer, a group of writers playing a practical joke, and, most bizarrely, to a sex maniac who had anonymously deposited his manuscripts in the Uruguayan National Library. What seems to have been ruled out in this speculation over authorship was the possibility of the novel having been written by a local *woman* writer, and critics even twenty years later were claiming that the novel was in fact "an excellent example of masculine literature" (Espada). Somers is reported to have enjoyed commenting on her own work (without revealing her identity as the author) in public literary discussions.

In later years, Somers frequently found herself having to answer questions by interviewers regarding the controversial sexual content of her work, ranging from paedophile stalkers, rape and masturbation, through a sublimated sexual encounter between a black man and the Virgin Mary (in the story "El derrumbamiento"), to prostitution and the presence of lesbian sexuality in a number of works. A good retrospective on these themes is the open letter she published in the *Revista iberoamericana* in 1992, entitled "Carta abierta desde Somersville" (An Open Letter from Somersville), where she argues that sexuality is important in her work because it is important in life, but that it should be placed into a web of existential concerns with liminal or boundary states in her writing including death, madness and metaphysical anguish.

From the outset, Somers' style caused as much controversy as her subject matter. She received a vituperative early review of the collection *El derrumbamiento* (The Landslide) from Mario Benedetti in 1953, accusing her of producing "an indigestible hotchpotch of textual influences" and of not knowing elemental rules of syntax and grammar. But Ángel Rama, in a famous review of 1963 entitled "La fascinación del horror", set the agenda for recent critical appreciation of her work when he described it as "uncanny, alien, disconcerting, repulsive" yet "incredibly fascinating", and he later went on to include Somers in his study of "raros y malditos" (the strange and the damned) in Uruguayan literature, citing her in particular as one of the few writers of the so-called Generación del '45 remaining faithful to the atmosphere of "phantasmagoric creativity" of the 1940s (Somers later denied that she belonged to the Generación del '45). Rama identified the literary origins of this Uruguayan tendency in a "secret" line of descent from the Franco-Uruguayan poet Comte de Lautréamont, via the European avant-garde of the 1920s and 1930s ("from Eliot to Kafka, from Joyce to Faulkner"). However, the emphasis on abjection, horror, repugnance, nausea, obscenity, and contagion, that runs throughout Somers' work, and the traces of this at the stylistic level, have led recent critics to examine her work through the lens of Georges Bataille, Julia Kristeva, and Jacques Derrida, although she owes her understanding of concepts such as abjection and dissemination as much to Louis-Ferdinand Céline, Martin Heidegger, and Sigmund Freud, as to post-structuralist theory. (Those interested in working out some of the philosophical and theoretical influences on Somers should look at one of her few works of literary analysis, "Diez relatos a la luz de sus probables vivenciales" (1979), which shows a rich engagement with theoretical psychoanalysis amd certain elements of post-structuralist thought, as well as a deep and on-going dialogue with the philosophy of Heidegger.)

Her third novel, *Un retrato para Dickens* (1969, A Portrait for Dickens), showed Somers' ability to manipulate a complex narrative structure imbued with several layers of intertextual reference. Two parallel stories in alternate chapters, one an elaboration of the Old Testament Book of Tobit or Tobias (part of the Catholic and Orthodox canon, but apocryphal in the Protestant tradition), and the other a Dickensian story concerning an orphaned girl brought up on the margins of society among alcoholics and prostitutes, culminate in a superficially comic section which revisits, from the perspective of a parrot Asmodeo (Ashmodai from the Book of Tobit), the principal points in the young girl's life. This section in fact throws an atrocious light over those events, and ends up engaging with profound metaphysical and ethical issues. The novel is also an excellent example of Somers' ability to place an abject realism in fruitful tension with metaphysical concerns and an experimental, ludic style, which are such fundamental features of her writing.

Somers' most important work is the extraordinary late fourth novel *Sólo los elefantes encuentran mandrágora* (1986), which was heralded as having all the characteristics of a posthumous work despite being published during the author's lifetime. As much a work of philosophy, autobiography, magic, alchemy, botany, psychoanalysis, medicine, feminism, politics, as a work of literature, this text consists of a series of remembered episodes written down by an elderly woman confined to a bed in a sanatorium in Montevideo, and compiled after her death by a fictional compiler, Victoria von Scherrer, who adds the occasional footnote to the text. The elderly woman has a life-threatening thoracic and pulmonary infection, from which immense amounts of lymphatic fluid are constantly being drained off, and this sense of bodily loss and dissemination governs the text (one of her many names is in fact Sembrando Flores, Scattering Flowers). The episodes remembered from childhood are organized into chromatic periods, each one characterized by varying colours in a loose alchemical sequence which becomes an increasingly important symbolic matrix as the novel progresses. These remembered episodes are interspersed with the present of narration and with extracts from a popular nineteenth-century serialized novel (significantly entitled *El manuscrito de una madre* [The Manuscript of a Mother]) which Sembrando Flores is reading alongside Heidegger's *Being and Time*.

The former text signals the problematic relationship of the mother figure – and women in general – to reading and writing, for the Spanish popular novel is one which Sembrando Flores' mother, as a young woman, was forced to read out loud to a local rich lady in exchange for fried egg-whites (without the yolks – the remains of the food given to the consumptive son of the family). This linking of forced reading and contagion establishes a network of references which give a symbolic character to abject bodily imagery in the novel, from sporadic engagement with Freud's analysis of the graphomanic memoirs of the "Magistrate of Saxony" (Daniel Paul Schreber), to literary accounts of the mandrake root as a magical homunculus, taking on a "pharmacological" role in the novel which critics have suggested is very similar to that of the *pharmakon*-as-writing in Derrida's interpretation of Plato. But in many ways this novel derives its engagement with deconstruction from a profound reading of Heidegger rather than from Derrida, and the references to the former philosopher's work are endemic throughout the text. The fictional transcriber herself comments that *Being and Time* is the true intertext of this novel:

> But the fact is that [Sembrando Flores] had open on her bedside table the last thing that she had been reading the night before, a chapter from *Being and Time* by Martin Heidegger, 'Fear as a Mode of State-of-Mind', and what is written there is no melodramatic form of fiction, but the coldest and most ontically delicate analysis of fear which has ever been undertaken: "that in the face of which we fear, fearing, and that about which we fear" . . . [T]he real bedtime book was this one, while [the melodramatic novel] . . . was nothing more than a distraction to escape from "that in the face of which we fear.
> (p. 345)

Beside these suggestive references, which ultimately constitute a carefully staged encounter between Freud, Heidegger, psychoanalysis, occult medicine, Marxism, and feminism, the text contains much astute political analysis of Uruguayan history, in particular of the role of the anarchist movement and the rise of militarism.

In the same year as *Los elefantes*, Somers published a fifth short novel or novella (she calls it a *nouvelle*) entitled *Viaje al corazón del día* (Journey to the Heart of Light), its title clearly alluding to Céline's *Voyage au bout de la nuit* and Conrad's *Heart of Darkness*. Subtitled "elegy for a secret love", this text concerns the discovery by the female protagonist, Laura Kadisja Hassam, of a boy (child of an illicit affair) hidden in the cellar of the farmstead where she is living. Brought up in isolation from most human contact, he is taught to read in childhood by Laura, who does not see him but passes him messages through a grille in the wall and names him Laurent (after her own name). Seven years later, on the death of the aunt who had been looking after Laurent, Laura returns to the farmstead to find a youth still waiting for her in the cellar, and the novel recounts the intense love affair that develops between them as she introduces him to the "heart of light" and learns from the intensity of his new-found discovery of the sensuousness of the world. While questioning Christian conceptions of sexuality as sin through a somewhat idealized Islamic filter, the text's focus on a perfect, secret love, and perhaps also on the female's sculpting of the male in opposition to the decapitated or otherwise mutilated women of her earlier work, attempts a dramatic, albeit ultimately tragic, reversal of the sign of abjection which governs so much of Somers' work. Given its year of publication, the novella could be read in many ways as the inversion and textual double of *Los elefantes*.

A final anthology of short stories, *La rebelión de la flor* (1988), was the last work published before the author's death in 1994.

GEOFFREY KANTARIS

Selected Works

La mujer desnuda. 1st edn published as 'La mujer desnuda'. *Clima* [Montevideo] 2–3 (1950); most recent edn *La mujer desnuda*. Montevideo: Arca, 1990.

El derrumbamiento. Montevideo: Editorial Salamanca, 1953.

La calle del viento norte y otros cuentos. Montevideo: Editorial Arca, 1963.

De miedo en miedo (Los manuscritos del río). Montevideo: Arca, 1965.

Todos los cuentos, 19531967. Narradores de Arca. Montevideo: Arca, 1967. 2 vols.

Un retrato para Dickens. Bolsilibros Arca #77. Montevideo: Editorial Arca, 1969.

Muerte por alacrán. Buenos Aires: Calicanto Editorial, 1978.

Tríptico darwiniano. Montevideo: Ediciones de La Torre, 1982.

Viaje al corazón del día: elegía por un secreto amor. Montevideo: Editorial Arca, 1986.

Sólo los elefantes encuentran mandrágora (Notas y Epílogo de Victoria von Scherrer). Buenos Aires: Editorial Legasa, 1986; reprint Barcelona: Ediciones Península, 1988.

La rebelión de la flor. Antología personal. Montevideo: Librería Linardi y Risso, 1988.

References and Further Reading

Araújo, Helena. "Escritura femenina: sobre un cuento de Armonía Somers". *Cuéntame tu vida (Revista de mujeres)* 5 (1981): 19–24.

——. "El modelo mariano (Tema y variaciones)". *Eco* 41(248) (June 1982): 117–45.

——. "El tema de la violación en Armonía Somers y Griselda Gambaro". *Plural* 15(179) (Aug. 1986): 21–3.

——. *La Scherezada Criolla: Ensayos sobre escritura femenina latinoamericana*. Bogotá: Universidad Nacional de Colombia, 1989.

"Armonía Somers: Los lobos esteparios". *Capítulo Oriental* 33 (1968): 523. (Review of *La mujer desnuda* published by *Clima*.)

Benedetti, Mario. *Literatura uruguaya siglo XX*. 2nd edn. Colección carabela. Montevideo: Editorial Alfa, 1969.

——. "Review of *El derrumbamiento* by Armonía Somers". *Número* 5(22) (1953): 102–3.

Campodónico, Miguel Angel. "Presentación de un capítulo de *Sólo los elefantes encuentran mandrágora*, Armonía Somers". *Maldoror* 16 (Nov. 1981): 4–15.

——. "Homenaje a Armonía Somers: Diálogo con Miguel Angel Campodónico". *Revista de la Biblioteca Nacional* 24 (1986): 45–61.

Cosse, Rómulo. "Armonía Somers: Monstruosidad y esplendor". *Fisión literaria: narrativa y proceso social*. Montevideo: Monte Sexto, 1990a, pp. 49–66.

——. (coordinador). *Armonía Somers, papeles críticos: cuarenta años de literatura*. Montevideo: Librería Linardi y Risso, 1990b.

Espada, Roberto de. "Armonía Somers o el dolor de la literatura". *Maldoror* 7 (1972): 62–6.

García Rey, José Manuel. "Armonía Somers: sondeo intuitivo y visceral del mundo". *Cuadernos Hispanoamericanos* 415 (Jan. 1985): 101–4.

——. and Fressia, A. "Maldición y exorcismo. Veintiuna preguntas a Armonía Somers". *Revista Sintaxis* 1(2) (Apr. 1976).

Kantaris, Elia Geoffrey. *The Subversive Psyche: Contemporary Women's Narrative from Argentina and Uruguay*. Oxford: Oxford University Press, 1996.

Niebylski, Dianna C. "Sick Bodies, Corrosive Humor: Armonía Somers". *Humoring Resistance: Laughter and the Excessive Body in*

Latin American Women's Fiction. Albany, NY: State University of New York Press, 2004.

Olivera-Williams, María Rosa. "'El derrumbamiento' de Armonía Somers y 'El ángel caído' de Cristina Peri Rossi: dos manifestaciones de la narrativa imaginaria". *Revista chilena de literatura* 42 (Aug. 1993), pp. 173–81.

Penco, Wilfredo. "Armonía Somers: El mito y sus laberintos". *Noticias* 3(82) (1979): 50–2.

——. "El amor en el centro del mundo" [reseña de *Viaje al corazón del día* de Armonía Somers]. *Casa de las Américas* 27(161) (1987): 125–7.

Perera San Martín, Nicasio. "Review of *Muerte por alacrán* by Armonía Somers". *Caravelle: Cahiers du Monde Hispanique et Luso Brésilien* 34 (1980): 259–62.

Picon Garfield, Evelyn. "'Yo soplo desde el páramo': la muerte en los cuentos de Armonía Somers". *Texto crítico* 3(6) (Jan.–Apr. 1977): 113–25.

——. *Women's Voices from Latin America: Interviews with Six Contemporary Authors*. Detroit, MI: Wayne State University Press, 1985.

"La metaforización de la soledad en los cuentos de Armonía Somers". *Hispamérica* 16(46–7) (1987): 179–88.

Rama, Angel. "La fascinación del horror: la insólita literatura de Somers". *Marcha* 1988 (27 Dec. 1963): 30.

——. "En la morgue con mis personajes (Encuesta: responde Armonía Somers)". *Marcha* (1964).

——. "Raros y malditos en la literatura uruguaya". *Marcha* 1319 (2 Sept. 1966): 30–1.

——. *La generación crítica, 1939–1969. Ensayo y testimonio*. Montevideo: Arca, 1972.

Rodríguez Monegal, Emir. "Onirismo, sexo y asco". *Marcha* (17 July 1953).

Rodríguez Villamil, Ana María. "Aspectos fantásticos en *La Mujer Desnuda* de Armonía Somers". *Río de la Plata: Culturas* 1 (1985): 147–63.

——. *Elementos fantásticos en la narrativa de Armonía Somers*. #142. Montevideo: Ediciones de la Banda Oriental, 1990.

Schipper, Minecke (ed.) *Unheard Words*. Trans. from Dutch by Barbara Potter Fasting. London: Allison and Busby, 1985 (1984).

Somers, Armonía. "Diez relatos a la luz de su probables vivenciales". In Miguel Ángel Campodónico (ed.), *Diez relatos y un epílogo*. Montevideo: Fundación de Cultura Universitaria, 1979, pp. 113–54.

——. "Carta abierta desde Somersville". *Revista iberoamericana* 58(160–1) (July–Dec. 1992): 1155–65.

STEIMBERG, ALICIA

Alicia Steimberg was born in 1933, in Buenos Aires, Argentina, into a family of first-generation Jewish immigrants from the Ukraine and Rumania on her mother's side. Her paternal grandparents emigrated from Russia to Argentina, where they settled on the Jewish agricultural colonies of the province of Entre Ríos. She has been a key figure in Argentine letters since the early 1970s and she continues to publish regularly. Many of her works have been translated into several languages including English. She received her formal training at the renowned Instituto de Lenguas Vivas in Buenos Aires where she trained as an English teacher and translator. She has long worked as a professional translator in a variety of capacities, but among some of her literary translations into Spanish are the work of Martín Amis and Lorrie Moore. In 1983, she received a Fulbright award and she participated in the International Writing Program and the University of Iowa. Her works have garnered numerous literary awards in Argentina such as the "Satiricón de oro" (1973), the prestigious Premio Planeta Biblioteca del Sur (1992) and the Buenos Aires Municipal Prize (1999). Steimberg conducts literary workshops in Buenos Aires, an activity she turned into a book titled *Aprender a escribir: fatigas y delicias de una escritora y sus alumnos* (2006, Learning to Write: The Difficulties and Delights of a Writer and her Pupils)

Perspectives on Jewishness

Alicia Steimberg's fiction provides ample space for critical inquiry and interpretation. Much of her work is informed by her own life experience with varying degrees of autobiographical content. While her literary corpus is as diverse as it is abundant, one common denominator is her work is the examination and representation of identity in its multiple manifestations (Jewish, Argentine, feminine, and so on). From the beginning, her literature has been marked by the consistent inclusion of Jewish themes, whether as the thematic core or as a supplementary component. Her first novel, *Músicos y relojeros* (1971, Musicians and Watchmakers), has become somewhat of a classic, enjoying multiple editions and translations. It narrates the story of a Jewish girl growing up in 1940s Buenos Aires and has been described as semi-autobiographical. The young character struggles with issues of identity as she tries to mediate the abyss between her home life among poor, secular Jewish immigrants and the larger Catholic world that surrounds her. Her experience with Jewishness is described in almost entirely negative terms. Being Jewish to the impressionable young girl means being an outsider. Each member of her family is odder than the next, which only adds to her feeling of not belonging either at home or at school. In spite of the seemingly gloomy environment, the tone of the novel is humorous. The narrator rather innocently and lightheartedly provides observations on the quirky nature of her family, rather than passing judgment on them. The topic of alienation and the desire to assimilate into the dominant Hispano-Catholic society is further developed in Steimberg's novel *Su espíritu inocente* (1981, Her Innocent Spirit), also narrated by a young girl. The protagonist, Julia, also finds Jewish tradition to be oppressive at worst and irrelevant at best. She is seduced by the seeming grandeur and eloquence of her classmates' Catholicism with all its orderliness, rituals, liturgies, iconography, and neatly kempt nuns. In turn, she finds Judaism to be embarrassing and confusing. Steimberg's now characteristic humor is also an integral characteristic of the novel. Early criticism of these two texts judged them to be examples of Jewish self-hatred (Senkman). Notwithstanding, the two novels are much richer in thematic content than such an appraisal indicates. More recent interpretations focus on the autobiographical elements, feminine discourse, and humor in the novels.

Steimberg won the coveted Premio Planeta with her 1992 novel *Cuando digo Magdalena* (Call Me Magdalena), which deals in a very different way with Jewish identity than the previous novels. This novel has received the greatest amount of critical attention, largely due to the innovative and experimental nature of the narrative. The text is fragmentary, disjointed and difficult to follow, which reflects the state of mind of the amnesiac narrator who is trying to piece together a story and rediscover her identity. The parallel narrative threads of Magdalena's psychoanalysis and that of a detective story provide some structure to the novel. Jewishness, here, is not central to the story (such as it is), but it is one piece of the puzzle Magdalena is attempting to place and thus assign meaning to it.

Like *Cuando digo Magdalena*, Jewishness is not at the core of Steimberg's 2000 novel *La selva* (The Rainforest) but it is there as a part of the protagonist's identity and surfaces in her sense of displacement. Also semi-autobiographical, the novel serves as an interesting study on perspective in relation to age when compared with *Músicos y relojeros* and *Su espíritu inocente*. Cecilia, a writer and widow in her late fifties, finds herself at a spa in the Brazilian rainforest where she has gone to rest and get away from her hectic life in Buenos Aires. The story revolves around her disparate attempts to write and meditations on her relationship with three key male figures in her life: her deceased husband, her drug-addicted and violently abusive son, and an American biologist she has met at the spa and with whom she begins to fall in love. Self-reflection and the search for inner fulfillment are at the forefront of the narrative. *La selva* follows a more traditional novelistic plot line than *Cuando digo Magdalena*. Nevertheless, there are a number of elements to the novel, such as dream sequences, time shifts, and intercalated stories which are characteristic of Steimberg's experimental style in nearly all her texts.

Experimentation, Humor, and Sexuality

Cuando digo Magdalena is clearly Steimberg's most experimental novel. Structurally it is difficult to classify and stretches the conventional limits of the novel. It is truly postmodern in its structure as a *pastiche* narrative comprised of surprisingly dissimilar textual components that draw on Argentine literary traditions as well as free verse poetry, theater, detective fiction, and memoir. Certainly, the novel is the culmination of Steimberg's narrative experimentation but it is not her first text to delve into genre-defying narrative style. Her *La loca 101* (1973, Madwoman 101) is an early example of Steimberg's innovative style. The text is also constructed of a hodge-podge of incongruent narrative fragments that have little or nothing to do with one another, except that they are all observations made by the narrator on the often violent, chaotic world that surrounds her as an inhabitant of Buenos Aires. As the title indicates, there is a major preoccupation with psychology and mental health, a recurring theme in Steimberg's work. Here, the narrative is based on the rather nonsensical ramblings of a woman perceived as being anything from daft to outright insane. Cats, vampires, aged lovers, Aladdin, and any number of other characters inhabit the world of the narrator, who consistently focuses on violence and blood in the telling of her stories. Steimberg makes psychoanalysis the focal point of her 1986 novel *El árbol del placer*. She pokes fun at the subculture of psychoanalysis in Buenos Aires but uses it as a vehicle for critiquing Argentine society in general. As with most of her fiction, Steimberg inserts a great deal of wry humor into her storytelling, which provides her novels with an ironic outlook and makes them highly entertaining. The novel that most stands out in Steimberg's œuvre as both experimental and atypical is *Amatista* (Amethyst). The novel was a finalist for the Sonrisa Vertical prize awarded by the Tusquets publishing house in Barcelona for erotic literature. Steimberg again returns to the therapist's office in this ingenious text, but rather than being a psychotherapist it is a sex therapist—called "señora"—who is one of the main characters. *Amatista* is an original narrative that has been praised as an example of feminine pornography that inverts the male-dominated power structure of conventional pornography by making the female protagonist the empowered figure (Foster). The sex therapist takes on the task of teaching her male client—a lawyer known only as "doctor" in the novel—to enhance his sexual desire and prolong pleasure by concentrating on masturbation techniques, which she often commands him to perform in her presence. Sex therapy and sexual fantasy mesh in the novel as the characters of the novel and those in their fantasies explore sexuality. There are a number of interesting aspects to the novel, among them is the way in which human sexuality and the sensuality of language are intertwined.

Steimberg is also the author of two volumes of short stories, *Como todas las mañanas* (1983, Like Any Other Morning) and *Vidas y vueltas* (1999. Lives and Turns), for which she was awarded the Buenos Aires Municipal Prize. In general, her stories conform to the conventions of the genre and explore many of the same issues found throughout her novels. Her short stories have been widely anthologized in numerous collections both in Spanish and in translation. In addition, she has written a book for adolescents—*Una tarde de invierno un submarino* (2001, Hot Chocolate on a Winter's Afternoon)—that contains amusing anecdotes and recipes for kids to try at home.

Criticism

Steimberg's work has been held in high regard among critics who have defined her work as innovative, experimental, postmodern, and feminist among other descriptions. While some critics focus on Jewish aspects in her work (Sosnowski, Barr, Schneider), others find her work to be postmodern and feminist (Tompkins, Foster, Flori). All these perspectives point to the profound richness of Steimberg's literature, her talent as an innovative and entertaining storyteller, and her status as a major figure in Argentine and Latin American fiction.

DARRELL B. LOCKHART

Selected Works

Músicos y relojeros. Buenos Aires: Centro Editor de América Latina, 1971.

La loca 101. Buenos Aires: Ediciones de la Flor, 1973.

Su espíritu inocente. Buenos Aires: Pomaire, 1981.

Como todas las mañanas. Buenos Aires: Celtia, 1983.

El árbol del placer. Buenos Aires: Emecé, 1986.

Amatista. Barcelona: Tusquets, 1989.

Cuando digo Magdalena. Buenos Aires: Planeta, 1992.

Musicians and Watchmakers. Trans. Andrea Labinger. Pittsburgh, PA: Latin American Literary Review Press, 1998.

Vidas y vueltas. Buenos Aires: Adriana Hidalgo, 1999.

La selva. Buenos Aires: Alfaguara, 2000.

Call Me Magdalena. Trans. Andrea Labinger. Lincoln, NB: University of Nebraska Press, 2001.

Aprender a escribir: fatigas y delicias de una escritora y sus alumnos. Buenos Aires: Aguilar, 2006.

The Rainforest. Trans. Andrea Labinger. Lincoln, NB: University of Nebraska Press, 2006.

References and Further Reading

Barr, Lois Baer. "Fighting with Freud, and Other Father Figures: Alicia Steimberg". In Lois Baer Barr, *Isaac Unbound: Patriarchal Traditions in the Latin American Jewish Novel*. Tempe, AZ: ASU Center for Latin American Studies, 1995, pp. 55–84.

Calabrese, Elisa T. "Mujeres, memoria e identidad en *Cuando digo Magdalena*, de Alicia Steimberg". *Confluencia* 11(2) (1996): 58–65.

Flori, Mónica. "Alicia Steimberg". In Mónica Flori, *Streams of Silver: Six Contemporary Women Writers from Argentina*. Lewisburg: Bucknell University Press, 1995, pp. 147–84.

Foster, D.W. "The Case for Feminine Pornography in Latin America". In David William Foster, *Sexual Textualities: Essays on Queer/ing Latin American Writing*. Austin, TX: University of Texas Press, 1997, pp. 39–63.

Gimbernat González, Ester. "*El árbol del placer*: retóricas de enfermedad". In Ester Gimbernat González, *Aventuras del desacuerdo: novelistas argentinas de los '80*. Buenos Aires: Danilo Albero Vergara, 1992, pp. 289–94.

Schneider, Judith Morganroth. "Alicia Steimberg: Inscriptions of a Jewish, Female Identity". *Yiddish* 9(1) (1993): 92–104.

Senkman, Leonardo. *La identidad judía en la literatura argentina*. Buenos Aires: Pardés, 1983, pp. 283–93.

Sosnowski, Saúl. "Alicia Steimebrg: enhebrando pequeñas historias". *Folio* 17 (1987): 104–10.

Tompkins, Cynthia. "Intertextualidad en *Amatista* y *Cuando digo Magdalena* de Alicia Steimberg". *Hispamérica* 26(76–7) (1997): 197–201.

——. "Aporía en *La selva* de Alicia Steimberg". *Hispamérica* 31(91) (2002): 107–10.

STORNI, ALFONSINA

Alfonsina Storni (1892–1938) was an Argentine poet and feminist whose bold strokes with the pen brought new insight into the human condition and the interior world of the individual. Storni's family originated in Lugano, Switzerland, and migrated to the San Juan province of Argentina in 1880. There, Storni's father and brothers ran a small brewing company. In 1891, Storni's parents returned to visit Switzerland with their two older children, María and Romeo. Alfonsina was born in Sala Capriasca, Switzerland, on May 29, 1892, though some biographers cite her date of birth as May 22, due to the fact that Storni's aunt (probably mistakenly) had Alfonsina's birth certificate legally changed to reflect her own recollection of the author's birth, forty-six years later (Jones 1979: 135).

The young Storni learned to speak Italian, but by 1896 the family had returned to San Juan province, where she quickly learned to read. In 1901, they moved to the port city of Rosario, where Alfonsina's mother, Paulina, opened a home school and the family attempted a small business, the "Café Suizo," near the train station. The 10-year-old Alfonsina often helped out at the café. After the business failed, the Storni sisters worked as seamstresses and Alfonsina was employed at a hat factory. Escape must have seemed wonderful for Alfonsina when the Manuel Cordero acting company arrived in Rosario when she was about 14 years old. Luckily, the creative Alfonsina was able to replace an actress who fell ill; she then traveled the country with the José Tallaví company—to Santa Fe, Córdoba, Mendoza, Santiago de Estero and Tucumán. Storni worked on plays such as Henrik Ibsen's *Ghosts*, *La loca de la casa* by Benito Pérez Galdós, and Florencio Sánchez's *Los muertos*.

Returning from her thespian adventure, Alfonsina joined her mother, who was living in Bustinza and had remarried after Alfonsina's father's death in 1906. Storni decided to embark upon a career as a rural schoolteacher, following in her mother's footsteps. In Coronda, she received her teaching license, obtained work as a dramatic arts teacher and became involved with the literary journals *Mundo Rosarino* and *Monos y Monadas*, where she published some of her first poems.

Having terminated a relationship with a married man in her late teen years, Storni decided to move to Buenos Aires, where her son Alejandro was born on April 21, 1912, and Alfonsina published her first short story in *Fray Mocho*. Benefiting from the freedoms of bustling Buenos Aires, Storni began a new life as a single mother and poet, often suffering economic hardship. In 1916, her first book of poems, *La inquietud del rosal*, was published and *Mundo Argentino* published her poem "Versos otoñales," which appears to show the influence of both Sor Juana's take on the Golden Age *carpe diem* poems and modernism's adherence to descriptive adornment. Storni was in good company in *Mundo Argentino*, for alongside her poems the work of modernists Rubén Darío (Nicaragua) and Amado Nervo (México) also appeared. Her confidence increasing, this same year, 1916, Storni began reading her poems in public. In 1917, she won the Premio Anual del Consejo Nacional de Mujeres, and in 1918 published her second book of poems, *El dulce daño*. In this era, the poet began frequenting literary salons and making friends with various modernist and Latin American *vanguardia* poets, among them Amado Nervo, who was in Buenos Aires after 1919 as a Mexican ambassador to Argentina. It was a year of mixed results for Storni, as in 1919 she was forced to temporarily rescind her teaching position in order to recover from nervous tension and stress, but at the same time she published *Irremediablemente* and was awarded a medal of membership of the Comité Argentino Pro Hogar de los Huérfanos Belgas for publicly having protested Germany's incursion into Belgium during the First World War. She soon began making periodic trips across the Río de la Plata to visit friends in Montevideo; she became acquainted with Uruguayan writers José Enrique Rodó and Julio Herrera y Reissig and befriended Manuel Ugarte and José Ingenieros (www.answers.com/topic/alfonsina-storni).

The 1920 publication of Storni's fourth book, *Languidez*, corresponds with her first visit to Montevideo and the forming of great friendships with Uruguayan authors Juana de Ibarborou and Horacio Quiroga. *Languidez*'s intensity and originality merited multiple poetry prizes, and Storni received both the First Municipal Poetry Prize and Second National Prize in Literature in Argentina. Her fame and popularity were sealed. She wrote articles for the Argentine press, at times using the pseudonym Tao Lao, and in the 1920s was a Professor of drama and diction at the Escuela Normal de Lenguas Vivas; she also taught at the Lavardén Municipal Children's Theater and the National Conservatory. In 1925, she published *Ocre* and became acquainted with Chilean author Gabriela Mistral, who wanted to meet Storni while visiting Buenos Aires.

Storni's incursions into theater were met with less success when in 1927 the premiere of *El amo del mundo: comedia en tres actos* was attended by the Argentinian president and his wife, and the next day was panned in the press. Storni twice failed to receive high praise for stage productions of her plays (*El amo del mundo* and *Dos farsas pirotécnicas*, 1932), but she continued to publish books of poems, including *Poemas de amor* (1926) and *Mundo de siete pozos* (1934). She was involved in the founding of the Argentine Writers' Society and was a vocal advocate for women's rights. In 1928, she traveled to Spain with her friend, actress Blanca Vega, and befriended various women writers, including Concha Meléndez.

Storni continued to be well accompanied in her literary activities, and she met Federico García Lorca when he visited Buenos Aires between October, 1933 and February, 1934. In the mid-1930s, however, Storni's health began to decline. A poet who often suffered from feelings of solitude and isolation, she endured invasive surgery for breast cancer on May 20, 1935. Shortly thereafter, two of her friends, Leopoldo Lugones and Horacio Quiroga, committed suicide. These startling setbacks inspired her to dedicate a poem to Quiroga.

In January, 1938, the Ministerio de Instrucción Pública invited Storni, Juana de Ibarborou and Gabriela Mistral to give a public lecture describing their creative processes; the talk took place in Colonia, Uruguay, after which Storni's *Mascarilla y trébol* (1938) and an *Antología poética* were published (1938). Despite increasing literary fame, Storni's health was failing, and she despaired as her cancer metastasized to the throat. On October 23, 1938, she traveled to Mar del Plata. She drafted and sent two farewell letters, one to her son, and the other to the Buenos Aires paper *La Nación*; her suicide note, this missive contained the famous poem "Voy a dormir" ("I Am Going to Sleep"). In the early morning hours of October 25, 1938, Alfonsina Storni walked into the sea, probably at La Perla beach in Mar del Plata, and committed suicide by drowning. One month later, on November 21, the Argentine Senate expressed the nation's appreciation of Storni, with Senator Alfredo Palacios praising the values of the spirit and lamenting that a fertile land such as Argentina had yet to construct a "hospitable atmosphere where this delicate plant called a poet can flourish" (Delgado 2001: 266).

Storni's death was commemorated when songwriters Ariel Ramírez and Félix Luna composed "Alfonsina y el Mar," which has been popularized by musicians Mercedes Sosa, Andrés Calamaro, and others. A commemorative monument designed by sculptor Luís Perlotti in 1942 marks the approximate spot where Storni is supposed to have entered the sea in Mar del Plata.

Early Work

Alfonsina Storni's poetic trajectory ranges from early works expressing sensuality and denouncing the limitations of feminine social roles, to great introspection and self-reflective works, to the discovery of new poetic forms in her later work. Storni's work is commonly read as located temporally and stylistically between the modernist movement typified by Rubén Darío, Leopoldo Lugones, and Horacio Quiroga, and the Latin American *vanguardia* of Vicente Huidobro and Pablo Neruda and surrealism of Julio Cortázar. Federico de Onís's 1934 *Antología de la poesía española e hispanoamericana* referred to Storni and the generation of authors born after 1896 as "postmodern". Storni's writing in the first half of her life employs a combination of romanticism, realism, and feminism, as the author expresses the realities of a woman's experience of life and love, openly protesting the unfair social conditions that women faced. Later Storni works breach an experimental, or quasi-*vanguardia* style with their exploration of human nature and poetic form. It is her consistent feminism that leads to Storni being read alongside her contemporaries Delmira Agustini, Gabriela Mistral, Juana de Ibarbourou, María Eugenia Vaz Ferreira and Dulce María Loynaz as one of the leading women writers of early twentieth-century Latin America. Storni paved the way for later-twentieth-century Argentinean feminist writers such as Victoria Ocampo, Griselda Gambaro, and Luisa Valenzuela.

Throughout her life, Storni's civic activism was motivated by an interest in labor issues, literary solidarity for writers, women's suffrage and women's and children's rights. During her decades in Buenos Aires, she penned articles on feminism, social justice, and middle-class labor issues. She regularly contributed to *La Nación* and organized the column "Feminidades" for *La Nota* (Kirkpatrick 1995).

She achieved early fame with the publication of her first books, *La inquietud del rosal* (1916), *El dulce daño* (1918) and *Irremediablemente* (1919). Her work's progressive originality is sometimes credited to influences culled during her visits to Europe. Storni's early verse mimetically reproduces the binding conditions of femininity in order to protest social demands for feminine obedience, passivity and purity. Her poem "Tú me quieres blanca" ("You Want Me White"—*El dulce daño*, 1918) is, along with "Hombre pequeñito" ("Little Little Man"—*Irremediablemente*, 1919), one of her most famous poems, and is widely anthologized. The poem brought her early fame, as women repeated the poem's daring protest of the hypocritical social demands for female virginity—a demand that is not placed on men. The speaking voice repeats "Tú me quieres alba, me quieres de espumas, me quieres de nácar" [You want me dawn, you want me of foam, you want me pearly] and ends by pointing to the inequality of a male demanding an ideal that he does not in turn provide. The poem asserts that only by going through his own purification process could the man possibly have the right to ask that a woman provide her virginity as prerequisite of her human worth. Storni's equally famous "Hombre pequeñito" (*Irremediablemente*, 1919) directly criticizes the feminine entrapment created by a masculine world. In a blatant accusation of male hypocrisy, the speaking voice repeats "Hombre pequeñito, hombre pequeñito, / Suelta a tu canario que quiere volar" [Little little man, little little man / Release your canary that wants to fly.]. The poem concludes "Hombre pequeñito, te amé media hora. / No me pidas más" [Little little man, I loved you for half an hour. / Don't ask me for more"]. By saying "I loved you for half an hour. / Don't ask me for more," the speaking voice dares to voice her need for solitude and the expression of free will; she also refers to the apparent falsity of romantic or erotic scenes that last but a moment, but according to social conventions of matrimony or male pleasure often involve feminine seduction or play-acting, which becomes tiresome when one is neither very interested nor, ultimately, satisfied.

Languidez

The 1925 collection *Languidez* provides some of the most complex, original and introspective work published in the Spanish language in the 1920s. We see that, if earlier Storni work expressed sensuality and frustrated desire, and protested the falsity and hypocrisy of femininity, then *Languidez* includes some poems that describe the conflicted ego's self-examination. Resultant emotions vacillate between female competition, self-castigation, guilt and reconciliation in what is ultimately a desire for creativity and companionship. We see this in poems such as "Carta lírica a otra mujer" (Lyrical Letter to Another Woman), "Partida" (Departure) and "Han venido" (They Have Come).

"Carta lírica a otra mujer" begins by addressing another woman in what could be a gesture of friendship as she imagines the other's face, small stature, and sweet disposition (lines 1–4). The speaker appears to praise the other woman's femininity, but in verse 20, the tone changes to chastise the other woman as possessing "el hombre que adoraba" (the man that I adored), thus unwittingly killing all hope that the speaker may have had, presumably for reconciliation with the man. The speaker punctuates her protest of her own state of suffering, calling the other woman "Vos, su criatura" (You, his creature, line 24).

This ending marks a self-aggressive impulse, as the poetic speaking voice internalizes the lack of the loved other, invoking this absence in a castigation of the imagined other woman, even though she cannot be directly blamed for the speaker's jealousy. At the same time as this destructive sentiment weaves its way through the poem, it relies on a constructed sisterhood made possible by the apostrophic, direct address to the other woman—who is the embodiment of an elsewhere, unattainable feminine ideal that excludes the speaker.

The poem "Partida" expresses a loosening from social restrictions as the speaking voice frees itself of social ideals via the sea's ferocity. In the poem, the speaker unites with the sea and sun, sinking into the sea in order to celebrate a chaotic liberation. She says that the "ciela rueda por el lecho" [sky spins through the seabed, line 56] and exclaims that she is similar to the sun in that "¡Giro, giro giro!" [I spin, I spin, I spin!, line 64]. At the poem's close, the voice seeks the frenzy of indeterminacy, where she may become one with nature. Rather than describe jealousy or the frenzied nature of human relationships, here the poetic voice chooses to imagine beyond the limits of human mortality by gyrating with the elements; this work prefigures the author's own death.

In an acme of expressiveness beyond feminine rejection and fantasies about elemental reunions seen in "Carta lírica a otra mujer" and "Partida," "Han venido" exposes the creative individual's reflections about human and familial solidarity, the ephemeral nature of existence, and the spatial and domestic relationships that mirror the gendered world that limited females in Storni's early twentieth-century world. "Han venido" (*Languidez*, 1925) unites all these perspectives in a haunting expression of the constantly alternating solitude and solidarity that pervade female relationships, especially between women who know one another well. "Han venido" illustrates dichotomies of plenitude and absence, intellect and sentiment, exterior and interior space, light and darkness, warmth and cold, nature and the home. Using a sparse style with minimalist description, the speaker begins saying that on this day, her mother and sisters have come to see her, an event which has interrupted a long solitude during which she was accompanied by just her verses, her pride, "almost nothing" (line 4). She describes subtle changes in her sisters: the eldest, who has grown and is filled with illusions; the youngest, to whom she remarks "La vida es dulce. Todo mal acaba . . ." [Life is sweet. All bad things come to an end . . . line 8]. The constant is the speaker's all-seeing mother, who smiles, places both hands on the speaker's shoulders, and looks fixedly into her eyes; this moment of recognition and communication causes tears to spring to the speaker's eyes. The remainder of the poem costructs a contrast between the female realms of domesticity and memory with the more traditionally masculine territory of nature, liberty, and movement/progression, with the imagination capable of moving between these zones. The mother and sisters partake of a comforting domestic space; with all of the windows open so that they can see the spring sky, they share a meal and reminisce about old things. The situation is abruptly punctuated as the youngest directs everyone's attention outside as she observes: "the swallows are passing by". The youngest has been drawn to the sign of spring's arrival, which the reader may be aware brings hope and the continued nesting of the swallows, which are known to return to familiar spaces. Ironically, it is the youngest who first points out to the older women what also is a sign of time passing. We can read various moments in "Han venido" as reflecting on the loneliness and solitude and the writing life, the limits and comfort of familiarity, the possibility of female solidarity, the recognition of language's breakdown when faced with human complexity, and the unfettered freedom inherent to the imagination.

Later Works: An Abbreviated Life

While "Han venido" is a sentimental and philosophical acme in Storni's expressive work, her fifth through eighth books of poetry expand her feminist themes and develop new content and formal styles. *Ocre* (1925) and *Poemas de amor* (1926) express the irony and bitterness of unequal romantic relationships with men and celebrate the strength of confident, intellectual women in history. In *Mundo de siete pozos* (1934) and *Mascarilla y trébol* (1938), Storni delves into darker themes of human nature, civilization, death, and structural experimentation. Constructions of human civilization are intellectualized and often compared to the human body; this darker, intellectual work responds to changing political realities such as the 1930 military coup in Argentina and rising fascism in Europe.

Storni's last book, *Antología poética* (1938), gathers her best poems in a collection published just before her suicide. The work speaks of an artist committed to expressing the plenitude of human experience and to challenging the social restrictions placed on women. Her last poem, "Voy a dormir," sent to *La Nación* on the eve of her death, indicates her desire for peace and need to escape the poor health and depression that had plagued her: "I am going to sleep, dear nurse / lay me down / Put a lamp at my head". Rather than a light at her head, Mar del Plata has erected a monument to Storni at La Perla beach; its carved image is of a woman of flowing hair and garments, hands extended as she faces the sea. The 1925

Storni poem "Dolor" (Pain), which is inscribed on the monument's plaque, describes wanting to be just such an upright figure, passing like an element of nature between the sky and beach, and feeling "the perennial forgetting of the sea".

JULI A. KROLL

Selected Works

La inquietud del rosal. Prólogo de Juan Julián Lastra. Buenos Aires: Librería "La Facultad," 1916.

El dulce daño. Buenos Aires: Cooperativa Editorial Limitada, 1918.

Irremediablemente. Buenos Aires: Cooperativa Editorial Limitada, 1919.

Languidez. Buenos Aires: Sociedad Editorial Latinoamericana, 1920.

Ocre. Buenos Aires: Babel, 1925.

Poemas de amor. In *Obra poética completa*. Buenos Aires: Meridión, 1961. Orig. published 1926.

El amo del mundo: Comedia en tres actos. Buenos Aires: *Bambalinas: Revista teatral*, 1927.

Dos farsas pirotécnicas. Buenos Aires: Cooperativa Editorial Buenos Aires; Cabaut & Cía, 1932.

Mundo de siete pozos. Buenos Aires: Tor, 1934.

Mascarilla y trébol. Buenos Aires: Editorial El Ateneo, 1938.

Antología poética. Buenos Aires: Espasa-Calpe Argentina, 1938.

References and Further Reading

Delgado, Josefina. *Alfonsina Storni: Una biografía esencial*. Buenos Aires: Planeta, 2001.

Galán, Ana Silvia and Gliemmo, Graciela. *La otra Alfonsina*. Buenos Aires: Aguilar, 2002.

Gociol, Judith. *Alfonsina Storni: Con-textos*. Buenos Aires: Ediciones Biblioteca Nacional, 1998.

Gómez Paz, Julieta. *Leyendo a Alfonsina Storni*. Buenos Aires: Losada, 1966.

Jones, Sonia. *Alfonsina Storni*. Boston, MA: Twayne, 1979.

Kirkpatrick, Gwen. "The Creation of Alfonsina Storni". In Marjorie Agosín (ed.), *A Dream of Light and Shadow: Portraits of Latin American Women Writers*. Albuquerque, NM: University of New Mexico, 1995, pp. 95–117.

Marr, Matthew J. "Formal Subversion and Aesthetic Harmony in *Mascarilla y trébol*: A Reconsideration of Alfonsina Storni's Late Poetics". *Romance Quarterly* 49(1) (2002): 50–60.

Martínez-Tolentino, Jaime. *La crítica literaria sobre Alfonsina Storni* (1945–80). Kassel: Reichenberg, 1997.

Nacidit-Perdomo, Ylonka. *Alfonsina Storni: a través de sus imágenes y metáforas*. Santo Domingo: Luís Rafael Sánchez, 1992.

de Onís, Federico. *Antología de la poesía española e hispánica*. Madrid: Librería y Casa Editorial Hernández, 1934.

Pérez Blanco, Lucrecio. *Homenaje a Alfonsina Storni*. Málaga: Academia Iberoamericana de Poesía, Capítulo de Málaga, 1996.

Phillips, Rachel. *Alfonsina Storni: From Poetess to Poet*. London: Tamesis Books, 1975.

Smith-Soto, Mark I. *El arte de Alfonsina Storni*. Bogotá: Ediciones Tercer Mundo, 1986.

Teitler, Nathalie. "Redefining the Female Body: Alfonsina Storni and the Modernist Tradition". *Bulletin of Spanish Studies: Hispanic Studies and Research on Spain, Portugal, and Latin America* 79(2–3) (2002): 171–92.

SUÁREZ, CLEMENTINA

Clementina Suárez (1902–91), murdered by an intruder in her Tegucigalpa home at the age of 89, is one of very few well-known Honduran women poets. She published her first poetry collection, *Corazón sangrante* (Bleeding Heart) in 1930, however, she did not receive due respect for her cultural work until her later years. In 1957, the Salvadoran Ministry of Culture published *Creciendo con la hierba* (Growing with the Grass), demonstrating the esteem granted Suárez outside Honduran borders. Only several years later, in 1969, after the so-called Soccer War between El Salvador and Honduras disrupted the publication of two of her poetry collections in El Salvador, did the Autonomous University of Honduras honor her by bringing out two books by and about Suárez. The first was an anthology of new and previously published verse, *El poeta y sus señas* (The Poet and Her Signs). The second was *Clementina Suárez*, a compilation of articles, biographical sketches, book reviews, homages and portraits of the poet. In 1970, she received Honduras' most prestigious award, the Ramón Rosa National Literature Award. In the two decades between receiving Honduras' highest literary award and her untimely death in Tegucigalpa in 1991, Suárez was recognized in the Spanish-speaking world, through various awards and official posts, as an important poet and promoter of Central American art. Throughout her life, Suárez represented the life possibilities and impossibilities, or improbabilities, for literary and upper class, women in Honduras.

Clementina Suárez was born in Juticalpa, Olancho, Honduras, to a wealthy family. Her parents, Luis Suárez and Amelia Zelaya, allowed her and her sisters many liberties that were unseemly for Honduran high society, particularly for women. As noted by her biographer, Suárez took advantage of her father's unconventional parenting; he took her with him to bars, for example, and her mother's nonchalance. From an early age, she rebelled against privileged families' and society's mores. For instance, she traveled alone throughout Central American and to Cuba, Argentina, Spain, New York, China and the Soviet Union. In a time when it was frowned upon for a woman of her social standing to do so, she lived alone in the cities she frequented; and spent substantial amounts of time in self-imposed exile in El Salvador and a few years in Mexico. True to her rebellious and unconventional ways, Suárez gave birth to two children out of wedlock, married and divorced twice, in addition to carrying on affairs with literati and artists. Suárez was also an assiduous art promoter, opening some of the first art galleries in Central America, and one in Mexico, where she displayed the work of Central American artists, including that of her second husband, Salvadoran José Mejía Vides, and Costa Rican, Francisco Amighetti. In return for her fervent patronage of the plastic arts, an impressive number of artists rendered her portrait. Her work in the promotion of art also earned her official recognition: in the 1950s, she served as cultural attaché to El Salvador and worked in Honduras' Ministry of Education. At the same time that Suárez gained a reputation as a poet and cultural promoter, her "liberated" personal life was fodder for gossip. For example, she was rumored to have read her poetry in see-through clothing. In turn, her "wanton" life has obfuscated studies of her poetic œuvre, but her life amounted to more than a series of scandals.

In actuality, Clementina Suárez, as is her Salvadoran contemporary Claudia Lars [pseudonym for Carmen Brannon (1899–1974)], is a pioneering voice in Central American women's poetic production. Her poetry, generally written in free verse in simple, direct language challenges Latin American society's conservatism, specifically its patriarchal attitudes toward women and their sexuality. As it integrates meditations on women's many roles: sexual, social, economic wherein they are sexual beings, wives, mothers, daughters, and workers, for instance, Suárez's poems often function as poetic critiques of social inequities and economic stratification. Her poetic production first enters the realm of politics in her 1937 collection, *Veleros*, a time in which Central America, specifically, was trying to survive the depression, undergoing an upsurge in political activism (many of the region's Leftist parties were established then) and experiencing the beginnings of what would turn out to be very long dictatorships (Tiburcio Carias in Honduras, Maximiliano Hernández Martínez in El Salvador, and the Somozas in Nicaragua, to name a few). In addition to *Veleros'* poems, Suárez directly demonstrated her political leanings in poems such as "Poema del hombre y su esperanza" (A Poem about Man and His Hope) and "Una obrera muerta" (A Dead Female Worker) published in *El poeta y sus señales*. But notably, unlike many contemporary Central American poets, Suárez did not subscribe to a particular political dogma or political party.

Although Suárez's incursions into poetry that reveals poetic speakers' outrage at social injustice and desire for change is important, it is her erotic poetry that highlights her influence on the development of Central American letters. Many years before the 1960s–1980s boom of Central American women's erotic poetry, represented by poets such as Guatemalan Ana María Rodas (1937), Nicaraguan Gioconda Belli (1948) and Costa Rican Ana Istarú (1960), Suárez dared to describe and exalt female erotic experiences in frank language, to defend women's right to these experiences, and to demand equality between the sexes. Many of Suárez's first poetic, and narrative, texts—including, *Corazón sangrante* (1930, Bleeding Heart), *Iniciales* (1931, Beginnings), *Los templos de fuego* (1931, Temples of Fire), *De mis sábados el ultimo* (prose) (1931, The Last of My Saturdays), and *Engranajes* (1935, Gears)—deal with feminine sexuality explicitly. As noted above, often, Suárez's texts are sensual meditations of everyday life and social critiques, frequently expressing disappointment and melancholy and joy when faced with love lost and won. Suárez's erotic poems' speakers take a range of positions vis-à-vis their lovers. For instance in 1931's "Explicaciones" (*Templos de fuego*), Suárez's poetic speaker is a Scheherazade sure of her certain knowledge who mocks that king she is to entertain; while in other poems with more mystical impulses, her poetic speakers desire to become one with their lovers. The majority of Suárez's poetry can be labeled love, or erotic, poetry, and literary critics cite *Creciendo con la hierba*'s (1957, Growing with the Grass) love poems as the culmination of Suárez's poetic production.

In *Creciendo con la hierba*, which can be read as a collection of eight poems as well as as one poem divided into eight parts, Suárez explores the spiritual and physical elements of erotic love. The first poems tend towards the abstract as they ponder the meaning and role of love in all human beings' lives. As the collection progresses, the poetic imagery becomes more explicitly physical, or carnal. The poetic speaker contemplates her desire for an erotic love that is enjoyable to both lovers and that is unfettered by social, moral, and even spiritual, constraints. At the end of this 1957 text, the poetic speaker imagines herself merging with a female collectivity and invites her lover to join her in her new vision of an unlimited sexuality. Thus, the female lover challenges the expectations of mid-twentieth century Latin American women for she disobeys the role of sexual passivity and disinterest and instead assumes an attitude of female empowerment. As *Creciendo con la hierba* amply illustrates, for Clementina Suárez, human beings' sexual lives involve more than momentary sexual experiences but rather permeate the everyday and, through a fuller understanding between the sexes, transform individuals and society at large. Thus, sexual equality is an essential element of social equality and leads to personal and national betterment.

The last discrete poetry collection Suárez published, *Canto a la encontrada patria y su héroe* (Song to the Found Motherland and Its Hero), is structured similarly to *Creciendo con la hierba*. It consists of thirteen short poems that can be read as autonomous poems and as part of a larger poetic meditation on individuals' intimate, natural connections to his/her motherland. The poetic speaker here identifies with the *patria* and with a proponent of the ill-fated Central American Union and one of Honduras' founding fathers, Francisco Morazán (1792–1842). In the aforementioned *El poeta y sus señales*, Suárez further delves into political questions, for instance in "Combate," the poetic speaker aligns herself with the people's social struggles and declares her poetry a weapon in defense of hope. And she also continues to explore the dominant elements, noted above, of her poetic production.

Despite Clementina Suárez's important contributions to Honduran and Latin American letters, her poetry has not received the necessary attention. The majority of articles and reviews of her poetic works tend to present Suárez as a great poet and a strong, independent woman who lived her life on her own terms. But, with few exceptions, such as the work of critics Janet Gold and Helen Umaña, in-depth analyses of her poetry are absent. That said, Gold's comprehensive biography and literary study, *Clementina Suárez: Her Life and Poetry*, must be acknowledged as a major scholarly achievement. Her research should motivate other scholars to further investigate Suárez's cultural work in the isthmus. Clearly, Suárez's œuvre, and its relation and place in Central and Latin American literature warrants continued study.

YVETTE APARICIO

Selected Works

Corazón sangrante. Tegucigalpa: Tipografía Nacional, 1930.
De mis sábados el último. Mexico: Libros Mexicanos, 1931.
Iniciales. Mexico: Libros Mexicanos, 1931
Los templos de fuego. Mexico: Libros Mexicanos, 1931.
Engranajes. San José, C.R.: Borrasé, 1935.
Veleros: 30 poemas. Havana: Hermes, 1937.
De la desilusión a la esperanza. Tegucigalpa: Tipografía Nacional, 1944.
Creciendo con la hierba. San Salvador: Ministerio de Cultura, 1957.
Canto a la encontrada patria y su héroe. Tegucigalpa: n.p., 1958.
El poeta y sus señales: antología. Tegucigalpa: Universidad Nacional Autónoma de Honduras, 1969.
Antología poética. Tegucigalpa: Secretaría de Cultura y Turismo, 1984.
Con mis versos saludo a las generaciones futuras. Ed. Rigoberto Paredes. Tegucigalpa: Ediciones Librería Paradiso, 1988.

References and Further Reading

Aparicio, Yvette. "La búsqueda por la plenitud erótica: *Creciendo con la hierba* de Clementina Suárez". *Afrodita en el trópico: erotismo y construcción del sujeto femenino en obras de autoras centroamericanas*. Potomac, MD: Scripta Humanistica, 1999, pp. 225–43.

Carrera, Julieta. *La mujer en América escribe* ... Mexico: Ediciones Alonso, 1956.

Clementina Suárez. Tegucigalpa: Universidad Autónoma de Honduras, 1969.

Gold, Janet N. *Clementina Suárez: Her Life and Poetry*. Gainesville, FL: University Press of Florida, 1995.

Pino del Rosario, Mari. "Clementina Suárez (12 May 1902–9 December 1991)". In María A. Salgado (ed.), *Modern Spanish American Poets: Second Series. Dictionary of Literary Biography*. Detroit: Gale, 2004, pp. 316–20

Soriano, Juanita. "Una poetisa hondureña: Clementina Suárez". *Armas y letras: Revista de la Universidad de Nuevo León* 2 (April/June 1959): 40–58.

Sosa, Roberto. *Diálogo de sombras*. Tegucigalpa: Editorial Guaymuras, 1993.

Umaña, Helen. "Una teoría del amor en la poesía de Clementina Suárez". *Literatura hondureña contemporánea (ensayos)*. Tegucigalpa: Editorial Guaymuras, 1986.

SUÁREZ, KARLA

Karla Suárez, born in Havana, Cuba, on October 28, 1969, was trained in Cuba as a computer engineer. She belongs to a group of writers who challenged, in the late 1990s, the traditional space dedicated to women in Cuban society. According to studies by Luisa Campuzano, director of the Centre for Women's Studies of the Casa de las Américas, Suárez broaches taboo subjects in her prose and uses writing as a privileged space for reflection and doubts. Coincidentally, the Centre was created in 1996, the same year as the first publication by Suárez of a short story in a Cuban anthology. In fact, Suárez offers an original approach to the Cuban woman, in her attempt to reconcile a society in evolution and the changing moral values that are associated with it.

Karla Suárez published her first complete collection of short stories, *Espuma*, at the young age of 30, published by Ediciones Letras Cubanas in her hometown. Since then her short stories have been included in anthologies in Spain (*Nuevos Narradores Cubanos*, Editorial Siruela, 2000; *Líneas Aéreas*, Lengua de Trapo, 1999); Italy, as well as in literary journals in Mexico, Cuba and Argentina. Her short story *Aniversario* (Anniversary) was adapted for Cuban theatre in 1996 and two others were adapted for Cuban television in 2002 (*El ojo de la noche* and *En esta casa hay un fantasma*). A second collection, *Carroza para actores* (Float for Actors), was published in Colombia in 2001. An English translation of one of her stories "The Eye of the Night" was included in *Open your eyes and soar: Cuban women writing now,* edited (and also translated) by Mary G. Berg and published in 2003. Suárez was invited in 2006 to be writer-in-residence of the *Agence régionale pour l'écrit et le livre* in Aquitaine, France.

Since 1998, she has lived in Rome and, more recently, Paris, and published two novels to much critical acclaim. *Silencios* (Silences) won the Fifth Annual Lengua de Trapo Prize for a First Novel written in Spanish. *Silencios* was published in Germany by Rowohlt in 2001 and has been published in a paperback version in France (Éditions Metailié, 2005). As was the case with Suárez' second novel, *La viajera* (The Female Traveller), translations promptly followed; French (Éditions Métailié, 2002 and 2005 respectively), then Italian (Besa Editrice, 2003) and Brasilian (Ediçóes Asa). The French translation of *Silencios* was short-listed in 2004 for the *Prix des Amériques Insulaires et de la Guyane*.

In her first novel, *Silencios,* Suárez raises various usually unvoiced issues in post-Revolutionary Cuban literature and society such as emigration, racism, divorce, censorship, drugs, alcoholism, pedophilia, homosexuality, and sexual abuse. The author tells the story of a young Cuban from childhood to adolescence in an essentially dysfunctional family. The narrator remains anonymous throughout this feminine *Bildungsroman*, emphasizing the universality of her difficult and often hostile environment. Although nameless, the protagonist is not without nicknames such as *marimacho* (a derogatory term for masculine women) because she does not fit the quite rigid mould offered to her by tradition. Along with other problematical circumstances, this leads the young protagonist to a profound hatred of her body that comes to be a symbol of the uncomfortable position of Cuban women in the revolution. Women had been promised important advances but had encountered unexpected difficulties on the road to the conception of the "New Woman" to parallel the so-called—purely masculine—"New Man" put forward by revolutionary leaders.

However, the remarkable feminine body also reveals itself a weapon in the protagonist's domination of her childhood rivals, momentarily inverting the long-established power structure that leads to the selection by Suárez of the title *Silence* for the novel. In one chapter, Suárez appropriates the time-honoured (and literary) ritual of the *Arabian Nights*, the protagonist puts into effect a subterfuge by which she teaches the "bad" boys from school (ironically called *El Ruso*, the Russian) that her theoretically "masculine" body still holds a mysterious attraction by allowing the Russian to touch her genitalia. Once he is subjugated, the protagonist stabs the youngster with a pen, is pushed over a ledge and breaks her femur. Discovering herself in a cast, she chooses to remain mute about the incident: her role, the confrontation, and the constant familial conflict that surrounds her. She also refuses to reveal the rape that she is subjected to in a later episode of the novel by an adolescent called *El Poeta* (the poet). This generalized lack of communication results in a progressive desertion (for various reasons) of the family household by its various members, leaving the protagonist alone in her choice to remain. In choosing to relate the story of speechlessness in writing, Suárez generates a daring statement about the necessity to reconsider the situation of women in Cuba.

Suárez' second novel, *La Viajera* (as of date of submission, unpublished in English), also has a woman protagonist and departs from the *Bildungsroman* theme of the first novel although it preserves a woman-centred plot. The story describes a traveller / protagonist named Circe and is narrated from two differing points of view, the traveller's journal (which imparts important flashbacks) and the consequent narration offered by the friend she visits in Rome, Lucia. The encounter of the two women is the foundation of the novel.

La Viajera's narrative begins chronologically with the departure of Circe from Cuba and the inauguration of her journal in which she wishes to rememorate the happenings of her travels. This journal and the act of writing eventually become essential to her existence as "the only way to preserve time". The decision to emigrate, or, as Circe discloses, to "stay" in Brazil, is one which is wrought with grave implications, which the narrators contend with implicitly and explicitly throughout the novel. The journey takes the protagonist, Circe, from Cuba to Brazil, then to Mexico, Madrid (where she has a child), Paris, Rome, and, finally, Greece.

Suárez bases her character's travels on all the journeys throughout history and especially with the classical Greek tradition, allotting names such as Circe, Ulysses (Circe's son), a final destination of an unspecified Greek island and an expedition that, through its vagaries, causes the protagonist to question identity and thus come to self-discovery. In effect, the voyage is one of a modern (and occasionally comical) exploration for a "city" with which Circe will feel some affinity and wish to remain. If this novel symbolizes well the writer's complex separation from her place of birth, it does not fall into the all-too-easy trap of condemnation of Fidel Castro's governance (never unambiguously mentioned) but indeed questions the personal decision of the narrators for leaving. Intriguingly (and contrarily to other anti-Castro "exiled" writers such as Zoé Valdés, for example), there are no concretely "Cuban" reasons (politically) offered for the decision not to return, except for an ironic measure of consternation when faced with the zealotry of certain Cuban solidarity organizations who are suspected of not allowing for the shades of grey that make up the spectrum of Cuban emigrants.

In the aftermath of the Cold War and a generalized dearth of women writers published in Cuba in the 1970s and 1980s (Campuzano), the generation of writers to which Suárez belongs has often been overlooked by recent criticism. However, if the numerous successful publications and awards are any indication, Karla Suárez and her cohort are up and coming writers. With her profound grasp of the feminine psyche, which she expresses in an ingenious and often elegant manner, Karla Suárez has become one of the foremost contemporary Cuban women writers and the development of her prose augurs of fertile prospects.

SOPHIE M. LAVOIE

Selected Works

Espuma. Editorial Letras Cubanas, Cuba, 1999. Colombia: Editorial Norma, 2002.

Silencios. Spain: Editorial Lengua de Trapo, 1999. Trans. into Italian, German, Portuguese, and French.

Carroza para actores. Colombia: Editorial Norma, 2001.

"The Eye of Night". In Mary Berg (ed., trans.), *Open your Eyes and Soar: Cuban Women Writing Now.* Buffalo, NY: White Pine Press, 2003.

La viajera. Spain: Roca Editorial, 2005. Trans. into French, Portuguese, and Italian.

References and Further Reading

Campuzano, Luisa. "Cuban Women Writers at the End of the 90s: A Thematic/Bibliographic Map". In Mary Berg, (ed.), *Open Your Eyes and Soar, Cuban Women Writers Now.* Buffalo, NY: White Pine Press, 2003, pp. 9–17.

Campuzano, Luisa. *Literatura de mujeres y cambio social: Narradoras cubanas de hoy.* Havana: Unión 8, 2004.

Valle, Amir. "Karla Suárez: 'No creo que el mundo este condenado'". *La Jiribilla, Revista digital de cultura cubana*, 17, August 2001. http://www.lajiribilla.cu/2001/n17_agosto/485_17.html (accessed January 15, 2006)

SUBERCASEAUX, ELIZABETH

A reporter, journalist and writer, Elizabeth Subercaseaux was born in an upper-class family in Santiago de Chile in 1945. Since childhood she was fascinated by literature and read world classics from Stendhal to Beauvoir. After her secondary studies she moved to Spain in the 1970s where she worked for a number of journals (*ABC, Vanguardia*) and later she worked as a correspondent for the BBC. Upon her return to Chile, she was the founder of *El Peque,* a magazine for children. She worked for several journals as a reporter and contributed articles regularly (*Cosas, Apsi, Sic*). She also taught journalism at University of Chile's School of Journalism in Santiago. Since 1990 Subercaseaux has lived in the US, however, she spends a lot of time in Chile which remains the main focus of her work.

Subercaseaux is a journalist of first order. In the past twenty years she has written over two thousand journalistic pieces and commentaries, but her preferred genre is the interview. She has interviewed a number of political figures, such as Hillary Rodham Clinton, Carlos Menem, Patricio Aylwin, and literary celebrities, namely Gabriel García Márquez, José Donoso, Manuel Puig and Laura Esquivel, among others (cf. Kostopoulos, 1999). During the 1970s and 1980s Chilean journalists like Elizabeth Subercaseaux played a major role in mobilizing public opinion against the Pinochet dictatorship. In her book of interviews with Pinochet (1989, *Ego Sum Pinochet*) together with Raquel Correa she succeeded in pressing him on several key points of his presidency, such as the *desaparecidos*. This book, and her biography of Chile's current president, Michelle Bachelet, the first woman in South America to be elected to the office in her own right: *Michelle. Desde la cárcel a la presidencia de Chile*, 2006, have placed Subercaseaux among the best-known journalists in Latin America. Bachelet knows both sides of power; she was detained together with her mother during the Pinochet regime and later went into exile. Upon her return she worked as a physician and started her political career that culminated in her election to the highest office.

Elizabeth Subercaseaux also has excelled as a fiction writer, as an original voice in the among Chilean women writers in the past few decades. Her critical and ironic treatment of her subjects did not always win her the appreciation of the conservative circles of the literary establishment; but her work has always been well received by the public at large. In her fiction she deals with the same topics she explores with her interviewees: social injustice, corruption, human rights, and the condition of women. Her first book, *Silendra* (1986) is inspired by the abhorrent number of *desaparecidos* in Chile and the effect their disappearance had on their families. In this work the writer chronicles the silencing of women who face the violence caused by the dictatorship. Her following book, *Canto de una raíz lejana* (1988, Song of a Distant Root, translated into English by John Hassett) is equally bleak. This is one of the rare books by Subercaseaux which is not set in Chile. A novel akin to Juan Rulfo's work it is a moving representation of the misery, solitude and abandonment of Mexican peasants. "Tapihue is a village whose name does not appear in the papers, nor is it found on the country's map, because the Captain ordered it to be erased" (p. 9). The main character, Salustio, is a self-styled utopian visionary who dreams of a village where freedom, equality and justice would thrive and in his search for such a place he meets many intriguing figures that suffer from oppression. The publication of this book was supported by a National Endowment for the Arts grant. Contrary to the countryside setting of the *Canto. . .*, *El general azul* (1991, The Blue General) explores a very different urban, middle-class environment. Nevertheless, it is also a study of the registers of fear and violence. The military are perpetrators of the violence, but they end up being its victims as well (the protagonist commits suicide), because once unleashed it cannot be controlled.

In her best-known works, such as *La comezón de ser mujer* (1994, The Itch of Being Female), and *Las diez cosas que una mujer en Chile no debe hacer jamás* (1995, Ten Things that a Chilean Woman Should Never Do), Subercaseaux focuses on the experiences of women and on the way patriarchy affects them. Patriarchy is a grave problem in Chile, a conservative country. The writer says that it affects—though in different ways—women of all classes. While poking fun at the characters' behavior (of both genders), Subercaseaux makes a parallel between patriarchal domination and political oppression. As Barbara Mujica notes in her review of *Matrimonio a la chilena* (1997, Marriage in Chile) which also treats the same topic, namely patriarchal oppression of women, and in which the author—once again—includes women of all classes: "Subercaseaux has a gift for reproducing the dialect, mindset, values, and customs of upper-class Chileans" (*Americas* 50, 5. 1998: 62). This is why her writing rings true and is not demagogical or simplistic when she condemns the hypocrisy of the upper classes, although machismo transcends class boundaries. Subercaseaux suggests that the outdated legal system that does not offer recourse for the protection of women and their children is also a culprit in perpetuating social injustice to women. Her book, *La rebelión de las nanas* (2000, The Rebellion of the Nannies) depicts the subhuman treatment of nannies and maids by upper-class families who employ them. The nannies organize a protest and become victims of the forces of political oppression of the Pinochet regime. Subercaseaux is well known for her opposition to oppression and the dictatorship in Chile. Her position is clearly shown in *Mi querido Papá* (2001, My Dear Father), in the form of a letter written to a general by his 17-year-old son. Using a young narrator, the writer juxtaposes the innocence of the sender of the letter with the hypocrisy of the political system that is a taboo subject. Her next novel, *Un hombre en la vereda* (2003, A Man on the Sidewalk), is a thriller that also treats a taboo subject in Chile: the life of homosexuals. *Reporteras* (Reporters) which appeared in 2005 is a moving novel that chronicles the life of reporters and the dangers of the job. The topic gives Subercaseaux an opportunity to reveal her opinions on current political events, such as the two wars in Iraq and the disastrous social and political conditions in Afghanistan, hardly changed in the post-Taliban era. In 2006, *Reporteras* was turned into a television series, entitled *Reporteras urbanas* (Urban Reporters) directed by Tatiana Gaviola. In 2007, she is publishing two more political thrillers, *Asesinato en La Moneda* (Murder in the Moneda), followed by *Asesinato en Zapallar* (Murder in Zapallar). She also has a finished book that is yet to be published, titled *La eterna edad del agua*. (The Eternal Age of the Water).

Elizabeth Subercaseaux's work is well known to readers beyond Chile. She has been on tours presenting her work at several US universities. In many schools and universities her works are included in the Latin American literature curriculum. Recently, together with Malú Sierra, another well-known Chilean journalist, Subercaseaux wrote her latest book which consists of a series of exclusive interviews with Evo Morales and chronicles the life of the first indigenous president of Bolivia. In these interviews that lasted a month and started every day at 5 a.m., Morales told them stories of his life, about his childhood as a shepherd, about his union struggles, about his beliefs and about how he became the president of his country. (Cf. Aristóteles España: "Interview with Elizabeth Subercaseaux" *La Pata de Liebre*: www.lapatadeliebre.cl.) According to Subercaseaux, Morales is very different from other politicians: he is transparent, he does not lie, and he is the "least diplomatic politician ever".

The prolific writer is currently developing two new projects: a biography of her great great grandmother, composer Clara Schuman; and another novel, entitled *Enedina* in which she (re)turns to the literary representation of her roots in the Chilean countryside where she grew up. This novel returns to some of the spaces depicted in her first books, *Silendra* and *El canto de la raíz lejana*.

In addition to her work as a novelist, Subercaseaux keeps working as a journalist. She continues to contribute to *Vanidades Continental,* she writes a weekly column for *La Nación,* one of the leading newspapers in Santiago; and collaborates with *Al Día*, a Spanish language newspaper in Philadelphia. Her subjects cover everything from the threats of Al Qaeda to healthy eating habits. She spends time both in Philadelphia and in Chile.

SILVIA NAGY-ZEKMI

Selected Works

La comezón de ser mujer. Santiago: Planeta, 1994.
Las diez cosas que una mujer en Chile no debe hacer jamás. Santiago de Chile: Planeta, 1995
Gabriel Valdés, señales de la historia. Santiago: Aguilar Chilena, 1998.
Las diez cosas que un hombre en Chile debe hacer de todas maneras. Santiago de Chile: Catalonia, 2005
Michelle Desde la cárcel a la presidencia de Chile Santiago de Chile: Catalonia, 2006.

Co-authored Works

Subercaseaux, Elizábeth with Raquel Correa and Malú Sierra. *Los generales del régimen*. Santiago de Chile: Ed. Aconcagua, 1983.
——. with Raquel Correa. *Ego Sum Pinochet.* Santiago de Chile: Ed. Zig-zag, 1989
——. with Malú Sierra. *Evo Morales.* Forthcoming 2007.

Fiction

Silendra. Santiago de Chile: Ornitorrinco, 1986.

Del lado de acá. Santiago de Chile: Galinost, 1986.
Canto de una raíz lejana. Santiago de Chile: Planeta, 1988.
El general azul. Santiago de Chile: Grupo Editorial Zeta, 1991.
Matrimonio a la chilena. Santiago de Chile: Aguilar Chilena, 1997.
Eva en el mundo de los jaguares. Santiago de Chile: Planeta, 1998.
Una semana de octubre. Buenos Aires: Grijalbo, 1999.
La rebelión de las nanas Santiago de Chile, 2000.
Mi querido Papá. Santiago de Chile: Sudamericana, 2001.
Un hombre en la vereda. Santiago de Chile: Sudamericana, 2003.
Reporteras. Santiago: Catalonia, 2005.
Asesinato en Zapallar Santiago de Chile: Planeta, 2007
Asesinato en la Moneda. Santiago de Chile: Planeta, 2007.
La eterna edad del agua. To be published.
Enedina. In process.

Texts Published in English

Selections from *Silendra*, *The Secret Weavers*, ed. Marjorie Agosín, Boston, MA: White Pine Press, 1991.
Song of a Distant Root. Trans. John Hassett. Pittsburgh, PA: Latin American Literary Review Press, 2001
Michelle: From Prisoner to President. Miami, FL: Santillana, 2006.

References and Further Reading

España, Aristóteles. "Entrevista con Elizabeth Subercaseaux, periodista y escritora chilena radicada en EEUU". *Pata de Liebre.* http://www.lapatadeliebre.cl/index.php?id=12&tx_ttnews%5Btt_news%5D=57&tx_ttnews%5BbackPid%5D=41&cHash=0512cebb9d
Güemes, César. "Nunca pensé que Pinochet fuera invencible; nadie lo es". *La Jornada.* September 18, 2000. http://www.jornada.unam.mx/2000/09/18/03an1clt.html
Kostopoulous, Celeste. "Elizabeth Subercaseaux". In Patricia Rubio (ed.), *Escritoras chilenas.* Vol. III. Santiago de Chile: Ed. Cuarto Propio, 1999, pp. 484–99.
Mora, Gabriela. "Silendra, ciclo cuentístico". *Revista Chilena de Literatura* 36 (1990) 113–19.
Osorio, José. "Elizabeth Subercaseaux y su mirada del Chile cultural y político". Entrevista. *Letras de Chile.* 2003. http://www.letrasdechile.cl/modules.php?name=News&file=article&sid=71
Rivera, Angélica. "Sociedad chilena con ojos críticos". *Las Últimas noticias*, May 22, 1997: 32.
Vera Lamperein, Lina. "Elizabeth Subercaseaux". In *Presencia femenina en la literatura nacional. Una trayectoria apasionante.* Santiago de Chile: Cuarto Propio, 1994, p. 232.

T

TELLES, LYGIA FAGUNDES

Lygia Fagundes Telles (b. 1923), is a novelist and short story writer who is very well known and acknowledged both in Brazil and abroad. She may be considered to be the *Grande Dame* of contemporary Brazilian literature and has won numerous national and international prizes. The most prestigious international prize she has won is the *Prêmio Camões* (Camoes Prize) 2005 in Portugal. Awarded annually by the Portuguese National Library Foundation and the Brazilian National Book Department, it is frequently regarded as the equivalent of the Nobel Prize in Literature for Portuguese writers. Her literary work comprises about twenty books, which have been published worldwide.

Lygia Fagundes Telles was born in the city of São Paulo on April 19, 1923, the daughter of the district attorney Dr. Durval de Azevedo Fagundes and Maria do Rosário de Azevedo Fagundes, who always supported her during her professional career. Due to her father's professional mobility, she spent her childhood in various small towns in the interior of the State of São Paulo.

When she was a child, Telles enjoyed being told stories by other children and her mother's maids, because this aroused her interest in the various styles and modes of expression of the Portuguese language, and inspired her imagination. This was very decisive in the development of her narrative art. It also furthered her fascination for the mysterious side of life, the dramatic and tragic aspects of human existence, which then became the basic elements of her writing.

In the 1930s, she returned with her family to the city of São Paulo, taking up her studies at the *Instituto de Educação Caetano de Campos* (Institute of Education Caetano de Campos), graduating there in 1939. Having always been attracted to the creative process in literature, she published her first book of narratives, *Porão e Sobrados* (1938), at the age of 15, containing twelve short stories, which she later excluded from her bibliography.

In 1940, she continued her studies, majoring in physical education at the *Escola Superior de Educação Física* (College of Physical Education). One year later she started to study law at the *Faculdade do Largo São Francisco* (Law School of the University of São Paulo), graduating in 1945.

Her official literary debut was in 1944 when she published her second collection of short stories *Praia Viva* (1944, Lively Beach). This was the same year when Clarice Lispector, another outstanding Brazilian writer, published her first novel *Perto do Coração Selvagem* (1944, Near the Wild Heart). These two women writers are completely different from each other apart from having the same objectives in their creative work: to testify the human condition in a time of worldwide crisis, transformation, and disillusionment during World War II. Another collection of short stories by Telles, *O Cacto Vermelho* (1949, The Red Cactus), followed. It was awarded the Afonso Arinos Prize from the Brazilian Academy of Letters.

In 1950, she married Goffredo da Silva Telles, who had been her professor of International Law at São Paulo University, and in 1954 her only son was born, Goffredo Neto, who later became a film producer. In the 1960s they separated and she later divorced her husband and started to work as a government official at the Social Security Institute of the State of São Paulo, a job she kept until retirement in 1991. She also worked as a journalist in the daily newspaper *A Manhã* (The Morning).

In 1954, her first novel *Ciranda de Pedra* (1954, The Marble Dance, 1986) was published. Later it was made into a *telenovela* (TV series, 1981). According to the critic Antonio Cândido, this novel marked her intellectual maturity as a writer. A woman's life is described in a very discreet and sensitive way, a life which starts in a traumatic family situation and results in various love affairs which end up in a frustrating experience. The main character tries to overcome her painful childhood, the separation of her parents and the insanity of her mother, but does not succeed.

In the 1950s, Telles was in close contact with the famous Brazilian *modernistas* (Modernist writers) Mário and Oswald de Andrade, the painters Tarsila do Amaral and Anita Malfatti, and the composer Heitor Villa Lobos. These outstanding Brazilian artists clearly influenced her attitude towards literature and arts.

In 1962, she married Paulo Emílio Salles Gomes, a university professor at the University of São Paulo (USP), a film expert and critic of cinema, novel writer and founder of the *Cinemateca Brasileira* (Brazilian Institute of Cinema), which he directed until his death in 1977. In partnership with her husband, Telles wrote the book *Capitu,* a free adaptation of the novel *Dom Casmurro* by Machado de Assis, which was published as late as 1993.

In 1963, her second novel *Verão no Aquário* (1963, Summer in the Aquarium) was published, dealing with the crucial problems within a family, the lack of mutual understanding and the main protagonist as a victim of the degenerative process of a society in crisis. It shows a depressing atmosphere within a decadent family in which the development of the female protagonist has been oppressed since childhood.

In 1964, Telles published two collections of short stories, *História escolhidas* (1964, Selected Stories) and *O jardim selvagem* (1964, The Wild Garden). There followed several new editions: *Antes do Baile Verde* (1970, Before the Green Ball), *Seminário dos Ratos* (1977, Seminar of Rats), *Filhos Pródigos* (1978, Prodigal Sons), and re-editions of collections of short stories. The collection of *Antes do Baile Verde* won her the "Best Foreign Women Writers Grand Prix in Cannes" (France), in 1969, before publication.

In 1973, her third novel *As meninas* (1973, The Girl in the Photograph, translated into English in 1982), was published in São Paulo. This book won many prizes and she became internationally known. Many literary critics consider this novel to be one of her best. It deals with the political and social changes in Brazil in the 1960s, which are presented and questioned by three female student protagonists. Its plot deals much more with the political reality of Brazil than the preceding ones because it was written during the military dictatorship, which lasted from 1964 to 1984.

Three young women, defined as *meninas*, represent three different social classes: Ana Clara, from the working class, has suffered from a series of negative experiences such as drug addiction; Lia, a political activist, dreams of the revolution; the ingenuous Lorena, from a bourgeois family, cannot cope with her inner conflicts. None are able to communicate their problems and none are aware of the things they have in common. They live in a religious boarding school, which in former times was considered a safe place to protect young girls from the risks they face in the big city, especially the risk of meeting young men. But the image of such a school has meanwhile changed: the three girls are rather exposed like all the rest of humanity to fear, politics, sex and drugs. It is a disturbing book in its reflection of the chaotic conditions of human existence in the twentieth century. This novel has been translated into various languages.

In 1977, *Seminário de Ratos* (1977, Seminar of Mice, translated into English as Tigrela and other stories, 1986) was published, another collection of short stories which received the Brazilian Pen Club prize. In the same year she became director of the *Cinemateca Brasileira* in São Paulo, following her late husband. In this function she traveled to Europe, the United States, China and the former USSR. She held this position until 1981.

In 1980, the novel *A Disciplina do Amor* (1980, The Discipline of Love) followed. In 1982 she was elected member of the *Academia Paulista de Letras* (Academy of Letters of São Paulo) and in 1985 she entered the *Academia Brasileira de Letras* (Brazilian Academy of Letters), being only the second woman writer, after Rachel de Queiroz (1977), to occupy this prestigious seat. The Academy has now four female members. Among them is the well-known Brazilian writer, Nélida Piñon, who became President of the Academy in 1995. Several documentaries were made to honor Telles, who had become very famous and popular by this time.

Her novel *As Horas Nuas* (1989, The Naked Hours), translated into French and German soon after the first edition, is composed in a very ironic tone and may be defined by its total disparity between the logical concept of life and real life. *A Noite Escura e Mais Eu* (1995, The Dark Night and I Besides) was another collection of short stories reflecting on death. Her novel *As meninas,* first published in 1973 and reprinted thirty-two times, was also made into a movie with the same title in 1995.

Lygia Fagundes Telles' most recent collection of short stories, *Invenção e memória* (1998, Inventions of Memory), was published by her new editor Rocco in Rio de Janeiro, which acquired the editorial rights of all her work.

In 2000, Lygia Fagundes Telles won the Prêmio Jabuti with her collection of short stories *Invenção de Memória*, which was followed by *Durante aquele estranho chá: perdidos e achados* (2002, During that Strange Tea: Lost and Found) in 2002.

Recently she has been very busy in revising some of her narrative œuvre and reediting it with Rocco. This includes works such as *Ciranda de Pedra* (1954), 31st edition in 1998, *Verão no Aquário* (1963) 11th edition in 1998; *Antes do Baile Verde* (1970), 16th edition in 1999; *As Meninas* (1973), 32nd edition in 1998, and *A Disciplina do Amor* (1980), 9th edition in 1998. She does not believe that an author cannot touch the text after it is published. Nevertheless she insisted on removing her early work from her bibliography. Her belief is that times change so much and the reality from yesterday does not necessarily fit with today's understanding of life.

She is a very productive person, publishing novels, short stories, essays, adapting her books for television, cinema, and theater. Among them there are some for the Brazilian TV channel *Globo*, including the following: *Caso Especial* (Special Case); *O Jardim Selvagem* (1978); telenovela—*Ciranda de Pedra* (1981); *Série Retratos de mulher* (Pictures of Woman) with the short-story "O moço do saxofone", which was adapted by Telles herself under the title "Era uma vez Valdete" (1993).

In 1995, the novel *As meninas* became the script for a movie with the same name, directed by Emiliano Ribeiro. In 1990, her son Goffredo Neto produced the documentary film *Narrarte* about his mother's life and work.

Telles is still an active writer and most interested in making Brazilian literature internationally better known by participating in congresses, debates and seminars. Her short stories are integrated both in national and international anthologies. One important role held by Fagundes Telles is ambassador of the cultural achievements of her country. Her goal is to contribute to a better understanding of Brazilian literature on an international level.

Among the national and international prizes she has won are: Prêmio Afonso Arinos of the Brazilian Academy of Letters, 1949; Prêmio Instituto Nacional do Livro, 1958; Prêmio Jabuti – Câmara Brasileira do Livro, 1965 and 1973; Prêmio Semaine Internationale de la Femme – Cannes, 1969; Prêmio Guimarães Rosa, 1971; Prêmio Pen Clube do Brasil, 1977; Grande Prêmio da Crítica – APCA, 2000; Prêmio Camões, 2005.

Narrative Art and Stylistic Devices

Lygia Fagundes Telles has published various novels and short stories, which are outstanding in their psychological sensitivity and their striving for analytical intelligence and accuracy in the usage of words and metaphors, qualities which helped her to perceive subtle gestures and reactions.

The first remarkable collection of short stories is *Praia Viva* (1944), in which Telles depicts unusual situations of everyday life in a direct stylistic form with short and clear sentences, which was characteristic of the narrative prose of the 1940s and 1950s. The influence of the journalistic language and cinematographic technique coming from the United States can be traced there.

These short stories already present the main topics of Telles' literary work: the inability to communicate between the individual and the world outside, between the visible and the invisible face of reality, the social hypocrisy, and the drama of rejected people who are prisoners of themselves and their loneliness.

Other innovations in her writing are technical devices such as the change of perspective and the polyphony of narrative voices which may be traced in her mature art of writing, which she had accomplished by 1973 in her third novel *As meninas*.

In this novel an obvious change can be noted in portraying the female protagonists in contrast to her earlier fictional works. There is much more self-confidence and authentic behavior to be found in these three female characters even when they are facing major problems. Telles discusses in *As meninas* the most burning problems of our time: the decadence of the social elite, the reduction of individual space in a consumer society, the lack of communication among people at a time of mass media and information, and the addiction to alcohol and sex because of people's lack of perspective.

Her metaphoric language is extremely unusual, experimental and very authentic. In the narrative structure of the novel the author avoids any traditional patterns of narrative technique. Otto Maria Carpeaux, a critic of Brazilian literature, compares Lygia Fagundes Telles to Katherine Mansfield, saying that she is able to create an atmospheric refinement, like Katherine Mansfield, not only in her short stories but extending it also to her novels.

An aging and alcohol-addicted actress and a clairvoyant tomcat, having been reborn various times, are the main protagonists of the novel *Horas Nuas* (1989), who have various lives in common. In this novel the dimension of chronological time is completely dissolved: the perception of the temporal components of the past, present, and future mix in a chaotic continuum without beginning or end. Time has become circular, eternal and repetitive. There is a mixture of various different narrative perspectives and crucial points, which shift all the time. The inner chaotic state of the protagonists is either revealed or sometimes also camouflaged by means of oscillating between authentic being and appearance.

Another characteristic of this novel is the deconstruction of the traditional meaning of logic as a possible link between man and his knowledge of the "truth" of the world in which he lives. This refers mainly to the meaning of life and the comprehension of the invisible behind the visible to which man is exposed.

Horas Nuas has absolutely no message, because in this crazy world there is nothing stable or reliable in the system of traditional values; everything is in process and therefore questionable: love, marriage, family, vocation, professional career, success and many other things. Rosa Ambrósio, an aging actress, and Gregório, the cat, are the main protagonists who move in this fictional universe, displaying their inner life and emotions and transforming themselves in a permanent metamorphosis.

In contrast to her earlier novels, various other female protagonists pervade the text, all of them being absorbed in their proper identity. In them we can recognize their different cultural values and distinguish them in their psychological and ideological profiles.

Telles the art of suspense dominates in her narrative, her style is a mixture of subtlety and strength, a writing that suggests more than it displays and always creates a certain atmosphere emanating from the people and objects, which make cruelty, envy, jealousy and destructive solitude appear in the interstices of the narrative. All of them are negative emotions which afflict the human mind.

From this ability to create atmosphere in her prose writing, Lygia Fagundes Telles succeeds in oscillating between dreamlike imagination and various levels of consciousness, often revealing the mysterious sides of life. The universe of her protagonists is often invaded by metamorphic and fantastic elements entering their minds and bodies, which fascinate the reader.

Telles wants to reveal the crazy side of human existence, certain that words are incapable or insufficient to express the essence of human beings and therefore striving permanently for adequate words because they are the only material a writer can dispose of in her fictional universe.

One of the characteristics of Telles' writing is the social variety from which she chooses her protagonists for her stories: from prostitutes to actresses, upstart crows to miserable and marginalized people, from adolescents to old people. These characters are presented in their own language. Their fictionalized language appears to be colloquial but there is always a subtext containing emotional irony and ambiguous meaning. This approach makes her books very lively and passionate, and this attitude demands a compassionate and alert reader.

In Telles' fiction the ambiguity of meaning may open up a rift in which basic ideas of human experience can be traced: disagreement between obligation and pleasure, desire and object of desire, expectation and consequence, dream and reality, the possible and the impossible, the real and the fantastic. This rift can only be perceived with the imagination opening up to a metaphysical space, and this is exactly the art of Telles' making visible otherwise invisible things. Her narrative is basically a narrative of mental states although she does not ignore historical and social items either.

In many interviews Telles has been asked about the meaning of literature and the main task of an author. Her idea of an author's task in her professional life is to build bridges and heal the lack of communication in the community. What is the social function of a writer? To write for those who want to hear from the author words and opinions they do not dare or cannot express themselves. A writer should be compassionate, encourage people in despair and strengthen the self-confidence of the readers. Her attitude towards the meaning of writing literature is above all a humanist one.

GERHILD REISNER

Selected Works

Short Stories

Praia Viva. São Paulo: Livraria Martins Editora, 1944.
Histórias do Desencontro. Prêmio Instituto Nacional de Livro. Rio de Janeiro: Livraria José Olympio Editora, 1958.
O jardim selvagem. Prêmio Jabuti, da Câmara Brasileira do Livro. São Paulo, 1965.
Antes do baile verde. Prêmio Guimarães Rosa. Rio de Janeiro: Bloch Editores, 1970.
Invencões e memória. Rio de Janeiro: Editora Rocco, 2000.

Novels

Ciranda de pedra. Rio de Janeiro: Edições O Cruzeiro, 1954.
Verão no aquário. São Paulo: Livraria Martins Editora, 1963.
As meninas. Rio de Janeiro: Livraria José Olympio Editora, 1973.
A Disciplina do Amor. Rio de Janeiro: Editora Rocco, 1980.
As horas nuas. Rio de Janeiro: Nova Fronteira, 1989.

Anthologies

Seleta. Ed. Nelly Novaes Coelho. Rio de Janeiro and Brasilia: Livraria José Olympio Editora, 1973.
Os melhores contos de Lygia F. Telles. Seleção e prefácio de Eduardo Portella. Rio de Janeiro and São Paulo: Editora Global, 1984.
Histórias escolhidas. Prêmio Boa Leitura. São Paulo: Livraria Martins Editora, 1964.

Website

Wikipedia, http://pt.wikipedia.org/wiki/Lygia_Fagundes_Telles
Cultura & Arte. www.estado.br

Films

Já não se faz amor como antigamente, directed by John Herbert, 1976.
As meninas, directed by Emiliano Ribeiro, 1976.
Narrarte, directed by Goffredo Neto, 1990.

Television

TV *Globo: Caso Especial* (Special Case) – *O Jardim Selvagem* (1978).
telenovela – Ciranda de Pedra (1981).

References and Further Reading

Angelini, P.R. Escudero. *A Intertextualide em Dois Contos Femininos. CLTL*, 8 (1982): 107–15.
Carrozza, Elsa. *Esse incrível amor.* São Paulo: Hucitec, 1992.
Coelho, Nelly Novaes de. *Dicionário Crítico de Escritoras Brasileiras.* São Paulo: Escrituras, 2002.
——. *A Literatura Feminina no Brasil Contemporâneo.* São Paulo: Editora Siciliana, 1993.
Coutinho, Afrânio and Sousa, J. Galante de. *Enciclopédia de Literatura Brasileira.* São Paulo: Global Editora, Fundação Biblioteca Nacional, Academia Brasileira de Letras, 2001, 2 vols.
De Franceschi, A.F. (ed.). *Cadernos de Literatura*, 5. São Paulo: Instituto Moreira Salles, 1998.
Pinto, Cristina Ferreira. *O Bildungsroman feminino: quatro exemplos brasileiros.* São Paulo: Perspectiva, 1990.
Silva, Vera Maria Tietzmann. *A metamorfose nos contos de Lygia Fagundes Telles.* Rio de Janeiro: Presença Edicões, 1985.
——. *A ficção intertextual de Lygia Fagundes Telles.* Goiânia: Centro editorial e gráfico da Universidade Federal de Goiás, 1992.
Série Retratos de mulher (Pictures of Woman) with the short story "O moço do saxofone", adapted by Fagundes Telles under the title "Era uma vez Valdete" (1993).
Tolman, J.H. *New Fiction: L. F. T. Review*, 30 (1981): 65–70.

TESTIMONIAL LITERATURE

Definition

Testimonial literature crosses traditional boundaries between literature, ethnography, journalism, and historical document. Testimonies from Latin America, or *testimonios*, originate in a first-hand experience of social or political injustice or turmoil from the point of view of those who have lived through the injustice. They are texts that recount an individual's or various individuals' personal contact with events of collective importance, or recount a life experience characterized by a marginalization shared by others. They are therefore explicitly or implicitly collective. Thus, most definitions of the genre clearly distinguish between testimonial writing and autobiography or biography, two genres originating in lives of privileged men who stand out as individuals and whose experience is not necessarily meant to represent others'. Testimonial writing also means raising the reader's consciousness and potentially serves as a tool for political activism. (See Kimberly Nance's *Can Literature Promote Justice?* for one discussion of how well *testimonio* can stimulate political action.) The author hopes to stimulate empathy and change, whether the intended audience is a member of the same group or a privileged reader from Latin America or beyond. Moreover, many testimonial texts work to rewrite dominant nationalist rhetoric, or are used to reconstruct notions of a particular national identity.

Either the author writes her own testimony or, in mediated *testimonios*, tells her story to a journalist, ethnographer, or other writer who edits and transcribes the conversations. Thus, testimonial writing often preserves aspects of oral discourse. The vast majority of the women's *testimonios* based on interviews are transcribed by women. *Testimonio*'s attention to unofficial and suppressed versions of history make this genre particularly relevant to women's writing, although *testimonio* is by no means limited to women authors from the region. At the same time, until recently, women authors have had greater representation among published *testimonios* than they do among published literary works in general.

Because of the many possible variations on *testimonio*'s combination of oral storytelling and writing, its overlap with several genres, and the political or social stakes behind the personal stories, a specific definition of *testimonio* as a genre has created much debate. If one begins to approximate a definition through *testimonio*'s structure, the majority of testimonial literature, by men or women, consists of an individual narrator's story, albeit with the collective implications noted above. Nevertheless, many *testimonios* are compilations of various life stories or interviews gathered by the editor, such as Ana Gutiérrez's collection of *testimonios* by domestic workers in Peru, *Se necesita muchacha* (1983), several books of interviews of Cuban and Central American revolutionary women conducted by Margaret Randall in the 1970s and 1980s, and Elena

Poniatowska's collected *testimonios* by civil rights activists (*Fuerte es el silencio*, 1980) and by earthquake survivors (*Nada, nadie*, 1988, Nothing, Nobody). Poniatowska's *La noche de Tlatelolco* (1971, Massacre in Mexico) creates a collage from fragments of many testimonies, creating a dialogue where there was none.

In the prologues to mediated or edited testimonies, editors and transcribers usually assure their fidelity to the author's manner of expression, including any errors, at the same time the editor organizes the original material for coherence. An interesting exception to this rule is Rosalina Ferreira Basseti's *Testemunha de uma vida* (1987), a working-class woman's life story that the editor left in its original form without punctuation, correction of phonological spellings, or division into chapters. Until more recent *testimonios*, the editor or transcriber typically eliminated his or her questions to create a seamless monologue. More recent *testimonios* do not eliminate those questions or the presence of other people, and sometimes include the interviewer's thoughts as the conversation takes place. Such texts emphasize collaboration and strive for greater transparency regarding any influence the relationship between the two women might have on the finished text. Examples are: Marta Diana's compilation of Argentine women guerrillas' testimonies, and of testimonies by people close to the militants who did not survive, *Mujeres guerrilleras: la militancia de los setenta en el testimonio de sus protagonistas femeninas* (1996); Rosa Isolde Reuque Paillalef's *When a Flower Is Reborn: The Life and Times of a Mapuche Feminist* (2002), published originally in English translation because a publisher could not be found in Chile; and Pilar Valenzuela's *Koshi shinanya ainbo: el testimonio de una mujer shipiba* (2005), a bilingual text in Spanish and Shipiba.

Another variation is the *novela testimonial* that combines lived experience with explicitly fictionalized material based on one or more real people, for example, Poniatowska's well-known story of a rebellious, working-class woman who fought in the Mexican Revolution, *Hasta no verte, Jesús mío* (1969), and Tununa Mercado's intensely psychological account of her exile from Argentina, *En estado de memoria* (1998). It is the structural variation of the *novela testimonial* that points to deeper issues regarding *testimonio*'s definition and purpose. The *novela testimonial* especially complicates testimonial literature's definition regarding authenticity and the narrator's role as truthful witness, which are addressed in the section below on scholarly debate.

History

In the Cuba of the 1960s, testimonial writing naturally found a context in which to flourish, where national history and its actors were reconsidered in light of revolutionary ideals. The Cuban ethnographer Miguel Barnet's *Biografía de un cimarrón* (1966, Biography of a Runaway Slave), based on interviews with a 103-year-old former slave, has become a founding text of the genre. Also, in 1970, Cuba institutionalized the genre with the first Casa de las Américas prize awarded to testimonial literature, *La guerrilla tupamara* (The Tupamaros) by the Uruguayan journalist María Esther Gilio. Important examples of *testimonio* predate the Cuban Revolution, however, and are notably texts by women: *Quarto de Despejo* (1960) from Brazil by Carolina Maria de Jesus, and *Benita* (1940) from Mexico by Benita Galeana.

One can find the roots of testimonial writing in the conquest period. Renato Prada Oropeza has stated that "testimoniar" (to give testimony) was Latin American literature's first mission ("De lo testimonial al testimonio: notas para un deslinde del discurso-testimonio," in Jara and Vidal 1986: 7–21). Prada Oropeza here refers to Latin American literature's origins in the letters, chronicles, diaries, and histories by Spanish, Portuguese, and later Latin American authors, documents that become textual acts of self-legitimation before an authority figure, of witnessing and naming, of relating one's knowledge of a world unknown to the reader, and of America telling its own story from its own perspective. Here one can consider Bernal Díaz del Castillo's revision of Hernán Cortés's conquest of Mexico (1632). Another text to mention is Bartolomé de Las Casas's adoption and adaptation of Columbus's diaries to support Las Casas's attack on Spanish abuse of the indigenous populations, the version of Columbus's diaries now commonly read. Just as these texts seek authority through the weight of an authentic eye witness, so does Carrió de Vandera through the possibly fictitious indigenous persona of Calixto Bustamante who narrates his *Lazarillo de ciego caminantes* (1773), and so does Miguel Hernández through the voice of the gaucho in *Martín Fierro* (1872, 1879).

These precursors differ, however, from what is now defined as testimonial discourse in that the authors enjoyed a certain privileged social status or adopted the voice or interests of those outside that status to legitimate their own authority. Testimonial precursors by women are thus particularly interesting because even those women privileged enough to have access to the written word shared marginalized status. The writings and confessions of nuns are the most numerous women's texts from the colonial period and are also relevant to *testimonio*'s key concerns. In "*Si me permiten hablar*: la lucha por el poder interpretativo" (in Beverley and Achugar 1992: 109–16), Jean Franco has pointed out the requirement that nuns write their confessions arose from the patriarchy's dependence on women's (and indigenous populations') participation in its ideology. Women's voices were necessary to further legitimate the structures of power. Sor Juana Inés de la Cruz's autobiographical *Respuesta a Sor Filotea* shows how these texts could be negotiated to use the master's weapons against him, questioning the patriarchal ideology that authorized the text itself, a gesture akin to testimonial literature's subversion of officially sanctioned truths. Jumping forward to the 19th century, Juana Manuela Gorriti's writings about her life and others' in the Argentina, Bolivia, and Peru marked by civil and international wars are also worth noting here. Personal accounts of the Mexican Revolution comprise another testimonial precursor. Herlinda Barrientos and María Dolores Cárdenas's experiences riding with Zapata and Villa included in *Con Zapata y Villa: tres relatos testimoniales* (1991) and Nellie Campobello's vignettes of her childhood experiences of the Revolution in *Cartucho* (1931) are examples.

Yet something else distinguishes these precursors from *testimonio* beginning with *Benita* and *Quarto de Despejo*, continuing through the explosion of testimonial writing in the 1960s and beyond. Many testimonial authors are women not heard before: poor, black or indigenous, and in the case of Benita

Galeana, newly literate. In addition, in the narrative a collective consciousness against the system responsible for the denounced injustices coexists with evidence of the author's extraordinary characteristics as an individual. *Testimonio* emphasizes an experience relevant to collective identity with the objective of creating change or raising consciousness. For this reason, after the explosion in testimonial writing in the 1960s propelled by the Cuban Revolution and political movements of the era, Central American civil conflicts, US intervention, and Southern Cone dictatorships of the 1970s and 1980s motivated the production of another important wave of *testimonio*. Members of indigenous communities have been among the authors of this wave from the beginning since certain regimes have specially targeted them. The political urgency of these contexts often altered the intended audience for texts by survivors of repression; these texts often sought international awareness and solidarity and were often written in exile. This is how Latin American testimonial literature came to have a growing readership in the US and why some *testimonios* were originally published in English, such as Alicia Partnoy's well-known *The Little School* (1986) or Emma Sepúlveda's collection of testimonies by Chilean *arpilleristas*, *We Chile* (1996). This wave also strengthened the collective nature of the narratives since many authors have expressed their desire to speak for those who did not survive.

Example Texts

Two important, early *testimonios* are Benita Galeana's *Benita* (1940) and Carolina Maria de Jesus's *Quarto de Despejo* (1960). Galeana was a militant activist in the Mexican Communist Party who, as she tells it, became involved through her husband's militancy. She learned to read and write as an adult and criticized the Communist Party for leaving her illiterate. Her testimony gathers moments from her childhood during the Mexican Revolution (though she barely addresses the Revolution directly), domestic violence, the birth of her daughter, her difficult journey to Mexico City, her economic survival and relationships with two quite different men, and her militancy and experiences in jail. One characteristic of Galeana's narrative is the contrast between moments of naiveté and biting critique of authority's hypocrisy, between loyalty to and criticism of the Communist Party, between humor and serious desperation, and between vulnerability and fierce independence. Carolina Maria de Jesus was a black slum dweller on the outskirts of São Paulo. She benefited enough from her book's instant success that she bought a house outside the *favela*, though she later fell on hard times and her popularity sank with that of populism after the rise of dictatorship in 1964. Jesus's testimony, as originally published, consists of diary entries selected by a journalist who happened upon her while investigating another story and found out she had been keeping a diary for years. Her book was described as a "diary-report" and it indeed interweaves an insider's perspective and poetic description of life in the "junk room" (*quarto de despejo*) with which she compares the slum, and a report on her neighbors' doings that distances herself from them, in part as defense from their complaints against her.

Domitila Barrios de Chungara's *Si me permiten hablar* (1978), as told to and edited by the Brazilian sociologist Moema Viezzer, and Rigoberta Menchú's *Me llamo Rigoberta Menchú y así me nació la conciencia* (1983), as told to and edited by the Venezuelan anthropologist Elisabeth Burgos-Debray, are probably the best-known women's *testimonios* from Latin America. Both Barrios de Chungara and Menchú are indigenous (Aymara and Quiché Mayan respectively), both emphasize from the first pages that their stories are not just personal but collective, both describe the alienating effect mainstream education in Spanish can have on indigenous communities, and both describe strong relationships with their fathers who were activists and supported their education. Barrios de Chungara was a mine worker's wife at the Siglo XX and organized a committee of the workers' wives. She spent a brutal period in prison for her activism. The testimony is striking for the details about working-class conditions in Bolivia and for the intersections between class and gender issues, such as when she explains women's work to activist *compañeros* or the famous scene at the International Women's Conference in Mexico where she in no uncertain terms identifies the limits of sisterhood across class divisions. Barrios de Chungara stresses that her story is for the working class, not just intellectuals. Menchú's testimony resists easy consumption by intellectuals in a different fashion, through her references to what she cannot tell to an audience of readers from outside her Mayan community. Secrets empower her community and Menchú as narrator, even as she shares many insights into Quiché customs, conditions, and survival strategies. Menchú told her story in exile from the genocide against Mayan communities in Guatemala, which she fled after becoming active in the Committee for Peasant Unity and losing parents and siblings in horrifyingly cruel circumstances.

More recent examples of *testimonios* are Yolanda Colom's account of her time as a guerrilla in Guatemala in *Mujeres en la alborada* (1998) and María de los Reyes Castillo Bueno's *Reyita, sencillamente: testimonio de una negra cubana nonagenaria* (1997) as told to and transcribed by her daughter Daisy.

Scholarly Debate

Just as testimonial writing crosses the boundaries of genre, so does scholarship on testimonial texts. Since mediated testimonial writing overlaps with ethnographic practice, post-structuralist anthropologists' self-reflection on field work and the production of life stories offer relevant perspectives on testimonial literature. (See for instance James Clifford and George Marcus's edited volume *Writing Culture: The Poetics and Politics of Ethnography*, 1986, and also Gluck and Patai 1991.) Also, studies of Holocaust survivors' memories provide a useful perspective on narratives of trauma, especially for testimonies of dictatorships in Southern Cone countries with sizeable populations descended from Jewish immigrants or refugees. (See for instance Shoshana Felman and Dori Laub's *Testimony: Crises of Witnessing in Literature, Psychoanalysis, and History*, 1992.) Most work on Latin American *testimonio* emerges from literary and cultural studies. In those areas there are book-length studies on *testimonio*, but most scholarly work has been in the form of essays, leading to substantive collections of articles on testimonial writing. (See Arias 2003; Beverley and Achugar 1992; Gugelberger 1996; Gugelberger and Kearney 1991; and Jara and Vidal 1986.)

The most heated academic discussions have centered on *testimonio*'s veracity and narrative authority: how to communicate the truth of an experience presented as radically different from most readers' lives, how to verify the testimony's accuracy, and what and who determines the legitimacy of the speaker and of how she tells her story. Testimony's verisimilitude authorizes its existence as an accusation or as evidence of obscured injustices. At the same time, it is a form of writing that reflects the same narrative choices that other authors make, and are authorized to make. On the one hand, transparent truth takes on ethical importance when official discourse negates the truth of exploitation or political repression. "Lying" would be betrayal. On the other hand, denying the testimonial author who is marginalized the authority to tell her story the way that best negotiates her situation risks repeating the silencing *testimonio* means to rectify.

Thus, early scholarship on *testimonio* often emphasized its resistance to fiction, while work since the mid-1990s has grappled more with the author's autonomy over her own story and the written medium's effects. In one of the first book-length studies of the genre, *Testimonio hispanoamericano*, Elzbieta Sklodowska uses the two broad categories of mediated testimonies and their "pre-texts," which include unmediated testimonies. Sklodowska's scheme emphasizes mediation as the organizing factor, since that mediation and the editing involved constitute a source of contention over truth and the *testimonio*'s validity as a means toward political change. Sklodowska begins with a series of binary oppositions whose limitations she recognizes, but whose terminology she finds hard to avoid as a preliminary approximation since they reflect "formaciones discursivas ya consagradas": *lo ficticio–lo factual*; *literariedad–no literariedad*; *fabulación–relación*; *ambiguación–desambiguación*". Therefore, based on these binary opposites, for some critics keeping *testimonio* and literature separate protects literature from contamination by inferior style, political propaganda, and temporary fads. For others, the aesthetic concerns associated with literature seem inappropriate to mix with the urgency of authorizing the reality and truth of marginalized accounts denied by official history. Early on, John Beverley viewed the *testimonio* as threatening or questioning bourgeois literary discourse in a productive manner that created both a representation of and a means to subaltern resistance and struggle. According to Beverley, *testimonio*'s importance lay in its alternative status, its separation from literature, although the later work of this critic who has written extensively on testimonial literature has reflected recent trends that reconsider this strict separation.

While fact and fiction's opposition were a starting point for discussion of *testimonio*, not all early scholarship viewed *testimonio* and literature as opposites. Hugo Achugar distinguishes literature from fiction by defining literature as an "elaboración ideológico-formal," which would certainly include mediated *testimonio* ("Historias paralelas/historias ejemplares: La historia y la voz del otro," in Beverley and Achugar 1992: 49–71). Achugar therefore calls *testimonio* literature because *testimonio*'s documentary aspirations resist fiction. More recently, Sklodowska has characterized testimonial texts as a "peculiar mixture of experience, creation, manipulation and invention, more akin, perhaps, to a novel, than to a scientific document" ("The Poetics of Remembering, the Politics of Forgetting: Rereading *I, Rigoberta Menchú*," in Arias 2001: 256). Claudia Ferman notes testimonial discourse's value as a framework for literature: "reading and analyzing *testimonio* deconstructs the literary tradition as the canon knows it and exposes the social fabric on which its circulation and reproduction relies" ("Textual Truth, Historical Truth, and Media Truth: Everybody Speaks about the Menchús," in Arias 2001: 162).

These quotations by Sklodowska and Ferman come from their comments on the controversy surrounding Rigoberta Menchú's 1983 testimony after the US anthropologist David Stoll published a book in late 1998 that questioned some facts of Menchú's life story as she told it, though not the reality of genocide against the Mayans. Menchú stood by the integrity of her story as she experienced it and interpreted it in 1983, reiterating what is stated in the first pages of her book: the testimony is not just hers but many people's. The flurry of critical attention in the US came in part from Menchú's status as Nobel Peace Prize laureate but also showed the importance *testimonio* had gained in academic circles of various fields and how invested US readers had become in real-life stories, whether those stories supported or questioned readers' opinions on culture and politics. While some scholars reproached Menchú's apparent misrepresentation, others defended her right to tell the truth as she sees it rather than as others see it. (See Arias 2001 for details of the debate and an array of arguments. See also Bueno's 1999 essay for observations on US reception of *testimonio*, including Menchú's.) Sklodowska's and Ferman's comments are examples of how the Menchú controversy intensified developing scholarly interest in the literariness and art of *testimonio* as natural outcomes of its narrative process. The turn to *testimonio*'s process explains the choice to include the interviewer's presence in the texts mentioned earlier by Diana, Reuque Paillalef, and Valenzuela. The controversy also highlighted the inherently contradictory position of many testimonial narrators who simultaneously represent many voices and experience unique circumstances that enable them to publish their stories.

Women's Testimonial Writing and a Feminist Perspective

Authority and narrative autonomy, alternate versions of history, and speaking collectively are familiar topics to those who work on feminist theory. Yet, relatively few critics have focused the issues explained above on specifically women's writing or have used a feminist perspective, even though *testimonios* by women have been studied in the broader discussion of *testimonio*. Women's testimonies lend authority and agency to the female transcriber and reader since they portray women as protagonists of history, a significant rationale in itself for expanding feminist readings to the genre. As is the case with *testimonio* in general, most scholarship on women's *testimonio* exists in the form of essays. Doris Sommer's essays on Rigoberta Menchú's plural narrative voice and on Jesusa Palancares's narrative resistance to easy appropriation in *Hasta no verte, Jesús mío* have made important contributions to a feminist perspective on *testimonio*. Three early essays on specifically women's *testimonio* are in Gugelberger and Kearney's 1991 edited volume. Two books, one edited by Emma Sepúlveda and Joy Logan (1995), and one by Joanna Bartow, have focused on women's testimonial writing.

The stigma of bourgeois feminism as a privilege divorced from the urgent realities recounted in testimonies, like the resistance to reading *testimonio* through a literary lens, may account in part for relatively little work in this area. Reading *testimonio* with feminist issues in mind can, however, provide a response to US and European feminist theories' history of homogenizing women's experience, a history more difficult to carry out when confronted with Latin America's poverty, racial politics, political instability, and regional variations. Latin American feminism, moreover, has from early on been divided along class lines between grassroots *movimientos de mujeres* and middle and upper-class feminism. From an anthropological perspective, Daphne Patai also replies negatively to the title of her own article, "U.S. Academics and Third World Women: is Ethical Research Possible?" (in Gluck and Patai 1991: 137–53). Sepúlveda notes international solidarity among feminists as important to *testimonio* while recognizing its problems, and that *testimonio* is important for the study of the relationship between first and third-world discourses. While these critics focus on the relationship between First World and Third World, an external dynamic fundamental to *testimonio*'s purposes, similar internal tensions exist within Latin America when speaking across divisions of privilege. The international division of labor becomes a local division within Latin America.

Alternatively, homogenization of women's experience finds its parallel in the danger of homogenizing other groups represented in testimonial texts and packaging their identities for readers' consumption. Thus feminist work on questions of self-representation in relation to accepted boundaries of identity contributes to debates on testimonial literature. Questions of authenticity and truth become particularly complicated when the author's self-representation must constantly shift between representativity and uniqueness, between anticipated reader expectations and the author's own perceptions. (See Shaw 1996 and Bartow for further discussion of this issue.) Theory on *testimonio* and the circumstances that testimonial narrators must negotiate do not necessarily make the leap from questioning genre boundaries to questioning some gender boundaries.

Despite the complexity of women's alliances across cultures, races, and social class, collective womanhood also occasionally appears acknowledged by the informants. Patai, outspokenly critical of a naive, utopian feminist ethnography, notes that most of the women she interviewed in Brazil recognized "some sort of bond with other women," including potential readers, despite differences (*Brazilian Women Speak,* 4). The language of several women's testimonies indeed stresses the "we" over the "I," as Sommer discusses throughout "'Not Just a Personal Story.'" In that essay, Sommer distinguishes the "impersonal" collective "I" from autobiography's conflation of history and extraordinary figures. She also uses the ideas of metaphor and metonymy to contrast the two, whereby in *testimonio* the relationships women constantly identify underlie the narrative they use to describe themselves in the singular, a move that Bartow points out is relevant to characteristics of *women's* autobiography. Similarly, Sepúlveda sees *testimonio* as crossing boundaries of genre that question autobiography's construction of a "rational, privileged, and masculine entity" as the only valued identity (Sepúlveda and Logan 1995: 12). For her it is the collective emphasis especially seen in women's testimonial writing that separates *testimonio* from autobiography.

JOANNA R. BARTOW

References and Further Reading

Barrientos, Herlinda, Cárdenas, María Dolores and Cedillo Guillermo González. *Con Zapata y Villa: tres relatos testimoniales*. Mexico: Instituto Nacional de Estudios Históricos, 1991.

Burgos, Elizabeth. *Me llamo Rigoberta Menchú y así me nació la conciencia*. La Habana: Casa de las Américas, 1983. *I... Rigoberta Menchú: An Indian Woman in Guatemala*. Trans. Ann Wright. London: Verso, 1984.

Campobello, Nellie. *Cartucho; relatos de la lucha en el norte de Mexico.* Mexico: Ediciones Integrales, 1931. *Cartucho; and My Mother's Hands*. Trans. Doris Meyer and Irene Matthews. Intro. Elena Poniatowska. Austin, TX: University of Texas Press, 1988.

Colom, Yolanda. *Mujeres en la alborada*. Guatemala City: Artemis y Edinter, 1998.

Diana, Marta. *Mujeres guerrilleras: la militancia de los setenta en el testimonio de sus protagonistas femeninas*. Buenos Aires: Planeta, 1996.

Galeana, Benita. *Benita*. Mexico: Editorial Extemporaneos, 1974. *Benita*. Trans. Amy Diane Prince. Pittsburgh, PA: Latin American Literary Review Press, 1994.

Jesus, Carolina Maria de. *Quarto de Despejo: Diário de uma Favelada*. Ed. Audálio Dantas. Rio de Janeiro: Paulo de Azevedo, 1963. *The Unedited Diaries of Carolina Maria de Jesus*. Eds. Robert M. Levine and José Carlos Sebe Bom Meihy. Trans. Nancy P. S. Naro and Cristina Mehrtens. New Brunswick, NJ: Rutgers University Press, 1999.

Menchú, Rigoberta. *Rigoberta: la nieta de los mayas*. In collaboration with Dante Liano and Gianni Minà. Mexico: Aguilar, 1998.

Mercado, Tununa. *En estado de memoria. In a State of Memory*. Trans. Peter Kahn. Lincoln, NB: University of Nebraska Press, 2001.

Patai, Daphne. *Brazilian Women Speak: Contemporary Life Stories*. New Brunswick, NJ: Rutgers University Press, 1988.

Poniatowska, Elena. *Hasta no verte, Jesús mío*. México, D.F.: Era, 1969. *Here's To You, Jesusa!* Trans. Deanna Heikkinen. New York: Farrar, Straus and Giroux, 2001.

Reuque Paillalef, Rosa Isolde. *When a Flower Is Reborn: The Life and Times of a Mapuche Feminist*. Ed. Florencia E. Mallon. Durham, NC: Duke University Press, 2002.

Rubiera Castillo, Daisy. *Reyita, sencillamente: testimonio de una negra cubana nonagenaria*. Havana: Instituto Cubano del Libro, 1997. *Reyita*. Trans. Anne McLean. Durham, NC: Duke University Press, 2000.

Viezzer, Moema. *Si me permiten hablar*. Mexico: Siglo XXI, 1978. *Let Me Speak!* Trans. Victoria Ortiz. Monthly Review Press, 1979.

References

Arias, Arturo (ed.) *The Rigoberta Menchú Controversy*. With a response by David Stoll. Minneapolis, MN: University of Minnesota Press, 2001.

Bartow, Joanna R. *Subject to Change: The Lessons of Latin American Women's Testimonio for Truth, Fiction, and Theory*. Chapel Hill, NC: University of North Carolina Press, 1999.

Beverley, John and Achugar, Hugo (eds) *La voz del otro: testimonio, subalternidad y verdad narrativa*. Pittsburgh, PA: Latinoamericana Editores, 1992.

Bueno, Eva Paulino. "Carolina Maria de Jesus in the Context of Testimonios: Race, Sexuality, and Exclusion". *Criticism* 41(2) (Spring 1999): 257–84.

Gluck, Sherna Berger and Patai, Daphne (eds) *Women's Words: The Feminist Practice of Oral History*. New York: Routledge, 1991.

Gugelberger, Georg M. *The Real Thing: Testimonial Discourse and Latin America*. Durham, NC: Duke University Press, 1996.

Gugelberger, Georg M. and Kearney, Michael. *Voices of the Voiceless in Testimonial Literature, Part I*. Special issue of *Latin American Perspectives* 18(3) (Summer 1991).

Jara, René and Vidal, Hernán (eds) *Testimonio y literatura*. Minneapolis, MN: Institute for the Study of Ideologies and Literature, 1986.

Levine, Robert M. and Meihy, José Carlos Sebe Bom. *The Life and Death of Carolina Maria de Jesus*. Albuquerque, NM: University of New Mexico Press, 1995.

Nance, Kimberly. *Can Literature Promote Justice?: Trauma Narrative and Social Action in Latin American Testimonio*. Nashville, TN: Vanderbilt University Press, 2006.

Sepúlveda, Emma and Logan, Joy (eds) *El testimonio femenino como escritura contestataria*. Santiago de Chile: Asteriön, 1995.

Shaw, Deborah. "Jesusa Palancares as Individual Subject in Elena Poniatowska's *Hasta no verte, Jesús mío*". *Bulletin of Hispanic Studies* 73 (1996): 191–204.

Sklodowska, Elzbieta. *Testimonio hispanoamericano: historia, teoría, práctica*. New York: Peter Lang, 1992.

Sommer, Doris. "'Not Just a Personal Story': Women's *Testimonios* and the Plural Self". In Bella Brodzki and Celeste Schenck (eds), *Life/Lines: Theorizing Women's Autobiography*. Ithaca, NY: Cornell University Press, 1988, pp. 107–30.

——. "Taking a Life: Hot Pursuit and Cold Rewards in a Mexican Testimonial Novel". *Signs* 20(4) (1995): 913–40. Revised in "Hot Pursuits and Cold Rewards of Mexicanness," *Proceed with Caution, When Engaged by Minority Writing in the Americas*. Boston, MA: Harvard University Press, 1999, pp. 138–59.

TOLEDO, AIDA

Aida Toledo is a poet, narrator, and writer currently teaching at the University of Alabama, but she was born in Guatemala in 1952. Her creative work is marked by a tone of great intimate sensuality that combines a stimulating and provocative feminist perspective, allowing her to excel as one of the most personal voices in Central American lyrical production. Trained as an educator, she has taught in school and university settings. In the 1980s her work with deaf-mute children was noteworthy, and it was then that she completed her degree at the University of San Carlos, with a thesis on Guatemalan writer Ricardo Estrada. At the university she taught classes on theory, essay, and poetry in the Literature Department.

She became known as a poet in 1990 with her book *Brutal batalla de silencios* (Brutal Battle of Silences) which would be followed by her 1994 work, *Realidad más extraña que el sueño* (Reality Stranger Than Dream), winner of the September 15th Central American Permanent Contest. *Realidad* ... is a three part volume in which classical themes are reworked with deep poetic irony. The poem "Pudiste haber sido normal" (You Could Have Been Normal) that appears in the first part of the collection recreates the experience of her reading in an autobiographical tone and mentions the influence of what she read on her education as a poet. There is an omnipresent rejection of submission to the guidelines of a traditional society that represses women. Gustavo Adolfo Bécquer, Rubén Darío, Pablo Neruda and Sor Juana stimulate her creative imagery, removing her from domestic conformity. In "Qué será de mí?" (What Will Become of Me?) she reflects on her identity and the place her reality occupies. She evokes the instance of death with a feeling of curiosity that confronts the afterlife and interpellates gods and beings of eternal power. In the first part of the book there is a poem "Bondades de la cibernética" (The Kindness of Cybernetics) which will later become the name of a collection of poems she wrote along with another writer. This poem reflects upon the creator's space in the light of her own ego as an everyday woman defined by social customs. Her homage to classical universal themes is noteworthy, mainly in the second and third parts of her collection, entitled "Minotaura" (Minotauress) and "El Tejido" (The Weaving). In "Minotaura," she is impregnated by Theseus and the Minotaur, while in "El Tejido" it is Penelope who helps her celebrate the feminine talent for resistance. At this point, her poem "Condecoración a Penélope" (Decorating Penelope) reclaims the invention of weaving as a device to establish a poetics of individuality. The poem "Penélope actualizada" (Penelope Actualized) refers to this idea, indicating that a modern-day Penelope is capable of inventing new ruses. The theme of woman as defender of her own space and identity is elaborated in this poet's perspective.

"Cuando Pittsburgh no cesa de ser Pittsburgh" (When Pittsburgh Doesn't Stop Being Pittsburgh) appeared in 1997 and was a key collection in Aída Toledo's work, since it contains a new focus on her life experience. Her career took an intellectual turn when she decided to pursue her Master's and Doctoral degrees in Pittsburgh and to develop her essayistic academic career. At the same time, her poems matured, integrating the new experiences of solitude and mainly her sensation of rootlessness, connected to a deep nostalgia. The first part of her collection, "Una noche de nieve más larga que mi infancia" (A Snowy Night Longer Than My Childhood) evokes the past days of childhood, calling on and recalling her family members as poetic characters that contrast with the winter cold of the US city. The theme of the double also appears in the work through her finding of a same being that forms part of her present and past. Aída plays with being a child and being an adult, while also evoking the childhood of her own daughter at a distance. Life in the US is initially a place of hardship in which her poetic monologues build up the place of her daughter's absent childhood. The second part of the book, "Más allá del espejo" (Beyond the Mirror) focuses on Aída, who views herself in an existential aspect that plays with a gaze directed at her own body. In the last part of the book, "Estúpida la inmovilidad de las nubes" (Stupid the Stillness of Clouds), the space of the present becomes even more unrecognizable. For the poet, the snow represents a dialogue with her new academic intellectual reality in which she had decided to plunge into, one which her poetic ego resists in a certain way. The loss of the juvenile and intuitive ego and the birth of an intellectualized and rationalist parallel identity established in literary experience becomes the crux of maturity in this poet's work.

The 1998 book, *Bondades de la cibernética / The Kindness of Cybernetics* appeared in a Spanish and English edition, a shared project with the researcher Janet Gold. The work has two parts and containts two collections of poems, one from the veteran Aída Toledo one debuting Janet Gold's work. In the second part of the book is Aida's anthology, entitled "Ella/La Misma" (She/The Same), a collection of works from her earlier three books. Her latest poetry collection of 2003, titled "Con la lengua pegada al paladar" (With Tongue Cleft to Palate), she won the Quetzaltenango Hispanic-American Floral Games

Competition and continues to work on her poetry with an intimate feminist voice of great charisma.

Toledo was also established as a short-story writer when her collection of short stories "Pezóculos" (an invented word that combines the words pezón, "nipple", and monóculos, "monocles") appeared in 2001. Its suggestive title indicates a subversive vision that questions canonical formulas of traditional definition. First come fourteen short stories in which female characters are set as the main protagonists. The role of women and the social pressures which confront the feminine condition persist in these stories, steeped in an intense tone of bitterness and impotence that gestures of resistance try to make up for. At the end of the book is the final part, from which the book's title comes, and which contains ten individual texts where poetic prose predominates. This prose reflects on identity and the act of writing. In Toledo's creative vision, there is a concern for the space of the unspeakable. She realizes the limitations of texts when she cannot manage to say fully what she feels. This concern is also tied to the lived time in which things remain to be said, in which feelings mix with memory. These philosophical and existential reflections are tied to her academic background, in which her literary essays on Miguel Ángel Asturias and Guatemalan literature are noteworthy. She is also known for her role as an editor, anthologist, and promoter of young Latin American writers.

ANA MERINO, TRANS. DEREK PETREY

Selected Works

Poetry

Brutal batalla de silencios. Guatemala: Ministry of Culture Publisher, 1990.

Realidad más extraña que el sueño. Guatemala: Ministry of Culture Publisher, 1994.

Cuando Pittsburgh no cesa de ser Pittsburgh. Guatemala: Del Pensamiento Publisher, 1997.

Bondades de la cibernética/Kindness of Cybernetics, bilingual edition. Guatemala: Landívar University-Colloquia-El Cadejo Publisher, 1998.

Por los bordes, bilingual edition (Spanish-Kekchí). Guatemala: Fondo de Cultura Económica-Helvetas-Comunidad de Escritores, 2003.

Con la lengua pegada al paladar. Guatemala: Centro Cultural de España-Ediciones del Cadejo, 2006.

Poetry Selection. Guatemala City: El Cadejo Ediciones, 2006. Sound Recording: Poetry CD-ROM.

Stories

Dis-cuentos. (Dis-counts / Dis-stories) Anthology of Short Stories. Guatemala: Facultad de Humanidades, 1988.

Pezóculos. Guatemala: Palo de Hormigo Publisher, 2001.

TORRES, ANA TERESA

Life and Literary Formation

Ana Teresa Torres (b. 1945) was born in and raised in the urban center of Caracas. After completing a traditional middle-class elementary and secondary education, she went on to university studies in psychology at the Universidad Católica Andrés Bello, and took a graduate degree in Clinical Psychology. For several years she continued her career in the field of mental health, working for the Venezuelan Ministry of Health, doing clinical research and becoming officially certified as a psychoanalyst by the government.

From 1970 to 1993, she pursued dual interests in psychology and literature. During this time, Torres saw patients as part of a private practice in psychotherapy. She also worked with new mothers and children in the Maternidad Concepción Palacios (Maternity and Conception Palace) and the National Institute of Children's Psychology.

In 1989, Torres left her work with the government and together with a group of colleagues, founded the Sociedad Psicoanalítica de Caracas (Psychoanalytical Society of Caracas). She continues to this day as the director of its editorial foundation, *Trópicos*. She has served as an instructor of psychology at the UCAB and other universities.

During her time as a working psychoanalyst, Torres was always interested in the production of literature as well. Her first short story "Los quehaceres de la tarde" (Afternoon Chores) appeared in 1973, and won a special mention in a short story contest offered by the newspaper *El Nacional*. In 1984, Torres won this annual short story contest with the story "Retrato frente al mar" (Portrait by the Sea).

Torres' first novel, *El exilio del tiempo* (Time's Exile) appeared in 1990, winning multiple local, regional and national awards. Torres then followed the success of the book with five more novels, including a very popular recent police procedural/ mystery *El corazón del otro* (Someone Else's Heart) published in 2005.

Torres is extremely active in the literary community both in and outside of Venezuela. She is a frequent judge of literary competitions, both for short narrative, novels and movie scripts, she participates as an invited speaker at universities in Venezuela, the US and Europe and was the recipient, with Yolanda Pantin, of a Rockefeller Foundation Grant to write a critical anthology of women writers in Venezuela.

Work

Torres has written both novels and short stories, but has described herself as more comfortable with the longer form. She has repeatedly expressed the need for the length of a novel. Torres has described in interviews her preference for the space, time, depth and extra dimensions a novel provides which allow her to completely describe the universe she has created.

Torres' novels vary in theme from historical, to erotic, to mysteries. She tells interviewers that she constantly seeks change as an intellectual exercise. Until the very recent success of the thriller *Someone Else's Heart*, Torres' most famous work was the historical novel *Doña Inés contra el olvido*, which tells the story of the dispute over ownership of a piece of land in the late 1700s and early 1800s in Venezuela, through the perspective of the titular Doña Inés. In the narrative, Doña Inés recounts how she is taken to court over land rights by her late husband's child, a former slave, and therefore a mulatto. Even after the widow dies, her ghost continues the tale interwoven with historical events through the twentieth century. The narrative therefore, spans three centuries, as Inés, from her perspective as a colonial criolla, comments on the span of Venezuelan history. Inés narrates the transition from dictatorship to democracy, the days of slavery to the modern-day Venezuelan ethnicity of "café con leche". The novel is therefore sweeping in scope and filled with detail. The narration is directed from the voice of Doña Inés to a series of interlocutors (both living and dead) through history within the novel.

Torres' interest in fictionalizing both the past, and the particular condition of women through time was evident in her first two works, *El exilio del tiempo* and *Doña Inés* which both examined the past through the lens of colonial family dynamics and personal histories. Her third novel *Vagas desapariciones* (Vague Disappearances) also looks at the past, but through the lens of a modern psychiatric office. In a departure from previous novels, the narration centers on a series of patients, both men and women, as they pass through the office, rather than the experiences of a single narrator or even one family. This allows Torres to explore other socio-cultural strata, rather than just the privileged classes shown in her earlier works. What the third novel has in common with the others, however, is the large cast of characters. Like *Doña Inés,* the reader is introduced to dozens of players and a wide social spectrum, each with a distinct past.

Indeed, one of the distinctive elements of each of Torres' novels is the depth of detail and width of scope of the narration. In Torres' fourth work *Malena de cinco mundos* (Malena in Five Worlds), the protagonist is reincarnated five times in five different time periods, each inhabited by a new cast of characters. In her fifth novel *Los últimos espectadores del acorazado Potemkin* (The Last Spectatators of the Ironclad *Potemkin*), Torres uses multiple levels of narration and perspective to provide depth and detail. In the erotic novel *La favorita del señor* (The Lord's favorite), it is the detailed experiences of a young girl growing up in a harem that provide the sensual and interior complexity for the reader.

Criticism

Torres' work has been both critically well received and popular with the general public in Venezuela and abroad. Her latest novel, a police procedural, has in particular been a best seller and very popular in Venezuela.

Much criticism has focused on the highly regarded novel *Doña Inés contra el olvido*. Critics such as Elizabeth Montes note the power of orality in the work, as the nearly illiterate protagonist seeks to reinsert her story into the dominant, male, written discourse of the nation. Critics see the protagonist of the novel as a combatant on the front lines, seeking to fight for the place of marginalized and forgotten groups in the history of Latin America. As such she has been seen as a figure of power and resistance, representative of more than just women, but also native groups, ethnic minorities and others. The tension in the novel between the slave-owning Inés and her antagonist, the mulatto child of her husband and a slave, has been shown to highlight both the inequality of power relationships in the span of Latin American history, and the marginality of both groups within the nation's story. The construction of history, and the powers who control the main discourses of history are seen to be the recurrent and most important themes in all of Torres' work.

Critics like Julio Ortega also note the tendency of Torres to delve deeply into the internal life of all of her characters. Usually attributing this tendency to her dual professions as psychoanalyst and author, critics note Torres' fascination with the primal energies of emotion as motivators for her characters. Indeed, some critics, in particular those outside Venezuela, like A. Jack Shreve, have found the truest value in the detail in Torres' work and in her finely drawn characters.

Much attention has also been paid by Luz Marina Rivas and others to the self-referential nature of the narration and structure of Torres' work. From the metafictional narrations, to the extended meditations on the place of literature in history, most of the novels by Torres concern the nature of writing itself. Again, to many critics, this self-awareness is attributable to Torres' training in the field of psychology.

ELIZABETH GACKSTETTER NICHOLS

Selected Works

"Los quehaceres de la tarde". *El Nacional.* 19 August, 1973.
"Al paso ni a Colombia". *Extramuros.* October, 1974.
"Retrato frente al mar". *El Nacional.* 3 August 1984.
"El vestido santo". *Imagen* 100–196 (1993).
Cuentos Completos. Mérida: Ediciones El otro, el mismo, 2002.

Novels

El exilio del tiempo. Caracas: Monte Avila, 1990.
Doña Inés contra el olvido. Caracas: Monte Avila, 1992.
Doña Inés versus Oblivion. Baton Rouge, LA: Louisiana State University Press, 2000.
Vagas desapariciones. Caracas: Grijalbo, 1995.
Malena de cinco mundos. Washington, DC: Literal Books, 1997.
Los últimos espectadores del acorazado Potemkin. Caracas: Monte Avila, 1999.
La favorita del señor. Caracas: Editorial Blanca Pantin, 2001.
El corazón del otro. Caracas: Alfadil Ediciones, 2005.

Literary Criticism

El hilo de la voz: Antología crítica de escritoras venezolanas del siglo xx. (with Yolanda Pantin) Caracas: Fundación Polar, 2003.

References and Further Reading

Acosta-Lugo, Maribel. "Oblivion and Power in Julia Alvarez, Cristina Garcia, Ana Teresa Torres, and Ana Lydia Vega." Diss. University of Conneticut, 2004.

Barra, Nathalie. "La mujer hispanoamericana hacia el nuevo milenio". In *La nueva mujer en la escritura de autoras hispánicas.* Montevideo: Instituto Literario y Cultural Hispánico. Colección Estudios Hispánicos. Vol. IV, pp. 27–39.

——. "La postmodernidad literaria venezolana: *El exilio de tiempo* de Ana Teresa Torres" *Escritura y desafío: Narradoras venezolanas del siglo xx.* Caracas: Monte Avila, pp. 125–33.

Mújica, Bárbara. "Doña Inés versus Oblivion". *Books of the Americas: Reviews and Interviews from Americas Magazine, 1990–1995.* Organization of American States. Washington, DC, 1997, pp. 254–5.

Ortega, Julio. "Ana Teresa Torres y la voz dirimente". In *El principio radical de lo Nuevo: Posmodernidad, identidad y novela en América Latina.* México: Fondo de Cultura Económica, pp. 225–40.

Pacheco, Carlos. "Textos en la frontera: autobiografía, ficción y escritura de mujeres". *Literatura venezolana hoy.* Frankfurt/Main–Madrid: Vervuert Verlag, Iberoamericana, pp. 127–37.

Rivas, Luz Marina. "La intrahistoria en tres autoras venezolanas: Torres, Antillano y Mata Gil, reinventando los espacios". *La historia de la mirada: La conciencia Histórica y la intrahistoria en la narrativa de Ana Teresa Torres, Laura Antillano y Milagros Mata Gil.* Ciudad Bolívar: Universidad Nacional de Guayana. Fondo de publicaciones del Centro de Estudios Literarios. pp. 53–63.

——. "Metaficción e historia en la escritura de Ana Teresa Torres". *Cifra Nueva: Revista de Cultura* 5(6) (1997): 163–82.

Tompkins, Cynthia. "La re-escritura de la historia en Doña Inés contra el olvido de Ana Teresa Torres". *Escritura y desafío: narrativa venezolana escrita por mujeres*. Caracas: Monte Avila, 1995.

TORRES MOLINA, SUSANA

Susana Torres Molina, born in Buenos Aires, Argentina in 1946, is an accomplished author, director, lighting designer, actress and writer whose unparalleled approach to drama has significantly expanded the margins of Latin American theater. She began her theater career as an actress, participating in plays such as *Libertad y otras intoxicaciones* (1967, Freedom and Other intoxications) and *Señor Frankenstein* (1968, Mister Frankenstein), productions sponsored by the enormously influential Di Tella Institute. She also had the opportunity to work with important directors such as Beatriz Matar, in *El baño de los pájaros* (1977, Bird Bath), and Laura Yussem, in *Boda blanca* (1981, White Wedding).

Torres Molina's groundbreaking play *Extraño juguete* (1977, Strange Toy) received first prize at the Primer Encuentro de Teatro Joven (Buenos Aires, 1981). In 1980, her short film *Pettoruti* was awarded first prize from Fondo Nacional de las Artes for *Lina y Tina* (1980), the first and second prize at the International Festival in Valladolid as well as the second prize in the International Festival de Huesca, Spain. Argentina's dictatorial regime (1976–83), in 1978, forced Torres Molina, her husband at the time—playwright and actor Eduardo Pavlovsky—and their three children into exile in Madrid where they resided until 1981. While in Spain, she restaged and performed *Extraño juguete* under the direction of renowned actress Norma Aleandro.

Some of her recent works as a writer and director include: *Soles* (1982) (Suns); *Inventario* (1983) (Inventory) co-written with Carlos Somigliana, Hebe Serebrinsky and Peñarol Méndez for Teatro Abierto's third annual festival; *Espiral de fuego* (1985, Spiral of Fire); *Amantísima* (1988, Beloved); *Unió Mystica* (1991, Mystic Union); *. . . y a otra cosa mariposa* (1981, Over and Done with It) read at the 3rd International Women Playwrights Conference in Adelaide, Australia; *Canto de sirenas* (1995, Mermaid's Song); *Ensayo* (monologue for the multiple award winning show) *A corazón abierto* (1996, Essay); *Paraísos perdidos* (1997, Lost Paradise); *Manifiesto* (unstaged, 1998) (Manifest); *No sé tú* (1999, Maybe You); *Nada entre los dientes* (monologue, 1999) (Nothing Between the Teeth); *Cero* (1999, Zero); *Hormigas en el bidet* (1999, Ants in the Bidet); *Una noche cualquiera* (unstaged, 1999, Any Other Night), winner of the XVIII Theatre Award "Hermanos Machado" in Seville, Spain; *Lo que no se nombra* (2000, The Unnameable), winner of the IV Concurso Nacional de Obras Breves in 2001, and *Ella* (2005, She), first prize winner of the Concurso de Obras Teatrales del Fondo Nacional de las Artes. Most recently, Torres Molina has collaborated with directors Daniel Marcove and Rubén Pires in *Como si nada* (2000, As if Nothing), a piece performed in *La mayor, la menor y el del medio* (The Oldest, The Youngest and The One in the Middle), and in *Sorteo* (Raffle), staged at the 2001 Teatroxlaidentidad Festival (Theatre for Identity). Also staged in 2001 were *Fría como azulejo de cocina* (Cold as Kitchen Tile), directed by Antonio Celico, a production based on selections from *Dueña y Señora* (short stories, 1982) (Mistress and Lady), and *Azul Metalizado* (Metallic Blue), directed by Guillermo Guío. Moreover, in 2002, Torres Molina staged and directed *Serie: Actos privados* (Series: Private Acts), a three-play show featuring *Nada entre los dientes* (1999), *Turning Point* (2002), and *Modus operandi* (2002). *Estática* (2002) (Static) was a finalist for the "Casa de America" award.

In addition to writing, directing, and participating in all forms of theatre production, Torres Molina has authored television, film, dance scripts, and collaborated with renowned musicians and singers. She also conducts workshops on performance, dramaturgy, and acting. Some of her creative research workshops involved HIV-positive inmates from the Devoto penitentiary (1999) and doctors from the Hospital Alvarez (2002).

Torres Molina's distinctive interpretation of reality and poignant sense of humor appeal to a generation of Argentine women playwrights—like Diana Raznovich and Cristina Escofet—interested in dismantling conventional categories of gender through the depiction of the experience of being a woman in a repressive male-centered society. Most important to the author, as seen in the vast repertoire of unconventional characters, is the deconstruction of prescribed gender roles and masculine hierarchies that perpetuate social and sexual stereotypes.

Strange Toy is a game-structured play in which two middle-aged spinsters, Perla and Angélica, receive an unexpected visit from a lingerie salesman. Role-playing and the erotic playfulness of the dialogue lead to the sexual arousal of the sadomasochist vendor, who seems to enjoy the spinsters' physical and emotional abuse. As the play unfolds, the dynamics of the game intensify, climaxing in a scene in which the man interrupts his performance to relieve himself. It is only at this point that the viewer realizes all has been a charade prearranged by the two well-off, bored matrons in search of a thrill. In this metatheatrical piece, Torres Molina not only renders a poignant critique of the overwhelmingly repressive conditions imposed by Argentina's dictatorial regime, but also exposes the manipulative ploys of the upper class willing to pay for their own enjoyment. Frustration, anger, fear, irony, and a heavy dose of sarcasm are the main elements of this theatrical game in which emotions and feelings are manipulated for the thrill of an affluent consumer. As Denise DiPuccio states

> Completely divested of control over their emotional lives, these rich women cannot feel happiness or sadness unless they pay for it. A virtual emotional buffet of mental states (including happiness, sadness, terror, sexuality, maternity, anger, boredom, and exhaustion), is laid bare for purchase and consumption by the two sisters.
> (1995, p. 157)

Transforming every discourse of power into an irreverent parody, the playwright raises the spectators' awareness of the consumerist vein of modern culture, while simultaneously reflecting upon the perpetual acting and role-playing required to fulfill societal expectations within our own daily routine.

In *Over and Done With It*, Torres Molina continues to debunk institutionalized categorizations of sex and gender by focusing on the behavior, language and dynamics of four *porteño* (people from Buenos Aires) male friends through the span of a lifetime. The originality of this *tour de force* script lies in fact that the roles of El Flaco (Skinny), El Inglés (The Brit), Cerdín (Fatso) and Pajarito (Finch), be strictly played by actresses. Indeed, as Jean Graham-Jones examines, "The reading, and appreciation, of this play lies in the fact that both sexes are present throughout the performance, thus providing a constant humanization to counter the dehumanizing process of sexist mythologizing" (1995, p. 100). Through a witty and sarcastic dialogue heavily influenced by *porteño* slang and mannerisms that best capture the characteristic demeanor of the Argentine male, the dramatist underscores the performance quality of gender as a social construct.

Significant to the playwright's feminist discourse, and perhaps, more evident in *Over and Done with It* than in *Strange Toy*, is the representation of the body as an instrument with which to subvert the patriarchal prescriptions of gender in relation to space and social behavior. Set as a paradigm of resistance, the body becomes a repository to recycle postmodern constructs of beauty, sexuality, eroticism and power. For Jean Graham-Jones, the powerful impression conveyed by the four women playing the males roles creates a distancing effect that alienates the text from its actors, thus forcing the spectator to re-evaluate both content and actions. According to Graham-Jones: "Each time Woman is objectified and thus dehumanized in the text, this would-be dehumanization is counteracted by the very physical human presence of the women portraying these characters, their social condition as women reinforced and even exaggerated by costuming and makeup" (1995, p. 100).

Since the 1980s, Torres Molina's theatrical discourse has shifted from the European and the Argentine tradition developing into a more personal style. As the dramatist has acknowledged, some of her influences come from the image-based spectacle of Butô or Butoh (The Dance of Shadows), a particular form of contemporary Japanese dance involving music, movement, and repeated or ritualistic symbolic actions performed by characters in white make-up and almost naked bodies.

Beloved is a visually stunning piece that moves away from the conventions of dramatic speech to follow "a theatrical trend known as 'teatro de imágenes' (theater of images), in which strong, expressionistic images and metaphor take precedence over conventional, causal structure and dialogue" (Bixler 1998: 216). Stage devices, costumes, and lighting design are integrated to create an intense spectacle in which the language of the body predominates over the dramatic text. With *Beloved*, Torres Molina sets the pace for a more self-reflective and insightful dramatic text, one in which archetypal voices acquire the corporeal physicality of bodies, though never reaching the individuality of a fully developed character. Detached from a unanimous meaning, the poetic image regains its expressive freedom, thus enhancing the lyrical as well as the visual language of the play.

Mystic Union also subscribes to such a theatrical style and technique by further exploring the ritualistic and the cyclic nature of the feminine self. Its theme, however, revolves around the feelings of anger, sadness and anguish of three women – the wife, the prostitute, and the lover – who have contracted HIV. The confessional tone of the play brings forth the intimacies of a feminine collective whose secret desires and expectations will never be fulfilled. By confronting their fears of death or infection, these women desperately seek to find meaning behind their own existence, each one revealing different levels of frustration, anger, and passion. A disquieting trip through the empire of the senses, *Mystic Union* guides the spectator to the core of the human soul, exposing its thirst for eternity and communion.

Mermaids' Song is a four-part monologue-poem, in which physical movement, sound and unconventional spatial arrangements are masterfully combined to enhance the enigmatic quality of the text. Within the realm of a limbic region, we witness the formative experience of a soul that seeks the perfection of divinity. As an incarnation of Humanity, this mythical creature wanders through the paths of "Desire," "Loneliness," "Senses," and "Passion," seeking to liberate the mundane aspects of the soul. Mirroring the aesthetics and the elucidation of religious texts like the Bible or the teachings of Buddha, the language of this parabolic play conveys a profound message of solidarity and compassion.

With *She*, Torres Molina reverts to a more traditional dramatic discourse. This eleven-scene piece presents the conflict between two men who find themselves trapped by their feelings of love and lust for the same woman. Through situations that oscillate from the real to the absurd, the plot discloses the pathetic ploys of a husband who psychologically manipulates his wife's lover as he seeks to match his own masculinity against that of his rival. The unseen overpowering SHE becomes a central character, a victim and an accomplice of this twisted game of power in which nothing is indeed what it seems. Torres Molina's insightful vision and constant experimentation with theatrical performance not only challenge more realistic and conventional forms of playwriting, but also expand the margins of contemporary theater.

María Claudia André

Selected Works

Dueña y señora. Buenos Aires: Editorial La Campana, 1982.

Extraño juguete. Buenos Aires: Ediciones Búsqueda, 1987.

Y a otra cosa mariposa. Buenos Aires: Ediciones Búsqueda, 1988.

"Y a otra cosa mariposa". In Nora Eidelberg and María Mercedes Jaramillo (eds), *Voces en Escena Antología de Dramaturgas Latinoamericanas*. Medellín: Ed. Universidad de Antioquía, 1991.

"Nada entre los dientes," in *Monólogos de dos continents: Catorce textos teatrales de reconocidos autores españoles y argentinos*. Buenos Aires: Ed. Corregidor, 1999.

Una noche cualquiera. Sevilla: Edición del Area de Cultura del Ayuntamiento de Sevilla, 2000.

"Sorteo". Co-written play edited in *Teatro por la Identidad*. Buenos Aires: Eudeba, 2001.

"*Espiral de fuego*" and "*Canto de sirenas.*" Buenos Aires: Teatro Vivo, 2002.

"Lo que no se nombra". In *Noticia del día. 14 obras teatrales de dramaturgos argentinos y españoles*. Madrid: Ed. La Avispa, 2002.

"Ella". In Jorge Dubatti (ed.), *Nuevo Teatro Argentino*. Buenos Aires: Interzona Latinoamericana, 2003.

"Ella". In Graciela de Díaz Araujo (ed.), *Dramaturgas Argentinas*. Buenos Aires: Ed. La abeja, 2003.

"Estática". Premio Dramaturgia Innovadora. Madrid: Edición Casa de América, 2003.

"Ella". In María Claudia André (ed.), *Antología de escritoras argentinas contemporáneas*. Buenos Aires: Biblos, 2004.

References and Further Reading

Bauman, Kevin. "Metatexts, Women and Sexuality: The Facts and (PH) allacies in Torres Molina's *Extraño Juguete*". *Romance Languages Annual* 2 (1990): 330–5.

Bixler, Jaqueline E. "For Women only? The Theatre of Susana Torres Molina". In Catherine Larson and Margarita Vargas (eds), *Latin American Women Dramatists: Theater, Texts, and Theories*. Bloomington, IN: Indiana University Press, 1998.

DiPuccio, Denise. "Radical and Materialist Relationships in Torres Molina's 'Extraño Juguete'". *Letras Femeninas* 21(1–2) (Spring–Fall, 1995): 153–64.

Eidelberg, Nora. "Susana Torres Molina: destacada teatrista argentina". *Alba de América* 7–12(13) (July 1989): 391–3.

Foster, David. "Identidades polifomórficas y planteo metateatral en *Extraño juguete* de Susana Torres Molina". *Alba de América*. 7–12(13) (July 1989): 75–86.

Graham-Jones, Jean. "Myths, Masks, and Machismo: *Un trabajo fabuloso* by Ricardo Halac and *Y a otra cosa mariposa* by Susana Torres Molina". *Gestos: Teoría y práctica del teatro hispanico* 10–20 (November 1995): 91–106.

TRABA, MARTA

To discuss Marta Traba (1923–83) is to speak of not just a writer, but also an individual with a profound literary sense and a keen critical perception, be it in the realm of literature or art. And, it is to speak of a prolific, dedicated, and active life cut short by tragedy.

Some of Traba's biographers point out that her wordsmithing abilities and globe-trotting nature are family legacies. Her maternal and paternal family roots can be traced back to Spain, in both the north-central Basque region and the northwestern area of Galicia. Indeed, Traba's brother claims to have traced the family genealogy to the town of Traba, near La Coruña, Spain. Regardless of the exact starting point, both sets of grandparents eventually emigrated to Argentina. Traba's father, Francisco Traba, was a journalist and also served on the editorial staff of the Argentine literary magazine *Caras y Caretas* (Faces and Masks). Her mother, Marta Taín, was a writer, principally of prose and poetry, who also worked with *Plus Ultra* (Extra Addition), the artistic supplement to *Caras y Caretas*.

Marta Traba was born into this intellectually rich environment in San Isidro, Buenos Aires, Argentina on January 25, 1923. Her mother gave birth at home, with the assistance of her sister and a neighbor. Most sources list 1930 as the birth year, but her cousin acknowledges that beginning in her teens, Traba altered it; due to her diminutive size, the deception was never questioned. In an interview with Magdalena García Pinto, Traba recalls, with wry humor, that "A esa revista (*Leoplán*) debo toda mi cultura literaria, mi pasión por la novela y mi astigmatismo. Todo Tolstoi, Dostoievski, Gorki, Turgueniev, Goncharov, Dickens, Victor Hugo, fueron devorados a esa edad" [To that magazine (*Leoplán*) I owe all of my literary foundation, my passion for the novel, and my astigmatism. All of Tolstoy, Dostoyevsky, Gorki, Turgenev, Goncharov, Dickens, Victor Hugo were devoured at that age].

With such auspicious beginnings, it is no surprise that Traba went on have a varied academic career. After finishing her high schooling in only two years, she went on to earn her Bachelor's degree in Philosophy and Letters from the University of Buenos Aires. Shortly thereafter, she traveled to Europe, where she furthered her studies in Art History and Esthetics at some of the most esteemed art institutions, including the Sorbonne and the Louvre School in Paris, and the School of the Arts in Rome. In 1954, with her journalist husband Alberto Zalamea, and her first son Gustavo (b. 1951), she ventured to Colombia. Her second son Fernando was born a few years later (in 1959); and, she also began in earnest to combine her esthetic eye for art criticism with her love of literary endeavors.

Up to the time of her death, Traba published at a steady pace, both in the art and literary worlds. She also joined the international lecture circuit as a sought-after speaker in Art History and Literary Theory, for example in Mexico, Colombia, Venezuela, Uruguay, Puerto Rico, and the United States, to name just a few. Traba also earned the position of "Visiting Professor" in many prestigious US institutions, such as Harvard University, Princeton University, Middlebury College, the Massachusetts Institute of Technology, and the University of Maryland.

Sadly, it was this propensity for participating in international conferences (and not the cancer against which she had fought a year earlier) that led to her death in the pre-dawn hours of November 27, 1983. Of the 194 individuals on Avianca flight 11, 183 perished in an accident just outside Madrid, Spain. Among the lost were Marta Traba, her second husband, whom she married in 1969, noted literary critic Ángel Rama, and several other well-known writers and artists. They were en route to attend *La Primera Conferencia de Cultura Hispanoamericana* (The First Conference of Hispano-American Culture) in Bogotá, Colombia. Although immediately after the crash there was speculation of foul play, the cockpit recordings indicate that it was human error. The pilots transposed two numbers in the altimeter's altitude alarm system (inputting 2,328 feet instead of 3,228); thus, the plane was traveling too low to clear the hillside of Mejorada del Campo.

There is no small irony in the fact that this conference was being held in Colombia, a country with which Traba had experienced past difficulties. In 1967, Traba had been teaching at the University of Bogotá. When she criticized the military's occupation of the university, Colombian President Carlos Lleras Restrepo wanted to expel her from the country. Due to her popularity, however, he had to soften his edict, which resulted in the ruling that she could stay in the country, but could no longer teach at the university. She chose exile. Given this background, it was indeed an auspicious moment in 1983 when both she and Rama had been personally invited to attend *La Primera Conferencia de Cultura Hispanoamericana* by the then president of Colombia, Belisario Betancur, who also extended to her Colombian citizenship when she faced deportation from the United States. Unfortunately, a turning point in Traba's relationship with Colombia was irrevocably lost.

The Art World

In spite of her later issues with Colombia, it was there that she truly established a name for herself in the art world. Although she began publishing art criticism articles in Argentina, in the *Ver y Estimar* (Look and Judge) magazine edited by noted art critic Jorge Romero Brest, she is most widely known for the work she accomplished while in Colombia. In the mid-1950s, when she moved to Colombia after her European studies, she worked as a professor of Art History at the University of Bogotá and founded *Prisma* (Prism), a magazine dedicated to the arts. By the mid-1960s she was named the Cultural Director of the University of Bogotá and was put in charge of the Museum of Modern Art in Bogotá, which opened on July 27, 1965. Such was her continued renown and involvement in the art world that in 1983 she was asked to be a guest curator for the permanent installment of the Latin American art collection at the Art Museum of the Americas in Washington, DC.

As evidenced, Traba voiced her theories of art history and art criticism tirelessly through a variety of mediums: courses, lectures, conferences, television appearances, magazines (some of which she founded), guides to art exhibits, and of course, books. In all, she published twenty-two texts on the subject, of which *Siglo XX en las artes plásticas latinoamericanas: una guía* (The Twentieth Century in Latin American Plastic Arts: A Guide) and *Art of Latin America: 1900–1980* are considered to be standards in the field.

Certainly, Traba had an erudite background in the arts and was able to reference works from the most established European masters to myriad lesser-known contemporary artists from around the globe, and everything in between. Yet, she would treat art / artists from all categories with the same level of examination and detail. She had a reputation for not just accepting the standard or established evaluation of a work/ artist without first considering it on her own, which often led to conflicts and debates. As Betancur states in the "Foreword" to *Art in Latin America*: *1900–1980*: "In seeking to define those individual identities that, taken together, constitute a common identity, she was harsh in dealing with both mediocrity and injustice" (p. x). Regardless of the situation, however, Traba's depth and breadth of artistic knowledge combined with her intellectual confidence allowed her to defend her positions admirably.

Key to her viewpoint, also, was her recognition of Latin America's art on its own terms, a Pan-Americanism, as some critics have termed it. This task is monumental in its undertaking, especially when considering the number of countries involved, their individual traditions, and their separate modes of expression. Thus, she became a strong observer of younger Latin American artists such as Alejandro Obregón and Fernando Botero, who could be categorized within an internationalist modernism. This was simultaneously perceived by some as being critical of established artists like Gónzalo Ariza and Ignacio Gómez Jaramillo, who could then be categorized as nationalists. While Traba could appreciate the latter within their context of past glories, she also recognized the need not just to rest on one's laurels.

In addition, Traba was one of the first to question the relationship between artistic culture / expression and the demands of development. She theorized the pressures of economic development, especially those of international origins, and criticized the homogenization process that this entailed, especially as the influence of the United States in the Hemisphere grew in the 1960s and 1970s. This led to her creation of an "art of resistance" theory in which she lambasted the prioritized role of technology in industrialized nations, and thus, their artistic expression. Certainly, she was a keen observer of her time; and, as such, she viewed each time with astuteness. More important, perhaps, was her ability for self-evaluation, as evidenced by how she would reevaluate some of her own positions, altering them if need be. For example, early in her career, she theorized that art did not need to reflect reality, that art for art's sake was enough; later in career, however, she focused on the need for art to communicate a contextualized message and cultural identity. She also reexamined her analysis of the Mexican muralist movement, which at first she criticized but later repositioned favorably as one of the most important Latin American artistic movements.

The World of Words

Traba's aptitude for self-reflection and expression is also readily seen in her essays and works of fiction, which she worked on at the same time as she developed her works of art history and criticism. It is, perhaps, a logically simultaneous action: both the plastic arts and the literary ones are forms of artistic expression born out of their cultural, political, and socio-economic contexts. Indeed, a characteristic of Traba's writing is the attention to detail and description, almost as if she were painting with words. Although she published one volume of poetry (*Historia natural de la alegría* (1951, A Natural History of Happiness)), one collection of essays (*El son se quedó en Cuba: cuatro artículos y una conferencia* (1966, The Son Stayed in Cuba: Four Articles and One Lecture)), and two collections of short stories (*Pasó así* (1968, It Happened Like This) and *De la mañana a la noche: cuentos norteamericanos* (1986, From Morning to Evening: North American Stories)), she stated often that she wished to be known for her contributions as a novelist.

This reputation is certainly deserved, as her novels are considered to be testimonials that are both highly personal, echoing her life's path, and intensely global, reflecting her keen observations of and increasingly more critical reactions to contemporary events. In general, several major themes can be traced through her works of fiction: the value and importance of love, communication, and humanity in the face of that which would destroy them. Central to this is the fundamental need for basic human rights and the obligation to protest their abuse by hegemonic powers. Protagonists, as well as the author, are on a constant journey for justice.

In her first novel, *Las ceremonias del verano* (1966, The Ceremonies of Summer), which won the coveted Havana "Casa de las Américas" Prize, Traba takes up these themes via the imagery of the traveler on a journey, one that autobiographically mirrors Traba's own life and environs. *Homérica latina* (1979, Latin Homeric) follows this theme and is often referred to as an odyssey at both the personal level of the individual and the continental level of Latin America. *Conversación al sur* (1981, Conversation Towards the South) traces the personal relationship between two women against the backdrop of strained military control in Argentina, Chile, and Uruguay. Within this novel, dialog combats silence, protest battles fear, and hope defies grim reality. Nevertheless, the ending of the novel is abrupt and positive closure is denied; such closure must take place, therefore, not in the fictional world, but in reality.

Traba continues with her denouncement of abuses of power, such as politically-motivated kidnappings, disappearances, torture, and murder, in *En cualquier lugar* (1984, In Any Place), a novel which is often referred to as the companion or twin of *Conversación al sur*. Yet, within the midst of the horrors depicted, Traba also plants the seeds of hope for recuperation and resurrection via her main protagonist, Alicia. Yet, such hope must battle the enemy of exile. Such separation is key in Traba's works, and indeed, mirrors her own experiences. Exile, whether forced or voluntary, is a condition of abandonment that marks identity through fragmentation and absence. Within this particular novel, this is reiterated through the blurring of narrative location and the disjointedness of dialog.

As an author, she also explored the role of memory, as exemplified in the posthumous *Casa sin fin* (1988, House without End), which can be considered an extension of the previous two novels. In particular, the everyday events of life are recalled in a manner that prioritizes moments that are all too often considered casual, if not insignificant. Yet, these often forgotten daily activities are what may restore balance to a life disrupted, if not destroyed, by abuse. This is not to say that Traba supports "forget and move on" as a means of recuperation. To the contrary, through this novel, and in particular its disjointed narrative style and its multiple interpretations of "home," she plants the idea that the persistence of life can be both a path through the chaos left behind by abusive societies and a form of denouncement of said abuses.

Honesty based on personal experience is also a fundamental component of Traba's writing, a characteristic that she prioritized in both her art-related texts and her literary endeavors. Indeed, she incorporated many elements from her own life in all of her works. Some characters hide their true age behind their small size, as she did; others search for a permanent location to make their own, a clear reaction to her family's propensity for moving (between 1923–48, she lived in fourteen different homes) and her own adult experiences with exile and a sense of being uprooted; and still others bear remarkable similarities to friends and family members, even with the same names. The situations and individuals are based on her reality; Traba felt that as an author, she had to write what she knew and she had to be committed to the truth.

Criticism of the Critic

Thus, Traba, was a polemic, almost rebellious, figure, even though in her mind, she was relaying naught but an honest truth. She had the tendency to infuriate the established *inteligencia* of the art and literary worlds, not to mention the power brokers of government. In an interview with artist Beatriz González, Traba highlights this bellicose nature, but defends it:

> I don't like to get into fights, but I have to, because it is my duty. I would prefer to live in a just society and serve it with meekness, loyalty, and passion ... My incredible struggles are always against forces that could reduce me to dust ... I should like to go on being Joan of Arc, ever Joan of Arc.
>
> (*Art of Latin America* p. xi)

Traba felt that, as a responsible member of society, it was her obligation not just to write what she perceived, but also to act upon it, even if doing so pushed against or through boundaries. This actually led to her "exile in protest" from Colombia in 1967, as referenced earlier. And, later, it is conjectured that her adamant beliefs, coupled with Leftist tendencies, led to the denial by the US Department of Immigration and Naturalization of her 1982 application for permanent residency in the US. Nevertheless, and regardless of the location of her home, she fought against those who would silence her, those who would silence the intellectual freedom of speech that she held dear.

Indeed, critics of her literary works often note that there is a voice of judgment in her narratives and a call to action. Mexican author Elena Poniatowska even labeled Traba's novels "novels of oppression". If this is so, then it is not the oppression of one individual that is being judged, but the oppression of society in general and the reader is pushed to react. The motif of the knock at the door, which is repeated throughout *Conversación al sur*, serves as an example. Within the context of the narration, the door is first opened to the unexpected guest, then left unanswered due to fear, and finally, brutally kicked in by force. The reader cannot help but empathize and, more importantly, wonder whose door may be approached next. Traba's message is clear: one becomes the next victim if one does not confront the horrors of life and act defiantly against them.

And it was an active life of defiance that Marta Traba lived. Although she was born an Argentine and died as a Colombian, she lived her life in numerous European and American countries. She learned from her studies, her life experiences, and her globe-trotting exile; she cast a critical eye on the development and impact of Latin American art in the face of modernization and globalization; and she wrote essays and fiction with an astute sense of the importance of the word in a society marked by violence. In sum, Marta Traba became a dedicated citizen of the world, and as such, she loved it, critiqued it, fought for the recognition of its individuality, and, ultimately, left behind not just a legacy of art appreciation and literary profundity, but also the legacy of her life's actions: a legacy of both word and deed.

DAWN SLACK

Selected Works

Art Criticism

Colombia: Latin American Art Today. Washington, DC: Ediciones de la Unión Panamericana, 1959.

Seis artistas contempoáneos colombianos: Obregón, Ramírez, Botero, Grau, Wiedeman, Negret. (Six Contemporary Colombian Artists: Obregón, Ramírez, Botero, Grau, Wiedeman, Negret). Bogotá: Editorial de Antares, 1963.

Los cuatro monstruos cardinales: Bacon, Cuevas, Dubuffet, De Kooning. (The Four Cardinal Monsters: Bacon, Cuevas, Dubuffet, De Kooning). Mexico City: Era, 1964.

Siglo XX en las artes plásticas latinoamericanas: una guía. (The Twentieth Century in Latin American Plastic Arts: A Guide). Washington, DC: Endowment for the Arts and Humanities and Museo de Arte Latinoamericano de la OEA, 1982–83.

Art of Latin America: 1900–1980. New York: The Johns Hopkins University Press and the Inter-American Development Bank, 1994.

Literature

Historia natural de la alegría. Buenos Aires: Editorial Losada, 1951.

Las ceremonias del verano. La Habana: Colección de los premios de Casa de las Américas, 1966.

El son se quedó en Cuba: cuatro artículos y una conferencia. Bogotá: Ediciones Reflexión, 1966.

Los laberintos insolados. Barcelona: Editorial Seix Barral, 1967.
Pasó así. Montevideo: Monte Sexto, 1968.
La jugada del sexto día. Santiago de Chile: Editorial Universitaria, 1970.
Homérica latina. Bogotá: Carlos Valencia Editores, 1979.
Conversación al sur. Mexico City: Siglo XXI, 1981.
En cualquier lugar. Bogotá: Siglo XXI, 1984.
De la mañana a la noche: cuentos norteamericanos. Montevideo: Monte Sexto, 1986.
Mothers and Shadows. Trans. Jo Labanji. London: Reader's International, 1986. Trans. of *Conversación al sur*. Mexico City: Siglo XXI, 1981.
Casa sin fin. Montevideo: Monte Sexto, 1988.

References and Further Reading

Agosín, Margorie (ed.). *A Dream of Light and Shadow: Portrait of Latin American Women Writers*. Albuquerque, NM: University of New Mexico Press, 1995.
Alazraki, Jaime. "¿Muerte accidental o asesinato político?" *Texto crítico* X(31–2) (Jan.–Aug. 1985): 109–13.
Bayón, Damián. "El espléndido no-conformismo de Marta Traba". *Sin Nombre* XIV(3) (April–June, 1984): 92–6.
Betancur, Belisario. "Foreword". In Marta Traba (ed.), *Art of Latin América: 1900–1980*. Washington, DC: Banco Interamericano de Desarrollo; Baltimore, MD: Johns Hopkins UP, 1994, pp. vii–xiv.
Castillo, Debra. *Talking Back: Toward a Latin American Feminist Literary Criticism*. Ithaca, NY: Cornell University Press, 1992.
Correas de Zapata, Celia. "Marta Traba". Trans. John Benson. In Diane E. Martinez, (ed.), *Spanish American Writers*. Westport, CT: Greenwood Press, 1990.
Domenella, Ana Rosa. "Homenaje múltiple". *Cuadernos Americanos* 1(43) (Jan–February, 1994): 196–204.
Franco, Jean. "Self-Destructing Heroines". *The Minnesota Review* 22 (Spring, 1984): 105–15.
García Pinto, Magdalena. "Entrevista: Marta Traba". *Hispamérica* XIII: 38 (1984): 37–46.
González, Patricia Elena and Ortega, Eliana *La sartén por el mango: Encuentro de escritoras latinoamericanas*. 2nd edn. Río Piedras: Ediciones Huracán, 1986.
Kantaris, Elia G. *The Subversive Psyche: Contemporary Women's Narrative from Argentina and Uruguay*. New York: Clarendon Press, 1995.
Partnoy, Alicia (ed.) *You Can't Drown the Fire: Latin American Women Writing in Exile*. Pittsburgh, PA: Cleis P, 1988.
Pacheco, José Emilio. "La generación crítica". *Texto crítico* X(31–2) (1985): 75–81.
Poniatowska, Elena. "Marta Traba o el salto al vacío". *Revista Iberoamericana* 60(132–3) (July–December, 1985): 883–97.
Verlichak, Victoria. *Marta Traba: una terquedad furibunda*. Buenos Aires: Universidad Nacional de Tres de Febrero – Funcación Proa, 2001.

TRISTÁN, FLORA

Flora Tristán was the *nom de plume* of Flora Célestine Thérèse Henriette Tristán y Moscoso, a Franco-Peruvian writer and political activist who was born in Paris on April 7, 1803. Her father, Mariano de Tristán y Moscoso, was a Peruvian aristocrat and a colonel in the Spanish army; her mother, Anne-Pierre Laisnay, was French. During her lifetime, Tristan defined her national identity as a hybrid that was half-Peruvian, half-French. She was known on both sides of the Atlantic for her work as a travel writer and a utopian social critic. Today she is remembered as an early feminist and a political activist who anticipated Marx's ideas about class struggle and the proletarian revolution.

Flora Tristan's desire to validate the Latin American side of her identity was evident throughout her life. In her personal correspondence, she recalls her father's friendship with Simón Bolívar and Simón Rodríguez, although she was only four years old when her father died of a stroke in 1807. When Flora Tristán was 16 years old, she started to work in André Chazal's lithography studio as an apprentice. According to Tristán, she married Chazal in 1821, at the insistence of her mother, who was anxious to end the family's economic hardship through her daughter's marriage. The union between Tristán and Chazal proved to be extremely unhappy, and Flora Tristán spent half of her life trying to escape or hide from what appears to have been a violent husband. She separated from Chazal in 1825 and spent part of her life defending the need to legalize divorce.

In 1833, Tristán left her two young children in the care of a friend and she undertook a long trip to Peru to claim her father's inheritance. On her return from Peru and as a response to Tristán's petition for the legalization of divorce (1837), Chazal tried to kill Tristán by shooting her in a busy Paris street. Tristán was wounded but survived the attack, gaining sensational visibility in French and Latin American intellectual circles. As a result of this failed murder attempt, Chazal was sent to jail for twenty years and Tristán obtained complete custody of her two children, Ernesto Camilo and Alina María. After Tristán's death, Alina married Clovis Gauguin, becoming the mother of the French Impressionist painter, Paul Gauguin. Mario Vargas Llosa in his double biographical novel, *El Paraíso en la otra esquina* (2005, The Way to Paradise) contrasts the lives of Flora Tristán and her equally famous grandson by fictionalizing Flora Tristán's voyage to Peru in 1833, and Paul Gauguin's trip to Tahiti in 1891.

Visions of Peru

Although *Pérégrinations d'une paria (1833–34)* (1838, Peregrinations of a Pariah) is the only one of Tristán's books that has Peru as its main topic, it now occupies an almost canonical status in Peruvian cultural history. Tristán's acute observations about the post-independence period in Peru from the perspective of a woman traveler in search of her roots captured the attention of Latin American scholars since the book's publication. At the same time, the prologue's dedication to her Peruvian "compatriots" allows us to conclude that Tristán wrote the book with both Latin American and European readers in mind.

Tristán's astute remarks on gender issues have turned *Pérégrinations d'une paria* into an icon for Peruvian feminist scholars who are particularly drawn to her depictions of *rabonas* (soldier women), *tapadas* (veiled women), and *limeñas*. Although she was extremely critical of Peruvian customs and traditions, seeing them as evidence of a barbarism that she wanted to Europeanize, Tristán celebrated the freedom that city women experienced in Lima. She claimed that Peruvian women were less domestic than their French counterparts thanks to the colonial *saya y manto,* a long dress that covered women's bodies in their totality except for one eye. This apparel, asserted Tristán, allowed women to circulate anonymously throughout the city, escaping the repressive gaze of patriarchal society. In this sense, the trip to Peru proved to be life changing for Tristán, putting her in contact with other ideologies of femininity that would help her question, on her return to France, the European domestic· stereotype of the angel of the house.

Gender and Travel

Flora Tristán went to Valparaíso and Peru aboard the ship *Le Mexicain* in a trip that lasted four and half months. In preparation for the trip, she started to correspond with her aristocratic uncle in 1929. In one of the letters she made the mistake of telling him that her parents' union had never been official and that she did not have a legal certificate to prove their union. When Tristán came to Arequipa, her uncle welcomed her into his home but used Tristán's argument about the illegitimacy of her birth to deny her the inheritance. The death of her paternal grandmother, shortly before her arrival in Arequipa, aggravated Tristán's state of affairs, and she soon found herself in a difficult situation with no advocates in a financial dispute that increasingly isolated Tristán from her Peruvian relatives.

When Flora Tristán returned to Paris, she published *Pérégrinations d'une paria (1833–1834)*, an autobiographical fictionalization of her travel experiences in Peru. As soon as copies of the travelogue reached Arequipa, both the book and Tristán's effigy were burned in the main square by angry readers who objected to her crude depiction of Peruvian customs. Tristán's negative views of life in the Andes, and of the upper classes in particular, were read as a revenge against her uncle for not recognizing her as one of his own. Although the trip to Peru was a turning point for Tristán's career as a political activist and a travel writer, the publication caused her uncle to cancel the allowance, making her economic situation in Paris even more difficult.

In 1835, Tristán published *Nécessité de faire un bon accueil aux femmes étrangères* (Of the Necessity to Properly Welcome Foreign Women), an autobiographical pamphlet in which she discussed nineteenth-century attitudes towards women travelers. She criticized society for not welcoming these women and for a lack of hospitable laws to ensure their safety. Tristán's observations about gender and travel were vastly based on her personal experiences, drawing heavily from her own trips to Lima, Paris and London. She made the first trip to the "monster city" (London) in 1826 as a governess for a well-to-do French family, and the last one in 1839 once she became more established as a writer.

Following the publication of a romantic novel, *Méphis ou le prolétaire* (1838, Méphis or the proletarian), Tristán wrote a second travel narrative titled *Promenades dans Londres* (1840, London Journals) in which she fictionalized her urban incursions into the poorest London neighborhoods. She wrote her travel book from the position of a social observer and critic who chose to narrate the plight of other social "pariahs" such as the Jewish poor, Irish proletarians, prisoners, and factory workers. Of particular importance are Tristán's observations about prostitutes in which she tried to rescue street women from their role as contaminated human beings. She claimed that prostitution was not the consequence of biological degeneracy in women, but of an unequal distribution of wealth along gender lines, in societies that closed all doors to women except matrimony.

In Search of a Political Identity

At the end of her trip to Peru, Tristán had a long interview with Francisca Zubiaga de Gamarra, known as *La Mariscala*, one of the most powerful and charismatic political women of the nineteenth century. *La Mariscala* had ruled Peru for four years, as the combative wife of Mariscal Agustín Gamarra, and she was both admired and despised by her Peruvian compatriots. The last chapter of *Pérégrinations* is a narrative account of the meeting between these two remarkable women who exchanged ideas about the difficulties of reconciling femininity and political power in a chaotic society that was suspicious of women's political activism. The meeting with *La Mariscala* who became a role model for non-domestic women in the nineteenth century was a turning point for Tristán's later political career.

Tristán left Peru in 1834 unable to collect the inheritance that she had set out to claim. However, she took back with her something far more valuable: the realization that there were other gender ideologies circulating in the nineteenth century, and that women could defy the European ideology of the spheres (public/private) by becoming political activists, writers and/or revolutionaries. At least in the area of gender building, Latin American women seemed to be ahead of their European sisters. On the other hand, Tristán's ideas about race in *Pérégrinations,* particularly her depiction of African slaves, were far more problematic, leading to accusations of racism by some literary critics.

Flora Tristán belonged to a generation of romantic women writers who were influenced by the utopian thought of the Saint-Simonians under the leadership of Prosper Enfantin. However, some of her biographers have pointed out that she differed from the leading utopian thinkers of the day in the way she placed women's equality with men ahead of their celebration of feminine difference. She also differed from Christian Feminists in her fierce defense of anticlericalism.

Tristán had a difficult relationship with Georges Sand, the other famous Romantic writer of her generation. In *Pérégrinations*, Tristán criticized her indirectly for hiding her female identity as a writer behind a male pseudonym, claiming that this was detrimental to the feminist cause. On the other hand, Georges Sand censored Tristán when she said that Tristán's daughter, Alina, was less combative and confrontational than her difficult mother.

After the scandal caused by the initial unfavorable reception of *Pérégrinations* in Peru, Flora Tristán was largely forgotten by Peruvian readers until Carolina Freyre de Jaimes gave a conference about Tristán in 1875, at Lima's Literary Circle. It was not until 1925 that Emilia Romero did a complete translation of the two volumes of the Peruvian travelogue although up to that point *Pérégrinations* had been circulating in French. Tristán's fictionalized portrait of *La Mariscala* initiated a long tradition of biographical texts on the life of this character that included works by Clorinda Matto de Turner and Abraham Valdelomar.

In 1945, Magda Portal wrote a book about Tristán entitled *Flora Tristán, la precursora* in which she underlined Tristán's significance as a feminist and a socialist. The importance that Tristán had for a whole generation of women writers and activists in Peru crystallized in the opening of the *Centro de la*

Mujer Peruana Flora Tristán in Lima in 1979, a feminist cultural center that is still in operation today.

Towards the end of Tristán's intellectual life, class took predominance over gender as the main category that defines identity. In *Union Ouvrière* (1843, The Worker's Union) she argued for the creation of what she called "palaces" for workers in which the needs of the poor and the elderly would be attended to. She convinced workers to become unionized by contributing a small amount of money to a union that would fight for their rights in the context of the industrial revolution. While she was encouraging workers to organize, she kept a diary of her political activities that was published in 1973 entitled *Le Tour de France*. She died on November 14, 1844 of an undiagnosed illness and was buried in the cemetery of Chartreux in Bordeaux. In 1848 when the radical revolution that she did not live to see erupted in France, the workers she helped to mobilize collected money to build a monument at the cemetery in celebration of her memory.

ANA PELUFFO

Selected Works

Nécessité de faire un bon accueil aux femmes étrangères. Paris: Dalauney, 1836

Pérégrinations d'une paria (1833–1834). 1838. Arles, France: Acte Sud, 2004. *Peregrinations of a Pariah: 1833–1834*. Trans. Jean Hawkes. Boston: Beacon Press, 1987. Spanish trans. Emilia Romero. *Peregrinaciones de una paria*. Lima: Antártica, 1946.

Méphis ou le prolétaire. 2 vols. Paris: L'advocat, 1838.

Promenades dans Londres. 1840. Paris: Maspero, 1983. English translation: *Flora Tristan's London Journal: A Survey of London Life in the 1830s*. Trans. Dennis Palmer and Giselle Pincetl. London: G. Prior, 1980.

Union Ouvrière. 1843. Paris: Editions d'Histoire Sociale, 1967. *The Worker's Union*. Trans. Beverly Livingston. Urbana, IL: University of Illinois Press, 1983.

Le tour de France, journal 1843–1844. 2nd edn. 2 vols. Text with notes by Jules Puech, preface by Millet Collinet, a new introduction by Stéphane Michaud. Paris: Maspero, 1980.

Lettres. Edited and collected by Stéphane Michaud. Paris: Seuil, 1980.

References and Further Reading

Basadre, Jorge. "Introduction". In Flora Tristán, *Peregrinaciones de una paria*. Lima: Antártica, 1946, pp. v–xxiii.

Beik, Doris and Beik, Paul (eds) *Flora Tristan: Utopian Feminist*. Bloomington, IN: Indiana University Press, 1993.

Dijkstra, Sandra. *Flora Tristan: Pioneer Feminist and Socialist*. Berkeley, CA: Californian Center for Social History, 1984.

Goldberg Moses, Claire and Rabine, Leslie Wahl. *Feminism, Socialism and French Romanticism*. Bloomington, IN: Indiana University Press, 1993.

Grogan, Susan. *Flora Tristan: Life Stories*. London: Routledge, 1998.

Matto de Turner, Clorinda. "La Mariscala". In *Tradiciones cuzqueñas, biografías, leyendas y hojas sueltas*. Cuzco: Rozas, 1954, pp. 181–8.

Moses, Claire Goldberg. *French Feminism in the Nineteenth Century*. Albany, NY: State University of New York, 1984.

Peluffo, Ana. "El *ennui* y la invención de la barbarie en Flora Tristán y Etiènne de Sartiges". In Ignacio Sánchez Prado (ed.), *América Latina: Giro Óptico*, pp. 369–87.

——. "La Mariscala de Flora Tristán". *Lágrimas andinas: Sentimentalismo, género y virtud republicana en Clorinda Matto de Turner*. Pittsburgh, PA: Instituto Internacional de Literatura Iberoamericana, 2005, pp. 120–7.

Portal, Magda. *Flora Tristan, Precursora*. Lima: La equidad, 1983.

Puech, Jules L. *La vie et l'oeuvre de Flora Tristan, 1803–1844*. Paris: M. Rivière, 1925.

Sánchez, Luis Alberto. *Una mujer sola contra el mundo: Flora Tristán, la paria*. Lima: Ediciones Nuevo Mundo, 1961.

Valdelomar, Abraham. *La Mariscala: Doña Francisca Zubiaga y Bernales de Gamara*. Lima: Imprenta de la penitenciaría, 1914.

Vargas Llosa, Mario. *El paraíso en la otra esquina*. Bogotá: Alfaguara, 2003. English trans.: *The Way to Paradise*. Trans. Natasha Wimmer. London: Faber, 2004.

U

UREÑA DE HENRÍQUEZ, SALOMÉ

Salomé Ureña de Henríquez (1850–97), know as "la musa de la patria," or "the muse" to her countrymen, is probably the Dominican Republic's most important female poet. Unfortunately, a thorough and comprehensive study of her poetry has yet to be published and as one of the island nation's first female poets, she warrants more attention from critics and scholars. Her fervent and patriotic poems, which she began writing at age 15, have made her one of the Republic's most important national icons.

Born in Santo Domingo on October 21, 1850, Ureña de Henríquez descended from two of the island's oldest families. Nicolás Ureña de Mendoza, her father, was a famous lawyer and senator as well as a poet, educator and essayist. Gregoria Díaz y León, her mother, was the member of an old land aristocracy and was primarily responsible for Ureña de Henríquez's early years of education.

At a very young age, Ureña de Henríquez exhibited a keen interest in reading and at the time only elementary schools were open to women. Her father, however, was determined to provide Ureña de Henríquez with the best education possible and he took it upon himself to design a plan for her schooling that would take her through her secondary school years. Trained in the classics as well as mathematics, botany and English and French literature, she found herself excelling in poetry. Ureña de Henríquez began writing poetry at the age of 15 and she published her first work at the age of 17 under the pseudonym "Herminia", which she dropped soon afterward when an article on French fashions appeared under the same name in a popular Dominican newspaper of the time.

Ureña de Henríquez's thirst for knowledge was unbounded and she dedicated the latter part of her teenage years to scientific and literary pursuits. It was during this time that she came under the tutelage of Francisco Henríquez y Caravajal, a well-known Dominican intellectual, with whom she eventually fell in love. In 1880, the two married and the couple would go on to have four children, three of whom survived: Pedro, Camila and Maximiliano. In due time, all three children would become important Dominican scholars and intellectuals both in their homeland and abroad.

Ureña de Henríquez's relationship with Francisco Henríquez, who after her death was president of the Republic for a short period in 1916, served as a catalyst for the poet's intellectual pursuits. Francisco introduced young Ureña de Henríquez to the leading intellectuals of the time and she soon became the close friend and pupil of the Puerto Rican intellectual and educator, Eugenio María de Hostos. In 1879, Hostos came to the Dominican Republic to help establish a school for teachers, the *Escuela Normal de Santo Domingo* (The Normal School of Santo Domingo). The friendship that formed between the two would eventually affect Ureña de Henríquez's role as an educator. In November of 1881, Salomé Ureña de Henríquez founded the *Instituto de Señoritas* (School for Young Ladies), the country's first institution for higher education for young women. The school enrolled fourteen students in 1881 and had its first graduation of six young women on April 17, 1887. Ureña de Henríquez was able to run the school until 1893 when it had to close because she was too weak to run it any longer. Soon after her death, the school was reopened by the government under the name of the *Instituto Salomé Ureña* (The Salomé Ureña Institute). In 1892, when Ureña de Henríquez gave birth to her daughter Camila, she became ill with pneumonia and never fully recovered. She retreated to the Northern town of Puerto Plata where she composed what is said to be her last poem, "Mi Pedro," written in honor of her son Pedro and his intellectual promise. On March 6, 1897, she died in Santo Domingo, shortly after returning from Puerto Plata.

Ureña de Henríquez lived during one of the most unstable periods of the Dominican Republic's history. As a child and a young girl, she witnessed the political turmoil that consumed her homeland leaving the impressionable young girl with plenty of fodder to fuel the patriotic themes of her poetry. She grew up in Santo Domingo shortly after the end of the Haitian rule of her country. Much of the political unrest that marked her youth also threatened the possibility of a Haitian return to power. The Dominicans, fearing another takeover by the Haitians, allowed the Spanish to regain control of the government (the only Spanish colony to gain its independence from Spain and then ask to be re-annexed). Ureña de Henríquez was only 11 years old when Spain reclaimed control of the government and it wasn't until 1865 that independence was restored. She would see more than twenty different governments between 1865 and her death, much of which inspired her to write poems that would see her country free from foreign powers and the threat of dictators.

There are three major themes that dominate Salomé Ureña de Henríquez's poetry. The first relates to her patriotic fervor, marked by the poet's desire to see her country in a stable and healthy state. Some poems include: "La fe en el porvenir" (Faith in the Future) "Mi ofrenda a la patria" (My Offering to my Country) "Gloria del progreso" (The Glory of Progress) and "Ruinas" (Ruins). The second comprises the sentimental and the personal, characterized by her commitment to nature and her family as in her poems "El ave y el nido," (The Bird and the Nest) "Mi Pedro," (My Pedro) "La llegada del invierno" (Winter's Arrival) and "En horas de angustia" (During the Hours of Anguish). A third theme is clearly marked by her desire to glorify the indigenous heritage of the island nation. Her long narrative poem "Anacaona" is a perfect example of Ureña de Henríquez's *indianismo* or nativism. "Anacaona" is by far her most ambitious work as she tries to revive the nation's historical origins by bringing to life the Taino race who were destroyed by the Spaniards while conquering the island.

While Salomé Ureña never really wrote much, peace and progress were the themes of her work from 1873–80. In the early 1880s, Salomé found herself lost and betrayed by her faith in patriotic politics and so she decided to dedicate her time to educating young women. Her relationship with Eugenio María de Hostos, Puerto Rican intellectual and her mentor, helped introduce *positivism* to the Dominican Republic. In Hostos, she found a soulmate and together they fought to espouse the ideas of progress and to offer Dominican women a modern, scientific education. Both envisioned work and education as necessary catalysts for the liberation of women from domestic slavery. And in this respect, Salomé Ureña shared the same concerns for her fellow women as did the Latin American proto-feminists of her time, Peruvian Clorinda Matos de Turner and Puerto Rican Ana Roqué de Puprey.

Critical studies of Salomé Ureña de Henríquez's work are few considering the poet's importance in the Republic's literary history. Eugenio María de Hostos was one of Ureña de Henríquez's first critics and he found himself drawn to her patriotic poems and themes. In 1920, her son Pedro Henríquez Ureña wrote the prologue to her *Poesías escogidas* (Selected Poems) which has served as the foundation of most of the biographical studies written on her. The most detailed and thorough analysis of Salomé Ureña de Henríquez's poetry appears in the introduction to her *Poesías completas* (Complete Collection of Poems) (1950) written by Joaquín Balaguer. In his introduction, Balaguer skillfully examines Ureña de Henríquez's poetic style and praises it for being technically flawless.

While contemporary Dominican scholars recognize the importance of Salomé Ureña de Henríquez as a leading literary and political figure, only a handful have truly dedicated their time to better understanding her place in Dominican literary history. José Alcántara Almánzar's *Estudios de poesía dominicana* (Studies in Dominican Poetry) (1979) and his *Narrativa y sociedad en Hispanoamérica* (Narrative and Society in Spanish-America) (1984) are two of the most comprehensive works that examine Salomé Ureña de Henríquez's positivist philosophies present in her poetry and it is probably the only Marxist critique of the poet's bourgeois ideologies (Paravisini-Gebert 530).

Catharina Vallejo's essay "Trascendencia poética del binarismo de lo público y lo doméstico en la obra de Salomé Ureña de Henríquez," appears in the collection *Poética de escritoras hispanoamericanas al alba del próximo milenio* (The Poetics of Spanish-American Women Writers at the Dawn of a New Millenium) (1998). In her essay, Vallejo carefully examines the binary relationship between public and domestic spaces that exists in Ureña de Henríquez's poetry. Her study asserts that she was the first Dominican poet to launch herself outside the realm of domesticity. Moreover, Vallejo's study confirms that her role was pivotal in the formation of a female presence in the public Dominican arena, as seen in her writing and patriotism, while, at the same time, reaffirming in her writing that the female subject is a loving and caring one.

Ironically, one of the most relevant and satisfying studies of Salomé Ureña de Henríquez's life and work appears in the form of a novel. Julia Alvarez's *In the Name of Salomé*, published in 2000, tells of Ureña de Henríquez and her daughter Camila's story, a university professor in the United States. The novel is set in the politically chaotic Dominican Republic of the nineteenth century, on three North American campuses and in Communist Cuba of the 1960s. *In the Name of Salomé*, although a novel, allows us to dive into the Caribbean waters of the young Salomé Ureña de Henríquez as she struggles to understand her place in nineteenth-century Dominican society. In Alvarez's novel, readers can hear the voice of the young Ureña de Henríquez fighting to create a space for women in Dominican society, educating Dominican girls to be teachers as well as patriots. In addition, the novel brings us closer to understanding why her shy and almost anonymous daughter, Camila, dedicated her life to educating young upper-class American girls at private universities in the United States.

H. J. MANZARI

Selected Works

Poesías. Santo Domingo: Sociedad Amigos del País, 1880

Poesías completas. Edición comemorativa del centenario de su nacimiento, 1850–1950. Prol. Joaquín Balaguer. Ciudad Trujillo: Impresora Dominicana, 1950.

Poesías escogidas. Prol. Pedro Henríquez Ureña. Madrid: n.p., 1920.

Poesías escogidas. Prol. Pedro Henríquez Ureña. Ciudad Trujillo: Librería Dominicana, 1960.

Cantos a la patria. Santo Domingo: Publicaciones América, 1970.

Poesías completas. Santo Domingo: Ediciones de la Fundación Corripio, 1989.

References and Further Reading

Alvarez, Julia. *In the Name of Salomé*. Chapel Hill, NC: Algonquin Books, 2000.

Gimbernat González, Ester. "Salomé Ureña, patriota y letrada". in *La voz de la mujer en la literatura hispanoamericana fin-de-siglo*. San José: Universidad de Costa Rica, 1999.

Henríquez Ureña, Pedro. *Obra dominicana*. Santo Domingo: Sociedad Dominicana de Bibliófilos, 1988.

Herrera, César A. *La poesía de Salomé Ureña en su función social patriótica*. Ciudad Trujillo: Impresora Dominicana, 1951.

Juliá, Julio Jaime. *Las discípulas de Salomé Ureña escriben*. Santo Domingo: Editorial Ciguapa, 2001.

Medrano, Marianela. *Seis mujeres poetas: en homenaje a Salomé Ureña*. Santo Domingo: Publicaciones de la Universidad Autónoma de Santo Domingo, 1989.

Rivera Martínez, Mildred. "La poesía de Salomé Ureña: Modos poéticos en la época modernista en la República Dominicana". *Journal of the Pacific Northwest Council on Foreign Languages* 9 (1988): 113–19.

Rojas-Trempe, L. and Vallejo, Catharina. *Poéticas de escritoras hispanoamericanas al alba del próximo milenio*. Miami, FL: Ediciones Universal, 1998.

Vicioso, Sherezada. *Salomé Ureña de Henríquez (1850–1897): a cien años de un magisterio*. Santo Domingo: Comisión Permanente de la Feria Nacional del Libro, 1997.

V

VALDÉS, ZOÉ

Zoé Valdés is Cuban of Chinese descent. She was born in Havana, on May 2, 1959, i.e. the year of Castro's triumph in the Cuban Revolution. Since her father abandoned their family very early, she was reared by her mother and her grandmother. Her upbringing may have influenced her work, which invariably presents a woman's world and her concerns, relegating male characters to marginal and often questionable positions. Valdés spent four years studying physical education at the Pedagógico Superior and two more working towards a degree in Spanish philology at the University of Havana. Together with her first husband, she worked at the Cuban Delegation for UNESCO, between 1984 and 1988. Valdés also worked as a film scriptwriter at the Cultural Office of the Cuban Embassy in Paris, and as an assistant director of the *Revista de Cine Cubano* in the Cuban Institute of Arts and Cinematographic Industry (ICAIC) between 1990 and 1995. Eventually disenchanted with Fidel Castro's regime, she left Cuba and moved to France on 22 January 1995. She was granted Spanish citizenship by King Juan Carlos in December 1997. Nevertheless, she has remained in Paris with her daughter Attys Luna and her second husband, film-maker Ricardo Vega. There, she was awarded the Chevalier's Order of Arts and Letters. In her very fruitful career Zoé Valdés has received numerous awards, such as the Premio Carlos Ortiz for *Todo para una sombra* (1985), the Roque Dalton prize for *Respuesta para vivir* (1986), the Juan March Cencillo Short Novel prize for *La hija del embajador* (1995), and she was a finalist for the Premio Planeta for *Te di la vida entera* in 1996. She also received the Premio de Novela Fernando Lara for her novel *Lobas de mar* (2003) and the III Premio de Novela Ciudad de Torrevieja for *La eternidad del instante* in 2004.

Valdés has participated in numerous cultural events, from poetry competitions and international film festivals to literary events. To name just a few, she has worked in the Latino Festival in New York (1990 and 1991), in the Competition for the Still-Unpublished Cinematographic Scripts at the XIII International Festival of New Latin American Cinema, and at the IV International Festival of Poetry in Medellín, Colombia (1994). She also served on the jury at the Cannes Film Festival (1998), and as a judge for Premio Planeta in 1998 and 1999. Her many fiction and non-fiction pieces have appeared in numerous European newspapers and magazines. Valdés has writtend for *El País*, *ELLE*, *Vogue*, *El Mundo, El Semanal, Qúe leer* in Spain, and *Le Monde, Libération, Le Nouvel Observateur, Beaux Arts, Les Inrockuptibles* in France.

Zoé Valdés is one of those controversial writers who inspire admiration in many and aversion in others. While countless readers enjoy her direct style, humor, and abundant eroticism, others criticize her for what they see as repetitiveness, quantity over quality (she publishes roughly one novel per year), crudeness, pornography, and megalomania in her interviews. This criticism comes in large part from within Cuba, suggesting, more likely, tensions caused by political differences. As one of the most prolific and widely read women writers of the moment, Valdés differs from other Cuban writers of her generation. Unlike most of "the novísimos," meaning the generation of writers born in the 1950s, Valdés does not ignore the sociopolitical context. Her texts obsessively revolve around Cuba with its historical circumstances and multiple social shortcomings. They present the island either as a lock-up riddled with propaganda and poverty, a society which destroys any signs of dignity in its citizens, or as an idyllic pre-revolutionary place of the past. The Havana prior to the revolution appears replete with desire, erotic pleasure, abundance, nightlife, and the influence of European bohemia. (This motif reappears with particular force in her recent novel, *Los misterios de la Havana.*) Nevertheless, this prosperity gives way to isolation, obscurantism, and collective disillusionment following Castro's coming to power. For example, the novels *Te di la vida entera* and *La nada cotidiana* show the deterioration of an agonizing nation, its people's disenchantment with socialism, the moral degeneration of Cuban youth, prostitution disguised as tourism and, finally, absurdly miserable living conditions. For instance, in *Te di la vida entera*, sentimental romance clashes with revolutionary penury, exposing an ailing society, where moral values are eradicated systematically by the faulty sociopolitical system.

Valdés's literary world is divided between Cuba and North America (or Cuba and China, presented in *La eternidad del instante*), a demarcation which has a decisive bearing on the lives of her characters. The border opens up only in rare historical moments such as, for example, with the start of revolution (when many immediately escaped abroad to await political changes) or in the "special period" after the fall of the Soviet Union (between 1990 and 1995), when exiled Cubans could finally visit their families. Valdés's own family has lived dispersed in different parts of the world as well; the writer has established herself in Paris, her siblings have resided in New Jersey and Miami, and their mother was forced to remain in Cuba, being able to join Valdés only two years before her death. It is no surprise that Valdés's literary characters have similar experiences, suffering from detachment and loneliness. Parents are separated from their children (*Te di la vida entera, Café nostalgia*), siblings live apart, resenting their brothers and sisters who were lucky enough to grow up with their parents (*Café nostalgia*), women lose their men (*Te di la vida entera*) and finally, friends are reduced to sporadic contact through correspondence only (various novels). Those who are forced to remain on the island wait hopelessly for the return of loved ones, whereas exiles try in vain to establish their lives elsewhere, always longing for the homeland and lost relationships (*Café Nostalgia, La hija del embajador*).

Perhaps the most interesting aspect of Valdés's writing is her focus on woman's experiences. Her narratives are feminist on several levels, as they center on woman's life and her position within a family and society, as well as her sexuality. For example, *Bailar con la vida*, a novel with numerous autobiographical elements, is replete with strong eroticism as it narrates the life of a somewhat disenchanted writer who finds herself in a crisis of professional identity. Valdés's novels portray the female body as a receptor of culture and politics but also as the heroine's most empowering tool for her self-definition. Aside from analyzing economic problems and their consequences, her texts invariably highlight women's *jouissance*. Desire and its fulfillment allow the heroines to reappropriate a body ridden with propaganda, and even to rename it—as in *La nada cotidiana* where the heroine rejects the politically charged name given by her father, Patria, in favor of Yocandra. Valdés's female characters are usually open to sexual experimentation, which serves as a tool to escape a mundane existence and to explore their embodied identity. Her recent female characters from *Lobas de mar*, two pirates who lived in the seventeenth and eighteenth centuries, Ann Bonny and Mary Read, exemplify female empowerment in the distinctly masculine environment of Caribbean pirates. Their wit, intelligence, bravery, and last but not least, the bond that they develop, corroborates Valdés's unwavering interest in women's issues.

In an interview with Itziar Bilbao, Valdés states that she is not afraid of the body, thus endorsing her unique style marked by an utterly frank sexuality. For Valdés, corporeality is an instrument to learn about the world and the site of resistance against patriarchal (male and state) power. Pleasure and sensuality defy the official discourse which taints even the most basic social cells. Standing in stark contrast to the establishment and its prerogatives, woman's body becomes a metaphor for a personalized, individualistic nation, as it engenders new discourses from a woman's perspective. Similarly, Valdés's poetry explores the female body and its biological processes, such as, for instance, reproduction and pregnancy. Experiencing corporeality is intrinsically linked with the five senses, which in Valdés's opinion, are intensified among islanders and accompanied by the sixth one—sensuality. The significance of this statement is reflected in the structure of *Café nostalgia,* which is divided into five chapters, each referring to one of the senses, together with a sixth chapter representing woman's desire.

One of Zoé Valdés's leitmotifs is the presence and the significance of the sea. It carries multifold meanings depending on the text, but it invariably gives Cubans a sense of national specificity. Valdés's unique trademark, however, is the recurrence of references to popular culture, particularly film and music. She draws comparisons between her characters by evoking film protagonists, such as Kubrick's Lolita and Scarlett O'Hara from *Gone with the Wind* or famous actors themselves, such as Anthony Perkins, Al Pacino, Humphrey Bogart, Ingrid Bergman, Jean Gabin, Alain Delon, Pedro Almodóvar, Juliette Binoche, or Catherine Deneuve, among others. Her cinematographic references come from Hollywood and Europe but, curiously, as Miguel Ángel González-Abellellás has noted, they never evoke Latin American or, even more so, Cuban cinematography (2000: 46). Music—in traditional and popular rhythms of bolero, son, and guaracha to mention few—populates Valdés's pages as well. Even the title of *Te di la vida entera* is a line from Benny Moré's *Camarera de amor*. Different verses from various songs by, for example, Pedro Vargas, Eliseo Grenet, Rodrigo Pratts, and José Quiñones appear within the narrative, as well as at the beginning of every chapter in the book.

Perhaps Valdés's most acclaimed novel to this day is *La nada cotidiana*, whose protagonist, Patria/Yocandra, negotiates her existence in the penury of post-revolutionary Cuba. Her job is limiting and unrewarding and her personal life continues between her ex-husband, "The Traitor" and a young director, "The Nihilist". Disenchanted with her reality and resigned to her restrictive sociopolitical circumstances, the heroine finds fulfillment in the arms of the Nihilist. In this highly sensual relationship, Yocandra asserts her own needs in terms of her own bodily pleasure, negotiating sexual boundaries with the partner and making her own sexual needs known. The force of her empowered femininity is perhaps what has contributed to the novel's success; the discourse of desire is no longer redistributed by male characters but instead it becomes the tool in woman's self-exploration and growth.

ALDONA BIALOWAS POBUTSKY

Selected Works

Novels

Sangre azul. Habana: Editorial Letras Cubanas, 1993 (also published by Emecé, Barcelona, España, 1996 and by Actes-Sud, Paris, France, 1996).

La nada cotidiana. Paris: Actes-Sud, París, 1995 (also published by Emecé, Barcelona, España, 1995; Amman Verlag, Switzerland and Germany, 1995; Zanzíbar, Italy, 1995; and other countries, such as Holland, the US, Portugal, Brazil, Greece, Great Britain, Turkey, Australia, Finland and Sweden).

La hija del embajador. Palma de Mallorca: Ediciones Bitzoc, 1995 (also published by Actes-Sud (La sous-developpée)), Paris, France in 1996).

Te di la vida entera. Barcelona: Planeta, 1996 (translated into German, French, Italian, Portuguese, Finnish, Swedish, Turkish, Polish, Yugoslavian and Russian).

Cólera de ángeles. Paris: Ediciones Textuel, 1996 (also published by Lumen in Barcelona, España, 1996).
Café Nostalgia. Barcelona: Planeta, 1997.
Querido primer novio. Barcelona: Planeta, 1999.
El pie de mi padre. Francia: Gallimard, 2000.
Querido primer novio. Francia: Actes-Sud, 2000.
Milagro en Miami. Barcelona: Planeta, 2001.
Lobas del mar. Editorial Planeta: 2003.
La eternidad del instante. Planeta: 2004.
Los misterios de la Havana. Mexico: Plaza y Janes, 2004.
Bailar con la vida. Planeta: 2006

Children's Literature

Los aretes de la luna. España: Everest, León, 1999.

Short Stories

"Mujer de alguien". In Mirta Yáñez and Marilyn Bobes (eds), *Estatuas de sal. Cuentistas cubanas contemporáneas. Panorama crítico (1959–1995).* Habana: Ediciones Unión, 1996.
Traficantes de belleza. Barcelona: Planeta, 1998.

Poetry

Respuestas para vivir. Havana: Editorial Letras Cubanas, 1986.
Todo para una sombra. Barcelona: Editorial Taifa, 1986.
Vagón para fumadores. Barcelona: Lumen, 1986 (also published by Actes-Sud, Arles, 1999).
Los poemas de la Habana. Paris: Editorial Antoine Soriano, 1997 (bilingual edition).
Cuerdas para el lince. Barcelona: Lumen, 1999.
Breve beso de la espera. 2002.

Essay

"Del poema al guión (capítulo), ensayos escritos por especialistas cubanos y americanos". 1992.
En fin, el mar ... (Cartas de balseros) (Ensayo testimonio), Ediciones Bitzoc, Palma de Mallorca, 1996.

References and Further Reading

González-Abellás, Miguel Angel. "'Aquella isla': Introducción al universo narrativo de Zoé Valdés". *Hispania* 83(1) (2000): 42–50.
Itziar Bilbao "Zoé Valdés. Coming to America." *EXITO Magazine* Nov. (1997)
www.fiu.edu/~fcf/Zoévaldes112097.html (accessed 5 June 2003).
Mateo del Pino, Angeles and Gutiérrez, José Ismael. "Zoé Valdés". *Hispamérica* 33(98) (2004): 49–60.
Ortiz Cerebro, Cristina. "La narrativa de Zoé Valdés: Hacia una reconfiguración de la na(rra-)ción cubana". *Chasqui* 27(2) (1998): 116–28.
Pobutsky, Aldona Bialowas. "Sex and Excess in Communist Cuba: *Te di la vida entera* de Zoé Valdés". *Hispanic Journal* 27(2) (2006): 137–46.

VALDÉS-GINEBRA, ARMINDA

Arminda Valdés-Ginebra was born in 1923 in Güines, a province of Havana. She completed a degree in Social Work and later received her doctorate in Pedagogy at the University of Havana. She also pursued studies in drama, journalism, and psychology. Primarily a poet, she has also written books on drama and short stories for children. Prevented from leaving Cuba for eight and a half years, Valdés-Ginebra finally went into exile in 1979. She spent a short time in Madrid, Spain, and then, in 1979 established her permanent residence in New York.

Valdés-Ginebra has won the following prizes: Rociana del Condado (Huelva, Spain) in 1987 for her collection *Absorto en el Anagrama* (Absorbed in the Anagram), Agustín Acosta (GALA, Miami, USA) twice in 1991 and 1992 for *Sombras imaginarias* (Imaginary Shadows) and for *Equilibrio del ansia* (Equilibrium of the Yearning) respectively; and Quinto Concurso Internacional Antológico de Santa Mónica (California, USA) in 1994 for *Todo en torno al amor* (Everything about Love). Valdés-Ginebra is a member of the Ibero-American Academy of Poetry.

Poet

Valdés-Ginebra's poetic discourse represents a dynamic contrast of light and shadows, life and death, presence and absence, and dream and reality that conveys a sentiment of estrangement. Through her poetry, experience and memories are combined to create an ambience of chiaroscuro which uncovers the passing of time. Her language carefully oscillates between suggestiveness and concreteness, between telluric representation and skillful irrational imagery, intentionally attempting to bridge the gap between the domains of intuition and of objective reality.

Her early collections are defined by a search for a distinctive and personal lyrical voice. Valdés-Ginebra's poetic expression links linguistic codes and metaphors with existential motifs, rooted in her acknowledgment of finitude but projected towards transcendence, as depicted in *Sombras imaginarias* (Imaginary Shadows). Anguish, desolation, solitude, and uneasiness are a constant in her verses: "I see you, although you are only a shadow / and in my dream I miss you". These feelings are overcome by her desire to live and her dedication to poetry. Valdés-Ginebra understands the poet developing within the poem, not outside it. In the process of creation, images and metaphors are intertwined with personal philosophical ideas and metaphysical intuitions. As Odón Betanzos Palacios observed, Valdés-Ginebra's poetry "represents one of the great achievements in contemporary Cuban poetry: originality, intense lyricism, novelty of spirit, freshness of something new, ample registry, search for innovative literary devices".

Vigilia del aliento (Vigil of Courage) reflects Valdés-Ginebra's admiration for José Martí, poet and apostle of the Cuban fight for freedom. His figure and defense of the Cuban spirit and independence open and close this collection, symbolizing the beginning and end of a process that denounces the repressive Castro regime. A multitude of images emerge in Valdés-Ginebra's poems to communicate the helplessness of people and the painful anguish and longing of those who went into exile. The contemplation of a distant Cuba evokes a sense of unreality, since her memories of a happy past are impossible to actualize while the tragedy of political subjection and imprisonment continues. With very popular verses, Valdés-Ginebra establishes the dilemma of the emotional ambivalence of those exiled: "To be who they were before and not to be the same / that is the aspiration. / To be the owners yet exist as tenants". Through the freedom of imagination, she returns to Cuba, manifesting her love for the island while criticizing its distressing asphyxia. The book's touching tone both mirrors the poet's intense pain for people exiled and expresses her hope for a political change that will allow the resurgence of a new Cuba.

In her collection *Sigo zurciendo las medias de mi hijo* (I Continue Darning My Son's Socks), Valdés-Ginebra's poetry becomes enriched with a powerful tenderness spurred by the memory of her son's tragic death. From the very first poem, reality and nightmare are interwoven in a forged child's world resembling a fairy tale to illustrate the recovery of her son's presence and happiness. The games he used to play, his fondness for theatrics, his skates, his longing for a bicycle, a day at the beach ... elucidate the emotional leitmotiv of the maternal affliction and formulate a pathetic *ubi sunt?* In her extraordinary poem "Boy with the Eggplant," Valdés-Ginebra describes, with pain balanced by love, how toys and boots miss the child and her feeling of the overwhelming void. The poet realizes, however, that remembering him entails a reencounter of mother and son. Anguish and affection define the defeat of her life and the absurdity of death, both lovingly entwined in her poetic discourse: "Dead children continue being children". For Orlirio Fuentes, this book "presents an uninhabited life, an empty body ... saved by the grace of the encounter, by the transmutation of the person into a memory, into an echo touched by death".

Renuevo tras la lluvia (Renewal after the Rain) and *Equilibrio del ansia* (Equilibrium of Yearning) compose a volume depicting two very different sentiments. In the first collection, existential tedium, pessimism and pain dominate to transmit a psychological fatigue and insomnia resulting from personal fragmentation: "It hurts the sky from up above / the light, the sphere revolving and estranging vertigo / torn off toward fingernail, shell, and root". Distress accompanies awareness and acknowledgment of being a "broken seed" who lives futilely: "I am tired of carrying my name". The consideration of life without meaning brings momentary defeat, an attitude of anguish, incompleteness and tardiness for love and for her son that, however, leaves room for tenderness and hope. Poetry also becomes a senseless activity to conciliate emotion and expression: "Dreams and nightmares assault me / striking me in the contours / of the idea". The tone in the second collection, *Equilibrio del ansia* (Equilibrium of Yearning), is very different. As the title conveys, a balance has been reached and serenity and optimism affirm the apparent passing of time. Several poems describe the poet's intuition of new adventures and the permanence of being, as well as a self-rejuvenation in Nature with images of springs, creeks, drizzles, sunsets: "I am elementary young. / Fresh water celebrated in the cliffs, / a scent just born in the creases". In Nature, love also persists as well as serenity and compassion. However, a climate of secrecy and unreality also hovers over memories and dreams in other poems: "My shadow and I completing / what is sinuous. / My contour elongating / under avid cerebrums / towards premises of doubtful / answers".

This atmosphere of enigmatic vagueness, complemented with a powerful and vivid creativity is a defining element of Valdés-Ginebra's poetic endeavor. Her discourse strives to blend symbols and images with the objective of connecting disparate realities. Writing is her salvation, acting to penetrate the mystery behind the dimensions of memory, love and suffering with the intuition of an underlying meaning that enables transcendence. This symbiotic coalescence of ambiences represents a new form of expressive freedom for Valdés-Ginebra, manifested by her metamorphosis into an emblematic butterfly that "recreates in forthcoming places, / reverberates in creations".

FRANCISCO J. PEÑAS-BERMEJO

Selected Works

Júbilo alcanzado. Prólogo de Andrés Eloy Blanco. La Habana: Editorial Vaillant, 1962.
Huella vertical. La Habana: Editorial Vaillant, 1965.
Poemas presurosos en España. Edición no venal, 1979.
Por una primavera. Edición no venal, 1979.
Absorto en el Anagrama. Nueva York: Editorial Mensaje, 1987.
Sombras imaginarias. Madrid: Betania, 1989.
Vigilia del aliento. Madrid: Betania, 1990.
Sigo zurciendo las medias de mi hijo. Madrid: Betania, 1991.
Renuevo tras la lluvia. Equilibrio del ansia. New York: Serena Bay Books, 1993.

References and Further Reading

Betanzos Palacios, Odón. "Algunas notas críticas en torno a la obra poética de Arminda Valdés Ginebra". *Sigo zurciendo las medias de mi hijo*. Madrid: Betania, 1991, pp. 47–9.
Campbell, John T. (ed.) *World of Poetry Anthology*. San Francisco, CA: World of Poetry, 1991.
El Puente 24, 1982.
Espina, Darío. *Poetisas cubanas contemporáneas*. Miami, FL: Academia Poética de Miami, 1990.
Fuentes, Orlirio. "Arminda Valdés-Ginebra, *Sigo zurciendo las medias de mi hijo*." *La Nuez* 4(12) (1991): 29.
Lázaro, Felipe (ed.) *Poesía cubana contemporánea. Antología*. Madrid: Catoblepas, 1986.
——. *Poetas cubanos en Nueva York*. Madrid: Betania, 1988.
Le Riverend (ed.) *Colectivo de Poetas Q-21*. Newark, NJ: Q-21, 1981.
——. *Diccionario biográfico de poetas cubanos en el exilio (Contemporáneos)*. Newark, NJ: Q-21, 1988.
Ligulappi, Óscar A. (ed.) *Patria Plural, El alba del hombre, Suma de amor y América poética*. Río de la Plata, Argentina: El Editor Interamericano, 1989, 1990, 1991, 1992.
Peñas-Bermejo, Francisco J. "Arminda Valdés Ginebra". In Francisco J. Peñas-Bermejo (ed.), *Poetas cubanos marginados*. El Ferrol: S.C.V-I., 1998, pp. 24–5, 83–103.

VALDIVIESO, MERCEDES

Mercedes Valdivieso's (1924–93) writing is characterized by its break from traditional visions of woman in Chilean society. In her most successful novels, Valdivieso creates women characters who defy canonical representations of the feminine and dare to escape the mores of a patriarchal society.

Valdivieso was born in Santiago de Chile on March 1, 1924. Her father was a physician and after his death, when she was 7 years old, her mother graduated as a medical doctor and practiced the profession until retirement. Her mother became an important role model in Valdivieso's life, as revealed in several aspects of her writing. Valdivieso attended a Catholic elementary school, completed her secondary education at El Colegio Universitario Inglés, and earned a degree in Literature from the Universidad de Chile. Divorced from her first husband, with whom she had two children, she married the writer Jaime Valdivieso. In the United States, where she moved with her husband, she obtained a Master's degree in Latin American

Literature from the University of Houston in 1968 and taught at Saint Thomas University and Rice University. Once retired, and after having lived in the United States for 23 years, she returned to her native country. She died in Santiago de Chile on August 3, 1993.

Mercedes Valdivieso's first novel, *La Brecha*, was originally published in Chile in 1961 and later translated to English and published in the United States (*Breakthrough,* 1988). Fernando Alegría, one of the leading literary critics of the time wrote the prologue to *La Brecha*'s first edition. The book received favorable reviews in major Chilean newspapers, *El Mecurio* and *La Nación,* which valued the originality with which it addressed women's concerns, and the novel became a best seller.

La Brecha narrates the experience of an upper middle-class woman who defies her traditional surroundings by taking the bold step of breaking up her conventional and loveless marriage, thus, leading her to confront the economic and social challenges of being a single mother. "I got married as everyone else does. Everybody agreed that a husband was absolutely indispensable," states the first person narrator of *La Brecha* on the first page. *La Brecha* fits within the framework of a number of women writers' novels that attained considerable success in Latin America from the 1940s to the 1960s. These narratives challenged a discourse that enclosed women into the private realm by exalting marriage and maternal bliss as the only acceptable choices in a woman's life. Significant among these type of narrative were novels by the Argentinian writers Silvina Bullrich and Martha Lynch. Silvina Bullrich in *Bodas de Cristal* (1951) and Martha Lynch in *La Señora Ordoñez* (1967) create alienated female characters that, although aware of their unhappiness in love, are unable to listen to their own desires as their ideas and goals are in constant flux responding to the pressures and opinions of their husbands, their lovers or their environs. *La Brecha* differs from these other novels because the unnamed protagonist breaks free of matrimony; refuses to marry the man she falls in love with, and is capable of feeling happy and fulfilled in a new life not defined by marriage. Thus, the protagonist is able to escape what Joanne S. Frye has called "the feminine text" in woman's existence; the need to abide to passivity or succumb to solitude, desperation or even suicide (1986: 78).

La Tierra que les di (1963) and *Las noches y un día* (1971) depict the decadence of the landowner class in Chile. *La Tierra que les dí* conveys a sense of nostalgia for a world that is breaking down. It narrates the story of a powerful and wealthy matriarch who, in spite of her fortune, raises her ten children strictly. As adults, her children refuse to continue the family's tradition of hard work and austerity, squandering their inheritance in a life of luxury and squalor. The novel is a reflection on the decay and failure of a once dominant social class that has recklessly wasted the immense wealth and resources of the country. In *Las noches y un día*, the two male protagonists live in a dilapidated house that once was a grand mansion. The elder had led a life of pleasure in his youth. In his old age, lonely and disenchanted, he wanders the city at nights. Mateo, his nephew, breaks loose from the political cynicism of his family, joins the Popular Front (a coalition of leftist parties) and becomes an activist. When the Popular Front loses the presidential elections in 1964, a sense of doom overcomes him and his life starts to fall apart. His devastating pessimism could be interpreted as a sign of a malaise that represents the fruitlessness of his social class.

When Jaime Valdivieso was invited to visit China in 1960 by the Association of Chinese Journalists, his wife, Mercedes, joined him and they spent a month visiting the country. Four years later she went back to China and stayed there for almost a year when she was invited to teach at the University of Peking.

Her novel *Los ojos de bambú* (1964) is the culmination of both experiences. In its prologue, the author emphasizes her admiration for China's ancient civilization and she states her sympathy for the Revolution that brought the Communists to power in 1949. She also notes that the Revolution was able to put an end to thousands of years of oppression suffered by the Chinese people. Nevertheless, through the dilemma that the protagonist, Clara, confronts, Valdivieso expresses her own uneasiness about several aspects of the new system. Clara is a painter invited by the Chinese government to convey to the world the Revolution's endeavors. Although she is provided with a perfect environment to work in, she feels hindered in her efforts to express her personal impressions. Through a variety of characters who represent the official position of the regime, it becomes obvious to her that there is no space in China for personal distinctiveness, or freedom of artistic expression. According to her hosts, there is a choice to be made between individualistic ambitions or a collective effort for the common good. Feeling disenchanted and thwarted and after an agonizing deliberation, Clara finally decides to return to her country before the expiration of her contract. Thus, Valdivieso expresses her disillusionment with the China she encountered during her time there. However, in the epilogue, Valdivieso states that she believes that the problems she perceived and describes in her novel are just stages in an historical development that will eventually lead to the liberation of human kind.

Her last novel, *Maldita yo entre las mujeres* (1991), received significant critical attention. The novel is a rewriting of the story of Catalina de los Ríos y Lisperguer (1604–65) known as "La Quintrala", an almost mythical character in the narratives that create the colonial history of Chile. ("Quintrala" is a red-leaved parasitic plant that kills the tree to which it attaches itself. Catalina had red hair, green eyes and a dark complexion.) Benjamin Vicuña Mackena, a prominent historian of the nineteenth century, wrote a historical essay in 1877 about "La Quintrala" and her powerful family, noting their "obscure" origins, a mixture of German, Spanish and Mapuche Indian. He linked the intemperance of the female descendants of the family and the cruelty of La Quintrala to their Mapuche blood. Instead, the male descendants of the family are glorified in his essay for their valor in the war, their shrewdness in business and their success in love. Vicuña Mackena's history manipulated concepts of gender and race in line with a model of a white Chilean nation promoted by the leading class of his time. Women had a subordinate role to play in that ideal society. They were responsible for the education of the children in the values of patriotism and the protection of the family from any undesirable elements.

Maldita yo entre las mujeres reclaims Catalina's story from a feminist perspective and provides a historical re-evaluation of the Indian cultures. In the novel, Catalina's first person narration is set against a polyphony of voices that articulate the discursive context of seventeenth-century Chile. Catalina's voice recovers a rebellious genealogy of women that originated with her great grandmother, the *cacica*, Elvira de Talagante, a Mapuche Indian who refused to marry her German lover when he made her pregnant with Catalina's grandmother. Her great-grandmother's cultural inheritance comes to Catalina through her Indian nanny, a woman who has lived through three generations, and is thus represented as the keeper of the shamanistic traditions of the Mapuche people symbolizing the persistent influence of the Indian culture. The novel's language mimics seventeenth-century Spanish and invites the reader into a ghostly world that erases the boundaries between reality and reverie. In the epilogue to the novel Valdivieso declares that her narrative restores the history of Catalina de los Ríos to the author's time. In so doing she creates an alternative history of the mythical Quintrala which challenges the ideas about women construed in the past.

Besides her novelistic production Valdivieso has published a considerable number of scholarly papers, many of them dedicated to feminine and feminist subjects. From *La Brecha* to *Maldita yo entre las mujeres* Mercedes Valdivieso has exhibited a significant development of her craft as well as an increasing awareness and insight into the treatment of gender issues. Her ability to embrace not only gender but racial and ethnic subjects in *Maldtita yo entre las mujeres* challenged longstanding claims of cultural and racial homogeneity in Chilean society. Additionally, her œuvre reveals a deep understanding of and commitment to the social and cultural issues of her native Chile and of her time.

Aída Apter-Cragnolino

Selected Works

La tierra que les di. Santiago de Chile: Zig-Zag, 1963.

Los ojos de bambú. Santiago de Chile: Zig-Zag, 1965.

Las noches y un día. Barcelona: Seix Barral, 1971.

La Brecha. Prólogo de Margot Glantz. Pittsburgh, PA: Latin American Literary Review, 1986.

Breakthrough. Trans. Graciela S. Daichman. Pittsburgh, PA: Latin American Review Press, 1988.

Maldita yo entre las mujeres. Santiago de Chile: Editorial Planeta Chilena, 1991.

References and Further Reading

Alone. "*La Brecha*. Novela por Mercedes Valdivieso". *El Mercurio*. Santiago de Chile, 11 June 1961.

Del Solar, Hernán. "*La Brecha*." *La Nación*. Santiago de Chile, 1 May 1961.

Fry, Joanne. *Living Stories. Telling Lives. Women and the Novel in Contemporary Experience*. Ann Arbor, MI: The University of Michigan State, 1986.

Fuente, José de la. "La narrativa de Mercedes Valdivieso; De *La Brecha* a la Tatamai". *Literatura y Lingüística*. 5 (1992): 39–51.

Labarca Garat, Gustavo. *Los ojos de bambú*. *La Nación*, 21 March 1965.

Llanos, Bernardita. "Tradición e historia en la narrativa femenina: Petit y Valdivieso frente a La Quintrala". *Revista Iberoamericana* 60(8) (1994): 1025–37.

Malverde-Disselkoen, Ivette. "De *La Ultima Niebla* y *La amortajada* a *La Brecha*. *Nuevo Texto Crítico*". 2(4) 1989: 69–78.

Marichien, Euler Carmona: "Mercedes Valdivieso". In Patricia Rubio (ed.), *Escritoras chilenas. Novela y cuento*. Santiago de Chile: Cuarto Propio, 1999, pp. 343–55.

Mora, Gabriela. "Discurso histórico y discurso novelesco: A propósito de La Quintrala". *Inti: Revista de Literatura Hispánica* (Autumn 1994–Spring 1995): 61–73.

Ojeda, Cecilia. "Una reinterpretación de La Quintrala en la historia chilena: *Maldita yo entre las mujeres* de Mercedes Valdivieso". *Confluencia. Revista Hispánica de Cultura y Literatura* 13(2) (Spring, 1998): 92–6.

Rojo, Sara. "La Quintrala El contra-mito de la mujer chilena?" *Literatura y Libros* (3 May 1992): 1–2.

Vicuña Mackena, Benjamín. *Los Lisperguer y la Quintrala*. 2nd edn. Crítica de Jaime Eyzaguirre. Santiago de Chile: Empresa editora Zig-Zag, 1950.

Ward, Ronda. "A Colonial Woman in a Republican's Chilean History: Benjamín Vicuña Mackena and La Quintrala". *Journal of Women's History* 13(1) (Spring 2001): 1–18.

VALENZUELA, LUISA

Luisa Valenzuela was born in 1938 in Buenos Aires, Argentina. Her mother, Mercedes Levinson, was a writer and a well-known figure in the literary society in Buenos Aires. Authors like Jorge Luis Borges, Juan Goyanarte, Eduardo Mallea, and Ernesto Sábato, among others, were frequent visitors to their home. Valenzuela started her career as a journalist when she was very young, working for newspapers *La Nación* and *El Mundo*. She also published a few short stories before 1958, when she moved to France. While living in Normandy, her interest in the local folklore inspired some of the fiction she published. She moved to Paris in the early 1960s, and wrote for the French radio and television network. During her years in France she became acquainted with the artistic movement known as "pataphysics," led by Alfred Jarry, and defined as "the art of imaginary solutions". She was deeply influenced by its playful nature, wordplay, and use of the absurd. This influence can be seen in most of her narrative. Her first novel, *Hay que sonreír* (1966, Clara), was published while she was living in Paris. Inspired by the miserable lives of French prostitutes, the story gives an excellent example of the condition of women in a patriarchal society, the psychological consequences of being sexually and emotionally restrained by patriarchal and religious mores.

In 1964, Valenzuela returned to Buenos Aires to continue her journalist career at *La Nación* and *Crisis*, a cutting edge literary magazine. Two years later, she published *Los heréticos* (The Heretics), her first collection of short stories in which the author explores, with a heavy dose of sarcasm and humor, the thin line between religion and heresy. In 1969, she was awarded a Fulbright scholarship to participate in a program for international writers in Iowa, where she published *El gato eficaz* (1972, The Effective Cat). With this text, she abandoned linear writing and began developing an experimental style based on irony and wordplay that has characterized her writing since then.

During the 1970s, Valenzuela traveled to Spain, the United States, France, and Mexico, and these travels deeply influenced her work. During this period, the censorship and repression of the military régime completely changed Argentinean reality, a situation fully represented in her writings published at the time. Violence and tension clearly appear in her collection of short stories *Aquí Pasan Cosas Raras* (1975, Strange Things Happen Here). In the prologue, Valenzuela noted that the text may be read as a vivid chronicle of the country's paranoia, and that many of her stories were inspired in conversations she overheard in the cafés in Buenos Aires. In "Visión de reojo," "Camino al Ministerio," and "Unlimited Rapes Argentina," the abnormal is presented as ordinary, either by stream of consciousness of deranged protagonists, or through the fraudulent accounts of a perverse narrator. Using two basic components of the grotesque: irony and dark humor, the novelist was able to bypass government censorship and express, at the moment, what she had to say. In *Como en la Guerra* (1977, He Who Searches), Valenzuela continues to develop this hyperrealistic style. The connecting thread of this novel takes readers from Barcelona to Mexico and Argentina; however, its plot deals mostly with Argentine history, its disappeared children and its middle class.

In 1979, Valenzuela moved to New York to be writer-in-residence at Columbia University, where she gave workshops in English and Spanish. She received a fellowship at the New York Institute for the Humanities as well as the Fund for Free Expression, and a member of the Freedom to Write Committee for the PEN American Center. In addition, she worked with Amnesty International and Americas Watch. *Cola de lagartija* (Lizard's Tail) and *Cambio de armas* (Other Weapons) appeared in 1983, and this same year, she was awarded the Guggenheim Scholarship. *Cola de lagartija* is a fictional biography of José López Rega, minister of Social Welfare during the presidency of Isabel Martínez de Perón. López Rega survived multiple murder attempts by the military and unscrupulous politicians. Apart from presenting a critical perspective on the country's political history, the novel demonstrates the mechanisms of power and corruption in Latin American politics in the twentieth century.

In 1989, Valenzuela returned to Argentina to find a country deeply affected by years of military and social repression, as well as a deep financial crisis. According to the author, her return was partly motivated by a question of language: "I have always written in Spanish, but if I had stayed there longer, I would have had to start writing in English" (Bach 1995: 27). This same year she published *Realidad nacional desde la cama* (1990, Bedside Manners), and a year later, *Novela negra con argentinos* (1991, Black Novel with Argentines), an intense story that portrays the pathetic reality of two exiled Argentine writers in New York. This psychological novel incorporates vital elements from the detective or hard-boiled literature, such as crime, eroticism, and suspense. The plot exploits these elements to the limit as the murder of an innocent woman is presented as a gratuitous act, totally unjustified. Pushing things further, the level of eroticism reaches that of sexual perversion—dealing with masochism, sadism, torture and prostitution—and the suspense is never resolved, thus conveying the idea that both the crime and the criminal will go unpunished. *Novela negra* is a complex allegory of the events that took place in the concentration camps in Argentina under the military dictatorship during the 1970s. The unjustified violence against the population, the indiscriminate murder of prisoners, and the impunity of those responsible, not only provide a frame to the narrative structure, but also present a clear referent of the political horrors of the traumatic period also known as the Dirty War (1976–83). These two novels were followed in 1993 by *Simetrías* (Symmetries), a collection of short stories in which the author deals with the many faces of oppression and the lasting effects of exposure to the language of patriarchy. In her latest narrative, *La travesía* (2001, The Voyage), Valenzuela continues to explore some of the themes already introduced in *Novela negra.* In addition to narrative, she has written several essays; some of these were recently edited in *Peligrosas palabras* (2000, Dangerous Words), and *Escritura y secreto* (2002, Writing and Secrecy) among other essay collections. Currently Valenzuela lectures, travels and writes about reality, life and the need for the oppressed to find their own voices.

Luisa Valenzuela is an acclaimed fiction writer; her works explore the themes of exile, memories and language. In her writings she clearly transmits her concern regarding expression (the body, words, the erotic) and the idea of exile and national identity. She leads the reader to question government, patriarchal language, and the literature of the canon. She parodies genres, such as fairy tales, that have been widely accepted and recognized. She sees the fairy tale as a strong influence on both civilization and colonization, the two processes that have forged the Western world and modernity, and so she reformulates them in a clearly political manner.

Patriarchal societies traditionally have been terrified of witches because of their sexuality and their supposed ability to curse. Valenzuela sees the witch as not only a subversive and fascinating character, but also as the symbol of the sexuality that liberates women. The witch in Valenzuela's fiction is a representative of powerful women. She recognizes the importance of female sexuality that patriarchal discourse considers dangerous and subversive and has tried to destroy, together with feminine discourse. Valenzuela has also written about national and cultural identities, especially marginal literatures in which there is a crossing of established borders, such as historical and social traditions and sexual roles and identities.

She deconstructs the language of the establishment when she points at the metaphor as an instrument of power, especially in the "official language" of repressive governments, i.e., the way that the military régime in Argentina described the country as a seriously ill body that needed to be cured, or when expressions like "disappearances" and "the disappeared" were used instead of "kidnappings" and "the dead". Her views coincide with those of many other feminists who argue that language is not a system of communication that represents reality as it is, but a social construct expressing a specific point of view, usually that of the dominant society. Valenzuela believes that women need to write about eroticism and erotic literature, since most of what has been published in this genre has been written by men, and much of it is a vehicle to express male domination. She frequently has emphasized the similarity between sexual oppression and political oppression, and sees it as the duty of the woman writer to re-name things and to create her own language, while at the same time recovering her sexuality and her power.

Valenzuela's narrative evolves and changes constantly, questioning what has been historically defined and accepted. Her work usually revolves around what have been referred to as "her favorite demons": women, power, words, and desire.

Her fiction has been analyzed from a social point of view, as well as using psychological analysis, feminism, historicism, postmodernism, and semiotics. It has even been studied using Ilya Prigogine's chaos theory, since chaotic structures change over time, alternating phases of order and disorder, and in its turn disorder generates the spontaneous reorganization of the system. Her constant concern with language and with the realities and cultural structures shaped by words, as well as with the idea of power and the way it is abused, leads her to constantly explore the relationships between the oppressors and those they oppress and the social and psychological conditioning caused by relationships defined by the abuse of power.

GIANNA MARTELLA

Selected Works

Hay que Sonreír. Buenos Aires: Américalee, 1966. Translated as *Clara: Thirteen Stories and a Novel*. New York: Harcourt Brace Jovanovich, 1976.

Los heréticos. Buenos Aires: Paidós, 1967. Translated as *He Who Searches.* Elmwood Park, IL: Dalkey Archive Press, 1979.

El gato eficaz. México: Mortiz, 1972.

Aquí pasan cosas raras. Buenos Aires: Ediciones de la Flor, 1975. (Translated as *Strange Things Happen Here: Twenty-Six Stories and a Novel.* New York: Harcourt Brace Jovanovich, 1979.)

Como en la guerra. Buenos Aires: Editorial Sudamericana, 1977.

Cambio de Armas. Hanover, NH: Ediciones del Norte, 1982. Translated as *Other Weapons*. Hanover, NH: Ediciones del Norte, 1985.

Donde viven las águilas. Buenos Aires: Celtia, 1983.

Novela negra con argentinos. Barcelona: Plaza y Janés, 1990. Translated as *Black Novel with Argentines*. New York: Simon and Schuster, 1992.

Realidad nacional desde la cama. Buenos Aires: Grupo Editorial Latinoamericana, 1990. Translated as *Bedside Manners*. London and New York: High Risk Books, 1995.

Simetrías. Buenos Aires: Editorial Sudamericana, 1993.

Cuentos Completos y Uno Más. Buenos Aires: Alfaguara, 1998.

Peligrosas Palabras. Buenos Aires: Temas Grupo Editorial, 2001.

La travesía. Buenos Aires: Grupo Editorial Norma, 2001.

References and Further Reading

André, María C. "Luisa Valenzuela: Tras la alquimia del lenguaje". In Priscilla Gac-Artigas (ed.), *Reflexiones: ensayos sobre escritoras hispanoamericanas contemporáneas.* Vol. II. New Jersey: Ediciones Nuevo Espacio, 2002, pp. 343–57.

Bach, Caleb. "Un viaje introspectivo con la escritora Luisa Valenzuela". *Américas* 47 (1995): 22–7.

Díaz, Gwendolyn (ed.) *Luisa Valenzuela sin máscara*. Buenos Aires: Feminaria Editora, 2002.

——. and Lagos, María Inés (eds) *La Palabra en Vilo: Narrativa de Luisa Valenzuela*. Santiago de Chile: Editorial Cuarto Propio, 1996.

Magnarelli, Sharon. *Reflections/Refractions: Reading Luisa Valenzuela.* New York: Peter Lang, 1988.

Martínez, Nelly. *El silencio que habla: Aproximación a la obra de Luisa Valenzuela*. Buenos Aires: Corregidor, 1994.

VALLBONA, RIMA DE

Rima de Vallbona (b. 1931) was born in San José, Costa Rica and moved to the United States in 1956. She obtained her M.A. degree in 1962 from the University of Costa Rica and her Doctorate in Modern Languages from Middlebury College, Vermont, in 1981.

Vallbona became a member of the faculty of Saint Thomas University in Houston, Texas, in 1964. She was the organizer and first Chair of the Spanish Department and later served as Chair of the Modern Languages Department. She held the title of Cullen Foundation Spanish Professor for several years and became Professor Emeritus of Spanish upon her retirement in 1995. She is a member of numerous national and international organizations related to literature, culture and education including: Instituto Internacional de Literatura Iberoamericana, National Writers Association, Latin American Writers Institute Inc. and the Costa Rican Association of Women Writers (ACE). She currently lives in the Houston area and continues to do research and publish creative texts and critical literary essays.

As an author, Rima de Vallbona is well recognized with three volumes of critical essays dedicated to her literary works in addition to many critical essays published in a variety of literary journals; there are also several theses and dissertations on her literary output. She is the recipient of prestigious awards, including the 1968 Aquileo Echeverría National Novel Award, the 1977 Jorge Luis Borges Short Story Award (Argentina), the 1978 Agripina Montes del Valle Novel Award (Colombia), the 1978 Professor Lilia Ramos Children's Poetry Award (Uruguay) and the 1984 Ancora Award for *Las sombras que perseguimos* (The Shadows We Pursue), considered the best work of fiction in Costa Rica. King Juan Carlos I of Spain awarded her the Civil Service Medal in 1989 for her cultural work in the Hispanic World. She received "Honorable Mention" in the Short Story Contest of American Markets Newsletter, the "Editor's Choice Award" of International Library of Poetry in 2000, and the 2003 Prize in an Open Contest of B.A.W.L (Bay Area Writers League).

Although Vallbona has published her works in Spanish, many of her short stories have also appeared in English, French, German and Portuguese. They have been published in literary journals and some have been included in anthologies in Costa Rica, France, Germany, México, Spain, the Dominican Republic, the United States, Uruguay, and Venezuela.

Influences and Themes

Critics claim that Rima de Vallbona creates works that have a social and aesthetic double function through an artistically conceived discourse. Unlike many of her contemporaries, she does not explore the exploited/exploiter topic often identified with Latin American literature. Instead she chooses more universal themes and creates works that are individual yet actively contribute to finding solutions to social, political and cultural problems of the time, particularly those relating to the destiny of women in contemporary society. The author's preoccupation with the victimization of women in a patriarchal society dominated by *machismo* and a sexuality that demeans the sublime feeling of love is present in the novels and short stories. Vallbona's narrative is existentialist in nature and the characters often agonize to find a purpose for life. In these texts the writing is a result of the constant confrontation between the self and the conscience. Some critics have associated the struggle of the protagonists of Vallbona's three novels to that of the characters in the works of Miguel de Unamuno, Spain's prolific writer of the Generation of '98. At the same time, the labyrinths that represent the lives of many of the characters are reminiscent of Borges' labyrinths.

The thematic scope in Vallbona's works is broad and includes the questioning of the meaning of life and the reigning ideology, the feelings of solitude and loneliness of human beings, the search for faith, the importance of the act of writing as a liberating act, the denouncement of vices and injustices such as racism, poverty and the suffering of children. The author also explores bold and controversial topics such as homosexuality and masturbation. Yet Vallbona's main inclination is the portrayal of the condition of women by creating imaginary situations in her novels and short stories that present women in all spheres: the private or domestic, the public or professional and the social.

The protagonists of the author's three novels question the social order and, through their imagination, achieve freedom, and in the process attempt to understand and interpret the universe. In *La sombra que perseguimos*, Vallbona explores the racial injustices and the social position of women, but the complexity and uniqueness of the text stems from the treatment of the writing process. Some of the short stories, such as "Penelope's Silver Wedding Anniversary" found in *Mujeres y agonías* (Women and Agonies) provide an example of Vallbona's dedication to represent the world of women. In this case the female character is trapped in a life assigned to her by the patriarchal society, and she attempts to escape through real experiences. Penelope uses knitting, a domestic activity normally seen as a pastime, to meditate and forge her destiny. Such an activity empowers the character to liberate herself from her present agonizing and meaningless existence as she marks her twenty-fifth wedding anniversary, and allows her to prepare herself as she reaches her own paradise. In order to provide an often symbolic distinction between the oppressed existence, marked by monotony and denial, and the paradise for which the female characters yearn, Vallbona skillfully uses narrative strategies such as the inclusion of names of foods, images that represent mostly unpleasant yet common odors and noises, marital disillusions and the use of hyphenated words.

Although not all of the female characters in Vallbona's works are confined to the domestic sphere, they are often seen in relation to the roles assigned to them by the patriarchal society. Therefore, their identity is defined by the relationship they have with others (as wife, mother, daughter and sister). As is common in contemporary narrative, these women yearn for self-realization, which for Vallbona's characters may be to find spiritual peace within; or it may require challenging traditional institutions, such as marriage, in order to make life somewhat bearable and meaningful. However, critics have concluded that Vallbona's narrative does not easily fit the feminist framework because these characters do not respond to a political change; instead, they often look for changes within themselves. Nonetheless, the innovation of her writings places the author among the first to challenge the traditions in contemporary Costa Rican literature.

Vallbona is a writer who participates in a contemporary and universal dialogue and her works form part of what many critics call *la nueva narrativa latinoamericana*, or (neo)narrative, a new manifestation of realism that surfaced in Latin America in the 1960s. The novelty of this type of (meta)narrative lies in its focus on the act of narrating/writing and the function of literature, so that aspects of narrative usually considered secondary to the story are now presented as process and theme. In addition, these texts often bear autobiographical traits made more evident in the case where the narrator is also a writer and often the creator of the text at hand. The result is a text that presents a varying amalgamation of genres associated with fiction and nonfiction, therefore challenging the traditional structure of any given literary genre.

MARISA HERRERA POSTLEWATE

Selected Works

Noche en vela. San José: Editorial Costa Rica, 1968.

Polvo del camino. San José: Editorial Autores Unidos, 1971.

Yolanda Oreamuno. Presentada por Rima de Vallbona. San José, Costa Rica: Ministerio de Cultura, Juventud y Deportes, Departamento de Publicaciones, 1972.

La salamandra rosada. Montevideo: Editorial Géminis, 1979.

"Trayectoria actual de la poesía femenina en Costa Rica". *Káñina: Revista de Artes y Letras de la Universidad de Costa Rica* 5(2) (1981): 18–27.

Mujeres y agonías. Houston: Arte Público Press, 1982.

Las sombras que perseguimos. San José: Editorial Costa Rica, 1983.

Baraja de soledades. Barcelona: Ediciones Rondas, 1983.

Vallbona, Rima de, Sandra Cisneros and others. *Woman of her Word: Hispanic Women Write*. Houston, TX: Arte Público Press, 1983.

"Introducción". In *Los elementos terrestres*. San José: Editorial Costa Rica, 1984.

La ruta de su evasión, de Yolanda Oreamuno: escritura proustiana suplementada. S.l.: s.n., 1987.

Cosecha de pecadores. San José: Editorial Costa Rica, 1988.

"Erotismo, remembranzas tropicales y misterio en María la noche de Ana Cristina Rossi". In *Mujer y sociedad en América: IV Simposio Internacional*. Vol. 1. Westminster, CA; Mexicali: Inst. Literario y Cultural Hispánico; Univ. Autónoma de Baja, California, 1988, pp. 117–35.

El arcángel del perdón. Buenos Aires: Ayala Palacios Ediciones Universitarias, 1990.

"Penelope's Silver Wedding Anniversary". In Celia Correas de Zapata (ed.), *Short Stories by Latin American Women: The Magic and the Real*. Houston, TX: Arte Público Press, 1990.

Mundo, demonio y mujer. Houston, TX: Arte Público Press, 1991. Trans. L. Lorca de Tagle as *Flowering Inferno: Tales of Singing Hearts*. Pittsburgh, PA: Latin American Review Press, 1994.

Los infiernos de la mujer y algo más. Madrid: Ediciones Torremozas, 1992.

"Introducción y notas". In *Vida i sucesos de la Monja Alférez*. Tempe, AZ: ASU Center for Latin American Studies, 1992.

"Rima [Gretel Rothe] de Vallbona". *Alba de America: Revista Literaria* 11(20–1) (1993): 69–78.

La narrativa de Yolanda Oreamuno. San José, Costa Rica: Editorial Costa Rica, 1996.

Tormy: La prodigiosa gata de Donaldito. San José: Ediciones Perro Azul, 1997.

"Espinas y laureles del quehacer literario en Hispanoamérica". In Juana Alcira Arancibia and Luis A. Jiménez (eds), *Protestas, interrogantes y agonías en la obra de Rima de Vallbona*. Westminster, CA: Instituto Literario y Cultural Hispánico, 1997. 343–83.

"Prólogo". In *Por el carnaval de la vida: cuentos*. San José, Costa Rica: Ediciones Perro Azul, 1998.

"Juicio de Dios: cuento". In Rafael T. Corbalán and Gerardo Piña-Rosales (eds), *Acentos femeninos y marco estético del nuevo milenio*. New

York: City University of New York, the Graduate School and University Center, 2000.

Tejedoras de sueños versus realidad. Madrid: Ediciones Torremozas, 2003.

"Re-visión diacrónica de textos escritos por mujeres del Nuevo Mundo". In Juana Alcira Arancibia (ed.), *La mujer en la literatura del mundo hispánico*. Westminster, CA: Instituto Literario y Cultural Hispánico, 2005, pp. 11–42.

A la deriva del tiempo y de la historia. San José, Costa Rica: EUNED, 2007.

References and Further Reading

Andrist, Debra D. "Reversiones y reversos de Rima de Vallbona: 'Beto y Betina.'" *Revista de Filología y Lingüística de la Universidad de Costa Rica* 1 (1995) (Supplement): 71–4.

Arancibia, Juana Alcira and Jiménez, Luis A. (eds) *Protestas, interrogantes y agonías en la obra de Rima de Vallbona*. Westminster, CA: Instituto Literario y Cultural Hispánico, 1997.

Chase, Cida S. "El mundo femenino en algunos cuentos de Rima de Vallbona". *Revista Iberoamericana* 53(138–9) (1987): 403–18.

——. "Sueño e imaginación en la obra de Rima de Vallbona". *Alba de América: Revista Literaria* 23(43–4) (2004): 167–79.

Chen Sham, Jorge (ed.) *Nuevos acercamientos a la obra de Rima de Vallbona*. Houston, TX, San José, Costa Rica: University of St. Thomas; Universidad de Costa Rica, 1999.

——. "Culpa y exilio en Mundo, demonio y mujer: Las transformaciones diaspóricas del sujeto". *Diáspora: Journal of the Annual Afro-Hispanic Literature and Culture Conference*11 (2001): 138–46.

——. *Radiografías del sujeto agónico: Culpa y transcendencia en la novelística deRima de Vallbona*. San José, Costa Rica: Perro Azul; 2001.

——. "Representación de la infancia en el Bildungsroman costarricense: Ana Cristina Rossi y Rima de Vallbona". In Juana Alcira Arancibia (ed.), *La mujer en la literatura del mundo hispánico*. Westminster, CA: Instituto Literario Cultural Hispánico; 2005, pp. 307–15.

Correa, Rafael E. "Rima de Vallbona y el lector: Texto y espacios desiderados". *Alba de América* 8(14–15) (1990): 85–91.

Cruz, Julia. "La anonimia en algunos relatos de Rima de Vallbona". *Diáspora: Journal of the Annual Afro-Hispanic Literature and Culture Conference* 11 (2001):133–7.

Rosas, Yolanda. "Hacia una identidad en *Cosecha de pecadores* de Rima de Vallbona". *The Americas Review: A Review of Hispanic Literature and Art of the USA* 19(3–4): (1991): 134–45.

VAN STEEN, EDLA

Brazilian author Edla Van Steen was born in 1936 in Florianópolis, Santa Catarina. She has spent most of her life in either Santa Catarina or São Paulo. Having worked as a journalist, scriptwriter, and author of short stories, novels and theatrical works, her literary style reflects the variety of her experience. Her works have been translated into a number of other languages and she has been awarded the Prêmio Molière e Mabembe, the Prêmio Coelho Neto, and the Prêmio Nacional. Her bibliography includes more than 20 volumes. She is married to legendary theater critic Sábato Magaldi.

Edla Van Steen's style incorporates many innovative forms that are influenced by stage and screen, as well as journalism. Her themes focus heavily on aspects of both heterosexual and homosexual love and eroticism. She has tackled a variety of feminine issues in her works, including sexual exploitation, rape, dehumanization, and the second class status of the Brazilian woman. The differences between men and women are also recurring themes.

"As desventuras de João" (or "The Misadventures of João"—available also as *A Bag of Stories*) is an ideal illustration of her portrayal of the male/female dichotomy. Helena and João engage in a clandestine love affair after spending many years apart. It is Helena who makes the initial contact out of longing and João accepts, driven by his sexual fantasies for Helena. The male/female dichotomy is the focus of the story, with both characters offering the extremes of gender difference and sexual convention. More than half of the short story focuses on the initial phone conversation. Helena lives in the past, drawing on memories of caring and tenderness, and becoming more emotional and sentimental. João, isolated in his office, dwells on the carnal with dreams of sex play and lovemaking. For her, it is an emotional adventure; for him, an escape from his secretary, co-workers, and clients. When the two finally end their phone conversation and meet, the affair itself is far less exciting than the thought of the affair. With Van Steen's description and lyrical rhythm, the lead-up to the actual affair is presented like foreplay and intercourse, and the actual consummation is a comical "anticlimax". João tries to rush and ends up unable to "perform". He apologizes repeatedly and Helena tries to change the subject. They lay intertwined for a few minutes and Helena, in true feminine fashion, asks João what he is thinking and hopes that he is thinking about his passion for her. In perfect masculine disconnect, he replies that he is thinking about a cup of coffee. The two lovers go their separate ways, but not before Van Steen reverses the gender roles. It is Helena who promises that she will call soon, but they both know that it will not happen.

In *Cheiro de amor* (1996, Scent of Love), we follow the life of a woman via entries in her diary and from the observations of a reporter. The woman was married at 14 because she was pregnant with the child of a 30-year old doctor. She spends much of her married life as the dutiful wife. She directs an orphanage and, characteristic of Van Steen's use of the erotic, our protagonist experiences her very first orgasm during a sexual assault by one of the orphans. This eventually leads her to begin affairs with her husband's brother and with a veterinarian who is conducting experiments on their family farm. She finally develops breast cancer and her husband kills her out of mercy to avoid further suffering. We see in *Cheiro de amor* the unconventional modern woman who defies the patriarchal structure of society and is subsequently punished by nature with a feminine illness. Her suffering is only ended by her husband's "merciful" act.

Madrugada (1992, Early Morning) is set in the city of São Paulo and the entire work takes place from dusk to dawn. The imagery is clear and colorful, almost cinematic in its detailed descriptions. David George says in the Foreword that Van Steen's work "filters the universal themes of death and renewal through the lens of Brazil's urgent social problems". This is a collection of vignettes about night and death and, in the stories, Brazil's social class structure is the primary focus of analysis. The poor are extremely poor and the rich have much more than is necessary for survival. Her journalistic approach to economic disparity is raw and real. To weave these tales together, Van Steen uses the voice of a female figure, Brenda. Brenda is a transvestite, a stripper, a petty thief, and a lover.

Torn between love (dependence) and independence, Brenda grapples with life on many levels. Her hatred for men motivates her to be independent and care only for herself. She wants to create her own existence as an independent woman, and not a mere extension of a man's life. A strong sense of duty is detailed in Brenda's thoughts, but her outer actions demonstrate that her independence is winning out and she finds validity through her own actions and not by connecting herself with a man. Van Steen also uses Brenda as a means of deconstructing notions of gender and sexual stereotypes. Brenda dresses as a man each night and then strips to reveal her true feminine self. This act clothes Brenda with a sense of pride and power, knowing that she can be as much a man as a woman.

In another story, "Ela e ele"—"She and He" (from the short story collection *A ira das águas—The Wrath of the Waters*), we see again the couple meeting after a long hiatus. This time, unlike "As desventuras de João," the man and the woman meet in his apartment, not in his office. But once again, the amount of life and of experience each had since they last met proves to be too much. He cannot perform sexually, and the couple separate, feeling that their relationship can never be revived. He cannot understand why he failed. She protests she cannot stay any longer because she did not tell her daughter she would be late. One sentence reveals an important facet of the female character that she shares with many others in Van Steen's fiction, "Não tenho mais paciência com homem". [I no longer have any patience with men]. Indeed, when their sexual encounter fails, she does not allow him to accompany her to the lobby. He stays in the apartment, alone, and recognizes that he is "o canalha de sempre" [the same despicable fellow], "o conquistador que perdia a mais infame das batalhas" [the seducer who lost the most infamous of all battles].

Edla Van Steen is a gifted writer because she manages to incorporate various forms and themes and weaves them together to leave an imprint in the mind of the reader. Her social commentary is journalistic and bold in its depiction of her country's social ills; yet her cinematic style enhances the journalistic photographs of each scene in her stories. Van Steen is a contemporary feminist and outspoken cultural critic.

Edla Van Steen has also authored several children's books and has translated a number of foreign authors into Portuguese.

BRYAN KENNEDY

Selected Works

Novels and Short Stories

Cio. São Paulo: Von Schmidt, 1965.
Memórias do medo. São Paulo: Melhoramentos, 1974.
Antes do amanhecer. São Paulo: Moderna, 1977.
Corações mordidos. São Paulo: Global, 1983.
Até sempre. São Paulo: Global, 1985.
Village of the Ghost Bells. Austin, TX: Texas University Press, 1991 (trans. *Corações mordidos*).
A Bag of Stories. Pittsburgh, PA: Latin American Literary Review, 1991 (translation of a number of Van Steen's early short stories from various collections).
Madrugada. Rio de Janeiro: Rocco, 1992.
Cheiro de amor. São Paulo: Global, 1996.
Early Morning. Pittsburgh, PA: Latin American Literary Review, 1996 (trans. *Madrugada*).
O presente. São Paulo: Global, 2000.
Scent of Love. Pittsburgh, PA: Latin American Literary Review, 2001 (trans. *Cheiro de amor*).
No silêncio das nuvens. São Paulo: Global, 2001.
A ira das águas. São Paulo: Global, 2004.

Theater

O último encontro. São Paulo: Arte Aplicada, 1989.
À mão armada. Rio de Janeiro: Caliban, 1996.
Bolo de nozes. Belo Horizonte: Hamdan, 1998.
Mina de ouro. Unpublished, 1999.
Amor de estrela. Unpublished, 1999.

Children's literature

Manto de nuvem. São Paulo: Nacional, 1985.
Por acaso. São Paulo: Global, 1996.
O gato barbudo. São Paulo: Global, 2000.
O presente. São Paulo: Global, 2001

Literary Translations

Mansfield, Katherine. *Aula de canto*. São Paulo: Global, 1984. (translation of a number of Mansfield's short stories from various collections).
Stevenson, Robert Louis. *O médico e o monstro*. São Paulo: Scipione, 1987. (translation of *The Strange Case of Dr. Jekyll and Mr. Hyde*).

Theatrical Translations and Adaptations

O encontro de Descartes com Pascal. Jean Claude Brisville. Performed in São Paulo and Rio de Janeiro, production of Italo Rossi and Daniel Dantas, 1987. Unpublished (translation of *L'entretien de M. Descartes avec M. Pascal*).
Três Anas. Arnold Wesker. Not performed and unpublished, 1987 (translation of *Annie Wobbler*).
Solness, o construtor. Henrik Ibsen. Performed in São Paulo, production of Paulo Autran. Unpublished, 1988 (translation of *Byggmester Solness*).
Max. Manfred Karge. Production of Walderez de Barros. Unpublished, 1990 (translation of *Jackie wie Hose*).
As parceiras. Claude Rullier. Not performed and unpublished, 1990 (translation of *Annabelle et Zina*).
Senhorita Julia. A. Strindberg. Production of William Pereira, Andréa Beltrão and José Mayer. Unpublished, 1991 (translation of *Miss Julie* [*Fröken Julie*]).
Cala a boca e solte dos dentes. Terence McNally. Not performed and unpublished, 1994 (translation of *Lips Together, Teeth Apart*).
A última carta. Nicolas Martin. Production of Gianni Ratto. Adaptation for the Theater, unpublished, 1994.
Encontro no supermercado. Shula Meggido. Production of Teresa Raquel. Adaptation for the Theater, unpublished, 1995.
Da manhã à meia noite. Georg Kaiser. Not performed and unpublished, 1995 (translation of *Von morgens bis mitternachts* [*From Morn to Midnight*]).
O doente imaginário. Molière. Performed in São Paulo, production of Italo Rossi and Moacyr Góes. Porto Alegre: Impressões do Brasil, 1996 (translation of *Le Malade imaginaire*).
A dama do mar. Henrik Ibsen. Production of Ulisses Cruz. Unpublished, 1996 (translation of *The Lady from the Sea*).
Vida no teatro. David Mamet. Production of Francisco Medeiros and Umberto Magnani. Unpublished, 1996 (translation of *A Life in the Theater*).
Três irmãs. Anton Chekov. Production of Enrique Diaz, Maria Padilha, Cláudia Abreu and Júlia Lemmertz. Unpublished, 1998 (translation of *The Three Sisters* [три сестры]).
Strip-teases. Joan Brossa. Production of Daniel Dantas. Unpublished, 2000 (translation of *Striptease de butxaca Strip-tease català*).

Art collections

Marcelo Grassman: 70 anos. São Paulo: Arte Aplicada, 1995.
Poetas da forma e da cor. São Paulo: Arte Aplicada, 1997.

Anthologies

Chame o ladrão: contos policiais. São Paulo: Edições Populares, 1978.
O conto da mulher brasileira. São Paulo: Vertente, 1978.
O papel do amor. São Paulo: Papel Simão e Livraria Cultura, 1979.
Erotismo no conto brasileiro. Rio de Janeiro: Civilização Brasileira, 1980.
21 dedos de prosa. Florianópolis: ACES e Cambirela Editores, 1980.
Pelo telefone. São Paulo: Edição Especial TELESP, 1981.
O prazer é todo meu. Rio de Janeiro: Record, 1984.
A posse da terra: escritor brasileiro hoje. Lisboa: Imprensa Nacional/Casa de Moeda, 1983.
Criança brinca, não brinca? Rio de Janeiro: Rhodia/Livraria Cultura, 1985.
Espelho mágico. Rio de Janeiro: Guanabara, 1985.
Histórias de amor infeliz. Rio de Janeiro: Nórdica, 1985.
Contos paulistas. São Paulo: Mercado Aberto, 1988.
Memórias de Hollywood. São Paulo: Nobel, 1988.
Este amor Catarina. Florianópolis: UFSC, 1996.
Uma situação delicada e outras histórias. São Paulo: Lazuli e SESC, 1997.
Brasil: receitas de crier e cozinhar. Rio de Janeiro: Bertrand Brasil, 1997.
Onze em campo e um banco de primeira. Rio de Janeiro: Relume Dumará, 1998.
Os cem melhores contos brasileiros do século. Rio de Janeiro: Objetiva, 2000.
Blumenauaçu 3: antologia de escritores catarinenses. Florianópolis: Cultura em Movimento, 2002.
Feminino. São Paulo: Lazuli, 2003.
Contos de escritoras brasileiras. São Paulo: Martins Fontes, 2003.
Conto com você. São Paulo: Global, 2003.

Short Stories

Nowe Opowiadana Brazylijskie. Krakow, 1982.
The Literary Review. Summer 1984. Madison, NJ: Ingram Periodicals, 1984.
Brazilian Literature. Kenneth Jackson and Yvette Miller (eds) Pittsburgh, PA: Latin American Literary Review, 1986.
Erkundungen. Berlin: Verlag Volk und Welt, 1988.
Sudden Fiction International. Robert Shapard and James Thomas (eds). New York: W.W. Norton, 1989.
Der Lauf Der Sonne in Den Gemässigten Zonen. Berlin: Diá, 1991.
One Hundred Years After Tomorrow: Brazilian Women's Fiction in the 20th Century. Darlene Sadlier (ed.). Bloomington, IN: Indiana University Press, 1992.
Something to Declare: Selections from International Literature. Toronto: Oxford University Press, 1994.
Das Grosse Brasilien-Lesebuch. Munich: Goldmann Verlag, 1994.
O novo conto brasileiro. Malcolm Silverman, (ed.) Boston, MA: McGraw-Hill, 2002.

References and Further Reading

George, David. "Foreword". *A Bag of Stories*. Pittsburgh, PA: Latin American Review, 1991.
——. "Foreword". *Early Morning*. Pittsburgh, PA: Latin American Review, 1996.
——. "Foreword". *Scent of Love*. Pittsburgh, PA: Latin American Review, 2001.
——. "Foreword". *Village of the Ghost Bells*. Austin, TX: Texas University Press, 1991.
Sadlier, Darlene (ed.) *One Hundred Years After Tomorrow: Brazilian Women's Fiction in the 20th Century*. Bloomington, IN: Indiana University Press, 1992, pp. 180–93.
Silverman, Malcolm. *O novo conto brasileiro*. 3rd edn. Boston, MA: McGraw-Hill, 2002, 91-103.

VARELA, BLANCA

Blanca Varela (b. 1926) is a Peruvian poet and journalist. She is one of the most recognized poets of the "1950s generation". As many Latin American intellectuals did, Varela traveled to Europe in order to study and develop artistically as a poet. Varela stayed in Europe for many years and later moved to the United States where she worked as a translator. She married and later divorced the famed Peruvian painter Fernando de Szyszlo. Back in Peru, Varela worked in many different places. She worked as a part-time journalist and translator, and as the director of the Peruvian branch of the Fondo de Cultura Económica, the Mexican Publishing house.

Her interest in poetry developed during her college years in Lima. While studying at the San Marcos University, she befriended José María Arguedas and Emilio Adolfo Westphalen who inspired her to pursue her intellectual interests. Later in Paris her horizons as a poet expanded as she discovered the Surrealism of the postwar era and met Carlos Paz, the renowned Mexican intellectual. In Paris, the Surrealist atmosphere and Paz's inspiring energy encouraged her to make poetry an integral part of her life. Paz has an enormous influence on Varela and he believes that Varela is a lyricist with an unlimited potential. He writes in his introduction to Varelas' *Ese puerto existe* (That Port Exists) that Varela's poetry is the most revealing consciousness of her time (16).

Early Poetry

Varela began to write at an early age. She felt the impulse to write and to express her feelings, which tormented her during her waking hours. At age 12, due to a religious conflict with her confessor, she struggled to find a personal answer to the disquieting questions she had about the world. At that age, she felt that her own feelings could not be expressed fully in everyday language. She wanted to develop a personal speech so that it could reveal her inner feelings to the world. Varela confessed that she wanted to know about "esa realidad que me rodeaba, que no comprendía y que no me gustaba demasiado" [that reality that was around me, which I did not understand and did not like much] (O'Hara 1998: 112). Although the themes of her work changed as Varela matures as a poet, the idea of the incomprehensibility of the world has remained one of her most enduring themes.

Her first collection of poems, *Ese puerto existe y otros poemas* (That Port Exists and Other Poems), embodies a series of preoccupations with dreams, lights and the surrealist imagery which she sees as dominant in her environment. Her poems in this collection reflect a transition from her early existence to her life as an adult. Her work shows what José Miguel Oviedo has called "un tono de rebelde insatisfación" [an attitude of dissenting dissatisfaction] (1979: 104) which materializes in visions of birds, dreams, and the city. These visions, however, are hasty and short-lived. Varela's metaphors in "El día" (The Day), for example, refer to the swiftness and purity of time and the poet sees sunrise as an untainted and amorphous body. The imagery in these poems also reveals a persona with a close affinity to nature. In "Puerto Supe" (Port Supe), fear and astonishment on seeing the beach and the ocean for the first time reveal a troubled infancy in the coastal plains of Peru.

The lyrics are full of dread and wonder and they reflect the poet's amazement at the power of nature as seen in the energy of the ocean. Varela finishes the poem with a note of hope to assuage these childhood fears. Even though the new sights at the beach overwhelm the speaker, she knows she has found her roots but also new sorrows. It is in the Peruvian coast where the poet finds those new roots, the place of personal solitude.

Existential Poetry

In *Canto Villano* (Wicked Song), Varela's work shows a sign of maturity. Gone are the lights and the storms of "Puerto Supe," and now the poet switches her interest to mankind and the vicissitudes which mold human existence. In "Curriculum Vitae," there are some echoes of her own persona as a shy poet, but also an afterthought about what eludes or characterizes the life of an intellectual, namely fame, work and recognition. The lyrics reflect Varela's own life as a poet. The poet concedes to a nameless third person that she has won the race, but she warns that the real prize is "otra carrera" [other pursuit] and requires only one competitor: oneself. Another existential category is found in "Casa de Cuervos" (House of Crows) where the themes of motherhood and the cycle of life worry the poet. Evoking her own offspring, the speaker cannot avoid sharing her suffering with the world.

In *Ejercicios Materiales* (Material Exercises), we have a mature poet perhaps reflecting the preoccupations of her own age. This work illustrates a qualitative change and reflects remembrances of times past, the deterioration of the human body and the preoccupation with death. Varela looks back to her past life while examining the present and wondering about the future. In these poems there is a strong negative view of human life, especially human reproduction. It seems that age and decay, the eternal and opposite twins of beauty, are engendered continually throughout time in an endless repetition. The biographical revelations in these poems have not escaped the critics. As Silvia Bermúdez has noted, Varela makes her *Ejercicios* (Exercises) stand as the refuge of her being, as she laments the human corruption around her (2001: 118). In "Crónica" (Chronic), there is also grieving but not about physical decay, but about moral dishonesty. There is false fame, vice and celebration of evil. The poet feels that "los cerdos" [the pigs] have become heroes, to reproduce, kill and procreate again. It is this corrupt world which is weighed against a more familiar place. We learn that as a counterpart to this violence and that world of iniquity, there is a secure place far away in the desert. That simple place is later identified as home.

The Fatalistic Imagery

The lyrics in *Claroscuro* (Chiaroscuro) refine the recurring images of the cruel world, birth and the renewal of human obsolescence, but also praise the human capacity to confront these challenges. The poet affirms the enduring human spirit in different temporal settings. She unifies different temporal experiences in a human being which embodies the past, the present and the future. This juxtaposition of different temporalities, however, must expire as human life does. Varela ends her verses with a challenge to death. Death is watching and waiting, but the poet is ready for her destiny.

Varela's obsession with dreams and lights, although imbued with some mysticism and fatalistic images, must be seen in a social context. It is not the ivory tower or the bourgeois persona but the hard reality that prompts Varela to invent alternative ways to understand the complexity of the world. Reality for her, as Américo Ferrari indicates, is "lo verdadero y lo falso" [the real and falsehood] (1986: 136) which the poet tries to understand with a clean conscience, without holding back, a job that Varela does superbly. This is perhaps why Varela's themes and concerns in her work show a great idealistic range.

In general, Varela's metaphysical categories are imbued with childhood fears, surrealistic images, maternal worries, animals, dissatisfaction and human obsolescence. There is, however, a unifying principle running through her poetry. It is the redemptive, cathartic, mystic force present in her lyrics. It is deep, mysterious, and unreachable yet alive with human wonder and social urgency. Her literary production, spanning more than forty years, has lacked the recognition which has brought fame to other contemporary poets. This is perhaps due to her aversion to self-promotion, her voluntary absence in literary contests and her lack of inclination for public appearances. In October, 2006, however, Varela won the prestigious García Lorca Prize of Poetry given by the city of Málaga in Spain.

JORGE J. BARRUETO

Selected Works

Ese Puerto Existe y otro poemas. Xalapa, México: Universidad Veracruzana, 1959.

Luz de día. Lima: Ediciones de La Rama Florida, 1963.

"Antes de escribir estas líneas". *Cuadernos Hispanoamericanos* 417 (1985): 84–7.

Canto Villano/Poesía Reunida, 1949–1983. México: Fondo de Cultura Económica, 1986.

Ejecicios Materiales. Lima: Jaime Campodónico, 1993.

El libro de barro. Madrid: Ediciones del Tapir, 1993.

Concierto animal. Lima: Ediciones Peisa, 1999.

References and Further Reading

Bermúdez, Silvia. "Extrañamiento y escritura: Blanca Varela y sus Ejercicios materiales". *Journal of Iberian and Latin American Studies* 7(2) (2001): 117–27.

Borso, Vittoria. "La poesía del eco en la escritura de los años 80: Blanca Varela, Giovana Pollarolo and Carmen Ollé". In Karl Kohut, José Morales Saravia and Sonia V. Rose (eds), *Literatura Peruana Hoy: Crisis y Creación*. Frankfurt: Vervuert, 1998, pp. 196–217.

Ferrari, Américo. "Varela: explorando los 'bordes espeluznantes.'" *Hueso Húmero* 21 (1986): 134–43.

Kristal, Efraín. "Entrevista con Blanca Varela". *Mester* 24(2) (1995): 133–50.

O'Hara, Edgar. "El recuerdo del recuerdo". *Partición de los bienes: conversaciones sobre poesía*. Lima: Lluvia Editores, 1998, pp. 101–17.

Oviedo, José Miguel. "Blanca Varela, o la persistencia de la memoria". *ECO* 36 (1979): 100–12.

Paz, Carlos. "Destiempos de Blanca Varela". *Puerta al Campo*. Barcelona: Seix Barral, 1972, pp. 94–9.

VEGA, ANA LYDIA

Ana Lydia Vega was born in Santurce, Puerto Rico, on December 6, 1946. Her parents were her first influence. Both parents were musicians and her mother was a public school teacher. Her father was a lover of poetry and participated in improvisation competitions. Her mother was a pianist and encouraged her love of education.

Vega began her studies at the University of Puerto Rico in 1964 and later obtained the doctoral degree in Provence, France. Vega pursued an academic career as a professor of both French literature and Caribbean studies at the University of Puerto Rico. She has also been an invited professor at Cornell University and the City College of New York. She was awarded the Premio Emilio S. Belaval (1978), Premio Casa de las Américas (1982), Premio Juan Rulfo (1984), the Guggenheim Fellowship (1989), and Premio de la Cámara Puertorriqueña del Libro (1997).

Vega's works deal with issues of the disenfranchised and in general the social and cultural problems that affect the Caribbean islands. She engages her characters in social, racial, and gender stereotypical settings in order to reveal their hardships and dilemmas, simultaneously deconstructing the misconceptions these engender. The language is innovative and permeated with sayings, colloquialisms, regionalism, street language, and spanglish among others. The popular language combined with satire and irony adds a humorous flavor to serious themes such as: race, class, sexism, and exploitation. The use of multilingualism (Spanish, French, Creole, and English) reflects the languages spoken in this area and the North American presence in the Caribbean.

Vega focuses on the people, the history, and the commonality among the people of the Caribbean. She questions written history by narrating stories based on the experiences of the people. Her works are imbued with a discourse of parody and humor that compels the reader to contemplate important issues such as national and racial identity, gender roles, and emigration among others. As she appeals to the idiosyncrasies that embody the Caribbean community, she facilitates a relationship and identification with the text for the reader. Her works include the collections of short stories *Vírgenes y mártires* (1981), *Encancaranublado y otros cuentos de naufragio* (1982), *Pasión de historia y otras historias de pasión* (1987), *Falsas crónicas del sur* (1991), and the collections of essays, *El tramo ancla: ensayos puertorriqueños de hoy* (1988), *La felicidad ja ja ja ja y la Universidad* (1989), and *Esperando a Loló y otros delirios* (1994).

From the collection *Vírgenes y mártires*, the short story "Pollito Chicken," for which she won the Premio Emilio S. Belaval, exemplifies the confused dual identity faced by many Puerto Ricans. This short story has attracted many reviews because some Nuyoricans disapproved of the portrayal of the protagonist as one who shuns her identity. In an interview with Carmen Dolores Hernández, Vega makes it clear that this is not a commentary on Nuyoricans. She also claims that it is her most popular story because of the problem of the language/s which seems to be more prevalent around different parts of the world today. The bilingual title, a song taught to children at an early age, represents the North American presence in the island as well as the factor of emigration to the mainland. The protagonist, a Puerto Rican woman who has been living in the United States for ten years, attempts to assimilate into the North American society through total immersion and rejection of her identity and the Spanish language. Seeking to integrate into the North American society she fails to ascknowledge that here she is considered inferior. This commingling of cultures eventually results in a clash. This individual who appeared to be lost in trying to "fit in", reveals her personal conflict with her identity. At an intimate moment, the protagonist instinctively shouts out in her first language sentiments of political independence, "Viva Puerto Rico libre". The theme of Puerto Rican national identity which appeared to be null and void in the life of this woman is momentarily reaffirmed and the internal tussle quelled.

In the collection *Encancaranublado y otros cuentos de naufragio*, Vega reproduces the defects and squabbles common to the people of Caribbean in order to demonstrate the need for regional unity. The story "El día de los hechos" deals with a historical event that has its origins in the racism reflective of the colonialist epoch's emphasis on white superiority. The story centers on the massacre of Haitians by Dominicans in 1937 during Rafael Trujillo's (1930–61) dictatorship in the two-nation island. A Dominican who leaves his country in a rowing boat for Puerto Rico is visited and killed by a Haitian who came to avenge the betrayal that led to the killing of his father during the massacre. The atrocities of the massacre are elaborated and the central theme of brother killing brother in the story is highlighted. As if balancing the responsibility of these two nations, the narrator speaks from a neutral corner, Puerto Rico, and blames both for lack of comradeship.

The story "Caso omiso" from the collection *Pasión de historia y otras historias de pasión* addresses the theme of domestic violence. The title refers to the lack of attention given to domestic violence. The protagonist is an older woman who has an affair with a teenage boy while separating from her physically abusive husband. Although she thrives on the obsession demonstrated by the teenager and it appears that she is an independent woman, in actuality she is subservient to her ex-husband. This ambivalence of identities is referred to by Eda B. Henao as an internalization of portions of different cultures. On the one hand, the woman asserts herself and plays the role of aggressor with the young man, on the other, she is very much afraid of her ex-husband who appears sporadically to assure himself that she does not have another man. The attainment of a certain level of sexual freedom may be viewed as a feminist attribute, however, she remains shackled to ideas formulated in sexism.

In the collection *Falsas crónicas del sur,* the story "Cuento en camino" is an account of a woman who travels to Europe to write a novel about another Puerto Rican woman who was murdered by her ex-lover. Paradoxically, the writer herself is killed by her ex-lover and the story ends with another woman implying that more remains to be said. Vega suggests that the role of women writers has not been completely satisfied and although one may be silenced, another assumes the responsibility, thereby giving voice to the silenced. The deaths symbolize the obstacles that women writers face. However, the title of the short story "Cuento en camino" alludes to a story about to be told; although it is not clear who will tell the story, it is evident that a woman acknowledges that the story is incomplete. The death of the writer does not close the door to the information that must be dispersed. The title and ending radiate with hope for women writers who are willing to take on the challenge of telling the stories of the silenced.

The story "El baúl de Miss Florence: Fragmentos para un novelón romántico," in the collection *Falsas crónicas del sur,* highlights the women's perspective of history. The title implies that chronicles have been misrepresented and that another interpretation is needed. An English tutor is the protagonist of the story which takes place during the time of slavery in Puerto Rico. Many of the stories in this collection are narrated by women and cover historical issues. Vega challenges the traditional depiction of women and disputes the official stories which have misrepresented women. She proposes and applauds a woman's explication of and inclusion in history.

In conclusion, Vega scrutinizes the values that are constructing Puerto Rican society. She examines these tainted constructions through her characters that represent the different walks of life. She penetrates the reality of different aspects of popular culture through a humorous language and exposes the misconceptions and distortions rooted in colonialism and the North American presence. By addressing these issues she offers another perspective from which to view reality and construct national values. Ultimately, she offers a mirror to the reader by probing issues of identity and national culture.

DIANA PARDO

Selected Works

Interviews

Hernández, Carmen Dolores. "A Sense of Space, a Sense of Speech: a Conversation with Ana Lydia Vega". *Hopscotch: A Cultural Review* 2(2) (2000): 52–9.

Hernández, Elizabeth. "Women and Writing in Puerto Rico: an Interview with Ana Lydia Vega". *Callaloo* 17(3) (1994).

Short Fiction

Vírgenes y mártires, in collaboration with Carmen Lugo Filippi. Río Piedras, Puerto Rico: Antillana, 1981.

Encancaranublado y otros cuentos de naufragio. Havana: Casa de las Américas, 1982.

Pasión de historia y otras historias de pasión. Buenos Aires: Ediciones de La Flor, 1987.

La felicidad ja ja ja ja y la Universidad. Río Piedras, Puerto Rico: Universidad de Puerto Rico, 1989.

Falsas crónicas del sur, illustrated by Walter Torres. Río Piedras: Editorial de la Universidad de Puerto Rico, 1991; as *True and False Romances: Stories and a Novella,* trans. Andrew Hurley, London: Serpent's Tail, 1994.

Cuentos calientes. México City: UNAM, 1992.

Esperando a Loló y otros delirios generacionales. San Juan, Puerto Rico: Editorial de la Universidad de Puerto Rico, 1994.

References and Further Reading

Cruz, María I. Acosta. "Historia y escritura femenina en Olga Nolla, Magali García Ramis, Rosario Ferré y Ana Lydia Vega". *Revista Iberoamericana* 59 (1993): 265–77.

Fernández Olmos, Margarite. "From a Woman's Perspective: the Short Stories of Rosario Ferré and Ana Lydia Vega". In *Contemporary Women Authors of Latin América,* Brooklyn, NY: Brooklyn College Press. 1983.

González, Anibal. "Ana Lydia Pluravega: unidad y multiplicidad caribeñas en la obra de Ana Lydia Vega". *Revista Iberoamericana* 56(162–3) (1993).

Henao, Eda B. *The Colonial Subject's Search for Nation, Culture, and Identity in the works of Julia Álvarez, Rosario Ferré, and Ana Lydia Vega*. Lewiston, NY: Edwin Mellen Press, 2004.

Ramos Rosado, Marie. *La mujer negra en la literatura puertorriqueña: cuentística de los setenta*. San Juan, Puerto Rico: Editorial de la Universidad de Puerto Rico, 1999.

Vélez, Diana L. "Pollito Chicken: Split Subjectivity, National Identity and the Articulation of Female Sexuality in a Narrative by Ana Lydia Vega". *The Americas Review* 14(2) (1986).

——. "We are (not) in this Together: The Caribbean Imaginary in *Encancaranublado* by Ana Lydia Vega". *Callaloo* 17(3) (1994): 826–33.

VICUÑA, CECILIA

An internationally acclaimed poet, filmmaker and artist, Cecilia Vicuña has long explored the messages and meanings of seemingly ordinary objects and their connections to the spirit of humanity and the natural world.

Vicuña was born in Chile, on July 22, 1948. Growing up in the outskirts of Santiago, alongside the Andes Mountains, the flow between art and daily life seemed completely integrated because most of her family members were artists, philosophers, or poets. Her mother, Norma Ramírez Arenas, worked as a tour guide and her father, Jorge Vicuña Lagarrique, practiced law. Vicuña recalls being left alone a great deal to play with light, shadows, and water at a nearby irrigation canal. Once the young Vicuña discovered the art of reading and writing, she made passionate attempts to articulate the sounds of water, the presence of indigenous languages, and the meanings of the occasional radio program. This early fascination for the emotional field of language and art remains present not only in her creative work but also in the workshops for children that she now organizes to encourage young people to get involved in the creative process of community building.

In 1971, Vicuña completed the M.F.A. program at the University of Chile, and from 1972 to 1973, she continued her at the Slade School of Fine Arts at the University College of London. While in the United Kingdom, a violent military coup in her native country ousted President-elect Salvador Allende and led to the formation of a bureaucratic authoritarian regime. Given her support of Popular Unity, Allende's party, Vicuña urgently sought exile. With other artists and intellectuals, she co-founded Artists for Democracy in 1974. She later moved to Bogotá, Colombia, and, in 1980, settled in New York City where she met the Argentine artist César Paternosto, also exiled from his native country and to whom she would be married for twenty-five years.

Vicuña's insistence on the sensorial nature of language and the communal spirit of the artistic experience has infused her poetry and visual art with a unique imprint. She was awarded the Human Rights Exile Award from the Fund for Free Expression in 1985; the Arts International Award from the Lila Wallace–Reader's Digest Fund in 1992; the 1995–96 Lee Krasner–Jackson Pollock Award; and the 1995–95 Fund for Poetry Award, among others. Her artwork has been exhibited at highly prestigious cultural institutions throughout Europe,

South America and the United States (the Institute of Contemporary Arts in London, the Museo Nacional de Bellas Artes in Chile, the Whitney Museum of American Art Biennial Exhibition and the Museum of Modern Art in New York, to name a few). Vicuña regularly reads her work and lectures on indigenous cultures of the Andes at universities and cultural organizations worldwide.

Creative Migrations

"Everything is falling apart because of the lack of connections," Vicuña explains in her *Quipoem* (1997). In this work, she offers a journal of debris of her native Chile, a self-professed "diary of a life in litter" that brings to mind the human rights violations and abuses brought about by the regime of Chilean General Augusto Pinochet – which lasted from 1973 to 1990 and during which thousands of people were systematically tortured, executed and buried following the overthrow of Allende on September 11, 1973. Vicuña's earliest poetic works, such as *Sabor a Mí* (1973, A Taste of Me), had responded to the experience of cultural displacement and exile through a series of autobiographical reflections and collage-style presentations of material objects. An earlier version of the book of poems, although recommended for publication by the Universidad Católica de Valparaíso, was allegedly rejected for its erotic content. Responding to the images and discourses emanating from the recently formed dictatorship in Chile, Vicuña created different versions of the same title. The final version, as published, ultimately consisted of photographs of Vicuña's paintings and artistic installations completed in Chile and the United Kingdom.

In *Precario / Precarious* (1983), Vicuña would connect images of seemingly insignificant objects and places to nature and human life. The book of visual and textual poems also documents a series of artistic installations that the poet found, placed, or built into various surroundings throughout Latin America. The positioning of ordinary objects like strings and fabrics serves as metaphors for other times, cultures, and spaces, as if to reveal hidden messages that exist silently but survive gracefully. "Poetry inhabits certain places where the cliffs need only a signal to bring them alive," she writes. "Two or three lines, a mark, and silence begins to speak". Here, the act of honor and trying to understand the meaning of a moment of silence leads to an awareness of the plight of those suppressed by the forces of authoritarianism, of humanity's unfinished dreams, and of the radical nature of "hope". The spiritual bent to this search, which Vicuña has described as the result of a force that impelled her to make small offerings to the Earth and which infused in her "a desire to expand," alludes to Pablo Neruda's ascent to the heights of Macchu Picchu in this compatriot's magnum opus, the *Canto general* (General Song).

Palabrarmas, published in 1984, takes its cues from Vicente Huidobro's *creacionismo*, as it combines semantic units to form new words and dissects images from words in order to reveal essences and hidden truths. The title of the book is itself an example of the linguistic strategies employed in poetry to counter the banality of official discourses that hide news of the disappeared within the cover, as the poet combines *palabra* [word] and *armas* [weapons] while also conveying the idea of working the land and the visions with which our human community arms itself.

In *Unraveling Words and the Weaving of Water* (1992) and *Cloud-Net* (1999), the multiple levels of poems are like divinations that, in a cyclical manner, summon the indigenous heritage of the Andean region and the Americas. *Cloud-net*, an installation initiated in 1998 that established connections between the work of the loom and the earth, or weaving and agriculture, was exhibited and performed at several museums in the United States. This project culminated with the compilation and subsequent publication of photographs of Vicuña's artistic mapping of these cultural spaces and weavings, as well as meditations and reflective quotations.

Armed with radical optimism, Vicuña's writing locates the connecting point between "people themselves, people and nature," finding visions of hope in *precarios* (small installations that serve as prayers, recalling insecure moments); in *quipus*, compilations of strings used by the Incas to narrate history; in *kijllu*, stones marked by the Mapuche Indians to symbolize the communications between the world above and below; and in the spinning and weaving of yarn. Vicuña's work has also unraveled the creative migrations of the global diaspora, with many poems attempting to recover indigenous wisdom in the aftermath of colonization and the neo-colonial enterprises of globalization.

Sé mi ya, or The Seed Project

Most recently, Vicuña has returned to *The Seed Project*, a community arts endeavor that she began as a young girl in Chile in 1971 (when she began to gather local and native seeds in danger of extinction) and which continues to enable young people "to connect with each other, to share experiences and stories". Vowing "to create a work in life and in poetry and art, by writing and drawing seeds, and planting them as well," Vicuña proposed a day of the seed to Chilean President Salvador Allende. Replying with a laugh, Allende allegedly told her, "maybe by the year two thousand". In 2000, the Chilean Ministry of Education invited Vicuña to return to the country in order to perform and create an artistic installation based on this very project. It was here that the poetic and artistic "Seed Speaking," an allusion to the creation of new experiences and relationships in democracy, was born. Today, the project hinges loosely on the word "diaspora," which means to plant, to seed, or to create something with new life. *The Seed Project* has been performed throughout the world, having been performed recently at various sites in Argentina, Brazil, Chile, the United States and Uruguay. Through her art and poetry, Vicuña asks participants of this ongoing community project "to care for the earth, and the survival of seeds". Appropriating the word for "seed" in Spanish, she creates new narratives. From the pronouncement of *semilla*, then, comes "Sé mi ya" (which Vicuña translates as "Be my readiness"), a phrase that one speaks with urgency as if to reveal the inclinations of the moment, the yearning for liberation from injustices, the desire for new directions. During a workshop, Vicuña works together with participants on the creation of poems that conceive a new set of relationships to the human and natural world. By engaging seeds as "the words of the Earth" and inspiring community interaction through creative work, Vicuña's work invites her audience, readers, and communities at large to perform as members of a larger public project, or as cultural agents whose actions challenge the pervasiveness of despair and seek to inspire social change.

Scholarly Directions

Vicuña's poetry, performances, and installations are multivalent indeed. Understandably, scholars must emphasize the urgent conditions under which the author produced her early work. At the same time, the transcendental nature of the themes, issues, and dates engaged provide scholars with an array of questions that will amplify the scope of humanistic knowledge on the rhetoric of human rights and environmentalism as well as their implicit connections to questions of memory and collective identity. Scholars like M. Catherine Zegher and Jill S. Kuhnheim have analyzed the significance of authorial voice and the repressed, of image and text, linking these to the realm of female subjectivity and the framework of postcolonial experience. Other scholars explore Vicuña's ties to indigenous spirituality and the complexities of this engagement in the age of globalization. Many of the author's works—from her scripts for children's television programs in Chile to her contributions on anthologies and museum catalogues that highlight indigenous literature and art in the Americas—have not yet been studied. Given that much of Vicuña's work with small presses is currently out of print, scholars may encounter limited access to some materials. Perhaps because of the diverse nature of Vicuña's literary and artistic endeavors, it appears that scholars may have only begun to explore the multifaceted dimensions of what is already a most impressive œuvre.

REGINA A. ROOT

Selected Works

Sabor a Mi. Bilingual edition, trans. Felipe Ehrenberg and the author. Devon: Beau Geste Press, 1973.

Siete poemas. Bogotá, Colombia: Ediciones Centro Colombo Americano, 1979.

Luxumei o el Traspié de la Doctrina. Mexico City, Mexico: Editorial Oasis, 1983.

PALABRARmas. Buenos Aires, Argentina: Ediciones El Imaginero, 1984.

Samara. Bogotá, Colombia: Ediciones Embalaje and the Museo Rayo, 1986.

Co-editor with Magda Bogin. *The Selected Poems of Rosario Castellanos*. Saint Paul, MN: Graywolf Press, 1988.

Unravelling Words and the Weaving of Water. Ed. Eliot Weinberger, and trans. Suzanne Jill Levine. Saint Paul, MN: Graywolf Press, 1992.

Word and Thread. Trans. Rosa Alcalá. Edinburgh: Morning Star Publications, 1996.

The Precarious, the Art and Poetry of Cecilia Vicuña/Quipoem. M. Catherine de Zegher, ed. Ester Allen, trans. Hanover, NH and London: University Press of New England, 1997.

(ed.) *UI. Four Mapuche Poets: An Anthology*. New York: Latin American Literary Review Press, 1998.

Instan. Berkeley, CA: Kelsey St. Press, 2002.

Website

Semiya. Website dedicated to one segment of *The Seed Project*. Initiated in 2003 and maintained by the Graduate School of Library and Information Science at the University of Illinois at Urbana-Champaign. http://www.inquiry.uiuc.edu/seeds/history.htm

References and Further Reading

Bianchi, Soledad. "Pasaron desde aquel ayer ya tantos años, o acerca de Cecilia Vicuña y la *Tribu No*". *Revista de Crítica Literaria Latinoamericana* 12(29) (1989): 87–94.

De Zegher, M. Catherine. "Cecilia Vicuña's Ouvrage: Knot a Not, Notes as Knots". In Griselda Pollock (ed.), *Generations and Geographies in the Visual Arts: Feminist Readings*. London and New York: Routledge, 1996, pp. 197–216.

Kuhnheim, Jill. "Image and Text: Reading Outside Language". in *Textual Disruptions: Spanish American Poetry at the End of the Twentieth Century*. Austin, TX: University of Texas Press, 2004, pp. 50–62.

Lippard, Lucy. "Spinning the Common Thread". In M. Catherine de Zegher (ed.), *The Precarious: The Art and Poetry of Cecilia Vicuña/Quipoem*. Hanover, NH and London: University Press of New England, 1996, pp. 7–15.

Méndez-Ramírez, Hugo. "Cryptic Weaving". In M. Catherine de Zegher (ed.), *The Precarious: The Art and Poetry of Cecilia Vicuña/Quipoem*. Hanover, NH and London: University Press of New England. 1996, pp. 59–71.

VILALTA, MARUXA

Maruxa Vilalta was born on September 23, 1932, in Barcelona. Her father, Antonio Vilalta y Vidal, was a lawyer and municipal official in Barcelona and her mother, María Soteras Maurí, a professor of law. The family left Spain because of the Civil War and, after living in Brussels for three years, moved to Mexico City in 1939 where Maruxa began and completed her education. She first earned her bachelor of French at the *Liceo Franco Mexicano* and later a Masters of Spanish Arts from la Universidad Nacional Autónoma de México (UNAM). She later continued her studies at Cambridge.

Vilalta began her writing career as a novelist with the publication of *El castigo* (The Punishment) in 1957. Two more novels followed: *Los desorientados* (1958, The Confused) and *Dos colores para el paisaje* (1961, Two Colors for a View). A collection of short stories *El otro día, la muerte* (The Next Day, Death) was published in 1974. She has also been an editor for the newspaper *Excélsior* and a stage director on Mexican television on the programs *Mujeres que trabajan* (Women Who Work) and *El libro de hoy* (Contemporary Book).

Vilalta, in interviews, describes writing as an expression of freedom and theatre as the genre which interests her most. Her works have been translated into various languages and performed in many Spanish-speaking countries as well as the United States, Yugoslavia, the former Czechoslovakia, France, Morocco and Canada. She has also directed the works of other playwrights. Her own works have been collected and published in four volumes by the *Fondo de Cultura Económica* (Mexico) and include: *Los desorientados* (1960, The confused), an adaptation of her novel by the same name, *Un país feliz* (1964, A Happy Country), *Soliloquio del tiempo* (1964, Time's Soliloquy), *Un día loco* (1964, A Crazy Day) and *La última letra* (1964, The Last Letter). *El 9* (1965, Number 9), was included in an anthology of the best short works of the year, *Best Short Plays* (1973) edited by Stanley Richards; *Cuestión de narices*

(1966, A Matter of Noses) won the award for best best group and best director, Ramón Dagés, at the Manresa Festival in 1974; *Esta noche juntos, amándonos tanto* (1970, Together Tonight, Loving Each Other So Much) won the Juan Ruiz de Alarcón award for best work of the year and another for best work at the Festival de las Máscara in Morelia. *Nada como el piso 16* (1976, Nothing Like the Sixteenth Floor) won the Juan Ruiz de Alarcón award for best work of the year as well as Best Work of the Year from the Unión de Críticos y Cronistas. *Historia de él* (1978, History of him) was also awarded Best Work of the Year with the Premio Juan Ruiz de Alarcón as well as Work of the Year with the Premio El Fígaro. Other works include: *Una mujer, dos hombres y un balazo* (1981, A Woman, Two Men and a Gunshot), *Pequeña historia de horror (y de amor desenfrenado)* (1985, A Little Tale of Horror (and Unbridled Love)), *Una voz en el desierto, Vida de San Jerónimo* (1991, A Voice in the Desert. Life of St. Jerome) which won won the award for best work of creative research by the Asociación Mexicana de Críticos del Teatro (AMCT – Mexican Theatre Critics Association) as well as an award by the Agrupación de Periodistas Teatrales (Theatre Journalists Society). *Francisco de Asís* (1992, Francis of Assisi) won Best Work of Theatre Research from AMCT; *Jesucristo entre nosotros* (1994, Jesus Christ Among Us). *Ignacio y los jesuitas* (Ignatius and the Jesuits) debuted in 1997 and was performed again in 2000 and 2001.

In addition to being awarded Best Work of the Year 10 times, Vilalta is recognized as a *Creadora Artística* (artistic creator) by the Sistema Nacional de Creadores de Arte (National Society of Creators of Art) in 1994. Aside from awards for particular theatrical works, she has recieved honors and distinctions from a variety of groups: Diploma del Instituto Mexicano de Cultura, 1963, Diploma del Departamento del Distrito Federal, Programa Cultural de la XIX Olimpiada, 1968 and Diploma as Vicepresident of the Colegio de Literatura, 1968. She received an award for literary merit from the Círculo de Letras Nuevos Horizontes in Managua, 1972, Diploma as an honorary Socio from the Unión Feminina de Periodistas y Escritoras, 1974, as well as being named Woman of the Decade (1970–80) by the same group. Las *Novenas Jornadas de Teatro Latinoamericano,* organized by the University of Tennessee and the Centro Cultural Espacio 1900 with the support of the Secretary of Cultura in Puebla, were dedicated to her successful career as a playwright. Vilalta is also a member of the Pen Club, the Sociedad General de Escritores de México, the Sociedad Mexicana de Geografía y Estadística and the Asociación de Escritores de México.

As Sharon Magnarelli points out, criticism of the works of Vilalta is varied. Joan Rea Boorman has labeled her works as "theatre of disruption"; Carlos Solórzano and Tamara Holzapfel have classified her plays as a mixture of theatre of the absurd and epic theatre; L. H. Quackenbush has labeled her work as existentialist while Daniel Zacalain has classified it as absurdist theatre. But, according to Magnarelli, Vilalta does not see; herself as part of any school; she believes that her works are always influenced by the political and follow in the steps of Ionesco (1998, p. 37).

In general, themes such as lack of communication and a zeal for evasion combine with political criticism to protest social injustice in defense of the individual. The plays of Vilalta are carefully constructed with an emphasis on the form of the message in an attempt to achieve a more universal context in which to understand the problems of Latin America and its people. One example would be the play *Un país feliz* in which Vilalta, employing a storyline essentially realist in nature and a foreign protagonist, denounces the state of dependency in which Latin America suffers.

The use of historical events and protagonists distinguishes Vilalta's work among other contemporary playwrights in Latin America. In works such as *Una voz en el desierto. Vida de San Jerónimo, Francisco de Asís, Jesucristo entre nosotros* and *Ignacio y los jesuitas*, Vilalta uses stories of a historical and religious nature to present the reader and audience with contemporary sociopolitical criticism.

In 1999, during a conference in the lecture hall at the Centro Nacional de las Artes (Center for the National Arts), in México city, Vilalta has herself stated that psychology is one of her main areas of focus in her work:

> Todos tenemos problemas existenciales y eso se puede apreciar en la obra *Esta noche juntos,* que trata de un par de viejos que se autodestruyen, y en *Pequeña historia de horror (y un amor desenfrenado)* que habla de la vida de un psicópata. En mis obras me importa mucho desnudar psicológicamente el espectador, abrir sus emociones, sensaciones y pensamientos.
>
> [We all have existential problems and one can see this in the work *Esta noche juntos* that is about an old couple who destroy themselves and each other, and, in *Pequeña historia de horror (y un amor desenfrenado)* that presents the life of a psychopath. It is important to me that my works expose the audience psychologically opening their emotions, feelings and thoughts. Violence, both physical and emotional, is another theme that appears frequently in my work.]

At that same conference, Vilalta describes the characters of her plays as taking on a life of their own at some point in the process of writing. "Llega un momento en que hay mucha vida en ellos, de manera que se comportan como quieren y así definen la historia; yo soy tan sólo un escribano" [There comes a moment in which they [the characters] are so full of life that it is they who direct the story being told leaving me to merely record it on paper.] She also speaks of the importance of using humor, often pointed and corrosive, to convey her message:

> Si con las obras yo le digo al público no hagan esto, seguramente me responderán ¿y por qué no lo voy a hacer? En cambio, si les muestro a un hombre y una mujer conduciéndose de una manera excesiva pero con humor, nada más con verlos la gente podrá hacer su lectura sobre lo que debe o no debe hacer.
>
> [If, in my works, I tell the audience not to do something, surely they would respond, why not? On the other hand if I show them a man and a woman carrying on in an excessive way but with humor, the audience can draw their own conclusions.]

In conclusion, although her works present socio-political criticism of some of the contemporary problems people face, Vilalta's plays also show the responsbility that individuals have in the creation of these problems. The circular structure of many of her plays underlines the idea that without changing the individual it will be impossible to change society and vice versa.

MARIA R. MATZ AND W. KEITH WOODALL

Selected Works

Primera antología de obras en un acto. México: Colección Teatro Mexicano, 1959.
Los desorientados. México: Libro Mex, 1960.
Segunda antología de obras en un acto. México: Imp. de Lujo, 1960.
Tercera antología de obras en un acto. México: Colección Teatro Mexicano, 1960.
Dos colores para el paisaje. México: Libro Mex, 1961.
Soliloquio del tiempo. México: Ecuador, 1964.
Un país feliz. México: Ecuador, 1965.
Trio: soliloquio del tiempo; un dia loco; la ultima letra. México: Rafael Peregrina, 1965.
Los desorientados: obra en tres actos. México: Ecuador, 1966.
Cuestion de narices: farsa tragica en dos actos. México: UNAM, 1967.
Esta noche juntos, amándonos tanto (farsa trágica sin intermedios). México: OPIC, 1970.
5 obras de teatro. México: SEP, 1970.
El otro día, la muerte. México: J. Mortiz, 1974.
Nada como el piso 16. México: J. Mortiz, 1977.
Historia de él: obra en 17 cuadros. México: UNAM Departamento de Teatro, 1979.
Dos obras de teatro. México: UNAM, 1984.
Pequeña historia de horror (y de amor desenfrenado): (obra en dos actos). México, D.F.: UAM, Unidad Xochimilco, 1986.
Teatro. México: FCE, 1990.
Francisco de Asís:obra en 14 cuadros. México: FCE, 1993.
El barco ebrio: obra en un acto. México: CONACULCA, 1995.
Jesucristo entre nosotros. México: FCE, 1995.
En blanco y negro: Ignacio y los jesuitas: obra en 12 cuadros. México: FCE, 1997.
A Contemporary Mexican Mystery Play: The Life of Saint Jerome, a Voice in the Wilderness. Lewiston, NY: Edwin Mellen Press, 2006.

References and Further Reading

Cajiao Salas, Teresa, and Vargas, Margarita. *El Teatro en México. 3 vols. 1990–1991, 1992–1993, 1994–1995*. Mexico: Centro de Investigación Teatral Rodolfo Usigli, Instituto Nacional de Bellas Artes, 1993, 1995, 1996.
——. *Women Writing Women: An Anthology of Spanish-American Theater of the 1980s*. Albany, NY: State University of New York Press, 1997.
Knapp Jones, Willis. *Latin American Women Dramatist*. Bloomington, IN: Indiana University Press, 1998.
Magnarelli, Sharon. "La historia puesta en escena: 1910, de Maruja Vilalta". *Revista Teatro XXI*, Facultad de Filosofía y Letras, Universidad de Buenos Aires, 8(14) (2002).
——. "Una voz en el desierto". In Catherine Larson and Margarita Vargas (eds), *Latin American Women Dramatists*. Bloomington, IN: Indiana University Press, 1998.
Reuben, María Elena. *Bibliografía de Maruxa Vilalta. 2004* http://www.geocities.com/maruxavilalta/BIBLIMV.pdf

VILARIÑO, IDEA

The poet, literary critic, translator, composer and professor of literature Idea Vilariño was born in Montevideo, Uruguay on August 18, 1920. The daughter of the anarchist poet Leandro Vilariño, she began writing before the age of 6 and, as a student, was commissioned to write love poems for her classmates. She began publishing her poetry in 1945 with *La suplicante* (The Imploring [One]). A key figure in Uruguay's Generation of 45, she co-directed the journal *Número* (1949–55) and collaborated in *Clinamen*, *Marcha*, *Brecha* and *Asir*. She taught literature at the Liceo de Nueva Helvecia, the Instituto Alfredo Vásquez Acevedo and the Universidad de la República. A popular and critically acclaimed writer in her homeland, her opposition to the process of juror selection has led her to refuse important prizes (including the Premio Nacional de Literatura in 1966 and two Guggenheim fellowships), and her natural aversion to self-promotion has prevented her from agreeing to interviews about her work; among the rare exceptions are a 1971 interview in which she responded (in writing) to questions posed by her ardent supporter Mario Benedetti (included in *Los poetas comunicantes* (1972; The Communicating Poets)); the 1997 video *Idea*, in which she responds to those of Rosario Peyrou and Pablo Rocca; and an interview with Elena Poniatowska, who visited her at home in Montevideo in 2004.

Among the honors she has accepted are the Premio a la labor intelectual José Enrique Rodó (José Enrique Rodó Prize for Intellectual Work) and the Haydée Santamaría medal in 1994; she has also served as a juror for Cuba's Casa de las Américas awards in 1966 and 1984. In 2005, she received the Premio Juan José Morosoli de Oro for her body of work and was recognized as an Illustrious Citizen of Montevideo in a ceremony attended by Benedetti. The last of a number of anthologies, *En lo más implacable de la noche* (2003; In the Most Implacable of the Night) was awarded the Premio de poesía José Lezama Lima by Casa de las Américas. She has been invited to speak in several countries throughout Latin America and Europe.

Poetry

Critics have focused on the apparent "obsessions" of Vilariño's poetry: love and its absence, eroticism and death (and the connection between the two). Her tone is viewed as pessimistic, even nihilistic, as her poetic subject rejects the pain and futility of worldly life and laments the inexistence of God. The driving force of rhythm combines with a simple, unadorned style, nearly bereft of punctuation from her second collection onwards. Her first collection, *La suplicante*, contained just five poems and was published under her first name only. This brief introduction to the poet's work establishes themes, images and devices to which she would return repeatedly throughout her career: preoccupations with solitude, nostalgia for childhood, passionate love, eroticism and death; images of the sea; the frequent use of anaphora and alliteration. Though carefully constructed rhythmic compositions, the poems have the appearance of free verse and a breathless, stream-of-consciousness quality, as though thoughts are often left unfinished. The next few years brought to light a series of similarly brief collections including *Cielo cielo* (1947, Heaven Heaven), also consisting of five poems and attributed simply to "Idea," though it possesses a darker and more somber tone; *Paraíso perdido 1945–1948* (1949, Paradise Lost 1945–48), which contains many of the poems from the previous two augmented by the title poem; and *Por aire sucio* (Through Dirty Air), which appeared in 1950 (and again, in a substantially altered version, in 1951) and reflects the poet's experience of a serious illness that began that same year. The latter volume follows previous patterns as it also contains two previously published poems, though the overall tone and subject matter are dramatically different: the gentle nature imagery seen in her earliest poetry has given way to that of punishing light (first glimpsed in *Paraíso perdido*), pain, sorrow and an oppressive solitude. Familiar recourses – repetition of sounds, words, and entire verses; plays on words involving the confusion of articles and the combining of two words into one, dating back to *Cielo cielo* – are employed to express a dark vision of confinement and isolation.

Poems from *Por aire sucio* made their way both into *Nocturnos* (Nocturnes), first published in 1955 and similar in tone and imagery to its predecessor, though the poems have taken on a more compact form; as well as into her most famous work, *Poemas de amor* (1957, Love Poems; an augmented edition was published in 1962). This best-selling collection was originally presented in the author's handwriting and was dedicated to Juan Carlos Onetti, with whom she shared a tumultuous relationship (and who dedicated his novel *Los adioses* [1954, The Goodbyes] to her). The poetic subject in this collection relates her experience of loneliness, constant waiting, absence, loss and a fundamental lack of understanding in poems characterized, once again, by repetition and enumeration. *Pobre mundo* (1966, Poor World) strikes a very different note, branching out into political and ecological themes, and moving between nature images reminiscent of her first collection and tributes to figures such as Che Guevara, Martin Luther King, Jr. and John F. Kennedy. 1980's *No*, dedicated to then-husband Jorge Liberati, marks a stylistic departure as the poems (each bearing a number in lieu of a title) are extremely compact, with lines frequently comprising only one or two words. The images, though relatively few, are familiar to readers of her poetry since *La suplicante*, but she continues to experiment with structure: a series of poems near the end of the book is composed entirely of extended similes beginning with "Como ..." (like ...). In addition to her poetry collections, Vilariño has provided lyrics for songs recorded by famous Uruguayan musicians such as Daniel Viglietti, Los Olimareños and Alfredo Zitarrosa; her most famous composition is the anthem "Los Orientales". Her songs were collected in *Canciones* (1993, Songs).

Prior to *En lo más implacable de la noche*, Vilariño regularly published anthologies of her work including *Treinta poemas* (Thirty Poems) in 1967; *Poesía* (1970, Poetry); *Segunda antología* (1980, Second Anthology), *Nocturnos del pobre amor* (1989, Nocturnes of Poor Love), which compiles poems from *Poemas de amor*, *No*, *Nocturnos* and *Pobre Mundo*; *Poesía (1945–1990)*, published in 1994 and augmented by additional poems written before the publication of *La suplicante*; and, *Poesía completa*, 2002. In addition, her work has been included in anthologies such as *Seis poetisas hispanoamericanas del Siglo XX* (Six Spanish American Poetesses of the Twentieth Century), *A Chorus for Peace: A Global Anthology of Poetry by Women* (2002), *Women's Writing in Latin America: An Anthology* (1991), and *Women Writers in Twentieth-Century Spain and Spanish America* (1993). English-speaking students of Spanish can find her work in anthologies including *Temas: Invitación a la literatura hispánica* (1994; Themes: Invitation to Hispanic Literature).

Other Works

Among many other critical studies, Vilariño provided the prologue to Julio Herrera y Reissig's *Poesía completa y prosa selecta* (1978, Complete Poetry and Select Prose) and published a study of her fellow Uruguayan's work in 1950. Her *Conocimiento de Darío* (1988, Knowledge of Darío), for which she received both the Premio Nacional de la Crítica Bartolomé de Hidago and the Premio Ensayo given by the Ministerio de Educación y Cultura, explores many controversial aspects of the Nicaraguan poet's life, views and works in a wide-ranging study of the man and his poetry; another book on Darío, *La masa sonora del poema* (1986, The Sonorous Mass of the Poem) is a rigorous investigation of the rhythmic organization of a handful of his poems. She has produced several critical works on the tango, including *Las letras de tango* (1965, Tango Lyrics) and the anthology *El tango cantado* (1981, The Tango Sung); in her prologue to the latter, she laments the lack of serious studies of the form and praises the artistry of Carlos Gardel. Other works of criticism include 1958's *Grupos simétricos en poesía* (Symmetrical Groups in Poetry). In 2001, she compiled *Antología Poética de Mujeres Hispanoamericanas* (Poetic Anthology of Spanish American Women), noting in her prologue the scarcity of poems by female authors in previous anthologies. Her prize-winning work as a translator includes several of Shakespeare's best-known plays, including *Hamlet* (1974) and *Julius Caesar* (1975), as well as works by T.S. Eliot, Graham Greene, and others. Her interest in the theatre is evident in her collaboration as translator and seamstress for the Teatro del Pueblo (People's Theatre), in which her sister Poema was also involved, and her collaboration with Mercedes Rein on a play based on tango lyrics, *Mano a mano* (Hand to Hand). In addition to her many publications, her decades-long affair with Onetti produced a large body of correspondence to be published only after her passing.

STACY HOULT

Selected Works

Conocimiento de Darío. Montevideo: ARCA Editorial, 1988.
Canciones. Montevideo: Ediciones de la Banda Oriental, 1993.
Poesía completa. Intro. Luis Gregorich. Montevideo: Cal y canto, 2002.

References and Further Reading

Benedetti, Mario. "Idea Vilariño: el amor y la muerte, esas certezas". In *Los poetas comunicantes*. Montevideo: Biblioteca de Marcha, 1972, pp. 251–63.

Berry-Bravo, Judy. *Texts and Contexts of Idea Vilariño's Poetry*. York, SC: Spanish Literature Publications Company, 1994.

Crelis Secco, Susana. *Idea Vilariño: Poesía e identidad*. México: Universidad Nacional Autónoma de México e Instituto Nacional de Bellas Artes, 1990.

Poniatowska, Elena. "Esencial y desesperada: entrevista con Idea Vilariño". *Masiosare/La Jornada de México*, 8 Aug. 2004. http://www.rodelu.net/2004/semana36cultur45c.htm (accessed 10 July 2006).

Rodriguez Monegal, Emir. "El mundo poetico de Idea Vilariño: la nueva poesia uruguaya (1945–55)". *Marcha* 824 (1956): 21–3.

http://www.archivodeprensa.edu.uy/r_monegal/bibliografia/prensa/artpren/marcha/marcha_824.htm (accessed 10 July 2006)

San Román, Gustavo. "Expression and Silence in the Poetry of Juana de Ibarbourou and Idea Vilariño". In Catherine Davies (ed.), *Women Writers in Twentieth-Century Spain and Spanish America*. New York: The Edwin Mellen Press, 1993, pp. 157–75.

VITALE, IDA

The poet, critic, journalist, translator and professor of literature Ida Vitale was born in Montevideo, Uruguay, on November 2, 1923. An only child, she was not permitted to attend school until the third grade and, as a young person, was sustained principally by novels (ranging from classic fairy tales to Dickens and *War and Peace*), discovering poetry and Latin American literature only later. An interest in the botanical imagery that would appear in many of her poems was formed through learning the scientific names of plants from her grandmother. Among her earliest influences was the Spanish poet José Bergamín, with whom she studied and to whom she has rendered homage in the pages of *Letras libres*.

An important member of the innovative group of intellectuals known as the "Generación del, '45", she collaborated in many journals associated with the circle, which included her first husband, the literary critic Angel Rama (with whom she had two children, Amparo and Claudio). She co-directed *Clinamen* with Rama, Manuel A. Claps, Victor Bachetta *et al.* and collaborated regularly in *Marcha*. Her first book of poetry, *La luz de esta memoria* (The Light of this Memory), was published in 1949. She published regularly and taught literature in Uruguay until 1973; along with her second husband, the poet Enrique Fierro, she lived in exile in Mexico between 1974 and 1984, during which time she was part of the editorial board of *Maldoror*. After returning to Uruguay, she became director of the cultural page of *Jaque*. She and Fierro divide their time between Montevideo, Mexico and Austin, Texas, where he teaches; each contributed one poem to their 1994 collaboration *Paz por dos* (Peace Times Two). She continues to publish both poetry and prose and is a sought-after critical voice, having given an interview about Felisberto Hernández in *Aperturas sobre el extrañamiento* (Openings onto Alienation, 1993) and contributed critical pieces to journals, including *Vuelta* and *Unomásuno* (from Mexico) and Nicaragua's *El pez y la serpiente*, throughout her career. She has also been active in numerous international literary congresses and festivals.

Poetry

Her complete works up to 1984 (*La luz de esta memoria*; *Palabra dada* (1953; Word Given), *Cada uno en su noche* (1960; Each in His Night), *Oidor andante* (1972; Walking Hear), and *Jardín de sílice* (1980; Garden of Silica)) are compiled in reverse chronological order in *Sueños de la constancia* (1988; Dreams of Constancy). Another anthology, *Obra poética I* (Poetic Works I), was published in 1992 but includes only works written up to 1980. A number of poems from the early collections are also gathered in the last section, entitled "Fieles" (Faithful Ones), of 2002's *Reducción del infinito* (Reduction of the Infinite). (An anthology entitled *Fieles* had previously been released in 1977 and 1982.) *Reducción* provides an invaluable overview of the stylistic and thematic directions her poetry has taken in later years, including forays into environmental and political poetry, while showcasing innovations in the treatment of images and preoccupations present since *La luz de esta memoria*. "Fieles" includes works from the previously cited books as well as *Parvo reino* (1984; Small Kingdom) and the poetry/prose anthology *Procura de lo imposible* (1998; Striving for the Impossible). *Serie del sinsonte* (1992; Series of the Mockingbird) is incorporated into the fourth section, "Breve mesta" (Brief Mix). Other collections include *Paso a paso* (1963; Step by Step), *Elegías en otoño* (1982; Elegies in Autumn), *Entresaca* (1984; Select), *Jardines imaginarios* (1996; Imaginary Gardens) and *Trema* (2005; Trema). Among the anthologies in which her work appears is the 2005 textbook *Nos tomamos la palabra: Antología crítica de textos de escritoras latinoamericanas contemporáneas* (... Critical Anthology of Texts by Contemporary Latin American (Women] Writers).

Critics of Vitale's poetry have noted the clear, precise and refined quality of her writing, the attention to the details of daily life, the simplicity and essentiality of her expression, her affinity for humor and plays on words, and her frequent use of such devices as alliteration, oxymoron and antithesis. Among her avowed influences are the Spanish poets of the Generation of 1927; the Argentine Oliverio Girondo; and fellow Uruguayans such as María Eugenia Vaz Ferreira. She has affirmed her adherence to Juan Ramón Jiménez's method of self-correction, setting aside her work until she is able to view it objectively. Formally, her works vary from the handful of sonnets found in *Reducción* to free verse, with most pieces incorporating at least some rhyme, nearly always assonant, and many showing some regularity in verse length. The use of blank spaces to shape thoughts, emphasize ideas and heighten emotional impact is particularly effective. Her typically objective tone, heightened by the frequent use of infinitives, is interrupted at times by the appearance of the first person singular or plural, and more frequently by the presence of a poetic object marked as familiar by the use of "tu". True to her professed belief that poetry should not degenerate into propaganda, she has preferred to avoid the obvious as she does the openly autobiographical, creating ambiguous, mysterious and sometimes darkly hermetic meditations on love, life, poetry and the world around her. Inspiration is drawn from a broad spectrum of sources, as evidenced by the myriad allusions and epigraphs from figures such as Hopkins, Eliot, Keats, Mallarmé, Jiménez, Leopardi and Bergamín.

Key themes include death and destruction, language and its limits, the natural world, changing seasons and the passing of time, memory, and disillusionment with the loss of magic in modern life. Among the most frequent recurring images are colors, given a rich symbolism in her poetry and prose; animals and plants, treated with a remarkable specificity and sensitivity; seeds, representing origins; fire and the sun; cold and snow; pits (and related images of climbing and/or falling); blank pages and similar surfaces such as blackboards, empty beaches, and fields; and religious figures, particularly angels. Her explorations of the daily reality of dying combine a tone of resignation with a cautious optimism toward the possibility of rebirth. Words are seen as both filled with possibility and promise and fraught with the danger of disappointment. Their powerful potential is evident in repeated appearance of beckoning blank surfaces, and of the acts of writing and singing. Her treatment of nature is characterized by a careful attention to often overlooked beings; scientific terminology is employed alongside creative and imaginative treatments of animal psychology. The passage of time is torturous as humanity is persecuted (and subsequently comforted) by the elements of the hot and cold seasons in equal measure. The relentless, solitary striving that she sees as the lot of all persons is depicted as the laborious climb from the bottom of a black pit. Freudian imagery is present in poems in which the poetic subject is haunted by vague memories of childhood and adolescence, a period in which the poet believes a person's most important experiences take place.

Prose Works

Her wide-ranging critical activity includes the prologues to the Cuban poet Eliseo Diego's *Divertimentos y Versiones* (1967, Distractions and Versions) and to the letters of Marina Alcoforado (*Cartas de amor de la religiosa portuguesa* (1968, Love Letters of the Portuguese Nun); essays on writers ranging from Cervantes to Antonio Machado; profiles of Bergamín and Clarice Lispector and a defense of Emilio Salgari's novels of adventure, among many other pieces, in *Letras libres;* and an article on symbolism in Juan Carlos Onetti in *Texto crítico*. Outside of her criticism and journalistic work, four genre-defying works comprise Vitale's prose production. *Léxico de afinidades* (1994, Lexicon of Affinities) is an alphabetically ordered collection of musings on disparate topics, in prose and in verse, varying in length from a single line to several pages. Among the terms that, as the author explains in her introduction, "sing" to her are the names of plants and animals, poets and artists, and familiar themes such as death, time and memory. A series of short stories, many structured as fables or parables, make up *Donde vuela el camaleón* (2000, Where the Chameleon Flies). Vitale's interest in reinterpreting mythology (as seen in repeated references to Ariadne, Daedalus and others in her poetry) is evident in her histories of minotaurs and Danae, while other pieces are set in an ancient or contemporary world marked by tension and conflict. Many familiar poetic recourses, such as alliteration and the use of colors as names for characters, are in evidence in this collection. Other prose publications include 2003's *De plantas y animales* (On Plants and Animals), a scholarly work containing tributes to a wide range of living creatures, and *El ABC de Byobu* (2004; The ABC of Byobu), another fragmented series of poetic prose pieces revolving around the central character of Byobu. Vitale's emphasis on freedom of expression, unlimited by form or genre, reflects her reading in a wide range of areas and is one of the distinguishing characteristics of her prolific and highly respected body of work.

STACY HOULT

Selected Works

Sueños de la constancia. México: Fondo de Cultura Económica, 1988.
Léxico de afinidades. México: Editorial Vuelta, 1994.
Donde vuela el camaleón. México: Ediciones Sin Nombre: Casa Juan Pablos (Universidad Nacional Autónoma de México), 2000.
Reducción del infinito. Barcelona: Tusquets Editores, 2002.

References and Further Reading

Fressia, Alfredo. "Los colores del aire". *Banda hispánica: Jornal de poesía*. http://www.revista.agulha.nom.br/bh2vitale.htm (accessed 10 July 2006).
——. "Nueva poesía de Ida Vitale: la ética de un canto". *Banda hispânica: Jornal de poesía*. http://www.revista.agulha.nom.br/bh13vitale.htm (accesed 10 July 2006).
García Pinto, Magdalena. "Ida Vitale". In Trudy Balch and Magdalena García Pinto (eds), *Women Writers of Latin America: Intimate Histories*. Austin, TX: University of Texas Press, 1991.
González Duenas, Daniel, and Toledo, Alejandro. "Ida Vitale y Enrique Fierro: Léxico de afinidades mexicanas". In Jose Angel Leyva (ed.), *Versoconverso: Poetas entrevistan poetas*. México: Alforja, Arte y Literatura, A.C., 2000.
Mascaro, Roberto. "La poesía es irremplazable". *El País Cultural* 209 (1993) http://letras-uruguay.espaciolatino.com/vitale/irremplazable.htm (accessed 27 July 2006).
Ramond, Michèle. "La noche alquímica de Ida Vitale". *Nuevo texto crítico* 3(5) (1990): 143–52.
Roque Difilippo, Aldo. "Ida Vitale: la llamada de la poesía". *Letralia: Tierra de Letras* 134 (2005) http://www.letralia.com/134/entrevistas01.htm (accessed 10 July 2006).

WALSH, MARÍA ELENA

María Elena Walsh, one of Argentina's greatest contemporary writers, was born on February 1, 1930, in Ramos Mejía, a suburb of Buenos Aires, Argentina. Her father came from an Irish and English family, while her mother's family was from Spain. In an interview by the Argentine critic and writer Mempo Giardinelli, Walsh has explained that her literary vocation began in childhood, first, when listening to narrative poetry and nursery rhymes, and afterwards while reading novels and stories like those by Dickens, Verne, Cervantes, Lewis Carroll, Andersen, Saki, or Jonathan Swift. She has also mentioned an early influence of popular forms, such as some tango lyrics with a melodramatic plot, as well as some local and universal folk tales, like those from *The Arabian Nights*, or those retold by Perrault or collected by the Brothers Grimm.

María Elena Walsh studied art at the Escuela Nacional de Bellas Artes. In 1947, when she was 17 years old, she published her first book, *Otoño imperdonable*, a collection of poems that expressed her adolescent feelings with a surprisingly mature technique. When in 1948 Juan Ramón Jiménez, the Spanish poet and future Nobel Prize winner, travelled to Buenos Aires, he was very impressed by Walsh's poetry. Jiménez and his wife Zenobia Camprubí, who had been exiled from Spain in 1936, had been living in the United States since 1939. In 1948, they were both teaching at the University of Maryland. At Buenos Aires, they invited Walsh and two other young poets to stay for some time at their Maryland home, but Walsh was the only one to accept their offer. Evidently, Jiménez's intention was to become a literary mentor for this promising poet, and, thanks to him, Walsh was able to attend classes at the University of Maryland and to meet writers and artists like Ezra Pound, Pedro Salinas or Salvador Dalí. But Walsh's learning experience was not an easy one, and in some of her articles she has written about Jiménez's harsh criticism and about a personal sense of inadequacy. Today, it is inevitable to attribute some of Walsh's uncomfortable feelings to an asymmetry that was well beyond both writers' individual personalities, considering the inevitable power clash between Jiménez, a strong-willed, older, famous, male mentor and poet, born in Spain, a colonizing country; and Walsh, a young, aspiring female disciple, born in Argentina, one of Spain's old colonies.

In 1952, Walsh went to Paris, where she lived for four years. There, she formed the musical duo "Leda y María", with another Argentine poet and composer, Leda Valladares, performing Argentine and Spanish folklore. Still in Paris, Walsh began to create music and literature for children.

Since her return to Argentina in 1956, she has published a large number of books. Her work includes short stories for children; a comic novel for children, *Dailan Kifki* (1966), and an autobiographic novel for adults, *Novios de antaño* (1990). She has written poems for children and for adults, and has published numerous essays collections in her books *Desventuras en el País-Jardín-de-Infantes* (1993) and *Diario Brujo* (1999). She has also recorded songs for children and adults and participated as a writer and performer in several theatre and television productions and programmes. During the tragic Argentine military dictatorship (1976–83), her works were banned from school reading lists and libraries and from radio and television programmes. She counterattacked with a magnificent anticensorship piece, "Desventuras en el País-Jardín-de-Infantes", published by the newspaper *El Clarín* (August 16, 1979), that now lends its title to her first collection of essays.

María Elena Walsh's stories for children are characterized by humour and laughter, by a sense of the absurd, and by an intense social awareness, which revalues marginal beings, particularly women, the eccentric and the physically or mentally deviant. Her works are subversive in confronting power, but they are not simple denouncing stories, since Walsh is able to express her personal sense of the precariousness of history and human existence. Only happiness, laughter and art might be able to save her unforgettable and vulnerable characters. In "El país de la geometría", for example, the protagonist, King Compass, is in search of a utopian entity, the mysterious "Round Flower". For a long time he searches in vain. When he finally stops worrying, he begins to enjoy life. In that moment, his dancing turns draw a series of beautiful round flowers on the floor (Domínguez Colavita, *Teoría del cuento infantil*). In another story, "La sirena y el capitán", Alahí is a beautiful pre-Columbian mermaid who lives happily near the

Paraná River until her perfect existence is shattered by the arrival of the Spanish "conquistadores". In this text, several oppositions emerge: nature versus civilization; woman versus man; art/beauty/happiness versus violence/power/money; Latin America versus Spain; and especially words and music versus silence or "noise". Because it is a story for children, the ending is a happy one: birds, butterflies and other animals finally save the mermaid, allowing her to survive and to continue singing for "whoever is capable of listening to her" (Domínguez Colavita, *Teoría del cuento infantil*).

María Elena Walsh's novel for children, *Dailan Kifki*, is a story about an elephant, full of humour and surprises. Her novel for adults, *Novios de antaño*, instead, combines nostalgia with social and gender awareness. Maybe the most interesting thing about this text is its ambiguity. Gender opposition is not homogenous or linear, since not all her male characters share a masculine point of view, and not all her women characters share a feminine point of view. Walsh considers her book a "crónica sumamente adulterada de mi primera época de vida" (p. 282). It is in fact, a hybrid novel that transcends several frontiers: fiction mixes with autobiography; childhood personal memories with social history; and fictional discourse with epistolary documents, specifically a series of letters written decades ago by María Elena Walsh's grandmother.

Analysis of Walsh's poetry shows deep thematic and structural relationships between her poems for adults and her poems for children. Her main poetry books for adults are: *Otoño imperdonable*, *Juguemos en el mundo* (1969), and *Cancionero contra el mal de ojo* (1976). Her most famous poetry books for children are: *Tutú Marambá* (1960), *El reino del revés* (1965), and *Zoo loco* (1965). From a referential point of view, both sets of texts present similar themes: the excluded, women, friendship, the sorrows of distance and exile, and the negative consequences of authoritarianism and repression. Also, both sets of poems show a tendency towards a strong narrative content. From an emotional point of view, Walsh knows how to combine anger and nostalgia. From a cognitive point of view, many of her poems sarcastically address the reader or a fictional character in an effort to demolish discrimination and pompous solemnity with the arms of irony and laughter. From a meta-literary point of view, several of her poems are a sort of poetics, being literary texts that speak about literature and literary creation (see "Arte caótica" and "Cantar canciones", *Cancionero contra el mal de ojo*, 9–14; 28). The common element between Walsh's poetry for children and her poetry for adults is the relevance she assigns to poetic form, specifically to several types of parallelisms, or repetitions of certain structures: semantic parallelisms, like her series of atmospheric elements (rocío, cielo, viento, nieve, nube, escarcha) in "¿Quién?" (*Tutú Marambá*); morphosyntactic parallelisms, like her series of gerunds (resuscitando, cantando, llorando, cantando, desesperando, cantando) in "Como la cigarra" (*Cancionero contra el mal de ojo*, 31); and phonological parallelisms, such as rhymes, metrical patterns, or alliterations. But her poetic constructions are never schematic, since even inside tightly organized structures, there are usually elements that break the proposed pattern (Domínguez Colavita–Suardiaz, "El paralelismo en la poesía de María Elena Walsh. La paradoja poética: regla y ruptura").

Most of María Elena Walsh's essays should be read with a bitter smile, because of their humorous mixture of hopeful idealism and disenchanted realism. Her book *Desventuras en el País-Jardín-de-Infantes* is divided into four sections. The first, "Los años de plomo", includes several of her most interesting articles, like her piece against censorship and others that also speak about culture, literature, political oppression, dictatorship and freedom of thought ("Desventuras en el País-Jardín-de-Infantes", "La Feria del Libro o *La Casada Infiel*" and "El año próximo seremos breves"). There is an article about the bibliophobia that Walsh views as characteristic of Argentine culture ("Infancia y bibliofobia"). This section is also important for understanding Walsh's feminist ideals and the style of her attacks on patriarchal society and patriarchal discourse, since her feminism is never limited to the injustice of the conception of the male as norm, but inserted in a wider perspective that describes, contextualizes and demolishes different forms of authoritarianism, violence, prejudice, discrimination and ignorance ("Feminismo y no violencia", "¿Corrupción de menores?", "Sepa por qué usted es machista", "Respuesta a la amada inmóvil"). The other three sections of her first book of essays are: "Apuntes juveniles", with articles about her youthful experience in the United States; "Según pasan las décadas", mainly articles about literature and music; and "Puntadas y nudos en democracia", a series of articles with a strong political orientation ("Tu ausencia, tu presencia, de Marta Oyhanarte de Sivak", "Lo mejor que nos está pasando", "La Pena de Muerte"). Her second book of essays, *Diario Brujo*, is a sarcastic but also a very comic and fresh analysis of her basic themes. Here, she chooses to criticize masculine gangs, several kinds of media abuse, and different discriminatory ways of treating the handicapped, the poor and the ill; she offers personal insights on Jorge Luis Borges, Eva Perón and Juan Ramón Jiménez; and she tells us once again that art, books and literature are essential to life. As a curiosity and an example of Walsh's perpetual crossing of literary frontiers, it is interesting to point out that one of these "essays" is a poem in memory of José Luis Cabezas, an Argentinean news photographer who was kidnapped, tortured and murdered in 1997 while investigating a case of personal and institutional corruption.

Like other authors who have written for children, María Elena Walsh has been excluded or marginalized from some canonical Argentine literary histories. In her 1993 interview with Mempo Giardinelli, she specified that children's literature "no entra en el Parnaso", in the sense that it is not a consecrated academic category, like poetry or the novel. Aside from this, in Argentina María Elena Walsh is so famous as a "children's author" that critics and the public sometimes forget that she has also produced extraordinary poems and essays and one novel for adults. Fortunately, new critical approaches to her literature are beginning to study María Elena Walsh simply as a great and original contemporary Latin American author. In this sense, it is possible to insert her texts in at least two strong Latin American literary traditions. The first is a tradition that started with the "cronistas", characterized by certain themes like the encounter with the "other", a sense of perpetual wonder, and a vision of Latin America as a paradise. Walsh's story "La sirena y el capitán" belongs to this particular tradition. The second is an irreverent tradition characterized by satire, humour and denunciation that goes back to Fernández de Lizardi and reappears—with a sort of utopian twist—in most of Walsh's narrative, poetic, and dramatic texts. Maybe this unique combination of two literary traditions that rarely mix can explain some of the fascination and the very personal flavour of María Elena Walsh's works.

FEDERICA DOMÍNGUEZ COLAVITA

Selected Works

Poems and Novels for Adults

Otoño imperdonable [poems]. Buenos Aires: Author Edition, 1947.
Apenas viaje [poems]. Buenos Aires: El Balcón de Madera, 1948.
Baladas con ángel [poems]. Buenos Aires: Losada, 1951.
Casi milagro [poems, plaquette]. Montevideo: Cuadernos Julio Herrera y Reissig, 1956.
Hecho a mano [poems]. Buenos Aires: Fariña Editores, 1965.
Juguemos en el mundo [poems]. Buenos Aires: Sudamericana, 1969.
Cancionero contra el mal de ojo [poems]. Buenos Aires: Sudamericana, 1976.
A la madre: poemas elegidos por María Elena Walsh [poems from other authors selected by María Elena Walsh]. Buenos Aires: Sudamericana, 1981.
Los poemas [poems]. Buenos Aires: Sudamericana, 1984.
Novios de antaño: 1930–1940 [novel]. Buenos Aires: Sudamericana, 1990.

Essays

Desventuras en el País-Jardín-de-Infantes [an anthology of her essays]. Buenos Aires: Sudamericana, 1993.
Diario brujo (1995–1999). Buenos Aires: Espasa-Calpe, 1999.

Poems, Short Stories and Novels for Children

La Familia Polillal. Buenos Aires: Editorial Abril, 1960.
La Mona Jacinta. Buenos Aires: Editorial Abril, 1960.
Tutú Marambá [poems for children]. Buenos Aires: Author's edition, 1960; Fariña Editores, 1964; Sudamericana, 1969 and 1980; and Espasa-Calpe, 1994.
Circo de Bichos. Buenos Aires: Editorial Abril, 1961.
Tres morrongos. Buenos Aires: Editorial Abril, 1961.
El reino del revés [poems for children]. Buenos Aires: Fariña Editores, 1965.
Zoo loco [poems for children]. Buenos Aires: Fariña Editores, 1965; and Sudamericana 1970.
Cuentopos de Gulubú [short stories for children]. Buenos Aires: Fariña Editores, 1966; and Sudamericana 1974.
Dailan Kifki [a short novel for children]. Buenos Aires: Fariña Editores, 1966 (translated into French, Italian and Swedish).
Versos para cebollitas [poems for children]. Buenos Aires: Fariña Editores, 1966.
Aire libre [reading book for elementary school, 2nd grade] Buenos Aires: Editorial Estrada, 1967.
Versos folklóricos para cebollitas [selection of folk poems]. Buenos Aires: Fariña Editores, 1967.
Versos tradicionales para cebollitas [selection of folk poems]. Buenos Aires: Sudamericana, 1967.
El diablo inglés [a short story for children]. Buenos Aires: Editorial Estrada, 1970; Hyspamerica, 1985; Sudamericana, 1992.
Angelito [a short story for children]. Buenos Aires: Editorial Estrada, 1974; Hyspamerica, 1985; Sudamericana, 1992.
El país de la geometría [a short story for children]. Buenos Aires: Editorial Estrada, 1974; Hyspamerica, 1985; Sudamericana, 1992.
La sirena y el capitán [a short story for children]. Buenos Aires: Editorial Estrada, 1974; Hyspamerica, 1985; Sudamericana, 1992.
Chaucha y palito [short stories for children]. Buenos Aires: Sudamericana, 1977.
Bisa vuela. Buenos Aires: Hyspamérica, 1985.
La nube traicionera [free version of Georges Sand's "Le nuage rose"]. Buenos Aires: Sudamericana, 1989.
Pocopán. Buenos Aires: Espasa-Calpe, 1996.
Manuelita ¿Dónde vas? Buenos Aires: Espasa-Calpe, 1997.
Don Fresquete. Buenos Aires: Espasa-Calpe, 1996.
El enanito y las siete Blancanieves. Buenos Aires: Espasa-Calpe, 1996.
La foca loca. Buenos Aires: Espasa-Calpe, 1996.
El gatopato y la princesa Monilda. Buenos Aires: Espasa-Calpe, 1996.
Historia de una princesa, su papá y ... Buenos Aires: Espasa-Calpe, 1996.
Martín Pescador y el delfín domador. Buenos Aires: Espasa-Calpe, 1996.
El paquete de Osofete. Buenos Aires: Espasa-Calpe, 1996.
La plaplá. Buenos Aires: Espasa-Calpe, 1996.
Un gato de la luna. Buenos Aires: Espasa-Calpe, 1996.
Una jirafa filarmónica. Buenos Aires: Espasa-Calpe, 1996.
El brujito de Gulubú. Buenos Aires: Espasa-Calpe, 1998.
Manuelita la tortuga. Buenos Aires: Espasa-Calpe, 1998.
El Mono Liso. Buenos Aires: Espasa-Calpe, 1998.
Osías el osito. Buenos Aires: Espasa-Calpe, 1998.
Colección AlfaWalsh, [a collection of 12 titles that include María Elena Walsh's works for children]. Buenos Aires: Alfaguara, 2000.

References and Further Reading

Bach, Caleb. "A Child's Wisdom in a Poet's Heart". *Américas* 47.3 (1995): 12–17.
Domínguez Colavita, Federica and Suardiaz, Delia E. "El paralelismo en la poesía de María Elena Walsh. La paradoja poética: regla y ruptura." *Revista/Review Interamericana* 19(3)–4 (1989): 41–9.
——. *Teoría del cuento infantil*. Buenos Aires: Plus Ultra, 1990.
Dujovne Ortiz, Alicia. *María Elena Walsh*. Madrid: Ediciones Júcar, 1982.
Facio, Sara. *María Elena Walsh. Retrato(s) de una artista libre*. Buenos Aires: La Azotea, 1999.
Foster, David William. "María Elena Walsh: Children's Literature and the Feminist Voice". *Cultural Diversity in Latin American Literature*. Albuquerque, NM: University of New Mexico Press, 1994.
Giardinelli, Mempo. "María Elena Walsh. El cuento infantil no entra en el Parnaso". *Así se escribe un cuento*. Buenos Aires: BEAS, 1993, 163–71.
Luraschi, Ilse Adriana and Sibbald, Kay. *María Elena Walsh, o El desafío de la limitación*. Buenos Aires: Sudamericana, 1993.
Origgi, Alicia. "El placer de crear, con integridad". *Imaginaria*, 9, Buenos Aires, February 23, 2000 (http://www.imaginaria.com.ar/01/9/walsh1.htm).
Pujol, Sergio Alejandro. *Como la cigarra: biografía de María Elena Walsh*. Buenos Aires: Beas Ediciones, 1993
Sotelo, Roberto. "La obra de M. E. Walsh: Bibliografía, discografía, premios, etc". *Imaginaria*, 19, Buenos Aires, February 23, 2000 (http://www.imaginaria.com.ar /01/9/walsh1.htm).

WIESSE ROMERO, MARÍA JESÚS

María Jesús Wiesse Romero (1894–1964), considered one of the most important Peruvian women writers of the twentieth century, was born in Lima, Peru, on November 19, 1894. She was the daughter of Teresa Romero and Carlos Wiesse (1859–1945). From an early age she had the opportunity to travel abroad due to her father's academic and diplomatic responsibilities. Consequently, she was exposed to foreign languages, and the writings of influential authors. María Wiesse's father was a renowned historian who taught courses in Peruvian history, aesthetics, contemporary philosophy, and sociology, at the main university in Lima, Peru, the Universidad Mayor de San Marcos. In 1896, when María Wiesse was two years old, her family moved to Switzerland where she started her elementary education in a private Catholic institution in the city of Herne (García y García 1925: 124). There is a confusion as to where she completed her secondary studies. Some sources say that she completed her studies in Lima; other sources claim that she completed them in London. During her formative years, Wiesse received education in music, and displayed an intrinsic appreciation for art, classical music and literature. While she lived in Europe, she was recognized by her teachers and peers as a promising young writer and critic.

From Journalism to Activism

Due to her exposure to other languages and cultures, Wiesse was fluent in English, French, and Spanish. She returned to Peru in 1914, at the age of 20. In 1916, she worked as a journalist for the local newspaper *La Crónica*. The following years, she decided to work for other national newspapers such as *El Perú,* and *El Día*. She was also a regular contributor to several national and international literary journals, cultural magazines, and other newspapers including *Actualidades, Amauta, La Familia, Variedades, El Mercurio Peruano, Mundial,* and *Antara*. Wiesse was the founder and the director of the literary journal *La Familia,* which was recognized as an intellectual space for writers and artists alike. In some of her writings, she used the pseudonym of "Myriam". Wiesse was often a guest speaker at several universities and in renowned literary circles. For example, she gave lectures on diverse topics such as women in society and the history of music. Her writings reflected a vast understanding of and a critical eye for social issues, cultural aesthetics, philosophy, Peruvian civilization, and teaching methodologies. During the years after 1916, her solidarity with the workers' struggle to obtain better working conditions and less working hours became a central topic in her writings. In 1919, she witnessed the legalization of the eight-hour shift. Wiesse became an active participant of the *indigenista* movement, advocating justice and recognition for the indigenous peoples of Latin America.

At the age of 28, she married the painter José Sabogal (1888–1956) with whom she shared a passion for Peruvian and indigenous artistic expressions. She often included photoreproductions of Sabogal's paintings and wood carved frame-representations called *maderas* in her publications. They were very active contributors in José Carlos Mariátegui's *vanguardista* journal *Amauta*. Wiesse published critical essays, short stories, and book reviews in almost every issue of *Amauta*, where her own books were also reviewed by her colleagues. These facts show the commitment and the participation of both Wiesse and Sabogal in the production and shaping of this very important and world-renowned journal of contemporary literature, art, criticism, and ideology. Other women who participated in the *Amauta* group were Magda Portal (writer, poet and activist), Angela Ramos (journalist), Alicia del Prado (political leader and activist), Blanca del Prado (political leader and activist), Carmen Saco (sculptor), and Julia Codesido (painter).

In 1923, Wiesse and Sabogal traveled to Cuba and Mexico, a trip that inspired her book *Croquis de viaje* (1923, Travel Sketches). Wiesse, like many other writers who were part of the *Amauta* group, supported socialist ideals, and helped develop, along with José Carlos Mariátegui, the founding of the Socialist Party in 1928. In this process, Wiesse along with other *Amauta* members such as Magda Portal (1900–89), were singled out and accused by the government of Augusto B. Leguía, of planning a communist conspiracy against him. Many of these *Amauta* contributors were forced to leave Peru or face imprisonment. In spite of her political persecution, Wiesse continued writing against all social injustices.

A Fictional Writer

María Wiesse's literary production shows a diverse array of literary genres: narrative, poetry, drama, and critical essays. Within the narrative genre, she is the author of several novels, legends, biographies, and short stories—for both children and adults. In 1946, she was the editor of the first anthology of love poetry from Peru. Furthermore, her interest as a pedagogue led her to write several pedagogic books on elementary education as well. In the realm of literary and cultural studies, she wrote critical essays on film, art, music, literature, as well as numerous book reviews. These texts are valuable in that they show Wiesse's thoughts and visionary insights on culture and modernity during the first half of the twentieth century.

Regarding her writing style, the beautifully woven description of her novels paints a narrative that the reader can easily relate to and learn from. With a direct, yet very descriptive narration, Wiesse uses recognizable urban settings of Lima, and middle class characters that represent the presence of Andean immigrants in the city, and also the interaction of other mixed races. According to Armando Bazán, Wiesse looks carefully at the weakest side of the lighter skinned Peruvians so as to fill it with irony (*De voces, sueños y osadías,* p. 134). This is the case of her novels *La huachafita* (1927, The Tacky Girl), *Diarios sin fecha* (1948, Undated Diaries), and *Tríptico* (1953, Triptych).

In her short stories, Wiesse incorporates characters of everyday life, creating a setting that plays with light, shadows, and darkness in order to dramatize the polarization of different points of view among its characters. For example, in her short story "Dos hombres" (1927, Two Men), a routine encounter between friends reveals the profound and contradictory differences between two men and their point of view on "art and knowledge" and "love and passion". Both these men, younger than 32 and close friends, share an evening of realization while walking home. One is Miguel Elguera, an artist sculptor who is represented as an intellectual leader, who is knowledgeable yet simple and direct when it comes to naming his artistic creations. The other, Carlos Oliver, a doctor of medicine who follows his heart when it comes to his practice and decides to serve the poor. A romantic encounter displayed by two lovers sitting by a fountain triggers an argument between these two friends—"is love that important as to give your life for the love of a woman?" The sculptor emphatically stated that never. The doctor, on the contrary, mumbled that he certainly would. This powerful statement that ends Wiesse's short story makes the reader reflect on common stereotypes regarding artists and scientists. For example, it is believed that artists are more inclined to show their feelings, and are more open to show them through their works. On the other hand, scientists are believed to be more pragmatic and commonly devoted to their studies. By reversing or altering these associations, Wiesse brings out the possibility of different preferences and personalities within the same gender. The detailed description of each character emphasizes the artist as being more assertive and less emotional, and the scientist as timid, naive, and more romantic. Therefore, Wiesse suggests in this short story that regardless of their gender, people can also have interests and characteristics that do not necessarily match the expectations of a traditional society that separates personal traits by gender, profession, or creed.

The Voice of a Critic

As a critic, María Wiesse is an independent thinker. Her critical essays comment on a variety of topics including, film, art, drama, music, and social issues among others. An avid supporter of cinematography, Wiesse valued film as an artistic expression and she is clearly opposed to its commercialization by the Hollywood industry. For example, in her essay "*Los problemas del cinema*" (1928, Problems in the Cinema), Wiesse anticipated very early in the twentieth century, the industrialization of cinema as the great danger of this modern artistic expression. In this respect, she affirms that film producers no longer worry about the artistic component, but rather concentrate in the marketing of the film as a commercial product (p. 24). Wiesse's critical evaluation of the cinema can be seen as a prophecy that has become a reality within the Hollywood "industry". In the same essay, Wiesse expresses her admiration for Charles Chaplin's films, and evaluates his innovative techniques as being part of the new spirit that has broken away from the old cinematographic formulas and procedures.

One recurrent topic in Wiesse's essays is the one related to modernization, and the ever-increasing participation of women in the public sphere. Such is the case of women in sports, journalism, law, and clerical office work among others. In "Señales de nuestro tiempo," for example, Wiesse justifies the changes in women's appearance and clothing as a good and much needed process in order to facilitate their active roles in a modern society. While others see the short skirt and the shorter hair as a sign of "frivolity," or vanity, Wiesse contends that in fact these changes reflect women's desire to free themselves from social patriarchal constraints, to acquire emancipation, and to obtain equal civil rights with men (p. 11). María Wiesse's active participation in cultural activities, and in academics, is an example of women increasing activism in social, and literary endeavors.

Final Considerations

In spite of María Wiesse's vast literary production, and the recognition she has gained in Peru as an accomplished writer and critic, there is still a need for more studies that will facilitate the analysis of Wiesse's texts as an example of Latin American women writers of the first half of the twentieth century. Several of Wiesse's articles have been published in journals and magazines of the period but are still untouched by literary critics, and other early evaluations of her texts have yet to be revised. Maria Wiesse died in Lima, on July 29, 1964; however, the life and the thoughts of this extraordinary woman transcended time and became true.

MYRIAM GONZALES-SMITH

Selected Works

Santa Rosa de Lima. Lima: Librería Francesa y Casa Editorial "E. Rosay," 1922.

Croquis de viaje. Lima: Librería Francesa y Casa Editorial "E. Rosay," 1923.

Nocturnos. Lima: Imprenta Lux, 1925.

Glosas franciscanas. Lima: Imprenta Lux, 1926.

"Señales de nuestro tiempo". *Amauta* 1 (Dec. 1926): 11–12.

La huachafita. Lima: Imprenta Lux, 1927.

"Dos hombres". *Amauta: Revista mensual de doctrina, literatura, arte y polémica* 2 (Dec. 1927): 35–36.

"El forastero". *Amauta* 2 (Apr. 1928): 17–21.

"Los problemas del cinema". *Amauta* 2 (Feb. 1928): 24–5.

Trébol de cuatro hojas. Lima: Co. de Impresiones y Publicidad, 1932.

Quipus: relatos peruanos para niños. Lima: Imprenta "La Voce d'Italia," 1936.

La romántica vida de Mariano Melgar. Lima: Taller Gráfico de "P. Barrientos C.," 1939

Aves nocturnas. Lima: Taller Gráfico de P. Barrientos C., 1941.

Antología de la poesía amorosa peruana. Lima: Ediciones Hora del Hombre, 1946.

José Carlos Mariátegui: Etapas de su vida. Lima: Ediciones "Hora del Hombre," 1946.

El mar y los piratas. Lima: Co. de Impresiones y Publicidad, 1947.

El pez de oro y otras historias absurdas. Lima: Imprenta Lux, 1958.

References and Further Reading

Bustamante, Cecilia. "Intelectuales peruanas de la generación de José Carlos Mariátegui". *Socialismo y Participación* 14 (1981): 115.

Gamiz Natalia. *Mujeres de América: Bosquejo antológico del paisaje espiritual femenino*. México: Editorial Continental, 1946.

García y García, Elvira. *La mujer peruana a través de los siglos: Serie historiada de estudios y observaciones*. Vol. 2. Lima: Americana, 1925.

Guardia, Sara Beatriz. *Mujeres peruanas: El otro lado de la historia*. 3rd edn. Lima: Editorial Minerva, 1995.

"María Wiesse Romero: La crítica certera". In *De voces, sueños y osadías: Mujeres ejemplares del Perú*. Lima: CPDR, Centro de Producción y Documentación Radiofónica "El día del pueblo," 1995, pp. 131–4.

Milla Batres, Carlos. *Diccionario histórico y biográfico del Perú*. Lima: Lima Batres, 1986.

Núñez, Estuardo. *La literatura peruana en el siglo XX: (1900–1965)*. México: Editorial Pormaca, 1965.

Rice Cortina, Lynn Ellen. *Spanish-American Women Writers: A Bibliographical Research Checklist*. New York: Garland Press, 1983.

Romero de Valle, Emilia. *Diccionario manual de literatura peruana y materias afines*. Lima: UNMS, 1966.

Smith, Myriam. "El entorno socio-político y artístico en el Perú (1920–30)". In Re-thinking the vanguardia: The Poetry and Politics of Magda Portal. Diss. University of California Santa Barbara, 2000, pp. 22–76.

Tamayo Vargas, Augusto. "Corrientes contemporáneas en la literatura del Perú". *Literatura peruana* 2 (1954): 332–57.

Villavicencio, Maritza. *Del silencio a la palabra: mujeres peruanas en los Siglos XIX–XX*. Lima: Ediciones Flora Tristán, 1992.

Y

YÁÑEZ, FLORA

The novelist and short-story writer María Flora Yáñez Bianchi de Echeverría (1898–1982) was born in Santiago, Chile, into an intellectual family that included her father Eliodoro Yáñez, founder of the newspaper *La nación*, and her brother, the writer Juan Emar. Yáñez, educated in Santiago and in the Sorbonne in Paris, wrote over a span of five decades, beginning with articles in *El Mercurio*, *El diario ilustrado* and *La atenea*. From 1933 to 1980, Yáñez wrote eight novels, two collections of short stories, and two autobiographical works. *La piedra* (1952, The Stone) won the Premio Municipal de Novela, and *Visiones de infancia* (1947, Visions of Childhood) won the Premio Atenea. Yáñez's literary fame opened the door to interaction with some of the most prominent writers of the time: María Luisa Bombal, Federico García Lorca, Juana de Ibarbourou, Pablo Neruda, Victoria Ocampo, and Alfonsina Storni.

Novels

Like other writers of her generation, Yáñez made her début in the spirit of the *criollista* genre, depicting the environment and events in her native Chile. Yáñez's first novel, *El abrazo de la tierra* (1933, The Earth's Embrace) and the two that followed, *Mundo en sombra* (1935, World in Shadow) and *Espejo sin imagen* (1936, Mirror without Image) fall within this category. Yáñez would later write in her memoirs that she wished she had begun her literary career in a different way. In Yáñez's prologue to the anthology *Cuento chileno moderno* (1956, Modern Chilean Short Story), she celebrates writers who left behind the *criollista* period in favor of more complicated characters and plots, and sees *criollismo* only as a necessary bridge to reach more universal themes and modernist techniques such as the stream of consciousness and the interior monologue. Although not favored by Yáñez, these early novels clearly show the beginnings of the psychological complexity that would characterize her later works. Written under the pseudonym of Mari Yan, the novels depict characters who struggle to come to terms with themselves and the environment in which they live, and the reader is introduced to themes that are present throughout Yáñez's works: a profound connection between protagonists and the natural world, the constant search for meaning in life and in relationships, and a tension between tradition and modernity.

Las cenizas (1942, Ashes) marks the first of Yáñez's novels to reflect the struggles of the modern condition, a topic that would permeate the works of the rest of her career. The themes touched upon in the three earlier novels are deepened here. Feelings of alienation are reflected in the protagonist, Marcela, who longs for a different life. She loses herself in daydreams, wanderings, and in intense appreciation and observation of nature, all of which serve as distractions while she waits for something to happen to make her feel alive. Yáñez gives her characters a sense of serenity and tranquility as they age – they grow to cope with and accept their isolation. Accompanying this serenity, however, is the realization that no one can ever come to truly know another.

A sense of longing and waiting (*espera*) will continue to be prominent themes throughout Yáñez's works as she creates in each novel a protagonist who seeks out someone who will wake them from their sonambulant state. In *El último faro* (1968, The Last Beacon), Miguel Arias searches for someone who will serve as a compass or a "beacon" to him, to guide him as he struggles to find a sense of purpose in his life, and to move him beyond the threshold (*umbral*) of his closed, interior world and into the divine experience that is the connection with another human being. In *El peldaño* (1974, The Stair), Nora talks of Julio introducing a little bit of light into her life, as if a door had begun to open inside of her. When such a relationship is established, it has a transformative effect, but like all of the relationships in Yáñez's novels, the transformation, as well as the bond, are fleeting. Indeed, despite the illumination, the path is never well defined. Nothing is certain, except for the impulse to move forward and to break free of the confines of one's circumstances.

The natural world, which bears witness to, reflects, and outlives the human drama unfolding around it, provides some solace in the face of the protagonists' struggles. In *Las cenizas*, Marcela exclaims that life is worth living even if it is for the springtime aroma of honey that awakens the spirit. Children especially appreciate nature's wonders (Gabriel in *Mundo en sombra*), and inherent to an adult protagonist's nostalgic journey back to childhood is the memory of a deep identification with nature, as Olivia experiences in *¿Dónde está el trigo y el vino?* (1962, Where Are the Wheat and the Wine?).

Short Stories

Yáñez's short story collections, *El estanque* (1945, The Pond) and *Juan Estrella* (1954, John Star), feature similar existential struggles. The three stories in *El estanque* include symbolic references to water and its representation of the soul and the mystery of life. At the end of "El estanque," the most allegorical of all of Yáñez's stories, Alina tries to reach Gerardo through a glassy pond, but she realizes that they will always be on opposite sides, and that she will have to stay on one side – alone. Although alluded to in many of her novels, the tension between tradition and modernity is front and center in the short story "Mil novecientos cincuenta y tres" (Nineteen Fifty-Three). Isabel feels lost in the aggressive and tyrannical throngs of people in the city, and observes that those, including herself, who have maintained a sense of decency feel lost at sea (*náufragos*), a metaphor that Yáñez uses in her novels as well to refer to a character's anxiety and isolation.

The idea of childhood as a time of immature actions that one comes to regret later as an adult is present in the title story of *Juan Estrella*. The protagonist, Carmen, recalls a transitional moment between childhood and the adult world when her friend Juan Estrella saved a drowning girl, fell in love with her, and then abandoned her. Carmen, who witnessed these events as a child, saw that Juan violated a sacred bond in this abandonment, and years later when she comes across him in the street – a physically and emotionally broken man – his appearance and demeanor seem to speak to this violation, as if he were paying for his sins of years ago.

Visiones de Infancia

Towards the end of her life, Yáñez expressed a desire to have elaborated more upon the snapshots of her childhood that are the short autobiographical pieces found in *Visiones de infancia*, but she says that they capture the spontaneity of her writing at the time. Among these stories, one reads about Yáñez's first fear (an earthquake), the death of her sister Inés, and her family's trips. In these pieces, Yáñez depicts childhood as a magical place populated by enigmatic, brilliant adults who exert a strong influence on the young people around them. Childhood is a time to create fictitious worlds and to hear about them through stories. It's a dangerous time too – when illness takes away young cousins and friends, and a time when one tries to decipher the rules of behavior. Above all, it's a time for enchantment, invention, and hope in the face of an uncertain future.

LISA MERSCHEL

Selected Works

El abrazo de la tierra. Santiago de Chile: Universitaria, 1933.
Mundo en sombra. Santiago de Chile: Universo, 1935.
Espejo sin imagen. Santiago de Chile: Nascimiento, 1936.
Las cenizas. Santiago de Chile: Casa Nacional del Niño, 1942.
El estanque. Santiago de Chile: La Semana Literaria, 1945.
Visiones de infancia. Santiago de Chile: Zig-Zag, 1947.
La piedra. Santiago de Chile: Zig-Zag, 1952.
Juan Estrella. Madrid: Samarán, 1954.
Antología del cuento chileno. Santiago de Chile: Del Pacífico, 1958.
¿Dónde está el trigo y el vino? Santiago de Chile: Zig-Zag, 1962.
El último faro. Santiago de Chile: Del Pacífico, 1968.
El peldaño. Santiago de Chile: Gabriela Mistral, 1974.
Historia de mi vida: fragmentos. Santiago de Chile: Nascimiento, 1980.

References and Further Reading

Orozco Vera, María Jesús. *La narrativa femenina chilena (1923–1980): escritura y enajenación*. Zaragoza, Spain: Anubar, 1995.

YÁNEZ COSSÍO, ALICIA

Born in Quito in 1928, Alicia Yánez Cossío is widely acknowledged as one of Ecuador's foremost contemporary novelists. One of a family of ten siblings, she was educated at Catholic schools in Quito. With the support of a grant from the Instituto de Cultura Hispánica, she studied journalism in Spain from 1952–53. She lived in Cuba from 1956–61. Her first novel, *Bruna, soroche y los tíos*, was published in 1972. She has published ten novels, as well as two collections of short stories and several children's books. Early in her career, she published several collections of poetry, the first of these, *Luciolas*, in 1949. Two of her novels, *Bruna, soroche y los tíos* and *La cofradía del mullo del vestido de la Virgen Pipona* have been translated into English. Her short stories have been widely anthologized, and several of her stories have been published in English translation. She was for many years a teacher of language and literature and also directed creative writing workshops for children. In 1990, she was awarded a Medal of Cultural Achievement of the First Class by the Ecuadorian government. She is a member of the Ecuadorian Academy of the Spanish Language.

Yánez Cossío's novels employ diverse narrative strategies, among them exaggeration, multiple narrators, and a flexible sense of time. Her principal themes include the role of women, the power of the Church, the nature of representation, and the interpretation of the past. Her work addresses the racial, gender, class, and ethnic tensions that characterize Ecuadorian society. Yánez Cossío is critical both of blind adherence to tradition and of a full-scale surrender to modern consumerism. Yánez Cossío's narrative has also addressed the power of the religious icon in popular faith. Her short fiction has addressed many of the same themes as her novels. *El beso y otras fricciones*, from which most anthologized stories are drawn, represents Yánez Cossío's foray into science fiction. Her stories for children, often written initially for her own grandchildren, are playful and imaginative. *Retratos cubanos* is a series of linked short stories that draw on the years the author spent in Cuba, during and immediately following the Cuban Revolution.

Yánez Cossío's first novel, *Bruna, soroche y los tíos*, has been described as an early (and under-recognized) example of magical realism. The manuscript, which as Rojas-Trempe notes, was first entered in a contest sponsored by the Ecuadorian *Casa de la Cultura* in 1965, went on to win the national novel contest sponsored by *El Universo* in 1971. Since its publication in 1972, the novel has undergone many reprintings. The novel's protagonist, Bruna, lives in a sleepy, tradition-bound city, plagued by *soroche* – altitude sickness – and superstition. Bruna, a 20-year-old secretary, resists the overpowering inertia that entraps both her relatives and her classmates. *Bruna* is a family saga, tracing the Catovil family from its origins at the moment of conquest, when a native princess was abducted and transformed into an illustrious forebear; her surname, Illacatu, was distorted generation by generation, becoming first Villa-Cató and finally Catovil, just as her skin was bleached in the portrait commissioned by her husband. Unable to accommodate herself to her new circumstances, she finally stabbed her husband with a pair of scissors and strangled herself with her own hair.

Bruna is a multi-vocal novel, as the narrative is punctuated with commentary by unnamed speakers who gossip about, question, or critique the actions of others. The violence, even melodrama, of parts of the novel is counterbalanced with accounts of magical or fantastic events – sinners turned to fish for bathing on Good Friday; a treasure chest that runs off under its own power; the uncle who continues to collect matchboxes after he dies, his flesh becoming transparent but his presence remaining as much with his family as ever. Only by leaving the city is Bruna able to achieve a degree of freedom, and as she leaves, the city itself seems to disappear. A scrap of paper blows to her feet, a leaf torn at random from the Bible, bearing a verse related to the destruction of Sodom and Gomorrah. (The motif of the wind-blown document will be taken up again in later novels.) The half-remembered verse echoes Bruna's aunt's obsessive, fanatical religion and the rigid atmosphere of stasis and retribution that define the sleeping city. Yet it would be wrong to characterize the novel as wholly dark. One of the striking aspects of Yánez Cossío's work is the balance of unsparing social critique, linguistic and conceptual playfulness, and joy.

Yánez Cossío's second novel, *Yo vendo unos ojos negros* (1979), again addresses the constraints of women's social and economic roles, as well as the lack of suitable, stable employment, but without the fantastic element that is so evident in *Bruna*. The title is drawn from a popular song. The narrative style is more directly realistic, and less experimental, than that of many of Yánez Cossío's texts. *Yo vendo unos ojos negros* presents a critique of commercialism in which the protagonist María, her marriage no longer viable, attempts to become a door-to-door cosmetics saleswoman. In its insistence on María's need for economic and personal independence, the novel carries a clear feminist tone. María's struggle centers on the "organic" need for survival; she longs, ultimately, for a greater wholeness, one that might bridge the gap between male and female.

By contrast, *Más allá de las islas* (1980) employs a mythical, almost other-worldly tone in the representation of its characters' lives and, more particularly, their deaths. The islands of the title are the Galapagos Islands, and the characters include scientists, pirates, tourists, and colonists. The novel takes place in an indeterminate present, yet the action is also situated historically according to specific references, such as those to Liberal leader, Eloy Alfaro. In one instance, as if to guard against any possibility that the reader might interpret the use of island wildlife for target practice by troops as strictly fictional, a footnote places the abuse during the military junta in power in 1979. The narrative is multi-layered, at once lyrical and pragmatic. Each chapter focuses on the ways in which individual characters meet death and are transformed, yet the reality of daily life (rattletrap buses, scarce food, infidelities) continues. Although individual characters reappear from chapter to chapter, the novel is essentially a series of eight linked stories, each with its own protagonist, each tracing that protagonist's avoidance of and finally encounter with an ambiguously personified Death. This complex text has received less critical attention than Yánez Cossío's other novels, but merits more in-depth analysis.

La cofradía del mullo del vestido de la Virgen Pipona (1985) offers an uncommon view of gender construction combined with a consideration of collective memory and national history. The novel is set in a small town inhabited by rival clans: the wealthy Benavides and the disenfranchised Pandos. Doña Carmen Benavides is the head of the powerful sisterhood that controls the worship of the town's miraculous icon. The Pandos are exemplified by the four old men who occupy a park bench in the center of town, rolling cigarettes and recalling the town's past. The detailed recollections of the four old Pandos anchor the narrative, providing background information that situates the novel historically and geographically.

The sisterhood's dominance and subsequent loss of authority parallel the shifts in political power in the town, as revolutionary violence becomes more prevalent (much of it occasioned by the short-sighted manipulations of the sisterhood) and the Benavides men ultimately replace their wives in the exercise of power. The Virgin of the title literally holds the town's history in her belly, for her robes hide the documents that prove precisely how the Pandos were swindled out of their lands by an earlier generation of the Benavides family. The Virgin's belly, however, is more than a convenient hiding place. The Virgin becomes a pawn in national politics, and the documents are lost during a skirmish between the townspeople and the army. The Virgin's belly is later padded with a small pillow. The changing shape of the Virgin is part of a complex understanding of gender construction, as the physical presence of the wooden icon is both fixed (eternal, idealized) and malleable.

La casa del sano placer (1989) takes place in the same town as *La Virgen Pipona,* although few of the characters of the earlier novel reappear. It is the story of Doña Rita Benavides, sister of Doña Carmen, and the brothel she establishes in her home, next door to her pious and imperious sister. Doña Rita sets out to develop a new sort of brothel, one in which the prostitutes are held to the highest standards of hygiene, training, and decency in the impersonal exercise of their profession. The novel shares the element of oral language evident in both *Bruna* and *La Virgen Pipona*. Large portions of the novel consist of unattributed dialogue in which each sentence begins—as if truncated by a bystander repeating it at second hand—with the word *que,* which might here be translated as "that" or "because". Much of the novel takes on the tone of a story overheard and then passed on, a novel in gossip and hearsay. Doña Rita, as powerful and strong-willed as her sister, is not as fully developed or compelling a character as Doña Carmen. Her hold on her tiny empire, however, unravels as quickly, after the outraged ladies of the town stage a cooking strike and the peace of the town is destroyed. The final impossibility of Doña Rita's strange, utopian project is underscored when she is trampled to death by the fleeing prostitutes, who follow a honey-voiced missionary charlatan who has saved them from the angry mob.

In *El Cristo feo* (1995) Yánez Cossío examines traditional assumptions about social class, aesthetics, religion, and gender. The gradual transformation of a wooden crucifix offers the protagonist, Ordalisa, the opportunity to transform herself into an artist at the same time that she begins to question her prior subordination. Ordalisa works as a maid for a well-off couple whose lives have sunk into boredom and routine. Her daily life is constrained by the living conditions of the domestic servant. At first, she occupies a single windowless room with a shared bathroom, making the daily baths her employer demands nearly impossible. When she moves to her employers' home, a move that both saves time and offers her much more comfortable surroundings, she is also more vulnerable to being interrupted during her time off. Disappointed by the ugliness of the Christ figure, one of the few objects inherited from her mother, Ordalisa begins to remake it, guided by a voice, associated with the icon, whose identity remains undefined. The novel invites a reconsideration of the artistic process and of the process of revision. The transformative process extends beyond the carved wooden figure, for Ordalisa is transformed as well: she gradually removes her own external layers of submission and humility at the same time that she comes to see the figure hidden behind the excess wood of the original statue.

Aprendiendo a morir (1997) is a historical novel of straightforward structure, narrated in the third person by a distanced, omniscient narrator who describes the life of Santa Mariana de Jesus in a largely compassionate tone. The novel is based on information contained in the archives of Mariana's beatification process, a process begun in 1771. While nearly all of the characters are drawn from the historical record, the novel holds two fictional characters: Xacinto de la Hoz, *converso* refugee from the Inquisition, and the sacristan Sandoval. Taking refuge in Quito, Xacinto de la Hoz becomes a neighbor of Mariana's and a skeptical witness to the privations and sufferings to which the future saint subjected herself even in childhood. The subtlety of Yánez Cossío's treatment of the Catholic Church and its role in Ecuadorian society is again in evidence. The limited spiritual options available to Mariana—viewed from birth as destined for sainthood—are portrayed critically, while Mariana herself is portrayed in an almost neutral, factual light. The tone of the novel conveys a portion of Mariana's innocence as well, approaching the girl's perspective in the representation of her attempts to find a suitable spiritual expression. Mariana further becomes a part of the historical record as well as of the popular memory of the city of Quito. Unlike the female icon of *La Virgen Pipona*, in which the female body represents, in part, the community's access to the past, in *Aprendiendo a morir*, a specific body is the focus of representation. As an intervention in the cultural discourse surrounding the saint, Yánez Cossío's novel also participates in the memorialization of Mariana.

Y amarle pude (2000), Yánez Cossío's second historical novel, retells the life of poet Dolores Veintimilla, precursor of Ecuadorian Romanticism who committed suicide in 1857. The title of the novel is drawn from the first line of Veitimilla's poem "Quejas," a plaintive lament that closes with the speaker's determination to forget the faithless lover. Abandoned by her husband, Veintimilla committed suicide after her defense of a man condemned to death brought on public vituperation. Yánez Cossío's spare novel incorporates the few extant poems written by Veintimilla, and offers another condemnation of religious fanaticism as well as a troubling portrait of an isolated woman today obscured behind the limited information available to common knowledge or lost in the gaps in the historical record.

Sé que vienen a matarme (2001) is a biography in novel form of conservative leader, Gabriel García Moreno (1821–75). Twice president of Ecuador (1861–65 and 1869–75), García Moreno was closely identified with highland and Catholic interests and remains a controversial figure. He was assassinated on the steps of the Presidential Palace in 1875. The novel is narrated in a distanced, impersonal style, taking Gabriel from his childhood in Guayaquil to the moment of his death. The protagonist is named only once in the novel, and then only by first name. His identity, however, is clear from the outset, as the title—"I know they are coming to kill me"—quotes García Moreno himself. The deceptively objective stance of the unidentified narrator produces a subtle but unmistakable critique of García Moreno and his admirers. The conclusion is pessimistic: the tyrant is dead, but the cycle of bloody revolutions, corruption, and individual revenge continues.

Concierto de sombras (2004) is both a novel and a memoir, a text narrated in the second person (and occasionally the first person plural) that treats childhood memories of convent schooling and family history, and the overlapping, interwoven character of recollections in the recreation of a personal past. Echoes of earlier texts, such as the "sleeping city" of *Bruna*, invite the reader to identify the novel's "you" with the author herself. Yet the second person also keeps the reader at arm's length. The distancing offered by the use of the second person, however, is effective in underscoring that this, too, is a narrative construct, not an uncomplicated retelling of an author's life. The slippage between first and second person is significant, subtly highlighting the instability of memory. The narrative oscillates between a seemingly interminable flight unexpectedly shared with a childhood friend and the memories that reencounter awakens. The origin of Yánez Cossío's own writing practice is portrayed as linked to the "tigress" that represents her loneliness, an image that returns throughout the narrative, index of both the necessity and the difficulty of writing. The text closes with a postscript that enumerates Yánez Cossío's books, describes their origins and reception, and lists various editions—sometimes noting errors in dedications, unhappy cover choices, or poor distribution. Even here, however, the intrinsic slipperiness of the memoir is in evidence; the poetic is not absent, and the tiger is again present at the end.

Concierto de sombras has in places an elegiac tone and reads almost as a farewell to the world of letters; Yánez Cossío initially conceived *Concierto* as her final book. It was not, however, to be her last novel. In 2006, Yánez Cossío published *Esclavos de Chatham*, her second novel to be set in the Galapagos Islands. The novel returns as well to the theme of tyranny, developed in *Sé que vienen a matarme*. *Esclavos de Chatham* relates the sufferings, rebellion, and trial of a group of presumed criminals who came ashore in Guayaquil in 1904 and were subsequently revealed to be refugees from an intolerable situation. Based on historical investigations by Octavio Latorre, the novel portrays the tyranny exercised by Manuel J. Cobos on Chatham Island (now known as San Cristóbal). *Esclavos de Chatham* alludes to the ecological richness and scientific importance of the archipelago, but the most striking features of the novel are the brutal punishments inflicted by Cobos on his workers—more properly prisoners or slaves—the cool, matter-of-fact tone of the narration, and the clarity of the language. The satire and humor of Yánez Cossío's earlier texts are absent, yet the individual characters, although often minimally delineated, become real through repetition. The novel presents, in episodic, somewhat fragmentary fashion, a series of testimonies, as Cobos' victims—also his assassins—one by one stand trial.

Yánez Cossío's varied body of work engages a wide range of social and political themes, always with a deep skepticism toward received dogmas of any ideological stripe. Impatient with hypocrisy, posturing, and inflexible ideologies, Yánez Cossío writes with a sharp satirical sensibility tempered by a compassionate awareness of human foibles. The necessity, if not always the difficulty, of writing are evident throughout Yánez Cossío's body of work, a group of texts remarkable both for its variety and for its overall coherence. While many of her themes have remained constant, her treatment of those themes has been complex and varied.

AMALIA GLADHART

Selected Works

De la sangre y el tiempo. Quito: Imprenta Fernández, 1964.

Bruna, soroche y los tío. Quito: Casa de la Cultura Ecuatoriana, 1972; reprinted, Bogotá: Ediciones Paulinas, 1974; reprinted, Quito: Colegio Técnico "Don Bosco," 1980; reprinted, Quito: Libresa, 1991; reprinted, Bogotá: Oveja Negra, 1997, 2000.

Poesía. Quito: Casa de la Cultura Ecuatoriana, 1974.

El beso y otras fricciones: cuentos. Bogotá: Ediciones Paulinas, 1975; reprinted, Bogotá: Oveja Negra, 1999.

Yo vendo unos ojos negros. Quito: Casa de la Cultura Ecuatoriana, 1979; 2nd edn. Quito: Colegio Técnico "Don Bosco," 1980.

Más allá de las islas. Quito: Colegio Técnico "Don Bosco," 1980.

La cofradía del mullo del vestido de la virgen pipona. Quito: Planeta, 1985; reprinted, Quito: Planeta, 1987; reprinted, Quito: Paradiso Editores, 2002.

La casa del sano placer. Quito: Planeta, 1989; reprinted, Bogotá: Oveja Negra, 1997.

El cristo feo. Quito: Abrapalabra Editores, 1995; reprinted, Bogotá: Oveja Negra, 2000.

Aprendiendo a morir. Quito: Planeta del Ecuador, 1997.

Retratos cubanos, 1957–1961: cuentos. Quito: Seix Barral/Planeta del Ecuador, 1998.

Y amarle pude. Quito: Planeta del Ecuador, 2000.

Sé que vienen a matarme. Quito: Paradiso Editores, 2001.

Concierto de sombras. Quito: Paradiso Editores, 2004.

Esclavos de Chatham. Cuenca: Editorial Sano Placer, 2006.

Books for Children

El viaje de la abuela. Quito: Libresa, 1996.

Pocapena. Quito: SINAB, 1997.

Niños escritores: talleres de literatura infantil para padres, profesores y niños. Bogotá: Oveja Negra, 1999.

La canoa de la abuela. Pocapena. Quito: Alfaguara, 2000.

Anthologized Stories

"Viaje imprevisto" and "El botón naranja". *Antología de narradoras ecuatorianas*. Ed. Miguel Donoso Pareja. Quito: Libresa, 1997, pp. 181–3, 184–8.

"Uno menos". *Cuentos ecuatorianos*. Ed. César Dávila Andrade. Madrid: Editorial Popular/UNESCO, 1999.

"Quimo". *Cuentan las mujeres*. Ed. Cecilia Ansaldo. Quito: Planeta del Ecuador, 2001, 63–70.

Works Translated into English

"Sabotage". In Doris Meyer and Margarite Fernández Olmos (eds), *Contemporary Women Authors of Latin America: New Translations*. Brooklyn, NY: Brooklyn College Press, 1983, pp. 250–3.

"Sabotage". In Gabriella Ibieta (ed.), *Latin American Writers: Thirty Stories*. New York: St. Martin's Press, 1993, pp. 288–92.

"The Mayor's Wife" (Chapter 13 from *La casa del sano placer*). In Susan E. Benner and Kathy S. Leonard (eds and trans.), *Fire from the Andes: Short Fiction by Women from Bolivia, Ecuador, and Peru*. Albuquerque, NM: University of New Mexico Press, 1998, pp. 103–10.

Bruna and Her Sisters in the Sleeping City. Trans. Kenneth J. A. Wishnia. Evanston, IL: Northwestern University Press, 1999.

"The IWM 1000". In Celia Correas de Zapata (ed.), *Short Stories by Latin American Women: The Magic and the Real*. Houston, TX: Arte Público, 1990, pp. 208–12; reprinted, New York: Modern Library, 2003, pp. 229–33.

The Potbellied Virgin. Trans. Amalia Gladhart. Austin, TX: University of Texas Press, 2006.

References and Further Reading

Gerdes, Dick. "An Embattled Society: Orality Versus Writing in Alicia Yánez Cossío's *La cofradía del mullo del vestido de la Virgen Pipona*". *Latin American Literary Review* 18(36) (1990): 50–8.

Gladhart, Amalia. "Padding the Virgin's Belly: Articulations of Gender and Memory in Alicia Yánez Cossío's *La cofradía del mullo del vestido de la Virgen Pipona*". *Bulletin of Hispanic Studies* 74 (1997): 235–44.

Handelsman, Michael. "En busca de una mujer nueva: rebelión y resistencia en *Yo vendo unos ojos negros* de Alicia Yánez Cossío". *Revista Iberoamericana* 54(144–5) (July–Dec. 1988): 893–901.

Rojas-Trempe, Lady. "Alicia Yánez Cossío". In Adelaida López de Martínez and Gloria Da Cunha-Giabbai (eds), *Narradoras ecuatorianas de hoy*. San Juan: Editorial de la Universidad de Puerto Rico, 2000, pp. 31–71.

Wishnia, Kenneth J. A. "Two Contemporary Novelists: Dialogic Cycles of History in Eliécer Cárdenas's *Polvo y ceniza* (*Dust and Ashes*) and Alicia Yánez Cossío's *Bruna, soroche y los tíos* (*Bruna and Her Family*)". *Twentieth-Century Ecuadorian Narrative: New Readings in the Context of the Americas*. Lewisburg, VA: Bucknell University Press, 1999, pp. 103–25.

Z

ZAMORA, DAISY

Daisy Zamora (b. 1950) is a woman committed to three causes: Nicaragua, poetry, and the female experience. Her writing strives to reflect the ordinariness of the everyday and the extreme moments. Most of her life's work, both as a writer and a cultural ambassador, demonstrates her deep concern for social welfare. Zamora's activism champions the struggle of the oppressed, whether those groups are marginalized socio-politically or economically. A polished and elegant professional, Zamora uses her status to speak on behalf of the common Central American woman. While some might attribute Zamora's celebrity to her physical attractiveness, she grounds her arguments logically in historical fact, drawing from her intimate knowledge of Nicaraguan poetry and politics. Always she espouses regional autonomy and individual liberty, yet her approach to achieving these goals varies according to the medium. Her poems exhibit a radical and sensual tone, whereas her essays and speeches highlight Zamora's intellectual, reserved character. This duality stems from her upbringing as a member of Nicaragua's elite class and the violent revolution that disrupted her destiny as a high society matron.

Daisy Zamora was born in Managua to an affluent, liberal family. She comes from a long line of influential Nicaraguan notables whose contributions to the nation are documented in the scientific, artistic, political, and educational realms. Zamora has nurtured sundry hobbies, although known primarily for her poetry and political beliefs, she also is an accomplished painter and psychologist. She received a religious education befitting a young woman of her status, attending Catholic convent schools. Nevertheless, her generation rebelled against conservative dogma and totalitarian control.

Zamora, as a woman, defied the patriarchal hypocrisy she witnessed in her country's dictatorships and male-dominated religious institutions. Her writing bears the mark of a staunch feminist, proud of her femininity yet firm in her belief that a woman's work matters; indeed, she embraced the philosophy of gender equality fused with nonconformist tenacity while in college. University campuses also provided the perfect environment for transforming young, passionate intellectuals like Zamora into freedom fighters against the totalitarian regime. This popular resistance group drew members from varying socio-economic classes. A fervent opposition to the despotic Somoza government that had dominated Nicaraguan politics since Anastasio Somoza García's 1930's presidency united the rebel Sandinistas, whose name (FSLN, Frente Sandinista de Liberación Nacional) honored fallen compatriot Augusto César Sandino. Zamora's diverse studies at the Nicaraguan Universidad Centroamericana, the Instituto Centroamericana de Administración de Empresas, the Academia Dante Alighieri and the Escuela Nacional de Bellas Artes in addition to her family's long involvement in the country's political development primed her to take a firm stance in favor of her beloved homeland.

Revolutionary Feminist

As a student of the arts, Zamora recognized that her lyrical talent could serve the struggle. She joined forces in 1960 with the tightly-knit "Ventana" writers group founded by Sergio Ramírez and also identified with the women poets (specifically, Gioconda Belli, Michele Najlis, Ana Ilce Gómez, Vidaluz Meneses, and Rosario Murillo) known as the "Generación Traicionada". Although she never sacrificed the intimacy and purity evident in her poetic voice, a deeper sensitivity to the collective experience began transforming her approach. Her poetry became a forum for clandestine insurgence. Nevertheless, she never abandoned her equally strong commitment to the women's movement and to refining her personal aesthetic.

After joining the FSLN in 1973, Zamora literally became the voice of a generation once taking on the role of program director and announcer for Radio Sandino in 1979. A deep admiration for the National Sandinista Liberation Front permeates her writing. The revolution not only embedded itself thematically in her texts but also transformed her approach to the poetic form. The unusual poem "Radio Sandino" serves as the most emblematic example. Not only does the text include snippets of Zamora's own experience as the opposition's underground broadcaster but more innovatively combines visually on the page a cacophonous mix of speakers. The individual voice shifts by way of typographic variations between letters in bold, italics, or all capital; punctuation marks such as parenthesis and quotation marks also establish tone or speaker, as do the organization of the lines in staccato bulleted points or descending, crescendo stanzas. "Radio Sandino" also alludes to prominent national figures such as Ernesto Cardenal, with whom Zamora formed a mentoring relationship while serving together with him in the Ministry of Culture. Zamora credits that agency's grassroots poetry workshops with drastic reductions in Nicaraguan illiteracy and the continuation of a world-renowned literary tradition, alongside whose most notable representative, Rubén Darío, she proudly aligns her own poetic production.

Zamora suffered the consequences of insurgency. Her participation in the guerrilla campaign ripped her from her native soil. Possible repercussions for her idealist zeal included kidnapping, torture, and assassination. Zamora was fortunate to endure a less violent, albeit still emotionally painful, form of punishment. Her prominence in the Sandinista hierarchy coupled with her outspoken, uncompromising faith in the movement made her a target for retribution. Exile permitted her to continue the fight from a safe distance.

Temporary residences in neighboring Central American countries such as Honduras, Panama, and Costa Rica further allowed Zamora to spread an anti-imperialist ideology and to forge relationships with fellow-minded women writers who viewed authoritative despots backed by foreign superpowers as embodiments of the same patriarchal domination Central American women confront on a daily basis. Such archetypal portraits of womanly strength abound in Zamora's poems. A strong female "I" weaves together the seemingly mundane experiences of such female stock characters as the seamstress and the waitress, the mother and the daughter, the homemaker and the waitress, the soldier and the poet. This speaker observes the daily actions of this collective sorority, describing with loving detail the tremendous and insignificant moments in a woman's life; she focuses on pregnancy and loss, service and repose, lovemaking and warfare.

Sensual Imagery

Critics highlight the presence of the female body in Zamora's writing. Far from satisfying a sexual fetishism, corporal imagery symbolizes feminist protest and personal freedom, poetic beautify and subversive desire. Oftentimes, this woman's body appears alongside an organic discourse that celebrates the earth mother and a female creative capacity, in the form of a poem or a child. The erotic feminism of Zamora's generation evolves parallel to the leftist rebellions of the time. Scholars point to the body as a metaphorical territory that female writers must rescue from the masculine grip. Aside from the obvious sexual liberation, comes an acceptance of feminine intimacy as an authoritative poetic voice; lastly, this carnal motif sparks a more profound metaphysical transcendence. Zamora's focus on hands or feet relates to her search for the individual within the collective experience. Her attention to changing female body parts like a swelling pregnant belly, reflect as much a celebration of the female experience as her interest in the universal woman's mental evolution.

International Spokesperson

Presently Zamora continues her advocacy and creative production. She has conducted literary seminars at the Universidad Centroamericana in Managua, emphasizing the Hispanic female writer and the early Spanish American literary history. Her participation in the Bill Moyers *Language of Life* for the American Public Broadcasting Series opened her to a global audience. Residing in the United States further grants the opportunity to reach out linguistically to a broad, English-speaking audience, and her fluency in English lets her collaborate closely with the translators. Zamora uses this medium to inform the international community of the need for meaningful arts, increased education, and protection of basic human rights.

JANA F. GUTIÉRREZ

Selected Works

La violenta espuma: Poemas 1968–1978. Managua: Ministerio de Cultura, 1982.
En limpio se escribe la vida. Managua: Editorial Nueva Nicaragua, 1988.
"Intervención de Daisy Zamora". *Tragaluz*, 2(15) (1986): 20–2.
"La mujer nicaragüense en la poesía". *Revista Iberoamericana*, 57(157) (1991): 933–54.
La mujer nicaragüense en la poesía: Antología. Managua: Editorial Nueva Nicaragua, 1992.
Riverbed of Memory. Trans. Barbara Paschke. San Francisco, CA: City Lights, 1992.
Clean Slate: New and Selected Poems. Trans. Margaret Randall. Willimantic, CT: Curbstone Press, 1993.
A cada quien la vida: 1989–1993. Managua: Editorial Vanguardia, 1994.
Life for Each. Trans. Dinah Livingstone. London: Katabasis, 1994.
The Violent Foam: New and Selected Poems. Trans. George Evans. Willimantic, CT: Curbstone Press, 2002.
Fiel al corazón: Poemas de amor. Managua: Ediciones Centroamericanas Anama, 2005

References and Further Reading

Moyers, Bill D. (ed.) *The Language of Life: A Festival of Poets*. New York: Doubleday, 1995.
Oralia Preble-Niemi (ed.) *Afrodita en el trópico: Erotismo y construcción del sujeto femenino en obras de autoras centroamericanas*. Potomac, MD: Scripta Humanística, 1999.
Randall, Margaret. *Sandino's Daughters Revisited: Feminism in Nicaragua*. New Brunswick, NJ: Rutgers University Press, 1994.
Vilariño, Idea. *Antología poética de mujeres hispanoamericanas: Siglo XX*. Montevideo: Ediciones de la Banda Oriental, 2001.
Woodward, Ralph Lee. *Central America: A Nation Divided*. New York: Oxford University Press, 1999.

ZAVALA, IRIS MILAGROS

Iris Milagros Zavala (1936) is a poet, novelist, essayist. A doctor in Arts and Philosophy from the University of Salamanca with a thesis on the theater of Unamuno, an innovative study that was the beginning of intense intellectual labor, labor that is reflected in the publication of more than forty books, a hundred articles in Spanish, English, and French on literature, literary theory, philosophy and more than a hundred conferences and seminars in Europe (Germany, Spain, France,

England, Italy, Poland), North America (Duke University, Harvard, Columbia), Hispanic America (Argentina, Bolivia, Cuba, Mexico) and Canada. Zavala is a plural interdisciplinary historian of ideas, historian of literature, linguist. Her subject matter addresses border issues, interdisciplinary themes, the Baroque, the Colonial World, the eighteenth century, from end-of-century writers (Darío, Unamuno, Valle-Inclán, Alejandro Sawa) to Mikhail Bakhtin and Jacques Lacan. Among her latest books is worth mentioning *Escuchar a Bajtín* (1996), *Bajtín y sus apócrifos* (ed., Introd.) (1996), *Hacia una ilusión del acto ético* (1997), *El rapto de América y el síntoma de la modernidad* (2000), *El bolero. Historia de un amor* (1991, 2000), *En otra lengua. La mujer en la España del siglo XX* (2003) and her recent *Leer el Quijote. Siete tesis sobre ética y literatura* (2005).

Her concern for feminism is expressed in the consolidation of the *Breve historia feminista de la literatura española*, which comprises five volumes, based on the following themes: Vol. 1, *Teoría feminista: discursos y diferencia* (ed. with M. Díaz Diocarez); Vol. II, *La mujer en la literatura española* (in Spanish) (1995); Vol. III, *La mujer en la literatura española* (in Spanish) (from the eighteenth century until the present) (1996); Vol. IV, *La literatura escrita por mujer* (from the Middle Ages to the eighteenth century) (1997); and Vol. V, *La literatura escrita por mujer* (the nineteenth and twentieth centuries) (1998). These volumes include numerous and plural approaches to the literary reading of female Spanish writers' works by famous national and international scholars.

From *Kiliagonía* to *El sueño del amor* . . . A Journey through the Caribbean

Iris Zavala's career in the academic field as a theorist on culture and literature is well known. This wide range of ideas is reflected in the novels published up to the present: *Kiliagonía* (1980), *Nocturna mas no funesta* (1985), *El libro de Apolonia o de las islas* (1993) and *El sueño del amor* (1998). Consequently, they could well be considered in their ensemble as a body in itself, in so far as the characters or voices in her texts fantastically appear and reappear directly through their voices or through indirect mention of others: Apolonia, the slave character of Ana de Lansós, the nun in *Nocturna mas no funesta*, is a common character in two of the stories. What is more, the geographic scenery is the same: they are the islands in the Caribbean Sea, especially Puerto Rico. Finally, as a composition orchestrated on diverse historical planes, they can be read as a single, plural and multiple text.

In *Kiliagonía o el poder del sueño*, her first novel, the insistence on a lyrical discourse is present, a poem-novel in which history finds itself submerged and of which we barely have concrete references beyond the inclusion of dates that immediately place us in the making of history, significant dates for the island of Puerto Rico: 1492, 1834, 1898. The discourses of *Kiliagonía* criss-cross between fables of mythology, philosophy, and poetry through the voices reaching us of different women: Lupe, Lola, Suncha. One of the narrators, Paloma, is responsible for making digressions, a strategy that allows her to multiply time. There are plenty of labyrinth metaphors, mirrors, cities with empty houses, fountains where the reflections break, and multiplication of time and space comparable to feminine dreams.

Her second novel, *Nocturna mas no funesta* is a story set in the seventeenth century in a Carmelite convent and is organized around a set of strategies grouped into two opposing systems. On one hand, the autobiographical space of the nun Ana de Lansós who exposes her feelings and thoughts through a set of letters and the inclusion of fragments of her diary. On the other hand, the inquisitorial reports, its questions and judgements mold its legal discourse, so that she is accused and sentenced for heresy. The variety of discourses intertwining the letters permits a series of journeys toward the past and the future, crossing three times. Ana de Lansós writes to herself through a captain to whom she writes love letters, through Georges Sand, through Roland Barthes, through the Mexican Sor Juana Inés de la Cruz, through the Nicaraguan poet Rubén Darío, through Simone de Beauvoir. Exemplarily parodying each of these writer's styles, Zavala stages in writing the theory she maintains in her Bakhtinian studies, projecting it into this literary work. The second discursive theory includes the nun's diary, into which she empties her feelings and emotions, and finally, a folder of the author's notes, and other elements such as fragmentary texts written on subway and bus tickets are interspersed. The models, like a palimpsest, hidden in the construction of the novel's central character are already advertised by name. Ana is part of Juana and a part of Mariana, the two nuns that fuse together in this Carmelite: Mariana de Alcanforado, a Portuguese nun to whom some famous love letters to the Marqués de Chamill are attributed, and Juana Inés de la Cruz. Intellect and passion. The two women become indistinguishable. The title, taken from some of Sor Juana's verses dedicated to the Marqués de La Laguna, reaffirm the influences: "Nocturna mas no funesta / de noche mi pluma escribe" (from the philosophic poem *El primer sueño*). Reappearing next to the character of Ana de Lansós is Apolonia, her black companion, descendant of an African king and queen, who lived in Ana's house and played with her during childhood.

Apolonia will be the protagonist of the novel *El libro de Apolonia o de las islas*. Apolonia, the protagonist of her third novel, breaks the slave model offered by official history. Not only does she read, but she is also educated and shares in the anxieties of her friend. Apolonia is the narrator of the Caribbean's history and of her own. From a hermetic and less lyrical prose, Zavala leads us through the Caribbean play with spatialization and playing with language, so close to the Latin American Neo-baroque period. Apolonia's journey adds another itinerary: through the interspersion of a multitude of discourses, she fulfills her trip to Puerto Rico. There, catalogues, reports of travelers, ecclesiastic texts, documents, controversial voices, dreams, oral tradition, visual elements, direct and indirect quotations, poems, metaphysical questions, edicts and, as Zavala indicates, "conjectures supporting cultural criticism using the imagination as an instrument" follow. The bodies of history circulate throughout the story of the novel with their names, dates, dreams and concretions. Apolonia, with her voice, unites and divides the elements, weaving them toward the past and present in a permanent displacement through the story's and history's time. The social discourses condense the multiplicity of their accents, emphasizing the intercultural, inter-textual and inter-discursive relationship. The voices are orchestrated in new registers expressed in word-play and experimentation.

Her latest novel, *El sueño del amor*, sends us on a voyage of love or presenting love as a voyage, speaks to us about love as a mirage, as an absence, knowing that, deep down, all Love is the construction of something impossible. Euridice, accompanied by the feminine voices of Amparo, Tatiana, Eliana, Euridice and Iris, is woman's voice reconstructing the H/history of the Caribbean. *El sueño del amor* offers an unpredictable reader's agreement, from the heteroglottism and polyphony inherent in all Zavala's works, and the readers will travel through a mass of unpredictable directions with an air of confusion and vertigo. Indeed, *El sueño del amor* does not just confront two discourses, it is not just a yearning for the Cuban Revolution or Fidel, this would be reducing the novel to a simple collection of anecdotes which would decentralize it from other, more important thoughts, or thoughts as important as the one about the revolutionary anecdote that marked Latin American history.

Poetic Variations

Barrio doliente (1961) is her first book of poetry. The book is divided into four sections: Jahvé, Christ, Man, and Race. Each of these parts corresponds with a figure of the conscience: Jahvé, figure of anger; Jesus Christ, the figure of hope; Man, the figure of deceit; and Race, the figure of salvation.

Her second book of poems *Poemas prescindibles*, is a work of defiant style within the countercultural canons of 1978. This book produces a radical lyric proposal compared to her first book of poems. Through experimental wordplay and unusual linguistic connections, her writing is characterized by a subversive force. Her aim is to give a voice to those who do not have one, through denunciation and exposure. The poetic voice abandons the first person in order to be expressed by a voice describing urban sceneries and situations of social injustice.

In her third book of poems, *Escritura desatada*, which includes poems written between 1970 and 1972, the intimate relationship between ethics and literature, which will be some of the themes and obsessions of all her writing, clearly appears. In *Escritura desatada*, reference is made to resisting the classic rules of literature.

Her last book of poems is *Que nadie muera sin amar al mar*, an anthology which includes poems from her previous books. The 36 poetic compositions about the sea are new and are those which lend the title to this book. In these poems the direction pursued in her previous books is abandoned, in the sense of "political commitment," and the poetic subject in first person addresses the sea, the sailor, and the wind.

Throughout her career, she has won numerous awards: Condecoración del Rey Juan Carlos I de España, Encomienda, Lazo de la Dama de la Orden del Mérito Civil (1988) (in recognition for her career as a critic), the *Medalla de Honor*, on behalf of the Institute for Puerto Rican Culture, in Puerto Rico (1994), the Doctorado Honoris Causa, from the University of Puerto Rico (1996), the Medalla de Oro from the Puerto Rican Atheneum (1998) y the Doctorado Honoris Causa, from the University of Málaga (2002, 2004). She has also been awarded numerous prizes, among which we can highlight the Premio Nacional de Literatura, Puerto Rico, for *Unamuno y su teatro de la conciencia* (1964); Premio Nacional de Literatura, Puerto Rico, for *Ideología y Política en la novela española del siglo XIX* (1972), Premio del Instituto de Literatura, Puerto Rico, for *Rubén Darío bajo el signo del cisne* (1990); Premio del Pen Club for *El bolero, Historia de un amor* (1992) and *Premio del Pen Club* for *El libro de Apolonia o de las islas* (1994). Her latest important award was the Premio María Zambrano de Pensamiento, in 2006.

ZULEMA MORET

Selected Works

Narrative

Kiliagonía. México, Premiá, 1980; trans. Chiliagony. Bloomington, IN: Indiana University, Third Woman Press, 1985.

Nocturna mas no funesta. Barcelona: Montesinos, 1987, 2nd edn. 2003.

El Libro de Apolonia o de las islas. San Juan de Puerto Rico: Instituto de Cultura Puertorriqueña, 1993.

El sueño del amor. Barcelona: Univ. de Puerto Rico: Montesinos, 1998.

Poetry

Barro Doliente. Santander: La Isla de los Ratones, 1964.

Poemas prescindibles. Puerto Rico: Anti-ediciones Villa Miseria, 1971.

Escritura desatada. Puerto Rico: Ediciones Puerto, 1974.

Que nadie muera sin amar al mar. Madrid: Visor, 1983.

References and Further Reading

Albornoz, Aurora de. "Reencuentro con unas palabras". *La Torre: Revista de la Universidad de Puerto Rico* 4(16) (Oct.–Dec. 1990): 517–20.

Antrophos, Número Monográfico "Iris Zavala: Una poética del imaginario social". (Barcelona) 145 (June 1993).

Bados Ciria, Concepción. "*Nocturna más no funesta*, de Iris M. Zavala: Cómo descolonizar los discursos coloniales". In María José Alvarez Maurín, Manuel Broncano, and José Luis Chamosa (eds), *Letras en el espejo II: Ensayos de literatura americana comparada*. León: Universidade de León, 1997.

de Vicente Hernando, César. "Los caminos de una imaginación emancipadora. Sobre *El sueño del amor*". *Revista Quimera* 184 (Oct. 1999): 60–4.

Manzano, Julia. "Disonancia y utopía en *El sueño del amor* de Iris M. Zavala". *Revista La Página* 39 (Oct. 2000): 55–61.

Moret, Zulema. "De Apolonia al sueño del amor, un solo viaje que se continúa". *Hispamérica: Revista de Literatura* 32(96) (Dec. 2003): 97–102.

Umpierre Herrera, Luz María. *Nuevas aproximaciones críticas a la literatura puertorriqueña contemporánea*. Río Piedras, Puerto Rico: Editorial Cultural, 1983.

Index